Lecture Notes in Computer Science 8237

Commenced Publication in 1973
Founding and Former Series Editors:
Gerhard Goos, Juris Hartmanis, and Jan van Leeuwen

AF180426

Halimah Badioze Zaman   Peter Robinson
Patrick Olivier   Timothy K. Shih
Sergio Velastin (Eds.)

Advances in Visual Informatics

Third International Visual Informatics Conference, IVIC 2013
Selangor, Malaysia, November 13-15, 2013
Proceedings

Springer

Volume Editors

Halimah Badioze Zaman
Universiti Kebangsaan Malaysia, Bangi, Malaysia
E-mail: pengarah@ivi.ukm.my

Peter Robinson
University of Cambridge, UK
E-mail: pr10@cam.ac.uk

Patrick Olivier
Newcastle University, Newcastle upon Tyne, UK
E-mail: patrick.olivier@ncl.ac.uk

Timothy K. Shih
National Central University, Jhongli, Taiwan
E-mail: timothyshih@gmail.com

Sergio Velastin
Universidad de Santiago de Chile
and Kingston University, London, UK
E-mail: sergio.velastin@kingston.ac.uk

ISSN 0302-9743 e-ISSN 1611-3349
ISBN 978-3-319-02957-3 e-ISBN 978-3-319-02958-0
DOI 10.1007/978-3-319-02958-0
Springer Cham Heidelberg New York Dordrecht London

Library of Congress Control Number: Applied for

CR Subject Classification (1998): I.4, I.5, I.2.10, I.3.5, I.3.7, I.7.5, F.2.2

LNCS Sublibrary: SL 6 – Image Processing, Computer Vision, Pattern Recognition, and Graphics

Typesetting: Camera-ready by author, data conversion by Scientific Publishing Services, Chennai, India
Printed on acid-free paper
Springer is part of Springer Science+Business Media (www.springer.com)

Preface

Visual informatics, currently a multidisciplinary field, is already well accepted among researchers and industry in computer science, information technology and engineering. The basic areas of research such as computer vision, image processing and pattern recognition, computer graphics and simulation, virtual reality, visualization and social computing have been applied in various domains such as education, medical and health, finance, agriculture, and security. Centers of Excellence (CoE) in the field of visual informatics are being established in various institutions of higher learning (IHLs) around the world (Europe, USA, and UK). The Institute of Visual Informatics (IVI), established at Universiti Kebangsaan Malaysia (UKM) or *The National University of Malaysia,* is the outcome of the first Visual Informatics Conference (IVIC) held in 2009. The institute, which conducts research in the basic areas mentioned earlier, runs both masters and doctoral (PhD) degree research programs. The end of 2013 saw the birth of our first batch of masters and PhD graduate students. We are indeed indebted to the international fraternity from the last two IVIC conferences (2009 and 2011), who have given so much support that has resulted in the establishment of the institute. It is our hope that the institute will one day become an international center of excellence in the field of visual informatics through partnerships and networking established at this conference.

The Visual Informatics Research Group and the Institute of Visual Informatics (IVI) at UKM decided to host the Third International Visual Informatics Conference (IVIC 2013) to bring together experts in this important and exciting research area so that more concerted efforts can be undertaken globally. Like the first and second IVIC conferences, this conference was conducted collaboratively by the visual informatics fraternity from several public and private universities and industry from various parts of the world. This third conference was co-sponsored by the Malaysian Information Technology Society (MITS), Multimedia Development Corporation (MDeC), Malaysian Research Education Network (MyREN), Malaysian Institute of Microelectronic Systems (MIMOS), and ICT Cluster of the National Professor's Council of Malaysia (MPN). The conference was co-chaired by five professors from the UK, Chile, Taiwan, and Malaysia.

The theme of the conference, "Visual Informatics: Sustaining 21st Century Creativity and Innovation" reflects the importance of creativity and innovation in the twenty-first century. It also portrayed the shared belief of the organizers (both locally and globally) on the importance of forming a creative and innovative product through cutting-edge and frontier research. It is particularly appropriate in this slow economic trend around the world that creativity and innovation has never been more important in order to accelerate global economic growth. Thus, the theme of the conference was relevant, apt, and timely. Since

IVIC is intended to be a long-standing conference, we decided that from this conference onward, the title of the proceedings would be *Advances in Visual Informatics.*

The conference focused on four tracks: Computer Vision and Engineering, Computer Graphics and Simulation, Virtual and Augmented Reality, and Visualization and Social Computing related to the basic areas of visual informatics. It commenced for two days (November 13 and 14, 2013) and ended with a one-day workshop (November 15, 2013). There were four keynote speakers and 69 paper presentations based on topics covered by the four main tracks. The reviewing of the papers was conducted by experts who represented more than 150 Program Committee members from Asia, Europe, Oceania, and USA. Each paper was reviewed by three reviewers and the rejection rate was 50%. The reviewing process was managed using an electronic conference management system created by the Computer&Information Technology Center of UKM.

On behalf of the Organizing and Program Committee of IVIC 2013, we thank all authors for their submissions and camera-ready copies of papers, and all participants for their thought-provoking ideas and active participation in the conference. We also thank the vice-chancellor of UKM (host university), and vice-chancellors and deans of all IT faculties of the IHLs for their support in organizing this conference. We also acknowledge the sponsors, members of the Organizing Committees, Program Committee members, support committees and individuals who gave their continuous help and support in making the conference a success. We fervently believe that IVIC will grow from strength to strength and we also hope that one day, it will be held in different host countries in Asia, Europe, Oceania, the UK, or USA. Finally, we hope that IVIC will continue to provide a stimulating and enriching platform for research and innovations that will contribute to peace and better human well-being.

We would like to make a special mention of appreciation in memory of a dear friend, *Professor Maria Petrou* of Imperial College, London, UK, who was a strong supporter of the last two IVIC conferences. She was a member of the Advisory Board of the Institute of Visual Informatics and co-chair of the last two IVIC conferences. Her death is a great loss to the field of visual informatics, specifically in visual pattern recognition and image processing.

November 2013

Halimah Badioze Zaman
Peter Robinson
Patrick Olivier
Timothy K. Shih
Sergio Velastin

Organization

The Third International Visual Informatics Conference (IVIC 2013) was organized by the Visual Informatics Research Group and Institute of Visual Informatics, Universiti Kebangsaan Malaysia (UKM), in collaboration with 15 local public and private universities in Malaysia, Malaysian Information Technology Society (MITS), Multimedia Development Corporation (MDeC), Malaysian Institute of Microelectronic Systems (MIMOS), Malaysian Research Educational Network (MYREN) and ICT Cluster of the National Professors' Council (MPN).

Local Executive Committee

General Chair

Halimah Badioze Zaman (UKM)

Deputy Chair

Zainab Abu Bakar (UiTM)

Secretary

Azizah Jaafar (UKM)

Assistant Secretary

Nazlena Mohamad Ali (UKM)

Treasurer

Azlina Ahmad (UKM)

Assistant Treasurer I

Azreen Azman (UPM)

Assistant Treasurer II

Syaimak Abdul Shukor (UKM)

Program Committee

Program Co-chairs

Halimah Badioze Zaman	Universiti Kebangsaan Malaysia, Malaysia
Peter Robinson	University of Cambridge, UK
Patrick Olivier	University of Newcastle Upon-Tyne, UK

Timothy Shih	National Central University, Taiwan
Sergio Velastin	Universidad de Santiago de Chile/Kingston University, UK

Program Committee and Additional Reviewers

Europe and USA

Alan F. Smeaton
Emanuele Trucco
Qingde Li
Tony Pridmore
Jianguo Zhang
Nick Holliman
Neil A. Gordon
Erich Neuhold
Jose Borbinha
Khurshid Ahmad
Marta Fairén
Jing Hua

Asia and Oceania

Abdul Razak Hamdan
Abdul Wahab Abdul Rahman
Abid Yahya
Abu Osman Md Tap
Adzhar Kamaludin
Ahmad Shukri Muhammad Noor
Aida Mustapha
Ali Alshock
Alvin W. Yeo
Andi Putra
Ariffin Abdul Mutalib
Asadullah Shah
Ashok Sivaji
Awang Ibrahim
Azizah Jaafar
Azizi Ab Aziz
Azlina Ahmad
Azlinah Mohamed
Aznan Zuhid Saidin
Azreen Azman
Azrina Kamarudin
Azrul Jantan
Bahari Belaton
Chan Chee Seng
Chen Chwen Jen
Daud Mohamad
Dayang Nurfatimah Awang Iskandar
Dayang Rohaya Awang Rambli
Edmund Ng Giap Weng
Edwin Mit
Effirul Ikhwan Ramlan
Elankovan A. Sundararajan
Evi Mansor
Faaizah Shahbodin
Faieza Abdul Aziz
Fatimah Khalid
Fauzi Saman
Haliyana Khalid
Hamid Abdulla Jallb Al-Tulea
Hamidah Ibrahim
Harold Thwaites
Hasiah Mohamad @Omar
Haslina Arshad
Hazmi Zaki
Hazmilah Hasan
Hector Chimeremeze Okere
Husnayati Hussin
Hyowon Lee
Idyawati Hussein
Izwan Ismail
Jamaluddin Ibrahim
Jasni Ahmad
Jasni Mohamad Zain
Juliana Abu Bakar

Kimberly Chu
Kiran Kaur Ap Gurmit Singh
Lalili Farhana Md Ibrahim
Lili Nurliyana Abdullah
Lilly Suriani Affendey
Loo Chu Kiong
M. Iqbal Saripan
Maher Arebey
Maheran Mohd Jaffar
Maizatul Akmar Ismail
Maizatul Mohd Yatim
Masitah Ghazali
Masrah Azrifah Azmi
Mazlina Abdul Majid
Md. Mamun Ibne Reaz
Mei Choo Ang
Mohamad Hanif Md Saad
Mohammad Ali Saghafi
Mohammad Tariqul Islam
Mohd Akhmal Abdul Manaf
Mohd Hazali Mohamed Halip
Mohd Khatim
Mohd Nizam Saad
Mohd Nordin Abdul Rahman
Mohd Shamsuri Md saad
Mohd Sharhan
Mohd Syaheezam Asyraq Yamin
Mohd Taufik Abdullah
Mohd Yahaya
Mohd Yunus Nayan
Mohd. Faizal Jamlos
Mohd. Murtadha Mohamad
Muhammad Taufik Abdullah
Muriati Mukhtar
Murni Mahmud
Muthukkaruppan Annamalai
Nasiroh Omar
Nasriah Zakaria
Nazean Jomhari
Nazlena Mohamad Ali
Nik Nailah Abdullah
Noor Elaiza Abdul Khalid
Noor Faezah Mohd Yatim
Noor Maizura Mohd Noor
Noorhidawati Abdullah
Nor Aniza Abdullah
Noraidah Sahari@Ashaari
Norasiken Bakar
Nordin Abu Bakar
Norhayati Mohd. Ali
Norlaila Md Nor
Norliza Mohd Noor
Norrozila Sulaiman
Norshita Nayan
Norshuhada Shiratuddin
Nur Zuraifah Othman
Nurazzah Abd Rahman
Nurfadhlina Mohd. Sharef
Nurhizam Safie Mohd Satar
Nursuriati Jamil
Peter Ho Chiung Ching
Rabiah Abdul Kadir
Rathiah Hashim
Razidah Ismail
Riaza Mohd Rias
Ridha Omar
Riza Sulaiman
Rodina Ahmad
Rodziah Atan
Roslina Ibrahim
Rosnafisah Sulaiman
Rosziati Ibrahim
Ruzaini Abdullah Arshah
Sa'adah Hasan
Safiah sidek
Saidatina Fatimah Ismail
Salwani Abdullah
Sameem Abdul Kareem
Samsul Ariffin Abdul Karim
Shahrul Azman Mohd Noah
Shamala K. Subramaniam
Sharifah Md. Yasin
Shinji Tsuzuki
Shukor Abd Razak
Shyamala Doraisamy
Sim Kok Swee
Siti Mahfuzah Sarif
Siti Mariyam Shamsuddin
Siti Salwa Salleh
Siti Salwah Salim

Sobihatun Nur Abdul Salam
Sofianiza Abd Malik
Suhaily Hafizha Suparafto
Suman K. Mitra
Sushil Kulkarni
Suzaimah Ramli
Suziah Sulaiman
Syahrul Junaini
Syaimak Abdul Shukor
Syed Abdul Rahman Al-Haddad Syed Mohamed
Syed Nasir Alsagoff Syed Zakaria
Tengku Siti Meriam Tengku Wook
Theng Yin Leng
Theng Yin Leng
Wan Adilah Wan Adnan
Wan Fatimah Wan Ahmad
Wan Zuha Wan Hasan
Wee Mee Chin
Wenyu Liu
Wong Hock Tze
Wong Kok Sheik
Wong Yin
Wou Onn Choo
Zainab Abu Bakar
Zainab Awang Ngah
Zanariah Abdul Majid
Zanariah Jano
Zulikha Ali Othman
Zulikha Jamaludin

Local Arrangements Committee

Technical Committee

Chair Members

Halimah Badioze Zaman (UKM)
Zainab Abu Bakar (UiTM)
Azizah Jaafar (UKM)
Nazlena Mohamad Ali (UKM)
Azlina Ahmad (UKM)
Riza Sulaiman (UKM)
Norasiken Bakar (UTEM)
Murni Mahmud (UIA)
Fatimah Ahmad (UPNM)
Syed Nasir Alsagoff Syed Zakaria (UPNM)
Azreen Azman (UPM)
Ang Mei Choo (UKM)
Zainal Arif Abdul Rahman (UM)
Syaimak Abdul Shukor (UKM)
Shahrul Azman Mohd Noah (UKM)
Noraidah Sahari @ Ashaari (UKM)
Muriati Mukhtar (UKM)
Wan Fatimah Wan Ahmad (UTP)
Suziah Sulaiman (UTP)
Dayang Rohaya Awang Rambli (UTP)
Riaza Rias (UiTM)
M. Iqbal Saripan (UPM)
Roslina Ibrahim (UTM)
Choo Wou Onn (Taylor)
Elankovan Sundarajan (UKM)
Mohd Hanif Md Saad (UKM)
Tengku Siti Meriam Tengku Wook (UKM)
Shahnorbanun Sahran (UKM)
Nursuriati Jamil (UiTM)
Shahnorbanun Sahran (UKM)
Haslina Arshad (UKM)
Norshuhada Shiratuddin (UUM)

Publicity

Chair Members

Ang Mei Choo (UKM)
Norshita Mat Nayan (UKM)
Norasiken Bakar (UTEM)
M. Iqbal Saripan (UPM)
Bahari Belaton (USM)
Wan Fatimah Wan Ahmad (UTP)
Roslina Ibrahim (UTM)
Choo Wou Onn (Taylor)
Hazali Mohd Halip (UPNM)
Tay Yong Haur (UTAR)
Riaza Rias (UiTM)
Zetti Azian Taip (UKM)
Mohd Sharhan Abdul Ghani (UKM)

Logistics

Chair Members

Riza Sulaiman (UKM)
Elankovan Sundarajan (UKM)
Syed Nasir Alsagoff Syed Zakaria (UPNM)

Financial

Head Members

Halimah Badioze Zaman (UKM)
Azlina Ahmad (UKM)

Workshop

Chair Members

Riza Sulaiman (UKM)
Norasiken Bakar (UTEM)
Mohd Hanif Md Saad (UKM)
Choo Wou Onn (UTAR)

Secretariat

Nurul Aini Kasran (UKM)
Aw Kien Sin (UKM)
Rose Khairunnisa (UKM)
Ahmad Faizal Khalil (UKM)
Pauzi Ibrahim (UKM)
Osama Kuder Nseaf (UKM)

Conference Management System

UKM Conference System, Computer and Information Technology Center, UKM

Sponsoring Institutions

Universiti Kebangsaan Malaysia (UKM)
Universiti Putra Malaysia (UPM)
Universiti Sains Malaysia (USM)
Universiti Teknologi PETRONAS (UTP)
Universiti Teknologi MARA (UiTM)
Universiti Pertahanan Nasional Malaysia (UPNM)
Universiti Teknologi Malaysia (UTM)
Universiti Islam Antarabangsa Malaysia (UIAM)
Universiti Malaysia Sarawak (UNIMAS)
Universiti Malaya (UM)
Universiti Utara Malaysia (UUM)
Universiti Teknikal Malaysia (UTeM)
Universiti Tunku Abdul Rahman (UTAR)
Taylor's University (Taylor)
Multimedia University (MMU)
Malaysian Information Technology Society (MITS)
Multimedia Corporation Malaysia (MDeC)
Malaysian Research Educational Network (MYREN)
Malaysian Institute of Microelectronics (MIMOS)
National Professors' Council (MPN)

Table of Contents

Keynotes

Computer Vision and Engineering

Computer Graphic and Simulation

Virtual and Augmented Reality

Visualisation and Social Computing

Toward a 3D Hand Gesture Multi-threaded Programming Environment

Raul A. Herrera-Acuña[1], Vasileios Argyriou[1], and Sergio A. Velastin[1,2]

[1] Digital Imaging Research Centre, Kingston University, London, UK
[2] Department of Informatic Engineering, Universidad de Santiago de Chile, Chile
R.Herrera@kingston.ac.uk, Vasileios.Argyriou@kingston.ac.uk, sergio.velastin@ieee.org

Abstract. Software programming for concurrent execution is not a simple task. The main issue related to this work is the lack of visibility of the multiple and parallel execution over the threads. Multi core processor technology is a reality nowadays and the only way to use modern hardware at its full capacity lays in the use of concurrent software. In this paper, we present a new 3D framework, based on hand gestures that manipulate multiple threads of execution and to deal with the visibility issues, using a 3D programming environment.

Keywords: Hand gesture interaction, 3D programming, multithreaded programming, human-computer interaction.

1 Introduction

Three-dimensional graphical interaction has become more frequent in the last decades in many applications. Attempts to overcome the issues related to providing a bridge between the real environment and the computer interfaces have become an important topic in human computer interaction research. The significance of these Human-Computer interaction problems have been addressed by several researchers in the last few years, highlighting the importance of creating new communication methods between humans and computers, replacing traditional methods and devices [1, 2, 3].

Due to the video game industry, the need to provide new levels of experience and higher interaction between the users and the systems results in significant novel contributions in the area of user interfaces. Also, most of the video game innovations have been used in other research areas such as graphics processing, interaction devices, tracking algorithms, body motion capture, etc., making that technology accessible to common people [4]. These technologies are leading mainly to interaction using the body of the user, especially hand gesture based interaction, because of the flexibility and the intuitive use of the hands in the interaction and the manipulation of 3D objects in 3D space. Gesture based systems are related to hand gesture controls and they have become very popular nowadays, especially in hand-held portable systems such as laptops, mobile phones and gaming devices [5]. In many cases just having a two dimensional interaction is not enough to perform naturally specific tasks, especially when these activities are performed in three

H. Badioze Zaman et al. (Eds.): IVIC 2013, LNCS 8237, pp. 1–12, 2013.

dimensions in everyday life. Advances in depth capturing devices have provided novel approaches to interface systems, as Microsoft Kinect has shown lately [6]. The work presented by Frati [7] suggested Kinect for hand gesture recognition and to use the same device in the field of wearable haptic technology (as a compensation for the lack of sensitivity of wearable haptic devices), seem to lead in a straightforward way to the development of hand-gesture based interactive systems.

Even when the technology to create a gesture based interfaces is available, it is necessary to consider how to represent the information. Multidimensional representation of information is not a new area [8]. There have been multiple efforts associated with managing databases in more than two dimensions to improve the search/retrieval of information and data modeling [9]. These representations are based on On-Line Analytical Processing (OLAP) and the same for all the derivations to construct databases, queries and data mining. One interesting aspect related to 3D databases is cube modeling and all the possible applications of that model. The possibility to represent multiple sources of information as a unique tri-dimensional entity provides the ability to manage data that could be impossible in a traditional interpretation, allowing relationship management and mapping of "hidden" information [10]. Actually, all these models are managed under traditional interfaces, creating and manipulating all those models just using line commands and simple graphic representations (e.g. disconnected tables). Instead, using a graphic 3D model to represent those data cubes seems to be the most natural way to interact with them. A 3D representation of those cubes will provide a better understanding of how the information in "each side" is related as a whole concept and the possibility of visually interacting with this cube (i.e. selecting rows, rotating sides and retrieving information using just gesture based interaction) will increase productivity and efficiency in manipulating and modeling all these type of entities. An experiment related to hand gesture interaction and cube database interface was presented in [11], showing the usability of this combined interaction approach.

This data interaction mechanism can be extended to have a real impact on the computer and software development community. A novel research area for 3D hand gesture technology is multi-threading programming, since the representation of multiple lines of simultaneous code execution can be better represented and understood in a three dimensional graphic environment than in simple sequential code. The complexity of generating applications using multiple threads and multiple core systems lays generally in the lack of view of how the final program is going to work. The issues related to the working environments in developing applications for multiple processors/threads are not new and there have been advances, especially in the area of graphic processing indicating further the need of novel and advanced interactive mechanisms [12, 13, 14]. Using graphic icons to represent data elements and functions helps to clarify the purpose of this type in programming and some environments successfully have been able to represent these tools in a fairly accurate and intuitive way [15]. Most of them lack a 3D representation, which as it has been indicated increases the understanding of the encapsulated information and the productivity during the utilization of multiple sources of information, especially in complex tasks such as multi-threading programming [16].

In this work we present a novel approach for generating multi-thread code using hand gesture interaction in a 3D environment introducing the concept of multidimensional programming and design. Among the other advantages of 3D software development, the proposed framework allows the user to navigate in a more human friendly code generation environment, while the proposed human computer interaction mechanism takes advantage of all the features and concepts of 3D interaction systems. In the following section an analysis of previous work is presented, showing the progress in the related areas. Then the proposed environment is analyzed providing details of the novel interaction framework for software development. Finally, an evaluation methodology of the proposed interaction methodology is discussed and conclusions are presented.

2 Previous Work

The creation of a 3D environment for multi thread hand-gesture based programming lies in the cross path of several different computer science research areas.

2.1 3D Interaction

Contemporary software engineering environments are evolving from the typical text editors to visual environments, where it is possible to interact directly with the graphic elements to create new applications. In the current human-computer interaction systems, there are still remnants of non-graphical elements that could be replaced by better representations. Those components are not enough to provide the necessary flexibility and clarity to understand many aspects of what they represent. That could be improved and better acquired with a 3D graphical user interface. Some aspects of data could clarify ideas in the context of metaphors being part of the representation [17]. Also, connections between 2D data and 3D objects could improve their understanding and functionality. The interaction with data is nowadays mostly limited to traditional 2D environments and representations. Also, if there is a graphic representation of information, they contain just a few graphic definitions (e.g. tables or data sheets), but these interface systems are not interactive and natural enough [18].

New interface paradigms have highlighted the need of improvements on the way we interact with information. MIT's Tangible Media Group [3] presents an alternative to replacing the text-driven systems in geographic information systems (GIS). This approach allows direct manipulation of geographical data, where the user can modify and analyse surfaces as part of the interface using tangible objects, (such as blocks, trees, hills, etc.), integrated with augmented reality, depicting changes of specific terrain characteristics. A 3D display provides the user a visualization of the feedback of their actions, using the "tangible bits" paradigm and digital elevation models of a surface. For example, *Illuminating Clay* uses a laser based scanner to capture a physical clay model using triangulation, which is calibrated with a projector, both of them above the model. *SanScape*, uses infrared illumination beneath the work surface; the interaction with the surface is captured with a monochrome infrared camera and the feedback can be seen on the surface due to a projector above the surface. These systems use GIS algorithms specially adapted to work with the hardware configurations. These systems were tested in a real urban design and the results showed that this kind of systems can make the designers' work easier and faster. The main problem of implementing this kind of interfaces is the high cost of the devices used and the difficulty to configure all the hardware and software for a single application. Also, the usability tests were not performed in real industrial environments. Despite that, these advances have defined a start point for new generation interfaces.

2.2 Multi-threading Programming

The possibility to improve the speed of performing complicated tasks focusing on their parallelisation has being explored during the last years. That was also important during the early years of computer science, where the processors just worked with one core. Nowadays, multi-threaded programming is necessary to use the full capacity of the available multi core processors with built-in capability to perform concurrent tasks. As stated by Lee [19] in his work about the inherent problems of multi-threads, the task of generating multi-thread applications is a complex one. His work describes how the lack of visibility of the code of parallel processing can become a significant problem, mainly for object-oriented programming, where the synchronization of the messages between objects is fundamental to achieve a defined task. In his proposal to fix this issue, a software engineering process was used to avoid wrong modelling and "language design flaws". Also, he suggested the use of stronger design patterns in concurrent computation, such as the ones used in database systems. In this work it was proposed to use other parallelization models, based on "rendezvous directors", which consist of a graphical method to label components corresponding to specific execution threads. However, the main problem with threads is not the threads themselves, but the lack of visibility of the components during the design and programming process which cause several of the problems mentioned above.

Another issue related to the multi-threading is the standardization of the programming models for parallel computing in heterogeneous systems. The MERGE framework presented by Lindeman [20] addresses this problem by an intense use of "libraries" to deal with tasks and the data distribution between the different components of heterogeneous systems, using a unified programming approach instead of the classic static/dynamic compilation method. This dynamic approach allows the programmer to designate specific tasks to architectures without knowing exactly which machine is going to be carrying out each task. The framework uses the library knowledge of the architecture to distribute the work between the components of the system. This approach addresses several issues related to the parallel programming in multiple machines, but is not a real solution when the parallel computing is done in just one of the processors and task assignment is defined by configuration hardcode, which generates the problem of lack of visibility of the different components in the application. Under that perspective, the use of a graphic-based environment becomes more suitable to solve programming issues of multi-core processors.

The approach for multi threads presented by Harrow [22] looked at the need of visualization of concurrent executions and provides an approach to modelling the working threads in real time and their progress in the system, but still uses as a starting point written code, which is prone to errors. Also, it does not provide any multiple views, because the threads work overlaps. The availability of a 3D graphic framework to see how the program is constructed seems to become more desirable.

The combination of a 3D visual interface and a 3D gesture based interaction system seems to be an attractive and interesting way to solve the problems previously discussed about concurrent programming. The proposed approach of this framework is presented in the following section.

3 Proposed Framework

The multi-thread framework that we propose is divided into different key elements related mainly to the interaction capabilities and the interface mechanisms. In a previous work [21] a metaphor to generate a 3D programming framework was presented. In this new version, after the experience gained working with 3D user interfaces and several experiments, a new approach has been established. In the following sections these elements are explained and analysed in more detail.

3.1 3D Gestures and 3D Metaphors for Multi-threading Programming

At this stage it is necessary to explain the importance of using this approach in a programming environment before describing the framework. The use of 3D interaction is possibly the most debatable issue in our proposal, but there are several reasons related to previous works in the area of human-computer interaction that support this approach. There are several studies on designing systems that can support 3D interaction, resulting in an increase of their capabilities including natural gestures and giving to the users more confidence and comfort when they interact with then. For example, the advances shown in touch tabletops and alternative 3D interaction devices [23] support the proposed framework. Additionally, such interaction devices can improve their performance by combining traditional information representation, especially in traditional interaction devices such keyboards and mice. However, the advances are becoming more pronounced toward more "human friendly" interactive systems, where the traditional external devices are practically completely eliminated from the interaction process. Particularly, the advances in infrared motion capturing devices, which provide the possibility of interacting directly with systems using bare hands, have been demonstrated recently. These devices have been extensively used in entertainment, mainly in the video games industry, and are slowly entering other development areas, especially those related to hand gesture based interaction frameworks [7]. This is due to the simplicity to understand interactions that are part of everyday human activity, such as grabbing and moving objects in a given space. These actions and gestures can be easily applied to interfaces related to graphic-based programming. The idea to use 3D metaphors to represent a program is not new, especially in robot programming, where several tasks are performed in real environments and an iconic representation is utilized to simplify the related tasks [24]. These ideas are also applicable to multi objective linear programming and 3D programming for dynamic systems. Consequently, we might argue that there is an interesting possibility to use the proposed methodology for multi-thread programming.

3.2 Gestures for Interaction

Since the interaction with the system is directly based on 3D hand gestures and using 3D objects as metaphors, three basic interactions are defined.

Rotation
Rotations in the system are based on simply moving the hand in the defined working area. This action only works in the workspace of the framework and its main utility is to shift between the different available threads in the program. The movement of the threads is around the vertical axis, rotating from left to right or vice versa with a predefined 3D space assigned to each thread. The action is performed by sliding the hand over the work area and it is possible to perform it either from left to right or from right to left. Also, it is possible to perform it only if there are no other actions or gestures performed at that time by the user.

Selection
The selection process is required to choose and add programming elements into a given thread. These elements are in a specific area of the screen, out of the workspace. The selection process is done in two steps: first, hovering over the selected item and then "pushing" to confirm the selected element. Then the element can float following the hand position allowing the user to move it in the workspace and add it to the program at the desired location.

Release
The release process is performed in a similar way to the selection, but in the work space. It consists of a stage where the user hovers the palm over the desired end location and a stage that pushes the element towards the screen to release it. Also, at that moment, the system is able to give the option to access features of the given element and "unlock" other actions once the process is finished, such as rotations or a new selection.

3.3 Multithread Interfacing Framework Analysis

The gesture definitions given above make the process of 'constructing' a program clearer, but also it is necessary to clarify some specific elements related to the working environment of the proposed framework.

Metaphors analysis
There are metaphors needed to represent as much as possible real actions based on 3D elements. The hand gestures analysed previously and the graphic icons must facilitate

the tasks of the programmer instead of making it more difficult. This can be achieved by understanding the application area and automatically adapting to it [25]. In our initial approach, the framework is shown in the Fig. 1. This figure represents an approximated view of the main interface window, with the basic working elements. It can be seen that the framework is divided in 3 basic areas: *the iconic toolbox*, where each 3D icon represents a specific function or operator (such as start/main, mathematic addition, while/for loop, etc); *the status box* to provide feedback to the user, and online help about the action being performed and finally, *the working space*, where the program will be constructed. Each part of this interface is further analysed below.

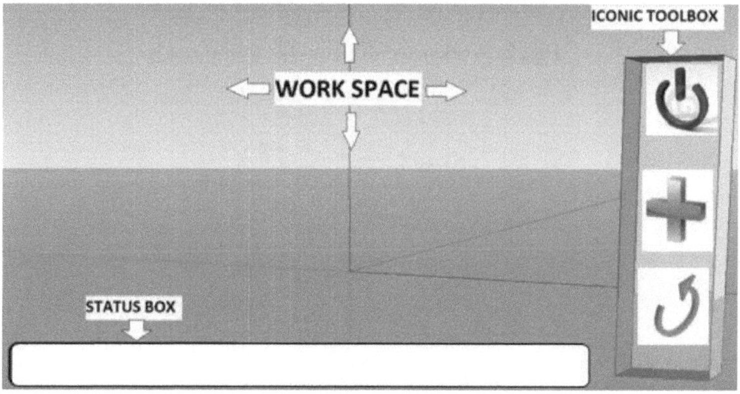

Fig. 1. Screenshot of the proposed framework

Main 3D Workspace

The main 3D workspace was presented in the previous section and corresponds to the area where the program will be created and this space will be further divided according the number of threads created. For example, for a program with four threads, the space will be divided equally into four areas as shown in Fig. 2. As can be seen, the workspace is divided to give each thread a specific working area where the graphic elements can be inserted to develop the application. This is the place where the rotation and release actions can take place. The separation between the threads is transparent and implicit once the program was started and the threads were defined. It needs to be mentioned that only one thread is active at a given time and to move to the next one the rotation gesture needs to be performed first.

3D iconic toolbox

The 3D iconic toolbox is the place on the screen where the iconic elements are stored. Contrary to the workspace, this screen area does not rotate, even if the icons are three dimensional. There is an option to scroll up and down if there is not enough space by moving the hand up and down, but this option is not available in the case shown here just for simplicity. As an example, we present three basic metaphors using 3D icons/models for the Start, Add and Loop processes. These metaphors can be combined and the icons/models can be adjusted based on the application domain, providing friendlier metaphors.

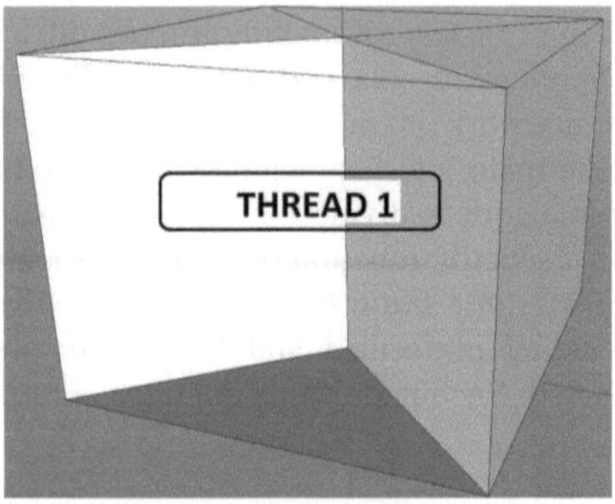

Fig. 2. Workspace division for four threads

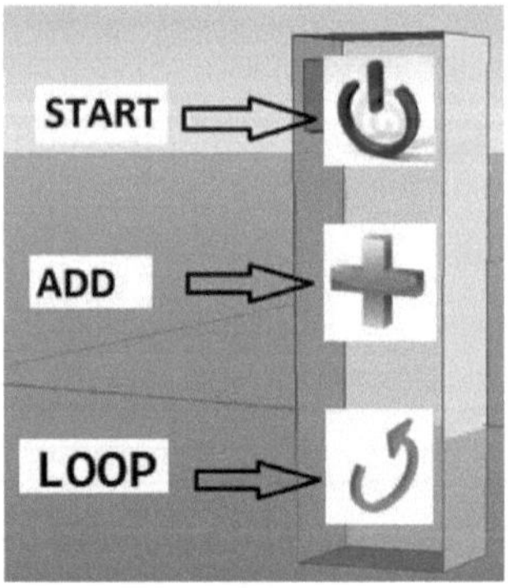

Fig. 3. Iconic toolbox for start/main, addition and while/for loop metaphors

The Start icon is used to start and initialise the application, defining for example the number of threads that will be used. The Add icon provides the possibility to add two variables or two specific numbers or a combination of them. The Loop icon is able to perform a predefined amount of iterations of a set of metaphors, similar to the "for-loop" in a traditional programming language.

Status box

The status box is a 2D static element, indicating important information and data associated to the process, such as current thread in use, function being performed and possible manipulation and syntactic errors providing online help and suggestions. It is located at the lower part of the interface, as was shown above in Fig. 1.

Application development process

The process to develop a program can be fairly simple and an example is provided to demonstrate the whole procedure. The initial step of the process is to select and move the Start 3D icon to the workplace. This metaphor provides the option to select the number of threads that will be used in this program. Once the thread selection process is completed, another can be started by selecting one of the icons in the toolbox. The working area will be now already split based on the number of threads with the start icon on top. The process of adding elements to each thread is similar i.e. selecting and moving them in the working area with the current thread to be initially the first one. According the function of each icon, they have different capabilities, such as a container in the case of the "loop" icon. The connection between some icons is implicit or based on the metaphors that represent variables. A final view of a 3D multithread program can be seen in Fig. 4.

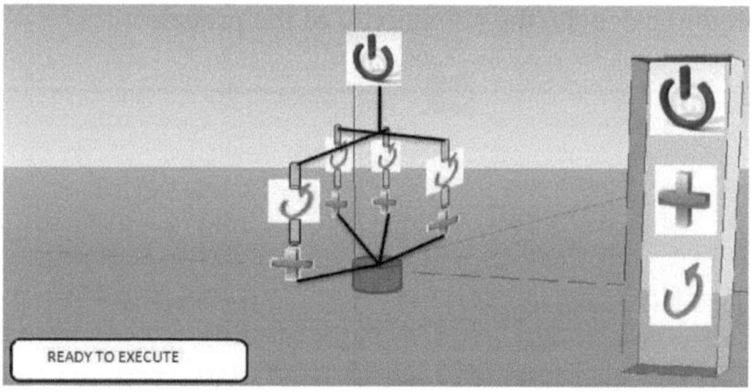

Fig. 4. Ideal view of a 3D multi-thread program

4 Evaluation Methodology

The evaluation process of the proposed framework is based on a simulated example that involves tasks focusing on the development of a specific multi-thread program. This experiment will provide the required information about two specific areas: performance and user satisfaction allowing both objective and subjective evaluations. Additionally a comparative study with the traditional development interfaces for multi thread applications is provided.

4.1 Suggested Experiment

The experiment needs to provide mechanisms to evaluate all the features of the proposed framework and it is necessary to evaluate them using an example simple enough to be understood both by people who do or do not have any experience on multi-thread programming. Based on these requirements, the task of adding a large amount of numbers (>1000000) using 4 threads was selected. The pseudo code for that task is presented in Fig. 5. This experiment covers the all main aspects related to multi thread programming allowing the complete evaluation of the framework. The evaluation points will be described in the next section.

4.2 Objective and Subjective Evaluation Metrics

The objective of the experiment is to provide a comparative study between a traditional multi-thread application development and the same application generated using the new proposed system. Therefore, it is necessary to evaluate two groups of parameters: objective and subjective ones.

Objective metrics

The objective metrics are directly related to the time required for the programmers to complete the specific task correctly and also the complexity of the developed code (e.g. time or cycles required to execute the task). The first evaluation metric can be applied directly, while the second one depends on the definition of the specific example that is used. The proposed experiment is simple to evaluate, but profiling tools are required to calculate the complexity of the process.

```
// Global Variables
LL =1000000
REPS = 1;
global_sum=0.0;
aa[LL];
mutex_sum;

// Function that adds the elements of an array
void sum
{
    i0 = TID*(N/NT), i1 = i0 + (N/NT);
    localSum=0.0;
    for (r =0; r<REPS; r++)
        for (i=i0; i<i1; i++)
            localSum += aa[i];

    mutex_sum.lock();
    global_sum = global_sum + localSum;
    mutex_sum.unlock();
}
```

```
main()
{
    // Initialization
    for(t=0; t<LL; t++)
    {
        aa[t]=t+1;
    }
    // Create 4 Threads
    thread_vector = new thread[4];
    NT=4;
    for (t=0; t<NT; t++)
    {
        thread_vector [t] = thread(sum, t, LL, NT);
    }

    // Join the Threads
    for (t=0; t<NT; t++)
    {
        thrds[t].join();
    }

    // Display the result
    print global_sum
}
```

Fig. 5. Multi thread pseudo code to test in the framework

Subjective metrics

The subjective metrics are related with the personal experience of each user and the related issues and preferences about the interface and performance. To evaluate these metrics, we can use a questionnaire such as the one used in the evaluation of users satisfaction proposed by Lewis [26]. The questionnaire is divided in three sections, with a range of evaluation mark from 1 (extremely bad) to 5 (extremely good). The sections of the questionnaire are described as follows.

General interaction section (S1): This section corresponds to questions related to the interaction in general. The questions of this section are:

Was the interaction easy to understand? (Q1)
Was it easy to manipulate? (Q2)
Is the navigation system intuitive? (Q3)

Interface rate section (S2): This section presents an evaluation of several aspects of the interface and user satisfaction. The evaluated topics are:

Interface (Q4)
Performance (Q5)

Functionality (Q6)
Objective Completed (Q7)
User Experience (Q8)
Selection of hand gestures for interaction (Q9)

Comparative section (S3): In this section, the subject is asked to compare the proposed framework with the traditional multi-thread programming interfaces. In case that the subject does not know multi-thread programming using traditional programming languages, the pseudo code will be provided.

5 Conclusions

In this paper a new approach for multi-threaded programming was presented. This approach deals principally with the lack of visibility in concurrent programming models, using a full 3D graphic interaction system, instead of the tradition code-based programming approach, where each element and the program itself are represented with 3D metaphors. Also, to improve the manipulation and construction of programs, 3D hand gesture interaction has been introduced, providing an improvement to the user experience, due to the physical manipulation of elements. Also, we presented a methodology to evaluate the features and the efficiency of the whole framework used to perform the required tasks and keeping the user satisfied. Future work will concentrate on a richer set of interaction modes and visualisation tools especially for more complex multi-threaded applications.

References

1. Harris, M., Buxton, B., Freeman, W.T., Ishii, H., Lucente, M., Sinclair, M.J.: Interfaces for humans (panel): natural interaction, tangible data, and beyond. In: SIGGRAPH 1998 Conference Abstracts and Applications, pp. 200–202 (1998)
2. Fishkin, K.P.: A taxonomy for and analysis of tangible interfaces. Personal and Ubiquitous Computing 8(5), 347–358 (2004)
3. Ratti, C., Wang, Y., Ishii, H., Piper, B., Frenchman, D.: Tangible User Interfaces (TUIs): a novel paradigm for GIS. Transactions in GIS 8(4), 407–421 (2004)
4. Barr, P., Noble, J., Biddle, R.: Video game values: Human-computer interaction and games. Interactive Computers 19(2), 180–195 (2007)
5. Boussemart, Y., Rioux, F., Rudzicz, F., Wozniewski, M., Cooperstock, J.R.: A framework for 3D visualisation and manipulation in an immersive space using an untethered bimanual gestural interface. In: Proceedings of the ACM Symposium on Virtual Reality Software and Technology, pp. 162–165 (2004)
6. Guettard, E., Jandziak, S., Lombard, C., Podevin, N., Varane, V., Dumont, P.: Virtual reality from the keyboard/mouse couple to Kinect. Annals of Physical and Rehabilitation Medicine 54(10, suppl. 1), 239 (2011)
7. Frati, V., Prattichizzo, D.: Using Kinect for hand tracking and rendering in wearable haptics. In: IEEE World Haptics Conference (WHC), pp. 317–321 (2011)
8. Stefanidis, K., Koutrika, G., Pitoura, E.: A survey on representation, composition and application of preferences in database systems. ACM Trans. Database Syst. 36(4) (2011)

9. Agrawal, R., Gupta, A., Sarawagi, S.: Modeling multidimensional databases. In: Proceedings of 13th. Int. Conf. on Data Engineering (ICDE), pp. 232–243 (1997)
10. Vassiliadis, P.: Modeling multidimensional databases, cubes and cube operations. In: Proceedings of the 10th International Conference on Scientific and Statistical Database Management, pp. 53–62 (1998)
11. Herrera-Acuña, R., Argyriou, V., Velastin, S.A.: Graphical interfaces for development exploiting the third dimension using Kinect. In: Proceedings of the 9th International Conference on Intelligent Environments, vol. 17, pp. 356–367 (2013)
12. Wang, P.H., Collins, J.D., Chinya, G.N., Jiang, H., Tian, X., Girkar, M., Yang, N.Y., Lueh, G., Wang, H.: EXOCHI: architecture and Programming Environment for a Heterogeneous Multi-core Multithreaded System. ACM SIGPLAN Notices 42(6), 156–166 (2007)
13. Ryoo, S., Rodrigues, C.I., Baghsorkhi, S.S., Stone, S.S., Kirk, D.B., Hwu, W.W.: Optimization principles and application performance evaluation of a multithreaded GPU using CUDA, pp. 73–82 (2008)
14. Nickolls, J., Buck, I., Garland, M., Skadron, K.: Scalable parallel programming with CUDA. Queue 6(2), 40–53 (2008)
15. Dolbeau, R., Bihan, S., Bodin, F.: HMPP: A hybrid multi-core parallel programming environment. In: Workshop on General Purpose Processing on Graphics Processing Units (2007)
16. Kumar, N., Benbasat, I.: The effect of relationship encoding, task type, and complexity on information representation: An empirical evaluation of 2D and 3D line graphs. MIS Quarterly 28(2), 255–281 (2004)
17. Clerici, S., Zoltan, C., Prestigiacomo, G.: NiMoToons: a Totally Graphic Workbench for Program Tuning and Experimentation. Electronic Notes in Theoretical Computer Science 258(1), 93–107 (2009)
18. Rotard, M., Weiskopf, D., Ertl, T.: A combined introductory course on human-computer interaction and computer graphics. Computers & Graphics 29, 267–272 (2005)
19. Lee, E.A.: The problem with threads. Computer 39(5), 33–42 (2006)
20. Linderman, M.D., et al.: Merge: a programming model for heterogeneous multi-core systems. ACM SIGOPS Operating Systems Review 42(2), 287–296 (2008)
21. Herrera-Acuña, R., Fidas, C., Argyriou, V., Velastin, S.A.: Toward a Two-Handed Gesture-Based Visual 3D Interactive Object-Oriented Environment for Software Development. In: Proceedings of IEEE 8th Int. Conf. on Intelligent Environments (IE), pp. 359–362 (2012)
22. Harrow Jr., J.: Runtime checking of multithreaded applications with visual threads. In: Havelund, K., Penix, J., Visser, W. (eds.) SPIN 2000. LNCS, vol. 1885, pp. 331–342. Springer, Heidelberg (2000)
23. Underkoffler, J., Ishii, H.: Illuminating light: an optical design tool with a luminous-tangible interface. In: Proceedings of the SIGCHI Conference on Human Factors in Computing Systems, pp. 542–549 (1998)
24. Biggs, G., MacDonald, B.: A survey of robot programming systems. In: Proceedings of the Australasian Conference on Robotics and Automation, pp. 1–3 (2003)
25. Hurtienne, J., Stößel, C., Sturm, C., Maus, A., Rötting, M., Langdon, P., Clarkson, J.: Physical gestures for abstract concepts: Inclusive design with primary metaphors. Interacting with Computers 22(6), 475–484 (2010)
26. Lewis, J.R.: IBM computer usability satisfaction questionnaires: psychometric evaluation and instructions for use. International Journal of Human-Computer Interaction 7(1), 57–78 (1993)

A Conversational Collaborative Filtering Approach to Recommendation

Eoin Hurrell[1] and Alan F. Smeaton[1,2]

[1] CLARITY: Centre for Sensor Web Technologies and School of Computing,
[2] INSIGHT: Big Data and Analytics Research Centre and School of Computing,
Dublin City University, Glasnevin, Dublin 9, Ireland
alan.smeaton@dcu.ie

Abstract. Recent work has shown the value of treating recommendation as a conversation between user and system, which conversational recommenders have done by allowing feedback like "not as expensive as this" on recommendations. This allows a more natural alternative to content-based information access. Our research focuses on creating a viable conversational methodology for collaborative-filtering recommendation which can apply to any kind of information, especially visual. Since collaborative filtering does not have an intrinsic understanding of the items it suggests, i.e. it doesn't understand the content, it has no obvious mechanism for conversation. Here we develop a means by which a recommender driven purely by collaborative filtering can sustain a conversation with a user and in our evaluation we show that it enables finding multimedia items that the user wants without requiring domain knowledge.

1 Introduction

Information retrieval is a pursuit that people have been following since before the use of the Internet but with the arrival of the rich information sources that the Internet brings information retrieval is now a far more commonplace activity. Approaches to information retrieval are multi-faceted and complex and there are multiple tools available which can support us in our information seeking. Search is often regarded as being synonymous with information retrieval but it is not the only option, some of the others being browsing, summarisation, personalisation and recommendation.

Recommendation involves finding items that users might like based on what is understood of their interests. One of the biggest challenges in recommendation is capturing a person's unique characteristics in order to model them better and give better recommendations. It can be difficult to determine if recommendations are optimal when the user can only indicate a degree of success tangentially, which they do by sharing their rating of an item they have experience of. It has been shown that users are willing to interact more with recommenders if it is more transparent and therefore fosters more trust in the results [16]. Such interactivity can be hugely beneficial, so the question that drove us was how

H. Badioze Zaman et al. (Eds.): IVIC 2013, LNCS 8237, pp. 13–24, 2013.

can we best capture these characteristics in order to embody both their interests and their current context. The usual interface to recommender systems will list predictions of items which users may be interested in [13], and this offers little incitement to elicit user feedback.

In any given list a user can only rate the items they have experience of, with no opportunity for feedback on unknown items. In addition, a recommendation list can be ambiguous as it is not clear what can be done with it to positively influence the recommendation or even to exert agency within the process. Because of this, while recommendation is ubiquitously part of the online shopping experience it is most frequently seen as an accessory function; users are familiar with the "customers who bought this also bought" panel as the primary manifestation of recommender systems. Ratings and reviews, which play a key part in recommendation are frequently seen as "sharing opinions with other users" rather than "helping the system learn about you". Researchers have provided contemporary re-imaginings of dedicated recommendation systems to better allow people to browse shop items of interest to them, including "conversational" systems that engage users to elicit feedback using methods like asking or proposing items [15].

Item suggestions remain an automated background task that contributes additional information to an otherwise directed task like online shopping. Recent research has taken to exploring methods by which recommendation could be the focus of a system [2], allowing users to more freely exercise their will based on preferences. Methods like critiquing items based on their properties [8] and interactive recommendation [10] have formed the basis for "conversational" approaches which allow for exploration and an active approach to recommendation thus reducing the pressure on eliciting information by making it a primary focus.

These methods of critiquing and interacting are useful in establishing that computer-driven recommendation, with its background in predicting a user's interest *a priori*, can benefit from the direct interaction that happens when people suggest things to each other. Conceptually, if users have a way with which to engage with the system in more ways than just sharing opinions on what has been seen, we have the opportunity to learn more about them. This flexibility results in a much shorter time to produce accurate recommendations [10] and more diverse results [9].

In the work we report here, we explore a new approach to conversation within recommendation as applied to visual item, namely movies. We have developed a way to generate conversation around a large dataset, letting users navigate their recommendations in situations where metadata about items is not present. An application called MovieQuiz, which allows users to quickly navigate the dataset to alter the initial recommendation given to them, is used as a basis for an evaluation of our approach. We recorded user interactions, ratings and responses to a follow-up survey for the purposes of evaluation and we show the ways in which our interactions can improve a user's ability to find good recommendations.

2 Background

Recommendation is traditionally regarded as an information retrieval problem in one of two broad forms [14], collaborative-filtering (CF) and content-based (CB) recommendation, both of which have been studied extensively [4,13]. CF recommendation attempts to mimic "word of mouth" suggestions, those recommendations users would expect to hear from their friends, by finding people like themselves whose similar tastes can be used to offer likely good items. CB recommendation, by contrast, attempts to classify a user's interests using machine learning and metadata about the items a user likes, in order to find good suggestions.

Content-based recommendation [12] covers any form of recommendation where the algorithm uses intrinsic data from the items it recommends. The drawback of doing this is the requirement that all of the possible items are well-described with metadata before recommendation begins, which comes with the advantage of giving good recommendations from a sparse amount of user data. Case-based recommendation (CBR) [3] attempts to leverage knowledge about prospective items and users interests. In CBR there are a series of known "cases", suggestions that were acceptable in the past, that are then offered to users based on their metadata. CBR is suited to domains such as product suggestion where the items can be described or identified by a well-defined set of metadata such as price, age or colour [18].

Collaborative-filtering [14] (CF) is widely-favoured commercially and offers a number of advantages. It uses only the rating information of items to recommend, either by grouping a user with others who have similar tastes (user-based CF), or uses ratings as a means to describe items having similar rating patterns yielding good recommendations for the people who rated them (item-based CF). With this, as the number of people rating items increases the probability that a match will be found for a new user also increases. By not requiring item metadata for its algorithms, CF is generally useful for recommendation without the need for specialised design for the items it uses.

Recent research has highlighted the need to treat the recommendation process as conversation, an interaction between the user and a system they should trust [19]. In such research, conventional recommendation is paralleled with a conversation, outlining a respectful process that does not place cognitive load on the user by respecting other content it appears with. This shift in approach will highlight that users' rating information provides a better recommendation, rather than being just a mechanism for the user to share opinions with a community. Work on ways to make a conversation between a user and a system possible have centred around case-based recommendation. Leveraging the well-described items in a case-base interaction of the form "I what something like this but less expensive, or a different colour", called critiquing, has been explored [8] with some success, as has "preference-based" [10]. Recent research with case-based conversational recommenders concludes that users prefer a level of control that mirrors their domain knowledge, i.e. someone who knows nothing of cameras will not know what feedback to provide on lens aperture, say [6]. There have also been explorations of recommendation as a game [1] or from a Human Computer Interaction perspective [11].

Here we present a new approach that is influenced by the case-based approach, without depending on an understanding of the domain by either the user or the system. Interaction is through a new type of explicit one-item relevance feedback [7], designed not for search but for CF recommendation.

3 Design and System Outline

Our approach centres around the idea of users choosing their area of interest. We hypothesise that using only the number of ratings and the average rating of items we can reduce the set of items to recommend from in order to offer better recommendations. We provide a means to give feedback based on the reaction, either reasoned or reactionary, of "I don't think I'd like that" or "I'm interested in that". While this reasoning is fussy, imprecise, and difficult to capture it is nonetheless an important part of decision-making for users. In contrast to early work on case-based conversation [10] this is not the same a expressing "I'm interested in more like this", rather the process proceeds like a conversation in which indicating a preference produces potentially entirely new recommendations. Our approach also differentiates a person's *immediate* interests, i.e. in this interactive session's preference indications, from their *continuing* or on-going interests, collected when they rate items.

The strength of CF recommendation lies in using rating information to understand users in comparison to others, to place them in a neighbourhood of peers or find items similar to the ones they like. Our approach uses this understanding of items through ratings, by focusing on how popular an item is, and how well it is rated. The popularity of an item ($Pop(i)$) for our purpose is its rating coverage, i.e. the number of people who have rated it, while the measure of how well rated it is comes from the average rating:

$$Pop(i) = \sum ratings(i)$$

$$Rated(i) = Avg(ratings(i))$$

$$Point(i) = (Pop(i), Rated(i))$$

From this, any item in the collection can be represented on a graph of popularity against average rating. This graph is a representation of the collection that is equally valid in all areas to user tastes. That is to say that aficionados of items such as books or film can understand there are audiences for both well-rated niche items and items that everyone has seen but wouldn't be their favourite.

Our approach works iteratively which makes it attractive for recommending image-based objects [5]. A session begins with the user having access to the entire collection of items. Two indicative movies are randomly picked from the collection, one to represent popular items and another to represent highly rated ones. The *popular* indicative movie is chosen from the movies with at least half the average number of ratings, while the *highly rated* one is chosen from movies with at least half the average rating of the collection. These are chosen from the movies considered to be *of interest* to the user, the set that they are working to decrease at each iteration. The two options are shown to the user to ask "Which do you prefer?" Additionally, a list of recommendations from the collection is generated and the top five are shown below the question, both to give users a sense that their interaction is having a meaningful effect and to show them new suggestions they may be interested in. Once the user chooses an option, the set of items from which recommendations and interface choices are generated, is partitioned. We use bounding here, which has been explored in search tasks [17] but not in recommendation, especially as a means by which conversation can occur. Here we use lower rather than upper bounds, to signify *least acceptable value*.

A new pair of options, with a list of recommendations, is posed to the user. The degree to which the items are partitioned depends on the density of the collection and our aim is to reduce the set to produce visible change in recommendations through every action. This continues until the user stops answering questions or there are less than ten items to choose from, at which point all ten are presented.

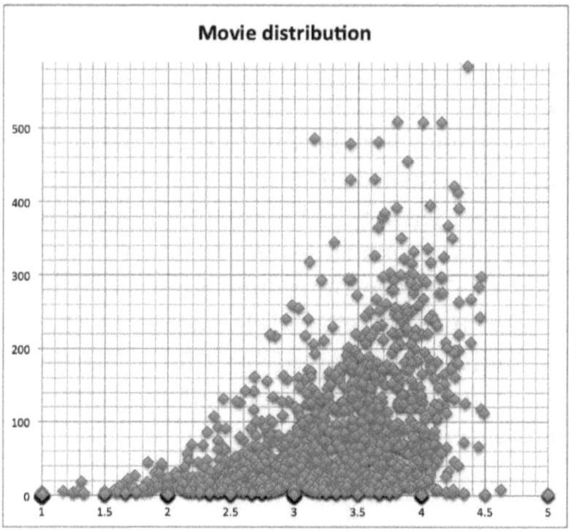

Fig. 1. Distribution of items in the MovieLens dataset plotted using our measurements

We guide the user through a series of decisions that subdivides the recommendation space according to preferences using a pair of lower bounds, reducing the portion of the collection we dub *of-interest* . This differs from critiquing, where the conversation is based on domain-specific traits. Our approach therefore works with items that do not have descriptive metadata, making it useful in situations where none exists.

4 The MovieQuiz Application

We developed an application to evaluate our method using the MovieLens 100K dataset which contains 100,000 ratings from 1,000 users on 1,700 movies. We use this as the seeding data for recommendations, with actual user interaction and rating data collected from other live users. Our example application uses movies, where "blockbuster" films and "indie hits" represent equally valued possible recommendations. Prior to engaging with the conversational interface users were asked to rate 10 of the most-popular films from a presented list.

We use a k-NN item-based collaborative-filtering algorithm to form recommendations. This algorithm is used for traditional recommendation and we adapt it here for our conversational approach as detailed above, to recommend from a subset. The adaptation is conceptually straightforward, in that we modify it to recommend only films with an average rating greater than or equal to X and with Y ratings, where X and Y are determined by the user's interactions with the conversational interface on a per-session basis. Any recommendation algorithm that can be so altered could be used for this approach.

In order to enable traversal of large datasets by the user, the affordance of the interface we develop must allow interaction while informing the user of the current best recommendations. Our basic layout, as shown in Figure 3, is to prompt the user with two candidate preferences. Not shown below the choices is a list of the top five recommended films from the collection according to the current partitioning. Users are given the title and genres of the movie, along with a poster and links to searches for the film on IMDB[1] and YouTube[2].

Experimentally, and as can be seen in Figure 1, the MovieLens dataset shows a skew toward items with higher ratings. This results in users needing to express a preference for high ratings numerous times at the start of a session before any significant changes are seen to their recommendations. For this reason we place greater weight on an interest in films with high ratings at the beginning of the process, incrementing the high rating bound by 2.5 on the first action and 0.5 after that. The popularity bound was incremented by 150 ratings per action, selecting popular over high-rated.

5 Evaluation

5.1 Interaction Analysis

We generated a detailed log for each user to help understand their actions within the system, and to explore the effectiveness of our approach. For any given rating we examined where the user would see that item on a static list of recommendations, to determine if interaction helped the user find the item more easily and what the average prediction error of ratings was, i.e. the degree to which interaction corrected the algorithm's model of the user. We also considered the

[1] `http://www.imdb.com`

[2] `http://www.youtube.com`

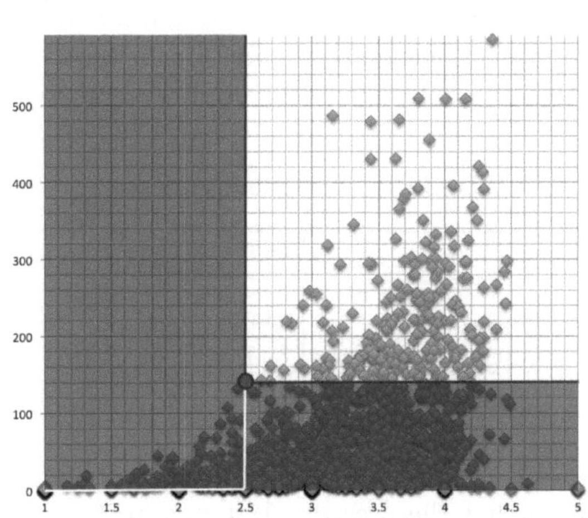

Fig. 2. The collection dissected according to the user's choices in the system

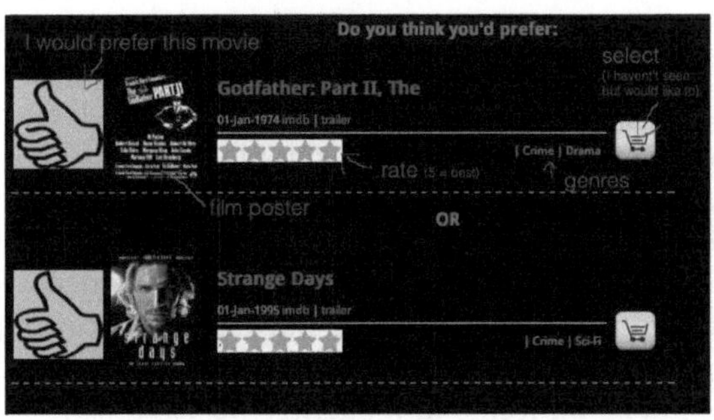

Fig. 3. The MovieQuiz application

average number of *moves* or interactions needed to get to an item that a user rated, a measure of user effort and system efficiency not unlike query difficulty.

We gathered 4,153 intra-conversation ratings from 251 people, and recorded the details of their 2,415 moves within the system. The average number of sessions (complete sets of interactions from start to end) each user had was two, with 9.6 average moves per user. The average user rated 20 items over the course of their sessions, having initially rated 10 items from a non-interactive list before starting (which were excluded from our analysis). Our set of tests involved an examination of where the items that users rated would appear on a flat list of recommendations. In order to test this for each user we used the same item-based collaborative filtering algorithm used in the MovieQuiz application and generated a list of 100 recommendations for them given their initial 10 ratings, made prior to using the interactive interface. Of the 4,153 ratings given while interacting with the system, the recommender algorithm alone lacked sufficient information to recommend 3,704 of the items within the users' top 100. These ratings were therefore excluded from the mean and standard deviation figures generated in Table 1. We also generated figures for the number of moves taken to get to an item worth rating, average rating, and error of predicted rating given by the algorithm.

Table 1. Interaction Analysis

Data	Mean	Std. Dev.
Moves-to-rate	2.33	2.26
Rating	3.60	0.41
Prediction Error	3.27	1.15
List place	77.9	22.3

Our findings, presented in Table 1, show a number of things. If the algorithm recommended an item that the user rated, it was in 78th place on the list on average, with a large deviation. This was the case for only 449 items, the rest being below 100th place on the list. If the recommendations were listed in groups or pages of ten as search results are, then it would take seven actions of "next page" before the user found their item, compared to an average of 2.3 actions in our approach. It follows that our approach would enable users to find the items they were looking for with greater effectiveness. We then looked at how usefully distinct the ratings were and found a reasonable accuracy as defined by RMSE (discussed later), though even so the average prediction error was 3.27, much larger than the RMSE, indicating that the items the user chose to rate were unexpected by the system. These unexpected items could not be accounted for through the algorithm alone and therefore our conversation helped the user find them. The average rating was 3.6 with a standard deviation of 0.4, indicating users expressed opinions on items in a slightly positive way.

Our collaborative-filtering conversation helped users find items that were of interest to them measurably more efficiently than a static recommendation using the same algorithm. We followed this with an exploration of user attitude toward the conversational approach.

5.2 User Survey

After our users had completed their trial use of the system 33 of the 251 users completed a short questionnaire about their prior usage. Of particular interest in the survey was whether users felt that the interaction improved their ability to find good recommendations and whether users without domain specific knowledge, or any knowledge of the items they were asked to judge, were at a disadvantage using the system. Previous research has found that users with greater domain knowledge prefer more fine-grained interaction and conversation from their recommender [6], so we were interested to see if this could be due to other conversational approaches hinging on domain-specific attribute feedback mechanisms such as "Like this but more expensive". The survey included the questions shown below, designed to enquire about users' knowledge levels and their comfort with the system, as a method of finding items and as a series of questions they could answer easily. Questions 1 to 8 were posed using a 5-point Likert scale.

1. How often do you watch movies, either at home or in the cinema?
2. Would you consider yourself knowledgeable about movies?
3. How many of the movies in the system did you recognise?
4. What did you think of the quality of the movies suggested by the system?
5. Did you feel the movie recommender offered a good selection of movies you otherwise wouldn't have heard of/seen?
6. What did you think of the "Which do you prefer" interface?
7. Do you think the interface helped you find good films?
8. How easy was it to state a preference between two movies in the movie quiz?
9. Did you find using the interface preferable to just being given a list of suggestions?
10. Would you use the interface in future, as part of Netflix or Amazon, as a way to help find movies?
11. Any other comments?

We found that users who responded had a wide range of experience and perceived knowledge about movies. The average score for question one, designed to show user experience with the domain area, was 3.27 on a scale of 1-to-5, with a standard deviation of 1.125, showing that while some were experienced, the average had a casual knowledge on the subject. Question two, on the user's own perceived knowledge of film, had an average of 3.33, with standard deviation of 1.163, indicating that for most movies they have at least some knowledge.

Next we looked at users' acceptance of the recommendations generated, finding that responders found the algorithm recommended fair quality films, with one user suggesting a "tag system" be used for genre-specific navigation, i.e. they would like some content-specific features. Users overall felt that the recommender helped them to discover a reasonably diverse set of films they probably wouldn't have seen otherwise, see Figure 4.

Finally, we looked at how users found the interface. Those asked stated they thought the interface was worthwhile with on average an only slightly greater than random chance of recognising films in the system (average score of 3.3, standard deviation of 0.95), suggesting that in a traditional conversational recommender they would have trouble giving feedback on any item features, and preferred a less interactive approach [6]. However with the approach to conversation we used, users felt that it helped them find good items and even without a high degree of domain knowledge they were able to offer feedback (Figure 6). Users preferred our interface to being offered a list of suggestions.

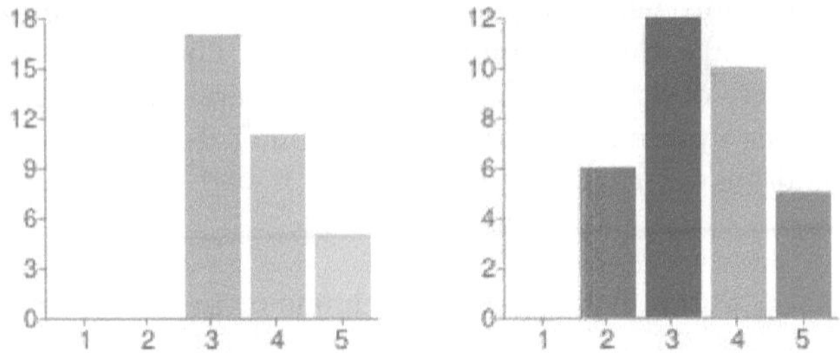

Fig. 4. "What did you think of the quality of the movies suggested by the system", and "did you feel the recommender offered a good selection of movies" ?

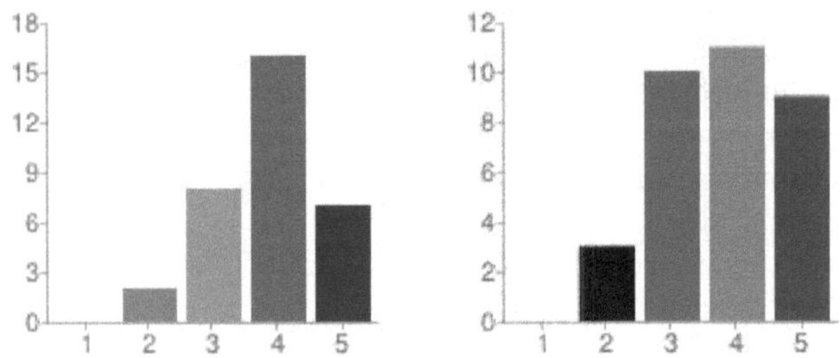

Fig. 5. "What did you think of the interface" and "Do you think the interface help you find good films ?"

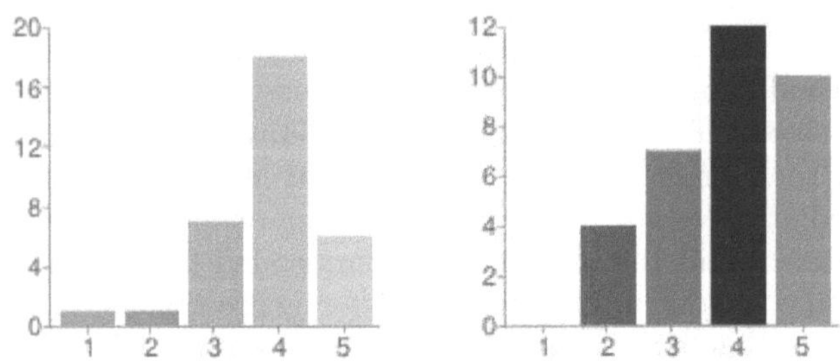

Fig. 6. "How easy was it to state a preference between two movies" and "Did you find using the interface preferable to just being given a list of suggestions ?"

6 Conclusion and Implications

We have shown that it is possible to offer conversation in a recommender system using only rating-derived data, a novel contribution that offsets the more usual reliance on metadata attributes for conversation. While the extent to which users can form information seeking strategies for answering the quiz interface is beyond the scope of this work we have found that users are satisfied with the mechanism we present for responding and finding items without confusion. Also clear is that the explicit information in the form of relative preference statements that can be harvested offer a possible new source of feedback to be harnessed to gain perspective on user information needs.

Finally we explored feedback from users of an application designed to prompt interaction, finding users greatly prefer an interactive interface to being given a list and had no trouble making choices to provide feedback and, in their mind as well as demonstratively, improving their suggestions.

Recent research has said that specific domain knowledge results in a preference for more interaction in recommendation, but here we have shown that a greater degree of interaction need not come with a domain-knowledge barrier, provided it does not hinge on domain specific attributes. Further work could be done to investigate if the variables used to identify an item, popularity and average rating, could be replaced with other valid variables, including possible metadata. Other vectors of investigation possible would include examining whether a hybrid system that limits the items being traversed by metadata, e.g. only films with the genre "action", would produce an improved recommendation.

From the user's perspective we offer an entirely new way to receive recommendations, which gives the system a lot of information quickly and transparently. By engaging the user in conversation we improve their ability to find items, in an open way. Given that privacy and the use of personal information are growing concerns in the public eye this transparent approach might also improve user satisfaction with how they are modelled in a recommender system, giving them transparent control of the process of modelling. By designing a conversational method for the least content-rich recommendation approach we have created a method that can in future be incorporated into any recommendation algorithm to allow for interaction without domain knowledge.

Acknowledgements. This work is supported by Science Foundation Ireland under grant numbers 07/CE/I1147 (CLARITY) and SFI/12/RC/2289 (INSIGHT).

References

1. Alon, N., Awerbuch, B., Azar, Y., Patt-Shamir, B.: Tell me who I am: An interactive recommendation system. Theory of Computing Systems 45, 261–279 (2009), doi:10.1007/s00224-008-9100-7
2. Averjanova, O., Ricci, F., Nguyen, Q.N.: Map-based interaction with a conversational mobile recommender system. In: The Second International Conference on Mobile Ubiquitous Computing, Systems, Services and Technologies, UBICOMM 2008, pp. 212–218 (October 2008)
3. Bridge, D., Göker, M.H., McGinty, L., Smyth, B.: Case-based recommender systems. Knowledge Engineering Review 20(3), 315–320 (2005)
4. de Mántaras, R.L., McSherry, D., Bridge, D.G., Leake, D.B., Smyth, B., Craw, S., Faltings, B., Maher, M.L., Cox, M.T., Forbus, K.D., Keane, M.T., Aamodt, A., Watson, I.D.: Retrieval, reuse, revision and retention in case-based reasoning. Knowledge Eng. Review 20(3), 215–240 (2005)
5. Hurrell, E., Smeaton, A.F., Smyth, B.: Interactivity and multimedia in case-based recommendation. In: Proceedings of the Twenty-Fifth International Florida Artificial Intelligence Research Society (FLAIRS) Conference, pp. 347–351. AAAI Press (2012)

6. Knijnenburg, B.P., Reijmer, N.J.M., Willemsen, M.C.: Each to his own: how different users call for different interaction methods in recommender systems. In: Proceedings of the Fifth ACM Conference on Recommender Systems, RecSys 2011, pp. 141–148. ACM, New York (2011)
7. Manning, C.D., Raghavan, P., Schtze, H.: Introduction to Information Retrieval. Cambridge University Press, New York (2008)
8. McCarthy, K., Reilly, J., McGinty, L., Smyth, B.: Thinking positively - explanatory feedback for conversational recommender systems. Technical report. In: Proceedings of the ECCBR 2004 Workshops (2004)
9. McGinty, L., Smyth, B.: On the role of diversity in conversational recommender systems. In: Ashley, K.D., Bridge, D.G. (eds.) ICCBR 2003. LNCS, vol. 2689, pp. 1065–1065. Springer, Heidelberg (2003)
10. Ginty, L.M., Smyth, B.: Evaluating preference-based feedback in recommender systems. In: O'Neill, M., Sutcliffe, R.F.E., Ryan, C., Eaton, M., Griffith, N.J.L. (eds.) AICS 2002. LNCS (LNAI), vol. 2464, pp. 209–214. Springer, Heidelberg (2002)
11. McNee, S.M., Riedl, J., Konstan, J.A.: Making recommendations better: an analytic model for human-recommender interaction. In: CHI Extended Abstracts on Human Factors in Computing Systems, CHI EA 2006, pp. 1103–1108. ACM, New York (2006)
12. Pazzani, M.J., Billsus, D.: Content-based recommendation systems. In: Brusilovsky, P., Kobsa, A., Nejdl, W. (eds.) Adaptive Web 2007. LNCS, vol. 4321, pp. 325–341. Springer, Heidelberg (2007)
13. Resnick, P., Varian, H.R.: Recommender systems. Communications of the ACM 40(3), 58 (1997)
14. Ricci, F., Rokach, L., Shapira, B., Kantor, P.B. (eds.): Recommender Systems Handbook. Springer (2011)
15. Shimazu, H.: Expertclerk: navigating shoppers' buying process with the combination of asking and proposing. In: Proceedings of the 17th International Joint Conference on Artificial Intelligence, vol. 2, pp. 1443–1448 (2001)
16. Sinha, S., Rashmi, K.S., Sinha, R.: Beyond algorithms: An HCI perspective on recommender systems (2001)
17. Smeaton, A.F., van Rijsbergen, C.J.: The nearest neighbour problem in information retrieval: An algorithm using upperbounds. In: Proceedings of the Fourth SIGIR Conference, pp. 83–87. ACM (1981)
18. Smyth, B.: Case-based recommendation. In: Brusilovsky, P., Kobsa, A., Nejdl, W. (eds.) Adaptive Web 2007. LNCS, vol. 4321, pp. 342–376. Springer, Heidelberg (2007)
19. Tunkelang, D.: Recommendations as a conversation with the user. In: ACM RecSys., pp. 11–12 (2011)

Orthogonal Nonnegative Matrix Factorization for Blind Image Separation

Andri Mirzal

Faculty of Computing N28-439-03,
Universiti Teknologi Malaysia,
81310 UTM Johor Bahru, Malaysia
Tel.: +60-755-32062
andrimirzal@utm.my

Abstract. This paper describes an application of orthogonal nonnegative matrix factorization (NMF) algorithm in blind image separation (BIS) problem. The algorithm itself has been presented in our previous work as an attempt to provide a simple and convergent algorithm for orthogonal NMF, a type of NMF proposed to improve clustering capability of the standard NMF. When we changed the application domain of the algorithm to the BIS problem, surprisingly good results were obtained; the reconstructed images were more similar to the original ones and pleasant to view compared to the results produced by other NMF algorithms. Good results were also obtained when another dataset that consists of unrelated images was used. This practical use along with its convergence guarantee and implementation simplicity demonstrate the benefits of our algorithm.

Keywords: nonnegative matrix factorization, convergent algorithm, blind image separation, orthogonality constraint.

1 Introduction

Orthogonal nonnegative matrix factorization (ONMF) is an NMF objective that imposes orthogonality constraints on its factors. This objective was first introduced by Ding at al. [1] as an attempt to improve clustering capability of the standard NMF (SNMF) proposed by Lee and Seung [2,3]. In ref. [4,5], we proposed a convergent algorithm for ONMF based on the work of Lin [6]. We also showed that our ONMF algorithm can outperform the SNMF algorithm in document clustering task.

In this paper, we will show that our ONMF algorithm can also be used in blind image separation (BIS) problem; a task of recovering original images from image mixtures. This finding, thus demonstrates another application domain of the algorithm.

2 BIS Problem Statement in NMF

Let $\mathbf{W} \in \mathbb{R}_+^{M \times R}$ denotes M-by-R nonnegative matrix which each of its column $\mathbf{w}_r$ contains an original image (for this purpose, every image must be of the

H. Badioze Zaman et al. (Eds.): IVIC 2013, LNCS 8237, pp. 25–35, 2013.

same size and has been reshaped into the corresponding vector). In this work, we assume that the mixing process is linear and involves only the original images. Thus, this process can be modeled with:

$$\mathbf{A} = \mathbf{WH},$$

where $\mathbf{H} \in \mathbb{R}_+^{R\times N}$ denotes column normalized nonnegative mixing matrix, i.e., $\sum_r h_{rn} = 1$, for $\forall n$. To recover $\mathbf{W}$ from $\mathbf{A}$, the NMF technique can be employed:

$$\mathbf{A} \approx \mathbf{BC}, \tag{1}$$

where $\mathbf{B} \in \mathbb{R}_+^{M\times R}$ and $\mathbf{C} \in \mathbb{R}_+^{R\times N}$ are nonnegative approximations to $\mathbf{W}$ and $\mathbf{H}$ respectively. Thus, the task of recovering the original images turns into the task of decomposing the mixture matrix $\mathbf{A}$ into basis matrix $\mathbf{B}$ and coefficient matrix $\mathbf{C}$ which can be done using NMF algorithms.

3 A Convergent Algorithm for ONMF

A brief description of the algorithm will be presented in this section. More details including convergence analysis and experimental results in document clustering can be found in ref. [4,5].

The algorithm was proposed to solve the following objective:

$$\begin{aligned} &\min_{\mathbf{B},\mathbf{C}} J(\mathbf{B},\mathbf{C}) = \frac{1}{2}\|\mathbf{A} - \mathbf{BC}\|_F^2 + \frac{\alpha}{2}\|\mathbf{CC}^T - \mathbf{I}\|_F^2 \\ &\text{s.t. } \mathbf{B} \geq \mathbf{0}, \mathbf{C} \geq \mathbf{0}, \end{aligned} \tag{2}$$

where $\|\mathbf{X}\|_F$ denotes the Frobenius norm of $\mathbf{X}$, the first component of the right hand side part denotes the SNMF objective, the second component denotes the orthogonality constraint imposed on the rows of $\mathbf{C}$, $\mathbf{I}$ denotes a compatible identity matrix, and α denotes a regularization parameter to adjust the degree of orthogonality of $\mathbf{C}$. Algorithm 1 shows the convergent algorithm proposed in [4,5] for finding a solution to the problem.

The following gives definitions for some notations used in the algorithm:

$$\bar{b}_{mr}^{(k)} \equiv \begin{cases} b_{mr}^{(k)} \text{ if } \nabla_{\mathbf{B}} J\big(\mathbf{B}^{(k)}, \mathbf{C}^{(k)}\big)_{mr} \geq 0 \\ \max(b_{mr}^{(k)}, \sigma) \text{ if } \nabla_{\mathbf{B}} J\big(\mathbf{B}^{(k)}, \mathbf{C}^{(k)}\big)_{mr} < 0 \end{cases},$$

$$\bar{c}_{rn}^{(k)} \equiv \begin{cases} c_{rn}^{(k)} \text{ if } \nabla_{\mathbf{C}} J\big(\mathbf{B}^{(k+1)}, \mathbf{C}^{(k)}\big)_{rn} \geq 0 \\ \max(c_{rn}^{(k)}, \sigma) \text{ if } \nabla_{\mathbf{C}} J\big(\mathbf{B}^{(k+1)}, \mathbf{C}^{(k)}\big)_{rn} < 0 \end{cases},$$

denote the modifications to avoid the zero locking with σ is a small positive number, $\bar{\mathbf{B}}$ and $\bar{\mathbf{C}}$ denote matrices that contain $\bar{b}_{mr}$ and $\bar{c}_{rn}$ respectively,

$$\nabla_{\mathbf{B}} J(\mathbf{B}^{(k)}, \mathbf{C}^{(k)}) = \mathbf{B}^{(k)}\mathbf{C}^{(k)}\mathbf{C}^{(k)T} - \mathbf{AC}^{(k)T},$$

Algorithm 1. A convergent algorithm for ONMF [4,5]

Initialization, $\mathbf{B}^{(0)} \geq \mathbf{0}$ and $\mathbf{C}^{(0)} \geq \mathbf{0}$.
for $k = 0, \ldots, K$ **do**

$$b_{mr}^{(k+1)} \longleftarrow b_{mr}^{(k)} - \frac{\bar{b}_{mr}^{(k)} \times \nabla_{\mathbf{B}} J(\mathbf{B}^{(k)}, \mathbf{C}^{(k)})_{mr}}{\mathbf{P}_{mr} + \delta}$$

$$\delta_{\mathbf{C}}^{k} \longleftarrow \delta$$

repeat

$$c_{rn}^{(k+1)} \longleftarrow c_{rn}^{(k)} - \frac{\bar{c}_{rn}^{(k)} \times \nabla_{\mathbf{C}} J(\mathbf{B}^{(k+1)}, \mathbf{C}^{(k)})_{rn}}{\mathbf{Q}_{rn} + \delta_{\mathbf{C}}^{(k)}}$$

$$\delta_{\mathbf{C}}^{(k)} \longleftarrow \delta_{\mathbf{C}}^{(k)} \times \text{step}$$

until $J\big(\mathbf{B}^{(k+1)}, \mathbf{C}^{(k+1)}\big) \leq J\big(\mathbf{B}^{(k+1)}, \mathbf{C}^{k}\big)$

end for

$$\nabla_{\mathbf{C}} J(\mathbf{B}^{(k+1)}, \mathbf{C}^{(k)}) = \mathbf{B}^{(k+1)T}\mathbf{B}^{(k+1)}\mathbf{C}^{(k)} - \mathbf{B}^{(k+1)T}\mathbf{A} + \alpha\mathbf{C}^{(k)}\mathbf{C}^{(k)T}\mathbf{C}^{(k)} - \alpha\mathbf{C}^{(k)},$$

$$\mathbf{P} = \bar{\mathbf{B}}^{(k)}\mathbf{C}^{(k)}\mathbf{C}^{(k)T},$$
$$\mathbf{Q} = \mathbf{B}^{(k+1)T}\mathbf{B}^{(k+1)}\bar{\mathbf{C}}^{(k)} + \alpha\bar{\mathbf{C}}^{(k)}\bar{\mathbf{C}}^{(k)T}\bar{\mathbf{C}}^{(k)},$$

δ denotes a small positive number to avoid division by zero, and step denotes a positive constant that determines how fast $\delta_{\mathbf{C}}^{(k)}$ grows in order to satisfy the nonincreasing property.

Numerically, as long as α is sufficiently small, then for each k-th iteration, the inner **repeat** – **until** loop will only be executed once. Since in practice usually α is set to be small, this inner loop can be opened to reduce the computational cost. The code below gives a quick implementation of the algorithm in Matlab codes for small α.

As shown, the computational complexity of the algorithm is $O(MNR)$ per iteration, thus is the same as the SNMF algorithm's.

```
function [B,C] = nmfOrtho(A,r)
[m,n] = size(A); alpha = 0.1; maxiter = 100;
B = rand(m,r);
C = rand(r,n);
sigma = 1.0e-9; delta = sigma;

for iteration = 1 : maxiter
  CCt   = C*C';
  gradB = B*CCt - A*C';
  Bm    = max(B,(gradB<0)*sigma);
  B     = B - Bm./(Bm*CCt+delta).*gradB;
```

```
    BtB    = B'*B;
    gradC = BtB*C + alpha1*CCt*C - alpha1*C - B'*A;
    Cm     = max(C,(gradC<0)*sigma);
    CmCmt = Cm*Cm';
    C      = C - Cm./(BtB*Cm + alpha1*CmCmt*Cm + delta).*gradC;
end
```

4 Experimental Results

The experiments were conducted using two image datasets. Each dataset consists of four images of 400x350 pixels. The first dataset is the dataset that contains related images, and the second contains unrelated images. Fig. 1 and 3 show the first and the second datasets respectively.

To create a mixture matrix **A** for each dataset, we generated a column normalized matrix $\mathbf{H} \in \mathbb{R}_{+}^{4\times 8}$ randomly. The resulting mixed images for the first and the second datasets are shown in fig. 2 and 4 respectively.

To recover the original images from the mixtures, the SNMF algorithm, the constrained NMF (CNMF) algorithm [7]—a widely used NMF algorithm in image unmixing research, extended Lee-Seung (ENMF) algorithm [8], and our ONMF algorithm were used. We also tried a block principal pivoting based NMF algorithm [9] which has a good convergence property and SMART algorithm [8] which was specially designed for blind source separation problem. However, we didn't include the results due to the poor performances in our datasets. The appendix shows the implementation of these algorithms with δ is defined as in algorithm 1, β in CNMF denotes the regularization parameter similar to α in ONMF, and η_B and η_C in ENMF denote the learning rates.

As there are parameters in CNMF, ONMF and ENMF, we repeatedly conducted the experiments using different parameter values until satisfactory results were obtained. Table 1 shows the values used in the experiments. The unmixed images are shown in fig. 5 and fig. 6 for dataset I and dataset II respectively.

For dataset I, ONMF produced the most pleasant images to view for all cases, followed by ENMF, CNMF and then SNMF. As shown in last row of fig. 5 every image produced by ONMF has minimum interference from other images resulting in the clearest images. ONMF also showed the best ability in detecting edges (boundaries of distinct regions) and distinct regions as both components are perceptually easiest to identify due to the more pronounced contrasts between

Table 1. Parameter values used in the experiments

Dataset	α	β	η_B	η_C
Dataset I	0.03	0.5	1	1
Dataset II	0.03	1	1	1

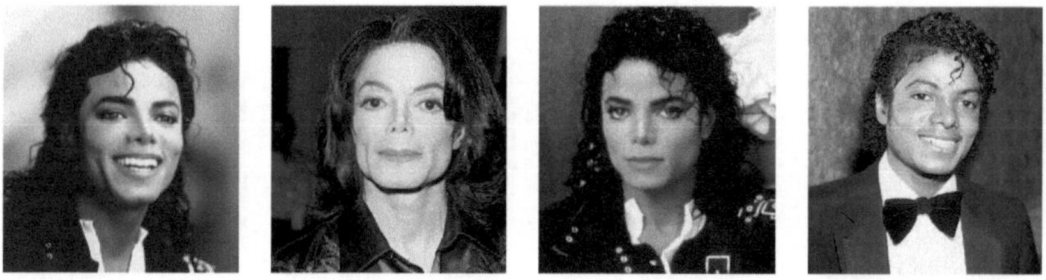

(a) (b) (c) (d)

Fig. 1. Dataset I: Related images

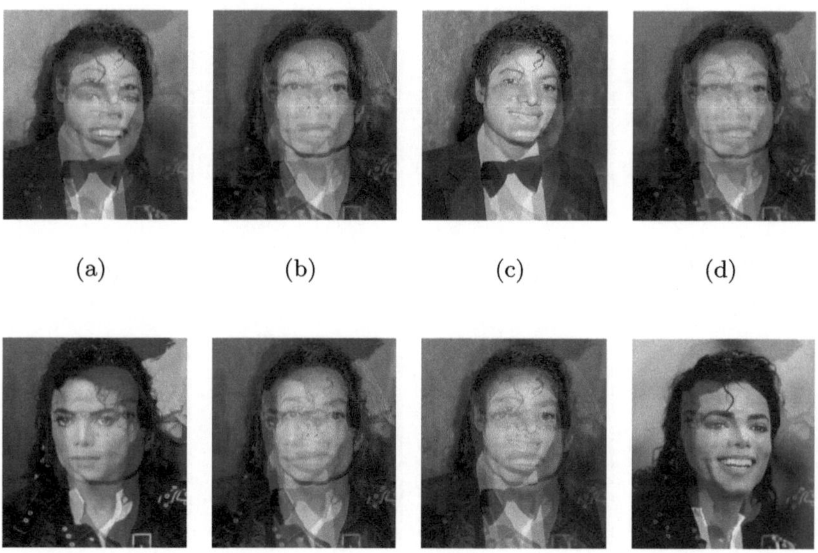

(a) (b) (c) (d)

(e) (f) (g) (h)

Fig. 2. Mixed images (dataset I)

(a) (b) (c) (d)

Fig. 3. Dataset II: Unrelated images

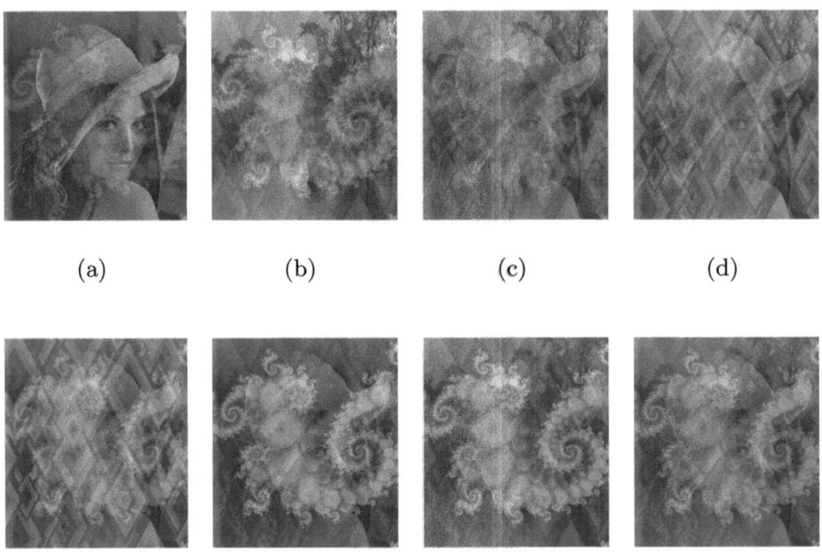

(a) (b) (c) (d)

(e) (f) (g) (h)

Fig. 4. Mixed images (dataset II)

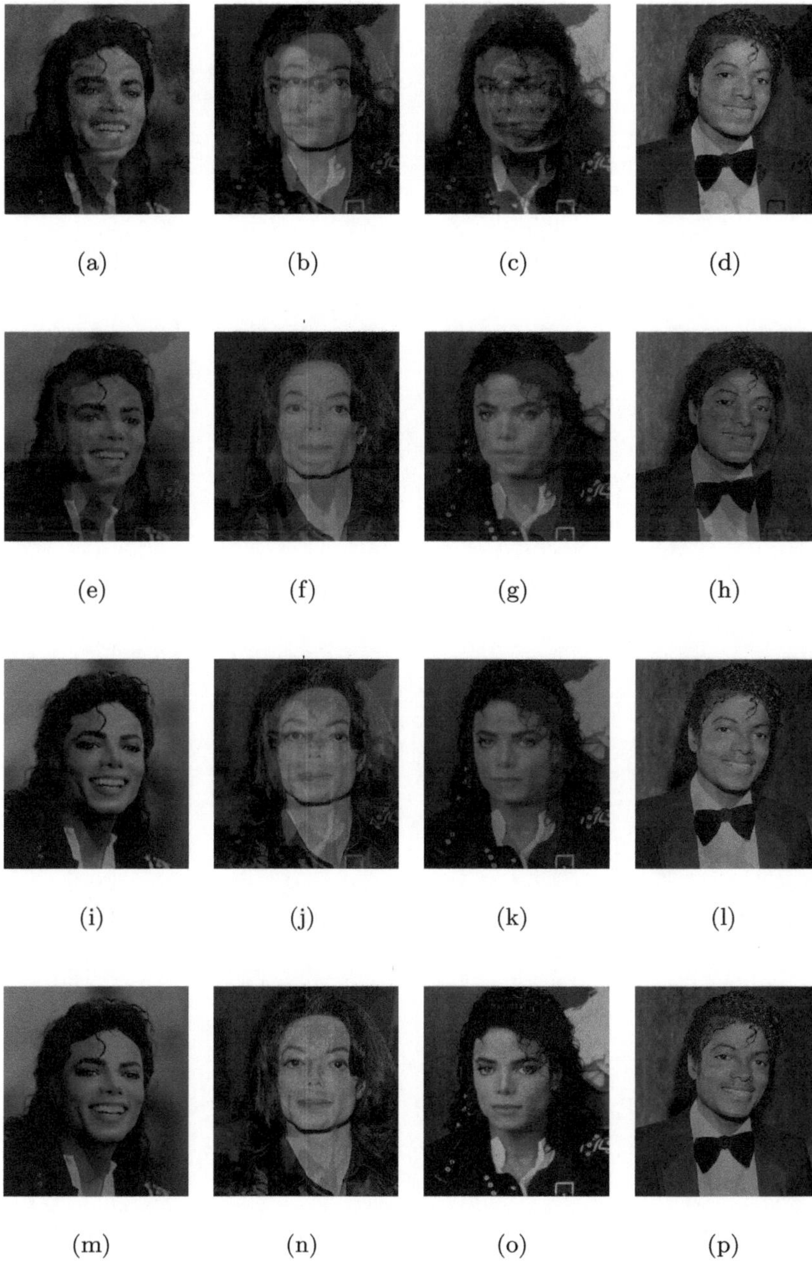

Fig. 5. Unmixed images for dataset I. The first, second, third, and fourth row correspond to SNMF, CNMF, ENMF, and ONMF respectively.

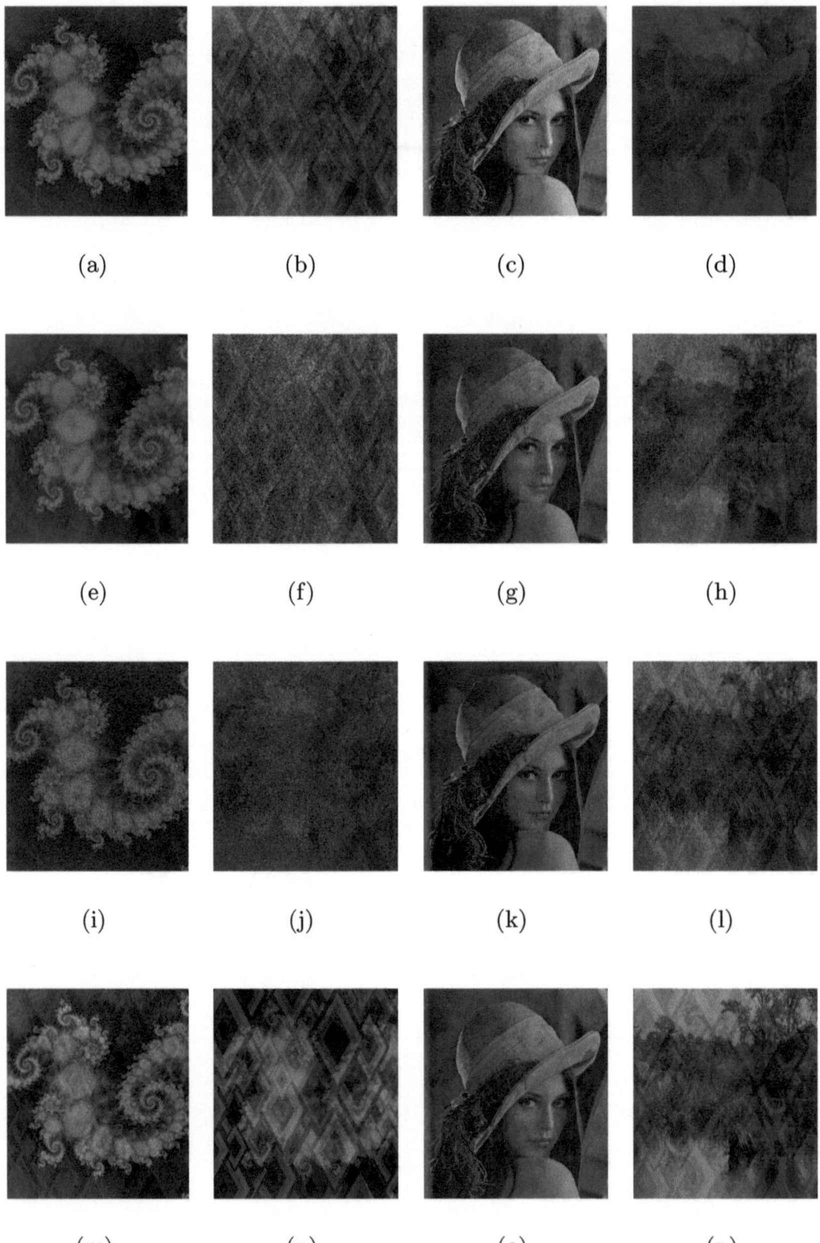

Fig. 6. Unmixed images for dataset II. The first, second, third, and fourth row correspond to SNMF, CNMF, ENMF, and ONMF respectively.

Table 2. SNR measures for dataset I

Algorithm	Fig 1	Fig 2	Fig 3	Fig 4	Total
SNMF	4.011	4.729	5.607	7.107	21.45
CNMF	3.909	5.322	5.487	4.530	19.25
ENMF	5.723	6.466	6.718	5.883	24.79
ONMF	**8.290**	**7.871**	**8.889**	**8.044**	**33.09**

Table 3. SNR measures for dataset II

Algorithm	Fig 1	Fig 2	Fig 3	Fig 4	Total
SNMF	5.338	3.361	**12.47**	3.086	24.26
CNMF	5.259	3.833	8.372	4.324	21.79
ENMF	5.891	4.165	10.56	5.010	25.63
ONMF	**7.364**	**5.654**	10.81	**6.915**	**30.74**

different regions and smoother pixels within a region. These facts can also be captured by using SNR (signal-to-noise-ratio). The following formula gives the definition of SNR.

$$\text{SNR} = -10 \log_{10} \frac{\|\mathbf{w}_r - \mathbf{b}_r\|_F^2}{\|\mathbf{w}_r\|_F^2},$$

where $\mathbf{w}_r$ and $\mathbf{b}_r$ denote r-th column of $\mathbf{W}$ and $\mathbf{B}$ respectively. Table 2 shows SNR measures between the original images and the reconstructed images. As shown, in term of SNR, ONMF confidently outperformed other algorithms as well.

In dataset II where the images are unrelated, the recovering tasks were more difficult to perform as the mixed images are less informative than the mixed images of dataset I (one can easily point out that there are four different images from fig. 2, but it's not clear how many images represented by fig. 4). Regardless, as shown in fig. 6 all NMF algorithms seemed to be successful in unmixing those images (except ENMF which seemed to fail to recover the second image). The quality of unmixing, however, is different as reflected by the SNR values shown in table 3. In this case, overall our algorithm performed the best. Only in the Lena image, SNMF outperformed our algorithm.

5 Conclusion

We have shown an application of our ONMF algorithm in image unmixing problem in which the algorithm could work well both in the dataset of related images and dataset of unrelated images. In the dataset of related images, our algorithm worked very well in which it produced very clear images and hence are pleasant to view. In the dataset of unrelated images, in overall the algorithm still performed the best. However, since the source images fig. 4 are less informative than the source images fig. 2, all algorithms produced rather unclear images compared to the reconstructions of the first dataset.

Our algorithm also had the best ability to detect boundaries between distinct regions which were often blurred in the results of other algorithms. The more pronounced contrasts between different regions and smoother pixels within a region were also observed in the results of our algorithm which contributed to the overall quality of the reconstruction.

When the unmixing performance was quantified using SNR, in general our algorithm could confidently outperform other algorithms since only in the Lena image, the algorithm failed to perform the best.

The good performance of the proposed algorithm in the BIS problem can be thought as a result of enforcing orthogonality in the coefficient matrix **C** which in the same time also enforcing independency in the basis matrix **B** so that each column of **B** tends to contain more information of individual image from the mixtures.

Acknowledgement. The author would like to thank the reviewers for useful comments. This research was supported by Ministry of Higher Education of Malaysia and Universiti Teknologi Malaysia under Research University Grant Q.J130000.2628.07J82.

References

1. Ding, C., Li, T., Peng, W., Park, H.: Orthogonal nonnegative matrix tri-factorizations for clustering. In: 12th ACM SIGKDD Intl Conf. on Knowledge Discovery and Data Mining, pp. 126–135 (2006)
2. Lee, D., Seung, H.: Learning the parts of objects by non-negative matrix factorization. Nature 401, pp. 788–791 (1999)
3. Lee, D., Seung, H.: Algorithms for non-negative matrix factorization. In: Proc. Advances in Neural Processing Information Systems, pp. 556–562 (2000)
4. Mirzal, A.: A convergent algorithm for orthogonal nonnegative matrix factorization. Submitted to J Computational and Applied Mathematics
5. Mirzal, A.: Nonnegative matrix factorizations for clustering and LSI: Theory and programming. LAP LAMBERT Academic Publishing, Germany (2011)
6. Lin, C.: On the convergence of multiplicative update algorithms for nonnegative matrix factorization. IEEE Transactions on Neural Networks 18(6), pp. 1589–1596 (2007)
7. Pauca, V., Piper, J., Plemmons, R.: Nonnegative matrix factorization for spectral data analysis. Linear Algebra and Its Applications 416(1), pp. 29–47 (2006)
8. Cichocki, A., Amari, S., Zdunek, R., Kompass, R., Hori, G., He, Z.: Extended smart algorithms for non-negative matrix factorization. In: 8th intl conf. on Artificial Intelligence and Soft Computing, Springer-Verlag, Berlin, Heidelberg, pp. 548–562 (2006)
9. Kim, J., Park, H.: Toward faster nonnegative matrix factorization: A new algorithm and comparisons. In: 8th IEEE Intl Conf. on Data Mining, pp. 353–362 (2008)

Appendix

Algorithm 2. The SNMF algorithm [3].

Initialization, $\mathbf{B}^{(0)} > \mathbf{0}$ **and** $\mathbf{C}^{(0)} > \mathbf{0}$.
for $k = 0, \ldots, K$ **do**

$$b_{mr}^{(k+1)} \longleftarrow b_{mr}^{(k)} \frac{(\mathbf{A}\mathbf{C}^{(k)T})_{mr}}{(\mathbf{B}^{(k)}\mathbf{C}^{(k)}\mathbf{C}^{(k)T})_{mr} + \delta}$$

$$c_{rn}^{(k+1)} \longleftarrow c_{rn}^{(k)} \frac{(\mathbf{B}^{(k+1)T}\mathbf{A})_{rn}}{(\mathbf{B}^{(k+1)T}\mathbf{B}^{(k+1)}\mathbf{C}^{(k)})_{rn} + \delta}$$

end for

Algorithm 3. The CNMF algorithm [7].

Initialization, $\mathbf{B}^{(0)} > \mathbf{0}$ **and** $\mathbf{C}^{(0)} > \mathbf{0}$.
for $k = 0, \ldots, K$ **do**

$$b_{mr}^{(k+1)} \longleftarrow b_{mr}^{(k)} \frac{(\mathbf{A}\mathbf{C}^{(k)T})_{mr}}{(\mathbf{B}^{(k)}\mathbf{C}^{(k)}\mathbf{C}^{(k)T})_{mr} + \delta}$$

$$c_{rn}^{(k+1)} \longleftarrow c_{rn}^{(k)} \frac{(\mathbf{B}^{(k+1)T}\mathbf{A})_{rn}}{(\mathbf{B}^{(k+1)T}\mathbf{B}^{(k+1)}\mathbf{C}^{(k)} + \beta\mathbf{C}^{(k)})_{rn} + \delta}$$

end for

Algorithm 4. The ENMF algorithm [8].

Initialization, $\mathbf{B}^{(0)} > \mathbf{0}$ **and** $\mathbf{C}^{(0)} > \mathbf{0}$.
for $k = 0, \ldots, K$ **do**

$$b_{mr}^{(k+1)} \longleftarrow b_{mr}^{(k)} - \eta_B b_{mr}^{(k)} \frac{(\mathbf{B}^{(k)}\mathbf{C}^{(k)T} - \mathbf{A}\mathbf{C}^{(k)T})_{mr}}{(\mathbf{B}^{(k)}\mathbf{C}^{(k)}\mathbf{C}^{(k)T})_{mr} + \delta}$$

$$c_{rn}^{(k+1)} \longleftarrow c_{rn}^{(k)} - \eta_C c_{rn}^{(k)} \frac{\left(\mathbf{B}^{(k+1)T}\left(\mathbf{B}^{(k+1)T}\mathbf{C}^{(k)} - \mathbf{A}\right)\right)_{rn}}{(\mathbf{B}^{(k+1)T}\mathbf{B}^{(k+1)}\mathbf{C}^{(k)})_{rn} + \delta}$$

end for

A Hybrid Robust Image Watermarking Scheme Using Integer Wavelet Transform, Singular Value Decomposition and Arnold Transform

Nasrin M. Makbol and Bee Ee Khoo

Universiti Sains Malaysia, School of Electronic and Electrical Engineering
14300, Seberang Perai Selatan, Nibong Tebal, Penang, Malaysia
Nasrin.ld08@student.usm.my,
BeeKhoo@eng.usm.my

Abstract. This paper presents new hybrid robust digital image watermarking scheme based on Integer Wavelet Transform (IWT), Singular Value Decomposition (SVD) and Arnold Transform (AT). The scheme employed the properties of those transforms to achieve the watermarking requirements (robustness, imperceptibility and security). The property of IWT which map integer to integer offers a high robustness and a good imperceptibility. The good stability and the descending order of singular values of S of SVD transform also contributed significantly in robustness and imperceptibility. Finally the scheme which applied scrambling of watermark by AT enhanced the security aspect of the scheme. The experimental results showed that the proposed scheme achieved good imperceptibility and high resistance against geometrical and non-geometrical attacks and outperformed some state of the art schemes.

Keywords: digital image watermarking, integer wavelet transform, singular value decomposition, arnold transform.

1 Introduction

A necessity to build secure methods for legal distribution of the digital content has been escalated due to the explosive growth in multimedia technology and its applications. Digital watermarking has attracted enormous attention as one of the secure technologies to protect the digital data from the tampering. It is used to hide a secret information (e.g.; text, image, number, etc.) by embedding it into a digital image, thus this information will be extracted or detected later. Different digital image watermarking techniques have been developed for different applications such as copyright protection, authentication, fingerprinting, etc. So, different requirements are achieved by each technique to serve the intended application such as robustness, imperceptibility, capacity and security. The robustness can be improved by increasing the embedding capacity but this may reduce the imperceptibility [3]. This continuous contradiction led the researchers to develop the watermarking techniques that

H. Badioze Zaman et al. (Eds.): IVIC 2013, LNCS 8237, pp. 36–47, 2013.

compromise between these requirements. Recently, improve the scheme robustness against the attacks while preserving the visual quality of the host image is the motivation to develop schemes that employ more than one transform. Such schemes are called hybrid schemes. The success of such schemes in achieving the desired goals depends on the successful selection of the involved transforms which will be selected according to their characteristics. How to employ the transforms's characteristics to achieve the requirements needed by the intended application will be the goal. Recently, many of robust hybrid image watermarking schemes based on SVD transform were developed. One essential advantages of SVD transform is keeping a minor changes even for a largest change in singular values due to attacks. On the other hand, due to the extensive computation if SVD is implemented alone, hybrid schemes based on SVD were developed [5], [8], [10] and [14]. Ganic et al. [5] and Lagzian et al. [8] followed the same embedding procedure. They embed the singular values of the gray scale watermark into the singular values of all one-level DWT sub-bands for Ganic et al. scheme and RDWT sub-bands for Lagzian et al. scheme. Lai et al. [10] and Makbol et al.[14] used the same embedding process with the presence of some differences. In Lai et al. scheme, DWT is used to decompose the host image. Then, the watermark is divided into two halves, each half will be embedded into the singular values of LH and HL sub-bands sequentially. While in Makbol et al. scheme, RDWT is used and four watermarks with size same as the host image are embedded in the four sub-bands. In all previous schemes, robustness was the target and it is the motivation to develop our present scheme in this paper. Digital image watermarking techniques can also be classified into two categories; transform domain techniques and spatial domain techniques. Other classifications are robust, fragile and semi-fragile and blind, semi-blind and non-blind [3].

In this study, a hybrid (IWT, SVD and AT) robust image watermarking scheme is developed. Robustness, imperceptibility and security are achieved nicely and strongly in the proposed scheme. That is due to the associated characteristics by the involved transforms. These characteristics are; mapping integers to integers by IWT, use of singular values S of SVD and their characteristics, and scrambling using AT. IWT achieved and improved the robustness and imperceptibility issues due to its property which ensure to process the data without rounding errors; in other words process them in their original form. The associated properties by S which are the good stability and their descending order into smaller values; helped to improve the imperceptibility and robustness because any update on these values leads to a small and non noticeable effect on the image visual quality. Finally, is the scrambling property using AT which improved the security issue and the robustness where it converts the watermark into a chaotic before embeds it and render it again in the extraction stage. The scheme, first applied a 1-level IWT to 512 × 512 Lena host image and decomposed it into four 256×256 sub-bands (LL, LH, HL, HH), then SVD was performed on each sub-band. Thereafter, a gray watermark image 256×256 was scrambled using AT before embedding it into the singular values S of each sub-band. The experimental results of the proposed scheme showed a good imperceptibility and a high resistance against geometrical and non-geometrical attacks (especially JPEG compression and noise attacks). Moreover, the proposed scheme is blind and scrambling watermark prior the embedding stage is significantly contributed to improve security. All of that is due to the acquired properties by the employed transforms. The experimental results of the proposed scheme is compared to the experimental results of our previous scheme; Makbol et al. scheme [14]. Another comparison based on some important criteria between the proposed scheme and some state of the art schemes [14], [5] and [8], is stated in the results section.

The rest of this paper is organized as follows. Section 2 presents a brief overview about each of the used transforms in the proposed scheme. The steps of embedding process and the extracting process of the proposed scheme are illustrated in section 3. The experimental setup and results are presented in section 4. The conclusion and the future work are presented in section 5.

2 The Proposed Scheme Transforms

2.1 Integer Wavelet Transform (IWT)

Lifting wavelet transform LWT is a flexible technique introduced by Sweldens to adapt wavelets to general settings [16]. Any lifting transform can be modified into a transform that maps integers to integers without rounding errors [1] and [16]. It is called the integer wavelet transform (IWT). IWT inherits the lifting transform's characteristics. It is also reversible so it ensures a perfect reconstruction property.

2.2 Singular Value Decomposition (SVD)

Singular Value Decomposition (SVD) is a numerical analysis tool that is widely used in many applications. It can analyze both of rectangular and square matrices by decomposing any matrix into three matrices as follows:

$$A = U_A S_A V_A^T \tag{1}$$

U_A and V_A are orthogonal matrices of sizes $N \times N$. S_A is a diagonal matrix of size $N \times N$. SVD has many characteristics, as follows:

1. The good stability of the singular values of S_A where they will not affected much if a small perturbation is added to them.
2. S_A specifies the luminance of the image while U_A and V_A represent the image geometry.
3. Singular values are in descending order so updating or ignoring these small singular values in the reconstruction stage, leads to a slightly and non noticeable effect on the image quality.

2.3 Arnold Transform

Arnold Transform (AT) is one of the most common image scrambling techniques. Applying AT on an image of size $N \times N$ will distribute its energy regularly and will result in a white noise image as follows [6]:

$$\begin{pmatrix} x' \\ y' \end{pmatrix} = \begin{pmatrix} 1 & 1 \\ 1 & 2 \end{pmatrix} \begin{pmatrix} x \\ y \end{pmatrix} (\bmod N) \tag{2}$$

(x, y) represents the original image pixel while (x', y') represents the transformed image pixel. N is the image size.

3 The Proposed Scheme (IWT-SVD)

3.1 The Watermark Embedding Procedure

A 256×256 Cameraman image is used as a watermark. It is exposed to the AT to scramble it before embedding and this leads to improve the security requirement. In the embedding process, a 512×512 Lena image is used as a cover image to include the watermarks where IWT is applied on it and decompose it into four sub-bands and then embeds the scrambled watermark four times. This will be clearly explained by the following embedding steps:

- First, one-level IWT is applied to decompose the cover image into four sub-bands (LL, HL, LH and HH). Each sub-band has half size of the host image due to the IWT decomposition process.
- Apply SVD on each sub-band that's getting from the previous step, as follows:

$$A^i = U^i S^i V^{iT} \tag{3}$$

where i refers to (LL, LH, HL, HH).

- Now, apply AT to scramble the watermark image.
- Embed the scrambled watermark image into the singular values S^i for each sub-band and again apply SVD to the altered singular values. This step can be expressed as follows:

$$S^i + \alpha W = U^i{}_W S^i{}_W V^{iT}{}_W \tag{4}$$

where i indicates (LL, LH, HL, HH). α is the scaling factor, $\alpha = 0.05$ for LL and $\alpha = 0.005$ for HL, LH and HH. $U^i{}_W$, $S^i{}_W$ and $V^i{}_W$ indicate the new SVD matrices that are getting after performing SVD again to result of the embedding process for each sub-band.

- Perform the new modified IWT coefficients for each sub-band. These new coefficients are developed by applying the equation in the step 2 by replacing $S^i{}_W$ instead of S^i, as follows:

$$A^{inew} = U^i S^i{}_W V^{iT} \tag{5}$$

- Finally, apply the inverse IWT on the four sets of the modified IWT coefficients to obtain the watermarked image.

$$A_W = IWT^{-1} \tag{6}$$

3.2 The Watermark Extracting Procedure

A watermarked 512×512 Lena image will be received by the receiver. It indicates as A^{*}_{W}, on the assumption that the watermarked image A_W (as indicated in the embedding stage) may have been exposed to any attack during the process of the transmitter. Then, it will be subjected to the extraction procedure steps to extract four scrambled watermarks; one from each sub-band (LL, LH, HL, HH). After that, apply an inverse AT on each scrambled watermark to return it back to its normal form. The extraction procedure steps are stated as follows:

- Use 1-level IWT to decompose the watermarked image A^{*}_{W} (possibly distorted) into four sub-bands LL, LH, HL, HH.
- Apply SVD on the all sub-bands, as follows:

$$A^{*}_{W} = U^{*i} S^{*i} V^{*iT} \quad (7)$$

where i refers (LL, LH, HL, HH).

- Compute

$$D^{*} = U^{i}_{W} S^{*i} V^{iT}_{W} \quad (8)$$

- Four scrambled watermarks (W^{*i}) are extracted using the secret key S^{i}, as follows:

$$W^{*i} = (D^{*i} - S^{*i}) / \alpha \quad (9)$$

W^{*i} is the extracted scrambled watermark from each sub-band.

- Finally, reconstruct the original watermarks by applying the inverse AT onto each of the extracted watermark; denotes W^{*i}.

4 Experimental Results and Comparative Analysis

The simulation of the proposed scheme IWT-SVD was implemented using MATLAB. A popular test image; Lena with a size 512×512 as a cover image and 256×256 Cameraman image as a watermark are used to evaluate the proposed scheme. The performance investigation of the proposed IWT-SVD scheme was in terms of imperceptibility and robustness against various attacks. The imperceptibility is a term used to evaluate the similarity between the cover image and the watermarked image. It can be expressed in terms of *PSNR* and it was 43.8738 dB for our proposed scheme for a gray scale Lena image 512×512. In the watermarking world, the minimum acceptable value of PSNR is 38 dB [11]. Fig.1 displays the host Lena image, the Cameraman watermark image and the watermarked Lena image.

The NC is used to measure the robustness by evaluating the similarity between the original watermark and the extracted watermark after attack. When the *NC* value is closer to 1 under applicable attacks, then the scheme is robust against those attacks. In general, the NC value is acceptable if it is 0.75 or higher. The robustness is the key requirement to develop the digital watermarking techniques. It is the resistance against geometrical attacks which are considered as malicious attacks and non geometrical attacks.

Table 1 shows and compares the NC values of the extracted watermarks of the proposed IWT-SVD scheme and our previous scheme, Makbol et al. scheme (RDWT-SVD) [14] when exposed to different types of attacks. Several non- geometrical and geometrical attacks are applied to the 512×512 Lena test image. Non-geometrical attacks (image processing attacks) such as noise addition (e.g. Pepper & salt noise, Gaussian noise and Speckle noise), filtering, gamma correction and JPEG compression attacks are applied, while cutting, shearing, scaling, rotation and translating attacks are selected as the geometrical attacks. The proposed scheme shows a high resistance in the all sub-bands.

Table 1. The robustness comparison of our proposed watermarking scheme with Makbol et al. scheme [14] in the all sub-bands against geometrical and non-geometrical attacks

	IWT - SVD (this paper)				RDWT - SVD [14]			
	LL	LH	HL	HH	LL	LH	HL	HH
Pepper & salt noise 0.5	**0.75**	**0.9044**	**0.9129**	**0.8868**	0.632	0.8853	0.8943	0.8086
Pepper & salt noise 0.3	**0.795**	**0.9083**	**0.9154**	**0.8912**	0.665	0.8893	0.8964	0.8112
Pepper & salt noise 0.1	**0.875**	**0.9202**	**0.92**	**0.9014**	0.783	0.9016	0.8917	0.8227
Pepper & salt noise 0.01	**0.972**	**0.9466**	**0.9075**	**0.9312**	0.951	0.8645	0.8247	0.8374
Pepper & salt noise 0.005	**0.984**	**0.959**	**0.9224**	**0.9464**	0.975	0.8699	0.868	0.8571
Pepper & salt noise 0.001	**0.997**	**0.979**	0.9734	**0.9625**	0.994	0.9637	0.9734	0.9002
Speckle noise 0.5	**0.81**	**0.9025**	**0.915**	**0.8863**	0.69	0.888	0.8971	0.8078
Speckle noise 0.3	**0.84**	**0.9077**	**0.9175**	**0.8878**	0.719	0.8924	0.8978	0.8107
Speckle noise 0.1	**0.894**	**0.9189**	**0.9234**	**0.8968**	0.81	0.9018	0.8981	0.8236
Speckle noise 0.01	**0.972**	**0.9344**	**0.8962**	**0.9288**	0.951	0.8385	0.8147	0.8315
Speckle noise 0.005	**0.983**	**0.9393**	**0.9101**	**0.9317**	0.972	0.8391	0.8516	0.7973
Speckle noise 0.001	**0.996**	**0.9695**	0.964	**0.9376**	0.993	0.957	**0.9662**	0.7958
Gaussian noise 0.5	**0.755**	**0.9029**	**0.9111**	**0.8858**	0.638	0.8879	0.8926	0.8085
Gaussian noise 0.3	**0.77**	**0.905**	**0.913**	**0.8904**	0.652	0.8865	0.8945	0.8056
Gaussian noise 0.1	**0.826**	**0.9094**	**0.9163**	**0.8936**	0.705	0.8941	0.8967	0.814

Table 1. *(Continued)*

Gaussian noise 0.01	**0.935**	**0.9339**	**0.9072**	**0.9149**	0.878	0.9002	0.8429	0.8307
Gaussian noise 0.005	**0.959**	**0.9389**	**0.8985**	**0.9229**	0.924	0.8664	0.8127	0.8283
Gaussian noise 0.001	**0.986**	**0.9436**	**0.925**	**0.9264**	0.979	0.8675	0.8853	0.7807
Gaussian filter (2,2)	**0.982**	0.7722	**0.9361**	**0.9556**	0.98	**0.9063**	0.8958	0.9148
Gaussian filter (3,3)	**0.988**	0.9404	**0.9703**	**0.9742**	0.987	**0.9652**	0.9608	0.9417
Gaussian filter (5,5)	**0.988**	0.9404	**0.9704**	**0.9738**	0.987	**0.9649**	0.9606	0.9418
Gaussian filter (7,7)	**0.988**	0.9404	**0.9704**	**0.9738**	0.987	**0.9649**	0.9606	0.9418
Gaussian filter (9,9)	**0.988**	0.9404	**0.9704**	**0.9738**	0.987	**0.9649**	0.9606	0.9418
Gaussian filter (11,11)	**0.988**	0.9404	**0.9704**	**0.9738**	0.987	**0.9649**	0.9606	0.9418
Median filter (2,2)	0.987	0.8108	0.9522	**0.9647**	**0.989**	**0.947**	**0.9531**	0.9328
Median filter (3,3)	0.981	0.9686	0.9697	**0.9686**	**0.982**	**0.9581**	**0.9663**	0.884
Median filter (5,5)	**0.956**	**0.9283**	**0.944**	0.9452	0.95	0.913	0.9268	**0.9845**
Median filter (7,7)	**0.929**	0.8164	**0.916**	0.8392	0.914	**0.8546**	0.8958	**0.9895**
Median filter (9,9)	**0.906**	0.7287	**0.9006**	0.9669	0.882	**0.8203**	0.8735	**0.9827**
Median filter (11,11)	**0.883**	0.733	**0.896**	0.6856	0.856	**0.7916**	0.8573	**0.9746**
Wiener filter (2,2)	0.991	**0.98**	0.9767	**0.9538**	**0.992**	0.9794	**0.9821**	0.9245
Wiener filter (3,3)	0.983	**0.9678**	**0.9641**	**0.9416**	**0.984**	0.9509	0.9609	0.9332
Wiener filter (5,5)	**0.975**	**0.9589**	0.9556	0.936	0.974	0.9404	**0.9561**	**0.9427**
Wiener filter (7,7)	**0.969**	**0.9567**	0.9527	0.9321	0.964	0.9384	**0.9545**	**0.9492**
Wiener filter (9,9)	**0.963**	**0.9559**	**0.9495**	0.9359	0.954	0.9381	0.9488	**0.9518**
Wiener filter (11,11)	**0.956**	**0.9558**	**0.9476**	0.9452	0.944	0.9364	0.9448	**0.9555**
JPEG compression Q=5	**0.969**	0.7351	**0.8013**	0.6533	0.952	**0.7666**	0.719	**0.7487**
JPEG compression Q=10	**0.987**	**0.8673**	**0.9055**	0.7543	0.972	0.8555	0.8328	**0.7902**

Table 1. (*Continued*)

JPEG compression Q=20	**0.993**	**0.9381**	**0.9494**	**0.8535**	0.983	0.9121	0.8929	0.8275
JPEG compression Q=25	**0.994**	**0.9544**	**0.9581**	0.8373	0.985	0.9242	0.9112	**0.8425**
JPEG compression Q=30	**0.994**	**0.9597**	**0.9635**	**0.8836**	0.987	0.9327	0.9222	0.8498
JPEG compression Q=40	**0.995**	**0.9693**	**0.9659**	**0.8902**	0.988	0.9411	0.9355	0.8653
JPEG compression Q=50	**0.996**	**0.973**	**0.9703**	**0.8654**	0.99	0.9487	0.9469	0.861
JPEG compression Q=70	**0.998**	**0.9806**	**0.9769**	0.8769	0.994	0.9644	0.967	**0.8863**
Gamma correction 1	**1.000**	0.9841	0.9912	**0.9857**	0.998	**0.9931**	**0.9942**	0.9225
Gamma correction 0.8	**0.995**	0.9871	0.9855	**0.9889**	**0.995**	**0.9944**	**0.995**	0.9284
Gamma correction 0.6	0.987	0.9847	0.9821	**0.986**	**0.989**	**0.9927**	**0.9927**	0.9263
Gamma correction 0.4	0.967	0.9829	0.9798	**0.983**	**0.974**	**0.9909**	**0.9902**	0.9234
Gamma correction 0.3	0.942	0.9827	0.979	**0.9815**	**0.955**	**0.99**	**0.9883**	0.9193
Gamma correction 0.1	0.679	0.9832	0.9751	**0.9795**	**0.738**	**0.9869**	**0.9829**	0.9032
Rotation 45	0.979	0.9673	0.9113	**0.9676**	**0.983**	**0.9823**	**0.9815**	0.8045
Rotation 2	0.979	0.7906	**0.9579**	**0.9498**	**0.981**	**0.8981**	0.9327	0.9389
Rotation 70	0.973	0.9594	0.9152	**0.9608**	**0.981**	**0.9668**	**0.9436**	0.8619
Rotation 110	0.977	0.967	0.9092	**0.9734**	**0.981**	**0.9686**	**0.9202**	0.9007
Rotation 50	0.979	0.9679	0.9457	**0.9397**	**0.985**	**0.985**	**0.9724**	0.7529
Rotation -50	0.982	0.9316	0.8974	**0.9475**	**0.984**	**0.9751**	**0.9376**	0.781
Rotation -270	**1**	0.9297	0.9213	**0.9857**	0.998	**0.9742**	**0.939**	0.9225
Rotation -2	0.978	0.8143	**0.9499**	**0.9603**	**0.98**	**0.9077**	0.9275	0.9415
Rotation -80	**0.98**	0.9373	0.9253	0.9815	0.978	**0.9507**	**0.9254**	0.9117
Scaling (0.5,2)	**0.971**	**0.8661**	**0.8512**	**0.8921**	0.948	0.8094	0.7467	0.8605
Scaling (0.25,4)	**0.807**	0.5373	**0.5193**	0.7981	0.788	**0.5588**	0.5137	**0.8529**
Scaling (2,0.5)	**0.996**	**0.9819**	**0.9789**	**0.9589**	0.992	0.9772	0.9716	0.9412
Scaling (0.125,8)	0.538	0.2558	0.2469	**0.8862**	**0.566**	**0.4578**	**0.3914**	0.7777
Scaling (4,0.25)	**0.996**	**0.9819**	**0.9791**	**0.9636**	0.993	0.979	0.9738	0.9428

Table 1. (*Continued*)

Scaling (8,0.125)	**0.996**	**0.9822**	**0.9791**	**0.9625**	0.993	0.9789	0.9739	0.9427
Cut 10 rows	**0.995**	0.8022	0.9814	**0.9847**	0.994	**0.9833**	**0.9928**	0.9228
Cut 10 columns	0.992	0.9872	0.9606	**0.986**	**0.993**	**0.9944**	**0.9882**	0.9277
Cut 20 rows	**0.99**	0.7908	0.9763	**0.9798**	0.989	**0.9819**	**0.99**	0.9137
Cut 20 columns	0.99	0.9796	0.9535	**0.98**	**0.992**	**0.9918**	**0.9853**	0.9262
Cut 30 rows	0.984	0.7749	0.9683	**0.9695**	**0.986**	**0.978**	**0.9865**	0.9112
Cut 30 columns	0.985	0.9717	0.9448	**0.9718**	**0.989**	**0.9887**	**0.9868**	0.9241
Translate (10,10)	**0.995**	**0.9897**	0.9821	**0.986**	0.994	0.9826	**0.9865**	0.923
Translate (10,20)	**0.992**	**0.9866**	0.9807	**0.9835**	0.991	0.9816	**0.9843**	0.9208
Translate (20,35)	**0.982**	**0.9808**	0.9694	**0.9817**	**0.989**	0.9799	**0.9788**	0.9208
Translate (35,40)	0.977	**0.9783**	0.9673	**0.9803**	**0.987**	0.976	**0.9771**	0.9127
Translate (40,40)	0.981	**0.9824**	0.9663	**0.9806**	**0.986**	0.9747	**0.9756**	0.9089
Translate (50,50)	0.981	**0.9819**	0.9649	**0.9801**	**0.982**	0.9708	**0.974**	0.9052
Shearing (0.2,0.2)	0.758	0.7283	**0.8365**	0.6277	**0.842**	**0.7485**	0.6623	0.8234
Shearing (1,0.2)	0.977	**0.9818**	0.9802	**0.9737**	**0.98**	0.9554	**0.9862**	0.8752
Shearing (0.2,1)	0.942	**0.8722**	0.7568	**0.804**	**0.957**	0.8621	**0.7273**	0.7813
Shearing (1,1)	0.969	0.9454	0.9567	**0.9548**	**0.977**	**0.9477**	**0.9725**	0.8676
Shearing (3,3)	0.708	0.4679	0.4424	0.5024	**0.865**	**0.713**	**0.6879**	**0.7342**
Shearing (5,5)	0.512	0.2443	0.191	0.2672	**0.726**	**0.4806**	**0.4722**	**0.5999**

In addition to our previous scheme; Makbol et al. scheme (RDWT-SVD) [14], the proposed IWT-SVD scheme compared with other state of the art schemes under different types of attacks. These were Lagzian et al. scheme (RDWT-SVD) [8] and Ganic et al. scheme (DWT-SVD) [5]. This comparison is shown in Table 2. The performance of the proposed scheme and Makbol's scheme surpassed the Lagzian's and Ganic's schemes. This could be seen in the Lagzian's and Ganic's schemes NC values where many values were lesser than 0.75; the negative values in the comparison table mean the extracted watermark is negative for the original watermark. The results of the proposed scheme and Makbol's scheme [14] were very close. After carefully looking at their results, we believed that the proposed scheme in this work is better than our previous scheme; Makbol's scheme [14]. The proposed scheme showed high resistance against nearly almost all non-geometrical attacks in the all sub-bands except the gamma correction attack, where only the HH sub-band in our proposed scheme showed more resistance against it. The proposed scheme also showed a good robustness against scale and translate geometrical attacks and the HH sub-band in our proposed scheme showed a good robustness against all geometrical attacks.

Table 2. Comparison of the robustness of our proposed watermarking scheme with previous schemes

Attack	IWT-SVD (this paper)				(RDWT-SVD) [14]				(DWT-SVD)[5]				(RDWT-SVD)[8]			
	LL	LH	HL	HH	LL	LH	HL	HH	LL	LH	HL	HH	LL	LH	HL	HH
Pepper&salt 0.001	0.997	0.979	0.9734	0.9625	0.994	0.9618	0.9689	0.8727	-	-	-	-	0.9860	0.6246	0.6038	0.6057
Gaussian noise 0.3	0.77	0.905	0.913	0.8904	0.6492	0.8890	0.8927	0.8102	0.865	0.207	0.271	0.277	-	-	-	-
Gauss. noise 0.005	0.959	0.9389	0.8985	0.9229	0.925	0.8617	0.8156	0.8230	-	-	-	-	0.6774	0.6388	0.6376	0.5836
Speckle noise 0.4	0.820	0.9043	0.9161	0.8872	0.704	0.8908	0.8980	0.8122	-	-	-	-	0.3281	0.6648	0.6838	0.6064
Rotation 50	0.979	0.9679	0.9457	0.9397	0.985	0.9850	0.9724	0.7529	-	-	-	-	0.5617	0.6803	-0.8282	0.0773
Rotation 20	0.977	0.9803	0.9619	0.9734	0.9805	0.9755	0.9742	0.9007	-0.353	-0.003	0.963	-0.335	-	-	-	-
JPEG comp. Q=40	0.995	0.9693	0.9659	0.8902	0.988	0.9411	0.9355	0.8653	-	-	-	-	0.9724	-0.2217	-0.4009	-0.4247
Median filter. (3x3)	0.981	0.9686	0.9697	0.9686	0.982	0.9581	0.9663	0.8840	-	-	-	-	0.7218	-0.6752	-0.7912	-0.7564
Cut 20	0.99	0.7908	0.9763	0.9798	0.989	0.9820	0.9900	0.9137	-	-	-	-	-0.8881	0.7097	0.0087	0.8292
Histogram equal.	0.986	0.9844	0.9848	0.9781	0.990	0.9865	0.9848	0.9084	0.586	0.657	0.716	0.823	0.5670	0.8138	0.8815	0.8220
JPEG Comp. Q=30	0.994	0.9597	0.9635	0.8836	0.982	0.8562	0.8753	0.8822	0.993	0.003	0.141	-0.381	-	-	-	-
Sharpening 80	0.950	0.9323	0.9355	0.9101	0.9255	0.9314	0.9244	0.9067	0.528	0.553	0.631	0.699 -	-	-	-	-
Scaling (zout=0.5,zin=2)	0.971	0.8661	0.8512	0.8921	0.949	0.6719	0.7038	0.8941	0.940	-0.258	-0.211	-0.437	-	-	-	-
Gamma correct. 0.6	0.98 7	0.9847	0.9821	0.986	0.9894	0.9927	0.9927	0.9263	-0.942	0.946	0.987	0.997	-	-	-	-

(a) (b) (c) (d)

Fig. 1. 1(a) Lena host image (512x512) 1(b) Gray watermark (256x256) 1(c)Scrambled watermark 1(d) Lena watermarked image (PSNR=43.8738)

The proposed scheme is blind, where none of the host image nor the watermark are required for the extraction process. This will help to achieve the security issue. Also, using of AT to scramble the watermark before the embedding process improved both of robustness and security issues. We tested the embedding capacity of our proposed scheme for the 512×512 Lena image after applying IWT to it and we got four sub-bands of 256×256, which represents the half size of the host image. This is due to IWT decomposition analysis. So, four Cameraman images of 256×256 were embedded into the sub-bands (each watermarks size was 256×256 to match with the produced embedding capacity by each sub-band). Table 3 summarizes the similarities, the differences, and some of the highlighted points of the proposed scheme and the other schemes [8,5,14]. From the comparison table, it is clear that the proposed scheme and Makbol et al. scheme [14] had accomplished a good security, but the proposed scheme had outperformed the Makbol's scheme due to the Arnold Ttransform. The proposed scheme's imperceptibility result was higher than Ganic et al. [5] and Lagzian et al. [8] but was not better than Makbol et al. [14]. It was 43.8738 dB for the gray Lena image 512×512 as shown in Table 3. In the watermarking world, this value is considered as a good and a high value [11]. The capacity issue has been covered nicely in our proposed scheme. It is considered as a high capacity scheme. The capacities carried out by Makbol's and Lagzian's schemes were higher than the capacity of the proposed IWT-SVD scheme and Ganic's scheme. That is due to the decomposition analysis of RDWT, IWT and DWT. Despite all of that, the proposed and Ganic schemes also considered as a high capacity schemes. Table 4 shows the extracted watermark for the proposed scheme under some attacks.

Table 3. Comparative analysis of our scheme with some of the previous schemes

Description	Existing schemes (DWT-SVD)[5]	(RDWT-SVD)[8]	(RDWT-SVD)[14]	Proposed scheme
Type of transforms	DWT+SVD	RDWT+SVD	RDWT+SVD	IWT+SVD+AT
Type of scheme	Non-blind	Non-blind	blind	blind
Embedding sub-bands	All	All	All	All
Watermark action before embedding	SVD	SVD	No action	Scrambling
Host image size	512×512	512×512	512×512	512×512
Watermark size	256×256	256×256	512×512	256×256
PSNR (Lena image)	34.42 dB	38.52 dB	54.0353 dB	43.8738 dB
Watermark image type	Gray	Gray	Gray	Gray
Scheme imperceptibility	++	+	++++	+++
Scheme security	++	++	+++	++++
Scheme capacity	++	++++	++++	++
Scheme robustness	++	++	+++	++++

5 Conclusion

A new hybrid robust image watermarking scheme based on IWT, SVD and Arnold Transform was proposed in this paper. The scheme utilized the properties of these transforms to achieve the imperceptibility, robustness and security watermarking requirements. The scheme utilized the good stability and the descending order of the singular values, that made any change on them do not affect the visual quality, the capability of IWT to preserve the perfect reconstruction because it maps integers to integers and the scrambling using Arnold Ttransform. Among all the compared techniques, the proposed IWT-SVD scheme proved its precedence since it was more robust against attacks. This high robustness was due to the properties of IWT, SVD and AT. The scheme was blind and it showed more security due to scrambling the watermark before embedding in addition to the blind issue. Furthermore, the proposed scheme showed a high imperceptibility because of the properties of IWT and SVD. A good capacity is also achieved by our proposed scheme.

One of the main challenges by SVD-based watermarking schemes is the false positive issue such as [12], [5], [10], [8] and [14]. There are solutions for this flaw [7], [13], [15], [2], [4] and [9]. The future work will be to improve this aspect of our proposed scheme.

Acknowledgment. This work is supported by Universiti Sains Malaysia (USM), Malaysia through research university (RU) grant scheme number (RU1001/PELECT/814105).

References

1. Calderbank, A., Daubechies, I., Sweldens, W., Yeo, B.L.: Wavelet transforms that map integers to integers. Appl. Comput. Harmon. Anal. 5(3), 332–369 (1998)
2. Chang, C.C., Tsai, P., Lin, C.C.: SVD-based digital image watermarking scheme. Pattern Recog. Lett. 26(10), 1577–1586 (2005)

3. Cox, I., Miller, M., Bloom, J., Fridrich, J., Kalker, T.: Digital watermarking and steganography, 2nd edn. Morgan Kaufmann Publishers Inc., San Francisco (2007)
4. Fan, M.Q., Wang, H.X., Li, S.K.: Restudy on SVD-based watermarking scheme. Appl. Math. Comput. 203(2), 926–930 (2008)
5. Ganic, E., Eskicioglu, A.M.: Robust embedding of visual watermarks using discrete wavelet transform and singular value decomposition. J. Electron. Imaging 14(4), 043004–043009 (2005)
6. Guo, Q., Liu, Z., Liu, S.: Color image encryption by using arnold and discrete fractional random transforms in IHS space. Opt. Laser Eng. 48(12), 1174–1181 (2010)
7. Gupta, A., Raval, M.: A robust and secure watermarking scheme based on singular values replacement. Sadhana 37, 425–440 (2012)
8. Lagzian, S., Soryani, M., Fathy, M.: Robust watermarking scheme based on RDWT SVD: embedding data in all sub-bands. In: International Symposium on Artificial Intelligence and Signal Processing (AISP), pp. 48–52 (2011)
9. Lai, C.C.: An improved SVD-based watermarking scheme using human visual characteristics. Opt. Commun. 284(4), 938–944 (2011)
10. Lai, C.C., Tsai, C.C.: Digital image watermarking using discrete wavelet transform and singular value decomposition. IEEE Trans. Instrum. Meas. 59(11), 3060–3063 (2010)
11. Lee, Y.P., Lee, J.C., Chen, W.K., Chang, K.C., Su, I.J., Chang, C.P.: High-payload image hiding with quality recovery using tri-way pixel-value differencing. Inf. Sci. 191, 214–225 (2012)
12. Liu, R., Tan, T.: An SVD-based watermarking scheme for protecting rightful ownership. IEEE Trans. Multimedia 4(1), 121–128 (2002)
13. Loukhaoukha, K., Chouinard, J.Y.: Hybrid watermarking algorithm based on SVD and lifting wavelet transform for ownership verification. In: Canadian Workshop on Information Theory, pp. 177–182 (2009)
14. Makbol, N.M., Khoo, B.E.: Robust blind image watermarking scheme based on redundant discrete wavelet transform and singular value decomposition. Int. J. Electron. Commun. (AEU) 67(2), 102–112 (2013)
15. Mohammad, A., Alhaj, A., Shaltaf, S.: An improved SVD-based watermarking scheme for protecting rightful ownership. Signal Process. 88(9), 2158–2180 (2008)
16. Sweldens, W.: The lifting scheme: A construction of second generation wavelets. SIAM J. Math. Anal. 29(2), 511–546 (1998)

Near-Optimal Moire Grating for Chaotic Dynamic Visual Cryptography

Rita Palivonaite[1], Algimantas Fedaravicius[2], Algiment Aleksa[1], and Minvydas Ragulskis[1]

[1] Research Group for Mathematical and Numerical Analaysis of Dynamical Systems Kaunas University of Technology, Studentu 50-222, Kaunas LT-51368, Lithuania
[2] Institute of Defence Technologies, Kaunas University of Technology, Kestucio 27, LT-44312, Lithuania

Abstract. Image hiding based on chaotic oscillations and near-optimal moire gratings is presented in this paper. The secret image is embedded into a single cover image. The encrypted secret image appears in a form of time-averaged moire fringes when the cover image is oscillated in a predefined direction, according to a chaotic law of motion. The criterion of the optimality of a moire grating is based on the absolute difference between the standard deviation of time-averaged images of near-optimal moire gratings in the background and in the zones associated to the secret image. Genetic algorithms are used for the identification of a nearoptimal set of moire gratings for image hiding applications. Numerical experiments are used to illustrate the functionality of the method.

Keywords: Visual cryptography, Time-averaged moire fringes, Chaotic oscillations.

1 Introduction

Visual cryptography is a cryptographic technique which allows visual information (pictures, text, etc.) to be encrypted in such a way that the decryption becomes a mechanical operation that does not require a computer. Visual cryptography was pioneered by Naor and Shamir (1994) [1]. They presented a visual secret sharing scheme, where an image is divided into *n* shares. Only one who has all *n* shares could reveal the secret image. Each share is printed on a separate transparency, and visual decryption is performed by overlaying all *n* shares.

Since 1994, many advances in visual cryptography have been done. Visual cryptography scheme for grey level images is proposed in [2], a necessary and sufficient conditions are given for such scheme to exist. Three methods for visual cryptography for gray level and color images is introduced in [3]. Efficient visua secret sharing scheme for color images by using pixel expansion is proposed by [4]. Probabilistic *k* out of *n* visual cryptographic schemes for grayscale and color images are presented in [5]. Visual secret sharing schemes for multiple images are demonstrated in [6–8]. Multi-secret image sharing scheme based on Boolea

H. Badioze Zaman et al. (Eds.): IVIC 2013, LNCS 8237, pp. 48–58, 2013.

operations is introduced in [9] where the proposed method not only keeps the secret images confidential but also increases the capacity of sharing multiple secrets. Algorithms of encryption based on random grids and multiple random grids are adopted for grayscale level and color images by [10, 11]. Multiple secret images are encrypted by circular random grids and presented by [12]. All these visual secret sharing schemes are based on the fact that the secret image is encrypted into two or more images (shares). The computer is used to embed the secret image into the background moire grating but the decryption of the secret image is completely visual and does not require the computer equipment [13, 14].

Single share technique is introduced in [15, 16]. This kind of encryption is based on time-averaging moire methods. The encrypted cover image has to be oscillated in order to produce time averaged moire fringes. These fringes are visualized when the encoded image is oscillated in a predefined direction, at a proper amplitude of harmonic oscillations. Moreover, different moire gratings can be used for the encryption of the secret image. Harmonic moire grating and harmonic oscillations are used in [15]. Stepped moire grating and triangular waveforms are used in [16].

It is important to note that the selection of the moire grating and type of oscillation must be pre-chosen before the secret image is encrypted into the cover image. Not every moire grating produces time-averaged fringes. It is shown by [15] that the stepped moire grating does not produce time-averaged moire fringes when the encoded image is harmonically oscillate even at appropriate amplitude and direction of oscillations. Image hiding technique based on time-average fringes produced by rectangular waveforms and near-optimal moire gratings is presented in [17]. Evolutionary algorithms are used here to find near optimal moire grating. The ability to embed a secret image into a single cover image opens a possibility

The ability to embed a secret image into a single cover image opens a possibility to exploit dynamic visual cryptography in vibration control applications [18]. But so far, only harmonic and rectangular waveforms had been considered for dynamic visual cryptography. It is clear that different type of complex nonlinear structures would perform chaotic vibrations even under harmonic loads. Thus, the main objective of this presentation is to develop a framework for chaotic dynamic visual cryptography. Moreover, it is completely unclear what types of moire gratings would be advantageous for chaotic oscillations. Therefore, the second objective of this paper is to identify a near optimal moire grating and to demonstrate its applicability for chaotic visual cryptography.

2 Optical Background

One-dimensional moire grating is considered in this paper. First of all we define requirements for the grayscale function F (x):

(i) Function F (x) is a periodic function $F(x + \lambda) = F(x)$, where λ is the pitch of grating.

(ii) All values of the grayscale function F (x) belongs to a closed interval $F(x) \in [0;1]$, where 0 corresponds to the black color; 1 – to white color; all inter mediate numerical values of the grating correspond to an appropriate grayscale level.

(iii) F (x) is an integrable function – it has only a finite number of discontinuity points in every finite interval [0;1]

(iv) The range of grayscale grating values spans through the whole grayscale interval.

We will use an m-pixels grayscale grating function Fm,n (x) in this paper. It is defined as follows:

$$F_{m,n}(x) = y_k \tag{1}$$

where x belongs to a closed interval $\left[\frac{(k-1)\lambda}{m} + j\lambda; \frac{k\lambda}{m} + j\lambda\right]$; $k = 1,2\ldots,m$; $j \in Z$ and y_k, k = 1,2. . . ,m are grayscale levels. Thus the size of a single pixel is λ/ m; m pixels fit into one period of the grayscale function.

For example, $F_{22,32}$ (x) represents a grayscale grating function which period is composed from 22 pixels and the grayscale level of every pixel can be selected from 32 different levels (all levels are in-between 0 and 1). Function $F_{22,32}$ (x) can be expanded into the Fourier series:

$$F(x) = \frac{a_0}{2} + \sum_{k=1}^{\infty}\left(a_k \cos\frac{2\pi kx}{\lambda} + b_k \sin\frac{2\pi kx}{\lambda}\right) \tag{2}$$

where a_k,$b_k \in R$; $k = 1,2,\ldots$. Parameters of the Fourier expansion of $F(x)$ read:

$a_0 = \frac{2}{m}\sum_{k=1}^{m} y_k$; $a_k = \frac{1}{k\lambda}\sum_{j=2}^{m}\left((y_{j-1} - y_j)\sin\frac{2(j-1)k\pi}{m}\right)$; and

$b_k = -\frac{1}{k\lambda}\sum_{j=2}^{m}\left((y_{j-1} - y_j)\cos\frac{2(j-1)k\pi}{m}\right)$; $k = 1,2,\ldots$.

Let us consider a situation when the described one-dimensional moire grating is oscillated in the direction of the x-axis and time-averaging optical techniques are used to register the time-averaged image. Time-averaging operator Hs describing the grayscale level of the time-averaged image is defined as [19]:

$$H_s(x \mid F; \xi_s) = \lim_{T\to\infty}\frac{1}{T}\int_0^T F(x - \xi_s(t))\,dt \tag{3}$$

where t is time; T is the exposure time; ξs (t) is a function describing dynamic deflection from the state of equilibrium; s ≥ 0 is a real parameter; x ∈ R. It is shown in [16] that if the density function Ps (x) of the time function ξs (t) is symmetric, then the time-averaged image of the moire grating oscillated according to the time function reads:

$$H_s(x \mid F; \xi_s) = \frac{a_0}{2} + \sum_{k=1}^{\infty}\left(\left(a_k \cos\frac{2\pi kx}{\lambda} + b_k \sin\frac{2\pi kx}{\lambda}\right)\right) P_s\left(\frac{2\pi ks}{\lambda}\right) \tag{4}$$

where the notation Ps is used for the Fourier transform of the density function Ps (x). In other words, the time-averaged image is the convolution of the static image (the cover image) and the point-spread function determining the oscillation of the original image [20, 21].

Let us require that ξ_σ (t) is a Gaussian normal ergodic process with zero mean and σ^2 variance. The standard deviation σ is used in the subscript instead of the parameter s in Eq. (3). Then, the density function Pσ (x) reads:

$$p_\sigma(x) = \frac{1}{\sqrt{2\pi}\sigma}\exp\left(-\frac{x^2}{2\sigma^2}\right) \tag{5}$$

and the Fourier transform of $p_\sigma(x)$ takes the form:

$$p_\sigma(\omega) = \exp\left(-\frac{1}{2}(\omega\sigma)^2\right) \tag{6}$$

Then, the time-averaged image of the moire grating oscillated by a Gaussian time function reads [22]:

$$H_s(x \mid F; \xi_\sigma) = \frac{1}{2} + \sum_{k=1}^{+\infty}\left(a_k\cos\left(\frac{2\pi kx}{\lambda}\right) + b_k\sin\left(\frac{2\pi kx}{\lambda}\right)\right)\cdot\exp\left(-\frac{1}{2}\left(\frac{2\pi k\sigma}{\lambda}\right)^2\right) \tag{7}$$

Equation 7 describes the formation of the time-averaged image as the exposure time tends to infinity and the oscillation of original moire grating is governed by the function ξ_σ (t).

The mean of a time-averaged grayscale function is defined as [17]:

$$E(H_s(x \mid F; \xi_s)) = \frac{1}{\lambda}\int_0^\lambda H_s(x \mid F; \xi_s)\,dx = \frac{a_0}{2} \tag{8}$$

Finally, the standard of a time-averaged grayscale grating function reads:

$$\sigma(H_s(x \mid F; \xi_s)) = \sqrt{\frac{1}{\lambda}\int_0^\lambda (H_s(x \mid F; \xi_s) - E(H_s(x \mid F; \xi_s)))^2\,dx} \tag{9}$$

In this paper we consider the oscillation of a grayscale grating function $F_{m,n}$ (x) according to the Gaussian time function. Therefore, the standard of such time-averaged image reads:

$$s = \sigma(H_s(x \mid F; \xi_s)) = \frac{\sqrt{2}}{2}\sqrt{\sum_{k=1}^{\infty}(a_k^2 + b_k^2)\exp\left(-\left(\frac{2\pi k\sigma}{\lambda}\right)^2\right)} \tag{10}$$

3 Perfect Grayscale Functions and Their Fitness Assessment

3.1 The Definition of a Perfect Grayscale Function

As mentioned previously, we will use an m-pixels grayscale grating function Fm,n(x). It is clear that unrestricted random selection of grayscale pixels' levels may result is such moire gratings which would be hardly applicable for image hiding applications.

Therefore we introduce four additional requirements. Grayscale functions satisfying these requirements will be entitled as perfect grayscale functions.

Requirement 1. Grayscale levels of pixels in the grating span over the whole grayscale interval [0;1]

Requirement 2. The average grayscale level in a period is equal to 0.5.

Requirement 3. The norm of the grayscale grating function must be greater than or equal to the half of the norm of the harmonic grayscale function: $\|F_{m,n}(x)\| \geq \left\|\frac{1}{2} + \frac{1}{2}\cos\left(\frac{2\pi}{\lambda}x\right)\right\| = \frac{1}{2\pi}$; where λ is the pitch of the harmonic grating; the norm is defined as follows [17]: $\|F(x)\| = \frac{1}{\lambda}\int_0^{\wedge}\left(F(x) - \frac{1}{2}\right)dx$.

Requirement 4. The main peak of the discrete Fourier amplitude spectrum at 2π/λ must be at least two times higher than all other peaks: c1 ≥ 2ck, for all k = 2,3,4,. . ., where $c_k = \sqrt{a_k^2 + b_k^2}$.

All four requirements are directly related to peculiarities of the visual decryption procedure based on the formation of time averaged moire fringes. Requirement requires using the whole range of grayscale levels in one pitch of the moire grating. Requirement 2 demands that the grayscale level of a time averaged moire fringe is equal to 0.5. Requirement 3 forbids grayscale functions with small variation around 0.5. Requirement 4 forces that the pitch of a grating be clearly visible by a naked eye.

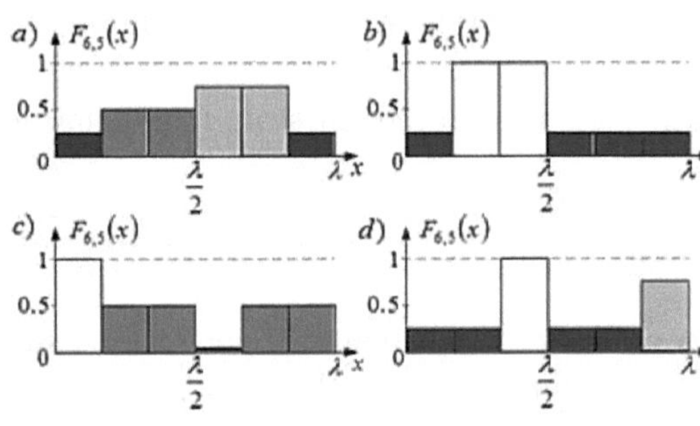

Fig. 1. Illustrations of non-perfect grayscale functions F6,5 (x): a) - the whole grayscale range is not used (Requirement 1 does not hold); b) - the average grayscale level in a pitch does not equal to 0.5 (Requirement 2 does not hold); c) - the norm of the grayscale functions is too small (Requirement 3 does not hold); d) - the secondary harmonic is too high (Requirement 4 does not hold)

It is obvious that not all grayscale functions fulfil these four requirements. Let us perform a simple computational experiment. We will find the number of perfect grayscale functions of $F_{6,5}(x)$ (6 pixels in a period; each pixel can acquire 5 discrete grayscale levels). Computational costs of full sorting algorithm are not high; the number of all possible $F_{6,5}(x)$ functions is 56 = 15625 (permutations with repetition). The percentage of $F_{6,5}(x)$ functions which meet according requirements are presented in Fig. 2. It can be noted that only about 1.728% of all grayscale grating functions $F_{6,5}(x)$ are perfect grayscale functions. We will use 22 pixels in the pitch of the grating and assume only 32 different discrete grayscale levels (instead of 256). Now, checking if a current $F_{6,5}(x)$ grayscale function is a perfect is a straightforward task (in opposite to the generation of the best perfect functions).

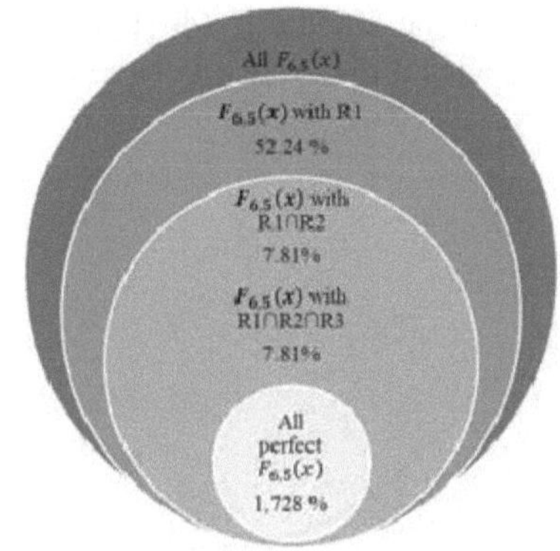

Fig. 2. Illustration of the percentage of F6,5 (x) functions which meet the requirements (R1 stands for Requirement 1, R2 stands for Requirement 2, R3 stands for Requirement 3)

3.2 The Definition of the Fitness Value for a Grayscale Function

The next step is the definition of the fitness function for every grayscale function $F_{22,32}(x)$. We did use a 22 pixels in a pitch stepped moire grating ($F_{22,2}(x)$) for the background and 20 pixels in a pitch stepped moire grating ($F_{20,2}(x)$) for the secret image in [17]. We will use the same principle now – except that grayscale functions will be $F_{22,32}(x)$ and $F_{20,32}(x)$. In fact, we need to define the fitness function only for $F_{22,32}(x)$ - the function $F_{20,32}(x)$ can be produced from $F_{22,32}(x)$ by deleting two pixels which grayscale levels are closest to 0.5.

It is well known that chaotic oscillations do not produce time-averaged moire fringes [16]. Anyway, the proposed visual cryptography scheme should be based on the differences between time-averaged images of $F_{22,32}(x)$ and $F_{20,32}(x)$ (even though time-averaged fringes would not form). The human eye does interpret a time-averaged moire fringe if its standard (Eq. 6) is less than 0.03 [18]. We fix this value for chaotic oscillations also and mark it as δ in Fig. 3.

First of all we compute the decay of the standard s of the time-averaged image formed by $F_{22,32}(x)$ at increasing standard σ of the Gaussian time function (Eq. 10). Note that Fourier expansions coefficients ak, bk for a concrete realization of $F_{22,32}(x)$ must be computed in advance.

This decay of the standard s is illustrated by a thick solid line in Fig. 3. Next we truncate $F_{22,32}(x)$ to $F_{20,32}(x)$ and compute the decay of s again (coefficients a_k, b_k must be recalculated again); it is illustrated by a thick dotted line in Figure 3.

As soon as one of the two lines intersect the level δ, we fix the optimal value of σ for the best visual reconstruction of the encoded image. Moreover, we compute the difference between standards of time-averaged-images produced by $F_{22,32}(x)$ to $F_{20,32}(x)$ (shown by a thin solid vertical line in Figure 3). This difference between standards is denoted as ϕ ($F_{22,32}(x)$) and is denoted as the fitness of a grayscale function. Note that the fitness value can be computed for any grayscale function (not necessarily the perfect function). Also, we do not know which line (the solid or the dashed line) will intersect the δ-level first; the most important is just the absolute value of the difference between the standards (ϕ ($F_{22,32}(x)$) ≥ 0). The higher is the fitness value, the better is the visual difference between the time averaged image of the background and the secret.

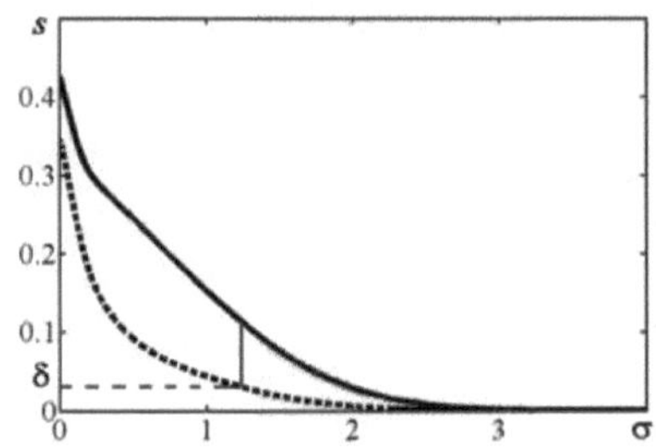

Fig. 3. Computation of the fitness value for F22,32 (x). Decay of the standards of the time-averaged images of F22,32 (x) and F22,32 (x) are illustrated in the thick solid line and the dashed solid line accordingly. The fitness value ϕ (F22,32 (x)) is shown in thin vertical solid line.

Now, the selection of the best perfect grayscale function is fully defined. Unfortunately, a brute force full sorting algorithm is simply impossible due to the limited computational resources. Naturally, the alternative task is to see near-optimal moire gratings and use evolutionary algorithms for that purpose.

4 The Structure of the Genetic Algorithm

We construct the genetic algorithm for the identification of a near-optimal perfect grayscale function in such a way that every chromosome represents one period of the function $F_{22,32}(x)$. The length of each chromosome is 22; every gene is an integer number between 0 and 31 and represents a grayscale level for the respective pixel. Since we operate with perfect moire gratings only, the modified fitness function Φ ($F_{22,32}(x)$) takes the following form:

$$\Phi\left(F_{22,32}\right)=\begin{cases}0 & \text{if } F_{22,32}\left(x\right) \text{ is not perfect}\\ \varphi\left(F_{22,32}\right) & \text{if } F_{22,32}\left(x\right) \text{ is perfect}\end{cases} \tag{11}$$

The initial population is composed of n randomly generated chromosomes wit values of genes uniformly distributed over the interval [0;31]. The fitness of each perfect chromosome is evaluated and an even number of chromosomes is selected to the mating population. A random roulette method for the selection of chromosomes is used. The chance that the chromosome will be selected to the mating population is proportional to its fitness value. All chromosomes are paired when process of mating is over. The crossover between two chromosomes is executed for all pairs in the mating population. We use one-point crossover method and the location of this point is random. The crossover coefficient κ characterizes a probability that the crossover procedure will be executed for a pair of chromosomes.

In order to avoid convergence to one local solution we use a mutation procedure. The mutation parameter μ ($0 < \mu < 1$) determines the probability for a chromosome to mutate. The quantity of chromosomes which are exposed to the mutation procedure is calculated as $nm = \text{round}(\mu \cdot n)$. Then nm chromosomes are selected randomly and one gene of each chromosome is changed by a random number $\text{mod}32\ (\tau + r)$; here τ is the gene value before the modification; r is a random integer uniformly distributed over the interval [0;31].

In general, the selection of parameters of evolutionary algorithms is an empirical process, though some common principles are described in [23, 24]. The following parameters of the evolutionary algorithm must be pre-selected: the crossover coefficient κ; the mutation parameter μ; the size of the population n and the number of generations. We will use recommendations for parameters as it was pre-selected for near optimal perfect grayscale gratings in [17]. As it is recommended we fix values of parameters of the evolutionary algorithm ($\kappa = 0.7$ and incremental increase of μ from 0.05 till 0.5), the size of the population is $n = 20000$ and the number of generations is 10. The evolutionary algorithm is executed 5 times; the best generated perfect grating is selected then.

The best result of finding near-optimal perfect grayscale grating function $F_{22,32}(x)$ is presented in Fig. 4 part (a). We will use this perfect grayscale function for image hiding based on chaotic visual cryptography.

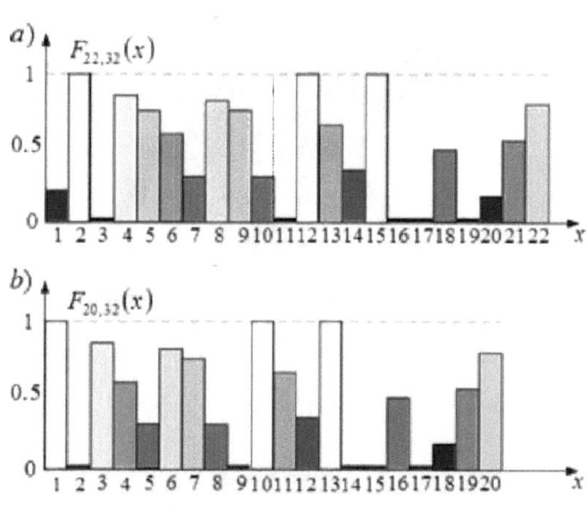

Fig. 4. Near-optimal perfect grayscale functions: a) $F_{22,32}(x)$ and b) $F_{20,32}(x)$

5 Near-Optimal Chaotic Visual Cryptography

5.1 The Structure of the Cover Image

As mentioned previously As mentioned previously, the main objective of this paper is to find a near-optimal perfect moire grating which can be adapted for image hiding based on time-averaged moire fringes produced by chaotic oscillations.

The structure of the encoded cover image is analogous to the one used in [15]. We have to select two moire gratings: the first for the secret image and the second for the background of the secret image. The pitch of the moire grating of the secret image is $\lambda 0 = 22 \cdot 0.27\text{mm} = 5.94$ mm and the pitch of the moire grating used for the background is $\lambda 1 = 20 \cdot 0.27\text{mm} = 5.40$ mm (the size of a pixel is assumed to be 0.27 mm for the monitor HP ZRW24; two different values 22 and 20 indicate the size of the pitches of moire gratings used for the secret image and for the background).

As mentioned previously, the encoding process is similar to the one presented in [15]. Stochastic phase deflection and phase regularization algorithms are used to embed the secret into the cover image.

5.2 Computational Experiments

The dichotomous image in Fig. 5 will be used as a secret image in computational experiments with chaotic visual cryptography. The encoded cover image is shown in Figure 6. A human eye cannot distinguish the secret from the background.

The secret image cannot be visualized using harmonic oscillations at any amplitude. But it can be revealed using chaotic oscillations at $\sigma = 2.2$. The pure grey moire fringes do not appear in a time-averaged image, but the difference between the background and the secret image is clearly visible (Fig. 7). Of course, the secret image is not leaked if σ is substantially different from 2.2, nor for other non-chaotic waveforms.

Fig. 5. The dichotomous secret image

Fig. 6. The encoded cover image

Fig. 7. Computational decryption of the secret image when the encoded image is oscillated chaotically by the Gaussian law at $\sigma = 2.2$

Fig. 8. Contrast enhancement of the decoded image

Though the boundaries between the secret image and the background are clearly visible in Figure 7, it would be advantageous to use contrast enhancement techniques for highlighting the leaked image [18]; the highlighted secret image is shown in Figure 8.

6 Conclusions

A computational proof for the applicability of dynamic visual cryptography for chaotic oscillations is presented in this paper. The proposed technique can be applied for optical control of chaotic oscillations. Experimental (real-world) implementation of such an optical control method is a definite object of future research.

Acknowledgments. This research was funded by a grant (No. MIP-100/2012) from the Research Council of Lithuania.

References

1. Naor, M., Shamir, A.: Visual cryptography. In: De Santis, A. (ed.) EUROCRYPT 1994. LNCS, vol. 950, pp. 1–12. Springer, Heidelberg (1995)
2. Blundo, C., De Santis, A., Naor, M.: Visual cryptography for grey level images. Inf. Process. Lett. 75(6), 255–259 (2000)

3. Hou, Y.C.: Visual cryptography for color images. Pattern Recognition 36(7), 1619–1629 (2003)
4. Shyu, S.J.: Efficient visual secret sharing scheme for color images. Pattern Recognition 39(5), 866–880 (2006)
5. Wang, D., Yi, F., Li, X.: Probabilistic visual secret sharing schemes for grey-scale images and color images. Information Sciences 181(11), 2189–2208 (2011)
6. Feng, J.B., Wu, H.C., Tsai, C.S., Chang, Y.F., Chu, Y.P.: Visual secret sharing for multiple secrets. Pattern Recognition 41(12), 3572–3581 (2008)
7. Shyu, S.J., Huang, S.Y., Lee, Y.K., Wang, R.Z., Chen, K.: Sharing multiple secrets in visual cryptography. Pattern Recognition 40(12), 3633–3651 (2007)
8. Lee, K.H., Chiu, P.L.: A high contrast and capacity efficient visual cryptography scheme for the encryption of multiple secret images. Optics Communications 284(12), 2730–2741 (2011)
9. Chen, T.H., Wu, C.S.: Efficient multi-secret image sharing based on Boolean operations. Signal Processing 91(1), 90–97 (2011)
10. Shyu, S.J.: Image encryption by random grids. Pattern Recognition 40(3), 1014–1031 (2007)
11. Shyu, S.J.: Image encryption by multiple random grids. Pattern Recognition 42(7), 1582–1596 (2009)
12. Chen, T.H., Li, K.C.: Multi-image encryption by circular random grids. Information Sciences 189, 255–265 (2012)
13. Wang, R.Z., Lan, Y.C., Lee, Y.K., Huang, S.Y., Shyu, S.J., Chia, T.L.: Incrementing visual cryptography using random grids. Optics Communications 283(21), 4242–4249 (2010)
14. Chen, Y.C., Tsai, D.S., Horng, G.: A new authentication based cheating prevention scheme in Naor–Shamir's visual cryptography. Journal of Visual Communication and Image Representation 23(8), 1225–1233 (2012)
15. Ragulskis, M., Aleksa, A.: Image hiding based on time-averaging moire. Optics Communications 282(14), 2752–2759 (2009)
16. Ragulskis, M., Aleksa, A., Navickas, Z.: Image hiding based on time-averaged fringes produced by non-harmonic oscillations. Journal of Optics A: Pure and Applied Optics 11(12), 125411 (2009)
17. Sakyte, E., Palivonaite, R., Aleksa, A., Ragulskis, M.: Image hiding based on near-optimal moire gratings. Optics Communications 284(16-17), 3954–3964 (2011)
18. Petrauskiene, V., Aleksa, A., Fedaravicius, A., Ragulskis, M.: Dynamic visual cryptography for optical control of vibration generation equipment. Optics and Lasers in Engineering 50(6), 869–876 (2012)
19. Ragulskis, M., Navickas, Z.: Hash function construction based on time averaged moire. Discrete and Continuous Dynamical Systems - Series B 8(4), 1007–1020 (2007)
20. Fujji, H., Asakura, T.: Effect of the point spread function on the average contrast of image speckle patterns. Optics Communications 21, 80–84 (1977)
21. Braat, J.J.M., van Haver, S., Janssen, A.J.E.M., Dirksen, P.: Assessment of optical systems by means of point-spread functions. Progress in Optics 51(6), 349–468 (2008)
22. Ragulskis, M., Sanjuan, M.A., Saunoriene, L.: Applicability of time-average moire techniques for chaotic oscillations. Physical Review E 79(3), 036208 (2007)
23. Holland, J.H.: Adaptation in Natural and Artificial Systems: An Introductory Analysis with Application to Biology, Control, and Artificial Intelligence, 2nd edn. The MIT Press, Cambridge (1992)
24. Whitley, D.: A genetic algorithm tutorial. Statistics Computing 4(2), 65–85 (1994)

A Robust Subset-ICP Method for Point Set Registration

Junfen Chen, Bahari Belaton, and Zheng Pan

School of Computer Sciences, Universiti Sains Malaysia, Penang, 11800, Malaysia
{Chenjunfenusm,panzheng}@gmail.com,
bahari@webmail.cs.usm.my

Abstract. Iterative Closest Point (ICP) is a popular point set registration method often used for rigid registration problems. Because of all points in ICP-based method are processed at each iteration to find their correspondences, the method's performance is bounded by this constraint. This paper introduces an alternative ICP-based method by considering only subset of points whose boundaries are determined by the context of the inputs. These subsets can be used to sufficiently derive spatial mapping of point's correspondences between the source and target set even if points have been missing or modified slightly in the target set. A brief description of this method is followed by a comparative analysis of its performance against two ICP-based methods, followed by some experiments on its subset's sensitivity and robustness against noise.

Keywords: Iterative Closest Point (ICP), Correspondences, Transformation, Registration error, Subset, Expectation Maximization (EM).

1 Introduction

This paper describes an ICP-based method for point set registration by employing partial points instead of the whole set to find point correspondences. First, we examine ICP-based methods currently available in the literature to identify improvements and what weaknesses exist with such ICP-based variants. Next, the method of subset ICP that produces spatial mapping of point's correspondences based only on the partial points is described. By using subset of points to set the boundaries for point registration, we achieve the following merits, (1) the point correspondence computation is reduced due to small mapping space with the order of complexity of $O(TN_1N_2)$ for each iteration, where $T=\frac{N_x}{N_1}=\frac{N_y}{N_2}$, and $N_1 \le N_x$, $N_2 \le N_y$ (N_1, N_2 is the cardinal of subsets X and Y respectively), (2) structural (shape) information is implicitly applied and (3) local minimum trap is avoided because the localization of closest points in the subset provide better estimate than those found in whole set. Such subset can be used to match ordered homologous points between the source and target set even if the points in the target have gone through slight modification or missing in some parts. We demonstrate the subset ICP algorithm, its Mathlab implementation, and briefly analyze its performance using sample data from [15] and [17].

H. Badioze Zaman et al. (Eds.): IVIC 2013, LNCS 8237, pp. 59–69, 2013.

The algorithm explained in the remainder of this paper was based on our previous work presented in [16]. This paper expanded that work in three areas, first it explains the methods clearly with example, second it provides comparative study against ICP's variants and CPD method, and finally it analyzes subset ICP method effectiveness in term of subset's cardinality sensitivity and it's robustness against noise.

2 Background

Point set registration is an important research topic in computer vision and image processing because of its applications in pattern recognition, shape reconstruction, object tracking and edge detection among others. With only the coordinate information of points, point set registration [1] is defined as to assign correspondences between two sets of points and to recover an optimal spatial mapping that matches one point set to the other so they are as close as possible to each other. Given two finite point sets $X=\{x_1,x_2,\cdots,x_{N_x}\}$ and $Y=\{y_1,y_2,\cdots,y_{N_y}\}$, where $x_i, y_i \in R^n$, N_x, N_y are the cardinalities of set X and Y respectively. The point set registration problem is to find a spatial transformation F, let $\sum \| x-F(y) \|^2 = \varepsilon, \varepsilon \geq 0$. Usually, point set Y is consecutively matched to set X by iterative mappings. The cardinality of set is defined as the number of points in set.

Iterative Closest Point (ICP) proposed in 1992 by Besl & McKay [2] and Chen & Medioni [3] is one of the most popular point set registration methods. It repeats two key steps until convergence is achieved: (1) to search for the correspondences based on the nearest distance criteria; (2) to determine a transformation based on current correspondence sets. However, it is an expensive computational algorithm because the correspondences need to be computed in each of iteration. Furthermore, the convergence is heavily depending on the initialization and it tends to converge to the local optimum.

Some variants of ICP intend to select the most representative points to form data set to reduce the computation complexity. Ezra et. al [4] pointed out that the number of iterations of ICP has a polynomial relationship to the number of input points under the root mean squared (RMS) distance and one-sided Hausdorff distance. A coarse-to-fine multi-resolution combined with the neighbor search technique [5] was introduced into ICP. A hierarchical selection point scheme was added into Picky ICP algorithm[6] that is an extension of ICP algorithm. Only every $2^t th$ point is selected to form "control point set" to perform Picky ICP, where $t+1$ is the number of hierarchical levels. However, local search instead of an exhaustive (global) one is performed to obtain the correspondence pairs, which may overlook some coherent information. Especially, it is difficult to tradeoff between the time and the accuracy requirements.

Other techniques to overcome the limitations of ICP include an evolutionary computation that was used to optimize the initial parameters of ICP. This method mainly motivated by the global optimization nature of evolutionary approaches [7]. Expectation Maximization (EM) algorithm combined ICP named as EM-ICP [8, 9] is used to handle noise and large data clouds. Multiple layer forward-feed neural network [10] is an alternative rigid point set registration method when the correspondences are estimated well. With Lie algebra viewpoint, a generalized ICP was proposed to deal with affine registration [11]. However, this method can neither reduce the computation cost nor avoid the risk of local minima. Rusinkiewicz & Levoy [12] presented an exhaustive and comparative summary for the state-of-the-art ICP variants.

Probabilistic methods such as Gaussian Mixture Model [1, 13], Robust Point Matching (RPM) [14, 15] are developed to solve point set registration problem. The probabilistic methods usually perform better than the conventional ICP, especially, in the presence of noise and outliers. However, the accurate registration results are at the cost of complex procedure and high computation complexity.

3 ICP-Based Registration Methods

In this section, subset ICP method is introduced first, where an example is used to demonstrate clearly its registration process. Next, two ICP-based methods respectively referred to as ICP-1 and ICP-2 are briefly explained. Their description is relevant for comparing the differences in the approach of finding correspondences and later in comparing the results in Section 3.1.

3.1 The Subset-ICP

Subset ICP algorithm starts by partitioning the source set X and the target set Y into multiple disjoints subsets, resulting in k pairs of subsets. The number of subset is determined by the size of the inputs but it is bounded by the minimum of cardinality of set X and Y. The algorithm works by iterating through the number of subset k and in each iteration, the algorithm performs a standard ICP method on each point in subset pair. Then, a spatial mapping in the form of rotation R and translation T are derived from current iteration, before they are applied to the target set Y. This process is repeated until a convergence or terminal condition is met. The registration procedure of subset-ICP is summarized in Fig 1.

```
Inputs : point set X with cardinality m and Y with cardinality n
Initialize R0 ← I, T0 ← 0, i ← 1
X is partitioned into k subsets, X = X1 + X2 + ... + Xk
Y is partitioned into k subsets, Y = Y1 + Y2 + ... + Yk, 1 < k < min(m,n)
While i < k and MSE(X ,Y) > threshold
    For all points in subset Xi and Yi
       Calculate the correspondences based on Euclidean distance in subset Xi and Yi
       Compute and Update transformation Ri and Ti
       Apply Ri and Ti to set Y and all its subsets Y1, Y2, ..., Yk
       Accumulate rotation R and translation T
    End ICP-iteration
    Calculate MSE for X and Y
End subset-iteration
Outputs : rotation R and translation T that matches all points in set Y
```

Fig. 1. Pseudo-code of subset-ICP algorithm

Fig. 2 illustrates the working of subset ICP for a simple example where only translation is needed to register point set X and Y. Assuming we have an input set $X = \{1, 2, 3, 4\}$ and $Y = \{5, 6, 7, 8\}$ with equal cardinality i.e. $m = n = 4$. In this case, both X and Y is uniformly partitioned into two subsets, $k = 2$ such as $X_1=\{1, 2\}$, $X_2=\{3, 4\}$ and $Y_1=\{5, 6\}$,$Y_2=\{7, 8\}$. Note that an arbitrary choice of partition can be chosen (as we later show in subsection 3.2), however we should avoided the two worse cases, that is when the subset contains a single point or when there is only a single subset. At first iteration, i.e. $k = 1$ the closest points of $X_1 = \{1, 2\}$ to Y_1 are the points $\{5, 5\}$ respectively hence, the neighbor set is $N_X(Y) = \{5\}$. In this example, the translation T is derived from the mean values of the set, thus given their values are 1.5 and 5, T = 1.5-5 = -3.5. Applying translation to set Y we updated the values for subsets $Y_1 = \{1.5, 2.5\}$ and $Y_2 = \{3.5, 4.5\}$. Since the MSE of X and Y is not met, the same process is repeated for subset pair $X_2 = \{3, 4\}$ and $Y_2 = \{3.5, 4.5\}$. Now the neighbor set is $N_X(Y) = \{3.5, 4.5\}$, with the mean values of 3.5 and 4, thus the translation is $T = 3.5\text{-}4 = -0.5$.Updating Y with T we get $Y_1 = \{1, 2\}$ and $Y_2 = \{3, 4\}$, which are exactly matching the points in set X. This also denotes that convergence has been met and thus ending the procedure.

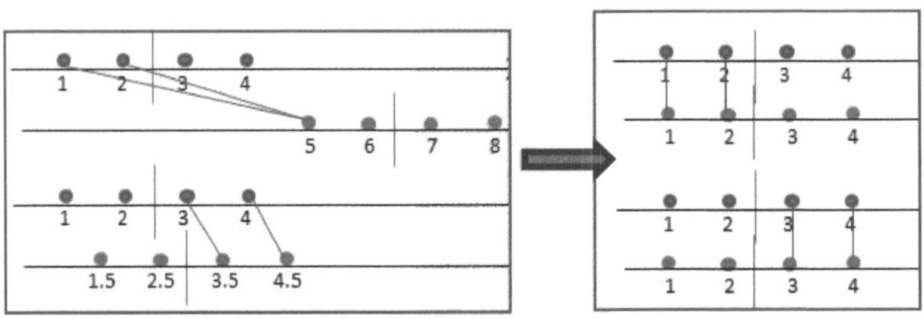

Fig. 2. The registration procedure of subset-ICP on the given data

3.2 Two ICP-Based Algorithms

ICP-1: ICP-1 is the original ICP algorithm from [2]. Two point sets are given which describe the shape of an object. For each point of one set, search for its closest points in another set to form the correspondence set. Based on the first set and its correspondences set, the rotation matrix and translation vector are computed using optimization combined with statistical technique, such as PCA. The correspondences and the transformation are updated iteratively until the stop conditions are satisfied.

ICP-2: ICP-2 is an improved version of ICP as presented in [6]. ICP-2 improves the solution set in ICP-1 by removing redundant points that satisfied the nearest point's condition. It only kept one point with the shortest distance [6]. For instance, if a point b from the source set is the closest point to four other points in template set, says a1, a2, a3, and a4, point a2 is chosen as the winner if it has the shortest distance to point b, i.e $d(\mathrm{a}2,\mathrm{b}) = \min\{d(\mathrm{a}1,\mathrm{b}), d(\mathrm{a}2,\mathrm{b}), d(\mathrm{a}3,\mathrm{b}), d(\mathrm{a}4,\mathrm{b})\}$.

The main difference between ICP-1 and ICP-2 is whether the mapping relation between the template set and the correspondences set is bijection (also known as one-to-one mapping) or not.

4 Experiments

In this section, experiments are carried out on 2D data to analyze subset ICP's performance with respect to its accuracy, robustness and computational time. Elephant shape is taken from part B of CE-Shape-1 [17], whereas the fish and blessing data are taken from [15]. In our experiments, when there are no outliers, the cardinality of the target point set is equal to the cardinality of the template point set. The performance measure is the global mean square error (MSE) on all points instead of the correspondence pairs. We also qualitatively show the results in visual form to complement the quantitative analysis.

4.1 Comparing ICP-Based Point Registration Methods

Fig. 3 shows the registration results of ICP-1, ICP-2 and subset-ICP when tested against three cases of fish data as described below:

- Case 1: the source data (in blue pentagram marks) is synthesized by a slight linear transformation
- Case 2: the source data is produced by the larger rigid transformation.
- Case 3: Gaussian noises added into the source data to deteriorate its shape

The template shape is presented as red circle where its points are kept unchanged in the experiments.

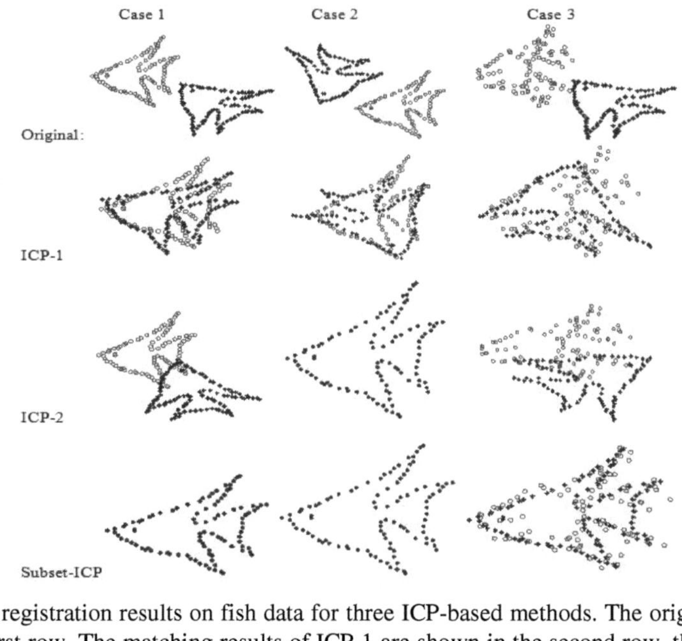

Fig. 3. The registration results on fish data for three ICP-based methods. The original data sets are in the first row. The matching results of ICP-1 are shown in the second row, those of ICP-2 are in the third row, and the last row is the subset-ICP registration results. Note that the transformed source data is still depicted by the blue pentagram marks

Table 1. The Mean Square Errors and execution time of three methods on fish data

	MSE (cm)			Time (seconds)		
	ICP-1	ICP-2	Subset-ICP	ICP-1	ICP-2	Subset-ICP
Case 1	0.0854	0.0224	**4.545e-016**	0.0587	0.0690	**0.0121**
Case 2	0.3691	5.022e-016	**4.459e-016**	0.0294	0.0811	**0.0057**
Case 3	0.3484	0.5188	**0.044**	0.3927	**0.3048**	0.3574

The results in Fig.3 indicate that the subset ICP algorithm achieves significantly better matching accuracy than ICP-1 and ICP-2 algorithms, while it is also superior in term of MSE and execution time (Table 1) over the two algorithms. The higher MSE of the ICP-1 and ICP-2 algorithms are due to them falling into local minima. Subset ICP is also robust against Gaussian noise (Case 3) compare to ICP-1 and ICP-2. In Case 3, ICP-2 took less execution time than the other two algorithms but as shown in Fig.3 the result is only partially matched.

Further tests of the subset ICP algorithm were performed and compared against Coherent Point Drift (CPD) method – an efficient point set registration for both rigid and non-rigid points based on Gaussian Mixture Model [1]. Registration results from the two data sets are shown in Fig.4.

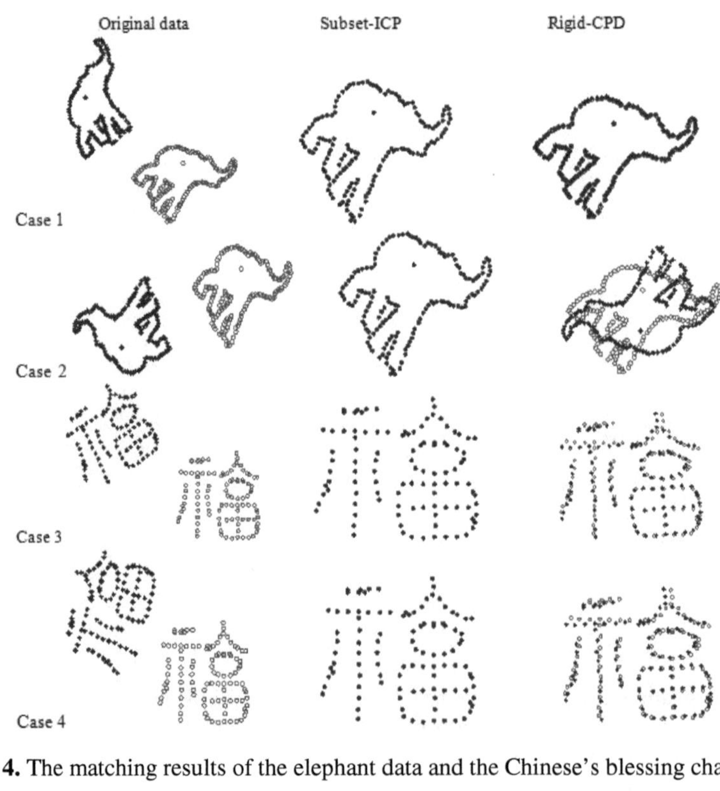

Fig. 4. The matching results of the elephant data and the Chinese's blessing character

For Chinese's blessing character, subset ICP algorithm achieves approximately the same level of accuracy as the rigid-CPD algorithm. However, for Case 2 of Elephant data, where its template has been rotated and translated slightly more than for Case 1 transformation, our method is able to register the template and source set properly.

4.2 Sensitivity Analysis of the Subset's Partition

The subset ICP method relies heavily on subset for registering points in its input set. Thus, it is interesting to study how sensitive is the subset's cardinality in influencing the algorithm's performance. Fig. 5 and Fig. 6 respectively show the MSE and execution time of the algorithm when tested with Elephant data where the cardinality of the subset is varied from 1 to 451.

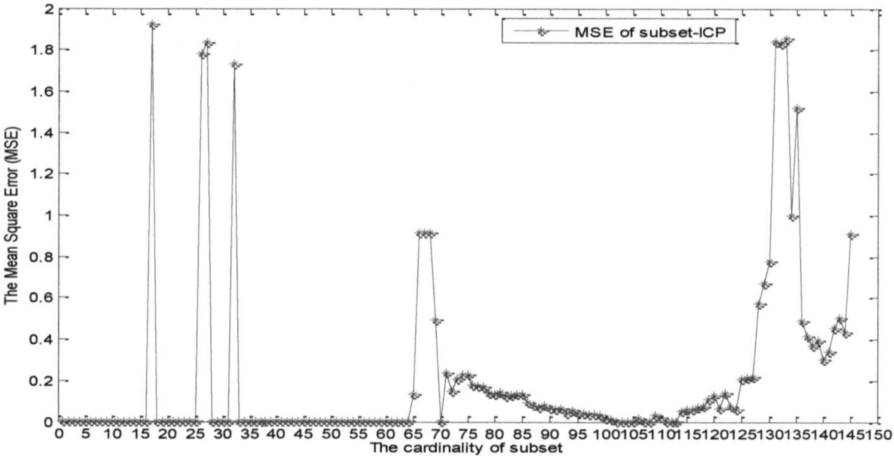

Fig. 5. The MSE of subset-ICP in the elephant data

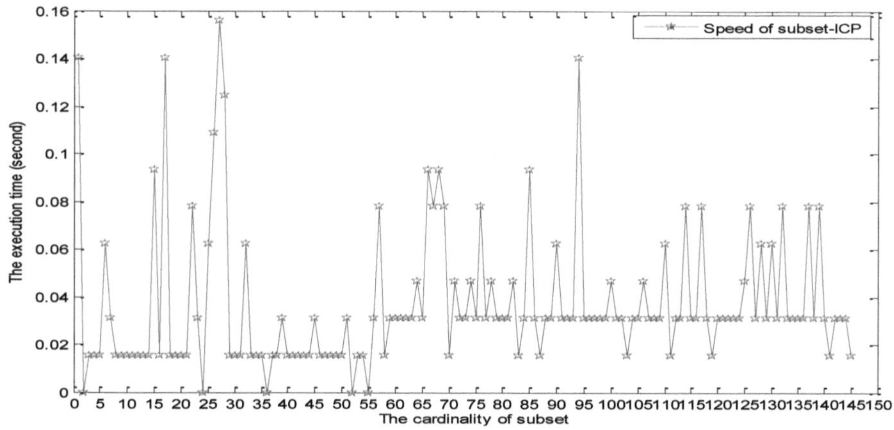

Fig. 6. The execution time of subset-ICP in the elephant data

The results provide the following general observations, first low MSE is recorded when the cardinality of the subset is small as illustrated in the initial graph's plot in Fig.5. In contrast, the opposite trend is exhibited when the size of subset is increased. A few exceptions to this pattern were also evidenced in the plot. For instance, for subset's cardinality 16 and 17 (and also for some other cardinal's values), there is a "spike" in the MSE plot thus nullifying the general pattern observed earlier. Fig.6 provides a confirmation on this observation for Case 2 with cardinal 17, where the two set were incorrectly matched. One possible answer to this flaw is due to the use of absolute orientation algorithm to find the least square distance between corresponding points. That is a larger error distance will have a large effect on the total score, this happen when the source point set is farther away from the template point set. Secondly, the graph plot in Fig.6 does not show any significant pattern between the cardinality of subset and their effect on execution time. This is expected because the convergence rate of the algorithm is predominantly determined by the quality of the selected points rather than by their quantity. Thus we may conclude that the algorithm is robust against the cardinality of subset, if the source point set is closer to the template point set, otherwise it is susceptible and hence sensitive to the cardinality of subset.

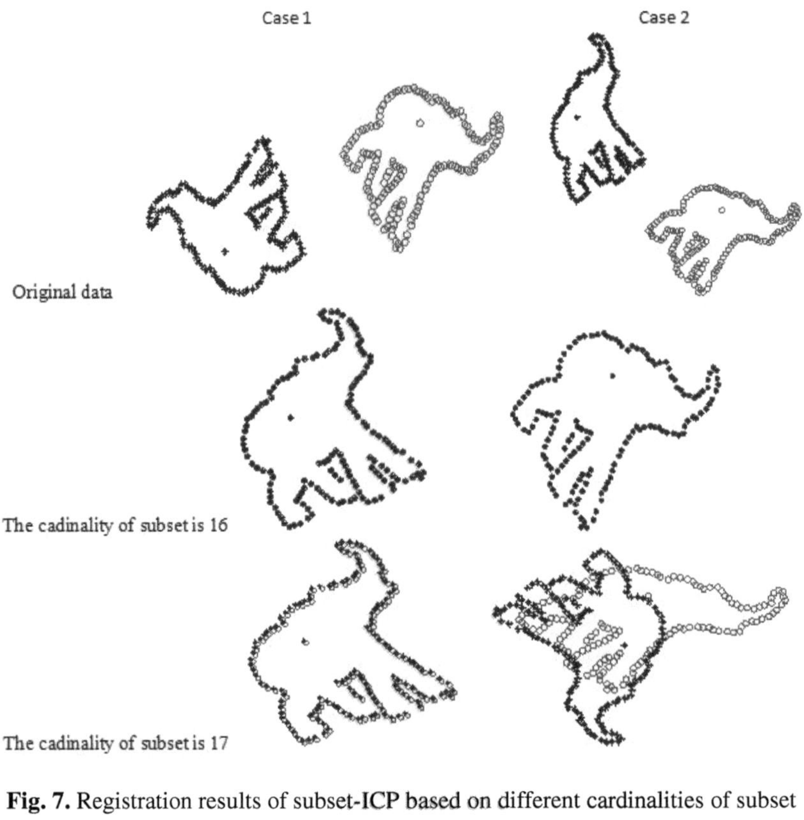

Fig. 7. Registration results of subset-ICP based on different cardinalities of subset

4.3 Noise Robustness

Robustness test evaluates the subset ICP's ability to cope against outlier points (often referred to as noise). In this test, different proportions of Gaussian noise were introduced into the fish's template data. In the experiments we fixed the subset's cardinal, and recorded the registration errors as shown in Table 2. The logarithmic scaling on *y*-axis allows the behaviour for small MSEs (of case b), to be seen in Fig.8.

Table 2. The MSE on fish data with different ratio Gaussian noise

r	0.02	0.05	0.1	0.15	0.2	0.3	0.4	0.5
a	3.85e-16	5.50e-16	5.37e-16	4.81e-16	6.86e-16	0.023	0.023	5.65e-16
b	6.50e-16	7.76e-16	6.59e-16	5.85e-16	9.62e-16	0.022	4.21e-16	7.60e-16

In Table 2, *r* is the noise proportion to the number of points on the fish's template data set. The letter *a* denotes, the noise data were appended at the back of the last point of the template data set. While letter *b* indicates the noise data were inserted in front of the first point of the template data set. Based on Table 2, we can see that the registration error is kept quite low with the increasing of Gaussian noise proportion.

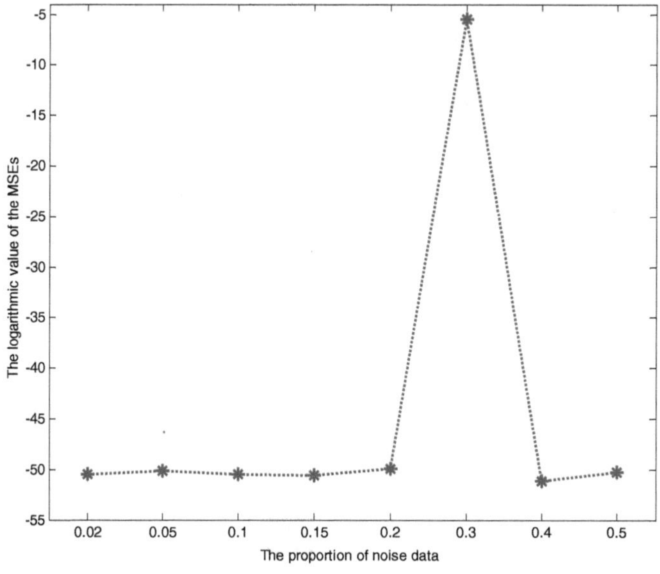

Fig. 8. MSE (in cm) of subset-ICP method as Gaussian noise proportion is varied (for case *b*)

In order to validate the influence of the outliers to the registration performance, a statistical t-test was performed. The *p* values of the error and execution time are shown in Table 3. Here the significant level is set to 0.05. If the *p* value is less than 0.05, this indicates the influence is statistically significant, otherwise, the influence is not statistically significant.

Table 3. The *p* values of t-test

Group	*P* value (for error)	*P* value (for speed)
A	5.92×10^{-11}	0.3026
B	3.3×10^{-6}	0.2647
C	7.14×10^{-7}	0.2683

As summarized in Table 3, the outliers affect significantly the registration error but the computation complexity is not significantly affected. The experimental results verify that for the sample data set used, subset IP method is robust against noise.

5 Conclusion

In this paper, a subset-based ICP method is proposed to handle rigid point set registration, which is an effective method for the larger rotation and less even without overlapping of two point sets. The merits of the proposed method stem from partial points instead of total points to find the correspondences. The registration performances are determined by the cardinality of subset when two point sets are fixed. In other words, the way of partition the entire data set influence heavily the success of the subset-ICP. Experiments are performed to indicate that subset-ICP method is an effective and robust registration method. More works will be done to prove and to explore how we can acquire an optimal partitioning scheme to generate subsets.

Acknowledgment. This work is supported by research project of Universiti Sains Malaysia (Grant number: 1001/PKOMP/817055), and the Postgraduate Research Grant Scheme of Universiti Sains Malaysia (Grant number: 1001/PKOMP/846050).

References

[1] Myronenko, A., Song, X.: Point Set Registration: Coherent Point Drift. IEEE Transactions on Pattern Analysis and Machine Intelligence 32(12), 2262–2275 (2010)

[2] Besl, P.J., McKay, N.D.: A Method for Registration of 3-D Shapes. IEEE Transactions on Pattern Analysis and Machine Intelligence 14(2), 239–256 (1992)

[3] Chen, Y., Medioni, G.: Object Modeling by Registration of Multiple Range Images. Image and Vision Computing 10(3), 145–155 (1992)

[4] Ezra, E., Sharir, M., Efrat, A.: On the performance of the ICP algorithm. Computational Geometry 41, 77–93 (2008)

[5] Jost, T., Hügli, H.: A Multi-Resolution ICP with Heuristic Closest Point Search for Fast and Robust 3D Registration of Range Images. In: Proceedings of the 4th International Conference on 3-D Digital Imaging and Modeling, pp. 427–433 (2003)

[6] Zinßer, T., Schmidt, J., Niemann, H.: A Refined ICP Algorithm for Robust 3-D Correspondence Estimation. In: Proceedings of the IEEE International Conference on Image Processing, pp. 695–698 (2003)

[7] Santamaría, J., Cordón, O., Damas, S.: A comparative study of state-of-the-art evolutionary image registration methods for 3D Modeling. Computer Vision and Image Understanding 115(9), 1340–1354 (2011)

[8] Granger, S., Pennec, X.: Multi-scale EM-ICP: A Fast and Robust Approach for Surface Registration. In: Heyden, A., Sparr, G., Nielsen, M., Johansen, P. (eds.) ECCV 2002, Part IV. LNCS, vol. 2353, pp. 418–432. Springer, Heidelberg (2002)

[9] Liu, Y.: Automatic registration of overlapping 3D point clouds using closest points. Image and Vision Computing 24(7), 762–781 (2006)

[10] Chen, J., Liao, I.Y., Belaton, B., Zaman, M.: A Neural Network-Based Registration Method for 3D Rigid Face Image. World Wide Web (2013), doi:10.1007/s11280-013-0213-9

[11] Du, S., Zheng, N., Ying, S., Liu, J.: Affine iterative closest point algorithm for point set registration. Pattern Recognition Letters 31, 791–799 (2010)

[12] Rusinkiewicz, S., Levoy, M.: Efficient variants of the ICP Algorithm. In: Proceedings of the 3th International Conference on 3-D Digital Imaging and Modeling, pp. 1–8 (2001)

[13] Rasoulian, A., Rohling, R., Abolmaesumi, P.: Group-Wise Registration of Point Sets for Statistical Shape Models. IEEE Transactions on Medical Imaging 31(11), 2025–2034 (2012)

[14] Gold, S., Rangarajan, A., Lu, C.-P., Mjolsness, E.: New Algorithms for 2D and 3D Point Matching: Pose Estimation and Correspondence. Pattern Recognition 31, 957–964 (1997)

[15] Chui, H., Rangarajan, A.: A new point matching algorithm for non-rigid registration. Computer Vision and Image Understanding 89, 114–141 (2003)

[16] Chen, J., Belaton, B.: An Improved Iterative Closest Point Algorithm for Rigid Point Registration. In: Proceedings of the International Conference on Machine Learning and Cybernetics (ICMLC), TianJin, pp. 481–485 (2013)

[17] Latecki, L.J., Lakämper, R., Eckhardt, U.: Shape descriptors for non rigid shapes with a single closed contour. In: Proceedings of the IEEE Conference on Computer Vision and Pattern Recognition, pp. 424–429 (2000)

Integrated Communication for Truck Monitoring in Solid Waste Collection Systems

Maher Arebey[1,*], M.A. Hannan[1], and Hassan Basri[2]

[1] Dept. of Electrical, Electronic & Systems Engineering
[2] Dept. of Civil and Structural Engineering
Universiti Kebangsaan Malaysia UKM,
43600 Bangi Selangor, Malaysia
maher@ukm.my

Abstract. This paper relates to a method of integration of RFID and communication technologies for solid waste bin and truck monitoring system. RFID, GPS, GPRS and Digital map along side camera technologies have been integrated and developed the brain and a truck intelligent monitoring system. A proposed kind of integrated theoretical framework using image processing approaches, hardware architecture and interface algorithm has been introduced between the technologies for the successful implementation of the proposed system. With this technique, bin and truck database have been developed such a way that the information on the bin and truck ID, date and time of waste collection, bin status, amount of waste and bin and truck GPS coordinates etc. are compiled and stored for monitoring and management activities. The outdoor field test demonstrates the performance of the developed system in solid waste collection. Important info was identified, collected, and automatically recorded upon the number of the bins.

Keywords: solid waste monitoring and management, rfid, gps, gprs, digital map, database.

1 Introduction

A collection of solid waste is the key element of any modern solid waste management system. Efficient collection operation means the optimum way of utilizing the trucks and bins during the collection. Automatically tracking the location of the truck and the bin is the key element to improve solid waste collection. The development of a system or prototype to automate the collection operation is based on monitoring the trucks and the bins during the collection operation [1] and [2].

Telematics are defined as the combination of modern information technologies and telecommunication. Typically, these systems rely on Global Positioning System (GPS), Global System for Mobile Communications (GSM), General packet radio service (GPRS) tracking and navigation. Waste management logistics is a fairly recent application of telematics. These are important tools for supporting SWM

* Corresponding author.

H. Badioze Zaman et al. (Eds.): IVIC 2013, LNCS 8237, pp. 70–80, 2013.

modeling systems that use computer-based technologies [3], [4] and [5]. It utilizes advanced communication technology and integrates with mapping technology to develop an intelligent system for SWM. The idea of developing such system is to create a visual presentation of the trucks and share information among residents and the SWM system operators, thereby making GPS and mapping a decision support tool that can realize the following benefits: increase the efficiency of solid waste collection, optimize routing, bin collection and transport of waste, maximize the collection area, and decrease fuel usage [6], [7], and [8].

Several researches have been conducted for integrating these technologies with mapping technology in SWM monitoring and tracking, the application has been applied in waste collection system to maximize the solid waste collection and management efficiency. Alam Flora is a waste collection company in Malaysia that utilizes GPS and GPRS to monitor and track its trucks during waste collection, in order to improve efficiency in the collection and reduce fuel consumption. Each truck is installed with a GPS device which is activated when the truck's engine starts thus initializing contact between the truck and the control centre. The GPS data is sent to the control centre via GPRS connection; the position of the truck is visualized on Google Map to provide the operator real-time monitoring and tracking of all trucks during waste collection [9].

Waste collection service requires three fundamental elements, the trucks, the bins, and the workers. To deploy those elements efficiently, a clear understanding of the main components of waste collection is necessary:

This research is focused on automating the collection operation, so all required data for efficient truck and bin monitoring system are collected and recorded from the truck and bin. Then, this data is sent and saved in the control centre automatically. The following is an example of the collection data collected and saved in the control centre.

1. Total number of collection bins per collection trip
2. Location of the truck all the time during the collection
3. A time when each bin was collected
4. Duration of bin collection
5. Bin level before and after collection

All data are collected and sent to the control centre in real time, allowing the operator in the control centre to react immediately in case of stop or break down. In a large collection area, the number of the truck and bin is optimized to enhance the collection operation.

This research integrates different advanced technologies to develop an intelligent solid waste bin and truck monitoring and management system to monitor the trucks and check the status of the bin during the collection operation. The data are collected from the truck and the bin, then sent via wireless communication to the central database where it is stored. Then, this information is used to update the digital map.

2 Systematic Design

Due to the harsh nature of waste management, trucks and bins face harsh environmental conditions, such as temperature, moisture, dirt, rain, and so on. Therefore, it was decided that the system components of truck and bin monitoring system must meet these challenges to monitor the waste collection efficiently. Furthermore, the selection of the RFID, GPRS modem, GPS receiver, and camera components must be closely guided to choose the best properties of hardware system that fit the monitoring system. This section describes the hardware components used in the developed system:

2.1 Radio Frequency Identification (RFID)

RFID is a technology that is designed to enable readers to capture data on tags and transmit it to a computer system without any physical connection at a range of radio frequency. An RFID system consists of three components: an antenna, transponders i.e. tag and transceiver i.e. reader. The antenna uses radio frequency waves to transmit a signal that activates the transponder. When activated, the tag transmits data back to the antenna [10]. Low-frequency RFID systems i.e. 30 KHz to 500 KHz have short transmission ranges, generally less than six feet. High-frequency RFID systems i.e. 850 MHz to 950 MHz and 2.4 GHz to 2.5 GHz offer longer transmission ranges, more than 90 feet [11]. The auto-ID technologies have been used to reduce the amount of time and labor needed to input data manually and to improve data accuracy unlike conventional inventory systems.

2.2 Global Positioning System (GPS)

GPS is a satellite-based navigation system formed by satellites placed into the orbit to record locations on the earth. The satellites periodically emit radio signals to GPS receivers to calculate and display accurate location, speed, and time, to compute two-dimensional or three-dimensional position information into a useful display format [12]. Today, GPS is extensively being used in a motor vehicle for providing emergency roadside assistance, determining the vehicle's position on an electronic map displaying and helping drivers to keep track of their position. The developed system used GPS to track the position of the truck and bin location [13].

2.3 GSM/GPRS Technology

GSM is an open, digital cellular technology used for transmitting mobile voice and data services with the transmission of SMS. GPRS is a wireless data service developed from the existing GSM system and can be associated with the Internet. It provides a link between mobile users and data network as well as high-speed wireless IP. GPRS can take up a number of wireless channels to transfer data at a rate up to 160 Kbps. GPRS network has a wide coverage and can truly achieve real-time sending and receiving [14].

2.4 Digital Map

Digital map integrates software and hardware for storage, collecting, managing, mapping, analyzing of data and showing all forms of geographical information in a computer-based system. It helps to analyze data visually and look patterns, trends, and relationships that might not be visible in tabular or written form [15]. Spatial data and associated attributes in the same coordinate system can be layered together for mapping and analysis. Digital map is different from other information systems, because it integrates common database operations such as query and statistical analysis with the advantages of visual and geographic analysis through maps [16].

3 System Communication

The communication between the trucks and the control centre is server and client communication. Before any data can be transmitted, a reliable connection must be obtained and acknowledged. Before any further explanation on how the system communicates and how the information is stored in the database. First, the concept of the communication between the server and the client is discussed. In the client-server, the client submits the request to the server. The server returns a response to the client. A response contains a completion status information on the request, and may contain any content requested by the client in its message body. Each TCP/IP-based networking application is assigned a specific port to monitor for incoming requests. Client programs that need to communicate with the server is connected to the server's assigned port. According to a standard protocol, the two systems exchange information once connected.

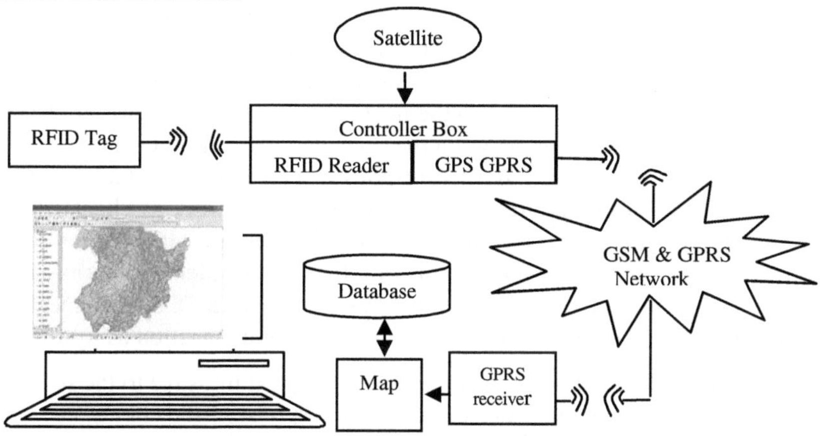

Fig. 1. Architecture of solid waste monitoring and management system

To achieve all system design requirements of sending and receiving the information between the truck and the control centre, a web server is used to store and to retrieve all data from the database. The web server is responsible for the entire communication process. The system is divided into two parts, the control centre and the controller box in the truck. The control centre is responsible for viewing the available information on the web server, whereas the controller box in the truck is responsible for sending and receiving the related information to the web server. Fig. 2 shows how the components of the system interact with each other, as well as the type of connection that should be selected carefully so as to make the connection reliable and consistent.

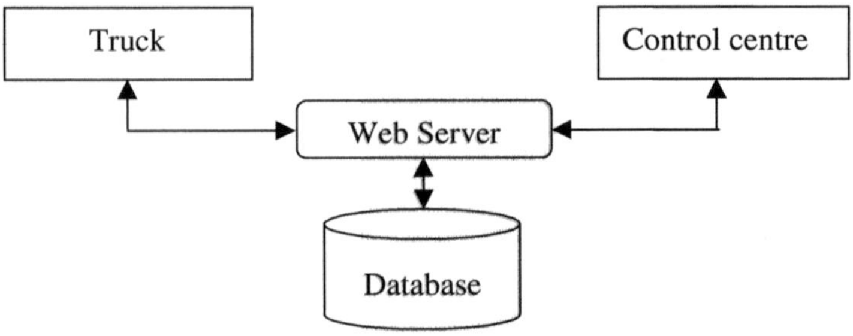

Fig. 2. Interaction of the system components

As explained earlier, the GPRS modem, with its GPRS feature, is seen as a special device, embedding and controlling the TCP/IP protocol stack inside itself. The protocol used to transfer data and information between the clients and the server is called the Transmission Control Protocol (TCP). TCP is a transport layer protocol in the internet protocol (TCP/IP protocol) suite. TCP and IP protocols are the core protocols of TCP/IP (hence, its name, TCP/IP).

All TCP based applications stand on the application layer ([17]. The communication between the clients and the server is achieved using HTTP connection protocol. HTTP connections are used with all the GPRS modems, without extra configuration. The server-side is implemented using HTTP. This is the chosen solution for the communication between the truck and the control centre.

HTTP functions are a request-response protocol in the client-server communication. In HTTP, the truck and the control centre work as clients. The client submits an HTTP request message to the server. The server, which stores content or provides resources, such as a list of drivers or a list of bin collected returns a response message to the client. The communication takes place over a TCP/IP connection. The protocol is basically stateless, a transaction consisting of connection as follows.

1. Request: The sending of the client with a request message to the server;
2. Response: The sending to the server of a response to the client;
3. Close: The closing of the connection by either both parties.

To build a direct communication, the truck gets a public IP to connect the server. The IP address, which is assigned from the Internet Service Provider (ISP) when connecting to the mobile network, is a dynamic IP. Therefore, the target is set to a fixed ID and sends the obtained IP to the server as registration. The client tries to connect to the GPRS. If it fails due to GPRS unavailability, then it logs the data in the non-volatile memory and waits for a certain fixed time period. Then, it tries to connect to the GPRS again. After a successful connection, the GPS data with truck ID number are sent to the server as a string. In this way, the truck communicates with the control centre by sending all the related information about the collection operation.

The data include the ID of the truck, latitude, longitude, coordinated universal time (UTC), date, speed, and number of satellite. The identification number (ID) number is used to authenticate the connection.

4 Digital Map Calibration

The received GPS data from the truck and bins need to be visualized on a map to show the location of the truck and collected bin during the collection operation. To visualize the position correctly on the map, raster images are needed, such as joint photographic experts group (JPEG) or portable network graphics (PNG). Some calibration is required as well. Screen capture from the Google map was used in this research. The images were used as backgrounds to develop the system.

Raster images have formats such as JPEG, BMP, and PNG. The structure of the information is stored as pixels. In the image format, the pixels are represented by (X,Y). In the top left corner is marked as (0,0) pixel, the value of X pixel increases from left to right direction, which is in the positive X axis and the value of Y pixel increases from top to bottom direction, which is in the negative Y axis.

When the controller box is activated, the GPS receiver starts to send the GPS data to the server side. The GPS receiver can relay the GPS messages which contain the position data to the computer using the NMEA 0183 protocol. GPS messages are data streams composed of short sentences in ASCII form. Every short sentence includes three parts, the frame header, the frame trailer, and the intra frame. The frame header determines the structure and content of the data frame. The frame header of each sentence is different, such as, "$GPGGA", "$GPGSA", "$GPGSV", and "$GPRMC". Usually, the location data, such as latitude, longitude, and time is acquired from "$GPRMC". In the test, the results obtained from the GPS are as follows, whereas Table 1 shows the GPS data format:

$GPRMC,044417.000,A,0255.7682,N,10147.2360,E,14.32,115.34,060111,,,A*50;

Table 1. GPS message format

	GPS Received data
$GPRMC	Recommended Minimum Specific GPS
044417	UTC_TIME,HHMMSS
0255.7682	Latitude
N	North latitude
10147.2360	Longitude
E	East Longitude

Coordinate transformation of the map means transferring from longitude, latitude coordinate system to X,Y coordinate system. This purpose is achieved in several ways. The method we chose is to calculate the coordinate of centre point and the rate of change in both latitude and longitude.

To represent the GPS coordinates latitude and longitude on the digital map, the relationship between the (X,Y) pixels and GPS data latitude and longitude are defined. As we know in the N/E hemisphere, the longitude increases in the positive X direction (left to right) and the latitude increases in the positive Y direction (bottom to top). Based on this information, if the value of Y is kept equal to 0, the latitude along the X axis does not increase. If the value of X kept to 0, the longitude along X axis does not increase as well.

Before the mapping begins, the latitude and longitude received on the server side are in the format of degrees and minutes are converted to decimal to represent the latitude and longitude precisely on the digital map.

0255.7682N=2.92947
10147.2360E=101.78726

To start mapping the truck position on the digital map, the degree per pixels is calculated. Converting from longitude, latitude coordinates to X, Y coordinate has four steps:

1. Define the latitude and longitude of the X, Y coordinates of the centre point in the digital map.
2. Set the latitude and longitude relative to digital map centre point.
3. Set the X,Y relative to the centre point.
4. The coordinates of digital map top left corner can then be used as the offset to get the actual X,Y points.

5 Field Testing

The field test will determine the benefit of using the RFID system, GPS, GPRS, and camera in monitoring the truck and identifying the bin during the collection operation. Some other issues related to the monitoring are investigated, such as the interval time to update the map and the size of the data that should be transferred from the truck to the server.

The developed system was tested under actual collection conditions in the Universiti Kebangsan Malaysia (UKM). The present field study used a rear-loader truck. The truck is used for 10 hours a day to collect and transport the waste to the landfill. A total of 160 bins distributed around the UKM campus must be collected three times a week. Three bins were attached with RFID tags and implemented to test the reading functionality of the RFID system and to determine the size of the images being sent to the control centre.

The developed system was tested in a series of experiments. The test was done in the following sequence:

i. Selecting the appropriate time interval to receive and to update the map during the collection operation
ii. Measuring the received data during the collection operation and compare it to the plan capacity of the GPRS used

5.1 Testing the Received Data versus the Interval Update Time

The developed prototype for the intelligent bin monitoring and tracking system used different interval time values to evaluate the time interval of sending the updated location of the truck during the collection operation. The test was performed during the collection operation when the truck demonstrated different speeds. When no bin collection was taking place, the speed of the truck was based on its location and the existing traffic. During bin collection, the speed of the truck is zero. The test was carried out according to the normal daily collection schedule, while several stops for collection were considered.

- **Data Transfer**

Real-time data transmission is the most challenging step in system development. During the early stages of system development, the quality of the image provides sufficient information about the bin level and describes the situation of the surrounding area as well as the GPRS bandwidth. The protocol that is responsible for sending and receiving data from the control centre is also considered. HTTP protocol was implemented in the system, which enhanced reliability every time information such as RFID data, truck location, and images of the bin are sent to the control centre.

- **Testing Procedure**

The tests were carried out at different speeds during the collection. All collected data during the collection operation are presented in Kbytes/hour. The size of the received data at the control centre is recorded along with the test duration. The tests were also carried out at different distances and at different image sizes to determine the influence of the received data and of the image sizes on system performance. Table 2 shows the time duration of the tests during the collection operation. The time interval provides updates on the status of the truck on the map and on the amount of the received data in the control centre during each test. As can be seen from the table, the update on the truck location based on the time interval clearly has affected the result. The image sizes also affected the performance in terms of transfer time.

Table 2. Data transfer measurement result with different interval time

Time (test duration) (Minute)	Interval time (Seconds)	Data transferred (Kbytes)	Data per minute (Kbytes/hour)	Average (Kbytes/hour)
45.34	5	1847	40.53	
15.30	5	623	40.9	
39.43	5	1577	39.7	40.05
12.35	5	502	39.9	
21.49	5	856	39.24	
46.40	10	925	19.82	
16.20	10	311	19.04	
41.8	10	717	17.43	18.95
43.0	10	794	18.47	
11.43	10	234	19.97	
36.49	40	239	6.49	
32.55	40	230	6.98	
43.12	40	264	6.11	6.35
16.56	40	97	5.72	
30	40	194	6.47	

Since waste collection is a daily operation, the time interval that updates the truck location has to be set to cope with the amount of data during truck and bin monitoring and for the tracking system to achieve the prototype development purpose. The interval time between 5 and 15 seems reasonable with the slow movement of the truck during waste collection.

The images of the collected bin were tested based on size and on the time taken to send the images to the control centre. The sizes of the images ranged from 30 to 200 KB. The images of the collected bin were tested at different sizes, as detailed in Table 3. The average transmission time was then calculated.

Table 3. The time measurement of different size of collected images

Image Size (Kbytes)	Transfer time (Seconds)					Average (Seconds)
30	25	22	21	20	26	22.8
50	55	40	50	43	33	44.2
100	90	92	88	92	91	90.6
150	111	109	112	116	110	111.6
200	155	167	154	144	151	154.2

Based on the GPRS connectivity, the recommended maximum size of the bin image to be sent to the control centre for further analysis is 100 KB. Images with sizes of 100 KB and more usually take more than 1 minute. With 3G availability, image size will not be an issue. The image resolution is really important in this research to capture sufficient information from the image to detect the correct level of the bin. Image resolution at 640 x 480 has been chosen for this project where the image size ranged from 25 to 50 KB with different bin levels.

The Celcom Company provides the service of GPRS and charges per data being transferred. The data plan at 1.5 GB costs around RM 50 per month. The truck collecting and transporting the waste to the dump station for 10 hours a day was considered. A total of 160 bins were distributed around the UKM campus, which are collected three times per week. The average data transferred for the time interval of 5 seconds was around 40.05 KB/min. The total transferred data per month was around 704 MB. Two images, exhibiting before and after collection, are taken for each bin, as explained earlier. The maximum size of the image is 50 KB, and both images of the bin are sent to the control centre. The total image size of each bin at 100 KB is sent to the control centre during the collection operation. With the bin collected three times a week, a total of 300 KB is expected to be sent weekly to the control centre. The total size of 187.5 MB for 160 bins is sent monthly to the control centre. The total amount of data that must be transferred monthly during the collection operation is around 891.5 MB which is acceptable based on the 1.5 GB data planning for the GPRS system.

The result of the test showed that the developed system of the intelligent solid waste bin and truck monitoring and the management based on RFID technology are fully operational during the collection operation. The driver was immediately identified by the system and the scheduled bin to be collected was successfully uploaded to the truck. All the bins were collected and represented on the map in the control centre. The movement of the truck during the collection operation was successfully recorded during the whole collection operation. Fig .3 shows the received data on the map during the collection. The red line shows the route of the truck being monitored and the location of the bins. The operator can monitor the truck during the collection operation at all time. The collection of the bins also monitored with digital map, the operator can monitor the time of the bins collection and also monitor the schedule of the collection.

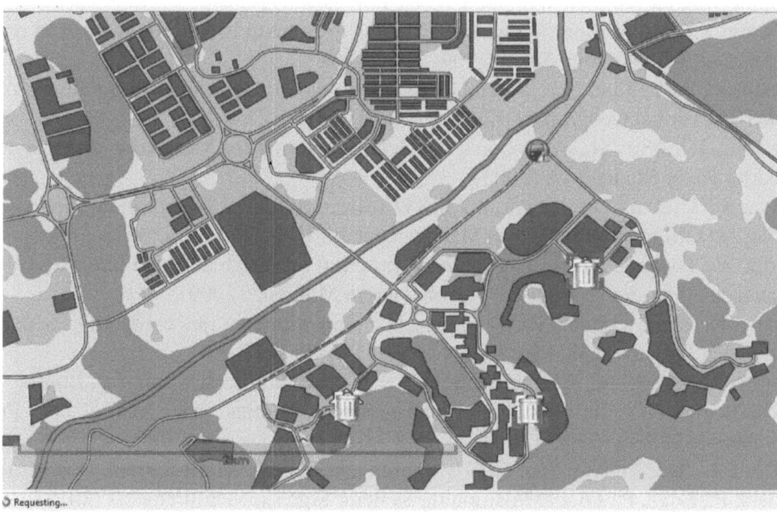

Fig. 3. The monitored truck and the distributed bin on the digital map

6 Conclusion

The outdoor field test shows the performance of the developed system in solid waste collection. Information was determined, collected, and automatically noted upon the number of the bins. The motion of the truck throughout the variety operation was also automatically noted and the position of the truck was currently in the repository and on the electronic map as well. Overall, the performance of the device was fantastic in terms of truck and bin checking and tracking. Container stage recognition throughout the variety was precisely carried out by the entire proposed image handling techniques. The overall feedback obtained from the waste management sellers and managers was really positive. The developed system was really efficient and can potentially save a substantial level of work hours on the handbook taking of the variety operation.

References

1. Arebey, M., et al.: Integrated technologies for solid waste bin monitoring system. Environmental Monitoring and Assessment 177(1-4), 399–408 (2011)
2. Hannan, M.A., et al.: Radio Frequency Identification (RFID) and communication technologies for solid waste bin and truck monitoring system. Waste Management 31(12), 2406–2413 (2011)
3. Blaakman, E.J., et al.: Integration of Remote Sensing in ECOSYS. Lelystad, The Netherlands, RIZA, Report No.011, p. 95 (1995)
4. Gong, P., Pu, R., Chen, J.: Mapping ecological land systems and classification uncertainty from digital elevation and forest cover data using neural networks. Photogrammetric Engineering and Remote Sensing 62(11), 1249–1260 (1996)
5. Cigdem, G.: Monitoring of a water basin area in istanbul using remote sensing data. Water Science and Technology 38(11), 209–216 (1998)
6. Atkinson, P.M., Tate, N.J.: Spatial Scale Problems and Geostatistical Solutions: A Review. The Professional Geographer 52(4), 607–623 (2000)
7. Le Vine, D., Wirt, M., Whitebook, B.: Grid Computing for Massively Multiplayer Games. Charles River Media, MA (2003)
8. Tavares, G., et al.: Optimisation of MSW collection routes for minimum fuel consumption using 3D GIS modelling. Waste Management 29(3), 1176–1185 (2009)
9. Flora, A.: Towards a clean environment, proposal on sustainable and integrated solid waste management system for universiti Kebangsaan Malaysia (2009)
10. Myny, K., et al.: Organic RFID transponder chip with data rate compatible with electronic product coding. Organic Electronics 11(7), 1176–1179 (2010)
11. Sarac, A., Absi, N., Dauzère-Pérès, S.: A literature review on the impact of RFID technologies on supply chain management. International Journal of Production Economics 128(1), 77–95 (2010)
12. Farrell, J.: Aided navigation: GPS with high rate sensors. McGraw-Hill, New York (2008)
13. Misra, P., Enge, P.: Global Positioning System: Signals, Measurements (2011)
14. Halonen, T., Romero, J., Melero, J.: GSM, GPRS and EDGE performance: evolution towards 3G/UMTS. Wiley (2004)
15. Greenfeld, J.S.: Matching GPS observations to locations on a digital map
16. Dawson, J.F., Thompson, E.J., Cousens, J.A.: Digital map system. Google Patents (1989)
17. Reverter, F., Gasulla, M., Pallas-Areny, R.: Capacitive level sensing for solid-waste collection. In: Proceedings of IEEE Sensors (2003)

A Geometrical Approach for Age-Invariant Face Recognition

Amal Seralkhatem Osman Ali[2], Vijanth Sagayan a/l Asirvadam[1], Aamir Saeed Malik[1], and Azrina Aziz[1]

[1] Centre of Intelligent Signals and Imaging Research
Department of Electric and Electronic Engineering
[2] Universiti Teknologi PETRONAS
31750 Tronoh, Perak, Malaysia
Amal61@gmail.com,
{vijanth_sagayan,aamir_saeed,azrina.aziz}@petronas.com.my

Abstract. Human faces undergo considerable amounts of variations with aging. While face recognition systems have proven to be sensitive to factors such as illumination and pose, their sensitivity to facial aging effects is yet to be studied. The FRVT (Face Recognition Vendor Test) report estimated a decrease in performance by approximately 5% for each year of age difference. Therefore, the development of age-invariant capability remains an important issue for robust face recognition. This research study proposed a geometrical model based on multiple triangular features for the purpose of handling the challenge of face age variations that affect the process of face recognition. The system is aimed to serve in real time applications where the test images are usually taken in random scales that may not be of the same scale as the probe image, along with orientation, lighting ,illumination, and pose variations. Multiple mathematical equations were developed and used in the process of forming distinct subject clusters. These clusters hold the results of applying the developed mathematical models over the FGNET face aging database. The system was able to achieve a maximum classification accuracy of above 99% when the system was tested over the entire FGNET database.

Keywords: frvt, age-invariant, geometrical model, triangular features, similarity proportion ratios, clustering, fgnet.

1 Introduction

Face recognition is a type of automated biometric identification method that recognizes individuals based on their facial features as basic elements of distinction. The research on face recognition has been dynamically going on in the recent years because face recognition is involved in many fields and disciplines such as access control, surveillance and security, criminal identification and digital library.

Automatic face detection and recognition have been a challenging problem in the field of computer vision for many years. Though humans accomplish the task in an

H. Badioze Zaman et al. (Eds.): IVIC 2013, LNCS 8237, pp. 81–96, 2013.

easy manner, the underlying computations within the human visual system are of remarkable complexity. The apparently insignificant task of finding and recognizing faces is the result of millions of years of regression and we are far from fully understanding how the brain performs it. Moreover, the capability to find faces visually in a scene and recognize them is critical for humans in their everyday events. Accordingly, the automation of this task would be beneficial for several applications including security, surveillance, gaze-based control, affective computing, speech recognition assistance, video compression and animation. Though, to date, no comprehensive solution has been anticipated that allows the automatic recognition of faces in real (un-affected) images [1]. In last decade, chief progresses occurred in the field of face recognition, with numerous systems capable of maintaining recognition rates superior to 90%. However real-world scenarios remain a challenge, because face acquisition procedure can experience a wide range of variations. Throughout a crime investigation, the community security agencies regularly need to match a probe image with registered database images, which may have major difference of facial features due to age deviations. Several efforts have been made to tackle this problem. Ling et al. [2] studied the aging effect on face recognition, O'Toole et al. [3] proposed a standard facial caricaturing algorithm using 3D face model, Ramanathan et al. [4] proposed a Bayesian age-difference classifier to be employed in applications such as passport renewal. These proposed techniques try to solve the problem by simulating the aging models; however, they are still far from hands-on use.

Unlike these complicated modelling methods, our system aims to perform a fast and robust aging face recognition based on a combination of geometrical and mathematical modelling. In this research study our goal is to develop a geometrical model that is age invariant. In our work we have explored the approach of using a mathematically developed geometrical model for maintaining the degree of similarity between six triangular features to address the problem of face recognition under age variations. The system to be developed is intended to operate in real time environment such as surveillance systems.

The remainder of this paper is organized as follows: Section 2 and section 3 represent the feature selection methods and the classifiers used during the experiments part. Section 4 introduces the proposed face recognition geometrical model where we define the mathematical relationships between our proposed triangular features, and our tendency in constructing the systems' facial features vectors. The results and discussion of experiments are presented in Section 5 and section 6 correspondingly. This is followed by conclusions in Section 7.

2 Feature Selection Methods

2.1 Correlation Feature Selection

The Correlation Feature Selection (CFS) [5] measure evaluates subsets of features on the basis of the following hypothesis: "Good feature subsets contain features highly correlated with the classification, yet uncorrelated to each other". The following equation gives the merit of a feature subset S consisting of k features:

$$\mathrm{Merit}_{Sk} = \frac{k\overline{r_{cf}}}{\sqrt{k + k(k-1)\overline{r_{ff}}}} \tag{1}$$

Here, $\overline{r_{cf}}$ is the average value of all feature-classification correlations, and $\overline{r_{ff}}$ is the average value of all feature-feature correlations. The CFS criterion is defined as follows:

$$CFS = \max_{S_k}\left[\frac{r_{cf1} + r_{cf2} + \cdots + r_{cfk}}{\sqrt{k + 2(r_{f1f2} + \cdots + r_{fifj} + \cdots + r_{fkf1}}}\right] \tag{2}$$

The r_{cfi} and r_{fifj} variables are referred to as correlations. Let xi be the set membership indicator function for feature fi; then the above equation can be rewritten as an optimization problem:

$$\mathrm{CFS} = \max_{x\in\{0,1\}^n}\left[\frac{(\sum_{i=1}^{n} a_i x_i)^2}{\sum_{i=1}^{n} x_i + \sum_{i\neq j} 2b_{ij}x_i x_j}\right] \tag{3}$$

2.2 Relief Attribute Evaluation Method

Relief-F is a feature selection strategy that chooses instances randomly, and changed the weights of the feature relevance based on the nearest neighbor. By its merits, Relief-F is one of the most successful strategies in feature selection. The nearest neighbor from the same class is a hit H, and from different class a miss, M(C) of class C. At the end W[f] is divided by m to get the average evaluation in [-1,1].

$$\mathrm{W[f]= W[f]\text{-}diff(f, E1, H)} + \sum_{C\neq \mathrm{class}(E_1)} P(C) \times \mathrm{diff}(f, E_1, M(C)) \tag{4}$$

The $\mathrm{diff}(f, E_1, E_2)$ function calculates the grade in which the values of feature f are different in examples E1 and E2.

2.3 Symmetrical Uncertainty Feature Selection Method

The algorithms find weights of discrete attributes basing on their correlation with continuous class attribute. The algorithm uses an information theoretic measure called symmetric uncertainty in order to evaluate the worth of constructed solutions. There are a number of benefits of this measure i.e. it is symmetric in nature therefore SU(i,j) is same as that of SU(j,i) hence it reduces the number of comparisons required, where i and j represent two independent variables, it is not influenced by multi-valued attributes as that is in the case of information gain, and its values are normalized. Following is the equation for symmetric uncertainty.

$$\mathrm{SU(X,Y)} = 2 \times \left[IG \times \frac{X\backslash Y}{H(X)+H(Y)}\right] \tag{5}$$

Where IG(X|Y) is the information gain of feature X, that is an independent attribute and Y is the class attribute. H(X) is the entropy of feature X and H(Y) is the entropy of feature Y. Information gain has a desired property, i.e. it is symmetric. The amount of Information given by a feature Y about another feature X is effectively the same as that of the information given of feature X and the feature Y.

3 Classification Algorithms

3.1 Naïve Bays Classifier

A Naïve Bays classifier [8] is a simple probabilistic classifier based on applying Bays rule. Bays theorem provides a means of calculating the posterior probability, P (b|x), from P (b), P(x), and P (x|b). Naïve Bays classifier assumes that the effect of the value of a predictor (x) on a particular class (c) is independent of the values of other predictors. This hypothesis is called class conditional independence.

$$P(x|b)= (P(x|b)P(b))/P(x) \tag{6}$$

$$P(b|x)= P(x_1|b)x\ P(x_2|b)x.....x\ P(x_n|b)Xp(b) \tag{7}$$

- *P*(*b*|*x*) is the posterior probability of class (target) given predictor (attribute).
- *P*(*b*) is the prior probability of class.
- *P*(*x*|*b*) is the likelihood which is the probability of predictor given class.
- *P(x)* is the prior probability of predictor.

3.2 Support Vector Machine (SVM)

In machine learning, support vector machines (SVMs, also support vector networks) are supervised learning models with associated learning algorithms that analyze data and recognize patterns, used for classification and regression analysis. The basic SVM takes a set of input data and predicts, for each given input, which of two possible classes forms the output, making it a non-probabilistic binary linear classifier. Given a set of training examples, each marked as belonging to one of two categories, an SVM training algorithm builds a model that assigns new examples into one category or the other. An SVM model is a representation of the examples as points in space, mapped so that the examples of the separate categories are divided by a clear gap that is as wide as possible. New examples are then mapped into that same space and predicted to belong to a category based on which side of the gap they fall on.

In addition to performing linear classification, SVMs can efficiently perform non-linear classification using what is called the kernel trick, implicitly mapping their inputs into high-dimensional feature spaces.

3.3 K-Means Clustering

In data mining, k-means clustering is a method of cluster analysis which aims to partition n observations into k clusters in which each observation belongs to the cluster with the nearest mean. This results in a partitioning of the data space into Voronoi cells.

The problem is computationally difficult (NP-hard); however, there are efficient heuristic algorithms that are commonly employed and converge quickly to a local optimum. These are usually similar to the expectation-maximization algorithm for mixtures of Gaussian distributions via an iterative refinement approach employed by both algorithms. Additionally, they both use cluster centers to model the data; however, k-means clustering tends to find clusters of comparable spatial extent, while the expectation-maximization mechanism allows clusters to have different shapes.

3.4 K-Nearest Neighbors Classifier

In pattern recognition, the k-nearest neighbor algorithm (k-NN) is a non-parametric method for classifying objects based on closest training examples in the feature space. k-NN is a type of instance-based learning, or lazy learning where the function is only approximated locally and all computation is deferred until classification. The k-nearest neighbor algorithm is amongst the simplest of all machine learning algorithms: an object is classified by a majority vote of its neighbors, with the object being assigned to the class most common amongst its k nearest neighbors (k is a positive integer, typically small). If k = 1, then the object is simply assigned to the class of its nearest neighbor.

The same method can be used for regression, by simply assigning the property value for the object to be the average of the values of its k nearest neighbors. It can be useful to weight the contributions of the neighbors, so that the nearer neighbors contribute more to the average than the more distant ones. (A common weighting scheme is to give each neighbor a weight of 1/d, where d is the distance to the neighbor. This scheme is a generalization of linear interpolation.)

The neighbors are taken from a set of objects for which the correct classification (or, in the case of regression, the value of the property) is known. This can be thought of as the training set for the algorithm, though no explicit training step is required. The k-nearest neighbor algorithm is sensitive to the local structure of the data. Nearest neighbor rules in effect implicitly compute the decision boundary. It is also possible to compute the decision boundary explicitly, and to do so efficiently, so that the computational complexity is a function of the boundary complexity.

4 Proposed Geometrical Model

The proposed system decomposed multiple stages. Face detection is the first stage at the beginning of each face recognition system. In our system a commercial version of the conventional Viola and Jones face detector [12] is employed to detect and crop the face area that contains the main features (Eyes, Mouth, Nose, and chine). Viola and Jones detector is robust and effective in real time applications. After detecting the face area twelve facial features points are to be localized in order to extract six different triangular areas around the main facial features. Following the parameters of the triangular features i.e. (areas and perimeters) are calculated. Then those parameters are passed to a number of equations to create features vectors for the sample image. In the following those stages are illustrated in details.

4.1 Facial Features Points Localization and Triangular Features Detection

Craniofacial anthropometry which is the science that involves measurement of the skull and face, citrine landmarks and measurements are known to identify human facial characters and growth pattern. In our study we consider twelve of these land marks mostly the ones that form the circumscription of the main facial features. Those facial feature points are normally localized using Active Appearance Model (AAM) [13] which designates 64 distinctive facial points. In our model the AAM is reduced to 12 facial features points using the algorithm proposed in [13]. Craniofacial anthropometry refers to those facial features points with scientific notation to discriminate between them as follows:

- **En (endocanthion)**: the inner corner of the eye fissure where the eyelids meet. In our model these points are given the numbers 6 and 8.
- **G (glabella)**: the most prominent point in the median sagittal plane between the supraorbital. In our model these point is given the number 9.
- **ridges.ex (exocanthion)**: the outer corner of the eye fissure where the eyelids meet. In our model these points are given the numbers 5 and 7.
- **Gn (gnathion)**: in the midline, the lowest point on the lower border of the chin.

In our model this point is given the number 2.

Following six triangles are formed between the facial points and they are given the notation triangle$_1$ through triangle6, as illustrated in Fig. (2.a) through (2.f)

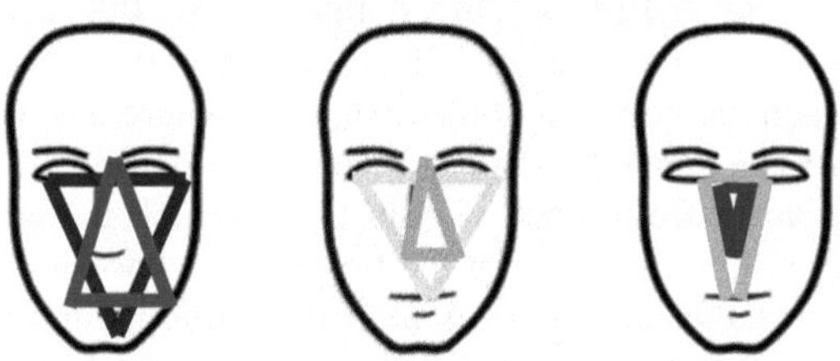

Fig. 1. (a) Triangle$_1$ and Triangle$_5$ *(dotted*

Fig. 1. (b) Triangle$_3$ and Triangle$_4$

Fig. 1. (c) Triangle$_2$ and Triangle$_6$

4.2 Calculating the Triangular Features Parameters

After localizing the facial features points, the system will gain knowledge of the triangular vertices coordinates. After that Euclidean distances between each triangle coordinates will be calculated, which will enable the system to calculate perimeters and areas of each triangular feature. Those parameters (areas and perimeters are given the notation *A* and *P* for areas and perimeters successively followed by a subscript representing the triangle designation. For example (*Ai, Pi*) represent the area and perimeter of triangle number one. Finally those parameters are used as inputs to some mathematical equations which will be discussed next, to form the features vectors for each sample image.

4.3 Deriving the Mathematical Model

In the geometry science it is known that Triangles are similar if they have the same shape, but not necessarily the same size [14]. This scientific fact inspired us to draw mathematical relationships between the six triangular features extracted during the previous stage. The Human population reached 7 Billion people around the world and thus, it is impractical to use a one-to-one comparison process for the purpose of face recognition using the measurements of our triangular features. As a different approach we were able to make use of the proportional ratio between the different triangles representing the facial features which led to fifteen different mathematical equations representing the degree of similarity between each two triangles. Based on the aforementioned geometrical theory regarding the similarity of triangles, any two triangles are considered similar even if they are of different sizes if the following mathematical relationship represented by "Eq. (1)" is satisfied:

$$A_i / A_j = p_j^2 / p_i^2. \tag{8}$$

Where A, and P represent triangles areas and perimeters successively, i and j are designations of the two triangles subject of the mathematical relationship. Eq. (8) is used to drive what is called triangles similarity proportion, which is a measurement of degree of similarity between two triangles, and it is represented by "Eq. (2)". TSP represents the triangles similarity proportion relationship.

$$TSP = A_i x p_j^2 / A_j x p_i^2. \tag{9}$$

The statistical analysis of the data collected in term of triangular features areas and perimeters had shown clearly that there is no significant difference between these measurements of different individuals. As a different approach we were able to make use of the similarity proportional ratio between the different triangles representing the facial features which led to fifteen different mathematical equations representing the degree of similarity between each two triangles. Those equation were derived using equation (9) by simply applying the formula between each two triangles, and substituting subscripts i and j by the designations of the two triangles. "Eq. (10)" through, "Eq. (24)" represents the fifteen relationships between the six triangular features as listed in Table 1:

Table 1. Similarity Proportions Relationships between the Triangular Features

Eq. 10, 13, 16, 19, 22	Eq. 11, 14, 17, 20,23	Eq. 12, 15, 18, 21, 24
$(T_1,T_2)=(A_1* P_2^2/A_2*P_1^2)$	$(T_1,T_3)=(A_1*P_3^2/A_3*P_1^2)$	$(T_1,T_4)=(A_1*P_4^2/A_4*P_1^2)$
$(T_1,T_5)=(A_1* P_5^2/A_5*P_1^2)$	$(T_1,T_6)=(A_1*P_6^2/A_6*P_1^2)$	$(T_2,T_3)=(A_2*P_3^2/A_3*P_2^2)$
$(T_2,T_4)=(A_2* P_4^2/A_4*P_2^2)$	$(T_2,T_5)=(A_2*P_5^2/A_5*P_2^2)$	$(T_2,T_6)=(A_2*P_6^2/A_6*P_2^2)$
$(T_3,T_4)=(A_3* P_4^2/A_4*P_3^2)$	$(T_3,T_5)=(A_3*P_5^2/A_5*P_3^2)$	$(T_3,T_6)=(A_3*P_6^2/A_6*P_3^2)$
$(T_4,T_5)=(A_4* P_5^2/A_5*P_4^2)$	$(T_4,T_6)=(A_4*P_6^2/A_6*P_4^2)$	$(T_5,T_6)=(A_5*P_6^2/A_6*P_5^2)$

For each sample image enrolled in the system those fifteen relationships will be calculated and stored in a vector which will be considered as a feature vector of this specific sample image. When multiple sample images are related to the same subject, the feature vectors of these sample images will be stored in a matrix to form a class for each subject.

5 Experiments

We performed our experiments on a public aging database FG-NET [15] containing 1,002 high resolution color or gray scale face images of 82 subjects from multiple races with large variation of lighting, expression, and pose. The image size is approximately 400 x 500 in pixels. The age range is from 0 to 69 years (on average, 12 images per subject). The FG-NET database was divided into three subsets as follows:

1. FGnet-8 consists of all the data collected at ages between 0 and 8. It includes 290 facial images from 74 subjects, among which 580 intra-person pairs and 6000 inter-person pairs are randomly generated for verification.
2. FGnet-18 consists of all the data collected at ages between 8 and 18. It includes 311 facial images from 79 subjects, among which 577 intra-person pairs and 6000 inter-person pairs are randomly generated for verification.
3. FGnet-adult consists of all the data collected at ages 18 or above and roughly frontal. It includes 272 images from 62 subjects, among which 665 intrapersonal pairs and about 6000 intra-personal pairs are randomly generated for verification.

The aim of using the aforementioned protocol for dividing the FGNET database was to determine which features contribute more in discriminating between the classes for each age range. To accomplish this goal a number of feature ranking and selection methods namely: The Correlation Feature Selection (CFS) method, ReliefF Attribute Evaluation method, Symmetrical Uncertainty feature selection method were employed to select a subset of the most significant features among the fifteenth extracted features for each age spam. After that a number of classifiers were used to evaluate the performance of the system namely: K-means KNN (K-Nearest Niebuhr), Random Forest, Naïve Bayes, and Bayes Net classifiers; when the system was tested on each of the FGNET subsets. In the next section the resultant features subsets when each of the aforementioned feature selection methods are used are illustrated, and classification results are illustrated to evaluate performance of the system .

6 Results and Discussion

6.1 Classification Results

Classification results of the developed facial geometrical system, when the system was tested on the entire FGNET database and each of the FGNET subsets separately are illustrated in terms of classification accuracy, and error rate. **Table 2** through **Table 5** illustrate the classification result of testing the system over the FGNET-8, FGNET-18, FGNET-Adult, and the entire FGNET database successively.

Table 2. FGNET-8 Subset Classification Results

Classifier	Accuracy (%)	Error rate (%)
KNN	96.0563	3.9437
Naïve Bayes	21.69	78.3099
K-means	5.6338	94.3662
SVM	3.3803	96.6197

Table 3. FGNET-18 Subset Classification Results

Classifier	Accuracy (%)	Error rate (%)
KNN	89.1008	10.8992
Naïve Bayes	24.2507	75.7493
SVM	4.3597	95.6403
K-means	5.1771	94.8229

Table 4. FGNET-Adult Subset Classification Results

Classifier	Accuracy (%)	Error rate (%)
KNN	96.0563	3.9437
Naïve Bayes	21.6901	78.3099
K-means	5.6338	94.3662
SVM	3.3803	96.6197

Table 5. FGNET-Adult Subset Classification Results

Classifier	Accuracy (%)	Error rate (%)
KNN	99.1701	0.8299
K-means	4.1494	95.8506
Naïve Bayes	9.5436	90.4564
SVM	17.2891	82.7109

It can be seen from the classification results that the best accuracy was achieved when the system was tested over the entire FGNET database using KNN classifier with a maximum accuracy of over 99%. Performance of the KNN classifier was relatively high for all FGNET subsets, which is due to the ability of the KNN classifier of handling large number of classes. On contrast the other three classifiers have shown poor performance over all of the FGNET subsets.

6.2 Feature Selection Results

6.2.1 FGNET Complete Set Feature Selection Results

Fig. 1 shows the ranking of the fifteen developed features. Features ranking was performed using ReliefF Attribute Evaluator feature selection method. The top five

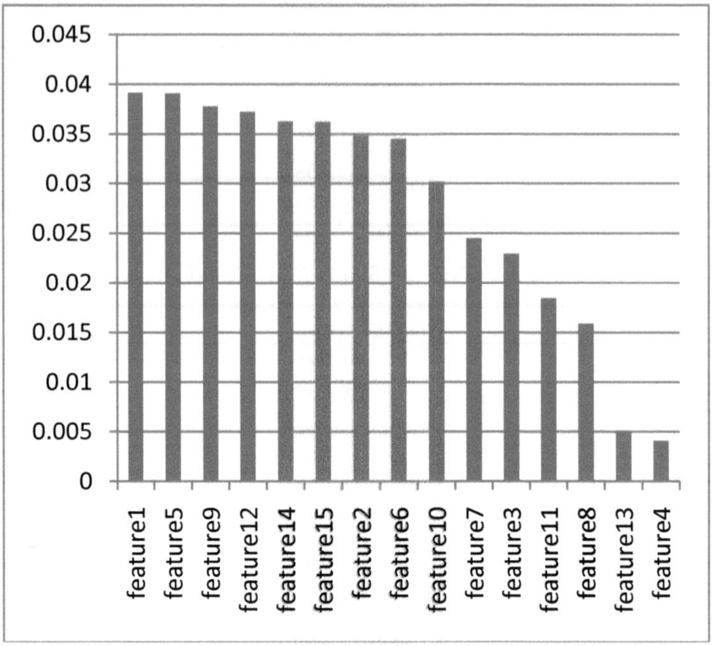

Fig. 1. ReliefF Attribute Evaluator FGNET

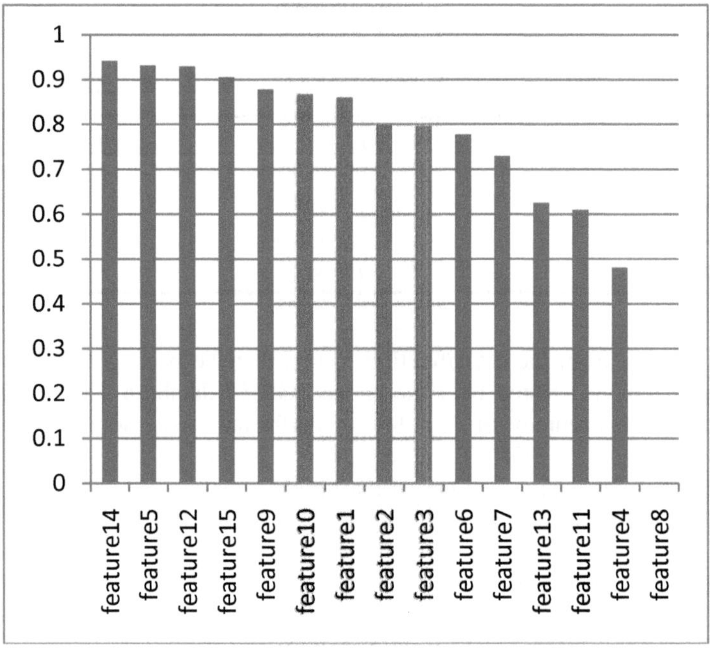

Fig. 2. Symmetrical Uncertainty Attribute Evaluator FGNET

are successively: Feature1, Feature5, Feature9, Feature12, Feature14, and the most important feature is feaure1 which is represented by equation (10). Symmetrical Uncertainty Attribute Evaluator feature selection method on the other hand produced different top features set where the most important feature is feature14 represented by equation (23), and the top five features are feature14, feature5, feature12, feature15, and feature9 as illustrated in Fig. 2 .

6.2.2 FGNET-8 Feature Selection Results

Features ranking and selection results were comparatively different when the system was tested on the FGNET-8 subset than the results when the system was tested on the entire FGNET database in particular the results achieved by ReliefF Attribute Evaluator feature selection method. As it can be seen in Fig. 3 and Fig. 4. When using ReliefF Attribute Evaluator feature selection method the top five are successively: Feature12, Feature14, Feature5, Feature15, Feature2, and the most

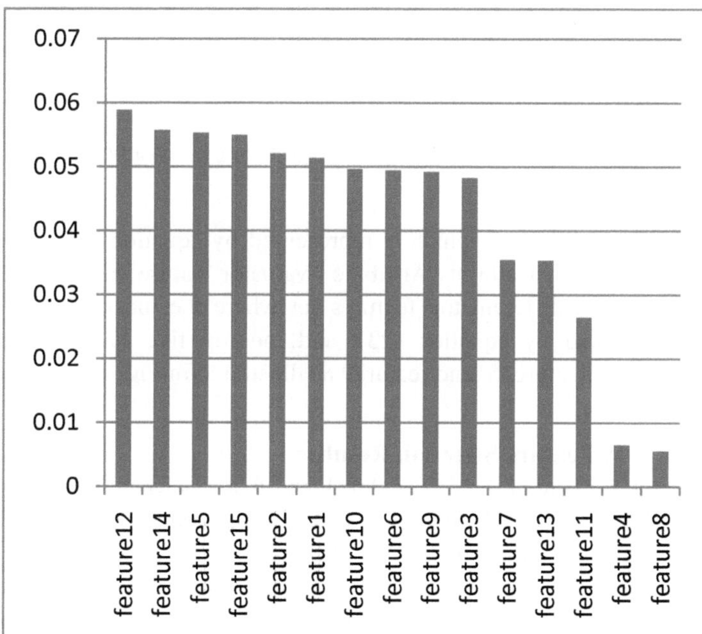

Fig. 3. ReliefF Attribute Evaluator FGNET-8

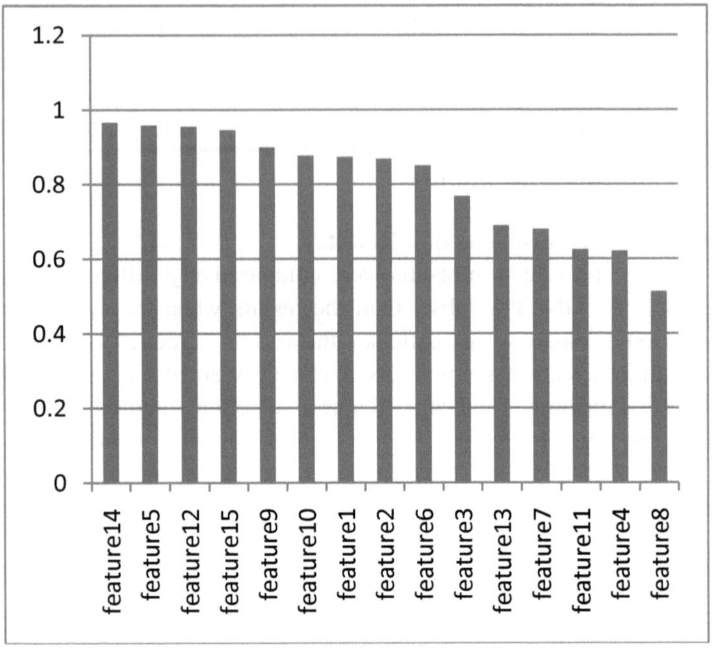

Fig. 4. Symmetrical Uncertainty Attribute Evaluator FGNET-8

important feature is feaure12 which is represented by equation (21) as illustrated in figure 3. Symmetrical Uncertainty Attribute Evaluator feature selection method on the other hand produced different top features set where the most important feature is feature14 represented by equation (23), and the top five features are feature14, feature5, feature12, feature15, and feature9 as illustrated in Fig. 4 .

6.2.3 FGNET-18 Feature Selection Results

Fig. 5 shows the ranking of the fifteen developed features when the system was tested over the FGNET-18 subset. Features ranking was performed using ReliefF Attribute Evaluator feature selection method. The top five are successively: Feature1, Feature12, Feature6, Feature15, Feature2, and the most important feature is feaure1 which is represented by equation (10). Symmetrical Uncertainty Attribute Evaluator feature selection method on the other hand produced different top features set where the most important feature is feature14 represented by equation (23), and the top five features are feature14, feature5, feature12, feature15, and feature9 as illustrated in Fig. 6 .

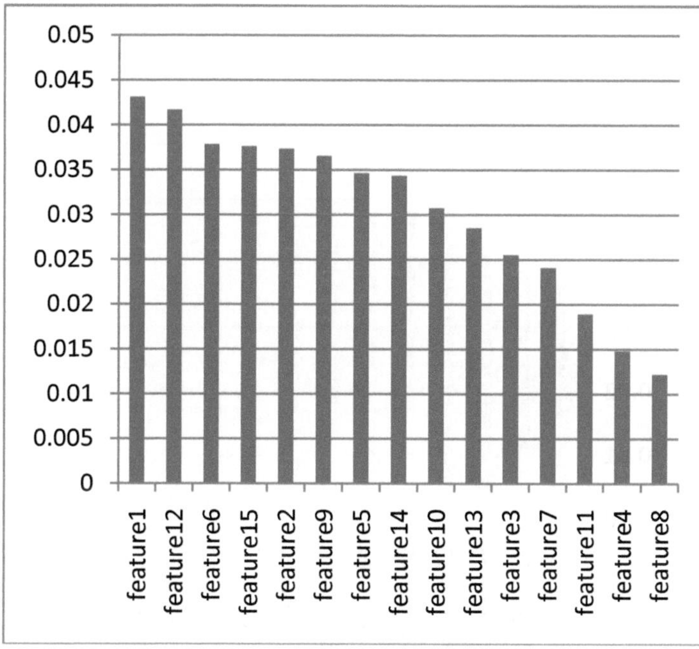

Fig. 5. ReliefF Attribute Evaluator FGNET-18

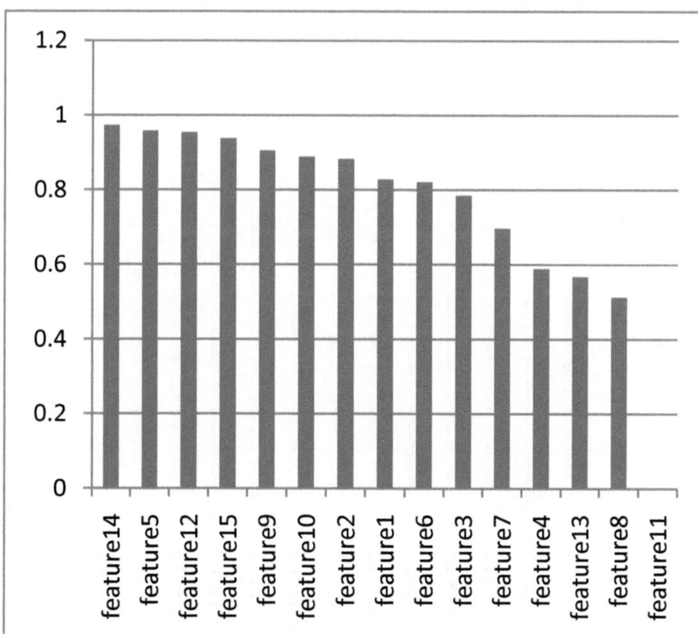

Fig. 6. Symmetrical Uncertainty Attribute Evaluator FGNET-18

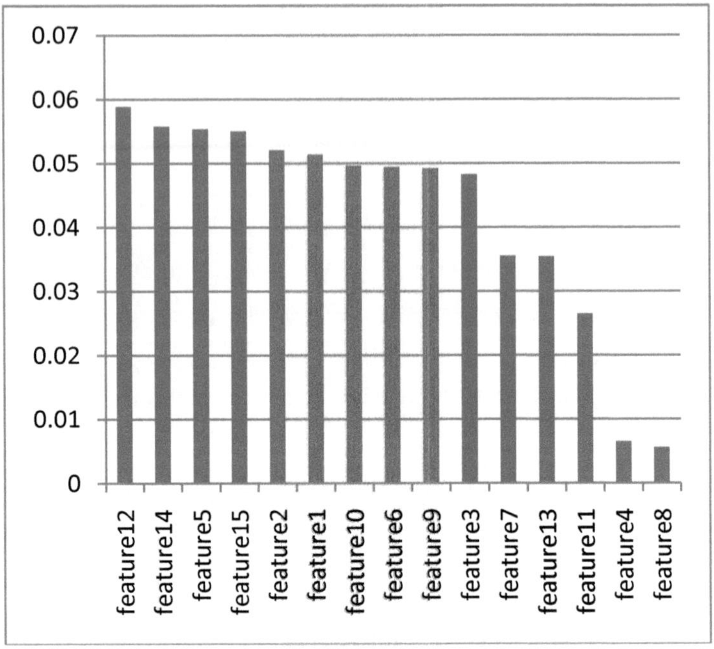

Fig. 7. ReliefF Attribute Evaluator FGNET-Adult

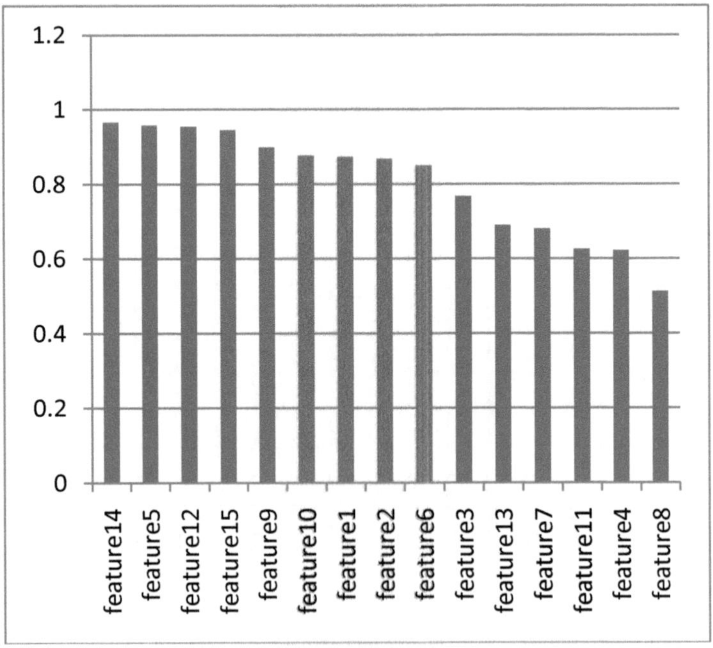

Fig. 8. Symmetrical Uncertainty Attribute Evaluator FGNET-Adult

6.2.3 FGNET-Adult Feature Selection Results

As it can be seen in Fig. 7 and Fig. 8. When using ReliefF Attribute Evaluator feature selection method the top five are successively: Feature12, Feature14, Feature5, Feature15, Feature2, and the most important feature is feaure12 which is represented by equation (21) as illustrated in figure 7. Symmetrical Uncertainty Attribute Evaluator feature selection method on the other hand produced different top features set where the most important feature is feature14 represented by equation (23), and the top five features are feature14, feature5, feature12, feature15, and feature9 as illustrated in Fig. 8.

7 Conclusion and Future Work

This research study proposed new geometrical features that are formed by connecting some of the facial features points defined in the anthropometric science. The main goal was to develop mathematical relationships among triangular features to accommodate for the aging variations conditions that may affect any face recognition system. The performance of the system was evaluated mainly in term of classification accuracy, and the maximum classification accuracy was reported when the KNN classifier was used to test the system over the entire FGNET database. Also a number of feature selection and ranking methods were used to study the importance of features in different age spans . In our future work we are planning to test the performance of the system when different feature selection methods are used in conjunction with multiple classification methods.

Acknowledgments. The authors gratefully acknowledge the support provided by Universiti Teknologi PETRONAS, Malaysia. Also the authors wish to express their gratitude to the Dean of the Centre for Graduate Studies Associate Prof Dr. Mohd Fadzil Hassan at the Universiti Teknologi PETRONAS for participating in the excremental part of this research work and for his continuous support to the research innovation in at the Universiti Teknologi PETRONAS.

References

1. Kachare, N.B., Inamdar, V.S.: Survey of Face Recognition Techniques. International Journal of Computer Applications (0975 - 8887) 1(19) (2010)
2. Ling, H., Soatto, S., Ramanathan, N., Jacobs, D.W.: Study of Face Recognition as People Age. In: Proc. 11th Int'l Conf. Computer Vision, pp. 1–8 (2007)
3. O'Toole, A., Vetter, T., Volz, H., Salter, M.: Three-dimensional caricatures of human heads: distinctiveness and the perception of facial age. Perception 26, 719–732 (1997)
4. Ramanathan, N., Chellappa, R.: Face Verification across Age Progression. IEEE Trans. Image Processing 15(11), 3394–3361 (2006)
5. Hall, M.A.: Correlation-based Feature Selection for Machine Learning. Department of Computer Science, Hamilton, New Zealand
6. Kononenko, I.: Estimating Attributes: Analysis and Extensions of RELIEF. In: European Conference on Machine Learning, pp. 171–182 (1994)

7. Ali, S.I., Shahzad, W.: A Feature Subset Selection Method based on Symmetric Uncertainty and Ant Colony Optimization. International Journal of Computer Applications (0975 – 8887) 60(11) (December 2012)
8. Leung, K.M.: Naive Bayesian Classifier, Polytechnic University Department Of Computer Science / Finance and Risk Engineering, Copyright c, mleung@poly.edu (2007)
9. Cortes, C., Vapnik, V.N.: Support-Vector Networks. Machine Learning 20 (1995)
10. Viola, P., Jones, M.J.: Robust Real time Face Detection. International Journal of Computer Vision (2004)
11. MacQueen, J.B.: Some Methods for classification and Analysis of Multivariate Observations. In: Proceedings of 5th Berkeley Symposium on Mathematical Statistics and Probability 1, pp. 281–297. MR 0214227. Zbl 0214.46201. University of California Press (1967) (retrieved April 7, 2009)
12. Cootes, T.F., Edwards, G.J., Taylor, C.J.: Active appearance models. In: Burkhardt, H., Neumann, B. (eds.) ECCV 1998. LNCS, vol. 1407, pp. 484–498. Springer, Heidelberg (1998)
13. Bremner, D., Demaine, E., Erickson, J., Iacono, J., Langerman, S., Morin, P., Toussaint, G.: Output-sensitive algorithms for computing nearest-neighbor decision boundaries. Discrete and Computational Geometry 33(4), 593–604 (2005), doi:10.1007/s00454-004-1152-0
14. McCartin, B.J.: Mysteries of the equilateral triangle. Applied Mathematics Kettering University (2010)
15. Everett, M.G., Borgatti, S.P.: The centrality of groups and classes. Journal of Mathematical Sociology 23(3), 181–201 (1999)
16. FG-NET Aging Database (2010), `http://www.fgnet.rsunit.com`

Face Verification Using Multiple Localized Face Features

Mohd. Ridzuwary Mohd. Zainal, Hafizah Husain,
Salina Abdul Samad, and Aini Hussain

Universiti Kebangsaan Malaysia, Selangor, Malaysia
{ridzwary,hafizah,salina,aini}@eng.ukm.my

Abstract. In this paper, we described face verification execution using different feature extraction methods on different regions of the face. We chose two feature extraction methods which are the Discrete Cosine Transform (DCT) and the Local Binary Pattern (LBP). Classification is done separately on for each region using Support Vector Machine. The final verification decision is calculated by combining the classification scores of the face region. The results show that generally, LBP gives better results than DCT on our dataset and parameter settings but both methods did not extract good discriminating features on the nose region.

Keywords: Face verification, local binary pattern, discrete cosine transform, support vector machine.

1 Introduction

Identity verification focuses on the task of determining the authenticity of a person's identity. The purpose of verification is to ensure that only the right people can access a particular area or resource. One way to verify an identity is by looking and comparing a person's face. Automatic face verification systems are machines that are designed to authenticate identities. There are numerous applications that can benefit from automatic face verification systems. Examples are access control for doors, password enhancement for computer access, and web-based authentication for secure online transactions.

To perform verification, the system must acquire the persons face features as input. An ideal face feature is one that can discriminate each person correctly. Many research have been accomplished to find an effective method to extract from or transform the face image to the best features to represent the face for automatic face verification systems [1]. Generally, there are several different approaches to perform face feature extraction. One is by taking geometrical measurements of the visible features on the face. Another approach, which is also known as the holistic approach, processes the face image as a whole into the desired feature form. The holistic approach can also be narrowed down to focus on smaller parts of the face called the local features. Even though these categorizations exist, feature extraction methods can be adapted to use an approach that differs from what it was originally intended. Feature extraction methods can also be combined to form a hybrid feature that may gain better discriminating characteristics.

H. Badioze Zaman et al. (Eds.): IVIC 2013, LNCS 8237, pp. 97–103, 2013.

An example of a face feature extraction method is the Principle Component Analysis (PCA) [2]. PCA is a feature transform that is commonly mentioned for face verification and face recognition. PCA attempts to project the face image to a feature subspace with basis vectors that correspond to the maximum variance direction in the original face image space. Its dimensional reduction property also helps to manage the high dimensional nature of face images. Although PCA was originally introduced as a holistic face feature transform, it can also be used in a more localized manner. For example, [3] used PCA on regions around the eyes, nose and mouth. A current trend of using PCA involves a hybrid or combinations with other feature extraction methods [4].

Hybrid or fusion of features has also been proposed in literature. An example would be the fusion of Discrete Cosine Transform (DCT) and Local Binary Pattern (LBP) as a single feature to represent face [5]. In their research, Chen and Chen used the fused feature and Support Vector Machine (SVM) classification to achieve a 95.5% recognition rate for their data set.

There are many methods that are proposed to represent face features for face verification. Most research literature attempts to define the whole face with a single feature extraction method but the human face is not an object with similar shape and contour across its region. For example, the eye region has many visible features like lines and creases but the nose region has less definitive features yet its protruding shape makes it more susceptible to varying illuminations. Different parts of the face may be better represented with certain types of feature extraction method than others.

Following this argument, we experimented on face verification technique using different feature extraction methods on different parts of the face. The classification results of the different regions are combined to get the final verification decision. In this paper, we chose to experiment using DCT and LBP as face features and classify the features using SVM.

2 Methodology

Face images are acquired from the extended Yale Face Database B which contains 16128 images of 28 human subjects under 9 poses and 64 illumination conditions [5]. For the experiments accomplished in this paper, only the front facing images that have been manually aligned and cropped are used [6].

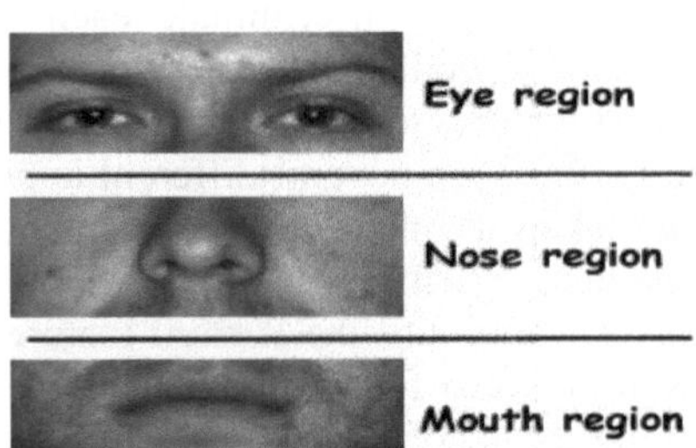

Fig. 1. Separation of the face image into three regions

The face image is divided into three separate regions with each containing the eyes, the nose, and the mouth. Fig. 1 shows how the separation is done. For each region the different features are extracted and support vectors are calculated based on each region. The classification score is calculated separately and are finally combined to verify the faces.

2.1 Discrete Cosine Transform

The DCT transforms a finite signal into a representation of cosine function coefficients. The DCT used in this paper is the two dimensional DCT (2D-DCT) that is based on the DCT-II type. The 2D-DCT is defined as

$$F(u,v) = \alpha(u)\alpha(v)\sum_{x=0}^{M-1}\sum_{y=0}^{N-1} f(x,y) \times \cos\left(\frac{\pi(2x+1)u}{2M}\right)\cos\left(\frac{\pi(2y+1)v}{2N}\right) \quad (1)$$

Where

$$\alpha(u) = \begin{cases} \frac{1}{\sqrt{M}}, & u = 0 \\ \sqrt{\frac{2}{M}}, & u = 1,2,\dots,M-1 \end{cases} \quad (2)$$

$$\alpha(v) = \begin{cases} \frac{1}{\sqrt{N}}, & v = 0 \\ \sqrt{\frac{2}{N}}, & v = 1,2,\dots,N-1 \end{cases} \quad (3)$$

The DCT has the characteristics of having a good data compression property, efficient computation and by using certain normalization techniques, can be robust against facial geometry and illumination variations. [7]

2.2 Local Binary Pattern

LBP tries to summarize the grey value relation between an image pixel and its surrounding [8]. For a given pixel position (x_c, y_c) in an image, its Local Binary Pattern is defined as a set of binary comparisons of pixel intensities between the given pixel and its eight surrounding pixels. The resulting 8-bit word is called an LBP code and is expressed in decimal form by

$$LBP(x_c, y_c) = \sum_{n=0}^{7} s(i_n - i_c)2^n \quad (4)$$

Where i_c corresponds to the grey value of the central pixel, i_n corresponds to the grey values of the 8 surrounding pixels, and s is defined as:

$$s(x) = \begin{cases} 1 \text{ if } x < 0 \\ 0 \text{ if } x \geq 0 \end{cases} \quad (5)$$

Fig. 2 shows an example how pixel intensity values are compared to the central pixel value resulting in binary values. The binary digits are read clockwise from the upper left corner to form an 8-bit word which can be converted into a decimal value.

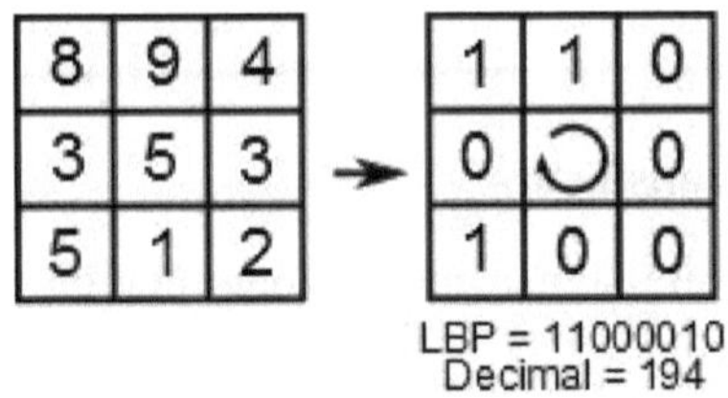

Fig. 2. Transforming pixel intensities into LBP code

2.3 Support Vector Machine

SVM is a binary classification method that classifies patterns by finding the optimal decision boundary or separating hyperplane between two classes. Several vectors from both classes are chosen to determine the position of the hyperplane and act as supports that hold the hyperplane in place, hence the term support vectors.

In this experiment, we train the SVM using linear SVM for each face region separately and then combine the classification results to calculate the final verification decision using equal weights. Multi-class classification is done via the "one versus the rest" approach.

3 Results and Discussion

The face verification experiment uses the combination of the different chosen feature extraction methods on different face regions. For comparison, raw image i.e. image that has not been put through feature extraction is also used as a feature type. Since three different features are used with three different face regions, a total of 27 different combinations of features are produced.

False Acceptance Rate (FAR) and False Rejection Rate (FRR) are used for evaluation. They are calculated by equations:

$$FAR = \frac{\mathrm{FA}}{\mathrm{N}_{false}} \times 100\% \tag{6}$$

$$FRR = \frac{\mathrm{FR}}{\mathrm{N}_{true}} \times 100\% \tag{7}$$

where *FAR* is defined as the ratio of the number of faces falsely accepted as true (*FA*) to the total number of imposter faces(N_{False}) while *FRR* is defined as the number of true faces falsely rejected as impostors (*FR*) to the total number of true faces (N_{True}). A high FAR means that more impostors are accepted by system and a high FRR means that more genuine users are locked out of the system.

Table 1. Face verification results with different feature combinations

Eye Region	Nose Region	Mouth Region	FAR (%)	FRR (%)
Raw	Raw	Raw	7.00	20.00
DCT	DCT	DCT	2.00	16.00
LBP	LBP	LBP	0.00	24.00
Raw	Raw	DCT	5.00	16.00
Raw	Raw	LBP	1.11	42.00
Raw	DCT	Raw	4.22	28.00
Raw	DCT	DCT	4.00	26.00
Raw	DCT	LBP	1.11	42.00
Raw	LBP	Raw	3.78	26.00
Raw	LBP	DCT	3.56	26.00
Raw	LBP	LBP	0.67	38.00
DCT	Raw	Raw	4.00	28.00
DCT	Raw	DCT	2.00	16.00
DCT	Raw	LBP	1.00	36.00
DCT	DCT	Raw	4.00	16.00
DCT	DCT	LBP	1.00	28.00
DCT	LBP	Raw	2.00	12.00
DCT	LBP	DCT	2.00	16.00
DCT	LBP	LBP	1.00	28.00
LBP	Raw	Raw	2.00	16.00
LBP	Raw	DCT	0.00	28.00
LBP	Raw	LBP	0.00	28.00
LBP	DCT	Raw	1.00	16.00
LBP	DCT	DCT	0.00	28.00
LBP	DCT	LBP	0.00	24.00
LBP	LBP	Raw	0.00	12.00
LBP	LBP	DCT	0.00	28.00

The columns Eye, Nose, and Mouth in Table 1 each indicates what type of feature was used for the eye region, nose region and mouth region respectively. For the purpose of discussing the results, we will use the notation Eye-Nose-Mouth to refer to the different feature combinations; i.e. Raw-LBP-DCT refers to the combination of raw feature for the eye region, LBP for the nose region and DCT for the mouth region.

The top three rows in the table shows the verification results for images that has only raw data, only DCT features and only LBP features respectively as features. The rest of the table shows the results for when two or more feature combinations are used.

The highest FAR value is given by the combination of Raw-Raw-Raw which shows that the unprocessed face images are not suitable for face verification. Changing one of the features with LBP or DCT seems to lower the FAR value which is an improvement. On the other hand, some of those combinations give a higher FRR.

Combinations that give the higher FRR values of above 30% mostly have the mouth region represented using LBP while combinations that give the lower FRR values of below 20% have the eyes represented using DCT. In terms of only FAR, combinations that uses Raw features for the eyes yield the highest values while combinations that uses LBP for the eyes gives the lowest values.

A change feature in the nose region may not give varying results. For example, the combinations DCT-Raw-DCT, DCT-LBP-DCT and DCT-DCT-DCT gives the same results which are FAR = 2% and FRR = 16%.

If we observe in terms of FAR and FRR average with respect to face regions, LBP gives the overall best performance, followed by DCT and Raw. Yet, for the FRR average with respect to the mouth region, LBP gives the worse performance. This may indicate that within the parameter constraints of this experiment, if LBP is used for the mouth region, the combined feature may not display the similarities of faces from the same person.

4 Conclusion

The results of a face verification experiment using different feature extraction methods for different parts of the face are shared in this paper. We have shown that it is possible to use different feature for different parts of the face to obtain a newer combination feature. Different feature combination will also give different performance results. Overall, using DCT and LBP to represent face features is significantly better than using raw image data. The result of this experiment can be improved since both DCT and LBP each has its own performance enhancement techniques that we have not touched in this paper.

References

1. Zhao, W., Chellappa, R., Phillips, P.J., Rosenfeld, A.: Face recognition: A literature survey. ACM Computing Surveys (CSUR) 35(4), 399–458 (2003)
2. Turk, M., Pentland, A.: Eigenfaces for Recognition. Journal of Cognitive Neuroscience 3(1), 71–86 (1991)

3. King, I., Xu, L.: Localized principal component analysis learning for face feature extraction and recognition. In: Proceedings to the Workshop on 3D Computer Vision, pp. 124–128 (1997)
4. Jaiswal, A., Kumar, N., Agrawal, R.K.: A Hybrid of Principal Component Analysis and Partial Least Squares for Face Recognition across Pose. In: Alvarez, L., Mejail, M., Gomez, L., Jacobo, J. (eds.) CIARP 2012. LNCS, vol. 7441, pp. 67–73. Springer, Heidelberg (2012)
5. Georghiades, A.S., Belhumeur, P.N., Kriegman, D.J.: From Few to Many: Illumination Cone Models for Face Recognition under Variable Lighting and Pose. IEEE Trans. Pattern Anal. Mach. Intelligence 23(6), 643–660 (2001)
6. Lee, K.C., Ho, J., Kriegman, D.: Acquiring Linear Subspaces for Face Recognition under Variable Lighting. IEEE Trans. Pattern Anal. Mach. Intelligence 27(5), 684–698 (2005)
7. Chadha, A.R., Vaidya, P.P., Roja, M.M.: Face recognition using discrete cosine transform for global and local features. In: 2011 International Conference on Recent Advancements in Electrical, Electronics and Control Engineering (ICONRAEeCE), pp. 502–505. IEEE (2011)
8. Ojala, T., Pietikäinen, M., Harwood, D.: A comparative study of texture measures with classification based on feature distributions. Pattern Recognition 29 (1996)

Adaptive Motion Pattern Analysis for Machine Vision Based Moving Detection from UAV Aerial Images

A.F.M. Saifuddin Saif, Anton Satria Prabuwono, and Zainal Rasyid Mahayuddin

Faculty of Information Science and Technology,
University Kebangsaan Malaysia, Selangor, Malaysia
rashedcse25@yahoo.com, {antonsatria,zainalr}@ftsm.ukm.my

Abstract. In order to detect moving object from UAV aerial images motion analysis has started to get attention in recent years where motion of the objects along with moving camera needs to be estimated and compensated by using detection algorithm. Moving object detection from UAV aerial images based on motion analysis involves modeling the pixel value changes over time. Moving object detection with moving cameras from UAV aerial images is still an unsolved issue due to not considering irregular motion of camera and improper estimation of noise, object motion changes and finally unfixed moving object direction. This paper presents a low complexity based motion analysis framework for moving object detection along with camera motion estimation by considering motion change of moving object and unfixed moving object direction. Based on the experimental results it is expected that proposed motion vector estimation performs well for both invariant motion and invariant moving object direction.

Keywords: machine vision, motion analysis, moving object detection.

1 Introduction

The first and enabling steps in in automated exploration of UAV video is moving object detection. Motion analysis based moving detection from aerial images has become an exciting research area due to promote searching objects in hills or other obstacles which can reduce the need for manual image analysis by less human efforts from live UAV video streaming. Most of previous motion based moving object detection approaches consider only moving object motion for detection. Most of previous research does not include motion of camera estimation with robust modeling of noise. This paper proposes use an adaptive motion pattern analysis for moving object detection from UAV aerial images under a unified computational framework.

Motion estimation is necessary to handle noise from camera. Motion estimation research makes use of parameters of video image. Considering of dithering or influencing factors, proper motion estimation is valuable for correct object detection

H. Badioze Zaman et al. (Eds.): IVIC 2013, LNCS 8237, pp. 104–114, 2013.

from UAV aerial images. The essential difference between motion patterns created by parallax and by moving objects is as follows [11]:

(a)Motion pattern of moving object is generated by the intrinsic properties of the objects and static environment constraints on the ground plane.
(b)Motion pattern of parallax is caused by the camera motion, as each motion vector on a 3D structure should be along with epipolar line that is determined by camera's translation. Each motion flow may contain multiple moving objects in sequence or in parallel, but their motion should comply with motion pattern.

This paper presents motion pattern analysis based on moving object motion estimation along with camera motion estimation and compensation. For noise removal a preprocessing step is used for better detection results.

2 Related Work

There are many approaches for motion pattern analysis.Such as,(a)Lagrangian particle dynamics approach is used to segment high density crowd flows and further track each marked objects [11].(b)Clustering based approach is proposed to segment and represent the motion flow in crowded scenes [11].Both two methods apply preclustering steps. As the scene may contain different motion patterns at one location within a period of time, preclustering before knowing the local structure of motion patterns may destroy such structure.Through the modelling of object and camera motion, the detection task becomes easy & thus also can handle noise. But to establish model is difficult for most of time [12].

In general motion detection algorithms are classified broadly into two main categories: feature based and optical flow based. For accurate tracking, the motion must be accurately detected using suitable methods, but they are affected by a number of practical problems such as motion change over time, unfixed direction of moving object. In [2], the authors proposed motion based object detection method to identify candidate object pixels. But their proposed method works only on structural object. In [8], the authors proposed framework based on shadow detection using invariant shape matching of corner features. But their method depends mainly on lighting condition where shadow based segmentation algorithm can not identify object on clocked shadows. In [5], framework proposed by the authors detect moving object based on clustering single points obtained from motion estimation. But their estimation does not include noise and proper camera motion estimation. For this reason their motion estimation can not be adapted with unfixed motion changes and unfixed moving object detection. In [4], the authors proposed moving object detection by distinguishing motion from background using image registration. But for object appearance similarity and variation of motion change make moving object detection more difficult. In [6], the authors proposed detection framework where they claimed to overcome the challenges of object orientation. But their proposed method rejects most of the object background for their input aerial image which is unrealistic.

While in [7], the authors claimed the same achievement of detecting moving object with invariant object orientation but the number and size of motion block they consider, increase computer complexity for real time vision based moving object detection. In [7], proposed framework by the authors is unable to differentiate different object in the same scene. In [9], the authors worked on the variation of poses due to motion changes in the camera, but due to their fixed assumption of object motion, their proposed method also does not work well for invariant motion changes. In [3], the authors proposed method based on SIFT (Scalar invariant feature transform),but due to use high resolution input images for experiment ,their proposed method does not work well in the real time object detection from UAV aerial images. In [1], proposed method by the authors work well for low resolution images. Due to assume constant motion moving object their proposed method also does not work well for invariant motion change of moving object.

Common motion detection technique such as background substraction or frame differencing cannot work on the aligned image perfectly [12]. It is due to existence of background noise caused by alignment imprecision or other undesirable artifacts. In [12], the authors proposed MODAT framework to detect moving. Due to absence of noise removal steps, their proposed MODAT framework also can not be considered as robust and adaptive to motion changes. Therefore a dynamic background noise removal technique is needed for motion detection to detect object.

In [11], the authors proposed a geometric interpretation of motion pattern in 4D space to detect and segment motion pattern. But because of their assumption of pure plane approximation proposed method does not work well. When two or multiple objects are close together their proposed method are unable to separate individual objects motion. In [13], the authors proposed motion vector processing method using camera motion estimation. But for same motion of more than one object, their proposed method does not work well.

Traditional problem of motion based moving object detection is the dependency on lot of parameters which increase computational complexity. None of the existing literature concentrates on decreasing parameter dependency. This paper concentrates on decreasing parameter dependency for motion based moving object detection from UAV aerial image by proposing a new framework for adaptive motion analysis along with camera motion estimation.

3 Research Methodology

3.1 Preprocessing

UAV aerial images are mixed by various kinds of noise because of object and camera motion. The noises include Gaussian noise, salt noise and so on. These noises will bring errors to latter motion estimation, and therefore influence the effect of object detection algorithm [14].

For preprocessing this paper uses wavelet denoising method based on Bayesian estimation method [13]. The overall process for the noise estimation is as follows:

(a)Estimate the difference between noise coefficient and real image coefficients after wavelet transform.
(b)A threshold needs to be estimated to separate the coefficient of noise from signal.
(c)Finally, Wavelet coefficient of noise is eliminated to attain denoising effect.

Let $g = x + \varepsilon$, Where g = observation image; x = real image; ε = Gaussian white noise with zero mean; Variance= σ^2.

The wavelet transform is

$$y = w + n$$

Where y and w are the Corresponding Wavelet Coefficient of g and x.

Assume the distribution of coefficient w is Laplacian distribution,

$$p(x) = \frac{1}{\sqrt{2\sigma}} \exp(-\frac{\sqrt{2}x}{\sigma}) \tag{1}$$

Probability density functions of noise coefficient is defined as follow,

$$p_n(n) = \frac{1}{\sqrt{2\pi\sigma_n}} \exp(-\frac{n^2}{2\sigma_n^2}) \tag{2}$$

MAP Estimation is Performed Here to Find w that Makes Posterior Probability Density on Conditions of Knowing Observation Information [15].

According to Bayesian rules, MAP estimation is

$$\hat{w}(y) = \arg\max_{w}(p_n(y-w).p_w(w)) \tag{3}$$

Combining (1), (2) and (3),

$$\hat{w}(y) = sign(y)\left(|y| - \frac{\sqrt{2}\sigma^2}{\sigma}\right) \tag{4}$$

The variance of noise according to Donoho robust median estimation is

$$\sigma_n^2 = median(|\ y(i)\ |)\,/\,0.6745,\ y(i) \in D_1^3$$

3.2 Proposed Motion Analysis

This research proposes motion based moving object detection has 5 Basic steps.

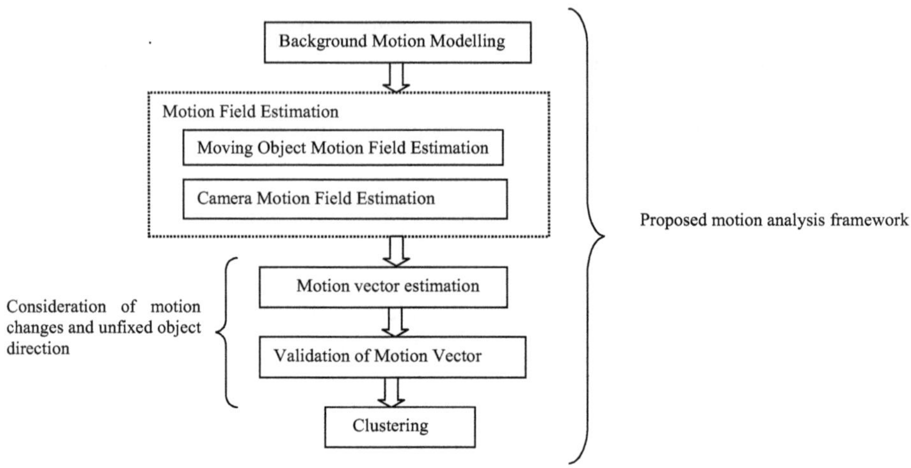

Fig. 1. Proposed framework for motion analysis

3.2.1 Background Motion Modeling

As this paper considers that UAV motion will change time to time, so background motion also not uniform. A proper background motion is needed to model where motion of moving objects and background should be different. This paper uses Gaussian mixture model (GMM) in this case.

A multivariate normal distribution is formed with the combination of Gaussian mixture model (GMM) in Equation 5.

$$\rho_m(X) = \frac{1}{(2\pi)^{\frac{n}{2}} |\Sigma|^{\frac{1}{2}}} \exp(-\frac{1}{2}(X - \mu_m)^T \Sigma^{-1}{}_m (X - \mu_m)) \tag{5}$$

Where M=Number of Gaussian distribution;

π_m = weight of each component;

Σ_m =covariance matrix.

To adapt motion changes parameters M, π_m, μ_m and Σ_m are needed to estimated to update the proposed motion model.

The following equations can be used to update these parameters,

$$\hat{\pi} \leftarrow \hat{\pi}_m + \alpha(o_m^{(t)} - \hat{\pi}_m) - \alpha c_T \tag{4}$$

$$\hat{\mu}_m \leftarrow \hat{\mu}_m + o_m^{(t)} \left(\frac{\alpha}{\hat{\pi}_m}\right) \delta_m \tag{6}$$

$$\hat{\sigma}_m \leftarrow \sigma + o_m^{(t)} \left(\frac{\alpha}{\hat{\pi}_m}\right)(\delta^T{}_m \delta_m - \hat{\sigma}_m) \tag{7}$$

Where $\delta_m = X - \hat{\mu}_m$;

α=*Constant (1/T);*

$o_m^{(t)}$ =1 if the new observation matches one of the components in the mixture model and set to 0 for the else;

Equation 5 to 7 describes a mixture model which includes both background motion and foreground motion of a pixel by different components. To separate the background motion from foreground motion the following equation can be used where background motion distribution can have a higher weight and lower variance and components can be sorted according to $\hat{\pi} / \hat{\sigma}$ from big to small.

$$B = \arg\min\left(\sum_{m=1}^{b} \hat{\pi}_m > (1 - c_f) \right) \tag{8}$$

The top B distribution is selected to describe the background motion where c_f = number of times motion of a particular pixel belongs to foreground. If top B components in the mixture model do not contain new optical value x_t , in t time in the position (x_0, y_0) , in that case that motion will be considered as foreground motion and the video frame will be considered as foreground which can be segmented later and can be referred as moving objects.

3.2.2 Motion Field Estimation

Through motion estimation field research, this paper presents relationship parameters for object motion and camera motion to compensate the result of motion estimation. The main challenge in global UAV camera motion estimation is to deal with uncertainty of dithering and other influencing factor.

Let, x_g , y_g two global estimation vector which is decided by various motion parameters such as altitude,velocity,course,rotation,camera zooming and camera panning.

A quadratic function proposed in [13] can be used here for simple camera motions and uav motion.

$$\left.\begin{aligned} x_g &= m_1 + m_3 x + m_5 y + m_7 x^2 + m_7 xy \\ x_g &= m_1 + m_3 x + m_5 y + m_7 x^2 + m_7 xy \end{aligned}\right\} \tag{9}$$

3.2.3 Motion Vector Estimation

The basic principal of frame matching is to compare each block of current frame with former frame or latter frame and compute the block motion vector as MV which is called as block displacement [13].Rules of block matching can also follow here. There are many simple distance measurement can be used for motion vector estimation. For example, SAD (Sum of Absolute Difference), MAD (Minimum absolute difference), MSE (Mean squared errors). SAD is used to estimate motion vector for a large number of image block and computer complexity is also lest. This research uses SAD for motion vector estimation.

If $\{B^m \mid 1 \le v \le M\}$ be the group of structure blocks from a given video frame. For each structure block B_m is a subgroup consists of the best L matches found in the reference frame. These matches can be denoted in the following equation,

$$\left.\begin{aligned} A &= \{(\mathrm{MV}, d_j^m) \mid 1 \le j \le L\}, \\ A &= \{(\mathrm{MV}, d_j^m) \mid 1 \le j \le L\} \end{aligned}\right\} \tag{10}$$

Where MV=Motion vector;

d_j^m = SAD distance. Now let

For reliable measurement of motion vector estimation SAD can be denoted in the following equation

$$d_-^m = \min d_j^m , d_+^m = Ave(d_j^m)_j \tag{11}$$

3.2.4 Validation of Motion Vector

This research uses this motion vector validating steps because of the following three reasons.

1. Estimated motion vector based on SAD reduce motion vectors of background block which makes the motion vector of objects more highlighted. So a judgment is necessary to the results of estimation of motion blocks.

2. As this research considers distribution of motion vector as reliability measurement, so it becomes a challenge to estimate motion vector correctly.
3. After choosing an accurate motion vector, there might be other motion vector closest distance from SAD. Difficulties increase when more of these motion vectors heading different directions, the possibility of getting more uncertainty also increase.

A threshold can separate invalid motion vectors from the effective one. As there is a possibility to have more than one motion vectors based on different direction, the diversity of different direction can results in false detection. So in accordance with setting a dynamic threshold, this research emphasizes to model more than one subsets of best matches.

$$\text{Threshold,} \quad d_0^m = d_-^m + \alpha.(d_+^m - d_-^m) \tag{12}$$

$$\text{Best few motion vectors,} \quad A = \{(V_k^m, d_k^m) \mid d_k^m < d_0^m\} \tag{13}$$

Mean motion vector $\overline{MV} = (\bar{x}, \bar{y})$ of A is as follows.

$$\left.\begin{aligned} \bar{x} &= \left\{x - x_g, x - x_g < d_0^m\right\}, \\ \bar{y} &= \left\{y - y_g, y - y_g < d_0^m\right\} \end{aligned}\right\} \tag{14}$$

3.2.5 Clustering

After selection of motion vector, a clustering scheme needs to develop to give a physical meaning of moving object detection from UAV aerial images. There are many approaches for clustering, such as center and density based approach, spatiotemporal clustering approach. This research uses centers and density based clustering approach which involves the following steps,

- Drawing a circle satisfying equation (14).
- A data set needs to form to measure density reachable with the search range.
- From one center reachable for all density reachable objects are combined to form a layer.

As the number of background motion vectors are huge this paper considers that most of the time mean motion vectors of moving object is greater that mean motion vector for background i.e. $|\overline{MV}|_{object} > |\overline{MV}|_{background}$ .Highest value of mean motion vector for moving object is considered as the starting point , $|\overline{MV}|_{\max}$ .If S is denoted as search range, first density reachable cluster is denoted as SR1 and sequentially is SR2, SR3….SRN to form Layer denoted as L1, L2…LN until all $|\overline{MV}|$ be done. In clustering approach more processing can be done to achieve more good results.

4 Experiments and Discussion

This paper proposes an aerial video image from DAPRA VIVID dataset [4] .The image size is 160x107 and frame rate is 1.57 fps.

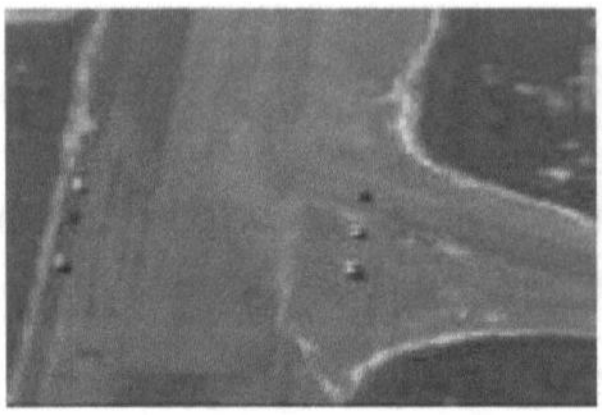

Fig. 2. Before denoise

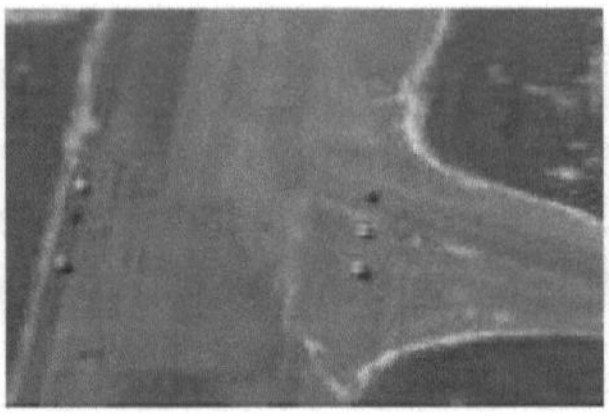

Fig. 3. After denoise

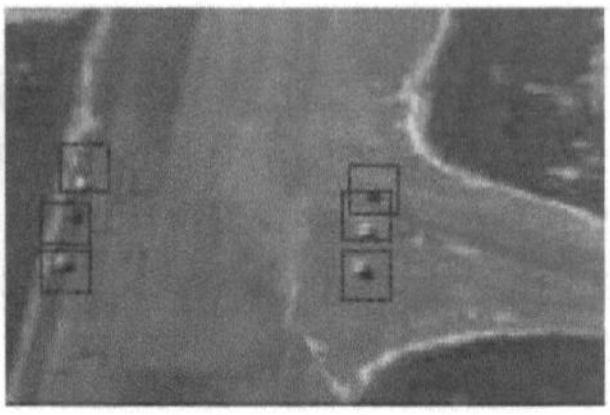

Fig. 4. Object detection

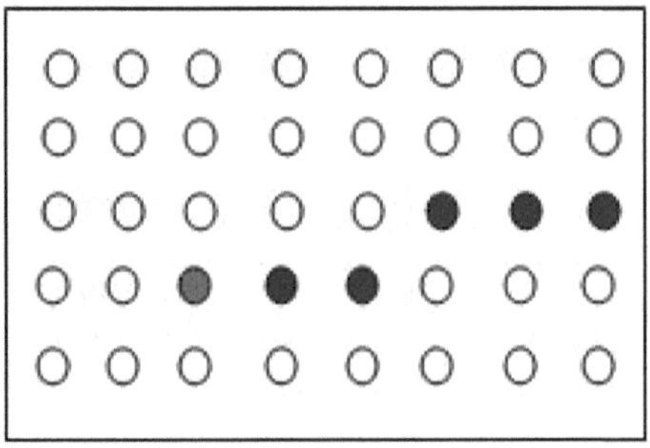

Fig. 5. Moving object motion vector (Red color) and background motion vector (White color) from Fig (3).

Fig. 2 shows an image before denoise, Fig. 3 shows the same image after removing noise and finally Fig. 4 shows final object detection based on the framework proposed in this paper. Fig. 5 shows motion vector estimation scenario for both moving object and background from Fig. 3.Estimation of motion field along with the camera motion field estimation based on the proposed motion analysis framework works well under unfixed motion changes and invariant moving object direction. Another achievement of this research that proposed framework does not need any prior knowledge of moving objects and dependency of less motion parameters which reduce the computation complexity.

5 Conclusion

The important part of the proposed framework is to give a dynamic solution for moving object detection with moving cameras with low complexity based motion analysis framework. This research uses multivariate normal distribution with the combination of Gaussian mixture model (GMM) to build background motion model. After that foreground motion is separated from background motion which is considered as motion block for moving objects. After estimating reliable motion vector for moving objects this paper proposes to use validation steps based on threshold for better results. Finally clustering is done to give a physical meaning of moving object detection from UAV aerial images. The proposed framework in this paper overcomes the traditional problem of dependency on lot of parameters for motion based moving object detection from UAV aerial images which reduces computer complexity.

Acknowledgement. This research is supported by Ministry of Higher Education Malaysia research grant scheme of FRGS/1/2012/SG05/UKM/02/12 and ERGS/1/2012/STG07/UKM/02/7.

References

1. Pollard, T., Antone, M.: Detecting and tracking all moving objects in wide-area aerial video. In: 2012 IEEE Computer Society Conference on Computer Vision and Pattern Recognition Workshops (CVPRW), pp. 15–22 (2012)
2. Zezhong, Z., Xiaoting, W., Guoqing, Z., Ling, J.: Vehicle detection based on morphology from highway aerial images. In: 2012 IEEE International Geoscience and Remote Sensing Symposium (IGARSS), pp. 5997–6000 (2012)
3. Moranduzzo, T., Melgani, F.: A SIFT-SVM method for detecting cars in UAV images. In: 2012 IEEE International Geoscience and Remote Sensing Symposium (IGARSS), pp. 6868–6871 (2012)
4. Cheraghi, S.A., Sheikh, U.U.: Moving object detection using image registration for a moving camera platform. In: 2012 IEEE International Conference on Control System, Computing and Engineering (ICCSCE), pp. 355–359 (2012)
5. Pingting, L., Fuqiang, L., Xiaofeng, L., Yingqian, Y.: Stationary vehicle detection in aerial surveillance with a UAV. In: 2012 8th International Conference on Information Science and Digital Content Technology (ICIDT), pp. 567–570 (2012)
6. Gleason, J., Nefian, A.V., Bouyssounousse, X., Fong, T., Bebis, G.: Vehicle detection from aerial imagery. In: 2011 IEEE International Conference on Robotics and Automation (ICRA), pp. 2065–2070 (2011)
7. Gąszczak, A., Breckon, T.P., Han, J.: Real-time people and vehicle detection from UAV imagery (2011)
8. Sheng, W.: Vehicle Detection on Aerial Images by Extracting Corner Features for Rotational Invariant Shape Matching. In: 2011 IEEE 11th International Conference on Computer and Information Technology (CIT), pp. 171–175 (2011)
9. Oreifej, O., Mehran, R., Shah, M.: Human identity recognition in aerial images, pp. 709–716 (2010)
10. Breckon, T.P., Barnes, S.E., Eichner, M.L., Wahren, K.: Autonomous Real-time Vehicle Detection from a Medium-Level UAV. In: 24th International Conference on Unmanned Air Vehicle Systems, pp. 29.21-29.29 (2009)

11. Qian, Y., Medioni, G.: Motion pattern interpretation and detection for tracking moving vehicles in airborne video. In: IEEE Conference on Computer Vision and Pattern Recognition, CVPR 2009, pp. 2671–2678 (2009)
12. Ibrahim, A.W.N., Pang Wee, C., Seet, G.L.G., Lau, W.S.M., Czajewski, W.: Moving Objects Detection and Tracking Framework for UAV-based Surveillance. In: 2010 Fourth Pacific-Rim Symposium on Image and Video Technology (PSIVT), pp. 456–461 (2010)
13. Jiang, Z., Ding, W., Li, H.: Aerial video image object detection and tracing based on motion vector compensation and statistic analysis. In: Asia Pacific Conference on Postgraduate Research in Microelectronics & Electronics, PrimeAsia 2009, pp. 302–305 (2009)
14. Mahmoudi, M., Sapiro, G.: Fast image and video denoising via nonlocal means of similar neighborhoods. IEEE Signal Processing Letters 12, 839–842 (2005)
15. Jaakkola, T.S., Jordan, M.I.: Bayesian parameter estimation via variational methods. Statistics and Computing 10, 25–37 (2000)

An Engineering Design Support Tool Based on TRIZ

Mei Choo Ang[1,2], Kok Weng Ng[3], Siti Azfanizam Ahmad[4], and Amelia Natasya Abdul Wahab[5]

[1] Institute of Visual Informatics, Universiti Kebangsaan Malaysia, Bangi, Malaysia
[2] School of Mechanical Engineering, University of Birmingham, United Kingdom
[3] Design Engineering Section, Industrial Design Centre, Sirim Berhad, Bukit Jalil, Malaysia
[4] Faculty of Engineering, Universiti Putra Malaysia, Malaysia
[5] Faculty of Information Science and Technology, Universiti Kebangsaan Malaysia, Bangi, Malaysia

amc@ukm.my, kwng@sirim.my, azfa@eng.upm.edu.my, amelia@ftsm.ukm.my

Abstract. TRIZ contradiction matrix was built after years of study on patent information. Designers using TRIZ contradiction matrix have to identify the improving and worsening features of their design problems and determine the inventive principles to solve their design problems. It is common to identify multiple improving and worsening features and with some features more important than the others. With the updated 2003 and 2010 TRIZ contradiction matrix introduced, more features have been added and hence, there is a need for a software tool based on these TRIZ matrices. This paper presents an engineering design support tool based on TRIZ that allows considerations for multiple improving and worsening features and allows designers to prioritise these features using weights to solve their design problems as well as the option to choose the version of TRIZ they prefer.

Keywords: TRIZ, contradiction matrix, support tool, product design.

1 Introduction

TRIZ has been one of the established methodologies that help designers to solve design problems [1] and has been utilized by many multinational enterprises including Samsung, Intel and many more. The TRIZ engineering contradiction matrix is a methodology that is developed on the basis that in most engineering design problems, any improvement made on a design feature usually will cause one or more of other design features to worsen [2]. Though the bulk of TRIZ research has concluded in 1985 [3] but the patent information kept expanding as more new patents are filed daily. Hence, Mann claimed to improve the contradiction matrix based on his analysis work on new patents and expand the classical contradiction matrix from 39 improving and worsening features to 48 [4] and then later to 50 [3]. However, the number of inventive principles stays the same at 40 in total. The next section describes more about TRIZ and how it was developed.

H. Badioze Zaman et al. (Eds.): IVIC 2013, LNCS 8237, pp. 115–127, 2013.

2 TRIZ

TRIZ is the Russian acronym for "Teoriya Resheniya Izobretatelskikh Zadatch" or Theory of Inventive Problem Solving. TRIZ was developed in the former Soviet Union by Genrikh Altshuller [2] based on years of study on patent information from 1946. The TRIZ contradiction matrix was developed to assist designers to solve design problems based on one or more pairs of contradicting features. However, the task of identifying these contradicting features is not easy [5]. In real design problems, the features that the designer wanted to improve and the features that are anticipated to worsen usually do not match those 39 features listed in the matrix. Hence, the designer has to select the improving and worsening features among the 39 features that are the nearest to those features faced in the real design problems. In addition to that, the TRIZ contradiction matrix is recommended to be applied at the root cause level of a design problem. This recommendation is presumably to avoid having too many improving features and worsening features to identify for the designer. Large number of improving and worsening features usually led to a large number of recommended inventive principles. The task in solving a design problem based on a large number of recommended inventive principles will be more difficult and confusing [6] as the inventive principles of TRIZ are ambiguous and abstract [7]. Table 1(a) illustrates the list of all the 39 features in the classical TRIZ contradiction matrix while Table 1(b) shows the updated 2003 and 2010 features. Table 2 illustrates the 40 inventive principles of classical TRIZ contradiction matrix.

The ambiguity and the abstractness of the inventive principles in TRIZ have its strengths and weaknesses. Inventive principles such as "The other way round" and "Blessing in Disguise" are obviously vague but it allows the designer the flexibility to interpret them into creative and variation of design solutions. However, to a novice designer, it would be much more difficult for them come up with a feasible design solution. Hence, there is a need to have some examples of possible interpretations of these inventive principles to help designers especially novice designers that have difficulty in translating the inventive principles.

3 Updating of Classical TRIZ

As the research work on classical TRIZ by Altshuller has concluded in 1985, there were predications that the classical TRIZ need to be updated. One of the reasons for the need to update the classical TRIZ contradiction matrix is because the number patents filed between 1985 and now has increased exponentially [4].

Hence, the addition of millions of patents information has changed the solution trends and this led the work by Mann [3, 4] to create an updated version of TRIZ contradiction matrix. The updated version of TRIZ contradiction matrices did not only have more features, the recommended inventive principles to solve the contradicting features are also different for some of the contradicting features when compared to the classical TRIZ contradiction matrix. However, the updated TRIZ contradiction matrix still utilises the same 40 inventive principles.

Table 1. (a). The list of improving and worsening features in classical TRIZ and **(b).** The list of improving and worsening features for 2003 and 2010 TRIZ

Improving and Worsening Features for Classical TRIZ Contradiction Matrix
1: Weight of moving object
2: Weight of stationary object
3: Length/Angle of moving object
4: Length/Angle of stationary object
5: Area of moving object
6: Area of stationary object
7: Volume of moving object
8: Volume of stationary object
9: Speed
10: Force/Torque
11: Stress/Pressure
12: Shape
13: Stability of the object
14: Strength
15: Duration of action of moving object
16: Duration of action of stationary object
17: Temperature
18: Illumination intensity
19: Energy used by moving object
20: Energy used by stationary object
21: Power
22: Loss of Energy
23: Loss of Substance
24: Loss of Information
25: Loss of Time
26: Amount of substance
27: Reliability/Robustness
28: Measurement accuracy/Measuring Precision
29: Manufacturing precision/Consistency
30: Other harmful effects acting on system
31: Other harmful effects generated by system
32: Manufacturability/Ease of manufacture
33: Trainability/Operability/Controllability/Ease of operation
34: Reparability / Ease of repair
35: Adaptability/versatility
36: Device complexity
37: Ability to detect/Measure/Difficulty of detecting
38: Automation/Extent of automation
39: Productivity

(a)

Improving and Worsening Features for TRIZ Contradiction Matrix 2003 (in shading) and 2010 (in shading and white cells)
1: Weight of moving object
2: Weight of stationary object
3: Length/Angle of moving object
4: Length/Angle of stationary object
5: Area of moving object
6: Area of stationary object
7: Volume of moving object
8: Volume of stationary object
9: Shape
10: Amount of substance
11: Amount of information
12: Duration of action of moving object
13: Duration of action of stationary object
14: Speed
15: Force/Torque
16: Energy used by moving object
17: Energy used by stationary object
18: Power
19: Stress/Pressure
20: Strength
21: Stability of the object
22: Temperature
23: Illumination intensity
24: Function Efficiency
25: Loss of Substance
26: Loss of Time
27: Loss of Energy
28: Loss of Information
29: Noise
30: Harmful Emission
31: Other harmful effects generated by system
32: Adaptability/versatility
33: Compatibility/Connectivity
34: Trainability/Operability/Controllability/Ease of operation
35: Reliability/Robustness
36: Reparability / Ease of repair
37: Security
38: Safety/Vulnerability
39: Aesthetics/Appearance
40: Other harmful effects acting on system
41: Manufacturability/Ease of manufacture
42: Manufacturing precision/Consistency
43: Automation/Extent of automation
44: Productivity
45: Device complexity
46: Control Complexity
47: Positive Intangible Factors
48: Negative Intangible Factors
49: Ability to detect/Measure/Difficulty of detecting
50: Measurement accuracy/Measuring Precision

(b)

Table 2. The list of 40 inventive principles in classical TRIZ

TRIZ Inventive Principles	
1. Segmentation	21. Skipping
2. Taking Out	22. "Blessing in Disguise"
3. Local Quality	23. Feedback
4. Asymmetry	24. "Intermediary"
5. Merging	25. Self-Service
6. Universality	26. Copying
7. "Nested Doll"	27. Cheap Short-Living Objects
8. Anti-Weight	28. Mechanics Substitution
9. Preliminary Anti-Action	29. Pneumatics and Hydraulics
10. Preliminary Action	30. Flexible Shells and Tin Flims
11. Beforehand Cushioning	31. Porous Materials
12. Equipotentiality	32. Colour Changes
13. "The other way round"	33. Homogeneity
14. Spheroidality - Curvature	34. Discarding and Recovering
15. Dynamisation	35. Parameter Changes
16. Partial or Excessive Actions	36. Phase Transitions
17. Another Dimension	37. Thermal Expansion
18. Mechanical Vibration	38. Strong Oxidants
19. Periodic Action	39. Inert Atmosphere
20. Continuity of Useful Action	40. Composite Materials

Mann had created two versions of the updated TRIZ contradiction matrix, one in 2003 [4] and another one in 2010 [3] on the basis of the change in solution trends due to substantial addition of patents filing from 2003 to 2010. Both of these updated TRIZ contradiction matrices also differ in the recommendation of inventive principles for some of the contradicting features.

4 Differences between Classical TRIZ and the Updated TRIZ

As shown in Table 1(a) and 1(b), both the updated TRIZ contradiction matrix of 2003 [4] and TRIZ contradiction matrix of 2010 [3] are similar except in the 2010 matrix has an addition of two features, namely the positive intangibles and negative intangibles [3]. The updated matrix of 2003 and 2010 has all the features in the classical matrix with addition of 9 more features in 2003 matrix while the 2010 matrix has 11 more features. The recommended inventive principles for only some contradicting features remain the same but quite a number of contradicting features has different recommended inventive principles when compared to each other. The arrangement of the features has also been changed in the updated 2003 and 2010 matrix.

In classical TRIZ matrix, a lot of contradicting features have no recommended inventive principles to solve certain design problems. This is one of the key issues of the TRIZ classical contradiction matrix. A designer using TRIZ matrix is very dependent on the recommended inventive principles that TRIZ matrix proposes. As with all TRIZ contradiction matrix (classical and updated ones), the diagonal cells of the contradiction matrix table has no recommended inventive principle. This means there is no possible solutions from TRIZ when you wanted to improve a feature, in which also cause the same feature to worsen. In the classical TRIZ matrix, the number of cells that has no recommended inventive principles is 275 or 18.08% of the matrix. That almost contribute a fifth of a chance that classical TRIZ cannot assist a designer to his design problems. The updated 2003 matrix has only 48 cells out of 2304 cells or 2.08% that has no recommended inventive principles (only the diagonal cells have no recommended inventive principles) while the updated 2010 matrix has 50 empty cells out of 2500 cells or 2% empty cells. The updated 2010 matrix has more number of empty cells because it is a bigger matrix with 50 features and only the diagonal cells are empty. Fig. 1 illustrates the entire classical contradiction matrix. The red cells are the empty cells or cells that have no recommended inventive principles while the orange cells are the diagonal cells which also have no recommended inventive principles. The light blue cells are the improving (vertical) and worsening features (horizontal). The numbers in the white cells are inventive principle numbers and these numbers are shown along with the inventive principles listed in Table 2.

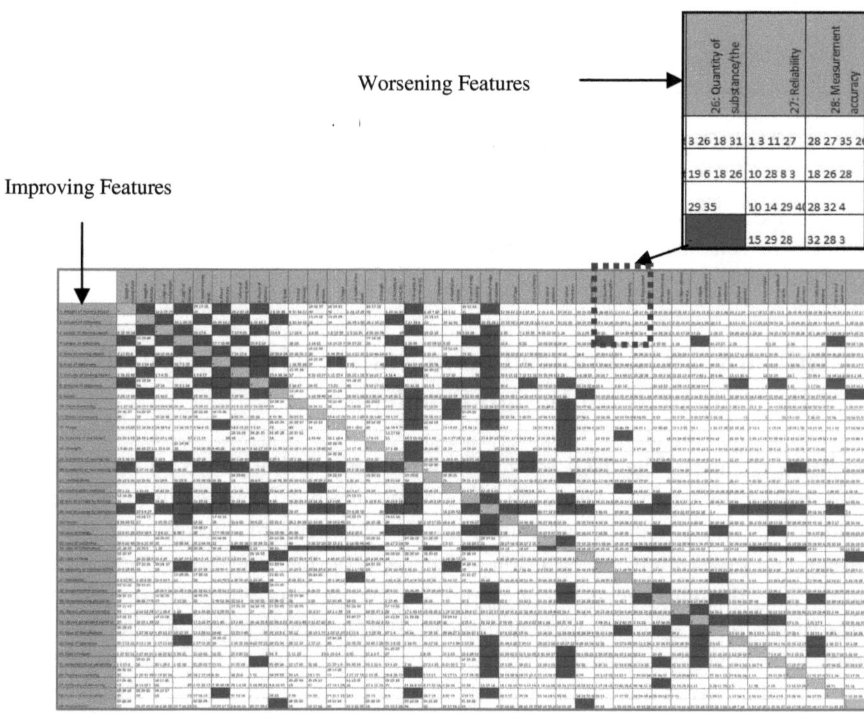

Fig. 1. The classical TRIZ contradiction matrix (the red cells are empty cells or cells that have no recommended inventive principles while the orange cells are diagonal cells which are also empty)

Both the updated 2003 and 2010 TRIZ contradiction matrix as shown in Fig. 2 were developed by Mann [3, 4]. Since there are differences in the recommended inventive principles between all three matrices, there is no work conducted to properly verify and validate how effective are these updated matrices. The updated versions of the TRIZ matrix have significant advantages of having recommended inventive principles available for all contradicting features and for having more improving and worsening features. Nevertheless, designers can utilise all three matrices to assist their creativity and innovation to derive better design solutions. The current way of utilising these contradiction matrices to solve design problems are manual and rather cumbersome as these matrices are printed in large piece of papers.

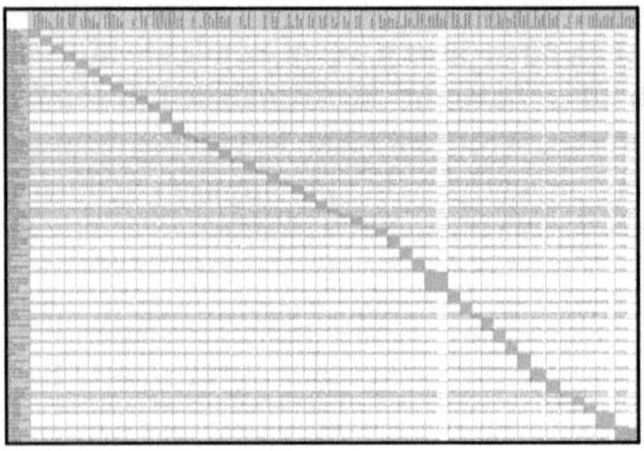

2003 TRIZ Contradiction Matrix

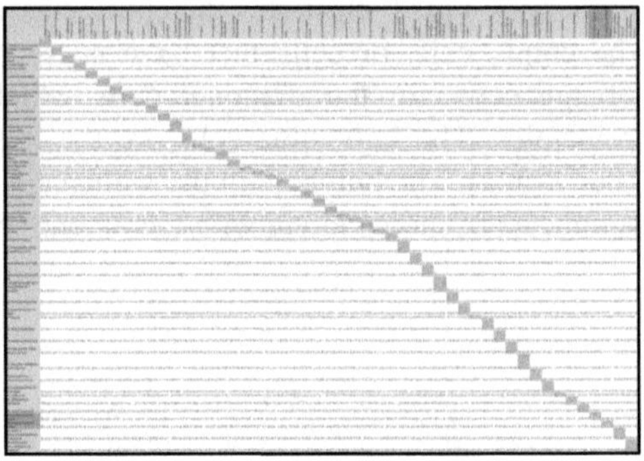

2010 TRIZ Contradiction Matrix
(note the additional features in green)

Fig. 2. The updated 2003 (left) and 2010 (right) TRIZ contradiction matrix (note that there are no red cells or cells that have no recommended inventive principles but the diagonal empty cells are still there)

5 Utilising TRIZ Contradiction Matrix with Trade-Offs Manually to Solve Design Problems

As mentioned earlier, the TRIZ contradiction matrix is known to be difficult to use and can be confusing to the user [6]. One of the main difficulties in using the TRIZ contradiction matrix can be attributed to the problem of interpreting the design requirements, constraints or criterion to the appropriate improving and worsening features. The designer need to interpret the design requirements, constraints and criteria to the nearest or try to match these design requirements to the best related features.

Table 3 illustrates an example of how difficult it is to use the TRIZ contradiction matrix without the support of a software tool. In a typical design problem, it is common to identify several improving features and worsening features. It is difficult to identify a single improving feature with a single worsening feature in typical design problem unless it is a very simple design problem. The difficulties of using TRIZ contradiction matrix will be aggravated further when prioritised features or trade-offs are allowed in which there will be weights assignments. As shown in Table 3 with an example that requires the improvement of two features, namely the shape and the adaptability/versatility features with the two worsening features, namely force/torque and loss of substance. The inventive principles proposed by the classical TRIZ contradiction matrix are 2, 3, 5, 10, 10, 13, 15, 15, 17, 20, 29, 35, 35, 37, and 40. Some of the inventive principles are repeatedly recommended. These inventive principles are obtained based on the classical TRIZ contradiction matrix. Different list of inventive principles will be obtained if the updated 2003 or 2010 contradiction matrices were used. The inventive principles 10, 15, and 35 are recommended twice. From the list of inventive principles, those recommended twice would be considered as having a higher potential of solving the design problem and those with higher weights will also have higher priorities. Table 4 illustrates the inventive principles recommended and the ranking of them based on frequency of recommendation along with the weights. The example has shown that it is not an easy task to interpret the inventive principles and maybe interpreted differently by different designers. Nevertheless, these principles provide some ideas to the designer in deriving design solutions. In addition to that, it is obvious that the more improving and worsening features, the more complex the application of the TRIZ contradiction matrix and a computerised software tool is needed.

Table 3. An example of how classical TRIZ contradiction matrix with prioritisation or trade-offs is used

Weight			0.5		0.75
	Worsening feature **Improving feature**		***15: Force/ Torque***		***25. Loss of Substance***
	⋮	....	⋮	....	⋮
0.5	***9: Shape***		35 10 37 40		35 29 3 5
	⋮	....	⋮	....	⋮
0.75	***32: Adaptability / versatility***		15 17 20		15 10 2 13

Table 4. The effects of weights on the ranking of the recommended inventive principles

Recommended Inventive Principle	Frequency of Recommendation	Aggregated Score (Frequency x Weight)
15. Dynamisation	2	1 x 0.75 x 0.5 + 1 x 0.75 x 0.75= 0.9375
10. Preliminary Action	2	1 x 0.5 x 0.5 + 1 x 0.75 x 0.75 = 0.8125
35. Parameter Changes	2	1 x 0.5 x 0.5 + 1 x 0.5 x 0.75 = 0.625
2. Taking Out	1	1 x 0.75 x 0.75 = 0.5625
13. "The other way round"	1	1 x 0.75 x 0.75 = 0.5625
3. Local Quality	1	1 x 0.5 x 0.75 = 0.375
17. Another Dimension	1	1 x 0.75 x 0.5 = 0.375
20. Continuity of Useful Action	1	1 x 0.75 x 0.5 = 0.375
29. Pneumatics and Hydraulics	1	1 x 0.5 x 0.75 = 0.375
5. Merging	1	1 x 0.5 x 0.75 = 0.375
37. Thermal Expansion	1	1 x 0.5 x 0.5 = 0.25
40. Composite Materials	1	1 x 0.5 x 0.5 = 0.25

Even though computerised tools are available for designers to find the best inventive principles to solve a design problem, these tools only handle one improving feature to one worsening feature and do not allow trade-offs. The importance of weights in the TRIZ contradiction matrix is shown in Table 4. Without weights, there are three inventive principles at the top ranking with the same frequency of recommendation and cannot be distinguished accordingly. Hence, the designer has to evaluate and explore all three of them first. When more improving and worsening features are involved, the number of inventive principles with the same ranking may increase significantly. Such recommendations will consume the designer a huge amount of time to evaluate and explore. In this paper, we proposed an option to assign four level of weight of 0.25, 0.5, 0.75, and 1 to each of the improving feature and worsening feature depending on the designer preference as shown in Table 3. The assignment of weights provide a prioritisation of the improving and worsening features, which will provide a flexibility to the designer to compromise on some of the features. This weight will allow trade-offs between improving and worsening features which is consistent with the reality in design [7]. In view of some designers that prefer not to have trade-offs, this software tool also allows designers to disable the assignment of weights.

6 An Engineering Design Support Tool Based on TRIZ

6.1 The Derivation and Development of the Engineering Support Tool Based on TRIZ

The software tool to support designer in utilizing TRIZ contradiction matrix with trade-offs to solve design problems need to consider three factors highlighted earlier in the paper:

1. There are 3 versions of TRIZ technical contradiction matrix in the literature
2. The tool should be able to consider multiple improving and worsening features
3. Most design involves trade-offs or prioritisation.

In view of these factors, an engineering design support software tool was derived. The tool allows a designer to choose the version of TRIZ contradiction matrix that he wishes to use. The software tool provides options for the designer to select the version of TRIZ contradiction matrix before deciding on the improving and worsening features. The number of improving and worsening features available for the designer to select would be dictated by the version of TRIZ contradiction matrix that he chooses. If the classical TRIZ contradiction matrix is selected, only 39 improving and worsening features will be available. Fig. 3 illustrates the graphical user interface of the software tool and the assignment of the weights using pull down and select menu.

The software tool was developed using Visual Basic 6. The TRIZ contradiction matrix data of three different versions were saved in three separate comma-separated

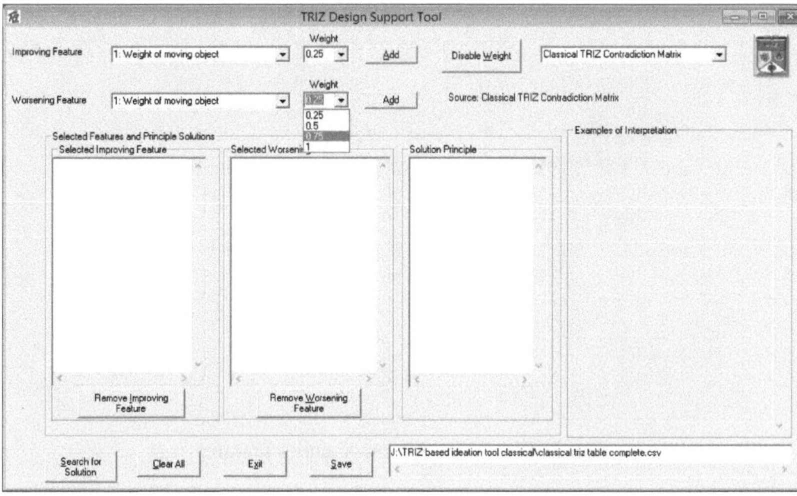

Fig. 3. The graphical user interface of the Engineering Design Support Tool based on TRIZ

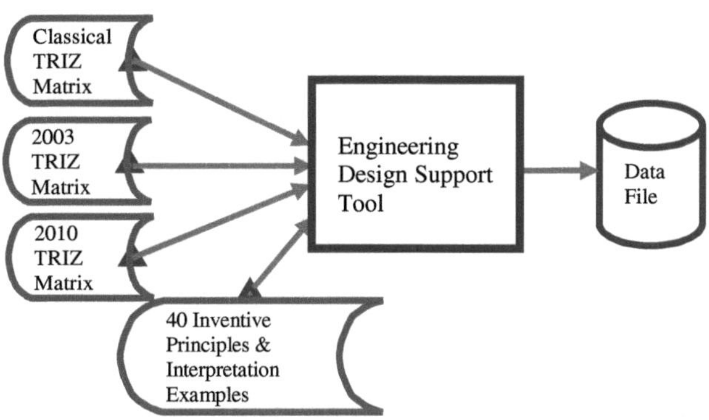

Fig. 4. The architecture of the Engineering Design Support Tool based on TRIZ

value (*csv*) file. Depending on which version of TRIZ contradiction matrix the designer wanted to use, the program will open and extract the appropriate *csv* file. The inventive principles and the interpretation of the inventive principles are stored in another *csv* file where during the search for design solutions, this file will be opened and searched. The program will allow the designer to save their search data and results in a text file. Fig. 4 shows the architecture of the software tool.

When the software tool is initially launched, there is no improving and worsening features selected and the designer is required to select them using the pull down menu as shown in Fig. 5. The default TRIZ matrix initially launched is the classical TRIZ contradiction matrix but the designer can choose the other version of TRIZ contradiction matrix as shown in Fig. 6.

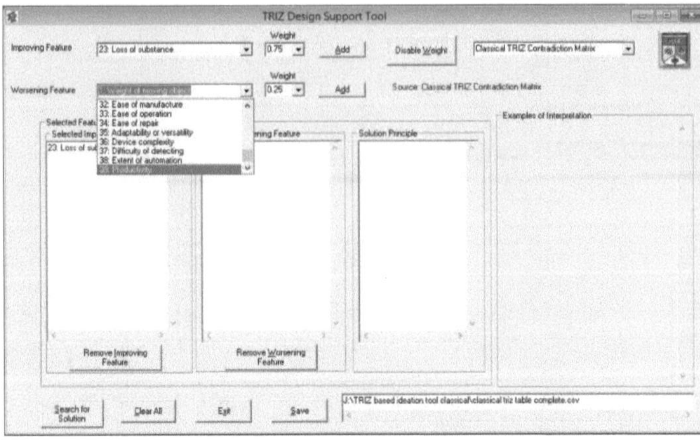

Fig. 5. The selection of worsening features

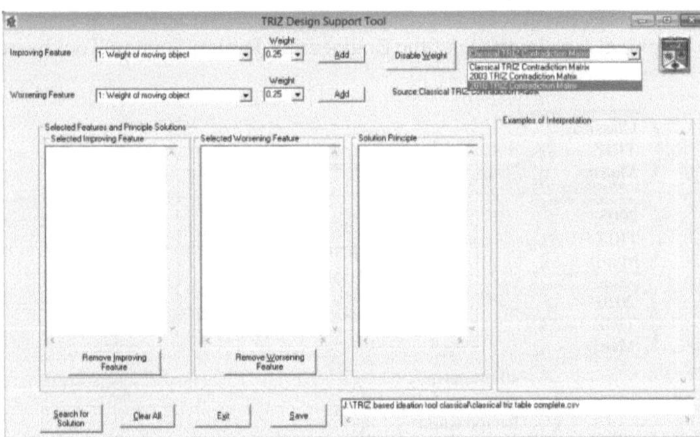

Fig. 6. The selection of the version of TRIZ contradiction matrix

6.2 Case Study: Design of a Pipe Transporting Wood-Based Material Using the Engineering Support Tool Based on TRIZ

In order to verify the effectiveness of the software tool, the tool was utilised in a case study. In this case study, a designer wanted to design a pipe to transport wood-based products using water as the medium (refer to Fig. 7). The flowing of water carries the wood-based products in the pipe and due to consistent knocking and rubbing of these wood-based products, it is common for the pipes to crack and leak after several weeks. Hence, the new pipe needs to withstand the rubbing and knocking of the wood-based products and last much longer than the existing one. However, cost is a major concern in this problem. The new design should have a minimum impact on cost. Using the engineering design support tool, the designer has decided to apply two improving features with two corresponding worsening features and utilise the classical TRIZ contradiction matrix as tabulated in Table 5.

Table 5. The improving and worsening features as well as their reasoning for the design of pipe in transporting wood-based product case study

Improving feature	Weight	Worsening Feature	Weight	Reasoning
23: Loss of Substance	1	**9: Speed**	0.5	The problem of water leaking from the pipe after weeks of operation need to be improved. Reducing the water flow rate is one way to reduce the knocking and rubbing of the wood-based product.
31: Other harmful effects generated by system	0.5	**39: Productivity**	0.5	Need to reduce (or improve) the harmful effect of knocking and rubbing against the pipe from the wood-based product. If less wood-based products are transported at one time, this will reduce the harmful effects but affects the productivity.

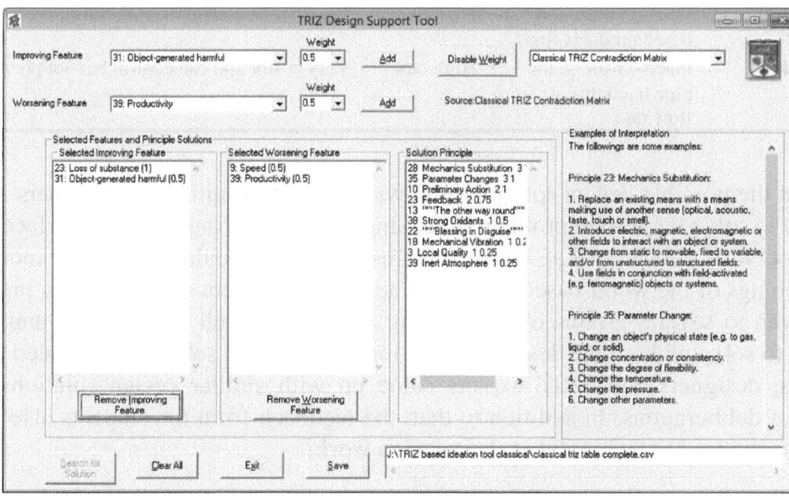

Fig. 7. The use of the Engineering Design Support Tool based on TRIZ to solve the leaking pipe design problem

The weight selected for the loss of substance is the highest (1.0) compared to the others because it is a confirmed problem. The other features were given the weight of 0.5 because of the uncertainty in their contributions to the design problem. Unlike the leaking of water which is observed and confirmed, the cause of the leak due to the knocking and rubbing of the wood-based material can only be a possibility because internal stress or manufacturing defects can also cause the pipe to fail. In this case study, these worsening features were identified based on assumptions and logics, thus these features can only be a possibility.

When the engineering design support tool was used to process these improving and worsening features as shown in Fig. 7, the inventive principles recommended to solve the leaking pipe problem are as shown in Table 6. Based on these inventive principles, the designers were able to come up with the possible design solutions which are also shown in Table 6.

Table 6. The design solutions from the classical TRIZ contradiction matrix based on the recommended inventive principles

Recommended Inventive Principle	Possible Design Solution	Feasibility Study	Further Description/ Explanation
Mechanics Substitution	Change the material of the pipe	High cost	Such change will involve suppliers and replacing all pipes will be costly.
	Change the wood-based products	Not possible	These products are made to the preference of the customer. No design change allowed.
	Coat with polyurea	Reasonable Cost	Spray the existing and the new pipe with polyurea coating.
Parameter Change	Make the pipe thicker	High cost	Again this involves suppliers and all pipes need to be replaced.
	Remove sharp edges of the wood-based product	Not possible	These products are made to the preference of the customer. No design change allowed.
	Change the mode of transportation	High cost	New transportation mode may not be suitable and it will be costly.
Preliminary Action	Cushion the wood-based products first	High cost	Very labour intensive and costly.
Feedback	Place sensor on the pipe to control water flow rate	High cost	Very costly and can control but not prevent.

From the possible design solutions and with the cost in mind, the designers finally decided to solve the design problem of leaking pipe by coating the inner surface of all new pipe with a material known as polyurea [8] which could absorb the knockings and rubbings of the wood-based product. The design problem of this leaking pipe was also given to several groups of engineering students as well as designers and TRIZ experts to solve without the design support tool. The design solutions presented by the students, designers and TRIZ experts came up with similar design solutions after weeks of deliberations. In addition to that, the feedback from the students also found this software tool to be helpful in their design work.

7 Conclusions

This paper has shown that there are three versions of TRIZ contradiction matrix available and apparently all three have their strengths and deficiencies. From designers' perspective, all three versions of TRIZ contradiction matrix can be very helpful to designers but with the newer version adding more features, the task of designing has become more challenging. Hence, the engineering design support tool based on TRIZ was derived and developed to assist designers to design better. In addition to that, this software tool also have the flexibility to allow designers to prioritise the improving and worsening features using weights and select which version of TRIZ contradiction matrix they wish.

The engineering design support tool based on TRIZ was demonstrated to be useful and effective in a case study that involved in designing new pipe for transporting wood-based products. The existing pipe was found to be leaking in operation after weeks and the new design needed to take into consideration about cost. The engineering support tool based on TRIZ recommended mechanics substitution inventive principle to solve the problem and the final solution was to coat the pipe with a layer of polyurea.

Acknowledgment. The authors would like to thank Universiti Kebangsaan Malaysia for sponsoring this research by using the funding of the research project ERGS/1/2011/STG/UKM/02/44.

References

1. Mann, D.L.: Hands-on systematic innovation. CREAX Press, Leper (2002)
2. Pham, D.T., Liu, H.: An I-CHING-TRIZ-inspired approach to design concept generation. In: Proc. ASME 2009 Int. Design Eng. Technical Conf. & Computers and Information in Eng. Conf. (IDETC/CIE 2009). Pinehurst Technologies, Inc., San Diego (2009)
3. Mann, D.L.: Matrix 2010: Re-updating the TRIZ contradiction matrix. IFR Press, Devon (2009)
4. Mann, D.L., Dewulf, S., Zlotin, B., Zusman, A.: Matrix 2003: Updating the TRIZ contradiction matrix. CREAX Press, Leper (2003)
5. Pham, D.T., Liu, H.: A new TRIZ-based approach to design concept generation. In: Int. Conf. on Manufacturing Research. Liverpool John Moores University, Liverpool (2006)
6. Pham, D.T., Ng, K.W., Ang, M.C.: Applying TRIZ to support designers in a descriptive design framework. In: Proc. of the ASME 2009 Int. Design Engineering Tech. Conf. & Computers and Information in Engineering Conf. (IDETC/CIE 2009), San Diego, California, USA (2009)
7. Otto, K., Antonsson, E.: Trade-off strategies in engineering design. Research in Engineering Design 3, 87–103 (1991)
8. Knight, W.J.: Polyurea Spray Coatings: An introduction. Journal of Protective Coatings and Linings 18, 48–52 (2001)

Enhancing an Automated Inspection System on Printed Circuit Boards Using Affine-SIFT and TRIZ Techniques

Amirhossein Aghamohammadi[1], Mei Choo Ang[1], Anton Satria Prabuwono[2], Marzieh Mogharrebi[1], and Kok Weng Ng[3]

[1] Institute of Visual Informatics (IVI)
[2] Faculty of Information Science and Technology, National University of Malaysia (UKM)
[3] Design Engineering Section, Industrial Design Centre, Sirim Berhad, Bukit Jalil, Kuala Lumpur, Malaysia
{amir.h.moh,mogharrebi.marzieh}@gmail.com, amc@ukm.my, antonsatria@ftsm.ukm.my, kwng@sirim.my

Abstract. Automated visual inspection is an important step to assure the quality of printed circuit boards (PCB). Component placement errors such as missing, misaligned or incorrectly rotated component are major causes of defects on surface mount PCB. This paper proposes a novel automated visual inspection method for PCB. The proposed method uses a sequence of image processing techniques inspired by the theory of inventive problem solving (TRIZ) with Affine-SIFT image matching techniques to enhance the component placement inspection. Only analytic discussions are presented in this paper to support the potential of the proposed method.

Keywords: automated visual inspection, printed circuit board, image matching, affine-sift, theory of inventive problem solving.

1 Introduction

Electronics manufacturers have been keen to implement automated solutions to inspect the quality of their products [1]. Among the automated solutions, automated visual inspection systems have been a popular choice for off-line and real-time inspection, monitoring and quality assurance processes [2]. These automated visual inspection systems are used to replace the tedious and time-consuming manual quality checking tasks carried out by human experts [3].

Printed circuit board (PCB) assembly is a main activity in electronic manufacturing sector. Since the PCB involves higher levels of component density, the component placement inspection process become unprecedentedly tight and time-consuming [4]. Various inspection methods for PCB components have been proposed based on wavelet theory [5], X-ray imaging [1] and automatic visual/optical inspection (AOI) [6]. AOI-based methods are considered to be extensively applied for PCB inspection [7] among these various inspection methods. In AOI-based methods, image matching technique is one of the main steps for component placement inspection [4]. Basically, the matching process involves the comparison of a PCB reference image as a template

H. Badioze Zaman et al. (Eds.): IVIC 2013, LNCS 8237, pp. 128–137, 2013.

and the PCBs under inspection. Direct subtracting of the template from the image under inspection followed by an elimination procedure is widely used to detect the defects (missing, misaligned or incorrectly rotated component) on a PCB. This approach can tackle the component checking task. However, inspection problems for misaligned components and incorrect rotated components are still difficult to be solved and inspection run-time is relatively too long [4]. Therefore, finding an appropriate inspection method is still needed to improve the efficiency and reduce inspection run-time [27].

This paper proposes an automated visual inspection system for PCB components. The proposed method uses a sequence of image processing techniques inspired by the theory of inventive problem solving (TRIZ) and Affine-SIFT image matching techniques to overcome PCB component inspection problem. The TRIZ inventive principle solutions were used to decide on the image processing techniques for the proposed automated visual inspection system to enhance PCB inspection process while the Affine-SIFT technique is applied to find any mismatch components on PCB. The proposed method will be analysed and compared with three other methods to justify its potential.

The following sections provide a brief introduction for TRIZ theory, image matching and Affine-SIFT algorithms. Section 2 reviews some existing PCB inspection systems. Section 3 describes the proposed method. Section 4 presents the discussion and comparison of the proposed method. Finally, the conclusion of the paper is given in Section 5.

1.1 Theory of Inventive Problem Solving

Teoriya Resheniya Izobretatelskikh Zadatch (TRIZ) is known as the theory of inventive problem solving and it was created by Genrich Altshuller in 1985 [9]. TRIZ has a total of 40 inventive principles derived from patents. These 40 inventive principles are very abstract and their interpretations are very subjective. TRIZ is used to help designers or developers to design or solve their problems. TRIZ has been applied, not only for design problems but also for business and software development problems. In addition to that, TRIZ theory is also extensively applied to enhance various processes in manufacturing. Some of the recent TRIZ applications are in the application of optimisation [8] and [10] that includes the optimisation of PCB assembly process [8].

1.2 Fully Affine Invariant Comparison (Affine-SIFT)

Image matching process is intended to establish the correspondences among similar objects and elements in different images. The image matching process is a basic and fundamental step in computer vision, pattern recognition and image processing applications such as object identification [11], two-dimensional (2D) and three-dimension (3D) reconstruction [12], object moving tracking [13], content–based image retrieval (CBIR) [14], and image registration [15] and [16].

Performing shape and object matching in images is a difficult task. This is because images of an object can be captured with different cameras and viewpoints.

These different camera viewpoints induce apparent distortion of the object image. Thus, a desired object matching system must be invariant with respect to such distortions.

There are many algorithms that have been proposed to overcome the invariant difficulty. Amidst these algorithms, the scale-invariant feature transform (SIFT) descriptor has been shown to be superior to many other algorithms [17]. Lowe [17] has proposed the SIFT to image scaling and rotation and partially invariant to illumination and viewpoint changes.

Affine-SIFT is an improved algorithm from SIFT that is fully affine invariant where the SIFT is partially invariant [18]. Affine-SIFT consider all images views obtained by the longitude and latitude angles and then matching by using SIFT algorithm. There is a new notion called transition tilt that is designed to quantify the amount of tilt between two such images. Fig. 1 shows the major steps of the Affine-SIFT algorithm [11] and [19].

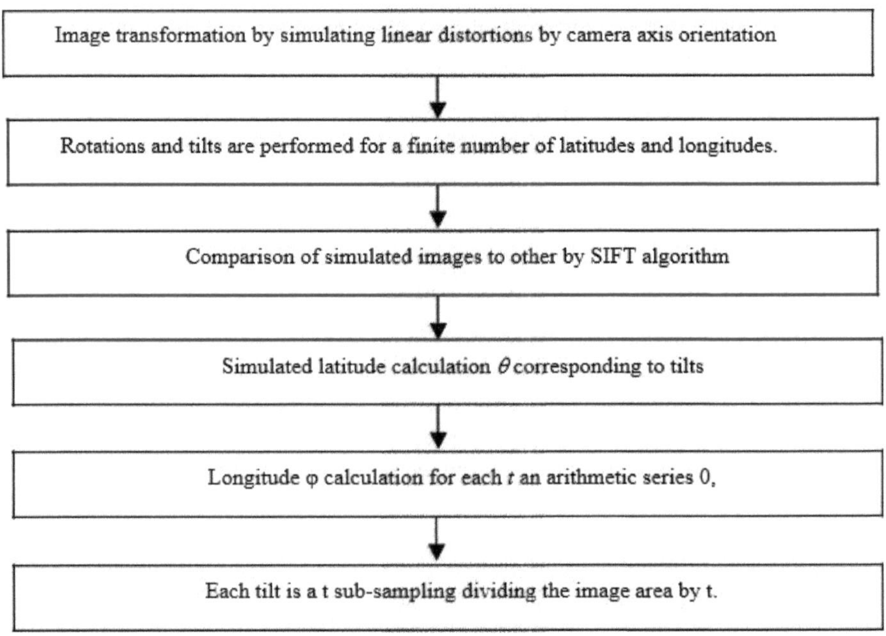

Fig. 1. Affine-SIFT algorithm [11, 19]

2 Related Works

There are different techniques applied in PCB inspection research which include trends to use artificial intelligence [20], such as evolutionary computation [21] and swarm intelligence [22] techniques. Among these techniques, image matching-based techniques have been extensively considered due to good performance [23] and [24]. Hence, in this section, we concentrate on the review of recent image matching in PCB inspection methods.

Template matching method was proposed for component placement inspection of PCB surface mount device (SMD) process by Cho [25]. The methodology was based on matching of component on input image with its standard image by template matching algorithm to discriminate mismatch assembled components. For a fast inspection, wavelet-based transformation was applied to reduce the image size as well as the calculation time. According to their presented results, template matching technique was effective in detecting the mismatched components on PCB.

A multi-templates matching (MTM) technique was developed for PCB components placement inspection by Dong [21]. The proposed approach was based on using chaotic species based particle swarm optimization (SPSO) and it was applied to the multi-template matching (MTM) process to determine the existence, location and alignment of a component within a captured image in the PCB. In order to evaluate the efficiency, they presented a comparison of their proposed method with other inspection methods. According to their presented results, their proposed method was able to find matching components efficiently though the processing-time was relatively long.

Wu [4] proposed an automatic visual inspection on PCB. Missing, misaligned and wrongly rotated components detection were as the main focus in his paper. They proposed an approach that includes the normalized cross correlation (NCC) based multi-template matching (MTM) method. Their proposed method was also focused on automatic object searching techniques for locating multiple components on a PCB. The searching process was accomplished by using the proposed accelerated species based particle swarm optimization (ASPSO) method and the genetic algorithm (GA). Their results indicated that the ASPSO proposed algorithm was able to reduce the computational time and it was effective in template matching. However, their proposed system did not consider PCBs inspection without fiducial marks.

A speed-up robust feature (SURF) approach was proposed to match PCB images by Dong [23]. Integrated strategies and Hough Transform (HT) techniques were used to build the matches and reject the wrong components matches. Based on their obtained results, the proposed algorithm could achieve a much better matching rate when compared to the ordinary SURF. However, the additional orientations have produced more descriptors causing it consume additional time for feature description and matching.

In research work, we tried to link the inventive principles of TRIZ to the established image processing processes to define a novel automated visual inspection system for PCB component placement inspection with no fiducial marks. Affine-SIFT algorithm was chosen for this system since it is a robust method.

3 Methodology

The focus of this research is to investigate an innovative approach to help manufacturers to enhance the PCB product inspection process. We propose a strategy to enhance the PCB component placement inspection based on TRIZ theory and Affine-SIFT techniques with the aim to reduce run-time and enhancing inspection accuracy. Fig. 2 shows the proposed methodology which is link TRIZ and Affine-SIFT techniques.

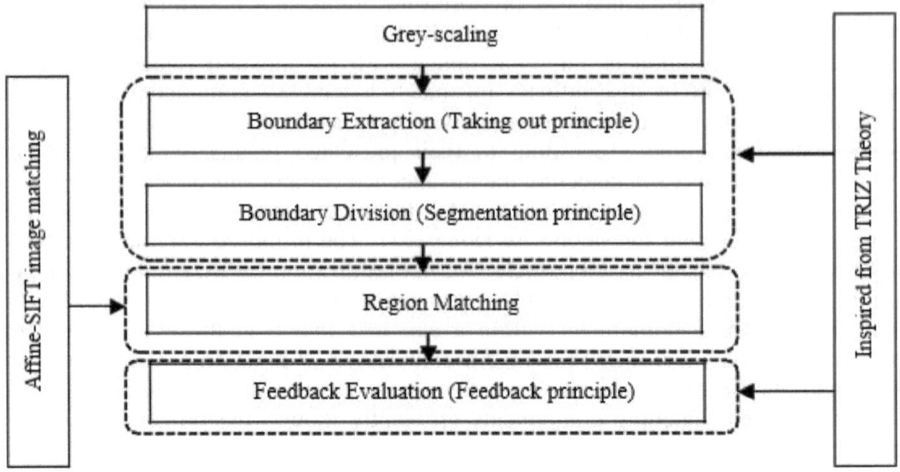

Fig. 2. The links of TRIZ and Affine-SIFT techniques in the proposed system

In order to enhance the automated inspection system, TRIZ-inspired principles are applied. In this case, only three principles are utilised. The principle number, name and description being applied in this paper are presented in Table 1. The 'taking out', 'segmentation' and the 'feedback' principles are derived based on the description of the inventive principles and an in depth study on how optimization algorithms work.

Table 1. The three adopted inventive principles of TRIZ.

Principle No	Principle Name	Description of principles	Applying TRIZ principles in PCB Inspection problem
1.	Taking out	Separate an interfering part or property from an object, or single out the only necessary part (or property) of an object	This principle suggests taking out and extracting each component region. The extracted region involves components such as resistor, capacitor and other electronic components.
2.	Segmentation	Divide an object into independent parts	After each component extraction, the region is segmented to sub-regions. This principle is utilized to facilitate robust matching.
3.	Feed back	Introduce feedback (referring back, cross-checking) to improve a process or action.	This principle suggests using feedback signal to inform the inspection system. The system should be sensitive to feedback from image matching. If a feedback from image matching (component comparison) process indicated a mismatch, the image matching process for other components would stop immediately.

The following section describes each step of the proposed method which is integration of TRIZ and Affine-SIFT techniques.

Step 1. Gray-scaling convert color image to gray color. Fig. 3 shows grayed image after gray-scaling step.

Fig. 3. Gray-scaling image

Step 2. Boundary extraction is performed to "taking out" the components boundaries. The extraction step is accomplished by boundary extraction function. This step is inspired from 'taking out' TRIZ principle. Fig. 4 illustrates an extracted boundary of a component.

Fig. 4. Boundary extraction of component

Step 3. In order to improve the accuracy in component placement detection, each extracted component is divided to sub regions. This step was inspired form the 'segmentation' TRIZ principle. Fig. 5 shows a divided boundary of a resistor component.

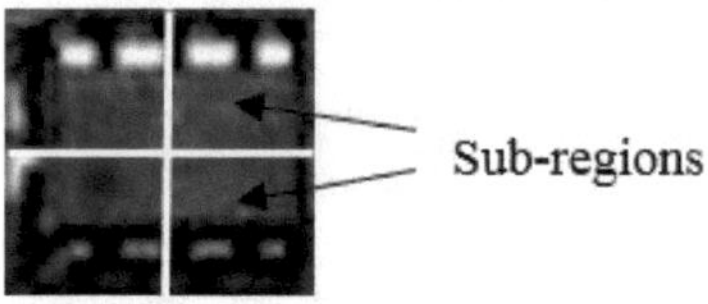

Fig. 5. Boundary division

Step 4. Matching process is the main step in our proposed method. In this step, each image is divided to regions before it is compared with the corresponding templates. Affine-SIFT algorithm applies in this matching process.

Step 5. Finally, the feedbacks from matching process are collected in order to make decision whether the PCB under inspection involves component placement defects or not. In this case, if there is any faulty component placement, all the processes are instantly interrupted and then PCB would be rejected. The feedback process is performed by if-else structure.

4 Discussion and Comparisons

The TRIZ theory is an innovative problem solving approach and it has been applied to inspire creativity. The recent application of using TRIZ with Bees algorithm in PCB assembly problem [8] showed that the TRIZ can be used to inspire the improvement of PCB assembly process. Their success has inspired us to propose the utilisation of TRIZ to look into the enhancement of the automated inspection system for PCB assembly. In our proposed system, based on TRIZ, we managed to link TRIZ inventive principles such as 'taking out', 'segmentation' and 'feedback' to the established image processing techniques such as boundary extraction, boundary division and feedback. The links to these principles assist us decide on established image processing techniques to be included to solve component placement inspection problem.

In addition to that, the Affine-SIFT image matching approach was chosen for the purpose of comparing the PCB under inspection with a template (with no defect). Based on this approach, incomplete and uncorrected component placement can be determined without special fiducial marks on PCB. Affine-SIFT algorithm is an improved version of SIFT algorithm which can efficiently detect the defects with shorter time [18]. Affine-SIFT is computationally expensive but the results are more accurate when compared to SIFT & SURF. In order to validate the efficiency of Affine-SIFT algorithm, we compared the result of some image matching methods (refer Table 2). Table 2 shows the number of corrected components matching on PCB images. The results for SIFT and Affine-SIFT algorithms are collected after testing images from online demo by Jean [28].

Table 2. Comparison of image matching techniques [28]

	Hessian-Affine	Harris-Affine	SIFT	SURF	Affine-SIFT
Number of corrected components matching	9	13	15	19	28

As shown in Table 2, Affine-SIFT, SURF, SIFT, Harris-Affine, Hessian-Affine find respectively 28, 19, 15, 13 and 9 correct matches. The comparison showed that Affine-SIFT method is considered as the best algorithm at the aspect of the affine invariant [26]. Therefore, the Affine-SIFT method is selected for incorrect component placement detection on PCB.

Finally, the comparison of the proposed and other PCB inspection methods was presented to prove the efficiency of our proposed system. Images matching in different viewpoints and image rotation condition, essentiality of existing fiducial marks on PCB and processing-time evaluation factors were considered to justify our proposed method is more robust in compared to other methods. Table 3 shows the comparison of proposed method and other inspection methods on PCB component placement inspection.

Table 3. Comparison of PCB component placement inspection techniques

Authors	Technique	Image matching in different viewpoints and image rotation condition	Essentiality of existing fiducial mark on PCB	Processing-time evaluation
Wu et al. (2009) [26]	Chaotic-base Particle Optimization (CSPSO)	No	Yes	Fast. Proposed method has outstanding iterative speed and need uniform distribution to increase the speed.
Cho and Park (2010) [25]	Wavelet-based transformation template matching algorithm	No	Yes	Fast. High speed in the inspection process.
Dong et al. (2012) [23]	Speeded Up Robust Features (SURF)	Yes	No*	Longer time. Longer time for feature description and matching.
Proposed method	TRIZ and Affine-SIFT algorithm	Yes	No*	Shorter time. It is expected to be relatively shorter time when Affine-SIFT is compared to SURF algorithm.

*This is preferable as no fiducial limitation.

As illustrated by Dong [23], the PCB is occasionally incorrectly located under a camera. In order to implement robust inspection system, the system must consider different viewpoint and rotation conditions especially during matching process. Hence, our proposed method has to consider these factors to overcome varying conditions such as different viewpoints and rotation conditions.

Furthermore, fiducial marks could cause problems in PCB inspection as highlighted by Dong [23]. Since, many inspection methods were based on fiducial marks to perform faulty component placement detection; these fiducial marks will constrain the inspection process. If PCB has no fiducial marks, then it becomes difficult to identify the faulty component during the component matching process. Thus, our proposed method is not relying on the need to have fiducial marks and it can be efficiently used in component placement inspection on PCB.

5 Conclusion

Automated visual inspection of printed circuit board (PCB) is an important step in PCB manufacturing to assure quality and to reduce manufacturing scrap costs and rework. The purpose of this paper is to propose the use of Affine-SIFT image matching algorithm and established image processing techniques inspired by TRIZ theory for automated visual inspection of PCB components without using special fiducial marks. Comparative analysis and discussions on the automated visual inspection system based on Affine-based method and established image processing techniques inspired by TRIZ showed that the proposed system is an effective and robust method to match the PCB images and detect incomplete or incorrect component placement on PCB without using fiducial marks. The proposed system has the potential to enhance the component placement inspection process.

Acknowledgments. The authors would like to thank Universiti Kebangsaan Malaysia and Ministry of Higher Education for sponsoring this research by using the funding of the research project UKM-TT-07-FRGS0249-2010.

References

1. Chuang, S.-F., Chang, W.-T., Lin, C.-C., Tarng, Y.-S.: Misalignment inspection of multilayer PCBs with an automated X-ray machine vision system. The International Journal of Advanced Manufacturing Technology 51, 995–1008 (2010)
2. Perng, D.-B., Liu, H.-W., Chang, C.-C.: Automated SMD LED inspection using machine vision. The International Journal of Advanced Manufacturing Technology 57, 1065–1077 (2011)
3. Zeng, Z., Ma, L.Z., Zheng, Z.Y.: Automated extraction of PCB components based on specularity using layered illumination. Journal of Intelligent Manufacturing 22, 919–932 (2011)
4. Wu, C.-H., Wang, D.-Z., Ip, A., Wang, D.-W., Chan, C.-Y., Wang, H.-F.: A particle swarm optimization approach for components placement inspection on printed circuit boards. Journal of Intelligent Manufacturing 20, 535–549 (2009)
5. Chu, C., Wang, C., Jiang, B.: An Automatic Image Enhancement Framework for Industrial Products Inspection. In: Proceedings of the Institute of Industrial Engineers Asian Conference, pp. 73–78. Springer (2013)
6. Mogharrebi, M., Prabuwono, A.S., Sahran, S., Aghamohammadi, A.: Missing Component Detection on PCB Using Neural Networks. In: Zheng, D. (ed.) Advances in Electrical Engineering & Electrical Machines. LNEE, vol. 134, pp. 387–394. Springer, Heidelberg (2012)
7. Mar, N.S.S., Yarlagadda, P., Fookes, C.: Design and development of automatic visual inspection system for PCB manufacturing. Robotics and Computer-Integrated Manufacturing 27, 949–962 (2011)
8. Ang, M.C., Pham, D.T., Soroka, A.J., Ng, K.W.: PCB assembly optimisation using the Bees Algorithm enhanced with TRIZ operators. In: IECON 2010 - 36th Annual Conference on IEEE Industrial Electronics Society, pp. 2708–2713 (2010)
9. Altshuller, G.: The innovation algorithm: TRIZ, systematic innovation and technical creativity. Technical Innovation Ctr, Worcester (1999)

10. Ahmad, S.A., Pham, D.T., Ng, K.W., Ang, M.C.: TRIZ-inspired Asymmetrical Search Neighborhood in the Bees Algorithm. In: 2012 Sixth Asia Modelling Symposium (AMS). IEEE (2012)
11. Yu, G., Morel, J.-M.: A fully affine invariant image comparison method. In: IEEE International Conference on Acoustics, Speech and Signal Processing, ICASSP 2009. IEEE (2009)
12. Newcombe, R.A., Davison, A.J.: Live dense reconstruction with a single moving camera. In: 2010 IEEE Conference on Computer Vision and Pattern Recognition (CVPR). IEEE (2010)
13. Ta, D.-N., Chen, W.-C., Gelfand, N., Pulli, K.: SURFTrac: Efficient tracking and continuous object recognition using local feature descriptors. In: IEEE Conference on Computer Vision and Pattern Recognition, CVPR 2009. IEEE (2009)
14. Doubek, P., Matas, J., Perdoch, M., Chum, O.: Image matching and retrieval by repetitive patterns. In: 2010 20th International Conference on Pattern Recognition (ICPR). IEEE (2010)
15. Morel, J., Yu, G.: Is SIFT scale invariant? Inverse Problems and Imaging 5, 115–136 (2011)
16. Morel, J.-M., Yu, G.: ASIFT: A new framework for fully affine invariant image comparison. SIAM Journal on Imaging Sciences 2, 438–469 (2009)
17. Lowe, D.G.: Object recognition from local scale-invariant features. In: The Proceedings of the Seventh IEEE International Conference on Computer Vision. IEEE (1999)
18. Oji, R.: An Automatic Algorithm for Object Recognition and Detection Based on ASIFT Keypoints, arXiv preprint arXiv:1211.5829 (2012)
19. Yu, G., Morel, J.-M.: ASIFT: An Algorithm for Fully Affine Invariant Comparison. Image Processing On Line (2011)
20. Su, Y.-Y., Srihari, K.: Placement sequence identification using artificial neural networks in surface mount PCB assembly. The International Journal of Advanced Manufacturing Technology 11, 285–299 (1996)
21. Dong, N., Wu, C.-H., Ip, W.-H., Chen, Z.-Q., Yung, K.-L.: Chaotic species based particle swarm optimization algorithms and its application in PCB components detection. Expert Systems with Applications (2012)
22. Wu, H., Kuang, Y., Ouyang, G., Xie, H., Zhang, X.: Optimize Position and Path Planning of Automated Optical Inspection. Journal of Computational Information Systems 8, 2957–2963 (2012)
23. Dong, Z.-J., Ye, F., Li, D., Huang, J.-X.: PCB matching based on SURF. Circuit World 38, 153–162 (2012)
24. Crispin, A., Rankov, V.: Automated inspection of PCB components using a genetic algorithm template-matching approach. The International Journal of Advanced Manufacturing Technology 35, 293–300 (2007)
25. Cho, H.-J., Park, T.-H.: Wavelet transform based image template matching for automatic component inspection. The International Journal of Advanced Manufacturing Technology 50, 1033–1039 (2010)
26. Wu, C., Dong, N., Ip, W., Chen, Z., Yung, K.: Applying Chaotic Particle Swarm Optimization to the Template Matching Problem. In: Cai, Z., Li, Z., Kang, Z., Liu, Y. (eds.) ISICA 2009. LNCS, vol. 5821, pp. 411–421. Springer, Heidelberg (2009)
27. Xie, F., Uitdenbogerd, A., Song, A.: Detecting PCB component placement defects by genetic programming. In: Congress on Evolutionary Computation (CEC), pp. 1138–1145. IEEE (2013)
28. Jean, M.M., Guoshen, Y.: SIFT and ASIFT — online demo: try if your images match! (2011), `http://www.cmap.polytechnique.fr/~yu/research/ASIFT/demo.html`, `http://demo.ipol.im/demo/my_affine_sift/`

Effective Method of Mobile Human Computer Interface for Military Operation Training

Fatin Farhana Abd. Khalid, Syed Nasir Alsagoff, and Mohd. Hazali Mohamed Halip

Department of Computer Science, National Defence University of Malaysia,
Sungai Besi Camp, Kuala Lumpur, 57000 Malaysia
fatin.farhana@live.com,
{syednasir,hazali}@upnm.edu.my

Abstract. In this paper, we evaluate the various methods of Human Computer Interface (HCI) for mobile command and control for military operation. For example, within a forest, field of observation and communication are limited. Thus, the design of user interface for command and control system for military operation is important to ensure delivery of command and control is directly received to all soldiers who involved in the operation. This will ensure the effectiveness of mobile human computer interface for soldiers can be used for military operation in different kind of environment.

Keywords: mobile device, silent signals, human computer interface, haptic, command and control, communication.

1 Introduction

All the commands and controls in terms of the restructuring movements for army are very important. Normally, all the command and control are sent through visually and verbally. [1] At present, all the command and control are having modernization process with Future Soldier System technology. Before the soldiers can use it, we must evaluate the various methods to make sure the soldiers will not misunderstood and information of Common Operating Picture (COP) in real time will be channel to the section leader quickly and accurately. With the topography and forest in Malaysia that encompasses a wide variety of flora and fauna, command and control are very difficult to maintain. [2] As a result, various problems were faced by the army such as misguided, misunderstood, lost verbal command due to noise and confusion, limited view in forest environment for visual command and loss of security and confidentiality due the noise factor. [2]

In the battle against the enemy, the implementation of effective tactics and strategies are very important to ensure the smooth running of the war operations and on schedule. Yet, the problems encounter during this operation is the presentation of the information is unclear, ineffective and dubious safety. Therefore, with the existence of an application system, it can be used in assisting the section leader in a small unit army to communicate silently with his soldiers either deliver instructions to assault and making movements through Human Computer Interface (HCI) method.

H. Badioze Zaman et al. (Eds.): IVIC 2013, LNCS 8237, pp. 138–145, 2013.

1.1 Background of Study

The purpose of the attack is carried out the importance of making move to destroy the enemy or to capture the enemy. It is implemented by fire and movement. This attack can be done during the day or night. It may be made with noisy raid with the help of fire or silent. Silent attack is only feasible when limited visibility conditions, such as at night and in closed areas. Attacking is categorized into two types, an immediate attack and a planned attack. This is depends on the state of the enemy's defense preparations which is involving preparations to destroy the attacking team. [2]

During the shooting situation in the battlefield, communication between members of section troop of army with the section leader is very important. Military hand and arm signals are used during an assault to the enemy and when voice communication is difficult or not possible.

Silent signal or hand signal and an arm are the act of communication. This communication involves hands, arms and body posture. Firstly, by using hand without making a sound, the signal is transmitted through the section leader to every soldier. Section leader have to make sure that the section members receive and understand the hand signals used. Section leader should be focused during this signal delivery and must repeat the signal several times to the members section so that each of information to be conveyed is reached. Besides that, the section leader have to make sure he is standing in a strategic place so that all members can see the movements he is done. [3]

This communication is used by the armed forces to communicate with other combat forces when communication devices such as radio set cannot be used. The silent signal over the phone in the field of human computer interfaces is also intended to prevent information leakage that could damage the entire operation if using voice.

1.2 Objective of Study

The objective of this study is to evaluate the various methods of Human Computer Interface (HCI) for military operation and to ensure the effectiveness of mobile human computer interface for soldiers that can be used for military operation in different kind of environment.

1.3 Scope of Study

This study will be for small unit army only. The project scope involving the use of small screen Android operating system mobile device with 3 inch LCD display and has 240 x 320 pixels resolution.

1.4 Significance of Study

It will increase the capability including the offensive and defensive capabilities and survivability of the soldiers. It is also can be a starting point for Future Soldier Program which is a modernization exercise designed to prepare the soldiers for the future.

2 Literature Review

In general, the HCI involves interaction between human as a user and computer. For example, using the keyboard and mouse are the most popular among all types of HCI. These tools are used in carrying out the delivery of instruction and delivery information between computer and user. The presence of virtual reality and the use of computer tools such as smart phones and tablets have gone beyond all the existing limitations. [4] Development of HCI technology is emerging as one of the new strategy in software development with the emergence of various applications. These days, power of computing capability of mobile devices is rising. This technology can support image based interaction and can allow users to produce creative content.

Haptic technology is a tactile feedback technology which takes advantage of the sense of touch by applying forces, vibrations or motions to the user. [5] The tactile input method is a push type input method using buttons and keys. [6] Haptic is relating to or based on the sense of touch. It allows user to touch, fell, manipulate, create and alter simulated three-dimensional objects in a virtual environment. It is activated by actuators that apply forces to the skin for touch feedback and controllers and enable user to feel something happening in the computer's mind through a typical interface.

Haptic force feedback significantly improves task performance, perceived task performance, and perceived virtual presence in the collaborative distributed environment. [7]

3 Mobile Human Computer Interface

Our system will have three features that completed the whole system flow for soldiers as they are receiving commands from the section leader.

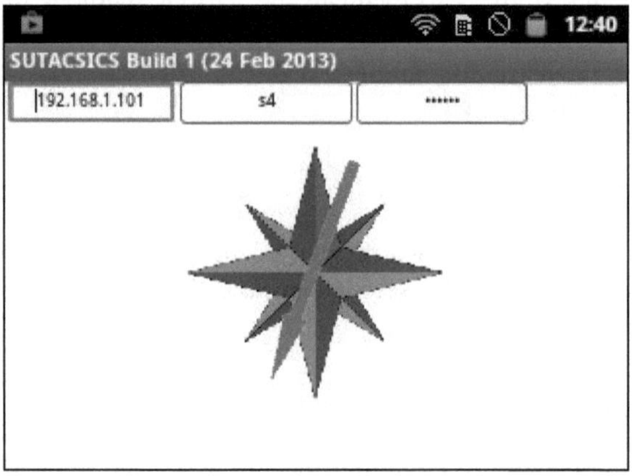

Fig. 1. System interface that consists of all command and control features for section members (soldiers)

- Voice alert - To notify command orders received and give alert for the soldiers' next movement.
- Haptic – Vibration alert to grab the soldier's attention and informing to perform the command orders.
- Command / order display – To display commands directly on the mobile screen.

4 Testing

4.1 Testing Procedure

The army soldiers have to ensure having complete equipment and wear all the equipment properly before commencing the operations as shown in Figure 2.

Fig. 2. Full set military orders consist of military camouflage uniform, helmet, boot, porches and belt

The uniform reflects orders and discipline and calls for subordination. They will be wearing full set military orders including military camouflage uniform suit to protect their skin and body and boot to comfort their foots and legs. The porches functioning as a bag pack to carry small equipment such as a high capacity power bank to increase operating hours and extending the mobile devices' battery life. They are wearing a helmet to put the mobile devices right in front of their eyes. In addition, the compass that built in the system will be more effective when it is put on their head, as shown in Figure 3 rather than holding on the hands which lead to many reflects movements that can distract the compass direction.

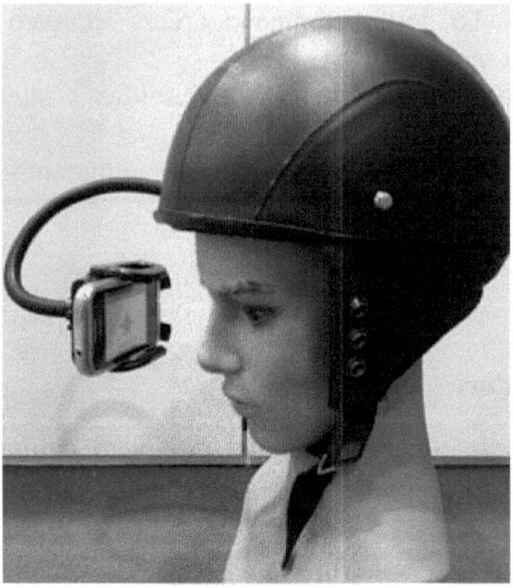

Fig. 3. Picture of a mannequin wearing a helmet with mobile device attached

4.2 Testing Procedure

The research testing of the system prototype has been done in a small forest field. This is a simulated exercise to assess the effectiveness of this mobile human computer interface method whether the soldiers can understand and effectively perform the orders given or not. The soldiers will be given regular commands such as "ATTACK", "DEFEND", "MOVE LEFT, "MOVE RIGHT" and so on. There will be no scenarios involved as this is just a movement exercise.

Fig. 4. Small forest field as the testing area

The experiment involved a team with 10 members. Each member is given a mobile device. After that a command will be sending to everybody at the same time. Time to response and accuracy of response are calculated and analyzed.

When we are sending the commands, all the man will be receiving commands in verbal, visual and haptic form. The command is sending to everybody to make sure they are not missed the command given at one time. If he did not listen to the voice alert, he can be notified by the vibration and indicator to look at the screen and perform the movement.

During the test, the server side interface in Figure 5 display the list of command, movement and location to send to the soldiers who carrying the mobile devices.

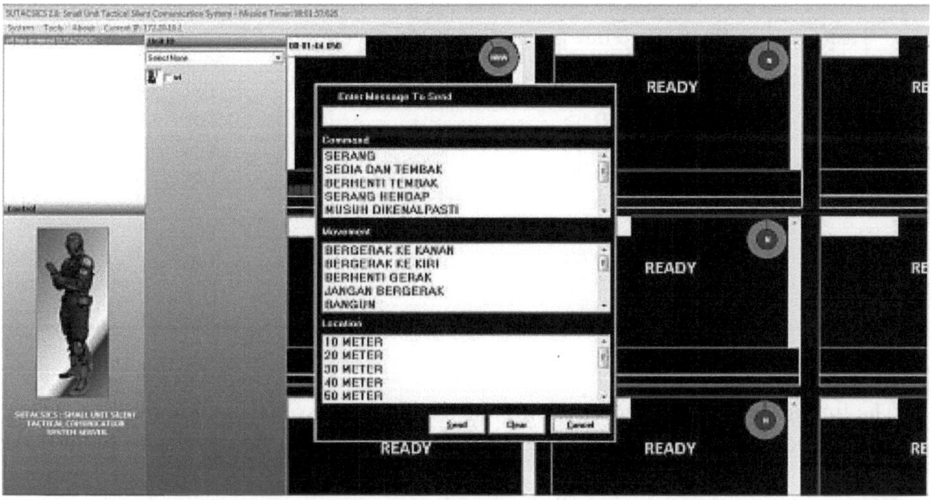

Fig. 5. Interface of system server application

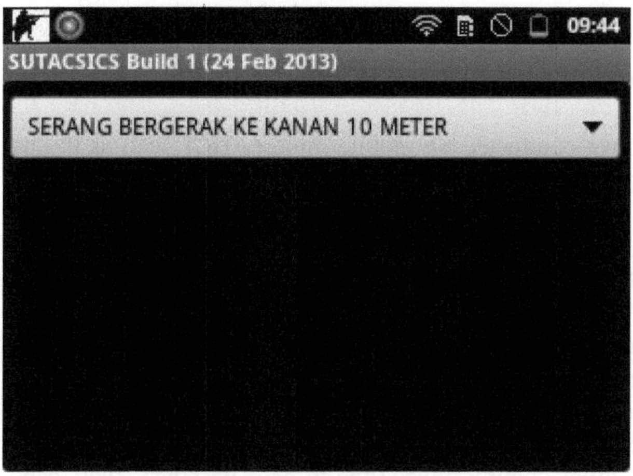

Fig. 6. Interface of command display

Mobile devices vibrated once the soldiers receiving any messages which include any command, movement or location that they should do.

4.3 Result

The time to response has been calculated and recorded as shown in Table 1. We are assuming the accuracy of response in between 0.5 seconds to 1.5 seconds is good enough.

Table 1. Table below shows the result of response time and accuracy of response by 10 men involved in the simulation exercise

Task	Response Time (seconds)	Accuracy of Response (Yes/No)
1	0.23	Yes
2	0.92	Yes
3	0.65	Yes
4	0.54	Yes
5	0.79	Yes
6	0.56	Yes
7	0.98	Yes
8	0.62	Yes
9	0.57	Yes
10	0.14	Yes

The limitations we had facing during the testing process is the soldier need to know the command direction accurately so that they had to place the devices to be in front all the time.

We are also having some challenges with the network communication instability because the range that can be covered up by the router and phone is in smaller range area only.

5 Conclusion and Future Work

Other studies have conducted on mobile military HCI such as the use of augmented reality, but none has focused on the effectiveness of the soldiers in an actual training environment.

Among the survey within the members who has been in the experiment test, this system can help section leader in commanding the members of the section in silent and no longer use the hand signals. Furthermore, this system can help section leader in plotting strategy against enemy attacks by delivering instructions to the members section quickly.

Mobile human computer interface is also seen to ensure delivery of command and control is directly received to all the section members simultaneously without having to make individual submissions (one-to-one passing) that can cause risk of information received is not the same as the information transmitted. By being able to send text commands, it minimizes the security issues from visual signal interception by the enemy and the loss of the element of surprise from the interception of verbal commands.

Next, this system can help the section members to be more understood of each order received without any confusion. Section leader does not need to be concerned with each delivery order to the members section because there is a safety element that uses encryption methods. Finally, this system is capable of assisting the section leader in the delivering orders to attack members of the section in a larger range in between 500 meters with integrated support of WIFI and radio communication devices.

In the future we are going to explore and investigate a more stabilize network communication, system stability and finding a proper testing areas. More experiment will be conducted in the different level of forest environment which included the primary forest and secondary forest.

References

1. Alsagoff, S.N.: Optimal command and control method for Malaysian army small units in a Malaysian forest environment: small unit tactical management system (SUTaMs). In: Zaman, H.B., Robinson, P., Petrou, M., Olivier, P., Shih, T.K., Velastin, S., Nyström, I. (eds.) IVIC 2011, Part II. LNCS, vol. 7067, pp. 419–427. Springer, Heidelberg (2011)
2. Ibrahim, M.S.: Kegunaan Future Soldier System Tentera Darat (FSS TD) Dalam Konteks Peperangan Gerila. Maktab Turus Angkatan Tentera Malaysia (2012)
3. Headquarters Department of the Army: Visual Signals, Washington, DC (1987)
4. Sharma, R., Pavlovic, V.I., Huang, T.S.: Toward multimodal human-computer interface. Proceedings of the IEEE 86(5), 853–869 (1998)
5. Hayward, V., Astley, O.R., Cruz-Hernandez, M., Grant, D., Robles-De-La-Torre, G.: Haptic interfaces and devices. Sensor Review 24(1), 16–29 (2004)
6. Song, T.H., Jeong, S.M., Kim, M.K., Kwon, K.H., Jeon, J.W.: Sensible interface using multi-sensors in mobile device. In: Proceedings of the 7th International Conference on Advances in Mobile Computing and Multimedia, pp. 637–641. ACM (2009)
7. Kuber, R., Yu, W., O'Modhrain, M.S.: Evaluation of haptic html mappings derived from a novel methodology. ACM Transactions on Accessible Computing (TACCESS) 3(4), 12 (2011)

A Simple Standalone Sign Based Recognition Translator without Using Super Computer Processing

Sandy Siu Ying Ko, Wei Lun Ng, Chee Kyun Ng, and Nor Kamariah Noordin

Department of Computer and Communication Systems Engineering,
Faculty of Engineering, University Putra Malaysia,
UPM Serdang, 43400 Selangor, Malaysia
{sandy1ing,william_2909}@hotmail.com,
{mpnck,nknordin}@eng.upm.edu.my

Abstract. In this paper, the design and development of a simple standalone sign based recognition translator without the use of supercomputer processing is presented. The main components for digital signal processing (DSP) and data storage in this translator system are peripheral interface controller (PIC) microcontroller and secure digital (SD) card respectively. The PIC 18F4620 is chosen as system's DSP because it is able to interface with the SD card. The input of sign gestures is being recognized and translated into text message such that people can understand its meanings. A flex sensor is attached to each finger in a data glove which has the capability to measure the finger sign. The five fingers per hand can create many different signs that can be translated into different text messages. The attached PIC 18F4620 microcontroller in the data glove receives the data associated with a given sign. These data are then diagnosed and translated by matching with the predefined data in the SD card data storage device by using deterministic matching model. When the data is matched, the matched predefined data will be sent to the microcontroller to display its text message on an on-board LCD module. The developed standalone translating system is flexible and adaptive as it can be reprogrammable according to the users that have special disabilities without any aid from a supercomputer.

Keywords: Sign language, recognition system, PIC microcontroller, SD card.

1 Introduction

Current technologies have extended our capabilities to overcome our physical limitations and interact with our environment in new ways. There are many cases in which different technologies can enable access or interaction for disabled people. For example, there are provisions of audible or touch alternatives for visually impaired people; interactive configurable learning devices to enable its use by people with learning difficulties; lifts and chair-lifts for people with mobility impairments; as well as provision of alternative ways of finding and manipulating information [1], [2].

Disabled people with communication difficulties as well as physical or learning impairments are doubly underprivileged in society. Thanks to new emerged

H. Badioze Zaman et al. (Eds.): IVIC 2013, LNCS 8237, pp. 146–156, 2013.

technologies in all industrialized and developed countries, there are much more communication project are launched with the aim to helping those with severe communication problems to express themselves. For human generally, being able to communicate means being able to send, transform and receive information. Of disabled people, those who are deaf, speech-impaired or who have certain motor disabilities have particular difficulty in sending information [3]. Hence, sign language is the natural way of communication for these disabled people all over the world [4]. Many researches and projects had been carried out to develop more utilities of the sign language.

A number of sign language translators have now been developed in various countries. Beyond issues of sign language utilization, they are mainly intended to provide a better means of communication between deaf or mute person and people that do not understand sign language. A translator device should be feasible in the next few years, which may provide immediate practical benefits to the deaf community, and leads to a sustainable program of research comparable to early speech recognition efforts [5].

A system is being developed in Greece for recognizing Greek sign language modules either signs or finger-spelled words, formed in isolation or combined into sentences. Greek Sign Language (GSL) is the natural way of communication between deaf people in Greece. The idea comes from the findings that most of the deaf people face a great difficulty in spelling Greek spoken words. The developed system is capable of recognizing finger-spelled words. It could also be used as a trainer for deaf students during their attempt to learn Greek spoken words [6]. However, the method used in building the recognition system is Hidden Markov Method (HMM), which requires complex processing with the computer assistance [7].

The objective this paper is to present the design and development of a simple and low cost translator for sign based recognition system without the use of supercomputer processing. The taken approach is to ensure the system is capable of translating and delivering text messages. The data of the finger sign gestures are collected from the hand glove using flex sensors to form a data glove system. These data are then analyzed by a programmable integrated circuit (PIC) 18F4620 microcontroller that attached at the data glove system. The received data consists of various voltage levels which will be converted into digital data. A standard secure digital (SD) card is used as data storage. The deterministic matching model is used to match the received data with the predefined data stored in SD card. The predefined data are the data library collected from the individual finger signs. When the data is matched, a message data will be sent to microcontroller display text message on an on-board Liquid Crystal Display (LCD) module.

2 System Design and Development

In this section, the system design and development of the standalone sign based recognition translator is described. The system consists of three main components: data glove, data storage and translator. The full process of the translating system is shown in Fig. 1.

The data glove system consists of hand glove and PIC 18F4620 microcontroller. The data glove uses flex sensors to collect the sign based gesture data [8]. The PIC 18F4620 microcontroller is used to perform DSP, which analyzes and translate the sign gestures into digital data [9]. The SD card data storage is used to store the predefined sign and command data for different finger signs data. The translator consists of a LCD module that will display text message according to the matched predefined sign data stored in SD card via PIC 18F4620 microcontroller.

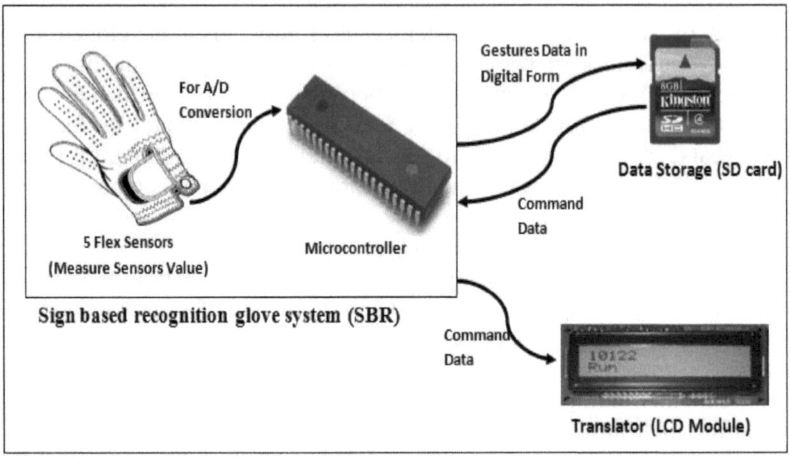

Fig. 1. The translating system overview

2.1 Data Glove

The data glove is a hand glove with five flex sensors attached to it. The flex sensor measures the change of resistance value based on the finger bending degree. Its resistance value varies from 10 KΩ (0° bending) to a maximum of 40 KΩ (90° bending). A basic flex sensor circuit consists of voltage divider (flex sensor and resistors) and impedance buffer (operational amplifier), as shown in Fig. 2.

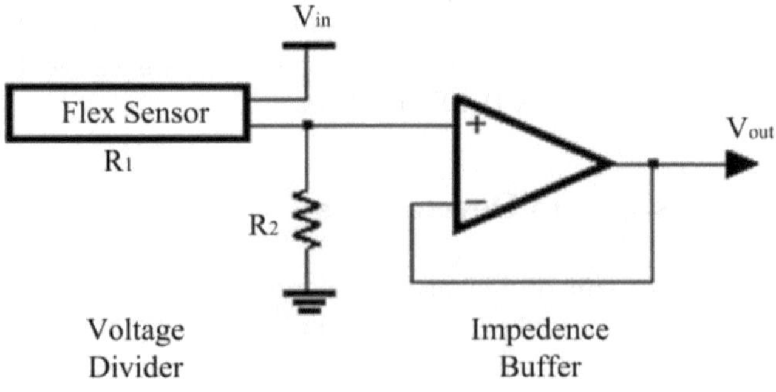

Fig. 2. Basic flex sensor circuit

The output voltage of the op-amp, V_{out} can be determined as

$$V_{out} = V_{in}\left(R_2 /(R_1 + R_2)\right) \tag{1}$$

where R_1 is the resistance of the flex sensor when bent, R_2 is the resistance of a resistor, and V_{in} is the power supplied to the circuit. The changed voltage value in the flex sensor circuit is the main data for the finger-sign recognition. The microcontroller PIC 18F4620 is used to perform the analog to digital conversion (ADC) operation, as a part of DSP. PIC18F4620 is chosen as it is able to interface with the SD card.

2.2 Data Storage

Data storage houses all the required data used by the system. The data storage is located in the SD card and it is inserted into a special card holder with external contacts to the PIC18F4620 microcontroller. There are two types of data which stored in the "data.txt" file in the SD card as shown in Fig. 3. The first type is the numeric value of predefined sign data that is necessary to recognize the received data from data glove. The second type is the message alphabet text data which represent the corresponding message to the predefined sign numeric value data.

One of the communication protocols for the SD memory card system is a serial peripheral interface (SPI) protocol. The SPI bus is a synchronous serial bus standard named by Motorola that operates in full duplex mode. Devices on an SPI bus operate in a master - slave mode, where the master device initiates the data transfer, selects a slave, and provides a clock for the slaves. The selected slave responds and sends its data to the master at each clock pulse. This simple interface is also called a "four-wire" interface [10], [11].

The SD memory card SPI channel consists of four signals: data out, DO (Card to PIC data signal), data in, DI (PIC to card data signal), clock, CLK (PIC to card clock signal), and chip select, CS (PIC to card Chip Select Signal). When the SD card operates in SPI mode, only seven pins are used as shown in Fig. 4. Three pins (pins 3, 4, and 6) are used for the power supply, leaving four pins (pins 1, 2, 5, and 7) for the SPI mode of operation. At power-up, the SD card defaults to the SD bus protocol. The card is switched to SPI mode if the CS signal is asserted during reception of the reset command. The host may reset a card by switching the power supply off and then on again. The PIC C compiler provides a library of commands for initializing, reading, and writing to SD card [11].

```
110,060,076,091,072-Hospital
114,064,080,097,104-Water
131,060,073,089,071-Food
113,065,111,125,112-Sleep
130,110,075,092,072-Toilet
```

Fig. 3. The samples of predefined data stored in the data.txt file

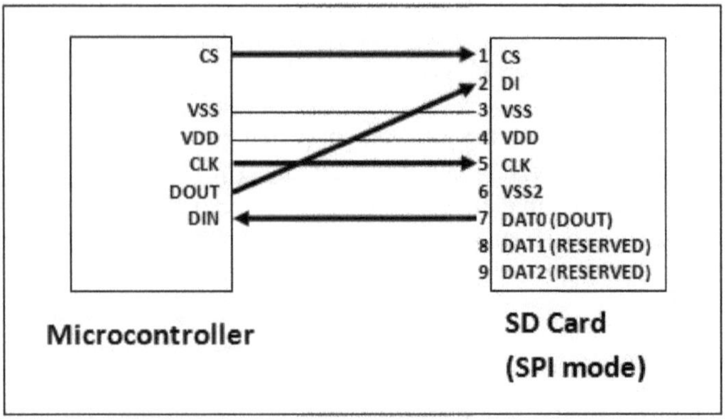

Fig. 4. The interface of the microcontroller and an SD card using SPI bus

2.3 Deterministic Matching Model

The deterministic matching model is an algorithm that compares the obtained sign gesture data from the data glove system to the predefined recognition gesture data stored in the SD card. The deterministic model works by margin matching algorithm. Direct matching is not being used as it is impossible to direct comparison result. The margin matching works by creating a margin of the received data. Assuming the received sign gesture data in digital form is 154. A margin is created by adding and subtracting the received data say margin of 5. Therefore the margin for the received data would be 149-159. By using decision methods (if-else function), the correct matching could be obtained. Higher margin creates large chances of matched whereas a smaller margin creates lower chances of matched. If a matched was found, the corresponding message data will be issued. However, if no match was found, the PIC will read another set of sign gesture input repeatedly until thc data is matched. The deterministic matching model can be explained with an example by considering a data string as shown in Table 1. This table shows an example of the received data glove signal data, predefined sign recognition data and margin ranged data of the corresponding message. If a match is found, the message data will be transmitted from the data storage to the translator via the microcontroller to display the corresponding text message 'ZERO' on an on-board LCD module.

Table 1. The data string of the deterministic model for recognizing a text message of 'ZERO'

	F0	F1	F2	F3	F4
Received data	153	175	171	132	150
Predefined data	155	172	173	132	146
Margin value	150 – 160	167 – 177	168 – 178	127 – 137	141 – 151

2.4 Translator

The translator consists of a LCD module. It requires a microcontroller to enable communication with the data storage. The microcontroller helps in controlling and configuring the LCD module. Figure 5 shows the interfacing of microcontroller and the

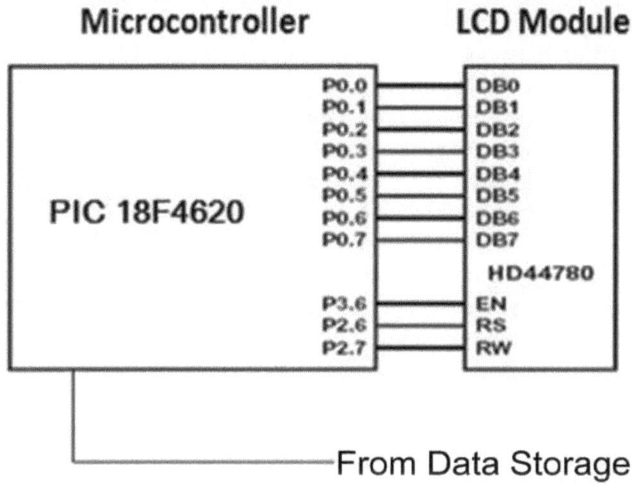

Fig. 5. The interface between microcontroller and LCD module

LCD module using serial communication which is an interface where information transfers in or out one bit at a time. The Hitachi HD44780 LCD controller supports eight downloadable characters. These characters are normally random garbage on power up. Also, the downloaded characters will be lost when the unit loses power, and will need to be programmed again. In this research, the model of 16 x 2 is used. Thus, the display provides a16-pin connector for interfacing. The mikroC LCD library provides a large number of functions to control text-based LCDs with 4-bit and 8-bit data interfaces, and for graphics LCDs. The most common is the 4-bit-interface text-based LCDs. The mikroC functions for these LCDs are available in the mikroC manual.

The operation of LCD module is illustrated as follows. First and foremost, interfacing with microcontroller makes LCD module capable of receiving bit values from microcontroller. It will get the message data from the microcontroller. The message data is the bit values that use to display corresponding message. In order to display text on the LCD screen, it must be configured. The LCD controller is told what sort of LCD screen is being used as well as the data bus format and the font. The various commands available can be found on the Hitachi HD44780 data sheet [12]. After the LCD screen is configured, the texts are written to the LCD screen. The message is then outputted to the LCD screen. After a message is displayed, the LCD module will again get message data from microcontroller and the operation is continued.

3 Implementation Results

Basically, how the sign based recognition system translator works is based on predefined data. The data stored on the SD card is used to keep a bank of predefined data. It is necessary to get the predefined data from the predefined sign gestures before they are being stored in the data storage. Figure 6 shows the source code for data matching using deterministic model. It involves reading the character data from

```
//data matching using deterministic model
      //use margin value = 5
      if(compare[0]-5<=sensor[0] && sensor[0]<=compare[0]+5 &&
      compare[1]-5<=sensor[1] && sensor[1]<=compare[1]+5 &&
      compare[2]-5<=sensor[2] && sensor[2]<=compare[2]+5 &&
      compare[3]-5<=sensor[3] && sensor[3]<=compare[3]+5 &&
      compare[4]-5<=sensor[4] && sensor[4]<=compare[4]+5)
         {
         lcd_putc("\fdata is match!");  //data is matched
         output_high(buzzer);     //alert the buzzer
         lcd_putc("\fMsg:  ");
         delay_ms(3000);
         output_low(buzzer);
      m = fatgetc(&stream); //read the corresponding message data
      while (m != '\r' && m != EOF)
         {
          printf(lcd_putc,"%c", m);     //output the message on LCD
          m = fatgetc(&stream);
          }
      return;
          }
      else
         {
         while (m != '\n')
           {
             m = fatgetc(&stream);
             if (m == EOF)      //data is not matched
             {
             lcd_putc("\fpls try again");
             delay_ms(5000);
             return;
             }
             }
          }
          } //back to the main function
```

Fig. 6. The source code for data matching using deterministic model

the data file that is stored in SD card, convert them to integer data, and then compare them with the sign gesture data that obtained from the DSP by using margin value.

The matching is started by reading line by line from the data file. If the matching is not successful with the first line of data stored in the SD card file, then it continues with the second line, and so forth. If the matching is successful, the corresponding message data are read and outputted. Otherwise, the comparison function will prompt for another sensor inputs and the process is repeated again.

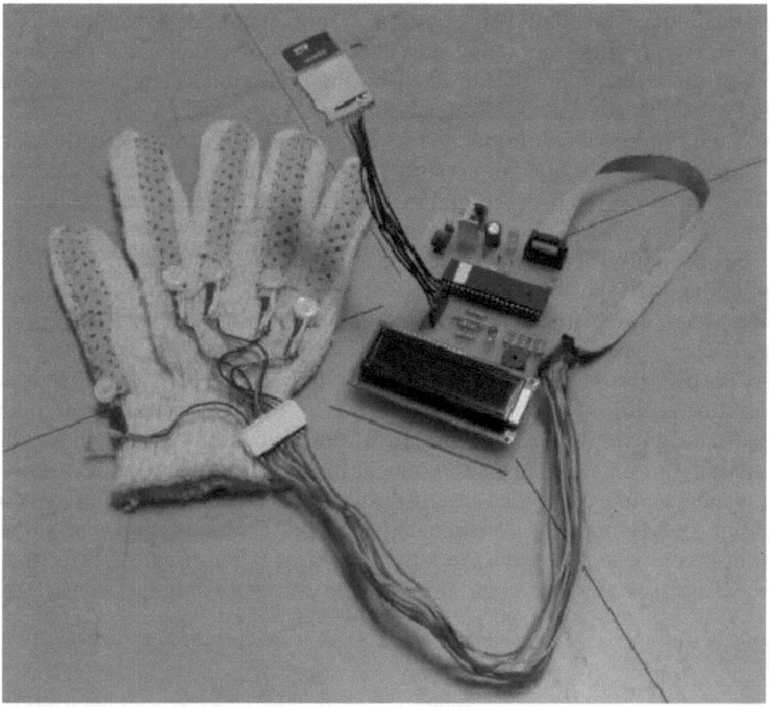

Fig. 7. The completed prototype of the developed standalone sign based recognition system

Table 2. The collected predefined data for five different sign gestures

No.	Sign Gesture	F0	F1	F2	F3	F4	Message
(1)	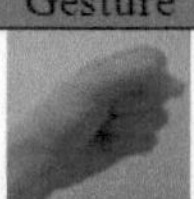	110	60	76	91	72	**Hospital**
(2)	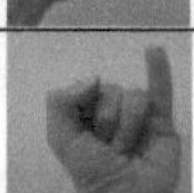	114	64	80	97	104	**Water**
(3)	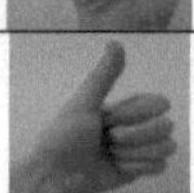	131	60	73	89	71	**Food**
(4)	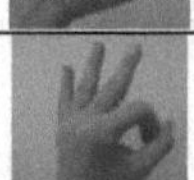	113	65	111	125	112	**Sleep**
(5)	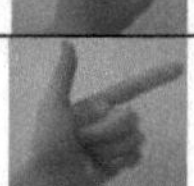	130	110	75	92	72	**Toilet**

The standalone sign based recognition system has been developed as shown in Fig. 7. Five sign gestures are being introduced for this research and thus there will be five sets of predefined data. Table 2 shows the predefined data that are obtained for the sign gesture of 'Hospital', 'Water', 'Food', 'Toilet' and 'Sleep'. It is obtained by recording the output value of attached flex sensor at each finger. For instance, Fig. 8 shows the screen shots of various sign gestures, (sign 1) and (sign 3). Figure 8(a) shows how the predefined data can be obtained from the sign gesture (sign 1) which represent message "hospital". The predefined data are then written to the SD card by using the program code write_sd.c. Figure 8(b) shows the result when the corresponding sign gesture (sign 3) is being recognized by matching with the predefined data stored in SD card, and then being translated into the corresponding message before displayed on the on-board LCD screen.

A few experiments are tested out to view the accuracy of developed standalone sign based recognition system. The performance evaluation has been conducted by using the data glove system with three different types of sensors, bidirectional flex sensor, unidirectional flex sensor and optical based sensor, to view the accuracy of the system. The accuracy of the system can be evaluated by using two methods; the matching performances are evaluated with and without using margin value. The system has been tested 10 times, in which the user is required to perform five set of predefined sign gestures that could translate the corresponding message.

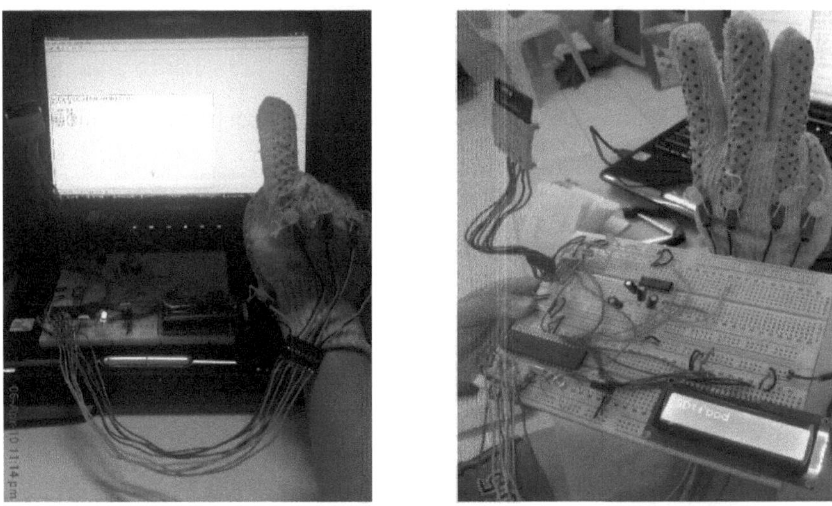

(a) (b)

Fig. 8. Screen shots of (a) sign gesture (sign 1) generates predefined data and (b) sign gesture (sign 3) translates to message "food"

Figure 9 shows the system accuracy performance without and with a margin value of 5. Five sign gestures are tested by using three types of sensors. The success percentage for each sign gesture is compared by using different type of sensors. Without the use of margin value, the system is not that accurate because it is hard to get exactly the same value with the predefined sign recognition gesture data compared to the system with a margin value of 5.

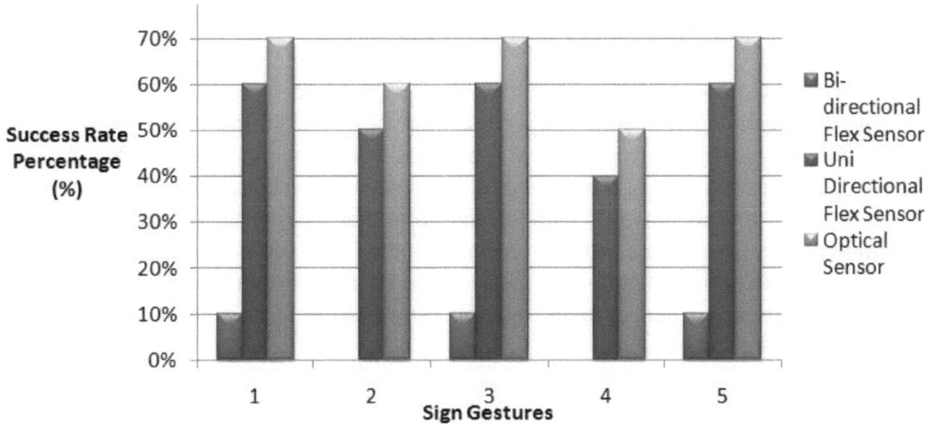

(a)

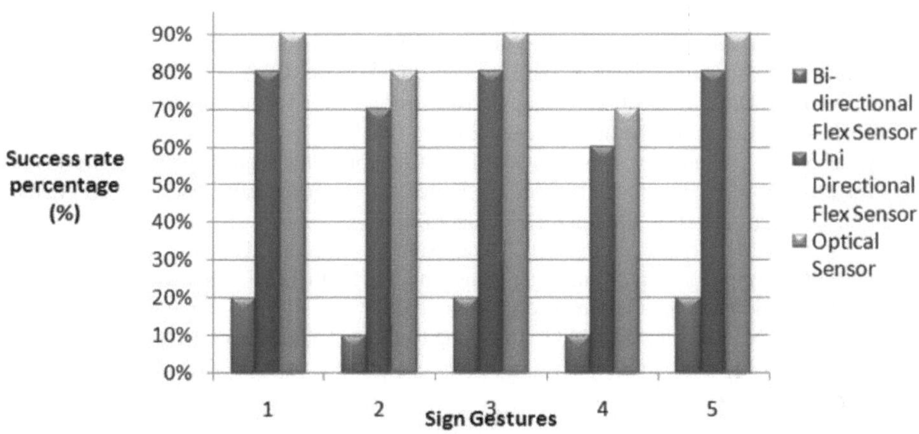

(b)

Fig. 9. The system accuracy performances for (a) without and (b) with using a margin value of 5

In terms of different types of sensor are used, the optical sensor has the best performance as it shows the highest rate of successful percentage. The unidirectional flex sensor has a better performance compared to the bidirectional flex sensor. The bidirectional flex sensor shows the worst performance as it is too sensitive even with little bending changes of the sensor. By comparing unidirectional and bidirectional flex sensor, the results show the trade off between the cost and performance. As the bidirectional flex sensor has lower cost, it shows poorer performance than the more expensive unidirectional flex sensor. However, by using optical sensor, it is able to provide better accuracy performance with lower cost compared to flex sensor.

4 Conclusions

In this paper, a simple and low cost standalone sign based recognition system that is capable of translating sign gestures without the use of the supercomputer processing has been presented. The recognition system is based on the signals that sensors receive and transmit to the gesture recognition system. Another advantage of this data glove is being able to be work without any computer assistance. It requires only an SD memory card to store all the command data and related information. This promotes the flexibility feature of the sign based recognition translator. Also, the developed system is cheaper than any other translating system as it does not use supercomputer for processing.

References

1. Delin, A.: Disability in Context. Resource Disability Portfolio Guide 1. Resource: The Council for Museums, Archives and Libraries (2003) ISBN 1-903743-14-1
2. Poole, N.: Using Technology. Resource Disability Portfolio Guide 7. Resource: The Council for Museums, Archives and Libraries (2003) ISBN 1-903743-20-6
3. Hawkridge, D.G., Vincent, T., Hales, G.: New Information Technology in the Education of Disabled Children and Adults. College Hill Pr. (1985)
4. Crasborn, O., Windhouwer, M.: ISOcat Data Categories for Signed Language Resources. In: Efthimiou, E., Kouroupetroglou, G., Fotinea, S.-E. (eds.) GW 2011. LNCS (LNAI), vol. 7206, pp. 118–128. Springer, Heidelberg (2012)
5. Mcguire, R.M., Hern, J., Starner, T., Henderson, V., Brashear, H., Ross, D.S.: Towards a One-Way American Sign Language Translator. In: Sixth IEEE International Conference on Automatic Face and Gesture Recognition (2004)
6. Vassilia, P.N., Konstantinos, M.G.: Listening to Deaf: A Greek Sign Language Translator. In: 2nd IEEE Information and Communication Technologies (ICTTA 2006), vol. 1, pp. 859–863 (2006)
7. Bilal, S., Akmeliawati, R., Shafie, A.A., Salami, M.J.E.: Hidden Markov Model for Human to Computer Interaction: A Study on Human Hand Gesture Recognition. Artificial Intelligence Review (2011), doi:10.1007/s10462-011-9292-0
8. Min, S., Oh, S., Kim, G., Yoon, T., Lim, C., Lee, Y., Jung, K.: Simple Glove-Based Korean Finger Spelling Recognition System. In: Gervasi, O., Gavrilova, M. (eds.) ICCSA 2007, Part I. LNCS, vol. 4705, pp. 1063–1073. Springer, Heidelberg (2007)
9. Borjian, R., Khamesee, M.B., Melek, W.: Feasibility Study on Echo Control of a Prosthetic Knee: Sensors and Wireless Communication. Microsystem Technologies 16, 257–265 (2010)
10. Ibrahim, D.: Advanced PIC Microcontroller Projects in C: From USB to ZIGBEE with the PIC 18F Series. Newnes, Elsevier (2008)
11. SD Memory Card Specifications: Part 1 Physical Layer Specification. SD Group, Matsushita Electric Industrial Co., Ltd. (MEI), SanDisk Corporation, Toshiba Corporation, Version 1.01 (2001)
12. Borowik, B.: Interfacing PIC Microcontrollers to Peripherial Devices. Intelligent Systems, Control and Automation: Science and Engineering 49 (2011), doi:10.1007/978-94-007-1119-8_12

Enhanced Image Super-Resolution Technique Using Convolutional Neural Network

Kah Keong Chua and Yong Haur Tay

Centre for Computing and Intelligent Systems
Universiti Tunku Abdul Rahman
Kuala Lumpur, Malaysia
chua.kah.keong@gmail.com,
tayyh@utar.edu.my

Abstract. A framework for image super resolution using Convolutional Neural Network (CNN) was developed. In this paper, we focus on verifying the performance of Convolutional Neural Network compared to other methods. CNN generally outperforms other super resolution methods. The training images were collected from various categories, i.e. flowers, buildings, animals, vehicles, human and cuisine. The neural network trained with multiple categories of training images made the CNN more robust towards different test scenarios. Common image degradation, i.e. motion blur and noise, can be reduced when the CNN is provided with proper training samples.

Keywords: Image Super Resolution, Convolutional Neural Network, motion blur, image denoising.

1 Introduction

Super-Resolution is the process of recovering a high resolution (HR) image from single or multiple low resolution (LR) images.

Various approaches for solving super-resolution problem have been proposed. Foremost attempt worked in the frequency domain by Tsai and Huang [1]. In order to overcome the image artefacts e.g. jagged edges and blurred contours, new methods and algorithms have been proposed to upscale the images [4] [5] [6]. Interpolation-based approach reconstructs high-resolution (HR) image by projecting the low-resolution (LR) images obtained to the respective referencing image, then followed by blending all the accessible information from each image to form the result [2] [3].

A neural network can be trained to estimate non-linear functions and perform parallel computation, minimizing the processing time of super-resolution systems [4]. Most of the learning-based super-resolution works in analysing and processing huge datasets from a particular image class, such as faces or alphabets [5]. Throughout the time consuming training process, the weight factors are adjusted and fine-tuned in every epoch [5] [10] [11].

H. Badioze Zaman et al. (Eds.): IVIC 2013, LNCS 8237, pp. 157–164, 2013.

Over the years, neural network based image up-scaling methods gained their popularity due to the flexibility and learning capability of the network. The nature of a neural network which allows fine tuning after the training completed greatly improve the adaptation of the network.

In a nutshell, the contribution of our work in this paper is to perform low level image processing using neural network, i.e. image super resolution, by creating a framework to test the behaviour of neural network based on different types of training samples provided, in contrast with several methods in image super-resolution.

2 Convolutional Neural Network

Convolutional Neural Network (CNN) is a feed-forward back-propagation multilayer perceptron model. CNN works on a supervised back-propagation learning technique during the training phase of the network. CNN generally consists of input layer, convolutional layer, hidden layer and output layer. Each layer has multiple numbers of neurons, which vary according to the complexity of the network.

The learning process takes place in the perceptron by altering the weight factors after each training epoch. Weight factors are adjusted accordingly by calculating the mean error of the expected result in contrary with the output result. The aim of training a neural network is to search for a set of weight factors which links the provided input with the expected output. The process of optimizing the number of hidden layers and amount of neurons used in each layer greatly affects the performance of the entire network. In addition, the neural network ought to be validated throughout the training to avoid over-fitting.

3 System Overview

The CNN used for this research has been configured to match the requirement of the network. The CNN is a feed-forward artificial neural network which consists of convolutional layer for feature extraction, hidden layer and output layer. It is a typical one hidden layer of 50 hidden neurons which has hyperbolic tangent (tanh) activation function, while the output is logistic regression layer. The network considers the desired pixel alongside with eight neighbouring pixels as reference, and then outputs four up-scaled pixels. The process is repeated on the adjacent pixel, throughout the entire image. The figure below shows the architecture of the proposed CNN system:

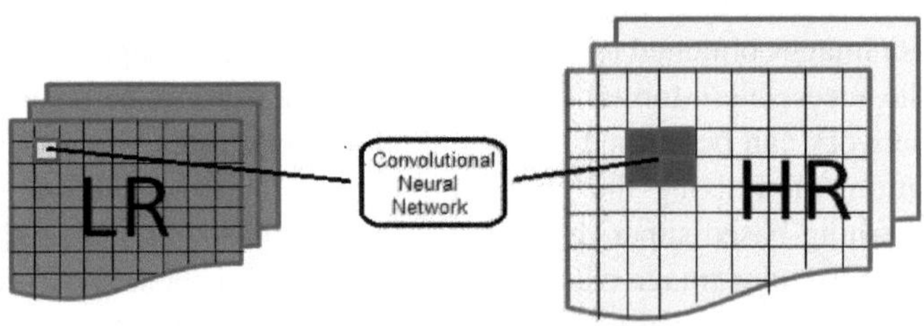

Fig. 1. Architecture of the proposed CNN system

4 Creation of Training and Testing Sets

We obtained the training images from morgueFile online archive for dataset creation. We chose the images from different categories and background settings as these sample images provide wide range of texture combination.

The downloaded images are 256x256 pixels and 512x512 pixels, which correspond to low resolution (LR) and high resolution (HR) images respectively. These images are in RGB colour space and samples are extracted from all three colour channels.

From all the dataset generated, it is then further divided into training set; validate set and testing set, at the ratio of 6:2:2.

For the purpose of benchmarking, the following algorithms are tested here: Nearest Neighbour, bi-cubic interpolation, an edge-oriented interpolation introduced by Chen et.al. [7], an improved version of New Edge-Directed Interpolation (NEDI) [8], as well as the Fast Curvature Based Interpolation (FBCI) [3] and Iterative Curvature Based Interpolation (ICBI) [3] proposed by Giachetti and Asuni. These methods are obtained then regenerated using the evaluation scripts and experimental setup which are available at the website [14].

5 Experiment Framework and Result

For the testing framework, all the methods will undergo a 2x image upscale process, in this case they are enlarged from 256x256 pixels to 512x512 pixels. The up- scaled image will then be compared to the original high resolution image to yield quantitative results. The difference of the images will be measured using Peak Signal-to-Noise Ratio (PSNR) as well as Structural Similarity Index (SSIM). The formulae are defined as follow:

For images $A = \{a_1 \dots a_M\}$, $B = \{b_1 \dots b_M\}$, where M represents the number of pixels, a and b are pixels for their respective images:

$$MSE(A, B) = \frac{1}{M}\sum_{i=1}^{M}(a_i - b_i)^2 \tag{1}$$

PSNR is calculated from all three colour channels. For images $A = \{a_1 \dots a_M\}$, $B = \{b_1 \dots b_M\}$, where MAX is the maximum possible pixel value, a and b are pixels for their respective images:

$$PSNR(A, B) = 10 \log_{10}(\frac{MAX^2}{MSE(A, B)}) \tag{2}$$

Structural Similarity is calculated according to the change in luminance, contrast and structure of an image. Luminance is the average pixel intensity; the contrast is the variance between the reference and distorted image, while structure is obtained by calculating the cross-correlation of the two images [15]. The measurement for SSIM is in range of 0 to 1; results that are closer to 1 represent higher resemblance of both images.

MLP will be trained using different sets of samples to tackle the problem effectively. The first training set will consist of sample from multiple sources, varies from flowers, buildings, animals, human and cuisine. This training set is customized at such that, in order to provide a more robust MLP network which will not suffer from performance loss when it comes to different scenarios.

Moreover, several training sets are created solely on image samples from similar categories, For example, different flowers will be sampled for flower training set. MLP_gen is the neural network trained with samples obtained from multiple sources, while MLP_sp solely trained with the samples from same category. CNN is trained using the same samples with MLP_gen as the result shows that general training samples perform equally well as specific ones.

In addition, another two special training sets are created to tackle common problems encountered in image capturing, namely image noise and motion blur. MLP_noise and CNN_noise contain noisy image samples from multiple sources, while motion blur effect is applied on the samples in MLP_motion and CNN_motion.

Table 1. Test results on zebra and tiger

Methods	**Animal: Tiger**		**Animal: Zebra**	
	PSNR	SSIM	PSNR	SSIM
N. Neighbour	32.38	0.61	31.85	0.70
Bicubic	33.00	0.67	33.07	0.77
Chen et.al.	32.31	0.60	31.85	0.71
NEDI	32.35	0.61	32.00	0.72
FCBI	32.32	0.61	31.76	0.71
ICBI	32.48	0.63	32.04	0.73
MLP_gen	34.40	**0.84**	35.38	0.87
MLP_sp	**34.62**	0.83	**35.92**	**0.90**
CNN	**36.58**	**0.88**	**36.27**	**0.91**

Table 2. Test results on buildings and flowers

Methods	**Buildings**		**Flowers**	
	PSNR	SSIM	PSNR	SSIM
N. Neighbour	33.26	0.74	34.02	0.81
Bicubic	33.83	0.78	34.99	0.88
Chen et.al.	33.23	0.74	34.03	0.83
NEDI	33.25	0.74	34.18	0.84
FCBI	32.97	0.74	33.80	0.84
ICBI	33.17	0.76	34.17	0.86
MLP_gen	**35.30**	**0.84**	36.22	0.90
MLP_sp	34.55	0.72	**37.38**	**0.92**
CNN	**36.93**	**0.84**	**37.88**	**0.92**

Table 3. Test results on noisy images

Methods	MLP_noise		CNN_noise	
	PSNR	SSIM	PSNR	SSIM
Buildings	33.39	0.71	34.67	**0.82**
Flowers	33.50	0.75	33.65	0.77
Random textures	31.60	0.69	32.08	0.75
Tiger	33.03	0.69	35.65	**0.80**
Colour vases	32.92	0.71	33.01	**0.83**
Zebra	33.59	0.76	35.57	**0.85**

Table 4. Test results on motion blurred images

Methods	MLP_motion		CNN_motion	
	PSNR	SSIM	PSNR	SSIM
Buildings	32.98	0.73	35.69	**0.80**
Flowers	32.55	0.64	33.37	0.69
Random textures	31.28	0.74	31.98	0.75
Tiger	32.54	0.73	34.41	0.77
Colour vases	32.81	0.77	35.08	**0.82**
Zebra	32.34	0.79	36.29	**0.81**

Table 1 and 2 are the PSNR and SSIM of several image up-scaling methods. Table 3 shows the summary of the comparison of MLP and CNN in noisy images, while Table 4 is the comparison for motion blurred images. Typical values for PSNR are between 30 to 50dB, where higher value indicates better result. SSIM values range from 0 to 1, where higher resemblance of output and original image provides higher values. In Table 1 and 2, CNN generally outperforms MLP and other methods. Meanwhile in Table 3 and 4, the performance of CNN is again proven to be better by yielding higher SSIM values.

6 Discussion

6.1 Comparison of Different Up-Scaling Method Results

The simulation results show that MLP and CNN generally perform better than ordinary image up-scaling methods. In most of the cases, MLP and CNN yield very high PSNR results. SSIM index shows significant resemblance of original reference images and the up-scaled images from CNN.

Image up-scaled using Nearest Neighbour gives very jagged edges, losing much of the detail on tiger's fur. Bi-cubic interpolation, however gives better result but tends to over smooth the image, resulting in blurry image. NEDI however provides better edges but still facing the blurring effect. Meanwhile, method proposed by Chen et. al. and FCBI introduces unwanted artefacts to the image, and it is solved by using the ICBI method proposed by Giachetti and Asuni. The results obtained from CNN provide a clearer image without introducing artefacts and jagged edges, while maintaining the details on tiger's fur.

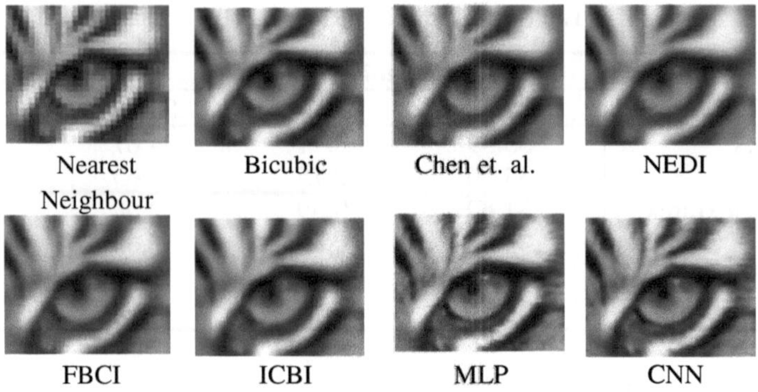

Fig. 2. Comparison between different types of image up-scaling methods

6.2 Comparison between CNN and MLP

Referring to the difference of images obtained in Figure 4, the colour of the images is inversed and scaled so that comparison can be easily made. The brighter region represents the area where up-scaled image closely resembles the reference image, while darker colour indicates there is noticeable difference between the two images. By comparing the CNN to MLP, with both trained with same samples, CNN can upscale the image provided accurately for most of the regions, but suffers from slight performance loss at most of the edges in the image, while MLP has major degradation at the edges.

The advantage of a neural network based image up-scaling method is the flexibility and adaptive nature of the network, which enables it to provide accurate results when the network is well trained. Utilizing the adaptive nature of CNN, the system is pre-trained with two different filters, namely noise reduction and motion reduction, in order to tackle different image artefacts effectively.

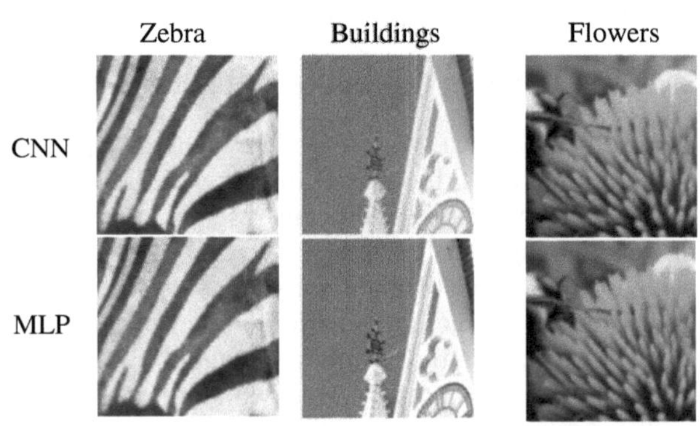

Fig. 3. Comparison of CNN and MLP

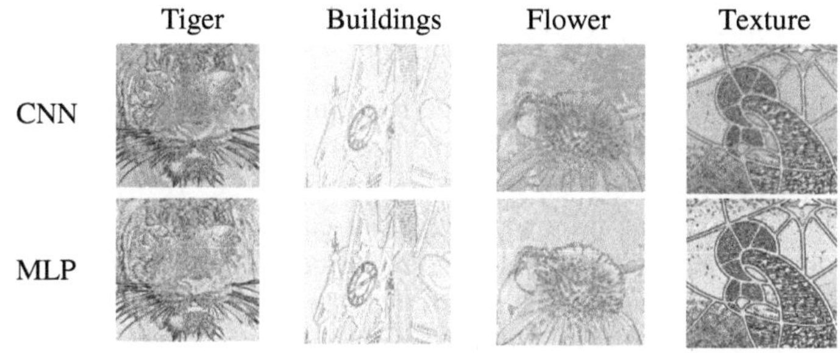

Fig. 4. The difference of original reference image and up-scaled images

6.3 Motion Blurred and Noisy Images

In CNN_noise, we can clearly notice that noise in the test image is greatly reduced, however not fully eliminated. Meanwhile, CNN_motion managed to minimize the blurry edges caused by motion blur. Noise and motion blur often cause image degradation and the loss of crucial information, especially in surveillance images. According to the experiments carried out, neural-network based image super-resolution has the ability to restore and up-scale the degraded images; hence retrieves back most of the important information.

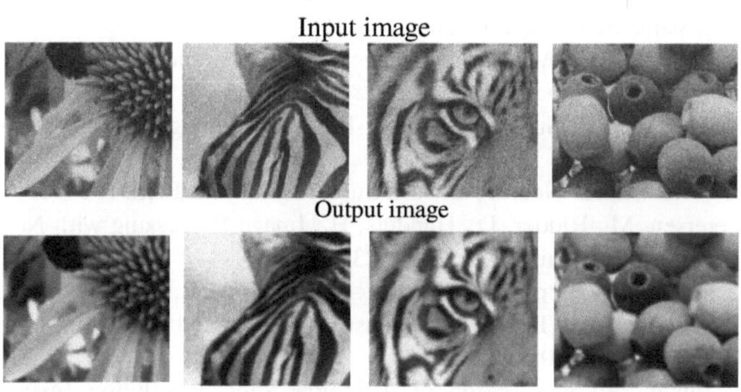

Fig. 5. Comparison of noisy input and up-scaled output images

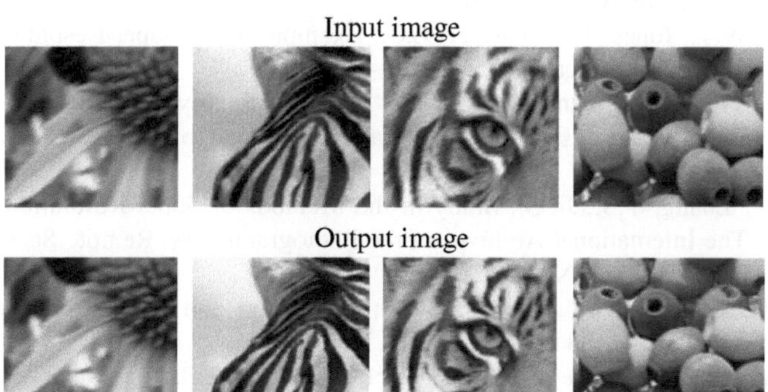

Fig. 6. Comparison of motion blurred input images and up-scaled output images

7 Conclusions and Future Works

To sum it all, CNN can be modelled to perform image super resolution, and it outperforms other super resolution methods. The neural network trained with single type of samples performs splendidly on images of similar type. However it is not robust against images beyond the training samples or category. Meanwhile, a more robust neural network, trained with samples from various categories, can handle different images accurately without introducing artefacts. In addition, the adaptation ability is a major advantage of neural network, utilizing this feature by pre-training some filters greatly help in artefacts reduction. In the future, this CNN system can be expanded to tackle more blur conditions, i.e. zoom-blur and unfocused blur, as well as rain drop and fog reduction. In addition, the system can be modelled into recognition engine with super-resolution capability.

References

1. Asuni, N., Giachetti, A.: Accuracy Improvements and Artifacts Removal in Edge Based Image Interpolation. In: Proc. 3rd Int. Conf. Comput. Vis. Theory Appl. (VISAPP), pp. 58–65 (2008)
2. Giachetti, A., Asuni, N.: Real-Time Artifact-Free Image Upscaling. IEEE Transactions on Image Proccessing 20(10), 2760–2768 (2011)
3. Tsai, R.Y., Huang, T.S.: Multiframe Image Restoration and Registration. JAI Press Inc., London (1984)
4. Tian, J., Ma, K.-K.: A Survey on Super-Resolution Imaging. Springer-Verlag London (2011)
5. Torrieri, D., Bakhru, K.: Neural Network Superresolution. IEEE, 1594–1598 (1997)
6. Egmont-Petersen, M., Ridder, D., Handels, H.: Image Processing with Neural Networks - A Review. Pattern Recognition 35, 2279–2301 (2002)
7. Sherrod, P.: DTREG, `http://www.dtreg.com/mlfn.htm`
8. Chen, M.J., Huang, C.H., Lee, W.L.: A Fast Edge-Oriented Algorithm for Digital Images. Image Vis. Comput. 20, 805–812 (2002)
9. Elad, M., Fueur, A.: Restoration of a SIngle Super-Resolution Image from Several BLurred, Noise and Undersampled Measured Images. IEEE Transactions on Image Processing 6(12), 1646–1658 (1997)
10. Freeman, W.T., Jones, T.R., Pasztor, E.C.: Example-based Super-Resolution. IEEE Computer Graphics and Applications 22(2), 56–65 (2002)
11. Sudheer Babu, R., Sreenivasa Murthy, K.E.: A Survey on the Methods of Super-Resolution Image Reconstruction. International Journal of Computer Application 15(2) (February 2011)
12. Liu, H.Y., Zhang, Y.S., Ji, S.: Study in the Methods of Super-Resolution Image Reconstruction. The International Archives of the Photogrammetry, Remote Sensing and Spatial Information Sciences XXXVII(B2) (2008)
13. Baker, S., Kanade, T.: Limits on Super Resolution and How to Break Them. IEEE TPAMI 24(9), 1167–1183 (2002)
14. ICBI Page, `http://www.andreagiachetti.it/icbi`
15. The SSIM Index for Image Quality Assessment, `https://ece.uwaterloo.ca/~z70wang/research/ssim/`

Segmentation of the Lung Anatomy for High Resolution Computed Tomography (HRCT) Thorax Images

Norliza Mohd. Noor[1], Omar Mohd. Rijal[2], Joel Than Chia Ming[1], Faizol Ahmad Roseli[2], Hossien Ebrahimian[2], Rosminah M. Kassim[3], and Ashari Yunus[4]

[1] UTM Razak School of Engineering and Advanced Technology, Universiti Teknologi Malaysia, Kuala Lumpur, Malaysia
[2] Institute of Mathematical Sciences, University of Malaya, Kuala Lumpur, Malaysia
[3] Department of Diagnostic Imaging, Kuala Lumpur Hospital, Malaysia
[4] Institute of Respiratory Medicine, Malaysia
norliza@utm.my

Abstract. In diagnosing interstitial lung disease (ILD) using HRCT Thorax images, the radiologists required to view large volume of images (30 slices scanned at 10 mm interval or 300 slices scanned at 1 mm interval). However, in the development of scoring index to assess the severity of the disease, viewing 3 to 5 slices at the predetermined levels of the lung is suffice for the radiologist. To develop an algorithm to determine the severity of the ILD, it is important for the computer aided system to capture the main anatomy of the chest, namely the lung and heart at these 5 predetermined levels. In this paper, an automatic segmentation algorithm is proposed to obtain the shape of the heart and lung. In determine the quality of the segmentation, ground truth or manual tracing of the lung and heart boundary done by senior radiologist was compared with the result from the proposed automatic segmentation. This paper discussed five segmentation quality measurements that are used to measure the performance of the proposed segmentation algorithm, namely, the volume overlap error rate (VOE), relative volumetric agreement (RVA), average symmetric surface distance (ASSD), root mean square surface distance (RMSD) and Hausdorff distance (HD). The results showed that the proposed segmentation algorithm produced good quality segmentation for both right and left lung and may be used in the development of computer aided system application.

Keywords: Interstitial lung disease, high resolution computed tomography (HRCT), segmentation quality.

1 Introduction

Interstitial lung disease (ILD) is gaining more attention due to the increasing cases reported worldwide. Although it covers only 15% of the recognized pulmonary diseases [1], issues such as the low survival rate [2] leads to the deeper study on the disease. ILD is a progressive disease which is only can be controlled or stagnated.

H. Badioze Zaman et al. (Eds.): IVIC 2013, LNCS 8237, pp. 165–175, 2013.

It will cause the reduction of lung volume hence affect the lung capability and patient physical ability as well. Severe cases had been reported to cause lung collapse and mortality [3]. Current practice on the ILD diagnosis includes patient history, physical examination, radiologists' findings and lung biopsy.

HRCT thorax is the most common imaging modalities used in the identification of any lung pathology due to its capability to produce a stack of very thin slices of images [4]. Investigating the pathology signs in the image can identify the presence of disease, the disease pattern and severity, which is crucial for medication and therapy planning. Different sub-category of ILD has different pattern/features in the HRCT image.

Modern HRCT scanner capable to produced up to 300 slices for single patient. The enormous number of images to be observed by radiologist costs a lot of time, which later may lead to other human error in reporting the case. In addition to that, different radiologists may have different opinion on the same set of images based on their experiences and unique judgment. To reduce time consumption and lower the human error risk, together to avoid inconsistency among different radiologists, a scoring index has been proposed in recent years. The scoring index requires the radiologists to investigate several changes or features which indicates the presence of ILD in only few selected slices instead of the whole set of image. The slices are selected based on the lung anatomy, representing the entire lung area from top (apices) to the bottom (diaphragm). In this study, we used five slices at predetermined levels based on our consultation with the experienced radiologists. The slices are taken and labeled as below;

i. Level 1 (L1) – aortic arch
ii. Level 2 (L2) – trachea carina
iii. Level 3 (L3) – pulmonary hilar
iv. Level 4 (L4) – pulmonary venous confluence
v. Level 5 (L5) – 1-2cm above right hemi-diaphragm

Segmenting body anatomy is increasingly popular and employed for different subjective purposes. Previous studies showed that the segmentation of the specific organs or tissues mainly contributes in diagnosing and monitoring the presence of any disease, and also complement the surgery preparation [5], [6]. The variations of the anatomy among different cases due to the intersections of different structures and pathological abnormalities, limit the performance of an algorithm [7].

Generally, a segmentation procedure can be divided into two, region-based and contour-based methods. Region-based approach deals directly with the local information of an object, such as texture and gray levels. It includes thresholding, filtering and morphological operation. Contour-based segmentation utilizes the boundary representation of an object, and further processes are based on the contour manipulation. Current trend on segmentation algorithm have seen that the combinations of both approaches are preferred. For a fully automated system, the model-based procedure with the combination of statistical shape model and some deformation segmentation yields optimal results [8], [9],10].

This study is motivated by the work of Lim, Jeong and Ho [11] who has proposed an algorithm which make use of the multilevel thresholding and morphology operation to obtain a search range of an object's shape, followed by the gradient-label mapping and labeling-based search algorithm to get the final object region.

In developing an algorithm to assess the severity of the ILD, it is important for computer aided system to be able to capture the main anatomy of the chest, namely the right lung, the left lung and the heart. In this paper a segmentation algorithm to detect the three main anatomy of the lung is proposed. The results from the proposed segmentation algorithm are then compared with the ground truth images prepared by senior radiologist to measure the segmentation quality.

2 Data Collection

HRCT Thorax images of 96 patients were collected from the Department of Diagnostic Imaging of Kuala Lumpur Hospital that consists of 15 healthy individuals (normal cases), 28 ILD cases and 53 other lung related diseases (non-ILD). The ILD cases were not restricted to any specific subcategory disease. The images were scanned using Siemens SomatomPlus4 CT scanner, and observed by the respective radiologists by Syngo Fast View version VX57G27. Each slice was obtained at 10 – 30 mm intervals of patients in supine position will full suspended inspiration.

The segmentation algorithm was developed using the normal cases and tested with all cases combined. A senior radiologist did the manual tracing of the heart, right lung and left lung on ten patients using level 5 image slice picked at random from the 96 patients to produce the ground truth images.

3 Methodology

The procedure begins with the segmentation of the lung and the heart, which is motivated by the approach presented in [12]. It involved global thresholding, morphology operation and connected-component analysis. The quality of the segmentation results is measured via 5 supervised evaluation methods, which were inspired by [6]. These methods compared the segmentation results with the ground truth images which were manually segmented by the experience radiologists.

3.1 Lung and Airway Segmentation

The flow chart of the proposed lung segmentation algorithm is shown in Figure 1. The Otsu thresholding was applied in order to segment the lung area based on the intensity level. Lung tissue is characterized as having darker pixel (HU value equal to -1000). Otsu thresholding assigned the group of dark pixels to 0 and others to 1. This output was inverted so that the 0 pixels become 1 and vice versa. It is important to highlight that the dark pixels is our reference pixel while the brighter pixels are the unwanted area.

Next, any area that consists of less than 700 pixels was removed assuming that the lung regions are large. Morphology closing is applied to the remaining regions so that any adjacent region is connected. This step aims to regroup pixels that belong to the same tissue/organ/anatomy which were separated by the previous thresholding step.

Connected component analysis was applied to the remaining regions via 8-neighbourhood approach. The labeled regions consist of several areas including non-lung regions such as the background outside the patient's body. To extract the lung regions, another rule were defined as follow;

Rule 1. Labeled components attached to the image frame are assumed to be the background.

Rule 2. Lung region consists of the two largest labeled components in the image. For each region, area and eccentricity measure (Ecc) were calculated. The regions that have the two largest area and eccentricity measure of $0.5 < \text{Ecc} < 0.9$ were selected as right lung and left lung.

Morphology dilation was employed to the extracted lung region in order to regain as accurate as possible the original shape and size of the lung. Finally, any holes present in the lung area were filled through flood-fill algorithm.

To decide which is right and left lung, the location of the centroid of each segmented lung regions were observed. The one having centroid with lower value in x-axis of the image is assumed to be the right lung while the other is the left lung. The output of the segmented right lung and left lung images were stored separately as bitmap file.

3.2 Heart Segmentation

Using similar approach to segment the lung, the heart area located between right and left lung (approximately in the middle of the HRCT image) was segmented. However, Otsu thresholding cannot separate the heart region due to its intensity similarity to other surrounding tissues. Thus, manual thresholding was incorporated where the histogram of the image was studied to obtain the range of intensity that constitutes the heart region.

Morphology closing operation was implemented to the threshold image to close any gap between pixels and erosion process was applied to separate connected regions. Any holes present in the remaining regions were filled similar as in section 3.1.

Next, the largest labeled component was extracted by assuming that the largest component represented are the heart region. Morphology dilation was applied in order to regain as close as possible the original shape and size of the heart area. Figure 2 shows the flow chart for heart segmentation algorithm. The output of the segmented heart images is also stored as bitmap file.

3.3 Ground Truth

A system to capture the manual tracing done by the radiologist was developed in MATLAB GUI environment. The result of the radiologist manual tracing is in bitmap file and named as ground truth image.

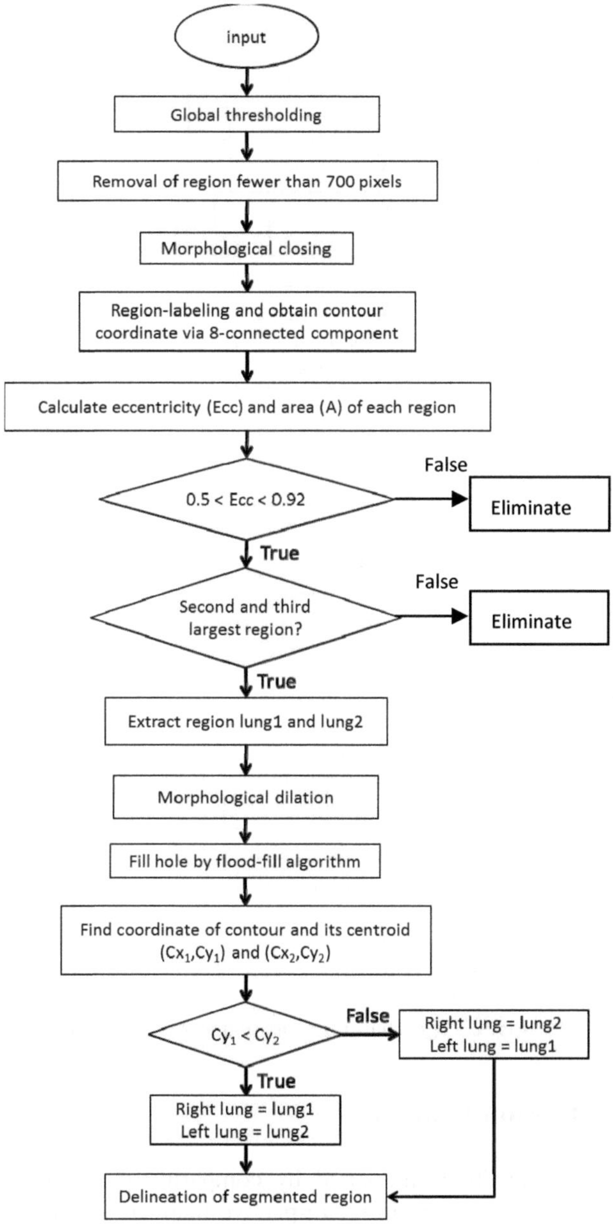

Fig. 1. The segmentation of the right and left lung

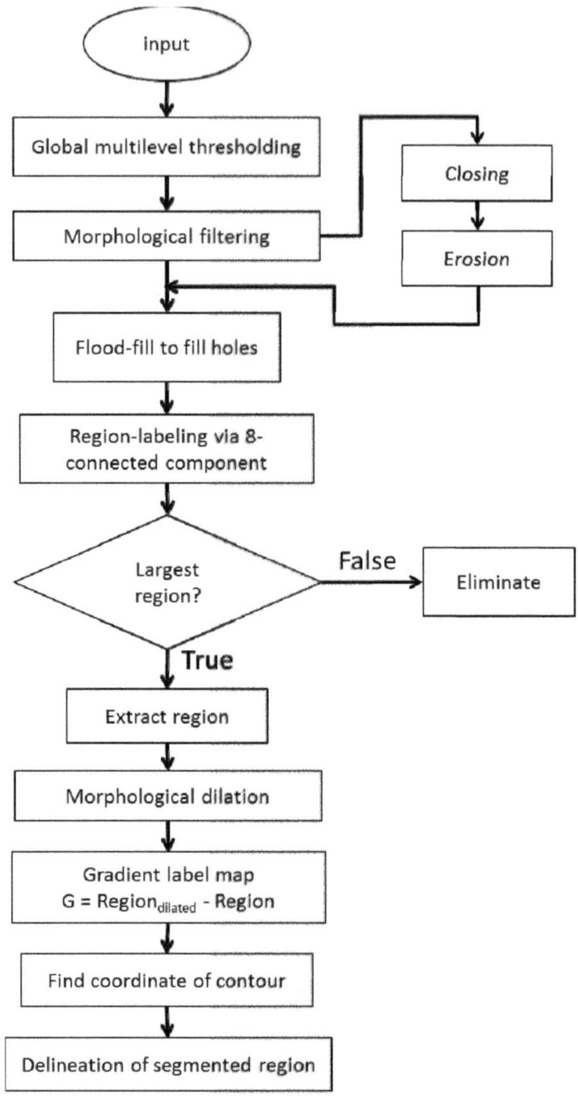

Fig. 2. Flow chart for heart segmentation algorithm

4 Segmentation Quality

The segmentation quality is measured by comparing the segmented image to the ground-truth image. The expert in the respective field (in this study will be the senior radiologist) manually defines the ground-truth or reference image (some called gold standard) by manually traced the boundary for each lung and the heart anatomy. The comparison was measured and the scores are given according to the detected deviations. Even though there are many measures that can be used in the evaluation, in this study, five metrics were considered as follows [6];

i) Volume Overlap Error rate (VOE)

Volume overlap rate is defined as the ratio of intersection to the union between the segmented region and the reference region (ground truth or gold standard). It is also known as Jaccard or Tanimoto coefficient. The overlap error rate is defined as in (1). Perfect segmentation leads to a 0% score while 100% error rate means there is no overlap at all.

$$\text{Volume Overlap Error rate} = \left(1 - \frac{A \cap B}{A \cup B}\right) x100\% \tag{1}$$

where A is the segmentation result and B is the reference image.

ii) Relative Volumetric Agreement (RVA)

This metric measures the area similarity between segmentation result and the reference region. It evaluates the similarity in size between both regions. The larger value of agreement indicates that the higher similarity of size between the segmented region and the gold standard

iii) Average Symmetric Surface Distance (ASSD)

It is used to assess the accuracy of the segmented shape corresponds to the reference region. The average distance of all contour points of the segmented shape to the closest contour point of the reference region is calculated. The smaller value denotes the higher similarity between both regions. It is also known as mean absolute distance (MAD).

Assuming that *S(A)* represents the set of surface pixels of *A* and *S(B)* denotes the surface pixels of *B*, the average symmetric surface distance (ASSD) is given by;

$$ASSD(A,B) = k\left(\sum_{s_A \in S(A)} d(s_A, S(B)) + \sum_{s_B \in S(B)} d(s_B, S(A))\right)$$

where $k = \dfrac{1}{|S(A)| + |S(B)|}$

and $d(s_A, S(B)) = \min_{s_B \in S(B)} \|s_A - s_B\|$ denotes the shortest distance of an arbitrary voxel, s_A to *S(B)* and $||.||$ indicates the Euclidean distance measure. Notice that the same process is repeated from voxel s_B to *S(A)* to provide symmetry analysis.

iv) Root Mean Square Surface Distance (RMSD)

Similar with ASD, however, the Euclidean Distance between both S(A) and S(B) ($d(c_A, C(B))$ and $d(c_B, C(A))$) are squared before being stored. Eq.5 is modified as follows;

$$RMSD(A,B) = \sqrt{\frac{1}{|S(A)|+|S(B)|}} \times \left(\sum_{s_A \in S(A)} d^2(s_A, S(B)) + \sum_{s_B \in S(B)} d^2(s_B, S(A)) \right)$$

where the definition hold the same as in ASD.

v) Hausdorff Distance (HD)

This metric measure how different of two images to each other, and is also known as Hausdorff distances. Similar to ASD and RMSD, MSD considers only the contour pixels of each set. General expression of the Hausdorff distance, or in our case, known as MSD, is shown as follow;

$$MSD(A,B) = \max\left\{ \max_{s_A \in S(A)} d(s_A, S(B)), \max_{s_B \in S(B)} d(s_B, S(A)) \right\}$$

Note that the distance of both directions, $d(s_A, S(B))$ and $d(s_B, S(A))$ are considered to provide symmetry analysis.

5 Results and Discussion

Figure 3, Figure 4, and Figure 5 show some sample the results of segmentation of the heart, right lung and the left lung using the proposed method for normal lung, ILD and non-ILD HRCT Thorax images. Based on visual inspection, both lung were successfully segmented for all 5 predetermined levels, however the same cannot be said for heart segmentation. In determine the segmentation quality of the proposed algorithm five metrics as proposed in Section 4 were used in this study. The segmented image of the heart, right lung and the left lung are compared one to one with the ground truth images of the same patient's anatomy. Five measurements of segmentation quality was derived and shown in Table 1 for heart, right lung, and left lung.VOE, ASSD, RMSD and HD metrics should have low value for segmentation to have good quality. RVA metric on the other hand defined that high value represent higher similarity. Results shown in Table 1 show that right lung and left lung have lower value than heart segmentation for VOE, ASSD, RMSD and HD and higher value for RVA implying that the segmentation for right lung and left lung has higher quality than the segmentation result for the heart boundary. The findings correspond to the visual inspection done by the radiologist. Further work need to be done to improve the segmentation quality for heart.

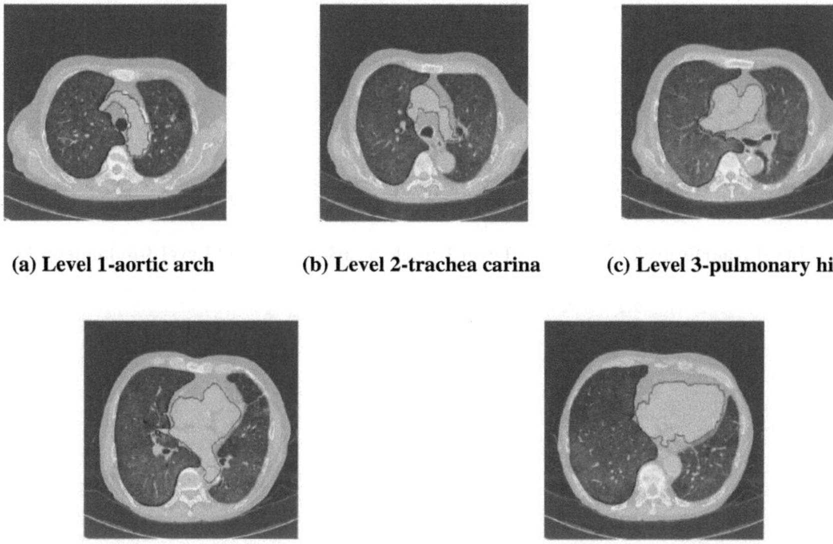

(a) Level 1-aortic arch (b) Level 2-trachea carina (c) Level 3-pulmonary hila

(d) Level 4-pulmonary venous confluence e) Level 5-1-2 cm above right hemi-diaphragm

Fig. 3. Segmented image superimposed with the original image for five levels (a) - (e) of HRCT Thorax for ILD cases

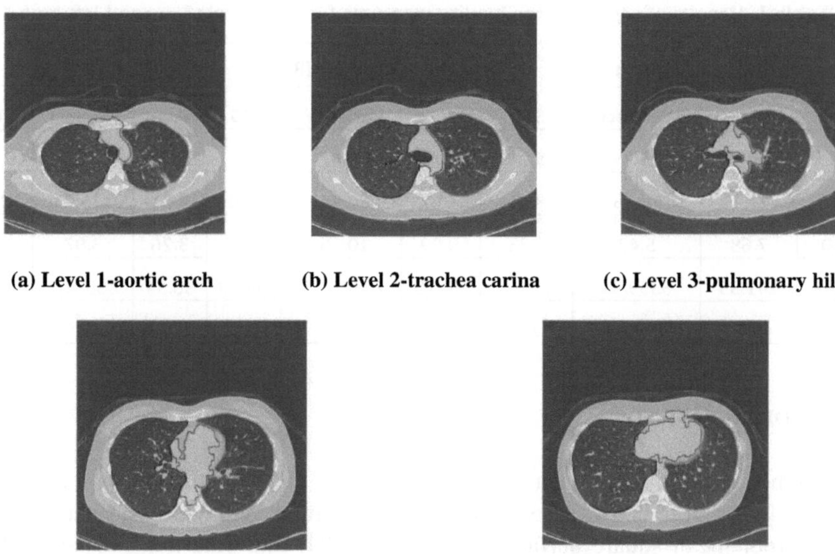

(a) Level 1-aortic arch (b) Level 2-trachea carina (c) Level 3-pulmonary hilar

(d) Level 4-pulmonary venous confluence (e) Level 5-1-2 cm above right hemi-diaphragm

Fig. 4. Segmented image superimposed with the original image for five levels (a) - (e) of HRCT Thorax for non-ILD cases

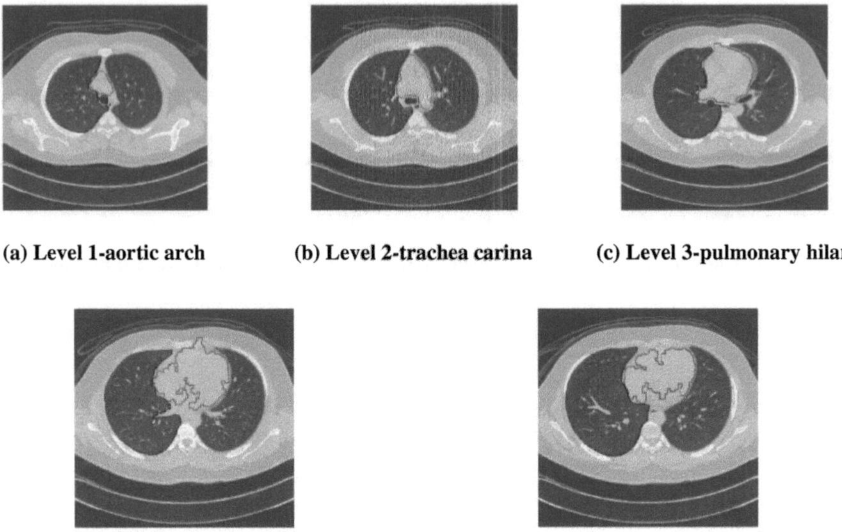

(a) Level 1-aortic arch (b) Level 2-trachea carina (c) Level 3-pulmonary hilar

(d) Level 4-pulmonary venous confluence (e) Level 5-1-2 cm above right hemi-diaphragm

Fig. 5. Segmented image superimposed with the original image for five levels (a) - (e) of HRCT Thorax for normal cases

Table 1. Results of segmentation quality measures for heart, right lung and left lung

	Heart			Right Lung (RL)			Left Lung (LL)		
Heart	Mean	Variance	STD	Mean	Variance	STD	Mean	Variance	STD
VOE	18.75	25.35	5.04	6.73	64.42	8.03	10.56	87.23	9.34
RVA	-12.19	70.73	8.41	2.62	80.99	9.00	4.31	111.95	10.58
ASSD	7.68	5.42	2.33	2.99	10.66	3.27	3.26	3.97	1.99
RMSD	141.33	5359.91	73.21	40.70	20885.22	144.52	30.54	3867.06	62.19
HD	40.61	127.98	11.31	10.19	155.76	12.48	13.97	234.95	15.33

6 Conclusion

Five segmentation quality measurements that are the volume overlap error rate (VOE), relative volumetric agreement (RVA), average symmetric surface distance (ASSD), root mean square surface distance (RMSD) and Hausdorff distance (HD) were used to determine the segmentation quality for the lung anatomy. The results showed that the proposed segmentation algorithm produced good quality segmentation for right and left lung and may be used in the development of computer aided system application. However, further work need to be done to improve the segmentation quality for the heart.

Acknowledgement. We acknowledge the contribution from Dato' Dr. Abdul Razak bin Abdul Muttalif, The Insitute of Respiratory Medicine, Kuala Lumpur, and Dr. Hajjah Zaleha binti Abd. Manaf, Head of Radiology Department (Diagnostic Imaging), Kuala Lumpur Hospital. This research is funded under UTM research grant (GUP 00H43).

References

1. Gulatia, M.: Diagnostic assessment of patients with interstitial lung disease. Prim. Care Respir. J. 20(2), 120–127 (2011)
2. Bjorker, A., Ryu, J.H., Edwin, M.K., Myers, J.L., Tazelaar, H.D., Schroeder, D.R., Offord, K.P.: Prognostic significance of histopathologic subsets in idiopathic pulmonary fibrosis. Am. J. Respir. Crit. Care Med. 157(1), 199–203 (1998)
3. Arzhaeva, Y., et al.: Computer-aided detection of interstitial abnormalities in chest radiographs using a reference standard based on computed tomography. Med. Phys. 34, 4798–4809 (2007)
4. Raghu, G., Brown, K.K.: Interstitial Lung Disease: Clinical evaluation and keys to an accurate diagnosis. Clinical Chest Med. 25, 409–419 (2004)
5. Nakashini, M., Demura, Y., Mizuno, S., Ameshima, S., Chiba, Y., Miyamori, I., Itoh, H., Kitaichi, M., Ishizaki, T.: Changes in HRCT findings in patients with respiratory bronchiolitis-associated interstitial lung disease after smoking cessation. European Respiratory Journal 29(3), 453–461 (2007)
6. Heimann, T., Van Ginneken, B., Styner, M.A., Aurich, Y., Bauer, C., Becker, C., Beichel, R., Bekes, G., et al.: Comparison and evaluation of methods for liver segmentation from CT datasets. IEEE Trans. Medical Imaging 28(8), 1251–1265 (2009)
7. Gletsos, M., Mougiakakou, S.G., Matsopoulos, G.K., Nikita, K.S., Nikita, A., Kelekis, D.: A computer-aided diagnostic system to characterize CT focal liver lesions: Design and optimization of a neural network classifier. IEEE Trans. Inf. Technol. Biomed. 7(3), 153–162 (2003)
8. Rangayyan, R.M., Vu, R.H., Boag, G.S.: Automatic delineation of the diaphragm in computed tomographic images. Journal of Digital Imaging 21, 134–147 (2008)
9. Kainmüller, D., Lange, T., Lamecker, H.: Shape constrained automatic segmentation of the liver based on a heuristic intensity model. In: Proc. MICCAI Workshop 3-D Segmentation Clinic: A Grand Challenge, pp. 109–116 (2007)
10. Heimann, T., Meinzer, H.-P., Wolf, I.: A statistical deformable model for the segmentation of liver CT volumes. In: Proc. MICCAI Workshop 3-D Segmentation in the Clinic: A Grand Challenge, pp. 161–166 (2007)
11. Saddi, K.A., Rousson, M., Chefd'hotel, C., Cheriet, F.: Global-to-local shape matching for liver segmentation in CT imaging. In: Proc. MICCAI Workshop 3-D Segmentation Clinic: A Grand Challenge, pp. 207–214 (2007)
12. Lim, S.J., Jeong, Y.Y., Ho, Y.S.: Automatic liver segmentation for volume measurement in CT images. Journal of Visual Communication and Image Representation 17(4), 860–875 (2006)

Comparison of Edge Detection Technique for Lane Analysis by Improved Hough Transform

Muhamad Lazim Talib[1], Xio Rui[2], Kamarul Hawari Ghazali[2], Norulzahrah Mohd. Zainudin[1], and Suzaimah Ramli[1]

[1] Jabatan Sains Komputer, Fakulti Sains dan Teknologi Pertahanan, Universiti Pertahanan Nasional Malaysia
[2] Fakulti Elektrik dan Elektronik, Universiti Malaysia Pahang
{lazim,norulzahrah,suzaimah}@upnm.edu.my, {kamarul,rui}@ump.edu.my

Abstract. Lane detection system for car driver assisted becomes an important study to be implemented for safety purposes. It used to lessen possibility of traffic accidents, to monitor the position of a car effectively and to contribute for further development of autonomous navigation technology. In this paper, we proposed an improved Hough transform technique to detect road lane where a comparison has been made on edge detection technique of Canny, Sobel and Roberts. The improved Hough Transform used to extract the features of structured roads. The close field-of-view scope adopts a straight line model to accelerate the speed of data calculation and to find the fitting line. Prior-knowledge is used in lane finding process to efficiently decrease Hough space efficiently, thus enhancing its robustness by improving the processing speed. The algorithm gave good result in detecting straight and smooth curvature lane on highway even when the lane was affected by shadow. The data of road lane has been taken in a video format. Experiment has been done by making a comparison of edge detection technique and we find that the best method that produces high accuracy of detection is by using canny edge detector.

Keywords: edge detection, lane analysis, hough transforms.

1 Introduction

Malaysia is paying a heavy price due to road accidents, and the cost to the economy last year was about RM9.3bil (Malaysia Road Safety Department, 2010). Recent statistic shows that the number of fatalities in Malaysia increased to 6,872 deaths in in last year. Bukit Aman Internal Security and Public Order Department revealed that the total number of road accidents has increased to 414,421.(MUFORS; 2011) In a separate online survey by the community project Malaysians Unite for Road Safety (MUFORS), 61.6% of the respondents believed that human error like improper Vehicle's deviation or unintentional lane change is one of the main causes for road carnages. Changing lanes in traffic can be complex and dangerous, and such detection

H. Badioze Zaman et al. (Eds.): IVIC 2013, LNCS 8237, pp. 176–183, 2013.

system may reduce the probability of a vehicle straying out of lane. To prevent a vehicle veering out of lane, technique for driving assistance is vitally important, particularly Lane Markings Detection System which has very significant market potential and high practical value.

One of the common techniques to detect lane is Hough Transform. There are a few step need to be taken before implementing Hough Transform to detect lane. One of the steps is finding edge of the lane. Edges Detection has been of a fundamental importance of image segmentation. Edges are strong intensity contrasts area in image, sharp, discontinuities intensity between neighbouring pixels, which usually identified between target object and background or different regions. The main contribution of detecting edges is that it filters out useless information and significantly simplifies data, while at the same time preserving the important structural objects in the image. The result output transferred to a binary image where each pixel is marked as either an edge pixel or a non-edge pixel.

2 Literature Review

Extensive techniques have been developed to detect lane markings in the related field of autonomous vehicles and driver support technologies. This chapter presents an overview of the foremost techniques used by these researchers. Review image-processing methods used in traffic applications and then grouping them according to the type of technologies were applied. An evaluation of the advantages and disadvantages from general needs attempted to carry out. The evaluation result will help to position our work in the context of previous research and creating a 'research space'.

RGB colour model does not correspond to the way that people recognize colours. Therefore, the HSI and HSV colour models are more common used. The previous paper [1] and [4] has shown that HSI colour spaces may offer advantages in terms of robustness against changes in illumination. The performance of RGB and HSI in identifying the road and road sign has been verified in this research [3].The conclusion declare that the HSI colour model is much more suited for traffic image detection because it has hue property that is immune to lighting condition and HSI colour segmentation process shows more correctness than colour identification made by the RGB colour segmentation.

In reference [6] which is carried out by colour analysis of road scene images using HSI colour model, full colour images are converted into HSI colour representation. The Hue component describes the colour itself in the form of an angle between (0, 360) the range of the S component is (0, 1). The Intensity range is between (0,1) and 0 means black, 1 means white. In HSI-based analysis, simple thresholds with saturation and intensity values avoid influences of brightness of road. HIS colour model has relative simpler thresholds but problems with HSI colour segmentation arise when the illumination has a non-white colour such as yellow or red that is found in most street lights which can affect the camera's observation, as a result, possibly fall outside the required colour range.

Many other approaches to image interpretation are based on edges, since analysis based on edge detection is insensitive to change in the overall illumination level. Edge detection highlights image contrast. Detecting contrast, which is difference in intensity, can emphasize the boundaries of features within an image, since this is where image contrast occurs.

Lane edges in an image are the boundary between two lanes. Edge detection methods are available in the literatures such as [7] and [8] detectors calculate the first directional derivative to ascertain the locations of the edges. The Canny detector [9], which is a Gaussian edge detector, is one of the most popular edge detectors in the literature and it has been widely used in many applications.

3 Methodology

Overall research methodology is depicted in Fig. 1. Data of road lane has been taken using video recording Panasonic and has been save in .mpg format.

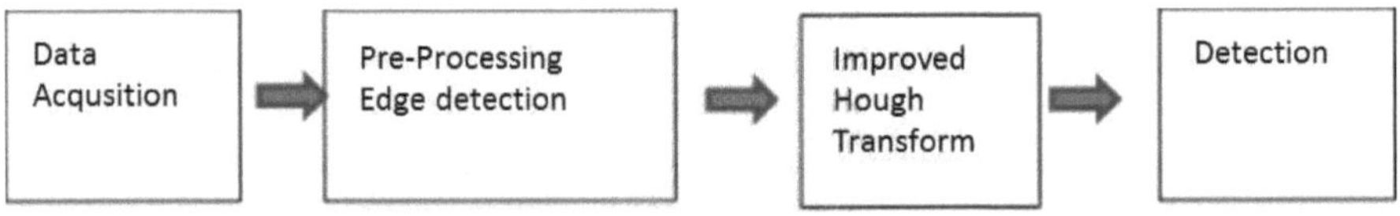

Fig. 1. Research Methodology

Fig. 2. A representation of data acquisition

Various condition of data has been considered such as different weather condition, and different time. The selection of a suitable experimental data is the first of a series difficult problems faced in developing a lane detection system. The type and quality of data collected directly affect the subsequent processing method and outcome. 48 test videos have been selected in this experiment, each approximately 20 seconds long – in total about 24,000 frames. The video recorded under real-time driving situation. The fixed CMOS camera was installed between the front windscreen and the rear-view mirror, seen the Fig. 2.

In order to detect the lane marking, the lane marking pixels must be extracted first. The strong contrast between lane markings and road surface is used to extract the lane marking edges. A single row level of grey-scale sampling based on a number of image sequences was analysed. An extraction scheme based on the EXTENDED-MAXIMA transform (E- MAXIMA) is introduced to obtain the feature extraction result, which was applied to decrease its noise and remove interference points as much as possible. Image minima and maxima are important morphological features as they often mark relevant image objects: minima for dark objects and maxima for bright objects so it's perfectly match with road characters where lane markings represent maxima region in images. Extraneous objects can be eliminated from images by H-maxima transformation; considering the intensity between road surface and lane markers has a strong image contrast. In grey scale colour map light-colours have higher value, dark-colour values is approximated to 0. H-H-extrema transformations provide a function to filter the image H-extrema using a contrast criterion. More precisely, the h-maxima transformation suppresses all maxima whose depth is lower or equal to a given threshold level h (Soille 2004). All other objects in the image with pixel values below this threshold turn to the black background in binary image. As an example of road surface shown in the Fig. 3. The regional H-extrema is used to extract the textures by marking the H-extrema region and non-H-extrema region with 0 and 1. The h-maxima transformation can be defined by the formula (1).

$$HMAXh(g)=R\_P^\wedge\lambda\ (g-t) \quad (1)$$

Where g expresses an intensity image; the h-maxima transform H is used for suppressing all maxima in the intensity image; t means threshold. R represents the reconstruction. R_P^λ is the morphological reconstruction by g.

Fig. 3. A cross section in road-surface image

Majority of edge detection techniques can be categorized into two groups: search-based and zero-crossing based [2]. The search-based method detects the edges by looking for the maximum and minimum in the first derivative of the image. The zero-crossing method searches for zero crossings in the second derivative of the image to find edges.

For an image $z= f(x, y)$, in x direction, y direction and α direction, first-order directional derivative can be shown in formula (2).

$$f_x(x,y) = \frac{\partial f(x,y)}{\partial x}$$

$$f_y(x,y) = \frac{\partial f(x,y)}{\partial y} \tag{2}$$

$$f_\alpha(x,y) = f_x(x,y)\sin\alpha + f_y(x,y)\cos\alpha$$

Image z in x direction, y direction and α direction by second-order derivative can be expressed as shown in formula (3).

$$f_{xx}(x,y) = \frac{\partial^2 f(x,y)}{\partial x^2}$$

$$f_y(x,y) = \frac{\partial^2 f(x,y)}{\partial y^2} \tag{3}$$

$$f_\alpha'(x,y) = f_{xx}(x,y)\sin^2\alpha + f_{yy}(x,y)\cos^2\alpha + 2\,f_{xy}\,(x,y)\sin\alpha\cos\alpha$$

In digital image, above differential operations can be replaced by the direction of difference functions, and first-order directional derivative given as shown in formula (4).

$$\Delta_x f(i,j) = f(i,j) - f(i-1,j)$$

$$\Delta_y f(i,j) = f(i,j) - f(i,j-1) \tag{4}$$

The corresponding second-order derivatives are defined by formula (5).

$$\Delta_\alpha f(i,j) = \Delta_x f(i,j)\sin\alpha - \Delta_y f(i,j)\cos\alpha$$

$$\Delta_x^2 f(i,j) = \Delta_x f(i+1,j) - \Delta_x f(i,j)$$

$$\Delta_y^2 f(i,j) = \Delta_y f(i,j+1) - \Delta_y f(i,j)$$

$$\Delta_{xy}^2 f(i,j) = \Delta_x f(i,j+1) - \Delta_y f(i,j)$$

$$\Delta_{yx}^2 f(i,j) = \Delta_y f(i+1,j) - \Delta_x f(i,j) \tag{5}$$

$$\Delta_\alpha^2 f(i,j) = \Delta_x^2 f(i,j)\sin^2\alpha + 2\Delta_{xy}^2 f(i,j)\sin\alpha\cos\alpha + \Delta_y^2 f(i,j) cos^2\alpha$$

Therefore, the derivation of each pixel can be calculated by grey scale values within a neighbourhood around the pixel.

4 Result and Discussion

Edge detection threshold values range is -1020 ~1020 for all grey scale range 0~255. To identify which threshold is the best suited to a lane detection task, the experiment indicates that using threshold form 0.01 to 0.06 the width of lane marking edges can reach 1~ 2 pixels. Applied this level of thresholds value can archived the purpose of thinning edges, also obtained edges enhancement effect. Hence the threshold values 0.06, 0.01 and Auto have been presented here in order to explore how does make effect on image with threshold value increasing. Fig. 4. can be seen that if the threshold value is 0.01, then more edge details are detected which compared to higher threshold value 0.06, less edge details can be acquired. Outcome denotes that auto threshold can give suitable enough detection result not only to find precise regions but it is also noise insensitive. The lane marking edges are salient relatively on road surface which can be recognized by all four operators with threshold in three levels.

Roberts cross operator in Fig. 4. indicates the edge positioning is not accurate in Threshold = 0.01 and 0.06. However, specifying the threshold value as auto get comparatively better result.

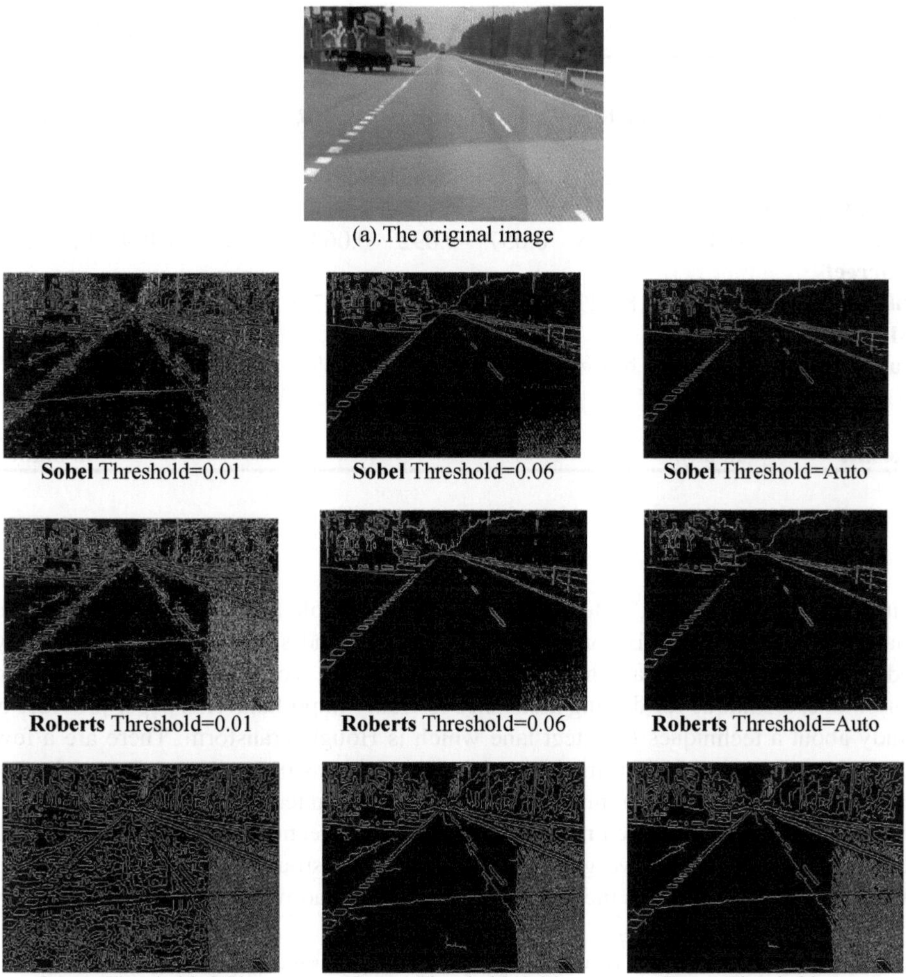

(a).The original image

Sobel Threshold=0.01 | **Sobel** Threshold=0.06 | **Sobel** Threshold=Auto

Roberts Threshold=0.01 | **Roberts** Threshold=0.06 | **Roberts** Threshold=Auto

Canny Threshold=0.01 | **Canny** Threshold=0.06 | **Canny** Threshold=Auto

Fig. 4. Result Comparison between Sobel, Roberts and Canny

The Canny detector is competitive to weak edge but slightly sensitive, more easily to get influence by extraneous boundaries other than lane markings once edge gradient can be determined.

Table 1 shows a comparison of the four classical derivative operators on average running time to extract the edge features, where the same video data are processed by the same Hough detection algorithm but based on different edge operators to compare the correct rates at day and night times. Correct rates of edge operators are statistics number by how many lines can be detected by Hough. It also reflected the edge operators affected on lane detection result. The comparative result on the performance of edge detection denotes that the Sobel operator sustains slightly high accuracy at day time and it is more suitable for lane detection purpose, it is suited well to filter out useless noise and inexpensive computation time.

Table 1. Comparison of classical derivative operators on average running time

Edge Detectors	**Sobel**		**Prewitt**		**Roberts**		**Canny**	
	day	night	day	night	day	night	day	night
Computation time	0.055	0.118	0.057	0.092	0.063	0.098	0.409	0.2498
Correct rates	98.6%	87.2%	98.2%	86.9%	98.17%	86.3%	97.4%	96.7%
Missing rates	0.02%	8.4%	0.02%	8.8%	0.02%	8.82%	0.02%	1.8%
Result	Optimal in day							Optimal in night

5 Conclusion

Lane Markings Detection System has very significant role for in our driving safety as changing lanes in traffic is complex and dangerous, and such detection system may reduce the probability of a vehicle straying out of lane. To prevent a vehicle veering out of lane, technique for driving assistance is vitally important. This paper provides a Study about a techniques to detect lane which is Hough Transform. There are a few step need to be taken before implementing Hough Transform to detect lane. . In this paper, we have proposed an improved Hough Transform technique to detect road lane where a comparison has been made on edge detection technique of Canny, Sobel and Roberts. The algorithm gave good result in detecting straight and smooth curvature lane on highway even when the lane was affected by shadow.

Acknowledgments. This research is funded by Research Acculturation Grant Scheme (RAGS).

References

1. Soille, P.: Morphological image analysis, 2nd edn., pp. 201–204. Springer, New York (2004) ISBN: 3540429883
2. Zhai, L., Dong, S., et al.: Recent methods and applications on image edge detection. In: International Workshop on Education Technology and Training and 2008 International Workshop on Geoscience and Remote Sensing, ETT and GRS 2008, vol. 1, pp. 332–335. IEEE (2008)
3. Jau, U.L., Teh, C.S., et al.: A comparison of RGB and HSI colour segmentation in real-time video images: A preliminary study on road sign detection. In: International Symposium on Information Technology, ITSim 2008, vol. 4, pp. 1–6. IEEE (2008)
4. Tan, C., Hong, T., et al.: Colour model-based real-time learning for road following. In: IEEE Intelligent Transportation Systems Conference, ITSC 2006, pp. 939–944. IEEE (2006)
5. He, W., Wang, X., et al.: Monocular based lane-change on scaled-down autonomous vehicles. In: 2011 IEEE Intelligent Vehicles Symposium (IV), pp. 144–149. IEEE (2011)
6. Sun, T.Y., Tsai, S.J., et al.: HSI colour model based Lane-Marking detection. In: 2006 IEEE Intelligent Transportation Systems Conference, pp. 1168–1172. IEEE (2006)
7. Sobel, I.: Neighborhood coding of binary images for fast contour following and general binary array processing. Computer Graphics and Image Processing 8(1), 127–135 (1978)
8. Prewitt, J.M.S.: Object enhancement and extraction, picture processing and psychopictorics. Academic Press, New York (1970)
9. Canny, J.: A computational approach to edge detection. IEEE Transactions on Pattern Analysis and Machine Intelligence PAMI-8(6), 679–698 (1986)

Adaptive Region Growing for Automated Oil Palm Fruit Quality Recognition

LaylaWantgli Shrif Amosh[1,*], Siti Norul Huda Sheikh Abdullah[1], Che Radiziah Che Mohd.[2], and Jinjuli Jameson[1]

[1] Pattern Recognition Research Group,
Center for Artificial Intelligence Technology,
Faculty of Information Science and Technology,
Universiti Kebangsaan Malaysia, 43600, Bangi, Selangor, Malaysia
[2] School of Bioscience and Biotechnology,
Faculty of Science and Technology,
Universiti Kebangsaan Malaysia, 43600, Bangi, Selangor, Malaysia
laylawantgleshreaf@yahoo.com, mimi@ftsm.ukm.my,
jpadasian237@gmail.com, cradziah@ukm.my

Abstract. Besides rubber and rice, oil palm or Elaeis Guineensis remains as one of the most important plantation crops in Malaysia. Unfortunately, the lack of experience in oil palm fruit grading among the plucking farmers results in wrong estimation when harvesting. This affects production, negatively. Meanwhile, region growing conventional image segmentation techniques need manually or fixed initial seed selection which, actually, increases the computational cost, as well as, implementation time. Hence, the main goal of this study is to improve the seed region growing algorithm in order to gain higher accuracy in segmenting color information for oil palm fruit image. This study presents n-Seed Region Growing (n-SRG) for color image segmentation by choosing adaptive numbers of seed. The data sample consists of 80 images which comprises and two ripeness classes (ripe and unripe).The proposed work has out-performed the k-mean clustering method with 86% and 80% of average accuracy rates correspondingly.

Keywords: color image segmentation, seed region growing, automated visual inspection.

1 Introduction

Oil palm, Elaeis guineensis, is local to Africa [1] and has its primary commercial value in oil, which can be obtained from the mesocarp of the kernel and fruit for palm oil. The oil palm fruit is used fundamentally in foodstuff such as cooking oil and margarine, as well as in soap, detergent and cosmetics. The oil palm tree carries fruit from fourth year onward and can be harvested for 40-50 years. It requires humid

* Corresponding author.

H. Badioze Zaman et al. (Eds.): IVIC 2013, LNCS 8237, pp. 184–192, 2013.

climate to grow. Oil palm tree grows up to 20 meters in height and grows best at temperatures of 24-27 degree Celsius. Nowadays, they flourish and grow in the western part of Africa, Malaysia and Indonesia and most recently in Brazil and Colombia. Fig. 1(a) shows the sample image on an oil palm tree and Fig.1 (b) shows the oil palm fresh fruit bunches (OPFFB) on the tree.

Fig. 1. Sample of (a) oil palm tree and (b) oil palm fresh fruit bunch (OPFFB)

In agriculture, the color of crops, forests and flowers in images can be evaluated according to their ripeness, size and quality. Automated grading systems have become the topic of interest for many researchers in Malaysia. In the last few years, there have been several reports published on oil palm fruit research which were done using different kind of methods and approaches. However, up until now, there are limited numbers of research focuses on image processing and intelligent system to automate or consistently classify some human expert tasks such as diagnosing paddy disease using texture analysis [2]. Therefore, this paper aims to introduce the adaptive region growing approach for color segmentation of the oil palm fresh fruit bunch. The summary of the previous studies in automated oil palm fruit bunch grading system is shown in Table 1. Meanwhile, Table 2 shows the review of the implementation of region growing algorithm in earlier studies.

Table 1. Summary of the previous studies in automated oil palm fruit bunch grading system

Author	Article Title	Methods & Classes	Results
Alfatni et al ., 2008	Oil palm fruit bunch grading system using RGB digital number	RGB, saturation and intensity imaging technique by using ripe, unripe and overripe classes.	The system performance achieved 90% accuracy of classification.
May et al., 2011	Automated oil palm fruit grading system using artificial intelligence	Fuzzy logic and RGB color using under ripe, ripe and overripe classes	The ripeness of the palm oil with three classes about 86.67%

Table 1. *(Continued)*

Author	Article Title	Methods & Classes	Results
Jamil et al., 2009	Automated grading of palm oil fresh fruit bunches (FFB) using neuro-fuzzy technique	Fuzzy logic and Hebbian using Ripe-unripe-overripe	The accuracy achieved 73.3%
Jaffar et al., 2009	Photogrammetric grading of oil palm fresh fruit bunches	K-means clustering using unripe and ripe categories eventually sorts them out physically	The testing results proved increasing the efficiency of degree and quality harvesting.
Roseleena et al., 2011	Assessment of palm oil fresh fruit bunches using photogrammetric grading system	LAB color space using unripe and ripe categories with two camera eventually sorts them out physically.	The fruit classification ability of the system about 90% accuracy

Table 2. Review of the implementation of region growing algorithm

Author	Article Title	Method/Type of Images	Seed Selection
Adams et al., 1994	Seeded region growing	Region growing using greyscale	Manually
Fan et al., 2001	Automatic image segmentation by integrating color-edge extraction and seeded region growing	Region growing with color image	Automatically
Tang J., 2010	A color image segmentation algorithm based on region growing	Watershed region growing	Automatically

Table 2. *(Continued)*

Author	Article Title	Method/Type of Images	Seed Selection
Verma et al., 2011	A simple single seeded region growing algorithm for color image segmentation using centroid of region growing	Region growing with color image	Automatically
Sanders, 2005	Seeded region growing using multiple seed points	Region growing in gray and color image	Manually

This study focused on n-seed region growing (n-SRG) and motivated by the work of Jaffar et al. in [4]. This paper is organized into four sections. In section 2, we discuss about our proposed work. The experimental result is presented in section 3. We conclude this paper in the final section.

2 Proposed Work

The sample data consists of 80 images for easy category with different background collected from Universiti Putra Malaysia benchmark dataset by Alfatni et al. [3]. The image has been reformatted into JPEG format and resized to pixel dimensions using a digital camera. Two categories of ripeness are considered in this work (Unripe-Ripe). Every category has 40 images. We divide them into two sets; 15 for training and 25 for testing per class and a total of images for evaluation. This system works in an uncontrolled environment. A sample of the collected palm oil fresh fruit bunch is shown in Fig. 2.

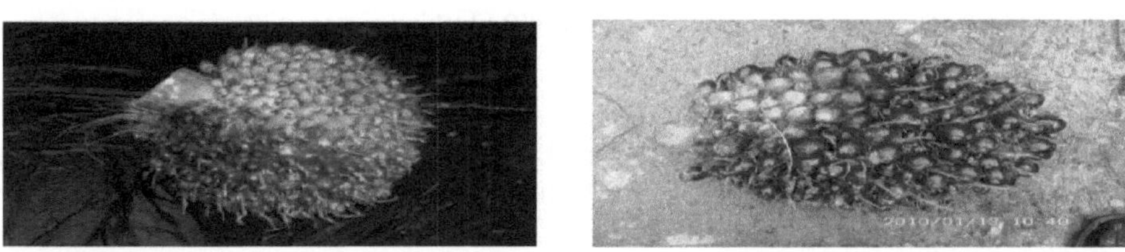

Fig. 2. Sample of oil palm fresh fruit bunches dataset collected from UPM with different background

In order to achieve the aims of the study, a framework for OFFFB plucking system which consists of six phases have been proposed as shown in Fig.3. The frameworks divided into three classes which are pre-processing, training and testing.

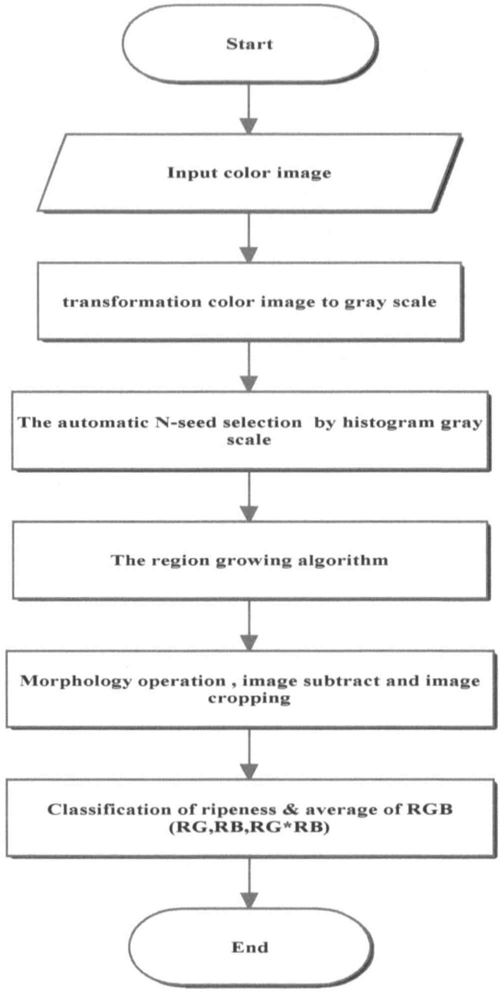

Fig. 3. The proposed framework for OPFFB plucking system with six phases

2.1 Image Pre-processing

The goal of this part is to remove the background noises of the OPFFB images in order to increase the accuracy of OPFFB plucking system. This step includes image enhancement, de-noising and image filtering. In this study, there are two pre-processing techniques that have been applied which are image cropping and conversion of color image to grayscale.

The purpose of image cropping is to reduce the size of the image before it will be sent for processing in order to reduce the calculation time. There are the two types of cropping method which is automatic and manual cropping. In this study, we used automatic cropping. The color image has been converted to gray level and the histogram of grayscale is calculated in the next step. The main objective in this stage is to find the first seed point from the histogram grayscale.

In the first step, the number of seeds is defined. Then, the histogram of image is divided into n-sub division. Next, the maximum pixel intensity within each n-division is searched. With the corresponding n-pixel maximum intensities, it will be set as the n-seed pixels. Lastly, the growing regions based on n-seed location are searched using SRG process. In [4], it was mentioned that using three clusters is more convenient than using five clusters. Hence, three seed points (n=3) were used in this study.

The proposed system started with finding the threshold values from pre-determined n-seed points; T1, T2 and T3 are the first, second and third threshold values which indicate maximum, medium and minimum values. Only the pixel values with maximum frequency of pixel intensity values within the histogram is selected as the seed point, S1, S2 and S3. The corresponding image results after applying T1, T2 and T3 threshold values and S1, S2and S3 are depicted in Fig. 4.

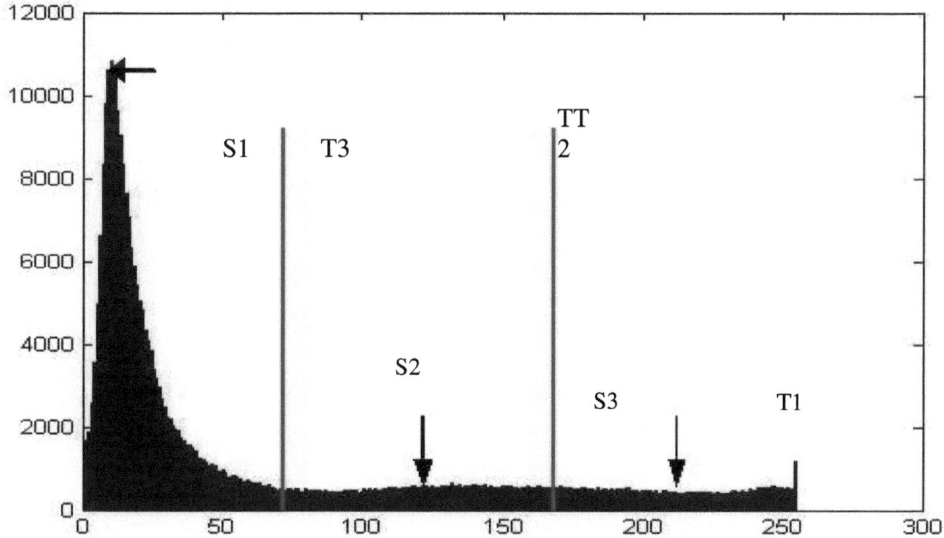

Fig. 4. The histogram of thresholding for n=3

The final phase in this study is to crop the image with the purpose of reducing computation time of selecting the color from the source image.

(a) (b) (c)

Fig. 5. The final n-seed color for proposed work (a) seed color 1, (b) seed color 2 and (c) seed color 3

2.2 Calculation of the Average RGB Color

The color values were then computed to find the value for R/G and R/B. To confirm the variance among unripe and ripe categories, a larger value of these ratios were used to compute the R/G*R/B. The average accuracy for all testing data sets in different classes ripe and unripe have been calculated using sum of average RG*RB in all values of classes between maximum and minimum values in RG*RB values. n is the sum of numbers values * 100 to find the percentage. Fig. 6 shows the range of average RGB in segmentation n-seed using ripeness easy dataset. It also shows the graph of mean value for ripe and unripe classes of OPFFB.

Ripeness	Easy data		
	Average RG Value	Average RB Value	Average RG*RB Value
Ripe	2.27< RG < 4.21	2.26< RB < 6.82	5.26< RG*RB < 28.08
Unripe	2.22< RG < 4.21	2.31< RB < 3.63	5.21< RG*RB < 9.16

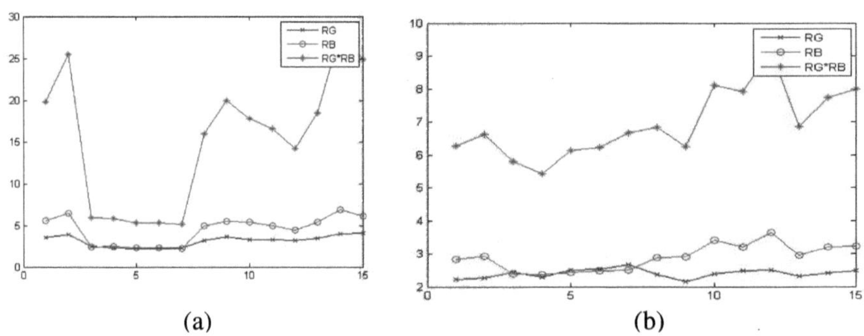

Fig. 6. The mean RGB value for (a) ripe and (b) unripe oil palm

3 Experiment Results

The objective in this study is to improve palm oil plucking and identification performance using adaptive region growing by separating n-seed colors to find other colors. The average time required processing the image by the system (running time) in easy dataset for k-means and proposed work are 5.8 and 4 seconds respectively. An experiment was conducted to choose the n-SRG is proposed in this study. Our proposed work is compared with the k-mean clustering method and the performance achieved is 86% and 80% correspondingly. The comparison of result is shown in Fig. 7.

Methods	Dataset	Total	Correct	%	Average (%)
Clustering	Ripe	25	21	84	80
	Unripe	25	19	76	
Proposed	Ripe	25	23	92	86
	Unripe	25	20	80	

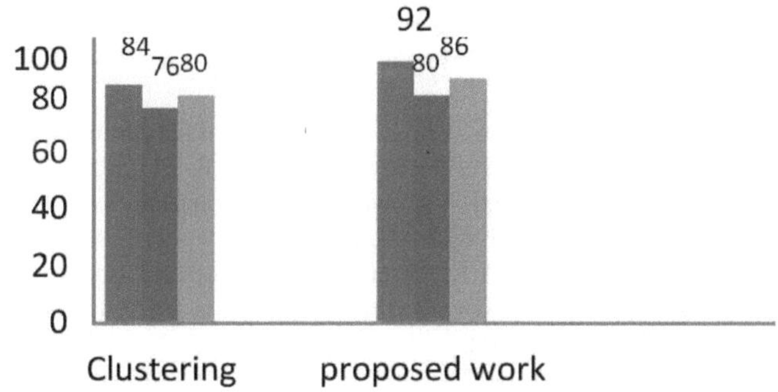

Fig. 7. Experiment result: (a) table of average rates based on clustering method and our proposed method and (b) comparison of the accuracy rate for clustering and our proposed method

4 Conclusion

In this study, an adaptive region growing for automated oil palm fruit quality recognition has been proposed. Basically, the proposed framework for bunches of fresh oil palm (OPFFB) plucking has six phases comprising the following: color image capturing, image transformation from color image to grayscale, image segmentation using proposed n-SRG and finally image ripeness classification using ratio color index production rule. The result demonstrates the significance of the proposed algorithms. The color ratio have to be used to differentiate the ripeness class in the segmented images of bunches of fresh oil palm. In conclusion, the proposed work has outperformed the k-mean clustering method. It is essential for the researchers to support the efforts of improving the welfare of farmers through improved applied technology in agriculture. Furthermore, the method described and implemented in this study can be the key for improvement of any fully automated oil palm or other agricultural products plucking system based on color images as the relationship to their ripeness classes.

Acknowledgments. The authors would like to thank Allayarham Sheikh Abdullah and his family for their helps and support during the collection of dataset phase. The oil palm fruit were taken from the oil palm plantation located at Chengal Lempong, Kuantan,Malaysia. This research is part of Fundamental Research Grant Scheme No. FRGS/1/2012/SG05/UKM/02/8 entitled "Generic Object Localization Algorithm for Image Segmentation".

References

1. Pippet, J.: Oil palm in Rural Development Series hand book, 57 p. Dept. of Agriculture, Port Moresby (1987)
2. Kurniawakti, N.N., Sheikh Abdullah, S.N.H., Abdullah, S., Abdullah, S.: Texture Analysis for Diagnosing Paddy Diseases. In: International Conference on Electrical Engineering and Informatics, vol. I, pp. 23–27 (2009)
3. Alfatni, M.S.M., Shariff, A.R.M., Shafri, H.Z.M., Saaed, O.M.B., Eshanta, O.M.: Oil palm fruit bunch grading system using red, green and blue digital number. Journal of Applied Sciences 8(8), 1444–1452 (2008)
4. Jaffar, A., Jaafar, R., Jamil, N., Low, C.Y., Abdullah, B.: Photogrammetri grading of oil palm fresh fruit bunches. Int. J. Mech. Mechatron. Eng. 9, 18–24 (2009)
5. Adams, R., Bischof, L.: Seeded region growing. IEEE Transactions on Pattern Analysis and Machine Intelligence 16(6), 641–647 (1994)
6. Fan, J., Yau, D.K., Elmagarmid, A.K., Aref, W.G.: Automatic image segmentation by integrating color-edge extraction and seeded region growing. IEEE Transactions on Image Processing 10(10), 1454–1466 (2001)
7. Jamil, N., Mohamed, A., Abdullah, S.: Automated grading of palm oil fresh bunches (FFB) using neuro-fuzzy technique. In: Soft Computing and Pattern Recognition, SOCPAR 2009, pp. 245–249 (2009)
8. May, Z., Amaran, M.H.: In Automated Ripeness Assessment of Oil Palm Fruit Using RGB and Fuzzy Logic Technique. In: Mathematical Methods and Techniques in Engineering and Environmental Science, Universiti Teknologi PETRONAS, pp. 52–59 (2011)
9. Roseleena, J., Nursuriati, J., Ahmed, J., Low, C.Y.: Assessment of palm oil fresh fruit bunches using photogrammetric grading system. International Food Research Journal 18(3), 999–1005 (2011)
10. Tang, J.: Color Image segmentation algorithm based on region growing. In: International Conference on Computer Engineering and Technology, vol. 6, pp. 634–637 (2010)
11. Verma, O.P., Hanmandlu, M., Susan, S., Kulkarni, M., Jain, P.K.: A Simple Single Seeded Region Growing Algorithm for Color Image Segmentation using Adaptive Thresholding. In: International Conference on Communication Systems and Network Technologies, pp. 500–503 (2011)
12. Sanders, I.: Seeded region growing using multiple seed points. In: Proceedings of the Sixteenth Annual Symposium of the Pattern Recognition Association of South Africa, pp. 177–182 (2005)

Performances of Invariant Feature Detectors in Real-Time Video Applications

M. Hedayati, W. Mimi Diyana W. Zaki, Aini Hussain, and Mohd. Asyraf Zulkifley

Department of Electrical, Electronic and Systems Engineering,
Faculty of Engineering and Built Environment, Universiti Kebangsaan Malaysia

Abstract. This paper reviews and compares the performance of five well-known detectors, SIFT, SURF, ORB, MSER and STAR, when combined in combination of with using three common descriptors, SIFT, SURF and ORB. To validate the results, these descriptors' performances are verified using three scenarios that differ with respect to changes in scale, light variation and rotation. The results show that the SIFT and SURF detectors possess the most stable features, with an overall accuracy of 80% under various conditions. Among the tested descriptors, SURF provides the best description of each keypoint.

Keywords: SIFT, SURF, ORB, MSER.

1 Introduction

Today, invariant features detectors have been employed in various applications such as object recognition, object modelling and robot localization. These detectors extract the natural features of objects and match similar regions in a scene. In general there are three steps involved to utilize features of image as feature detection, description and matching.

Generally, features are distinct characteristics of an object that make the object recognisable to an observer. These features can be a single pixel or small area with distinguishing characteristics and should be invariant with regard to geometric and photometric transformation.

To identify distinguishable features, the pixel information for each keypoint must be extracted. This information is required to characterize each keypoint. In addition, this description must be highly resistant to environmental challenges such as illumination change. This information, which reveals how the intensities are distributed around each keypoint, are called "descriptors". Descriptors are highly useful in feature matching algorithms. Numerous descriptors have been proposed in the literature. Li & Allinson [1] categorized descriptors into four main categories as filter-based descriptors [2], distribution-based descriptors [3], [4] and 55], textons [6] and derivative descriptors [7].

Feature matching is necessary to evaluate the similarities between two images [8]. The matching technique directly compares an incoming descriptor for one feature with all possible descriptors in the database to find features shared by two different

H. Badioze Zaman et al. (Eds.): IVIC 2013, LNCS 8237, pp. 193–205, 2013.

images. This technique can be classified into three different methods, the threshold model, the nearest neighbor model and the nearest neighbor distance ratio method [1]. The threshold method matches a candidate point with a reference point if the distance between the two points is less than a specified threshold; the nearest neighbor model identifies the point that is the shortest distance from the reference point; and the nearest neighbor distance ratio method uses the ratio of the distances between the reference point and the nearest and second-nearest neighbors to match the candidate point with the reference point [1]. This paper briefly reviews some well-known feature detectors (i.e., SIFT, SURF, ORB, MSER and STAR) and evaluates their performances with three well-known descriptors, SURF, SIFT and ORB.

The remainder of this paper is organised as follows: Section 2 (Basic terms) explains the general terms used papers describing invariant feature detectors; Section 3 (Invariant feature detectors) reviews most well-known feature detector algorithms in detail; Section 4 (Evaluation methodology) describes the techniques and materials used to compare the selected detectors; Section 5 (Results and discussion) analyses and compares the final result; and the final section states the conclusion based on this analysis.

2 Basic Terms

Most invariant detectors share a common structure for building the features block of an object. This section briefly explains the terms frequently used to construct the local detectors and descriptors.

2.1 Corner Detection

When searching for keypoint features in images, corners seem to be a notable solution. The most commonly used definition of a corner is provided by Harris & Stephens [9]. The Harris corner detector [9] exhibits a strong immutability to rotation and illumination changes [10]. The Harris detector is a well-modified version of the earlier Moravec method [11], which works based on an auto correlation function that detects changes in intensity by shifting a small window in various directions, as represented by Equation 1:

$$E_{x,y} = \sum_{u,v} W_{u,v} \left[I_{x+u,y+v} - I_{u,v} \right]^2 . \tag{1}$$

In the above equation, w represents the window function, $I_{(x,y)}$ represents the current pixel position, and $I_{(u,v)}$ represents the small shift of the point. Therefore, the auto correlation function, which is also known as the second moment matrix, can be derived from Equation 1 by considering the small shift in (x, y) Equation 2:

$$M = \sum_{x,y} w(x,y) \begin{bmatrix} I_x^2 & I_x I_y \\ I_x I_y & I_y^2 \end{bmatrix}. \tag{2}$$

If α and β are considered eigenvalues of M , these values will be proportional to the auto correlation curvature. Therefore, the following assumptions apply:

1. If both α and β are small, then the point is considered flat.
2. If one eigenvalue is high and another eigenvalue is low, then the point is considered the edge.
3. If both α and β are large, then the point can be considered a corner.

Hessian-based detectors: Hessian detectors are similar to Harris detectors. Hessian detectors use second derivatives based on Hessian matrix Equation 3. The Hessian-based detectors provide an effective response to the blobs and ridges area [10]:

$$M_h = \begin{bmatrix} I_{xx}(P) & I_{xy}(P) \\ I_{xy}(P) & I_{yy}(P) \end{bmatrix}. \tag{3}$$

Where I_{xx} and I_{yy} are the second derivatives of the image intensity I at point p , and I_{xy} is the mixed derivative.

2.2 Multi-scale Space Theory

Mathematically, objects have no scale. However, in reality, objects manifest on a wide-ranging scale. Therefore, the features and behaviour of an object can be changed by varying the scale. For example, it is inefficient to extract the features of leaves at a distance measured in nanometres or several kilometres away. With respect to this concern, the multi-scale representation of image is introduced [12] and [13]. The quadtree, introduced by Klinger [14], is one of the earliest multi-scale representations of an image. This tree-like representation model divides the image recursively into smaller regions. The pyramid is another well-known scale representation model that functions based on sub-sampling and smoothing a grey image on different scales. The Gaussian and Laplacian pyramids are two main sub-sampling operations: a Gaussian pyramid's scales are generated by a Gaussian kernel, and a Laplacian pyramid is obtained by constructing differences between adjacent levels in the Gaussian pyramid.

Scale-space representation is another successful multi scale representation. It generates a one-parameter family of derived signals [15]. Mathematically, the scale-space representation of an image is constructed from the convolution of a scale operator with an input image. As proven by Koenderink [16] and Lindeberg [12], under different assumptions, the only suitable scale-space kernel is the Gaussian function. This representation, which convolves the Gaussian kernel with an input image, results from the Laplacian of Gaussian (LoG) operation, which can be expressed as:

$$L(x, y, \sigma) = G(x, y, \sigma) * I(x, y) . \tag{4}$$

Where L is the LOG, G is the Gaussian kernel, I is the input image, and $*$ is the convolution operator. Difference of Gaussians (DoG), which is widely used for edge detection, can produce the LOG form by subtracting two nearby Gaussian scales (Fig 1).

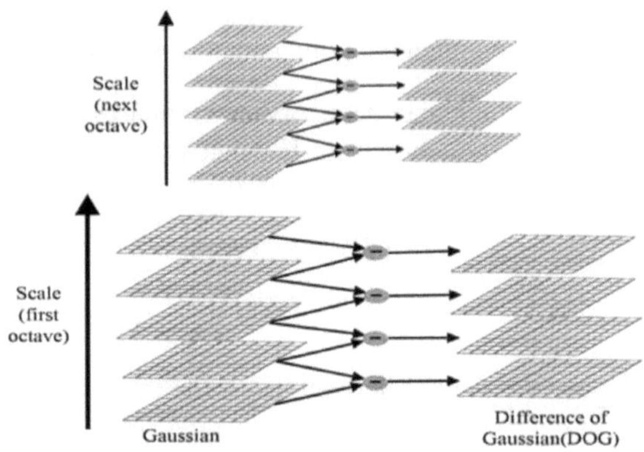

Fig. 1. The computation of the DoG. Adjacent Gaussian images are subtracted to produce the Difference of Gaussian images on the right.

2.3 Suppression

Non-maximum suppression (NMS) or brief suppression is important for edge detection and corner detection. NMS will set all pixels in the current neighbourhood window that are lower than the maximum value in that window to zero. NMS usually involves the following four steps [17]:

1. Let $I_{(x, y)}$ be the pixel intensity at point x and y .
2. Calculate the gradient and the magnitude of the image intensity at (x, y).
3. Estimate the magnitude of the gradient along the direction of the gradient with respect to the area neighbouring (x, y).
4. If (x, y) is not the maximum point along the direction of gradient, then it is not the interest point.

To find the maximum point in scale space, NMS can be applied to a selected pixel along its native scale and with respect to the intervals above and below the pixel, as shown in Fig 2.

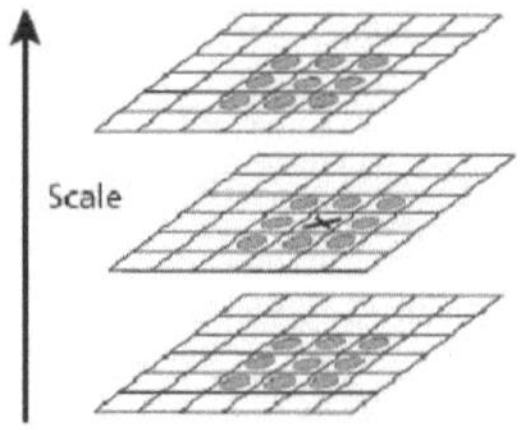

Fig. 2. The marked pixel is selected as the maxima if it is greater than the surrounding pixels in its interval and the intervals above and below it

2.4 Orientation Assignment

The main goal of orientation assignment is to enable features to be invariant with regard to frame rotation. The orientation assignment is usually defined as a property of descriptors rather than a characteristic of feature detectors. The methods introduced by Lowe [18], Bay [4] and Taylors [19] are three of the most well-known method used for assigning the orientation of keypoints.

2.5 Integral Image

Rectangular features can be computed rapidly using an intermediate representation of an image that is known as the integral image. The integral image was first introduced by Viloa and Jones [20] to achieve optimal computation speed when calculating the set of five rectangular features, as shown in Fig 3.

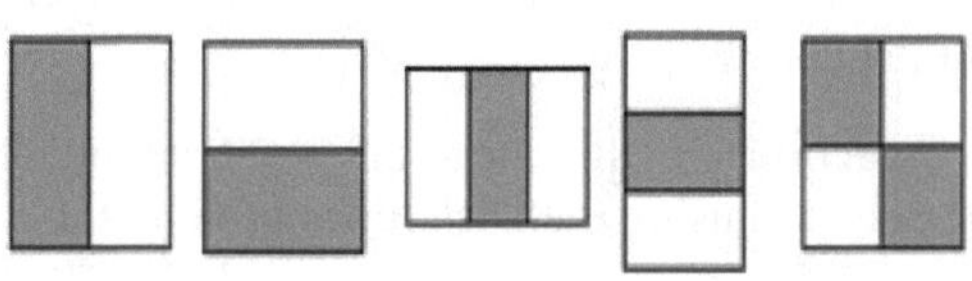

Fig. 3. The set of rectangular filters used by Viloa & Jones[19]

The integral image, by $ii(x, y)$, at point x, y, contains the sum of the pixels above and to the left of x, y as:

$$ii(x, y) = \sum_{x' \leq x,\, y' \leq y} i(x', xy') . \tag{5}$$

Where $i(x, y)$ is the original image.

Using the integral image, the sum of pixel values within a rectangular region of the image can be calculated with four array references within a specified duration. As evident from Fig 4, to compute the sum of region A, the following four references are required: $L4 + L1 - (L2 + L3)$.

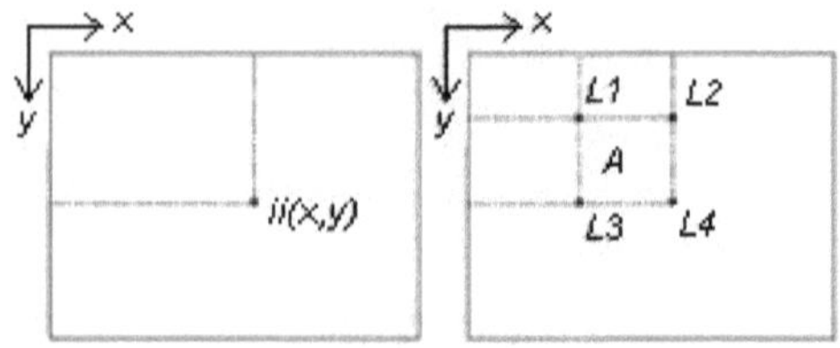

Fig. 4. The left image shows the construction of the integral image. The right image shows the computation of region using the four array references: $L4 + L1 - (L2 + L3)$.

3 Invariant Feature Detectors

Many studies have been dedicated to extracting invariant features. Harris and Hessian affine region detectors are two of the famous affine region detectors introduced by Mikolajczyk and Schmid [21]. This model detects the interest point with a Harris detector or a Hessian matrix in the scale-space and then determines an elliptical region for each point. This model entails four main steps. First, the interest point with a Harris or a Hessian detector at different scales is detected. Second, the affine region is normalised to the circular shape. Third, the second moment matrix is applied to each point to determine its shape. Fourth, if the eigenvalues of the second moment matrix for the new point are not equal, the process is repeated [10].

The Scale Invariant Feature Transform (SIFT) feature detector is another well-known invariant feature detector that was introduced by Lowe [3] and [18]. Lowe used scale space and a Harris detector to find highly distinct features in an image that are highly invariant with regard to image scale and rotation and partly invariant with regard to illumination changes. This model used three main steps to extract a set of image features, i.e., scale-space extrema detection, keypoint localisation and orientation assignment [3] and [22].

Scale-space extrema detection: In this step, all potential interest points across all possible scales will be detected using the Difference of Gaussians (DOG).

Keypoint localisation: Lowe used two stages of elimination to select distinctive features and to eliminate poorly localised features. In the first stage, a three-dimensional quadric function is used to determine the location of extrema in each subspace and to then eliminate unstable features by detecting the corners using Harris detectors [18].

Orientation assignment: To have keypoints that are invariant with regard to image rotation, each feature must be assigned to a proper direction. To achieve this goal, the Magnetite gradient and orientation of each sample image is computed using pixel differences. From these two parameters, the ordination histogram is built by sorting the gradient information into 36 bins, each of which covers 10 degrees of rotation. Histogram entries are weighted by the gradient magnitude and a Gaussian function, for which σ is equal to 1.5 times the scale of the keypoint. The peaks in the orientation histogram indicate the direction of each keypoint; the highest peaks which within 80% are used to assign keypoints with those directions.

Speeded-Up Robust Feature (SURF), which was proposed by Bay et al. [4], is an improvement over SIFT in terms of processing speed [23]. The computational reduction is achieved by implementing integral images, which simplify the process of locating the points of interest. The Hessian matrix or second-order partial differential is easily determined using the integral image. The author of that study claimed that the performance of SURF is similar to that of SIFT. SURF features are obtained as follows:

1. *Points of interest detection:* A Hessian matrix is used to obtain the second-order gradient of the image. The scale-space approach is used to obtain the points in the case of size fluctuation. Instead of using the pyramid-down approach by iteratively scaling down the size by applying a Gaussian filter, SURF employed the up-scaling method, which enhances the image resolution rather than reducing the image size. This allows for multiple layers in pyramid image processing to be processed with the same speed and even simultaneously [4].
2. *Keypoint localisation:* First, all corners that are lower than a predefined threshold will be removed. Then, NMS is applied to $3 \times 3 \times 3$ neighbouring pixels over three scale spaces. Finally, the maximum of the Hessian matrix's determinant is obtained by interpolating it in scale space using Brown's [24] 3D quadratic method.
3. *Orientation assignment:* The SURF detector used a Haar wavelet to assign each accepted point an orientation and a distinct representation. A square region around each keypoint, which is the neighbourhood region that will affect the keypoint's performance, will be constructed. This region is divided into equal 4×4 square sub-regions. To identify each keypoint's direction, the Haar wavelet responses are calculated at 5×5 sample points. Then, in each sub-region, the wavelet responses dx and dy are summed and represented as a new orientation vector. The longest vector represents the highest possibility of each keypoint orientation.

However, the computational speed improvement is marginal, which inspired Agrawal [25] to introduce scale-invariant centre-surround detectors (CenSurE). The main advantage of this detector is its low computational burden, which results from approximating the shape of a circle with a rotated square. A keypoint is detected by applying bi-level kernels to the original image. Then, local extrema are detected using a simple threshold, and the Harris measure is subsequently applied to filter the candidate points. These processes will eliminate local extrema, which indicate weak corner responses.

Maximally Stable Extremal Regions (MSER) [26] represent one of the simplest and most effective invariant feature detectors. MSER detects the maximum and minimum points using watershed-like thresholding. The keypoints are obtained by considering all of the possible intensity thresholds of an image, starting from 0 (white pixel) and ending at 255 (black pixel). Therefore, the maximum regions are extracted from a set of connected components. The minimum regions are obtained analogously by reversing the threshold decision. These maximum and minimum points remain stable over a wide range of thresholds. Hence, they are invariant with regard to changes in the image scale, the rotation and the illumination. Kristensen and Maclean [27] have obtained a real-time implementation of MSER using a FPGA board.

The oriented FAST and Rotated BRIEF (ORB) detector is one of the newest local feature detectors, which was introduced by Rublee et al. [28]. This approach is based on FAST detector methodology [29], which detects the keypoints at an early stage. FAST detects the keypoints by thresholding the centre pixel and its neighbouring pixels located at a circular distance from the centre. The detected corner is then filtered by the Harris approach to eliminate weak features. ORB applies a multi-scale and pyramidal approach to the image to produce scale-invariant features. An invariant orientation has also been obtained by Rublee et al. [25], who used intensity centroid theory, which was introduced by Rosin [30]. The intensity centroid theory assumes that the intensity of a corner is balanced when anchored at its centre.

4 Evaluation Methodology

For performance comparisons, five well-known detectors with three different descriptors are analysed. Usually, two performance criteria are examined to measure detector performance, i.e., accuracy and computational speed. Accuracy indicates how well the matching process between the keypoints performs, and computational speed analyses the computational power and time required to perform the task. However, this paper focuses on the accuracy. Rather than focusing on the performance of each keypoint, we calculate accuracy by measuring the matching process for the entire object under various projection angles of the target object. The homography approach is used to determine the projection using object boundary information. In general, homography relates two images with different spaces but a similar planar surface. A homography matrix provides information about the camera rotation and translation that can be used to register the location of a two-dimensional or a three-dimensional object in the image or video (Fig 5).

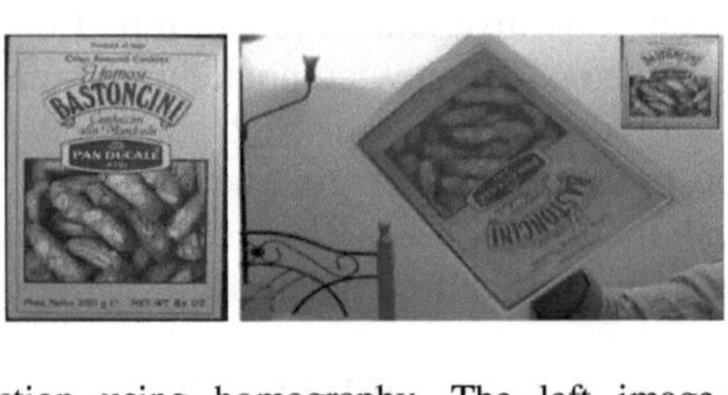

Fig. 5. Boundary detection using homography. The left image represents the original orientation of the object. The right image shows the detected object from a different orientation.

Table 1 illustrates the five detectors and descriptors used for this experiment, i.e., SIFT, SURF, STAR, MSER and ORB. These detectors are combined with three different descriptors, i.e., SIFT, SURF and ORB, to produce a distinct representation for the purposes of matching. Therefore, 15 combinations of detectors and descriptors are evaluated.

Table 1. Detectors and descriptors used for performance evaluation

	Methods				
Descriptors	SIFT, SURF, ORB				
Detectors	SIFT	SURF	STAR	MSER	ORB
Matching	Euclidean distance				Hamming distance

4.1 Video Database

Three videos consisting of the same object in different environments are used to validate the detectors' performance. These videos are selected to evaluate the matching performance in relation to changes in orientation, illumination and scale. We sampled the videos to select 40 frames from each video to quantify the performance. The video selection is conducted to verify each variable (orientation, illumination and scale) separately. An amateur' webcam is used to capture the video feed to simulate real world surroundings and environments. Therefore, effects such as changes in blur, shadow, scale and illumination occur within the videos. Fig 6 shows samples from each video.

5 Results and Discussion

Fig 7 shows the percentage of detection accuracy in relation to changes in illumination, rotation and scale. The following observation can be inferred from the graphs:

Descriptor: Fig 7 shows that the combination of SIFT and SURF detectors with a SIFT descriptor yields the best average result for all three cases. However, the SIFT descriptor does not work well with the STAR detector and generates the lowest accuracy of all other descriptors. In addition, the SURF descriptor performs moderately well with all detectors, as the variations in performance are small. SURF's average accuracy is the highest among all cases except the rotational change scenario, in which SIFT produces a slightly better accuracy. Fig 6 shows that the ORB descriptor works well with ORB and STAR detectors, but its performance declines with SIFT and SURF detectors.

Fig. 6. Test videos samples, from top to bottom: light variation, object rotation and scale changes

Detectors: Table 2 shows each detector's average accuracy for all three descriptors–SIFT, SURF and ORB; thus, this table indicates how well each detector adapts to different descriptors. The table also shows which detector remains most stable when placed in various surroundings. We can conclude that the SURF detector has the highest accuracy, with an overall 80% accuracy under three different cases, whereas the least accurate detector is STAR, with an average accuracy of 41%.

The computational time of each descriptor with respect to five different detectors is shown in Table 3. The computational speeds of the SIFT descriptor and detector are notably low compared with those of other methods and are therefore unsuitable for real-time applications. STAR is the fastest algorithm, but because of its low accuracy, it is not considered the optimal model. The two descriptors SURF and ORB have approximately identical computational times, with speeds of 1.53 and 1.45 seconds per frame, respectively, thus making them more suitable for real-time applications.

Table 2. The average accuracy for each detector for the three scenarios

	Light	Rotation	Scale
SIFT	85%	74%	75%
SURF	85%	78%	77%
STAR	58%	42%	22%
ORB	84%	77%	50%
MSER	80%	68%	65%

Table 3. The computational time of combination descriptors and detectors (seconds per frame)

	SIFT	SURF	ORB	Average
SIFT	6.5	2.60	2.13	3.80
SURF	6	2.50	2	3.50
STAR	1.1	0.28	0.58	0.65
ORB	4	1.8	1.7	2.50
MSER	1.5	0.45	0.83	0.93
Average	3.82	1.53	1.45	

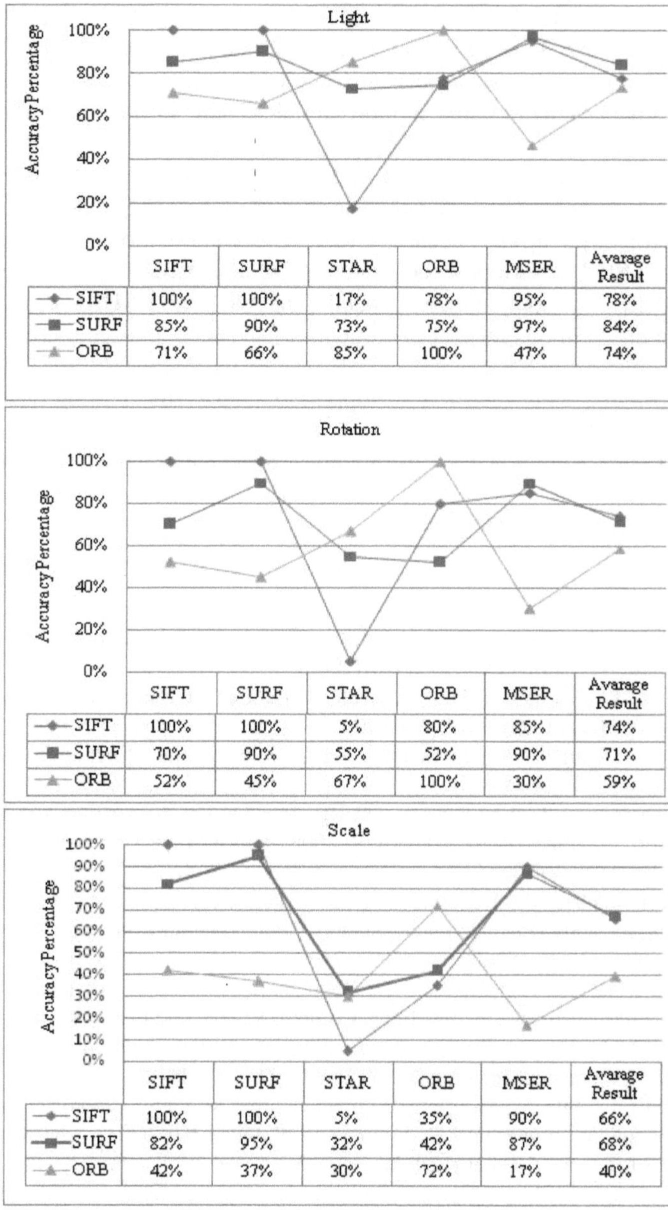

Fig. 7. Detection performance, from top to bottom : illumination changes, orientation changes and scale changes

6 Conclusion

This paper explains the basic building blocks of an invariant feature detector. We also review some of the well-known feature detectors and compare their performances.

Five different detectors (SIFT SURF, STAR, ORB and MSER) are assessed with three descriptors (SIFT, SURF and ORB) to compare the performances. Three different challenging situations are examined with respect to scale, orientation and illumination changes to achieve a more reliable real world implementation. The results indicate that the SURF descriptor provides the best representation of each keypoint compared with ORB and SIFT. The SURF detector is also the most stable feature detector, with an accuracy rate of least 80%, whereas STAR is the least stable feature detector, with a 41% accuracy rate. The computational time analysis also reveals that the SIFT descriptors and detectors are unsuitable for real-time application because of their low computational speed. The ORB and SURF descriptors yield better performances in this respect of computational speed and accuracy.

Acknowledgments. This research is supported in part by a Long Term Research Grant Scheme LRGS/TD/2011/UKM/ICT/03/03 by Kementerian Pengajian Tinggi Malaysia and DPP-2013-003 grant from Universiti Kebangsaan Malaysia (UKM).

References

1. Li, J., Allinson, N.: A comprehensive review of current local features for computer vision. Neurocomputing 71(10-12), 1771–1787 (2008)
2. Freeman, W.T., Adelson, E.H.: The Design and Use of Steerable Filters. IEEE Trans. Pattern Anal. Mach. Intell. 13(9), 891–906 (1991)
3. Lowe, D.G.: Distinctive Image Features from Scale-Invariant Keypoints. Int. J. Comput. Vision 60(2), 91–110 (2004)
4. Bay, H., Tuytelaars, T., Van Gool, L.: SURF: Speeded Up Robust Features. In: Leonardis, A., Bischof, H., Pinz, A. (eds.) ECCV 2006, Part I. LNCS, vol. 3951, pp. 404–417. Springer, Heidelberg (2006)
5. Ke, Y., Sukthankar, R.: PCA-SIFT: a more distinctive representation for local image descriptors. In: 2004 IEEE Computer Society Conference on Computer Vision and Pattern Recognition, vol. 2, pp. 506–513 (2004)
6. Leung, T., Malik, J.: Representing and Recognizing the Visual Appearance of Materials using Three-dimensional Textons. Int. J. Comput. Vision 43(1), 29–44 (2001)
7. Florack, L.M.J., et al.: General intensity transformations and differential invariants. Journal of Mathematical Imaging and Vision 4, 171–181 (1994)
8. Yan, B., Shi, F., Yue, J.: An Improved Image Corner Matching Approach. In: Huang, D.-S., Bevilacqua, V., Figueroa, J.C., Premaratne, P. (eds.) ICIC 2013. LNCS, vol. 7995, pp. 472–481. Springer, Heidelberg (2013)
9. Harris, C., Stephens, M.: A Combined Corner and Edge Detection. In: Proceedings of the Fourth Alvey Vision Conference, pp. 147–151 (1988)
10. Mikolajczyk, K., et al.: A Comparison of Affine Region Detectors. Int. J. Comput. Vision 65(1-2), 43–72 (2005)
11. Moravec, H.: Obstacle Avoidance and Navigation in the Real World by a Seeing Robot Rover, tech. report CMU-RI-TR-80-03, Robotics Institute, Carnegie Mellon University & doctoral dissertation, Stanford University (1980)
12. Lindeberg, T.: Scale-space Theory: A Basic Tool for Analysing Structures at Different Scales. J. of Applied Statistics 21(2), 224–270 (1994)

13. Witkin, A.P.,: Scale-space Filtering. In: Proceedings of the Eighth International Joint Conference on Artificial Intelligence, vol. 2, pp. 1019–1022 (1983)
14. Klinger, A.: Patterns and Search Statistics. In: Rustagi, J.S. (ed.) Optimizing Methods in Statistics. Academic Press, New York (1971)
15. Lindeberg, T.: Scale-space Theory: A Framework for Handling Image Structures at Multiple Scales. CERN School of Computing, Egmond aan Zee (1996)
16. Koenderink, J.: The Structure of Images. Biological Cybernetics 50(5), 363–370 (1984)
17. Devernay, F.: A Non-Maxima Suppression Method for Edge Detection with Sub-Pixel Accuracy, Institut National De Recherche En Informatique Et En Automatique (1995)
18. Lowe, D.G.: Object Recognition from Local Scale-Invariant Features. In: Proceedings of the International Conference on Computer Vision, vol. 2, pp. 1150–1157 (1999)
19. Taylor, S., Drummond, T.: Binary Histogrammed Intensity Patches for Efficient and Robust Matching. Int. J. Comput. Vision 94(2), 241–265 (2011)
20. Viola, P., Jones, M.: Rapid Object Detection Using a Boosted Cascade of Simple Features. In: 2001 IEEE Computer Society Conference on Computer Vision and Pattern Recognition, vol. 1, pp. 511–518 (2001)
21. Mikolajczyk, K., Schmid, C.: Scale & Affine Invariant Interest Point Detectors. Int. J. Comput. Vision 60(1), 63–86 (2004)
22. Zhuping, W., et al.: An Affine Invariant Feature Detection Method Based on SIFT and MSER. In: 2012 7th IEEE Conference on Industrial Electronics and Applications (ICIEA), pp. 69–72 (2012)
23. Mainali, P., et al.: SIFER: Scale-Invariant Feature Detector with Error Resilience. International Journal of Computer Vision 104(2), 172–197 (2013)
24. Brown, M., Lowe, D.: Invariant Features from Interest Point Groups (2002)
25. Agrawal, M., Konolige, K., Blas, M.R.: CenSurE: Center Surround Extremas for Realtime Feature Detection and Matching. In: Forsyth, D., Torr, P., Zisserman, A. (eds.) ECCV 2008, Part IV. LNCS, vol. 5305, pp. 102–115. Springer, Heidelberg (2008)
26. Matas, J., et al.: Robust wide baseline stereo from maximally stable extremal regions. In: Proceedings of the British Machine Vision Conference, vol. 1, pp. 384–393 (2002)
27. Kristensen, F., Maclean, W.J.: Real-Time Extraction of Maximally Stable Extremal Regions on an FPGA. In: IEEE International Symposium on Circuits and Systems, ISCAS 2007, pp. 165–168 (2007)
28. Rublee, E., et al.: ORB: An Efficient Alternative to SIFT or SURF. In: International Conference on Computer Vision (2011)
29. Trajkovic, M., Hedley, M.: Fast Corner Detection. Image and Vision Computing 16(2), 75–87 (1998)
30. Rosin, P.L.: Measuring Corner Properties. Computer Vision and Image Understanding, 291–307 (1999)

A Simulation Study on Factors Affecting Airwaves Using Factorial Design

Muhammad Abdulkarim[1,*], Afza Shafie[2], Wan Fatimah Wan Ahmad[1], and Radzuan Razali[2]

[1] Department of Computer & Information Sciences
[2] Department of Fundamental & Applied Sciences
Universiti Teknologi PETRONAS, Seri Iskandar, 31750 Tronoh, Perak, Malaysia
mmmhammmad@gmail.com, muhammad_g01387@utp.edu.my, {afza,fatimhd,radzuan_razali}@petronas.com.my

Abstract. In shallow water Sea Bed Logging (SBL) survey, air layer response from the Electro-Magnetic (EM) signals creates a disturbance known as the source-induced airwaves. The airwaves commonly denote the energy that propagates from the EM source via the atmosphere to the receiver on the seabed. As a result, the airwaves dominate the measured survey data, so that the sought-after signals from possible hydrocarbon layers in the subsurface can be totally masked. In this study, a 5x5 factorial design is used to analyze the effect of frequency, seawater conductivity, sediment conductivity, seawater depth and offset on the magnitude of airwaves. The result based on *F*-statistics, indicates that frequency has higher significant effect on the magnitude of the airwaves followed by the seawater depth, offset, seawater conductivity and sediment conductivity in that order.

Keywords: Airwaves; Factorial Design, F-Statistics, Sea Bed Logging, Shallow Water.

1 Introduction

Sea Bed Logging (SBL) survey is an offshore exploration method used to measure the response of earth's subsurface structures due to the imparted alternating electric current when external electromagnetic field is applied into sub-sea floor formations. The SBL technique has recently provide a means of remotely detecting the presence of high resistive sub-sea floor structures of the earth's interior such as the hydrocarbon reservoir. The following describes a typical SBL survey.

Commonly in practice, an electrode refers to a Horizontal Electric Dipole (HED) which serves as electromagnetic source is disposed approximately 30 – 50m above the seabed and connected to the survey recording vessel. The electrode is being charged by the power source on the survey vessel at selected magnitude of alternating

---

* Corresponding author.

H. Badioze Zaman et al. (Eds.): IVIC 2013, LNCS 8237, pp. 206–217, 2013.

current and transmission frequency or frequencies. At a selected source receiver distance (offset), an Ultra-low (~ 0.1 – 5Hz) transmission frequency is commonly passed through the seabed into the subsurface of the earth formation. Electric and magnetic sensors/receiver designed with a voltage measuring circuit are placed strategically either on the seabed or on a different survey vessel (see Figure 1). The imparted voltages recorded by the receivers on the seabed are then analyzed to presume the structural formations beneath the earth surface through their electrical properties [1 – 3].

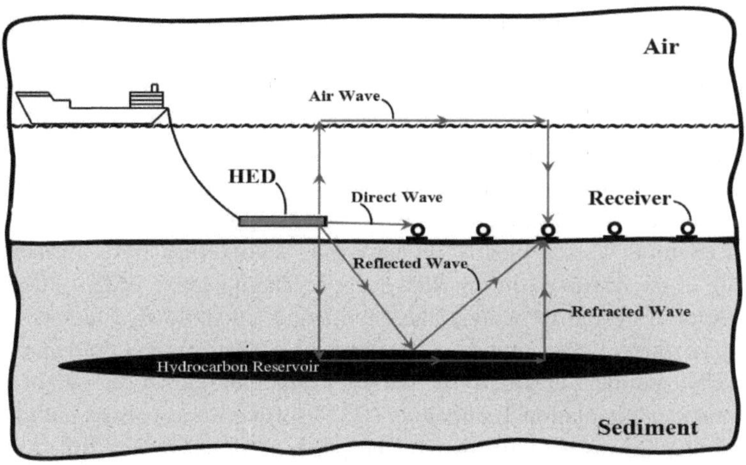

Fig. 1. Schematic Illustration of SBL Survey Environment

Theoretically, one of the main physics about the SBL is basically the knowledge that when the electromagnetic (EM) field is propagated through a conductive subsurface, the induced signal is mainly affected by spatial distribution of resistivity. Sediments filled with saltwater in a marine environments typically represent good conductors, whereas the example of resistive bodies that scatter the EM field include carbonates, hydrocarbon filled sediments, salt and volcanic rocks. Part of the electromagnetic field signal that were scattered by subsurface in-homogeneities propagates back to the seafloor where the signal is recorded by receivers equipped with electric and magnetic field sensors.

The data recorded in shallow water SBL survey are known to be affected by a noise called “airwaves". The noise component (airwaves) are generated predominantly by the vertically up going diffuse electromagnetic signal component that propagates in form of wave at the air/sea interface with speed of light and without attenuation before it diffuse back through the water layer vertically down where it is recorded by the electromagnetic receivers [4] as illustrated in Figure 1.

There are numerous modeling concepts developed to provide better understanding of systems having factors with nonlinear relationships like the airwaves. The numerical modeling conducted by [5] that used HED as the electromagnetic source, investigated the airwaves contribution to the SBL data. Their study identified far offset, transmission frequency and relatively shallow seawater depths to have important effect on the airwaves component. Even though, apart from the numerical modeling, no method of computing the airwaves was given in that study. Hankel transform was used by [6] to develop another 1D model through numerical airwaves calculations that resulted into a fast algorithm. The behaviour and physical insight of how airwaves build up in the water layer was not explained by the algorithm.

Study by [4] has also shown the effect of seawater depth would be important at large source-receiver separations, low frequencies, or in relatively shallow water. It was also pointed out that in principle, the method of modeling-and-subtraction can be used to suppress the airwave component. The effect can be incorporated into the theory if both water depth and source location are accurately determined [6]. Features of the effect of the air wave on the amplitude and phase was described by [2] and reported that the range at which the air wave dominates the response, and information on seabed resistivity is lost, increases with decreasing frequency and water depth.

The literatures above clearly suggest the factors that have influence on the magnitude of the airwaves during SBL survey. The objective of this study is to use a 5 by 5 factorial design to analyze the significance of these five factors each at five levels. The factors considered in this study are transmission frequency, seawater conductivity, sediment conductivity, seawater depth and offset. Series of simulations using Computer Simulation Technology (CST) software was carried out to acquire the shallow water airwaves study data. The paper is organized as follows; Section 2 discusses factorial design followed by methodology in section 3. The study results are presented in section 4 and section 5 is the conclusion.

2 Factorial Design

A factorial design is a robust analytical research tool for identifying the effects of multiple variables against a response variable. According to R.A. Fisher, factorial design has the advantage of reducing number of experiments or simulations to conduct by simultaneously studying the multiple factors. Furthermore, factorial design can be used to find the main effects from each independent factor and the interaction effects in the cases where all the factors need to be considered for explaining the response. However, because the factorial design provides only relative values, achieving the actual numerical values tends to be a difficult mathematics that require sum of values to be minimized similar to regressions. Nevertheless, the method of factorial design is essential for both laboratory and industrial experimental settings [7 – 9]. There are many different ways to design factorial analysis depending on the number on factors and their corresponding level. Note that in this text, the word experiment also means the simulated experiment.

2.1 The Study Design

The main purpose of this section is to introduce a general notation used in the study. The simulated experiment carefully considered five different factors with five levels each. Thus the experiment is called a 5 x 5 factorial design. The considered factors by this study are as follows: Frequency (FRQ), Sediment Conductivity (SDC), Sea Water Conductivity (SWC), Sea Water Depth (SWD), and Offset (OST). A measurement number (n) are made for each of the five factors combination and a random error term ℓ. The terminology used as response refers to a result of certain combination of a factor in single experiment as well as sum of the results obtained for the given factor combination. Table 1 provide the setup values for the completely randomized design with $n = 5$ repetitions per factor combination.

Table 1. Factors and Levels of the Study Data

Factor	Level 1	Level 2	Level 3	Level 4	Level 5
FRQ (Hz)	1.0	0.5	0.25	0.125	0.0625
SDC (Sm^{-1})	1.0	0.8	0.7	0.6	0.5
SWC (Sm^{-1})	3.0	3.5	4.0	4.5	5.0
SWD (m)	100	200	300	400	500
OST (m)	5000	10000	15000	20000	25000

The values in Table 1 provide the number of different factors and their corresponding levels considered in the study. Let A, B, C, D and E be the experimental factors representing the Frequency (FRQ), Sediment Conductivity (SDC), Sea Water Conductivity (SWC), Sea Water Depth (SWD), and Offset (OST) respectively. It is practical, not to say required, always using these names. Mathematically, the response for the model is:

$$\begin{aligned}
&Y_{ijklmn} = \mu + \\
&A_i + B_j + C_k + D_l + E_m + \\
&\gamma AB_{ij} + \gamma AC_{ik} + \gamma AD_{il} + \gamma AE_{im} + \gamma BC_{jk} + \gamma BD_{jl} + \gamma BE_{jm} + \gamma CD_{kl} + \gamma CE_{km} \gamma DE_{lm} + \\
&\gamma ABC_{ijk} + \gamma ABD_{ijl} + \gamma ABE_{ijm} + \gamma BCD_{jkl} + \gamma BCE_{jkm} + \gamma CDE_{klm} + \\
&\gamma ABCD_{ijkl} + \gamma ABCE_{ijkm} + \gamma BCDE_{jklm} + \\
&\gamma ABCDE_{ijklm} + \\
&\ell_{ijklmn}
\end{aligned} \tag{1}$$

Where μ is the mean response, the terms in the second line of equation 1 are the main effects and the term(s) in the third, fourth, fifth and sixth lines of equation 1 are the 1st, 2nd, 3rd and 4th order interactions respectively. The last term of equation 1 is the general random error. Note that, $i = j = k = l = m = n = 1, 2, \ldots, 5$ (see Table 1). The usual restrictions also apply as follow:

- Main Effects: sums are 0

$$\sum_i A_i = \sum_j B_j = \sum_k C_k = \sum_l D_l = \sum_m E_m = 0 \tag{2}$$

- Interactions: sum to 0 along each dimension represented

$$\forall i \quad \sum_j \gamma_{AB_{ij}} = \sum_k \gamma_{AC_{ik}} = \sum_l \gamma_{AD_{il}} = \sum_m \gamma_{AE_{im}} = \sum_j \gamma_{BC_{jk}} =$$
$$\sum_l \gamma_{BD_{jl}} = \sum_m \gamma_{BE_{jm}} = \sum_k \gamma_{CD_{kl}} = \sum_m \gamma_{CE_{km}} \sum_l \gamma_{DE_{lm}} = 0 \tag{3}$$

$$\sum_k \gamma_{ABC_{ijk}} = \sum_l \gamma_{ABD_{ijl}} = \sum_m \gamma_{ABE_{ijm}} = \sum_j \gamma_{BCD_{jkl}} = \sum_k \gamma_{BCE_{jkm}} \sum_m \gamma_{CDE_{klm}} = 0 \tag{4}$$

$$\sum_l \gamma_{ABCD_{ijkl}} = \sum_k \gamma_{ABCE_{ijkm}} = \sum_m \gamma_{BCDE_{jklm}} = 0 \tag{5}$$

$$\sum_m \gamma_{ABCDE_{ijklm}} = 0 \tag{6}$$

- Errors: sum to 0 among all replications of each experiment

$$\sum_n \ell_{ijklmn} \;, \quad \forall\, i, j, k, l, m \tag{7}$$

3 Methodology

The simulation protocols related to the study data acquisition are explained in this section. Computer Simulation Technology (CST) software was used in designing and solving the different models of SBL environment with defined parameters. Maxwell's grid equations are used as codes in the CST software by discretizing each Maxwell's equations at low frequency to show the resistivity contrast. The area simulated is 25Km. The transmitter is modeled as a short 1250A AC line current segment of length 270m located 30m above the sea bed. The Maxwell's electromagnetic field wave equation in vacuum in the absence of electric or magnetic sources is solved for the electric field vector ***E*** inside the computational domains.

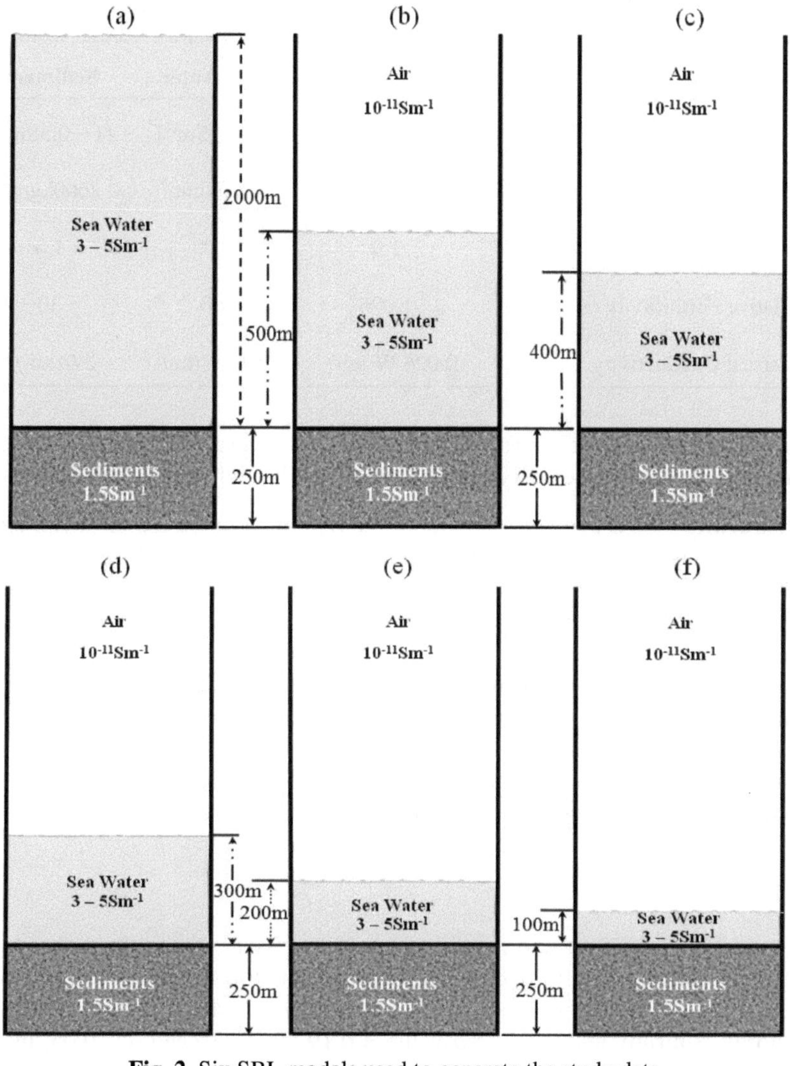

Fig. 2. Six SBL models used to generate the study data

Figure 2 (a) is a 1D SBL model depicting "No Air Layer Model" and Figure 2 (b) – (f) are "With Air Layer Models" configurations that were simulated to obtain the airwaves data. Note that the figures are not drawn to scale in this text; but in practice all have the same area. The only difference between "No Air Layer Model" and "With Air Layer Models" is the changing of the sea water depth and replacing the space with air layer. We changed the sea water depth at interval of 100m from 2000m down to 100m in order to obtain the airwaves data for the sea water depth of 500m down to 100m that was used in this study. This is because a study by [10] has shown that airwaves have significant effect on the SBL survey data within the depth of 100m to 500m. Table 2 present other physical values used for the simulation domains.

Table 2. Values assigned to the domains physical properties

Domain	Air	Sea Water	Sediment
Conductivity (σ)	1e-11Sm^{-1}	[3 − 5Sm^{-1}]	[1− 0.5Sm^{-1}]
Material Density (ρ)	1.293kgm^{-3}	1025kgm^{-3}	2600kgm^{-3}
Relative Permeability (μ_r)	1.0	0.99	1.0
Relative Permittivity (ε_r)	1.006	80	30
Thermal Conductivity	0.024 W(km)$^{-1}$	0.593 W(km)$^{-1}$	2W(km)$^{-1}$

The contribution of the airwaves to the SBL data were computed by the method for removing the air wave effect as patented by [11] through the following steps:

1. Constructing a SBL geometric model of the region having a top air layer, a middle sea water layer, and a bottom earth layer, with the model reflecting known bathymetry of the region and known conductivities of the air, seawater and earth;
2. Using the model to compute the electromagnetic field at all receiver locations for each source location;
3. Replacing the air layer in the model with sea water to create No-Air Layer model;
4. Computing the fields for the same source-receiver geometries for the No-Air Layer model; and
5. Computing the airwaves effect at each SWD by subtracting the No-Air Layer Model fields from the corresponding fields of the With-Air Layer Models.

3.1 Data Analysis

The homogeity of variance and normality test is necessary due to the nature factorial analysis [12]. Hence, the study data was first subjected to Kolmogorov–Smirnov test and Levene's test for the normality and homogeity of variance respectively. The Kolmogorov–Smirnov test shows a p-value = 0.19 which exceed α = 0.05, therefore, the null hypothesis was retained and we assume that the assumption of normality is met for the data. The result of this test is supported by the probability plot in Figure 6(f) showing the data points pretty close to the line of best fit, suggesting that the distribution doesn't deviate far from normal. The Levene's test of homogeity of variace indicates a p-value = 0.13 which is non-significant. Hence we can assume that the variance on independent variable across population of the study data is equal or homogeneous.

Analysis of Variance (ANOVA) approach was used in analyzing the factorial experiment. This allows studying the effect of each factor on the response variable, as well as the effects of interactions between factors on the response variable. The fundamental technique of ANOVA is based on partitioning of the total Sum of Squares (SS) into components related to the effects used in the model [13, 14].

$$SS_{Total} = SS_{Treatments} + SS_{Error} \tag{1}$$

The number of Degrees of Freedom (*DF*) can be partitioned in a similar way: one of these components (that for error) specify a chi-squared distribution which describes the associated sum of squares, while the same is true for "treatments" if there is no treatment effect.

$$DF_{Total} = DF_{Treatments} + DF_{Error} \tag{2}$$

The statistical significance was tested for by comparing the *F* test statistic as:

$$F = \frac{\dfrac{SS_{Treatment}}{r-1}}{\dfrac{SS_{Error}}{n-r}} \tag{3}$$

Where *r* is the number of treatments and *n* is the total number of cases to the *F*-distribution with $(r - 1)(n - r)$ degrees of freedom. The use of *F*-distribution has become a natural choice since the test statistic is a ratio of two scaled sums of squares each following a scaled chi-squared distribution with expected *F* value given as:

$$F = \frac{1 + \eta_t \sigma^2_{Treatment}}{\sigma^2_{Error}} \tag{4}$$

Where η_t is the sample size for the treatment, it has the value of 1 when there is no treatment effect. When the *F* values increase beyond 1 the evidence will gradually become more inconsistent with the null hypothesis. The two obvious experimental methods of increasing *F* value are increase of sample size and decrease of the error variance by tight experimental controls.

The textbook method of concluding test of hypothesis is by comparing the observed *F* value with critical *F* value determined from statistical tables. The critical *F* value is defined as the function of significance level (α), degrees of freedom for the numerator and the degrees of freedom for the denominator. The null hypothesis is to be rejected if $F_{Table} \geq F_{Critical}$ (α, numerator degrees of freedom, denominator degrees of freedom). The ANOVA *F*–test (of the null-hypothesis that all treatments have exactly the same effect) is recommended as a practical test, because of its robustness against many alternative distributions [15 – 17].

The study null and the alternative research hypotheses are as stated below:

- **H_0:** There will be no difference in airwave magnitude between the five levels of the main effects (i.e. FRQ, OST, SDC, SWC, and SWD) together with their interaction effects.
- **H_A:** There will be difference in airwave magnitude between the five levels of the main effects (i.e. FRQ, OST, SDC, SWC, and SWD) together with their interaction effects.

MATLAB software statistical tool kit method was utilized to calculate the probability (*p*-value) of a value of *F* greater than or equal to the observed value. The null hypothesis is rejected if this probability is less than or equal to the significance level ($\alpha = 0.05$). The two methods produce the same result.

4 Result and Discussion

Figures 3(a) – (e) presents the magnitude of airwaves plotted against the different levels of factors considered in this study. Data from the five different levels of FRQ corresponding to the five OST points are displayed in Figure 3(a). Firstly, the plot clearly shows that as the FRQ decreases the magnitude of the airwaves increases for all the offsets. This can be explain thus, the low frequency gives the up-going EM signal enough strength to reach the air/sea interface before diffusing back down vertically through the water layer to the sea bottom, where it is picked up by the EM receivers. Secondly, the separation between the five curves seems to be fairly equal.

Figure 3(b) displays the plot of five different levels of SWD corresponding to the five OST points. In this plot, it can be noticed that the magnitude of the airwaves decreases with the increase of both the SWD and the offset. Furthermore, the separation between the five curves seems are clearly unequal with the highest difference between the SWD of 100m and 200m. This is as a result of the less attenuation encountered by the up-going signal as the SWD is getting shallow.

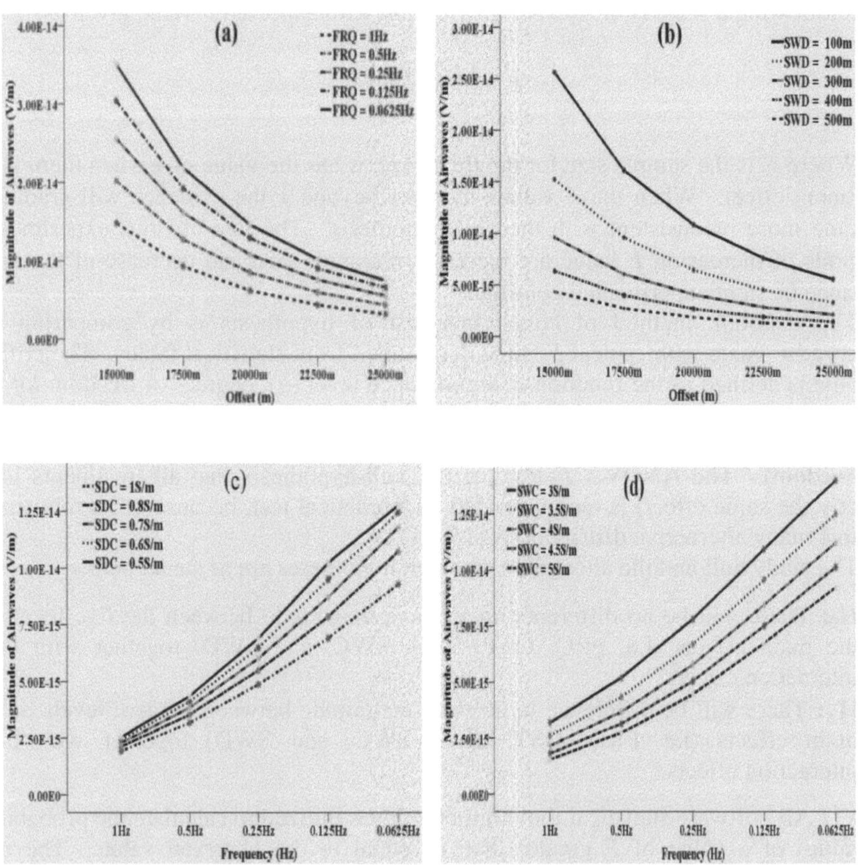

Fig. 3. Graphs of the Study Data (a – e) and the Probability Plot (f)

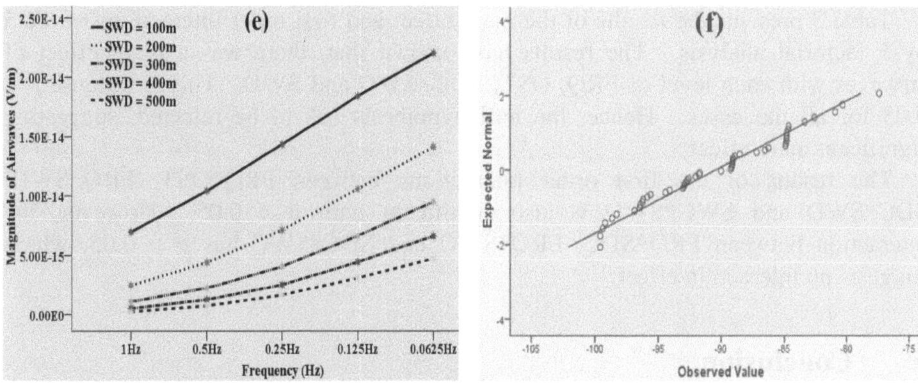

Fig. 3. *(Continued)*

Figure 3(c) displays the plot of five different levels of SDC together with the five levels of FRQ against the magnitude of the airwaves. This plot show that the increase of FRQ and SDC results in the increase of the magnitude of the airwaves.

Similarly, Figure 3(d) indicates that increase of FRQ and SWC also results in the increase of the magnitude of the airwaves even though the separation between the five curves seems to differ with FRQ and SWC having higher difference than the FRQ and SDC against magnitude of the airwaves. The data plot for the five different FRQ at five different SWD against the magnitude of the airwaves is presented in Figure 3(f). It can be observed that the increase of SWD and the decrease of FRQ greatly affect the magnitude of the airwaves especially in the 100m SWD. Therefore, this suggests that the FRQ, SDC, SWC, SWD and OST all have effect on the magnitude of the airwaves.

Table 3. The ANOVA Table

Source	*SS*	*DF*	*MS*	*F*	*Sig.*
FRQ	5.377E-26	4	1.344E-26	225.811	0.000
OST	3.579E-26	4	8.948E-27	150.302	0.000
SDC	1.783E-27	4	4.458E-28	7.488	0.000
SWC	4.245E-27	4	1.061E-27	17.827	0.000
SWD	6.176E-26	4	1.544E-26	259.365	0.000
FRQ*OST	5.753E-27	16	3.596E-28	6.040	0.000
FRQ*SDC	5.379E-28	16	3.362E-29	0.565	0.099
FRQ*SWC	5.008E-28	16	3.13E-29	0.526	0.145
FRQ*SWD	5.925E-27	16	3.703E-28	6.221	0.000
SDC*SWC	1.203E-28	16	7.519E-30	0.126	0.995
SDC*SWD	1.957E-27	16	1.223E-28	2.055	0.000
SWC*SWD	6.222E-28	16	3.889E-29	0.653	0.039
Error	5.953E-29	3518	1.692E-32		
Total	1.728E-25	3650			

Table 3 presents the results of the main effect and first order interactions of the 5 by 5 factorial analysis. The results have shown that, there was a main effect of airwaves with each level of FRQ, OST, SDC, SWC and SWD. This is because $p < 0.05$ for all the cases. Hence, the null hypothesis has to be rejected, suggesting significant main effect.

The results of the first order interactions between FRQ*OST, FRQ*SWD, SDC*SWD and SWC*SWD is also significant with $p < 0.05$. However, the interaction between FRQ*SDC, FRQ*SWC and SDC*SWC has $p > 0.05$, which suggests no interaction effect.

5 Conclusion

Factorial design was used in this study to analyze the effect of frequency, seawater conductivity, sediment conductivity, seawater depth and offset on the magnitude of airwaves. The result from the simulated data showed that indeed those factors have an effect on the magnitude of airwaves. The results based on the F-statistics from the simulated models of SBL environment suggested that frequency factor that affect the magnitude of the airwaves, followed by the seawater depth, offset, seawater conductivity and sediment conductivity in that order. Moreover, the study showed that factorial design has several important features. First, it has great flexibility for exploring or enhancing the "signal" (treatment) in our studies. Whenever we are interested in examining treatment variations, factorial designs should be strong candidates as the designs of choice. Second, factorial designs are efficient. Instead of conducting a series of independent studies we are effectively able to combine these studies into one. Hence, factorial designs are effective way to examine both main and interaction effects. Finally, further studies may want to look at some factorial design variations to get a deeper understanding of how it works.

Acknowledgments. This research is carried out under the PETRONAS Research Fund (PRF). The authors would like to acknowledge Universiti Teknologi PETRONAS for giving the opportunity to carry out this research work.

References

1. Constable, S., Srnka, L.J.: An introduction to marine controlled-source electromagnetic methods for hydrocarbon exploration. Geophysics 72, WA3 (2007)
2. Hesthammer, J., Boulaenko, M.: The potential of CSEM technology. GeoExpro 4, 52–58, and HGS Bulletin, 23–43 (December 2007)
3. Johansen, S.E., Amundsen, H.E.F., Røsten, T., Ellingsrud, S., Eidesmo, T., Bhuiyan, A.H.: Subsurface hydrocarbons detected by electromagnetic sounding. First Break 23(3), 31–36 (2005)
4. Eidesmo, T., Ellingsrud, S., MacGregor, L.M., Constable, S., Sinha, M.C., Johansen, S., Kong, F.N., Westerdahl, H.: Sea Bed Logging (SBL), a new method for remote and direct identification of hydrocarbon filled layers in deepwater areas. First Break 20(3) (March 2002)

5. Chave, A.D., Cox, C.S.: Theoretical numerical model study for offshore CESM exploration with a horizontal electric dipole source. Journal of Geophys. Res. 87, 5327–5338 (1982)
6. Anderson, W.L.: Numerical integration of related Hankel transforms of order 0 and 1 by adaptive digital filtering. Geophysics 44, 1287–1305 (1979)
7. Fisher, R.A.: Statistical methods for research workers. Oliver and Boyd, Edinburgh (1938, 7th printing) (1946, 10th printing)
8. Box, G.E.P., et al.: Statistics for Engineers: An Introduction to Design, Data Analysis, and Model Building. John Wiley & Sons, New York
9. Trochim, W.M.K.: Factorial Designs. Research Methods Knowledge Base (2006), `http://www.socialresearchmethods.net/kb/expfact.htm`
10. Muhammad, A., Afza, S., Noorhana, Y., Radzuan, R., Ahmad, W.F.W.: A Simulation Study to Identify the Sea Water Depth for the Presence of Air Waves in Sea Bed Logging. In: 2nd International Conference on Fundamental and Applied Sciences, AIP Conference Proceedings 1482, p. 140 (2012)
11. Xinyou, L., Srnka, L.J., Carazzone, J.J.: Method for Removing Air Wave Effect from Offshore Frequency Domain Controlled-Source Electromagnetic Data, U.S. Patent 7 277 806 (October 2, 2007)
12. Lopes, R.H.C., Reid, I., Hobson, P.R.: The two-dimensional Kolmogorov-Smirnov test. In: XI International Workshop on Advanced Computing and Analysis Techniques in Physics Research, Amsterdam, The Netherlands (2007)
13. Bailey, R.A.: Design of Comparative Experiments. Cambridge University Press (2008) ISBN 978-0-521-68357-9
14. Lentner, M., Thomas, B.: Experimental design and analysis, 2nd edn. Valley Book Company (1993) ISBN 0-9616255-2-X
15. Hinkelmann, K., Kempthorne, O.: Completely randomized design; Approximating the randomization test, vol. 1, sec. 6.6 (2008)
16. Hinkelmann, K., Kempthorne, O.: Completely randomized design; CRD with unequal numbers of replications, vol. 1, sec. 6.7 (2008)
17. Moore, D.S., McCabe, G.P.: Introduction to the Practice of Statistics, 4th edn., p. 763. W. H. Freeman and Company, New York (2003)

Game Design for Acquired Brain Injury Cognitive Rehabilitation: A Conceptual Framework

Ahmed Mohammed Elaklouk, Nor Azan Mat Zin, and Azrulhizam Shapii

School of Information Technology, Faculty of Information Science and Technology, Universiti Kebangsaan Malaysia (UKM), 43600 Bangi, Selangor, Malaysia
{a.aklouk,azan,azrul}@ftsm.ukm.my

Abstract. Acquired brain injury, such as traumatic brain injury and stroke, is the leading cause of long term disabilities in most countries. In rehabilitation, two critical issues are the increasing number of patients and heterogeneity of impairments lead to limit human resources, facilities resulting in high cost of rehabilitation treatment; and the patients' perceptions that traditional rehabilitation exercises are boring which lead them to neglect the prescribed exercises. Currently, there is no specific standard and guideline to deliver feasible and effective game-based rehabilitation intervention. Hence, in this paper, a conceptual framework is proposed to guide the designing of effective and efficient games for acquired brain injury cognitive rehabilitation. The conceptual framework is developed by investigating serious games and rehabilitation related frameworks and literatures.

Keywords: serious games, cognitive rehabilitation, game design, brain injury.

1 Background

Acquired brain injury (ABI), such as traumatic brain injury (TBI) and stroke, is the leading cause of long term disabilities in most countries. The frequently cognitive impairments occurring after sustaining an ABI includes mental process deterioration, attention impairments, memory deficits, and executive functions problems. These consequences dramatically affect patients' lives and limit the performance of their everyday activities [1].

The increasing rate of brain damaged victims who have been involved in serious accidents lead to limited human resources and facilities which burdened healthcare systems; for example, in the United States alone, 7% of the population or approximately 20 million persons are suffering from cognitive disabilities [2]. In addition, the heterogeneity of impairments that patients suffer from is a relevant factor for planning, developing and evaluating treatments. The severity and the consequences of brain injuries depend on the individual circumstances where the size and location of the lesion determine the rehabilitation treatment of each patient. Individualized rehabilitation tasks involve a higher cost of tailoring unique content for each patient. A study reported that, the health care costs for patients after sustaining brain injuries are among the highest compared with other healthcare services in many

H. Badioze Zaman et al. (Eds.): IVIC 2013, LNCS 8237, pp. 218–230, 2013.

countries [3]. For example, in the United States, $62.7 billion are estimated as annual cost for stroke patients. Without introducing vital new rehabilitation interventions, the outlook on rehabilitation for future patients is under rapid decline [4]. Therefore, with such substantial effect on the quality of life of millions of patients and on healthcare systems worldwide, further research into feasible and effective intervention for brain injuries rehabilitation is crucial.

On the other hand, studies in the field of epidemiology revealed that majority of patients (75%) with traumatic brain injuries are those less than 35 years of age [5], and this group is more inclined to play games on computers and/or handheld games devices compared to other age groups. Current research findings revealed that the brain has the ability to cure itself following an injury through repetitive, intensive and task oriented training [6] and [7]. However, brain damaged patients commonly reported that traditional rehabilitation exercises can be boring due to their repetitive nature and thus lead them to neglect the exercises required to repair neural and functional damages [8]. Patient's motivation is an important factor for rehabilitation success and is often utilized as a determining factor in the outcome of rehabilitation [9]. The therapists' main problem is to find a way to encourage patients to actively take part in a rehabilitation program [10] and [11]. Researchers showed evidence that playing computer games can motivate brain damaged patients [12] and [13].

However, providing patients with motivating and suitable games in the currently struggling economy requires efficient and effective solution for delivering motivating rehabilitation intervention. Hence, the rehabilitation program's delivery, scenarios and organization should be changed.

To our knowledge, currently there is no standard and guideline concerning how to design feasible and effective game based intervention that can sustain patients' engagement in cognitive rehabilitation exercises. Therefore, in order to address these issues, this paper defines a conceptual framework as guidance for designing games-based system for acquired brain injury cognitive rehabilitation. This can assist game developers and researchers in rehabilitation field on how games should be designed and delivered in rehabilitation context. The conceptual framework is developed through investigation of serious games and rehabilitation related frameworks and literatures.

2 Proposed Conceptual Framework for Designing Brain Injury Cognitive Rehabilitation Game

The proposed conceptual framework for designing brain injury cognitive rehabilitation game is illustrated in Fig. 1. The aim is to establish a conceptual framework that will be used by the game developer and practitioner when designing serious games for effective cognitive rehabilitation. Basically, the proposed framework consists of the four components: condition, process, activity, and outcome. Each one of these parts plays a crucial role in designing efficient and effective motivating game-based cognitive rehabilitation intervention for acquired brain injury. The following sections describe these components in detail.

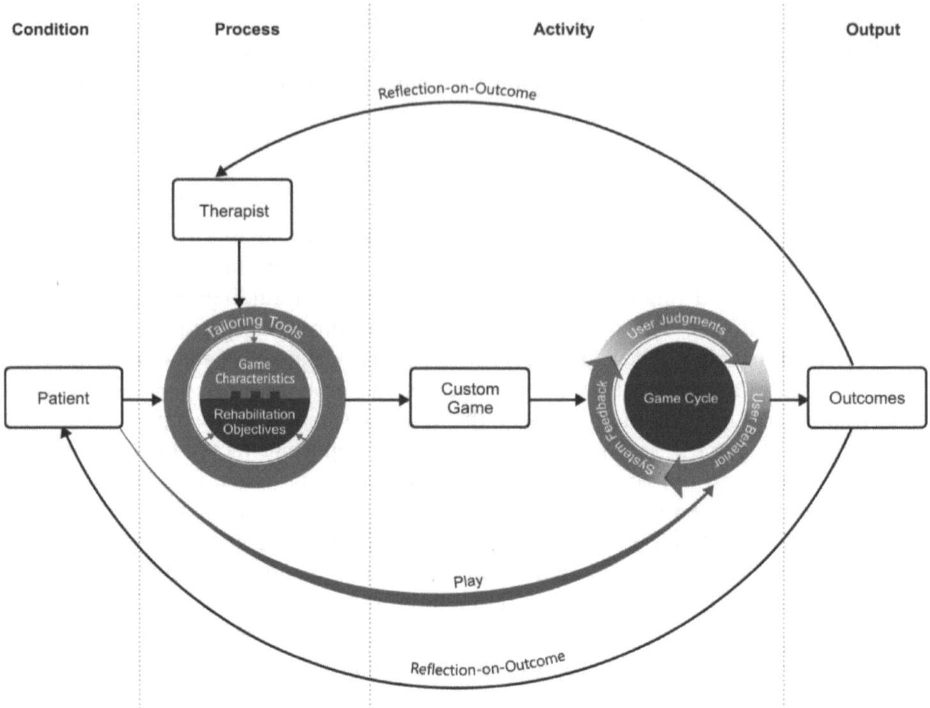

Fig. 1. A Conceptual framework for designing brain injury cognitive rehabilitation game

2.1 Condition

Perry et al. [4] reported that no study has been dedicated to brain injury rehabilitative game design based on factors that affect user function and motivation. Although there are many rehabilitative games contributions, new games interventions that better address the needs of the patient from therapeutic as well as motivational perspectives are required. Games will be instructionally effective if their specific characteristics are linked with specific instructional objectives [14]. Moreover, if a person has no interest in the instructional content, specific game's features can be used to trigger his motivation [15]. Hence, in the rehabilitation context, we can describe Effective Rehabilitation Game (ERG) according to the equation (1).

$$\text{ERG} = \text{IRO} + \text{GC}. \tag{1}$$

The IRO stands for Intended Rehabilitation Objective and GC stands for Game Characteristics. The IROs are the rehabilitation goals to be achieved from playing the serious game. Therefore, in this part (condition), these goals are defined through patient evaluation and assessment.

A crucial aspect in the care of patients is that brain injury consequences manifest differently in different patients. Furthermore, patients may have the same disorder but their responses to the disorder can be unique. Patient-centered practice is considered by some studies to improve health status and the efficiency of health care [16].

Understanding the patient's needs, priorities and preferences prior to technology selection can positively affect the matching between patient and technology. However, the main factor that accounts for the poor match is that of an inadequate evaluation and assessment of the patient's needs and preferences [1] and [17]. The only essential thing about design is how it relates to targeted people. However, very limited studies have investigated the relationship between the characteristics of people with intellectual disability and their special needs of the technology that fit them [18].

The difficulty of matching a patient to a technology is due not only to his unique combination of cognitive, sensory and physical abilities but also his expectations and reactions to the new technology interventions. These reactions arise from personal preferences, needs, abilities, and prior technology experiences [17].

Therefore, patient-centered evaluation is required to clarify the rehabilitation goal prior to planning interventions. This orientation is consistent with rehabilitation management models that consider the identification of a patient's problems, needs and mediators, relevant to target problems, as the first step before planning rehabilitation interventions [20]. Hence, in the condition part, an assessment (instruments) should be used by a therapist to collect relevant information during patient evaluation. Additionally, in the assessment process, a constellation of factors that influence patients' predispositions to the use of particular technology interventions must be understood. For instance, the preferences, needs and impairments of the patient as well as the environment in which the activity will take place need to be understood so that the most suitable game-based intervention can be provided and the most appropriate training strategies can be designed.

Cognitive assessment practice typically begins with simple tests such as the Mini Mental State Exam (MMSE). In case of MMSE poor performance, it is fundamental to conduct a more in-depth evaluation using the Neuropsychological Assessment (NA) [22]. The NA is usually conducted to assess the extent of deterioration to a particular skill, in order to determine the damaged brain area after sustaining brain injury. By applying NA tests, we can assess various cognitive domains such as executive function, attention, memory, perception, and other functions [21]. For example, the Wisconsin Card Sorting Test (WCST) is used to measure the "executive function" impairments that affect the person's ability to initiate, plan, monitor performance, anticipate consequences, set goals and respond adaptively. Furthermore, direct observations and interviews provide a useful method for evaluating cognitive impairments and skills. The rehabilitation professional may use information obtained by interviewing family members as well as caregivers about patient's everyday behavior, or by valuing the behavior of the patient using direct observation [23].

Investigation of personal and health related factors as well as environment may help in the identification of factors that influence patient's functional ability and recovery [26]. Unlike its predecessor the International Classification of Impairment Disability and Handicap (ICIDH), the International Classification of Functioning, Disability and Health (ICF) model of human functioning and disability focuses on the "components of health" instead of the "consequences of disease" [24]. The ICF can be used as a valuable framework to manage and classify patient's information and helps rehabilitation professional to identify aspects of a patient's condition that affect his/her recovery [25]. The most significant advantage of the ICF is in expanding thinking further rather than fixing particular impairments. ICF describes "disability and functioning" as outcomes resulting from the interactions between "health conditions" and "contextual factors". The contextual factors are classified into personal factors and environmental factors. There is formal acknowledgment of the ICF personal factors which recognize the importance of personal choices, interests, likes, and dislikes of the patient whose activities are being addressed in a rehabilitation program [24] and [25]. Therefore, game-based rehabilitation interventions are most effective when they are shaped to meet a patient's particular needs and preferences, not when they are prescribed as an isolated intervention of addressing particular cognitive and/or physical deficiencies. This process needs to begin with a comprehensive evaluation that gives the rehabilitation professionals the opportunity to assess the patient's ability, needs, preferences and expectation. The evaluation generates information that can assist with tailoring game interventions that enhance the quality of training and affect the self-esteem and motivation of patients, a point necessary for a patient's active involvement in the rehabilitation process.

2.2 Process

In game-based learning, Garris et al. [15] argued that, success in pairing game's characteristics with appropriate instructional practices can trigger individuals' motivational forces towards achieving the intended learning outcome. The challenge is to adapt these game's characteristics/features for instructional purposes to enter the game-cycle that motivates and sustains learner's engagement. Although many studies have noted the potential advantages that can be earned from incorporating game features/characteristics into instructional applications, the question that remains is "how will this incorporation (pairing) be done?"

Therefore, in a cognitive rehabilitation context, we will try to answer the question of how to incorporate game characteristics into rehabilitation programs. In other words, based on our proposed framework (process part), we will answer how rehabilitation professionals can provide patients with effective and efficient game interventions designed and customized to accommodate individual's skills and deficits and sustain his motivation.

In rehabilitation, a user-centered design approach is crucial [4]. While the evaluation from the "condition part" is concerned with considering patients' context, ability, needs, preferences and expectation, thus realistic therapy goals are defined by the end of the "condition part". This, in turn, can help in planning the most appropriate game interventions Therefore, rehabilitation professional can now use the "tailoring tools" to pair a game's characteristics with defined rehabilitation goals and, hence, create and deliver the appropriate game for an individual patient that is tailored to his needs and expectation.

Many studies discussed game characteristics [15] and [27]. Garris et al. [15] described game characteristics in terms of six categories:

- Fantasy: Imaginary or fantasy context, themes, or characters.
- Rules/Goals: Clear rules, goals, and feedback on progress towards the goals.
- Sensory Stimuli: Dramatic or novel visual and auditory stimuli.
- Challenge: Optimal level of activity and uncertain goal attainment.
- Mystery: Optimal level of informational complexity.
- Control: Active learner control.

Therapist's motivation for using gaming in rehabilitation is clearly the motivational benefit to the patient. Increased treatment adherence translates to increased functional outcomes [4]. Many potential benefits will be gained from incorporating these games' characteristics into instructional rehabilitation programs. This incorporation can provide a training environment in which the patient can practice rehabilitation tasks without real-world consequences, specifically in case of failure; this is crucial in a rehabilitation context. Moreover, games that can provide difficulty levels progressively, allows the patient to gain familiarity and improve his skills gradually and this can enhance his enjoyment and confidence. Patients with greater confidence are more resilient to the real-world difficulties, applying skills learned in game-based intervention.

Therefore, according to our proposed framework, the "Tailoring Tools" are responsible for mapping a game's characteristics with the intended rehabilitation objectives. For example, a "challenge" is a crucial characteristic of instructional games. Providing optimal challenge for a specific patient means that, the game difficulty matches the patient's ability in being neither too easy nor too difficult. To enable the optimal challenge, it is necessary to continuously adapt the game or create new game levels using "tailoring tools" to match the patient's current skills. This means "flow experience" will be increased, and the patient will strive towards the goal, and hence the intended rehabilitation outcomes can be achieved. Adequate flexibility to tailor and adapt game difficulty to the patient ability is required not for functional improvement, but also as a motivational incentive for cognitive and motor engagement [4]. The complexity of game environment depends on its "tailoring tools" and ability of these tools to map the intended rehabilitation objectives with various game characteristics (i.e., fantasy, rules/goals, sensory stimuli, challenge, mystery, and control) based on the needs and preferences of the patient.

Elaklouk et al. [32] and [33] determined principles of game design that are critical for brain damage rehabilitation and developed a game prototype called "Ship Game". Investigation of therapists' acceptance and intention to use "Ship Game" for acquired brain injury cognitive rehabilitation reported several crucial aspects that affect their intention to use game for rehabilitation.

One respondent stated that "If more rehabilitation goals are achieved, high acceptance will be realized." He also explained that therapists need a variety of game exercises with different levels of challenges to meet the diversity of patients' impairments.

Other feedback mentioned that in the process of developing a serious game, a series of issues must be taken into account; for example, the goal of rehabilitation should be reflected in the game architecture and this is why off-the-shelf games are unsuitable for rehabilitation. Therapists' fear of losing control over a game's therapeutic activities entail that the game tasks should be designed in such a way that the patient can focus on goal achievement as opposed to playing the game. In addition, they mentioned that before referring the game to patients, they should experience and control the exercises themselves so that the patients can actively practice the game exercises that are closely linked to their abilities, a link that is very important for their cognitive improvement.

In addition, respondents stated that it is important for therapists to have specific functions in games so that patients can get well-tailored treatment "Patients have to be trained based on what their therapists want to achieve". Therapists, who have prior game experience, suggest improving the functionality of the system in terms of bringing a greater number of individualized games into one platform with each possessing specific goals for every level and kind of impairment, to eventually result in the achievement of rehabilitation goals and the maximization of intention to use the system by therapists.

However, the developments of individualized game-based rehabilitation tasks imply a higher cost. For widespread use in clinical settings, ongoing costs for developing individualized game-based tasks need to be kept low. Additionally, the timeframe of in-patient rehabilitation is short in most countries. For example in the United States, stroke patients spend an average of 15 days in in-patient rehabilitation [3]. Hence, if the game development can be adjusted to the short period of stay of in-patient rehabilitation, game-based intervention could provide a strong alternative for individualized cognitive rehabilitation.

Moreover, over time, personal and environmental factors may change [28] along with therapy goals and demands throughout the process of rehabilitation [3]. Hence, rehabilitation interventions should be adapted to fit these changes.

Adaptive training that automatically modifies the current difficulty level to the patients' abilities may have had increments that were too large for some of the patients, and consequently, they may not advance as the others [29]. Furthermore, although a fully automated rehabilitation intervention which assesses the patient´s deficiencies and then uses this assessment to create an individualized rehabilitation plan is virtually possible, such intervention has a low chance to be medically accepted [4]. The rehabilitation professionals' experience in formulating and determining rehabilitation objectives and selecting exercises and facilities to attain those objectives has to be recognized. However, compromising between a fully automated rehabilitation intervention and a fully therapist-dependant rehabilitation intervention is probably the best alternative [4]. Reusable content that can be adapted for the patient context seems to be a cost-effective rehabilitation intervention [3].

In a physical rehabilitation context, while some researchers have built games to address particular deficits, these customized games take time to create, are expensive and they only cater to a small number of brain damaged patients. Environments with authoring tools that decrease time and expense enable therapists to quickly create games tailored to individuals with brain injury [30]. However, in cognitive rehabilitation, where there is diversity and heterogeneity of cognitive impairments, environment with "authoring tools" to create customizable game can be more cost-effective and can provide games that can meet the specific needs of brain-injured individuals. A study in game-based learning emphasized that user-friendly instructor oriented authoring tools seem to be indispensable for educational game development; these tools abstract the technical aspects, reduce the game development costs and enable instructor to deliver game based intervention that can fit the learner [31].

Furthermore, Garris et al. [15] argued that almost pure discovery-based learning does not exist. In other words, learners' self-directed knowledge construction on their own is unrealistic. They further mentioned that, although the goal of instructional games is to attain self-directed, self-motivated learners, the role of the instructor is critical for supporting learner's knowledge construction; and if overlooked, other supporting strategies, such as online help, should be available.

Therefore, in cognitive rehabilitation, while people have specific impairments and needs, it is critical to confirm the fact that cognitive rehabilitation must be paired with appropriate therapist support for effective rehabilitation to occur. If the patient does not receive needed support, the game-based intervention may become unused or used incorrectly. Hence, the therapist plays an essential role in patient's motivation and game system development. For any game-based intervention to be successful and effective, it should be incorporated by the therapist into his/her daily clinical practice. The therapist is the one who instructs, motivates, and assesses the patients and plays an important role in the patient's recovery. In our previous works [32] and [33], we conducted a four-week study and tested the game prototype "Ship Game" on patients. Some patients were observed to be more motivated as opposed to others. Seven of the patients who participated in our study commented that they prefer to play games at home. However, other participants who played the games at home stated that they prefer to play in sessions with their therapist, and they commented that if their therapist could monitor their home game play, they would be motivated to play at home.

However, rehabilitation professionals often do not possess advanced knowledge in game/software engineering to understand the underlying design and development. Hence, intuitive interactions with the game environment and its facilities/tools to tailor the game should be without the need of much technical knowledge. Moreover, the game system should be accepted by rehabilitation professionals who will use it for their patients' cognitive rehabilitation.

2.3 Activity

The output of the process part is a "custom game" as shown in Fig. 1 which is an input to the activity part whereby the game is ready to be played by patient. The game activity is tailored to keep the patient engaged. Retention of patient attention and his/her deep involvement depends on the effectiveness of the tailoring of these game activities by therapists. The game should involve activities that are appropriate for the target patient. The affective judgments that are constructed from the beginning and ongoing game play imply the direction and intensity of further behavior. Patients who have positive judgments are more actively engaged in game play, exert more effort and concentration, and are committed to continue the game activity and frequently return to game play. If the therapist succeeds in mapping the game's characteristics with the intended rehabilitation goal in the game, this will produce a repeating game cycle, and this, in turn, may help motivate the patient to engage in the rehabilitation intervention, ultimately leading to specific cognitive and affective outcomes.

The game-cycle is the key component triggered by specific game's characteristics/features; reflecting user engagement manner in the game activity. The game-cycle, as depicted in Fig. 1, consists of repeated loops of user judgment, user behavior and system feedback. The game-cycle is described by many literatures as loops of game play that lead to certain user judgments such as increased involvement, enjoyment, or confidence. These judgments lead to user behaviors such as greater persistence or intensity of effort, and these behaviors result in system feedback, which again triggers user judgment [15] and [19].

2.4 Output

Meaningful play, maintaining challenge appropriately, and handling failure positively are important [32] and [33]. Eventually however, tracking and presenting the patient's performance is what really motivates the patient's as well as the therapist's continual use of games.

The game play activities generate specific outcomes which can be indicated by the game achievement, which is the level of patient achievement in playing the game. This achievement can represent the game scores such as the total amount of assets collected, or the time taken to achieve the goal within the game. These game scores would indicate the level of the patient's skills and abilities while playing games and can serve the purpose of patient assessment. Hence, new game play activities should be modified and adapted to suit the patient's level.

In a game-based learning context, [34] introduced a time element to allow individuals to progress through the game, incrementing their knowledge and acquiring new levels of skill. This suggests that knowledge is acquired over time and individuals abilities and/or skills are increased through experience. Therefore, from one day to another, progressing to a new game level and small successes may motivate the patient. However, in the long run, patients would want to see that their achievements in the games and the time they spent on this type of treatment are really contributing to overall rehabilitation success. Therefore, presentation of the patient's performances over time motivates the patient to continue using it. Furthermore, tracking how much time the patient spends on the game treatment gives therapists invaluable information about their patients' progress and how the games are actually helping the patients, particularly those who are not in one-on-one rehabilitation sessions.

In addition, if patients can visually see their improvements over time on graphs or other visual statistical presentation, they will be more inclined towards the game treatment and will continue using it. Therefore, outcomes can be extended to describe "changes of patient's outcomes". In other words, automatic measures can be developed to track patient's cognitive performance over time to measure improvements in a given cognitive function. However, information about the sensitivity as well as reliability of automatic measurement systems is still absent. This gap needs a complex debriefing process and a comprehensive empirical study to validate any proposed automatic measure scientifically. A better solution to measure "changes of outcomes" would be to use validated instruments such as sound questionnaire and standardized clinical instruments previously discussed in the condition part.

Moreover, outcome can generally play a crucial role. According to the short time-frame of inpatient rehabilitation and the therapist's limited time, the individualized rehabilitation should effectively use this time without the need for many supervised rehabilitation sessions. Therapists would like to have data regarding what their patients do when they practice, these data will be used for patient monitoring and tracking. This promotes the possibility of unsupervised rehabilitation that can be continued after the patient is discharged from in-patient rehabilitation services. Thus, patients do not need long instructions and supervision by therapist. Available commercial games lack data recording function making it difficult for therapists to track and monitor the patient's exercising activity and progress.

Reflections on Outcomes: In Fig. 1, we showed that, the reflections on outcomes provide a link between the outcome and the therapist as well as the patient. Reflection is an important part of the rehabilitation process for the patient as well as for the therapist. According to the "active learning" concept, learning follows a cyclic loop instead of a linear pattern. For example, experiencing learning intervention, result in reflections, and these reflections lead to certain conclusions, which in turn lead to construct a plan for new actions, then experiencing again [35]. Reflection is a crucial part of this cycle. Without reflection, the cycle cannot produce new conclusions and actions [36]. In our proposed framework, reflections on outcomes objectives are twofold;

Firstly, with respect to the patient, it is vital to consider the patients' expectations regarding rehabilitation game activities and outcomes. People like to work at things that are important to them rather than at things that are important to others. Affective reactions comprise self-efficacy, attitudes, and feelings of confidence, preferences, and dispositions. These reactions are recognized as one type of outcomes; for example, attitude change is considered as one of the training objectives of an instructional intervention [15]. Moreover, besides the game playing activity itself, characteristics of individual, expectancies, interests, motives, outcomes and consequences should be considered in the development of game-based learning [19]. Game play produces expectations in the individual about the outcome of the game. These expectations affect individual motivation. In other words, a player who believes that he can reach certain outcomes and eventually does so is motivated to continue using the game and this can be an incentive for him to exert more effort to attain the intended game goal [19]. Hence, motivation and engagement in game-based trainings will be achieved, if patient believes in a potential success in game play. This perception strengthens the patient's confidence, and can be reflected through outcomes representing his performance in game experience.

Secondly, with respect to the therapist, reflecting on outcomes can provide an assessment of the patient's progress and his expectation. After the game has been designed, delivered, and then played by patient, therapist need to check the goal attainment by comparing outcomes with intended rehabilitation objectives and to assess the effectiveness of game interventions. Outcomes enable therapist to capture changes in skills, what the patient is able to do, his/her level of task performance and affective reactions. Therefore, outcomes can reflect patient progress towards a goal and his expectation. Hence, to satisfy rehabilitation effectiveness, reflection on outcome guides therapist to continuously adjust and modify the game to patient's current skills and expectation through therapist oriented tailoring tools offered by the game environment. This part provides useful information that enable rehabilitation professional to compare patient's performance with normative data and also provides the opportunity to compare task performance across patients and rehabilitation sessions to quantify patient's progress.

3 Conclusion and Future Work

In this paper, we proposed a conceptual framework for designing serious games for acquired brain injury cognitive rehabilitation. Every component of this framework plays a role to ensure the effectiveness of the game intervention produced. This framework can be a useful guide for serious game designers, developers and practitioners in designing effective and efficient rehabilitation gaming system that can significantly affect patients, therapists, and health care systems.

Incorporation of the potential technology with the therapist's daily clinical practice is a must. The proposed framework was developed based on the conventional rehabilitation procedures. In conventional rehabilitation, there is a great coordination between the patient and therapist. The therapist defines a treatment plan based on the patient's assessment, and selects appropriate exercises and techniques. The patient depends on the experienced planning of the therapist regarding training exercises for reducing deficits and increasing participation, while the therapist depends on the patient's cooperation in the established rehabilitation program. Therefore, the therapist has to be considered to ensure successful adoption of new technology. Hence, in our proposed framework, the therapist remains an integral part in planning game based rehabilitation intervention. By providing easy-to-use therapist-oriented tailoring tools, the game intervention can be tailored precisely to the ability and need of the patient, which in turn increases patient motivation and adherence to training in rehabilitation.

Researchers, who looked into available commercial games' therapeutic usefulness, revealed that these games are too fast, created for able-bodied game play and the lack of data recording function makes them unsuitable for rehabilitation. While other researchers have created games to address a particular deficit, these customized games take time to create, are expensive and only cater to a small number of brain-damaged patients. Environments with tailoring tools that decrease the time and expense enable therapists to quickly create games tailored to individuals with brain injury.

Therefore, user-friendly therapist oriented tailoring tools are important in rehabilitation games development, as they can deliver motivating intervention and reduce development costs. The challenge is developing a game tailoring environment customized to therapists. Hence, future work will be to demonstrate the framework implementation by designing and developing a system prototype for experimental use and evaluation.

References

1. LoPresti, E.F., Bodine, C., Lewis, C.: Assistive technology for cognition [Understanding the Needs of Persons with Disabilities]. IEEE Engineering in Medicine and Biology Magazine 27, 29–39 (2008)
2. Carmien, S., DePaula, R., Gorman, A., Kintsch, A.: Increasing workplace independence for people with cognitive disabilities by leveraging distributed cognition among caregivers and clients. In: Proceedings of the International ACM SIGGROUP Conference on Supporting Group Work, pp. 95–104. ACM (2003)
3. Koenig, S.: Individualized Virtual Reality Rehabilitation after Brain Injuries. PhD in Human Interface Technology. College of Engineering, University of Canterbury (2012)

4. Perry, J.C., Andureu, J., Cavallaro, F.I., Veneman, J., Carmien, S., Keller, T.: Effective game use in neurorehabilitation: user-centered perspectives. In: Handbook of Research on Improving Learning and Motivation through Educational Games. IGI Global (2010)
5. Tagliaferri, F., Compagnone, C., Korsic, M., Servadei, F., Kraus, J.: A systematic review of brain injury epidemiology in Europe. Acta Neurochirurgica 148, 255–268 (2006)
6. Panic, A.S.: Addressing patient motivation in virtual reality based neurocognitive rehabilitation. BA Thesis, Hogere Technische School Arnheim, Arnheim (2010)
7. Doidge, N., Bond, J.: The brain that changes itself. Brilliance Audio (2008)
8. Burdea, G.: Virtual rehabilitation-benefits and challenges. Methods of Information in Medicine-Methodik der Information in der Medizin 42, 519–523 (2003)
9. Maclean, N., Pound, P., Wolfe, C., Rudd, A.: The concept of patient motivation. Stroke 33, 444–448 (2002)
10. Burke, J., McNeill, M., Charles, D., Morrow, P., Crosbie, J., McDonough, S.: Designing engaging, playable games for rehabilitation. In: Proc. 8th Intl Conf. on Disability, Virtual Reality and Assoc. Technologies, Viña del Mar/Valparaíso, Chile, pp. 195–201 (August 2010)
11. Alankus, G., Lazar, A., May, M., Kelleher, C.: Towards customizable games for stroke rehabilitation. In: The 28th International Conference on Human Factors in Computing Systems, pp. 2113–2122. ACM (2010)
12. Rizzo, A.S., Kim, G.J.: A SWOT analysis of the field of virtual reality rehabilitation and therapy. Presence: Teleoperators & Virtual Environments 14, 119–146 (2005)
13. Burke, J.W., McNeill, M., Charles, D., Morrow, P., Crosbie, J., McDonough, S.: Serious games for upper limb rehabilitation following stroke. In: Conference in Games and Virtual Worlds for Serious Applications, VS-GAMES 2009, pp. 103–110. IEEE (2009)
14. Hays, R.T.: The effectiveness of instructional games: A literature review and discussion. DTIC Document (2005)
15. Garris, R., Ahlers, R., Driskell, J.E.: Games, motivation, and learning: A research and practice model. Simulation & Gaming 33, 441–467 (2002)
16. Oates, J., Weston, W.W., Jordan, J.: The impact of patient-centered care on outcomes. Fam. Pract. 49, 796–804 (2000)
17. Scherer, M.J., Glueckauf, R.: Assessing the benefits of assistive technologies for activities and participation. Rehabilitation Psychology 50, 132–141 (2005)
18. Zhang-Farrelly, J.: What are service providers' perceptions about the use and need of assistive technology by people in Ireland with intellectual disability in the context of providing a person centered service? (2011)
19. Mattheiss, E., Kickmeier-Rust, M., Steiner, C., Albert, D.: Motivation in Game-Based Learning: It's More than 'Flow'. In: Lernen im Digitalen Zeitalter, Potsdam, pp. 77–84 (2009)
20. Steiner, W.A., Ryser, L., Huber, E., Uebelhart, D., Aeschlimann, A., Stucki, G.: Use of the ICF model as a clinical problem-solving tool in physical therapy and rehabilitation medicine. Physical Therapy 82, 1098–1107 (2002)
21. Pimentel, É.M.L.: Role of neuropsychological assessment in the differential diagnosis of Alzheimer's disease and vascular dementia. Dementia & Neuropsychologia 3(3), 214–221 (2009)
22. Tsaousides, T., Gordon, W.A.: Cognitive rehabilitation following traumatic brain injury: assessment to treatment. Mount Sinai Journal of Medicine: A Journal of Translational and Personalized Medicine 76, 173–181 (2009)
23. Panic, A.S.: Research Project: Virtual Reality Based Neurocognitive Rehabilitation. Delft University of Technology (2010)

24. Rosenbaum, P., Stewart, D.: The World Health Organization International Classification of Functioning, Disability, and Health: a model to guide clinical thinking, practice and research in the field of cerebral palsy. In: Seminars in Pediatric Neurology, pp. 5–10. Elsevier (2004)
25. Belchior, P.D.C.: Cognitive training with video games to improve driving skills and driving safety among older adults. University of Florida (2007)
26. Karlsson, P.: ICF: a guide to assistive technology decision-making. In: ARATA 2010 National Conference, Hobart, Tasmania (2010), `http://www.arata.org.au/arataconf10` (retrieved)
27. Wilson, K.A., Bedwell, W.L., Lazzara, E.H., Salas, E., Burke, C.S., Estock, J.L., Orvis, K.L., Conkey, C.: Relationships Between Game Attributes and Learning Outcomes Review and Research Proposals. Simulation & Gaming 40, 217–266 (2009)
28. Scherer, M., Jutai, J., Fuhrer, M., Demers, L., Deruyter, F.: A framework for modelling the selection of assistive technology devices (ATDs). Disability & Rehabilitation: Assistive Technology 2, 1–8 (2007)
29. Jaeggi, S.M., Buschkuehl, M., Jonides, J., Shah, P.: Short-and long-term benefits of cognitive training. Proceedings of the National Academy of Sciences 108, 10081–10086 (2011)
30. Tam, S.: An Environment for Stroke Therapy Game Authoring (2010)
31. Torrente, J., Moreno-Ger, P., Fernández-Manjón, B., Sierra, J.L.: Instructor-oriented authoring tools for educational videogames. In: Eighth IEEE International Conference on Advanced Learning Technologies, ICALT 2008, pp. 516–518. IEEE (2008)
32. Elaklouk, A.M., Zin, N.A.M.: Games for cognitive rehabilitation. In: 5th International Conference on Computer Games Multimedia and Allied Technology (2012a)
33. Elaklouk, A.M., Zin, N.A.M.: Requirements for game-based cognitive intervention system for acquired brain Injury. The GSTF Journal on Computing, JoC (2012b)
34. Kearney, P., Pivec, M.: Recursive Loops of Game-Based Learning: a Conceptual model. In: World Conference on Educational Multimedia, Hypermedia and Telecommunications, pp. 2546–2553 (2007)
35. Kolb, D.A.: Experiential learning: Experience as the source of learning and development. Prentice-Hall, Englewood Cliffs (1984)
36. Paras, B.: Game, motivation, and effective learning: An integrated model for educational game design (2005)

Exploring the User Engagement in Interacting with Game Interfaces

Siti Zahidah Abdullah[1], Nazlena Mohamad Ali[1], and Hyowon Lee[2]

[1] Institute Visual Informatics, Universiti Kebangsaan Malaysia,
43600, Bangi, Selangor
[2] Singapore University of Technology and Design
Singapore
ctz1986@gmail.com, nazlena@ivi.ukm.my, hlee@sutd.edu.sg

Abstract. This research investigates and identifies the factors that influence positive user engagement while interacting with games interfaces. In this paper we provide a finding on our experiences with two case studies; 1) A study on the variation of flow experience in different gaming devices (mobile and non-mobile) using *Time Tunnel* game; and 2)A study of the user engagement by measuring the user experience while interacting with the game interface using *The Sims 3* game. From the results, we identify some issues arising from using different platforms such as flow experience on difference game devices, and different user experience and user engagement on game interface. These findings on games interfaces and user engagement offer many avenues for further research, such as manipulating the levels of user engagement through appropriate gaming interface design.

Keywords: flow, game engagement, game interface, user engagement, user experience, user interface design.

1 Introduction

User-interfaces in game are considered to be the software and hardware that the game player uses to understand the current game state and act in ways to influence or change that state. The user-interface can include controller buttons, mouse clicks, menus, status bars, and field of view [1]. The creation of the game world is also supported by the user-interface, which sets limits on both physical and social interactions in the game and provides an environment to explore, discover, and collect new things [2]. Barr et al. [3] argue that video games are within the domain of Human-Computer Interaction (HCI): they are software, running on computers, and used by people via the user-interface. They add that the study of video game interfaces can be strongly anchored in an understanding of values and value systems and the ways they relate to gameplay. The player experiences the interface as consistent, but the game play is varied; the player should experience the menu as a part of the game; sounds from the game provides meaningful feedback or stir a particular emotion; with an easy interface, players do not need to use a manual to

H. Badioze Zaman et al. (Eds.): IVIC 2013, LNCS 8237, pp. 231–240, 2013.

learn how to play it; the interface should be as non-intrusive to the player as possible [3]. Juul and Norton [1] similarly claim that game interface should be as easy as possible to use, while the gameplay should be challenging; the interface should be easy to learn, but the gameplay should be difficult to master. Various methods and approaches have been used to improve the interface ultimately for the users' satisfaction. It shows that interface has played an important role in game playability which is the rapid development of interface design and parallel to the currently booming game industry. Moreover, the user-interface of a game represents values of gameplay to the player.

This study is an early stage in our series of studies to examine whether the features in a user-interface can help the user engage with the game interaction better. Inputs from Game Flow theory [4] and model of user engagement [5] were used in identifying user engagement when interacting with the game interfaces. These could reveal interesting phenomena which have correlations with user engagement towards interacting with game interfaces. This paper is organised as follows: Section 2 describes the background work in game interfaces and game engagement. Section 3 explains the methods and procedures employed in our study, and then Section 4 discusses the results and findings from the study. Finally, Section 5 concludes the paper with a brief summary and the next step to follow.

2 Literature Review

2.1 Games Interfaces

Several recent studies in game methodologies had been done by previous researchers evaluating various aspects of game interfaces. Bucolo et al. [6] investigated on different input interfaces for a mobile phone games application. A standard mobile phone joystick interface is compared with a phone camera interface to detect the phone translation and tilt to control a ball's movement within various levels of difficulty in a virtual maze game. Results indicate that the joystick control provided the fastest completion times for each game, but with the lowest levels of user engagement. Shinkle [7], in her study on significance of affect in the digital games refer to engaging interfaces that characterize many arcade games, but most standard joysticks or joy pads tend to limit the player activity. She listed beauty, aesthetics, enjoyment, and fun as possible affective 'emotional factors' that motivate individuals to play games. Van Vugt et al. [8] found that task-related interface characters contributed to user engagement when controlled for various user perceptions. They found that perceived aesthetics and task-relevance further influenced user engagement.

Another research [9] focuses on the design of pleasurably playful interfaces within the context of an interactive art. The result shows that the framework that accounts for pleasure is a useful tool to aid in the design of playful interfaces. Furthermore, Xie et al. [10] investigated the relationship between interface style and school children's enjoyment and engagement while doing puzzles. They used three different user-interfaces: physical (traditional), graphical and tangible. Results indicated that the children's self-reports of enjoyment were similar for all three interface modalities. Various methods and approaches have been used to improve the interface in order to enhance the users' satisfaction. In this perspective, it shows that interface has played an important role in game playability which is related to gameplay or game engagement. Our study focuses on measuring the user experience to find out what the factors are those influence user engagements when a user interacts with the games interfaces.

2.2 Engagement in Gaming

Several recent studies on game engagement have introduced a number of factors that reliably influence the level of user engagement. For example, *usability* and *playability* aspects [11], *fun* and *play* [12], and *flow* and *immersion* aspect [4] [13] [14] [15][16][17] and [18]. Another aspect is more on *presence* and *involvement* [2] [18] and [20]. Mayes and Cotton [21] define engagement with respect to computer games as how *fun*, *involving*, and *motivating* a task is. Prensky [12] has listed the twelve characteristics that make computer games and videogames engaging for people (see Table 1)

Table 1. Twelve characteristics of game engagement

No.	12 characteristics
1.	Games are a form of fun. That gives us enjoyment and pleasure.
2.	Games are form of play. That gives us intense and passionate involvement.
3.	Games have rules. That gives us structure.
4.	Games have goals. That gives us motivation.
5.	Games are interactive. That gives us doing.
6.	Games are adaptive. That gives us flow.
7.	Games have outcomes and feedback. That gives us learning.
8.	Games have win states. That gives us ego gratification.
9.	Games have conflict/competition/challenge/opposition. That gives us adrenaline.
10.	Games have problem solving. That sparks our creativity.
11.	Games have interaction. That gives us social groups.
12.	Games have representation and story. That gives us emotion.

Source: Prensky[12]

Terms such as *fun*, *immersion*, *presence*, *usability*, and *playability* are most often used to explain user experience and user engagement in game design. A recent shift in computer game design represents a new trend in game development including element like *usability* [11], *playability* [12] and [23], *presence* [20], and *immersion* [23] in game interface. Thus engaging interface in gaming is most popular topic for many researchers in game study area. Therein lies the issues on game interface related to the game engagement; how people's engagement with games is changing as a result of new types of interfaces, hardware, and games [22]. In this study, we have used the terms such as flow theory by Csikszentmihalyi [24] and User Engagement Model by O'Brien and Toms [5] to measure the user engagement.

2.3 GameFlow Theory

Flow experience is a concept defined by Csikszentmihalyi [24] to describe the moments or states when someone is completely absorbed in an activity or task being carried out. This activity can be a work task or a leisure pursuit and indeed the user can become so absorbed that s/he is not aware whether it is work or play. The involvement in the activity makes it seem that nothing else seems to matter and the user does not notice that the time is passing because s/he is so immersed in the activity currently engaged in. The activities that can produce the sense of flow are varied, and can include creative art, athletic competition, engaging in hobbies, for example reading a novel, gardening or cooking. Input from flow theory [25] has been used in identifying the level of user engagement when using a software application. Flow theory also has been widely adopted in studies of gaming [4] [25] and [26]. Smith [25] argues that flow, a psychological state, contributes to the enjoyment of playing video games.

An optimal engagement is closely related to, or the same as optimal user experience or flow [24]. Thus, Sweetser and Wyeht [4] presented GameFlow as a possible concept of evaluating user experience in games. GameFlow is a model that can be used to measure games and player enjoyment [4]. The eight elements of the GameFlow consist of challenge, clear goal, control, concentration, feedback, immersion, player skills, and social interaction. Player enjoyment is the most important criteria for computer games to attract more users and gain their loyalty.

2.4 User Engagement

Engagement is a quality of user experience and a clearly important component of user experience. A model for defining user engagement was proposed by O'Brien and Toms [5] that is characterized by challenge, aesthetic and sensory appeal, feedback, novelty, interactivity, perceived control and time, awareness, motivation, interest, and affects.They define engagement through a multidisciplinary literature review and an exploratory study of users of web searching, online shopping, webcasting, and gaming applications, and provides the foundation for testing a conceptual model of engagement in various application areas and for developing methods to measure engaging user experiences in user interfaces. We use this model in our study.

3 Case Study

In this paper we provide a short overview of two case studies conducted to investigate and identify user engagement in interacting with games interfaces. In order to measure the user engagement, we need to measure the user experience while interacting with the application. This is because, an optimal engagement is closely related to, or the same as optimal of user experience [24].

3.1 Case Study 1

The objective of the study was to identify and measure the variation of flow experience in two different platforms of game interfaces. The *Time Tunnel*[1] game has been used in this study because this game was compatible with difference platforms we were interested in studying: desktop and mobile. Figure 1 shows the game interfaces in these two platforms.

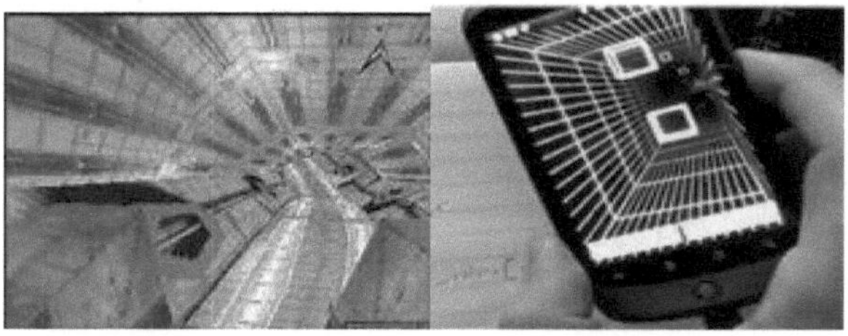

(a) (b)

Fig. 1. (a) *Time Tunnel* game on a desktop PC; (b) *Time Tunnel* game on a mobile phone

Procedure. The data were collected through a survey form in two methods which are online survey and conventional printed-out questionnaire form. Sixty three participants (N=63) have been involved in this experiment which is 31.74% are male and 68.25% are female. The questionnaires of the survey have been slightly altered from the GameFlow criteria identified in the previous work [4] that consists of two sections. GameFlow is a model that can be used to measure games and player enjoyment [4]. Section A captured demographic information and Section B on the actual gaming experiences. There were four type of platforms mentioned in the survey question to be chosen by the participant, which are: mobile platform (Mobile and Handheld) and non-mobile platform (PC and Console). The online survey forms have been posted in one of the selected gamers' forums and social network sites for two weeks. User name (if any) and their IP address were recorded to ensure there is no redundant input from the participant. Meanwhile, for the data collected from printed-out questionnaire form, participants were randomly selected from the university student body and invited for participation.

Collected data were analysed by using SPSS v11.0. An initial exploration involved descriptive analysis such as frequency, mean and standard deviation, and to ensure there is no missing data and also to analyse the rate of non-response for each item. Other than descriptive analysis, Paired Samples T-Test was used in grouping variable of non-mobile and mobile platforms. It computes the difference between the two variables for each case, and tests if the average difference is significantly different from zero by assuming the both variables are normally distributed.

Findings. From the survey result, most of the participants preferred PC as their main platform to play games. The data are represented in Table 2 and Table 3. We found

---

[1] *Time Tunnel* is an Adventure game published by U.S. Goldand released in 1985.

that the challenge criteria for mobile platform score were lower than non-mobile platform. The reason might be because of the limitation of features provided in the mobile platform such as control, graphic quality, refresh rate (fps) and processing capability. In terms of control, non-mobile platform such as PC and console could be enhanced by using controllers such as vibration joystick and seat, 3D glasses, and steering wheels. In term of graphic and processing power, non-mobile platform is much stronger compared to mobile platforms. The data shows some variation for GameFlow criteria for non-mobile platform and mobile platform, the mean averages for the mobile platforms were slightly lower than those for non-mobile platform for most of criteria.

Table 2. Mean for Non-Mobile Platform

Criteria	Mean
Immersion	2.868
Challenge	3.549
Player's Skill	3.428
Control	3.430
Clear Goals	3.603
Social Interaction	3.428

Table 3. Mean for Mobile Platform

Criteria	Mean
Immersion	2.743
Challenge	3.348
Player's Skill	3.238
Control	3.135
Clear Goals	3.301
Social Interaction	2.756

3.2 Case Study 2

The objective in this study was to explore the level of user experience specifically in game interface. We investigated whether and how the different design elements of a game interface positively or negatively influence the user engagement.

Procedure. We examined the user engagement through user interaction with the game interface using one of the most popular computer games called *The Sims* 3[2]. The questionnaire consisted of a five-point Likert scale with 1 (Strongly Disagree) and 5 (Strongly Agree). The user-interface part of the questionnaire was derived from previous study on measuring user experience in interface (see Table 4) and the measurement of game engagement was based on Game Experience Questionnaire (GEQ) used in [27]. An optimal engagement is closely related to, or the same as optimal user experience or flow [24]. Thus, we used GEQ to measure the user

[2] *The Sims 3* is a strategic life simulation computer game developed by The Sims Studio, published by Electronic Arts using Nintendo 3DS, released in 2009.

engagement in this experiment. Thirty five participants (N=35) were introduced to *The Sims 3* game and had some tutorials before the experiment began. During the experiment, participants were given an information sheet about the game, three specific tasks and a list of game controls. The goal of the game in this experiment was to keep the Sims characters happy, fed, clean, and nurtured.

Table 4. Assessment aspects of game interface

No.	Questions	Interface elements
1.	I like the interface used in this game	Graphics/Layout/
2.	I am interested in the *Sims* character	Images
3.	I experience using the menu as a part of the game	Menu/Buttons/
4.	It is easy to understand the menu	Icons
5.	The game control is easy	Control
6.	Sounds from the game gave me meaningful feedback	Feedback/Sounds/ Music
7.	I experience the game story as part of the game play	
8.	I am interested in the game story	Feedback

Findings. Results showed that the players gave different feedback on their experiences depending on their levels of expertise (novice vs. expert). From the observation, novice players seemed to be more impressed by the user interface, graphics and the presence element, while expert players more readily and more easily became immersed with the game. Understandably, novice players were more focusing on how to control the game, mastering the menu and trying hard to enjoy the game (playing the interface) implying the game interface as an important element to capture player attraction for the novice players. However, for the expert players we noticed that the game challenge and goals were the more important elements. Overall the participants acknowledged that they were satisfied with the game interface and were having a positive experience with the game.

4 Discussion

The results of our studies demonstrate that the work has interesting finding related to positive user experience while interacting with game interface. Based on these initial studies, we can see there are some connections between the ways game interface elements are designed in and the levels of user engagements.Through the studies, we identified that some of the interface elements (e.g., graphics and images, feedback, sounds and music) influenced the player experience with the game playing. Novice players were attracted to images and graphics that first caught their attention and helped them start engaging in playing the game.O'Brienand Toms [5] state some users become engaged by the layout or aesthetics of the interface. While in GameFlow study [4] by creating engaging new interfaces and controllers using advanced haptic interfaces makes players "be in the game".

Furthermore, feedback (e.g., sound effects, soundtracks, music) and control was also as important interface elements for drawing players into a game and keeping them engaged [4]. Feedback can give the information communicated to users about actions that have occurred and results that have been achieved. Players used sounds to keep track of background elements of the game that were separate from the ones currently on the screen and maintain the focus [5]. Sweetser and Wyeht [4] had included control as an element in the GameFlow and claimed that players should feel a sense of control over their characters or units and their movements and interactions in the game world. Moreover, O'Brien and Toms [5] mentioned that video gamers described control as their ability to direct some things in games. These interface elements captured players' attention and interest and moved them forward into engagement.

However, there are many different ways of playing and enjoying a game and thus influence the user engagement. In the context of our research, there were a few factors that can influence the user experience while playing the game instead of user interface. Examples include the game platform, game genre and different level of player experience (novice and expert). For future work; it would be interesting to investigate different types of game genre involving more participants with different levels of gaming experiences. We also note that the study needs to be carried out with more respondents and an increased variety of categories, such as gender, occupation, education level, and other demographic factors to get more reliable results.

Findings from this study can be used as starting point in looking at how to design engaging user interface in game to deliver the right game mechanics to the players, which capture their full attention, and results in an engaging user experience. This makes the domain of gaming design very interesting in understanding or formulating the kinds of user interface design guidelines or patterns to follow in game design. It also represents a new trend with a growing influence on future game interfaces design that goes out of conventional game consoles or PC but a variety of platforms with novel interaction modalities. Presenting attractive game interface elements was able to influence player satisfaction and enjoyment in gaming. We believe that there are design possibilities that game interfaces can influence to control the level of user engagement. These initial observations on games interfaces and user engagement offer many avenues for further research, such as manipulating engaging interfaces in gaming application, studying how the level of gaming expertise relates to different aspects of gaming interfaces, and examining how the different interaction platforms influence the level of engagement.

5 Conclusion

This study is an early stage to examine whether the features in user interface can help the user engage with the game interaction better. In summary, we tried to understand user engagement through the interface interaction in gaming application. In the context of gaming, different interaction platforms and difference levels of player experience do give different experiences while interacting with the games. Understanding the variation of user experience towards multiplatform gaming devices will provide us with more guidelines in gaming system interface development.

Besides, understanding the relationship between the elements of a gaming user-interface and their overall impact on user experience will be one of the key factors in designing more effective and engaging games interfaces in the coming years.

Acknowledgement. This research was supported by a university research grant (UKM-TT-03-FRGS0135-2010).

References

1. Juul, J., Norton, M.: Easy to use and incredibly difficult: on the mythical border between interface and gameplay. In: Proceedings of the 4th International Conference on Foundations of Digital Games, FDG 2009 (2009) ISBN: 978-1-60558-437-9
2. Takatalo, J., Hakkinen, J., Kaistinen, J., Nyman, G.: Presence, Involvement, and Flow in Digital Games. Evaluating User Experience in Games, Human-Computer Interaction Series, pp. 23–45 (2010), doi:10.1007/978-1-84882-963-3_3
3. Barr, P., Khaled, R., Noble, J., Biddle, R.: Videogame values: Human–computer interaction and games. Interacting with Computers 19(2), 180–195 (2007)
4. Sweetser, P., Wyeth, P.: 'GameFlow: A Model for Evaluating Player Enjoyment in Games' Magazine Computers in Entertainment (CIE). Theoretical and Practical Computer Applications in Entertainment 3(3) (July 2005)
5. O'Brien, H.L., Toms, E.G.: What is user engagement? A conceptual framework for defining user engagement with technology. Journal of the American Society for Information Science and Technology (2008)
6. Bucolo, S., Billinghurst, M., Sickinger, D.: User experiences with mobile phone camera game interfaces. In: Proceedings of the 4th International Conference on Mobile and Ubiquitous Multimedia, MUM 2005 (2005) ISBN: 0-473-10658-2
7. Shinkle, E.: Feel It, Don't Think: the Significance of Affect in the Study of Digital Games. In: DiGRA 2005: Changing Views: Worlds in Play, International Conference (2005)
8. Van Vugt, H.C., Konijn, E.A., Hoorn, J.F., Keur, I., Eliens, A.: Realism is not all! User engagement with task-related interface characters. Interacting with Computers 19(2), 267–280 (2007)
9. Costello, B., Edmonds, E.: A study in play, pleasure and interaction design. In: Proceedings of the 2007 Conference on Designing Pleasurable Products and Interfaces, DPPI 2007 (2007) ISBN: 978-1-59593-942-5
10. Xie, L., Antle, A.N., Motamedi, N.: Are Tangibles More Fun? Comparing Children's Enjoyment and Engagement Using Physical, Graphical and Tangible User Interfaces. In: Proceedings of the 2nd International Conference on Tangible and Embedded Interaction, TEI 2008 (2008) ISBN: 978-1-60558-004-3
11. Febretti, A., Garzotto, F.: Usability, playability, and long-term engagement in computer games. In: Proceedings of the 27th International Conference Extended Abstracts on Human Factors in Computing Systems, CHI EA 2009 (2009) (ISBN: 978-1-60558-247-4)
12. Prensky, M.: Fun, Play and Games: What Makes Games Engaging. Digital Game-Based Learning. McGraw-Hill (2001)
13. Douglas, Y., Hargadon, A.: The pleasure principle: immersion, engagement, flow. In: Proceedings of the Eleventh ACM on Hypertext and Hypermedia, pp. 153–160. ACM (2000)
14. Voiskounsky, A.E., Mitina, O.V., Avetisova, A.A.: Playing online games: Flow experience. PsychNology Journal 2(3), 259–281 (2004)
15. Brown, E., Cairns, P.: A grounded investigation of game immersion. In: Extended Abstracts on Human Factors in Computing Systems, CHI 2004, pp. 1297–1300. ACM (2004)

16. Cowley, B., Charles, D., Black, M., Hickey, R.: 'Toward an understanding of flow in video games. ACM Computer Entertainment 6(2) (April/June 2008), doi:10.1145/1371216.1371223
17. Zagal, J., Chan, S.S., Zhang, J.: Measuring Flow Experience of Computer Game Players. In: Americas Conference on Information Systems Proceeding, AMCIS 2010, paper 137 (2010), `http://aisel.aisnet.org/amcis2010/137`
18. Procci, K., Bowers, C.: An Examination of Flow and Immersion in Games. In: Proceedings of the Human Factors and an Ergonomics Society (2011), doi:10.1177/ 1071181311551455201155:2183
19. Weibel, D., Wissmath, B., Habegger, S., Steiner, Y., Groner, R.: Playing online games against computer-vs. human-controlled opponents: Effects on presence, flow, and enjoyment. Computers in Human Behavior 24(5), 2274–2291 (2008)
20. McMahan, A.: Immersion, engagement and presence. The video game theory reader, pp. 67–86 (2003)
21. Mayes, D.K., Cotton, J.E.: Measuring engagement in video games: A questionnaire. In: Proceedings of the Human Factors and Ergonomics Society 45th Annual Meeting, pp. 692–696 (2001)
22. Whitson, J., Eaket, C., Greenspan, B., Tran, M.: Neo-Immersion: Awareness and Engagement in Gameplay. In: Proceeding Future Play 2008 Proceedings of the 2008 Conference on Future Play: Research, Play, Share (2008) ISBN: 978-1-60558-218-4
23. Kuts, E.: Playful User Interfaces: Literature Review and Model for Analysis. In: Proceedings of DiGRA 2009. Breaking New Ground: Innovation in Games, Play, Practice and Theory (2009)
24. Csikszentmihalyi, M.: Flow: The Psychology of Optimal Experience. Harper Perennial, New York (1991)
25. Smith, B.P.: Flow and the enjoyment of video games. Unpublished dissertation. The University of Alabama, UMI3223325 (2006)
26. Zhang, J., Fang, X., Chan, S.S., Zagal, J.: Measuring Flow Experience of Computer Game Players. In: Proceedings of the Sixteenth Americas Conference on Information Systems, Paper 137 (2010)
27. Brockmyer, J.H., Fox, C.M., Curtiss, K.A., McBroom, E., Burkhart, K.M., Pidruzny, J.N.: The development of the Game Engagement Questionnaire: A measure of engagement in video game-playing. Journal of Experimental Social Psychology 45, 624–634 (2009)

Fast and Efficient Video Completion Using Object Prior Position

Sameh Zarif[1,2,*], Ibrahima Faye[1,3], and Dayang Rohaya[1,2]

[1] Centre of Intelligent Signal and Imaging Research (CISIR),
[2] Department of Computer and Information Sciences,
[3] Department of Fundamental and Applied Sciences
Universiti Teknologi Petronas, Malaysia
Sameh.shenoda@ci.menofia.edu.eg,
{ibrahima_faye,roharam}@petronas.com.my

Abstract. Reconstruction and repairing damaged parts after object removal of digital video is an important trend in artwork restoration. Video completion is an active subject in video processing, which deals with the recovery of the original data. Most previous video completion approaches consume more time in extensive search to find the best patch to restore the damaged frames. In addition to that, visual artifacts appear when the damaged area is large. In this paper, we present a fast and efficient video completion method without the extensive search process. The proposed method is based on the object prior positions and the temporal continuity of the video frames. The proposed method is fast and maintains the spatial and temporal consistency. In addition to that, it can handle the object size and posture change, non periodic motion, and non stationary background.

Keywords: Video inpainting, Video Completion, Object Removal, Texture Synthesis.

1 Introduction

Video completion is an interesting research topic in multimedia computing and video processing since 2000 because of its powerful ability to repair damaged video. In recent years, transforming cultural and historical artifacts such as photographs and old films into digital format has become an important trend. Most old video that have a historical value are very poor after digitization and often contain unstable luminance and damaged content. Old video are usually subject to degradation due to bad environment, dust and dirt, scratches, water, noise, compression or transmission, and others have logos. The purpose of video completion is to modify and repair damaged structures and texture areas in a non-detectable way for an observer not familiar with the original video. The challenges of video completion compared to image completion are the huge number of data to be restored and the spatial and temporal consistency between video frames that must be maintained [1-3].

* Corresponding author.

H. Badioze Zaman et al. (Eds.): IVIC 2013, LNCS 8237, pp. 241–252, 2013.

Image completion approaches combine both texture synthesis and inpainting techniques to reconstruct large holes in the image by inpainting unknown area on the image using both texture and structure information [4, 5]. Unfortunately, image completion methods that work on standalone images cannot be extended to sequences and videos frames without taking into account the temporal continuity with a robust tracking method. To design a video inpainting process, both the spatial and temporal continuity issues have to be considered since the human visual system is more sensitive to motion distortion [6].

There are numerous applications for video completion including video editing and film post production, wireless video transmission (e.g. recovering lost blocks), special effects (e.g. removal of unwanted objects), video restoration (e.g. scratch removal), removal of occlusions such as text, subtitle, logos, stamps; removal of information from aerial video like orientation and location. Other applications include annotation removal from medical and military sequences and video [1, 3, and 7].

In this paper we proposed a fast and efficient video completion method based on the object prior positions and the temporal continuity of video frames. We assume that, the scene is recorded by static camera and the object of interest is the first or last object entering the scene. The remaining of the paper is organized as follows. Section 2 gives an overview of the related video completion methods. In section 3 we present the proposed algorithm. Section 4 illustrates the results. Finally the conclusion is drawn in section 5.

2 Related Work

In recent years, researchers started to address the problems of video completion using number of standalone image completion algorithms to each video frame as independent image. One of the first efforts for video inpainting is made in Bertalmio et al. [8], which consider only the spatial information in video and perform the inpainting on a frame by frame basis, using the partial differential equations (PDE) based method in [9]. It fails to inpaint large regions in a video and does not utilize the temporal information. Jia et al. [10] proposed a method that aims to challenging the presence of occlusions in static camera scene. Layer segmentation and holography techniques are used to recover static background. Moving object pixels are repaired by sampling motion data to maintain temporal coherence. The object motion is restricted to be periodic and do no change in scale. Zhang et al. [11] presented a method that divide video frames into different non overlapping motion layers using graph cut algorithm. Image inpainting method repairs each layer separately. The inpainted information is propagated to other frames using the known motion parameters, and then all layers are combined to restore the completed video. This method does not take into account the temporal consistency between adjacent frames and is limited to rigid bodies.

Wexler et al. [12] proposed a space time video completion for stationary camera as a global optimization problem. It takes into account the spatial and temporal dimensions. It solves the inpainting problem by sampling a set of spatial-temporal patches from other frames to fill in the missing data. It optimizes the patch search process at different resolution levels using spatio-temporal pyramids and nearest neighbor algorithms. The damaged parts in a frame are completed using different region of the same video. Exhaustive searching strategy for finding appropriate patches leads to high computational load. This method handles only periodic moving objects that do not significantly change in scale. Patwardhan et al. [13] pioneered a video completion method for constrained camera motion and static background. The method constructs three mosaics for background, foreground and the corresponding optical flow based on the motion vectors. Extended exemplar based image inpainting in [14] is used to repair the background holes. The extracted texture synthesis patches from the neighbor frames are used to complete the remaining foreground hole. It fails when the object changes in size. Shih et al. [15] proposed a video completion method that divides the video frames into an intrinsic motion layer and an extrinsic motion layer. Exemplar based method in [14] is used to inpaint the damaged area in each layer by improving match strategy using modifications on data term. It can only handle videos that have consistent luminance and stable camera motion.

Vijay et al. [16] presented an object based video inpainting technique that separately completes the background and the foreground. Adaptive background replacement and the image inpainting method in [14] are used to complete the stationary background. The foreground object is formatted as an energy minimization problem. Dynamic programming and window based dissimilarity are introduced to select the optimal candidates and improve the motion continuity by solving the minimization problem. This method reduced the complexity, but still takes more time. Unnatural results appear when the object to be inpainted moves in non repetitive motion or have a shadow. Xia et al. [17] proposed an exemplar based video inpainting method that focuses on static background and moving foreground using Gaussian Mixture Model (GMM) to find best patches. The method does not do well when the background and the foreground are close to each other. Tang et al. [1] proposed a video inpainting technique to repair old damaged films. Local and global motion estimations are used to construct the motion map. A motion completion is used to repair the damaged motion information to obtain more reference data. Frame completion is used to complete the damaged areas in the video frames through patch pasting and frame adjustment. Visual defect and shadows appear if the damaged area is large. Mosleh et al. [18] proposed a video completion approach based on bandlet transform and exemplar based image inpainting in [14]. The completion process starts separating the moving objects from the background using the bi-layer video segmentation method in [19]. A precise optimization in Bandlet transform is used to complete the damaged background after removing the object of interest. Exemplar based image inpainting method is performed to repair the occluded part in the moving foreground. This method produces satisfying results but still takes time in the search strategy.

Most of the recent video completion techniques are based on the exemplar based image inpainting method in [14] by adapting the search space to the temporal properties between video frames. These methods suffer from the following major limitations. Searching the source patch in spatial and temporal frames is computationally expensive and will easily lead to error match, which will accumulate and propagate to other frames. Over 90 percent of the total computation time is spent on the search for match patch [20]. Large damaged areas cause visual artifacts in the result, and the methods are limited to non periodic motions and regular object sizes.

3 Proposed Work

The proposed video completion method is a fully automatic method based on the prior positions of the moving object and the temporal continuity of video frames to complete the damaged background after removing the object of interest. The goal of our proposed method is to fill the damaged area with the original information using the prior positions instead of searching and estimating data from the surrounding frames. Fig.1 presents the block diagram of the proposed method.

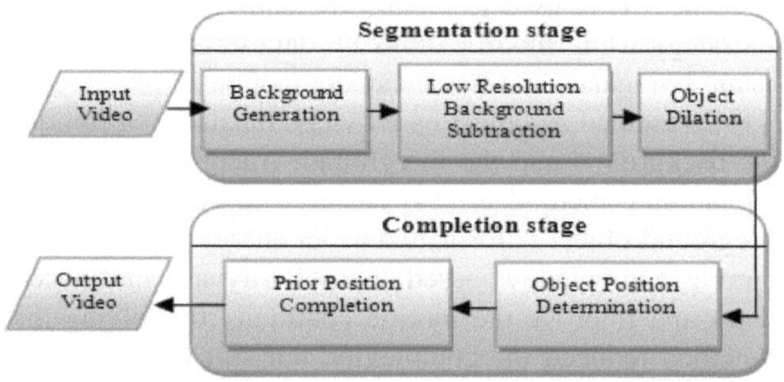

Fig. 1. Block diagram of the proposed video completion method

The proposed work consists of two stages to restore the damaged area. It addresses the time consuming problem which represents the most challenging part in video completion. The segmentation stage aims to separate the background from the foreground using low resolution background subtraction. The completion stage uses the object prior position to complete the damaged region.

3.1 Segmentation Stage

The object of interest in image inpainting is manually selected by the user. However, it is very difficult in video to manually select the object of interest in all video frames due to the huge number of video frames. Therefore, the first step in most of video completion techniques is detecting and tracking the moving objects. Accurate video completion methods depend on the quality of the moving objects extraction. The segmentation stage is a crucial part of the proposed work.

Background subtraction techniques are the most common for separating moving objects from the background when the camera is stationary. The proposed method starts by performing frames median to generate an accurate background model that is used in the background subtraction process. Frames median or temporal median determines the median pixel based on the total number of frames. The main problem of background subtraction techniques is that it is more sensitive to small motion or change derived from fake motion like lighting and tree leaf between frames, especially in outdoor scenes. Fake motions that derived from the non stationary background can cause failure of the segmentation stage. The proposed method handles the fake motion problem by doing the background subtraction on a low resolution version. The low resolution version is obtained by decreasing the frame spatial resolution using 2x2 block average. The frame size after applying the low resolution will be one quarter of the original size as illustrated in fig. 2. There are two advantages of using low resolution process before doing the background subtraction. First, it removes the fake motion derived from non stationary background. Second, it reduces the computational time of the segmentation stage.

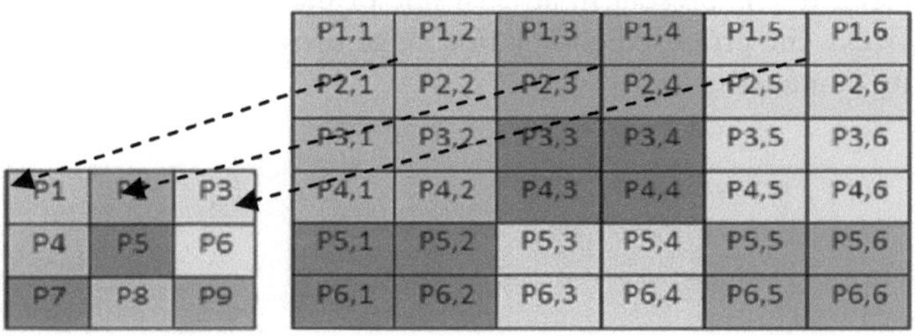

(a) (b)

Fig. 2. Low resolution process. (a) Result after low resolution, (b) original image

Background subtraction is performed by taking the absolute difference between the low resolution of each frame $F(x, y, t)$ and the low resolution of the computed background $B(x, y)$ as defined in equation 1. Motion mask between the background and the moving object is obtained by performing thresholding on the subtraction result as defined in equation 2.

$$D(x,y) = |F(x,y,t) - B(x,y)| \tag{1}$$

$$Mask(x,y) = \begin{cases} 1 & D(x,y) > Thr \\ 0 & Otherwise \end{cases} \tag{2}$$

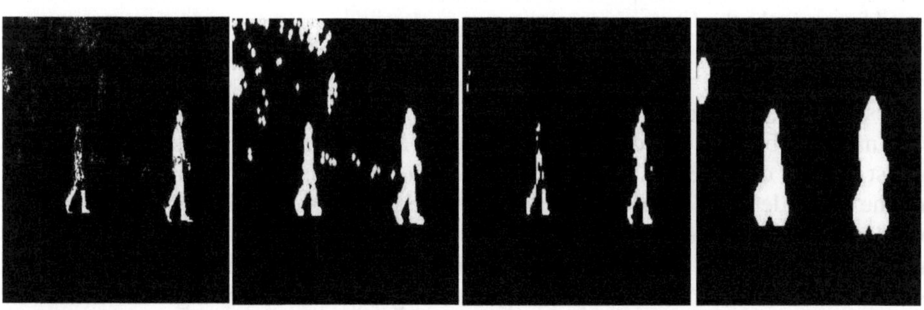

(a) (b) (c) (d)

Fig. 3. Segmentation stage. (a) traditional subtraction, (b) dilation of (a), (c) low resolution subtraction, and (d) dilation of (c).

After background subtraction using low resolution, the moving object appears long thin and have small hole. Morphological dilation is then performed to the mask image to fill in the gaps and merge the near isolated region. The initial resolution is then set back to start the completion stage. Fig.3 illustrates the results of the segmentation stage with and without low resolution.

3.2 Completion Stage

Video frames have advantages compared to a standalone image. Damaged information can be recovered if it is present in at least one of the other frames. To avoid extensive search process, the proposed completion stage uses the object prior position to complete the entire damaged area.

Fig. 4. Completion stage. Sample frames in the first row, motion mask in the second row, completed frames in the third row.

Fig. 4 presents the steps of the completion stage. The object position determination process uses connected component analysis to extract the smallest bounding box for each moving object detected in the motion mask and determine the position of the first or last moving object entering the scene. The prior position completion starts completing the entire detected object of interest from the previous completed frame. The prior position means that, the current position of the object of interest is available in the prior inpainted frame. The missing data in the first frame is completed using the available information located in the corresponding bounding box from the background model. In outdoor scene, sometimes the scene changes due to illumination variation, clutter motion or if the object stop moving. To maintain the gradual and sudden changes, the proposed completion method completes the remaining frames using the object prior position from the previous completed frame instead of the background model. The position of the object or damaged area in the second frame will be available in the first frame after completion and the missing region in the third frame will be available in the completed second frame. The computed background model is used once for the first frame and does not need to be updated. As illustrated in fig. 4, the quality of the proposed method does not depend on the quality of the computed background model. The solid box represents the object of interest, the dashed box represents the available corresponding box in the previous frame, and the dotted box represents the inpainted area in the current frame. The main advantage of using the prior position in the completion process is to avoid using extensive search process to find the best data from spatial and temporal frames. The method avoids flickering and ensures the temporal consistency and the smoothness of the completed areas.

4 Experimental Results

The proposed method has been implemented using MATLAB R2009a and tested on a PC with Pentium Dual Core 2.8 GHz CPU and 2 Gigabyte memory. To demonstrate its effectiveness, it is tested on a variety of video scenes recorded by a stationary camera. Each video scene illustrates the efficiency of the proposed method in addressing one of the inpainting challenges like object size change, processing time, non stationary background, and change in object posture. Table 1 summarizes the details of the examples used in this work.

Because of the changes in the inpainted frames in structure, texture, geometric attributes, and hole size, it is very difficult to evaluate the quality of the inpainting techniques by traditional objective evaluation such as Peak Signal to Noise Ratio (PSNR), Mean Squared Error (MSE), and Structural Similarity (SSIM). The quality of image and video inpainting depends on the human visual perception system rather than mathematical measures [7, 21, and 22].

The existing video completion methods are still few and the original video data are not available in most cases to make a comparison. To evaluate the proposed method, we apply it in the following challenges which constitute limitations for most of the related works:

- Non stationary background
- Object change in scale
- Object change in posture
- Static object occluding the object of interest
- Illumination changes
- Processing time

Non stationary background challenge, fig. 3 and 4 illustrate the efficiency of the proposed method in handling an outdoor scene containing non stationary background by using low resolution before background subtraction. Moving objects that significantly change in scale and posture constitute a very challenging problems in most of video completion methods. Fig. 5 demonstrates a real life scene having speed moving bike that changes in scale and a normal walking person. The results show that the proposed method successfully removed the moving bike and completed the background using object prior position. Fig. 6 shows an example of removing a foreground object that significantly changes in pose for video sequence which consists of multiple objects. The second row in fig. 6 illustrates that the proposed method works well when the moving object changes in pose and moves in non periodic motion.

Occlusion is a very challenging problem in video inpainting. The object of interest, in most of real life videos, may be occluded by other static objects from the background or other moving objects. The proposed method works well when the object of interest is occluded by a static object or occludes a static object. It fails when the object is occluded by, or occludes, other moving objects. Fig. 7 shows the efficiency of the proposed work in removing moving object occluded by long grass and reconstructs the grass again. Fig. 8 presents an example for moving jumping girl occluded by another girl who moves her hands.

Gradual and sudden illumination changes are real challenges that happened due to light and environment changes during the day hours, sudden switch of light, and shadows during the day hours. Most techniques that depend on the background model fail to repair the illumination changes. Some methods need to update the background model every few frames. These techniques take more time. Fig. 9 illustrates an example for indoor video scene that has sudden changes due to switching light on. The results that appear in the second row of fig. 9 are satisfactory but not perfect due to the shadow that appears when switching on the light.

Processing time is the most challenging problem in all video completion techniques. The processing time in most of the previous video completion methods are very high compared to the proposed method. The method in [7] and in [12] takes 17 minutes and 4 hours respectively to repair 100 frames at 320 x 240 resolution on P-4 machine. The method in [13] takes about 15 minutes to complete 50 frames video at 320 x 240 resolutions by using C++ and P-4 machine. The method in [16] takes 10 to 20 minutes to complete the example of the jumping girl mentioned in fig. 8. It uses MATLAB and P-4 with 4 Gigabyte memory machine. The complexity analysis and the processing time of the methods in [7, 12, 13, and 16] are located in [7, 16]. Table 1 illustrates the processing time of the proposed method. The big difference in the processing time is mainly because of the removal of the extensive patch search process which takes more time. Table 2 shows that, despite a bigger number of frames and a bigger resolution, the proposed method is still much faster than the others. The proposed method has a weakness in separating the moving objects when occlusion happens. It is limited to removing the first or last object entering the scene and also to static camera.

Table 1. Processing time of the proposed work

Figure	Resolution	No. of Frames	Completion time
4 and 6	480 x 270	405	25 Sec.
5	596 x 336	95	5 Sec.
7	480 x 270	360	20 Sec.
8	300 x 100	240	12 Sec.
9	480 x 270	90	4 Sec.

Table 2. Processing time comparison between the proposed work and the others

Method	Machine	No. of Frames	Resolution	Time
In [7]	Pentium 4	100	320 x 240	17 Min.
In [12]	Pentium 4	100	320 x 240	4 Hours
In [13]	Pentium 4	50	320 x 240	15 Min.
In [16]	Pentium 4	240	300 x 100	13 Min.
Proposed	Pentium 4	405	480 x 270	25 Sec.

Fig. 5. Bike removal. Original frames in the first row; completed frames in the second row.

Fig. 6. Object change in posture. Original frames in the first row; completed frames in the second row.

Fig. 7. Static occlusion example. Original frames in the first row; completed frames in the second row.

Fig. 8. Dynamic occlusion example. Original frames in the first row; completed frames in the second row.

Fig. 9. Sudden illumination change example. Original frames in the first row; completed frames in the second row.

5 Conclusion

In this work, we proposed a fast and efficient video completion method based on the prior position and temporal frames continuity. The proposed method effectively maintains the spatial and temporal consistency by using the original data from the prior completed frame. It also works well when the object size, the pose or the illumination change and when the background is non stationary. The experimental results showed a faster processing and high quality results. A future work will consist in extending the proposed method to the case where the object of interest is not the first or the last object entering the scene and also when including different occlusion problems.

References

1. Tang, N.C., Chiou-ting, Chih-wen, Hong-yuan.: Video Inpainting on Digitized Vintage Films via Maintaining Spatiotemporal Continuity. IEEE Trans. on Multimedia 13(4), 602–614 (2011)
2. Hongying, Z., Yadong, W.: An Efficient Scratches Detection and Inpainting Algorithm for Old Film Restoration. In: IEEE Inter. Conf. on Information Technology and Computer Science, pp. 75–78 (2009)
3. Zarif, S., Faye, I., Rohaya, D.: Fast and Efficient Multichannel Image Completion Using Local Similarity. In: IEEE 21st Inter. Conf. on Pattern Recognition, pp. 3116–3119 (2012)
4. Sun, D., Yuan, L., Zhang, Y., Pan, G.: Structure-aware Image Completion with Texture Propagation. In: IEEE 6th Inter. Conf. on Image and Graphics (ICIG), pp. 199–204 (2011)
5. Lu, Z., Huang, H., Li, L., Cheng, D.: A Novel Exemplar-Based Image Completion Scheme With Adaptive TV-Constraint. In: IEEE 4th Inter. Conf. on Genetic and Evolutionary Computing, pp. 94–97 (2010)
6. Raimbault, F., Kokaram, A.: Stereo Video Inpainting. In: Proceeding of SPIE, vol. 7863, pp. 320–333 (2011)
7. Jia, Y., Hu, S., Martin, R.: Video Completion Using Tracking and Fragment Merging. Proceeding of Pacific Graphics 21(8-10), 601–610 (2005)
8. Bertalmio, M., Bertozzi, A.L., Sapiro, G.: Navier-stokes, fluid dynamics and image and video inpainting. In: IEEE CVPR, vol. I, pp. 355–363 (2001)
9. Bertalmio, M., Sapiro, G., Caselles, V., Ballester.: Image Inpainting. In: Proceeding of the ACM SIGGRAPH Conf. on Computer Graphics, pp. 417–424 (2000)
10. Jia, J., Wu, T., Tang, C.: Video repairing. In: Proceeding IEEE Computer Vision and Pattern Recognition (CVPR), pp. 364–371 (2004)
11. Zhang, Y., Xiao, J., Shah, M.: Motion Layer Based Object Removal in Video. In: 7 IEEE Workshop on Application of Computer Vision, pp. 516–521 (2005)
12. Wexler, Y., Shechtmam, E.: Irani Space Time Completion of Video. IEEE Trans. on Pattern Analysis and Machine Intelligence 29, 463–476 (2007)
13. Patwardhan, K., Sapiro, G., Bertalmio, M.: Video Inpainting Under Constrained Camera Motion. IEEE Trans. on Image Processing 16(2), 545–553 (2007)
14. Criminisi, A., Perez, P., Toyama, K.: Region Filling and Object Removal by Examplar-based Inpainting. IEEE Trans. Image Processing 13(9), 1200–1212 (2004)
15. Shih, T.K., Tang, N.C., Hwang, J.N.: Exemplar Based Video Inpainting Without Ghost Shadow Artifacts by Maintaining Temporal Continuity. IEEE Trans. Circuit syst. Video Technol. 19(2), 347–360 (2009)

16. Vijay, M., Samson, S., Zhao, J.: Efficient Object Based Video Inpainting. Proceeding of Pattern Recognition Letters 30(2), 168–179 (2009)
17. Xia, A., Gui, Y., Yao, L., Ma, L., Lin, X.: Exemplar Based Object Removal in Video Using GMM. In: IEEE CMSP, pp. 366–370 (2011)
18. Mosleh, A., Bouguila, N., Hamza, A.: Video Completion Method Using Bandlet Transform. IEEE Trans. on Multimedia 14(6), 1591–1601 (2012)
19. Criminisi, A., Cross, G., Blake, A., Kolmogorov, V.: Bilayer Segmentation of live Video. In: IEEE Inter. Conf. on Computer Vision and Pattern Recognition, pp. 53–60 (2006)
20. Drori, I., Cohen, D., Yeshurun, H.: Fragment-based Image Completion. Proceedings of SIGGRAPH 22, 303–312 (2003)
21. Li, H., Wang, S., Zhang, W., Wu, M.: Image Inpainting Based on Scene Transform and Color Transform. Pattern Recognition Letters 31(7), 582–592 (2010)
22. Zarif, S., Faye, I., Rohaya, D.: Static Object Removal from Video Scene Using Local Similarity. In: IEEE 9th Inter. Colloquium on Signal Processing and its Applications, pp. 54–57 (2013)

Let's Play with Colours: BacaMAX User Interface for Dyslexic Children

Husniza Husni and Zulikha Jamaludin

School of Computing, College of Arts and Sciences,
Universiti Utara Malaysia, 06010 UUM Sintok, Kedah, Malaysia
{husniza,zulie}@uum.edu.my

Abstract. Reading difficulties are synonymous with dyslexic children, whose unique condition is due to dyslexia. One of the major theories of dyslexia is visual deficits which are not caused by the problems with the eyes but with the information processing that took place inside the brain. Hence, to assist dyslexic children reading we propose BacaMAX, a visually stimulating voice replay application designed carefully to ease them reading. The application is a result of years of study on dyslexic children and their colour choices. Bedside experiment with the children was carried out on a systematic background and a foreground colour scheme, specifically on syllables, words, and short sentences. This paper aims to deliberately discuss BacaMAX interface design that started with our beta version to the current improved version. Rapid application development is employed as the methodology to develop prototypes and user acceptance test is employed to test the prototypes on real users. As the result, all versions are presented and discussed.

Keywords: Interface design for dyslexic, reading application, visual stimuli and colours, dyslexia and reading.

1 Introduction

Dyslexia's secret that impedes reading abilities has been unveiled through research that shows pertinent deactivation in the parts of the brain that are normally used for reading. This unique condition can be clearly visualized through *functional magnetic resonance images* (fMRI) images, which also reveal that dyslexics are using a different pathway in the brain in order to read [1, 2].

Normally, three parts of the brain are activated for reading: the inferior frontal gyrus, the parieto-temporal, and the occipito-temporal. These three parts are located on the left side of the brain where the frontal gyrus sits on the anterior part (the front), the parieto-temporal is located somewhat in the middle part, and the occipito-temporal occupies the posterior part of the brain. The three parts combine together to form a system for reading where each of the parts play roles such as articulation and word analysis, and word form.

H. Badioze Zaman et al. (Eds.): IVIC 2013, LNCS 8237, pp. 253–263, 2013.

Dyslexics, however, did not activate the aforementioned brain parts for reading but rather activated a different route as illustrated in Fig. 1 (source from [1]). The fMRI images reveal that dyslexics are under activating the parieto-temporal and the occipito-temporal pathways where these two areas fail to be activated at all when dyslexics were asked to read. Therefore, due to the under activated reading areas of the brain that dyslexics have the difficulties to read and process text information.

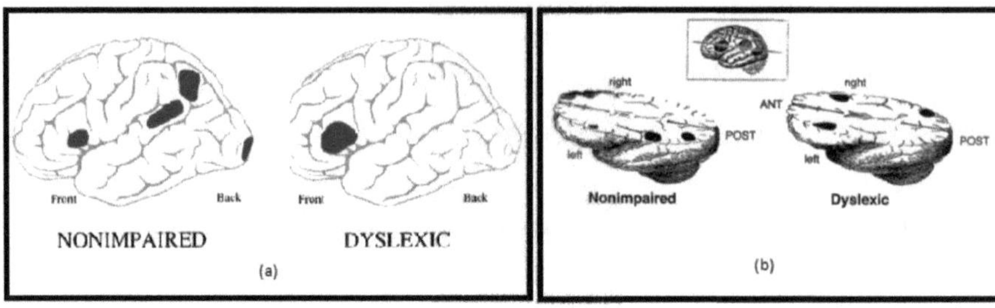

Fig. 1. The different activated reading pathways between normal reader and dyslexic reader (a). The normal reader activated areas on the left of the brain whereas dyslexic reader uses alternative pathways to read (b) [1].

The question is – what makes such conditions occur? What can technology offers to help them read and how? Therefore, this paper presents theories underlying dyslexia and deliberately discusses them in relation to BacaMAX, an application with its design specifically tailored to dyslexic children's requirements that aims to reduce their difficulties in reading.

2 Dyslexia and 'Twisted' Visual Cues

The universal theory of dyslexia is the phonological deficit theory [3-8], which says that the difficulties to read amongst dyslexics are caused by the impairment of the brain to process phonological input, as evidenced by the fMRI images. One of the causes for reading difficulties is due to problems with visual processing. It is important to note that the visual problems here do not refer to the physical problems of the eyes but instead, they are referring to the processing of visual cues sent by the eyes to the brain that supposedly targeting the reading pathways to be activated. Unfortunately for dyslexics, it didn't.

A number of theories have been put forward in relation with visual impairments namely visual deficits, temporal and timing difficulties, and low working memory. Table 1 highlights and briefly describes the three visual-related theories of dyslexia [9-11]. The theories presented in Table 1 serve as fundamental idea for designing a suitable interface for dyslexic children so that, somehow, their difficulties in reading can be reduced and thus, provide them a better means for reading.

Table 1. Visual-related theories that affect dyslexic children (DC)'s ability to read

Theories	Main cause	Description	Effects
Low working memory	Deficits in short term memory in the front lobus of the brain, right hemisphere (video), and left hemisphere (audio).	Memory processing involving 4 main components: 1) audio memory (including phonology); 2) visual memory (including orthography or the shape of words); 3) procedural or movement memory (a.k.a. habit memory, e.g. riding a bicycle); 4) semantic memory.	· inefficient use of working memory. · problems in translating visual information to phonological representation, thus limiting the ability to learn new words when reading.
Visual deficits	deficits in visual magnocellular system (a group of neurons as path for transferring electrical signals from eyes to the brain).	Dyslexics failed or have difficulties to process information sent from the eyes.	· unstable and vibrating binocular vision. · confusing the sequence of letters and causing weak memory for visual information.
Temporal or timing difficulties	·magnocellular differences (audio or visual). · only effects temporary processing.	Deficits in the part of the brain that controls sounds and rapid visual information.	· DC have difficulties in processing rapid sounds and visual information. · DC need more time to learn, process information, and give response.

Referring to Table 1, the difficulties to read that are caused by visual impairments, i.e. visual deficits and low working memory which can be potentially reduced by providing a specifically designed reading interface for them. Note that, temporal or timing difficulties also cause dyslexic children to have problems in visual information processing. Nevertheless, this theory does not conflict with the established statement that visual impairment, particularly referring to the *physical* problems of the eyes and vision, do not contribute to reading difficulties [12]. After all, the theories here suggest that phonological deficits occur due to the problems in processing visual information sent to the brain for reading. For some unique reasons, the information is sent to the wrong parts of the brain creating either a different pathway for reading or no activation at all.

Inspired by the nature of the visual-related problems for dyslexics, we therefore intend to focus the reading interface design such that it could ease, somehow, the visual cues (of text) submitted to the brain. The design is aimed to ease the information processing ability sent from the eye to the brain by providing stimulating visual presentation of text on screen for them read. This includes a set of identified requirements as depicted in Fig.2.

Using all 7 phases of Norman's Model and 4 components of Abowd and Beale.

Major* impairments (dyslexic children observed & interviewed)	Computer support	IxD Dimension	Affective dimension to include	Design example (result)
Easily distracted (weak focus for coherence)	- Limits distraction by simple interface design	**Form (F)**: large & minimum screen objects **Content (C)**: words to read **Bahaviour (B)**: - Choices for: 1. Word level 2. Number of words to display	- curiosity - relaxed	BUDU simple navigation
Cannot take cognitive load	- Animation - Following the sequence while writing the word is easier than reading the word prompted as in the flash card.	F: writing animation C: words to read B: choices for: 1. Word level 2. Pen size 3. Speed of animation	- curiosity (have to wait, digest each alphabet...) - awaiting - eagerness	budu pen animation
Very much effected with coloured words and background	- Utilize colour as adviced by Irlen Method for background colour - colour coded syllable	F: working with effective colours C: words to read, colour B: choices for: 1. Colour selection (background) 2. Syallabe 1st colour, 2nd colour is automatics from IxD theory of colour)	- joyfulness - astonishment - curiosity - fascination	bunga different coloured syallable
Alphabet confusion (consonant, vowel). Tends to substitute, eliminate, replace with other alphabets. e.g: b,d,p u,n,m,w Excellent with very different letters like k,t,g,s ... mostly consonant.	- Use carefully selected font type that don't mirror b d ← exact	F: layout, contrast, usage of white space C: words to read, colour B: choices for: 1. Font types not quirk: ×a a✓ ×g g✓ don't mirror: b d 2. Similar word selection	- satisfaction - curiosity	badai doesn't mirror b, and high contrast

*their minor impairments are not included in this paper due to page limitation

Fig. 2. A design specification for dyslexic children's reading application [13]. The specification outlines the dyslexic children's impairments and suggested some computer supports. Some of the examples are also presented.

As illustrated in Fig. 2, special consideration on their need to have suitable and adjustable background colours, different coloured fonts to highlight syllable boundaries in a word, as well as adjustable font types and sizes, for example, would ease the learning process. The suggestions for computer support mainly focusing on the interface design and presentation of text on screen for dyslexics to read are indeed important for developing reading application for them. Therefore as depicted in Fig. 2, the interaction design dimensions – forms, content, and behavior – are emphasized together with certain sample of design that would create positive affect on dyslexic children. Nevertheless, the design leads us to 'play' with colours to design an effective and affective reading application.

3 Playing with Colours

With the unique reading pathways for dyslexic children, experimenting with colours might result in an optimal design to increase the potential for these children to read thus easing the process of reading. After all, the good news about dyslexia is that it can be remedied. If not, the dyslexics can actually read by activating alternative brain pathways to read correctly, but slowly, as have been mentioned. Since reading is an important skill to be acquired, methods have been proposed and used to teach them to read such as the multi-sensory method [14, 15].

Although the conventional methods do wonders in teaching them skills they need to read, using computers seems both potential and promising as it facilitate a more interesting, fun environment allowing them to be more motivated and less intimidated to learn to read [16, 17]. Since using colours is important to create ease of reading, thus facilitating the visual cues, we chose to select colour schemes based on the Irlen method [18] for text background colours (see Fig. 3). As for the text colours, we opt to allow the children to select their own colour preferences that they feel most comfortable with. Interestingly, from our observation we have discovered that the children read better when using their own choice of favourite colours for the text.

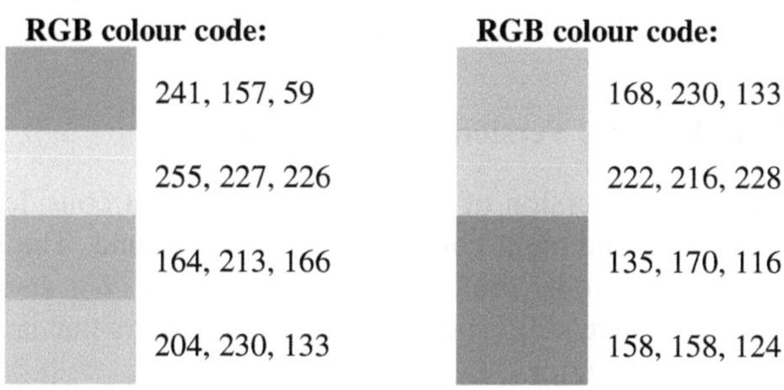

Fig. 3. The eight colours proposed by Irlen method [18] to be used as a way of 'treating' visual problems for dyslexics. The colours are presented together with their respective RGB colour code.

Since 2009, we have worked with dyslexic children of age 9 to 14. Their condition ranges from mild to severe dyslexia. We opt for personal bedside coaching and experiment since the children tend to lose attention very quickly. Although most studies [19, 20, 21] discovered 10-15 minutes attention span, we found that their attention span in reading Bahasa Melayu words is between 5 to 15 minutes, at most. The 5-minute attention span, specifically to the visuals being presented to them, is observed in those hyperactive dyslexics. Changing the visual contents such as colours and fonts size, or adding animation to the related texts help extends the duration.

We begin with coloured pencils and coloured papers and a set of vocabulary ranging from one to three syllables of all 23 syllable patterns of Bahasa Melayu. The first goal of this experiment was to show that different child has a different colour choices and that their choice can be used to improve their attention span and thus their reading ability. The second goal was to set an entry level in deciding on colours, fonts, and overall user interface for the computer prototype we intent to build.

4 BacaMAX

The experiments disclose problems that can easily be solved by colours. Of all the problems faced by the dyslexic children, seven problems with regards to reading can be mellowed. They are (1) syllable identification, (2) similar-sounding word confusion, (3) little interest in words and letters, (4) jumbling up letters or whole words, (5) reversal in reading words, (5) visually irritating glare from white paper or white background, and finally (7) their attention span.

Taking the results from our manual experiments with coloured pencils and coloured papers, we move on to developing the computer prototype, given a persona name, BacaMAX. Since 2009 we have had four versions of BacaMAX being tested by the children. Just like the experiments conducted on papers, experiments were conducted on a computer screen. With BacaMAX, the children have control over the background colour, syllable colour and font size. From each version, feedback from teachers and students were gathered in order to come out with improved versions. Figure 4, 5 and 6 elucidate the first three versions of BacaMAX.

4.1 BacaMAX: Beta Version, Version 1 and Version 2

Figure 4 illustrates the earliest version of BacaMAX (2009) that considers only one colour for the text, i.e. black, and eight colours for the background. The goal was to test on the types and sizes of fonts preferred by the children. We also wanted to confirm that Irlen colours [18] are still valid as background colours that are suitable in assisting reading among the dyslexics.

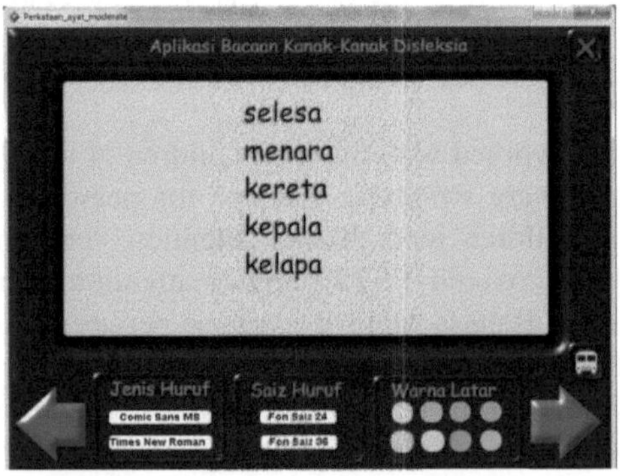

Fig. 4. The beta version of BacaMAX

Version 1 (2010) (illustrated in Fig. 5) is the modified version of BacaMAX that uses two distinct colours to represent each syllable in a word. The colours chosen are black and red, while the background colours remain the same eight. Black and red is the colour used by most books in early readings for normal children. The feedback that we gather was that the children prefer to have control on their choice of colours not only on the background but also on the syllable colours.

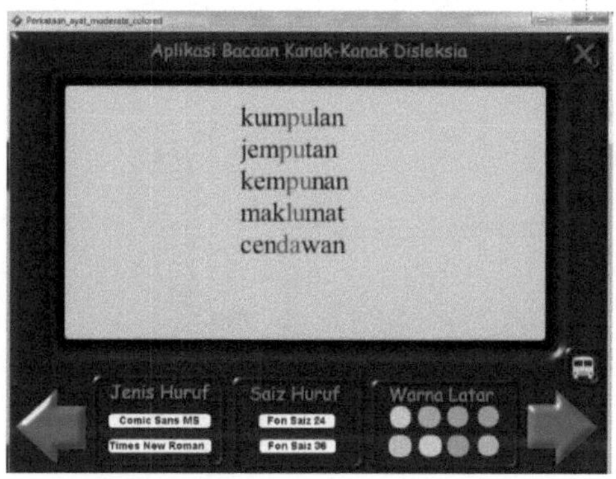

Fig. 5. BacaMAX's version 1

The improvement is reflected in version 2 of BacaMAX. In this version, the background colours still remain to be eight in total, are chosen as suggested in [18]. Another feature was added, i.e. the 'teacher' who is supposed to assist the children in case they need any help with the word. This version is a total makeover from version 1 where the minimalist concept is used in designing the user interface.

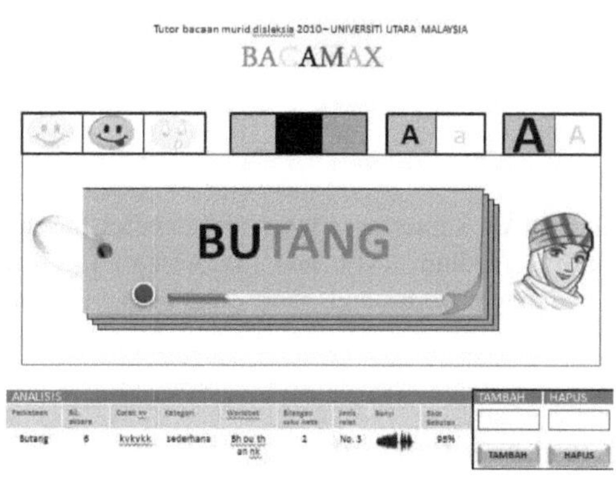

Fig. 6. The interface design for BacaMAX version 2. The smiley represents the difficulty level, the three colour represent the background and syllable colours, the A represents fonts size and fonts case (upper/lower).

4.2 BacaMAX: Version 3

In version 3, the concept designed for BacaMAX in version 2 is retained. However, the current version infused its design with a more child-friendly look. In version 3 a cute, green dinosaur called Dino is introduced while maintaining the minimalist concept with minimum text presented on the screen (Fig. 7). Dino is replacing the 'teacher', which is featured in the previous version, to function more like a 'help' button where users can click on its body to hear the correct reading of the words and sentences. The interface is designed in such a way that there are no other texts to read other than the word required.

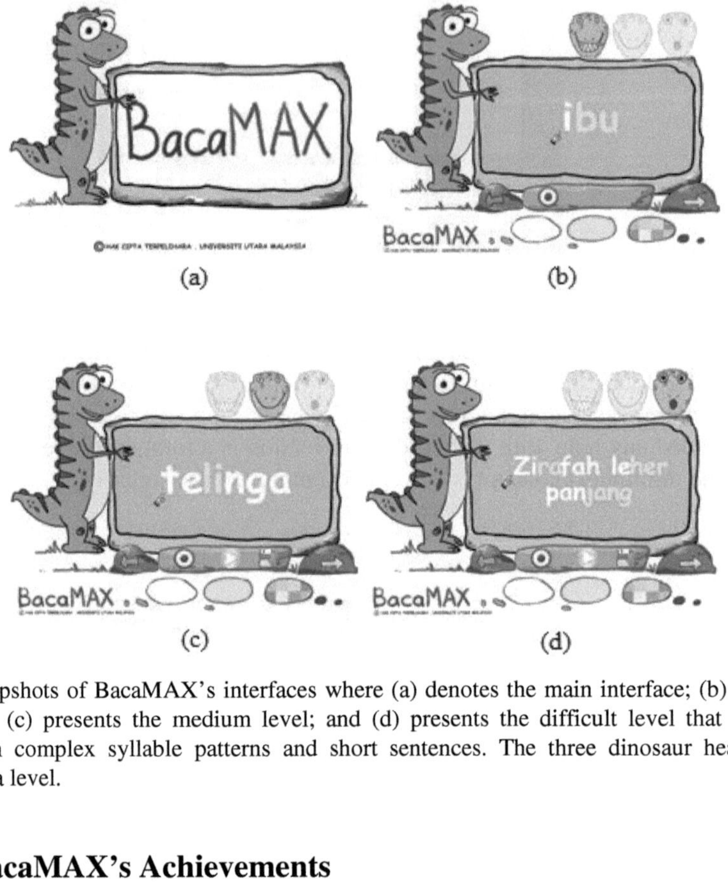

Fig. 7. Snapshots of BacaMAX's interfaces where (a) denotes the main interface; (b) presents level easy; (c) presents the medium level; and (d) presents the difficult level that involves words with complex syllable patterns and short sentences. The three dinosaur heads each represents a level.

5 BacaMAX's Achievements

Experiments with Version 3 of BacaMAX are still in progress at one of the schools in Kedah running a dyslexia class. Initial results of the experiment can be reported in terms of its general achievement in helping children reading words (and some sentences) in Bahasa Melayu. The achievement in terms of improvements in reading is clustered into seven problems mentioned earlier and listed in Table 2.

Table 2. Seven problems of which colour assistance facilitates some achievements

	Problems	Colour assistance	Achievement
1	Syllables identification	Different colour for different syllable (using their own colour choices)	*bu+nga* instead on *bun+ga*
2	Similar-sounding word confusion	Different colour for different syllable (using their own colour choices)	*duka, duga, buka*
3	Little interest in words and letters	Repeat same letter/word with different font colour/size/type	Increase attention span
4	Jumbling up letters or whole words	Use totally different syllable colour stroke and contrast for similar words	*kelapa* and *kepala* can be differentiated
5	Reversal in reading the words	Always use different colour for b/d/p when they appear in one word	Able to differentiate *b/d/p*
6	Glare from white paper or white background	Change paper colour/background on computer screen	Increase reading speed, with accuracy
7	Attention span	Combination of all the above	For hyper active dyslexic: from 5 to 10 minutes (100%) For normal dyslexics: no improvement in attention span

Yet to be observed specifically for readings are the (1) difficulties in acquiring phonic skills, (2) slow reading speed (with repetition in reading certain syllables), (3) inaccurate reading, in the case of omission of consonant/vowel/syllable/word, (4) frequent loss of the place when reading longer texts (an animation strategy would help), (5) an inability to skim through or scan over reading material, (6) a high degree of distractibility when reading, i.e. issues with gaining attention, (7) perceived distortion of text (this is for severe cases where words may seem to float off the page or run together)

Other than colour, animation is another viable strategy that can be ventured in order to assist dyslexic children in reading. Issues with frequent loss of the place when reading longer texts and distraction can be tackled with a smart animation strategy.

6 Conclusion

The design for BacaMAX's interface applies the concept of reading by colours proposed by Irlen for her exceptional effort to help people with reading disabilities to read. Since dyslexics are having difficulties, 'playing' with colours seems to be a potential solution that could leverage their reading, or at least ease their reading. The interface design, which emphasized on minimalist concept design, does indeed manage to ease reading for dyslexic children reading in Malay. Not only the interface has been designed exclusively for the children, the content and its presentation are designed specifically for them too. The words and simple sentences, which are grouped in three levels denoted by three dinosaur heads, are presented according to the syllable patterns. Here is where colours play their role – each syllable in a word is represented by a colour that is chosen by the children. BacaMAX has other features such as recording and voice replay, however only features related to colours are discussed in this paper. While further research remains necessary to include other explanatory factors, this study provides strong evidence that poor reading performance in dyslexia stems from visual processing deficit where colours can be of valuable help.

Acknowledgments. This research is financially funded by the Ministry of Higher Education Malaysia under the Fundamental Research Grant Scheme (FRGS).

References

1. Singleton, C.: Computer and Dyslexia: Implications for Policy and Practice, Dyslexia Computer Resource Centre, United Kingdom (2006)
2. Shaywitz, S.: Overcoming Dyslexia. A. A. Knopf Distributed by Random House, New York (2003)
3. Frost, J.: Phonemic Awareness, Spontaneous Writing, and Reading and Spelling Development from a Preventive Perspective. Reading and Writing: An Interdisciplinary Journal 14, 487–513 (2001)
4. Lundberg, I.: The Computer as a Tool of Remediation In the Education of Students with Reading Disabilities: A Theory-based Approach. Learning Disability Quarterly 18, 88–99 (1995)
5. Shaywitz, S.E.: Dyslexia, pp. 98–104. Scientific American (1996)
6. Snowling, M.J.: Dyslexia, 2nd edn. Blackwell Publishers, United Kingdom (2000)
7. Wolf, M.: What Time Tell: Towards a New Conceptualization of Developmental Dyslexia. Annals of Dyslexia 49, 3–28 (1999)
8. Ziegler, J.: Do Differences in Brain Activation Challenge the Universal Theories of Dyslexia? Brain and Language 98, 341–343 (2006)
9. Beneventi, H., Tonessen, F.E., Ersland, L., Hugdahl, K.: Executive Working Memory Processes in Dyslexia: Behavioral and fMRI Evidence. Scandinavian Journal of Psychology 51, 192–202 (2010)
10. Paulesu, E.: Is Developmental Dyslexia a Disconnection Syndrome? Evidence from PET Scanning. Brain. 119, 143–157 (1996)
11. Ramus, F., Rosen, S., Dakin, S.C., Day, B.L., Catellote, J.M., White, S., Frith, U.: Theories of Developmental Dyslexia: Insights from a Multiple Case Study of Dyslexic Adults. Brain 126, 841–865 (2003)
12. Stein, J., Walsh, V.: To See But Not to Read: The Magnocellular Theory of Dyslexia. TINS 20, 147–152 (1997)
13. Zulikha, J., Husniza, H., Fakhrul, A.A.: An IxD Support Model with Affective Characteristics for Dyslexic Children's Reading Application. In: Proceedings of International Conference on Computing and Informatics, pp. 141–146 (2011)
14. Handler, S.M., Fierson, W.M.: Learning Disabilities, Dyslexia, and Vision. Pediatrics 127, 818–856 (2011)
15. Birsh, J.R.: Multisensory Teaching of Basic Language Skills. Paul H. Brookes Pub. Co., Baltimore (2011)
16. Southeast Comprehensive Center: Multisensory Structured Language Programs for Students with Characteristics of Dyslexia, `http://secc.sedl.org/orc/rr/secc_rr_00059.pdf`

17. Lerner, J.: Learning Disabilities: Theories, Diagnosis, and Teaching Strategies. Houghton Mifflin Company, Boston (1997)
18. Irlen, H.: Reading by the Colors: Overcoming Dyslexia and Other Reading Disabilities through the Irlen Method. Perigee, New York (2005)
19. Lobier, M., et al.: The Visual Attention Span Deficit in Dyslexia is Visual and Not Verbal, Cortex (2011), doi:10.1016/j.cortex.2011.09.003
20. Bosse, M.L., Tainturier, M.J., Valdois, S.: Developmental Dyslexia: The Visual Attention Span Deficit Hypothesis. Cognition 104, 198–230 (2007)
21. Bosse, M.L., Valdois, S.: Influence of the Visual Attention Span on Child Reading Performance: A Cross-sectional Study. Journal of Research in Reading 32, 230–253 (2009)

Evaluation of Mobile Games Using Playability Heuristics

Sarmad Soomro, Wan Fatimah Wan Ahmad, and Suziah Sulaiman

Department of Computer & Information Sciences
Universiti Teknologi PETRONAS
Bandar Seri Iskandar
31750 Tronoh,
Perak Darul Ridzuan, Malaysia
sarmad.iu@gmail.com, {fatimhd,suziah}@petronas.com.my

Abstract. Touch screen mobile devices have begun to better facilitate different game playing while gaining greater attention among users. 'Playability' is an important element that measures the ease by which games can be played. It is evaluated by two common methods; heuristic evaluation, and playtesting. Several heuristics have been proposed to evaluate playability but users still face playability problems. This paper attempts to evaluate existing mobile games using the heuristic evaluation method in order to examine the extent in which the heuristics support playability. Two sets of existing playability heuristics were used in the study. Six android games of different genres were evaluated by fourteen test participants. The study result reveals that existing playability heuristics lack the capability of identifying playability problems. These problems are usability, mobility, gameplay, and the multiplayer function for touch screen mobile game applications. Thus, there is a need for a new set of playability heuristics that extensively cover all aspects of playability.

Keywords: heuristics, playability, heuristic evaluation, mobile games.

1 Introduction

Presently, video games are not only designed and developed for fun and entertainment but they also play an important role in education, military, medical, and business sectors. There are a number of gaming platforms available and widely used such as PC games, console games and mobile games. In recent years, mobile games have gained increasing attention as compared to other gaming platforms. The reason for the rapid growth of mobile games is the mobility of the mobile phone. Mobile games can be played "anytime-anywhere" [1] and [2]. These games are very popular among all ages, including children, teenagers, adults and senior citizens. The growth of mobile game use increases daily and thus it attracts game developing companies to produce and commercialize even more games. However, it is a challenging task for game developing companies to produce good-quality games.

Designing and developing a game are the initial stages in the production of a good-quality game that ensure the provision of adequate features. A good quality game must be fun, learnable, convenient, reliable and, more important, it should be easily

H. Badioze Zaman et al. (Eds.): IVIC 2013, LNCS 8237, pp. 264–274, 2013.

playable. To evaluate these factors of a proposed game, two common methods are widely used; playtesting and heuristic evaluation. Play-testing is a traditional method that is widely used for all gaming platforms. It is carried out to uncover design problems in the game's interface during the initial development stage and is usually called the 'alpha' version of the game. To conduct an effective evaluation, the game should be fully functional and playable.

A heuristic evaluation method was proposed by Neilsen & Molich (1990) [3] to test the usability of software applications. In this method, usability experts went through the software to uncover interface problems that may be faced by end-users. However, it is not necessary for any identified problem in the heuristic evaluation to be identical with problems users might face, as the method is predictive of such problems [4]. Nevertheless, heuristic evaluation with traditional 'usability' heuristics cannot be directly applied to the evaluation of video games because application software and video games are very different in context and usability heuristics do not cover all aspects of gaming such as fun, entertainment, and enjoyment [4], [5] and [6]. Heuristic evaluation has only recently received greater attention by game researchers and usability experts. Several game-domain heuristics have been proposed by researchers to investigate the playability of games [1], [2], [5], [7], [8], [9] and [10].

This paper investigates the extent to which existing playability heuristic for mobile games are useful in uncovering playability problems. We also investigate existing playability heuristics for mobile games that do not support different gaming genres. This study selected two existing sets of playability heuristic as proposed by Korhonen & Koivisto [1] and [2]. The first set of heuristics covers the game's usability, mobility and gameplay while the second evaluates the multiplayer feature of mobile games.

The organization of this paper is as follows: The second section covers the analysis of existing heuristics for video games. The third section presents the methodology for conducting the evaluation. The fourth section presents data analysis and results. The fifth section summarizes and discusses the results. The sixth section presents the study's conclusions as well as suggestions for future research.

2 Literature Review

A number of usability and domain-specific heuristics were proposed by several researchers in recent years. However, the development of heuristics does not prove their efficacy, as they must also be validated. In heuristic validation, each heuristic is evaluated according to its relevance in designating usability problems. In the common approach, each heuristic is compared with a playability problem and the rate of the problem's severity as to how well that heuristic defines a problem [4], [11], [12] and [13].

The first heuristics for video gaming were proposed by Malone in 1980 [14] and were basically concerned with designing an enjoyable user interface. The author categorized heuristics into three types: challenges, fantasy, and curiosity. Whereas the author subscribed challenges to goals, curiosity was described by the audio and visual effects that enhanced the fantasy, and fantasy itself was related to the allurement of the interface. However, these heuristics were insufficient and proved valid only for high level issues in the games. These heuristics also lacked the ability to identify playability issues.

Clanton proposed fifteen principles for video games in 1988 [15]. His main purpose was to facilitate game design in order to achieve user interest. Moreover, he recommended that Human-Computer interactions in computer gaming can be categorized according to the game's interface and mechanics in addition to Gameplay. Gameplay concerns functional aspects of the game; i.e., the 'things' a player needs to do to achieve the game's objectives. Game Mechanics describe the game's behavior. Game Interface refers to how the player controls objects in the game and how elements are illustrated on the screen. These principles can be considered heuristics in which each has a brief description.

Federoff compiled a list of playability heuristics considered the first specific heuristic schemata for video games due to its structure and modeling [5]. These heuristics were developed by inspecting usability literature and the performance of a field study for a game development company. Based on a literature review, observations and interviews, Federoff proposed a list of forty heuristics that focused on three features of computer gaming: "game interface", "game mechanics", and "game playability". Most of the proposed heuristics in his study focused on gameplay, engagement and storyline elements. Moreover, some usability aspects were widely covered as well. However, these heuristics were not validated, either due to a lack of results or the failure to publish results by the author.

Desurvire et al. [7] proposed heuristics for the evaluation of Playability (HEP). This list was comprehensive and based on the literature for productivity and playtesting methods. It reviewed heuristics that were specific for computer games. The authors divided these heuristics into four categories; game-play, game-story, game-mechanics and game-usability. These heuristics were validated by evaluating early game prototypes with a play-testing method and then comparing results to the HEP evaluation. The results of their study advocated HEP heuristics as efficient means for the identification of game-play and game-usability issues. However, they did not widely cover game-story and game-mechanic issues. Nevertheless, it did establish that HEP evaluation identified more playability problems when compared to a play-testing user study [7].

In 2006, Korhonen & Koivisto [1] proposed Playability Heuristics for Mobile Games. These heuristics were created by studying the mobile context, a literature review, and by a mobile game evaluation using existing playability heuristics. They presented twenty-nine heuristics divided into three categorize as follows: 'Game-Usability', 'Game-Mobility' and 'Game-Play'. 'Game-Play' defines a user's interaction with other objects in the game. 'Game-Mobility' defines how easily a player is involved in the game's venue and how it behaves under unclear conditions. 'Game-Usability' covers a player's interaction with the game's world and with other players. These heuristics widely covered important gaming features but also revealed some remaining playability problems that were unidentified up to that time which were not widely explored. Later in 2007, the authors proposed a new category consisting of eight heuristics for multiplayer games. These heuristic were found to be effective in identifying playability problems in multiplayer mobile games [2].

Despite the unidentified playability problems, heuristics did cover the core aspects of games and also identified serious playability problems. Due to intense testing, most heuristics were easily understood by simply reading the heading. In addition, authors stated that heuristic models were segmented so that each module could be evaluated separately.

Paavilainen [16] highlighted a few major issues with the cited heuristics and reported that some could be merged into one. For example, for Game-Usability heuristics such as "Control keys are consistent and follow standard conventions" and "Game controls are convenient and flexible" may be merged into one because both reflect each other. Another example was that of "There are no repetitive or boring Tasks" and "The game does not stagnate". These are similar and may be merged.

In 2007, Schaffer introduced heuristics for Game-Usability [8]. He argued that earlier heuristics lacked concrete examples which made them less defined. The heuristics proposed by Schaffer were based on the literature and his own expertise from the field of Human Computer Interaction. Schaffer divided his heuristics into five categories: General, Graphical User Interface, Gameplay, Control Mapping, and Level Design. These categories comprised a total of twenty-one heuristics with descriptions for each one.

Pinelle et al. [9] proposed a new set of heuristics to inspect usability issues in video games. They conclude that these heuristics were only applicable to game prototypes during the initial developmental phase. The author presented ten heuristics that covered usability aspects and the authors described how common usability problems could be avoided. However, these heuristics did not cover other features such as "game-play, mobility and multiplayer" features. Pinelle et al. introduced an additional ten usability heuristics for multiplayer gaming [17]. These heuristics were validated through evaluations of single player and multiplayer games.

In 2012, Soomro et. al. [18] conducted a 'user experience' based survey for mobile games. A questionnaire based on playability heuristics as proposed by Korhonen & Koivisto [1] and [2] was formulated. The purpose of the studies was to explore playability problems which users faced in their daily routing while playing mobile games. They proposed a further ten playability heuristics for mobile games.

We have reviewed those proposed heuristics for the evaluation of video games from 1982 to 2012. Some sets of heuristics covered only general usability issues and others covered fun and engagement issues in games. Each researcher focused on a specific aspect of the game while other aspects of gaming were not raised. This indicates that there is no general set of heuristics for the evaluation of video games with multiple platforms. The heuristics cited above are useful to some extent but they do not cover all aspects of video gaming.

Furthermore, the size of heuristic sets is also an important factor. Federoff [5] proposed forty heuristics and Desurvire et al. [19] proposed forty-three heuristics. Large heuristic sets have been considered problematic for evaluators as regards the ease of the evaluation because the user confronts difficulty when browsing through a large list of heuristics [20]. The literature also reported that small heuristic sets were ambiguous and thus, also problematic [9] because evaluators were confused when trying to identify and associate problems with more than one heuristic. Hence, evaluators did not discover the most viable heuristics for problem identification.

3 Methodology

In this study, two sets of playability heuristic (Table 1) were considered for the purposes of evaluation. These sets were designed for mobile game applications with respect to the mobile context. In addition, these heuristics supported different gaming genres and styles, such as single and multiplayer gaming.

Table 1. Playability Heuristics [1] – [2]

Category	Keyword	Heuristic
Usability[1]	GU1	Audio-visual representation supports the game
	GU2	Screen layout is efficient and visually pleasing
	GU3	Device UI and game UI are used for their own purposes
	GU4	Indicators are visible
	GU5	The player understands the terminology
	GU6	Navigation is consistent, logical, and minimalist
	GU7	Control keys are consistent and follow standard conventions
	GU8	Game controls are convenient and flexible
	GU9	The game gives feedback on the player's actions
	GU10	The player cannot make irreversible errors
	GU11	The player does not have to memorize things unnecessarily
	GU12	The game contains help
Mobility[1]	MO1	The game and play sessions can be started quickly
	MO2	The game accommodates with the surroundings
	MO3	Interruptions are handled responsibly
Gameplay[1]	GP1	The game provides clear goals or support player-created goals
	GP2	The player sees the progress in the game and can compare the results
	GP3	The players are rewarded and rewards are meaningful
	GP4	The players in in control
	GP5	Challenge, strategy, and pace are in balance
	GP6	The first-time experience is encouraging
	GP7	The game story supports the gameplay and is meaningful
	GP8	There are no repetitive or boring tasks
	GP9	The players can express themselves
	GP10	The game supports different playing styles
	GP11	The game does not stagnate
	GP12	The game is consistent
	GP13	The game uses orthogonal unit differentiation
	GP14	The player does not lose any hard-won possessions
Multiplayer[2]	MP1	The game supports communication
	MP2	There are reasons to communicate
	MP3	The game helps the player to find other players and game instances
	MP4	The game supports groups and communities
	MP5	The design minimizes deviant behavior
	MP6	The design hides the effects of the network

In order to evaluate mobile games by using selected playability heuristics, fourteen participants were recruited from the university. Each participant had experience with playing mobile and computer games and also attended the usability inspection course during their studies. The gaming style of each participant was different so they were divided into two groups. Some of the participants preferred single player games while others preferred multiplayer games. Before forming these groups, the necessary background data for each user was collected.

Six commercial Android games were selected from different game genres. The purpose for selecting different game genres was to test the scope of the given heuristics. The characteristics of the study's selected games are listed in Table 2. These selections were based on the highest internet ratings. All games were downloaded from Google's play store, some were free and some were paid versions.

Table 2. Game Characteristics

Game	Game Genre	Player Mode	Target Players	Devices	Evaluators
A	Action/Adventure	Single	15+ Male/Female	Mobile Devices	4
B	Puzzle/Strategy	Single	15+ Male/Female	Mobile Devices	4
C	Simulation	Single	15+ Male/Female	Mobile Devices	4
D	Arcade	Single	15+ Male/Female	Mobile Devices	4
E	Racing/Multiplayer	Multiplayer	15+ Male/Female	Mobile Devices	4
F	Shooter/Multiplayer	Multiplayer	15+ Male/Female	Mobile Devices	4

Before starting the evaluation, a brief introduction was given to participants regarding the evaluation process with the selected playability heuristics and how to report problems. In addition, other instructions were given as to the navigation keys for the mobile phone. The reason for the briefing was because users may not have been familiar with the mobile phone model chosen for the task. Participants were instructed to record (write) any identifiable problems in the report sheets provided for the purpose, along with problem severity as per given guidelines.

Evaluations were conducted over three days. Day one was divided into two sessions. In the first session, four participants evaluated Game A, and in second session, four participants evaluated Game B. Similarly, on the second day, four participants evaluated Game C and four participants evaluated Game D. On the third day, a single session was undertaken in which four participant evaluated games E and F. At the beginning of each session, participants received an android mobile phone on which the games were installed, a list of playability heuristics, and a problem report sheet. This approach was adopted from Korhonen [4].

From the onset, participants were free to play the game as they wished and were not instructed to achieve any particular goal. Each session lasted for an average of one and half hours. During the evaluation, participants were advised not to discuss identified problems with each other, which then allowed for a maximum number of distinctly identifiable problems. Participants describe problems in their own words and assigned such problems to a violated heuristic and also stated the severity of the problem (low, medium and critical). At the end of the session, problem report sheets were collected and each participant was interviewed regarding their evaluation experience.

4 Data Analysis and Results

Participants reported a total of one-hundred-twenty-one (121) problems in six games (Table 3). Forty-seven problems were found for Game-Play (Fig 1); thirty-nine problems were found in Game-Usability (Fig 2); seventeen problems were found for Game-Mobility (Fig 3); and eighteen problems were found for the Multiplayer function (Fig 4).

Table 3. Problems Identified

Game Feature	No. of Identified Problems	Weightage %
Gameplay	47	38.84%
Usability	39	32.23%
Mobility	17	14.04%
Multiplayer	18	14.87%
Total	121	100%

Game-Play is the core of any game and is considered a most critical phase of the evaluation due to its dynamic nature. Game-Play is very different for each game as players interact with respective game mechanics. Results from this phase of the evaluation cited the maximum number of problems identified related to game-play issues. Heuristics GP1 ('the game provides clear goals or supports player-created goals'); GP5 ('challenge, strategy and pace are in balance'); GP6 ('the first-time experience is encouraging'); and GP7 ('the game story supports the gameplay and is meaningful') were maximally violated. Problems violating these heuristics indicated that the games did not provide clear goals and the pace of game was unbalanced. Additionally, each of thirteen other heuristics were violated excepting one, GP9 ('the player can express themselves'). In addition, four new gameplay problems were identified, each of which did not have a proper heuristic. (See Fig. 1).

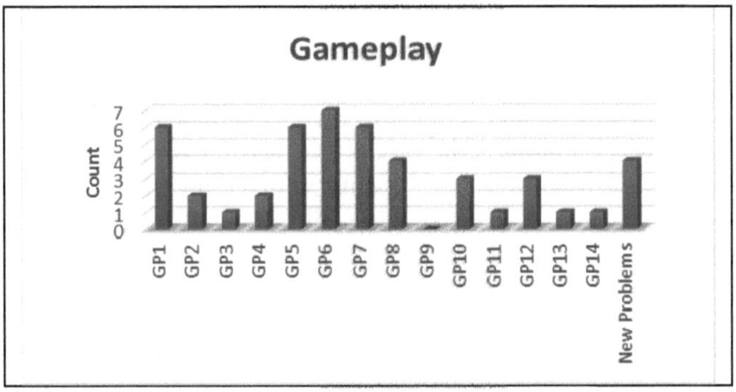

Fig. 1. Playability problems violating Gameplay Heuristics

Participants reported that 'Game-Usability' (GU) heuristics were much easier to understand and that they did not face similar problems while reporting as those they confronted during 'game-play' heuristics. A total number of thirty-nine problems were reported that violated game-usability heuristics. (See Fig. 2) Nine new usability issues were also identified and reported. It became obvious that the maximum number of problems identified regarding usability were new as they were not supported by extant usability heuristics, most of which were related to the touch screen interface.

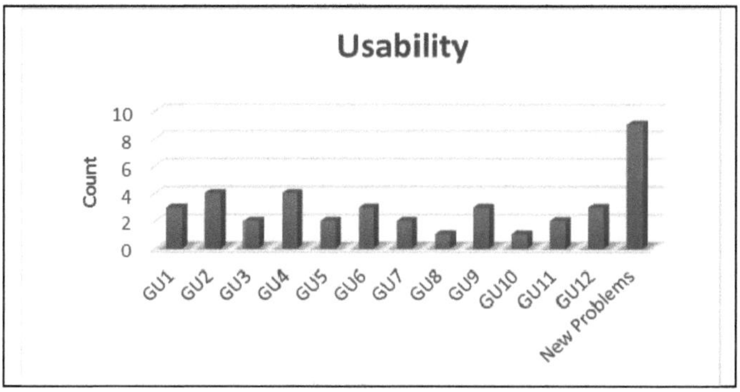

Fig. 2. Playability problems violated Game Usability Heuristics

'Mobility' heuristics were also violated. (See Fig. 3) Seventeen game mobility problems were reported by participants. In addition, three new problems were reported by participants, which were related to interruptions faced during game playing. Participants reported that the games were not able to handle internal interruptions occurring during the play operation; interruptions such as email, messaging and call alerts. Participants also reported that touch screen mobile phones were difficult to handle they you wanted to play while walking.

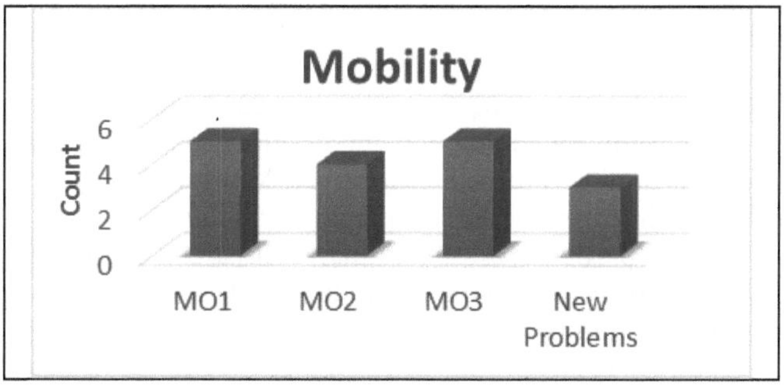

Fig. 3. Playability problems violated Mobility Heuristics

Four participants reported eighteen problems that violated 'multiplayer' heuristics, in addition to eleven problems that violated other existing heuristics. Seven new problems were also identified during the evaluation. (See Fig. 4) These latter problems were related to communication and the medium of connectivity between players. Participants added that it was very difficult to communicate with other players during the game because the games only supported a chat feature. Moreover, participants also reported that the games supported only the Wi-Fi medium of connectivity with other players which restricted the boundary of multiplayer gaming to a local area for wireless gaming.

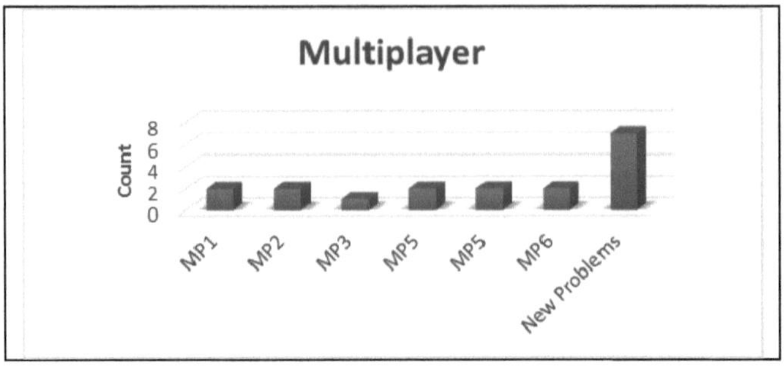

Fig. 4. Playability problems violated Game Multiplayer

5 Discussion

This study revealed the limits of existing sets of useful playability heuristics in the evaluation of mobile games. The results demonstrate that existing playability heuristics need to be refined even further. Although most heuristics are useful and support core aspects of gaming, new playability problems were identified. The studied heuristics remain valuable in the mobile context, nevertheless, new gameplay, usability, mobility and multiplayer problems were identified that are not supported by existing heuristics. The study also found a lack of 'touch screen' usability heuristics in existing playability heuristic sets. In the present era of new mobile technologies, touch screen interface issues cannot be ignored.

Additionally, current mobile phone technologies are very potent and capable of multitasking. Powerful CPUs, GPUs and instantaneous communication technology allow for mobile phones to perform greater gaming such as RPG and Racing Multiplayer. This study found that existing multiplayer heuristics are both acceptable and able to identify limited problems. However, Multiplayer heuristics remain in need of improvement with respect to current gaming technologies.

Moreover, some participants stated that heuristic terminology was sometimes unclear and that not a few heuristics appeared redundant, which then caused difficulties when assigning identified problems. In addition, such ambiguity in heuristics may cause biased results. It was also reported by participants that the heuristics list was far too large and thus also, too difficult to browse through while assigning identified problems.

The problems and issues identified in this study are supported by the literature review [16], [21] and [4] as other researchers have reported identical issues for playability. Furthermore, it is not yet established which playability heuristics are generically suitable for all games or applicable to different platforms. Moreover, usability experts do not yet know whether or not playability heuristics are useful or how they can best be utilized during evaluation. In addition, we revealed that experts used their own expertise and knowledge when identifying playability problems during evaluation. Nevertheless, the reason for developing heuristics is to provide guidelines for evaluators when assessing critical aspects of playability [4].

6 Conclusion and Future Work

This study evaluated six android games using a heuristic evaluation method. Two sets of existing playability heuristics were used to evaluate and validate the extent to which these heuristics are useful for mobile games. The results of this study indicate that existing playability heuristics lack certain abilities to identify all playability problems. Several new playability issues were discovered that are not supported by existing playability heuristics.

The results of this research suggest a need for a new set of playability heuristics for mobile games that supports innovative features and core aspects of the present gaming era. This study therefore recommends the development of a new set of playability heuristics that support touch screen usability and mobility issues for mobile phones. We therefore propose this as a goal for a future research paper.

References

1. Korhonen, H.: Playability Heuristics for Mobile Games. Human Factors, 9–16 (2006)
2. Korhonen, H., Koivisto, E.M.I.: Playability heuristics for mobile multi-player games. In: Proceedings of the 2nd International Conference on Digital Interactive Media in Entertainment and Arts, pp. 28–35. ACM (2007)
3. Nielsen, J., Molich, R.: Heuristic evaluation of user interfaces. In: Proceedings of the SIGCHI Conference on Human Factors in Computing Systems: Empowering People, pp. 249–256. ACM (1990)
4. Korhonen, H.: The explanatory power of playability heuristics. In: Proceedings of the 8th International Conference on, 1 (2011)
5. Federoff, M.A.: Heuristics and usability guidelines for the creation and evaluation of fun in video games. FUN in Video Games Thesis University Graduate School of Indiana University Dec. Master of, pp. 52 (2002)
6. Johnson, D., Wiles, J.: Effective affective user interface design in games. Ergonomics, 46 (2003)
7. Desurvire, H., Blvd, W., Rey, M., Caplan, M.: Using Heuristics to Evaluate the Playability of Games. Defense, 1509–1512 (2004)
8. Schaffer, N.: Heuristics for usability in games, pp. 1–30 (2007), `http://www.playerfriendly.com`
9. Pinelle, D., Wong, N., Stach, T.: Heuristic evaluation for games: usability principles for video game design. In: Proceeding of the Twenty-sixth Annual SIGCHI Conference on Human Factors in Computing Systems, pp. 1453–1462. ACM (2008)
10. Desurvire, H., Wiberg, C.: Game usability heuristics (PLAY) for evaluating and designing better games: The next iteration. In: Ozok, A.A., Zaphiris, P. (eds.) OCSC 2009. LNCS, vol. 5621, pp. 557–566. Springer, Heidelberg (2009)
11. Nielsen, J.: Enhancing the explanatory power of usability heuristics. In: Conference Companion on Human factors in Computing Systems, CHI 1994, pp. 152–158 (1994)

12. Somervell, J., Mccrickard, D.S.: Comparing Generic vs. Specific Heuristics: Illustrating a New UEM Comparison Technique. Source (2001)
13. Mankoff, J., Dey, A.K., Hsieh, G., Kientz, J., Lederer, S., Ames, M.: Heuristic evaluation of ambient displays. In: Cockton, G., Korhonen, P. (eds.) Proceedings of the Conference on Human Factors in Computing Systems CHI 2003, pp. 169–176. ACM Press (2003)
14. Malone, T.T.W.: Heuristics for designing enjoyable user interfaces: Lessons from computer games. Human Factors in Computer Systems, 63–68 (1982)
15. Clanton, C.: An Interpreted Demonstration of Computer Game Design. Most, 7–8 (1998)
16. Paavilainen, J.: Critical Review on Video Game Evaluation Heuristics: Social Games Perspective. Human Factors, 56–65 (2010)
17. Pinelle, D., Wong, N., Stach, T., Gutwin, C.: Usability heuristics for networked multiplayer games. In: Proceedings of the ACM 2009, pp. 169–178 (2009)
18. Soomro, S., Ahmad, W.F.W., Sulaiman, S.: A preliminary study on heuristics for mobile games. In: 2012 International Conference on Computer & Information Science (ICCIS), pp. 1030–1035. IEEE (2012)
19. Desurvire, H., Blvd, W., Rey, M., Caplan, M.: Using Heuristics to Evaluate the Playability of Games. Defense, 1509–1512 (2004)
20. Korhonen, H.: Expert Review Method in Game Evaluations – Comparison of Two Playability Heuristic Sets. Development, 74–81 (2009)
21. Korhonen, H.: Comparison of playtesting and expert review methods in mobile game evaluation. In: Proceedings of the 3rd International Conference on. pp. 18–27 (2010)

Children's Technology: How Do Children Want It?

Fariza Hanis Abdul Razak,
Khairiyah Salleh, and Noor Hidayah Azmi

Department of Information Technology, Faculty of Computer & Mathematical Sciences,
Universiti Teknologi MARA (UiTM),
40450 Shah Alam, Malaysia
fariza@tmsk.uitm.edu.my, khairiyah_salleh@yahoo.com,
noorhidayah84@gmail.com

Abstract. Though today's children have many chances to interact with IT technology, what they understand about technology from their point of view still needs to be explored. In this paper, we report how children view technology according to their perspectives. We used qualitative research methods that employed drawing activity and interviews. Seventeen 11-12 years old primary school children participated in the study and produced five drawings. From the study we found that the children actually wanted technology which is ubiquitous, wearable, natural in interaction and child-centred.

Keywords: children, children technology, participatory design, drawing, child-centred, child computer interaction.

1 Introduction

Children are changing. Today, children are more highly connected to the World Wide Web than children of previous generations [12]. They have had lifelong use of communications and media technologies such as instant messaging, text messaging, MP3 players, Smartphone, tablet computer technologies, social networking, earning them the nickname "digital natives" [10]. Grail Research Analysis describes these children as " ... proficient with and dependent on technology; media multi-taskers; and more accessible, on a more regular basis, through different communication channels.." [1]. Despite their proficiency and dependency on technology, they have never been considered seriously as a part of technology design team. In other words, they have not been invited to get involved in any technology design (active participation) from children. Very often they become users and testers. Technologists decide how to design for children and parents decide what technology to use for the children.

According to Ruland et al., designing for children brings different sets of demands and challenges, as children have different perceptions and make sense of the world around them differently from adults [17]. Their ideas on motivating and fun aspects of technological systems may likely be different from what the adults can anticipate as

H. Badioze Zaman et al. (Eds.): IVIC 2013, LNCS 8237, pp. 275–284, 2013.

the children expectation and how they make meaning in the computer applications may not be aligned to the designers' assumptions [5].

Due to this, we were motivated to undertake a design study which involved children both as informants and designers. It was our first attempt to understand technologies from children's point of views. In this paper we will highlight how these children actually perceive technology for them.

2 Child Computer Interaction

Human-computer interaction (HCI) community in its pursuit of developing user-centric interactive systems has propounded that the methodologies in the design and evaluation should be driven by knowledge of target users. It should not conveniently accept the central tenet that a single design fits all [9]. Traditional user-centred design has been criticized for focusing too much on HCI principles pertaining to adult users and neglecting on issues related to children [9, 19].

Traditionally children have been the focus of research rather than participants in the research itself [2, 16]. The assumptions and requirements of the adult researchers have taken precedence over the views and opinions of children themselves with adult researchers being content in the knowledge that they were once children and therefore know how children think, know their likes and dislikes, and have a shared view of the world around them [21]. It is through the introduction and adoption of user-centred and participatory research methods that this stance has been challenged, highlighting the importance of children's own ideas and opinions.

Children at different ages interact differently with technological systems due to their varied cognitive and emotional developmental needs, skills, and knowledge [9]. For example, younger children of between 3 and 7 years old do not have fully developed reasoning skills, so the products developed for them should be based on concrete concepts. On the other hand, older children of between 8 and 12 years old have started to develop a sense of logic, reasoning, and simple abstractions, so more complex and challenging concepts such as means-ends thinking can be integrated into the products. It is important to conceptualize and design the game to meet the characteristics and needs of a specific age group, as expanding to suit a bigger age audience will most likely make it suitable for no one [11]. In developmental games for children, user-centered design practices call for the involvement of children in the game design process, as it is agreed that children can provide useful insights [6].

A common mistake in designing products for children is not involving the potential users for which the games are intended due to the traditional power structure of the "all-knowing" adult and the "all-learning" child [4].

Druin demonstrated in her research that children can play the role of user, tester, informant, and partner in the technology design process [4]. She strongly advocated the competence of children in giving ideas and suggestions. Scaife et al. discovered that the children had well-articulated representations of their expectations of interactive software in general and had ideas about designs from specific to abstract [18]. In their research to evaluate concepts for new games, Hanna et al. posited that even in the early concept stages of the product development life-cycle, children could effectively evaluate the appeal and potential of game concepts [6].

As children are consumers of various entertainment technologies, nowadays their participation in game development and evaluation is a key factor. Children represent a heterogeneous user group having varying cognitive, emotional and social skills and require extremely careful design for experiments. According to Pyyko and Hellsten, different research methods have been adapted to involve children in computer product design of new children's technologies. When conducting user research with children, it is especially important to minimize the power structures and authority between adult and child and provide supportive natural and social environment to decrease impact of pleasing and scaring [14].

3 Methodology

3.1 Methods

We did a brainstorming session with a group of primary school children. In this session, we asked children to draw a technology for them. We employed drawing activity and interviews as our methods to gather children's perception on technology.

3.2 Participants

The selection of children was made through the purposive sampling where the children were selected because of some characteristics [13]. We chose children who had experiences in using different types of technologies, ranging from the Internet, social networks, gaming technologies, to mobile technologies. We also specified the child age to participate in our study. We used Facebook for the invitation and managed to get seventeen 11-12 years old children. All of them live in Kuala Lumpur. We purposely chose these group of children as these children have cognitively started to develop a sense of logic, reasoning, and simple abstractions, so more complex and challenging concepts such as means-ends thinking that can be integrated into the products [9].

3.3 Drawing Activity

The drawing activity was conducted to gain in depth understanding on children's technology from their points of views [15]. To do this, we asked them to pretend to be a technology designer and design a new technology that is suitable for them.

The drawing was supposed to be done in pairs, however, some of them were reluctant to do it together with their friends, thus, chose to do it alone.

In this activity the children spent around 30-40 minutes to finish their drawings. We provided them with the drawing papers, colour pencils and other stationeries. We just facilitated the session with little assistance from us. This was to ensure that the effect of us as observers on them could be minimized as much as possible. We encouraged them to create their own IT gadgets with their own needs, desires, and preferences based on their experiences, knowledge and creativity.

Fig. 1. Children drawing pictures

3.4 Interviews

After we collected the drawings from the children, first we tried to understand them based on our knowledge. However, we failed to understand the meaning of the gadget from the drawings. Thus, we decided to do follow-up interviews with the same participants to find out the meanings of their drawings. These interviews were done a week later.

4 Results

The first drawing is called iPPLe, an IT gadget which is suitable for young kids who like to be online wherever they go and comes in an apple shape. iPPLe has a touch screen and has social network applications such as Facebook and Twitter, Games, Browser, and other basic application includes Camera, Music and Calculator. The size of iPPLe is the same as nowadays tablets. The screen should be large and have high resolution images.

Fig. 2. First drawing - iPPLe

The second drawing is called YEAH, the IT spectacles gadget that comes with hand bracelet as the sensor together with Bluetooth necklace. The YEAH spectacles have a speaker on each side so that when a user wears the spectacles, he or she can see the video and at the same time hear the sound. The wristband is working through sensor waves for the interaction with the technology.

Fig. 3. Second drawing – YEAH

Basically, the children's idea is about on how to play guitar, and it also can be used in playing games. For example, the YEAH is an amazing spectacle when the user wears it, he/she could see and feels that they are really holding and play the guitar. Yet, the spectacles can also be used for watching movies and listening to music. The children thought of having this design in order to have convenient and comfortable position without holding the gadgets anymore where they can wear it as accessories too.

Fig. 4. Third drawing – THINAZ

The idea is the same with the first drawing -iPPLe, however with a different design. Thinaz looks the same with the IT gadget such as Samsung and Apple products. However Thinaz is more interesting than the existing tablets: it has different colours of shading with two tones. The shape is slightly different in which the children want an IT gadget that looks cute and adorable. Furthermore the function is still the same with iPPLe, where they want to be connected to the Internet to stay connected with their friends using Facebook, Twitter and YouTube. Meanwhile other applications such as camera, music and other phone setting should also be available.

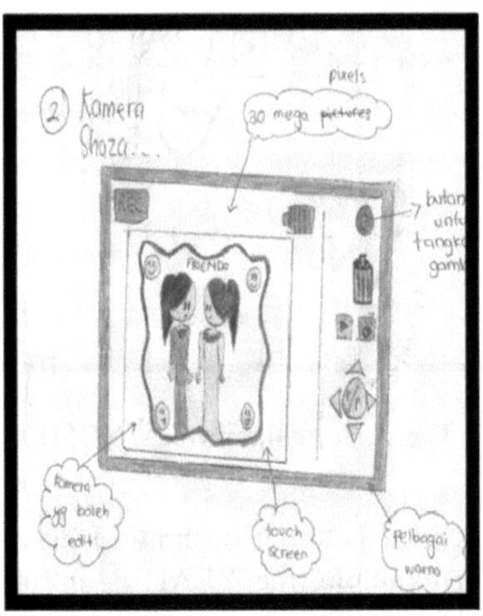

Fig. 5. Fourth drawing – Kamera Shaza

Kamera Shaza is a touch-screen digital camera being designed by the children, with better handling. They want a camera with a 30 megapixels (MP) to catch a good quality picture. These children also want a camera with an anti-shake and image stabilizers so that they do not have to worry about the quality of the pictures taken when the children are moving. They also want the camera to be embedded with an editing software so that they can immediately edit the pictures on the camera itself rather than doing it on the computer. The camera should come in many different colours for the users to choose from. The camera should also have a recording function in order to capture videos. Other camera functions should remain on this camera.

Fig. 6. Fifth drawing – Pie Phone

This drawing, Pie Phone, is a smartphone in a pie shape. This child who drew this preferred to have a different-shaped smartphone to the ones currently available in the market. The motto of this phone is "Make it Easy". The phone should be easy to use and should be waterproof. This phone should enable the users to go online anyway, anytime and get connected on Facebook and Twitter. It should also have pre- installed games and allow the users to download games as well.

5 Discussion

Based on our findings, we have identified two important issues: role of children and technology for children.

5.1 Role of Children

Literature suggests that older children can be a design informant for a project. In our study, we found that young children such as these primary schoolers are also capable to be a design informant. Traditional method to elicit user requirements is often done through oral interviews, however, this might not be appropriate for young children as their cognitive intelligence is just starting to develop at this age. Thus, based on our 4 years of experience working with children, we found that drawing is an effective method to help the children express not only their ideas creatively but also their user requirements. From the study, we also found that drawing not only brings fun to the children but also helps children become more creative.

5.2 Technology for Children

From the study, we can conclude that technology for children should be:

- ubiquitous

Children want their technology to be ubiquitous. All of the children's drawing highlight this requirement. Ubiquitous technology is often wireless, mobile, and networked, making its users more connected to the world around them and the people in it [22]. It also can be defined, to have access to a variety of digital devices and services, including computers connected to the Internet and mobile computing devices, whenever and wherever they need them [8, 20].

- wearable

Children also like their technology to be wearable. According to Buechley, the wearable technology can be defined as tech togs, or fashion electronics such as clothing and accessories incorporating computer and advanced electronic technologies [3]. For instance, the most ubiquitous wearable technology today is smartphone. It is always with us and always connected to software, apps, and services. Using the phone's processing power, sensors, storage and data capabilities, and services create huge new opportunities for wearable. Examples from our study are YEAH spectacles and Pie Phone.

- natural in interaction

Another important requirement is that the interaction between child and technology should be natural. From the study, the children want a touch interface. The interaction by using a fingertip on the screen is the preferred technique of their interaction because it is used at less effort and much easier to do it than conventional ways [7].

- child-centred

The technology is meant for the children, therefore, understanding of children is essential for the designers. Most of the designers still do not understand the needs of the children: what are they good at and what are they bad at? Being young, children are more often seen as active yet careless, reckless, forgetful or ignorant. Features such as anti-shake, anti-damage and waterproof should therefore be embedded in the design. Children love colours very much. This can be seen clearly in our results. It is contradictory to the existing children technologies such as PSP, XBOX and tablets which are mostly still in black colour and in a rectangular shape rather than real-life shapes such as bunny ears, apple, and pie.

6 Conclusion

Children have proved that they can contribute in a design team. They can be a design informant or perhaps later a designer if given a trust and an opportunity. Children technology should be ubiquitous, wearable, natural in interaction and child-centred.

References

1. Consumer of Tomorrow: Insight and Observations About Generation Z (November 2012), from Grail Research: http://www.grailresearch.com/pdf/ContenPodsPdf/Consumers_of_Tomorrow_Insights_and_Observations_About_Generation_Z.pdf (retrieved November 29, 2012)
2. Barker, J., Weller, S.: Is it Fun? Developing Children Centred Research Methods. International Journal of Sociology and Social Policy 23(1), 33–58 (2003)
3. Buechley, L., Eisenberg, M.: Fabric PCBs, Electronic Sequins, and Socket Buttons: Techniques for E-textile Craft. Journal of Personal and Ubiquitous Computing 13(2), 133–150 (2007)
4. Druin, A.: The Role of Children in the Design of New Technology. Behaviour and Information Technology (BIT) 21(1), 1–25 (2002)
5. Good, J., Robertson, J.: CASS: A Framework for Learner Centred Design with Children. International Journal of Artificial Intelligence in Education 16(4), 381–413 (2006)
6. Hanna, L., Neapolitan, D., Risden, K.: Evaluating computer game concepts with children. In: Proceedings of the 3rd International Conference on Interaction Design and Children (IDC 2004), pp. 49–56. ACM Press (2004)
7. Harper, S.: Is there design for all? Universal Access in the Information Society 6(1), 111–113 (2007)
8. Hill, E.J., Ferris, M., Martinson, V.: Does it Matter Where You Work? A Comparison of How Three Work Venues (Traditional Office, Virtual Office, and Home Office) Influence Aspects of Work and Personal/Family Life. Journal of Vocational Behavoiur 63, 220–241 (2003)
9. Markopoulos, P., Bekker, M.: On the assessment of usability testing methods for children. Interacting with Computers 15(2), 227–243 (2003)
10. Nesset, V., & Large, A. Children in the information technology design process. A Review of Theories and Their Applications, 140-162 (2004)
11. Oosterholt, R., Kusano, M., de Vries, G.: Interaction Design and Human Factors Support in the Development of a Personal Communicator for Children. In: Proceedings of the Human Factors and Computing Systems (CHI 1996), pp. 45–477. ACM (1996)
12. Palley, W., Gen, Z.: Digital in DNA. From JWT Inttelligence coversting cultural shifts into opportunities (September 21, 2012) http://www.jwtintelligence.com/wp-content/uploads/2012/04/F_INTERNAL_Gen_Z_0418122.pdf (retrieved November 23, 2012)
13. Patton, M.Q.: Qualitative Research and Evaluation Methods. Thousand Oaks, Sage (2002)
14. Pyykko, S., Hellsten, S., Weitzel, M., Rakkolainen, I.: Children's game experiences in different settings. In: Proceedings of Second 3DTV Conference, pp. 377–390. IEEE (2008)
15. Razak, F.H.A., Razak, N.A., Adnan, W.A.W.: Elderly mental model of reminder systems. In: APCHI 2012, pp. 193–200. ACM, Matsue (2012)
16. Read, J., Markopoulos, P.: Child-computer interaction. International Journal of Child-Computer Interaction 1, 2–6 (2013)
17. Ruland, C.M., Starren, J., Vatne, T.: Participatory design with children in the development of a support system for patient-centered care in pediatric oncology. Journal of Biomedical Informatics 41(4), 624–635 (2008)
18. Scaife, M., Rogers, Y., Aldrich, F., Davies, M.: Designing for or designing with? Informant design for interactive learning environments. In: Proceedings of the SIGCHI Conference on Human Factors in Computing Systems, pp. 343–350. ACM Press (1997)

19. Shneiderman, B., Plaisant, C.: Designing the User Interface: Strategies for Effective Human Computer Interaction. Addison-Wesley (2010)
20. Useem, J.: Welcome to the New Company Town, Fortune, pp. 62–70 (2000)
21. Valentine, G.: Being seen and heard? The ethical complexities of working with children and young people at home and school. Ethics Place and Environment 2, 141–155 (1999)
22. Weiser, M., Gold, R., Brown, J.S.: The Origins of ubiquitous computing research at PARC in the late of 1980s. IBM Systems Journal 36(7), 693–696 (1999)

An Interactive Rough Set Attribute Reduction Using Great Deluge Algorithm

Najmeh Sadat Jaddi and Salwani Abdullah

Data Mining and Optimization Research Group (DMO),
Center for Artificial Intelligence Technology,
Faculty of Information Science and Technology,
Universiti Kebangsaan Malaysia,
43600 Bangi, Selangor, Malaysia
najmehjaddi@gmail.com, salwani@ftsm.ukm.my

Abstract. Dimensionality reduction from an information system is a problem of eliminating unimportant attributes from the original set of attributes while avoiding loss of information in data mining process. In this process, a subset of attributes that is highly correlated with decision attributes is selected. In this paper, performance of the great deluge algorithm for rough set attribute reduction is investigated by comparing the method with other available approaches in the literature in terms of cardinality of obtained reducts (subsets), time required to obtain reducts, number of calculating dependency degree functions, number of rules generated by reducts, and the accuracy of the classification. An interactive interface is initially developed that user can easily select the parameters for reduction. This user interface is developed toward visual data mining. The carried out model has been tested on the standard datasets available in the UCI machine learning repository. Experimental results show the effectiveness of the method especially with relation to the time and accuracy of the classification using generated rules. The method outperformed other approaches in M-of-N, Exactly, and LED datasets with achieving 100% accuracy.

Keywords: interactive data mining, great deluge algorithm, rough set theory, attribute reduction, classification.

1 Introduction

Visual data mining is a new approach to deal with the fast rate of growing of information. With this rapid growth of high dimensional data in many domains (e.g. machine learning, pattern recognition, customer relation management and data mining), attribute reduction is considered as a necessary task of preprocessing techniques for learning process to extract rule-like knowledge from information system [1]. In recent years, the goal of many researches is to combine data mining algorithms with information visualization methods to use the advantages of both approaches [2], [3], [4], [5] and [6] . Interaction is important for useful visual data mining. The data analyst must be able to interact with the presented data and mining

H. Badioze Zaman et al. (Eds.): IVIC 2013, LNCS 8237, pp. 285–299, 2013.

parameters according to the requirements. Attribute reduction is a process of eliminating the irrelevant and redundant attributes. This process involves the metaheuristic algorithms to optimize the solution [7], [8], [9], [10] and [11]. Attribute reduction aids to increase the speed and quality of the learning algorithm. The quality of the learning algorithm is normally measured by accuracy of the classification [12]. Rough set theory [13] as a tool can solve this problem by discovering data dependencies using only data. This is the advantage of rough set theory that no additional information is required. Removing attributes that are highly related with other attributes (redundant) and searching for attributes that are strongly relevant to decision attribute with minimal information loss is the aim of rough set attribute reduction.

Many computational intelligence tools has been developed by Jensen and Shen [14], tabu search by Hedar et al. [15], genetic algorithm by Jensen and Shen [14], scatter search by Wang et al. [16], ant colony by Jensen and Shen [14, 17] and by Ke et al. [18] , great deluge by Abdullah and Jaddi [19] and [20] and by Mafarja and Abdullah [21] are some of the available and successful methods for attribute reduction. This research investigates the performance of the great deluge for rough set attribute reduction (GD-RSAR) [19]. The investigation is performed by comparing the method with other available methods in the literature. Comparisons are based on the number of attributes in reducts, running time, number of computing dependency degree functions and classification accuracy with the use of generated rules. The proposed method in this paper is tested on 13 available datasets in http://www.ics.uci.edu/~mlearn.

An interactive interface is produced as initial study toward visualization of attribute reduction process. The interface helps analysts to easily interact with the data mining process. The user can select the class attribute for the attribute reduction. The class attribute in datasets may take place as first or last attribute or may be placed in between of other conditional attributes. This is the cause of importance of selection of class attribute by the user.

The next section describes the summary of rough set attribute reduction concept, and basic structure of the standard great deluge algorithm. The attribute reduction method using GD-RSAR is described in section 3. Section 4 presents the user interface for interaction in details. The experimental results and their comparisons with other available approaches in the literature are illustrated in section 5. Section 6 provides the final remark and conclusion.

2 Preliminaries

This section provides a brief description of the basics and concepts of rough set theory for attribute reduction as well as basic structure of the standard great deluge algorithm.

2.1 Rough Set Theory

Let (U, A) be an information system where U (universe) is a nonempty set of finite objects and A be a nonempty finite set of attributes that $\alpha: U \rightarrow V_\alpha$ for each $\alpha \in A$. In a decision system, A is equal to the union of conditional attributes and decision attribute

($A=C \cup D$ where C is conditional attributes and D is the decision attribute). With any $P \subset A$ there is an equivalence relation IND (P) as in (1).

$$IND(P) = \{(x, y) \in U^2 | \forall\ \alpha \in P, \alpha(x) = \alpha(y)\} \tag{1}$$

The segment of U, produced by $IND(P)$ is named $U/IND(P)$ and can be presented as equation (2) where $A \otimes B = \{X \cap Y: \forall X \in A, \forall Y \in B, X \cap Y \neq \emptyset\}$.

$$U/IND(P) = \otimes \{\alpha \in P: U/IND(\{\alpha\})\} \tag{2}$$

If $(x, y) \in IND(P)$, then x and y can be indiscernible by attributes from P. The group of all equivalence classes of IND (P) that contains x is denoted by $[x]_P$.

Let $X \subseteq U$, the P-lower approximation, $\underline{P}X$ of set X is defined as: $\underline{P}X = \{x | [x]_p \subseteq X\}$ and P-upper approximation $\overline{P}X$ is specified as $\overline{P}X = \{x | [x]_p \cap X \neq \emptyset\}$. Let P and Q be equivalence relations over U then the positive region can be presented as relation (3).

$$POS_p(Q) = \bigcup_{X \in U/Q} \underline{P}X \tag{3}$$

The positive region consists of all objects in U that can be classified to class of U/Q using attributes P. An important issue in data analysis is finding dependencies among attributes. Dependency degree between P and Q is expressed by equation (4).

$$k = \gamma_P(Q) = \frac{|POS_P(Q)|}{|U|} \tag{4}$$

If $k = 1$, Q depends totally on P, If $0 < k < 1$, Q depends partially on P, and If $k = 0$ then Q does not depends on P. The attributes are selected using dependency degree measurement. A subset can be reduct if the condition $\gamma_R(D) = \gamma_C(D)$ is met (R is the reduct set, C is the conditional attribute set and D is the decision attribute set). Therefore, the reduced set gives the same dependency degree as the original set. Set of all reducts is defined as ralation (5).

$$\text{Red} = \{X: X \subseteq C, \gamma_R(D) = \gamma_C(D)\} \tag{5}$$

Normally, in an attribute reduction process the reduct with minimum cardinality which is called minimal reduct is searched.

2.2 Standard Great Deluge Algorithm

The basic idea of standard great deluge was presented by Dueck [22]. This is an alternative and enhanced form of the simulated annealing algorithm. The advantage of great deluge over simulated annealing is that great deluge is less dependent on parameters than simulated annealing. It requires only two easily understandable input parameters: computational time (the user is willing to spend) and satisfying estimated value of objective function.

A standard great deluge accepts the solution when its quality is improved. It also accepts the worse solutions by comparing the quality of the solution with some given lower boundary *Level* (for the case of maximization). At this point, the worse solution is accepted if quality of the solution is greater or equal to *Level*. At first, the *Level* is set to function value of initial solution but during running the *Level* is increased by fixed increasing rate which is initialized as β. The value of β is an input parameter in this technique.

During the search, the value of *Level* makes a part of the search space impossible and pushes the current solution into the remaining possible search area (as shown in Fig. 1 with considering the quality of initial solution is equal to 0). Increasing the value of *Level* is a control process which drives the search towards a wanted solution. In this case, the current solution has many chances to provide several successful moves inside the remaining neighborhood and improve its value before the value of *Level* meets the estimated quality function.

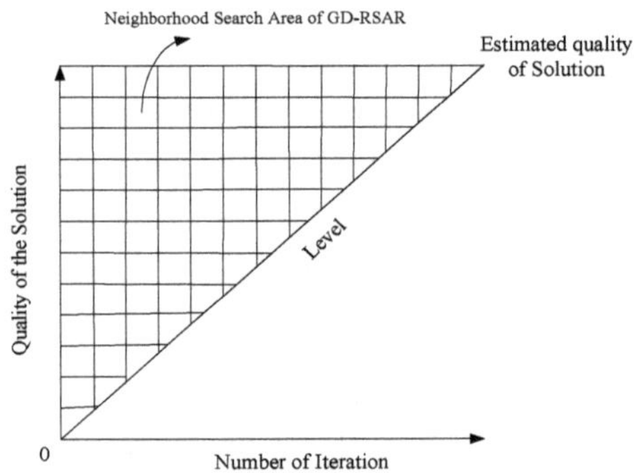

Fig. 1. The neighborhood search area of GD-RSAR

The usefulness of the algorithm has been shown by successful applications on various optimization problems [23], [24], [25] and [26].

3 GD-RSAR

GD-RSAR presented by Abdullah and Jaddi [19] suggests a great deluge based algorithm for solving attribute reduction problems. This algorithm follows the standard great deluge algorithm (in maximization approach). However, it employs many components which are described in the following subsections. The pseudo code of GD-RSAR is shown in Fig. 2.

At each iteration of searching process of GD-RSAR, the neighborhood structure with the help of GDList, constructs a trial solution and then with the use of solution quality measure, the quality of the trial solution is evaluated. After that, based on the quality of the trial solution, the best solution and the current solution are updated. The GDList is updated when the solution is updated as the best solution. The algorithm stops if one of the defined termination conditions is satisfied.

```
Set initial solution as Sol, obtained from constructive heuristic;
Set best solution, Sol_best ← Sol;
Calculate the initial and best cost function, γ Sol and γ Sol_best;
Set estimated quality of final solution, EstimatedQuality ← 1;
Set number of iteration, NumOfIte;
Set initial Level: Level ← γ Sol;
Set increasing rate β;
Set iteration ← 0;
do while (iteration < NumOfIte)
        Add or remove or replace one attribute to/from the current solution (Sol) to obtain a
    trial solution, Sol*;
        Evaluate trial solution, γ Sol*;
        if (γ Sol* > γ Sol_best)
           Sol ← Sol*; Sol_best ← Sol*;
           γ Sol ← γ Sol*; γ Sol_best ← γ Sol*;
         else
                if (γ Sol* == γ Sol_best)
                   Calculate |Sol*| , |Sol_best|;
                      If ( |Sol*| < |Sol_best| )
                        Sol ← Sol*; Sol_best ← Sol*;
                        γ Sol ← γ Sol*; γ Sol_best ← γ Sol*;
                  else
                     if (γ Sol* ≥ Level)
                           Sol ← Sol*; γ Sol ← γ Sol*;
                endif
         endif
         Level = Level + β;
         iteration++;
end do;
Calculate |Sol_best|;
return |Sol_best|, γ Sol_best, Sol_best;
```

Fig. 2. The pseudo code of the GD-RSAR

GD-RSAR presents solutions by using one-dimensional vector. Each cell in the vector contains the index of the attributes which is initially constructed by a constrictive heuristic. The length of initial solution is set based on user experience or with the use of the results found in the literature. The highest quality between randomly generated numbers of solutions is selected as initial solution. This number is set up by calculating 10 percent of the number of conditional attributes.

GDList is used to keep the sequence (history) of the best solutions (attributes) found so far. This sequence is to assist the great deluge algorithm to employ different neighborhood structures when it is creating a trial solution.

GD-RSAR involves three processes to generate trial solutions in a neighborhood of a current solution: 1) If the current solution has been assigned as the best solution by the previous iteration (working on the best solution) then one attribute with the lowest occurrence in the GDList is removed from the current solution. 2) If the current solution has been assigned as the worse solution by the previous iteration (working on the worse solution) then one attribute with the highest occurrence in the GDList is added to the current solution. 3) Otherwise, an alteration of an attribute is done by replacing it with another one randomly.

In GD-RSAR, the dependency degree $\gamma Sol\,(D)$ of decision attribute D is used to measure the quality of a solution *Sol*. To compare two solutions *Sol* and *Sol**, we say *Sol** is better than the *Sol* if one of the following conditions meets. Note that the cardinality (number of attributes) of set *Sol* is denoted as $|Sol|$.

- $\gamma\, Sol^*(D) > \gamma\, Sol\,(D)$
- $|Sol^*| < |Sol|$ if $\gamma\, Sol^*(D) = \gamma\, Sol\,(D)$

If the quality value of the *Sol** is greater than the quality value of the *Sol*, the *Sol** is directly assigned as the best solution. When quality values of the *Sol* and *Sol** are the same, one of these two solutions is assigned as the best solution under condition of the number of attributes. Definitely, the solution with less cardinality is assigned as the best solution.

GD-RSAR algorithm starts with an initialization part and continues with a *do-while* loop that during its iterations updates the current and the best solutions. As initialization, the number of iterations is denoted as *NumOfIte* and is assigned to 250 iterations (as used in Ke et al. [18]). In addition, estimated quality of the final solution is denoted as *EstimatedQuality* ad is set to one (maximum possibility for quality of solution). Initially, the *Level* is set to the quality of the initial solution, γ *Sol,* and is increased by increasing rate β at each iteration. The value of β is calculated by (5).

$$\beta = (EstimatedQuality - \gamma\, Sol) \,/\, NumOfIte \tag{5}$$

Firstly, in the *do-while* loop of the algorithm, the neighborhood structure employs GDList to generate a trial solution, *Sol**. After that, the quality of the solution is calculated ($\gamma\, Sol^*$). Then, $\gamma\, Sol^*$ is compared with the quality of the best solution $\gamma\, Sol_{best}$. If there is an improvement in quality function, the trial solution, *Sol**, is accepted and the current and the best solutions are updated. However, if there is no change in the quality function between these two solutions, then the cardinality of the solutions are compared. If ($|Sol^*| < |Sol|$), then the current solution and the best solution are updated. A worse solution is accepted as current solution if the quality of the trial solution, $\gamma\, Sol^*$, is greater than the *Level*. By inserting the best solution into GDList, when the best solution is updated, the GDList is updated as well. The process continues until one of the two stopping conditions is met. The stopping conditions are the number of iterations when it exceeds *NumOfIte* or the *Level* when it exceeds 1.

4 Visual Data Mining and Knowledge Discovery

The benefit of visual data mining is that the user is involved in the data mining process [27]. Visual data mining tries at join together the human in the data mining procedure. Fig. 3 describes the knowledge discovery process with the visualization part. The dashed lines and elements show visual analytic process. Note that the visual analytics procedure is interactive through interaction with the user of the system. Therefore an interactive user interface is required to give the user easy interaction. In the following subsection we describe the interface implemented for this aim. This user interface aids us toward an interactive visual data mining and knowledge discovery.

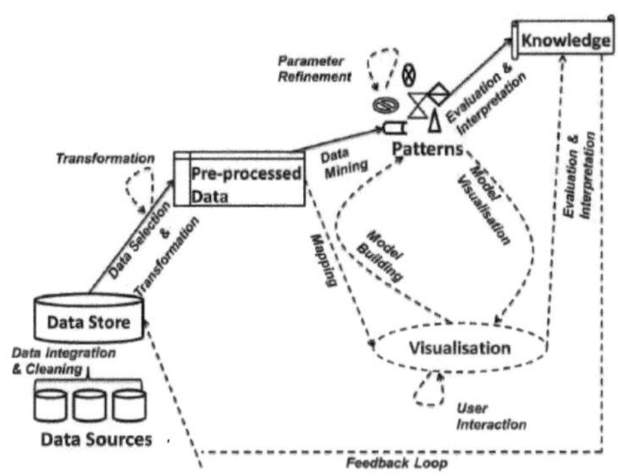

Fig. 3. The Overall process of visual data mining (taken from[28])

4.1 Interactive User Interface

For any data mining algorithms, such as classification, cluster analysis, decision tree, etc., an interactive processing between system and user is required. Toward this, interactive interface is necessary especially in visual data mining. In this paper, an initial design of interactive attribute reduction as preprocessing technique for any data mining task is developed (Fig. 4(a)). In this interface a combo box is designed for selecting the algorithm for attribute reduction which in current study we use the great deluge algorithm. The class attribute number is asked from the user to ensure which attribute is considered as class attribute. The user can select the dataset file which is in CSV format using “Select File” button. When this button is clicked a file chooser window is opened that makes the user able to select the appropriate file (Fig. 4(b)).

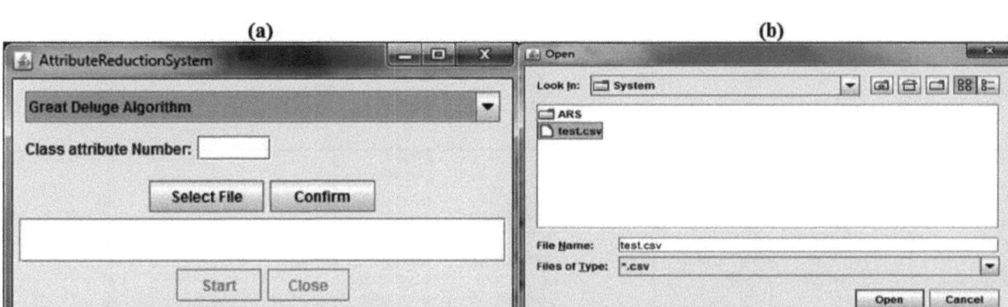

Fig. 4. The user interface for attribute reduction process: (a) main interface window, (b) File chooser window

When the CSV file is selected the file path is shown for the user to confirm it. If the selected file is not the file that user needs to be reduced then by selecting the "Select File" button can choose another one. When the confirm button is clicked the "Start" button is active and a message that guide user to click the "Start" button for starting process is exposed. After doing the process the results for the reduction process are shown in the text box.

If for any reason the user missed the inserting class attribute number or selecting the file a message will be appeared to notify the user about any mistake. Besides, if the selected file by the user is not in CSV format the user will be informed by a message.

In the design of this system the effort is for high usability. This system is simple yet easy to use for the user. By extending this system we can produce a visual classification, clustering or any other data mining task. This system is toward visual data mining approach.

5 Experimental Results

The algorithm was programmed using Java and the model was tested on 13 well-known datasets from UCI. The algorithm is less dependent on the parameters (with two parameters) compared to the methods such as TSAR with seven [15], GenRSAR and SimRSAR each one with three [14] and SSAR with five [16] parameters to be tuned in advance. AntRSAR [17] and ACOAR [18], with two parameters have the same number of parameters as great deluge.

5.1 Number of Attributes in Obtained Reducts

Table 1 provides a comparison of GD-RSAR results with the results of other works in the literature. We compare the presented approach with other attribute reduction methods that are available in the literature on the 13 instances from UCI machine learning repository. The records in Table 1 represent the number of attributes in the minimal reducts obtained by each method.

Table 1. Comparison results of number of reduced attributes

Datasets	No. attributes	GD-RSAR	TSAR	SimRSAR	AntRSAR	GenRSAR	ACOAR	SSAR	MGDAR
M-of-N	13	$6^{(10)}7^{(10)}$	6	6	6	$6^{(6)}7^{(12)}$	6	6	6
Exactly	13	$6^{(7)}7^{(10)}8^{(3)}$	6	6	6	$6^{(10)}7^{(10)}$	6	6	6
Exactly2	13	$10^{(14)}11^{(6)}$	10	10	10	$10^{(9)}11^{(11)}$	10	10	10
Heart	13	$9^{(4)}10^{(16)}$	6	$6^{(29)}\ 7^{(1)}$	$6^{(18)}\ 7^{(2)}$	$6^{(18)}7^{(2)}$	6	6	$6^{(14)}7^{(6)}$
Vote	16	$9^{(17)}10^{(3)}$	8	$8^{(15)}\ 9^{(15)}$	8	$8^{(2)}9^{(18)}$	8	8	8
Credit	20	$11^{(11)}12^{(9)}$	$8^{(13)}9^{(5)}10^{(2)}$	$8^{(18)}9^{(1)}11^{(1)}$	$8^{(12)}\ 9^{(4)}\ 10^{(4)}$	$10^{(6)}11^{(14}$	$8^{(16)}9^{(4)}$	$8^{(9)}\ 9^{(8)}\ 10^{(3)}$	$8^{(13)}9^{(3)}10^{(4)}$
Mushroom	22	$4^{(8)}5^{(9)}6^{(3)}$	$4^{(17)}\ 5^{(3}$	4	4	$5^{(1)}6^{(5)}7^{(14)}$	4	$4^{(12)}\ 5^{(8)}$	$4^{(7)}5^{(13)}$
LED	24	$8^{(14)}9^{(6)}$	5	5	$5^{(12)}\ 6^{(4)}\ 7^{(3)}$	$6^{(1)}7^{(3)}8^{(16)}$	5	5	5
Letters	25	$8^{(7)}9^{(13)}$	$8^{(17)}\ 9^{(3)}$	8	8	$8^{(8)}9^{(12}$	8	$8^{(5)}\ 9^{(15)}$	8(18)9(2)
Derm	34	$12^{(14)}13^{(6)}$	$6^{(14)}\ 7^{(6)}$	$6^{(12)}\ 7^{(8)}$	$6^{(17)}\ 7^{(3)}$	$10^{(6)}11^{(14)}$	6	6	6(11)7(9)
Derm2	34	$11^{(14)}12^{(6)}$	$8^{(2)}\ 9^{(14)}10^{(4)}$	$8^{(3)}\ 9^{(7)}$	$8^{(3)}\ 9^{(17)}$	$10^{(4)}11^{(16)}$	$8^{(4)}9^{(16)}$	$8^{(2)}\ 9^{(18)}$	$8^{(4)}9^{(12)}10^{(4)}$
WQ	38	$15^{(14)}16^{(6)}$	$12^{(1)}13^{(13)}14^{(6)}$	$13^{(16)}\ 14^{(4)}$	$12^{(2)}13^{(7)}14^{(11)}$	16	$12^{(4)}13^{(12)}14^{(4)}$	$13^{(4)}\ 14^{(16)}$	$12^{(1)}13^{(11)}14^{(8)}$
Lung	56	$4^{(5)}5^{(2)}6^{(13)}$	$4^{(6)}\ 5^{(13)}6^{(1)}$	$4^{(7)}5^{(12)}6^{(1)}$	4	$6^{(8)}7^{(12)}$	4	4	$4^{(6)}5^{(11)}6^{(3)}$

In Table 1 the superscripts in parentheses represent the number of runs that achieved the minimal reducts. The number of attributes without superscripts means that the method could obtain this number of attributes for all runs. Note that we have used the same number of runs (20 runs) as other methods except SimRSAR that has used 30, 30 and 10 runs for Heart, Vote and Derm2 datasets, respectively. Although in some of the datasets the obtained reducts have slightly higher cardinality (e.g. Heart and Derm datasets) than other approaches, in general the results of GD-RSAR show potential of this method. To have more detailed comparison, we continued our study in other areas as following subsections.

5.2 Running Time

The time taken for finding reducts by some methods (AntRSAR, SimRSAR, and GenRSAR) has been reported in Jensen and Shen [14]. Comparison of GD-RSAR with three reported methods is presented in Fig. 5.

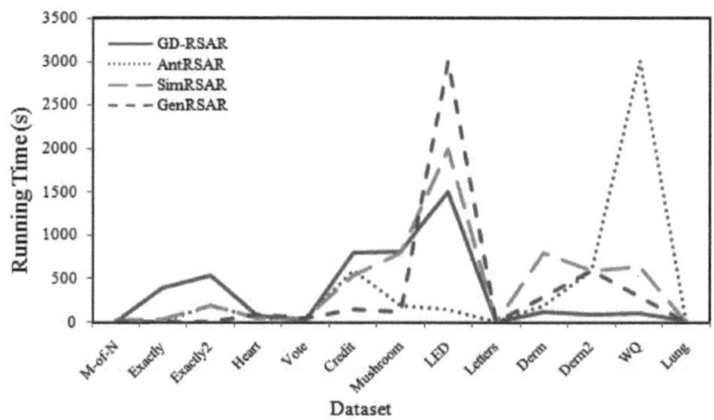

Fig. 5. Comparison of running time

This graph shows that the running time for GD-RSAR in most of the datasets is less than the other methods. It means that the method could obtain the reducts with spending less time compared with other methods. In this comparison, only Exactly, Exactly2 and Credit datasets needed slightly more time to discover the reducts. AntRSAR in WQ dataset and GenRSAR in LED dataset have spent a long time to discover the reducts. This might be the reason of finding reducts with lesser cardinality than GD-RSAR reducts.

As reported in Jensen and Shen [14], the rough order of techniques based on time is as: SimRSAR $\leq$ AntRSAR $\leq$ GenRSAR. With comparing GD-RSAR and SimRSAR (as best known algorithm in spending time) it can be found that GD-RSAR outperforms the SimRSAR in most of the datasets. Therefore, the order of algorithms can be extended as: GD-RSAR $\leq$ SimRSAR $\leq$ AntRSAR $\leq$ GenRSAR. Although GD-RSAR could not obtain the best reducts in some datasets in comparison with other methods, it could outperform others in terms of the time taken to generate reducts for most of the datasets. This advantage of finding reduct with consuming less time firstly is due to controlling the search space by the *Level* in great deluge algorithm. It makes the search space more promising and causes the solution to be found in a shorter time compared with other algorithms. The second reason might be the number of calculating dependency degree functions. The number of computing dependency degree which is a time-consuming process for the algorithms is investigated in next subsection as well.

5.3 Number of Computing Dependency Degree

By looking at the cost of the dependency degree computation especially if the number of attributes or the number of objects is a large number in a dataset, the significance of investigating number of calculating dependency degree functions in optimization of attribute reduction problem is appeared. In this part, we investigate the computational cost for the method as is shown in Table 2 and Fig. 6.

Table 2. Comparison of number of computing dependency degree

Datasets	No. Attributes	GD-RSAR	AntRSAR	GenRSAR	TSAR
M-of-N	13	**251**	12000	10000	702
Exactly	13	**251**	12000	10000	702
Exactly2	13	**251**	28000	10000	702
Heart	13	**251**	13000	10000	702
Vote	16	**251**	27000	10000	864
Credit	20	**252**	31000	10000	1080
Mushroom	22	**252**	11000	10000	1188
LED	24	**252**	17000	10000	1296
Letters	25	**252**	38000	10000	1350
Derm	34	**253**	34000	10000	1836
Derm2	34	**253**	50000	10000	1836
WQ	38	**253**	98000	10000	2052
Lung	56	**255**	28000	10000	3024

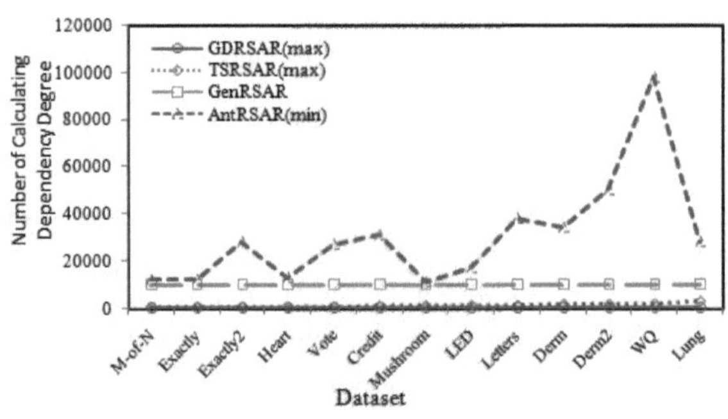

Fig. 6. Comparison of number of calculating dependency degree functions

In Hedar et al. [15], the number of calculating dependency degree functions used for GenRSAR, AntRSAR and TSAR is reported as following: (note that $|C|$ is cardinality of conditional attribute set)

- The exact number of function evaluation in GenRSAR is about 10,000.
- The minimum number of function evaluations in AntRSAR is $250|C|$ ($|R_{min}|$-2).
- The maximum number of function evaluations in TSAR is $54|C|$.

In comparison, GD-RSAR uses maximum 250 iterations and one calculating dependency degree function for each plus the number of function evaluation for generating initial solution which is calculated by 10|C|/100. Therefore, the maximum number of evaluation functions for GD-RSAR is 250+(10|C|/100).

Table 2 shows the results of applied formula for all tested datasets. Fig. 6 illustrates the estimate comparison of function evaluation in GD-RSAR with other reported methods. The best known results are presented in bold. It is obvious that the GD-RSAR could gain the first place in the number of calculating dependency degree functions.

5.4 Number of Rules and the Accuracy of the Classification

The reducts of GD-RSAR were tested by importing them into ROSETTA software to generate rules and find accuracy of the classification for all datasets. ROSETTA is a tool for analyzing data within the structure of rough set theory. This beneficial toolkit is available at http://www.lcb.uu.se/tools/rosetta/. The results of GD-RSAR were compared with genetic algorithm (GA), Johnson's algorithm and Holte's 1R that are available in ROSETTA. The 10-fold cross validation [1] was performed to evaluate the classification accuracy. Datasets were randomly divided into 10 subsamples. The single subsample was considered as validation data for testing the model and the rest (9 subsamples) were used as training sets. Then, the cross validation process was repeated 10 times (10 folds) and the 10 results from 10 folds were averaged to generate a single measure as predicted accuracy. So, the splitting percentage for testing and training set was 10% as testing set and 90% as training set. This process was performed for all the 13 datasets to generate rules and the predicted accuracies of the classification. The detail results are shown in Table 3. The best known results produced by GD-RSAR are presented in bold.

Table 3. Comparison of number of rules and classification accuracies

Datasets	**Great Deluge Algorithm**		**Genetic Algorithm**		**Johnson's Algorithm**		**Holte's 1R Algorithm**	
	Average number of rules	Accuracy %	Average number of rules	Accuracy %	Average number of rules	Accuracy %	Average number of rules	Accuracy %
M-of-N	64	**100**	8658	95	45	99	26	63
Exactly	64	**100**	28350	73	271	94	26	68
Exactly2	559	68	27167	74	441	79	26	73
Heart	195	50	1984	81	133	68	50	64
Vote	71	92	2517	95	54	95	48	90
Credit	527	58	47450	72	560	67	81	69
Mushroom	**52**	100	8872	100	85	100	112	89
LED	**40**	**100**	41908	98	316	99	48	63
Letters	**19**	0	1139	0	20	0	50	0
Derm	127	86	7485	94	92	89	129	48
Derm2	196	64	8378	92	98	88	138	48
WQ	136	55	48687	69	329	58	94	51
Lung	18	66	1387	71	12	69	156	73

The results of the generated rules of different algorithms are shown in Fig. 6. In the case of genetic algorithm, the results were shown in Fig. 7(a) because of having a big difference in numbers compared with the other algorithms. As it is obvious in Table 3 and Fig. 7(a), the average number of generated rules by GD-RSAR is extensively less than the number of generated rules by genetic algorithm for all datasets without exception. Table 3 and Fig. 7(b) show GD-RSAR outperformed Johnson's algorithm in 6 datasets and in comparison with Holte's 1R, GD-RSAR gone one better than some datasets such as Mushroom, LED, Letters and Lung.

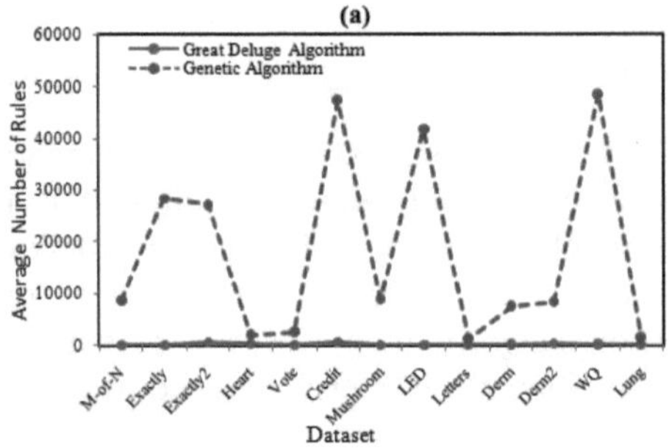

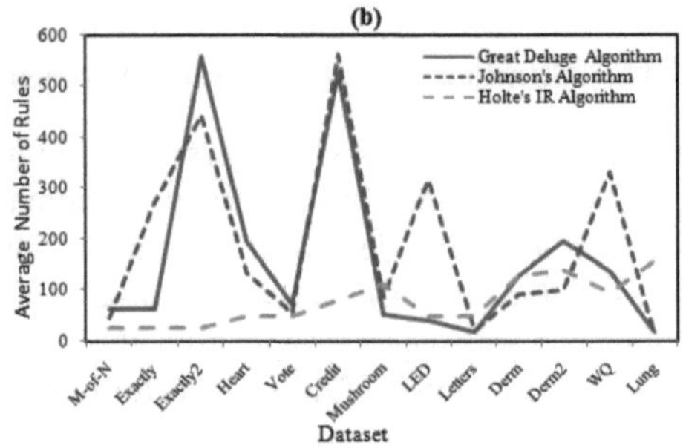

Fig. 7. Number of rules generated by GD-RSAR : (a) compared with genetic algorithm and (b) compared with GD-RSAR, Johnson's and Holte's 1R

Now, by looking at the Table 3 and Fig. 8 that compare the classification accuracy of GD-RSAR, GA, Johnson's and Holte's 1R algorithms, it can be observed that the GD-RSAR in three of datasets such as M-of-N, Exactly, and LED could reach to 100% accuracy but other algorithms could not. If we compare the classification accuracy of the GD-RSAR and Holte's 1R, GD-RSAR could obtain better result in most of the datasets which it can cover the inferiority of the number of rules in each datasets.

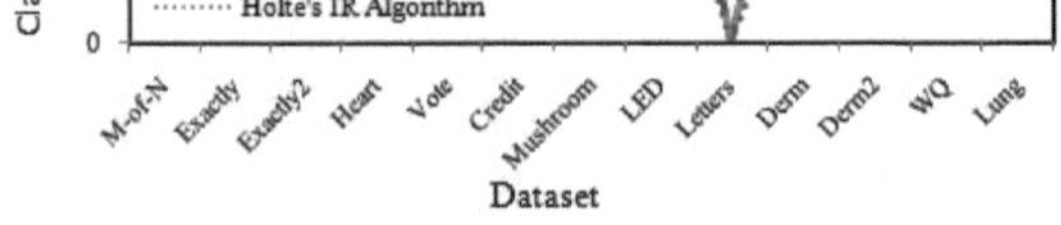

Fig. 8. Comparison of classification accuracies

Although, the reducts of GD-RSAR has slightly higher number of attributes, the reducts found have high quality in terms of accuracy of the classification using very low computational cost. In various real-world applications, low computational cost with only approximate optimal solutions is preferred. In this case our examined method can be easily adapted for datasets when the problem is the size of dataset.

6 Conclusion and Future Work

In this study, a comparison of the GD-RSAR with other available approaches in terms of number of parameters, cardinality of the reducts, running time required finding the reducts, number of calculating dependency degree functions, number of rules generated by the reducts and predicted classification accuracy was investigated. In these comparisons, experiments were carried out on UCI datasets. The result of the reducts cardinality showed a competitive result with other approaches. However it outperformed other methods in terms of running time and number of calculating dependency degree function. The results of the number of rules and classification accuracy showed that this method was able to obtain 100% accuracy for three datasets (i.e. M-of-N, Exactly, and LED) that other methods were not able to predict this accuracy. The rest of the datasets showed the accuracies between 50%-92% without taking into account Letters dataset which has the accuracy 0% due to its structure. These results for accuracy of the classification were achieved for the case of having less number of rules compared to other approaches in some of the datasets (i.e. Mushroom, LED, and Letters). In general, we can conclude that all these results confirm the effectiveness of this method due to generating high classification accuracy reducts in low computational cost.

Moreover, the developed user interface for attribute reduction increased the productivity and ability of use in real world problems. An enhanced of this user interface can be used for visual classification, visual clustering or in general visual data mining. This is subject to our future work.

References

1. Han, J., Kamber, M.: Data Mining: Concepts and Techniques. Morgan Kaufman Publishers, Oxford (2006)
2. Keim, D.A.: Visual exploration of large data sets. Commun. ACM 44, 38–44 (2001)
3. Havre, S., Hetzler, E., Whitney, P., Nowell, L.: ThemeRiver: visualizing thematic changes in large document collections. IEEE Transactions on Visualization and Computer Graphics 8, 9–20 (2002)
4. Stolte, C., Tang, D., Hanrahan, P.: Polaris: A System for Query, Analysis, and Visualization of Multidimensional Relational Databases. IEEE Transactions on Visualization and Computer Graphics 8, 52–65 (2002)
5. Abello, J., Korn, J.: MGV: a system for visualizing massive multidigraphs. IEEE Transactions on Visualization and Computer Graphics 8, 21–38 (2002)
6. Zhen, L., Xiangshi, R., Chaohai, Z.: User interface design of interactive data mining in parallel environment. In: Proceedings of the 2005 International Conference on Active Media Technology, AMT 2005, pp. 359–363 (2005)
7. Dash, M., Liu, H.: Consistency-based search in feature selection. Artificial Intelligence 151, 155–176 (2003)

8. Lihe, G.: A New Algorithm for Attribute Reduction Based on Discernibility Matrix. In: Cao, B.-Y. (ed.) Fuzzy Information and Engineering. ASC, vol. 40, pp. 373–381. Springer, Heidelberg (2007)
9. Kudo, Y., Murai, T.: A Heuristic Algorithm for Attribute Reduction Based on Discernibility and Equivalence by Attributes. In: Torra, V., Narukawa, Y., Inuiguchi, M. (eds.) MDAI 2009. LNCS, vol. 5861, pp. 351–359. Springer, Heidelberg (2009)
10. Li, H., Zhang, W., Xu, P., Wang, H.: Rough Set Attribute Reduction in Decision Systems. In: Wang, G.-Y., Peters, J.F., Skowron, A., Yao, Y. (eds.) RSKT 2006. LNCS (LNAI), vol. 4062, pp. 135–140. Springer, Heidelberg (2006)
11. Liu, H., Li, J., Wong, L.: A comparative study on feature selection and classification methods using gene expression profiles and proteomic patterns. In: Lathrop, R., Nakai, K., Miyano, S., Takagi, T., Kanehisa, M. (eds.) Genome Informatics 2002, vol. 13, pp. 51–60. Universal Academy Press, Tokyo (2002)
12. Hu, Q.-H., Li, X., Yu, D.-R.: Analysis on Classification Performance of Rough Set Based Reducts. In: Yang, Q., Webb, G. (eds.) PRICAI 2006. LNCS (LNAI), vol. 4099, pp. 423–433. Springer, Heidelberg (2006)
13. Pawlak, Z.: Rough sets. International Journal of Computer and Information Sciences 11, 341–356 (1982)
14. Jensen, R., Qiang, S.: Semantics-preserving dimensionality reduction: rough and fuzzy-rough-based approaches. IEEE Transactions on Knowledge and Data Engineering 16, 1457–1471 (2004)
15. Hedar, A.-R., Wang, J., Fukushima, M.: Tabu search for attribute reduction in rough set theory. Soft. Comput. 12, 909–918 (2008)
16. Jue, W., Hedar, A.R., Guihuan, Z., Shouyang, W.: Scatter Search for Rough Set Attribute Reduction. In: International Joint Conference on Computational Sciences and Optimization, CSO 2009, pp. 531–535 (2009)
17. Jensen, R., Shen, Q.: Finding Rough Set Reducts with Ant Colony Optimization. In: Workshop, U.K. (ed.) UK Workshop on Computational Intelligence, UK (2003)
18. Ke, L., Feng, Z., Ren, Z.: An efficient ant colony optimization approach to attribute reduction in rough set theory. Pattern Recogn. Lett. 29, 1351–1357 (2008)
19. Abdullah, S., Jaddi, N.S.: Great Deluge Algorithm for Rough Set Attribute Reduction. In: Zhang, Y., Cuzzocrea, A., Ma, J., Chung, K.-i., Arslan, T., Song, X. (eds.) DTA/BSBT 2010. CCIS, vol. 118, pp. 189–197. Springer, Heidelberg (2010)
20. Jaddi, N.S., Abdullah, S.: Nonlinear Great Deluge Algorithm for Rough Set Attribute Reduction. Journal of Information Science & Engineering 29, 49–62 (2013)
21. Mafarja, M., Abdullah, S.: Modified great deluge for attribute reduction in rough set theory. In: 2011 Eighth International Conference on Fuzzy Systems and Knowledge Discovery (FSKD), pp. 1464–1469 (2011)
22. Gunter, D.: New optimization heuristics (The Great Deluge Algorithm and Record to Record Travel). Computational Physic, 86–92 (1993)
23. Burke, E.K., Abdullah, S.: A Multi-start Large Neighbourhood Search Approach with Local Search Methods for Examination Timetabling. In: Long, D., Smith, S., Borrajo, D., McCluskey, L. (eds.) Proceedings of the International Conference on Automated Planning and Scheduling (ICAPS 2006), Cumbria, UK (2006)
24. Burke, E., Bykov, Y., Newall, J., Petrovic, S.: A time-predefined local search approach to exam timetabling problems. IIE Transactions 36, 509–528 (2004)
25. Landa-Silva, D., Obit, J.H.: Evolutionary Non-linear Great Deluge for University Course Timetabling. In: Corchado, E., Wu, X., Oja, E., Herrero, Á., Baruque, B. (eds.) HAIS 2009. LNCS, vol. 5572, pp. 269–276. Springer, Heidelberg (2009)

26. McMullan, P.: An Extended Implementation of the Great Deluge Algorithm for Course Timetabling. In: Shi, Y., van Albada, G.D., Dongarra, J., Sloot, P.M.A. (eds.) ICCS 2007, Part I. LNCS, vol. 4487, pp. 538–545. Springer, Heidelberg (2007)
27. Migut, M., Worring, M.: Visual exploration of classification models for various data types in risk assessment. Information Visualization (2012)
28. Stahl, F., Gabrys, B., Gaber, M.M., Berendsen, M.: An overview of interactive visual data mining techniques for knowledge discovery. Wiley Interdisciplinary Reviews: Data Mining and Knowledge Discovery 3, 239–256 (2013)

Reconstructing 3D Face Shapes from Single 2D Images Using an Adaptive Deformation Model

Ashraf Y.A. Maghari[1], Ibrahim Venkat[1], Iman Yi Liao[2], and Bahari Belaton[1]

[1] School of Computer Sciences, Universiti Sains Malaysia, Pinang, Malaysia
myashraf2@gmail.com
[2] School of Computer Science, University of Nottingham Malaysia Campus

Abstract. The Representational Power (RP) of an example-based model is its capability to depict a new 3D face for a given 2D face image. In this contribution, a novel approach is proposed to increase the RP of the 3D reconstruction PCA-based model by deforming a set of examples in the training dataset. By adding these deformed samples together with the original training samples we gain more RP. A 3D PCA-based model is adapted for each new input face image by deforming 3D faces in the training data set. This adapted model is used to reconstruct the 3D face shape for the given input 2D near frontal face image. Our experimental results justify that the proposed adaptive model considerably improves the RP of the conventional PCA-based model.

Keywords: Representational Power, Statistical facial modeling, 3D face reconstruction, PCA, TPS.

1 Introduction

Reconstruction of 3D face images from single 2D images is an open problem in the field of computer vision. The need for 3D face reconstruction has grown in applications such as virtual reality simulations, face recognition [8,9], and plastic surgery [6]. For example, in biometric identification, it has been shown that face recognition rate could be significantly improved by incorporating 3D face shapes with 2D face images [11]. The objective of 3D facial reconstruction systems is to recover the three dimensional shape of individuals from their 2D pictures or video sequences. However, accurate reconstruction of a person's 3D face model from his/her 2D face images still remains as a challenge.

There are many approaches for the reconstruction of 3D faces from single images. One of such early techniques being utilized is Shape-from-Shading (SFS) [1,23], which capitalizes the idea that the depth information is related to the intensity of a face image acquired through a given/chosen reflectance model. It has been shown that SFS suffers from poor global shape control.

Recently, Kemelmacher-Shlizerman and Basri proposed an approach that combines shading information with generic shape information derived from a single reference model by utilizing the global similarity of faces [13]. In this method the

H. Badioze Zaman et al. (Eds.): IVIC 2013, LNCS 8237, pp. 300–310, 2013.

involved fitting process requires boundary conditions and parameters to be adjusted during the reconstruction process. However, a 3D reference model which keeps shape similarities with the input image has not been considered in this method. Owing to this, inaccurate 3D shape estimation might be possible.

There are also conventional learning-based methods, such as neural networks [16] and typical statistical learning-based methods such as 3D Morphable Model (3DMM) [4]. The advancement of 3D scanning technology has led to the creation of more accurate 3D face exemplar models [18]. Example-based modeling allows more realistic face reconstruction than other methods [15]. However, the quality of face reconstruction using such models is affected by the chosen examples. For example, Kemelmacher-Shlizerman and Basri [13] have emphasized that learning a generic 3D face model requires large amounts of 3D faces. Furthermore, analytical results in [20] show that in many cases the representational power of the model may vary if the model is trained with a different sample though the same sample size is retained.

The PCA-based model proposed by Blanz et al. with relatively small sample size (100 faces) which was used for face recognition has obtained reasonable results [3]. Although in some statistical modeling methods both shape and texture are modeled separately using PCA (e.g. 3DMM), it has been suggested that shapes are more amenable than texture, as textures are subject to vast variation when compared to shape based features [12]. Therefore, the model we intend to propose in this contribution is based on modeling of shapes. When shapes are considered, the reconstruction of 3D face from 2D images using shape models is relatively simple. A popular method is a regularization based reconstruction where a few feature points are selected as the observations for reconstruction [12].

This study addresses the problem of increasing the Representational Power (RP) of the PCA-model to improve its capability in depicting a new 3D face from a given input face image. A 3D face shape modeling scheme is proposed to handle the vital model adaptation part of the PCA-based model. There are other methods that intend to create synthetic views in training sets for face recognition. These synthetic views includes different pose and expression [17]. However, this work is different and novel in the context of deforming 3D faces using the given input face for 3D face reconstruction.

The rest of the paper is organized as follows: Section 2 demonstrates the representational power of PCA model. Section 3 describes the methodology of the proposed adaptive 3D face shape modeling approach. Section 4 deals with the experimental evaluation and associated discussions. Section 5 concludes our research.

2 Representational Power of PCA Model

In this study, we define the RP of the PCA-based model as its capability in depicting a new 3D face of a given input face image. The capability of the PCA model can be measured by evaluating the quality of a reconstruction (with respect to its ground-truth). The most obvious and appropriate choice to compare two 3D surfaces is the Euclidean distance. The sum of the Euclidean distances over all vertices of the shapes weighted by the number of vertices is our measure:

$$Ed_w = \frac{\sum_{i=1}^{n} \sqrt{(s_i - s_{ri})^2}}{n}, \tag{1}$$

where Ed_w is the weighted Euclidean distance, s is the probe face shape, s_r is the reconstructed face shape, n is the number of vertices of the face shape.

As an example, Fig. 1 demonstrates the advantage of RP in terms of evaluating the quality of reconstruction. An original testing face shape is projected to PCA-based models learned from different training set sizes. As one can see in Fig. 1, the projection (representation) gets more realistic and more closer to the ground truth when Ed_w decreases, which means that the PCA model that represent a new 3D face with less Ed_w has more RP. In the next section, we propose a novel method that is able to improve the RP of the PCA model for the same training data set by reducing the Euclidean distance.

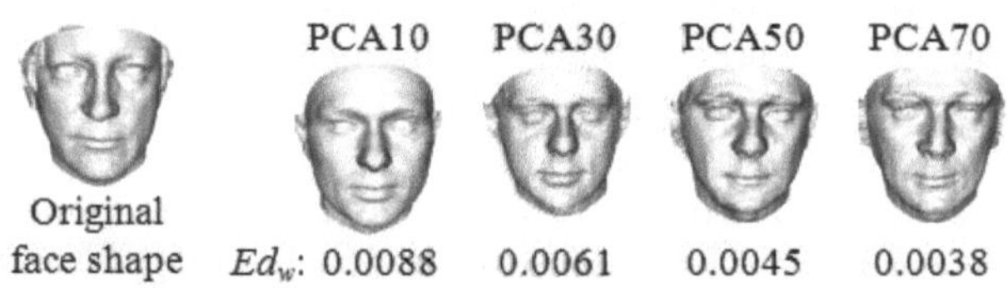

Fig. 1. Projecting the leftmost face shape to PCA models trained with different sample sizes. The RPs that represent the quality of projected face are shown below the shapes. PCA10 means the training set has 10 examples, PCA30 means the training set has 30 examples and so on

3 Adaptive 3D Face Shape Modeling

Fig. 2 shows the bird's eye view of the proposed scheme. It shows how a given input face gets reconstructed via a deformation synthesis mechanism.

Similar to Farkas [10] as referred by Knothe et al. [14] firstly we chose landmarks over facial regions such as eyes, nose, mouth and chin for the purpose of face alignment and deformation.

The input feature points are aligned using a standard algorithm called *Procrustes Analysis.* The concept of the Procrustes Analysis is similar to Iterative Closest Point (ICP) [2].

3.1 Deforming 3D Exemplar Faces

We use TPS to establish the mapping and interpolation for the deformation process. TPS is a commonly used basis function for representing coordinate mappings from rigid to nonrigid deformations. It is used for estimating a deformation function between two surfaces [17]. Let g_0 and g_1 be two 2D/3D shapes, and $P = (p_1, p_2, ..., p_m) \subset g_0$ and $V = (v_1, v_2, ..., v_m) \subset g_1$ be the correspondences (landmarks)

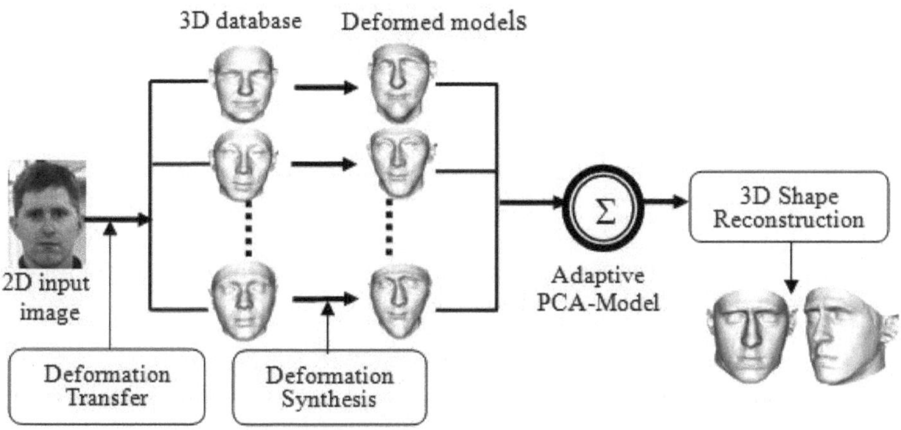

Fig. 2. Proposed scheme of the deformation model for 3D face shape reconstruction

between the two shapes, where m is the number of corresponding points. A warping function F that warps point set P to V is given by the following condition:

$$F(p_j) = v_j \ , \qquad j = 1, 2, ..., m \tag{2}$$

For the two corresponding sets of landmarks P and V, F is unique and has a minimal bending energy [7]. A TPS can minimize the following energy function

$$E_\lambda = \frac{1}{m} \sum_{i=1}^{m} |v_i - F(p_i)| + \lambda J \ , \qquad i = 1, ..., m \tag{3}$$

where v_i represents the ith 2D/3D point (landmark) of the input face (base points) and $p_i = (p_{i1}, ..., p_{id})$ is the ith point given in d-dimensions (in our case d could be 2D or 3D, p_i represent the set of points used to warp an image), m is the total number of corresponding points, J is a smoothness penalty function in d-dimensions, and λ is the smoothness parameter [24]. For the approximating case, minimizing Eq. (3) leads to the following matrix form.

$$PA + (K + m\lambda I)W = V, \quad P^T W = 0, \tag{4}$$

which actually performs the standard QR decomposition. Obviously, a QR decomposition of the matrix P produces an orthogonal matrix Q and an upper triangular matrix R such that $P = QR$ [24].

As an example, for the case $d = 2$ (2-dimension), the interpolation map is form R^2 *to* R^2, where $p_i = (x_i, y_i)$ and $v_i = (x'_i, y'_i)$. Let $r_{ij} = |p_i - p_j|$ be the distance between points i and j. Define matrices

$$K = \begin{bmatrix} 0 & U(r_{12}) & ... & U(r_{1m}) \\ U(r_{21}) & 0 & ... & U(r_{2m}) \\ ... & ... & ... & ... \\ U(r_{n1}) & U(r_{m2}) & ... & 0 \end{bmatrix}, \ m \times m \tag{5}$$

$$P = \begin{bmatrix} 1 & x_1 & y_1 \\ 1 & x_2 & y_2 \\ \dots & \dots & \dots \\ 1 & x_m & y_m \end{bmatrix}, \ m \times 3 \tag{6}$$

and

$$L = \left[\begin{array}{c|c} K & P \\ \hline P^T & O \end{array}\right], \ (m+3) \times (m+3) \tag{7}$$

where O is a 3×3 matrix of zeros. Let $Y = (V|0 \ \ 0 \ \ 0)^T$, a column vector of length $n+3$ and $W = (w_1, w_2, ..., w_m)$. For the interpolating case, TPS provides a linear system of equations [5] which is given by

$$L^{-1}Y = (W|a_1 \ \ a_x \ \ a_y)^T, \tag{8}$$

The element of $L^{-1}Y$ are used to define a function $F(x, y)$ everywhere in the plane:

$$F(x, y) = a_1 + a_x x + a_y y + \sum_{i=1}^{m} w_i U(|p_i - (x, y)|), \tag{9}$$

For simplifying, F can be written in the following matrix form:

$$F(p) = p.A + KW \ , \tag{10}$$

where $p \in g_0, A = (a_1 \ \ a_x \ \ a_y)$ is an affine transformation, W is a fixed m-dimensional column vector of non-affine warping parameters constrained to $P^T W = 0$ and K is m-dimensional row vector with $K_{ij} = U(|p_i - p_j|)$.

Some typical deformed 3D faces registered with reference to three typical 2D images using TPS are shown in Fig. 3.

3.2 Deformable Model Construction

Usually, each synthesized 3D model captures only some characteristics from its corresponding input face. This leads to a 3D morphable model that is a linear combination of 3D face shapes, some of which are obtained as a result of a deformation transfer mechanism from one input face to the neutral 3D example face shapes. The linear combination is controlled by shape parameters α where a new 3D shape can be generated using:

$$s = s_0 + \sum_{i=1}^{m} \alpha_i e_i \ , \tag{11}$$

where s_0 is the mean 3D shape, e_i represent the ith eigenvector of the covariance matrix, α_i is the coefficient of the shape eigenvector e_i and m is the number of significant eigenvectors. The coefficient of a face shape s can be calculated using the following equation

$$\alpha = E^T(s_i - s_0) \ , \tag{12}$$

where $E = [e_1, e_2, ..., e_m]$ are the eigenvectors of the covariance matrix. The projected new face shape can be precisely represented by applying Equation (11).

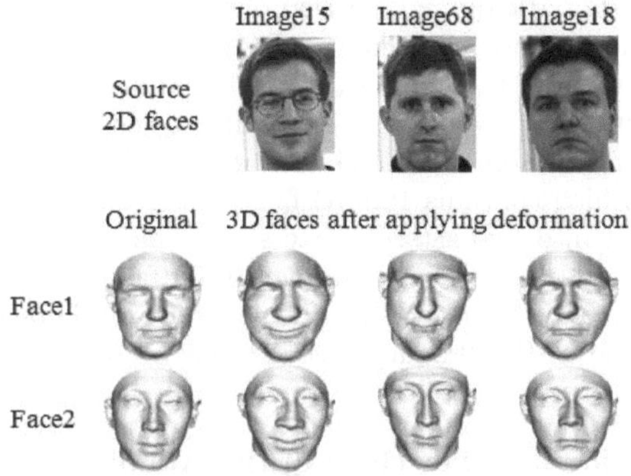

Fig. 3. Typical 3D-2D registration scheme based on the proposed deformation model. The top row shows three 2D face images. Column 1 (left most) shows original two 3D faces. The corresponding deformed faces are shown in columns 2, 3 and 4 (right most).

3.3 3D Face Reconstruction Based on Regularization

After training the 3D face model with the new training set (original training face shapes and deformed 3D face shapes), the well known regularized algorithm has been used for 3D face shape reconstruction. The regularized algorithm has been categorized as one of the existing four core methods for 3D facial reconstruction [15]. The manually selected feature points have been used to compute the 3D shape coefficients of the eigenvectors using equation (13). Then, these coefficients were used to reconstruct the 3D face shape using equation (11). Let t be the number of feature points that can be selected from the input 2D face image, $S_f = (p_1, p_2, ..., p_t) \in R^{2t}$ be the set of selected points on the 2D face image, whereas every point p_i has 2 axes viz., x and y, $S_{f0} \in R^{2t}$ be the t corresponding points on S_0 (the average 3D face shape) and $E_f \in R^{2t \times m}$ be the t corresponding columns on $E \in R^{3n \times m}$ (the matrix of row eigenvectors) where m and n respectively represent the first potential eigenvectors and the number of vertices of the eigenvectors. Then the coefficient α of a new 3D face shape can be derived as

$$\alpha = (E_f^T E_f + \lambda \Lambda^{-1})^{-1} E_f^T (S_f - S_{f0})) \;, \tag{13}$$

where Λ is a diagonal $m \times m$ matrix with diagonal elements being the eigenvalues and λ being the weighting factor. Then α is applied to equation (11) to obtain the whole 3D face shape.

4 Experiments and Discussion

In this section we intend to report the experimental evaluation aspects of the proposed adaptive PCA-based model in comparison to the standard PCA-based model. We have systematically categorized our experimental study in terms of two phases: In the first phase, the adaptive PCA-based model is evaluated quantitatively in comparison to the standard PCA-based model. In the second phase the model is qualitatively evaluated pertaining to the visualization aspect of the reconstructed faces from their 2D face images. The USF Human ID 3D Face database [4] which contains 100 3D faces has been used. The 100 3D face shapes were divided into two sets; 80 face shapes have been used for training and deforming purposes and the remaining 20 3D face shapes have been used for testing. Further to visually evaluate the accuracy of 3D reconstruction from single 2D images, the CMU-PIE database [22] has been used.

4.1 Representational Power (RP) of the Adaptive Model

As an example of 40 deformed faces, the adaptive PCA model has been trained with 120 3D face shapes which include 80 original training 3D face shapes and the 40 deformed face shapes while the standard PCA model has been trained with 80 original 3D face shapes. Fig. 4 shows the representation errors (Ed_w) found by the standard PCA-based model and the adaptive PCA-based model for 20 probe face shapes. We perceive that Ed_w of the new face shape actually represents the accuracy of representation. It can be seen that the adaptive PCA-based model reduces the representative errors when compared to the standard PCA-based model for all probe faces.

Moreover, the statistical t-Test has been applied to compare the two models. The α-value of the t-Test (level of significance) has been chosen to be 0.05 which means that the two models have been compared at a 95% confidence level. The average results of the 20 probe face shapes shown in Table 1 indicates that the adaptive PCA-based model outperforms the standard PCA-based model with a 95% confidence level, whereas the P-value of the t-Test corresponding to the two models is less than $\alpha = 0.05$ (level of significance). This indicates that there is a statistically significant difference between the representation errors of the two

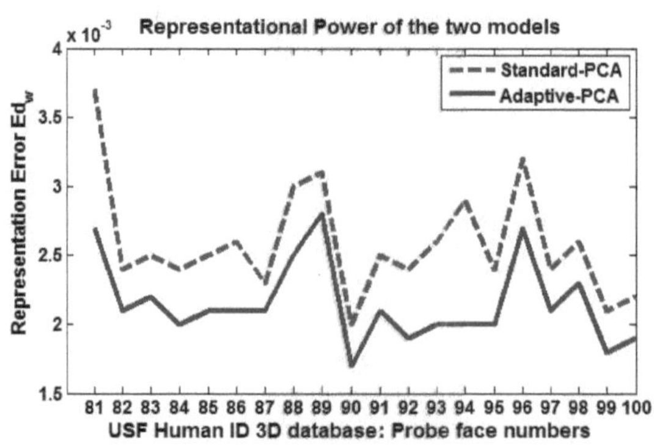

Fig. 4. Comparison between the standard-PCA and the adaptive-PCA in terms of *Representational Power*

Table 1. Comparative results between the representation errors of standard PCA-based model and the adaptive PCA-based model

Model	Mean Error	Std. Dev.	P-value of t-test
Standard Model	2.59×10^{-3}	4.07×10^{-4}	1.07×10^{-8}
Adaptive Model	2.15×10^{-3}	3.02×10^{-4}	

models and justifies that the proposed method yields better RP than that of the standard PCA-based model.

Three typical representations of probe face shapes represented using both models are visualized in Fig. 5. The represented 3D face models for some typical face images shown in Fig. 5 clearly demonstrate that sharp features of the facial components (eg. nose, lips) are well retained by the proposed adaptive PCA-based model when compared to the standard PCA-based model.

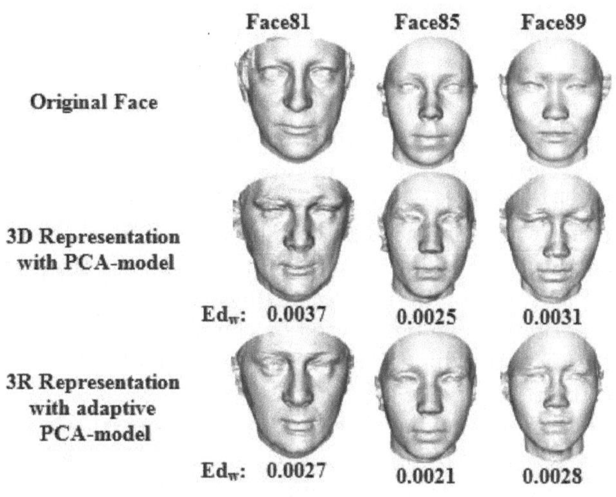

Fig. 5. Visual comparison of represented 3D face shapes using the standard PCA-based model and the adaptive PCA-based model

4.2 3D Face Shape Reconstruction from 2D Image

As an example, the adaptive PCA model has been trained with 90 3D face shapes including 80 original training 3D face shapes and the 10 deformed face shapes while the standard PCA model has been trained with 80 original 3D face shapes. This number of training faces was potentially suitable for building a 3D face reconstruction model where only limited number of feature points was used for 3D face reconstruction. The CMU-PIE database [22] have been used for testing the visual effects of the proposed model. We intend to reconstruct 3D models for the 2D images of CMU-PIE database. The comparisons between some typical 2D face images and their 3D reconstructions using standard PCA model and the adaptive PCA model are illustrated in Fig. 6. From the results

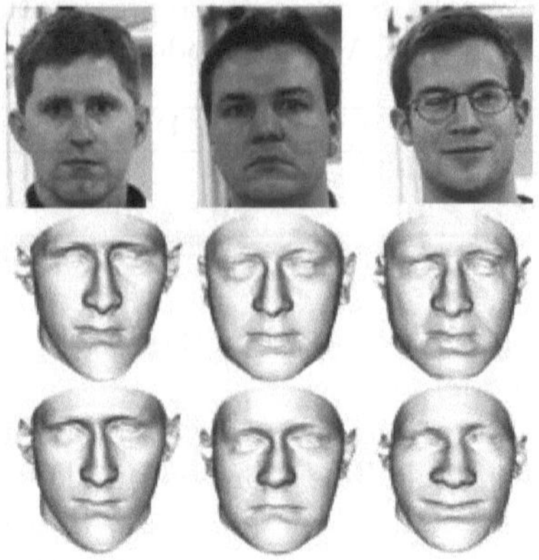

Fig. 6. Visual comparison. (a) Typical input 2D images; (b) 3D reconstruction using normal PCA-based model; (c) 3D reconstruction using adaptive PCA-based model.

in Fig. 6(c), one could notice some visual improvements in the reconstructed 3D face shapes. For example, in the middle face image of Fig. 6(c), the reconstructed 3D face shape has retained some expression of the input image (Fig. 6(a)) such as the facial grimace, chin features, and lips expressions. In the right most face image of the same figure, the 3D face shape has been reconstructed from the 2D image without losing the smile expression. This means that the capability of the model to depict a new 3D face can be improved when 3D exemplar training faces are deformed with the guidance of the input 2D image. However, in addition to the number of feature points used for 3D face shape reconstruction [19], the accuracy of reconstruction can be affected by the number and position of feature points used for deformation modeling, and proportion of deformed faces vs. the original faces in the training data.

Interestingly the proposed model is capable of reconstructing 3D faces from 2D face images by retaining facial expressions though the training samples what we have used contain only neutral expression. By this way we don't impose that the training samples should contain a variety of expressions as imposed by certain recent approaches (eg. Shu-Fan and Shang-Hong [25]).

All experiments were implemented on a workstation with processor Intel(R) Xeon(R) CPU E5620 @ 2.40GH. Assuming that the feature points are available, our MATLAB implementation of the algorithm (including deforming 10 faces, rebuilding the PCA-model and reconstructing the complete face shape vector) takes approximately 72 seconds. Compared with other methods, the proposed method is able to outperform those proposed in [3] and [25] in terms of efficiency. It is also comparably comparative with others such that proposed in [21] and [13].

5 Conclusion and Future Work

In this paper, a novel approach for the problem of 3D face reconstruction from single 2D face images have been proposed. A 3D deformable PCA-based model has been adapted for a given input 2D face image by deforming 3D faces in the training data set so as to gain significant RP. Then, the adapted PCA-based model is used to reconstruct a 3D face shape from the given input 2D image using a number of feature points. The experimental results demonstrate that the proposed deformation model scheme increases the representational power of the PCA-based model for any given input face image. However, deforming 3D face shapes using TPS tends to increase the computational cost of the proposed scheme compared to the standard PCA-based model. Hence, deformation techniques other than TPS would be considered for the future work to improve the deformation synthesis. Furthermore, we will study the effect of deformed faces number on the reconstruction accuracy.

References

1. Atick, J., Griffin, P., Redlich, A.: Statistical approach to shape from shading: Reconstruction of three-dimensional face surfaces from single two-dimensional images. Neural Computation 8(6), 1321–1340 (1996)
2. Besl, P., McKay, H.: A method for registration of 3D shapes. IEEE Transactions on Pattern Analysis and Machine Intelligence 14(2), 239–256 (1992)
3. Blanz, V., Vetter, T.: Face recognition based on fitting a 3D morphable model. IEEE Transactions on Pattern Analysis and Machine Intelligence 25(9), 1063–1074 (2003)
4. Blanz, V., Vetter, T.: A morphable model for the synthesis of 3D faces. In: Proceedings of the 26th Annual Conference on Computer Graphics and Interactive Techniques, SIGGRAPH 1999, pp. 187–194. ACM Press/Addison-Wesley Publishing Co., New York (1999), `http://dx.doi.org/10.1145/311535.311556`
5. Bookstein, F.L.: Principal warps: Thin-plate splines and the decomposition of deformations. IEEE Transactions on Pattern Analysis and Machine Intelligence 11(6), 567–585 (1989)
6. Bottino, A., De Simone, M., Laurentini, A., Sforza, C.: A new 3D tool for planning plastic surgery. IEEE Transactions on Bio-medical Engineering (2012)
7. Brown, B., Rusinkiewicz, S.: Non-rigid range-scan alignment using thin-plate splines. In: Proceedings of the 2nd International Symposium on 3D Data Processing, Visualization and Transmission, 3DPVT 2004, pp. 759–765. IEEE (2004)
8. Elyan, E., Ugail, H.: Reconstruction of 3D human facial images using partial differential equations. JCP, 1–8 (2007)
9. Fanany, M.I., Ohno, M., Kumazawa, I.: Face Reconstruction from Shading Using Smooth Projected Polygon Representation NN. In: Proceedings of the 15th International Conference on Vision Interface, Calgary, Canada, pp. 308–313 (May 2002)
10. Farkas, L.G.: Anthropometry of the head and face, 2nd edn. Raven Press (1994)
11. Hu, Y., Jiang, D., Yan, S., Zhang, L.: Automatic 3D reconstruction for face recognition. In: Proceedings of the Sixth IEEE International Conference on Automatic Face and Gesture Recognition, pp. 843–848. IEEE (2004)
12. Jiang, D., Hu, Y., Yan, S., Zhang, L., Zhang, H., Gao, W.: Efficient 3D reconstruction for face recognition. Pattern Recogn. 38, 787–798 (2005), `http://dx.doi.org/10.1016/j.patcog.2004.11.004`

13. Kemelmacher-Shlizerman, I., Basri, R.: 3D face reconstruction from a single image using a single reference face shape. IEEE Transactions on Pattern Analysis and Machine Intelligence 33(2), 394–405 (2011)
14. Knothe, R., Romdhani, S., Vetter, T.: Combining PCA and LFA for surface reconstruction from a sparse set of control points. In: 7th International Conference on Automatic Face and Gesture Recognition, FGR 2006, pp. 637–644. IEEE (2006)
15. Levine, M.D. (Chris) Yu, Y.: State-of-the-art of 3D facial reconstruction methods for face recognition based on a single 2D training image per person. Pattern Recogn. Lett. 30, 908–913 (2009), http://dl.acm.org/citation.cfm?id=1552570.1552692
16. Lin, C., Cheng, W., Liang, S.: Neural-network-based adaptive hybrid-reflectance model for 3D surface reconstruction. IEEE Transactions on Neural Networks 16(6), 1601–1615 (2005)
17. Lu, X., Jain, A.: Deformation modeling for robust 3D face matching. IEEE Transactions on Pattern Analysis and Machine Intelligence 30(8), 1346–1357 (2008)
18. Luximon, Y., Ball, R., Justice, L.: The 3D chinese head and face modeling. Computer-Aided Design 44(1), 40–47 (2012), digital Human Modeling in Product Design, http://www.sciencedirect.com/science/article/pii/S0010448511000133
19. Maghari, A.Y.A., Liao, I.Y., Belaton, B.: Effect of facial feature points selection on 3D face shape reconstruction using regularization. In: Huang, T., Zeng, Z., Li, C., Leung, C.S. (eds.) ICONIP 2012, Part V. LNCS, vol. 7667, pp. 516–524. Springer, Heidelberg (2012)
20. Maghari, A., Liao, I., Belaton, B.: Quantitative analysis on PCA-based statistical 3D face shape modeling. In: Computational Modelling of Objects Represented in Images III: Fundamentals, Methods and Applications, vol. 13 (2012)
21. Romdhani, S., Blanz, V., Vetter, T.: Face identification by fitting a 3D morphable model using linear shape and texture error functions. In: Heyden, A., Sparr, G., Nielsen, M., Johansen, P. (eds.) ECCV 2002, Part IV. LNCS, vol. 2353, pp. 3–19. Springer, Heidelberg (2002)
22. Sim, T., Baker, S., Bsat, M.: The CMU pose, illumination, and expression database. IEEE Transactions on Pattern Analysis and Machine Intelligence 25(12), 1615–1618 (2003)
23. Smith, W., Hancock, E.: Recovering facial shape using a statistical model of surface normal direction. IEEE Transactions on Pattern Analysis and Machine Intelligence 28(12), 1914–1930 (2006)
24. Wahba, G.: Spline models for observational data, vol. 59. Society for Industrial Mathematics (1990)
25. Wang, S.F., Lai, S.H.: Reconstructing 3D face model with associated expression deformation from a single face image via constructing a low-dimensional expression deformation manifold. IEEE Transactions on Pattern Analysis and Machine Intelligence 33(10), 2115–2121 (2011)

Understanding Big Picture and Its Challenges: Experts and Decision Makers Perspectives

Suraya Ya'acob[1], Nazlena Mohamad Ali[2], and Norshita Mat Nayan[2]

[1] Public Service Department of Malaysia
[2] Institut of Visual Informatics
Universiti Kebangsaan Malaysia,
43600 Bangi,
Selangor, Malaysia
surayayaacob@gmail.com, {nazlena,norshita}@ivi.ukm.my

Abstract. The big picture of an organization plays an important role in providing insight into the decision making process. Thus, the objectives of this paper are to investigate how experts and decision makers obtain the features of the big picture, and then identify related challenges (problems and issues). Data analysis and interpretation show that experts and decision makers gain the big picture through a process of collaboration. Basically there are four main sequences in the collaboration process of constructing the big picture. These are: (i) understanding the big picture requirements, (ii) extracting content from the tools, (iii) collaborating on pieces of information and (iv) using the collaborative information for decision making. In addition, the challenges of attaining the big picture were identified and then clustered into the 3 main components from the perspective of knowledge visualization (KV) on user perception, namely cognition, perception and communication. Data was collected using semi structured interviews following qualitative methods. The sketching technique was used in the one-to-one interviews to represent mental models which are important for later use in the design stage.

Keywords: big picture, knowledge visualization, cognition and perception.

1 Introduction

The visions and the outcomes of an organization are closely related to the decision making processes. As organizational decision making is increasingly complex and dynamic, the collaboration of decision makers and experts becomes an even more critical component for the quality of decision making in management [3].

Lamont explained that the big picture of an organization should provide insight and be the main drivers in decision-making[10] and [11] added that successfully coping with the big picture challenge positively reflects the process of knowledge integration between experts and decision makers, thus enhancing the quality of decision making. Through ten years of collaborative knowledge study, [24] has identified the big picture as one of the key problems in the process of expert/manager knowledge communication as shown in Fig. 1.

H. Badioze Zaman et al. (Eds.): IVIC 2013, LNCS 8237, pp. 311–322, 2013.

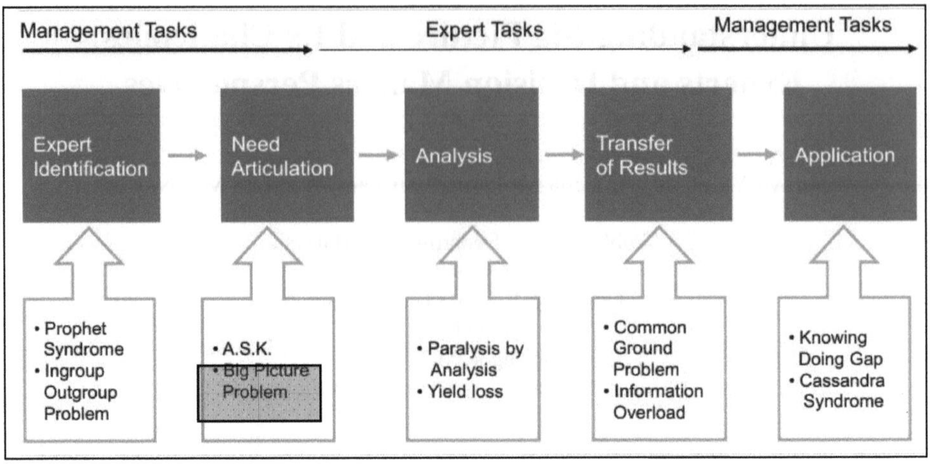

Fig. 1. Key Problems in the Process of Expert/Manager Knowledge Communication [24]

This research investigates big picture problems from the perspective of knowledge communication with computer support, specifically using visualization. The big picture has been described in terms of identifying its main drivers and the interconnections between various perspectives while paying sufficient attention to its relevant details [5].

Investigation into real organization practices has identified that Knowledge Management (KM) and Business Intelligence (BI) support decision makers to gain the big picture in an organization but unfortunately, 50%-70% of KM initiatives fail to fulfill the organization's needs [26] and 30% of BI applications fail to meet business requirements [21].

From the information and interface design perspectives, currently BI technologies and KM initiatives use the concept of Information Visualization (IV) to present information. Through the IV concept, the information will be mapped to a visual coding in terms of architecture, design and interaction. Thus visual techniques and mechanisms such as heat maps, bubble charts, fish eye views and timelines are widely used today as big picture tools [25]. This is because visual representations can utilize the natural capability of experts and decision makers who are better at pattern recognition compared to reading text to obtain the big picture. Further investigations through literature reviews and market studies reveal a gap in the use of visual representations to support organisations. Tergan & Grimm clarify that IV is focussed on coding textual to visual representations and should be synergized with the perceptive capacity of experts and decision makers [15].

Therefore the coding processes in computational environments through information architecture, design and interaction need to be enhanced to meet the cognition, perception and communication needs of experts and decision makers. In order to do that, this research further explores the field of Knowledge Visualization (KV), focusing on fostering knowledge through cognition, perception and communication perspectives [2] and demonstrating how it fulfills the needs in the field of IV.

2 Background of Work

Knowledge Visualization (KV) is an umbrella term for any domain using visual artifacts in sequence to deliver knowledge [15]. Zhang describe KV as an evolution. It started in the 1980s with Scientific Computing Visualization and within two decades, Information Visualization (IV) spread as an alternative solution for information overload [17]. Fig. 2 shows the evolution of Knowledge Visualization.

KV was introduced in 2004 and has been well accepted since then. Through an understanding of users, knowledge transfer and perception should be better, more efficient and should generate more knowledge.

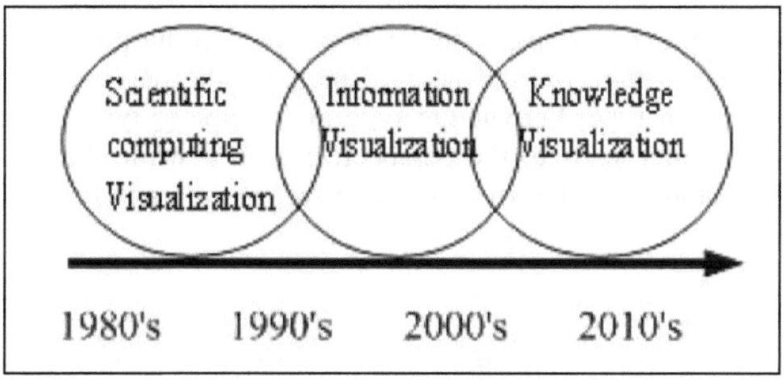

Fig. 2. Knowledge Visualization Evolution [17]

Specifically, Eppler defined KV as the use of visual representations to improve the transfer and creation of knowledge between at least two persons [13]. It is a new field in visualization with business and management as its core. It designates all graphic means that can be used to construct and convey complex insights. Beyond the mere transport of facts, KV aims to transfer insights, experiences, attitudes, values, expectations, perspectives, opinions and predictions, and this in a way that enables someone else to re-construct, remember and apply these insights correctly.

A related field and precursor to KV is information visualization (IV). IV is a rapidly advancing field of study both in terms of academic research and practical applications. [22] Defined IV as "the use of computer-supported, interactive, visual representations of abstract data to amplify cognition".

IV and KV are both exploiting our innate abilities to effectively process visual representations, but the way of using these abilities differs in both domains [15]. IV aims to explore large amounts of abstract (often numeric) data to derive new insights or simply make the stored data more accessible. KV, in contrast, aims to improve the transfer and creation of knowledge among people by giving them richer means of expressing what they know. While IV typically helps to improve information retrieval, access and presentation of large data sets, particularly in the interaction of humans and computers, KV, on the other hand, primarily aims at understanding users and augmenting knowledge-intensive communication between individuals.

IV has reached high technological standards and offers a variety of useful applications in different working, learning and problem solving scenarios. Focusing on techniques and visualization tools has resulted in IV lacking an understanding of the users. While the technical issues have been the focus, the prerequisites of the user for dealing adequately with IV and making sense of visualizations have not gained much attention in the past. It is important to develop new technologies in alignment with the changing demands of the user, because the user is the one who has to interact with the tools. Thus, it is necessary to include the experience and know-how of more user-oriented sciences from KV perspectives into IV tools design. On the other hand, the study of KV has focused more on understanding the users but the shortcomings are related to the lack of representational facilities of the visualization tools. Therefore, more synergistic approaches are needed.

To synergize KV and IV in a coherent manner, this research intends to use the design approach based on the Knowledge Visualization Framework [13] as a foundation. There are four main components in the framework; these are function type, knowledge type, recipient type and visualization type. In the process of identifying a suitable visualization design, this framework includes the perspectives of both users and tools. The function type, knowledge type and recipient type perspectives weigh more on the users which leads to the perspective of KV while the visualization type focuses more on the tools, leading to IV perspective, as shown in Fig. 3.

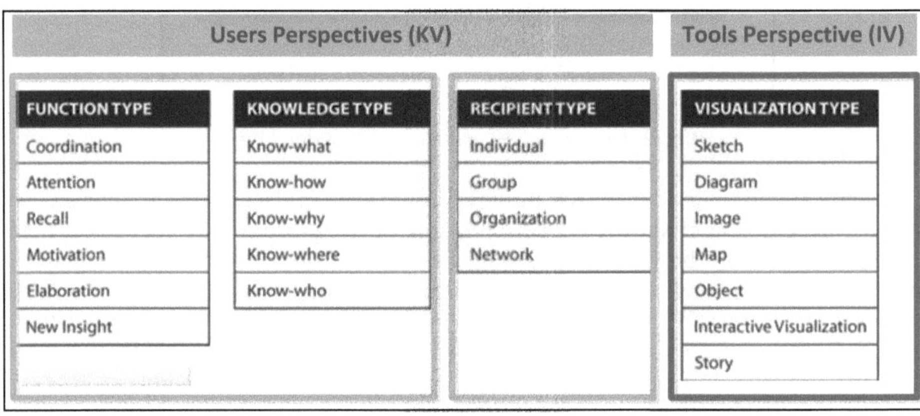

Fig. 3. Knowledge Visualization Framework [13]

However, this paper focuses on the recipient type perspective as in the KV concern, and in terms of knowledge, it only covers the perspective of context. As a preliminary study, the results will indicate the issues and challenges that arise from the users' perspectives (KV concept) in gaining the big picture. Explaining the function type and knowledge type perspectives will be done in another phase. Finally, through a process of dynamic identification [16], the principles of design for visualization tools will be identified within a user's perspective.

3 The Experimental Procedures

As mentioned above, this study intends to identify the challenges in establishing the big picture and to get an understanding about the big picture from the recipient's perspective.

3.1 The Objectives

There are two objectives for the data collection. Firstly is to investigate how experts and decision makers gain the big picture. Secondly is to identify the challenges (problems and issues) related to the big picture from experts and decision makers perspective.

3.2 The Respondents

For this study, the selection of respondents as recipients is based on the concept of knowledge communication. Using this domain concept, Eppler carried out his research among specialists (experts in the field) and decision makers (managers, clients or top management) [24]. As this research is designed to investigate big picture problems that originate from the field of knowledge communication, it uses the same pattern of expert-decision makers to select the recipients. In this case, the ICT Department (experts in the ICT field) and the Chief Information Officer (CIO) Unit (decision makers) were selected. Five recipients were interviewed from the ICT Department and CIO Unit in the Treasury, Ministry of Finance Malaysia as they met the requirements of the research sample:

(i) The respondents were at the Professional/Executives/Grade A level. Experts and decision makers are mostly within this level and this eliminates the issue of different education and work background.
(ii) The respondents had more than five years working experience. The data collection needed to obtain the perspective of experts and decision makers and how they integrate knowledge to form the big picture. Respondents with this range of work experience are mostly experts who influence decision making and some of them had been promoted to the management team (decision makers).

3.3 The Task and Setting

Data was collected using semi structured interviews, following qualitative methods. Interestingly, the sketching technique, introduced by Bischof [3], was used to facilitate one-to-one interviews. The visual representations through sketches may represent the respondents' mental models which are important for later use in the design stage. Besides, they support qualitative interviewing by providing an overarching structure which organizes information, coordinates the conversation and highlights key aspects. Before the interview, there was a session to introduce the objectives of the interview and to briefly explain the sketching concept that would be used during the interview. The interview was divided into three main components as shown below:

(i) Defining the Big Picture
The initial phase of the interview was to get a mutual understanding about the definition of the big picture. The respondents described the meaning of the big picture from their perspectives. Using big picture variables provided by [11], the interviewer included and explained additional facts. By building mutual understanding, indirectly the respondents will better understand the concept of the big picture that the study seeks to investigate.

(ii) Accessing the Job Scope
The respondents were then asked to list out their scope of work. From the list, the interviewer picked the most regular or unique job scope for further investigation.

(iii) Understanding the Big Picture from the Job Scope Perspective.
For the particular job scope selected, the respondents were asked to give a few examples of recurring problems. The interviewer then picked one of the problems as the new sketching subject. Respondents employed think-aloud through sketching techniques when describing the particular problem. All of the respondents were able to clearly describe the problem and fluently explained the main drivers, key points, information details and the relationships within the job scope.

4 Results

The results section has been divided according to the objectives of this user study. First, it presents how the big picture is constructed through knowledge integration and collaboration from multiple sources. Understanding the process contributes towards understanding the big picture concept. The second part describes the challenges, issues and problems faced by the experts and decision makers while gaining the big picture.

4.1 Construction of the Big Picture

To understand how these experts and decision makers construct the big picture, a list of the respondents' answers is given below:

- *Respondent 1 said it took him 8 years to gain the big picture of his organization. From time to time, he gained the knowledge through managing several of the company's projects. Each project gave him an insight from a different perspective. Nowadays, he can link them all and give weightage from every hand (key point).*
- *Respondent 4 mentioned that she needed at least 3 months to understand the job scope, to read and digest the workflow process, to search and understand the policies, circulars and to ask people for help if she could not get the information from the documents.*
- *Respondent 5 said that the time taken depended on the complexity of the big picture and the incoming task. If it was simple, then the process of getting it done was less complex. But when it was complex, she needed to gain more knowledge through previous cases, through files and the internet, and by asking the people inside and outside the agency before producing solutions.*

From the list above, it appears that experts and decision makers gain the big picture through a process. A process, as defined by the business dictionary [26], is a sequence of interdependent and linked key points which at every stage, consumes one or more resources (explicit and tacit knowledge) to convert the incoming issues to quality solutions (outcomes).

Furthermore, experts and decision makers combine and relate multiple data, information and knowledge (tacit and explicit) using various types of tools. [9] define the combination and relation of more than one data source as a collaboration process. As a collaboration process, the big picture challenge is about seeing and explaining the multiple connections of an issue. Experts and decision makers have to juggle simultaneously a multitude of causes, (indirect) implications, and contextual factors. In this view, the challenge of creating the big picture is also related to the capacity of systemic thinking and relates to cognitive capacity. Basically there are four main sequences in the collaboration process in order to construct the big picture:

- Understand the big picture requirements
- Extract the content/material from the tools.
- Collaborate on the pieces of information.
- Use the collaborative information for the decision making.

4.2 Challenges in Gaining the Big Picture

After understand that there are four main sequences in the collaboration process in order to construct the big picture, next step is to identify the challenges rely in each of the steps. There are basically four main challenges. The challenges have been group as (i) Pattern of the incoming issues, (ii) Level of abstraction and detail, (iii) Complexity and the key point changes and (iv) Tools usage.

The finding shows that there are wide gap and diversity of the requirements between experts and decision makers. Table 1 is the summary of the challenges for experts and decision makers while gaining the big picture.

Table 1. Challenges for Experts and Decision Makers in Formulating the Big Picture

No.	Challenges	The Expert	The Decision Maker
i.	**Pattern of incoming issues**		
a.	Field of Expertise	Mostly related to the experts' related field (focus)	Mostly involves the whole/various field(s) of expertise
b.	Issues similarities	Mostly the incoming issue is similar to previous cases.	Mostly the incoming issue is unique. It requires new solutions, ideas, innovations, decision making and evaluation.
c.	The need for a big picture solution	Less important: To initially understand the job scope.	More important: Emphasizes the need to sustain the big picture throughout the collaboration process.

Table 1. *(Continued)*

No.	Challenges	The Expert	The Decision Maker
d.	The usage	As a reminder /reference through the collaboration process.	Emphasizes the need to sustain the big picture to handle complexities of the collaboration.
ii.	**The Level of Abstraction and Detail**		
a.	Coverage	Within limited (one) job scope or expertise	From various expert fields
iii.	**The Complexity and the Level of Key Point Changes**		
a.	Key points	Low changes for the key points	High changes for the key points
b.	Perspectives	Considers a specific perspective (One perspective holds one or more key points)	Considers various perspectives (Each perspective holds one or more key points).
c.	Complexity	Less Complex	More complex
iv.	**Tools Usage**		
a.	The same usage	• Standard Operating Procedure (SOP) • Desktop Files ("Fail Meja") • Flow Chart • Manual Work Procedure • Policies	• Circulars ("pekeliling") • System (specific for the task) • Email • Contract Document • Minutes of Meetings • Search Engine/Internet
b.	Different for explicit tools	• Checklist • Work Procedure Kit • Video Tutorial • Demo – latest technology Portal • Simulations	• Related Systems/Applications • Table of Content (TOC) • Previous files • Formal letters • Site Map • BI Dashboard
c.	Different for tacit tools	• Skills Experience – benefit of salary increment if in the related specific field • Ask people (boss, subordinate, colleague) • Training	• Working Experience - advantage for higher position if there has been involvement in the various fields • Ask people – internal/external (organisation) • Expert views/ opinion/paperwork • Observation

5 Discussion

From the data collection analysis and interpretation, it was found that the data collection fulfilled the purposes: the two main objectives were clearly addressed.

Table 2. Summary of Big Picture Challenges

Cognition	Perception	Communication
Complexity of level of requirements • Experts: Less complex • DMs : More complex	Experts and DMs mostly use the same tools but with different coverage.	Manual searching process from sources is very time and energy consuming.
Unsure which information to delete as the working memory can only hold seven plus minus two components at one time. So users tend to hold as much as possible and this contributes to a higher cognitive load	**The different field coverage** • Experts: Related to their field of expertise (focus) • DMs: Involves the whole/various field(s) of expertise	**The need for the big picture** • Experts: For early tasks • DMs: Sustains the big picture to handle the complexities of the collaboration.
No supporting tools while doing the analysis. The analysis happens in the user's head	**Level of information abstraction** • Experts: more detailed (vertical) • DMs: more abstract (horizontal)	Difficulty in communicating complex working ideas (knowledge sharing)
Cognitive background through experience helps decision makers construct the big picture easily	**Perspectives considered** • Experts: Specific • DMs: Various	
	Issues Similarities • Experts: Similar • DMs: Unique	
The need for structure and organization of the information for better understanding.	**Level of Key Points changes** • Experts: Low changes • DMs: High changes	
	Not well guided to access the relevant information. Uncertainty regarding related information may lead to missing, forgetting or losing valuable information	

* DMs = Decision Makers

The first objective was to investigate how the experts and decision makers discern the big picture. This has been clearly answered through the interview's content extraction and analysis. Experts and decision makers gain the big picture through the collaborative process and the requirements of the incoming issue determine the complexity of the process. It also impacts the extraction of information from the tools in terms of usage, depth and coverage. A primary finding is that the process of gaining the big picture depicts the mental model and cognitive processes highlighted in Bloom's Taxonomy.

The second objective was to identify the challenges related to determining the big picture from the perspective of experts and decision makers. After discussions with experts and decision makers, the challenges have been identified not only from the problems or issues arising but also from the needs and requirements mentioned by them. The list of challenges has been clustered into three main components, namely cognition, perception and communication as highlighted in KV perspectives on user perception [1]. Table 2 presents a summary of the challenges, grouped according to the cognition, perception and communication components.

6 Conclusion

Based on the Design Principles for Visual Communication [20] and identification process [16], the next stage is to elaborate on and identify the design principles that will help experts and decision makers get the big picture. In order to meet the experts and decision makers' requirements in getting the big picture, the visual perception from the perspective of experts and decision makers (users) should be synergized with the visual coding perspective, thus the concept of IV should be mapped on to the concept of KV.

Regarding the information and interface design concepts, the mapping process is based on the basic components of IV and KV. Thus, three main components from KV (user) perspectives namely cognition, perception and communication will be synergized with the information architecture, design and interactive components from IV (visual coding) perspectives as shown in Table 3.

Table 3. Main Components for KV and IV

User Perceive (KV perspectives - human)	**Visual Coding (IV perspectives - technical)**
Cognition	Information Architecture
Perception	Design
Communication	Interactive

From the interpretations of the data collected, the challenges in gaining the big picture from the perspective of experts and decision makers (users) have been identified and clustered according to the three main KV components as mentioned above. Further, the forthcoming plan is to identify suitable IV components in order to fulfill the requirements of experts and decision makers.

Firstly, the navigation, structure, organization, management, relationship and strategy used in the information architecture components should reduce the cognitive load of experts and decision makers relevant to user cognition challenges and conditions. Secondly, the context and task variables for the information and visual design must suit the perception of experts and decision makers. Thirdly, the interactive mechanism, pre-structuring mental model and technology interactivity should resolve the communication issues of experts and decision makers.

References

[1] Bertschi, S.: Knowledge Visualization and Business Analysis: Meaning as Media. In: IEEE International Conference Information Visualization, vol. 13, pp. 480–485 (2009)

[2] Bresciani, S., Eppler, M.J.: Choosing Knowledge Visualizations to Augment Cognition: The Managers' View. In: IEEE International Conference Information Visualization, vol. 14, pp. 355–360 (2010)

[3] Bischof, N., Comi, A., Eppler, M.J.: Knowledge Visualization in Qualitative Methods - Or How Can I See What I Say? In: IEEE International Conference Information Visualization, vol. 15, pp. 371–376 (2011)

[4] Dillon, K.M., Talbot, P.J., Hillis, W.D.: Knowledge Visualization: Redesigning the Human-Computer Interface. Technology Review Journal 13(1), 37–55 (2005)

[5] Mengis, J., Eppler, M.J.: Seeing versus Arguing. The Moderating Role of Collaborative Visualization in Team Knowledge Integration. Journal of Universal Knowledge Management 1(3), 151–162 (2006)

[6] Eppler, M.J., Hoffmann, F., Bresciani, S.: New Business Models Through Collaborative Idea Generation. International Journal of Innovation Management 15(06), 1323–1341 (2011)

[7] Eppler, M.J., Mengis, J., Bresciani, S.: Seven Types of Visual Ambiguity: On the Merits and Risks of Multiple Interpretations of Collaborative Visualizations. In: IEEE International Conference of Information Visualization, vol. 12, pp. 391–396 (2008)

[8] Bresciani, S., Blackwell, A.F., Eppler, M.: A Collaborative Dimensions Framework: Understanding the mediating role of conceptual visualizations in collaborative knowledge work. In: IEEE Hawaii International Conference on System Sciences, vol. 41, pp. 364–364 (2008)

[9] Kolfschoten, G.L., Brazier, F.: Cognitive Load in Collaboration-Convergence. In: Hawaii International Conference on System Sciences, vol. 45, pp. 129–138 (2012)

[10] Liu, Z., Stasko, J.T.: Mental models, visual reasoning and interaction in information visualization: a top-down perspective. IEEE Transactions On Visualization and Computer Graphics 16(6), 999–1008 (2010)

[11] Mengis, J., Eppler, M.J.: Understanding and Managing Conversations from a Knowledge Perspective: An Analysis of the Roles and Rules of Face-to-face Conversations in Organizations. Organization Studies 29(10), 1287–1313 (2007)

[12] Miller, G.A.: The magical number seven, plus or minus two: some limits on our capacity for processing information. Psychological Review 101(2), 343–352 (1994)

[13] Burkhard, R.A.: Towards a framework and a model for knowledge visualization: Synergies between information and knowledge visualization. In: Tergan, S.-O., Keller, T. (eds.) Knowledge and Information Visualization. LNCS, vol. 3426, pp. 238–255. Springer, Heidelberg (2005)

[14] Sweller, J., Van Merrienboer, J.J.: Cognitive Load Theory and Complex Learning: Recent Developments and future directions. Educational Psychology Review 17(2), 147–177 (2005)
[15] Keller, T., Grimm, M.: The Impact of Dimensionality and Color Coding of Information Visualizations on Knowledge Acquisition. In: Tergan, S.-O., Keller, T. (eds.) Knowledge and Information Visualization. LNCS, vol. 3426, pp. 167–182. Springer, Heidelberg (2005)
[16] Ziemkiewicz, C., Kosara, R.: Implied Dynamics in Information Visualization. In: ACM Proceedings of the International Conference on Advanced Visual Interfaces, pp. 215–222 (2010)
[17] Zhang, J., Zhong, D., Zhang, J.: Knowledge Visualization; an effective way to improve learning. In: IEEE Education Technology and Computer Science ETCS 2010 Second International Workshop, vol. 1, pp. 598–601 (2010)
[18] Dillenbourg, P., Betrancourt, M.: Collaboration Load. In: Elen, E.J., Clark, R.E. (eds.) Dealing with Complexity in Learning Environments, pp. 142–163 (2006)
[19] Akrani, G.: Decision Making Proces. In: Management - Problem Solving. Study Notes in Education and Management (2010)
[20] Agrawala, M., Li, W., Berthouzoz, F.: Design Principles for Visual Communication. Communications of the ACM 54(4), 60–69 (2011)
[21] John, H., Sallam, R.L., Richardson, J.: Magic Quadrat for business intelligence platforms. In: Gartner for Business Leaders (February 2012)
[22] Card, S.K., Mackinlay, J.D., Schneiderman, B.: Information Visualization: Using Vision To Think. Morgan Kaufmann, San Francisco (1999)
[23] Schwartz, D.G.: Encyclopedia of Knowledge Management. IGI Global (2005)
[24] 10 years of Knowledge-Communication.Org; Results, Insights and Perspectives, http://issuu.com/mcminstitute/docs
[25] Resources of Information Visualization, http://www.infovis.org/
[26] Beyond the Podium: Delivering Training and Performance to a Digital World, http://www.jbp.com
[27] Business dictionary, http://www.businessdictionary.com/

Eyes on OSH – Usability Testing with Eye-Tracking and User Preference Rating

Norfarhana Abdollah, Soo Shi Tzuaan, and Ashok Sivaji

Product Quality & Reliability Engineering, MIMOS Berhad, Technology Park Malaysia, 57000, Kuala Lumpur, Malaysia
{norfarhana.abdollah,soo.st,ashok.sivaji}@mimos.my

Abstract. Occupational Safety and Health (OSH) is significant for all personnel engaged in work or employment. OSH websites is as well important as it should be relevant to educate the workers to be aware of any hazard or inconvenience act that may jeopardize their health and safety in workplace. This study is conducted to evaluate three OSH websites which are DOSH, NIOSH and OSHA using eye-tracker equipment to collect usability data. This paper is an extended version of our previous submitted paper which reported the details of methodology and results of usability testing conducted for these three websites. This paper reports the satisfaction results obtained from user's subjective preferences. The satisfaction data is represented into rating percentage and word clouds. This paper also concludes the results of OSH website usability in terms of user satisfaction and preferences with recommendations on further research on usability for OSH domain.

Keywords: usability testing, satisfaction, osh, effectiveness, efficiency, iso/iec 25010.

1 Introduction

Occupational Safety and Health (OSH) is a domain area concerned to protect the health, safety and welfare of all personnel engaged in work or employment. Cited from [1], Occupational Safety and Health Act 1970 is officially authorized with the purpose to guarantee safe and healthful working conditions for working men and women; by authorizing enforcement of the standards developed under the Act; by assisting and encouraging the governments in their efforts to assure safe and healthful working conditions; by providing for research, information, education, and training in the field of occupational safety and health; and for other purposes. Over years, various changes in workplace environment have taken into place such as globalization of many industries, work time scheduling, rapid growth of technology usage in workplace as well as various resources used and expanded. These changes may affect the workplace and workers in such ways that may cause hazard to them. Thus, OSH sets out responsibilities of workplace parties and their worker's rights by establishing procedures for dealing with workplace hazards.

H. Badioze Zaman et al. (Eds.): IVIC 2013, LNCS 8237, pp. 323–334, 2013.

Since OSH organizations play crucial role in educating workers regarding health and safety issues in workplace, OSH websites is unquestionably important as it should be an effective reference medium where all of the desired information pertaining to safety and health matters as workers can be accessed. Thus, the website should be usable enough in order for users to acquire the important information accordingly. Usable website will increase the likeliness of user to obtain all of their desired information and performing any related tasks effectively, efficiently and satisfyingly [2], [3] and [4].

To our knowledge to date, there is no study on usability testing conducted, reported or published regarding OSH websites. Thus we envisage this study will contribute to the knowledge of usability on OSH domain considering user experience while using the websites. This paper is an extension discussion of usability testing results obtained from usability evaluation for all of the three OSH websites in [5]. In this paper however, satisfaction results from the test performed will be discussed in further details.

2 Background of Study

2.1 OSH Websites

Occupational Safety and Health (OSH) website provides information pertaining to cultivate the knowledge of occupational safety and health practices for workers globally. In this study, two Malaysian based and one US based OSH websites have been chosen, namely Department of Occupational Safety and Health Malaysia (DOSH) [6], National Institute of Occupational Safety and Health Malaysia (NIOSH) [7], and Occupational Safety and Health Administration United States (OSHA) [8]. The purpose of choosing these three websites is to benchmark the local (Malaysian) OSH websites usability against international OSH website (US), similar to studies conducted by [2] and [4].

2.2 Usability Evaluation (Satisfaction Metric) for OSH Websites

Usability is defined as a subset of quality in use model consisting of effectiveness, efficiency and satisfaction for consistency with its established meaning [9]. ISO/IEC 25010 in [9] also defines effectiveness as accuracy and completeness which users achieved specified goals; efficiency as total resources expanded (time/material/financial etc.) in relation to accuracy and completeness with which users achieve goals; and satisfaction as the degree to which user needs are satisfied when the system is used in a specified context of use.

In this study, evaluation for usability in terms of satisfaction metric is applied to measure the degree of user's satisfaction while performing the task which includes their subjective preferences on the OSH websites. According to [10], since satisfaction is subjective to users, the measure can be determined by interviewing user directly, using written surveys that may include satisfaction scales and/or providing a means for users to fill in their open-ended comments. In this study, user's satisfaction were reported using two main methods; questionnaire analysis and word clouds. The reason of using two different techniques to measure satisfaction in this study is that by using ordinary questionnaire, users will normally tend to rate an interface highly even when they fail to complete many of the tasks [11]. This study attempts to use the word cloud to visually reference the degree of user's satisfaction towards the OSH websites. Word clouds are clouds generated by automatically analyzing document contents, which is also known as summarized representation of a document's text [12]. Word cloud is useful in order to get a first impression of long documents or to summarize a collection of documents, such as clustered or aggregated search results. This technique also provides a quick and simple visual reference of user's satisfaction [13]. Besides, the advantage of using this technique is that based on the word chosen by users from the checklist, testers may access their emotion towards using the OSH websites after the completion of each task by asking for their subjective comments, as suggested by [14].

3 Objectives and Scope

The main objective of this study is to evaluate the usability of three OSH websites which are DOSH, NIOSH and OSHA by using eye tracker, user feedback and moderator rating. Eye tracking method provides visual cues as in addition to the verbal results obtained from users during the testing. The usability were evaluated based on three metrics adapted from ISO/IEC 25010 namely effectiveness, efficiency and satisfaction.

The objective of this paper is to discuss on the user's satisfaction while performing Task 2 during Lab Based Usability Testing (LBUT) for these three websites. However, the testing does not cover the entire websites as the test mainly focusing on the landing pages. The scope of user is limited to 18 random samples that are all local (Malaysian). The study is only a subset of information retrieval task from the OSH websites, which is aligned to the objective of OSH related organizations to disseminate the information to the nation.

4 Methodology

During the testing, each 18 users were required to complete three tasks for each websites. Table 1 depicts the tasks performed by each of the users. The entire tests were observed by moderator. Conversations between moderator and users as well as user's eye fixation were recorded. Detailed methodology of test conducted is explained in [5].

Table 1. LBUT Task Descriptions

Tasks	Description
1	This is the landing page for the occupational safety and health website. Browse around for 3 minute to get familiar with the webpage.
2	You are interested in the programs organized by the occupational safety and health website. Without using the search box, find information regarding the latest available program.
3	You are interested in the news of the occupational safety and health website. Without using the search box, find information regarding the occupational safety related news

In this study, user's satisfaction were analyzed using two main methods; questionnaire analysis and word clouds. Measures of satisfaction using questionnaire require users to answer post-test question of "I can quickly find the information I need on this Website" after they perform Task 2. The questions and answers are structured using 7 point Likert scale. The scale ranged from 1 (strongly disagree) to 7 (strongly agree).

Besides the questionnaire, users were provided with a checklist adapted from [14]. The checklist is in the form of Microsoft Excel spreadsheet which can be used to generate and randomize word lists to prevent order effects. The users were required to choose words/adjectives that they think most described the websites and best defined their experience while using them. Based on the checklist, they were required to provide feedback by giving subjective comments for the adjectives that they have chosen during post-task interview. Subsequent testing, the chosen words/adjectives were coded into Microsoft Excel spreadsheet. The spreadsheet will automatically analyze the inserted data (adjectives chosen by participants) and generate word clouds accordingly. Word clouds generated from the checklist are used to illustrate the frequency of the adjectives chosen by users. The larger the size of the adjective and the greater the colour contrast indicates the higher frequency of occurrences. The results will be reported in detail in Results and Discussions section.

5 Results and Discussions

From the usability testing, effectiveness, efficiency and satisfaction results have been obtained. Table 2 illustrates the effectiveness and efficiency results and also heatmaps generated while performing Task 2 for all three websites. Note that the red rectangle indicates the target area where the latest program location supposed to be noticed by the users.

Table 2. Effectiveness, Efficiency Result and Heatmaps for Task 2

Website	Result for Task 2	
DOSH [6] 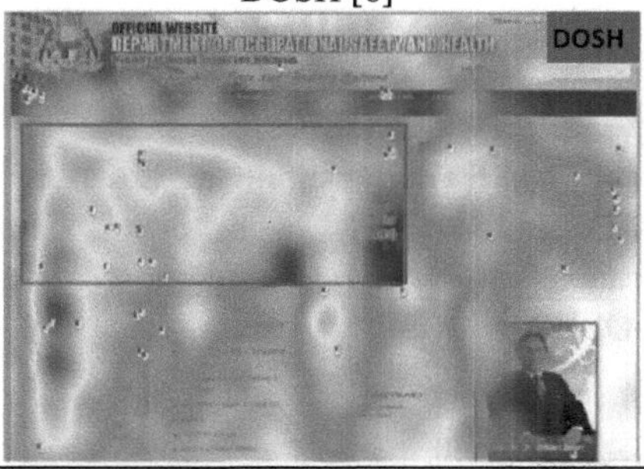	User Success Rate (%)	77
	User Efficiency Rate (%)	61
	Average Timing (second)	144
NIOSH [7] 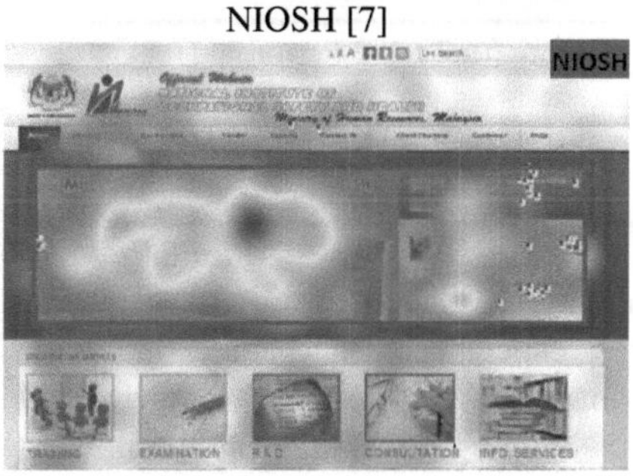	User Success Rate (%)	94
	User Efficiency Rate (%)	89
	Average Timing (second)	60
OSHA [8] 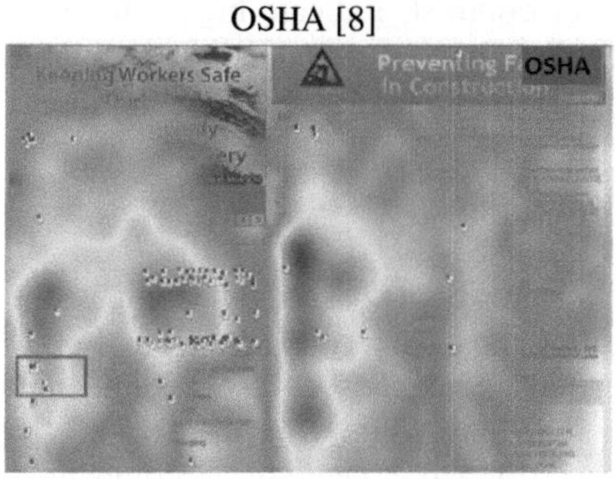	User Success Rate (%)	63
	User Efficiency Rate (%)	32
	Average Timing (second)	206

It could be observed that for NIOSH website, there is high density of the gazes within the rectangle area which indicates that most users managed to find the latest program in most of the area of the expected location. For DOSH website, an inverted 'L' pattern is observed where most users tend to look for the information towards the left vertical side of the page. However, for OSHA website, the target area is very small. There was significant fixation outside the area of interest. This shows that for Task 2, NIOSH website allows the users to perform their task most effectively while for OSHA website; users experienced significant difficulty in performing the task.

Similar to efficiency rate and timing result from Table 2, NIOSH website allowed users to complete the task in most minimum time, followed by DOSH and OSHA website. Note that the shorter time taken by users to perform the task indicates the higher efficiency of the website.

5.1 Satisfaction Results

Table 3 summarizes the satisfaction score obtained from questionnaire based on Task 2 performed by the users for DOSH, NIOSH and OSHA websites respectively. Satisfaction score of 76% obtained indicates that NIOSH is the most satisfying website, followed by DOSH with 58% and OSHA with 35%.

Table 3. Satisfaction Score for Task 2

Website	Satisfaction Score for Task 2 Performed (%)
DOSH	58
NIOSH	76
OSHA	35

Table 4 illustrates the satisfaction percentage score of all 18 subjects while performing Task 2 for these three websites respectively. The agree line starts from ‘somewhat agree’ as indicated using red dotted line. Note that ‘somewhat agree’ in Likert scale means subject agrees to some extend/degree. While Table 5 illustrates the word clouds of adjectives chosen for these three websites respectively. Note that the larger the font size and the greater the colour contrast, indicate higher frequency of selections by user. The adjectives chosen by user also indicate their subjective preferences of the websites which also interprets their experiences of using them.

5.2 Discussions

From the words/adjectives chosen, users were being asked of their subjective comments regarding each of the website after they performed the task. For DOSH website, 4 positive and 8 negative adjectives have been chosen. Users commented that DOSH website is confusing, even though there are users who also stated that the website displays the information straightforwardly and expectedly, accompanied with easy to use feature. From comments, 7 out of 18 users agree that they can quickly find the information they needed from the website. One user mentioned that since the latest available program information is placed on the top of the page make it more visible and easy to be spotted. Besides, the website also provides the label called ‘Latest’, as depicted in (a) in Fig. 1, makes it helpful to spot the required information. However, because of the slideshow which is located at the left side of the latest available program, with quite fast slide animation interval; 3-4 seconds which is too fast for decision making (4 of the users also commented on this), some of them failed to notice the ‘Latest’ label on the right side of it. Two users also commented that the

Table 4. Satisfaction Scores for DOSH, NIOSH and OSHA Websites

Website

DOSH

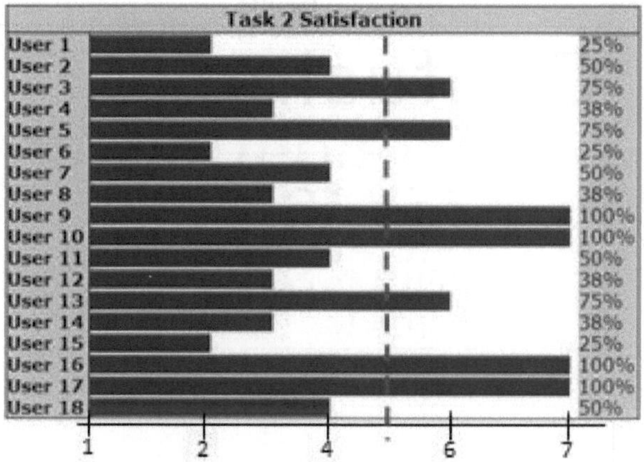

NIOSH

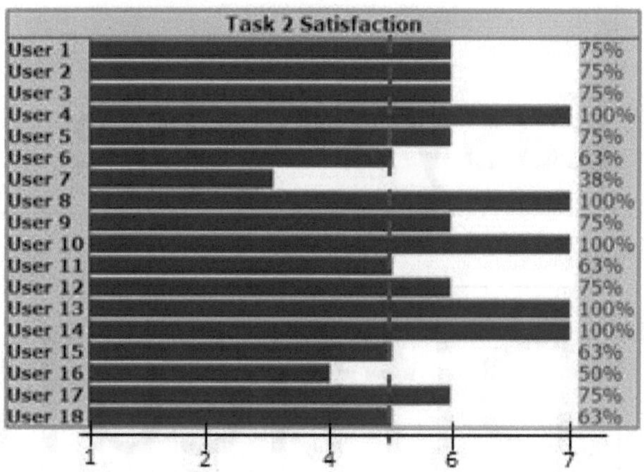

OSHA

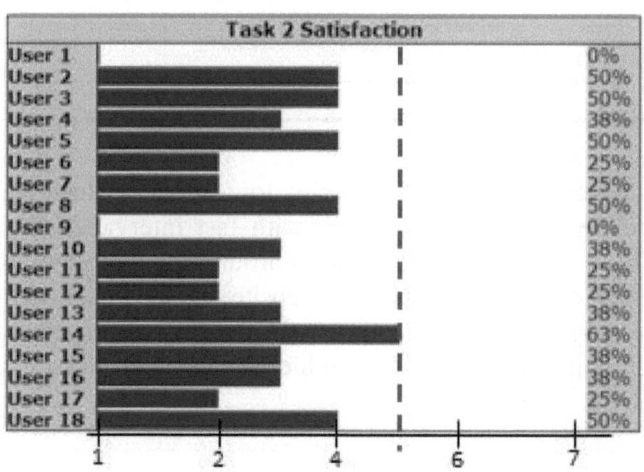

Table 5. Word Clouds generated for DOSH, NIOSH and OSHA Websites

Website
DOSH

NIOSH

OSHA

images in slideshow are unattractive, using low colour contrast and small fonts which make it harder for them to read, more with fast interval of the slideshow. This is depicted in (b) in Fig. 1. The information around the slideshow in DOSH website is also a bit wordy compared to NIOSH website, as shown in (b) in Fig. 2. This may distracted the subjects as they tend to read the text displayed compared to NIOSH website which emphasize more on graphics/images that make it more appealing and informative to the users.

Fig. 1. Slideshow for DOSH website [6]

From the word clouds generated for NIOSH website evaluation, 12 positive and 3 negative adjectives have been chosen. Most of the users agree that NIOSH website is easy to use and require minimal effort with content arrangement that is very accessible. In fact, 12 out of 18 users agree that they can quickly find the information they needed from the website. One user commented that since NIOSH website also provides a static highlighted box next to the slideshow, for the topic address in the slideshow as shown in (a) in Fig. 2, make it much comfortable to be read and the information much easier to be understood. The static box basically emphasized more on the information contained in the animation/slideshow provided. Overall, user's positive comments for NIOSH website indicates high satisfaction and positive user experience while using the website.

Fig. 2. Slideshow for NIOSH website [7]

For OSHA website, only 1 out of 18 users somewhat agree that they can find the required information they needed while performing Task 2. Other 5 users gave score of neutral, 5 disagree, 5 somewhat disagree and 2 totally disagree. From word clouds generated, most users agree that OSHA website is difficult to be used. This is most likely because of the content and information organization are mixed and cluttered and not being categorized accordingly. This is depicted using red boxes highlighted in Fig. 3. 7 users commented that they can hardly find any information on the OSHA website. One of the reasons for this is because the website is too wordy thus making user stressed out while reading to find the information. Other comment is that there are too many thumbnails or link in the form of words/sentences. This kind of thumbnail will complicate the user in order to differentiate between the information and hyperlink. Users also commented that this website provide too many information on one page where they need to read and scroll up and down frequently in order to find the information. Users also stated that it was hard to find the title of the latest program available. Furthermore, two users strongly disagreed or were not satisfied with the website by giving 0 score. They also commented that that the website is not user friendly at all.

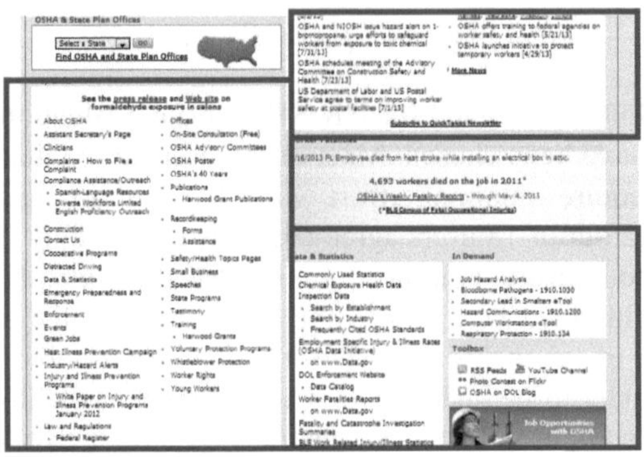

Fig. 3. Thumbnail/Wordy Hyperlinks in OSHA website [8]

Satisfaction score obtained from this evaluation can be concluded as conforming to the effectiveness and efficiency scores gained for Task 2. As discussed, users agree that NIOSH website is the most effective (degree of user successes to complete the task) and efficient (degree of timing/effort taken by user to complete the task) followed by DOSH and OSHA websites. In compliance with the effectiveness and efficiency results, NIOSH website also ranked as the most satisfying website followed by DOSH and OSHA websites respectively. Furthermore, heatmaps shown in Table 3 indicates that there is highest density within target area for NIOSH website, followed by DOSH and OSHA. Thus, the results indicate that the lesser effort and easier a website to be used by user to perform their task, the more satisfy user will be with their overall experiences.

6 Conclusion

This study used an eye-tracking device to capture users' eye movements as well as user preference rating in evaluating usability of OSH websites. Align with study conducted by [13], the word cloud technique provides a quick and simple visual reference of user's satisfaction towards the OSH websites. Besides, it has also useful to cater the situation of evaluating using normal questionnaire method where user typically tend to rate highly and give only positive comments [14]. The word cloud technique used in this study has successfully allowed testers to elicit user's subjective comments whether positive or negative regarding the websites based on the words chosen by them. Comments obtained from the evaluation indicate user's subjective emotions regarding their experience of using the websites.

Website that allows user to perform their desired task effectively and efficiently will likely fulfill user satisfaction as well thus will attract user to use the website again in the future. Results obtained indicates that users preferred NIOSH website the most compared to DOSH and OSHA as NIOSH website satisfy their needs, by allowing them to perform their required task effectively and efficiently. Align with study conducted by [5], it can be concluded that website design that hinder user to perform their desired task efficiently and effectively will consequently leave negative impression to the users, as they will not be satisfied with the overall experiences.

Upon benchmarking local websites again global international website, the results indicates that users of this study prefer local-based websites which are NIOSH and DOSH more compared to OSHA which is US based. Although our study shows that most users preferred the local OSH websites, it is important to identify certain limitations of this study. Firstly, only three tasks were selected and this is certainly not a representation of the entire websites. Secondly, only the landing page of the websites was tested. Besides, all of the users are all local which might also influence the results. Despite these limitations, the findings from the study will be useful for future research which may focus on evaluations of other types of tasks which may consist of greater testing coverage of the OSH website, as well as recruiting different background of users as to generate various types of results.

References

1. OSH Act: Occupational Safety and Health Administration (1970), `https://www.osha.gov/pls/oshaweb/owasrch.search_form?p_doc_type=OSHACT&p_toc_level=0&p_keyvalue=&p_status=CURRENT`
2. Sivaji, A., Mazlan, M.F., Shi–Tzuaan, S., Abdullah, A., Downe, A.G.: Importance of Incorporating Fundamental Usability with Social, Trust & Persuasive Elements for E-Commerce Website. In: IEE EXplore Business Engineering and Industrial Applications (ICBEIA), Kuala Lumpur, Malaysia, pp. 221–226 (2011)
3. Sivaji, A., Tzuaan, S.S.: Website user experience (UX) testing tool development using Open Source Software (OSS). In: 2012 Southeast Asian Network of Ergonomics Societies Conference (SEANES), vol. 1(6), pp. 9–12 (2012)
4. Goh, K.N., Chen, Y.Y., Lai, F.W., Daud, S.C., Sivaji, A., Soo, S.T.: A Comparison of Usability Testing Methods for an E-Commerce Website: A Case Study on a Malaysian Online Gift Shop. In: Tenth International Conference on Information Technology - New Generations (2013)
5. Rashid, S. , Soo, S.T., Sivaji, A., Sadhegi, N.H., Bahri, S.: Preliminary Usability Testing with Eye Tracking and FCAT Analysis on Occupational Safety and Health Websites, (2013)
6. Department of Occupational Safety and Health (DOSH), Malaysia, `http://www.dosh.gov.my/doshv2/` (accessed: March 26, 2013)

7. National Institute of Occupational Safety and Health (NIOSH), Malaysia, http://www.niosh.com.my/en/ (accessed: March 26, 2013)
8. Occupational Safety and Health Administration (OSHA), United State, http://www.osha.gov/index.html (accessed: March 26, 2013)
9. Systems and software engineering – Systems and software Quality Requirements and Evaluation (SQuaRE) – System and software quality models, Ref. No.: MS ISO/IEC 25010 (2011)
10. Shneiderman, B., Plaisant, C.: Designing the user interface:Strategies for Effective Human-Computer Interaction, 5th edn. Addison-Wesley, USA (2010)
11. Travis, D.: Discount Usability: Time to Push Back the Pendulum (2003), http://www.userfocus.co.uk/articles/discount.html
12. Kaptein, R., Hiemstra, D., Kamps, J.: How different are language models andWord clouds? In: Gurrin, C., He, Y., Kazai, G., Kruschwitz, U., Little, S., Roelleke, T., Rüger, S., van Rijsbergen, K. (eds.) ECIR 2010. LNCS, vol. 5993, pp. 556–568. Springer, Heidelberg (2010)
13. Abdollah, N., Ahmad, W.F.W., Akhir, E.A.P.: Development and usability study of multimedia courseware for slow learners: 'Komputer Saya'. In: 2012 International Conference on Computer & Information Science (ICCIS), June 12–14, vol. 2, pp. 1110–1114 (2012)
14. Travis, D.: Measuring satisfaction: Beyond the usability questionnaire (2009), http://www.userfocus.co.uk/articles/satisfaction.html

Simulations of PCB Assembly Optimisation Based on the Bees Algorithm with TRIZ-Inspired Operators

Mei Choo Ang[1,3], Kok Weng Ng[2], Duc Truong Pham[3], and Anthony Soroka[4]

[1] Institute of Visual Informatics, Universiti Kebangsaan Malaysia, Bangi, Malaysia
[2] Industrial Design Centre, Sirim Berhad, Malaysia
[3] School of Mechanical Engineering, University of Birmingham, United Kingdom
[4] Cardiff Business School, Cardiff University, United Kingdom
amc@ukm.my, kwng@sirim.my, d.t.pham@bham.ac.uk, sorokaaj@cardiff.ac.uk

Abstract. The process of assembling electronic components on a printed circuit board (PCB) with moving board time delay characteristic involves complex co-ordination of a component feeding system, a pick and place system and the positioning movement of the PCB board. Different component arrangements in the feeder system and different assembly paths influence the total assembly time. Reducing the total assembly time can deliver significant cost savings. In this research work, the application of simulation to component assembly enables process engineers to visualise, compare assembly paths and the arrangement of the feeders as well as to verify the total assembly time achieved. This allows the process engineers to make better decision on the planning of the PCB assembly process. The paper shows that simulation when coupled with optimisation techniques enable process engineers to make and plan improvements in PCB assembly times.

Keywords: simulation, TRIZ, pcb assembly, Bees Algorithm, optimisation.

1 Introduction

The automation of the assembly process for electronic components on a printed circuit board (PCB) with moving board time delay characteristic (MBTD) involves the complex co-ordination of a component feeding system, a pick and place system and the positioning movement of the PCB board. Hence, the planning of the component arrangement in the feeder system, the assembly path and the sequence of the assembly as well as the movement of the PCB board are crucial before the actual assembly process begins. Such planning allows the process engineers to establish the total assembly time and determine how many PCB boards can be assembled in a day. Such information enables manufacturers to determine whether it can fulfill the demands of their customers and whether they can keep their delivery promise.

Planning of PCB assembly processes is not a new research area and as such a lot of research work has been carried out by a number of researchers aiming to improve the total assembly time [1], [2], [3], [4], [5] and [6]. There are three types of PCB

H. Badioze Zaman et al. (Eds.): IVIC 2013, LNCS 8237, pp. 335–346, 2013.

assembly machine configurations [7] as shown in Fig. 1, these machines assemble surface-mount electronic components (SMC). Assembling these components is a time consuming process as the process involves many components which need to be placed at different locations and is therefore considered a critical process in the electronics industry [8].

	Configuration 1	**Configuration 2**	**Configuration 3**
Model of System	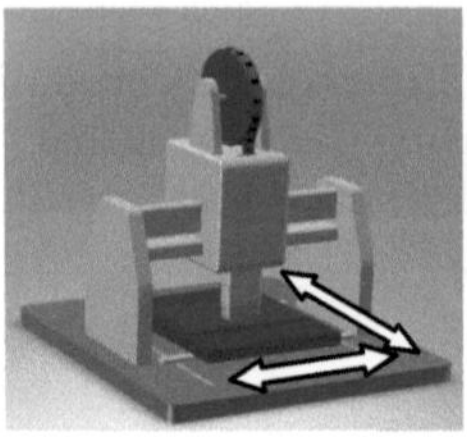	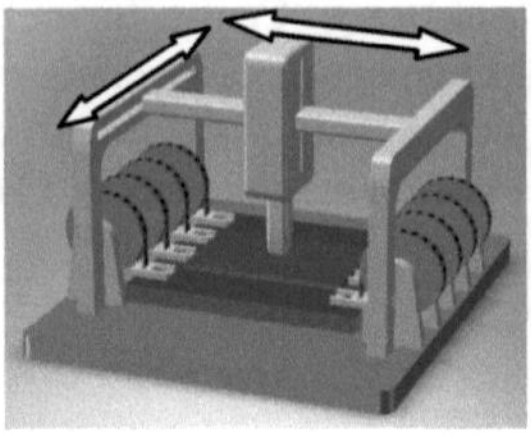	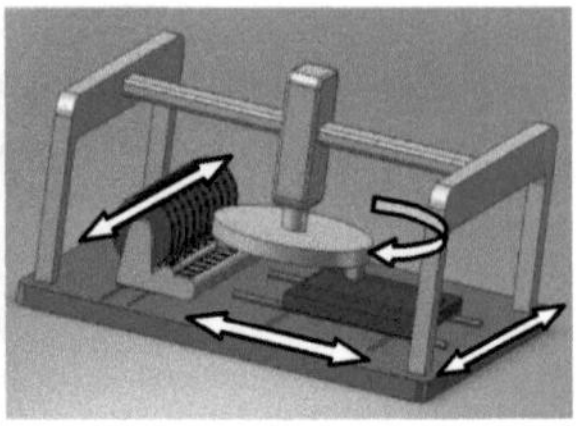
Model of problem	Travelling salesman	Pick and place	Moving board with time delay (MBTD)
Key characteristics of solution	1. The path to assemble the components	1. The feeder slot arrangement. 2. The shortest path to assemble the components.	1. The feeder slot arrangement. 2. The shortest path to assemble the components. 3. The number of heads on the assembly turret.

Fig. 1. The three configurations of the PCB Assembly machine [9]

As shown Fig. 1, all three types of configuration are different from each other where Configuration 1 has the simplest component assembly task. A PCB assembly machine with Configuration 1 has only the PCB mounting table moving in X-Y axis as the static feeder system feeds the components onto the PCB. Hence, the planning of SMC assembly for a machine with Configuration 1 is similar to the classic travelling salesman problem. This means that the main task of the PCB assembly planning for Configuration 1 is to find a shortest path to move from one point to another to place the components until all the points have been visited exactly once before returning to the starting point. One of the main disadvantages of PCB assembly machine with such a configuration is that only a single type of component can be assembled in one complete assembly cycle as it has only one feeder system. As the only movable mechanism in this machine is the mounting table which holds the PCB and can only move in X-Y axis. The total assembly time is only dependent on the component sequencing and the speed of the mounting table.

PCB assembly planning Configuration 2 can assemble multiple types of components as it has a multi-feeder system, which is commonly known as the Sequential Pick and Place Machine (PAP) [8]. Such a system has the PCB fix-mounted and with a multiple feeder system feeding the components to be picked and placed by the assembly arm. Machines with such configuration have the flexibility to assemble a broad range of PCB sizes. The total assembly time is dependent on the travelling speed and distance of the assembly arm. The traveling distance of the assembly arm is dependent on the location of the component feeders and the location of the components to be placed on the PCB. Hence, the sequencing of the component to be assembled and the arrangement of the feeders affects the total assembly time. The complexity of finding the shortest total assembly time is much higher than with Configuration 1. The process engineers that plan the assembly operations have to consider both factors, namely the component sequencing and the feeder arrangement to optimise the total assembly time. The speed of travel of the assembly arm that picks and places the components also affects the total assembly time.

Finally, the last configuration for the PCB assembly machine is Configuration 3 as shown in Fig. 1. This type of PCB assembly machine is known as the PCB Assembly Machine Moving Board with Time Delay (MBTD) [7] or Concurrent Chip Shooter (CS) Machine [8]. This type of assembly machine presents the most complex assembly problem in PCB assembly as the machine has three movable mechanisms [8]. The type of assembly machine consists of a multi-feeders system that holds multiple type of component, a rotary turret with one or more assembly heads and a X-Y axis moving table that holds the PCB (see Configuration 3 in Fig. 1). All three movable mechanisms have to be synchronised and move concurrently. Hence, the total assembly time for a CS is dependent on all three mechanisms and need to be optimised. The slowest of the three movable mechanisms will dictate the rate of assembly.

For this research work, we focused on the most complex of all three PCB assembly machine, namely the CS machine. The next section will explore in briefly about how a CS machine planning is performed particularly using the Bees algorithm with TRIZ-inspired operators and the role of simulation in the planning of PCB assembly.

2 The Planning of PCB Assembly for a Concurrent Chip Shooter Machine

The introduction to the three types of configuration for the PCB assembly machines in the previous section highlighted their difference particularly in the complexity of assembly. Due to the complexities involving synchronisation of three movable mechanisms, the Concurrent Chip Shooter (CS) machine presents a very challenging optimisation problem for the production engineer responsible for the assembly operations. Various methods and techniques have been used to assist in the optimisation of PCB assembly using a CS machine [10], [11], [12], [13] and [14]. Meta-heuristics and heuristics approaches such as the Bees Algorithms and Genetic Algorithms have performed very well in optimising the total assembly time for a CS machine [11], [15] and [16]. The ultimate aim of all the research work on optimising the total assembly time is to obtain the shortest total assembly time which will lead to a reduction in costs and improved productivity.

In order to do this component sequencing, feeder arrangement, and rate of rotation for the turret need to be synchronised to ensure the shortest total assembly. In order to optimise and synchronise all three mechanism, integrated approach to consider all three mechanisms is crucial in the formulation of a mathematical optimisation model. The mathematical optimisation formulation is shown in Table 1.

Table 1. Mathematical models derived from factors that affect the total assembly time

Factors Affecting Total PCB Assembly Time	Mathematical Representation/Notation		Remarks
PCB movement (due to moving Mounting Table in x-y)	$t_1(c_i,c_j)=\max\left(\frac{\lvert x_j-x_i\rvert}{v_x},\frac{\lvert y_j-y_i\rvert}{v_y}\right)$	(1)	$t_1(c_i,c_j)$ = time between placement of component *i* and component *j* $c_i(x_i, y_i)$ = component *i* with co-ordinate (x_i, y_i) $c_j(x_j, y_j)$ = component *j* with co-ordinate (x_j, y_j) v_x= the velocities of the X-Y table in the x-direction v_y= velocities of the X-Y table in the y-direction
Feeder movement	$t_2(f_i,f_j)=\frac{\sqrt{\lvert x_j^f-x_i^f\rvert^2+\lvert y_j^f-y_i^f\rvert^2}}{v_f}$	(2)	$t_2(f_i,f_j)$ = travelling time of the feeder carrier between feeder $f_i(x_i^f,y_i^f)$ and $f_j(x_j^f,y_j^f)$. v_f = speed of the feeder carrier $f_i(x_i^f,y_i^f)$ = feeder *i* $f_j(x_j^f,y_j^f)$ = feeder *j*
Turret movement	t_3	(3)	t_3 = turret indexing time (s/step)
Component Sequence	$C = \{c_1..., c_i, ..., c_{N-1}, c_N\}$	(4)	*C = component sequence from* c_1 *to* c_N c_i = *the ith component to be placed.* *N = total components to be inserted to PCB board.*
Feeder Assignment Sequence	$F = \{f_1..., f_j, ..., f_{R-1}, f_R\}$	(5)	*F = feeder assignment sequence from fl to* f_R. *fj = the feeder for the jth component type.* *R = Total number of feeders*

From the mathematical equations (1) to (2) and notations (3) to (5), the placement time can be deduced as equation (6) as shown in Table 2. Finally, the ultimate objective of the planning of PCB assembly is shown as equation (7) in Table 3.

Table 2. The mathematical model for the time needed to place a component, c_k

Placement time for component, c_k	$\tau_k=\max(t_1(c_{k-1},c_k),t_2(f_{k+g-1},f_{k+g}),t_3)$	(6)	τ_k = the time needed to place a component, c_k. $c_{k-1} = c_N$ when k=1. If f_l has $l > N$, where $l = k+g+1$ or $k+g$, then f_l is substituted by f_{l-N}. f_{l-N} = first component of the next board in the batch. g = gap between turret heads

Table 3. The mathematical model for minimising the total PCB assembly time

Minimise total assembly time	$T_{\text{Total}} = \sum_{k=1}^{N} \tau_k$	(7)	T_{total} = total assembly time for the components from k =1 to N on to PCB. τ_k = the time needed to place a single component, c_k.

As mentioned earlier, various methods and techniques including genetic algorithms and the Bees algorithms were applied to minimise the total assembly time. The shorter the assembly time, the better the result as this means more cost saving and higher productivity. Some researchers proposed to solve the PCB assembly problem for CS machine based on the three mechanisms separately while some did it by considering one or two mechanism first and finally a few consider these mechanism as an integrated problem [8]. Recent literature shows that the integrated approach is getting more popular as the integrated approach can be synced and considered all three mechanisms concurrently during optimisation based on the mathematical model presented above.

3 The Optimisation of Total PCB Assembly Time for a Concurrent Chip Shooter Machine (CS)

With the mathematical model for minimising the PCB assembly time determined, the optimisation of the total time assembly can be done using meta-heuristic approach such as the Bees Algorithm. In this research, we have used the Bees Algorithm along with TRIZ-inspired operators to optimise and determine the shortest total assembly time for CS machine with a twin assembly head turret (as illustrated in Fig. 2). The machine has 10 component feeders (holding 10 different components) and the aim was to assemble 50 components on to a PCB.

In order to minimise the total PCB assembly time, the Bees Algorithm was applied with three non-standard search operators inspired by TRIZ [11] to obtain an assembly time better than the results obtained in [3], [7], [8] and [16]. In this research work, further investigation focusing on the same PCB assembly problem of a CS machine with twin assembly head turret, 10 component feeders and 50 components was conducted. The detailed flow chart representing the Bees algorithm with 3 TRIZ-inspired operators are reported in [9] and [11].

The setting for the velocities for the mounting table that holds the PCB is 60mm/s for both X and Y directions. The speed of the carrier feeder is also 60mm/s and the feeders are located 15mm between one another in the Y-axis while their x-coordinates for the feeders are the same throughout and can be negligible. The t_3 is the turret indexing time and it is set at 0.25s/step as in [7].

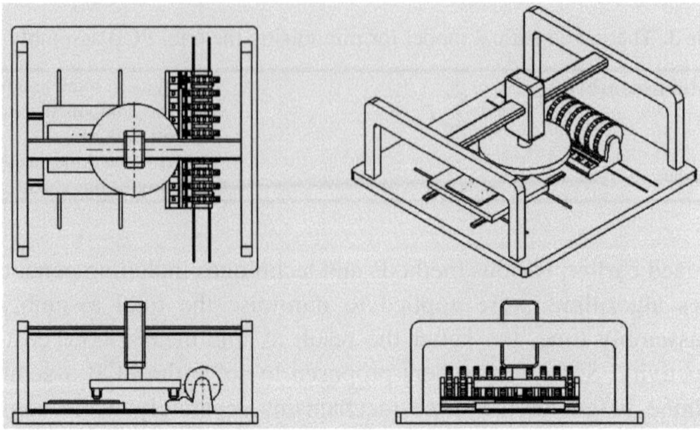

Fig. 2. The CS machine with twin assembly head turret and 10 component feeders [9]

Though finding the shortest assembly time is crucial in the planning of PCB assembly, the ability to simulate the assembly path and allow the process engineers to visualise the assembly process plays an important role in reducing errors and helps them to make better decisions. The next section elaborates the role and importance of simulation in the planning of PCB assembly.

4 Simulations of PCB Assembly Paths for a Concurrent Chip Shooter Machine (CS)

Though achieving the minimum PCB assembly time is crucial for cost-saving and higher productivity, obtaining a good time alone with the optimisation using the Bees algorithm with TRIZ-inspired operators is insufficient for a production engineer in producing a successful assembly plan. This is because the process engineers in planning PCB assembly need to simulate and analyse the simulation data to verify and validate data of the assembly time as well as to understand the assembly sequence more. In the case of assembling 50 components using a CS machine with a twin assembly turret, the assembly path obtained is shown in Fig. 3 and published in [11] with the total assembly time of 23.5833s.

Based on Fig. 3, the process engineer can visualise how the assembly path, the direction of the assembly process as well as the arrangement of the feeders for the components. The total assembly path length is 1350 mm. After 1000 iterations, the total number of evaluation is 23,686,899, which is rather high. However, the production engineer needs to look further into the simulation data in detail to see when exactly the total assembly time of 23.5833s is achieved, the number iterations required to achieve the time and other information about the optimised path.

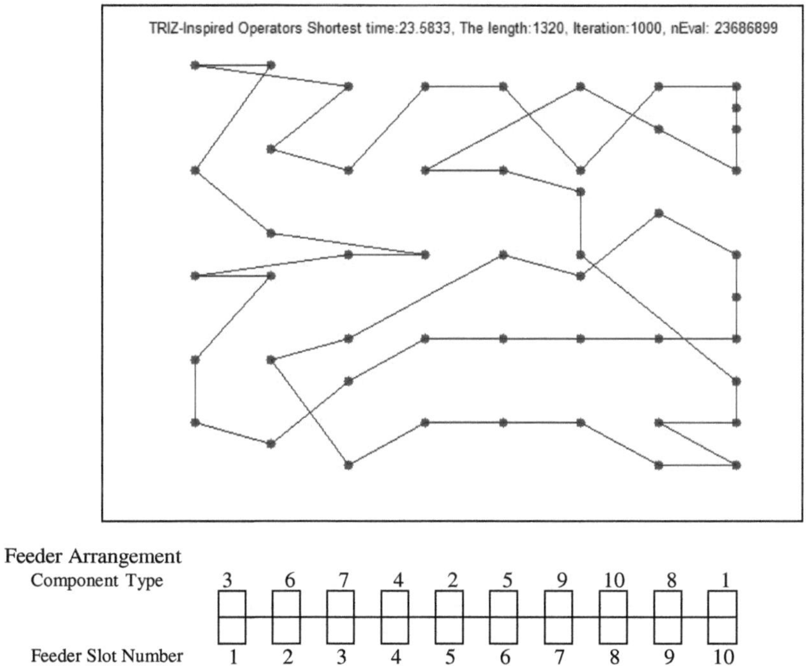

Fig. 3. The optimum path and the feeder arrangement for the assembly of 50 components obtained using the Bees algorithm with TRIZ-inspired operators for a CS machine with a twin assembly head turret and 10 component feeders [11] where the total assembly time is 23.5833s.

Further investigation on the optimisation of the PCB assembly of 50 components for a CS machine with a twin assembly head turret shows that there is an alternative assembly path and feeder arrangement to obtain the same assembly time of 23.5833s. Fig. 4 illustrates the alternative path which also led to the total PCB assembly time of 23.5833s with a different set of feeder arrangement. The total assembly path length is 1250mm but after 1000 iterations, the number of evaluation is 24,893,877, which is higher than the previous result shown in Fig. 3.

With similar total assembly time, the production engineer has to make a decision as to which of the assembly path and feeder arrangement is better. In such circumstances, the visualisation and the data from the simulation of the PCB assembly process plays a vital role to assist the engineer to make this decision. In addition to that, the process engineers also need to verify and validate the simulation data first to ensure both assembly paths feeder arrangement are correct.

4.1 Analysis and Discussions of Simulation Data from the Optimised Assembly Path and Feeder Arrangement

Assume the assembly path shown in Fig. 3 as Path A, the simulation data obtained for Path A is shown in Table 4. Similarly for assembly path shown in Fig.4, assume the path as Path B, the simulation data obtained for Path B is shown in Table 5.

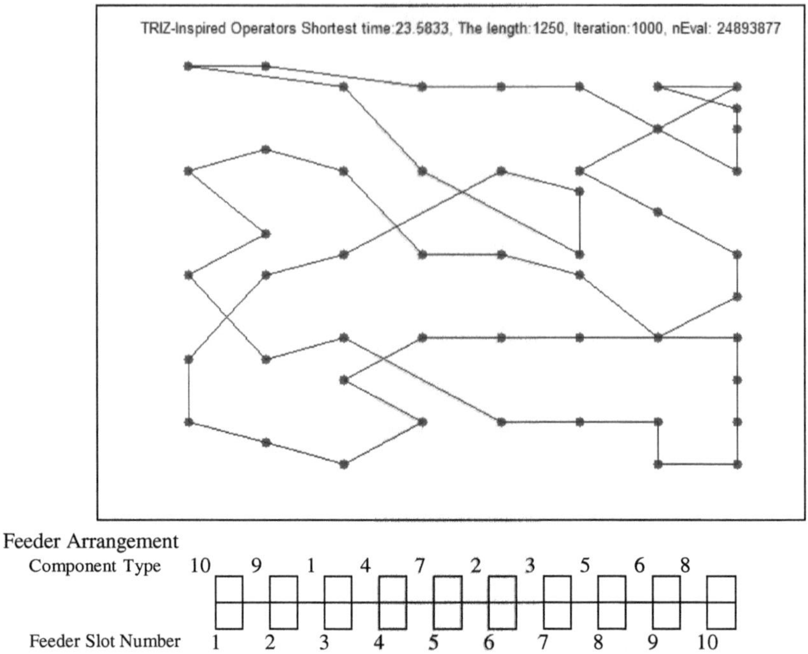

Fig. 4. The alternative optimum path and the feeder arrangement for the assembly of 50 components obtained using the Bees algorithm with TRIZ-inspired operators for a CS machine with a twin assembly head turret and 10 component feeders where the total assembly time is also 23.5833s.

The detailed investigation on the simulation data showed that both set of assembly paths and feeder arrangements are valid and hence, can be applied to assemble 50 components for the CS machine with a twin assembly head turret and 10 feeders. From the perspective of time saving, apparently even though very small, assembly Path B has a very slight longer assembly time than Path A. Though, such minute difference in assembly time maybe due to rounding up of decimal places, but if the total assembly time is accurate then Path A is better than Path B.

Only simulation data can reveal such information and minute differences in total assembly time can be important. This is because the assembly of PCB can go up to millions of PCB per month for certain electronic products such as mobile phones.

4.2 Analysis of Simulation Data Captured Throughout the Optimisation Process of Total PCB Assembly Time

The simulation data obtained also allowed the analysis and review of the convergence characteristics of the Bees algorithm with TRIZ-inspired operators. Based on two different sets of assembly path and feeder arrangement, the optimisation process for Path B appeared to converge much faster than the optimisation process for Path A (refer to Fig. 5).

Table 4. The simulation data for Path A in the assembly of 50 components obtained using the Bees algorithm with TRIZ-inspired operators for a CS machine with a twin assembly head turret and 10 component feeders where the total assembly time is 23.5833s.

Assembly Location		Component Type	Traveling time between placement of components due to movement of mounting table	Travelling time of feeder carrier between feeders	Turret indexing time	The actual assembly time needed (dictated by the longest time needed of either t_1 or t_2 or t_3)
x	y		t_1 (s)	t_2 (s)	t_3 (s)	t_{max} (s)
100	90	3	0.6666667	0.75	0.25	0.75
120	130	6	0.3333333	0.25	0.25	0.3333333
100	130	2	0.6666667	0.5	0.25	0.6666667
140	140	4	0.3333333	0.25	0.25	0.3333333
160	140	5	0.6666667	0.25	0.25	0.6666667
120	150	9	0.5	0.25	0.25	0.5
100	180	10	0.8333333	0.75	0.25	0.8333333
120	230	9	0.3333333	0.25	0.25	0.3333333
100	230	4	0.6666667	0.75	0.25	0.75
140	220	7	0.5	0.5	0.25	0.5
120	190	5	0.3333333	0.25	0.25	0.3333333
140	180	10	0.6666667	0.5	0.25	0.6666667
160	220	9	0.3333333	0.25	0.25	0.3333333
180	220	8	0.6666667	0.5	0.25	0.6666667
200	180	10	0.6666667	0.25	0.25	0.6666667
220	220	5	0.3333333	0.5	0.25	0.5
240	220	2	0.1666667	0.25	0.25	0.25
240	210	7	0.1666667	0.25	0.25	0.25
240	200	6	0.3333333	0	0.25	0.3333333
240	180	7	0.3333333	0.25	0.25	0.3333333
220	200	7	0.3333333	0	0.25	0.3333333
200	220	4	0.6666667	0	0.25	0.6666667
160	180	4	0.3333333	0.25	0.25	0.3333333
180	180	4	0.3333333	0.5	0.25	0.5
200	170	7	0.5	0.75	0.25	0.75
200	140	3	1	0.75	0.25	1
240	80	4	0.3333333	0	0.25	0.3333333
240	60	9	0.3333333	0.25	0.25	0.3333333
220	60	9	0.3333333	0.25	0.25	0.3333333
240	40	10	0.3333333	0.5	0.25	0.5
220	40	9	0.3333333	0.5	0.25	0.5
200	60	8	0.3333333	0.25	0.25	0.3333333
180	60	9	0.3333333	0.25	0.25	0.3333333
160	60	5	0.3333333	0.25	0.25	0.3333333
140	40	9	0.8333333	0.25	0.25	0.8333333
120	90	10	0.3333333	0.5	0.25	0.5
140	100	9	0.6666667	0.5	0.25	0.6666667
180	140	8	0.3333333	0	0.25	0.3333333
200	130	9	0.5	0.25	0.25	0.5
220	160	9	0.3333333	0.5	0.25	0.5
240	140	10	0.3333333	0.25	0.25	0.3333333
240	120	1	0.3333333	0.25	0.25	0.3333333
240	100	8	0.3333333	0.25	0.25	0.3333333
220	100	10	0.3333333	0.25	0.25	0.3333333
200	100	9	0.3333333	0.25	0.25	0.3333333
180	100	5	0.3333333	0.25	0.25	0.3333333
160	100	2	0.3333333	0.25	0.25	0.3333333
140	80	2	0.5	0.25	0.25	0.5
120	50	4	0.3333333	0.25	0.25	0.3333333
100	60	6	0.5	0.25	0.25	0.5
			Total Assembly Time (s)			23.5833327

As shown in Fig. 5, the total assembly time for Path B reached the minimum time of 23.583333s when the number of evaluations reached 11,867,130 at 497 iterations. For Path A, the total assembly time reached the minimum value of 23.583333s only when the number of evaluation achieved 16,906,938 at 716 iterations. This data showed that the optimisation process to achieve the minimum total assembly time for Path B was converged faster than Path A.

Table 5. The simulation data for Path B in the assembly of 50 components obtained using the Bees algorithm with TRIZ-inspired operators for a CS machine with a twin assembly head turret and 10 component feeders where the total assembly time is also 23.5833s.

Assembly Location		Component Type	Traveling time between placement of components due to movement of mounting table	Travelling time of feeder carrier between feeders	Turret indexing time	The actual assembly time needed (dictated by the longest time needed of either t_1 or t_2 or t_3)
x	y		t_1 (s)	t_2 (s)	t_3 (s)	t_{max} (s)
220	200	7	0.3333333	0.25	0.25	0.3333333
200	220	4	0.3333333	0.25	0.25	0.3333333
180	220	8	0.3333333	0	0.25	0.3333333
160	220	9	0.6666667	0.5	0.25	0.6666667
120	230	9	0.3333333	0.25	0.25	0.3333333
100	230	4	0.6666667	0.25	0.25	0.6666667
140	220	7	0.6666667	0.75	0.25	0.75
160	180	4	0.6666667	0.5	0.25	0.6666667
200	140	3	0.5	0.25	0.25	0.5
200	170	7	0.3333333	0	0.25	0.3333333
180	180	4	0.6666667	0.5	0.25	0.6666667
140	140	4	0.3333333	0.25	0.25	0.3333333
120	130	6	0.6666667	0.25	0.25	0.6666667
100	90	3	0.5	0.5	0.25	0.5
100	60	6	0.3333333	0.5	0.25	0.5
120	50	4	0.3333333	0.25	0.25	0.3333333
140	40	9	0.3333333	0.5	0.25	0.5
160	60	5	0.3333333	0	0.25	0.3333333
140	80	2	0.3333333	0.5	0.25	0.5
160	100	2	0.3333333	0.25	0.25	0.3333333
180	100	5	0.3333333	0.25	0.25	0.3333333
200	100	9	0.6666667	0.25	0.25	0.6666667
240	100	8	0.3333333	0.5	0.25	0.5
240	80	4	0.3333333	0.5	0.25	0.5
240	60	9	0.3333333	0.5	0.25	0.5
240	40	10	0.3333333	0	0.25	0.3333333
220	40	9	0.3333333	0.25	0.25	0.3333333
220	60	9	0.3333333	0.25	0.25	0.3333333
200	60	8	0.3333333	0	0.25	0.3333333
180	60	9	0.6666667	0.5	0.25	0.6666667
140	100	9	0.3333333	0.25	0.25	0.3333333
120	90	10	0.6666667	0.75	0.25	0.75
100	130	2	0.3333333	0.5	0.25	0.5
120	150	9	0.5	0.25	0.25	0.5
100	180	10	0.3333333	0.25	0.25	0.3333333
120	190	5	0.3333333	0.25	0.25	0.3333333
140	180	10	0.6666667	0.5	0.25	0.6666667
160	140	5	0.3333333	0.25	0.25	0.3333333
180	140	8	0.3333333	0.25	0.25	0.5
200	130	9	0.5	0.5	0.25	0.5
220	100	10	0.3333333	0.5	0.25	0.5
240	120	1	0.3333333	0.5	0.25	0.5
240	140	10	0.3333333	0.5	0.25	0.5
220	160	9	0.3333333	0.25	0.25	0.3333333
200	180	10	0.6666667	0.5	0.25	0.6666667
240	220	2	0.3333333	1	0.25	1
220	220	5	0.3333333	0.25	0.25	0.3333333
240	210	7	0.1666667	0.25	0.25	0.25
240	200	6	0.3333333	0	0.25	0.3333333
240	180	7	0.3333333	0.25	0.25	0.3333333
			Total Assembly Time (s)			23.5833329

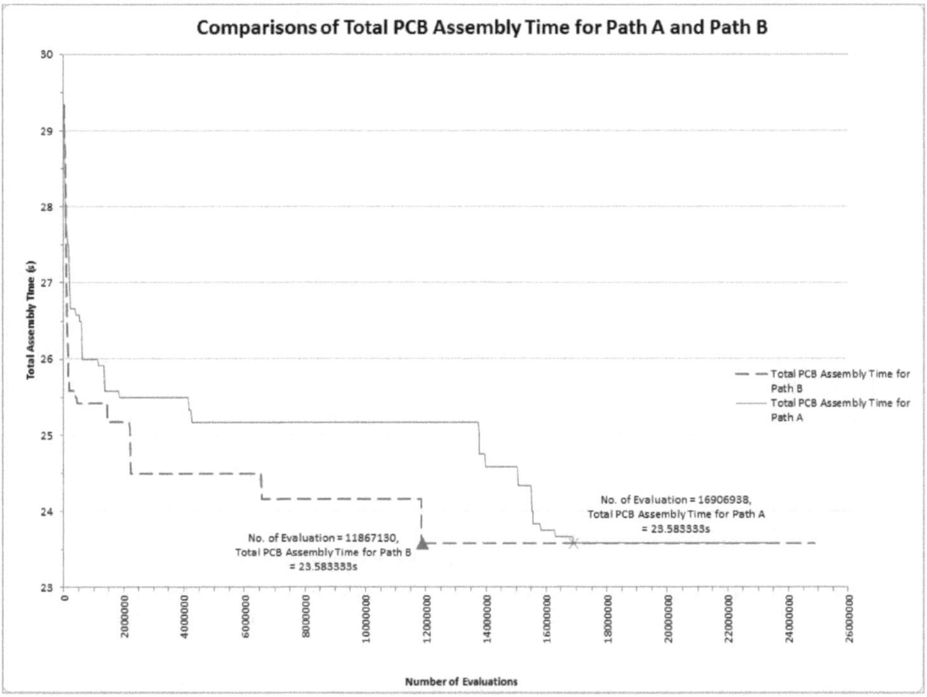

Fig. 5. Comparing Path A and Path B throughout the optimisation process using the Bees algorithm with TRIZ-inspired operators

5 Conclusions

This research work has shown that simulation is crucial in the planning of PCB assembly for a CS machine particularly in the verification and validation of the minimum assembly time obtained using an optimisation technique. For this research work, the planning of the assembly of 50 components using a CS machine with a twin assembly head turret and which is capable of dispensing 10 types of components was used as a case study. With the minimum assembly time of 23.58333s obtained using the Bees algorithm with TRIZ-inspired operators, two pair of assembly path and feeder arrangement were found to achieve the minimum assembly time of 23.58333s. The simulation data of optimisation process was investigated to verify and validate the validity of this assembly time of 23.58333s. The investigation showed that both results are valid but with the second assembly path and feeder arrangement to be slightly slower. However, the slight differences may be due to rounding up errors and hence should be further investigated to enable to process engineers to decide on which assembly path and feeder arrangement to adopt.

Acknowledgments. The authors would like to thank the Universiti Kebangsaan Malaysia and the Ministry of Higher Education, Malaysia for the support to continue the work through research grant UKM-TT-07-FRGS0249-2010.

References

1. Khoo, L.P., Ng, T.K.: A genetic algorithm-based planning system for PCB component placement. Int. Journal of Production Economics (1998)
2. Ong, N.-S., Khoo, L.P.: Genetic algorithm approach in PCB assembly. Integrated Manufacturing Systems 10, 256–265 (1999)
3. Ong, N.-S., Tan, W.-C.: Sequence placement planning for high-speed PCB assembly machine. Integrated Manufacturing Systems 13, 35 (2002)
4. Ho, W., Ji, P.: A hybrid genetic algorithm for component sequencing and feeder arrangement. Journal of Intelligent Manufacturing 15, 307–315 (2004)
5. Ho, W., Ji, P.: A genetic algorithm to optimise the component placement process in PCB assembly. The Int. Journal of Advanced Manufacturing Technology 26, 1397–1401 (2005)
6. Ho, W., Ji, P., Wu, Y.: A heuristic approach for component scheduling on a high-speed PCB assembly machine. Production Planning and Control 18, 655–665 (2007)
7. Leu, M.C., Wong, H., Ji, Z.: Planning of component placement/insertion sequence and feeder setup in PCB assembly using genetic algorithm. ASME Journal of Electronic Packaging 115, 424–432 (1993)
8. Ho, W., Ji, P.: Optimal Production Planning for PCB Assembly. Springer, London (2007)
9. Ang, M.C., Pham, D.T., Ng, K.W.: Application of the Bees Algorithm with TRIZ-inspired operators for PCB assembly planning. In: Proceedings of 5th International Virtual Conference on Innovative Production Machines and Systems (I*PROMS 2009). Cardiff University (2009)
10. Moyer, L.K., Gupta, S.M.: Simultaneous component sequencing and feeder assignment for high speed chip shooter machines. Journal of Electronics Manufacturing 6, 271–305 (1996)
11. Ang, M.C., Pham, D.T., Soroka, A.J., Ng, K.W.: PCB assembly optimisation using the Bees Algorithm enhanced with TRIZ operators. In: IECON 2010 - 36th Annual Conference on IEEE Industrial Electronics Society, pp. 2708–2713 (2010)
12. Souza, R., Lijun, W.: Intelligent optimization of component onsertion in multi-head concurrent operation PCBA machines. Journal of Intelligent Manufacturing 6, 235–243 (1995)
13. Ho, W., Ji, P.: Integrated component scheduling models for chip shooter machines. International Journal of Production Economics 123, 31–41 (2010)
14. Klomp, C., van de Klundert, J., Spieksma, F.C.R., Voogt, S.: The feeder rack assignment problem in PCB assembly: A case study. International Journal of Production Economics 64, 399–407 (2000)
15. Ho, W., Ji, P.: Component scheduling for chip shooter machines: A hybrid genetic algorithm approach. Computers and Operations Research 30, 2175–2189 (2003)
16. Pham, D.T., Otri, S., Haj Darwish, A.: Application of the Bees Algorithm to PCB assembly optimisation. In: Pham, D.T., Eldukhri, E.E., Soroka, A.J. (eds.) Proc. 3rd Virtual Int. Conf. on Innovative Production Machines and Systems (I*PROMS 2007), pp. 511–516. Whittles Pub. (2007)

Soft Key and Hard Key Mobile Input Devices on Player Experience for Mobile Gaming

Kimberly Chu[1,*], Tek Yong Lim[2], Chee Weng Khong[1], and Chui Yin Wong[1]

[1] Interface Design Department, Faculty of Creative Multimedia,
[2] Faculty of Computing and Informatics,
Multimedia University, Cyberjaya, Malaysia
{kimberly.chu,tylim,cwkhong,cywong}@mmu.edu.my

Abstract. Input devices come in different interaction modalities, structure, layout and controls on a mobile platform. However, there is limited information on the types of mobile input devices that affect player experience. Most of the information about the advantages and disadvantages of input devices are reported in isolation without involvement from mobile game application. This paper aims to explore player experience by comparing two different types of mobile input methods, namely hard keypad (HK) and soft keypad (SK), for mobile gaming. Interview was conducted and the results were analysed using content analysis as a way of understanding player experience of input devices for mobile games. The content analysis highlighted positive and negative feedback comprising of two main categories, *Features* and *Effects*. Overall, both qualitative and quantitative data collected revealed that HK was better than SK for mobile gaming.

Keywords: input devices, player experience, mobile games, soft key, hard key.

1 Introduction

Mobile games provide the richness of device interaction on the mobile phone environment. The main goal of a game is to entertain and engage the player by interacting with a set of rules that involve emotional, cognitive and physical activity. The first game that hits the mass market on the mobile phone was Snake. It was pre-installed in most Nokia phones in 1997 [1]. The success of Snake on Nokia phones led to a wide variety of mobile games being pre-installed on other phone manufacturers. The arrival of Java-based games on mobile phones came with colour screens, improved networking technologies and specifications continued to spur the uptake of mobile games in the mass market.

Most games are pre-installed by the device manufacturer, the growth in take up is also due to wide accessibility as users could download mobile games over the air from the developers portal, via a personal computer through USB cable, memory card, Bluetooth, or infrared. In 2008, Apple launched its App Store which enabled

* Corresponding author.

H. Badioze Zaman et al. (Eds.): IVIC 2013, LNCS 8237, pp. 347–357, 2013.

iPhone users to download games via 3G or wireless connection. Since then, the mobile games market has grown exponentially. Currently, mobile games are either pre-installed or downloadable via app stores such as Apple's App Store, GooglePlay (previously known as Android Marketplace) and Nokia Ovi Store.

Mobile gamers usually prefer to play casual or mini-games. Casual gamers engage with play when they are bored or while waiting for a friend, thus spending minimal time playing games compared to hard core gamer. Thus, the skill of a casual gamer would take a longer time to progress. Hardcore gamers on the other hand spend hours and days completing quests and engaging with multiplayer opponents. They take the time to understand the game rules, goals, cheats to increase their knowledge about the game they are playing. Hardcore gamers are also quite determined to pursue experience and complete quest levels as proficiently as possible. Although mobile users tend to be casual games in general, games such as Doom on Apple's iPhone are gaining popularity among hardcore gamers who are using mobile as a platform to play among each other [2].

The underlying basis of selecting mobile platform is because of the growth of mobile apps in the market, as well as a personalised item and gaming platform. Literature highlights that games are one of the most bought items in mobile apps store emphasizing the importance of this platform [3]. Having said this, the industry face usability issues due to platform fragmentation as not all games were installed into the same phone. Thus, this study helps to understand the player experience of input devices from a broader audience perspective. It is also interesting to note that there are some mobile games created as a result of certain input devices. For examples, Fruit Ninja by Halfbrick Studios and Monster Kill by Origin8 were created specifically for touch screen devices as they use the swipe input method. These games would not work on physical keypad phones.

2 Input Devices for Mobile Gaming

This section provides an in-depth understanding of interaction and related studies on the variety of input devices for mobile gaming. In Human-Computer Interaction (HCI), input devices are divided into two categories, which are switched-based and pointing devices [4]. Currently, the most commonly used input devices on mobile gaming are keypads that consist of numerical keypad, navigational keys that fall under switch-based, and touch screen under pointing devices. Within mobile keypads, there were two main input devices - hard keypad (HK) and soft keypad (SK). Although there are some studies about input devices, categorisation of the available input types for mobile games context were insufficient.

Apart from this, mobile gaming input interaction can also come in the form of tangible (physical hardware), intangible (virtual software) or a combination of both. For example, tangible input referred to a physical button while intangible input are generated through computing calculations on software for interaction between menus. For HK, the size, sensitivity and feedback is limited by the physical shape of the device. For SK, however, the availability of software customization offers a higher degree of flexibility such as button sounds, button sensitivity, and size.

2.1 Evaluating Input Devices on Player Experience

As pointed out by Brown [5] the guidelines related to the support of input devices on mobile devices are limited. With the lack of research to provide data pertaining to the relationship of input device and player experience, game designers, developers and input designers would require a broad range of evaluation to determine these issues, which would be costly to conduct. Player experience is a significant factor that can determine the success of a game. Games coupled with the right inputs would provide a positive experience that draw strong interest from its intended target market and raising the reputation of the developer. The definition of player experience is often associated with words such as fun, flow, fulfilment, enjoyment, engagement, satisfaction, playability and pleasure. However, Ribbens and Poels [6] highlighted that there is a lack on empirical research investigating player experiences and their interaction in input devices for mobile gaming.

Nacke [7] added that player experience is the evaluative process directed towards players. Player experience is an evaluation of a player's perspective to improve gaming while playability focuses on game design improvement. This study is interested at observing from the input device perspective and how such input methods impact the player experience through gameplay.

As games are created by game developers, they build games and construct rules for players to interact. Their goal would be to design games that provide excellent experience with the players in mind. However, the creation of a game does not depend solely on the ideas of designers and developers. This is where the role of beta testers comes in. Ermi and Mäyrä [8] said that because players were not designers, their contribution during the design process would be significant in improving the game. Generally beta testers provide a personal perspective when they evaluate a game because they report about their experience (fun to play) and usability (use of input, game menu). Beta testers are assigned to test in-game issues while quality assurance (QA) testers are tasked with fixing bugs or programming issues during game play. Thus, it is important to understand player experience at the interaction level.

The concept of player experience is fragmented due to different viewpoints and not defined as a cohesive integrated framework [9]. Sweetser and Wyeth [10] believe that there is no integrated model to evaluate input device enjoyment level in games. Bernhaupt, Eckschlager, and Tscheligi [11] add that there is no general framework on what methods should be used to assess the concept of interaction in games. Behaviourists have also discussed the effect of positive or negative reinforcement on players. For example, winning the game, attaining high score during gameplay, achieving game goals or acquiring experience are rewards that can affect a player's experience during gameplay. Hence, there are a lot of factors that can affect the outcome of player experience.

From the Cognitive Science perspective, it is possible to map out the potential problems that players would face by analysing the input device beforehand [12]. This allows researchers to find out more information on player experience in relation to the diversity of game input device layout and type. The differences in input device would have a causal effect that can be both positive and negative. Players have positive experience when they experience ease of use or encouragement and negative experience when they feel frustrated or distress while interacting with the input. Psychologically, a player experiences different emotional states while playing and this would affect his or her performance and personal preference. He or she could be experiencing difficulty in using a particular input, which would directly influence his or her performance.

The interaction process that leads one's experience is common to any individual, regardless of how different an individual may be because there is a set of common elements that lets them understand and communicate to each other [13]. A set of common elements ought to exist for input interaction, especially when it involves positive experiences. For users to make sense of the experience, they would internalise the information of the interaction felt to create a personal experience [14]. As it is a process which an individual might not present explicitly, players would need to recall the experience by reporting it. Hence, it is necessary to capture the information through communication and to recognise the influence of input on their experience. In this respect, developers and designers are constantly trying to understand how input can be fun and enjoyable to players while minimizing their negative experiences.

According to Jarvinen [15], player experience is the relationship between the game and the player with a focus on the player's cognition, emotion and psychological activities. When a player engages with the activities, they experience both verbal and non-verbal communication (facial or body expressions) as a result of the game. The positive or negative emotions would be depicted as either spoken or non-spoken behaviours through the players.

Greenstein [4] suggested that the selection of input device for a specific application should factor in task, user, environment and hardware. The characteristic of input devices should be compared with the requirements of the application (for example, games) to narrow down the list of possible devices. Quick [16] reported a remarkably high percentage of mobile users who own smart phones. As there are various types of phones available in the market, this study considered smart phones with a focus on its input devices. The advantages of each input device were noted with consideration given to the user population, task, environment and hardware configuration. However, occasionally it takes more than one device to satisfy the limitation imposed by another device.

3 Research Method

Qualitative method such as semi-structured interview was used to further understand player experience. The semi-structured interview was conducted to find out the categories of input devices that affect player experience during mobile gaming. This requires participants to state their experience on HK and SK inputs after game play. Questions regarding their playing experience were asked during the interviews. The interview sessions were conducted after game play so that players would not be distracted while playing the game.

There were 50 participants in total, of which 33 were male and 17 female. The participants were staff and students recruited through the Interface Design Program, Multimedia University. All participants have no prior experience with the game selection before. For input device selection, Shiratuddin and Zaibon [17] highlighted that navigation keys are the natural choice for mobile phone control because all mobile phones have the navigation capabilities. Therefore, this study employed interviews to solicit user feedback on navigational key layout on HK and SK. The phone models selected to carry out the experiment were Nokia N8 (SK) and Nokia E72 (HK) as seen in Figure 1. Nokia phones were selected due to variability of input device and phone availability. Additionally, the phones are selected because of the access and availability of resources.

Fig. 1. HK (left) and SK (right) phone models with selected game

Game play, game mechanics and game interface play a pivotal role to provide excellent usability and player experience. Literature on gaming mainly explores the gameplay and occasionally, game mechanics when evaluating games, but rarely focuses on the game interface. This study proposes to look into game interface particularly in evaluating different input devices that would affect player experience. The differences perceived by the participants would focus entirely on the input device.

According to Fritsch, Ritter and Schiller [18], the most played games on mobile phones are arcade games followed by Real Time Strategy (RTS), First Person Shooter (FPS), action and puzzle. Arcade games required basic controls and small learning curve to play in comparison with strategy or adventure games that usually tie in with the storyline. Arcade game genre also appeal to both male and female gender compared to racing games or sports genre which usually dominated by male players. Therefore, an arcade game called Capture was selected in this study due to its popularity among mobile gamers. Arcade game would require constant taps on the key more actively compared to other games genre.

To further understand player experience, a semi-structured interview was conducted. The interview was transcribed from digital video recording with extensive notes taken during the interview. The information gathered from the interview session was subjective, but the interview topics were designed in a way that only relevant comments with regard to the input devices and their experience would be involved. This interview focused on player experience of input devices hence, content analysis is used to extract information from a verbal material and objectively identify specified themes [19]. Content analysis can be analysed through qualitative and quantitative, hence the result will be divided to qualitative and quantitative result. As themes are located in a variety of written sentences, this study only considers the primary theme highlighted in a given sentence for analysis. Interview transcripts were then analysed systematically by reading and grouping key themes collected from the interview. Then, based on the content analysis, a set of categories related to the themes were arranged. After the interview, the set of categories were classified into related groups. Each category was then identified and defined.

4 Results

4.1 Quantitative Results

The results highlighted positive and negative comments with two main categories which are *Features* and *Effects*. Features highlight the structure of input characteristics and Effects highlight the variation of experience in consequences of players interacting on SK or HK. The categories included under Features were *Texture, Size, Sensitivity, Feedback, Shape, Spacing* and Effects were *Ease of use, Error, Comfort Familiarity, Interaction Styles* and *Realism.*

Table 1. HK Positive and Negative Comments

	Positive Comments (HK)	**Negative Comments (HK)**	**Total**
Features			
Texture	31	1	32
Size	8	18	26
Sensitivity	13	4	17
Feedback	13	1	14
Shape	7	4	11
Spacing	0	3	3
Effects			
Ease of use	23	1	24
Interaction Style	6	2	8
Comfort	4	3	7
Familiarity	6	0	6
Error	5	13	18
Realism	2	0	2
Total	**118**	**50**	**168**

The most mentioned comments obtained from *Features* for HK and SK were *Texture, Size, Sensitivity* and *Feedback.* As for the *Effect* of HK and SK input, the most mentioned comments were on *Ease of Use* and *Error.* This shows that the categories above were significant in affecting their experience. Overall, the total number of positive comments on HK (118) was higher than SK (67). For negative comments, the total for SK (91) was more than HK (50). This infers that players enjoy a better experience on HK compared with SK. The total of positive comments on both HK and SK (185) highlights there are more positive comments as majority of comments comes from HK. The total of negative comments on both HK and SK (141) highlights there are more negative comments as most comments comes from SK.

Table 2. SK Positive and Negative Comments

	Positive Comments (SK)	Negative Comments (SK)	Total
Features			
Sensitivity	9	18	27
Size	17	3	20
Feedback	7	18	24
Texture	0	11	11
Spacing	3	3	6
Shape	8	2	10
Effects			
Error	3	11	14
Ease of use	7	10	17
Interaction Style	5	8	13
Comfort	6	3	9
Familiarity	2	2	4
Realism	0	2	2
Total	**67**	**91**	**158**

4.2 Qualitative Results

Hard key Comments

For HK, the *Texture* aspect on keypad buttons and *Ease of Use* provided the participants a positive experience. HK received negative comments on the *Size* and *Error* category. For HK, the size of the keypad might have resulted in a reduced gaming experience.

"...prefer HK because I can feel the up/down/left/right button. The texture is very important to me because I can feel it, rather than seeing so I can focus on the game." (Participant 4 on HK *Texture*, positive)

Under *Features* category, they said because of *Texture* support, they could focus their attention on the game fully. Participants added that touch modality was used to insert the input command and visual modality to look at the screen when using HK. The texture on HK allowed participants to feel, resulting in more certainty during gameplay. When using HK, participants said by pressing hard on the keys which simultaneously help expressed their excitement and emotion during gameplay.

".. I feel that it is easier to control where I want to move. It is very easy to click button on HK especially when the moment I want to press the button is easy to control." (Participant 16 on HK *Ease of Use*, positive)

Under *Effects*, *Ease of use* positive comments were higher than negative comments. The positive comments placed emphasis on participant control of instantaneous fluency and smooth finger placement on HK. Participant felt it was effortless in pressing keys during gameplay, adding that this was a contributing factor to their playing experience. According to the participants, HK was easier to play with as they can control their movement easily and this directly affects their player experience.

"HK has a smaller navigation key which I feel limits my thumb movement... HK is hard to navigate because the size is small and I have big thumb." (Participant 6 on HK *Size*, negative)

Under *Features*, HK *Size* had a higher number of negative than positive comments. Participants said HK was rather small in size which made their finger movement feel cramped. Several participants, who preferred playing with both hands, suggested that the size of the HK would be more suitable for single-handed playing. One participant commented that his large thumbs affected his ability to use the keys during gameplay

"... in HK there are many mistakes when I am using it therefore I feel frustrated and angry with the HK. I make a few mistake and error because there are a few times I press the button that I don't want." (Participants 19 on HK *Error*, negative)

Under *Effects*, HK *Error* negative comments were higher than positive comments. Most of the HK comments described a poor game play experience due to error and lack of accuracy on HK. One of the frequent errors that occurred was when participants pressed the end call button by accident. The end call button action ends the game even when players are still halfway playing.

Soft key Comments

Through the classification, this study is able to determine their distinct positive and negative experiences for SK. For SK, the keypad *Size* gives them a positive experience. For SK, the *Sensitivity* and *Feedback* gives them a negative experience.

"The size of the input plays a big part for my enjoyment level." (Participant 17 on SK *Size*, positive)

For the *Features* category, SK *Size* received higher positive compared with negative comments. The bigger size on SK played a big part in their enjoyment level and participants reportedly have more freedom when pressing since they are not confined by small size. The distance between the buttons on SK was larger and participants said they preferred to play on bigger buttons. The bigger size offered by SK helped improved their assurance and subsequently, playing experience.

"SK is too sensitive and I have long nails therefore I need to be very alert when I use this kind of input..." (Participant 5 on SK *Sensitivity*, negative)

There were more negative comments on *Effects* for SK *Sensitivity* compared with positive, highlighting the lack of sensitivity when using SK keys to control the game. The input logic response relation to a key press affects the gameplay especially if the game requires speed as a winning criterion. Because SK is a capacitive-based touch screen, it will not be able to detect long fingernails accurately due to limited skin contact area. This would reduce the sensitivity of SK response during game play or seemingly being non-functional. In addition, the combo button on SK was reportedly not working during gameplay, resulting less enjoyable experience for the participant.

"I did not feel much vibration feedback while playing." (Participant 15 on SK *Feedback*, negative)

Similarly, on *Features* for SK *Feedback* received more negative than positive comments. A majority of the SK negative comments was about participants not sensing much vibration feedback during gameplay. However, some said vibration feature on SK could become a distraction and they preferred to play without it. Participants also reported they felt less focused during the game.

5 Discussion

On HK during game play, touch modality was used to control the input and visual modality to look at the game screen. The texture on HK makes the player feel more in control during gameplay [20]. Through this categorisation, it is noticeable that being able to focus with minimal involvement from other modalities, feeling in control and able to express could have an effect on more pleasurable experience. Additionally, *Ease of use* is a category that was also reported in a study by [5]. Comments on *Ease of use* were mainly positive with emphasis on HK control for instantaneous response and smooth movement.

Reason [21] has extensively analysed human errors and distinguishes between *mistakes* and *slips*. Majority of the errors were slips on HK, with most of the main errors on HK was when players accidentally pressed the end call button during gameplay. This action would end the game even if players were playing midway. The slips reduce the player's dexterity. They needed to press the keys more than once to make sure they press correctly. This was a source of frustration and annoyance that affected their experience.

For SK, with the larger key size, female players with long nails and males with larger fingers are able to play games the way they intended. The larger size also gives the player the feeling of an interface that is less confined as reported by [22]. Players highlighted that they preferred to play on bigger buttons because it helped improve their assurance and playing experience.

For sensitivity, SK is a capacitive based touch screen which would not be able to detect long fingernails reducing the sensitivity of SK response in this game [22]. SK was represented by a capacitive touch screen in this study as it is a widely available technology in the current smartphones such as Apple's iPhone and Nokia's N8. Some players said that SK did not sense their key press as expected and instead required them to press the keys longer resulting in slowed movement. The errors on SK occurred when players pressed the area in between the key or outside of the keypad area. Outside the keypad area for SK, there were no indications to inform their finger position. Players only notice that they committed an error when the game character did not move to where they wanted. In SK, player needs to hold their finger in an upward position, where unintentional slips sometimes create unwanted input commands.

6 Conclusion

In conclusion, this study has established that HK and SK input devices affect player experience. This study shows that input devices are essential factors in player experience and should not be taken lightly. Overall, positive comments on HK were higher than SK. This infers that players enjoy a better experience on HK compared with SK. Two main categories that predominantly affect player experience were Features and Effects. The most mentioned comments on HK and SK were features that include *Texture, Size, Sensitivity* and *Feedback.* As for the *Effect* of HK and SK input, the most mentioned comments were on *Ease of Use* and *Error.* This shows that the categories above were significant in affecting their experience. For future research, a similar interaction framework can be applied on other types of input devices such as accelerometer, gyroscope, microphone and camera for the mobile gaming platform. Further studies may perhaps examine the game designers' or developers' perspectives as this study focused on the players' perception. Having learned the several categories with positive or negative player experiences, the subsequent stage is to explore the categories in detail with further data collection and analysis on different pool of participants. Therefore, this study provides groundwork for future studies on other input device categories for mobile game play.

Acknowledgments. The authors would like to thank the participants from Interface Design Department, Faculty of Creative Multimedia, Multimedia University Malaysia, who were involved in this project.

References

1. Mobile Entertainment Forum, `http://www.dancewithshadows.com/tech/snake-nokia-game.asp`
2. Takahashi, D.: `http://games.venturebeat.com/2009/07/03/doom-resurrection-brings-hardcore-gaming-to-the-iphone/`
3. Newzoo, `http://www.newzoo.com/ENG/1632-Mobile_Games_Trend_Report.html`
4. Greenstein, J.S.: Pointing Devices. In: Helander, M.G., Landauer, T.K., Prabhu, P. (eds.) Handbook of Human Computer Interaction, North-Holland, Netherlands, pp. 1317–1348 (1997)

5. Brown, M., Kehoe, A., Kirakowski, J., Pitt, I.: Beyond the Gamepad: HCI and Game Controller Design and Evaluation. In: Evaluating User Experience in Games. Springer (2010)
6. Ribbens, W., Poels, Y.: Researching Player Experiences Through the Use of Different Qualitative Methods. In: DiGRA Digital Library-Proceedings 2009, DiGRA, London, pp. 1–10 (2009)
7. Nacke, L.: From Playability to a Hierarchical Game Usability Model. In: Proceedings of the Conference on Future Play 2009, Vancouver, BC Canada, pp. 11–12. ACM, New York (2009)
8. Ermi, L., Mäyrä, F.: http://gamestudies.org/0501/ermi_mayra/
9. Law, E.L.C., Roto, V., Hassenzahl, M., Vermeeren, A.P., Kort, J.: Understanding, scoping and defining user experience: a survey approach. In: Proceedings of the 27th International Conference on Human factors in Computing Systems (CHI 2009), pp. 719–728. ACM, New York (2009)
10. Sweetser, P., Wyeth, P.: GameFlow: A Model for Evaluating Player Enjoyment in Games. ACM Computers in Entertainment 3, Article 3A (2005)
11. Bernhaupt, R., Eckschlager, M., Tscheligi, M.: Methods for Evaluating Games – How to Measure Usability and User Experience in Games? In: Proceedings of the International Conference on Advances in Computer Entertainment Technology (ACE 2007), Salzburg, Austria, pp. 309–310. ACM Press, New York (2007)
12. Oatley, K., Jenkins, J.M.: Human emotions: Function and dysfunction. Annual Review of Psychology 43, 55–85 (1992)
13. Popper, K.R.: Knowledge and the body-mind problem: In Defence of Interaction. Routledge, Barcelona (1994)
14. McCarthy, J., Wright, P.: Technology as Experience. The MIT Press, Cambridge (2004)
15. Jarvinen, A., http://acta.uta.fi/english/teos.php?id=11046
16. Quick, C.: http://blog.nielsen.com/nielsenwire/online_mobile/with-smartphone-adoption-on-the-rise-opportunity-for-marketers-is-calling/
17. Shiratuddin, N., Zaibon, S.B.: Designing User Experience for Mobile Game-Based Learning. In: 2011 i-USEr, Kuala Lumpur, Malaysia, pp. 89–94 (2011)
18. Fritsch, T., Ritter, H., Schiller, J.: Mobile Phone Gaming (A Follow Survey of the Mobile Phone Gaming Sector and Its Users). In: Harper, R., Rauterberg, M., Combetto, M. (eds.) ICEC 2006. LNCS, vol. 4161, pp. 292–297. Springer, Heidelberg (2006)
19. Holsti, O.R.: Content Analysis for the Social Sciences and Humanities. Addison-Wesley, Reading (1969)
20. Hoggan, E., Brewster, S.A., Johnston, J.: Investigating the Effectiveness of Tactile Feedback for Mobile Touchscreens. In: Proc. CHI 2008 of Human Factors in Computing Systems, pp. 1573–1582. ACM Press, New York (2008)
21. Reason, J.: Human Error. Cambridge University Press, New York (1990)
22. Lee, S., Zhai, S.: The Performance of Touch Screen Soft Buttons. In: Proceedings of the 27th International Conference on Human Factors in Computing Systems, pp. 309–318. ACM, New York (2009)

An Endeavour to Detect Persons Using Stereo Cues

Rim Trabelsi[1,5], Fethi Smach[2], Issam Jabri[1], Fatma Abdelkefi[3], Hichem Snoussi[4], and Ammar Bouallegue[5]

[1] IResCoMath Unit, National Engineering School of Gabes, University of Gabes
rim.trabelsi@ymail.com,
issam.jabri@enig.rnu.tn

[2] ActivNetworks, 1 rue de Terre Neuve BP 127, 91944 Courtaboeuf Cedex, France
fethi.smach@gmail.com

[3] COSIM Laboratory, High School of Communications of Tunis, University of Carthage
fatma.abdelkefi@supcom.rnu.tn

[4] LM2S Laboratory, Charles Delaunay Institute, University of Technology of Troyes
Hichem.Snoussi@utt.fr

[5] SysCom Laboratory, National Engineering School of Tunis, University of Tunis ElManar
ammar.bouallegue@enit.rnu.tn

Abstract. The present work aims to exploit the new generation of 3D vision systems for detecting people. We present a challenge process dedicated to test the feasibility of detection over disparity maps by exploiting techniques used with monocular cues, specifically HOG/SVM. Disparity maps are extracted by a developed stereoscopic vision system using two passive sensors with an algorithm stack well adopted to real time constraint with lower processing speeds. This detection module can improve systems' perception ability in complex scenes under shadows, gradual/sudden illumination changes and animated texture. Another key point is to estimate their exact locations to predict intrusions in monitored areas. Results indicate a clear advantage of the proposed method to enhance the rate of performance up to 99.6%.

Keywords: Passive stereovision, Disparity maps, Pedestrian detection, HOG, SVM.

1 Introduction

Emulating the human visual system is the ultimate goal of machine vision. It aims to make vision systems, increasingly cognitive by designing models that have properties similar to visual perception. Developing a module able to detect people is of crucial importance in various fields such as robotics, surveillance and driving assistance. However, a major challenge is the ability to discern people from many other objects. This issue has attracted the attention of the machine vision community since the nineties, which allowed a diversity of approaches and solutions proposed [1][2]. Those systems model traditionally monocular cues over 2D images and videos. Techniques employed are often based on appearance and/or motion information [3][4]. Almost of defined methods prosecute a descriptor/classifier structure and try to find better combination.

H. Badioze Zaman et al. (Eds.): IVIC 2013, LNCS 8237, pp. 358–370, 2013.

All attempts are always looking forward to improve detection performance of the system in order to reduce false alarms while enhancing positive detections. This task is still challenging in complex environments with illumination changes and animated textures.

3D vision systems have been lately exploited in order to take advantage of depth information to overcome the shortcomings of 2D systems.At this level, many types of 3D sensors have been designed. However, multi-cameras-equipped sensors are more useful in outdoor areas; they are often denoted passive stereoscopic sensors. With such hardware, it's crucial to pass through a preparatory step aiming to calibrate and rectify the stereo pair [5]. This requires a mathematical model to describe projection from 3D onto the 2D image plane to simplify computing of 3D information by matching stereo pair images in order to educe disparity maps [6]. People detection, accordingly, is not well mastered yet. Indeed, misconstrue of extracting depth information are added to difficulties of its use for the detection and recognition process. Many works have succeed to applied depth map to object recognition. However, almost of them employ pre-calibrated stereoscopic sensors which produce depth map either with good quality but they are only effective in indoor [7][8] or with lower quality though rigid in outdoor [9][10]. Thereby, we present in this paper an attempt for outdoor people detection using 3D information over disparity maps by conceiving, firstly, a passive binocular stereoscopic sensor that we proceed to calibrate and rectify. In a second step, we realize a comparative study between local and global stereo correspondence approaches in order to choose the algorithm that gives a sufficient disparity map'quality and usable in real time systems. Then, we propose the reuse of detection and recognition techniques that have proven effective results on visual appearance information (intensity or color images) to test feasibility of detection over disparity maps which are more robust to illumination changes and can relay objects depth values.

This paper is organized as follows: in section 2, we provide an overview about binocular stereoscopic technique while emphasizing steps from calibration to stereo matching. In section 3, we describe the used recognition techniques. Then, the whole designed system is presented in section 4. Finally, experimental results and analysis are shown in section 5.

2 Disparity Extraction Using Stereovision

2.1 Overview

Both monocular (single view) and stereoscopic (multi-view) systems can be used to extract 3D data. Monocular vision is a difficult task. In fact, the third dimension cant be easily estimated from a single projection, on the camera's image plane, for several points from the real space. This requires taking into account the global structure of the image and camera motion [11][12]. However, stereoscopy is much less costly in terms of computation. It does not infer depth from weak or unverifiable photometric and statistical assumptions, nor does it require specific detailed objects models. The stereoscopy, also called stereovision, aims to extract 3D information from at least two images taken from two cameras separated by a baseline distance. In this work, we will use binocular stereoscopy system. This technique mimics the depth perception of human beings provided by two eyes. Its fundamental process involves mainly three steps: calibration, rectification and stereo matching.

2.2 Stereo Calibration and Epipolar Rectification

Sensors calibration is a crucial step for the success of the three-dimensional reconstruction process. It consists in modeling the whole vision system on both optical and mechanical sides. The mechanical side is to establish the relationship between sensors disposition and orientation with respect to the observed scene, while the optical side is to model the process by which the projection of the real scene on the projection plan of each camera [13]. It is a question of estimating the geometric transformations parameters: matrices of translation, rotation and change of scale, to return the form and the actual position of the real object. This is accomplished by the passage from the object reference frame in $\mathbb{R}^3$ to the reference frame of the projection planes of left and right cameras, expressed in $\mathbb{R}^2$. This passage is characterized by matrix of intrinsic parameters A, given by Eq. (1), where k_u and k_v are the horizonal and the vertical scale factors and u_0 and v_0 represent the coordinates of the principal points, as well as matrix of extrinsic parameters which refer to the rigid transformation of a point $M = (x, y, z)^t$ in $\mathfrak{R}_w$ (the world reference frame) into a point $M_c = (x_c, y_c, z_c)^t$ in $\mathfrak{R}_c$ (the camera reference frame), calculated according to the Eq. (2), depending on t: translation vector (of size 3) and R: rotation matrix (of size (3×3)) representing the position and the orientation of $\mathfrak{R}_c$ in $\mathfrak{R}_w$.

$$A = \begin{pmatrix} k_u & 0 & u_0 \\ 0 & k_v & v_0 \\ 0 & 0 & 1 \end{pmatrix} \tag{1}$$

$$\tilde{M_c} = \begin{pmatrix} R & t \\ 0^t & 1 \end{pmatrix} \tilde{M} \tag{2}$$

With a calibrated stereo sensor, it would be possible, from two homologous points, to estimate the resulting angle by intersection of the two light rays emitted by a point in the scene, and therefore estimate the position of this point according to the world reference frame $\mathfrak{R}_w$. A detailed study about methods and models of calibration has been developed in [14][15]. The calibration models for computer vision have traditionally used reference grids such as checkerboard patterns. The most efficient calibration method is Zhang's method. It consists in acquiring images of a pattern planar calibration placed at different orientations in front to the sensor [16]. Its advantage is that it includes the modeling of lens distortion based on the pinhole camera model. In fact, the lenses of the cameras, by their spherical symmetry, generate distortion, i.e deformation of the real image. This distortion is decomposed into a radial (k_i) and tangential (p_i) components as:

$$D = (k_1, k_2, p_1, p_2, k_3) \tag{3}$$

As for epipolar rectification of a stereo images, it aims to curtail the search space of matching simply to a straight line instead of a 2D plan [17]. Indeed, stereoscopic rectification can be brought back to an easy epipolar geometry where epipolar lines are parallel to each other and the corresponding pixel in the left image is located on the same row to the right image but in a different columns. This epipolar constraint is important to reduce the computation time of stereo matching stage as well as the number of wrong results.

2.3 Disparity Computing

Stereo correspondence algorithm aims to compute disparity which represents the relative displacements between the locations of homologous primitives in the left and the right images and to produce a disparity map, i.e., a disparity estimate at each pixel. A multitude of methods has been proposed (see [6][18] for a survey). However, finding corresponding points is always challenging mainly in complex conditions (specular surface, uniform area, repetitive texture, occultation, etc.). They can often be classified into local or global approaches. Local methods exploit the neighborhood of the pixel to be matched without taking into account the information contained in the rest of stereo pair. Whereas global methods consider all pixels of the image for the recursive estimation of the disparity. Local methods are known for their speed and lack of precision, while global methods are relatively slow but they provide better quality. The most effective algorithms from those families are the stereo-Block Matching which belongs to local approach and the stereo-Graph Cuts as a global one. The adaptation of Graph Cuts method for stereo matching is introduced for the first time by Roy et al. [19]. This technique proposed a constraint of local consistency which suggests that the disparity function is locally continuous. Close pixels in all directions have similar disparities. This local consistency constraint is combined with a constraint of similarity which depends on the variation of the intensity of matched pixels. Then, the proposed method in [19] aims to solve the optimal disparity function over the entire image. As to stereo-Block Matching, it is a correlation-based method. It consists in comparing a block surrounding each pixel in the left view to the candidate block located on the conjugated epipolar line of the right view. An evaluation metric is used to measure the difference between two blocks and compare with all other potential target blocks.

3 Recognition Process

3.1 HOG Descriptors

In order to calculate wealthier information to characterize the content of disparity images, we reuse HOG (Histogram of Oriented Gradients) descriptors which have proved a great performance with visual appearance specifically intensity images for people detection. Indeed, since their introduction by Dalal and Triggs [20] in 2005, they have proven unprecedented perfection for human detection. Recent studies and experiments have shown that they are still competitive [2][21]. For our purpose, we will try to assess the detection performance for this type of descriptors over 3D information. They are used to compute occurrences of gradient direction in a localized region of the image. Its principle is as follows: initially, the image is divided into adjacent small regions called cells that are grouped into blocks. The features vector is subsequently formed, for each block, the histograms of oriented gradients of cells.

3.2 Review of SVM Classification

SVM (Support Vector Machine) were developed in 1995 by Vladimir Vapnik [22]. In general, SVM can be used to solve discrimination problems, i.e. to decide to which class belongs a given sample, or regression problems, i.e. to predict the value of a variable. Here we shall merely investigate the case of binary discrimination [23]. The set is said to be linearly separable if there exist a vector w and a scalar b for decision functions as:

$$g(x) = w \otimes x + b\, ;\ \text{sgn(g(x))} = \begin{cases} 1 \text{ if x } \in \text{ Class 1} \\ -1 \text{ if x } \in \text{ Class 2} \end{cases} \quad (4)$$

where x is the feature vector to be classified,the general form is $u \otimes v = K(u, v)$. The kernel function K(u,v) accepts two input vectors with same dimension and gives their dot-product in high-dimensional feature space. The most common kernel functions are: Linear and RBF (Radial Basis Function). They can be expressed as follows:

$$K_{Linear}(u, v) = u.v \quad (5)$$

$$K_{RBF}(u, v) = e^{(-\gamma \|u-v\|^2)} \quad (6)$$

The algorithm in this case determines the optimal hyperplane which can separate the space of feature vectors into two sub-spaces, as in Fig. 1, one containing all the positive-example vectors, the other contains all the negative-example vectors.

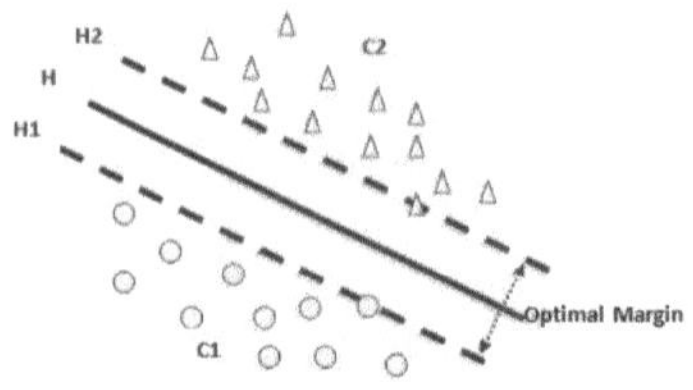

Fig. 1. Case of linearly separable data

The hyperplane is calculated in order to minimize the margin with the closest positive and negative samples. The equation of the hyperplane is defined as in [23]:

$$wx + b = 0 \quad (7)$$

where w is the normal to this hyperplane, $\frac{b}{\|\mathbf{w}\|}$ perpendicular distance from the origin to the plane in which $\|.\|$ defines the Euclidean norm. Assume that d_+ (respectively d_-) the smallest distance between the separating hyperplane and the closest element of the class $+1$ (respectively -1). We define the margin of the hyperplane for those prototypes as $d_+ + d_-$. Those elements fulfill:

$$x_i w + b \geq 1 \ for\ y_i = +1 \quad (8)$$

$$x_i w + b \geq -1 \ for\ y_i = -1 \quad (9)$$

Assume that :

$$y_i\,(x_i w + b) - 1 \geq 0 \tag{10}$$

where $i = 1..n$ with n is the size of the training set.

By considering the points belonging to the hyperplane H_1 (respectively H_2), those points fulfill $x_i w + b = 1$ (respectively $x_i w + b = -1$ for H_2), this hyperplane is at a distance of $\frac{|1-b|}{\|w\|}$ (respectively $\frac{|-1-b|}{\|w\|}$)from the origin. The margin between these two hyperplanes is $\frac{2}{\|w\|}$. Thus, determining the two hyperplanes equations that maximize the margin is equivalent to minimizing $\|w\|^2$ under the constraint of Eq. (10). It's a quadratic-programming problem under constraint, the use of Lagrange multipliers (α_i) leads to :

$$L_p(w, b, \alpha) = \frac{\|\mathbf{w}\|}{2}^2 - \sum_{i=1}^{n} \alpha_i y_i(\mathbf{x_i w} + b) + \sum_{i=1}^{n} \alpha_i \tag{11}$$

by canceling the partial derivatives of the Lagrangian we obtain:

$$\mathbf{w} = \sum_{k=1}^{n} \alpha_k y_k x_k \tag{12}$$

4 Designed System

The designed system described in Fig. 2 includes mainly two major phases, each one contains an online process and an offline process. As regards the online process, it runs as and when the main task that we seek to realize. Whereas the offline process enables, in front of the main task, to perform some costly operations in processing time and memory consumption.

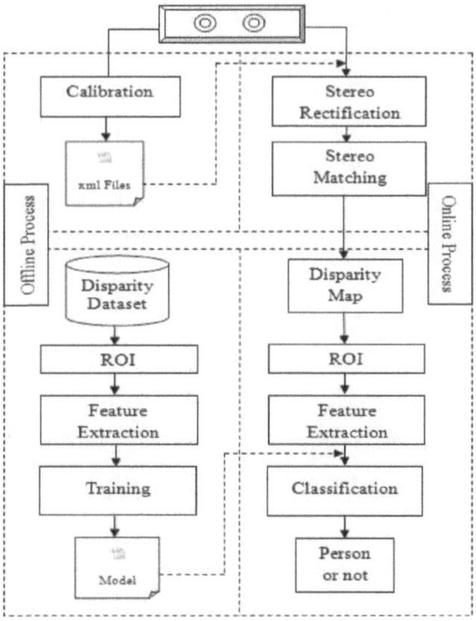

Fig. 2. Overall view of the designed system

The first step aims to compute disparity maps. At the beginning, we start by calibrating our binocular sensor. The obtained results will be saved to be reused later to complete the rectification of each pair of images captured. To highlight that, it's possible to go through a triangulation to construct depth maps, but we are content in this work to computing disparity maps since they reflect both all the same information. The second step involves using the obtained disparity images for people detection and recognition. Offline phase consists in describing and training a database containing positive and negative disparity images in order to extract a prediction model. This model will serve for the classification of detected objects during the main task. In what follows, we will detail our technical choices at each step.

5 Experimental Results and Analysis

5.1 Preprocessing Step

Concerning hardware, we choose to conceive our own sensor. In fact, commercialized stereoscopic sensors aren't yet well appealing; on the one hand their disparity map quality aren't well sufficient, in the other hand, their FoV (Field of View) aren't quite suitable for many application contexts. Moreover, they are very expensive which discourage their deployment to cover large area in video surveillance application. For this purpose, we are equipped with two homologous VGA CMOS sensor with a FPS (Frame Per Second) rate up to 30. We adopt a parallel configuration in such way that optical axes of both cameras are parallel. In addition, baseline distance separating sensors centers is of great importance. Its value depends necessarily on the FoV on each sensor. To fend the optimal value of this baseline, we adopt an adjustment between sensors so as to modify this distance and measure it each time while examining the result's quality. Based on our experiments, the value range of the baseline deemed as the most optimal is between $6.5cm$ and $7cm$. This choice leads to a simplification of stereoscopic processing. As we have already discussed in 2.2, to conceive a vision system based on the stereoscopy, it requires two preparatory steps: calibration and epipolar rectification. Using Zhang's technique, we obtain the spatial relationship between the two cameras and their intrinsic parameters as a set of matrices of intrinsic parameters A_1 and A_2 (Eq. 13), their distortion coefficients D_1 and D_2 (Eq. 14), the rotation matrix R (Eq. 15) and the translation vector t (Eq. 16) relating the two cameras.

$$
\begin{aligned}
A_1 &= \begin{bmatrix} 5.337e+002 & 0 & 1.805\mathrm{e}+002 \\ 0 & 5.337e+002 & -1.055\mathrm{e}+002 \\ 0 & 0 & 1 \end{bmatrix} \\
A_2 &= \begin{bmatrix} 5.337e+002 & 0 & 1.789\mathrm{e}+002 \\ 0 & 5.337e+002 & -1.068\mathrm{e}+002 \\ 0 & 0 & 1 \end{bmatrix}
\end{aligned}
\tag{13}
$$

$$
\begin{cases} D_1 = \begin{pmatrix} -2.268\mathrm{e}-001 & 2.875\mathrm{e}-001 & 0 & 0 & -2.707\mathrm{e}-001 \end{pmatrix} \\ D_2 = \begin{pmatrix} -2.203\mathrm{e}-001 & 1.448\mathrm{e}-001 & 0 & 0 & -3.631\mathrm{e}-002 \end{pmatrix} \end{cases}
\tag{14}
$$

$$R = \begin{bmatrix} 9.949e-001 & 3.095e-002 & 9.522e-002 \\ -3.279e-002 & 9.993e-001 & 1.780e-002 \\ -9.461e-002 & -2.084e-002 & 9.952e-001 \end{bmatrix} \quad (15)$$

$$t = \begin{pmatrix} 7.0153e+002 \\ 0 \\ 1.125e+002 \end{pmatrix} \quad (16)$$

By analogy with the formula Eq. (1) and Eq. (3), the horizonal and the vertical scaling factors are $k_u = 5.337e + 2$ and $k_v = 5.337e + 2$ and the coordinates of the principal points of the left and right cameras worth respectively $(1.805e + 2, -1.055e + 2)$ et $(1.789e + 2, -1.068e + 2)$. In addition, results prove that the model of sensors used doesn't take into account tangential distortion $(p_1 = p_2 = 0)$. Obtained matrices are then saved in XML files in order to be used later for rectification as long as mechanic configuration wasn't changed.

5.2 Stereo Correspondence Evaluation

In order to assess performances of local and global stereo correspondence approach, we opt to compare the stereo-Block Matching and the stereo-Graph Cuts algorithms. For this purpose, we use to follow method described in [19] to implement the stereo-Graph Cuts. Regarding stereo-Block Matching, we opt to the SAD evaluation metric given by Eq. (17) since it is the simplest one. It involves computing the absolute difference between each pixel in the block of the left image I_l and the corresponding pixel of the targeted block (of size W) in the right image I_r.

$$SAD = \sum_{(i,j)\in W} |I_l(i,j) - I_r(x+i, y+j)| \quad (17)$$

To evaluate and compare results of those algorithms, we use in a first step, stereo pair images associated with their ground truth. We take examples from the database of Middlebury [1] proposed by Scharstein and Szeliski [6]. For our tests, we will consider Tsukuba (384×288) and Cones (450×375) images. Results of disparity computing are summarized in Table 1. They are well and truly different not only in terms of disparity maps quality rendering but also in terms of WCET (Worst Case Execution Time) with a CPU implementation. The stereo-Graph Cuts algorithm gives disparity maps with high precision of edges and takes into account occlusions. Nevertheless, this algorithm is too heavy in terms of calculation requirements, its WCTE tends to ten minutes for a single image fault of its iterative criterion. Therefore,in such context, we choose to use stereo-Block Matching algorithm which is pretty fast with a CPU implementation. The drawback of stereo-Block Matching is the generation of invalid disparity values especially in uniform area. However, foreground objects generally have enough texture which make easy to obtain distance values. Moreover, the window width W (Eq. 17) is too important; if a large one is used, it will be costly in terms of time processing, whereas a small window increase the mismatch rate.

[1] http://vision.middlebury.edu/stereo/data/

Table 1. Results of disparity computing with Stereo-Graph Cuts and Stereo-Block Matching algorithms for Tsukuba and Cones stereo pairs

	" Tsukuba "	" Cones "
Left View		
Ground Truth	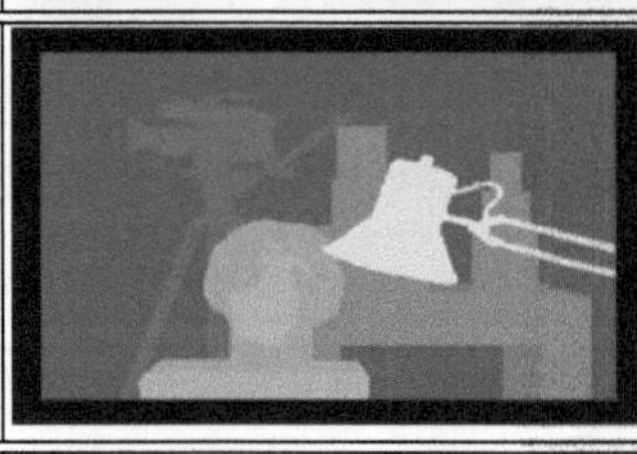	
Stereo Graph Cuts	 WCET=10mn	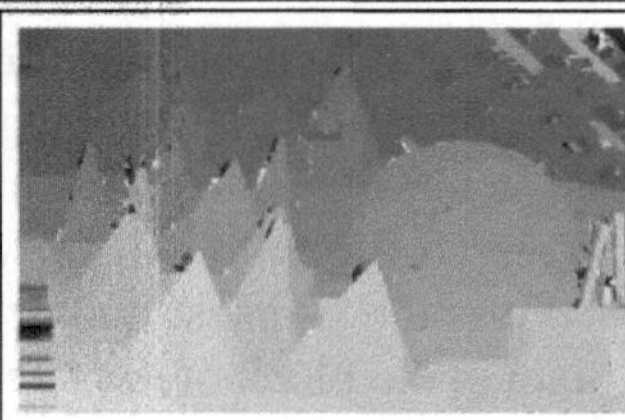 WCET=17mn
Stereo Block Matching	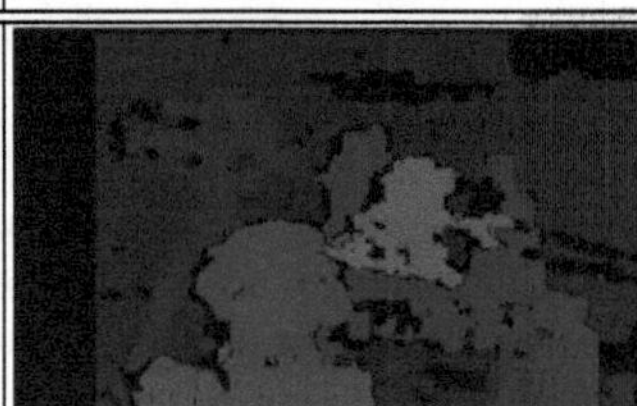 WCET=69.998ms	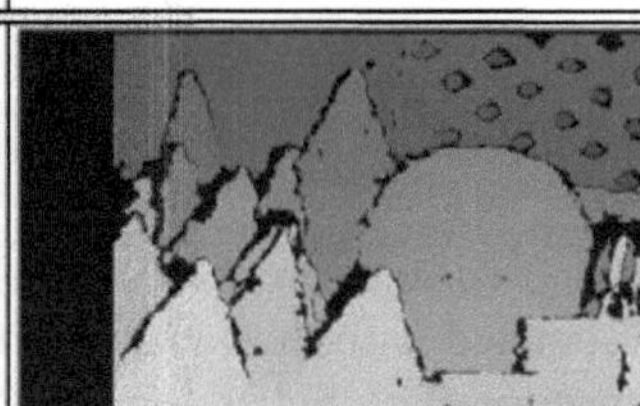 WCET=224.246ms

5.3 Classifier Evaluation and Testing

In order to evaluate the proposed method, we opt to the data-set of Shenzhen university [2]which contains 4637 positive depth images of size (144×176) and 192 negative ones. The images are taken at three different environments. People are captured in diverse positions with different manners of clothing and different scales. The data-set is accompanied with a configuration file that specifies information to help extracting ROI for each positive image. Resulting ROI, as in Fig. 3 are over-sampling at (64×128) to be prepared for the description in the following step as well as negative images (Fig. 4).

[2] `http://yushiqi.cn/research/depthdataset`

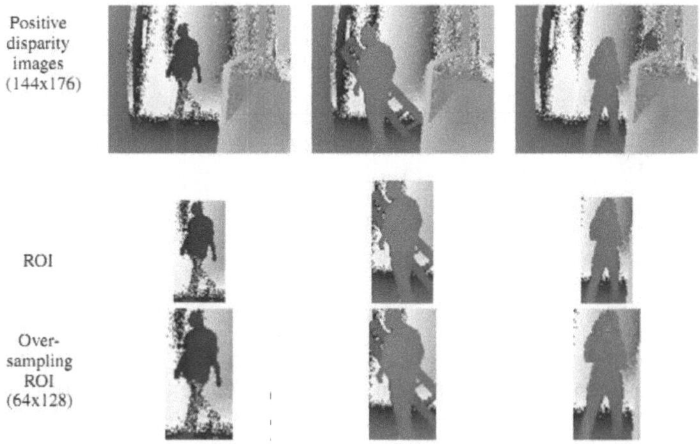

Fig. 3. Positive samples of disparity map with the extracted ROI

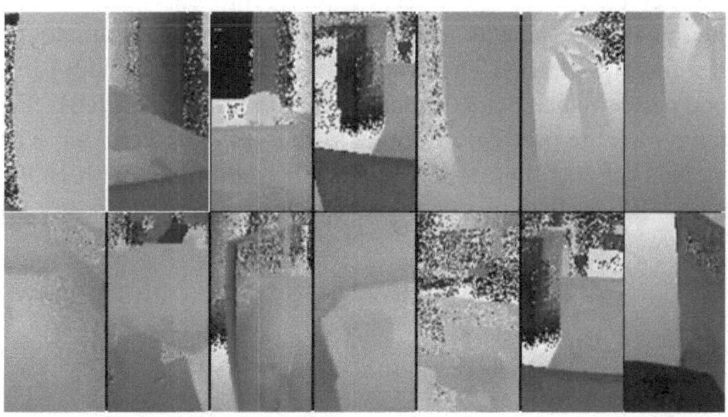

Fig. 4. Negative samples of disparity maps (64×128)

The study carried out by Dalal and Triggs [20] is very helpful to fix HOG parameters that fit our case. We choose subdivided ROI into blocs of 4 cells of size (8×8) with an horizontal overlap of 8. The orientation is divided into 8 bins which are spaced over $[0°, 180°]$. The feature vector obtained is combined with the class label (-1: for negative samples, 1: for positive samples). Exploiting all training samples, SVM classification process computes the optimal hyperplane as a decision model.

To extract the exact position of detected persons, we take advantage of computed intrinsic parameters to resituate depth value using the relation $Z = \frac{f \times B}{d}$ with f: focal length, b: baseline distance and d: disparity value. Fig. 5 shows a set of detection results on depth maps indicating distance value which they occupy in meters.

Fig. 5. Examples of persons detection with accuracy of the depth value

The purpose of recognition is, first, finding the positive examples, designated by the term <True Positive>, which corresponds in our case to the person that the system recognizes well as person. But we must also look at limiting the number of false alarms i.e. <False Positive>, which are objects that the system takes as persons whereas they aren't. To assess the performance of the structure HOG/SVM with disparity maps, we resort to ROC (Receiver Operating Curves) curve. It represents the rate of correct detections against the rate of false alarms. The closer ROC curve approximates the upper-left corner, the better the classifier is. Therefore, as shown on Fig. 6, both Linear and RBF SVM give a good performance but RBF outcompetes Linear SVM. RBF-SVM classifier are able to find not only the positive examples with a very good rate but with a very low false detection. This reflects that the SVM classifier combined with HOG descriptors allow the detection of people with a very good performance on disparity images.

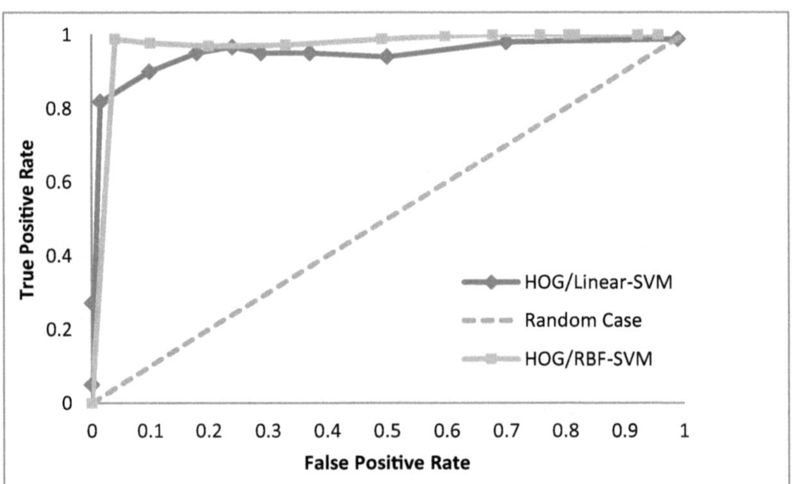

Fig. 6. ROC curves of Linear and RBF SVM classifiers

6 Conclusion

This paper presents an endeavour to detect people with stereoscopy. Firstly, we have developed a system that englobe an algorithm stack for stereo processing using two cheap CMOS cameras taking into consideration real time constraint with a CPU implementation. Secondly, we have used disparity maps obtained to test feasibility of person detection with HOG/SVM techniques employed with appearance information. Due to the robustness of those maps against illumination and texture variations, results show a great capability to increase detection performance. This is extremely encouraging, supporting the belief that the employ of disparity cue will find many uses in object recognition tasks.

References

1. Geronimo, D., Lopez, A.M., Graf, T.: Survey on pedestrian detection for advanced driver assistance systems. IEEE Transactions on Pattern Analysis and Machine Intelligence (2009)
2. Dollar, P., Wojek, C., Schiele, B., Perona, P.: Pedestrian Detection: A Benchmark. In: IEEE Conference on Computer Vision and Pattern Recognition, Miami Florida, USA (June 2009)
3. Cutler, R., Davis, L.S.: Robust real-time periodic motion detection, analysis, and applications. IEEE Transactions on Pattern Analysis and Machine Intelligence 22, 781–796 (2000)
4. Viola, P., Jones, M., Snow, D.: Detecting pedestrians using patterns of motion and appearance. In: International Conference on Computer Vision, Nice, France (2003)
5. Salvi, J., Armangue, X., Batlle, J.: A comparative review of camera calibrating methods with accuracy evaluation. Pattern Recognition 35(7), 1617–1635 (2002)
6. Scharstein, D., Szeliski, R.: A Taxonomy and Evaluation of Dense Two-Frame Stereo Correspondence Algorithms. International Journal of Computer Vision 47(1–3), 7–42 (2002)
7. Janoch, A., Karayev, S., Jia, Y., Barron, J., Fritz, M., Saenko, K., Darrell, T.: A category-level 3d object dataset: Putting the kinect to work. In: Consumer Depth Cameras for Computer Vision. Springer, London (2013)
8. Yu, W., Ashraf, A.B., Chang, Y.-J., Li, C., Chen, T.: 3d augmented markov random field for object recognition. In: IEEE International Conference on Image Processing, pp. 3889–3892 (2010)
9. Mitzel, D., Leibe, B.: Close-range human detection and tracking for head-mounted cameras (2012)
10. Molinier, T., Rossi, L., Akhloufi, M., Tison, Y., Pieri, A.: Estimation of fire volume by stereovision. In: SPIE-Image Processing: Machine Vision Applications, vol. 7877 (2011)
11. Li, P., Farin, D., Gunnewiek, R., With, P.D.: On Creating Depth Maps from Monoscopic Video using Structure From Motion. In: IEEE Workshop on Content Generation and Coding for 3D-Television (June 2006)
12. Howard, I.: Perceiving in Depth: Basic Mechanisms, vol. 1. Oxford University Press (March 2012)
13. Faugeras, O.: Three-dimensional computer-vision: a geometric viewpoint. MIT Press (1993)
14. Armangu, X., Salvi, J., Batlle, J.: A comparative review of camera calibrating methods with accuracy evaluation. Pattern Recognition 35, 1617–1635 (2000)
15. Weng, J., Cohen, P., Herniou, M.: Camera calibration with distortion models and accuracy evaluation. IEEE Transactions on Pattern Analysis and Machine Intelligence 14(10), 965–980 (1992)
16. Zhang, Z.: Flexible camera calibration by viewing a plane from unknown orientations. In: IEEE International Conference on Computer Vision, Corfu, Greece (September 1999)

17. Papadimitriou, D., Dennis, T.: Epipolar line estimation and rectification for stereo image pairs. IEEE International Transactions on Image Processing 5(4), 672–676 (1996)
18. Brown, M., Burschka, D., Hager, G.: Advances in Computational Stereo. IEEE Transactions on Pattern Analysis and Machine Intelligence 25(8), 993–1008 (2003)
19. Roy, S., Cox, I.: A maximum-flow formulation of the n-camera stereo correspondence problem. In: IEEE International Conference on Computer Vision, Bombay, India (January 1998)
20. Dalal, N., Triggs, B.: Histograms of Oriented Gradients for Human Detection. In: IEEE Conference on Computer Vision and Pattern Recognition, San Diego, CA, USA (June 2005)
21. Enzweiler, M., Gavrila, D.: Monocular Pedestrian Detection: Survey and Experiments. IEEE Transactions on Pattern Analysis and Machine Intelligence 31(12), 2179–2195 (2009)
22. Vapnik, V.N.: The nature of statistical learning theory. Springer-Verlag New York, Inc. (1995)
23. Smach, F., Lemaître, C., Gauthier, J.-P., Miteran, J., Atri, M.: Generalized Fourier Descriptors with Applications to Objects Recognition in SVM Context. Journal of Mathematical Imaging and Vision 30(1), 43–71 (2008)

Development of a Multimedia Courseware for Slow Learner Children with Reading Difficulties: MyLINUS

Wan Fatimah Wan Ahmad[1], Shahrina Md. Noordin[2], and Nor Syafiza Md. Shariffuldin[1]

[1] Computer & Information Sciences Department,
[2] Management & Humanities Department,
Universiti Teknologi PETRONAS,
31750 Tronoh, Perak Darul Ridzuan
{fatimhd,shahrina_mnordin}@petronas.com.my,
syafizashariffuldin@gmail.com

Abstract. This paper presents the development of a multimedia courseware namely 'My LINUS' as a medium in teaching and learning specially designed for slow learner with reading difficulties. The courseware will help slow learner children using an approach and a suitable technique/method with appropriate teaching materials essential for the learning process. The courseware integrates Literacy and Numeracy (LINUS) Syllabus officially prepared by the Ministry of Education for primary school children aged between 7 to 9 years old with the learning multimedia theme. The "MyLINUS" primarily consists of 2 sections for the modules and exercises. The modules consist of 3 sub-modules. Each module is designed to teach in certain domain starting from Module 1 till Module 3. Module 1 teaches the users on how to recognize and pronounce a letter. Module 2 teaches users on how to combine letters to form a word. Module 3 guides users on how to combine words and syllable to form complete sentences. A user acceptance test was conducted in two primary schools in Perak. The results help to support suitability and acceptability and the effectiveness of the courseware for further improvement. The findings of the evaluation indicate positive feedback about the courseware.

Keywords: multimedia, slow learner, linus, user acceptance.

1 Introduction

Slow learner is referred to a person who tends to take longer in understanding things than an average person, or someone who requires multiple explanations before they get a concept and not eligible for special education [1]. According to Yusha'u [2], the measured intelligence of a slow is between 75% to 90% of an average child and the rate at which they learn is 4/5 to 9/10 of the normal rate. Slow learners have difficulties in abstract thinking and their attention span is also short. A line of research revealed that multimedia courseware is able to help students in their learning process by attracting the learners, engaging longer learning retention time, making learners more independent and proactive in their learning and increasing their self-motivation.

H. Badioze Zaman et al. (Eds.): IVIC 2013, LNCS 8237, pp. 371–382, 2013.

The intention of using the technology is not to replace the traditional ways of teaching and learning, but rather to provide an additional aided learning tool for some areas that require more attention.

Postnote [3] revealed that the government statistics for 2008 showed 16% of the children failed to achieve the expected levels of reading skill by the age of 7, 13% by 11 years old and 31% by 14 years old – that is they cannot read and understand a short paragraph at a very basic level [3]. According to a report in 2009 released by National Union of the Teaching Profession (NUTP) Malaysia, a research was done in 143 primary schools where a total of 75,699 students were involved. The findings revealed that there were 3,690 (4.87%) students who were neither able to recognize letters nor mastering reading and writing skills. The study also indicated that a total of 48,250 students in Malaysia have difficulties in learning where 29,169 consisted of primary school children and the rest are secondary school children [4].

Multimedia-based learning is one of the approaches to increase children's attention during their teaching and learning process, which consequently could reduce the risk of reading difficulties in the future. Multimedia-based learning refers to the presentations involving words, pictures and animations that are intended to foster the learning process [5]. It helps in building mental representations from words and pictures which will effectively support the learning process of slow learner children [6]. Research done by Mayer similarly indicates that people learn better from multimedia elements such as pictures, animations and audios compared to from words alone [5]. A line of research concluded that computer usage could make children enjoy learning, emotionally involved with complex issues, and could find someone to talk to when feeling alone [6]. Computers will never replace the importance of playing and learning materials such as paint, flash cards, blocks and books but using computers in classroom could increase children's interest and help in engaging their attention toward acquiring knowledge.

2 Literature Review

The Literacy and Numeracy Screening (LINUS) was established by Ministry of Education through NKRA in 2009. The program aims to achieve 100% literacy and numeracy for all Malaysian school children (without learning difficulties) by the time they reach Primary 3. The objectives are to ensure all children will master reading, writing and arithmetic (3R) and are able to read and write in Bahasa Malaysia and to do basic mathematics by Year 4. There are three groups of students classified under the LINUS Program, which are "Arus Perdana" (literate and numerate), "Linus" (illiterate and innumerate) and "Linus Tegar" ("hard-core" illiterate and innumerate). Literacy is the student's capability to master in reading, writing and word arrangement including single sentence and compound sentence (using conjunctions) as well as applying the knowledge lesson for their everyday communication. Every year students will be screened three times which has been scheduled in March, June and September. This is to identify those who are still not meeting the group under "Arus Perdana" (literate and numerate). If the students still cannot achieve the expected levels of 3R skills at the end of their year 3, then the students will be taken for a check up to detect specific factor for learning disabilities in order to educate them under special education. Therefore, LINUS program also helps in detecting dyslexic students at an early stage. Hence, this will help the dyslexic students to receive a special education to support their learning process. This paper focuses on the *Literacy* part of the LINUS module for "Linus" (illiterate and innumerate) and "Linus Tegar" ("hard-core" illiterate and innumerate) students only.

According to Sorden [7], the cognitive theory in multimedia learning, which was introduced by Mayer has effectively maximized students' learning. It was found that students learn more effectively from words and pictures than from words alone. Hence, learners should engage with three important cognitive processes, which are selecting, organizing and integrating in multimedia learning [8].

i) **Selecting:** Applies to incoming verbal information to generate a text base and is applied to incoming visual information to generate an image base.
ii) **Organizing:** Applies in creating verbally based model, which is applied to image base to create a visually-based model.
iii) **Integrating:** Occurs when the learner builds connections between corresponding events in the verbally-based model and visually-based model.

However, modality principle states that students will learn better from animation and narration than animation and printed text [9]. Animation refers to a simulated motion picture illustrating movement of drawn objects [10]. By referring to the modality principle for multimedia learning, pictures presented together with audio will be more helpful compared to the pictures in printed text. Multimedia presentations involving both words and pictures should be created using auditory or spoken words, rather than written texts that are accompanied by the pictures [11]. The theoretical basis is that the learner's visual channel might become overloaded when words and pictures are both presented visually, that is, learners must process the on-screen text and the animation through the eyes, at least initially [11]. Thus, it increases the working memory storage capacity. The approach tries to engage users by narration and story–telling technique. Figure 1 shows an example of an existing courseware developed by Rukus Reader Corporation (2012) that applies the modality approach (Owen 2012). The courseware consists of stories for 3-8 years old children. The aim of the courseware is to teach them to improve their reading skills by using a story-telling approach.

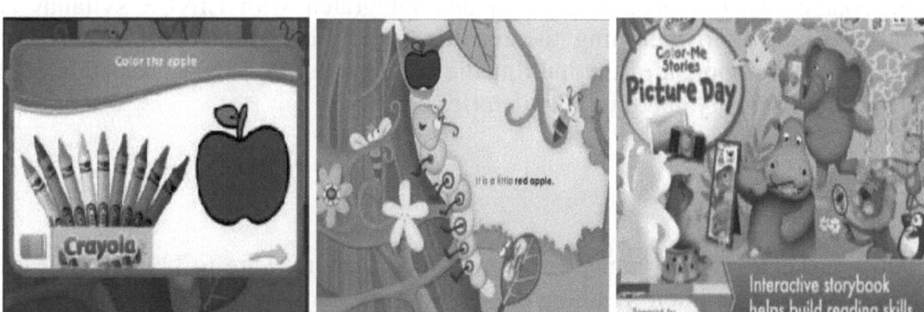

Fig. 1. Sample Existing Courseware - Color - Me Stories

Meanwhile, the theory of multi-sensory approach puts together three learning styles which are visual, auditory and kinesthetic to help a child to learn through more than one sense at one time [12]. In order to teach slow learner children, it is not just limited to visual and auditory but to engage the children in the teaching and learning process [13]. They have to see what the teacher does, listen to teacher's instructions and hand movements or shows something related to the teaching and learning process. The VAK Theory requires the learners to use all three modalities in order to receive and learn new information and experience. VAK learning style appears to be dominated by primary school children [12]. The best teaching approach for children is to involve the use of the child's senses especially the use of touch and movement [14]. It is believed that, the application of VAK Model Theory in learning using multimedia increases the learning retention time of the children [15]. Figure 2 shows an existing courseware game to master reading skills, developed by Focus Multimedia Corporation (2011). Focus Multimedia Corporation believes that children will learn and build critical reading skills through playing games such as climbing mountains, explore dark caves and puzzle move. Learning is made fun with CJ as the frog needs the users to use more than one sense at one time.

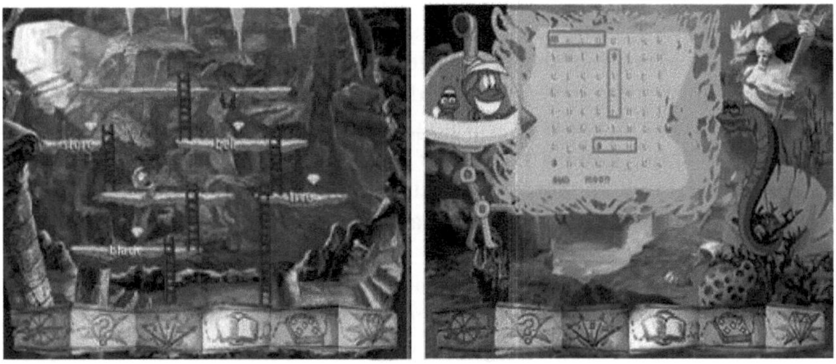

Fig. 2. Fun in Learning with CJ the frog

Generally, no child uses one style of learning exclusively, but they do have preferred learning styles. It is therefore important to incorporate various learning styles during lessons to enable the most efficient learning to take place [16].

The courseware has been developed and integrated with LINUS syllabus and dedicated to help in overcoming the reading difficulties problem of slow learner children. The development of the multimedia courseware, MyLINUS has adopted the cognitive, multi sensory and modality theories.

3 MyLINUS

The paper presents a development of a multimedia courseware to help slow learner children to overcome their reading difficulties problem in their learning process. ADDIE has been used in the development of the prototype. The tools used in the development include Adobe Flash Professional CS4, Adobe Photoshop CS4,

Photoscape and Audicity. The courseware, MyLINUS will help slow learner children by using a suitable technique/method with proper teaching materials. The courseware integrates, Literasi & Numerasi (LINUS) Syllabus prepared by the Ministry of Education for primary school children between 7 – 9 years old with the learning multimedia theme. MyLINUS is developed for slow learner children who are having reading difficulties. It is developed in Malay language since it is the medium of instruction used in schools. A game has also been designed where a student can learn and play game at the same time. The flowchart of the system architecture is depicted in Figure 3.

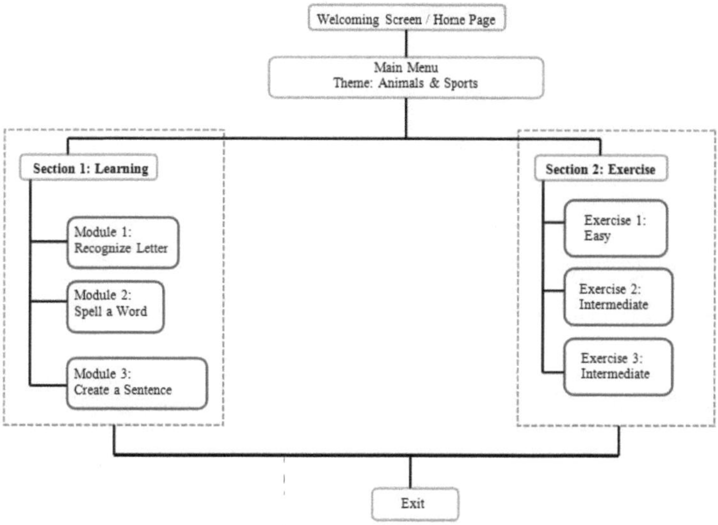

Fig. 3. Courseware Flow

Figure 4 shows the interfaces of the splash screen and main page of MyLinus. Users have the option to choose either to learn or test their IQ. Hence, students can choose either “Let’s Learn” or “Test My IQ”.

(a) Splash Screen (b) Main page

Fig. 4.

There are 3 modules in "Let's Learn": Module 1 consists of alphabets, Module 2 is the combination of letter to form word and Module 3 is on the combination of words and syllables to form a complete sentence. In "Test My IQ", student has to get 3 keys by solving the problems at 3 different places. Figures 5, 6 and 7 show the selected interfaces of modules 1, 2 and 3. Figure 8 shows the interface of game. There are three levels of exercise that users need to complete. Each exercise requires the users to recall what they learn in the first section ("Jom Belajar" section). Users need to complete the three locations by getting a key in order to complete the module.

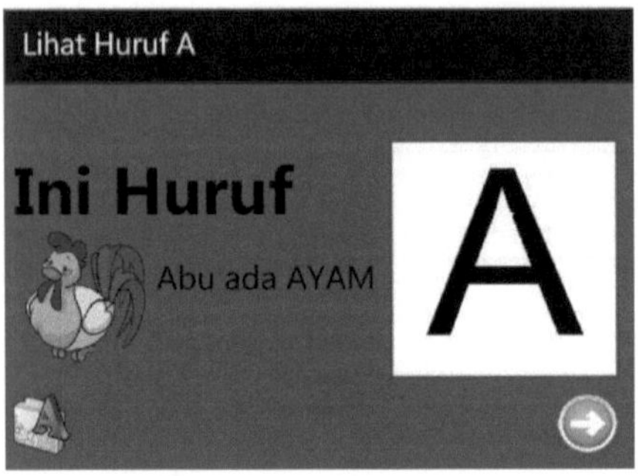

Fig. 5. Module 1: Recognizing Pronunciation of Letter

Fig. 6. Module 2: Words available for Animal Topic

Fig. 7. Module 3 Contents for Animal Topic

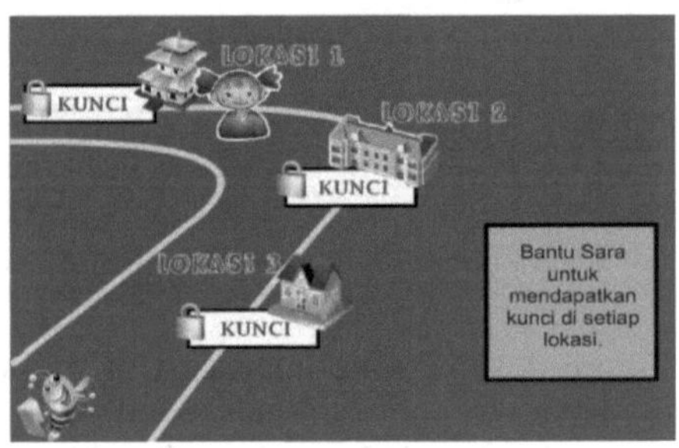

Fig. 8. Main Page of Exercise in the Game

4 User Acceptance Test

User acceptance test has been conducted on the developed courseware. There are two experiments that were conducted. The objective of the first experiment was to test on the efficient of the courseware in term of the features and contents, the ease of use of the courseware used by slow learners regardless of their level of abilities and also the users' interest towards this courseware. The second experiment evaluated the efficient of the courseware features and contents i terms of how easy to learn regardless of their abilities also the users' interest towards this courseware.

4.1 Efficiency

Efficiency is measured on the speed with of the users to be able to complete the tasks while experiencing the prototype [17]. The evaluation was conducted in 'Sekolah Kebangsaan Temong' which involved a total of ten users from "Linus" hard-core" illiterate and innumerate) and "Linus Tegar" (illiterate and innumerate) children. In this study, the efficient testing was conducted by looking at the length of time taken to execute the given exercises by the users. The purpose was to look at length of time in which each user spend to finish the exercise, whether by using this courseware may lessen the time taken to complete (increase of efficiency). If the time taken decreases, it means that the courseware is suitable for the users as they can learn easily within a shorter period of time. In addition, qualitative data was also collected based on observations of the interaction of users with courseware such as text, icon, button, picture, sound interaction and etc. This stage helps to detect if there are any problems arise which will slow the users during the learning process using "myLINUS" courseware. The findings from this session are as follows:

- **Time taken:** The lenght of time from starting till the end of each exercise until it is completed. There are three exercises provided to the user in the form of games, ranging from easy to difficult level. The recorded time includes the mistakes of the user because it is one of the limitations due to learning dificulties
- **Errors:** Mistakes made by users in terms of navigation and interaction while completing the tasks given.

Figures 9-10 shows the results on the time taken for the users to complete exercises 1 and 2. The results show that the users spent less time after a few with the numbers attempts were performed. Therefore, the more attempts the users try on the identical tasks, they will become more familiar and hence they will take less time to perform the task.

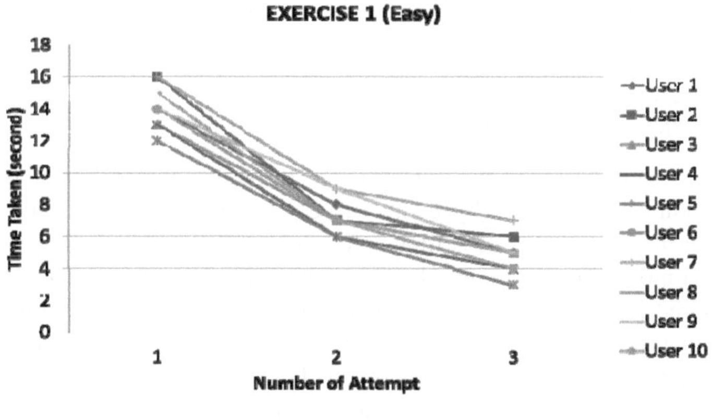

Fig. 9. Time taken for the users to complete exercise 1

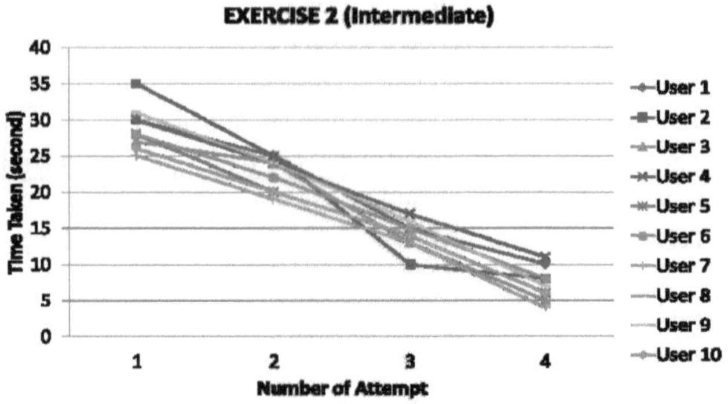

Fig. 10. Time taken for the users to complete exercise 2

Overall results indicate that the time taken to complete the exercises decrease along with the number of attempts performed by users on similar tasks. It indicates that MyLINUS is designed to assist the efficient aspects that are suitable for slow learners and the interactions developed are appropriate to their speed and abilities for the learning process.

4.2 Effectiveness

The second evaluation measured the effectiveness by taking the time difference taken between the current LINUS method and the developed "my LINUS" courseware using the same module contents and the same exercises. A total of six slow learner children Linus (illiterate and innumerate) and Linus Tegar ("hard-core" illiterate and innumerate) from Sekolah Kebangsaan Chegar Galah, Kuala Kangsar, Perak were involved in the experiment. This evaluation was conducted to measure which the ease of getting an access into the module and exercise, regardless of their ability levels. All users were asked to do three sets of the same modules and exercises two times using two different approaches:

i) Current LINUS method
ii) "My LINUS" courseware

Figures 11, 12 and 13 show the performance through comparison of time taken to complete modules 1, 2 and 3 by using LINUS textbook and MyLinus courseware. Results show that users took less time to complete the modules using "my LINUS" courseware compared to the textbook. This is because, by using textbook, users could get easily bored as textbooks merely contained static words and pictures. The results also show that the users were more interested in learning using the multimedia approach compared to the current approach. Users may interact with the computer through the sound and animation built in the courseware. As a result, users could increase their retention time and learnt actively using the developed courseware.

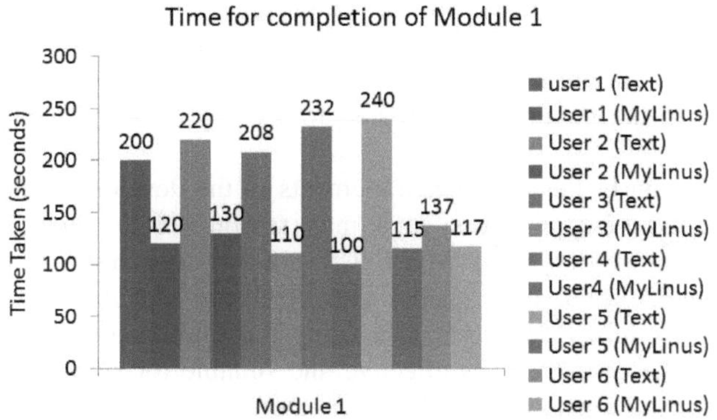

Fig. 11. Performance Comparison of Time taken to complete the textbook and module 1

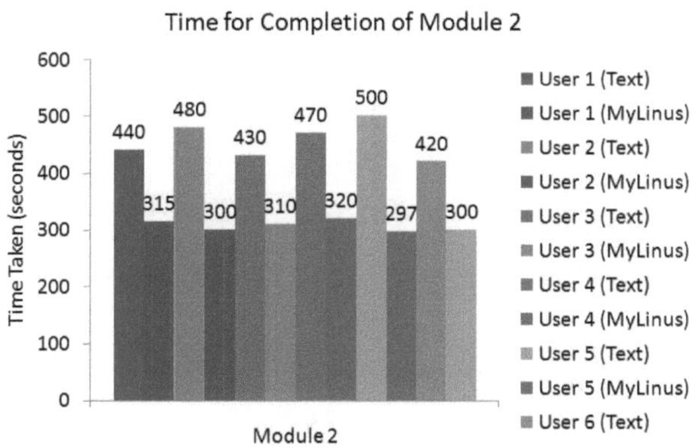

Fig. 12. Performance Comparison of Time taken for the users to complete module 2

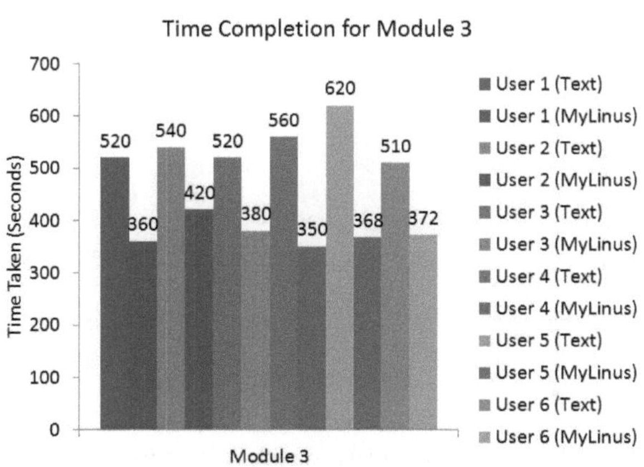

Fig. 13. Performance Comparison of Time taken for the users to complete module 3

Figures 14, 15 and 16 reveal similar findings. Users took less time to complete the same exercises provided using "my LINUS" courseware compared to the printed paper exercises (current LINUS method). Users showed more motivation to answer the questions using computers compared to writing in the printed paper from the textbook.

The integration of the multimedia elements in the developed courseware such as picture, text, audio and animation is the main reason why the time taken for modules and exercises completion using "MyLINUS" courseware is less than using the current LINUS method. The overall results show that the time taken to complete both modules and exercises decrease when using the multimedia learning approach. It indicates that the courseware is effective and suitable for slow learners in terms of interactions, speed and abilities in the learning process.

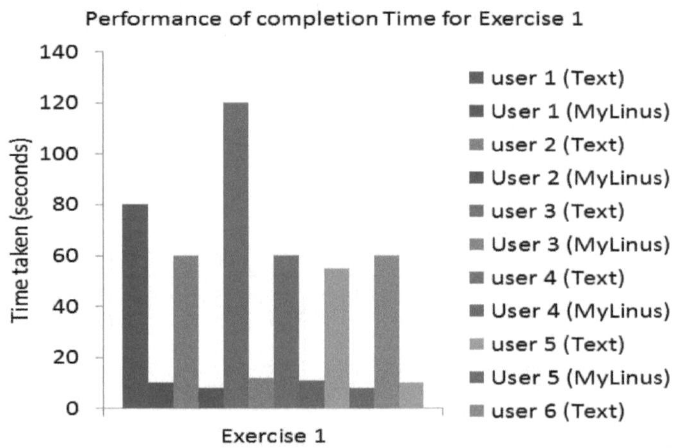

Fig. 14. Performance of Time taken for the users to complete Exercise 1

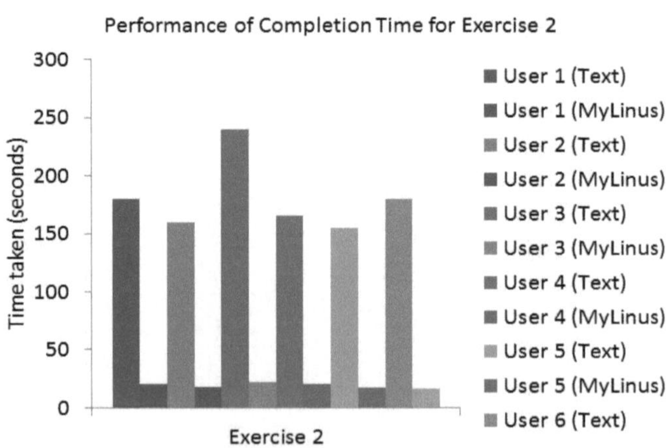

Fig. 15. Performance of Time taken for the users to complete Exercise 2

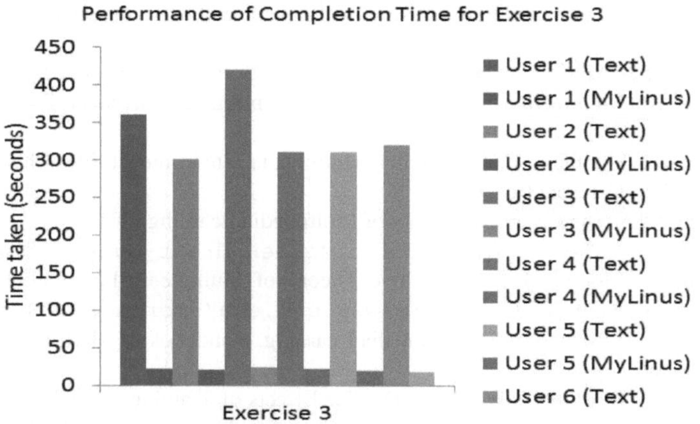

Fig. 16. Performance of Time taken for the users to complete Exercise 3

5 Conclusion

This paper describes development of a multimedia courseware and users' experience in testing "MyLINUS". It is capable of helping slow learner children overcome reading difficulties during the learning process. The development of this courseware is helpful as the approach and technique used are suitable for the slow learner learning levels. In addition, this courseware at the same time helps teachers in assisting slow learner children in today's learning environment. MyLINUS creates a much more fun way of learning and grasps the children's attention to focus and to stay interested in the module given during their learning process.

It is proven through the user acceptance test that MyLINUS is able to increase efficiency and effectiveness compared to the current LINUS method. Overall, the evaluations generated encouraging results where all users showed that MyLINUS suitable and has been accepted to meet the slow learners' needs e specifically for multimedia elements, contents and its usability.

This product can be further enhanced and made compatible in other platforms and not only limited to PC / laptop but also in smartphone and online usage. Operating system such as Android, iOS and Blackberry will create portability to this application. Further studies also need to add other functions and attractive elements that can help slow learner children to overcome reading difficulties in the learning process.

Acknowledgment. The authors would like to thank UTP and others who have been involved directly or indirectly in this research.

References

1. Shaw, S., Grimes, D., Bulman, J.: Educating slow learners: Are charter schools the last, best hope for their educational success? The Charter Schools Resource Journal 1(1) (2005)
2. Yusha'u, M.A.: Teaching slow learners in Mathematics: Yugal Remediation as alternative method. SER 13(2), 108–123 (2012)

3. Postnote. Teaching Children To Read. Parliamentary Office of Science and Technology, Number 345 (2009)
4. Sinar. 48,520 Murid Sekolah Rendah, Menengah Bermasalah Dalam Pembelajaran (2012)
5. Mayer, R.: Multimedia Learning, 2nd edn. Cambridge University Press, United States (2009)
6. Druin, A., Solomon, C.: Designing Multimedia Environment For Children. Katherine Schowalter, Canada (1996)
7. Sorden, S.D.: The Cognitive Theory of Multimedia Learning (2012), http://sorden.com/portfolio/sorden_draft_multimedia2012.pdf
8. Mayer, R., Moreno, R.: A cognitive Theory of Multimedia Learning: Implications for Design Prônciples (2002), http://www.unm.edu/~moreno/PDFS/chi.pdf
9. Mayer, R.: Introduction to Multimedia Learning. Handbook of Multimedia Learning, The Cambridge
10. Neill, A.L., Doolittle, P.E., Hicks, D.: The Effects of Training, Modality, and Redundancy on the Development of a Historical Inquiry Strategy in a Multimedia Learning Environment. Journal of Interactive Online Learning 8(3) (2009), http://www.ncolr.org/jiol
11. Doolittle, P.E.: Multimedia Learning: Empirical Results and Practical Applications (2002), http://scr.csc.noctrl.edu/courses/edn509/resources/readings/multimediaLearningEmpericalResults.pdf
12. Sharp, J., Bowker, R., Byrne, J.: VAK or VAK-uous? Towards the trivialisation of learning and the death of scholarship. Research Papers in Education 23(3), 293–314 (2008)
13. NYRC Handouts. Apply Adult Numeracy Methodologies to Develop Numeracy Skills (2010), http://www.ibsa.org.au/Portals/ibsa.org.au/docs/Resources/TAE%20VGC%20VGD%20LLN%20Resources/Readings%20Folder/CAE%20Learning%20styles%20.pdf (retrieved)
14. Devi U.: Brain Development, Teaching and Learning Styles (2002), http://www.educationallife.com/36-37.pdf
15. Chen, E.H.: A Review of Learning Theories from Visual Literacy. Journal of Educational Computing, Design & Online Learning 5, 1–8 (2004)
16. Duckett, I., Tatarkowski, M.: Learning Styles and their Application for Effective Learning. Quick Guide Effective Practice (2012)
17. Venkatesh, V., Morris, M.G., Davis, G.B., Davis, F.D.: User Acceptance of information Technology: Toward a Unified View. MIS Quarterly 27(3), 425–478 (2003)

Users' Expectation of Web Objects Location: Case Study of ASEAN Countries

Aslina Baharum and Azizah Jaafar

Institute of Visual Informatics, Universiti Kebangsaan Malaysia (UKM), 43600 Bangi, Selangor Malaysia
{cappuccino_aszz,azizahftsm}@yahoo.com

Abstract. A study conducted in 2006 had successfully determined that users could form a schema for the location of web objects on informational websites. This study investigates whether users' expectation has not changed since the previous study. Among the objects being examined include 'Logo'; 'Internal links'; 'Search'; 'Advertisement'; 'External links'; 'Site title'; 'Login'; 'Language'; 'Content' and 'Calendar'. Ninety-four participants from ten ASEAN countries were presented with a demographic questionnaire followed by a mock browser window consisted of six horizontal and seven vertical grid squares. They completed the survey on the expected location of each of the ten web objects. The study found that there were significant changes in user expectations in web object locations. The result supported the findings of the previous study that predicted the advances of technology significantly affect user's schema of the web objects' layout within a four-years minimum.

Keywords: expectation, user interface, web objects, schema and mental model.

1 Introduction

Websites are useful for information retrieval for public's medium tool. There is a wide range of applicable for websites other than information retrieval, such as online shopping, online counseling, online tutoring etc. With the thousands of users in countries around the world, the need of an efficient websites design is becoming increasingly vital. Interface of website is the first impression users will attracted to stay on. This fact had been stated by Fogg, Murable, Stanford & Tuber [1] revealed that "design look" of the website was one of the major aspects to determine the credibility of websites. Visual appeal tends to influence user mental model to revisits websites. Previously usability studies have reported design problems encounter by users while browsing websites [2] and [3]. One of the main reasons for this is, often web designers rely on web style guides rather considering user understanding of websites. Users expect certain web objects to be placed in certain locations for easy access.

In 2006, Shaikh & Lenz [7] conducted a survey to determine if user experience for locations of web objects has changed since 2001 (in five years). The study used undergraduate psychology students for the sample study following Bernard's [4]

H. Badioze Zaman et al. (Eds.): IVIC 2013, LNCS 8237, pp. 383–395, 2013.

methodology by evaluating expected location for the following web objects: 'Back to home', 'Internal links', 'Site search engine', 'Advertisements' and 'About us'. Based on Shaikh & Lenz's [7], changes were found on three objects ('Internal links', 'Search' and 'Advertisements').

Based on Internet usage statistics (www.internetworldstats.com/stats.htm) retrieved in March 26, 2013, Internet users were over 2 billion worldwide, with an increase of 566.4 percent from 2000 to 2012. With the rapidly growing number of websites on the Internet, searching for the best information increasingly becomes a search for the best information presentation on best possible technology information system [5] and [6].

It was concluded that users would locate information quickly and efficiently when they are satisfied and feel familiar when the location of web objects place in the site in where they would expect it [7], [8] and [17]. For e-commerce sites, placing these objects in expected locations would give an e-commerce site a competitive edge over those that do not place them in their expected location [9].

Since 2005, there has been no study to re-evaluate the effect of the location of web objects for websites. Since Shaikh & Lenz [7], technology has made many advances in the last four years and advances on the back-end can affect the layout of web objects on the front-end.

1.1 Beginning of Users' Schema

Schema or mental model is based on the creation of a mental representation of objects that are present in an environment. This model is often used to help explain the interaction of users with the websites. Various theories have been introduced to help researchers figure out model in the context of human behavior. People develop unconscious mental models to interact with the world live in. By studying mental models such as the order of objects [10] and [11], researchers will be able to better understand how a person interact with the environment. Mental model has been used in many contexts and for many purposes, where Craik first mentioned it in his 1943 book, "The Nature of Explanation" [12] and [13]. Then Johnson-Laird proposed mental models as a way of describing the process, which humans go through to solve deductive reasoning problems. His theory included the use of a set of diagrams to describe the various combinations of premises and possible conclusions [13] and [14]. Johnson-Laird started this idea and uses it to order things like space objects. Based on this idea, Norman [15] and Payne [16] incorporated this idea into Human Computer Interaction (HCI). HCI can be used to create interfaces and interaction methods that help people create a more accurate model of the mental system are interacting. In most studies, the mental model was deciphered based on the location of web objects [4], [7], [9], [17], [18], [19], [20] and [22].

Bernard [8] stated that the user has a schema or mental model of where web objects should be located. This was in correspondence with his study on 2001, which found the similar schemas between the novice and the experienced in US. So, it was suggested that users quickly develop common schemas for these web objects, which underscore the need to place them in their expected location.

Bernard & Shesadri [18], then found this was consistent with their study on global experience of user's mental models for e-commerce with websites web objects with Bernard's previous study [4] and [17] and his [9] study with e-commerce sites web objects in US. Seventy-six percent reported that their expectation for the locations of common e-commerce web objects is generally the same as to where they would prefer the objects to be located, again supporting the argument that website layouts should attempt to conform to user expectation [17].

A recent study of library websites of top world universities by Vasantha & Harinarayana [19] found the pattern of library web object placement was not different compared to e-commerce objects which means that the library web designer in developing countries can use the results of the study to design websites for facilitating easy navigation and retrieval of information.

1.2 Background of the Study

At the beginning, Bernard [17] chooses respondents who have one or more years of web experience. He continued his study in 2001 by comparing the novice and experienced user and he found similar schemas between both. Later in 2002, Bernard examined e-commerce buyer expectation for the location of common e-commerce web objects in US and found general consensus among respondents. This e-commerce web layout corresponded with Adkisson in same year on 75 leading e-commerce sites.

Bernard and Shesadri [18] expanded the study on four geographical areas, 61% North America, 12% Commonwealth, 17% Europe, 8% India and found that different regional cultures and conventions influenced by multinational and cross-regional web browsing have significantly shaped website layout expectations. In addition, Costa [20] who studied the effect of culture found a pattern similar to that of Bernard & Shesadri [18] with a group of universities of Lisbon and Coimbra, Portugal. The study stated that if the consistency holds true over time, then the need to localize user-interface for specific region would be less important, with the condition that users from those region have the same cultural background [19].

Nowadays, a larger, more diverse group of users access the Internet on a regular basis that need multinational cross-culture websites with user-centered interface. The traditional information organizations techniques and information retrieval tools have influenced in great deal in designing user-centered web interface [21]. There is a need to review the location of web objects after a few years, particularly every five years to see if there are any changes over the years. This study investigates culture on ASEAN countries, user expectations to improve the accuracy of regional multinational expectations.

2 Methodology

A methodology adapted from previous studies was used [4], [7], [9], [17], [18], [19], [20] and [22]. Respondents were presented with a demographic questionnaire followed by a page containing a depiction of web browser windows with dimension

1074 x 768 pixels. The mock browser window consisted of six horizontal and seven vertical grid squares adapted from Bernard & Shesadri [18] was used. Participants numbered the location based on web objects listed in Table 1, to where they expected the corresponding web objects to be normally located on a basic website. A total of 94 participants consisting of 60 males and 34 females from ten ASEAN countries (Fig. 1) completed the survey on the expected location of each of the ten web objects. Seventy-one percent of the participants were above the age of 30 and 80% indicated that they used the computer daily. All participants used English as their first or second language. This indicates that they are familiar with the English language websites. Criteria for the selection of participants were; (1) Respondent must be resident or have stayed more years in an ASEAN than in other country/countries, (2) Respondent must have computer literacy and at least be familiar with websites. The distribution of participants from different countries is shown in Fig. 1. The data for the study were collected from June 2012 to December 2012 using online and offline basis.

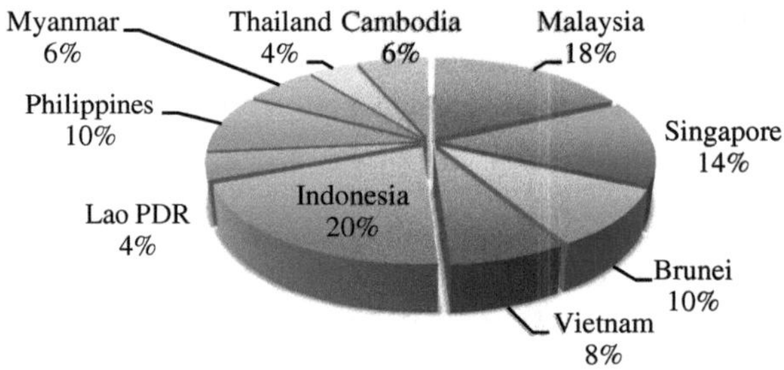

Fig. 1. Distribution of participants from different countries

Table 1. List of web objects

No.	Web objects
1.	Logo
2	Site title
3	Internal links
4	External links
5	Login
6	Language selection
7	Search
8	Content
9	Calendar
10	Advertisements

2.1 Web Objects Studied

Three fields had identified location web objects; on informational website, e-commerce websites and library websites (Table 2).

Based on previous studies, the present study used ten objects. Four objects from previous studies; first 'Internal links', second 'External links', third 'Search' and fourth 'Ads', were found to be important for informational websites. The fifth 'Login' object was identified as creating user profile membership record and security. 'Back home' object was identified as not necessary because all browsers have the 'Back home' already. Thus, sixth 'Logo' object was added to show website trademark and ownership to replace 'Back home' and 'Home link". Then, seventh 'Site title' object gives an overview about the websites. For the purpose of a multinational website, there is a need to have multiple languages for user preference, thus eight 'Language' object needs also to be added. Another two additional objects, ninth 'Content' object to identify where the locations will be, and finally, tenth 'Calendar' object for easy navigation for the user to know the latest news available.

Table 2. Web objects from previous fields of study

Websites [4, 7, 17]	E-commerce websites [9, 18, 20, 23]	Library websites [19]
Internal links	**Internal links**	OPAC
External links	**External links**	Ask us
Search	**Search**	**Search**
Advertisements	**Advertisements**	About us
Back home	Back home	Back home
Home link	Help	Help
About us	**Login**	**Login**
	Cart	
	Account	
	Product	

3 Results and Discussion

The location of the particular web objects was counted in such a way that it can be presented in 6 x 7 horizontal and vertical grids. The darker the shade, the greater the number of times that the particular web objects was found in that particular location. The frequencies are represented by increasingly darker shades (Fig. 2). The figures reveal that most respondents had an expected location for each of the presented web objects.

In 2006, Shaikh & Lenz [7] determined that users were able to form a schema for the location of web objects on informational websites. The current study investigates whether users' expectation have changed since 2005 data collection for 2006 study. Clearly changes were found in the expected location of 'Internal links' and 'Advertisements'. Also, another five objects were added based on requirements.

Fig. 2. Each grid represents the frequency of web object found in particular locations

3.1 'Home Link'/ 'Logo'

Shaikh & Lenz [7] found the expected location of the 'Home link' to be in the upper left corner of the website. The data collected in 2012 used 'Logo' object and indicated participants still have this expectation, which revealed a similar trend (Fig. 3).

The current study shows that 48% of the participants expected the 'Logo' object to be in the top-left corner of the website. Approximately 11% expected it to be in the center top and 10% expected it to be in the top right area as shown in Figure 3. Previous studies used the 'Back home' object that is no longer used due to the function already being included in the browser. This result also corresponded with results from most previous studies that used the 'Back home' object [4], [7], [9], [17], [18] and [20].

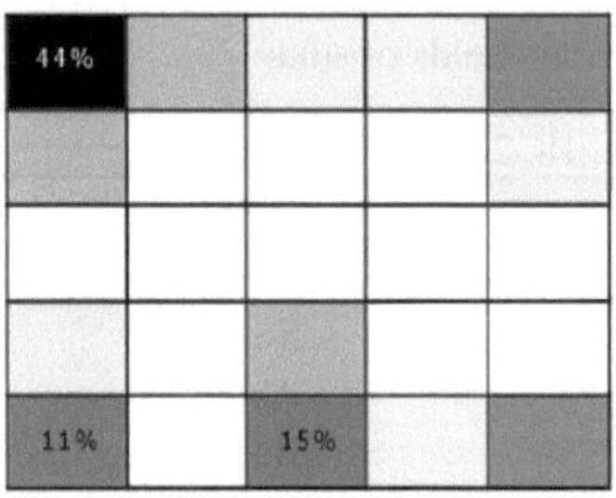

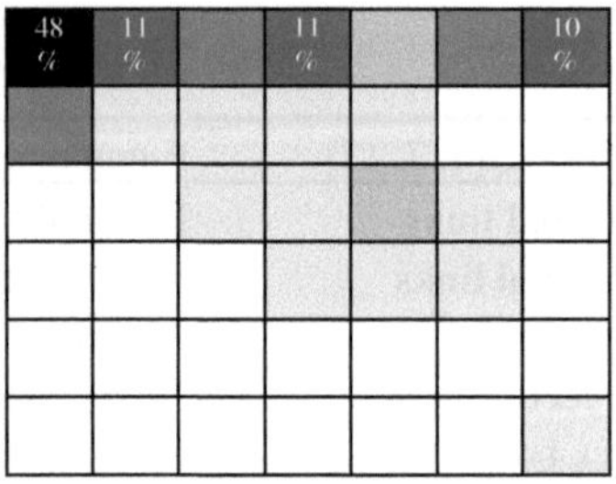

Fig. 3. Expected location of 'Back home' from Shaikh & Lenz [7] (left), 'Logo' from the current study (right)

3.2 'Internal Links'

Participants in the Shaikh & Lenz [7] study overwhelming expected the 'Internal links' to be located on the left side of the website. The current study finds a similar expectation among participants. However, the 2012 data also showed a tendency for users to choose locations along the top of website for 'Internal links', which corresponded with Shaikh & Lenz's [7] study that also found some users choose the top for 'Internal link' object location.

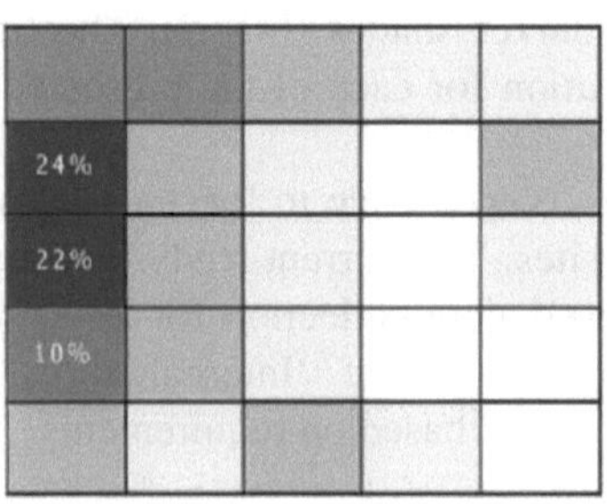

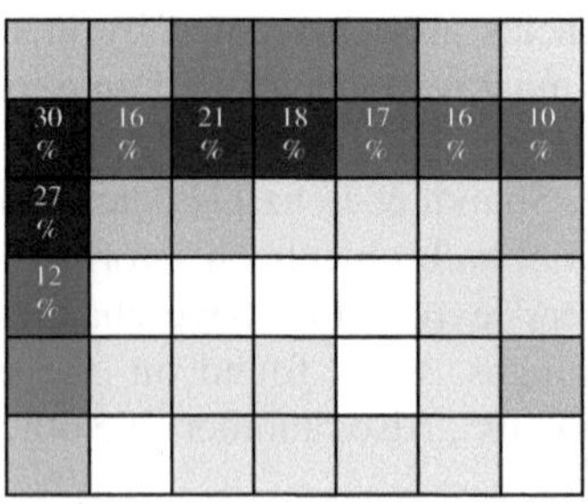

Fig. 4. Expected location of 'Internal links' from Shaikh & Lenz [7] (left) and the current study (right)

As shown in Figure 4, many participants in the current study expected to find the 'Internal links' object to be located in the top of the website or on the left side. The left side result was consistent with results found by the previous studies [9], [17] and [20]. The location of internal links has likely been affected by the increased use of DHTML or JavaScript menus. The technology that is more prevalent today is more conducive towards multi-level navigation being displayed across the top of the website [7] and [23].

3.3 'Search'

Information retrieval is the most important aspect of the web and has become a very common phenomenon. This information is delivered to users via 'Search' object. In the 2006 study conducted by Shaikh & Lenz [7], participants expected the 'Search' object to be located in the upper right corner of the website or near the upper left corner. The current study did not find the upper left trend; participants expected the 'Search' object to be located in the top-right of the website.

As seen in Figure 5, most of the participants in the current study expected it to be located on the top-right. This is consistent also with Vasantha & Harinarayana [19], who found information retrieval is the most important aspect of the web. As such, it has become a very common phenomenon. Almost 50% of the 75 library websites placed the 'Search' object at the top-right corner of the library websites [23].

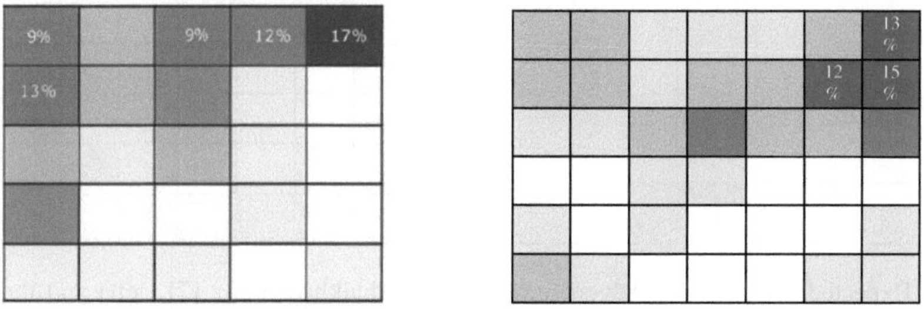

Fig. 5. Expected location of 'Search' from Shaikh & Lenz [7] (left) and the current study (right)

3.4 'Advertisements'

The previous study by Shaikh & Lenz [7] revealed that participants expected 'Advertisements' object to be located either at the center top or the right side of the website as shown in Figure 6 (left). Whereas, participants in the 2012 study showed a difference preference for either the right area or lower area of the website. However, in the 2006 study, participants were almost as likely to choose the right side of the website for the location of advertisements object.

The previous studies revealed that participants mostly expected 'Advertisements' object to be located in the upper or center area of the website. There is a pattern also in the right area and the bottom line of the website in Costa [20], which is consistent with this study as well. According to the Portuguese study, the years that separate the studies could make a big difference in terms of the advertisement content. If we look closer, the advertisement is the main financing model of most websites, even those outside the e-commerce category. The banner ads have been changing the format, content and location, as a need to capture the user's attention and reaction to the users "banner blindness" [23] and [24].

Nowadays, the online ads are almost everywhere so the differences shown by the studies could easily be explained. As technology has changed over the past few years, so have advertisements. In the early 2000s, ads were not as likely to be floating or intrusive in nature as they are today [19] and [23].

In addition, studies from Benway & Lane [25] have shown that banner advertisements are effective. Therefore, guidelines that recommend placing important items at the top of the page may be misguided. Spool et al. [26] found in usability tests that users turn to navigation bars after determining that the page does not contain the information they need. At this point the user tends to have scrolled to the top or the bottom of the page. Users may start viewing the page in the center, and examine the very top and bottom only of the page after they determine what they want is not located in the center. Therefore, it may not be advisable to place the "important" items at the top because the user may look there last [23] and [26].

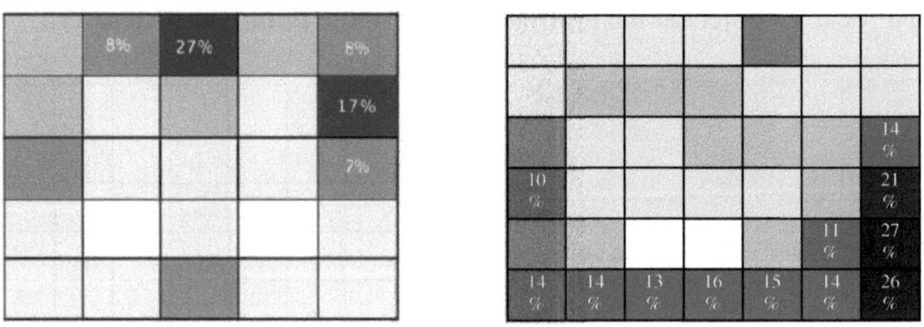

Fig. 6. Expected location of 'Advertisement' from Shaikh & Lenz [7] (left) and the current study (right)

3.5 Additional Web Objects

3.5.1 'External Links'

'External links' is the useful link or a hyperlink on a website that points to a page on a different website. Figure 7 indicates participants expected to find the 'External links' object in the footer area. Participants also expected it located either on the right or left side of the footer website. This result is nearly same as that found by Bernard [9] and [20]. The study by Bernard & Sheshadri [18] on e-commerce website with four different geographical (North America, Commonwealth, Europe & India) which found 'External links' should on left and right side.

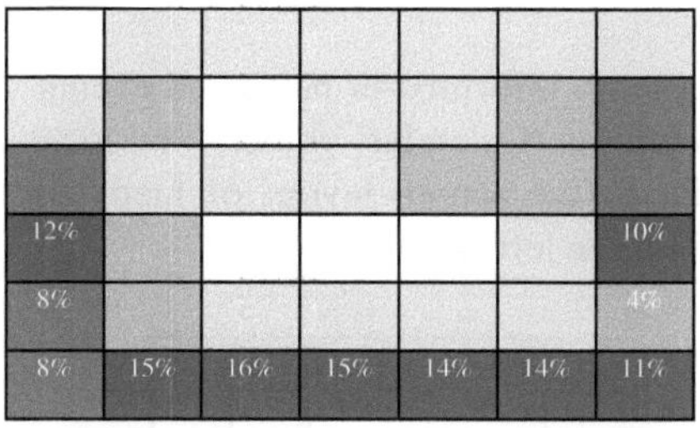

Fig. 7. Expected location of 'External links'

3.5.2 'Site Title'

'Site title' is used to identify and provide information about the website. Figure 8 reveals that participants expected the 'Site title' to be located on the top of the website. Participants were given the option of using just one or more of the squares; 43% used more than one square for this web object. The article posted by Atzl [27], clarified that a clearer title better conveys to the user what they can accomplish on that page. 'Site title' must be the correct title for each website. Page titles or 'Site title' must accurately reflect the page contents; otherwise, it will confuse users and make it extremely difficult for them to navigate the site [23].

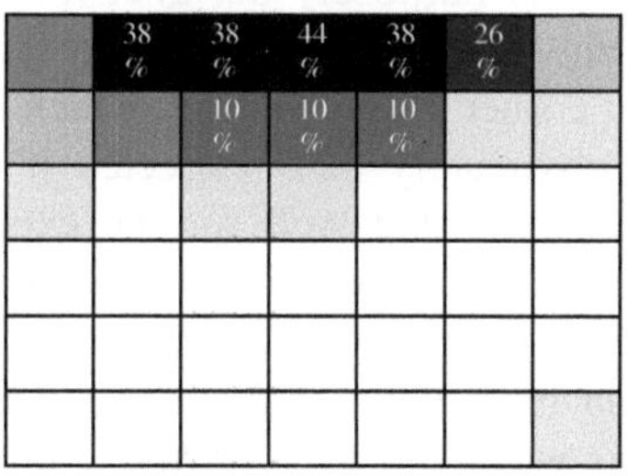

Fig. 8. Expected location of 'Site title'

3.5.3 'Login'

'Login' is the subscription-based part of the website. As seen in Figure 9, most participants expected the 'Login' object to be located at the top-right side of the website. The 'Login' link is usually placed at this location because this is an area where it is believed that visitors initially glance when they view a website [23]. Some studies have found this to be true [4] and [18], while others have not [9] and [19]. The observation of several categories of website reveals that the login objects is usually located in a visible interface area, but that it also depends on the website category [23].

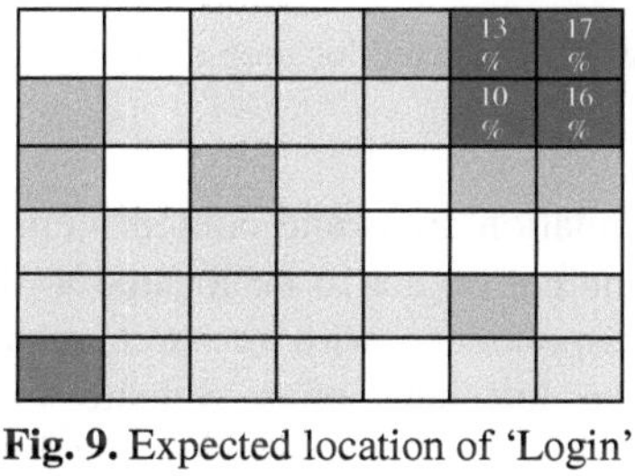

Fig. 9. Expected location of 'Login'

3.5.4 'Calendar'

'Calendar' is where the user is informed of news and events. As seen in Fig. 10, most of the participants expected the 'Calendar' object to be located at the right side of the website, which is similar to the screen layout of many online websites. But some expected it to be located on the left side.

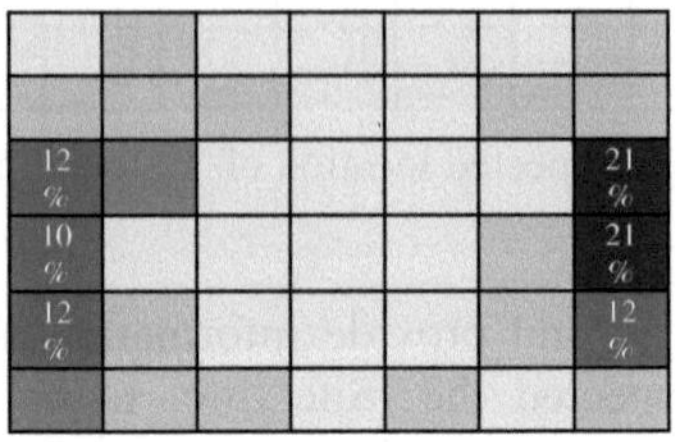

Fig. 10. Expected location of 'Calendar'

3.5.5 'Language'

'Language' is the requirement feature for user to choose languages options. As stated by Shaikh & Lenz [7], today a more diverse group of users access the Internet on a regular basis, so, this feature is purposely designed for multi-national and diverse cultures used. As shown in Fig. 11, participants (29%) expected the 'Language' object to be located at the top-right corner of the website, which is a fairly common location within other websites. Approximately 22% expected it to be in the top-left area. Clearly, this convention has translated well for the expected location of language selection for centric sites. Since, the expectation of placing this web object at this location is very strong, so it is suggested that it be placed in this location. Based on HCI Design Journal, written by Cullata [28], in accessibility problems, one of the good user interface solutions was to add a 'Language' option on the main page [23]. Furthermore, according to Nielsen's eye-tracking study over 20 users, that 69% of the time spent web browsing, users' more attention on the left side of a website.

Fig. 11. Expected location of 'Language'

3.5.6 'Content'

'Content' contains the information areas and content items. As seen in Fig. 12, most participants expected the content object to be located at the left to the center of the website. This finding correspondence with research results by Chapman [29] that discovered to place on the left side of a website for important content [23].

In addition, Dr. Nielsen's in his study of eye tracking stated that 69% of users times spend of their attention on the left side [23, 24]. This was also recommended locations for several style guides in general [23].

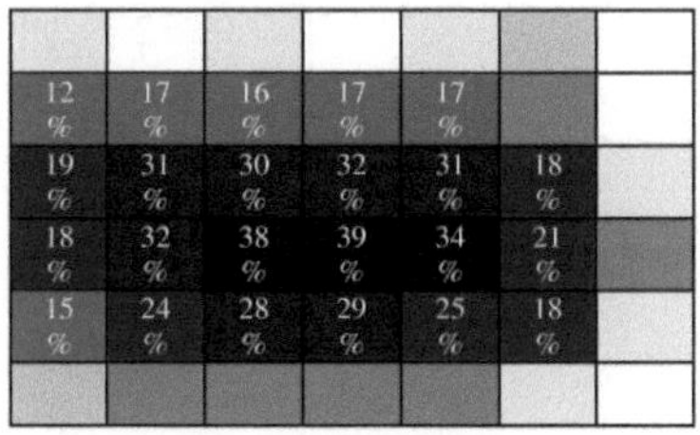

Fig. 12. Expected location of 'Content'

4 Conclusion

The study examined the placement of ten web objects in informational website. The result of the study can be summarized in Fig. 13 and Fig. 14 as follows:

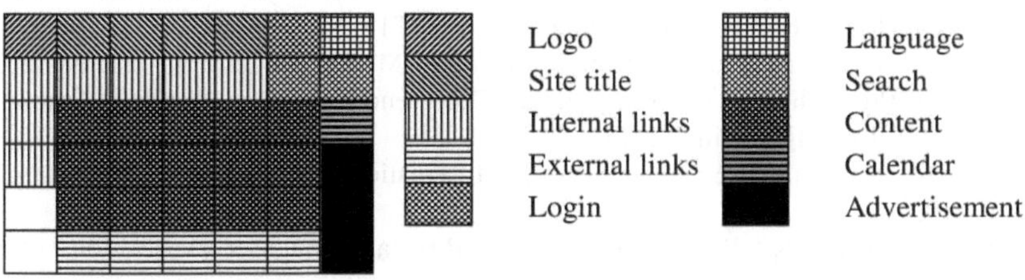

Fig. 13. Combined expectations

The study revealed that the 'Logo'/'Back to Home' object was the only one that corresponded with results of the previous study by Shaikh & Lenz [7]. Whereas 'Internal links' object found another option then the original left side corner of the website. An interesting aspect of the study is that the pattern revealed that as predicted technology and time do effect expectation and acceptance of users placement in web objects. This result strengthens the idea of Shaikh & Lenz [7] that users' schemas change to keep up with advances in technology. So, there is a need to review after four years or more.

As technology changes the face of the Internet, users' expectation seems to shift as well. The changes over the past few years have not been dramatic but reflect updates in technology and advertising schemes. With "Web 2.0" being the buzzword, all implications indicate that the layout of websites will continue to evolve to take advantage of technology that allows for faster download and more relevant content. Further research on the acceptance of expected placement of web objects with international audiences has also been conducted and will be discussed in other paper.

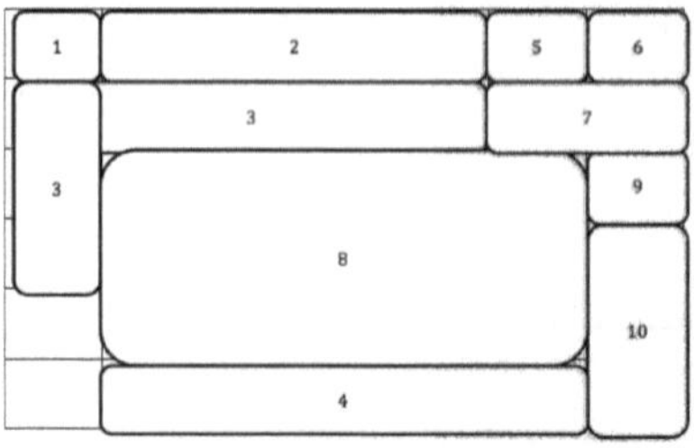

Fig. 14. Layout of the result

References

1. Fogg, B.J., Marable, L., Stanford, J., Tauber, E.R.: How Do People Evaluate A Website's Credibility? Result From A Large Study (2002)
2. Blummer, B.A.: A Literature Review Of Academic Library Web Page Studies. Journal of Web Librarianship 1(1), 45–64 (2007)
3. Brown, B., Sellen, A.: Exploring Users' Experience of the Web. Publishing Systems and Solutions Laboratory. HP Laboratories Bristol. First Monday 6(9) (2001)
4. Bernard, M.: User Expectations for the Location of Web Objects. Chi 2001 Extended Abstracts On Human Factors In Computer Systems, 171 (2001)
5. Aslina, B., Azizah, J.: Cultural Adaptivity Through Mental Model For Sustainable User Interface. In: Proceeding of The International Conference on Future Trends in Computing & Communication Engineering (2013)
6. McCarty, K.: Technology & Hospitality. In: International CHRIE, vol. 19(1), Virginia, USA (2010)
7. Shaikh, A.D., Lenz, K.: Where's the search? Re-examining user expectations of web objects. Usability News 8(1) (2006)
8. Brumfield, B., Cox, G., Delgado, N., Pulelo, M., Shifflett, K., Smith, D., Taylor, D.: Client-Side Web Development for Modern Browsers. Microsoft (2011)
9. Bernard, M.: Examining user expectations for the location of common e-commerce web objects. Usability News 4(1) (2002)
10. Johnson-Laird, P.N., Girotto, V., Legrenzi, P.: Mental models: a gentle guide for outsiders (1998)
11. Gorman, M.E., Carlson, W.B.: Interpreting Invention As A Cognitive Process: The Case Of Alexander Graham Bell, Thomas Edison, And The Telephone. Science, Technology, & Human Values 15, 131–164 (1990)
12. Craik, K.J.W.: The Nature of Explanation. Cambridge University Press, Cambridge (1943)
13. Davidson, M.J., Dove, L., Weltz, J.: Mental Models And Usability (1999)
14. Johnson-Laird, P.N.: Mental Models-Towards A Cognitive Science of Language, Inference and Consciousness. Harvard University Press, Cambridge (1983)
15. Norman, D.: Some Observations On Mental Models. In: Gentner, D., Stevens, A. (eds.) Mental Models, Lea (1983)
16. Payne, S.: A descriptive study of mental models. Behaviour and Information Technology 10(1), 3–21 (1991)
17. Bernard. M.L.: Examining user expectations of the location of web objects. ITG Internetworking 3.3 (2000)

18. Bernard, M., Sheshadri, A.: Preliminary examination of global expectations of users' mental models for e-commerce web layouts. Usability News 6(2) (2004)
19. Vasantha, R.N., Harinarayana, N.S.: Identifying the Location of Web Objects: A Study of Library Websites. In: 8th International Caliber, pp. 28–39. Goa Universit (2011)
20. Costa, C.: Cultural Factors and Usability User Expectations for the Location of E-Commerce Web Objects Case Study in Portugal (2010)
21. Rosenfield, L., Morville, P.: Information architecture for the World Wide Web, 2nd edn., p. 496. O'Reilly Media, Beijing (2002)
22. Adkisson, H.: Identifying de-facto standards for e-commerce web sites (Unpublished master thesis). University of Washington, Washington, US (2002)
23. Aslina, B., Azizah, J.: Investigating Adaptive Cultural Diversity Through Users' Mental Model For Sustainable User Interface. In: Visual Informatics International Seminar (2013)
24. Nielsen, J.: Will pain-text ads continue to rule? Jakob Nielsen's Alertbox (2003)
25. Benway, J.P., Lane, D.M.: Banner Blindness: Web Searchers Often Miss "Obvious" Links. ITG Newsletter 1.3, 1–10 (1998)
26. Spool, J.M., Scanlon, T., Schroeder, W., Snyder, C., DeAngelo, T.: Web Site Usability: A Designer's Guide. Morgan Kaufmann Publishers (1997)
27. Atzl, A.: What Is UI Design, and Why Does It Matter? Singlebrook Technology (2012)
28. Cullata, R.: Instructional Design. Developer of The Instructional Design Website. HCI Design Journal (2011)
29. Chapman, C.: 10 Usability Tips Based On Research Studies (2010)

Playability Assessment for Educational Computer Games: Pilot Study for Model Development

Hasiah Mohamed[1] and Azizah Jaafar[2]

[1] Faculty of Computer & Mathematical Sciences, Universiti Teknologi MARA, 23000 Dungun, Terengganu, Malaysia
[2] Institute of Visual Informatics, Universiti Kebangsaan Malaysia, 43600 Bangi, Selangor, Malaysia
hasia980@tganu.uitm.edu.my, aj@ivi.ukm.my

Abstract. This study used the partial least squares (PLS) and structural equation modeling (SEM) tool to examine evaluation constructs that are appropriate to evaluate educational computer games (ECG) by real users. The focus of the evaluation constructs are for evaluating ECG that still in the development process. There are five constructs that being derived from heuristic evaluation for ECG known as Playability Heuristic Evaluation for Educational Computer Games (PHEG) that being developed to evaluate ECG by expert evaluators. The constructs are interface (10), educational element (6), content (6), playability (7) and multimedia (8). Total numbers of items for the five constructs are 37. Statistical results confirm that all of the five constructs and 29 items are important to be included in evaluating ECG. The results, besides indicating the suitability of the PLS in statistical analysis, has also contributed to a better understanding of constructs needed in evaluating ECG that still in the development process that has not been tested. Findings are useful for game developers and educational technologist to have a validated model and questionnaire that can be used to evaluate ECG. The result of the evaluation using the proposed model can be used to enhance the ECG before it can be released. Limitations and suggestions for future research are also included.

Keywords: playability assessment for educational computer games, model, interface, usability.

1 Introduction

In application development process, evaluation plays an important and integral part. Evaluation can be carried out either during the development (formative) or once the development is completed (summative). Expert evaluators may involve in any stage either formative or summative and real users normally involve during summative evaluation. The involvement in summative evaluation process normally related to user perception on the usability of the games that already being released. Selection of evaluators depends on the types of application, evaluation techniques and tools. One of the popular applications nowadays is computer game. The popularity of computer

H. Badioze Zaman et al. (Eds.): IVIC 2013, LNCS 8237, pp. 396–407, 2013.

games lead to the advancement of computer game development to integrates educational elements in it. There are a lot of research have been conducted on the integration of computer game and educational elements in the perspective of impact, implication and effects [1]. The terms used for these applications are known as game based learning, computer games, educational computer games and digital game based learning [2],[3] and [4].

Integration of fun to be played by the users and ability to contribute to the teaching and learning process become vital elements in any educational games development process. In order to merge these elements, comprehensive evaluation technique is needed during the development process. One of the evaluation techniques that are normally used by expert evaluators is Heuristic Evaluation (HE). HE is used by expert evaluators to examine interface of any application during interactive design process. Experts' involvement in the evaluation process able to help developers to detect usability problem before the game can be released [5]. The ability and characteristics of HE has been used as a basis in developing specific heuristic technique to evaluate educational computer games (ECG). This technique is known as Playability Heuristic Evaluation for Educational Computer Game (PHEG) consists of five heuristics; interface (IN), educational element (ED), content (CN), playability (PL) and multimedia (MM) [5]. Experts that involve in the evaluation process are from various backgrounds based on the heuristics provided such as interface expert (for IN), educational technologies (for ED), subject matter experts (for CN), multimedia experts (for MM) and game developers (for PL).

Our goal is to propose a validated model that can be used in evaluating educational computer games that still in the development process. This paper reports the validated model known as ECG Evaluation Model that can be used by real (potential) users to evaluate educational computer games. This research is important to facilitate game developers to get users perceptions on the ECG that still in the development process.

The next section of this paper discusses the research context and conceptual model in relation to existing literature on educational computer game and relational constructs such as interface, educational element, content, playability and multimedia. This is followed by an explanation of the research method used and an assessment of goodness of measures, namely, the construct validity, convergent validity, discriminant validity and reliability of the constructs. Subsequent sections deal with data analysis, path analysis and hypotheses testing. The last section is on discussion and conclusion with suggestions for future research.

2 Background

2.1 Educational Computer Games

Computer games are often expected to be effective educational tools [7],[8] and [9]. Digital games have been recently considered as meaningful learning environments [10],[11] and [12]. Educational computer games (ECG) or game based learning

(GBL) can be defined as a mixture of educational content and computer games [13]. Games are the optimized environments for fun. In addition to fun, games provide interaction, feedback and collaboration. Integrating digital games in education, therefore, becomes more significant because it can provide engaging and motivating learning environments. The hybrid incorporation between education and game entertainment make the educational context more interesting to the players. In comparison between game and GBL, game has no external goal but is played because of fun [14] and GBL has an added characteristic which is the learning content [15].

It is thus not surprising that many educators have begun to examine whether games can contribute to students' interest and learning [12],[13],[16] and [17]. For last decade, many empirical studies have shown that games enhance students' motivation [18],[19] and [20]. In terms of cognitive load, it is often argued that learners' cognitive capacity during learning with games may become overloaded [21] and [22]. Games appear to intrinsically motivate users through environmental features [23] and [24]. There are six characteristics of digital games, such as fantasy, rules/goals, sensory stimuli, challenge, mystery, and control [25]. Game characteristics should be activated within an instructional context in order to enhance learning and game features, such as challenge, curiosity, fantasy, control, cooperation, competition and recognition, make learning fun [26].

2.2 Interface

Heuristic Evaluation (HE) [27] and [28] is one of the usability evaluation methods commonly used to determine the usability problems of an interface design software [29],[30] and [31]. HE contains nine guidelines in place [27] and has added one more to makes it ten [28]. Heuristic evaluation is a heuristic that is often used in evaluating a variety of software, applications and systems. HE main goal is to produce a list of usability problems where this list can be used for improvement [32]. Based on the review of the literature above, the hypothesis is:

H1. Interface has a direct positive effect on the evaluation of educational computer games.

2.3 Educational Elements

Previous researchers have developed specific heuristics to be used to evaluate the usability of educational software [29], [30], [31], [32], [33] and [34]. Development and implementation educational element heuristic in the evaluation process has shown the importance of the process in evaluating educational element. This is to ensure that the objectives of education-based software development can be achieved and beneficial to the users. Pedagogical expert involvement in the evaluation process play an important role to ensure the objectives of educational software development can be achieved. Heuristics and sub-heuristics for educational elements have been developed and used in evaluating educational based applications [30], [31], [33] and [34]. These heuristic was develop based on HE. Therefore, it is necessary to integrate educational elements in the process of evaluating educational computer games. But heuristics and sub-heuristics need to be streamlined so that it is appropriate and specific to the ECG. Therefore it is hypothesized that:

H2. Educational elements has a direct positive effect on the evaluation of educational computer games.

2.4 Content

In any educational-based application development, content must be presented properly. In evaluating content, 9 sub-heuristics have been identified [39] and later 8 sub-heuristic that relate to instructional design has been identified [40]. Other then that, four dimensions in evaluating web-based e-learning system which are learner interface, learning community, system content and personalization has been identified [41]. Design criteria, evaluation scale for eLearning system and four dimensions for evaluation scale which would enhance meaningful learning also being identified [42]. The four dimensions are instructional strategy, teaching materials, learning tool and learning interface.

The complete contents of the presentation materials mean that the application has a content and interactive mechanism sufficient to meet the educational goals of different types of students. Software is said to be complete when it supports a variety of learning activities, including tasks such as reading, creative writing, problem solving and self-assessment. Learning activities in an educational software may include some or a combination of tutorial activities, drill, instructional and simulation of the game. Hence, it is hypothesizes that:

H3. Content has a direct positive effect on the evaluation of educational computer games.

2.5 Playability

As for game evaluation, there are many techniques and methods being developed to evaluate the usability. Heuristics Evaluation, think aloud, cognitive walkthrough and usability testing are among the technique used to evaluate game [16], [19], [20], [21], [22] and [33]. Heuristics evaluation shown a huge potential to be a valuable evaluation tool for computer games since the development of heuristic related to computer games were recorded increasingly started on 1982 until 2008. First heuristics to evaluate educational games was developed in 1982 [25]. Later in 2002, [44] has created a list of heuristics based on her study at a game development company. Later in 2004 [45] created the list of heuristics that are best suited to evaluate general issues in early development phase with prototype or mock-up, known as Heuristic Evaluation for Playability (HEP). Alternative solutions for resolving the playability issues were generated by both the evaluator and the game designer. HEP has been defined based on four categories of games which is a set of problems and challenges faced by the players to win the game; games story including all the games plot and development character; game mechanics involving programming that provides structure where each unit can interact the environment and game usability-focused interface and emphasizes the elements that are used to interact with the game (mouse, keyboard, remote control, etc.). The above discussion leads to the hypothesis:

H4. Playability has a direct positive effect on the evaluation of educational computer games.

2.6 Multimedia

Technology in teaching and learning is often applied using several methods, which include drills, tutorials, simulations, games and problem solving. Methods of computer-aided teaching and learning developed and fine tuned with the advent of multimedia technology at the end of 1993. Multimedia technology is a technology that is associated with the integration of the use of various media such as text, audio, video, animations and photos to create a presentation. The use of visual-based instruction from said multimedia technology can enhance students' understanding of the materials and scientific experiment [47]. Similarly, the use of interactive animations in multimedia found to affect learning, however this effect depends on the level of a certain age students [46] and found that a coordinated text and pictures in a frame and presented simultaneously with the sound enhance learning [47]. Study shows that controlling the sequential learning is important to new students who are not proficient in any subject [48]. The above discussion leads to the hypothesis:

H5. Multimedia has a direct positive effect on the evaluation of educational computer games.

The literature also leads to the formulation of the research framework for examining the relationship between interface, educational elements, content, playability, multimedia and evaluation of educational computer games of real users as shown in Fig. 1.

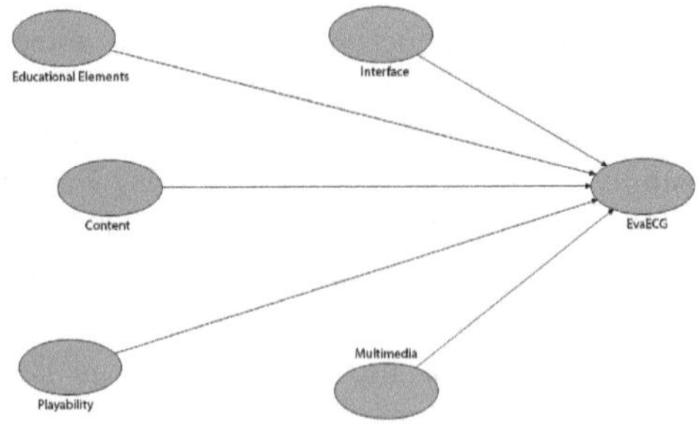

Fig. 1. Research framework

3 Research Method

Five hypotheses were discussed in the prior section. The research model aims to identify the factors affecting the evaluation of ECG. The factors include interface, educational elements, content, playability and multimedia [6]. To test the proposed research model, we conducted data collection process for pilot study and examined the proposed hypotheses using partial least squares (PLS).

3.1 Data Collection

All of the items in the questionnaire were developed by adopting sub-heuristic in PHEG technique [5]. All variables were measured using five-point Likert scales (1 = strongly disagree and 5 = strongly agree). The questionnaire was carefully pre-tested before data collection for pilot study. First, the constructs, items and structure of the questionnaire were thoroughly evaluated by five experts in related field (interface, educational element, content, playability and multimedia). Next, pre-testing process was conducted specifically for the wording of the questions. It was reviewed by 6 potential ECG users. Modification of the questionnaire based on user's comments and suggestion were done. This pilot study was conducted once the modification based on pre-testing is finished. Three universities were selected for data collection purposes; University A, B and C. The process of distribution and collection of questionnaires was carried out over a period of 1 month. A total of 150 questionnaires were distributed and 128 questionnaires were received and 115 valid questionnaires were used for this analysis which translates to about 76.67% response rate. Fig. 2 shows the research model.

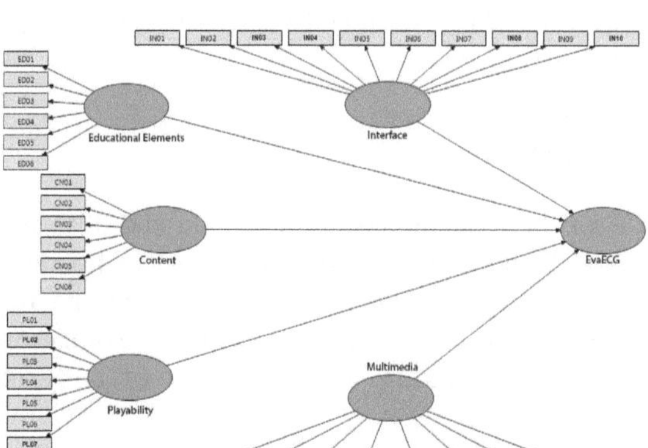

Fig. 2. Research Model

3.2 Measurement Model - Goodness of Measures

The two main criteria used for testing goodness of measures are validity and reliability. Reliability is a test of how consistently a measuring instrument measures whatever concept it is measuring, whereas validity is a test of how well an instrument that is developed measures the particular concept it is intended to measure [49]. Construct validity testifies to how well the results obtained from the use of the measure fit the theories around which the test is designed [49]. This can be assessed through convergent and discriminant validity. Respective loadings and cross loadings is use to assess if there are problems with any particular items. Cutoff value for loadings at 0.6 is consider as significant [49].

Convergent validity is the measure of the internal consistency. Factor loadings, composite reliability and average variance extracted (AVE) is used to assess convergence validity as suggested [49]. AVE measures the variance captured by the indicators relative to measurement error, and it should be greater than 0.50 to justify using a construct [51]. In PLS, test that can be used to determine the convergent validity of the measured constructs [52] are (1) Cronbach's alpha (CA) and composite reliability (CR) scores and (2) Average variance extracted (AVE). Nunally [53] suggests 0.7 as a benchmark for 'modest' CR.

The discriminant validity of the measures (the degree to which items differentiate among constructs or measure distinct concepts) was assessed by examining the correlations between the measures of potentially overlapping constructs. Items should load more strongly on their own constructs in the model and the average variance shared between each construct and its measures should be greater than the variance shared between the construct and other constructs Compeau [55].

3.3 Structural Model

Structural model of a model is assessed by Path coefficients (γ & β), *t*-values and the variance explained (R^2) in the dependent constructs. Support for each general hypothesis on both samples can be determined by examining the sign and statistical significance of the *t*-values.

4 Result and Discussion

Results shown that 68% of the respondents were female and 32% male. Most of the respondents were between 19 and 24 years old. Out of 115 respondents, 90% of them were Malays and 10% were non Malays. The majority of the respondents were familiar with system development but not familiar with the evaluation of the system. The next section examines the validity and reliability of construct followed by hypothesis testing.

4.1 The Measurement Model Analysis

In order to validate measurement model, content validity, convergent validity and discriminant validity were assessed. Content validity was done by interviewing five domain experts and pre-testing the survey instrument by 6 potential ECG users. Table 1 summarizes the result of internal reliability and convergent validity for constructs. The factor loading for all items in this study exceeded the recommended level of 0.60 [50]. The AVE which reflect the overall amount of variance in the indicators accounted for by the latent construct, were in range between 0.5252 to 0.6381, exceeding the recommended level 0.5 [50]. The CR which depict the degree to which the constructs indicator indicate the latent construct, range from 0.8463 to 0.9249 exceeding the recommended level of 0.7 [59]. As such we can conclude that the measurements are reliable.

Table 1. Internal Realibility and Convergent Validity

Model Construcs	**Measurement Items**	**Loadings**	**AVE**	**CR**	**CA**
Interface	IN01	0.6448	0.5270	0.8473	0.7751
	IN05	0.7327			
	IN06	0.7907			
	IN07	0.7385			
	IN09	0.7153			
Educational Elements	ED01	0.7093	0.5349	0.8723	0.8227
	ED02	0.8222			
	ED03	0.7459			
	ED04	0.6468			
	ED05	0.8129			
	ED06	0.6285			
Content	CN01	0.7601	0.5813	0.8927	0.8563
	CN02	0.7878			
	CN03	0.7280			
	CN04	0.7917			
	CN05	0.7885			
	CN06	0.7148			
Playability	PL01	0.6386	0.5252	0.8463	0.7724
	PL03	0.7885			
	PL04	0.7142			
	PL05	0.7249			
	PL06	0.7489			
Multimedia	MM01	0.8197	0.6381	0.9249	0.9049
	MM02	0.8181			
	MM03	0.8463			
	MM04	0.7773			
	MM06	0.7833			
	MM07	0.7180			
	MM08	0.8220			

4.2 The Structural Model

Based on the results in Table 1, the measurement model has good individual item reliability, convergent validity and discriminant validity. The latent variables are within acceptable level of error. Therefore, the measurement model demonstrates sufficient robustness needed to test the relationship among the latent variables and the dependent variable. With satisfactory robustness of the measurement model, the structural model is assessed next to test the research hypotheses.

A close look (Table 2) shows that multimedia was positively related (β = 0.309, p<0.01), interface was positively related (β = 0.145, p<0.01) and so was educational elements (β = 0.239, p<0.01) was positively related in evaluating educational computer games. Content and playability were also positively related (β = 0.264, p<0.01) and (β = 0.218, p<0.01). Thus, H1, H2, H3, H4 and H5 hypotheses of this study were supported. In this study it was found that multimedia was the most significant predictor of extent in evaluating educational computer games followed by content. Unfortunately, no previous research finding can be found to support the result.

Table 2. Path coefficients and hypothesis

Hypothesis	Relationship	Path Coefficient (β)	t value	Decision
H1	Interface -> EvaECG	0.172	8.644*	Supported
H2	Educational Elements -> EvaECG	0.239	13.01 *	Supported
H3	Content -> EvaECG	0.264	11.34*	Supported
H4	Playability -> EvaECG	0.218	11.04*	Supported
H5	Multimedia -> EvaECG	0.309	16.01*	Supported

*p<0.05 (t-value>1.96).

5 Conclusion

Motivated by the need to understand the evaluation construct to evaluate educational computer game, this study attempts to investigate the determinants and the relationship among the constructs. Five independent constructs; interface, educational element, content, playability and multimedia using partial least squares (PLS) in testing hypotheses. The result showed that the measures used exhibited both convergent and discriminant validity and next is the assessment of reliability of measures. Both the CA and CR values were at par with the criteria set up by other researchers. As such the measures on the model were shown to be reliable. Structural model is assessed to test the research hypotheses of the model. Result of the structural model shows that all of the hypotheses (H1, H2, H3, H4 and H5) were supported based on the t-value which are significant at p>0.05. In term of explanatory power which is refer to R^2, this value cannot be assessed because the dependent construct (Evaluation of ECG) does not have any indicator.

Thus, the results should assist game developers to evaluate ECG for real user and improvement of the ECG need to be done before the final release. The study also contributes to research methodology in evaluating educational computer games by describing in detail the rationale and the application of PLS estimation approach. It provides useful framework that other researchers might draw upon when conducting research of a similar nature under a similar data and model constraints. This study has some limitations. Evaluation of ECG construct does not has it owns items. This gives effect to the explanatory power of the structural model. Further study could be conducted by considering the above discussion, need to develop related items for this construct thus the analysis should be able to provide the variance explained (R^2) in the dependent constructs.

References

1. Yee Leng, E., et al.: Computer games development and appreciative learning approach in enhancing students' creative perception. Computers & Education 54(1), 146–161 (2010)
2. Kato, P.M.: Video games in health care: Closing the gap. Review of General Psychology 14(2), 113 (2010)
3. Robertson, J., Howells, C.: Computer game design: Opportunities for successful learning. Computers & Education 50(2), 559–578 (2008)
4. Papastergiou, M.: Exploring the potential of computer and video games for health and physical education: A literature review. Computers & Education 53(3), 603–622 (2009)
5. Mohamed, H., Jaafar, A.: Challenges in the evaluation of educational computer games. In: 2010 International Symposium on Information Technology (ITSim). IEEE (2010)
6. Hasiah, M.O., Azizah, J.: Heuristics evaluation in computer games. In: 2010 International Conference on Information Retrieval & Knowledge Management (CAMP). IEEE (2010)
7. Prensky, M.: Students as designers and creators of educational computer games: Who else? British Journal of Educational Technology 39(6), 1004–1019 (2008)
8. Oblinger, D.G.: The next generation of educational engagement. Journal of Interactive Media in Education (2004)
9. Hogle, J.G.: Considering games as cognitive tools: in search of effective "edutainment". ERIC Clearinghouse (1996)
10. Barab, S., et al.: Making learning fun: Quest Atlantis, a game without guns. Educational Technology Research and Development 53(1), 86–107 (2005)
11. Kiili, K.: Content creation challenges and flow experience in educational games: The IT-Emperor case. The Internet and Higher Education 8(3), 183–198 (2005)
12. Van Eck, R.: Digital game-based learning: It's not just the digital natives who are restless. EDUCAUSE Review 41(2), 16 (2006)
13. Prensky, M.: Digital game-based learning. McGraw-Hill, New York (2001)
14. Pohl, M., et al.: Designing game based learning-a participatory approach. In: World Conference on Educational Multimedia, Hypermedia and Telecommunications (2008)
15. Dondlinger, M.J.: Educational video game design: A review of the literature. Journal of Applied Educational Technology 4(1), 21–31 (2007)
16. Gee, J.P.: What video games have to teach us about learning and literacy. Palgrave Macmillan, New York (2003)
17. Gee, J.P.: Are video games good for learning? (2006), `http://cmslive.curriculum.edu.au/leader/default.asp?id=16866&issueID=10696` (cited Oktober 18, 2008)
18. Cordova, D.I., Lepper, M.R.: Intrinsic motivation and the process of learning: Beneficial effects of contextualization, personalization, and choice. Journal of Educational Psychology 88, 715–730 (1996)
19. Lopez-Morteo, G., López, G.: Computer support for learning mathematics: A learning environment based on recreational learning objects. Computers & Education 48(4), 618–641 (2007)
20. Tüzün, H., et al.: The effects of computer games on primary school students' achievement and motivation in geography learning. Computers & Education 52(1), 68–77 (2009)
21. von der Heiden, B., et al.: Learning by Playing: Potential of Serious Games to Increase Intellectual Capital. In: Enabling Innovation, pp. 375–388. Springer (2011)
22. Hillen, S.A., Breuer, K.U., Tennyson, R.D.: Gaming and learning: Theory, research, and practice. In: Challenges Facing Contemporary Didactics: Diversity of Students and the Role of New Media in Teaching and Learning, p. 185 (2011)

23. Thomas, P.J., Meech, J.F., Macredie, R.D.: A framework for the development of information appliances. ACM SIGICE Bulletin 21(1), 15–19 (1995)
24. Amory, A., et al.: Computer games as a learning resource. In: World Conference on Educational Multimedia, Hypermedia and Telecommunications (1998)
25. Garris, R., Ahlers, R., Driskell, J.E.: Games, motivation, and learning: A research and practice model. Simulation & Gaming 33(4), 441–467 (2002)
26. Malone, T.W., Lepper, M.R.: Making learning fun: A taxonomy of intrinsic motivations for learning. Aptitude, Learning, and Instruction 3, 223–253 (1987)
27. Nielsen, J., Molich, R.: Heuristic evaluation of user interfaces. In: Proceedings of the SIGCHI Conference on Human Factors in Computing Systems: Empowering People. ACM (1990)
28. Nielsen, J.: Heuristic evaluation. In: Nielsen, J., Mark, R.L. (eds.) Usability Inspection Methods. John Wiley & Sons, New York (1994)
29. Hvannberg, E.T., Law, E.L.-C., Lárusdóttir, M.K.: Heuristic evaluation: Comparing ways of finding and reporting usability problems. Interacting with Computers 19(2), 225–240 (2007)
30. Desurvire, H., Wiberg, C.: Master of the game: assessing approachability in future game design. In: Proceedings of ACM CHI 2008 Conference on Human Factors in Computing Systems (2008)
31. Ling, C., Salvendy, G.: Optimizing Heuristic Evaluation Process in E-Commerce: Use of the Taguchi Method. International Journal of Human-Computer Interaction 22(3), 271–287 (2007)
32. Ling, C., Salvendy, G.: Effect of evaluators' cognitive style on heuristic evaluation: Field dependent and field independent evaluators. International Journal of Human-Computer Studies 67(4), 382–393 (2009)
33. Nielsen, J., Molich, R.: Heuristics Evaluation of User Interfaces. In: Proceedings of Human Computer Interaction (1994)
34. Squires, D., Preece, J.: Usability and learning: Evaluating the potential of educational software. Computers & Education 27(1), 15–22 (1996)
35. Squires, D.: Usability and Educational Software Design: Special Issue of Interacting with Computers. Interacting with Computers 11(5), 463–466 (1999)
36. Squires, D., Preece, J.: Predicting quality in educational software: Evaluating for learning, usability and the synergy between them. Interacting with Computers 11(5), 467–483 (1999)
37. Reeves, T., et al.: Usability and instructional design heuristics for e-learning evaluation. In: World Conference on Educational Multimedia, Hypermedia and Telecommunications. AACE, Charlottesville (2002)
38. Evans, C., Sabry, K.: Evaluation of the interactivity of web-based learning systems: Principles and process. Innovations in Education and Teaching International 40(1), 89–99 (2003)
39. Albion, P.: Heuristic evaluation of educational multimedia: from theory to practice. In: Proceedings ASCILITE 1999: 16th Annual Conference of the Australasian Society for Computers in Learning in Tertiary Education: Responding to Diversity. Australasian Society for Computers in Learning in Tertiary Education, ASCILITE (1999)
40. Ssemugabi, S., de Villiers, R.: A comparative study of two usability evaluation methods using a web-based e-learning application (2007)
41. Shee, D.Y., Wang, Y.-S.: Multi-criteria evaluation of the web-based e-learning system: A methodology based on learner satisfaction and its applications. Computers & Education 50(3), 894–905 (2008)

42. Hsu, S.H., Wen, M.-H., Wu, M.-C.: Exploring user experiences as predictors of MMORPG addiction. Computers & Education 53(3), 990–999 (2009)
43. Malone, T.W.: Heuristics for designing enjoyable user interfaces: Lessons from computer games. In: Thomas, J.C., Schneider, M.L. (eds.) Human Factors in Computing Systems. Ablex Publishing Corporation, Norwood (1982)
44. Federoff, M.A.: Heuristics and Usability Guidelines for the Creation and Evaluation of Fun in Video Games. Indiana University (2002)
45. Desurvire, H., Caplan, M., Toth, J.A.: Using heuristics to evaluate the playability of games. In: Computer Human Interaction (CHI 2004), Vienna, Austria (2004)
46. Rieber, L.P., et al.: The role of meaning in interpreting graphical and textual feedback during a computer-based simulation. Computers & Education 27(1), 45–58 (1996)
47. Mayer, R.E., Moreno, R.: A cognitive theory of multimedia learning: Implications for design principles. In: Annual Meeting of the ACM SIGCHI Conference on Human Factors in Computing Systems, Los Angeles, CA (1998)
48. Barr, P., Noble, J., Biddle, R.: Video game values: Human-computer interaction and games. Interacting with Computers 19(2), 180–195 (2007)
49. Sekaran, U., Bougie, R.: Research methods for business: a skill building approach. Wiley, UK (2010)
50. Hair, J., Babin, B.J., Anderson, R.E.: Multivariate Data Analysis: A global perspective. Pearson, Upper Saddle River (2010)
51. Barclay, D., Higgins, C., Thompson, R.: The partial least squares (PLS) approach to causal modeling: personal computer adoption and use as an illustration. Technology Studies 2(2), 285–309 (1995)
52. Fornell, C., Larcker, D.F.: Evaluating structural equation models with unobservable variables and measurement error. Journal of Marketing Research, 39–50 (1981)
53. Nunnally, J.: Psychometric theory. McGraw-Hill, New York (1978)
54. Churchill Jr., G.A.: A paradigm for developing better measures of marketing constructs. Journal of Marketing Research, 64–73 (1979)
55. Compeau, D.R., Higgins, C.A.: Computer self-efficacy: Development of a measure and initial test. Mis Quarterly, 189–211 (1995)
56. Hair, J.F., et al.: Multivariate data analysis. Prentice Hall, Upper Saddle River (1998)
57. Nunnally, J.C., Bernstein, I.H.: Psychometric theory. McGraw, New York (1991, 1994)
58. Gefen, D., Straub, D.W., Boudreau, M.-C.: Structural equation modeling and regression: Guidelines for research practice. In: Communications of the Association for Information Systems. Citeseer (2000)

Preliminary Investigation on Creative Educational Content for Visually-impaired (VI) Learners

Nurulnadwan Aziz[1], Ariffin Abdul Mutalib[2], Siti Mahfuzah Sarif[3], and Mohd. Saifullizam Jaafar[4]

[1,2,3] School of Multimedia Technology and Communication
College of Arts and Science Universiti Utara Malaysia
06010 Sintok Kedah, Malaysia
[4] Faculty of Computer, Media, and Technology Management
TATI University College 24000 Kemaman Terengganu, Malaysia
nuruln746@tganu.uitm.edu.my, {am.ariffin,ctmahfuzah}@uum.edu.my, mslizam@gmail.com

Abstract. This paper reports on an ongoing research regarding the availability and the needs of creative content application for visually-impaired (VI) learners, particularly low vision children. Numerous assistive technologies (AT) products in terms of hardware and software have been found in previous studies. Conversely, studies in the development of creative content application especially in education are highly scarce. Furthermore, elicitation from literatures also reveals that the use of AT was problematic for low vision children. Hence, this study attempts to investigate the availability and the needs of creative educational content application for VI learners. Accordingly, semi-structured interviews have been conducted with experts from special needs field. The results indicate that the creative educational content application specifically developed for VI learners is not yet exist and the need for it is urgent.

Keywords: creative content, visually-impaired learners, computer-based learning application, courseware.

1 Introduction

"Learning is a common process for everybody" [1]. Over the years, effects on learning through multimedia application have been researched spiritedly [2]. Currently, learning with computer-generated visualization has become major interest [3] in learning activities especially among children. However, for people with restriction in visualization, learning could be one of the most challenging tasks in their life. Numerous previous studies discovered that normal tasks such as organizing personal care, reading, writing, and understand learning contents are crucial and problematic for VI people [4]. In addition, it was also found that educational contents specifically designed for VI learners are highly limited. This study acknowledges that there have been many AT products in terms of hardware and software available in the

H. Badioze Zaman et al. (Eds.): IVIC 2013, LNCS 8237, pp. 408–417, 2013.

market. In fact, most of the sophisticated tablets and smart phones are equipped with accessibility functions such as screen magnification and screen readers. All these are categorized as software or system. However, most of the AT products are expensive and are usually used by high income people [5] and [6].

On the other hand, another phenomenon that triggers the acceleration of this study is the current state of VI people. In regards to this, [7] reports that 285 million people in the world are VI, in which 246 million of them have low vision and 39 million of them are blind. Approximately 90% of the VI people live in developing countries. Meanwhile, as at December 2004 the Malaysian Social Welfare Department reported that there were 15,364 VI people officially registered, and then the number increased to 31,924 in December 2011 (Table 1). Referring to the facts in (Table 1) it could be deduced that from the year 2004 until 2011, the registered VI people in Malaysia drastically increased to be double.

Table 1. Registered VI people in Malaysia from 2004 until 2011

Types of disability	Year							
	2004	**2005**	**2006**	**2007**	**2008**	**2009**	**2010**	**2011**
VI people	15, 364	16,211	18,258	20,039	21,204	23,738	27,363	31,924

Due to the above fact, the government of Malaysia is taking serious efforts in ensuring the VI people have the rights particularly in acquiring formal education to ensure their achievements are not neglected [8]. In conjunction, the disabled children including VI in low income families are supported through the pilot project called TASKA OKU [9]. This clearly explains that equipping children especially the disabled with basic education is important to start since their early childhood life.

The facts in the previous section reveal that the number of PWDs keeps on increasing drastically including VI learners (Table 1). Therefore, exposing them to the world of education and technology is important because they should together be respected as a part of the resources for the country with the normal people. Unfortunately, [22] reveal that 80% of education materials such as textbook and courseware are provided for fully-sighted students. This is because the main learning styles preferred by normal students especially children is visual, followed by kinesthetic and further by auditory [23]. Due to that, VI learners have to adapt this situation into their learning activities even though they face problems in terms of information accessibility and ease of use. Thus, they feel frustrated and have no pleasure in learning [1], which could affect their quality of education.

On the other hand, [4], [7] and [18] acknowledge that PWDs especially children and young people deserve to have quality education similar with the non-disabled students. Due to this, equipping disabled children with education and life skills training through the utilization of content applications can help them in achieving a brighter future life. Besides, [4] reveal that in education, there is a large overlap in some activities and interests between VI students and fully-sighted students (Fig.1) such as physical education, music and dance lesson, computer and IT lessons, and Science, Mathematics, and English subjects. These deduces that VI students have similar interests with the fully sighted students even though they have restrictions in visualization. The study also found that VI learners including children and young people prefer to learn lessons which are related to practical activities. It means that they like activities that allow them to interact with other participants and have pleasure.

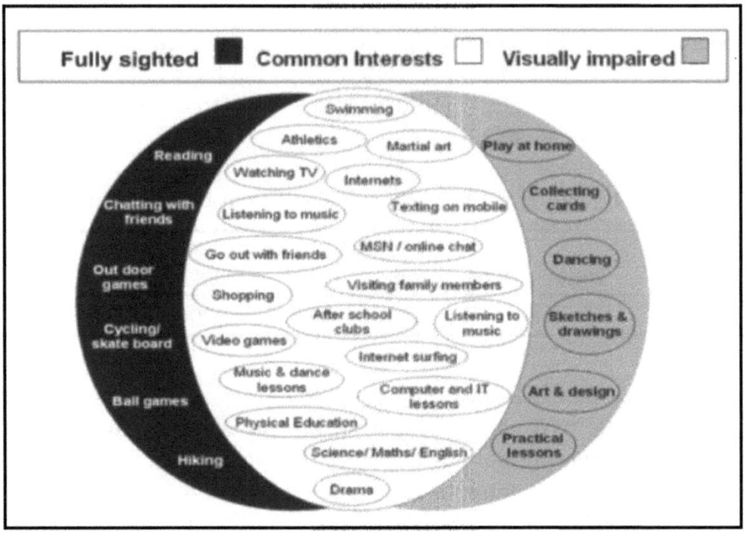

Fig. 1. Activities and interests between VI students and non-disabled students

However, due to their restricted abilities and lack of specially-designed technologies especially in content creation, the learning activities are not carried out smoothly [4]. In addition, [4] also found that there are certain activities in education that VI learners face difficulties and they have to struggle to achieve it because of their vision. Further, focus group interviews with children and young people of vision impairment found that geography is the most difficult subjects for them especially in reading maps. The study also found that most of the VI learners hate reading because of getting eyes strain after some reading and the use of low vision devices such as magnifying glasses was problematic for them. It is because the optical devices make them look different compared to their fully sighted peers. This agrees with [4] who exhibits Table 2 that indicates nine learning activities considered challenging for children and young people with VI.

In accordance, Malaysian government is also considering serious efforts in promoting the usages of technologies among the VI people. However, as discussed previously, the availability of computer application in the form of creative contents for VI people particularly in Malaysia is infancy and very expensive [10], [11] and [12]. In regards to that, the Malaysian Communication and Multimedia Act 1998, defines content as *"any sound, text, still picture, moving picture, or other audio-visual representation, tactile representation, or any combination of the preceding which is capable of being created, manipulated, stored, retrieved, and communicated electronically"* [5]. In addition, creative content can be classified into six clusters [5] as listed in Table 3.

Table 2. Learning activities

No.	Learning activities
1.	Reading maps in geographical subject
2.	Reading drama scripts
3.	Prolonged reading
4.	Handwriting
5.	Reading text messages
6.	Reading musical notes
7.	Reading story books and novels
8.	Reading colorful magazines
9.	Reading the board in the classroom

Table 3. Creative content cluster

Cluster	Example
Film and television	Movies, drama, documentary, and musical
Animation and modeling	Animated series/full length, architectural fly-through, virtual reality, and 3D models
Games	PC games, online games, and mobile games
Mobile	Games, animation, wall paper, screen savers, and music
Audio	Music and voice over

Through the great commitment, support, and concerted efforts from the Malaysian government, it seems that Malaysia's creative content has grown greatly since the past a few years (June, 2011). As a result, in efforts to achieve the high income country status, the Malaysian Government certainly recognizes the potential of creative content through its' Information Technology and Communication (ICT) sector and Economic Transformation Programme (ETP) [15]. In fact, in the 2013 budget speech, the Prime Minister of Malaysia encourages the researchers and developers to contribute in this sector by allocating research grants and funds to create and produce unique creative contents [9]. Simultaneously, this initiative also has been growing in most developing countries especially in assisting the disabled people [16], [17] and [18].

One of the creative content applications that can be exploited as an interesting learning content for VI learners is courseware. In accordance, preliminary investigation has been conducted with two main objectives which are: i) to gather the information regarding the availability of courseware for VI learners, and ii) to clarify the factors that lead to the needs of courseware for VI learners.

2 Methodology

This study is based on qualitative approach as it is concerns with the phenomenon related to VI learners as discussed in previous section. This is important in ensuring the richness of data are guaranteed. The technique that utilized in this study is semi-structured interview. It is a method that could provide exhaustive information regarding the subjects' experiences and perspective pertaining to the research topic. The procedure of the semi-structured interview is described in the following points.

2.1 Procedure of Semi-structured Interview

To achieve the stated objectives, a preliminary investigation has been conducted by involving five content experts as the respondents. All of them are from special needs field. They are Deputy Chief Director of Special Education Department from Ministry of Education (MOE), Executive Director of Malaysian Association for the Blind (MAB), VI teachers, and Coordinator of Special Education Department from special education primary school. Semi-structured interviews were carried out face-to-face in different time and place. In the interview, 12 questions as listed in Table 4 were asked in semi-structured format.

Table 4. List of interview question

No.	Items
Q1	Are the VI learners exposed to the utilization of computer?
Q2	Are the VI learners exposed to the utilization of AT?
Q3	What types of AT that are used by the VI learners in their learning activities?
Q4	Does the AT (hardware and software) help the VI learners in their learning activities?
Q5	Are the VI learners exposed to the courseware provided by MOE?
Q6	Do the courseware contain audio, graphics, animation, and video?
Q7	Do the courseware assist the VI learners during the learning process?
Q8	Is there any special courseware designed for VI learners provided by MOE?
Q9	Are the VI learners exposed to the courseware available in the market?
Q10	Are the courseware available in the market suitable for VI learners?
Q11	Is there any special courseware designed for VI learners available in the market?
Q12	Do you recommend for a proper courseware that is specifically designed for VI learners?

The questions were addressed to investigate the following conditions: (1) whether the VI learners have computer literacy, (2) whether the VI learners are familiar with the AT provided in schools, (3) to identify the current AT (hardware and software) that are used by VI learners in their learning activities, (4) whether the used of AT (hardware and software) could help the VI learners in their learning activities, (5) whether the VI learners are exposed to the courseware that are provided within course teaching; the interview was proceeded if the VI learners are exposed to the courseware, (6) whether the coursewares contain various media elements, as recommended by the design guidelines, (7) whether the courseware provided by MOE within text book are suitable to be utilized by VI learners, (8) whether the MOE has already provided courseware that are specifically designed for VI learners, (9) whether the VI learners are disclosed to the courseware that are available in the market, (10) whether the courseware that are available in the market are appropriate for VI learners, (11) whether the courseware for VI learners have already available in the market, (12) whether the courseware is needed to assist the VI learners in their learning process. In the end, the interviews managed to gather results as discussed in the next section.

3 Result Analysis

Table 5. Respondents' opinion on the availability and the needs of courseware for VI learners

Q	R1 (MOE)	R1 (MAB)	R1 (VI teacher)	R1 (VI teacher)	R1 (Coordinator)
1	√	√	√	√	√
2	√	√	√	√	√
3	√	√	√	√	√
4					
5	√	√	√	√	√
6	√	√	√	√	√
7					
8					
9		√			
10					
11					
12	√	√	√	√	√

Referring to Table 5, all respondents responded positively for questions 1, 2, and 3. In primary school, the VI learners were introduced to the basic Information and Communication Technology skills and utilization of assistive devices and assistive software such as braille machine, CCTV, magnifier, slate and stylus, and JAWS since they are in standard three through a module called *Kemahiran Asas Individu Masalah Penglihatan (KAIMal).* It contains three submodules namely (a) *Module1: Orientation and Mobility,* (b) *Module 2: Code Braille Skill and Utilization of Assistive Devices,* and (c) *Module 3: Basic ICT for Visual Impairment* [26]. Also, at MAB the organization offers some vocational training course such as computer literacy and computer programming for those VI persons who are interested (Q1) (Q2). The study also found that not only primary schools but most of the VI training centers in Malaysia have introduced their students to the courseware and software (Q3) (Q5) (Q9). These indicate that most of the VI learners are computer literate or at least they have been introduced to computer technologies since they were children. However, some of the ATs provided for them such as magnifying glass and CCTV were not 100% help them in their learning activities especially for low vision children (Q4). Statement from the Coordinator of Special Education Department from special education primary school indicates that the uses of CCTV was problematic for low vision children because it requires them to struggle seriously in getting the information due to limited display (i.e. alphabet by alphabet or word by word) (Q4). This makes them feel frustrated with the learning activities (Q4). This findings also agreed by [4] and [26] when they also found that the use of magnifying glasses and CCTV or other AT devices was problematic for VI learners either because of they incapable to buy that equipment, they missing the equipment, or psychologically they do not like to use AT as well as do not like to look different between their sighted peers.

For question 6 all respondents also agreed that the courseware were composed with various media elements. However, Table 5 also explains that majority of the respondents found that the courseware provided by MOE within text books and the courseware that are available in the market are not appropriate for VI learners even though they contain various media elements and activities (Q7) (Q10). This leads to question: *Why the courseware are not assisting the VI learners?* and further questions were asked: *if you say the courseware include audio, graphics, animation, and video, then what makes the courseware not assisting the VI learners?*. In addition, the Deputy Chief Director of Special Education Department addressed that there is no standard guideline or model engaged by MOE regarding the development of courseware for VI learners (Q8) (Q11). Most of the respondents also suggest that researchers should propose courseware that focus on how far it can convey knowledge, not only look fun and entertaining to non-disabled students without supporting the needs of VI students (Q12) especially in terms of multimedia element provided in the courseware. Hence, the results from the interviews indicate that the need for creative educational content application for low vision children is high and it is urgently necessary.

4 Discussion

In relation to the results discussed in the previous section, this study is attentive to the needs of courseware for VI learners for the reason of educational requirement towards student-centered learning (SCL) and problem-based learning (PBL). Both of these learning approaches have relationship to each other. The next subsection discusses details the implication of SCL and PBL to this study.

4.1 SCL

SCL or also known as flexible learning, experiential learning, or self-directed learning is a learning approach that focuses on the students' needs rather than others (e.g. teachers or educational administrators) [20]. SCL which is contrasted to teacher-centered learning (TCL), places the teacher as the learning facilitator. It provides full attention to students' needs, ability, interests, and learning styles which is corresponding with the content application (courseware) intended to propose in this study. On the other hand, SCL also encourage the students to access multiple sources of information directly such as books, online database, community members, and courseware [21]. However, for students with VI, the approach for them to acquire knowledge is definitely different from normal students even though the medium is similar. For that reason, this study attempts to come out with a courseware that is designed exclusively for VI learners by incorporating with SCL approach.

4.2 PBL

On the other hand, PBL means the students learn the subjects through experience and problem solving [19]. PBL is a student-centered approach, in which students learn through experience and realistic problem solving [27]. It is an instructional method that originates from medical education and has become increasingly popular across disciplines at multiple levels of education [28] and [31]. The basic characteristics of PBL is (i) the use of problem as the starting point of learning process, (ii) small group collaboration, (iii) flexible guidance of instructor, (iv) limited number of lectures, (v) student-initiated learning, and (vi) ample-time for self-study [30] and [32].

Meanwhile, the goals of PBL is to help the students to develop their (i) flexible knowledge, (ii) effective problem-solving skills, (iii) self-directed learning skills, (iv) effective collaboration skills, and (v) intrinsic motivation [30]. This implies that instructors or teachers have to act as facilitators rather than providing knowledge [30] to achieve those goals. Through the problem-solving and other characteristics of PBL, it trains the students to become active learners and responsible to their learning [27]. In accordance, it enables the students to understand the subject deeply [31].

PBL embraces on good principle of teaching and learning, in which it (i) promotes student-directed learning, (ii) promotes active and in-depth learning, (iii) taps into existing knowledge of student, (iii) supports reflection on teaching and learning process, (iv) develops mutually respectful learning skills, (v) involves well-timed feedback, and (vi) supports the self-assessment and peer-assessment of students [29].

In this study, by embedding the PBL approach in the proposed courseware, it could educate the VI learners to be more independent, self-motivated, producing interesting work, and become a challenging person [29].

5 Conclusion

In a nutshell, creative content related to computer-based learning application that is specifically designed for VI learners is not yet exist. Even though there are various types of courseware produced by MOE and available in the market, but it means nothing for VI learners. This is unfair because VI learners also deserve and have the rights to learn via computer technology applications. In addition, the findings and literatures also exposing that currently VI learners face difficulties in learning by using ATs device and software provided for them. This means that the need for educational content application is urgent. With the obtained results, in the previous section this study intends to propose a courseware that is able to fulfill the needs of VI learners in learning. More importantly, they could grasp and understand the knowledge delivered through the courseware by embedding SCL and PBL approach. Hence, this requires more steps that have to be investigated deeply.

References

1. Ariffin, A.M.: Conceptual Framework of Reality Learning Media (RLM) based on Entertaining and Fun Construct. PhD Thesis, Universiti Utara Malaysia (2009)
2. Riaza, M.R., Halimah, B.Z.: Looking at the Effects of Various Multimedia Approach in Student Learning: A Case Study. In: Proceedings of the 7th International Conference on Ubiquitous Information and Management and Communication. ACM Portal, New York (2013)
3. Riaza, M.R., Halimah, B.Z.: Can Different Types of Animation Enhance Recall and Transfer of Knowledge? A Case Study on a Computer Science Subject. ASEAN J. of Teach. & Learn. in Higher Edu., 32–43 (2012)
4. Khadka, J., Ryan, B., Margrain, T.H., Woodhouse, J.M., Davies, N.: Listening to Voices of Children with Visual Impairment: A Focus Group Study. British J. of Visual Impairment, 182–196 (2012)
5. Dawe, M.: Desperately Seeking Simplicity: How Young Adults with Cognitive Disabilities and Their Families Adopt Assistive Technologies. In: Proceedings of the SIGCHI Conference on Human Factors in Computing Systems, pp. 1143–1152 (2006)
6. Joyojeet, P., Manas, P., Rakesh, B.: Assistive Technology for Vision-Impairments: An Agenda for the ICTD Community. In: Proccedings of the International World Wide Web Conference, pp. 513–522 (2011)
7. World Health Organization, `http://www.who.int/mediacentre/factsheets/fs282/en/`
8. Melissa, N.G., Yen, A., See, C.M.: Employment of People with Disabilities in Malaysia: Drivers and Inhibitors. Int. J. of Special Edu., 112–124 (2011)
9. Mohd Najib, A.R.: The 2013 Budget Speech. News Paper Report. News Strait Time (2012)
10. Muhammad Haziq, L.A., Syariffanor, H., Shahril, P.: MyLexics: An Assistive Courseware for Dyslexic Children to Learn Basic Malay Language. Newsletter ACM SIGACCESS Accessibility and Computing, 3–9 (2009)
11. Aziz, N., Mohamad Roseli, N.H., Abdul Mutalib, A.: Assistive Courseware for Visually-Impaired. In: Badioze Zaman, H., Robinson, P., Petrou, M., Olivier, P., Schröder, H., Shih, T.K. (eds.) IVIC 2009. LNCS, vol. 5857, pp. 905–915. Springer, Heidelberg (2009)
12. Aziz, N., Mohamad Roseli, N.H., Abdul Mutalib, A.: Visually Impaired Children's Acceptances on Assistive Courseware. American J. of Applied Sciences, 1019–1026 (2011)
13. Malaysian Commisioner of Law Revision, `http://www.agc.gov.my/Akta/Vol.%2012/Act%20588.pdf`
14. June, R.: Promising Future for Creative Content Industry. News Paper Report. Business Time (2011)
15. Sakini, M.S.: Malaysia Creative Content Industry Has Grown Temendously, Says Info. News Paper Report. Bernama (2011)
16. Wong, M.E., Cohen, L.: School, Family and Other Influences on Assistive Technology Use: Access and Challenges for Students with Visual Impairment in Singapore. British J. of Visual Impairment, 130–144 (2011)
17. Judge, S., Robertson, Z., Hawley, M.S.: The Limitations of Speech Control: Perceptions of Provision of Speech-Driven Environmental Controls. J. of Assistive Tech., 4–11 (2011)
18. Savita, K.S., Nur Athirah, A.P.: Malay Sign Language Courseware for Hearing-Impaired Children in Malaysia. World Applied Scien. J., 59–64 (2011)

19. Larry, D.S.: Problem-Based Learning. School of Information Science and Technology, 1–12 (2003)
20. O'neil, G., McMahon, T.: Student-centred Learning: What Does It Mean for Students and Lectures? In: O'neil, G., Moore, S., McMullin, B. (eds.) Emerging Issues in the Practice of University Learning and Teaching, Dublin, AISHE, pp. 27–36 (2005)
21. Ellis, A.: Student-Centered Collaborative Learning via Face-to-Face and Asynchronous Online Communication: What's the Difference? In: Proceedings of the Annual Conference of the Australasian Society for Computers in Learning in Tertiary Education, pp. 169–178 (2001)
22. Rasmeet, K.C., Ahalya, S.: The Effect of Visual Impairment on Quality of Life of Children Aged 3-16 Years. The British Journal of Ophthalmology, 642–645 (2011)
23. Nor Azah, A.A., Roznim, M.R., Khairunnisa, R.: Preschool Multimedia Interactive Courseware: Classifying Object (Mengelaskan Objek) PMICMO. In: 2010 Second WRI World Congress on Software Engineering (2010)
24. United Nations Educational Scientific and Cultural Organization, `http://www.unesco.org/new/en/education/themes/leading-the-international-agenda/education-for-all/`
25. Vaquer, N.: A Voice and a Choice for Students with Special Needs. Philadelphia Social Innovations J., 1–3 (2011)
26. Malaysian Ministry of Education, `http://www.lmsipda.net/ppg_lms/file.php/1/MODUL_PPG_SEMESTER_1/PKU3101_Pengenalan_Kepada_Pendidikan_Khas.pdf`
27. Allen, D.E., Donham, R.S., Bernhardt, S.A.: Problem-Based Learning. New Directions for Teaching and Learning, 21–30 (2011)
28. Hung, W., Jonassen, D.H., Liu, R.: Problem-based Learning. In: Spector, J.M., Merrill, M.D., van Merrianboer, J., Driscoll, M.P. (eds.) Handbook of Research on Educational Communications and Technology, pp. 485–500. Taylor & Francis Group, New York (2008)
29. Kiley, M., Mullins, G., Peterson, R.F., Rogers: Leep Into...Problem-Based Learning. University of Adelaide, Australia (2000)
30. Hmelo-Silver, C.E.: Problem-based Learning: What and How Do Students Learn?, pp. 235–266 (2004)
31. Jolly, J., Jacob, C.: A Study of Problem-based Learning Approach for Undergraduate Students. Asian Social Science, 157–165 (2012)
32. Socklingam, N., Rotgans, J., Schmidt, H.G.: Student and Tutor Perceptions on Attributes of Effective Problems in Problem Based Learning. Higher Education, 1–6 (2010)

Handheld Augmented Reality Interaction Technique

Shahan Ahmad Chowdhury[1,*], Haslina Arshad[1], Behrang Parhizkar[2], and Waqas Khalid Obeidy[3]

[1,3] Faculty of Information Science and Technology
University Kebangsaan Malaysia, 43600 UKM, Bangi, Selangor, Malaysia
{bpy_07,waquaskhalid}@yahoo.com, has@ftsm.ukm.my
[2] School of Computer Science
The University of Nottingham, Malaysia Campus
hani.parhizkar@nottingham.edu.my

Abstract. Handheld devices are popular device for an Augmented Reality application. It has a basic hardware requirement for AR system. However it must be overcome some technical obstacle to realize its true power. One of the problems is interaction in handheld AR environment. Touch screen interaction is one of the common interaction methods in handheld AR but it is not easy to interact in touch screen with virtual object in handheld AR scene. Current research shows that Freeze Interaction technique shows its usefulness in handheld touch screen AR interaction. However it has a drawback such as, when users freeze their view it freezes the whole scene. When virtual object are updating continuously the real world-view is not being updated and remains as still picture. It can be a problem when users need to deal with current up-to date real world scene. To overcome current problem of Freeze Interaction technique we have implemented new freeze technique 'Freeze-Object' for more precise interaction. This paper presents a short review of handheld AR interaction technique and our proposed work.

Keywords: handheld augmented reality, interaction technique, touch screen interface.

1 Introduction

Augmented Reality (AR) is related to Virtual Reality (VR). Where VR is the fully computer generated virtual content, Augmented Reality is the combination of the real world and the virtual content [1]. It gives the users a chance to interact with virtual objects in real time. AR can provide users with sub immersive feeling by allowing interactions to occur between the real and virtual worlds [2]. There has been lots of research done to explore AR. Early AR was based on desktop computer and custom input output device and backpack with HMD (Head-Mounted Display). The time passed, the trend of AR device has switched from the backpack with HMD to low cost small handheld device such as PDA, Smartphone (Fig.1) [3].

* Corresponding author.

H. Badioze Zaman et al. (Eds.): IVIC 2013, LNCS 8237, pp. 418–426, 2013.

Fig. 1. Evolution of AR device

Handheld device have been identified as most promising devices for an Augmented Reality [4] and [5]. Smartphones or tablets are lightweight and have the entire basic hardware requirement for AR, such as display, camera, graphics, GPS compass and accelerometer [6]. Handheld AR has some important applications in the gaming [7] interactive marketing and advertising [8] education [9] and navigation [10]. However, some technical problem must be solved before AR can realize its true power. One of the major problems is allowing users to interact with the virtual object in augmented scene in handheld devices [8].

Touch screen interface is one of the widely used interaction methods in handheld augmented reality. Most of the handheld devices come with touch screen interface and they are replacing traditional input such as physical button, stylus input. However precise interaction in the touch screen interface is not easy. In handheld AR environment users need to hold their device with one hand and interact with other hand which needs accurate coordination between both hands, but in handheld environment it is difficult because hands can be shaky and it could lead unexpected error. Users often need to move their devices which make the problem more difficult. To overcome this problem researcher proposed few techniques. One of the novel techniques is freeze interaction technique. Freeze interaction techniques allow users to freeze their AR view and interact with the virtual content. In the past freeze interaction techniques have been shown to overcome the problem of camera shake and allows the users comfortable interaction, but it has a problem that the whole scene is frozen. The real world view from the camera remains still which may be a problem when users have to deal with current up to date real world scene [11], [12] and [13].

In this paper we propose a 'Freeze-Object' interaction technique for handheld AR. The proposed interaction method will allow the users to freeze their virtual object with live real view. Which will help the user to interact with virtual content in live real world scene and user do not have to look at the target continuously for tracking. Once they detect the target they can freeze the virtual object and can move the device to any direction with virtual object attach in the screen and can interact with the object in any background. In the rest of this paper, we review previous works related to our research and describe the proposed technique.

2 Handheld Augmented Reality

Handheld devices are ideal for augmented reality applications. Current handheld devices have graphical display, integrated camera, powerful processor and equipped with all the basic hardware needed for AR. As significant processing power and graphics became available on PDA's researchers began exploring AR application in handheld device, such as the AR-PDA project [14] and BatPortal [15]. These AR applications used thin client approach for showing virtual content generated from a server because early PDA's did not have enough processing power for stand-alone applications [16]. [17] Used ARToolKit in Windows CE platform and developed the first fully stand alone PDA AR Application. Later [16] ported ARToolKit to the Symbian platform and created a two-player AR game on current-generation Smartphones. Recent day's Smartphones have improved in every aspect relevant for AR, powerful processors, memory, improved input interfaces, larger and superior displays, more sensors and improved network capabilities and with the advent of iPhone and Android OS.

2.1 Handheld Augmented Reality Interaction

Handheld device has become popular alternative for Augmented Reality. Current tablet and Smartphones are lightweight and truly mobile. All the necessary hardware for AR is packaged in one device. Handheld device gives video see-through AR experience via powerful processor and various built-in sensors [8]. Since AR moved to handheld there need to be new interaction methods [4] and [18]. Compared to traditional HMD based AR, handheld AR interaction is different [18].

AR Interaction in handheld devices is called a magic lens because users use the device display to see the physical environment using camera lens [8] and [19]. Currently, handheld AR uses two types of interaction techniques.

- Tangible interaction
- Embodied interaction

Tangible Interaction

Tangible interaction is direct manipulation of physical object such as marker movement or hand gesture recognition. In tangible interaction user reaches into the AR scene and moves the known physical objects [20]. [21] Proposed tangible interaction for handheld AR. They use mobile phone as tangible input. Virtual object was controlled by phone joypad for selecting and releasing and phone motion used for translation the object. However tangible interaction is not compatible with handheld device since the user must focus on handheld device and TUI [22]. Tangible AR interactions assume that users both hands are free but it is not be the case with handheld AR. Unlike HMD based AR system, in handheld device input and screen are connected and user have to hold the device with one hand and only one hand are free for interaction [18].

Researchers also work on gestural interfaces for handheld device using computer vision based algorithm. As an example, [23] Implemented bare-hand based interaction in handheld AR environment. Their application detects user hand with handheld device camera and virtual object is rendered on users hand for interaction. User finds gestural interaction is more fun and engaging but research showed that gesture interaction is less suitable for handheld device [24]. Gestural interfaces on handheld devices also suffer from the more limited distance between the camera and the interacting appendage [22].

Embodied Interaction

Embodied interaction is based on device movement and touch screen interaction. Examples such as moving the device near to the scene or touch screen gesture [8]. [16] Developed AR tennis the first collaborative handheld AR application. In their application two player play tennis using mobile phone. User serves the virtual ball, pressing the key and hit it back by moving their phone in front. Each time the ball is hit phone plays sound and vibrates. Mendenhall et al. [25] developed handheld AR game NerdHerder which require the user's physical movement. Users need to move their handheld device over the marker to play the game.

Currently, touch interface is commonly available on the current generation of mobile devices and it is widely used in handheld AR. It has the advantage that no hardware is required beyond the mobile device itself. Previously touch based interaction was based on stylus input. Styles are magnetic pen used for interaction on the touch screen [26] and [27]. The downside of stylus is, it requires the user to have access additional hardware, and multi-touch input is not possible [22].

Recent handheld device use finger touch interaction. It is replacing traditional input method such as button, keypad and styles. However precise interaction with touch interface in handheld AR is not easy [12] and [11]. In handheld AR applications, the AR scene changes according to the device movement. This can cause errors even when the user keeps pressing at the same point on the screen. In some situation users have to hold the device in uncomfortable poses [28]. This makes interaction difficult.

3 Related Work

This section discussed related research of our proposed work. Handheld AR interaction metaphor is different than traditional mobile AR interaction [4]. Touch screen interface are common in Smartphone and also widely used in current handheld AR. Touch interaction is not easy in handheld AR. It causes shaky viewpoint because users have to hold the device with one hand and touch the interface with other hand [11] and [28]. Moreover current handheld device have ergonomic limitation. This problem could be solved by "freezing" method. Freeze Interaction method allows the user to freeze the AR scene and user can interact with virtual object in a more comfortable position [19]. Researchers have previously explored freezing methods in several applications. For example, [29] implemented freezing technique for oil refinery application to overcome jitter problem with ARToolkit. In oil refinery application freezing metaphor was important for the usability of the application and calibration phase of the authoring process. [30] Presented a 'Freeze-Frame' technique. Their technique allows the user to capture a snapshot (frame) of the environment in authoring applications using tablet PC. In their Freeze-Frame technique users are allowed to freeze the AR environment to work on it later [11] proposed similar technique 'Freeze-Set-Go' or FSG in mobile AR environment using UMPC (Ultra Mobile Pocket Computer). They investigate freezing method in annotation task. The freeze technique allows user to freeze their view and manipulate the virtual object while viewpoint stands still. When users are ready they unfroze the scene and it get updated with live camera view and tracking data. FSG interaction method shows its strength in shaky environment. [28] Implement the same technique as 'Freeze-Set-Go' in Smartphone named 'Freeze- View-Touch' interaction technique. To avoid losing the tracking of marker and object they utilize 'Freeze-Set-Go' interaction approach and offer users to freeze and manipulate virtual object in touch screen Smartphone.

However current freeze approaches have drawback. When user freeze AR scene it also freeze the real world-view. When virtual object are updating continuously real world-view remains as still picture until user unfreeze the scene. This will be a problem when users have to deal with current up to date real world scene, such as when users waking while using AR application or need to deal with different real world background. To overcome current problem we proposed a 'Freeze-Object' interaction technique to improve the Freeze technique for precise and comfortable interaction.

4 Freeze-Object Interaction

This section will provide a brief description of the concept of our work and development methodologies of the Freeze-Object interaction technique. From our review we realize that handheld devices are ideal for AR application, but to make it more interesting we need more precise interaction with virtual content. Touch screen is the major input in handheld mobile devices. However precise interaction is difficult in touch screen environment, using freeze interaction technique user may overcome this problem but current freeze technique freezes the whole AR scene like still picture. We proposed new improved freeze technique 'Freeze-Object' (FO) where users can freeze only the virtual objects with live real world view. FO interaction technique will allows the users to interact with virtual object in live real world scene and once the user freezes the object they can move their device to any direction without moving the marker or target image. After completion of task the user can unfreeze the edited virtual object on the target tracking image (see Fig.2). Compared to previous freeze techniques, the FO interaction technique will help the users to interact with virtual content with up to date real world view. Various application areas can benefit from new technique such as authoring tool, interior design, electrical wiring, maintenance and training.

To implement our proposed technique we used QUALCOMM vuforia vision based SDK[1] with android NDK. Our first attempt was using AndAR[2] open source augmented reality library. AndAR provide java API to the ARToolkit. ARToolkit tracks 3D position and orientation of square fiducial markers. However we found that, it is difficult to implement our new freeze technique using AndAR toolkit. OpenGL ES real-time computer graphics library is used for rendering virtual object. Proposed technique is built on Android platform based touch screen handheld device.

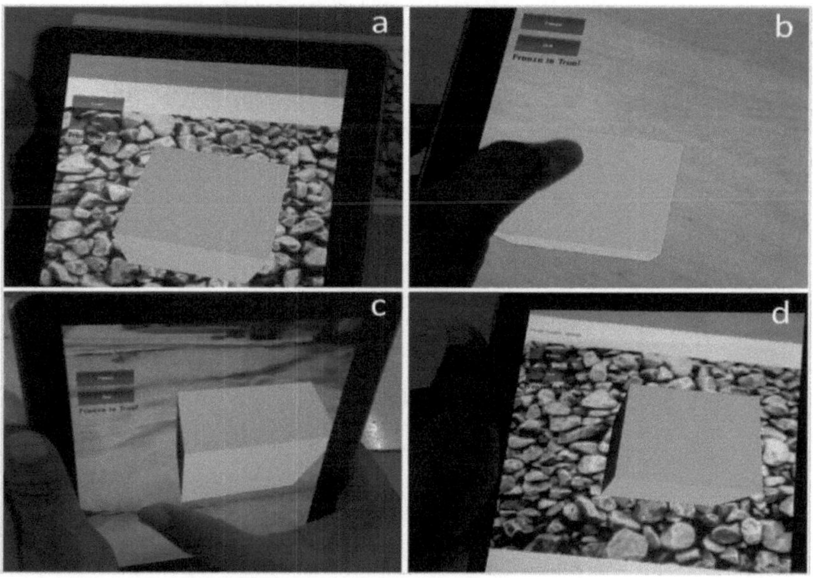

Fig. 2. a) Detecting target image and freezing a 3D virtual cube. b) Moving the 3D cube with touch. c) Moving 3D cube in different view. d) Unfreeze the virtual cube after manipulation.

To validate FO interaction technique quantitative comparative study will be conducted. Existing freeze technique and new freeze technique will be compared. The aim of this study is to identify the performance of improve technique such as accuracy of interaction, task completion time. Below is our project flow chart (Fig. 3).

1 https://developer.vuforia.com/
2 http://code.google.com/p/andar

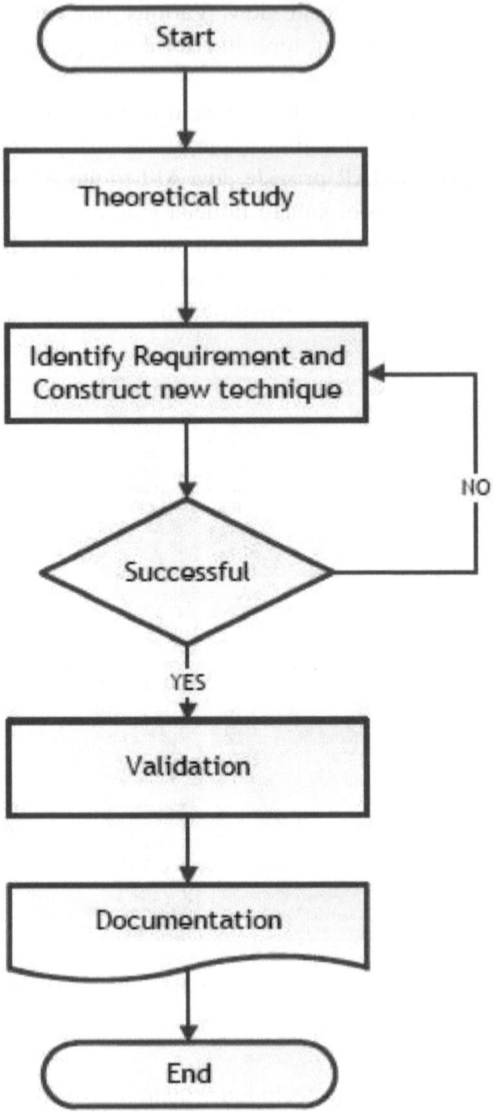

Fig. 3. Flow Chart

5 Conclusion

In this paper, existing handheld AR interaction techniques are reviewed and the author descried the proposed new improved Freeze interaction technique 'Freeze-Object' for more precise interaction in handheld AR environment. FO interaction technique can enhance the user's interaction with the virtual object in AR scene without tracking failure and moving the target image. FO interaction can be applied to a wide range of useful applications including AR authoring tool, interior design, electrical design, maintenance and training. In the future we will focus on improving FO interaction method and more complex interaction methods will be studied for touch screen based handheld AR interface.

Acknowledgement. The authors would like to thank all the participants involved in this work. It is part of the research project entitled A Real-Time Borderless Image Detection Tracking Technique for Mobile Augmented Reality System supported by the Research University Grant Universiti Kebangsaan Malaysia (GUP-2012-008).

References

1. Vallino, J.R.: Interactive Augmented Reality. Degree Doctor of Philosophy. University of Rochester, New York (1998)
2. Uematsu, Y., Saito, H.: Vision-Based Augmented Reality Applications. Computer Vision I-Tech, Vienna, Austria (2008)
3. Wagner, D., Schmalstieg, D.: Projects in VR Making Augmented Reality Practical on Mobile Phones, Part 1. IEEE Computer Graphics and Application 29(3), 12–15 (2009)
4. Henrysson, A., Marshally, J., Billinghurst, M.: Experiments in 3D Interaction for Mobile Phone AR. In: Proceedings of the 5th International Conference on Computer Graphics and Interactive Techniques in Australia and Southeast Asia (GRAPHITE 2007), pp. 187–194 (2007)
5. Arth, C., Schmalstieg, D.: Challenges of Large-Scale Augmented Reality on Smartphones. In: ISMAR 2011 Workshop: Enabling Large-Scale Outdoor Mixed Reality and Augmented Reality, Basel, Switzerland (October 26, 2011)
6. Schmalstieg, D.: Trends in Mobile Augmented Reality. In: IEEE Virtual Reality 2012 Tutorial, pp. 1–3 (2012)
7. Koceski, S., Koceska, N.: Interaction Between Players of Mobile Phone Game with Augmented Reality (AR) Interface. In: International Conference on User Science and Engineering (I-User 2011), pp. 245–250 (2011)
8. Gervautz, M., Schmalstieg, D.: Anywhere Interfaces Using Handheld Augmented Reality. Computer 45(7), 26–31 (2012)
9. Liu, T.-Y., Tan, T.-H., Chu, Y.-L.: QR Code and Augmented Reality-Supported Mobile English Learning System. In: Jiang, X., Ma, M.Y., Chen, C.W. (eds.) WMMP 2008. LNCS, vol. 5960, pp. 37–52. Springer, Heidelberg (2010)
10. de Sa, M., Churchill, E.F.: Mobile Augmented Reality: Exploring Design and Prototyping Techniques. In: MobileHCI 2012, pp. 221–230 (2012)
11. Lee, G.A., Yang, U., Dongsik, K.J., Kim, K.H., Kim, J.H., Choi, J.S.: Freeze-Set-Go Interaction Method for Handheld Mobile Augmented Reality Environments. In: Proceedings of the 16th ACM Symposium on Virtual Reality Software and Technology (VRST 2009), pp. 143–146 (2009)
12. Lee, G.A., Billinghurst, M.: A User Study on the Snap-To-Feature Interaction Method. In: IEEE International Symposium on Mixed and Augmented Reality, Basel, Switzerland (October 26, 2011)
13. Lee, G.A., Billinghurst, M.: Assistive Techniques for Precise Touch Interaction in Handheld Augmented Reality Environments. In: VRCAI 2012, Singapore, pp. 279–286 (2012)

14. Geiger, C., Kleinjohann, B., Reimann, C., Stichling, D.: Mobile AR4ALL. In: Proceedings of the Second IEEE and ACM International Symposium on Augmented Reality, ISAR 2001, New York (2001)
15. Ingram, D., Newman, J.: Augmented Reality in a Widearea Sentient Environment. In: Proceedings of the 2nd IEEE and ACM International Symposium on Augmented Reality (ISAR 2001), New York (2001)
16. Henrysson, A., Billinghurst, M., Ollila, M.: Face to Face Collaborative AR on Mobile Phones. In: Proceedings of the International Symposium on Mixed and Augmented Reality (ISMAR 2005), Vienna, Austria, October 5-8 (2005)
17. Wagner, D., Schmalstieg, D.: First Steps Towards Handheld Augmented Reality. In: Proceedings of the 7th IEEE International Symposium on Wearable Computers (ISWC 2003), p. 127 (2003)
18. Billinghurst, M., Kato, H., Myojin, S.: Advanced Interaction Techniques for Augmented Reality Applications. In: Shumaker, R. (ed.) VMR 2009. LNCS, vol. 5622, pp. 13–22. Springer, Heidelberg (2009)
19. Kurkovsky, S., Koshy, R., Novak, V., Szul, P.: Current Issues in Handheld Augmented Reality. In: Communications and Information Technology (ICCIT 2012), pp. 68–72 (2012)
20. Poupyrev, I., Tan, D., Billinghurst, M., Kato, H., Regenbrech, H., Tetsutani, N.: Tiles: A Mixed Reality Authoring Interface. In: Proc. 7th Conf. Human-Computer Interaction (INTERACT 2001), pp. 334–341 (2001)
21. Billinghurst, M., Henrysson, A.: Research Directions in Handheld AR. The International Journal of Virtual Reality 5(2), 51–58 (2006)
22. Van Olst, R.: 3D Manipulations in Handheld Augmented Reality Applications. Master Thesis. Graduate School of Natural Sciences Department of Information and Computing Sciences. Utrecht University (2012)
23. Choi, J., Park, H., Park, J., Park, J.I.: Bare-Hand-Based Augmented Reality Interface on Mobile Phone. In: IEEE International Symposium on Mixed and Augmented Reality 2011 Science and Technology Proceedings, Basel, Switzerland, October 26-29 (2011)
24. Hürst, W., van Wezel, C.: Multimodal Interaction Concepts for Mobile Augmented Reality Applications. In: Lee, K.-T., Tsai, W.-H., Liao, H.-Y.M., Chen, T., Hsieh, J.-W., Tseng, C.-C. (eds.) MMM 2011, Part II. LNCS, vol. 6524, pp. 157–167. Springer, Heidelberg (2011)
25. Mendenhall, S., Ha, V., Xu, Y., Tillery, P., Cohen, J., Sharp, J., Macintyre, B.: Nerdherder: Designing for Physical Actions in an Augmented Reality Puzzle Game. In: FDG 2012, Raleigh, NC, USA, May 29-June 1 (2012)
26. Yee, K.P.: Peephole Displays: Pen Interaction on Spatially Aware Handheld Computers. In: Proceedings of the SIGCHI Conference on Human Factors in Computing Systems, CHI 2003, pp 1–8 (2003)
27. Dang, N.T., Tavanti, M., Rankin, I., Cooper, M.: A Comparison of Different Input Devices for a 3d Environment. In: Proceedings of the 14th European Conference on Cognitive Ergonomics, ECCE 2007, pp. 153–160 (2007)
28. Bai, H., Lee, G.: Interaction Methods for Mobile Augmented Reality. In: Proceedings of the 13th International Conference of the NZ Chapter of the ACM's Special Interest Group on Human-Computer Interaction (CHINZ 2012), p. 101 (2012)
29. Abawi, D.F., Dörner, R., Haller, M., Zauner, J.: Efficient Mixed Reality Application Development. In: Proc. CVMP 2004 (European Conf. on Visual Media Production), London, UK, March 15-16, pp. 289–294 (2004)
30. Güven, S., Feiner, S., Oda, O.: Mobile Augmented Reality Interaction Techniques for Authoring Situated Media on-Site. In: Proceedings of Fifth IEEE and ACM International Symposium on Mixed and Augmented Reality, pp. 235–236. IEEE (2006)

Exploring Medical Family Tree Data Using Visual Data Mining

Wan Mohd. Nazmee Wan Zainon* and Abdullah Zawawi Talib

School of Computer Sciences, Universiti Sains Malaysia,
11800 USM, Penang, Malaysia
{nazmee,azht}@cs.usm.my

Abstract. Medical Family Tree can provide a branch-by-branch indication of the types of diseases that have been present in a family's past. Some of these diseases may be genetic in nature. By exploring a Medical Family Tree we can become more aware of any genetic factors that may put us at risk of developing genetically-linked diseases. The main purpose of this paper is to present a proposal on a study to explore the medical family data using visual data mining techniques. This article seeks to enable reader to basically understand how and why this type of research is being conducted and how it can be used to help medical practitioners in understanding family health and condition based on information gathered for family medical tree. Initial investigation suggest that visual data mining has huge potentials as it can visually help a lot people such as health practitioners, therapist, clinicians, social workers and others in various fields to understand the patient's family medical history and to look for recurring patterns of illness and behaviour.

Keywords: visual data mining, medical family tree, visual data representation.

1 Introduction

A family medical history - also called a medical family tree is a record of health information (including illnesses and medical conditions) about a person and their family members. Families have many factors in common, including their genes, environment, and lifestyle. Together, these factors can give clues to medical conditions that may run in a family. By noticing patterns of disorders among relatives, healthcare professionals can determine whether an individual, other family members, or future generations may be at an increased risk of developing a particular condition.

A family medical history can identify people with a higher-than-usual chance of having common disorders, such as heart disease, high blood pressure, stroke, certain cancers, and diabetes. These complex disorders are influenced by a combination of genetic factors, environmental conditions, and lifestyle choices. A family history also can provide information about the risk of rarer conditions caused by mutations in a single gene, such as cystic fibrosis and sickle cell anemia [1].

---

* Corresponding author.

H. Badioze Zaman et al. (Eds.): IVIC 2013, LNCS 8237, pp. 427–434, 2013.

This research plan to design a new data mining model and apply or proposed a visualization techniques in order to investigate familiar health risk factor data derived from family trees. The purpose of the analysis will be to highlight factors which could increase a person's risk of developing a particular health problem. This information could be used both to assess an individual's relative risk of developing a disease, and to target limited health care resources to those most at risk.

The basic idea of visual data exploration is to present the data in some visual form, allowing the human to get insight into the data, draw conclusions, and directly interact with the data. Visual data mining techniques have proven to be of high value in exploratory data analysis and they also have a high potential for exploring large dataset [10]. Visual data exploration is especially useful when little is known about the data and the exploration goals are vague. Since the user is directly involved in the exploration process, shifting and adjusting the exploration goals is automatically done if necessary.

2 Background and Related Work

2.1 Data Mining and Visualization

The amount of data stored on electronic media is growing exponentially fast. Today's data warehouses dwarf the biggest databases built a decade ago [2], and making sense of such data is becoming harder and more challenging.

Data mining, sometimes referred to as knowledge discovery [3], is at the intersection of multiple research areas, including Machine Learning [4], Statistics [5], Databases [6], and Visualization [7]. It is considers as a process of identifying new patterns and insights in data, whether it is for understanding the Human Genome to develop new drugs, or for understanding the online customers behavior at an electronic web store in order to provide a personalized one-to-one experience [8].

For data mining to be effective, it is important to include the human in the data exploration process and combine the flexibility, creativity, and general knowledge of the human with the enormous storage capacity and the computational power of today's computers [9].

In this context, visualization offers a powerful means of analysis that can help to uncover patterns and trends hidden in unknown data. Additionally, visualization provides a natural method of integrating multiple data sets and has been proven to be reliable and effective across a number of application domains. Still, visual methods cannot entirely replace analytic non visual mining algorithms. Rather, it is useful to combine multiple methods during data exploration processes [17].

The classical visualization pipeline for visual data mining is shown in Fig. 1. From Raw Data to producing a visual representation for a user to interact and acquire knowledge, there are several steps as shown in the figure. Research in all these areas is actively persued by scientists around the world.

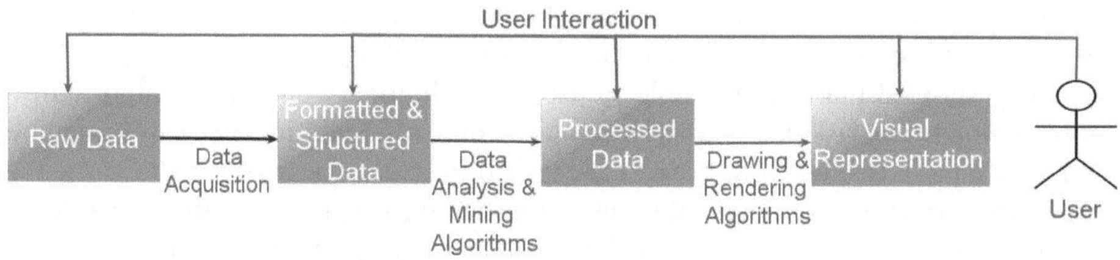

Fig. 1. Visualization Pipeline for Visual Data Mining

2.2 Medical Family Tree Data

Medical family tree is a record of illnesses and medical conditions affecting the patients and their family members. Similar to a family tree, a family medical history shows the relationships among members of the patient's family, but it also includes relevant health information for each person. It can be used to provide insight into the conditions that are common in the patient's family.

Family trees can be used to show the incidence of risk factors within a family. From the family trees risk factors can be extracted e.g. number of first and second degree relatives with colorectal cancer, number of first and second degree relatives with stomach cancer etc. The person's age at which the relevant cancer developed is also very important and this also can be extracted [1].

Various statistical and data mining techniques can be used in the process of knowledge discovery from the extracted family tree risk factor database in order to attempt to identify, which factors are important and what the contribution of each risk factor is, to a person developing a particular health condition [15]. From this discovered knowledge a model that assesses a person relative risk can be developed.

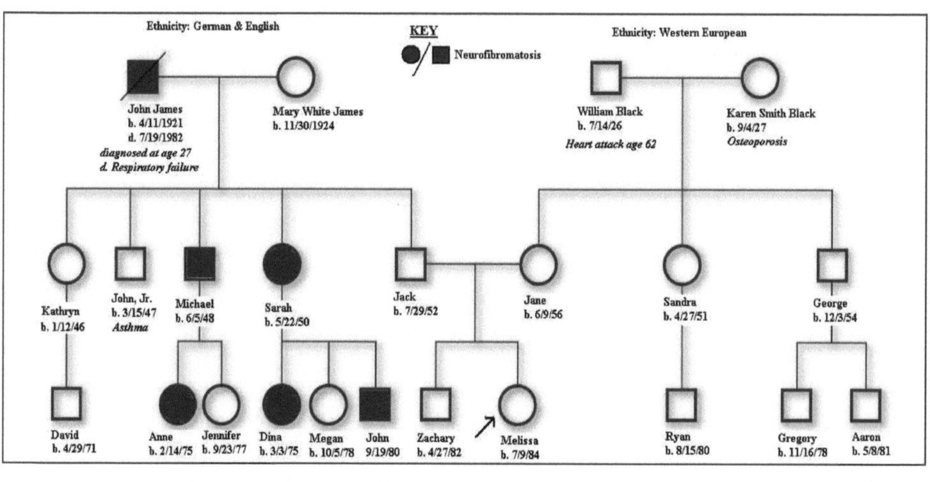

Fig. 2. An Example of Medical Family Tree Data [15]

Previous studies [1], [11] and [16] has shown that it is possible to get meaningful analysis of these extracted risk factor data by using Evolutionary Computing methods. This study showed that it is possible to use an evolutionary computing algorithm to highlight important risk factor contributions within a population of family member risk factor data extracted from breast cancer family trees. The analysis did show that there were a number of optimal solutions to the risk factors, however the research was limited in scope and there was a number of data issues particularly duplication and scarcity which could have affected the results.

Fig. 2. shows an example of medical family tree data. The visualizations of these data will allow the user to gain insight into the data and come up with new hypotheses. The verification of the hypotheses can also be done via visual data exploration but it may also be accomplished by automatic techniques from statistics or machine learning.

2.3 Visualizing Tree Structure Data

Tree-structured data is a specific kind of graph that is very important in many applications. Trees are simple, powerful, and elegant abstractions that have broad applicability in computer science and many other fields. For example, in the domain of the World-Wide Web, nodes represent web pages and links represent hyperlinks, and in biology nodes represent species, and links represent evolutionary descent. In the case of the internet, nodes could represent routers and links would imply direct network connectivity.

The size of the tree to view is usually considered as a key issue in tree visualization. Large trees sometimes pose several difficult problems. If the number of nodes is large, it can easily compromise performance or even reach the limits of the viewing platform. Many techniques have been proposed to show such tree structures

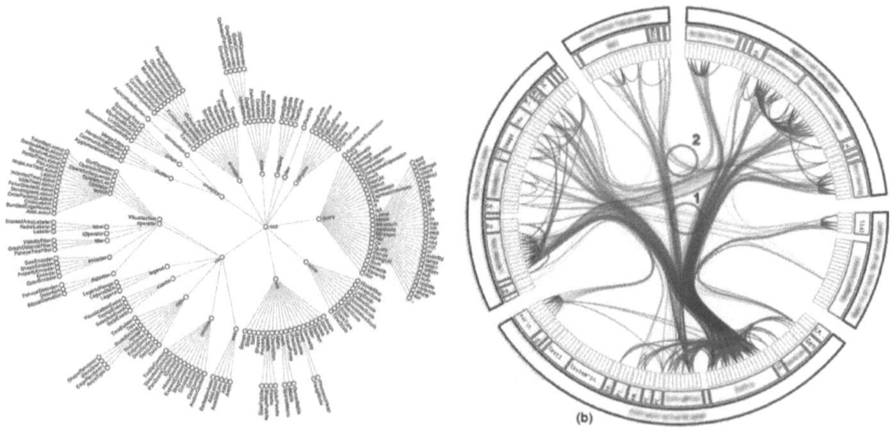

Fig. 3. Example of Visualization Techniques of Tree Structure Data: (a) Radial Tree and (b) Hierarchical Edge Bundles by Cornelissen et al. [18]

more effectively. Treemap, cone tree, hyperbolic tree, and spacetree are examples of techniques and applications that are being developed to tackle this issue. These techniques are considered to be some of the major contributors to this area. All of these visualization techniques do have their own advantages and disadvantages depending on what aspect of data being used and the user's preference in visualizing their data.

Our previous study on visualizing phologenetic tree data [13] and [14] has shown that by visualizing these tree structure data, more meaningful information can be extracted and it provide much needed help for the users in interpreting their tree data.

3 Research Objectives

Most of the existing data mining research focuses on finding the best models that can represent a particular set of data. For this research we propose the Integration of data mining and visualization techniques on medical family tree data that would established a new models/methods that would combine fast automatic data mining algorithms with the intuitive power of the human mind which will improve the quality and speed of the visual data mining process.

This research aims to study on Medical Family Tree Data Mining & Visualization. In more detail, it seeks to fulfill the following research objectives:

- To proposed a new data mining models that is suitable to predict health risk factor based on the data derived from medical family trees
- To devise a visualization methods that can visually explore these data which will help users (including the healthcare professionals) in making decision
- To design an interactive data mining and visualization application that will allow users to directly interact with medical family trees data.

4 Research Methodology

In order to achieve the research objectives as stated above, the research has conducted through the following step:

i. ***Preliminary Study*** - In this step various data mining techniques and tools has been explored with the focus especially to the ones that deal with medical or tree structure data.
ii. ***Develop New Data Mining Model*** - Based on the identified techniques and tools found in previous step, a new data mining model will be designed such that the information from the medical family tree data can be explored and properly harvested.
iii. ***Visualizing the New Model*** - Once a new data mining model has been developed, proper visualization techniques will be used/proposed so that the model can be presented in a graphical form. The graphical representation should be simple enough to be easily understood, but complete enough to reveal all the information presented in the model.

iv. ***Designing Visual Data Mining Application*** - An interactive data mining and visualization tools will be design based on the new data mining model and visualization techniques chosen.

v. ***Analyzing/Evaluating the Proposed Model and Application***- The effectiveness of the newly design data mining model and visualization techniques will be analyzed and evaluated by comparing it with current existing models. Evaluation is one the key points in any data mining process. It helps to predict on how well the final model will work in the future, and it is used to help in finding the model that can better represents the training data involved.

Fig. 4. shows the application architecture of the proposed research project. Based on this architecture, the accuracy of the results of the visual data mining application relies heavily on the new data mining model and the schema of the data warehouse. Based on the queries submitted to the data warehouse, the metadata will be evaluated based on the new data mining model and the results (in this case the medical problems associated with the family tree) will be known to the users.

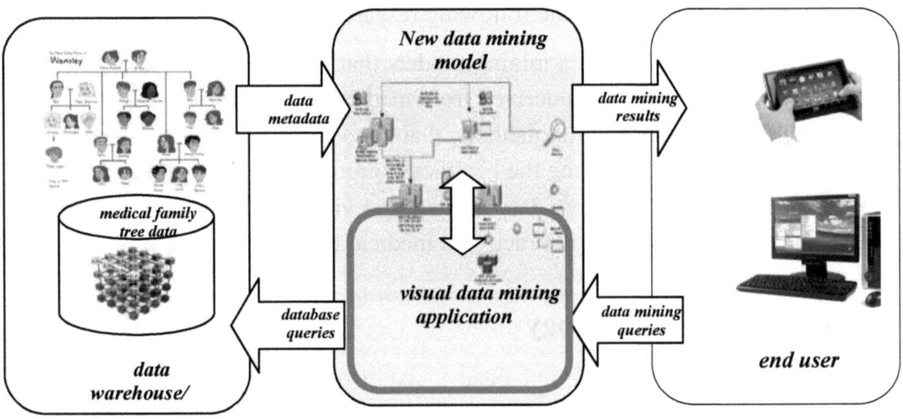

Fig. 4. Diagram showing the application architecture of the proposed research

5 Discussion, Conclusion and Future Work

The paper describes an attempt to visualise data mining process for medical family tree data. Visual data mining aims at putting the human user in the retrieval loop as far as possible. It is based on the concept that every relevant bit of information is visualised in the user interface.

The presented elements of visual data mining form only the basis of the approach. Various extensions are thinkable. Our future work will include evaluating the proposed framework and by comparing it with other well known data mining framework. Additionally, we are currently in the process of developing an interactive visual data mining application based on our proposed framework.

This work has provided us with an opportunity to explore the visualization of medical family tree data in detail. So far, the work has been successful and its results and achievement will hopefully contribute to the visualization community.

Knowing one's family medical history allows a person to take steps to reduce his or her risk. For people at an increased risk of certain cancers, healthcare professionals may recommend more frequent screening (such as mammography or colonoscopy) starting at an earlier age. Healthcare providers may also encourage regular checkups or testing for people with a medical condition that runs in their family. Additionally, lifestyle changes such as adopting a healthier diet, getting regular exercise, and quitting smoking help many people lower their chances of developing heart disease and other common illnesses.

Acknowledgments. The authors wish to thank Universiti Sains Malaysia (USM) for providing the funding (Research University (RUI) Grant - no: 1001/PKOMP/817071) through which this article was produced.

References

1. Gill, S.S.: Evolutionary Computing for Cancer Genetics Risk Assessment, MSc IMM dissertation, MACS, Heriot Watt University (2003)
2. Kimball, R., Mer, R.: The Data Webhouse Toolkit: Building the Web-Enabled Data Warehouse. John Wiley & Sons (2000)
3. Fayyad, U.M., Piatetsky-Shapiro, G., Smyth, P.: From data mining to knowledge discovery: An overview. In: Advances in Knowledge Discovery and Data Mining, ch. 1, pp. 1–34. AAAI Press, The MIT Press (1996)
4. Mitchell, T.M.: Machine Learning. McGraw-Hill (1997)
5. Friedman, J., Hastie, T., Tibshirani, R.: The Elements of Statistical Learning: Data Mining, Inference and Prediction, 2nd edn. Springer (2009)
6. Berthold, M.R., Dill, F., Kötter, T., Thiel, K.: Supporting creativity: Towards associative discovery of new insights. In: Washio, T., Suzuki, E., Ting, K.M., Inokuchi, A. (eds.) PAKDD 2008. LNCS (LNAI), vol. 5012, pp. 14–25. Springer, Heidelberg (2008)
7. Fry, B.: Visualizing Data: Exploring and Explaining Data with the Processing Environment. O'Reilly Media (2007)
8. Kohavi, R.: Data Mining and Visualization. In: Sixth Annual Symposium on Frontiers of Engineering, pp. 30–40. National Academy Press (2001)
9. Keim, D.A.: Information Visualization and Visual Data Mining. IEEE Transactions on Visualization and Computer Graphics 8(1), 1–8 (2002)
10. Pandey, B., Mishra, R.B.: Knowledge and intelligent computing system in medicine. Computers in Biology and Medicine 39(3), 215–230 (2009)
11. Bellazzi, R., Zupan, B.: Predictive data mining in clinical medicine: current issues and guidelines. International Journal of Medical Informatics 77(2), 81–97 (2008)

12. Souza, J., Matwin, S., Japkowicz, N.: Evaluating data mining models: A pattern language. Presented at PLoP 2002 (2002), http://jerry.cs.uiuc.edu/~plop/plop2002/final/PLoP2002_jtsouza0_1.pdf (retrieved February 18, 2012)
13. Zainon, W.M.N.W., Talib, A.Z., Belaton, B.: A New Framework for Phylogenetic Tree Visualization. In: Badioze Zaman, H., Robinson, P., Petrou, M., Olivier, P., Shih, T.K., Velastin, S., Nyström, I. (eds.) IVIC 2011, Part II. LNCS, vol. 7067, pp. 348–359. Springer, Heidelberg (2011)
14. Zainon, W.M.N.W., Talib, A.Z., Belaton, B.: Display-based Approaches for Phylogenetic Tree Visualization. In: Proceedings of the 2nd International Conference on Distributed Frameworks and Applications (DFmA 2010), Yogyakarta, Indonesia, pp. 53–59 (2010) ISBN: 978-602-9747-9-0-4
15. Altshuler, D., Clark, A.G.: Harvesting Medical Information from the Human Family Tree. Science 307(5712), 1052–1053 (2005)
16. Delen, D.: Analysis of cancer data: a data mining approach. Expert Systems 26(1), 100–112 (2009)
17. Kreuseler, M., Schumann, H.: A Flexible Approach for Visual Data Mining. IEEE Transactions on Visualization and Computer Graphics 8(1), 39–51 (2002)
18. Cornelissen, B., Holten, D., Zaidman, A., Moonen, L., van Wijk, J.J., van Deursen, A.: Understanding Execution Traces Using Massive Sequence and Circular Bundle Views. In: Proceedings of the 15th International Conference on Program Comprehension (ICPC), pp. 49–58. IEEE Computer Society (2007)

Interactivity and Animation Effects towards Student Enhancement of Learning in WAN Protocols

Nurul Hazra Abdul Salam, Riaza Mohd. Rias, Wan Kadijah Yusof, and Aisyah Abdul Manap

Fakulty of Computer and Mathematical Sciences, Universiti Teknologi MARA, 40450 Shah Alam Selangor, Malaysia
{hazra,riaza,wankhadijah}@tmsk.uitm.edu.my, aisyahmanap.13@gmail.com

Abstract. The development of multimedia educational software using available multimedia technologies has been proven as an effective tool to support teaching and learning process. It provides a good solution to the problem of introducing new learning and teaching techniques in education system. Therefore, this research is investigating a suitable technique to develop interactive multimedia application for effective learning. In this research, cognitive, constructive learning and metaphor of active learning theory was investigated as a potential technique that could be applied in this application. A statistical research study then follows which aims at finding out whether the animation and interactive environment in the courseware developed using learning techniques mentioned above can make learning more efficient and help student to increase their understanding in the subject of Data Communication & Networking. Collection and analysis of data was carried out quantitatively and qualitatively including survey on student learning tools preferences.

Keywords: animation, learning, wan, interactive, metaphor.

1 Introduction

Multimedia brings about a number of changes in education. For this recent year, amongst other applications of multimedia, educational applications have been important to multimedia technology in terms of developing tools and technology to support the desired applications. Until the advent of WWW, courseware was comprised of stand-alone packages. These generally implemented hypertext type systems themselves. Therefore, dynamic interactive courseware with animation is very popular and of great significance in teaching in primary and secondary schools [8].

There were various reasons, the basic one being that the courseware is attractive, dynamic, interactive and effective, since it can combine still and moving pictures, and audio with text graphics. If computer-based learning material is chosen to assist with individual student problems, it must be interactive, providing to find where the student needs help and providing that help [4].

H. Badioze Zaman et al. (Eds.): IVIC 2013, LNCS 8237, pp. 435–446, 2013.

Many studies [15], [2] and [18], meta-studies [6], and surveys [3] address the effectiveness (or ineffectiveness) of animations for learning. For a summary, we refer readers to a \state-of-the-art" survey [5] and we do concentrate on one: predictive (or active) versus passive animations. Although studies of animation effectiveness have been mixed, to us it seems that prediction based systems have generally had better results. The issue addressed in this study is learning Data Communication and Networking is not easy to be clearly absorbed by student using traditional learning methods; textual information. The study of computer networks can be challenging and students have to learn ever-changing technical and apply concepts covered in textbooks, lectures [19]. From TecheExam.net, it's provide the statistics of the hardest topic to study for CCNA *(Cisco Certified Network Associate)*. According to the statistics, it show that WAN protocols get the higher percentage based on the vote from the user.

The purpose of this research is to investigate and gather students' experiences who are enrolled in Data Communication and Networking on how multimedia interactive software could be assistance to them in their learning process, in term of performance and preference of 2D and 3D animation. This paper reports the effectiveness of interactive and animations in students' learning in a difficult topic of WAN protocols.

1.1 The Use of Animation

Animation is a graphic representation of drawings to show movement within those drawings. A series of drawings are linked together and have been slightly changed between individualized frames so when they are played back in rapid succession (24 frames per second) there appears to be seamless movement within the drawings [1]. The animations in a hypermedia system can be classified in the 2D, 3D, metamorphosis, combination of 2D and 3D [7]. It is seems like moving and real, which can gives emphasis in presentation to attract users' attention and engage the learner.

According to [7], animations may have the same ways of visualization as the objects. Visualization viewed as the graphical presentation of information with the goal providing the viewer with a qualitative understanding of the information contents [23]. Good visualization must be effective, accurate, efficient, aesthetics and adaptable. In order to design effective visualization it is necessary to know what the learner knows especially in the context of education. Multimedia learning environments must be shown to be educationally effective and to provide students the same or better quality of experience as they have with traditional teaching methods [28]. At best such systems will enhance and improve the students' quality of learning.

In the context of this study, we wanted to know if 3-D animation is any better than 2-D animation. Cockburn and McKenzie (2001) compared the use of 3-D interfaces with their traditional 2-D counterpart. The study describes the comparative evaluation of two document management systems that differ only in the number of dimensions used for displaying and interacting with the data. The primary purpose of this experiment was to see if there were any differences between the 2-D and 3-D interfaces in the efficiency of storing and retrieving web page thumbnail images.

Also, they wanted to know how performance in these tasks might be affected by increasing densities of data ('clutter') within the displays. The 3-D system supports users in sorting, organizing and retrieving 'thumbnail' representations of documents such as bookmarked web-pages. Results showed that the subjects were faster at storing and retrieving pages in the display when using 2-D interface, but not significantly so. Retrieval times significantly increased as the number of thumbnails increased. Despite the lack of significant differences between the 2-D and 3-D interfaces, subjective assessments showed a significant preference for 3-D interface.

Computer based multimedia material offers different means of supporting 3-D information representations [13] Viewing dynamic and 3-D animations is assumed to be a possible way of changing and improving students' incomplete mental models [14]. Nevertheless, based on various researchers [24] and [12], it is found that 3-D models may lead to cognitive overload problems in hypermedia-learning environments in particular. On the other hand, the findings of [12] research revealed that some representations of molecular 3-D structure are better understood and can be more readily used by students in solving tasks of different complexity. However, empirical studies that focus on the impact of 3-D visualization on learning are, to date, rare and inconsistent [27].

1.2 The Courseware

The use of metaphors in interactive learning environments considerably reduces the perceived complexity of user interface which is able to help student learn, remember, and enjoy the system completely. The main idea realized in the metaphor for this research is a 'window to the new world' [22]. 'The new world' is a three-dimensional world where all information objects have a shape and behavior. Many studies have shown that learning style plays an important role in the academic performance of students. Cognitive style refers to an individual's method of processing information. The key elements in an individual's personal psychology which are structured and organized by an individual's cognitive style are effect or feeling, behavior or doing, and cognition or knowing and this psychological process is reflected in the way that the person builds a generalized approach to learning [20]. Individual have learned when they have constructed new interpretations of the social, cultural, physical and intellectual environments in which they live [9]. One of principles to accomplish goal that facilitate constructivism theory is to use authentic task and activities that are personally relevant to learners.

The development of this application is concerning the combination of three learning concept namely cognitive, constructive and active learning. The user interface for this application were designed based on theme park metaphor, where it is suitable for teenagers, easy to use, understandable and the most important thing is that this colorful animated user interface will be able to attract students' interest to explore in depth about WAN protocols. The main screen shows the visualization of theme park where it displays some element of 2D animation and graphics such as moving roller coaster, floating boat, ferris wheel, moving swan in a lake, restaurant and restroom icons. There is a cute bear character which acts as a navigator and user will have to control this bear to navigate through the application using the keyboard. Students can view the animation, read the content and hear all the theories about WAN protocols including the subtopics of packet and circuit switching. The application is interactive in nature and students can view the animation as many times possible to strengthen their cognitive learning.

As for the 3D animated version, the metaphor used was that of a factory production system. The concept of constructivism was applied here where students can relate factory operation with the concepts of packet and circuit switching.

2 Method

The research framework for this study is referred and guided by [10] research framework. The framework contains the description of research control modes, content and output. Control modes of the research consist of two independent variables which are interactive learning scenario and non-interactive learning scenario. Pre-test will be given for non-interactive (passive interaction) group where method of learning is using traditional slides notes and teacher as transmitter. This group is also called as passive interaction group because students essentially provide only one way information delivery, where students might listen to the presenter (teacher) information with limited intellectual engagement.

Post-test will be given after the students have been given the task to explore interactive multimedia approach using 2D and 3D animation. This group is called as predictive, active interaction animation tools. The tools transform the students from a mere observer to an active participant. The content is the development of courseware based on ADDIE model. Then, the research output is to measure student‘s preferences and performances based on the scenario categorization.

A quiz section is included in the form of multiple choice question and drag and drop. Apart from static text and recorded voice, to increase the understanding of the user, 2D and 3D animation is added to visualize the process of circuit and packet switching.

2.1 Design

The experiment consists of four phases:

- There are 2 groups who are involved with the total of 45 students of first year students from the Faculty of Computer and Mathematical Sciences at UiTM, Shah Alam. These students were assumed to be homogenous in terms of age, education and cultural background. Group 1 and Group 2 have received the same theoretical training in classroom (lecture). There are 14 and 31 students in Group 1 and Group 2 respectively. Group 1 and group 2 students attend to lecture and classroom. They are also were given note in classroom.

- Then, both of these groups carried out pre-test. At this level students are required to answer some basic questions about WAN protocol. It is consists of close and open questions. Example the meaning of WAN, the objective of WAN and others. The objective for this step is to measure the background knowledge of students about WAN protocols.
- Next, each group were given task to learn about WAN application of animation. For the group1, the students were given task to learn about WAN through application with 2D animation while group 2 explored and viewed the application with 3D animation. All the text contents in the two versions were the same and in accordance with the syllabus for the subject taught at the faculty.
- Lastly, both groups were given 1 hour to view the learning materials and they need to answer subjective and multiple choice questions in post-test. Post-test were carried out to check the gain scores of acquired knowledge using these two approach, 2D and 3D animation.

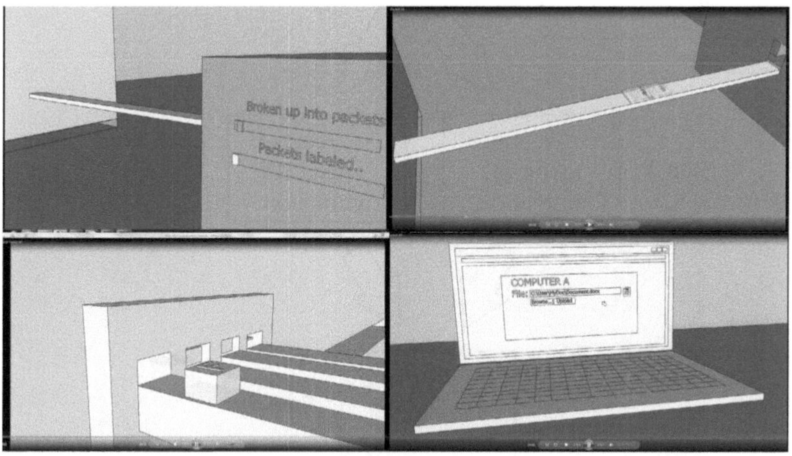

Fig. 1. Snapshot of interactive application: 3D animation

Fig. 2. Snapshots of 2D animation

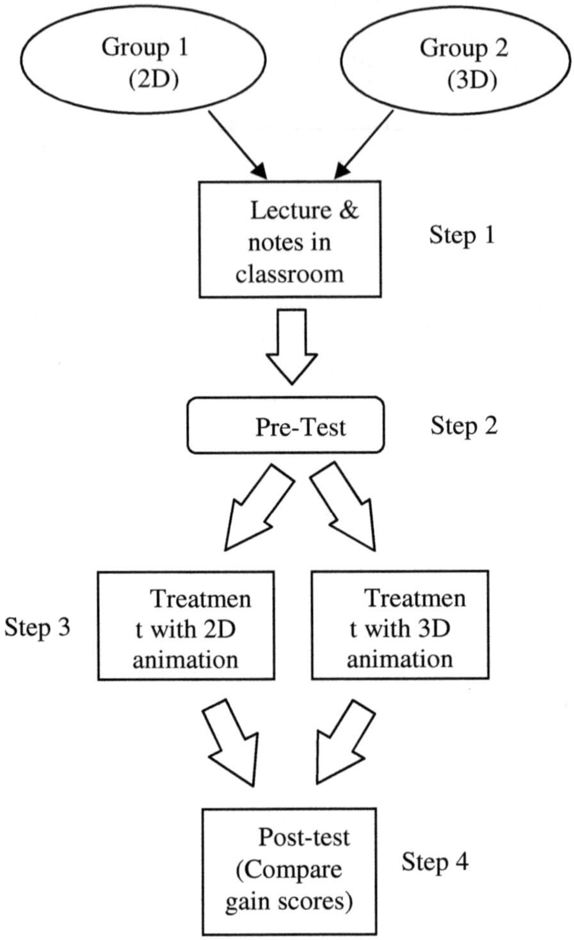

Fig. 3. Flow of the experiment

3 Result

The results of gain scores (gain defines as post-test minus pre-test) between two groups were statistically analyzed using T-test since there are two different sample sets involved in this evaluation. Gain scores appear to be a natural measure of growth for education and can be useful indicators of progress after experimental treatment.

Hypothesis: The gain scores for 3-D (Group 2) is equal to 2-D (Group 1).

Table 1. Result on knowledge gain

Dimension	Mean	Std.Deviation	N	t-value	p-value
2D Animation	2.286	2.8670	14	2.983	0.011
3D Animation	3.823	2.4985	31	8.518	0.000

Based on the One-sample t-test in Table 1, there is a significant different for visual dimension between 2-D and 3-D animated groups on the gain scores (post-test score – pre-test score) since the $p<0.05$. This implies that is rejected and therefore there is significance difference in the post test score between 2D and 3D animated group. When the mean scores test is observed, the mean gain scores is higher for students who viewed the 3-D version (3.823) as compared to students who viewed the 2-D version (2.286). This finding indicates there is a positive gain in knowledge through the use of interactive multimedia application for both groups. However, comparing these two animation techniques, the result shows that students demonstrated slightly higher learning performance after learning with 3D animation application compared with 2D animation.

Table 2. Maximum, minimum and mean score for 2D and 3D animation

	2D ANIMATION		3D ANIMATION	
	PRE	**POST**	**PRE**	**POST**
Maximum	10	13	10.5	14
Minimum	6	7	3.5	6.5
Mean	8.78	9.07	6.90	11.72

Table 2 shows the scores differences between 2D and 3D animation. Maximum scores for both groups are same, 14 while mean scores for 2D and 3D group are 9.07 and 11.72 respectively. From the result we can conclude that most of the students have successfully enhanced their learning in WAN topics through the assistance of this interactive multimedia courseware. It can be observed in higher scores after experiment, compared to lower pre-test scores where they were taught using conventional method. As 3D animation resemble the real thing and the effects is more powerful, it might seem that student who learned using 3D animation after teaching should have greater ability to understand the concept, able to solve the post-test questions and performed the best.

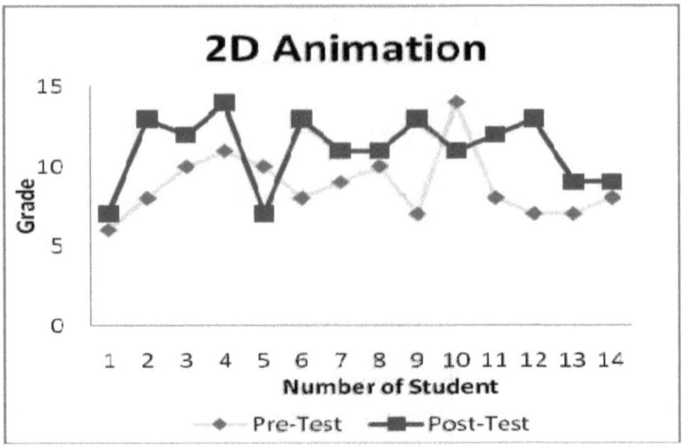

Fig. 4. Students Score for Pre-Test and Post-Test on 2D Animation

Fig. 4 shows that, the score on 2D animation between pre-test and post-test. Most of the students scored high for the post-test compare to pretest. There are only two student score high for pretest compare to post-test.

While for the 3D animation, we noticed that from Fig. 5, most of the students scored high in post-test compare to pre-test. The difference score between pre-test and post-test for most students are significantly different. Only 3 students scored high for pre-test compare to post-test and one student got the same score for both tests.

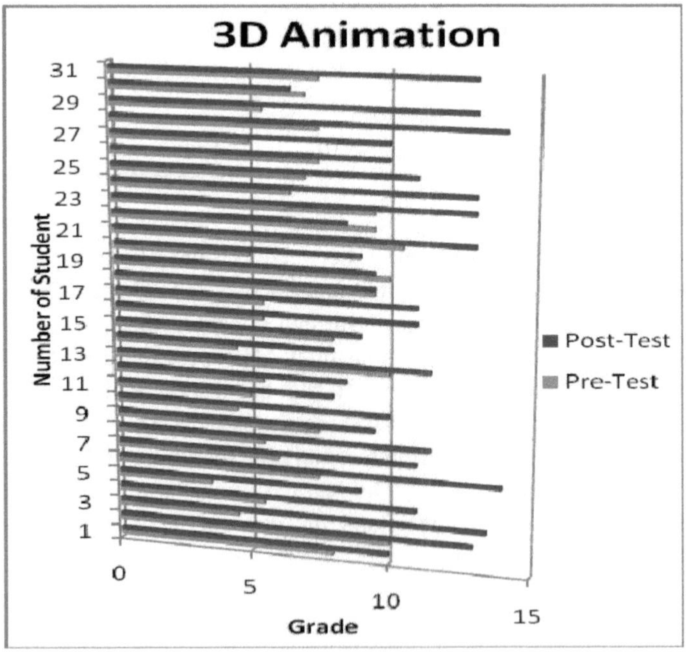

Fig. 5. Students Score for Pre-Test and Post-Test on 3D Animation

In order to answer the research question on user satisfaction and preference concerning the use of supplemental tools in teaching and comparison between 2D and 3D animation, a questionnaire was given to the students. Data were collected from 30 students who enrolled for subject Data Communication and Network where they were exposed to the interactive application using 2D and 3D animations.

A questionnaire was developed based on QUIS and it covered the overall reactions to the software, learnability, usability and user interface. 22 statements in the questionnaire focused on three research areas; overall satisfaction with six adjective pairs, various learnability aspects including navigational ease, interactivity, easiness of quiz, enjoyment factor and preference using 2D animation or 3D animation in learning, and investigated the usability and user interface such as the use of colors, text and functionality of each menu item. For each question, respondents required to indicate their response according to the rating based on Likert scale, ranged from 0 to 9, with 0 representing a negative adjective and 9 representing a positive adjective.

Findings from the feedback received showed that the respondents rated their experience with WAN application quite high. Minimum mean score is 6.28 which is the response from the overall reaction whether the application has inadequate power or adequate power of quality and explanatory. The highest mean score is shown in Section 3 with 7.84 indicating that the use of attractive colors and sound in application is important in student's preference. The rating for 'fun in learning and explore' is at the second highest with mean scores 7.8. The attractive bear character, interesting metaphor and interactive animations might affects the user's feeling and emotions, as most of them were agree to evaluate themselves as fun in their exploration.

The result also showed for animation approaches, the level of satisfaction appeared to be higher on 2D animation (7.36) compared with 3D animation (6.56).This satisfaction scores for 3D animation is not a dissatisfied level as it is still above 5.0. Some of the students evaluated fairly themselves as if they found it was a bit confusing and unhelpful in their learning. For overall reaction, most students evaluated this application as wonderful (7.72) and satisfying. Quizzes and interactivity of the application affects the student's preference positively, with means scores of 7.12 and 6.76 respectively.

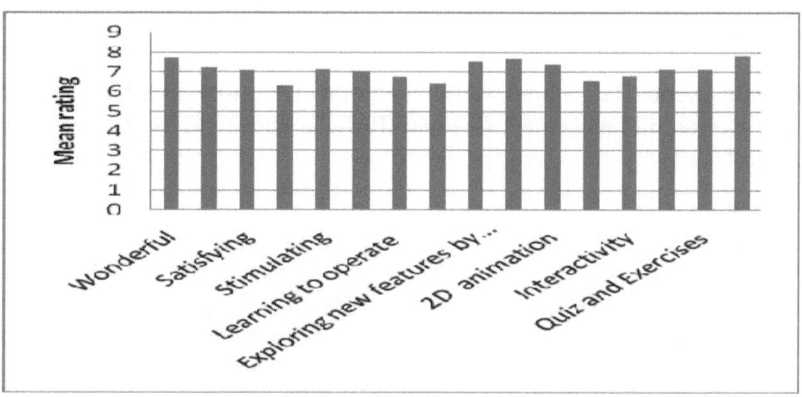

Fig. 6. Average rating of students' preference

4 Discussion and Conclusion

Wide Area Network (WAN) is known as one of the toughest topic for student in computer science. Therefore it is important that one try to master the topic. In order to make the WAN protocols easier to learn, many techniques have been introduced such as learning through animation, objective question, cross word game and word search game. These techniques are then applied to various learning media to make the learning experience more effective. From this research, several findings and results are obtained.

The observation of the result has proven that interactive multimedia application is an effective tool as an addition to traditional method to help students in learning difficult subjects. The result of the study reveals the effectiveness of interactive application based on better result obtained by the student after being taught using lecturing method and also using application to supplement and enhance their performance. Comparing between 2D and 3D animation, in term of performance, the student's result analysis proven that 3D gives slightly more impact on improving their learning process. This result is in accordance with findings from [27]. 3D is a good and effective visualization technique that can be easily interpreted into student's knowledge base.

However, findings on user preference indicated the opposite where students have significantly lower preference or satisfaction using 3D as compared to 2D animation. Therefore, 2D and 3D animation are both important educative function in contributing better experiences to students as well as improving their learning skills. University should encourages all instructors to implement both traditional and multimedia approaches in their teaching in order to help students understand better, remember longer and fun in learning.

In literature, it is found that learning with animation, and use of metaphors in interactive learning environments can enhance user understanding on a topic [13, 14]. The use of interactive animation is expected to attract student's interest, stimulate their creativity while improving their understanding of that particular subject. It can be concluded that this study has demonstrates the educational benefits of using interactive multimedia application either in 2D or 3D in teaching core topic of Data Communication and Networking.

Acknowledgement. The authors would like to thank the Research Increment Faculty (RIF) and Research Management Institute (RMI) at Universiti Teknologi MARA for their support.

References

1. Anderson: Wikipedia, the free encyclopedia (2010) `http://en.wikipedia.org/wiki/Animation` (retrieved August 31, 2010)
2. Lawrence, A.W., Badre, A.M., Stasko, J.T.: Empirically evaluating the use of animations to teach algorithms. In: Proceedings of the 1994 IEEE Symposium on Visual Languages, pp. 48–54. IEEE (1994)

3. Tversky, B., Morrison, J.B.: Animation: Can it facilitate? International Journal of Human Computer Studies 57(4), 247–262 (2002)
4. Aris, B., Ahmad, M.H., Shiong, K.B., Ali, M.B., Harun, J., Tasir, Z.: Learning "Goal Programming" Using an Interactive Multimedia Courseware: Design Factors and Students' Preferences. Department of Educational Multimedia Faculty of Education Universiti Teknologi Malaysia (2006)
5. Shaer, C.A., Cooper, M., Edwards, H.S.: Algorithm visualization: A report on the state of the field. In: SIGCSE 2007: Proceedings of the Thirty-eighth SIGCSE Technical Symposium on Computer Science Education, SIGSCE, pp. 150–154 (March 2007)
6. Hundhausen, C.D., Douglas, S.A., Stasko, J.T.: A meta-study of software visualization effectiveness. Journal of Visual Languages and Computing 13(3), 259–290 (2002)
7. Cipolla-Ficarra, F.V., Cipolla-Ficarra, M.: Computer Animation and Communicability in Multimedia System: A Trichotomy Evaluation. In: Damiani, E., Jeong, J., Howlett, R.J., Jain, L.C. (eds.) New Directions in Intelligent Interactive Multimedia Systems and Services - 2. SCI, vol. 226, pp. 103–115. Springer, Heidelberg (2009)
8. Chen, M., Yu, C., Min, L., Hu, G.: Development of an Animation-making Software Applied in Education, Engineering & Research Center for Information Technology on Education, HuaZhong Normal University Wuhan 430079, Hubei (2009)
9. Dick, W., Carey, L.: The Systematic Design of Instruction, 4th edn. Haper Collins College Publishers, New York (1996)
10. Eng Hong, L., et al.: The Leaner Control Feature in Multimedia Learning Courseware Towards Learners with Different Cognitive Styles: A Proposed Research Framework. In: Third International Malaysian Educational Technology Convention (2009)
11. Felder, R.M., Solomon, B.A.: Learning styles and strategies (2007), `http://www.ncsu.edu/felder-public/ILSdir/styles.htm` (retrieved August 31, 2010)
12. Fred, P., Alexander, R., John, S.: Cognitive Load Theory and Instructional Design: Recent Developments 38(1) (2003)
13. Huk, T.: Who benefits from learning with 3D models? The case of spatial ability 22(6), 392–404 (December 2006)
14. Wu, H.K., Shah, P.: Exploring visuospatial thinking in chemistry learning 88(3), 465–492 (May 2004)
15. Stasko, J., Badre, A., Lewis, C.: Do algorithm animations assist learning?: an empirical study and analysis. In: Proceedings of the INTERCHI 1993 Conference on Human Factors in Computing Systems, INTERCHI, pp. 61–66 (May 1993)
16. Knicolas, K., Nizar, A., Ece, Y.: Using Computer Network Simulation Tools as Supplements to Computer Network Curriculum. In: Frontiers in Education (FIE 2000), October 18-21, pp. 13–16 (2000)
17. Kyparisia, P., Mabbott, Bull, Grigoriadou: Designing learner-controlled educational interactions based on learning/cognitive style and learner behavior. Department of Informatics and Telecommunications, University of Athens, Panepistimiopolis, GR-15784 Athens, Greece (2006)
18. Byrne, M.D., Catrambone, R., Stasko, J.T.: Evaluating animations as student aids in learning computer algorithms. Computers and Education 33(4), 253–278 (1999)
19. Morozov, M., Markov, A.: How to make Courseware for School Interesting: New Metaphor in Educational Multimedia (2000)
20. Matthew, O., Wei, P., Elke, A.: Clutter Reduction in Multi-Dimensional Data Visualization Using Dimension Reordering. In: IEEE Symposium on Information Visualization 2004, October 10-12, pp. 89–96 (2004)

21. Overview of Learning Styles-Advanogy.com (2003-2007) (retrieved September 27, 2010)
22. Papanikolaou, K.A., Grigoriadou, M., Kornilakis, H., Magoulas, G.D.: Personalizing the interaction in a Web-based educational hypermedia system: the case of INSPIRE. Proceedings of the User-Modeling and User-Adapted Interaction 13(3), 213–267 (2003)
23. Papanikolaou, K.A., Grigoriadou, M.: Modelling and externalising learners' interaction behaviour. In: Proceedings of Workshop on Learner Modelling for Reflection, International Conference on Artificial Intelligence in Education, Amsterdam, Netherlands, pp. 52–61 (2005)
24. Peter, G., Katharina, S., Ricarhd, C.: Designing Instructional Examples to Reduce Intrinsic Cognitive Load: Molar versus Modular Presentation of Solution Procedures 32(1-2), 33–58 (2004)
25. Rafaeli, S., Ariel, Y.: Assessing Interactivity in Computer-Mediated Research. In: Joinson, A.N., McKenna, K.Y.A., Postmes, T., Rieps, U.D. (eds.) The Oxford Handbook of Internet Psychology, pp. 71–88. Oxford University Press (2007)
26. Revelle, G., Zuckerman, O., Druin, A., Bolas, M.: Tangible user interfaces for children. Extended abstract of the Conference on Human Factors in Computing Systems, Portland, Oregon (2005)
27. Rias, R.M., Zaman, H.B.: Can different types of animation enchance recall and transer of knowledge? A case study on a computer science subject. AJTLHE: ASEAN Journal of Teaching and Learning in Higher Education 4(1), 32–43 (2012) ISSN 1985-5826
28. Richards, D., Kelaiah, I.: Usability Attributes in Virtual Learning Environment. In: IE 2012, Proceedings of the 8th Australasian Conference on Interactive Entertainment: Playing the System, Auckland, New Zealand, July 21-22 (2012)
29. Steinke, M., Huk, T., Floto, C.: Helping teachers develop computer animations for improving learning in science education. In: Crawford, C., et al. (eds.) Proceedings of the Society for Information Technology and Teacher Education International Conference 2003, pp. 3022–3025. AACE, Chesapeake (2003)
30. Terrell, L.P.: History of Interactive Education and Training. The CEO Refresher (2003), `http://www.refresher.com/!history2.html`
31. Triantafillou, E., Pomportsis, A., Demetriadis, S.: The design and the formative evaluation of an adaptive educational system based on cognitive styles. Computers and Education 41, 87–103 (2003)
32. Tversky, B., Morrison, J., Betrancourt, M.: Animation: can it facilitate. International Journal of Human-Computer Studies, 247–262 (2002)
33. Weber, G., Brusilovsky, P.: ELM-ART: An Adaptive Versatile System for Web-Based Instruction. International Journal of AI in Education 12(4), 351–384 (2001)
34. Woodcock, A., Burns, J., Mount, S., Newman, R., Gaura, E.: Animating pervasive computing. In: Proceedings of the 23rd Annual International Conference on Design of Communication, SIGDOC 2005, pp. 116–122. ACM, New York (2005)
35. Woolf, B.P., Hall, W.: Multimedia Pedagogues: Interactive System for Teaching and Learning. IEEE Computer, Special Issue on Multimedia 28(5), 74–80 (1995)
36. Shang, Y., Shi, H., Chen, S.-S.: An Intelligent Distributed Environment for Active Learning. University of Missouri-Columbia (2001)

Increasing the Tracking Efficiency of Mobile Augmented Reality Using a Hybrid Tracking Technique

Waqas Khalid Obeidy[1], Haslina Arshad[1], Shahan Ahmad Chowdhury[1], Behrang Parhizkar[2], and Jiungyao Huang[3]

[1] School of Information Technology,
Faculty of Information Science and Technology,
Universiti Kebangsaan Malaysia, Bangi, Selangor
{waquaskhalid,haslinarshad,bpy_07}@yahoo.com
[2] School of Computer Science,
The University of Nottingham
hani.parhizkar@nottingham.edu.my
[3] Department of Computer Science & Information Engineering,
National Taipei University
jiungyao@gmail.com

Abstract. Traditional vision tracking approaches have failed to support the fast tracking required by Mobile Augmented Reality (MAR) for a real-time interactive effect. The main problem addressed by this research is the tracking problem in MAR where the computational load is a major issue. In this paper we proposed a more efficient visual tracking technique based on fast detectors and small binary descriptors which are capable of providing both; scale and rotation invariance. We also propose a new hybrid tracking technique which can speed up the overall performance of MAR by reducing the detection rate of the tracking process. The hybrid technique is based on the usage of inertial sensors such as accelerometer, gyroscopes and gravitational vectors which can readily improve the efficiency of any vision based feature tracking system that uses computer vision. The preliminary tests carried out during the course of the study produced very promising results.

Keywords: Mobile Augmented Reality, Hybrid Tracking, Feature Detection, Computer Vision.

1 Introduction

During the past recent years, a large number of researches have been carried out to explore the secrets of Augmented Reality (AR). Early AR was based on desktop computer and custom input output devices and backpack with Head Mounted Devices (HMD). With the passage of time, the trend of display in AR switched from the backpack with HMD to low cost small handheld devices such as tablet PC's, PDA's and Smart phones. Today's smart phones contains display systems, cameras, graphics, GPS compasses and accelerometers which are enough to serve the basic requirements for AR. However, some major technical obstacles must be tackled before AR can

H. Badioze Zaman et al. (Eds.): IVIC 2013, LNCS 8237, pp. 447–457, 2013.

claim its true potential as a technology in any field. One of those major obstacles lies in the area of tracking where AR demands seamless & speedy detection of objects in real time.

Both AR as well as Virtual Reality (VR) need accurate real-time 6DOF pose tracking of devices such as tangible interface objects, head-mounted displays etc. Handheld devices such as PDAs and mobile phones enforce many restrictions on tracking which are not experienced on stationary and mobile PC-based setups. Smart phones provide a different environment for AR which provides an unstable view point when users hold the device with one hand, move around and touch the interface with other hand [1]. To observe large environment users have to move the device frequently which can cause marker tracking failure. AR researchers in recent years have been working hard in order to achieve robustness and accuracy in the tracking environment of both; desktop systems and mobile systems (Fig. 1). Tracking from natural features is not a simple problem and generally requires very high computational power. Therefore it is very difficult to use natural feature tracking in mobile applications of AR, which runs with limited computational resources, such as on Tablet PCs [2].

Feature detection is used for different purposes and therefore performance is evaluated in terms of location, accuracy and speed. Often natural feature tracking approaches uses FAST, SIFT or SURF features for tracking and pose estimation. FAST features can be computed very fast but are not scale invariant, on the other hand SURF and SIFT features demand much computational power (especially for mobile devices) [3]. However, usage of inertial sensors such as accelerometer; gyroscopes and gravitational vectors can readily improve the efficiency of a feature based tracking system which uses computer vision. The idea of this research is to integrate the feature based computer vision tracking technique with the phones built-in inertial sensors data to develop a robust hybrid tracking technique. The hybrid technique will be implemented in an indoor environment using an android smart phone and its tracking efficiency will be tested based on its tracking time, speed & accuracy. The specific steps taken in order to carry out this research are:

- A Review of the existing Mobile AR and vision based tracking techniques including recent development in the areas of feature detectors & descriptors such as SIFT, FAST, SURF, BRIEF, ORB, BRISK and FREAK [4,5,6,7,8,9,10].
- Development of a hybrid mobile tracking technique based on suitable vision based tracking techniques and phones inertial sensors to increase the tracking efficiency of Mobile AR.

2 Related Work

A great deal of research effort has been directed towards the development of augmented reality in recent years. Most of the works done in the field revolves around the areas of tracking, registration, rendering and occlusion issues. Various techniques have been applied to produce a quality AR experience for users using different platforms in various domains.

AR is perceived to have evolved from the bases of Virtual Reality (VR) technology. Vallino[11] stated clearly that AR is the seamless combination of virtual objects and the real world where the users are given a chance to interact with the objects in real time. One of the first augmented reality systems was developed by Ivan Sutherland in 1960 [12]. Since then, large number of researches has been carried out to explore the secrets of AR. As stated earlier, early AR was based on desktop computer and custom input output devices and backpack with HMD's. With the passage of time, the trend of display in AR has switched from the backpack with HMD to low cost small handheld device such as monitors, PDA's, Smart phones [13](Fig. 1).

Smart phones are developed for a comparatively larger consumer base which is mobile. They are surprisingly robust and powerful although their appearance is very fragile. Almost all of the smart phones available today include a built in camera which automatically serves for computer vision approaches [14]. Camera and image sensor characteristics like frame size, update rate etc. greatly influences the quality of tracking process [15]. Generally in mobile devices, the quality of AR is lower than AR in PC platforms because the computer vision's quality is based on camera and image sensor characteristics [16]. Thus, in order to achieve the required performance of AR applications, careful selection of algorithms and tracking techniques is needed. This is because PC's which acts as a high end device have greater computing capabilities than the smart phones. This limits mobile devices solely to the application of simple algorithms to solve complex issues of tracking, registration and rendering of augmented reality contents.

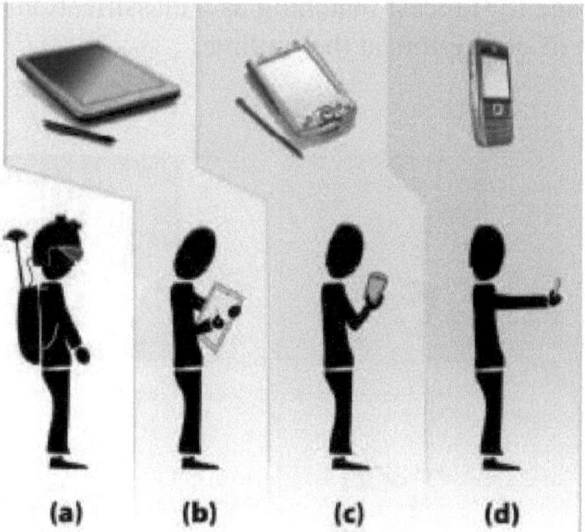

Fig. 1. Symbolic evolution of Mobile AR: (a) HMD Backpacks, (b) UMPC's, (c) Handhelds, (d) Mobile phones

In order to either align or register any virtual information with the physical objects that are to be annotated, AR requires very accurate position and orientation tracking. The process of locating a user's position and•orientation in an environment is critical to AR as more realistic results can be obtained when the registration of real and synthetic is accurate. A common approach in visual tracking is to make use of passive (printed marker) or active (light-emitting diode) markers. In a marker based Mobile Augmented Reality system, tracking done using fiducial markers is a common strategic practice to achieve robustness and computational efficiency at the same time [13]. As we examined the widely used opensource ARToolkit, we realized that most of the markers are surrounded with thick black borders which facilitate their tracking by improving the concentration of ARToolKit in searching its interest region (Fig. 2).

Since 1990's numerous attempts have been made to solve the pose estimation problems without the use of fiducials or the borders in computer based augmented reality where the heavy load of tracking processes is handled by the powerful computer processors. Such examples can be seen by [17]. Some AR researchers have also tried to focus upon online markerless AR systems where no priory information of the environment is available and the system gathers its information online [18, 3]. Visual markerless tracking algorithms are capable of providing realistic real-time camera tracking information based on different approaches such as natural edge detection, planar methods, feature detection etc. This consumes a huge amount of processing power posing difficulties on the AR rendering tasks.

Tracking from natural features is a complex problem and usually demands high computational power. Across large view changes it is very difficult to compute the descriptors that are invariant. Scholars such as Skrypnyk and Lowe [19] came up with a classic system based on the SIFT descriptor for object localization in the context of AR [20,21]. However, it is also possible to select the features from a technique or mapped from the environment at runtime online [22]. Using a decision tree and trade increased memory usage [23] recast matching as a classification problem by avoiding complex computation of descriptors at the runtime.

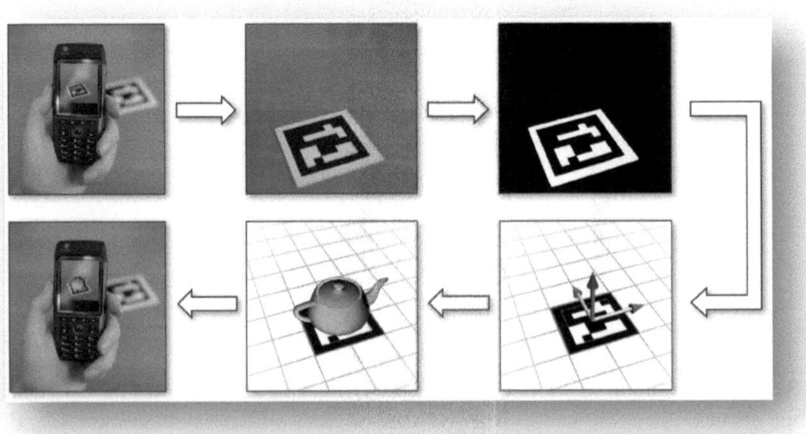

Fig. 2. General fiducial marker tracking workflow of an AR application (Wagner & Schmalstieg, 2007)

Often natural feature tracking approaches use FAST or SIFT features for feature detection. However, FAST features can be computed very fast but are not scale invariant, on the other hand SIFT features are multi scaled and need too much computational power (especially for mobile devices). An approach using SURF features for tracking by [6] can be computed much faster than SIFT features but it is not accurate. A different approach for tracking with a built-in camera of a mobile phone was carried out by [3]. They used a combination of SIFT and Ferns features to create descriptors based on a fast classification method.

The challenge of tracking in mobile handheld AR is to reduce the computational load. This can be achieved by improving the tracking process by using a hybrid tracking system that makes use of more than one kind of tracking techniques and instruments. The idea of a hybrid tracking technique, combining a visual tracking system and inertial sensors is not a new idea. It has already been implemented in augmented reality using Head Mounted Display (HMD). Year 2002 saw a great move forward in the field of hybrid tracking when Naimark et al. [24] successfully predicted marker position by combining fiducial markers with inertial sensors. Two years later, Jiang et al. [25] found the features of the real scene with the help of inertial sensors and his computer vision algorithm was able to reduce the drift caused by gyroscope in previous works. Due to the advancements in the technology, coming years saw a shift in researchers working on HMD devices to the handheld and mobile devices. This was the time when Hol et al. [26], Reitmayr and Drummond [27], Seo et al. [28] and Lee et al. [29] proposed their work related to tracking in mobile AR in outdoor environment. Reitmayr and Drummond [23] worked on the initialization of tracking poses and showed that the use of sensors like GPS along with the computer vision techniques are capable of reducing the tracking failure recovery time. Soe et al. [28] and Lee et al. [29] also worked on increasing the accuracy of feature detection where they found that GPS proved a good solution only in the large environments. Lee et al. [29] suggested that accuracy of the initialization process can be improved by the use of sensors with the help of gyroscopes and accelerometers and not by the user assistance. Researchers such as Mulloni who are very active in the researches for Mobile AR published their work [30] and showed that the combination of sensors which could provide data related to the gravitational force would prove beneficial in indoor tracking environments. Recent works [31, 32] also states that efficiency and robustness of tracking can now be improved tremendously with the help of strong inbuilt sensors available in almost every phone today.

3 Proposed Work

A comparative review of typical techniques used in the natural feature tracking development has already been carried out during the course of study to understand the concepts of Mobile AR, marker and image detection, description and matching. We have realized that there are many existing methods available for hybrid tracking in augmented reality. However there also exist many issues on efficiency and robustness of those tracking techniques. Therefore, in order to propose a robust hybrid tracking techniques which combines the vision based techniques along with the inertial sensors available in the android phone; we have constructed a detailed methodology for this research. The proposed hybrid technique is capable of offering a wide range of applications in various domains including manufacturing, teaching, medical and biological imaging. It can improve the radiological diagnostic services which can increase access for the people and lower the cost of healthcare industry. Our hypothesis shows that feature tracking using interest points when hybrid with inertial sensors can reduce the computational power thus creating an efficient hybrid tracking technique for mobile handheld AR. Similar to the earlier sensor fusion works, we rely on visual tracking techniques and subsequently aiding them with the inertial sensor data.

During the initial steps of our research, we have identified and analyzed numerous natural feature tracking techniques based on different feature detectors and descriptors such as SIFT, FAST, SURF, BRIEF, ORB, BRISK and FREAK. We also focused our research to identify different sensor based and hybrid techniques available for real time tracking. A special focus is shed on the efficiency of the feasible techniques and the platform related issues. These studies allowed us to come out with feature detectors, descriptors and matchers that will be used in natural feature tracking and sensors that will be integrated with them in the hybrid tracking system. The developed hybrid technique includes the following stages; video image input, feature detection, feature description, feature matching, outlier removals, camera pose detection and rendering of the virtual objects on top of the real scenes. However, our special attention will be focused onto the visual tracking module which consist of video image input, feature detection, feature description, feature matching, outlier removals. Inertial sensors will be integrated with these modules to make the tracking process more efficient.

The advantage of key feature points is that they substantially reduce the search space and computation time required for finding correspondences between two scenes. This allows the system to focus the computations on areas that are more likely relevant for the description and matching process. From our literature search we have found out that the traditional process of visual tracking itself needs strict restructuring if we wish to perform it in mobile platforms. We have proposed a new restructured visual tracking model based on suitable techniques for feature tracking on mobile platforms. It is named as the visual tracking module (Fig. 3). This module uses FAST features detected at different scales in order to provide scale invariance similar to the SIFT multiscale detector but is 20 times faster with minimal expense of memory. Similarly use of newly developed binary descriptors are capable of creating distinctive descriptors of very small sizes. FREAK and BRISK are novel rotation invariant binary descriptors that far surpass the industry standards and its vector competitors including SIFT and SURF. Since FREAK is marginally faster than BRISK, we would recommend using FREAK in order to speed up the tracking process. For matching the descriptor currently we rely on the brute-force (BF) matcher. BF matcher looks for each descriptor in the first set and the closest descriptor in the second set by performing an exhaustive search. Lastly we perform the outlier removal process to overcome the mismatches occurred during the matching process. We perform simple ration-tests and homography estimation technique based on RANSAC method to improve our matching results even more.

After the development of visual tracking module we shifted our focus to the Hybrid Technique Construction. Here the visual tracking module is coupled with the available inertial sensors including the accelerometer, gyroscope and gravitational sensors. Inertial sensors are capable of helping the overall tracking process by reducing the number of frames consumed by visual tracking based on the inertial data provided by the sensors, hence making tracking even more efficient.

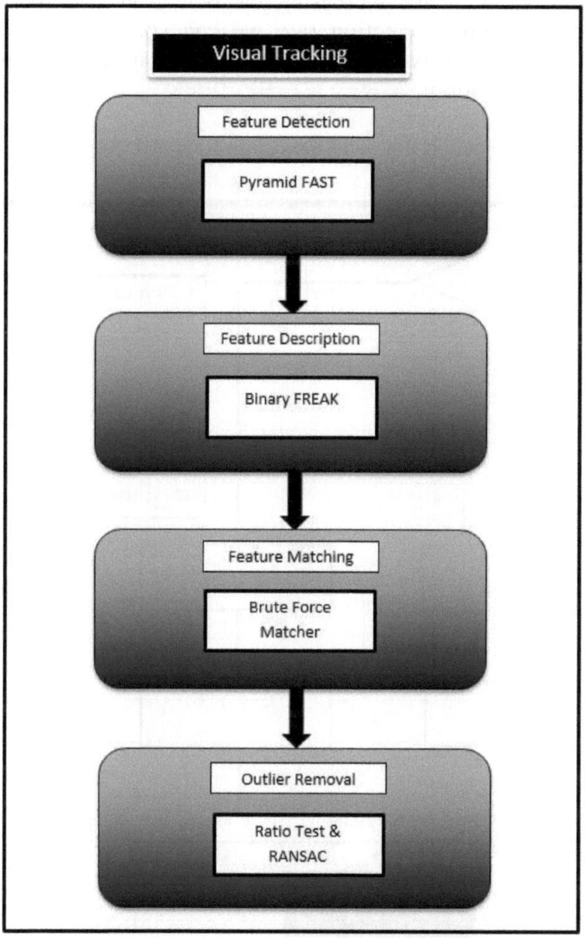

Fig. 3. Visual Tracking Module Structure

To address this, we propose a new hybrid technique which allows inertial sensors to speed up the overall tracking process (Fig. 4). We assume that there is a certain amount of translation and rotation due to the user's movement which can be known with the help of the inertial sensors. This data can then be set as the threshold value to reinitiate the visual tracking when required. Inertial tracking will continue its tracking process until it reaches a standard threshold value and frame count value, hence resting the visual tracking process and increasing the efficiency of the overall tracking process. We will conduct a user study in order to generate a standard threshold value in the near future to find out suitable values for different users performing different tasks. The above process allows visual tracking to less frequently take place during a given time by allowing inertial tracking to take over for the remaining time.

We can assume that if in a traditional setup visual tracking takes place 20 times per second, the new hybrid tracking technique will let visual tracking take place only a minimum of 3 times per second or gradually increase the number when it detects certain device movement, hence increasing the detection rate. We believe that by reducing the visual tracking detection rate we can speed up the total frame rate required for real-time interactive effect. Our assumption can be summarized in the form of the following equation:

Total Frame Rate = (VT Detection Rate + IT Detection Rate) + Pose Estimation + Rendering

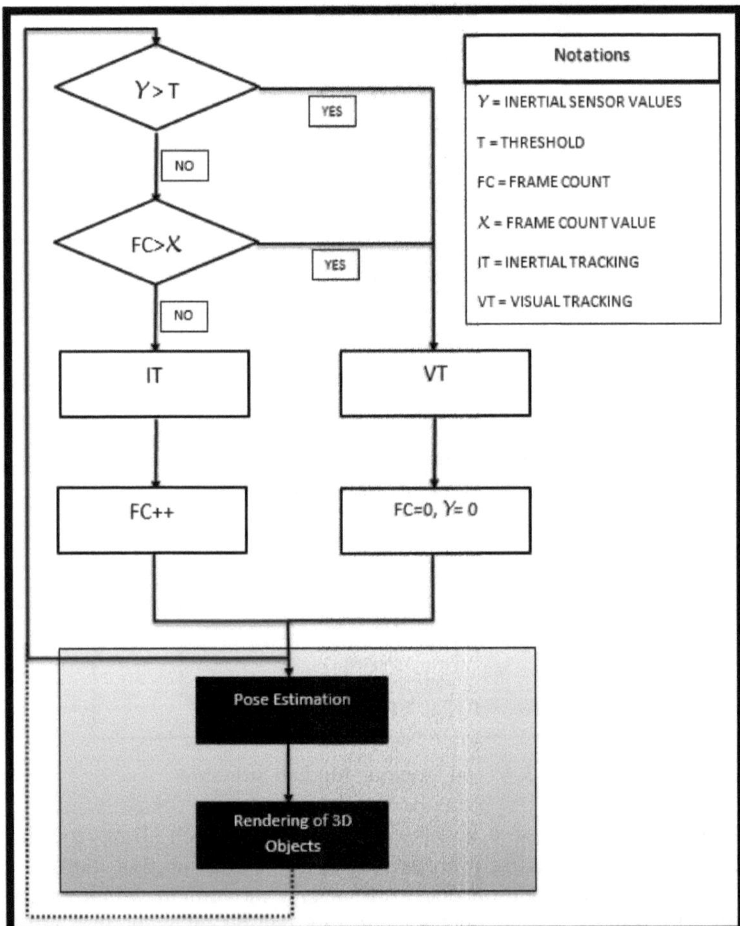

Fig. 4. Hybrid Tracking Technique Structure

This hybrid technique shows promising results for efficiency in mobile augmented reality tracking. It also helps the overall mobile augmented reality experience of users by lessening the load of tracking and allowing better pose estimation and rendering. In this work we have focused strictly onto the tracking processes and its detection rate. Although the processes of pose estimation and rendering are important for a complete AR experience but they are out of this papers scope and will be discussed in our upcoming works.

4 Implementation and Results

The last phase of this research involves implementation and validation of the hybrid technique. The hybrid technique is implemented in the form of a mobile AR application used in an indoor environment. It is then validated based on its efficiency i.e. time, speed and accuracy. We have used the PyramidFAST, FREAK, BF Matcher and RANSAC implementations from the latest 2.4.5 OpenCV implementations. SIFT and SURF algorithms are patented but can still be used from the non-free module of OpenCV's implementation for noncommercial and research purposes. In order to access the sensors of the phone we can make use of the standard SensorManager class provided by android development kit. The preliminary results of various visual tracking techniques implemented during the course of the development of the hybrid technique were very encouraging. FAST detector with multi scales performed at least 15 times faster than the normal SIFT DOG detector. Similarly FREAK outperformed all its competitors by clocking just 30ms for both extracting the descriptor and matching it without any errors. This assures us that we are capable of achieving better results in our future tests of the developed Hybrid tracking technique.

5 Conclusion

The foundation of this research contributes to the mobile Augmented Reality knowledge and tracking advancement. The main problem addressed by this research is the tracking problem in mobile handheld AR where the computational load is an issue. By heavily relying on state of the art approaches of FAST and FREAK features we expect to achieve higher frame rates and tilt values. Important advantages of using these descriptors are that they substantially reduce the search space and computation time required for finding correspondences between two scenes and focus the computation on areas that are more likely relevant for the matching process. In addition to that this work also shows how inertial sensors can provide accurate pose predictions and the computational load required for the vision processing can be reduced decreasing search windows or processing at lower frame rates. It is also capable of improving the radiological diagnostic services which can increase access for the people and lower the cost of healthcare. Once further tested, this hybrid technique will be used in a wide range of applications including medical, biological imaging and healthcare services.

References

1. Bai, H., Lee, G.: Interaction Methods for Mobile Augmented Reality. In: Proceedings of the 13th International Conference of the NZ Chapter of the ACM's Special Interest Group on Human-Computer Interaction (CHINZ 2012), p. 101 (2012)
2. Wagner, D., Schmalstieg, D.: ARToolKitPlus for Pose Tracking on Mobile Devices. In: Computer Vision Winter Workshop, pp. 1-8 (2007)
3. Wagner, D., Reitmayr, G., Mulloni, A., Drummond, T., Schmalstieg, D.: Pose tracking from natural features on mobile phones. In: Int. Symp. on Mixed and Augmented Reality, pp. 125–134 (2008)
4. Lowe, D.: Distinctive image features from scale-invariant keypoints. Int. Journal of Computer Vision 60(2), 91–110 (2004)
5. Rosten, E., Drummond, T.: Fusing Points and Lines for High Performance Tracking. In: Proceedings of the Tenth IEEE International Conference on Computer Vision, vol. 2 (2005)
6. Bay, H., Ess, A., Tuytelaars, T., Van Gool, L.: Speeded-up robust features. Computer Vision and Image Understanding 110(3), 346–359 (2008)
7. Calonder, M., Lepetit, V., Strecha, C., Fua, P.: BRIEF: Binary robust independent elementary features. In: Daniilidis, K., Maragos, P., Paragios, N. (eds.) ECCV 2010, Part IV. LNCS, vol. 6314, pp. 778–792. Springer, Heidelberg (2010)
8. Rublee, E., Rabaud, V., Konolige, K., Bradski, G.: Orb: an efficient alternative to sift or surf (2011)
9. Leutenegger, S., Chli, M., Siegwart, R.: Brisk: Binary robust invariant scalable keypoints (2011)
10. Alahi, A., Ortiz, R., Vandergheynst, P.: FREAK: Fast Retina Keypoint. In: IEEE Conference on Computer Vision and Pattern Recognition (2012)
11. Vallino, J.R.: Interactive Augmented Reality. Thesis Doctor of Philosophy, Department of Computer Science, University of Rochester (1998)
12. Sutherland, I.E.: The Ultimate Display. In: Proceedings of the IFIP Congress, New York, vol. 2, pp. 506–508 (1965)
13. Rosenblum, L., Julier, S.: Projects in VR, Making Augmented Reality Practical on Mobile Phones, Part 1, pp. 1–4 (2009)
14. Zheng, Ni, L.M.: Smart Phone and Next-Generation Mobile Computing. Morgan Kaufmann Publishers, San Francisco (2006)
15. Wagner, D., Schmalstieg, D.: History and Future of Tracking for Mobile Phone Augmented Reality. In: International Symposium on Ubiquitous Virtual Reality (ISUVR 2009), pp. 1–4 (2009)
16. Koch, D., Walther, D., Edgington, C.: Detection and tracking of objects in underwater video. In: Proceedings of the IEEE Computer Society Conference on Computer Vision and Pattern Recognition (2004)
17. Klein, G., Murray, D.W.: Parallel tracking and mapping for small AR workspaces. In: Proceedings of the International Symposium on Mixed and Augmented Reality, ISMAR (2007)
18. Klein, G., Murray, D.: Parallel tracking and mapping on a camera phone. In: International Symposium on Mixed and Augmented Reality (2009)
19. Skrypnyk, I., Lowe, D.: Scene modeling, recognition and tracking with invariant image features. In: Proc. of ISMAR 2004, pp. 110–119 (2004)
20. Davison, A.J., Mayol, W.W., Murray, D.W.: Real-time localization and mapping with wearable active vision. In: Proc. of ISMAR, pp. 18–27 (2003)

21. Klein, G., Drummond, T.: Robust visual tracking for noninstrumented augmented reality. In: Proc. of ISMAR, pp. 113–122 (2003)
22. Bleser, G., Stricker, D.: Advanced tracking through efficient image processing and visual-inertial sensor fusion. In: Proc. of IEEE VR, pp. 137–144 (2008)
23. Lepetit, V., Lagger, P., Fua, P.: Randomized trees for real-time keypoint recognition. In: Proc. CVPR, pp. 775–781 (2005)
24. Naimark, L., Foxlin, E.: Circular Data Matrix Fiducial System and Robust Image Processing for a Wearable Vision-Inertial Self-Tracker. In: Proceedings of the 1st International Symposium on Mixed and Augmented Reality (ISMAR), pp. 27–36. IEEE Computer Society, Washington, DC (2002)
25. Jiang, B., Neumann, U., Suya, Y.: A robust hybrid tracking system for outdoor augmented reality. In: Proceedings of Virtual Reality, pp. 3–275 (2004)
26. Hol, J.D., Schon, T.B., Gustafsson, F., Slycke, P.J.: Sensor Fusion for Augmented Reality. In: 9th International Conference on Information Fusion, pp. 1–6 (2006)
27. Reitmayr, G., Drummond, T.W.: Initialization for Visual Tracking in Urban Environments, pp. 161–172 (2007)
28. Seo, B.-K., Kim, K., Park, J.: A tracking framework for augmented reality tours on cultural heritage sites. In: 9th ACM SIGGRAPH Conf. on Virtual-Reality Continuum and its Applications in Industry, pp. 169–174 (2010)
29. Lee, G.A., Yang, U., Kim, Y., Jo, D., Kim, H., Kim, J.H., Choi, J.: Freeze-Set-Go Interaction Method for Handheld Mobile Augmented Reality Environments. In: VRST 2009 Proceedings of the 16th ACM Symposium on Virtual Reality Software and Technology, pp. 143–146 (2009)
30. Seichter, H., Schmalstieg, D.: Handheld augmented reality indoor navigation with activity-based instructions. In: 13th Int'l Conf. on Human-Computer Interaction with Mobile Devices and Services (2011)
31. Kurkovsky, S., Koshy, R., Novak, V., Szul, P.: Current issues in handheld augmented reality. In: International Conference on Communications and Information Technology (ICCIT), pp. 68–72 (2011)
32. Siltanen, S.: Theory and applications of marker-based augmented reality (2012)

MMUGait Database and Baseline Results

Hu Ng[1,*], Chiung Ching Ho[1], Wooi-Haw Tan[2], Hau-Lee Tong[1], Kok-Why Ng[1], Timothy Tzen-Vun Yap[1], Pei-Fen Chong[1], Lay-Kun Tan[3], Junaidi Abdullah[1], and Chikkannan Eswaran[1]

[1] Faculty of Computing and Informatics, Multimedia Univeristy, 63100 Cyberjaya, Malaysia

[2] Faculty of Engineering, Multimedia Univeristy, 63100 Cyberjaya, Malaysia

[3] Sekolah Menengah Seksyen 3 Bandar Kinrara, 47180 Puchong, Malaysia

{nghu,twhaw,hltong,ccho,kwng,timothy,pfchong, junaidi,eswaran}@mmu.edu.my

Abstract. This paper describes the acquisition setup and development of a new gait database, MMUGait DB. The database was captured in side and oblique views, where 82 subjects participated under normal walking conditions and 19 subjects walking under 11 covariate factors. The database includes 'sarong' and 'kain samping' as changes of apparel, which are the traditional costumes for ethnic Malays in South East Asia. Classification experiments were carried out on MMUGait DB and the baseline results are presented for validation purposes.

Keywords: gait database, gait biometrics, segmentation, classification.

1 Introduction

Biometrics is an approach to identify individuals through their physical and behavioral characteristics such as gait, fingerprint, face, iris and spoken speech. These characteristics are known as the biometric identifiers that are both distinctive and do not change over time for any individual. Gait is an emerging biometric that has gained public recognition and high acceptance as one the security assessment tools. This is mainly because gait does not require any intervention from the user or close contact with the capturing device. Besides that, it is still competent to recognize people from a distance even if other biometrics identifiers are intentionally obscured, for example: hand gloves to cover finger print and mask to cover face.

Since 1998, many gait datasets [1], [2], [3], [4] and [5] have been developed for performance evaluation of the gait recognition systems. While good gait datasets are available, we argue that all of them have neglected one important challenge: none of the male subjects are wearing long fabrics that cover the legs. Most of the currently available datasets contain male subjects that are predominantly wearing trousers.

* Corresponding author.

H. Badioze Zaman et al. (Eds.): IVIC 2013, LNCS 8237, pp. 458–469, 2013.

The closest comparison is the Soton dataset [1]; where there are two female subjects (out of 115 subjects) wearing long blouse and Indian traditional garment ('shalwar kameez'). Apart from the Soton dataset, the other comparable dataset is the OU-ISIR Treadmill Database B [2], which involves short skirt as a covariate factor for the participants. However, the short skirt is only partially covering the legs while the knees are still clearly visible. The main reason why subjects were previously not recorded wearing long fabrics is to avoid the legs from being occluded. This limitation is imposed as most model-based gait recognition systems [7], [8] and [9] require the labeling of the legs manually during the features extraction process. The occluded legs will cause the failure of generating the hip and knees trajectories correctly and hence result in a low Correct Classification Rate (CCR). However, our system does not detect each of the lower limbs. Therefore, it can handle occluded silhouette.

In reality males do wear long fabrics such as 'sarong' and 'kain samping' worn by the ethnic Malays in South East Asia, long 'dhoti' by ethnic Indians in Southern Asia and 'kilt' by the Scots in Europe. These reasons motivated the authors to build a gait dataset with subjects wearing long fabrics in the form of 'sarong' and 'kain samping'. A further motivation is to prove that our gait recognition system will still perform well even when the legs are non-detectable.

The rest of this paper is organized as follows. Section 2 reviews the existing gait databases. In Section 3, the MMUGait database setup and development is presented. In Section 4, the proposed gait recognition system is briefly explained. Section 5 discusses experimental setups and the corresponding results. Lastly, Section 6 concludes the paper.

2 Existing Gait Databases Reviews

The existing major gait databases are summarized in Table 1.

Table 1. Existing major gait databases

Database	Covariates Factors	Number of Subjects	Number of Walking Sequences
UCSD DB [3]	1 view with personal clothing	6	42
Soton Large DB [1]	2 views with personal clothing	115	2,163
Soton Small DB [1]	2 views with 15 covariate factors (apparel, bags & speed)	11	3,178
HumanID Gait Challenge DB [4]	2 views with 5 covariate factors (apparel, bags, surface & time)	122	1,870
CASIA Dataset A [5]	3 views with personal clothing	20	240
CASIA Dataset B [5]	11 views with 3 covariate factors (apparel & bag)	124	13,640
OU-ISIR Treadmill Dataset A [2]	1 view with 9 covariate factors (speed)	34	612
OU-ISIR Treadmill Dataset B [2]	1 view with 32 covariate factors (apparel & bag)	68	2,746

The University of California San Diego (UCSD) gait dataset [3] is the first gait dataset that was captured in 1998. However, it is limited to six subjects with 42 outdoor walking sequences. In 2002, University of Southampton released the Soton dataset [1] that comprises the Large DB with 115 subjects and the Small DB with 11 subjects involving 15 covariate factors. In 2001, CASIA dataset A [4] that was captured in 3 view angles (side-view, 45° and 90°) was available for public use. In 2005, the HumanID Gait Challenge [4] that comprises 122 subjects with 5 major covariate factors was made publicly available. In the same year, CASIA dataset B [4] that captures 11 different view angles and 3 covariate factors was disclosed. In 2012, Osaka University released databases that contain subjects walking on treadmills: OU-ISIR Treadmill Dataset A and B [5]. Treadmill Dataset A involves 34 subjects with nine different walking speeds. Treadmill Dataset B involves 64 subjects with 32 combinations of clothing variation. Although the OU-ISIR Treadmill Dataset A and B contains similar clothing variations as the MMUGait Database, Lee et al. [6] demonstrated that there are differences in optical flow between subjects walking on treadmill and solid ground.

MMUGait DB contains 82 subjects recorded under normal condition for reliable performance evaluation on the large population and 19 subjects recorded with 11 covariate factors to emphasis the evaluation of the exploratory factor analysis of gait recognition. It contains side-view and oblique-view videos, the extracted silhouette frames, subject still face images, and ancillary data like subject specific information, camera setups and floor measurements.

3 The MMUGait Database

MMUGait database (MMUGait DB) is part of the MMU GASPFA database [10]. It was captured and recorded in the Set and Background Studio located in the Faculty of Creative Multimedia, Multimedia University. The acquisition was done over a period of four days in December, 2011 and involved 82 subjects. Ethical approval was obtained from the subjects by signing an approval consent form prior to volunteering. The recording of MMUGait DB was done in an indoor environment with green backdrop and white solid surface. Details of the development of database are discusses in the following subsections.

3.1 Acquisition of the MMUGait DB

Two SONY HDR-XR160E full HD video camera recorders (camcorders) were used during the recording. The recorded videos are in MPEG Transport Stream (MTS) format with resolution of 1920 (Height) x 1080 (Width) pixels. The video stream was captured using progressive scan with a frame rate of 50 frames per seconds (fps). The camcorders captured the walking sequence from two different view angles, which were side-view (frontal parallel) and 60° oblique-view.

The subjects walked back-and-forth on a track continuously and captured in both directions. Both ends of the walking track were the turning point that subjects must turn around and repeat the walking sequence in another direction. Fig.1a and Fig.1b show the acquisition environment and the recording layout respectively.

82 subjects took part in the recording of the MMUGait DB. They were from different genders, nationalities and age groups. For the gender class, 15 subjects were female, while the remaining 67 were male. Fig.2a and Fig.2b show the distribution of nationalities and age groups respectively.

There are two categories of dataset collected in this phase. The first set (MMUGait Large DB) contains 82 subjects that walked for at least 20 sequences in both directions with personal clothing (own shoes and own cloth). On the other hand, the second set (MMUGait Covariate DB) contains 19 subjects that walked in both directions wearing different types of clothes, shoes and carrying bags, with varying walking speed. This set includes 11 covariant factors, which are 'sarong', 'kain samping', personal clothing, carrying hand bag, slung barrel bag over shoulder), carrying barrel bag, carrying rucksack, walking slowly, walking quickly, walking in flip flops and bare feet. In total, there were approximately 110 sequences per subject.

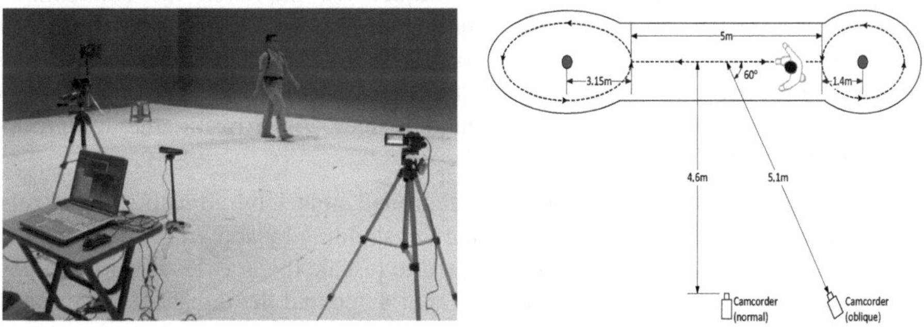

(a) (b)

Fig. 1. (a) The acquisition environment. (b) The recording layout.

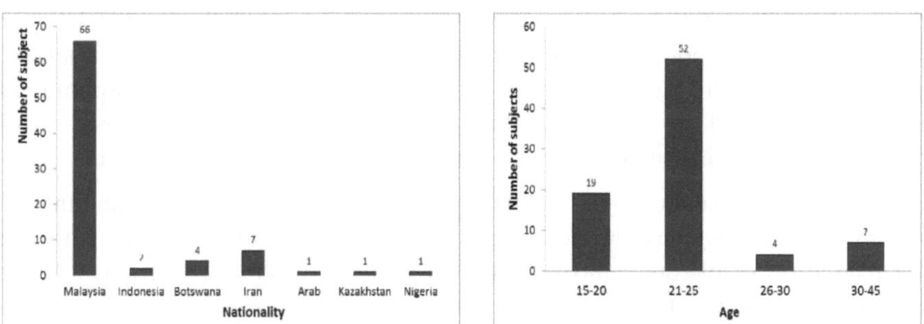

(a) (b)

Fig. 2. (a) Distribution of nationalities. (b) Distribution of age.

To the best of our knowledge, this is the first paper that introduces gait database with ethnic Malays' traditional costumes, which are common attire for ethnic Malays in South East Asia, especially during Friday prayers and religious festivals. In this case, we recorded subjects with 'kain samping' and 'sarong' as covariate factors as changes in apparel. We believe that it can act as a benchmark database for performance evaluation by other gait recognition systems.

3.2 Data Processing

The original video format filmed was in MPEG transport stream format (MTS) with 50 frames per second (FPS). For further processing, all the recorded videos were converted to Audio Video Interleave (AVI) format with resolution of 1920 (High)*1080(Width) pixels. After that, the videos were extracted into individual frames in Joint Photographic Experts Group (JPEG) format.

3.3 Silhouette Generation

The silhouette generation processes are described as follows:

Step 1: To extract human silhouette from each frame as the region of interest (ROI) by employing background subtraction technique. We improved the conventional background subtraction technique by summing up the gray level results from (a) background image subtracted by foreground image, and (b) foreground image subtracted by background image. This new technique is able to amplify the difference between the foreground and the background images. As a result, the foreground object is more distinct from the background.

Step 2: To increase the contrast of the foreground object by adjusting the pixels' intensity. The process is obtained via optimal thresholding by applying Otsu's method [11]. Once the threshold was found, it was used to rescale the gray level values to new values such that values between the lowest input value and the threshold were scaled to values between 0 and 1.

Step 3: Convert the rescaled foreground object image to binary image by using another threshold obtained from Otsu's method. In this case, if a pixel value was below the threshold, it was set to zero; otherwise it was set to one in the binary image.

Step 4: Apply the morphological operations with a 7x7 diamond shape structuring element are applied to enhance the generated foreground object. Morphological opening was applied to separate the shadow into isolated regions, while morphological closing is used to close the small gaps in the foreground object.

Step 5: To eliminate pseudo objects in the image, connected component labeling was applied to label all regions in the image. Subsequently, those regions with area smaller than 1500 pixels are removed. Fig.3 shows the resulting images at different stages of silhouette generation.

4 Gait Recognition System

We present a hybrid gait recognition system which combine model-free approach to extract subject's height, width, step-size and crotch height as the static features and model-based approach to extract joint angular trajectories as the dynamic features. The processes are discusses in the following subsections.

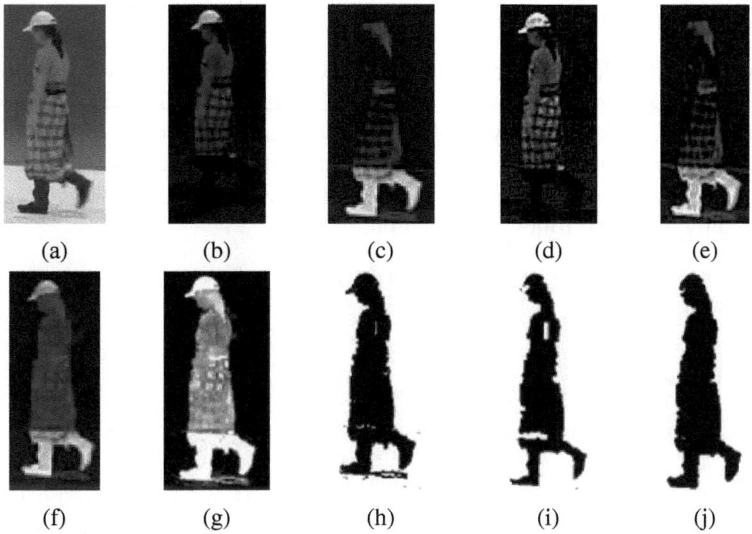

Fig. 3. (a) Foreground image. (b) Color image of foreground subtracts background. (c) Color image of background subtracts foreground. (d) Gray level image of b. (e) Gray level of c. (f) Addition of d and e. (g) Foreground object after intensity adjustment. (h) Binary image of foreground object. (i) Foreground object after morphological opening. (j) Extracted silhouette.

4.1 View-point Normalization

To normalize the oblique walking sequence into the side-view plane, the perspective correction technique is employed. First, all silhouettes in a walking sequence are superimposed into a single image, as shown in Fig.4a.

Next, line X and Y are drawn horizontally based on the highest and lowest point among the silhouettes. As the normal gait cycle is periodic, a sinusoidal line is formed when the highest points of all silhouettes in a walking sequence are connected. Line Z is then drawn by connecting the first peak and the last peak of the sinusoidal line.

The perspective correction technique consists of two stages: vertical and horizontal adjustments. For vertical adjustment, each silhouette is vertically stretched from line Z towards line X. In addition, each silhouette is also vertically stretched from the bottom towards line Y. Details of the normalization technique can be referred to [12]. Fig.4b shows superimposed silhouettes after perspective correction.

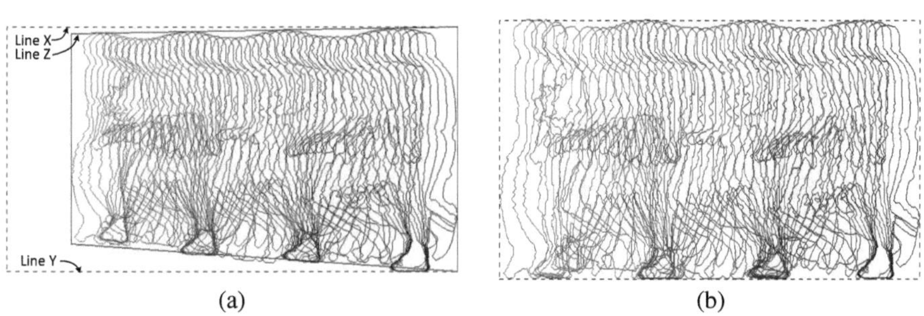

Fig. 4. (a) Superimposed silhouettes from one walking sequence. (b) Superimposed silhouettes after perspective correction.

4.2 Gait Feature Extraction

Referring to a priori knowledge of the body proportions [13], the vertical position of hip, knee and ankle are estimated as 0.48*H*, 0.285*H* and 0.039*H* with referring to the body height *H*. The lower body joints that define the pivot points in human gait are then identified and the joint trajectories are computed. Details of the gait feature extraction technique can be referred to [12]. The joint angular trajectory (θ) can be determined by using the following equation:

$$\phi_1 = \tan^{-1}\left(\frac{p2_x - p1_x}{p2_y - p1_y}\right) \tag{1}$$

$$\phi_2 = \tan^{-1}\left(\frac{p3_x - p1_x}{p3_y - p1_y}\right) \tag{2}$$

$$\theta = \phi_1 + \phi_2 \tag{3}$$

where $p1_x$, $p2_x$ and $p3_x$ are the x-coordinates of joint p1, p2 and p3, respectively, and $p1_y$, $p2_y$ and $p3_y$ are the y-coordinates of joint p1, p2 and p3, respectively. Fig.5a illustrates the joint angular trajectory is determined from two joints.

In our gait system, five joint angular trajectories have been extracted, as there are the five main joints on the limbs. These angular trajectories are hip angular trajectory (θ_1), front knee angular trajectory (θ_2), back knee angular trajectory (θ_3), front ankle angular trajectory (θ_4) and back ankle angular trajectory (θ_5).

The height and width of the human silhouette is measured. The Euclidean distance between the ankles is used to represent the subject's step-size (*S*). Then, the Euclidean distance between the ground and the subject's crotch is being calculated as crotch height (*CH*). If the crotch height is found lower than the height of knee, we will assume that it is equal to zero, as the crotch is considered occluded.

As the presence of outliers in the extracted features would hinder the classification process, Gaussian filter with sigma values (σ) equal to 2.5 is applied to remove them. In order to normalize the extracted features from various dimensions to be independent and standardized Linear scaling technique [14] has been applied to normalize each feature component to the range between 0 and 1. Fig.5b shows a sample of a human silhouette with the nine extracted gait features.

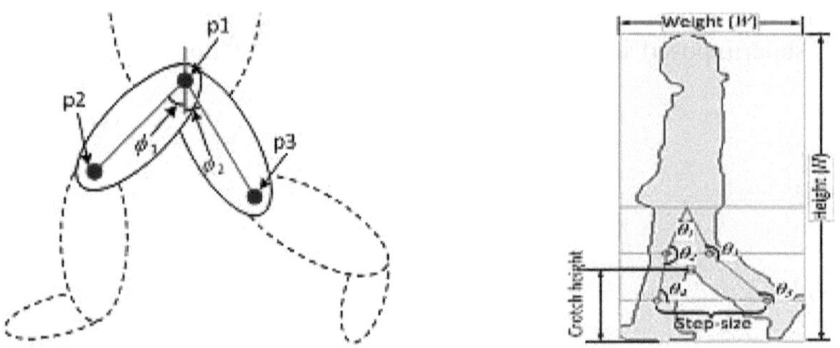

(a) (b)

Fig. 5. (a) Joint angular trajectory computation. (b) Nine extracted gait features.

4.3 Feature Vector and Features Selection

To construct the feature vector, maximum hip angular trajectory (θ_1^{max}) was determined during a walking sequence. When θ_1^{max} was identified, the corresponding S, W, H, θ_2, θ_3, θ_4, θ_5 and CH were also determined. To better describe the human gait, 24 features were used to construct the feature vector as shown:

$$F = \{\theta_1^{\max}, S, W, H, \theta_2, \theta_3, \theta_4, \theta_5, CH, A^W, A^H, A^{CH}, A^{\theta_1}, A^{\theta_2}, A^{\theta_3}, A^{\theta_4}, A^{\theta_5}, A^S, R^{AH}, R^{ACH}, R^{AS}, R^{CH}, R^H, R^S\}$$

where A^W, A^H, A^{CH}, $A^{\theta 1}$, $A^{\theta 2}$, $A^{\theta 3}$, $A^{\theta 4}$, $A^{\theta 5}$ and A^S are the average of the local maxima detected for width, height, crotch height, hip angular trajectory, front knee angular trajectory, back knee angular trajectory, front ankle angular trajectory, back ankle angular trajectory and step-size, respectively; R^{AH}, R^{ACH}, R^{AS}, R^{CH}, R^H and R^S are the ratio of A^H, A^{CH}, A^S, CH, H and S to W, respectively.

The performance of a recognition system is determined by the effectiveness of the selected features, which can maximize inter-class variance. In our work, Ranker [15] is used to rank features by their individual evaluations, which helps to identify those extracted features that contribute positively in the recognition process. Based on the scores obtained, all twenty four features have exhibited positive contribution. Thus, all of them are used in our system. Fig.6 shows examples of successful joint detection from self-occluded silhouettes and silhouettes with external occlusion.

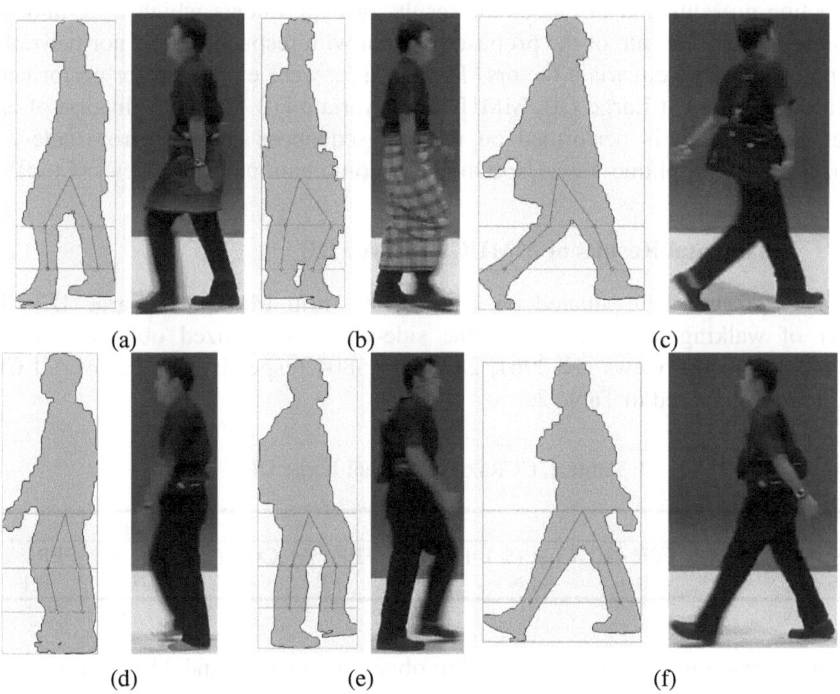

(a) (b) (c)

(d) (e) (f)

Fig. 6. Examples of joints detection on occluded human silhouettes. a) Wearing 'kain samping'. b) Wearing 'sarong'. c) Barrel bag slung over shoulder. d) Walking in bare feet. e) Carrying rucksack. f) Carrying barrel bag by hand.

4.4 Classification Technique

To study the performance of our approach in gait recognition system, multi-class Support Vector Machine (SVM) with Radial Basis Function (RBF) kernel was applied to evaluate the performance of the proposed gait recognition system. This is because RBF has proven to perform better than other SVM's kernels [16]. For this paper, the SVM technique was implemented by applying LIBSVM package [17]. The kernel's parameters such as *g* (gamma) and regularization parameter *C* were trained as to find the best correct classification rate. Three quality measures were used in the experiment: correct classification rate (CCR), true positive rate (TPR) and false positive rate (FPR).

Ten folds cross validation was employed for this work, where the walking sequences from the gait databases were randomly divided into ten disjoint subsets, nine subsets used for analysis training and one subset is used for validation. The cross-validation process was iterated for 10 turns with features vectors of each disjointed subset channeled into classifiers as the validation test. Then, the mean correct classification rate can be obtained by averaging the cross validation results.

5 Experimental Results and Discussion

This section presents and discusses the results of experiments which were aimed to assess the recognition rate of the proposed system with respect to view normalization, large population and covariate factors. Two datasets were employed for performance evaluation; MMUGait Large DB, MMUGait Covariate DB. In the evaluation of each dataset, the analysis is performed on walking sequences captured from side-view (Side), normalized oblique-view (NorOb) and a combination of both views (Com).

5.1 Experimental Results of MMUGait Large DB

The performance was evaluated on 80 subjects from MMUGait Large DB. The number of walking sequences from the side-view, normalized oblique-view and combination of both views are 2961, 2843 and 5804 respectively. The overall CCR results are summarized in Table 2.

Table 2. CCRs of MMUGait Large DB

Side			NorOb			Com		
CCR (%)	TPR (%)	FPR (%)	CCR (%)	TPR (%)	FPR (%)	CCR (%)	TPR (%)	FPR (%)
95.4	95.4	0.1	91.6	91.6	0.1	93.2	93.2	0.1

The gait recognition system managed to obtain high CCRs and TPRs (above 91%) in the large population recognition. The system achieved low FPRs (0.1%).

5.2 Experimental Results of MMUGait Covariate DB

The performance was evaluated on 19 subjects from MMUGait Covariate DB. The number of walking sequences from the side-view, normalized oblique-view and combination of both views are 3780, 3713 and 7493 respectively. The overall CCR results are summarized in Table 3.

Table 3. CCRs of MMUGait Covariate DB

Side			NorOb			Com		
CCR (%)	TPR (%)	FPR (%)	CCR (%)	TPR (%)	FPR (%)	CCR (%)	TPR (%)	FPR (%)
96.0	96.0	0.2	93.6	93.6	0.4	94.2	94.2	0.3

For group covariate factor analysis, the database categorized into five groups: Group 1 (G1) different speeds; Group 2 (G2) variety of footwear; Group 3 (G3) various objects carrying; Group 4 (G4) various type of clothes; Group 5 (G5) personal clothing without carrying any object. The overall CCR results for group and individual covariate factor are summarized in Tables 4 and 5 respectively.

Table 4. CCRs of group covariate factors for the MMUGait Covariate DB

	Side			NorOb			Com		
	CCR (%)	TPR (%)	FPR (%)	CCR (%)	TPR (%)	FPR %)	CCR (%)	TPR (%)	FPR (%)
G1 (speed)	95.9	95.9	0.2	94.2	94.2	0.3	95.1	95.1	0.3
G2 (shoes)	95.8	95.8	0.2	94.4	94.4	0.3	95.0	95.0	0.3
G3 (carrying)	97.7	97.7	0.1	95.0	95.0	0.3	95.7	95.7	0.2
G4 (apparel)	95.5	95.5	0.3	94.2	94.2	0.3	94.3	94.3	0.3
G5 (personal clothing)	96.6	96.6	0.2	94.2	94.2	0.3	95.2	95.2	0.3

Table 5. CCRs of individual covariate factor from MMUGait Covariate DB

	Side			NorOb			Com		
	CCR (%)	TPR (%)	FPR (%)	CCR (%)	TPR (%)	FPR (%)	CCR (%)	TPR (%)	FPR (%)
Wearing 'sarong'	95.1	95.1	0.3	93.7	93.7	0.3	93.7	93.7	0.4
Wearing 'kain samping'	97.1	97.1	0.2	96.4	96.4	0.2	96.3	96.3	0.2
Carrying handbag	98.2	98.2	0.1	95.5	95.5	0.3	96.1	96.1	0.2
Slung barrel bag	97.7	97.7	0.1	94.1	94.1	0.3	96.4	96.4	0.2
Carrying barrel bag	96.8	96.8	0.2	93.6	93.6	0.4	95.0	95.0	0.3
Carrying rucksack	98.1	98.1	0.1	96.0	96.0	0.2	96.4	96.4	0.2
Walking slowly	97.3	97.3	0.2	95.3	95.3	0.3	95.6	95.6	0.3
Walking quickly	95.3	95.3	0.3	93.7	93.7	0.3	94.4	94.4	0.3
Walking in flip flops	96.6	96.6	0.2	93.9	93.9	0.3	95.1	95.1	0.3
Walking with barefeet	95.2	95.2	0.3	94.9	94.9	0.3	95.2	95.2	0.3

In general, our gait recognition system managed to obtain high CCRs and TPRs (above 94%) in the experiments. The system achieved low FPRs, which are in the range of 0.1 % to 0.4%.

From Table 4, it can be observed that our system is robust to covariant factors as it has resulted in high CCRs. For that reason, we found that Group G1 generated high CCR as the duration of the walking cycle was not included as a feature. Similarly, the high CCRs generated from group G2, G3 and G4 shows that changes of shoe types, occlusion by bags or apparel did not affect the extracted feature.

From Table 5, it can be observed that our system managed to provide high CCRs even when the subjects were wearing long fabrics. Nevertheless, this factor has resulted in the lowest CCR as it was not possible to identify the crotch height due to the occlusion by the 'sarong'.

6 Conclusions

We managed to develop a new gait database that consists of 'sarong' and 'kain samping' as the changes of apparel. Our automated multi-view gait recognition system is able to extract gait features from silhouette effectively. It can detect the body joints even from self-occluded silhouettes or those occluded by apparel or bags. In addition, the high CCRs and TPRs, low FPRs also show that it is robust and can achieve good performance either in gait databases with various covariate factors or large population of subjects and multiple view angles.

The authors are planning to allow public access to the MMUGait DB in the near future. We believe that the walking sequences with special apparels will be invaluable for performance evaluation of other gait recognition systems.

Acknowledgments. The authors would like to thank all the anonymous participants, voluntarily helpers and the university in this research work. We would also like to thank the management of the university and all the helpers that make this dataset collection possible.

References

1. Shutler, J., Grant, M., Nixon, M.S., Carter, J.: On a Large Sequence-based Human Gait Database. In: Proc. of 4th International Conference on Recent Advances in Soft Computing, Nottingham, UK, pp. 66–71 (2002)
2. Makihara, Y., Mannami, H., Tsuji, A., Hossain, M.A., Sugiura, K., Mori, A., Yagi, Y.: The OU-ISIR Gait Database Comprising the Treadmill Dataset. IPSJ Trans. on Computer Vision and Applications 4, 53–62 (2012)
3. Little, J., Boyd, J.: Recognizing People by Their Gait: The Shape of Motion. Videre: Journal of Computer Vision Research 1(2), 1–32 (1998)
4. Sarkar, S., Phillips, P.J., Liu, Z., Vega, I.R., Grother, P., Bowyer, K.W.: The Humanid Gait Challenge Problem: Data Sets, Performance, and Analysis. IEEE Transactions on Pattern Analysis and Machine Intelligence 27(2), 162–177 (2005)

5. Yu, S., Tan, D., Tan, T.: A Framework for Evaluating the Effect of View Angle, Clothing and Carrying Condition on Gait Recognition. In: Proc. of International Conference on Pattern Recognition, vol. 4, pp. 441–444 (2006)
6. Lee, S.J., Hidler, J.: Biometrics of Overground Vs. Treadmill Walking in Healthy Individuals. Journal of Applied Physiology 104(3), 747–755 (2008)
7. Yam, C., Nixon, M.S., Carter, J.N.: Automated Person Recognition by Walking and Running via Model-Based Approaches. Pattern Recognition 37(5), 1057–1072 (2004)
8. Wagg, K., Nixon, M.S.: On Automated Model-Based Extraction and Analysis of Gait. In: Proc. of 6th IEEE International Conference on Automatic Face and Gesture Recognition, pp. 11–16 (2004)
9. Bouchrika, I., Nixon, M.S.: Model-based Features Extraction for Gait Analysis and Recognition. In: Proc. of Mirage: Computer and Vision/Computer Graphics Collaboration Techniques and Applications, pp. 150–160 (2007)
10. Ho, C.C., Ng, H., Tan, W.H., Ng, K.W., Tong, H.L., Yap, T.T.V., Chong, P.F., Eswaran, C., Junaidi, A.: MMU GASPFA: A COTS multimodal biometric database. Pattern Recognition Letters 34(15), 2043–2050 (2013)
11. Otsu, N.: A Threshold Selection Method from Gray-level Histograms. Automatica 11(285-296), 23–27 (1975)
12. Ng, H., Tan, W.H., Junaidi, A.: Multi-view Gait Based Human Identification System with Covariate Analysis. International Arab Journal of Information Technology 10(5), 519–526 (2013)
13. Dempster, W.T., Gaughran, G.R.L.: Properties of Body Segments Based on Size and Weight. American Journal of Anatomy 120, 33–54 (1967)
14. Aksoy, S., Haralick, R.: Feature Normalization and Likelihood-based Similarity Measures for Image Retrieval. Pattern Recognition Letters 22(5), 563–582 (2001)
15. Hall, M., Frank, E., Holmes, G., Pfahringer, B., Reutemann, P., Witten, I.: The WEKA Data Mining Software: An Update. ACM SIGKDD Explorations Newsletter 11(1), 10–18 (2009)
16. Byun, H., Lee, S.W.: A Survey on Pattern Recognition Applications of Support Vector Machines. International Journal of Pattern Recognition and Artificial Intelligence 17(03), 459–486 (2003)
17. Chang, C.C., Lin, C.J.: LIBSVM: A Library for Support Vector Machines (2001), Software available at `http://www.csie.ntu.edu.tw/~cjlin/libsvm`

Color-Spatial Person Re-identification by a Voting Matching Scheme

Mohammad Ali Saghafi[1], Aini Hussain[1], Halimah Badioze Zaman[2], and Mohamad Hanif Md. Saad[1]

[1] Smart Engineering System Research Group (SESRG), Faculty of Engineering and Built Environment
[2] Institute of Visual Informatics, University Kebangsaan Malaysia (UKM), 43600 Bangi, Selangor, Malaysia
{asaghafi,aini,hanif}@eng.ukm.my, hbz@ftsm.ukm.my

Abstract. This paper introduces a novel and fast method for person re-identification using features extracted from the appearance of individuals observed in non-overlapped fields of views in a network of surveillance cameras. The proposed method involves segmentation of silhouettes into meaningful regions, which is close to human visual categorization of colorful clothes, consequently obtaining better performance in various poses. The spatial features extracted from these areas that include color features contribute to the robustness of the method due to illumination changes. In addition, the use of the voting scheme reduces the computational complexity of the algorithm, thus yielding a fast algorithm.

Keywords: re-identification, appearance-based, spatial feature, illumination.

1 Introduction

Person re-identification is the process of detecting a person of interest in different scenes with disjoint fields of view [1]. Based on this definition and on a variety of applications, several scenarios can be designed and implemented to perform re-identification. Although the applications are diverse, the re-identification steps are almost the same. First, individuals in all frames must be detected and segmented from the background. Second, the features must be extracted from the segmented parts. Third, the exploited features of the probe and of the queries must be compared based on a criterion. The differences between methods are based on the way in which the frames are being segmented and also the features which are being used for comparison and the measures that are used for matching purposes.

Re-identification is essential especially in surveillance and in intelligent monitoring applications. The current characteristic of state-of-the-art surveillance systems is wide area coverage using a limited number of closed circuit TVs (CCTVs). Consequently, some areas will have no CCTV coverage. Depending on the size of the areas to be monitored, the number of discontinued views can reach hundreds, especially in airports or in shopping malls in which tracking an individual in specific

H. Badioze Zaman et al. (Eds.): IVIC 2013, LNCS 8237, pp. 470–482, 2013.

scenes can be difficult, if not impossible. As such, re-identification techniques seem crucial as a complementary option for these systems. However, the issues and the solutions depend on the environment being monitored, on the cameras being used, and on the areas where the cameras are installed. In most cases, real-time re-identification is ideal but the re-identification process is more challenging. To date, some proposed methods in the literature do not involve real-time re-identification and their applications are limited [2].

The methods proposed in the literature have not completely covered re-identification issues. Most systems designed for re-identification work are under pre-defined and specific conditions in which some assumptions are made to simplify the problem [3] and [4]. Various problems are common in almost all re-identification scenarios. Background elimination is one of the most challenging processes in re-identification work, requiring the analysis of video frames or images from different locations. In addition, moving clutters can cause a serious problem in the task of background elimination. Sometimes a frame can consist of more than one individual necessary to be detected and to be analyzed. In [5], the researchers considered the crowd of individuals in their scenarios for re-identification, while the study by [6] dealt with different poses and gestures of different people in different frames. The lighting conditions, as well, differ in different cameras though they may belong to the same manufacturer. Some cameras, for example, are installed indoors, while others are installed outdoors so the illumination of the frames in both locations varies. Most methods use color and texture as features for re-identification [1], [7] and [8] so changes in illumination in the images or in the frames cause the difficulty in exploiting stable and reliable color and texture features. Low quality and standard resolution of CCTVs also decreases the performance of appearance-based methods.

Therefore, we propose a novel method in this paper in which the extracted color and the spatial features are compared based on a voting scheme. Instead of simultaneously comparing all extracted features of the probe image and of the queries, comparison is done in consecutive steps. This method helps the system to quickly ignore unrelated queries without any computational complexity. Color features are used along with spatial features to make the feature vector more robust against illumination changes and pose variations. This paper has been outlined as following sections. Section 2 provides a brief review of related methods in person re-identification. Section 3 describes the proposed method. Section 4 presents the results. Lastly, Section 5 concludes the study.

2 Related Works

Two general categories of features can be utilized in re-identification, namely, the features extracted from the gait and the gesture of individuals [6] and the features that use appearance properties such as color and texture of individuals [7] and [8]. Models of re-identification methods are often based on one of the mentioned categories, while some methods are based on both [3]. In this paper, we used specific appearance-based features to construct our feature vectors. Hence, our review in this section is focused and is limited to appearance-based methods. As indicated above, the first step in the re-identification process is background/foreground segmentation. Mixture models are widely used for segmentation purposes [9], while a few studies adopt generative models such as STEL [10]. In the present research, we have used the latter. The histogram of oriented gradients (HoG) as a person detector, with the support vector machine (SVM) as classifier, has been applied by Bak et al. [11] as the person detector. The gradient information has also been used in the research by Hirzer et al. [10] to construct their descriptors.

In appearance-based methods, colors play salient roles in feature extraction. Thus, HSV or LAB color spaces are preferred because of their robustness in overcoming illumination changes. Color histograms are commonly used [7] and [8] for feature extraction. To extract more robust color features, MPEG7 color and texture descriptors had been employed by [4] and covariance descriptors by [11]. SIFT [13] and SURF [14] descriptors and their interest points had also been considered to compose feature vectors. For re-identification purposes, experiments had been conducted using graph-based [15] and probabilistic [2] models.

In addition to color features, spatial details had been helpful for the inclusion of features that are invariant against scale and pose variations. Some descriptors, such as covariance regions used by Bak et al. [11] and some MPEG7 descriptors, have spatial information inside. While histograms do not possess spatial information, spatiograms [16] can present spatial contents. The segmentation method for body parts or for the torso from the legs [1] has been used to exploit spatial information. Dividing the body to several patches and extracting their features [8] is another way of exploiting spatial data of the frames.

Some frameworks proposed in the literature attempted to formulate the re-identification process. For example, Presti et al. [17] presented a probabilistic framework to determine the match between a set of identities and observations. The probability density function was formulated as an exponential distribution of the Euclidean distance of descriptors. Satta et al. [8] proposed the multiple component matching (MCM) framework in which a set of templates $\{\boldsymbol{\tau}\}$ are defined for individuals and each τ_i corresponds to the M parts that can be the features extracted from the M patches of the bodies of individuals. In another research [18], the authors proposed the multiple component dissimilarity (MCD) framework as an alternative representing an individual by the vector of dissimilarity values.

Euclidean and Bhattacharyya distances [19] are two common measures for similarity measurements in re-identification. Bak et al. [11] implemented the pyramid matching scheme to match feature vectors. KD-tree [20] and nearest neighbor distance ratio [13] that include distance metric learning methods and discriminative models [2] and [12] are other tools that have been applied for similarity matching.

3 Overview of the Approach

In this paper, we adopt the MCM framework [8] as a general guideline. The color extraction method and the spatial features of frames are described in the succeeding sub-sections. Similarity of the extracted features was measured using the Bhattacharyya distance measure. In the MCM framework, we have the following vector of $\boldsymbol{N}$ templates:

$$\mathbf{T} = \{\mathbf{T}\mathit{1},\ldots,\mathbf{T}\mathit{N}\} \quad (1)$$

where N is the number of frames or images of individuals in the gallery set in which their similarities are compared with the probe frame. Each template $\mathbf{T}i$ corresponds to an individual. In this framework, each template consists of M parts considered in the expression below:

$$T_i = \{T_{i,1}, \ldots, T_{i,M}\} \quad (2)$$

This subdivision allows algorithms to compare only the corresponding areas in different frames or images. To decrease the computational cost and to rapidly implement the algorithm, we use the upper body information of the silhouettes and set M =1. After silhouette segmentation, the main parts comprise a set of the following N components:

$$T_{i,j} = \{f_{i,j}^1, \ldots, f_{i,j}^N\},\ f_{i,j}^k \in \mathbb{X} \quad (3)$$

Where, $\mathbb{X}$ denotes the feature vector space. Satta et al [8] defined N components as randomly selected patches and subsequently extracted feature vectors. However, contrary to Satta et al., we select the components more wisely by clustering the main parts to major colors using K-means which will be described later. Based on MCM framework, the last step of re-identification is to compare the components of gallery set image to their corresponding parts in the probe image.

3.1 Background Elimination and Segmentation

All experiments in this research were initially carried out using the video frames obtained in the SESRG laboratory for the SESRG dataset. We then used the standard data VIPeR dataset [21] for our experiments, and then the results of the experiments were compared.

In [1], the features were extracted from multiple video frames or images that were obtained from the person of interest (multi-shot) while in [8], a single frame or image was used (single-shot). In the present study, our method is categorized as a single-shot method because we only used one frame or image of each individual to extract features. We used ViBe [22] for the foreground/background segmentation of our own video dataset and STEL [10] for the VIPeR dataset. In the STEL model, we set S = 2 and C = 2. In our scenario, one frame of the probe person was compared with those of other individuals. The frames were acquired from two cameras with different parameters and lighting conditions. After background elimination, we used asymmetry axes previously proposed by Farenzena et al. [1] to compose the main parts of the silhouettes. The head, the torso, and the legs were segmented, but we only used the torsos of the individuals for comparison, while other parts such as the legs were discarded. This procedure may decrease the accuracy rate in some cases but in our experiments, this ignorance only had a minor effect. To avoid additional computations, the comparison of the legs was disregarded. To segment the body into main parts, we used HSV color spaces because of the robustness of the technique against illumination variations. Samples of the separated main parts of the silhouette are shown in Fig.1.

Fig. 1. Separation of the silhouette into main parts

3.2 Composing the Set of Components

After obtaining the segmented images with the separated main parts of the silhouettes, we composed the set of components from the main parts. Satta et al. [8] randomly selected patches in each part as components. In contrast, we selected the components more wisely by examining the clothes of individuals and explaining only their major colors. At first glance, visual perception is limited only to main colors and not on other specific details. We therefore designed our algorithm to select the components of the main parts based on this fact. We used the well-known K-means clustering algorithm to segment the main parts into their major colors and to consider them as components. Before clustering by the K-means algorithm to reduce the impact of illumination changes, we quantized the parts into 10 major colors based on hue channel values of the pixels (of the HSV color space). The values of the pixels were then substituted by the mean value of their respective quantized level. Afterwards, each part was divided into three or four colors (based on our experiments, these numbers were more efficient) using the K-means method. A simple measure was adopted [23] by defining the ratio of inter and intra-cluster distances to determine the number of clusters for the main parts. Moreover, for local minima avoidance, we first indicated primary centers for clusters, and then, based on the Lloyd algorithm [24], the cluster pixels and centers were updated. To cluster the colors, we used LAB color space because it separates the luminance channel from the pixel values. In this step, clustering the major colors of clothing, which are invariant from illumination changes, is highly important. Fig.2 shows the results of the extraction of the main components of the torsos. The clustered colors in the figure denote the RGB color space, while the K-means is denoted by the LAB channel values.

The selection of components in this manner increases the robustness of the method against varying poses of individuals in different frames because, in most cases, major colors of clothes can be viewed from different camera angles. Another advantage of this clustering method is that external accessories of individuals (e.g., bags or suitcases) are not only unwanted but can dominate a specific main component to themselves and play a distinctive role in re-identifying the individual bearing them. As shown in Fig.2 (a), the backpack or even carried objects and colorful patterns on shirts (b) are being clustered as separated components, helping in the discrimination of individuals.

a)

b)

Fig. 2. The component sets are combined of major colors of the torso a)VIPeR dataset b) our video gallery

3.3 Color and Spatial Feature Representation

Both color and spatial features are used in this study. We have segmented the main parts (torso and legs) and identified components that are depicted as major color clusters in Fig.2. We used the normalized HSV color histograms of clusters with (16, 8, 8) quantization levels, resulting in three or four histograms. The number of histograms depends on the number of clusters for each main part. In this case, we only have the segmented torsos. The spatial features in our research are exploited using spatial chromatic histograms (SCH) [25]. Before explaining the utilization of this feature, we describe the construction elements of SCH. The SCH descriptor is a combination of three elements $(\boldsymbol{h}_k, \boldsymbol{b}_k, \boldsymbol{\sigma}_k)$, namely, pixel ratio, relative center, and standard deviation of pixels in respective regions with the same colors. As defined in the previous section, the components were set of $\boldsymbol{f}_{i,j}^{k}$ feature vectors. Here, we indicate component spatial regions by $\boldsymbol{F}$ to preserve the symbolic compatibility with their feature vector. Hence, $\boldsymbol{F}^k = \{(\boldsymbol{x}, \boldsymbol{y}) \in \boldsymbol{k}\}$ denotes the pixels that belong to component $\boldsymbol{k}$. If the number of pixels in all components (i.e., the height and the width of the whole torso) is $\boldsymbol{n}\times\boldsymbol{m}$, the descriptor is defined as follows:

$$\boldsymbol{h}_{\boldsymbol{k}} = \frac{|F^k|}{n\times m} \tag{4}$$

Where, $|\boldsymbol{F}^{\boldsymbol{k}}|$ denotes the number of pixels in the $\boldsymbol{k}^{th}$ component. The relative center is defined based on relative coordinates $\boldsymbol{b}_{\boldsymbol{k}} := (\bar{x}_k, \bar{y}_k)$ of the region's pixels expressed as the following:

$$\bar{x}_k = \frac{1}{n}\frac{1}{|F^k|}\sum_{(x,y)\in F^k} x \tag{5}$$

$$\bar{y}_k = \frac{1}{m}\frac{1}{|F^k|}\sum_{(x,y)\in F^k} y \tag{6}$$

Finally the standard deviation for the pixels inside the components is expressed as:

$$\sigma_k = \sqrt{\frac{1}{|F^k|}\sum_{P\in F^k} d(P, b_k)^2} \tag{7}$$

Where, $\boldsymbol{P}$ denotes the relative coordinates of a generic point and $\boldsymbol{d}(\boldsymbol{P}, \boldsymbol{b}_{\boldsymbol{k}})$ is the Euclidean distance between the pixel and the relative center of component $\boldsymbol{k}$.

With the help of the SCH descriptor, we obtain the spatial details of the components along with their color data. As shown in the formulas, the parameters are normalized, consequently achieving invariance of the spatial information through different scales of silhouettes in different frames. The information is also partially robust against varying poses of individuals. After segmentation of the torso as the main part of each silhouette and with three or four clusters of major colors inside each part, we construct the components and the vector of color and of spatial features ($\boldsymbol{f}_{i,j}^{\boldsymbol{k}}$) for each component. The components and their color-spatial features are selected to achieve robustness in illumination changes, varying poses, and in scale variations. In the next section, the procedure for similarity matching is explained.

3.4 Similarity Matching

In this section, we describe the algorithm employed to compare color and spatial features for the identification of the best match in the gallery set with the probe image. As mentioned previously, one of the significant indices in evaluating re-identification algorithms is their rapid implementation. The speed of the algorithms is important because a practical re-identification system must be capable of functioning in real-time. To determine the best match with the probe image, we initially use the Bhattacharyya distance measure to extract the distance between the components of the probe image and those of other images in the gallery set. If ***H1*** and ***H2*** are the histograms of two components, their Bhattacharyya distances are defined as

$$d(H_1, H_2) = \sqrt{1 - \frac{1}{\bar{H}_1 \bar{H}_2 N^2} \sum_{i=1}^{N} H_1(i).H_2(i)} \tag{8}$$

Where, N is the total number of histogram bins and $\bar{H}$ is the average of all histogram bins. Each component of the probe image is compared separately with the gallery image components. The number of images that have the shortest distance to the probe components is sorted. If all components that are close to the probe are assigned to one query that query will be selected as the first match without any further processing, while the algorithm searches for succeeding matches. However, if the closest components belong to different images, which is usually the case, the algorithm determines if the first match of each component exists in the first three matches (this number is found experimentally) of other components. Images, with at least one of their components being close to one of the probe image components and the others in the first three matches of other probe components, are indicated.

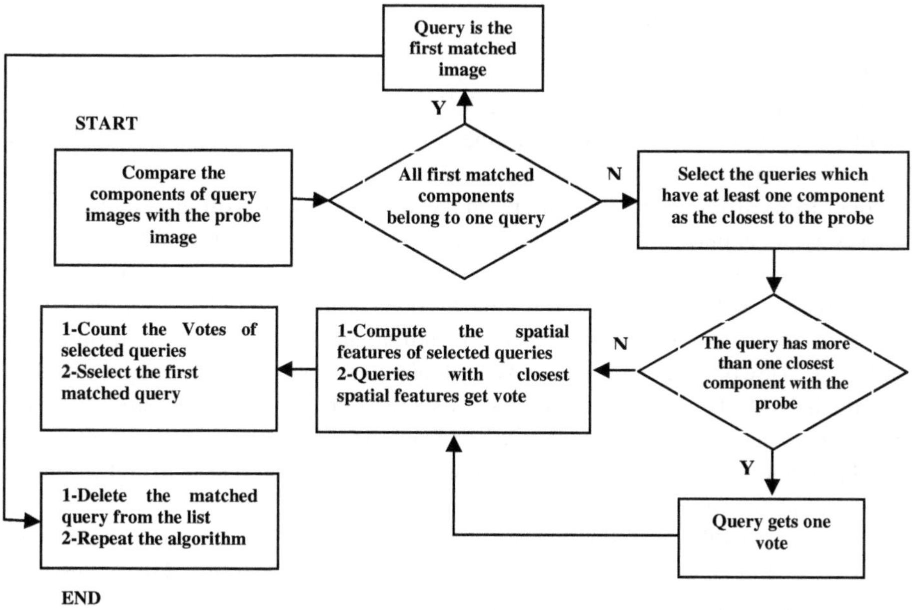

Fig. 3. Similarity matching procedure

After this step, the spatial information is processed and by implementing a voting scheme, the algorithm indicates matching ranks of the gallery images. Each image with more than one of its components achieving the first rank will obtain one vote. Subsequently, the pixel ratio, relative centers, and the standard deviation of probe components are compared with selected queries using the Euclidean distance. The closest component to the probe image is sorted and the closest distance obtains votes. By using this strategy, comparison of all spatial features of the images is unnecessary, consequently reducing the computational complexity of the algorithm. Finally, the query that has the most votes will be selected as the matched image and then, the algorithm will be repeated for the rest. Fig.3 shows the flowchart of the voting scheme for similarity matching.

4 Experimental Results

The performance of our system is compared with SDALF [1] and with that proposed by Satta et al. [8] using the VIPeR dataset [21]. We also applied the algorithm in our data recorded in the SESRG laboratories [26]. The dataset information used is detailed in the next section.

4.1 Dataset Description

For the experiments, two different datasets were used, namely, our own dataset from the SESRG data collection [26] and the VIPeR dataset [21]. We use a subset of the SESRG dataset comprises100 video frames of 50 individuals recorded in the SESRG laboratory using two cameras (one inside the laboratory and another along the corridor) from different manufacturers and with varied illumination conditions. The cameras were intentionally not calibrated prior to the recording of the videos to determine the robustness of our proposed method against camera parameters. After segmenting the video frames from the background using ViBe [22], we selected two frames of each individual and those of individuals under different illumination conditions, viewpoints, and poses. We obtained a total of 100 images of these individuals, with the images of one camera set as probe and those of another camera as the gallery set. The images were selected from video sequence with maximum pose and illumination variations. The images are first segmented and then fed to our re-identification system.

Meanwhile, another dataset that we chose to validate our algorithm with is the VIPeR dataset [21], comprising two viewpoints of 632 pedestrians. The inclusion of the VIPeR dataset in the evaluation of the algorithms is intended to obtain fair comparison with other two methods [1] and [8]. Besides, this dataset presents a potential challenge with its different poses of individuals and with its diverse illumination conditions at low resolution. Based on these characteristics, the VIPeR dataset can validate algorithm capabilities better compared with other available datasets. All algorithms are realized using Matlab® R2010a and ran on PC with 2.4 GHz processor.

4.2 Results and Comparison

The results are depicted as Cumulative Matching Curve (CMC) that demonstrates the percent of finding the correct match (true positives) within the first *n* ranks. To achieve comparable results, the dataset is split into two groups of 316 pedestrians and the image groups are selected as it is done in the two abovementioned research. The results show that our system slightly outperforms those obtained in SDALF [1] and those by Satta [8] in majority of the ranks. The CMC is also depicted for the video sequences recorded in our labs which can be seen in Fig.4 and Fig.5 below.

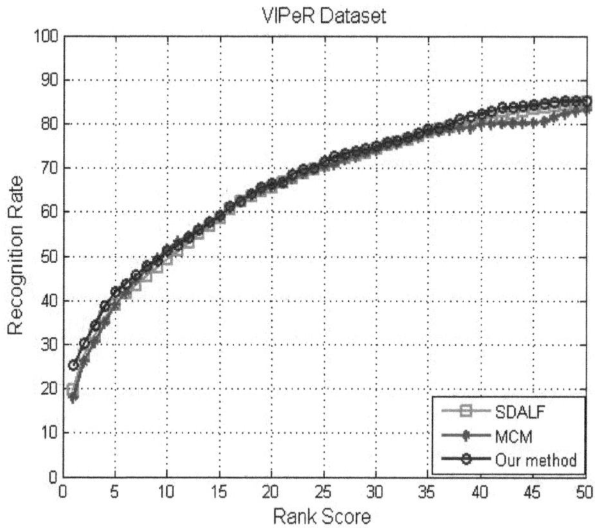

Fig. 4. Comparison of our method with SDALF [4] and MCM [5]

The recognition rate on the first 10 ranks of our video sequence images is as shown in Fig.5. As presented in the figure, the first correct matches (Rank 1) are recognized by the system that is about 30%.

The steep curve in the lower ranks is also considerable and shows the ability of the system to find the correct match in the first lower ranks. The better performance of the algorithm on our own dataset in comparison to VIPeR dataset is related to better resolution of our video frames but the pose and light conditions in our dataset is more challenging than in VIPeR dataset in most of the samples. This means the algorithm is considerably robust against illumination and pose variations.

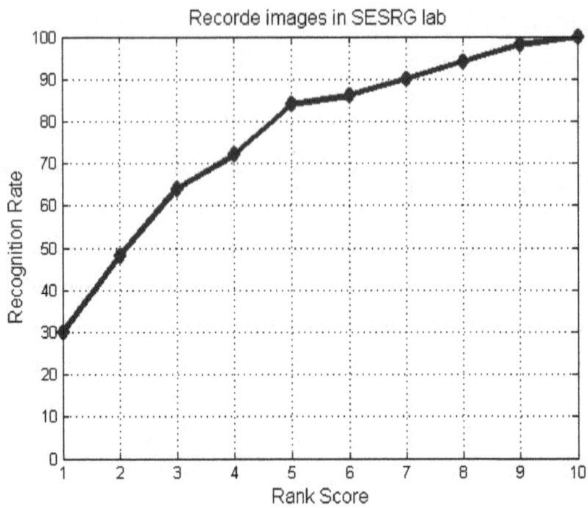

Fig. 5. Performance of proposed method on images of recorded videos in SESRG labs

5 Conclusion

In this paper, we proposed and implemented the HSV color histograms of extracted components along with SCH [25] descriptor. The method is based on MCM [8] framework but has a distinct manner of selecting components and features. The voting scheme that we used in this study helps to decrease the computational complexity of the algorithm. The similarity of the selection of components to human visual perception made the method more robust against illumination and pose variation. In addition, by using this type of component clustering the accessories that are carried by individuals contribute to the re-identification because they can be considered as separated clusters. The results show our method performs better than the two state-of-the-art researches exactly in the 1st rank score which has a significant importance in re-identification systems.

Acknowledgments. This work is supported by Malaysian government via grant LRGS/TD/2011/UKM/ICT/04/02 and DPP-2013-003.

References

1. Farenzena, M., Bazzani, L., Perina, A., Murino, V., Cristani, M.: Person re-identification by Symmetry-Driven Accumulation of Local Features. In: International Conference on Computer Vision and Pattern Recognition, CVPR, USA, pp. 2360–2367 (2010)
2. Zheng, W.-S., Gong, S., Xiang, T.: Person re-identification by probabilistic relative distance comparison. In: IEEE Conf. on CVPR, USA, pp. 649–656 (2011)
3. Gheissari, N., Sebastian, T.B., Tu, P.H., Rittscher, J., Hartley, R.: Person re-identification using spatiotemporal appearance. In: International Conference on Computer Vision and Pattern Recognition, CVPR, USA, pp. 1528–1535 (2006)

4. Bak, S., Corvee, E., Brémond, F., Thonnat, M.: Person Re-identification Using Haar-based and DCD-based Signature. In: 7th IEEE International Conference on Advanced Video and Signal Based Surveillance, USA, pp. 1–8 (2010)
5. Mazzon, R., Tahir, S.F., Cavallaro, A.: Person Re-Identification in Crowd. Pattern Recognition Letters 33(14), 1828–1837 (2012)
6. Skog, D.: Gait-based Re-identification of People in Urban Surveillance Video, Master thesis, Uppsala University, Department of Information Technology (2010)
7. Khan, A., Zhang, J., Wang, Y.: Appearance-Based Re-identification of People in Video. In: International Conference on Digital Image Computing: Techniques and Applications, DICTA 2010, Australia, pp. 357–362 (2010)
8. Satta, R., Fumera, G., Roli, F., Cristani, M., Murino, V.: A Multiple Component Matching Framework for Person Re-Identification. In: 16th Int. Conf. on Image Analysis and Processing, ICIAP, Italy, pp. 140–149 (2011)
9. Huang, C.H., Wu, Y.T., Shih, M.Y.: Unsupervised Pedestrian Re-identification for Loitering Detection. In: 3rd Pacific Rim Symposium on Advances in Image and Video Technology (2009)
10. Jojic, N., Perina, A., Cristani, M., Murino, V., Frey, B.: Stel component analysis: Modeling spatial correlations in image class structure. In: International Conference on Computer Vision and Pattern Recognition, CVPR, USA, pp. 2044–2051 (2009)
11. Bak, S., Corvee, E., Brémond, F., Thonnat, M.: Person Re-identification Using Spatial Covariance Regions of Human Body Parts. In: 7th IEEE International Conference on Advanced Video and Signal Based Surveillance, USA, pp. 435–440 (2010)
12. Hirzer, M., Beleznai, C., Roth, P.M., Bischof, H.: Person Re-Identification by Descriptive and Discriminative Classification. In: Heyden, A., Kahl, F. (eds.) SCIA 2011. LNCS, vol. 6688, pp. 91–102. Springer, Heidelberg (2011)
13. Schügerl, P., Sorschag, R., Bailer, W., Thallinger, G.: Object Re-detection Using SIFT and MPEG-7. In: Sebe, N., Liu, Y., Zhuang, Y.-T., Huang, T.S. (eds.) MCAM 2007. LNCS, vol. 4577, pp. 305–314. Springer, Heidelberg (2007)
14. De Oliveira, I.O., De Souza Pio, J.L.: People Re-identification in a camera network. In: 8th IEEE International Conference on Dependable, Autonomic and Secure Computing, DASC 2009, China, pp. 461–466 (2009)
15. Cong, D.-N.T., Khoudour, L., Achard, C., Phothisane, P.: People Re-identification by Means of a Camera Network Using a Graph-based Approach. In: IAPR Conference on Machine Vision Applications, MVA 2009, Japan, pp. 152–155 (2009)
16. Stanley, T., Rangarajan, S.: Spatiograms versus Histograms for Region-Based Tracking. In: IEEE Computer Society Conference on Computer Vision and Pattern Recognition, CVPR 2005, USA, vol. 2, pp. 1158–1163 (2005)
17. Lo Presti, L., Morana, M., La Cascia, M.: A Data Association Algorithm for People Re-Identification in Photo Sequences. In: IEEE International Symposium on Multimedia, Taiwan, pp. 318–323 (2010)
18. Satta, R., Fumera, G., Roli, F.: Fast person re-identification based on dissimilarity representations. Pattern Recognition Letters 33(14), 1838–1848 (2012)
19. Bhattacharyya, A.: On a measure of divergence between two statistical populations defined by their probability distribution. Bulletin of the Calcutta Mathematical Society 35, 99–110 (1943)
20. Hamdoun, O., Moutarde, F., Stanciulescu, B., Steux, B.: Person re-identification in multi-camera system by signature based on interest point descriptors collected on short video sequences. In: IEEE Conference on Distributed Smart Cameras, USA, pp. 1–6 (2008)

21. Gray, D., Brennan, S., Tao, H.: Evaluating appearance models for recognition, reacquisition and tracking. In: PETS (2007)
22. Barnich, O., Van Droogenbroeck, M.: ViBe: A universal background subtraction algorithm for video sequences. IEEE Transactions on Image Processing 20(6), 1709–1724 (2011)
23. Ray, S., Turi, R.H.: Determination of number of clusters in K-Means clustering and application in color Image Segmentation. Journal of Intelligent & Fuzzy Systems: Applications in Engineering and Technology 17(3), 297–311 (2006)
24. Gersho, A., Gray, R.M.: Vector quantisation and signal compression. Kluwer Academic Publishers (1992)
25. Cinque, L., Ciocca, G., Levialdi, S., Pellicano, A., Schettini, R.: Color-based image retrieval using spatial-chromatic histogram. Image and Vision Computing 19(13), 979–986 (2001)
26. Saad, M.H.M., Hussain, A., Kong, W., Tahir, N.M., Abdul Rahman, F.Y.: SESRG-InViSS: Image and Video Data Set for Human Pose, Action, Activity and Behavior Detection. In: International Conference on Systems Engineering and Technology, ICSET 2013 (2013)

Designing a Checklist for an E-Commerce Website Using Kansei Engineering

Kim Nee Goh[1], Yoke Yie Chen[1], Stephanie Cristal Daud[1], Ashok Sivaji[2], and Shi Tzuaan Soo[2]

[1] Computer and Information Sciences Department
Universiti Teknologi PETRONAS
Bandar Seri Iskandar, Tronoh,
31750, Perak, Malaysia
[2] Product Quality and Reliability Engineering
MIMOS Berhad,
Technology Park Malaysia,
57000, Kuala Lumpur, Malaysia
{gohkimnee,chenyokeyie}@petronas.com.my

Abstract. Usability has played a big role in refining the design of a website. Effective design of e-commerce web interfaces potentially increases perceived trust of its consumers. It is thus critical that e-commerce designers understand usability issues pertaining to e-commerce. However, usability looks only at functionalities and we have moved beyond usability towards user's emotions. The purpose of this study is to design a preliminary checklist using Kansei Engineering for an e-commerce perspective, which can contribute towards trust and purchase intention of consumers in the Malaysia context. A usability evaluation method was conducted, Feedback Capture after Task (FCAT) using the URANUS tool. It was performed on an online gift shop with a group of potential consumers with age range of 18-22. Using Kansei Engineering, we manage to extract words that are mentioned by the users, in which we have categorized it as per Kansei Concept. There are four categories, namely aesthetic, physical, sensational and operational. This research is deemed important in which future web designers could use as a guideline to design an e-commerce website that focuses on perceived trust and purchase intentions based on Kansei Engineering.

Keywords: Evaluation method, Feedback Capture after Task, Kansei Engineering, Kansei Concepts, Kansei Words.

1 Introduction

A study conducted by PayPal [1] revealed that the size of Malaysia online shopping was RM1.8 billion in 2010, estimated to be RM5 billion by 2014. Out of the RM14.8 billion, about RM825 million (45%) was spent on local business websites. This shows potential prospects in Malaysia's e-commerce. The majority of Malaysians purchasing online is in the age group of 21-40. The products bought online were flight tickets,

H. Badioze Zaman et al. (Eds.): IVIC 2013, LNCS 8237, pp. 483–496, 2013.

which constitutes 24% of the total product and services bought online, followed by bill payment (18%), entertainment (14%) and IT & Electronics (12%). The less favorable products to buy online were gifts and collectibles.

The importance of usability testing to evaluate e-commerce has been well defined [2] and [3]. User interface of computer applications affects how people interact with the website and also their perception towards the website. The overall goal of usability from a user perspective is to measure and improve effectiveness, efficiency and satisfaction [4]. Usability of an e-commerce website will provide users with satisfactory transaction effectively and efficiently. It helps to obtain a complete understanding of user's needs and to improve product development in order to provide a better user experience. Indeed, the usability of an e-commerce website is of utmost importance as it will affect consumer's trust towards the website and in turn their purchase intention [3]. However, as e-commerce sites intensify their effort to provide persuasive shopping experience for their users, it is then necessary to look beyond usefulness and functional usability [5]. Recently, study of e-commerce website design focuses on the consumer's feelings and emotions. In designing such an e-commerce website, Kansei Engineering methodology could be the most suitable method. Kansei Engineering is used to ensure the product or services evoke desirable emotional responses, which in turn potentially increases customer's satisfaction as trust and purchase intentions rely mostly on user's emotion.

The purpose of this study is to establish a preliminary e-commerce design checklist, using Kansei Engineering, which can contribute to trust and purchase intention of consumers in the Malaysia context. The study focuses on Malaysian age between 18-22, the group that has the most experience shopping online.

2 Related Works

Trust and satisfaction are the main determinants for successful business relationships in business to consumer electronic commerce [6]. Trust plays a vital role in any form of business that requires monetary transaction. Customer's satisfaction has a direct relationship to customer's purchase intention, repurchase intention and word of mouth marketing. Consumer satisfaction is a measure of how well the product or services provided by companies meets its consumer's expectations. A satisfied customer can expect higher purchase intention, repurchase intention and in effect promote the company to other potential consumers. Hence, there is clearly a need to study how an e-commerce website will influence consumer's trust and satisfaction.

Usability of a website is critical in determining the success or failure of a company [7]. However, many e-commerce applications still do not meet customers' usability requirements [2] and [8]. Customers judge the credibility of a website within the first 50 milliseconds. Therefore, the website needs to be designed with customer's behavior in mind. In this line, usability is an essential component of e-commerce strategy [9, 10]. Considering the importance of usability on e-commerce website, there were many studies conducted to understand how every aspect of an e-commerce website can influence customer's behavior. For example, Papadopoulou and Pelet

[11] studied how colors in an e-commerce website can affect consumer's mood and purchase intention. Work by Kamoun and Halaweh [12] investigated HCI factors that contributes to customer's security perception towards an e-commerce website. Their work has also re-emphasized on the importance of a good user interface design as an effective technique for increasing customer's trust and purchase intention. Sivaji et al. [3] showed the importance of applying Gestalt Principle, Fitts' Law and affordance across e-commerce websites. Since these elements are frequently present in a conventional shopping mall, online transactions were recommended to be virtualized. The study also showed that once fundamental usability principles have been applied to the website, other principles such as trust, social presence, online and offline communication elements needs to be incorporated.

Among all, user testing and heuristic evaluation method are most commonly used for e-commerce website [3] and [13]. To perform a more complete evaluation, most previous studies uses more than one evaluation method in evaluating their web application. For example, a combination of user testing (think aloud protocol) and inquiry methods (interview, questionnaire). These methods help in generating a list of usability problems; however it does not provide guidelines on how to resolve these problems. Therefore, usability evaluation must take into account discovering the usability problems and repairing them [13].

So far we have discussed points on customer satisfaction, trust, usability and credibility. These attributes are important in ensuring the success of an e-commerce website. Nielsen's heuristics are useful for cognitive functionality and usability. And as e-commerce grows, the importance of its website persuasiveness and appeal is apparent. Thus, it is important to know how will Kansei effect people's perception towards an e-commerce website.

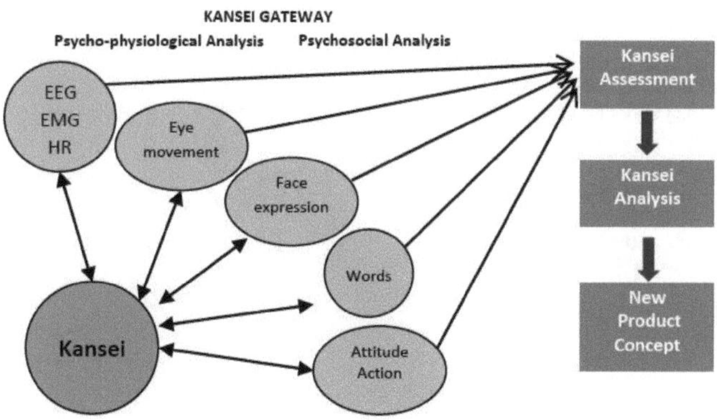

Fig. 1. Kansei gateways

As found in [14], Kansei is a Japanese term used in order to define a person's impression towards certain object, situation and surrounding. It uses the five senses, namely, vision, hearing, smell, taste and skin, for the brain to deduce a person's feelings, emotions and intuition. When a person's senses are triggered, psychological cognition that involves perception, judgment and memory will become apparent to a person. Thus, one of the methods to evaluate the impact the object, situation or surrounding has on someone is to ask the person to express their Kansei in words for the object, situation or surrounding they would like to encounter in the future. These are known as Kansei Words (KW) [15] and [16].

To enable a person to express their KW and measure the expressions, there are a few entrance points to a person. Fig. 1 shows the gateway in reaching Kansei [17].

In [14], the author gave examples where certain words are only used in certain context. For example, we use 'luxury' and 'elegant' for cars, rather than for clothing items. Therefore, context plays an important part in knowing the appropriate KW.

Studies have been done to understand KW for kitchen cabinet design [18], gift flower arrangement [19] and car instrument panel [20] but these are however product designs. A study has been done by [21] to know whether it is valid to incorporate Kansei Engineering into an e-commerce website. The author developed a model, known as Kansei Design Model (Fig. 2) and developed a prototype to test the model. The model is divided into 4 levels as shown in Fig. 2. In our research work, we are interested in L2, Establishing of Checklist, which are divided into three parts: 1. Synthesizing KW, 2. Selection of domain specific and 3. Development of checklist. In Section 4, we will present our results. However, [21] has proven that the incorporation of Kansei Engineering in web design is valid. In fact, [22] has developed a Kansei Web Design Guidelines (KWDG) as a reference for web designers to design websites catering to user's emotion. Although its practicality was not tested in a real world scenario, a website was developed based on the guidelines and a comparative analysis from the expert designer's perception and users were done. The positive results obtained suggested that it is highly feasible to incorporate KWDG into the real world.

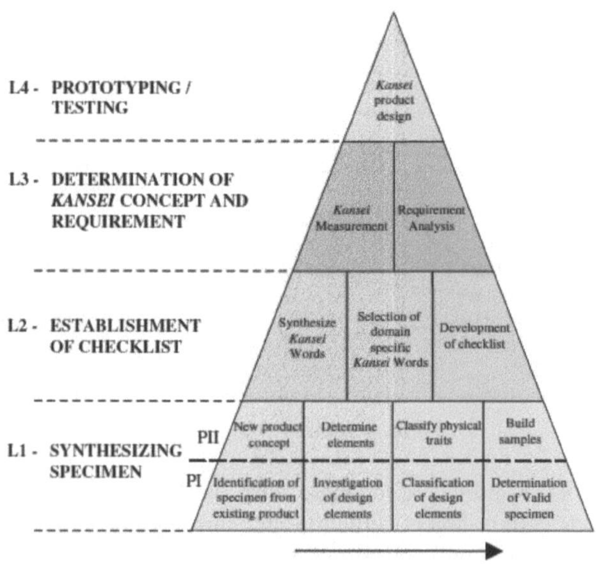

Fig. 2. Kansei Design Model

In this research, we would like to explore the appropriateness of Kansei Engineering for an e-commerce website, specifically selling gifts in Malaysia context. We will extract KW based on our usability testing. As shown in Fig. 1, our study involved various Kansei gateways such as eye movements, face expression, words, attitude action, the scope of this paper is on Kansei words (KW) only. An extension to this study involving the analysis on eye movements is published in [23].

3 Methodology

Six users were purposefully sampled from among the targeted web visitors to participate in the first user-based web usability testing at MIMOS Berhad UX Lab using the Tobii T60 Eye Tracker, Tobii Studio and URANUS [25]. All of them were male; with age range from 18-22. They were chosen as users as the website we are testing is mainly targeted for male users who are keen on purchasing gifts online. With regards to the sample size for performing lab based usability testing, [25] and [26] found that based on a binomial probability, six users will be needed to discover between 85% - 90% of the problems, given that the occurrence of the problem is 30%. Although this sample size does not represent the Malaysian demography, it is sufficient to detect significant usability problems. Another study by [27], also suggested 6 users if the research method involves qualitative eye tracking such as analyzing the gaze replays as opposed to solely depending on heat maps, which would require larger sample size.

The methodology was adapted from previous lab based usability testing studies and Kansei engineering [3], [15], [16], [17], [23], [24] and [28] and is shown in Fig. 3.

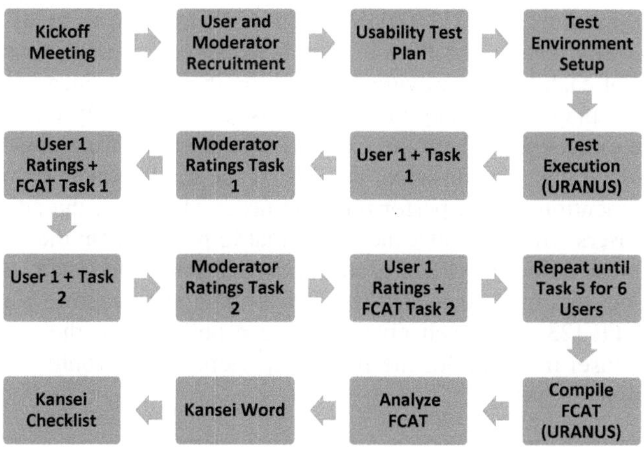

Fig. 3. Kansei Word and Checklist Development

The six users took turns to enter the UX Lab, guided by a moderator, to complete a list of five outlined test cases (tasks) as shown in Table 1. Each session lasted for the duration of one hour. The entire tests for all the six users were observed and the entire conversation between the users and the moderator were recorded. Table 1 lists the task that needs to be completed by each user.

Table 1. Tasks description

Tasks	Description
1	Next Friday is your partner's birthday; you wish to buy him/her a small gift. You have a budget of RM30 to buy a gift for your partner. What are the 2 gifts that you think is most suitable for your partner?
2	Read the description of each product.
3	Find the product comparison tool and compare the price of 'Love Letter Keychain' and '3D Character Keychain'.
4	You are a new user to this website. Create a new account for this website.
5	You do not wish to buy anything today. You want to log off the account.

From the usability testing conducted, four sets of qualitative data was obtained, namely textual feedback or also known as feedback capture after task (FCAT), verbalization or also known as retrospective think aloud (RTA), retrospective think aloud with eye movement (RTE) and observation. The complete results for the mentioned methods will be published in a future paper [23]. The scope of this paper however, is on the FCAT method, as it would result in the derivation of the Kansei words. This method is suitable, as it has been found that Malaysian users prefer to type their thoughts instead of verbalizing them due to the language and cultural barrier of the users [29]. The URANUS system [24] used in this study facilitates the end-to-end usability testing and FCAT. This is achieved by prompting the user after the completion of each task to provide feedback on their experiences. FCAT however does not involve playback of any videos but instead rely purely on their short-term memory of the experience. There are chances of users forgetting some of the issues they have faced. In this circumstance, the role of the moderator is to remind them of what they had mention during performing the tasks. However, the advantage of this method is that users will remember the issues that impacted them the most, hence it is expected that most of the important issues or words will be fed back. Since no video playback is done, this method is also the fastest method to capture Kansei words as compared to RTE [23]. For each given tasks, we believe that the users are able to express their Kansei in words for the future experience they would like to encounter from the e-commerce website.

4 Results

After performing the test, the FCAT results are compiled and summarized in Table 2 - 6. The URANUS tool [24] that was used in this study facilitates the FCAT data collection in real time for all five tasks and for all six users.

Table 2. FCAT for Task 1

User	FCAT
1	Colors are just right, not too difficult to search for the product I wanted. Information given is enough to help me out with my choices. Clear view, not stressful and able to maintain interest of user browsing the website. Layout and background of website in calm. If possible, increase the number of variety of products.
2	List all products, sort all by price, give an option for user to type in their budget and show the relevant products, and show the most purchased products for this budget
3	The middle button opens to a new window instead of a new tab. couldn't maximize the new windows making browsing a little more harder
4	Design of the website is good. Product is easily found
5	Ok
6	The choices of gift are generally little to choose from. Sites are easy to use and hopefully the choices will increase

Table 3. FCAT for Task 2

User	FCAT
1	Delivery time should be mentioned. Extra information about the photo printing service, included or not. Enquire about the features, helpline/customer care service (e-mail).
2	Font needs to be slightly bigger for the product info and features
3	It's good that we can customize what we want to 'embroid' on the pouch, especially the part where I can upload a picture of what I want on the pouch
4	Product information was well displayed but when I am trying to preview the zooming of the product, the zooming was not accurate (zooming was off to the right).
5	Ok
6	Many info of the product was given even more than expected to be found. Would prefer a nicer font or bigger one for the important keywords.

Table 4. FCAT for Task 3

User	FCAT
1	Certain information is not necessary, e.g. Mobile number. Maybe can be included when confirm purchase of product. Address title in the last section of signing up was difficult to understand the actual meaning. Should have two separate buttons for 'Sign up' and 'Log in'
2	When the user's name is too long at the top right side, the vertical panel on the right side is pushed to the left(Facebook icon, etc.)
3	A compare button should be placed in the item description page too so that we can compare an item we're currently browsing with another."
4	I cannot find the product comparison tool. I had expected the product comparison tool to be below the product description.
5	Price difference is reasonably proportional to the crafting duration (effort taken to complete the order
6	When comparing 3 products, there is the right side bar distracting the product view even though it was visible; still it has to be cleared for better view. It's a new way of comparing the gift product to people this way

Table 5. FCAT for Task 4

User	FCAT
1	Comparison tool is hard to find, should be placed somewhere easy to look for when viewing the product. Maybe allow user to compare more than two items at a time, maximum of 4 items. Details of items compared should be clear.
2	When there's more than 2 products, the 3rd product is being blocked by the vertical advertisement
3	Maybe you should put something that indicates that you can sign up by clicking the log in button. Because not everyone would know that you must first go into the log in page to sign up.
4	Design of the registration form is good. Registration is easily made.
5	Ok
6	The additional address input was not really clear of its purpose, and the * for the required field is suggested to be bigger. I would suggest also a description of new field such as the address field popping out when the mouse is hovered over it. I would also expect to see a small welcoming note when I sign into the website. Theme color customization is preferred for me

Table 6. FCAT for Task 5

User	FCAT
1	Was easy to find the logout button. User's name was mentioned on top right of screen, indicating user was logged into the web.
2	Would like a prompt asking if "are you sure you would like to logout while your cart isn't empty?" something like that. An add to cart button is only found on the 1st item on the item list. The rest of the other items does not have the button. In the product item view, the add to cart button looks a bit weird
3	Nothing much. just something very basic and simple
4	Logout button easily found
5	Ok
6	Very clear button

5 Analysis and Discussion

5.1 Synthesizing Kansei Words

During the FCAT method, we obtained user feedbacks, which were useful in knowing what their perceptions were and how the 'would be' system should be like in the future. From here, we were able to extract their KW, where we categorize them into attributes and gather them based on Kansei Concepts. In most cases Kansei Concepts are segmented into the four areas, namely, aesthetic, physical, sensational and operational [17]. The comments can fall into either of the above-mentioned categories. Kansei words are mostly adjectives but can also include nouns, verbs or sentences [17]. From Table 2 - 6, we synthesize the KW. And use a semantic differential (SD) scale, whereby the positive side is weighted at 5 points decreasing by one point each into the negative side [17] as shown below:

GOOD 5 4 3 2 1 BAD

Based on the four areas, Table 7 shows the categories listed broken down into attributes and then categorized by Kansei Concepts.

Table 7. Categories based on Kansei Concepts

1. Aesthetic

Attribute: Browsing Experience	
Maintain Interest	Not Maintain Interest
Relaxed	Not Relaxed
Easier	Not Easier
Free Flow	Not Free Flow
Attractive	Not Attractive
Attribute: Interaction	
New	Not New
Unique	Not Unique
Intuitive	Not Intuitive
Attribute: Font for Important Information	
Nicer font	Not Having Nicer font
Attribute: Layout	
Professional	Not Professional
Consistent	Not Consistent

2. Physical

Attribute: Colors	
Just Right	Not Just Right
Clear	Not Clear
Customizable Themes	No Customizable Themes
Attribute: Information	
Sufficient Information	Not Sufficient Information
Well Displayed	Not Well Displayed
Accurate	Not Accurate
Detailed	Not Detailed
Relevant	Not Relevant
Timely	Not Timely
Informative Feedback	No Informative Feedback
Attribute: Interaction	
Timely	Not Timely
Attribute: Layout	
Clear View	Not Clear View
Accurate Resizing	No Accurate Resizing

Table 7. (*Continued*)

Attribute: Content	
Increase Variety of Products	Not Increase Variety of Products
Increase Number of Products	Not Increase Number of Products
Specify Delivery Time	Not Specify Delivery Time
Provide Extra Information about the photo printing service	Do Not Provide Extra Information about the photo printing service
Provide Means to Enquire about the features, helpline/customer care service(e-mail)."	Do Not Provide Means to Enquire about the features, helpline/customer care service (e-mail)."
Provide Means to Customize Gift with Personal Note or Image	Do Not Provide Means to Customize Gift with Personal Note or Image
Accurate	Not Accurate
Attribute: Content Presentation	
List All Products	Not List All Products
Sort By Price	Not Sort By Price
Show the most purchased products for this budget	Not Show the most purchased products for this budget
Larger font for product info and features	Not Having Larger font for product info and features

3. Sensational

Attribute: Layout	
Calm	Not Calm
Clear View	Not Clear View
Good Design	Not Good Design
Flexible	Not Flexible
Customizable	Not Customizable
Simple	Not Simple
Attribute: Background	
Calm	Not Calm
Good Design	Not Good Design

Table 7. (*Continued*)

Attribute: Controls / Command Buttons	
Good Placement	Not Good Placement
Clear	Not Clear
Concise	Not Concise
Specific Function	Not Specific Function

4. Operational

Attribute: Navigation	
Easy to Search	Not Easy to Search
Search by Product Budget	Not Search by Product Budget
Product is Easily Found	Product is Not Easily Found
Easy to Use	Not Easy to Use
Easy to Navigate	Not Easy to Navigate
Attribute: Interaction	
Tabbed Browsing	Not Tabbed Browsing
New Window Browsing	Not New Window Browsing
Easy to Use	Not Easy to Use
Easy to Interact	Not Easy to Interact
Compare more than two items at a time	Not able to compare more than two items at a time
Compare four items at a time	Not able to compare four items at a time
Attribute: Controls / Command Buttons	
Easily Found	Not Easily Found
Attribute: Information	
Easy to Understand	Not Easy to Understand

There are some points that are worth mentioning that can be drawn from Table 7. Under 'Aesthetic', we can see words like 'Relaxed', 'Easy' and 'Attractive', which evokes emotional feelings of the users, supporting Kansei. The feelings could either give a good impression of the website or vice versa. This can also be related to reducing cognitive workload of users and in turn their perception, where they understand a website better with less cognitive workload. Things easily understood are perceived as direct and good. Contents would also need to be 'Professional' and 'Consistent' as this is known to build trust and credibility of the website.

In 'Physical', under the' Information' category, we can extract KW words like 'Sufficient Information', 'Accurate', 'Detailed' and 'Timely'. Similar related words under 'Content' like 'Providing extra information' and 'Provide means to enquire' is relevant to what was stated previously under 'Information' category. Perceived trust elements of a website revolve around providing timely and adequate information to portray credibility. It also gives contentment for the users as they know information is suffice and relevant.

It was also interesting to note that users nowadays would want their interfaces to be 'Customizable'. This can be found under 'Sensational' category. Personalization allows users options to view information that are of interest to them rather than irrelevant information. The feeling of being in control while using a computer is important nowadays as developed technologies are now becoming more conforming to humans. This point can also relate to reducing cognitive workload and this is critical point worth noticing for developing personalized interfaces in the future.

Under 'Operational' category in 'Navigation' attribute, users mentioned words like 'Easy to search', 'Search by Product Budget', 'Product is Easily Found', 'Easy to Use' and 'Easy to Navigate'. These points are deemed important as it has the potential to convert web browsers to buyers. Of course, these are the same points that would be important in ensuring returning customers to a website.

This e-commerce design checklist based on FCAT study has brought to light a few important points in which we could build trust and purchase intentions of an e-commerce website by incorporating it in the future. There are many extensions that can be done to this work. Further mathematical analysis is necessary to strengthen our findings and sieve relevant points to be incorporated into a future website.

6 Conclusion

We manage to conduct FCAT test (which has been previously validated in [23]) with the users using URANUS (validated in [23], [24] and [28]). From the test, we manage to gather the KW and put it in categories based on the established and validated Kansei Concepts to develop an e-commerce design checklist (validated in [14], [15], [16], [17], [18], [19], [20], [21] and [22]). Study [17] has suggested compiling KW from magazines or books relating to a product, listening to customers or sales people's conversation or gathering expert's opinion or by theoretical study. Our approach in this study was unique in the sense that it is more user centric, whereby we have obtained KWs directly from performing user experience (UX) study on an e-commerce website. We believe gathering feedback directly from users (experimentally) from the target demography increases the reliability of the KW words as compared to compiling them from magazines and books. Future works would include using the design checklist found from this study to develop an e-commerce website by engaging a Kansei engineer that would analyze the data gathered, interpret the data and work in hand with web designer to incorporate these elements. We can also use this checklist to compare with existing competitor sites for benchmarking. We could also benchmark with other websites that have applied Kansei Concepts. It is hoped that this design checklist would increase trust and purchase intentions of Malaysian e-commerce users.

References

1. Marketing-Interactive, http://marketing-interactive.com/news/25946 (retrieved: August 21, 2013)
2. Li, F., Li, Y.: Usability evaluation of e-commerce on B2C websites in China. Procedia Engineering 15, 5299–5304 (2011)
3. Sivaji, A., Mazlan, M.F., Soo, S.T., Abdullah, A., Downe, A.G.: Importance of Incorporating Fundamental Usability with Social, Trust & Persuasive Elements for E-Commerce Website. In: IEEEXplore Business, Engineering and Industrial Applications (ICBEIA), pp. 221–226. IEEE Press, New York (2011)
4. Bevan, N.: Classifying and selecting UX and usability measures. In: Proceedings of the 5th COST294-MAUSE Open Workshop on Meaningful Measures: Valid Useful User Experience Measurement (VUUM) (2008)
5. Anitawati, M.L., Nor Laila, M.N.: Kansei Engineering: A study on Perception of Online Clothing Website. In: Proceedings of the 10th International Conference on Quality Management and Operation Development (2008)
6. Kim, D.J., Ferrin, D.L., Rao, H.R.: Trust and Satisfaction, Two Stepping Stones for Successful E-Commerce Relationships: A Longitudinal Exploration. J. Information Systems Research 20, 237–257 (2009)
7. Tezza, R., Bornia, A.C., Andrade, D.F.: Measuring web usability using item response theory: Principles, features and opportunities. J. Interacting with Computers 23, 167–175 (2011)
8. Offutt, J.: Quality attributes of Web software applications. In: IEEE Software: Special Issue on Software Engineering of Internet Software, pp. 25–32. IEEE Press, New York (2002)
9. Oneupweb, http://www.oneupweb.com (retrieved: August 21, 2013)
10. Shi, M.: Website Characteristics and Their Influences: A Review on Web Design. In: Association of Business Information Systems (ABIS) Refereed Proceedings (2011), http://www.abis-fbd.org/wp-content/uploads/2011/03/ABIS_2011_Proceedings.pdf#page=147 (retrieved)
11. Papadopoulou, P., Pelet, J.: The effect of colors of e-commerce websites on consumer mood, memorization and buying intention. In: MCIS 2009 Proceedings, Paper 116 (2009)
12. Kamoun, F., Halaweh, M.: User Interface Design and E-Commerce Security Perception: An Empirical Study. E-business Research 8 (2012)
13. Fernandez, A., Insfran, E., Abrahao, S.: Usability evaluation methods for the web: A systematic mapping study. Information and Software Technology 53, 789–817 (2011)
14. Anitawati, M.L.: Design & Emotion: The Kansei Engineering Methodology. Malaysian J. Computing, UPENA (2010)
15. Nagamachi, M.: The story of Kansei Engineering. Japanese Standard Association (2003)
16. Ishihara, I., Nishino, T., Matsubara, Y., Tsuchiya, T., Kanda, F., Inoue, K.: Kansei and Product Development. In: Nagamachi, M. (ed.), vol. 1 (2005)
17. Lokman, A.M., Nagamachi, M.: Kansei Engineering: A Beginners Perspective, 1st edn. UPENA (2009)
18. Nomura, J., Imamura, K., Enomoto, N., Nagamachi, M.: Virtual Space Decision Support System Using Kansei Engineering. Cyberworld, 273–288 (1998)
19. Ishihara, K., Ishihara, S., Nagamachi, M.: An Expert System that Incorporates Constraints into Gift Flower Arrangements. In: 8th International Conference on Industrial Management, China (2006)

20. Ishihara, S., Ishihara, K., Nagamachi, M.: Kansei Engineering Analysis on Car Instrument Panel. In: International Conference on Affective Human Factor Design, London (2001)
21. Lokman, A.M., Nagamachi, M.: Validation of Kansei Engineering Adoption in E-Commerce Web Design. J. of Kansei Engineering International 9, 1345–1928 (2009)
22. Hussin, S.N., Lokman, A.M.: Kansei Website Interface Design: Practicality and Accuracy of Kansei Web Design Guidelines. In: 2011 International Conference on User Science and Engineering (i-USEr), pp. 30–35. IEEE Press, New York (2011)
23. Goh, K.N., Chen, Y.Y., Lai, F.W., Daud, S.C., Sivaji, A., Soo, S.T.: A Comparison of Usability Testing Methods for an E-Commerce Website: A Case Study on a Malaysian Online Gift Shop. In: Proceedings of the 2013 10th International Conference on Information Technology: New Generations (ITNG 2013), pp. 143–150. IEEE Computer Society, Washington, DC (2013), http://dx.doi.org/10.1109/ITNG.2013.129, doi:10.1109/ITNG.2013.129
24. Sivaji, A., Soo, S.T.: Website User Experience (UX) Testing Tool Development using Open Source Software (OSS). In: IEEEXplore, Network of Ergonomics Societies Conference (SEANES) 2012 Southeast Asian, pp. 1–6. IEEE Press, New York (2012)
25. Sauro, J.: Why you only need to test with five users (explained), http://www.measuringusability.com/five-users.php
26. Sivaji, A., Mohd Nor, Z., Downe, A.G.: Comparison of the Lab Based Usability Testing and Exploratory Heuristic Evaluation: A Case Study on Human Factor Conference Website Usability. Malaysian J. Ergonomics, 57–71 (2011)
27. Pernice, K., Nielsem, J.: How to conduct eye tracking studies, http://nngroup.com.s3.amazonaws.com/media/reports/free/How_to_Conduct_Eyetracking_Studies.pdf
28. Sivaji, A., Abdullah, M.R., Downe, A.G., Ahmad, W.: Hybrid Usability Methodology: Integrating Heuristic Evaluation with Laboratory Testing across the Software Development Lifecycle. In: Proceedings of the 2013 10th International Conference on Information Technology: New Generations (ITNG 2013), pp. 375–383. IEEE Computer Society, Washington, DC (2013), http://dx.doi.org/10.1109/ITNG.2013.60, doi:10.1109/ITNG.2013.60
29. Sivaji, A., Wan Ahmad, W.F.: Benefits of complementing Eye Tracking analysis with Think Aloud protocol in a multilingual country with high power distance (Hofstede's model) for website user experience testing. In: Current Themes in Eye Tracking Research: Method and Application (2012) (in press)

Automatic Assessment for Engineering Drawing

Kim Nee Goh, Siti Rohkmah Mohd. Shukri, and Rofans Beleam Hilisebua Manao

Computer and Information Sciences Department
Universiti Teknologi PETRONAS
Bandar Seri Iskandar, 31750, Tronoh, Perak, Malaysia
{gohkimnee,sitirohkmah}@petronas.com.my, inbox@rofans.net

Abstract. Assessment of student's Engineering Drawing (ED) is always tedious, repetitive and time consuming. Image processing has been the common method to convert ED to be automatically assessed. This method is tedious as algorithms need to be developed for each shape to be assessed. Our research aims to create a software application that is able to perform automatic assessment for AutoCAD Drawing Exchange Format (DXF) files for undergraduate ED course. To achieve this goal, we have explored methods to convert DXF files into SVG format and develop a marking algorithm for the generated SVG files. The result shows that it is feasible to create software that automatically assesses ED without human intervention. Future implementation would include complex real-world ED.

Keywords: automatic assessment, engineering drawing, autocad, dxf, svg.

1 Introduction

An ED is a type of technical drawing, used to fully and clearly define requirements for engineered items. It is usually created in accordance with standardized conventions for layout, nomenclature, interpretation, appearance size and other criteria. ED is used to accurately and unambiguously capture all the geometric features of a particular engineering product or a component. Engineered items can take the form of a simple engine piston to a 30-floor building. The end goal of an ED is to convey all the required information to allow communication between the manufacturers that produces that component and engineers that needs the respective component. Most universities offer ED as an undergraduate course during the first or second year. Some engineers will end up solely doing work related to ED in their career.

A survey conducted in a Malaysian university revealed that there is indeed a potential demand for automatic ED assessment software. An instructor team composed of one lecturer and two tutors will have to assess as many as two weekly assignments submitted by 80 to 100 students. We estimated approximately 1000 assignments to be marked by the instructors every semester. Assuming each assignment requires 10 minutes for marking, the team will have to spend approximately 167 hours for assessment.

H. Badioze Zaman et al. (Eds.): IVIC 2013, LNCS 8237, pp. 497–507, 2013.

Assessing ED assignments has proven to be quite complex. Fig. 1 shows a partial view of a Floor Layout Plan that is created as part of a real assignment. Notice that there are quite a number of details to be observed in this assignment. Humans are prone to mistakes during examination. Although it is a doable task, it is time consuming, error-prone and at times not standardized. Thus, automation is a favorable method to ensure timely marking and standardized marking scheme.

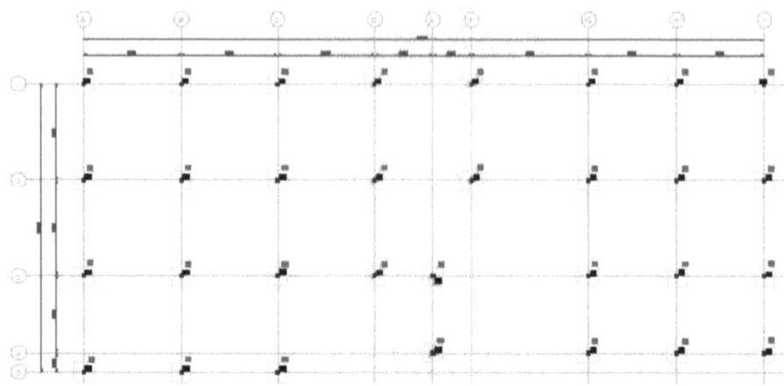

Fig. 1. Example of ED Assignment

Such software shall assist assessors to automate and standardize the grading of ED drawings. It can also significantly reduce the time to assess the students' assignments. While there are researches [1], [2] and [3] who automated the marking process in ED course, similar studies have been conducted in the field of programming [4], [5], [6] and [7] courses and mathematics [8].

AutoDesk AutoCAD is the most popular and widely used Computer Aided Design (CAD) tool for ED. Based on a survey done with the university faculty, it shows that AutoCAD is the most used tool for academic purpose with a 10 to 1 advantage over other software. AutoCAD file formats such as DXF or Drawing (DWG) are also professionally documented and it shall allow us to build the necessary APIs needed to read these files.

DXF is a file type composed by ASCII based codes thus making it easier to process than the other AutoCAD file formats. Another popular file type is DWG, which is built on bit codes, thus manipulation of such files are more complex. Scalable Vector Graphics (SVG) is Extensible Markup Language (XML) based, graphic vector file format that is recommended by the World Wide Web Consortium. As an XML based file, SVG is relatively easy to handle and process than DXF. We will explain in detail how the two file formats are related.

The novelty in our research lies on our approach. Our method on the other hand is relying on the flexibility offered by DXF file format that allows us to conveniently examine ED properties. We explore an already established method to do ED recognition instead of developing new algorithm to do the task. Prior researches [3], [9], [10], [11] and [12] tries to do automatic assessment of ED using image-processing method. This method treats ED as images and the researches find algorithms to detect shapes and edges in the image.

Our research aims to create a software application that is able to perform automatic assessment for AutoCAD DXF files for undergraduate level ED course. To achieve this goal, we have to explore methods to convert DXF files into SVG format and develop a marking algorithm for the generated SVG files.

2 Related Works

Marking student assignments is a fairly subjective task and the automated process comes with some limitations. Research by [1] suggested a hybrid between the manual and automatic assessment. The author said that assessment should not be based solely on the output's accuracy, but rather consider other means such as the way students create comments and organize their code. These factors are somehow beyond the reach of the automatic assessment software. Therefore, the author suggested a semi automated approach. Research by [1] proposed that in order to mark the subjective parts of student assignment, the software designed must also provide a medium to let a human assessor view and perform manual checking on the code. Both marking results from the manual and automatic assessment process shall then be combined to produce the final mark.

However, [2] suggested that a fully automatic approach is indeed possible. This would mean that humans would not be involved in the entire marking process. The author's study was based on a Programming course. The author suggested that automatic assessment should focused on examining the objective parts of the assignment without taking into account the subjective parts. The authors also suggested some alternatives to get the students to cope with this approach. The software designed allows students to retrieve their marks instantly after the first submission. Based on the retrieved marks, students can decide whether to resubmit the assignment. Survey results indicated that students taking the course were happy with the approach suggested.

In the early days of CAD's inception, researchers [9] and [13] are particularly interested in converting manually drawn engineering sketches into their equivalent digitized forms. While there are variations in the proposed methods, conversions are mostly done by first scanning the sketches into digital images and performing image processing based algorithm onto them to allow the computers to understand the entities that composed the drawings. As CAD gets more popular, researches then focus on finding more effective ways to understand and recognize ED, which are already in digitized form. Applications of such research are meant for the usage of ED for manufacturing where little human interventions are desired.

Researchers in [9] proposed a three-layered process to read hand-drawn ED sketches. The process starts by retrieving raster image, which is a digital image produced from scanning paper-based ED. To avoid confusion, the graphic components of the raster will be separated from the ED's character components. The pixels of the graphic components are then converted into geometric entities through vectorization process. The vectorization consists of: thinning, node regulation, line distinguishing, arrowhead recognition, and vector conformity. Their recognition algorithm treats characters differently. This is concluded with a help of human to fix and correct inaccuracies that might have taken place. This method, although practical and simple, but still relies on human to do the final judgment.

Research by [10] suggested that vectorization might not solve problems in reading ED as a whole. Instead, the authors suggested recognizing main ED entities as the main priority. According to [10], ED main entities are line types, circular arcs, blocs, hatched areas and dimensions. They also suggested four principles to read complex ED better:

1. Start from the simple graph into more complex entities
2. Use space logical relations to understand elements of ED
3. Only read ED that are equipped with complete information
4. Extract all the information before the recognition process is started

Besides vectorization, another method available to read ED is graphic class hierarchy. This method is based on the assumption that vectorization is not time efficient and lacking in quality [11]. Instead of performing vectorization, the researchers built C++ based classes, which consist of basic graphical objects. Using these classes, raster images are examined to determine its main component. Once the main component is detected, other components are gradually added through further detection processes. All components must take form in one of the classes set in the library. The research is proven to be very successful and in fact DXF format is also based on a similar, if not, the same graphic objects library.

Researchers in [12] proposed that ED reading could be separated into three levels, namely, low, high and intelligent interpretation. High-level graphic objects can be difficult to read, as there are many combinations of shapes that can take place. A hard coded implementation to resolve such complexities can be very difficult. Therefore the aforementioned researches have suggested the adoption of machine learning to resolve this matter.

According to AutoCAD official documentation [14], the DXF format is an ASCII based tag data representation of all the information contained in an AutoCAD drawing file that handily stores ED information as human readable. That documentation also gives a very clear outline on every single code and terms used in DXF, hence allowing developers to build software or APIs to communicate with this file format. There are several versions of popularly used SVG file. However, in this research we limit our study to the 2009 version.

We are particularly interested in investigating ways of converting DXF to SVG. A research done by [15] successfully revealed methods to logically group and understand DXF data. Despite not being able to map out every single data, their research has revealed a breakthrough to show that it is possible to convert DXF to SVG. Another study by [16] proved that bidirectional conversion between the two formats is possible. Their research proved that with a proper method, the conversion would not result in any data loss. The same study also critically compared the performance of SVG and DXF. Their study showed that to represent the same drawing or object, DXF's file size is 4 times bigger than the one produced using SVG. DXF will also take up 6 times longer loading time as compared to SVG.

We explore a method to convert DXF to SVG files as an ED consists of different shapes and would need to be handled by different algorithms. Assuming that there is no conversion done, we would have to find a specific algorithm for both, to read and perform assessment for different kind of shapes. On the other hand, if the DXF files are converted to SVG, we can focus on reading the files only, as SVG files are relatively easy to handle with its tags easily understood.

3 Results and Discussion

3.1 System Flowchart

As mentioned, marking student assignments is a subjective task. However, approach in [2] seems to be more comprehensive as it does not have to rely on subjective measurement to assess the students' submissions. With the addition of the DXF to SVG conversion, our software flowchart is as illustrated in Fig. 2.

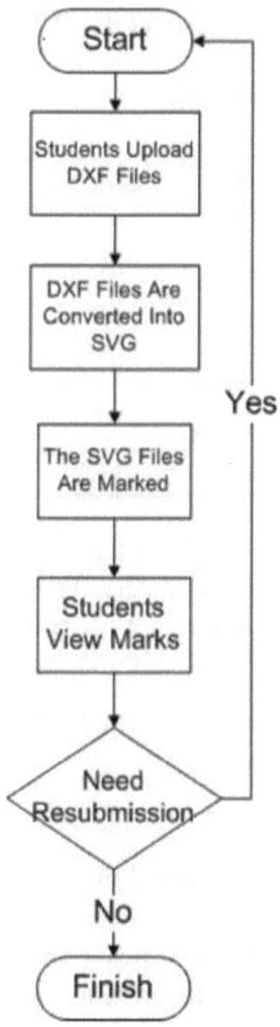

Fig. 2. Automated assessment of ED system flowchart

3.2 The Conversion Algorithm

Fig. 3 and Fig. 4 shows how the contents of SVG and DXF files look like when opened using a simple text editor. DXF files are divided into several section such HEADER, ENTITIES, OBJECT, etc. The section that needs to be looked up in particular to find the exact information of the drawing itself is located in the ENTITIES section. DXF groups its data based on certain identifier to logically link the data.

```
  0
SECTION
  2
ENTITIES
999
DXF created from EnergyPlus
999
Program Version,EnergyPlus 4.0.0.024, 8/23/2010
6:14 PM
999
Polygon Action,TRIANGULATE3DFACE
999
Color Scheme,Default
999
Text - True North
  0
TEXT
  8
...
```

Fig. 3. Partial View of Randomly Sampled DXF Code

```
<svg version="1.1" id="Layer_1"
xmlns="http://www.w3.org/2000/svg"
xmlns:xlink="http://www.w3.org/1999/xlink" x="0px"
y="0px" width="250px" height="250px" viewBox="0 0 250
250" enable-background="new 0 0 250 250"
xml:space="preserve"> ...
```

Fig. 4. Partial View of Randomly Sampled SVG Code

AutoCAD official documentation does not reveal methods to render or view their proprietary file formats. The documentation shows how to transfer data in AutoCAD generated files into other file format. Hence, to automatically assess ED DXF files, we must convert it into another file format. This is where SVG comes in handy. SVG is an open XML-based file format and its structure can be easily understood. SVG has its data contained inside an XML tag that has additional attributes to further describe extra properties of the data. SVG is also proven to be powerful especially in displaying 2D images because they are composed by vector instead of bitmaps. A set of Java classes were created to transform all set of data stored in DXF format to its SVG counterparts. We created several Java classes capable to transform some of the DXF data library. Here we demonstrate how to use one of the classes to convert a DXF drawing illustrating a circle, into SVG. Fig. 5 shall represent how a circle should look like in an ED.

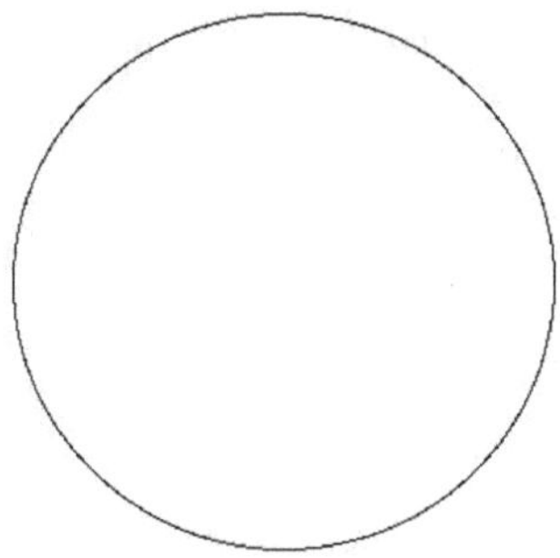

Fig. 5. A circle

In DXF format, this circle takes up 7000 lines of code to be represented. However, the only significant data is store in the ENTITIES section, as shown in Fig. 6.

```
...
SECTION
  2
ENTITIES
  0
CIRCLE
  5
188
330
1F
100
AcDbEntity
  8
0
100
AcDbCircle            → 1
 10
9.667172840374078     → 2
 20
13.48236319755094
 30                   → 3
0.0
 40
2.702626290815926
```

Fig. 6. Representation of the Circle in DXF file

In Fig. 6, 1 represents x-axis coordinate of the circle center point, 2 represents the y-axis coordinate and 3 represents the radius of the circle. Knowing these properties in DXF and how they are being represented in SVG will enable us to learn and develop a mechanism to convert this circle from its DXF format into SVG. Fig. 7 illustrates a flowchart on the algorithm of this mechanism.

As shown in Fig. 7, the system will first retrieve a DXF file from the student. A lookup alogrithm will be performed in order to find the "CIRCLE" which is located under the "ENTITIES" section. "HEADER" section is skipped as it does not contain critical information. The algorithm will then proceed to find "8", 1, 2 and 3 block codes, which contains the geometric circle of the circle. To complete the process, the algorithm will find "ENDSEC" section. The values obtained from the aforementioned block codes will then be stored inside the created SVG file.

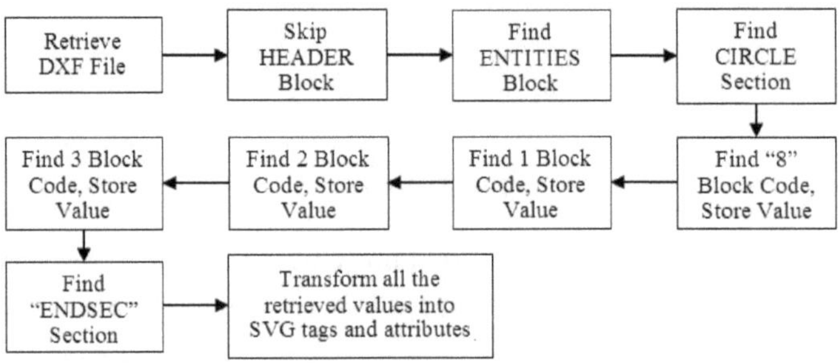

Fig. 7. Circle DXF to SVG Conversion Algorithm

Fig. 8 shows the resulted SVG file after conversion. XML tags in SVG file format are easily easily readable for developing web-based assessment system.

```
<svg xmlns="http://www.w3.org/2000/svg" version="1.1">
<circle cx="9.667172840374078" cy="13.48236319755094"
r="2.702626290815926" stroke="black" stroke-width="1"/>
</svg>
```

Fig. 8. SVG Resulted from the Conversion

After converting DXF into SVG, the circle will have 3 attributes. Cx is the x-coordinate for the circle's center point, whereas Cy is the y-coordinate of the circle. R is the radius of the circle.

3.3 The Marking Algorithm

Once the DXF files are converted into SVG, we implement an XPath algorithm to traverse both the student's submission and the prepared benchmark answer. The algorithm shall traverse into each of the generated SVG tag of the student's file and examine its attributes. The values will later be compared to the values of the similar tag from the benchmarked answer. For example in Table 1, we show two different SVG representation of a circle. One is from the tutor whereas the other is from the student. The student apparently made a mistake in the cx parameter. The algorithm shall detect the differences in the same SVG group tag.

Table 1. Illustration of Student's SVG and Tutor's SVG

Student	Tutor
<svg xmlns="http://www.w3. org/2000/svg" version="1.1"> <circle cx="**9.667172840374078** " cy="13.48236319755094 " r="2.702626290815926" stroke="black" stroke-width="1"/> </svg>	<svg xmlns="http://www.w3 .org/2000/svg" version="1.1"> <circle cx="**8.66717284037407 8**" cy="13.4823631975509 4" r="2.702626290815926 " stroke="black" stroke-width="1"/> </svg>

The algorithm will then subtract the value of each student's attributes with the tutor's answer. A proper grading scheme should be developed to award relevant grade based on the outcomes of the marking algorithm. Awarding grades would need to imitate methods of manual awarding implemented by tutors or lecturers. This should encompass checking a student's work based on correctness and creativity against the sample answer scheme provided.

3.4 Prototype

In this section, we present some screenshots of the preliminary prototype developed.

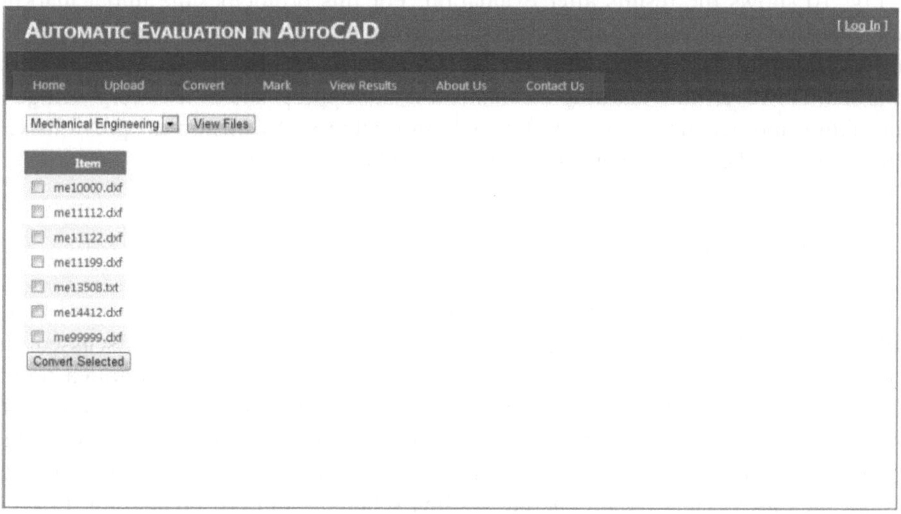

Fig. 9. Interface for 'Convert' to select files to be converted from DXF to SVG

Fig. 9 shows the system interface that will list the student files submitted through the system. The files are categorized based on programs eg. Mechanical Engineering, Civil Engineering. The tutor or lecturer can select the files to be converted from DXF to SVG. Once converted, the 'Mark' page will evaluate the student's work. There is a 'Upload' page that will allow students to login and upload their files for evaluation.

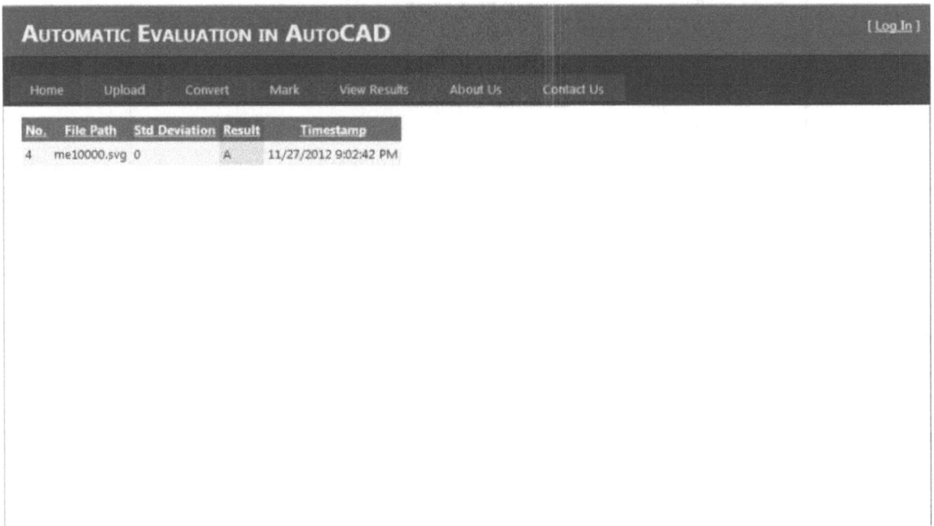

Fig. 10. 'View Results' page

Fig. 10 shows the results after evaluation. For this prototype, the initial marking and awarding marks uses standard deviation, to compare the student's answer with the answer scheme. The bigger the standard deviation, the lower the grade / marks awarded. However, this marking mechanism is not appropriate as it is very stringent, not taking into account creativity, but only correctness. As mentioned previously, a more proper and concrete marking scheme should be developed.

4 Conclusion

A prototype was developed to automatically assess EDs. This method proved that a fully automated assessment is highly possible. In this paper, we discussed the conversion of DXF to SVG file format and the marking algorithm. Although only a circle in ED was tested, it is a proof of concept that other shapes would feasibly work as well. Future works would include assessing real world and sophisticated drawings. We will also extend this work to perform conversion on the file format into an open format such as SVG. A more concrete grading scheme should be created for different levels of ED course for a standardized and fair assessment. Thorough usability testing of the complete system shall also be conducted. Time comparison between using this software versus assessors will be discussed in a future paper.

References

1. Jackson, D.: A Semi-Automated Approach to Online Assessment. In: 6th Innovation and Technology in Computer Science Education, pp. 164–167. ACM, New York (2000)
2. Saikkonen, R., Malmi, L., Korhonen, A.: Fully automatic assessment of programming exercise. SIGCSE Bull. 33(3), 133–136 (2001)
3. Othman, N.: Automated AutoCAD Drawing Assessment System for Engineering Graphics Course. B.Tech thesis, Universiti Teknologi PETRONAS, Malaysia (2007)
4. Ihantola, P., Ahoniemi, T., Karavirta, V., Seppälä, O.: Review of recent systems for automatic assessment of programming assignments. In: Proceedings of the 10th Koli Calling International Conference on Computing Education Research (Koli Calling 2010), pp. 86–93. ACM, New York (2010)
5. Ahoniemi, T., Reinikainen, T.: ALOHA - a grading tool for semi-automatic assessment of mass programming courses. In: Proceedings of the 6th Baltic Sea Conference on Computing Education Research: Koli Calling 2006 (Baltic Sea 2006), pp. 139–140. ACM, New York (2006)
6. Rajaguru, D., Rajeswari, A., Bhuvaneshwari, V., Vagheesan, K.: E-assessment of programming assignments in web service. In: 2012 International Conference on Advances in Engineering, Science and Management (ICAESM), pp. 484–489. IEEE Press, New York (2012)
7. Joy, M., Griffiths, N., Boyatt, R.: The boss online submission and assessment system. J. Educational Resources in Computing 5 (2005)
8. Rasila, A., Harjula, M., Zenger, K.: Automatic assessment of mathematics exercises: Experiences and future prospects. In: ReflekTori 2007, pp. 70–80 (2007)
9. Jin, L., Zhou, Z., Xiong, S., Chen, Y., Liu, M.: Practical technique in conversion of engineering drawings to CAD. In: Proceedings Instrumentation and Measurement Technology Conference, IMTC 1998, vol. 1, pp. 8–13. IEEE Press, New York (1998)
10. Ablameyko, S., Bereishik, V., Frantskevich, O., Homenko, M., Paramonova, N.: A system for automatic recognition of engineering drawing entities. In: Proceedings of 14th International Conference on Pattern Recognition, vol. 2, pp. 1157–1159. IEEE Press, New York (1998)
11. Dori, D., Liu, W.: Automated CAD conversion with the Machine Drawing Understanding System: concepts, algorithms, and performance. IEEE Transactions on Systems, Man and Cybernetics, Part A: Systems and Humans 29(4), 411–416 (1999)
12. Yan, L., Wenyin, L.: Engineering drawings recognition using a case-based approach. In: Proceedings of 7th International Conference on Document Analysis and Recognition, vol. 1, pp. 190–194. IEEE Press, New York (2003)
13. Pferd, W., Ramachandran, K.: Computer aided automatic digitizing of engineering drawings. In: The IEEE Computer Society's Second International Computer Software and Applications Conference, COMPSAC 1978, pp. 630–635. IEEE Press, New York (1978)
14. AutoCAD, `http://docs.autodesk.com/ACD/2010/ENU/AutoCAD%202010%20User%20Documentation/`
15. Ahmad, N., Haque, A.F.M.: Manufacturing Feature Recognition of Parts Using DXF File. In: 4th International Conference on Mechanical Engineering, pp. 111–115 (2001)
16. Fahiem, M.A., Farhan, S.: Representation of Engineering Drawings in SVG and DXF for Information Interexchange. In: 6th International Conference on Circuits, Systems, Electronics, Control & Signal Processing, pp. 592–596 (2007)

The Use of Personalized Digital Memory Book as a Reminiscence Therapy for Alzheimer's Disease (AD) Patients

Anis Hashim, Riaza Mohd. Rias, and Muhamad Fairus Kamaruzaman

Faculty of Computer and Mathematical Sciences, University Technology MARA, 40450 Shah Alam Selangor, Malaysia
anis_hasliza@yahoo.com, riaza@tmsk.uitm.edu.my

Abstract. Many researchers have been carried out in order to increase motivation and to stimulate the ability of memorizing among the Alzheimer's Disease (AD) patients. Modern therapy methods have begun to integrate with multimedia and computer technology in their therapy session for more desirable results. Memory book is an example of an application that is used to assist in the treatment of people who is suffering from the AD. With the advancement in computer technologies, the concept of traditional memory book has been transformed to an attractive, interactive as well as an effective digital memory book. This paper looks into the design and development of a personalized digital memory book specially catered for a 67 years old early stage Alzheimer's patient. The content included some information about the patient's family and a multimedia-based learning guide on how to perform prayer (solah). The Alzheimer's patient, who was previously a devoted Muslim, has now succumbed to her disease and has forgotten how to pray. The outcome from this study revealed that with the help of the personalized memory book, the patient was able to give positive response. Due to the promising result, this study should be continued with some improvement on its contents, user interface design and the hardware used.

Keywords: alzheimer's disease, memory book, multimedia, reminiscence therapy.

1 Introduction

The population suffering from chronic diseases, such as mild dementia, is increasing in out aging society [1]. These people facing difficulties in carrying out their daily life such as remembering their name, things they do daily and even finding their way [2]. As mentioned by Clare et al [3] and Kikhia, et al [2], people with dementia often rely on external memory aid such as calendars, alarms, diaries, timers and whiteboards to help them replacing their memory deficits.

According to National Institute of Neurological Disorders and Stroke [4], Alzheimer's Disease (AD) is an age-related, non-reversible brain disorder that develops over a period of years. At the beginning, people experience memory loss and

H. Badioze Zaman et al. (Eds.): IVIC 2013, LNCS 8237, pp. 508–515, 2013.

confusion, which may be mistaken for the kinds of memory changes that are sometimes associated with normal aging. As the disease becoming more serious, it will lead to behavior and personality changes, a decline in cognitive abilities such as decision-making and language skills, and problems recognizing family and friends.

Memories are important as it shapes the life of human being. The loss of memory can cause changes in personality and behavior. Besides that, AD patients are depending more on their caregivers with their daily activities. Nearly one half of individuals over the age of 85 show symptoms of AD. As for this matter, the needs to provide social support for people who are affected by this pervasive and complex disease are becoming increasingly important [5] and [6]. For persons suffering from dementia, memories can be confused and disconnected, while accompanied by difficulties of experiencing wholeness and meaning.

Reminiscence is a natural and valuable form of interaction for older people in general. It can give them a 'dignity', a sense of purpose, in going back over their lives and passing on valuable information to a younger generation [7]. People who are suffering from AD lose the capability to keep new memories. This deficiency has directly impact upon their ability to involve in a normal conversation.

Reminiscence Therapy (RT) that was introduced in 1980s has been named as one of the most popular psychosocial treatment in dementia care. The therapy activities involve discussion with another person or group about past events and experiences that able to stimulate feelings and memories [14]. For example making a personal scrapbook that contains photos and images of a person's life.

Pictures that bring back memories are an excellent aid to reminiscence process. A memory book is an example of a simple way to organize memories. Photographs, stories, significant documents, etc can be added into the memory book [8]. As mentioned by Gowans [9] that Reminiscence Therapy/Intervention is a proven means to stimulate long-term memory to motivate communication in people with AD and other forms of dementia. There are several practices which use physical support such as old photo albums, memoribilia, audio tapes/CD, videos and others.

Multimedia is making possible much more advanced, adaptive technology for persons with disabilities. The presence of several different media, together with sophisticated input and output devices, makes it much simpler to provide viable alternative presentation and input mode through which people with disabilities can gain access to the information and entertainment applications on their computer. Concerns have been expressed that developers should make every effort to ensure that their materials are accessible to all users [10].

Digital memory book is an example of multimedia application which is used to treat people with AD. Mulvena [11] stated that memory books has been used as a traditional reminiscent work where the caretaker or the family member compiles a personal scrapbook with images and souvenirs of a patient's life. Reminiscent therapy involves with sharing, discussing and evaluating the memories [8]. Thus, with the help of personalized digital memory book, AD patients can use the application over and over again to stimulate reminiscences. With the used of multimedia technology in, this memory book can appear more attractive and effective while adding more interactive features to the user. With the advancement in computer technology such as touch screen interface and tablet PCs, the memory book could be a more effective way to assist the AD patients.

2 The Methodology for Development

The development of memory book this application was involved with five stages. First stage concerned with identification of issues, scope, goals, objectives, target audiences and learning environment. During the second stage, storyboards and prototypes are prepared, as well as determine the user interface, graphic design and its contents. Third stage focuses on creating the contents and materials based on the second stage. Implementation stage or the fourth stage involved with testing the prototype. The prototype will be used and tested by the target group. Any issues that occurred during this phase will be identified and documented. The final stage concerned with getting the data and feedback. The application was developed in an iterative method, using the feedback from the caretaker, doctor and the patient.

2.1 The Patient

The prototype application was developed for Pn. Nik Binti Mohd Ali, 67 years old who is suffering from a mild AD. She lives in Terengganu, East Coast of Malaysia. Mohd. Yusri who is Pn.Nik's son is her caretaker. Mohd. Yusri has been assisting Pn. Nik with the application. Dr. Marami Satar is the doctor in charge to observe and evaluate the patient. Pn. Nik has always been a devoted Muslim. As the disease progressed, she has forgotten on how to perform prayer or solah. According to Dr, Marami Satar, the patient is suffering from AD and Parkinson's Disease based on her brain infection at the basal gaglia, but the characteristics of AD is more obvious.

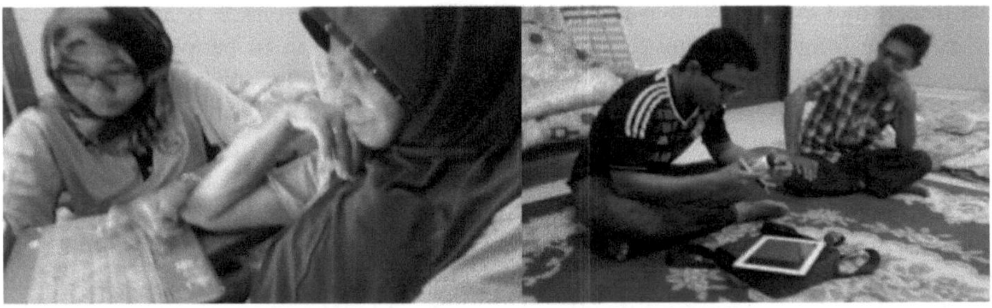

Fig. 1. The Figure above shows how the application was introduced and used by the patient. The caretaker was also accompanying the patient as part of training so he can help to operate the application later.

2.2 Description of the Application

The digital memory book application included four hierarchical levels. The first level has options where the patient could select to proceed to the next level. It contained three buttons to choose from. The patient will be assisted by the caretaker to choose the required choice. The second level was managed in such way to provide more details for each selection. Each button in first level has more options to choose from. When patient choose any of these three buttons, the patient would arrived at the third level. Only one option in this level that provides more options. The navigation between the levels was done hierarchically and bi-directional. The application also used few multimedia software, such as Adobe Photoshop to edit the pictures that has been taken and Adobe Flash was used to add animation to the application.

2.3 The Contents of the Application

The application is a personalized memory book that was designed according to the need of the user. The application includes the personal information of the patient and the family. It is included in the multimedia application on performing praying, from the beginning until the end of the process. The language used in this application is Malay Language (Bahasa Malaysia) as it is the most familiar language used by the patient. The contents were divided into three parts. First part is about 'Myself', the second is about 'My Family' and the third one is about 'Performing Prayer'.

2.4 The Development of the Digital Memory Book Application

The memory book is designed according to the need of the patient. Designing computer systems for the Alzheimer's patients should consider the existing limitations owing to their old age and to the impairments associated with their illness [12]. The first stage is analysis phase, where the main purpose of this phase was to consider all factors that related to the project and so it will produce a desirable result. The study involved a 67 years old Alzheimer's disease patient. To understand the need of the user, interviews were held with the caretaker and the doctor. From the information obtained, we have identified the issues and objectives for this application. The goal of this study is to build a prototype that focus on the process of performing praying.

Based on the information in the analysis stage, a conceptual design of the application was drafted by bearing in mind that the application should highlight simplicity and ease of use as the main goal. Storyboard was created to define the interface of the application. The layout has been carefully thought to make sure that the application is going to be as user friendly as it can. Factors such as the patient's age, patient's ability to use the computer and patient's knowledge on the computer was taken into consideration. Multimedia elements of text, sound, animation and graphics were added into the design to enhance the reminiscence of the patient. The figures below showed some of the interface that is used in the application.

Fig. 2. Front screen

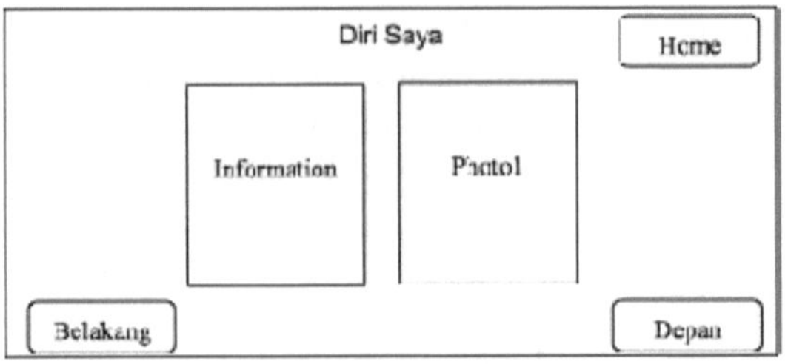

Fig. 3. Myself Screen

Fig. 4. Jom Solat (Performing Prayer) Screen

Development phase has been carried out after the design phase. In this phase, the contents will be arranged according to the storyboard. The application is kept as simple and easy to use as possible. Music is added to the application in order to make the application more interesting. Music by a local nasyid group was accompanying the application when button 'JomSolat' was hit. According to El Haj et al [15], autobiographical memories were remembered faster and more specific as compared to memories that were evoked in silence.

Fig. 5. Sample of photo editing

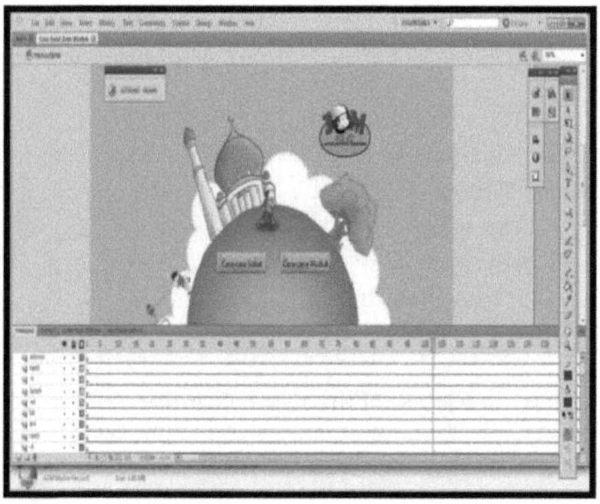

Fig. 6. Sample of animation added into the application

During the implementation phase, the prototype has been introduced to the patient. The patient went for four sessions within four weeks and during that period, she has been observed thoroughly by the doctor and her caretaker. The first experiment was conducted by the researcher. It lasted for almost one hour. The prototype consisted of three parts: Myself', 'My Family' and 'Performing Prayer'. The second, third and fourth experiments were conducted by the caretaker. Any issues occurred during the testing were identified and documented. The behaviour of the patient was observed and documented through the whole testing. After four weeks, the progress of the patient was evaluated. The outcome from the evaluation has been documented and analyzed.

The patient has been tested with her long term and short term memory. The result showed improvement with her short term memory by observing her performing the praying process. The patient was able to memorize the praying sequence after a few times learning from the application. The patient also has shown positive feedback after using the application. She showed some response for example, touching the touchpad of the laptop, trying to click on the next button, positive reaction when the audio was played and touched the screen of the laptop.

3 Screenshots

The Figures below are the screenshots of the project.

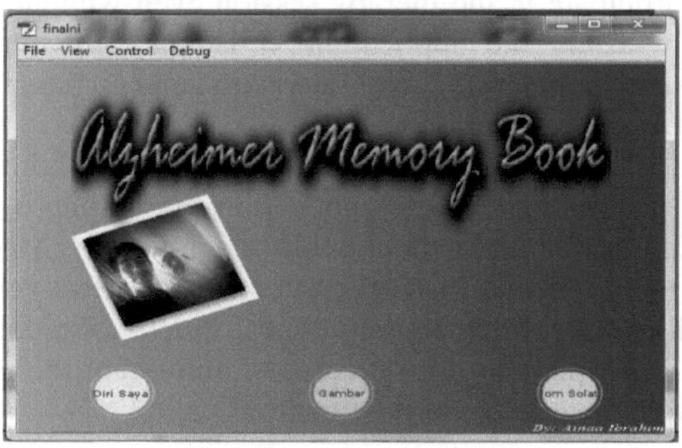

Fig. 7. Homepage Screen

Fig. 8. 'Diri Saya' Screen

Fig. 9. Example of 'Rukun Wuduk' and 'Contoh Solat'

4 Discussion and Conclusion

This paper described the design and implementation of personalized digital memory book that aimed to teach the user on how to perform prayer. This project used the collaboration of multimedia technology and the advancement of computer technology to make it more effective and interesting. One of the important factors in this study is to see the effectiveness of multimedia technology in improving the user's reminiscene gained from this therapy. Preliminary tests with the user showed that the application is able to attract the user's attention and gave positive responses. We have trained the caretaker on how to use the application. We observed the caretaker handling the session without our interference. From the observation, it showed that the patient's was motivated to participate in the therapy session even without our presence. The result shows that by using the application, it is not only improve the patient's reminiscene, but it also upgrade the social interaction and communication between the patient and her caretaker.

Future work involves with improving the user interaction with the application such as the use of touch screen display. The application can be improved by making it as easy to use as possible so that the patient could use it directly. More time needs to be allocated in testing the application in order to ensure its effectiveness to enhance the user's cognitive ability. According to the Clinical Practice Guidelines from Ministry of Health Malaysia [13], patients who received reminiscent therapy for eight weeks had significant improvement in cognitive function.

Acknowledgment. The authors would like to thank the Exploratory Research Grant Scheme (ERGS) and University Technology Mara (UiTM) for their supports.

References

1. Pollack, M.: Intelligent technology for an aging population: the use of AI to assist elders with cognitive impairments. AI Magazine 26(2), 9–24 (2005)
2. Kikhia, B., Hallberg, J., Bengtsson, J.E., Sävenstedt, S., Synnes, K.: Building digital life stories for memory support. Int. J. Computers in Healthcare 1(2), 161–176 (2010)
3. Clare, L.: We'll fight it as long as we can: Coping with the onset of Alzheimer's disease. Aging & Mental Health 6(2), 139–148 (2002)
4. NINDS Dementia Information Page (n.d.), `http://www.ninds.nih.gov/disorders/alzheimersdisease/alzheimersdisease.htm` (retrieved May 02, 2013)
5. Alzheimer's Association, `http://www.alz.org/what-is-dementia.asp` (retrieved April 19, 2013)
6. Cohone, T., Baecker, R., Marziali, E., Mindy, S.: Memories of a life: A design case study for Alzheimer's Disease. In: Lazar, J. (ed.) Universal Usability: Designing Computer Interfaces for Diverse Users, pp. 357–387. John Wiley & Sons, Chichester (2007)
7. Thompson, P.: The voice of the Past: Oral History. Oxford University Press, Oxford
8. Best Alzheimer's Product, Memory, Reminiscene, and Alzheimer's Disease (1978, 2008), `http://www.best-alzheimers-products.com/reminiscence-and-alzheimers-disease.html`
9. Gowans, G., Campbell, J., Alm, N., Dye, R., Astell, A., Ellis, M.: Designing a multimedia conversation aid for reminiscence therapy in dementia care environments. In: CHI 2004 Extended Abstracts on Human Factors in Computing Systems (CHI EA 2004), pp. 825–836. ACM, New York (2004)
10. Tannenbaum: Theoretical Foundations of Multimedia. Summary, ch. 1 (1996)
11. Mulvenna, M., Zheng, H., Wright, T.: Reminiscene Systems. In: Proceedings of First International Workshop on Reminiscence Systems (RSW 2009), pp. 2–4. CEUR (2009) ISBN 1613-0073
12. Sarne-Fleischmann, V., Tractinsky, N.: Development and Evaluation of a Personalised Multimedia System for Reminiscene Therapy in Alzheimer's patients. International Journal Social and Humanistic Computing 1(1) (2008)
13. 2nd Edition of Clinical Practice Guidelines on Management of Dementia. Ministry of Health Malaysia (November 2009)
14. Cotelli, M., Manenti, R., Zanetti, O.: Reminiscene therapy in demetia: A review. Maturitas 72(3), 203–205 (2012)
15. El Haj, M., Fasotti, L., Allain, P.: The involuntary nature of music-evoked autobiographical memories in Alzheimer's disease. Consciousness and Cognition 21(1), 238–246 (2012)

Application of Mobile Augmented Reality in a Computer Science Course

Nazatul Aini Abd. Majid

Faculty of Information Science and Technology,
Universiti Kebangsaan Malaysia (UKM),43600 Selangor, Malaysia
nazatul@ftsm.ukm.my

Abstract. Engaging learning environment for learning complex materials in higher education is difficult to perform because the contents are mostly theoretical and hard to visualize. This problem motivates the use of mobile augmented reality in this research. The objective of this research is to design and develop a mobile augmented reality application that can enhance the student's perception of the selected materials in computer organization and operating system course. The application was developed using three levels of knowledge (understand, apply, analyze) and involved the integration of video, audio, graphic and text information. The evaluation of the application using responses from 13 second year university students shows that this application can be used to enhance the students understanding and engage them in a group discussion for solving the given exercises. This application is expected to be a good start for learning complex materials in the selected course and can be extended to cover different levels of knowledge and subjects.

Keywords: mobile augmented reality, higher education, computer science.

1 Introduction

One of the most important content in computer organization and operating system course is Central Processing Unit (CPU), where CPU controls the operation of the computer and performs its data processing function; often simply referred to as processor [1]. The complexity of CPU presents great challenges to teach this component to the university students. A set of integrated educational simulators supporting teaching and learning of computer architecture has been developed and used to engage students to modern computer system architecture including CPU [2]. A new technology, augmented reality (AR), that has gained a growing interest from education industry, is a potential technique that can be used as an additional tool for engaging students in learning this complex material. This is because one of the benefits of AR is that it can enhance a user's perception of the real world with virtual objects [3]. AR can be used to improve the explanation of a complex concept by overlaying related information on the real object. Since the hand-held devices such as tablet, mobile phone can be used as a tool to view the information overlay, mobile AR has gained increased attention from academia and industry because the portability of

H. Badioze Zaman et al. (Eds.): IVIC 2013, LNCS 8237, pp. 516–525, 2013.

the mobile devices and ubiquitous nature of camera phone [4]. However, little or no work has been done towards systematic development of mobile AR applications for learning computer organization especially CPU. Therefore, the objective of this research is to design and develop a mobile augmented reality application that can enhance the student's perception of the selected materials in computer organization and operating system course.

2 Related Research

AR is a new technology that can play a significant role in improving teaching and learning. According to Azuma in 1997 [3], AR has been applied in many areas: medical, manufacturing and repair, annotation and visualization, robot path planning, entertainment and military aircraft. In 2001, Azuma et al [5] added three new groups: mobile, collaborative and commercial applications. The additional of these three areas have opened a lot of research opportunities to be explored in education industry. In terms of instructional approaches, Wu et al [6] have divided the usage of AR into three categories: (1) emphasizing the roles, (2) emphasizing the locations and (3) emphasizing the tasks. The first category is about emphasizing engaging learners into different roles in an AR environment [6]. For example, Dunleavy et al [7] developed *Alien Contact!* where students were given roles to complete outdoor tasks. The second category is about emphasizing learners' interactions with the physical environment [6]. For example, Lucia et al [8] developed *ACCampus,* a mobile augmented reality system which combines the world perceived by the phone camera with information concerning student location and community. The third category is about the design of learning tasks in AR environments. For example, Liu et al [9] developed *EULER* which students can use m-AR module for immersive learning activity to learn about wildlife rarely seen in wetlands. In this activity, students were given a set of questions. All these examples focus on outdoor activities. In terms of using AR in indoor environment in higher education, Table 1 summaries three examples.

Table 1. AR based education applications

No.	Projects	Display device	Tracking technologies	Area/Course	Instructional approaches
1	Construct3D (AR based geometry education tool) [10]	Head Mounted Display (HMD)	Personal Interaction Panel (PIP) [11]	Mathematics and geometry education	Roles based
2	AR-based Engineering Graphics Education System [12]	Computer screen/ smartphone	Marker based	Engineering Graphics Education	Task based
3	AR-Dehaes toolkit [13]	Computer screen	Marker based	Engineering Graphic	Task based

The first example is a roles based application where students can use see-through HMD to collaboratively, for example, inscribe a sphere in a cone [10]. The second and third examples are based on task approaches where students need to complete a set of exercises by viewing the 3D virtual models pop-up on the computer screen. The third example used visualization but the mobility of this application was limited because they did not focus on hand-held devices. However, the second example included two options in using the application, computer desktop or smartphone. In order to adopts portable technologies that are less obtrusive and enhance a sense of immersion [6], students can use their mobile devices to learn the complex materials by using AR based applications. Hence, this could lead to a methodology breakthrough as suggested by Cadavieco et al [14] that emphasize the combination of AR and mobile devices in learning. Thus, the use of mobile augmented reality that mixes the real world and the virtual world on hand-held devices such as smartphone and tablet is a viable option for teaching and learning complex materials. This research proposed mobile AR based application for learning CPU called AR-CPULearn.

3 Methodology

In order to identify the effectiveness of mobile augmented reality in learning selected topics in computer organization course, this research adopted Analysis, Design, Development, Implementation and Evaluation (ADDIE) methodology.

The first step is analysis where the requirements to develop the application were identified in terms of the contents, learning objects (real objects), virtual objects and elements (e.g. video, audio, 3D model and 2D image, text) that need to be included in the application. The contents were selected based on a specific topic in subject computer organization and operating system (TK2833). Since CPU is an important topic in this subject, a set of exercises based on this topic was identified.

The second step is to design the application. The application was designed to a specific learning activity which is doing exercise in class. In this exercise, there were four main parts so that the application was design to include four main buttons:

(1) Button A for introduction
(2) Button B for questions related to the main function of CPU
(3) Button C for questions related to the components on a motherboard
(4) Button D for questions related to how CPU works.

Questions for Button A, B, C and D were composed based on three selected levels in Bloom's taxonomy: understand, apply and analysis.

The third step is to develop the application. The related software in developing the application were:

- Eclipse Integrated Development Environment (IDE) for Android platform development using Java.
- Metaio Software Development Kit (SDK) for augmented reality development.
- GIMP for image editing.

The fourth step is to implement the developed application. The application was implemented in two hours lecture for computer organization and operating system course in a lecture room. Tablets were used as the hand-held devices to show the virtual objects. A set of question sheet was given to each group in the class. The application was installed in the tablets and each group was given a duration of time to discuss the exercise by using the tablet.

The fifth step is evaluation using a questionnaire. This phase is to evaluate whether the mobile augmented reality based application can assist students in achieving the learning outcome of the specific learning activity. The questionnaire was divided into two main parts. The first part used a five level Likert scale and the second part was to collect feedbacks from the students in terms of how AR can be used to achieve learning outcome and what elements should be included in the AR based application.

4 AR Design and Development

AR-CPULearn is based on the augmented reality framework developed by Metaio [15]. The framework for the application is shown in Fig. 1. There are four layers in this framework: (1) application, (2) high level Application Programming Interface (API), (3) Metaio SDK and (4) operating system (OS) [15].

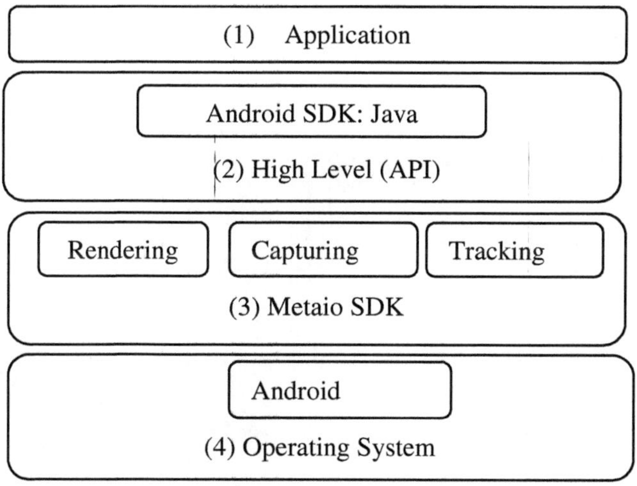

Fig. 1. The framework for AR based application

The application layer focuses on graphical user interface application and operation logic. This layer allows a direct access to the high level API layer. The API layer is a platform-specific programming interface that supports Java for Android SDK, Objective C for iOS SDK and C+++ for Windows. Android SDK based on Java was used in this research because AR-CPULearn was developed for Android platform. In this API layer, there are several classes and functions that can be used by the programmers to interact with the metaio SDK. Metaio SDK, the third layer, provides components for an augmented reality enabled application. There are three key components in metaio SDK: capturing, tracking and rendering. The capturing component configures a camera and provides an image from the camera. In the tracking component, the tracking configuration needs to be loaded first in order to specify a marker. The tracking component can then process the captured image from the capturing component in terms of its position, scale and orientation of the marker relative to the camera. When the marker is recognized, the rendering component loads a model or specified computer-generated information that has been configured on the screen. The fourth layer is OS layer which combines all components of the framework based on the selected platform [15].

AR-CPULearn is composed of these components (see Fig. 2):

- An augmented sheet that provides a marker for the application and a set of exercises. The marker for this application is an image of a motherboard. The appearance of the 3D model on top of the image as shown in Fig.2 is to indicate that the AR based application is working.
- A tablet as the hand held devices with the installed software. The screen shows the main menu of mobile augmented reality application for learning activity which contains five buttons, A, B, C, D and E. Button E is for non-academic contents.

The constraint in this exercise is that the real motherboard was not available, so that an image for a motherboard was used as a marker. When a student clicks button A, B, C, D or E and scans the motherboard, specified virtual objects will overlay on top of the motherboard.

Augmented sheet | Tablet with the installed software

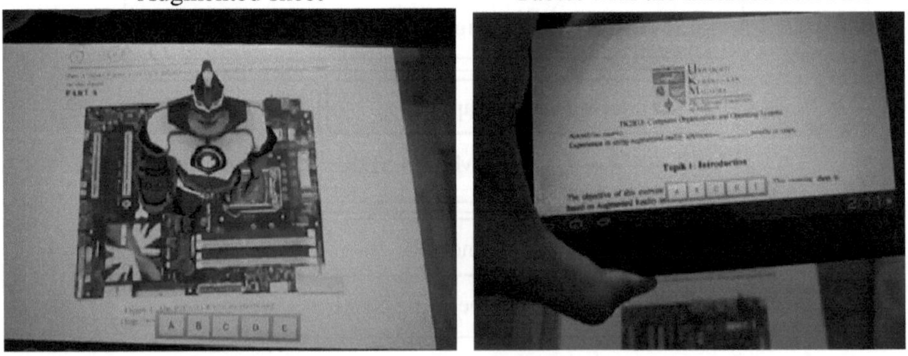

Fig. 2. AR-CPULearn application

As shown in Table 2, there are four exercises based on the AR content in AR-CPULearn. Firstly, when a student clicks button A for the first exercise, a video that introduces the subject will be overlaid on the screen of the tablet. The student needs to answer a few simple questions based on the video. Secondly, overlaid information for button B is images with audio for explaining the basic concept of CPU. This is to

Table 2. Description of the exercises

No.	Questions/level	Virtual object
Exercise 1 (Button A)	Understand	Video 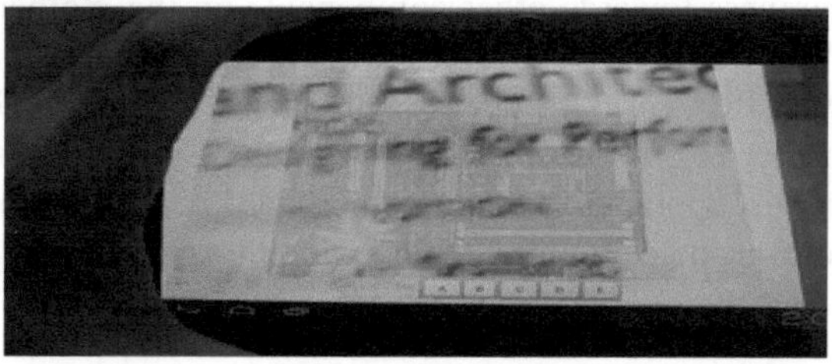
Exercise 2 (Button B)	Understand	2D image and audio 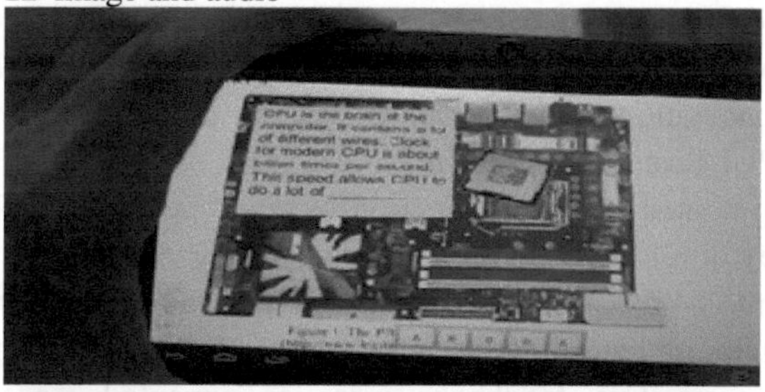
Exercise 3 (Button C)	Apply	2D image and audio 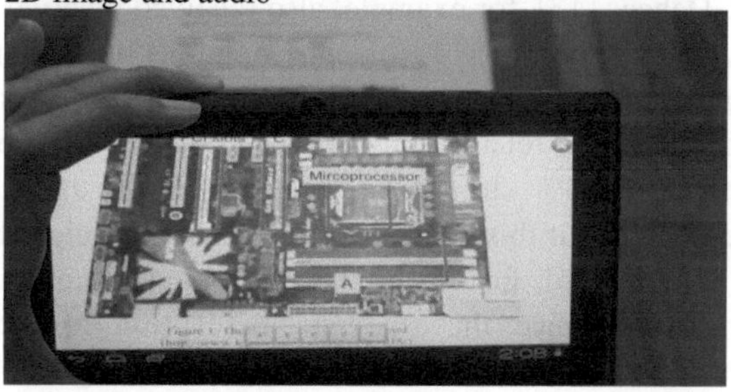
Exercise 4 (Button D)	Analyze	2D image and audio 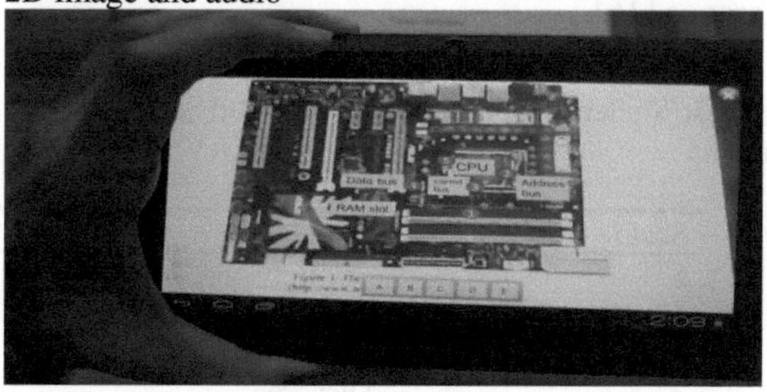

increase the observation of the students towards the location of the CPU and its function. Thirdly, overlaid information for button C is images with audio for explaining the main components on a motherboard. This is to increase the students' awareness towards other components on the motherboard that have connection with CPU. Fourthly, overlaid information for button D is images with audio for explaining how CPU works. Students will identify how CPU, memory and bus are working together in order to execute a program. Since the marker which is the learning object for this application is a motherboard, each group will discuss how to solve the questions by examining the overlay information on the motherboard (marker).

5 Results and Discussion

AR-CPULearn has been designed and developed in order to apply mobile augmented reality that can enhance the student's perception of the selected materials in computer organization and operating system course. The findings of evaluation of AR-CPULearn are depicted in Table 3, 4 and 5. The findings show that mobile augmented reality application received positive feedbacks from the students although they don't have any experience in using AR before. As shown in Table 3 for the first item, 84.6% of students agreed that augmented reality can be used to assist in achieving learning outcome. In fact, 15.4% of students strongly agreed with this item. This positive feedbacks were as expected since other AR based applications, AR-Dehaes [13], for example, also received positive feedbacks.

As shown in Table 4, students' opinions were changed slightly for the second item: augmented reality application in the exercise session in class helps me to better understand the relationship between components on the motherboard. For this item, although 30.8% strongly agree and 46.1% agree, there were 23.1% of students uncertain about this. This uncertain situation might be related to the use of the image of motherboard, instead of the real object. This might affect the research goal that aims to enhance the students' perception toward the material. A future study investigating the use of 3D markerless tracking technology would be very interesting because this new technology allows us to use any real world object as a tracking reference [16].

Table 3. Students' opinion for augmented reality can be used to assist in achieving learning outcome

Scale	Illumination	Percent
5	Strongly agree	15.4
4	Agree	84.6
3	Not certain	0
2	Disagree	0
1	Strongly disagree	0

Table 4. Students' opinion for augmented reality application in the exercise session in class helps me to better understand the relationship between components on the motherboard.

Scale	Illumination	Percent
5	Strongly agree	30.8
4	Agree	46.2
3	Not certain	23.1
2	Disagree	0
1	Strongly disagree	0

Table 5 shows the findings for the second part of the evaluations. In terms of how AR can be used to achieve learning outcome, two main points were given by the students: increase interest and increase understanding. The integration of video, audio and images can help the students engaged with the given tasks and this can lead to effective discussion within the group. Although the application based on images and text which are 2D information, the students can still get benefit from this activity. One of the students said that the application was easy to access. This might be related to the use of tablets that increases the mobility while doing the exercise. In terms of what elements should be included in the AR based application, most students agreed that images, video, audio and 3D model should be included. Although this application was lack of 3D models, the findings show that this application can still provide better understanding towards the topic. Azuma et al. [5] stated that the involvement of 2D information can give benefit for collaborative activities by having that information spread throughout the physical world.

Table 5. Students' opinions on the mobile augmented reality application

Items	Feedbacks
How AR can be used to achieve learning outcome for subject TK2833	• This application provides graphics and information about computers' component. Therefore, students will better understand the components. • The teaching is more efficient by using additional images provided by AR • Easy to access • AR can increase the students' interest to a specific course because students can interact with the provided teaching material or exercise. This can help in understanding the topic • Students can view clearly the available components (e.g. hardware) • AR can be used to explain functions in a computer • AR increases interest by using camera and real object • Do exercise in class
What elements should be included in the AR based application	• Images (should be more clear) • Video • Audio (should be more clear) • 3D model • Games

One of the learning impacts of the application is engaging learning environment for learning complex materials in this course. This can be observed during the implementation of the AR-CPULearn during class where each group engaged in a group discussion and solved the exercises collaboratively as shown in Fig. 3. This supports that AR environment can increase students' motivation and interest [17] where every student participate in the learning process. The question whether this application has improved the learning among students need to be further investigated by giving pre and post- test to the future students based on the AR course content.

Fig. 3. The implementation of the mobile augmented reality application during class

6 Conclusions

Application of mobile augmented reality called AR-CPULearn has been developed in this research where the results show that the students were interested in using the application. They have confidence that the application can assist them in achieving the learning outcome of the specific learning activity. AR-CPULearn was implemented as an exercise activity for computer organization and operating system students in higher education. The implementation of the application revealed that the use of mobile augmented reality can assist in engaging students in a group discussion for solving questions related to complex materials. The application of mobile augmented reality can be further improved by using real objects as the tracking reference. This can be done by using the new 3D tracking technology. This application is expected to be used as an additional tool to facilitate teaching and learning computer organization course because AR can enhance students' perception of the computer's components.

References

1. Stallings, W.: Computer Organization and Architecture, Designing for Performance, 9th edn. Pearson Education International, Inc. (2013)
2. Mustafa, B.: Modern computer architecture teaching and learning support: An experience in evaluation. In: 2011 International Conference on Information Society (i-Society), June 27-29, pp. 411–416 (2011)
3. Azuma, R.: A Survey of Augmented Reality. Teleoperators and Virtual Environments 6(4), 355–385 (1997)
4. Nee, A.Y.C., Ong, S.K., Chryssolouris, G., Mourtzis, D.: Augmented Reality Applications in Design and Manufacturing. CIRP Annals - Manufacturing Technology 61(2), 657–679 (2012)
5. Azuma, R., Baillot, Y., Behringer, R., Feiner, S., Julier, S., MacIntyre, B.: Recent advances in augmented reality. IEEE Computer Graphics and Applications 21(6), 34–47 (2001)
6. Wu, H.K., Lee, S.W.Y., Chang, H.Y., Liang, J.C.: Current status, opportunities and challenges of augmented reality in education. Computers & Education 62, 41–49 (2013)
7. Dunleavy, M., Dede, C., Mitchell, R.: Affordances and limitations of immersive participatory augmented reality simulations for teaching and learning. Journal of Science Education and Technology 18(1), 7–22 (2009)
8. De Lucia, A., Francese, R., Passero, I., Tortora, G.: A collaborative augmented campus based on location-aware mobile technology. International Journal of Distance Education Technologies 10(1), 55–73 (2012)
9. Liu, T.Y., Tan, T.H., Chu, Y.L.: Outdoor natural science learning with an RFID-supported immersive ubiquitous learning environment. Educational Technology & Society, 161–175 (2009)
10. Kaufmann, H., Schmalstieg, D.: Mathematics and geometry education with collaborative augmented reality. Computers and Graphics 27(3), 339–345 (2003)
11. Szalavári, Z., Gervautz, M.: The Personal Interaction Panel - A Two-handed Interface, for Augmented Reality. In: Proc. EUROGRAPHICS 1997 B, Hungary, pp. 335–346 (1997)
12. Heen, C., Kaiping, F., Chunliu, M., Siyuan, C., Zhongning, G., Yizhu, H.: Application of Augmented Reality in Engineering Graphics Education. In: 2011 International Symposium on IT in Medicine and Education (ITME), December 9-11, pp. 362–365 (2011)
13. Martín-Gutiérrez, J., Saorín, J.L., Contero, M., Raya, M.A., Pérez-López, D.C., Ortega, M.: Education: Design and validation of an augmented book for spatial abilities development in engineering students. Comput. Graph. 34(1), 77–91 (2010)
14. Cadavieco, J.F., de Fatima Goulão, M., Costales, A.F.: Using Augmented Reality and m-Learning to Optimize Students Performance in Higher Education. Procedia - Social and Behavioral Sciences 46, 2970–2977 (2012)
15. Overview over the UnifeyeSDKMobile framework, `http://docs.metaio.com/bin/view/Main/UnifeyeMobileIntroduction`
16. Markerless 3D, `http://dev.metaio.com/sdk/tracking-config/optical-tracking-technologies/markerless-3d/`
17. Sotiriou, S., Bogner, F.X.: Visualizing the Invisible: Augmented Reality as an Innovative Science Education Scheme. Advanced Science Letters 1(1), 114–122 (2008)

Design Method of Video Based Iris Recognition System (V-IRS)

Asama Kuder Nseaf[1], Azizah Jaafar[1], Haroon Rashid[2], Riza Sulaiman[3], and Rahmita Wirza O.K. Rahmat[4]

[1] Institute of Visual Informatics (IVI), Universiti Kebangsaan Malaysia, Malaysia
[2] Department of Electrical, Electronic and Systems Engineering, UniversitiKebangsaan Malaysia, Malaysia
[3] Institute of Visual Informatics (IVI), Universiti Kebangsaan Malaysia, Malaysia
[4] Fakulti Sains Komputer dan Teknologi Maklumat, Universiti Putra Malaysia, UniversitiKebangsaan Malaysia, JalanReko, 43600, Bangi, Selangor DarulEhsan, Malaysia, Universiti Putra Malaysia, UPM, 43400, Serdang, Selangor Darul Ehsan
osama_ftsm@yahoo.com, azizah@ivi.ukm.my, haroon@live.com.my, riza@ivi.ukm.my, rahmita@fsktm.upm.edu.my

Abstract. Reliable person recognition is crucial in all modern-day processes. Biometric systems have been arrayed by public and private organizations. Iris has been used as the most trusted physical attribute of human being as it is accurate, highly reliable, unchangeable and unique. Iris recognition is the identification for an individual based on iris features. In the past, many methods were used to enhance the efficiency of iris recognition systems (IRS). However, currently, the majority of existing systems substantially limit the position and motion of the subjects during the recognition process. This is largely due to the image acquisition process, rather than the specific pattern-matching algorithm applied during the recognition process. Therefore, the current study proposes an accurate method for identification of people using iris recognition system based on video streaming (V-IRS). The results of the study are expected to reveal that iris recognition on the move is an accurate and effective method to identifying people. The study concludes by highlighting the importance of the iris recognition system based on the subject moving.

Keywords: Accuracy, Biometric Technology, Features, Iris Recognition System.

1 Introduction

Humane verification has great importance all over the world. Rapid growth in the market of electronic [12] and computers [22] [16] made automatic individual identification easy by using biometric techniques such as: face recognition, fingerprints, hand geometry, iris, etc. Efficient ways of humane verification are recognition via DNA, face, fingerprint, signature, speech, and iris. Iris recognition is one of the most likely methodologies due to its high reliability for personal identification. Automated iris recognition is a non-hostile unique and great robust

H. Badioze Zaman et al. (Eds.): IVIC 2013, LNCS 8237, pp. 526–538, 2013.

technique for verification and identification of people. Interestingly, the spatial patterns that are apparent in the human iris are very distinctive to an individual. Even though, now fingerprints have taken over the market of biometrics, but iris recognition was forecasted to become the most significant biometric technique in the following decade [1]. Iris is defined as the circular part between sclera and pupil of the human eye. Some Iris images taken from a different database are illustrated in figure 1. For security in next future, iris recognition is the best solution. There are mainly three anticipated properties, i.e. uniqueness, stability and non-invasiveness.

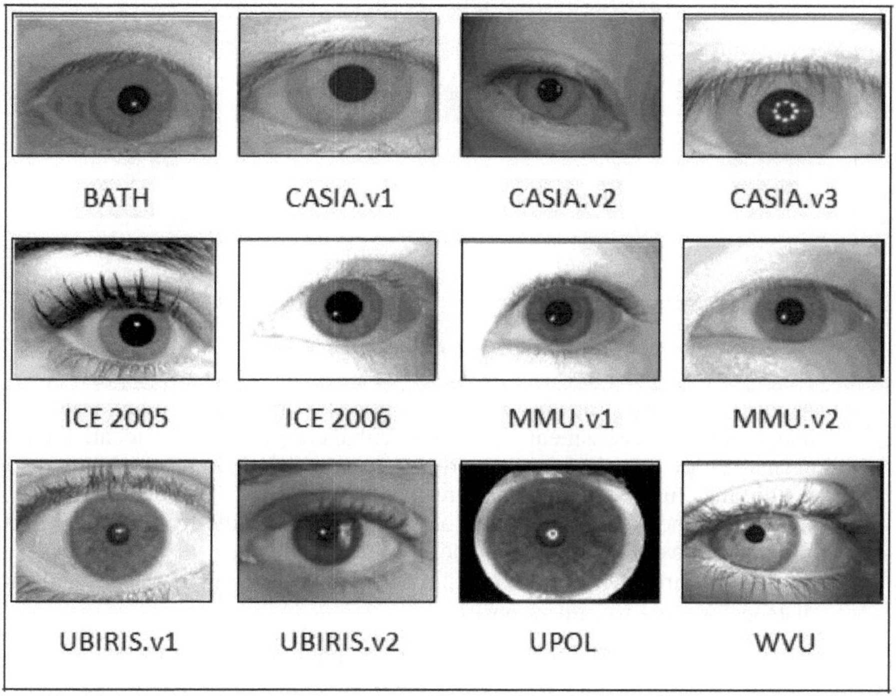

Fig. 1. Different iris images from different Database

Iris recognition was proposed by Flom and Safir for the first time in 1987 [3]. Pattern and acquisition of the iris recognition system have gained countless growth in research industry. At present, iris recognition system is a demanding research topic with research institutions, government and industry. Border crossing, identification of missing children, welfare distribution, and national identification card and immigration access control records are some of the examples of critical and sensitive applications for which iris recognition system is playing an important role to cater this need. Market demand is the main obstacle on the way of the present-day iris recognition system. Advancements in hardware and software have made iris recognition system easier to use, and now it has become "human-centered" from "machine-centered". It is trying to make the iris recognition system smarter and user friendly for future generations [4].

2 Video Based Iris Recognition System (V-IRS) Design Approach

A design approach of V-IRS can generally be categorized into three process elements, which are algorithm, camera and subject as shown in Fig. 2.

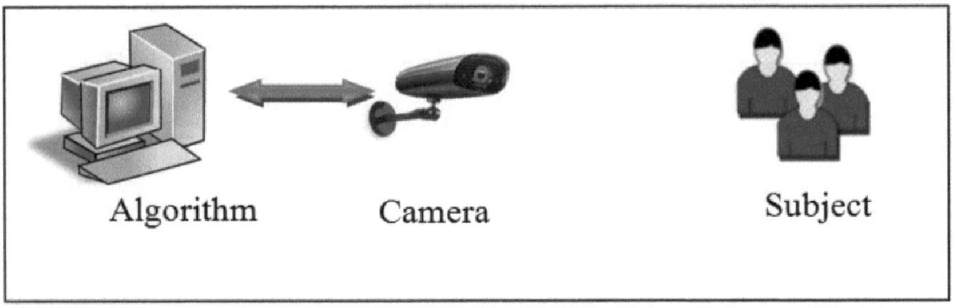

Fig. 2. Process elements of the V-IRS

- Algorithm – Deviations in unlived detection → iris detection and tracking → image quality assessment → image enhancement → iris localization → normalization → iris feature representation → iris feature extraction → iris feature matching → iris database retrieval.
- Camera – One or multi cameras, active camera with the feature of zoom/ tilt and pan or passive camera, long or close range lenses.
- Subject – Single or numerous subjects either moving or static with at a distance or close to camera position.

In enabling iris recognition to be acceptable for subjects, it is a must for the design principle of V-IRS to be human-centred rather than machine-centred. Because of being human-centered, there is no need for subjects to "stop, close, bend and stare."The subjects should be allowed to have flexible positions, and they are free to move during the iris recognition process. Therefore, the most important issue to be tackled in the new design method is that users do not need to liaise with iris system. Thus, acquiring and recognizing iris images can be achieved in an unobtrusive way and in real-time as a group of users are walking at a distance to iris cameras. It is important to configure the V-IRS with multiple active cameras with long-range in order to support the friendly HCI (Human-Computer Interaction). Moreover, it is a must for iris recognition algorithms to achieve other features, including speed, efficiency, robustness, security and adaptability to image quality. The major features characterizing V-IRS are listed as follows:

- Human-cantered iris recognition
- Self-adaptive machine intelligence
- User-friendly HCI
- Cooperative multi-camera system
- Active detection, tracking and identification
- Iris recognition on the move
- Accurate identification result
- Robust recognition performance
- Efficient recognition processes
- Fast matching engine
- Multi-user iris recognition at the same time
- High throughput
- Abnormal event report
- Self-protection

The performance targets of V-IRS are listed as follows:

- Number of users recognizable at the same time: 5 persons
- Head pose of users (Left/Right): –90o ~ 90o
- Head pose of users (Up/Down): –30o ~ 10o
- Standoff distance: 1~5 m
- Speed of movement: 2 m/s
- Recognizable zone (Height×Width×Depth): 1m×3m×2m
- Recognition time: <1 s
- False accept rate: <1/10,000,000
- Genuine accept rate: >99.9%
- Speed of iris matching: >100,000,000 records/second
- High throughput: 60 subjects/min
- Eyeglasses: Allowable

There are five aspects involved in iris recognition. They are optics, electronics, mechanics, image processing, and pattern recognition [12]. Both commercial applications and research problems are considered the two forces deriving the advanced applications of the V-IRS. For the last decade, both iris acquisition systems and iris recognition algorithms have witnessed a rapid development with a common aim of making iris recognition easier [16]. The following sections discuss in detail related information on procedures and processes that are identified as expected inputs to the design method of V-IRS that consists of several modules. These modules are being discussed base on the strengths of the past and present procedures which can be adapted and enhanced in the procedures of V-IRS design method.

3 Modules of V-IRS

An archetypal V-IRS includes mainly four modules. The first module which is called image acquisition is concerned with capturing the sequence of iris images from the subject by using cameras and sensors. There are three elements constituting up the image acquisition specifically; illumination, position and physical capture system and three main factors; the occlusion, lighting, number of pixels on the iris which all together have effect on the quality of the image quality [11]. Furthermore, a wide number of iris recognition systems needed stern cooperation from the user in acquiring the image. The method proposed by Ketchantang [5] acquired the entire sequence of images during enrolment and selects the best feasible images, thus, increasing the flexibility. Enrolment aids to provide strong identity management.

The second module, pre-processing includes several steps to be followed namely; detecting the iris livens, detecting the pupil and iris boundary, detecting the eyelid and removal and normalization. The first step, iris livens detection, is capable of differentiating the live subject from a photograph, a video playback, a glass eye or other artifacts. Biometric features can be forged and illegally used. There are several methods including Hough transformation, Integro-differential operator, gradient based edge detection which have been reported in previous research as the most well known methods used in localizing the portions of iris and the pupil from the eye image. Furthermore, the contours of upper and lower eyelids are fit which use the parabolic arcs and lead to detecting and removing the eyelid. In normalizing a form, mapping the extracted iris region is regarded an essential step. The methods used in localizing the irises are based on spring force, morphological operators, gradient, probability and moments. For instance, the iris localization method developed by Zhaofeng He [6] is based on spring force-driven iteration scheme using Hooke's law. Thus, the process of composing forces from all points can determine the centre and radius of pupil and iris. Furthermore, in applying the morphological operators to obtain iris boundaries, Mira and Mayer [7] showed that detecting the inner boundary was performed by applying threshold, image opening and closing operators. The iris localization method by GuodongGuo [8] is based on intensity gradient and texture difference. The intensity gradient uses integro-differential operator. The Kullback-Leibler divergence is used to measure the distance between two probability distributions derived from the inner and outer zones. H. Proenca and L.A.Alexandre [9] proposed a moment-based texture segmentation algorithm, using second order geometric moments of the image as texture features. The clustering algorithms like self-organizing maps, k means and fuzzy k means were used to segment the image to produce as output the clusters-labeled images. The experiments were conducted on UBIRIS database with accuracy of 98.02% and 97.88% for images captured in session 1 and session 2, respectively. The segmentation performance for 1214 good quality images and 663 noisy images was 98.02% and 97.88%, respectively.

The third module, feature extraction, is concerned with identifying the majority of prominent characteristics for classification including x-y coordinates, radius, shape and size of the pupil, intensity values, orientation of the pupil ellipse and ratio between average intensity of two pupils. Thus, encoding these features is important to format suitable for recognition.

The fourth module, recognition, obtains result by comparing these features with stored patterns [10]. Two types of variability; interclass and intra-class are used as metrics for classifying the patterns of the problems.

4 Camera Selection

The camera with WFOV captures any change in the viewing field, e.g. whether there is a face or not and more importantly provides temporal information, e.g., whether and when an eye region is ready for iris capturing by another camera. For these purposes, a video camera must be used for the WFOV camera. On the other hand, there is no need to use temporal or motion information in iris recognition [17] [18] [21] [10]. The traditional approaches first capture a short video sequence of iris and then choose one frame with the best quality [18] [10] [20].

5 Acquisition of Iris for V-IRS

Iris acquisition is very important but there are many aspects involve in it such as images quality, false acceptance and rejection and it badly effect on systems performance. The criteria related of key performance factor will be identified to insure the highest quality of image selected.

- The iris is fairly small (its diameter is about 1cm) but its resolution must be larger than 150 pixels in image. So DOF (depth of field) of iris acquisition system is limited.
- Many people especially Asians only exhibit abundant texture features under near infrared (NIR) lighting. So configuration of NIR lighting system is a big problem in iris acquisition.
- The iris should be optically on-axis and it is hard to detect and track iris due to its small size and head movement.
- When people wear eyeglasses it is challenging to capture qualified iris images due to specular reflections and dirty on eyeglasses.

The expansion of biometrics market in the late 1990s led to designating iris image acquisition apparatus and developing iris recognition (IR) products based on effective algorithms proposed in research community by some corporations such as Sarnoff, Panasonic, LG, and OKI etc. reflecting on the variation of the camera and user factors in iris recognition (Fig.2), it is evident that there are seven categories of iris acquisition systems in the history of iris recognition (Table 1) identified. This indicates that iris acquisition has been witnessing a dynamic evolution from passive to active, close-range to long-range, static to dynamic, single camera to multi-camera [4] [16]. Therefore, this evolution has assisted users to significantly reduce the constraints concerning the position and motion during iris recognition. It is expected that users will be satisfied to use smart iris recognition in the future. However, it is worth noting that advanced technologies in iris acquisition require a time period to be mature for practical applications. The mainstream iris acquisition systems in current commercial market still belong to the simplest category, i.e. Close-range IR.

Table 1. Characteristics of Iris recognition system acquisition [4]

Category	*Camera*	*Distance*	*Motion*	*User*	*Example Systems*	*Applications*
Close-range IR	Passive	Close-range	Static	Single	BM-ET330 (Panasonic) [7]. IrisAssess 4000 (LG) [8]. CASIA-IrisCamV1	Access control, Time & Attendance, Banking, Personal security, etc.
Active IR	Active	Close-range	Static	Single	IRISPASS-M (OK) [9]. CASIA-IrisCamV2 [12].	
IR at a distance	Passive	Long-range	Static	Single	Iris at Distance (Sarnoff) [10].	Pre-research for IR on move
Active IR at a distance	Active	Long-range	Static	Single	Mitsubishi [11]. CASIA-IrisCamV3	
Passive IR on move	Passive	Long-range	Movement to an access control point	Single	Iris on Move (Sarnoff) [13].	Border-crossing, Airport, Stadium, Park, Hall, etc.
Active IR on move	Active	Long-range	Movement to an access control point	Single		
IR for Surveillance	Active	Long-range	Free movement	Multiple		Covert Personal identification, Security surveillance, Watch-list, Homeland security, etc.

6 Algorithm of V-IRS

Researchers have demonstrated many algorithms and common ways to construct an Iris recognition system that can classify people via iris of the eye. Iris recognition algorithm transforms input iris image into identity after a number of steps:

- Segmentation
- Normalization
- Feature Extraction
- Encoding
- Matching

6.1 Segmentation

Isolating the actual iris region in a digital eye image is the first stage of iris recognition. Figure 3 shows that the iris region can be approximated by two circles, one for the iris/sclera boundary and another, interior to the first, for the iris/pupil boundary [19]. Removing noise from an eye image such as eyelid, eyelash and reflection is important in order to obtain high accuracy and matching. The eyelids and eyelashes normally include the upper and lower parts of the iris region. Also, specular reflections can occur within the iris region corrupting the iris pattern. These specular reflections will inevitably destroy the structure of the iris [23]. A technique is required to isolate and exclude these artifacts and locate the circular iris region.

In addition, the success of segmentation depends on the imaging quality of eye images [24]. The images in the CASIA-IrisV3-Lamp database display these specular reflections caused by imaging under natural light [25]. Moreover, it is expected that those individuals with darkly pigmented irises will display very low contrast between the pupil and iris region especially in case when imaged under natural light makes segmentation more difficult.

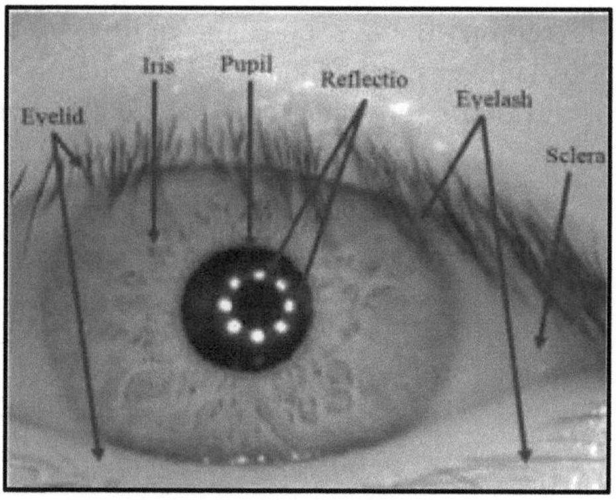

Fig. 3. The Original Iris Image [2]

According to Masek [13], the Hough transform is a standard computer vision algorithm that can determine the parameters of simple geometric objects, such as lines and circles, present in an image. He also added that the circular Hough transform canbe applied to deduce the radius and centre coordinates of the pupil and iris regions. Wildes et al., [26] [21] [27][28] Peihua Li & Xiaomin Liu, have employed an automatic segmentation algorithm based on the circular Hough transform. The Hough space maximum point will correspond to the radius and centre coordinates of the circle that is best defined by the edge points [29].

Daugman in 1994 [30] and his early publications in 1993 [17] gave in some detail a description of an operational iris recognition system. Therefore, Daugman's approach has become a standard reference model in the field of iris biometrics, which has greatly developed in the last two decades. Daugman [18] stated that the acquisition of the image should use near-infrared illumination in order to control this illumination, still, remains unintrusive to humans. Near-infrared illumination also assists to reveal the detailed structure of heavily pigmented (that is dark) irises. The built systems on Daugman's concepts require subjects to locate their eyes within the camera's view field. Asama et. al [22] came up with the study to enhance the accuracy of iris segmentation, by using Integro-differential Operator approach in the segmentation process with the aim of locating the iris region of eye image, by employing one centre of the iris and pupil.

6.2 Normalization

Normalization is a process that refers to preparing a localized iris image for feature extraction process, which is relatively independent of iris feature variations. In matching a computerized image, scaling is always a factor that needs a careful treatment. Typically, if the scale of all iris images is similar, the subsequent processing steps can be performed robustly as no need to account for more scale variations. It is suitable to transform an iris image into a standard size before performing feature extraction and image matching [33]. Another point of note is that the pupil region is not always concentric within the iris region, and is usually slightly nasal Daugman [31]. This must be taken into account if trying to normalize the 'doughnut' shaped iris region to have constant radius Masek [13], S. Sanderson [32]devised homogenous rubber sheet model by Daugman remaps each point within the iris region to a pair of polar coordinates (r,θ) where r is on the interval [0,1] and θ is angle [0,2π].

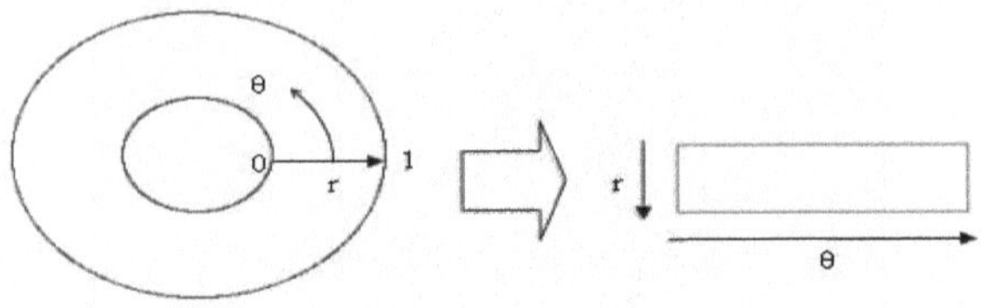

Fig. 4. Daugman's rubber sheet model

Daugman [17] developed a homogenous rubber-sheet like algorithm for the purpose of eliminating many of the inconsistencies from the above sources. These include rotation of the camera, rotation of the eye and head position, and varying image distance. This developed rubber-sheet algorithm is capable of converting the iris image from Cartesian coordinates to a polar coordinate system where the pupil center seems to be corresponding to the origin of the iris.

Image registration is defined as a process of aligning two images of the same scene. Typically, one image is regarded as the reference image whereas another image is known as the input image. The latter image is usually compared with the reference image. In attempting to provide further information about this, Wildes [21] conducted a detailed comparison between the two iris images. The researcher applied an area-based image registration technique as a tool of compensating for both eye scaling and rotation for the purpose of establishing the goodness of match.

According the system developed by Boles [34], scaling the iris images is the first step in achieving a constant diameter so that when comparing two images, one is regarded as the reference image. However, this system performs this differently to the other techniques. This is because normalization is not performed until attempts to match two iris regions are made. Unlike this, other techniques start performing normalization and saving the result for later comparisons. Once the two irises have the same dimensions, extracting the features from the iris region by storing the intensity values along virtual concentric circles, with origin at the centre of the pupil is conducted. Following this is selecting the normalization resolution to achieve almost the same number of data points extracted from each iris. This makes this system essentially similar to Daugman's rubber sheet model. However, the exceptional difference is that scaling performed is at match time, and is related to the comparing iris region, rather than scaling to some constant dimensions. Moreover, Boles did not explain how rotational invariance is obtained.

For the proposed non-linear normalization method proposed by Yuan and Shi [35], iris patterns follow a non-linear behavior because of the changes of pupil size.

6.3 Feature Extraction

According to Masek [13], it is a must to extract the most discriminating information available in an iris pattern to provide accurate recognition of individuals. In order tomake comparisons between templates, encoding the significant characteristics of the iris is essential. Most systems of the iris recognition benefit from a band pass decomposition of the iris image so that a biometric template can be created. Moreover, the template, resulted from the process of encoding these features will require a corresponding matching metric measuring similarity between two iris templates. This metric ought to give two ranges of values, one is known as intra-class comparisons, and another is known as inter-class comparisons, depending on generating or creating iris templates. Therefore, distinct and separate values given by these two states help make a decision with high confidence as to whether two templates are from the same iris, or from two different irises [13].

In addition, the texture of the external surface of the iris usually represents its unique pattern. To accurately identify individuals, representation of the iris patterns needs to focus on these features that are close enough in distance for similar patterns, and otherwise for different patterns. Thus, encoding these features is a must order to conduct the comparison among the iris images that are encoded. Besides, in most algorithms used in extracting the iris feature, filter banks are used to achieve the iris texture. Furthermore, encoding the filter output is performed using a bit vector code. In processing the image and recognizing the pattern, the process of extracting the features also functions as data reduction. As it is capable of transforming the input data into a set of feature vectors, it is not only capable of retaining the features of the input state, but also can minimize the size of the data [33].

There are many techniques used in different researches are stated as: wavelet encoding, gabor filter, log-gabor filter, Zero-crossings of the 1D Wavelet, Daugman's Algorithm, Wilder's Algorithm, Cumulative Sums, wavelet transform, Haar Wavelet and etc.

6.4 Iris Matching

The pattern matching is the last stage in an iris recognition system. To calculate the "distance" between two equal length image codes, the most common method is to compare two iris images [17] [36]. Hamming distance and Euclidean distance are two examples. In addition, correlation is another technique often used by some researchers.

6.4.1 Hamming Distance

The Hamming distance was first introduced by Richard Hamming in 1950 for error detecting and error counting. The Hamming distance is also the matching metric, which is applied by Daugman. It can be defined as the sum of the bitwise exclusive values of the two image codes that are divided by the total number of bits. The calculation of the Hamming distance is taken only with bits that are generated from the actual iris area [17]. Daugman's algorithm has been widely used in commercial iris recognition products.

Great progress has been achieved on iris recognition method since last decade. Testing results of both International Biometrics Group (FRR=2~5% @ FAR= 6^{10-}) [39] and Iris Challenge Evaluation in 2006 (FRR=1~3% @ FAR= 3^{10-}) [40]. Demonstrate that the state-of-the-art iris recognition algorithms perform well on most of qualified iris images.

6.4.2 Euclidean Distance

The Euclidean distance is another approach usually used to compare the feature vectors that represent two images. The Euclidean distance measures how similar a collection of values are between two templates. Sanchez-Avila and Sanchez-Reillo in 2005 [27] compared the Euclidean distance method with Hamming distance method, and found that the Hamming distance produced better results than Euclidean distance as well as other methods.

6.4.3 Normalized Correlation

Wildes et al. [38] benefit from the normalized correlation between the acquired representations of database for goodness of match. Normalized correlation is much better than the standard correlation. This is because it is capable of considering or accounting for local variations in image intensity that corrupt the calculation of the standard correlation.

7 Conclusions

Video based iris recognition system has been recognized as an optimistic future but prodigious attempts and work are needed on smart user interface and intelligent recognition algorithms. The next generation of iris recognition systems considers human as the centre in the process of designing ideologies. To advance the usability of iris recognition system, it is important to reduce the constraints on the position and motion of users. Moreover, algorithms require to achieve accuracy and robustness in iris localization, normalization and feature representation, secure in iris livens detection and faster in iris database retrieval.

The aim of this work in the current paper is to propose general idea of V-IRS design method base on better understanding on strengths and key problems of the past and present iris recognition system. Consequently, they provide possible solutions to yield an effective design method for-IRS. This design method will certainly determine the effectiveness of the developed V-IRS in the next research phase.

References

1. Jain, A.K., Bolle, R., Pankanti, S.: Biometrics: personal identification in networked society. Kluwer Academic Publishers (1999)
2. CASIA Iris Image Database, `http://www.cbsr.ia.ac.cn/irisdatabase.htm`
3. Flom, L., Safir, A.: Iris recognition system. Google Patents (1987)
4. Sun, Z., Dong, W., Tan, T.: Technology Roadmap for Smart Iris Recognition (2009)

5. Ketchantang, W., Derrode, S., Bourennane, S., Martin, L.: Video pupil tracking for iris based identification. In: Blanc-Talon, J., Philips, W., Popescu, D.C., Scheunders, P. (eds.) ACIVS 2005. LNCS, vol. 3708, pp. 1–8. Springer, Heidelberg (2005)
6. He, Z., Tan, T., Sun, Z.: Iris localization via pulling and pushing. In: 18th International Conference on Pattern Recognition, ICPR 2006, vol. 4, pp. 366–369. IEEE (2006)
7. De Mira Jr., J., Mayer, J.: Image feature extraction for application of biometric identification of iris-a morphological approach. In: XVI Brazilian Symposium on Computer Graphics and Image Processing, SIBGRAPI 2003, pp. 391–398. IEEE (2003)
8. Guo, G., Jones, M.J.: Iris extraction based on intensity gradient and texture difference. In: IEEE Workshop on Applications of Computer Vision, WACV 2008, pp. 1–6. IEEE (2008)
9. Proença, H., Alexandre, L.A.: UBIRIS: A Noisy Iris Image Database. In: Roli, F., Vitulano, S. (eds.) ICIAP 2005. LNCS, vol. 3617, pp. 970–977. Springer, Heidelberg (2005)
10. Ma, L., Tan, T., Wang, Y., Zhang, D.: Personal identification based on iris texture analysis. IEEE Transactions on Pattern Analysis and Machine Intelligence 25, 1519–1533 (2003)
11. Bowyer, K.W., Hollingsworth, K., Flynn, P.J.: Image understanding for iris biometrics: A survey. Computer Vision and Image Understanding 110, 281–307 (2008)
12. Kader, W.M., Rashid, H., Mamun, M., Bhuiyan, M.A.S.: Advancement of CMOS Schmitt Trigger Circuits. Modern Applied Science 6, 51 (2012)
13. Masek, L.: Recognition of human iris patterns for biometric identification. Master's thesis, University of Western Australia (2003)
14. Liu, X., Bowyer, K.W., Flynn, P.J.: Experimental evaluation of iris recognition. In: IEEE Computer Society Conference on Computer Vision and Pattern Recognition-Workshops, CVPR Workshops, p. 158. IEEE (2005)
15. Hollingsworth, K., Baker, S., Ring, S., Bowyer, K.W., Flynn, P.J.: Recent research results in iris biometrics. In: Proc. of SPIE, vol. 7306, p. 73061Y (2009)
16. Rashid, H., Mamun, M., Amin, M.S., Husain, H.: Design of a Low Voltage Schmitt Trigger in 0.18 um CMOS Process With Tunable Hysteresis. Modern Applied Science 7, 47 (2013)
17. Daugman, J.G.: High confidence visual recognition of persons by a test of statistical independence. IEEE Transactions on Pattern Analysis and Machine Intelligence 15, 1148–1161 (1993)
18. Daugman, J.: How iris recognition works. IEEE Transactions on Circuits and Systems for Video Technology 14, 21–30 (2004)
19. Nseaf, A.K.: Enhancement segmentation technique for iris recognition system based on hough transform. Master. University Kebangsaan Malaysia UKM, Bangi (2011)
20. Negin, M., Chmielewski Jr., T.A., Salganicoff, M., von Seelen, U.M., Venetainer, P.L., Zhang, G.G.: An iris biometric system for public and personal use. Computer 33, 70–75 (2000)
21. Wildes, R.P.: Iris recognition: an emerging biometric technology. Proceedings of the IEEE 85, 1348–1363 (1997)
22. Nsaef, A.K., Jaafar, A., Jassim, K.N.: Enhancement segmentation technique for iris recognition system based on Daugman's Integro-differential operator. In: 2012 International Symposium on Instrumentation & Measurement, Sensor Network and Automation (IMSNA), vol. 1, pp. 71–75. IEEE (2012)
23. He, Z., Tan, T., Sun, Z., Qiu, X.: Toward accurate and fast iris segmentation for iris biometrics. IEEE Transactions on Pattern Analysis and Machine Intelligence 31, 1670–1684 (2009)

24. Shamsi, M., Saad, P.B., Ibrahim, S.B., Kenari, A.R.: Fast algorithm for iris localization using Daugman circular integro differential operator. In: International Conference of Soft Computing and Pattern Recognition, SOCPAR 2009, pp. 393–398. IEEE (2009)
25. Ling, L.L., de Brito, D.F.: Fast and efficient iris image segmentation. Journal of Medical and Biological Engineering 30, 381–391 (2010)
26. Wildes, R.P., Asmuth, J.C., Green, G.L., Hsu, S.C., Kolczynski, R.J., Matey, J.R., McBride, S.E.: A system for automated iris recognition. In: Proceedings of the Second IEEE Workshop on Applications of Computer Vision, pp. 121–128. IEEE (1994)
27. Kong, W.K., Zhang, D.: Accurate iris segmentation based on novel reflection and eyelash detection model. In: Proceedings of 2001 International Symposium on Intelligent Multimedia, Video and Speech Processing, pp. 263–266. IEEE (2001)
28. Tisse, C.-L., Martin, L., Torres, L., Robert, M.: Person identification technique using human iris recognition. In: Proc. of Vision Interface. Citeseer (2002)
29. Li, P., Liu, X.: An incremental method for accurate iris segmentation. In: 19th International Conference on Pattern Recognition, ICPR 2008, pp. 1–4. IEEE (2008)
30. Daugman, J.G.: Biometric personal identification system based on iris analysis. Google Patents (1994)
31. Daugman, J.: How iris recognition works. In: Proceedings of the 2002 International Conference on Image Processing, vol. 1, 31, pp. I-33–I-36. IEEE (2002)
32. Sanderson, S., Erbetta, J.H.: Authentication for secure environments based on iris scanning technology (2000)
33. Zhou, S.: A novel approach to iris localization and code matching for iris recognition. Nova Southeastern University (2009)
34. Boles, W.W., Boashash, B.: A human identification technique using images of the iris and wavelet transform. IEEE Transactions on Signal Processing 46, 1185–1188 (1998)
35. Yuan, X., Shi, P.: A non-linear normalization model for iris recognition. In: Li, S.Z., Sun, Z., Tan, T., Pankanti, S., Chollet, G., Zhang, D. (eds.) IWBRS 2005. LNCS, vol. 3781, pp. 135–141. Springer, Heidelberg (2005)
36. Lim, S., Lee, K., Byeon, O., Kim, T.: Efficient iris recognition through improvement of feature vector and classifier. ETRI Journal 23, 61–70 (2001)
37. Sanchez-Avila, C., Sanchez-Reillo, R.: Two different approaches for iris recognition using Gabor filters and multiscale zero-crossing representation. Pattern Recognition 38, 231–240 (2005)
38. Wildes, R.P., Asmuth, J.C., Green, G.L., Hsu, S.C., Kolczynski, R.J., Matey, J.R., McBride, S.E.: A system for automated iris recognition. In: Proceedings of the Second IEEE Workshop on Applications of Computer Vision, pp. 121–128. IEEE (1994)
39. International Biometrics Group, Independent Testing of Iris Recognition Technology. Final Report (May 2005), http://www.biometricgroup.com/reports/public/ITIRT.html
40. Iris Challenge Evaluation, http://iris.nist.gov/ice/

Smart-Device-Based Augmented Reality (SDAR) Models to Support Interior Design: Rethinking "Screen" in Augmented Reality

Pei-Hsien Hsu, Sheng-Yang Huang, and Bao-Shuh Lin

National Chiao Tung University, Taiwan
phsu@arch.nctu.edu.tw

Abstract. As the viewing devices for augmented reality (AR) shift from head-mounted display to smart devices, screen becomes a design factor which affects the viewing experience and associated conceptions. In this paper, we present three models of smart-device-based augmented reality (SDAR) for applications in interior design. The objective is to provide a theoretical framework for the rethinking of augmented reality based on relationships among screen, body, space and information, leading to developments in SDAR-assisted design for interior design profession.

Keywords: augmented reality, AR-aided design, interior design, architecture, HCI.

1 Introduction

Advances in applied technologies do not merely count on the innovation of technologies per se. To establish a conceptual model which facilitates the comprehension and analytical thinking toward the use of technologies is equally important. It provides designers with a foundation to develop design strategies which lead to comprehensible and user-friendly technologies. It is argued that the application of smart-device-based augmented reality (SDAR) technology can benefit from a rethinking of conceptual models involved, and this can be done by re-examining the element of "screen", often ignored in such applications, and its physical-visual relationships with the viewer, along with types of information displayed. In addition, interior design as a professional field can utilize SDAR to assist design visualization and communication. However, the use of it in such a field is not fully explored. In this paper, we present a theoretical framework for the rethinking of SDAR, leading to design strategies of its applications in interior design.

1.1 Smart-Device-Based Augmented Reality

Augmented reality (AR in brief) is not a new technology. However, since its emergence in the 90', it had been a high-end technology which was only available in some laboratories, remote from the general public. As a nature of augmented reality based on its definition, it aims to achieve a coexistence of physical and virtual reality,

H. Badioze Zaman et al. (Eds.): IVIC 2013, LNCS 8237, pp. 539–548, 2013.

and this had been made possible by a special device — head-mounted display (HMD). In contrast, augmented reality has now become a common technology, and this is mainly attributed to the popularization of portable smart devices (i.e. smart phones and compact tablet PCs), which have built-in video cameras, high-resolution display and computational power adequate for data processing related to augmented reality. Today, with proper software, most of smart device owners are able to use this technology for various purposes without having to purchase a pricy HMD. In addition, with the announcement of AR glasses (e.g. Google Glasses), it can be anticipated that eyeglasses will become the next consumer-level devices for augmented reality. Nevertheless, it can also be assumed that smart devices will still be the dominant tool for the general purpose of augmented reality for the next years.

There are fundamental differences between smart-device-based augmented reality (SDAR) and HMD-based augmented reality (HMDAR) in terms of how images are perceived by the user, but the differences are often ignored in literatures and applications within the field. The key characteristic of AR display based on HMD is the disappearance of screen, which may be described as "immediacy" or "transparent mediation". [1] Although, in fact, there is a screen, see-through or not, in each HMD unit, it is normally not in the viewer's attention and is perceptually ignored. Thus, the process of mediation becomes transparent. By contrast, in the case of handheld SDAR, the viewer/user holds a portable device, of which the screen is in conscious awareness and this makes it fundamentally different from HMDAR. Such a difference is an analogy to the relationship between HMD-based virtual reality and desktop-based virtual reality (which is called "3D virtual environments" by some authors). Screen is addressed as an important design factor as desktop-based virtual reality (3DVEs) became prevalent. With the acknowledgement of "screen" and "frame", 3DVEs are distinguished from idealistic virtual reality and are furthermore linked to conventional screen-based media forms, such as animation and cinema, since they share the same screen-viewer relationship and therefore conceptual models of the old media and associated conventions in terms of their design may be borrowed. Such an acknowledgement leads to what Manovich describes as "cultural interface" [2] and what Bolter et al. describe as the "digital remediation of media". [1] Seeing desktop-based VR as another screen-based cultural form frees 3DVEs from a technology-oriented thinking and thus widens the field for its applications.

We argue that SDAR is fundamentally different from HMDAR not just in terms of devices utilized, but also in terms of the conceptions users may develop in their mind. The acknowledgement of screen and frame as additional factors should leads to different ways of conceptualizing the experience of augmented reality based on portable screens. New design strategies may also be developed as a result of the introduction of new design factors, similar to how 3DVEs evolved out of HMD-based VR. The objective of this paper

1.2 Augmented Reality for Interior Design

As a powerful visualization tool, the technology of augmented reality is suitable for various design fields. Through visualization based on AR, design proposals can be examined beforehand. In addition, as a nature of AR, it aligns computer-rendered virtual elements with particular parts of the physical world and displays the visual combination according to the viewer's current perspective. This makes it particularly useful for design fields involving built environments such as urban design, architecture and interior design. By replacing a portion of physical environment with proposed three-dimensional design made possible by AR technology, the difference between the current status of the environment and the simulated status — which in fact makes the "content" of a design, becomes evident.

In the research field of interior design, AR has been used to simulate "objects" inside architectural space, which often include furniture, fixtures and appliances. With the physical environment captured in real time and processed as a visual backdrop, 3D rendering of virtual objects is superimposed. The virtual objects may be manipulated in many ways. For instance, they can change, in response to the viewer's input, in position, orientation, size or material. Alteration in shape or switching between a selection of objects as design options is also feasible. AR, in this sense, serves not just as 3D visualization, but also an interactive and intuitive way to support design decisions — AR-assisted interior design.

While such application of AR for interior design has been proved useful, we argue that AR in this context should go beyond the simulation of objects and include the design of spatial enclosures (e.g. ceilings, walls and floors), which is normally neglected in previous developments for the same purpose of AR-assisted interior design. [3~5] Nevertheless, AR visualization of spatial enclosures leads to computer renderings that could cover the whole display area, which reflexively stops itself from being seen as augmented reality due to the absence of a key characteristic of AR — the coexistence of virtual and physical elements. To solve this problem, the very nature of SDAR based on the relationship between the element of screen, body and vision needs to be re-examined, and the definition of augmented reality in this particular context should be redefined. This task includes not only the re-examining of SDAR at a perceptual level [6], but also at a cognitive level and from a user-centric point of view.

2 Three Models of Augmented Reality Based on Smart Devices

2.1 AR vs. VR for Interior Design

There are apparent differences between AR and VR, and the major one is that VR seeks to achieve, in theory, a total replacement of the physical environment with computer-generated vision and other sensual inputs, whereas AR, on the other hand, aims to achieve a coexistence of physical and virtual world. That is, in AR, only a portion of the perceived world is replaced by digital inputs. It may be argued that such a different between them shows their similarities, rather than a conflict. Indeed, it is only the "degree of replacement" that makes the difference, and from this standpoint, AR can be regarded as a variation of VR. However, such a distinction leads to very different applications in design.

With VR, it is not difficult to create a world with rather realistic look in terms of lighting and textures, and a user does not need to physically go to a specific site to use it. This makes VR particularly useful for visualizing a new design which does not involve close coordination with existing environment. While with AR, a proposed three-dimensional design may be evaluated through two types of relationship: contrast between the two "versions" of the perceived environment, with and without the overlaid virtual elements, and the spatial-configurational relationship between virtual elements and the physical environment. Unlike VR, to be able obtain such a design simulation based on AR, viewers are required to engage their bodies directly with the simulated environment, and this on-location bodily engagement is helpful for the comprehension of spatial configuration and formal features, which is important to particular applications such as interior design.

Another major difference between AR and VR for interior design lies in their capability to display "components" of an interior space. AR is suitable for visualizing "objects" inside a space, whereas VR is suitable for "spatial enclosures" that define spaces, which also accommodate "objects". Such a difference leads to a question for us — is it possible to combine the two things below?

1. The capability of VR in visualizing spatial enclosures
2. The feature AR in terms of allowing a visible connection/comparison between the proposed 3D design and the existing environment

In addition, shifting from idealistic virtual reality to 3DVEs leads to an awareness of screen and frame as additional design factors, and a connection between virtual reality and conventional media such as cinema or television is thus established. Likewise, shifting from HMDAR to SDAR should bring out a possibility of treating screen and frame as new factors for the designing of AR applications based on portable display devices. Thus, a few questions can be asked:

1. How is the screen of SDAR comprehended by its user — what is the conceptual model?
2. Can metaphors be used to facilitate the forming of such a conceptual model?
3. What are the possible screen-body relationships, and do they create different conceptual models?

The questions listed above lead to "three models of SDAR" explained below.

2.2 Three SDAR Models

Based on the context of smart-device-based augmented reality, in which a user holds a portable smart device (smartphone/tablet PC) in hands, we identify three models. They define the relationships between the user and the screen and describe conceptual models/metaphors involved. They three models are: ***Filtered Reality***, ***Parallel Reality***, and ***Projective Reality***.

"**Filtered Reality**" (Fig. 1(a).) is the most typical model for smart-device-based augmented reality. The user holds a portable device in front of the face, and the screen is relatively close to the eyes so that it roughly covers the field of view. The screen is generally kept in the same position relative to the body of the user, and therefore the obtained AR vision based on this setting is similar to a HMD-based setting. The frame of the display screen is somewhat visible. It is, however, not in the center of the user's

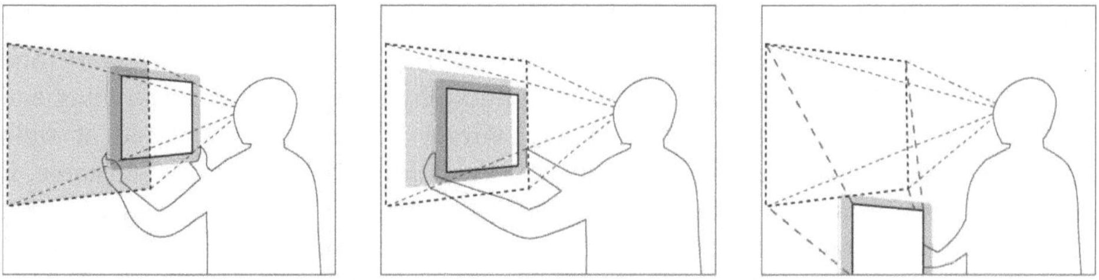

(a) (b) (c)

Fig. 1. Three models of smart-device-based augmented reality (SDAR): (a) Filtered Reality model; (b) Parallel Reality model; (c) Projective Reality model

attention and can be generally ignored. Holding a screen, in contrast, is a conscious action, and we argue that with a proper design metaphor, this action can become part of a comprehendible setting leading to a conceptual model. As the name — filtered reality — suggests, the screen in this context can be seen as a piece of special filter which is see-through and at the same time adds a layer of information, 2D or 3D, on the top of physical environment video-captured in real time. Through such a special filter, vision is manipulated. This is not too different from how filters work in conventional media — e.g. we can add a piece of effect filter in front of a camera to alter the vision or overlay a piece of printed film on a book page to add additional information.

"**Parallel Reality**" (Fig. 1(b).) is basically the same as Filtered Reality in terms of the relationship between the screen and the user's body, except that the eyes-screen distance in this model is relative longer than it is in the previous model. This extra distance results in an important distinction: in Parallel Reality, the display screen only occupies a portion of the field of view, rather than the whole. Consequently, a digitally mediated vision which only partially occupies the field of view allows the coexistence o f two types of vision inside the viewing spectrum: vision that comes directly from the physical environment and vision that comes from the screen. Based on such coexistence, it is therefore possible to display a "full-virtual" content inside the screen while retaining a "pseudo" AR relationship, if there is spatial "registration" between the virtual content and the physical environment.

Although a digitally mediated display with full virtual contents is normally regarded as virtual reality (or 3DVEs), we argue that the coexistence of virtuality and physicality, which occurs outside the screen itself, still satisfies the conditions that define augmented reality — merging of virtual and physical worlds, registration and interactivity.[7] In addition, by looking at a screen with its frame visible, placed in the center of the field of view, the viewer perceptually see through the frame into a virtual world. In this sense, the screen can be conceptualized as a special "window" leading to a parallel/overlapping reality, similar to a "parallel universe" or "alternate reality", as described in sci-fi fictions or metaphysics. "The other world" may share some common properties with "this world" in various aspects. On the other hand, it may also have its own textures, lighting, time, forms, spaces and so on.

"**Projective Reality**" (Fig. 1(c).) combines the emerging "micro projection" technology with smart-device-based AR. By integrating a micro projector and a smart device, virtual images from a smart device can be projected onto the surfaces of a physical environment. Through such projection, the coexistence of virtuality and physicality is thus made possible.[8,9] In addition, by using a proper positioning and tracking mechanism (e.g. visual tracking), virtual images can be placed at right locations in the physical environment, even if the holding of the device is unstable. It is also possible to project images which match the shapes of objects in space so that they only fall on particular areas of the physical environment. Dynamic effects or illusive deformation can thus be given to otherwise static objects, and this relationship is normally described as "projection/video mapping". [10] By projecting images onto spatial enclosures, screen and frame are removed from the viewer's field of view. Augmented reality takes place on the surfaces of physical environment, rather than through the screen. Consequently, screen becomes a handling part for the projector, and on a conceptual level, overlaid images are similar to decals.

The idea of combing augmented reality and image projection is not new. Conceptually, augmented reality can be achieved by overlapping virtual images on the surfaces of a physical environment through projection. In fact, such a combination is often described as "spatial augmented reality". [11] However, previous applications are mostly based on the use of fixed projectors, and therefore the projection is normally for specific locations. We argue that, with a light-weight micro projector, the projector itself and a smart device can be integrated into one unit, which retains good mobility and intuitive operations, and this distinguishes Projective Reality from a general spatial augmented reality.

A comparison between the three models, in terms of screen/frame-body relationships and conceptions involved, is summarized in Table 1. It should be noted that, although these three models can all be understood as augmented reality, coexistence of virtuality and physicality, which is an essential quality of augmented reality, occurs in different ways in these models. In Filtered Reality, such coexistence takes place inside the screen, whereas in Parallel reality, this takes place between the screen and physical environments. In Projective Reality, it is on the surfaces of physical environments par se where such coexistence takes place.

Table 1. Comparison between the three SDAR models

Model	Frame	Screen	Conception
Filtered Reality	In frame	Translucent Full spectrum In front of face, close	Looking through a filter hold in hands
Parallel Reality	Out of frame	Transparent Partial spectrum In front of face, away	Looking through a window hold in hands
Projective Reality	No frame	Invisible Not in view Not in front of face	Video projector, Dynamic decals

3 SDAR-Assisted Interior Design

Combining SDAR technology and proper information contents, including 2D and 3D virtual elements, smart devices can serve as useful tools to support tasks related to interior design. The three SDAR models defined above describe 3 sets of relationships between the user, the screen, the frame, the content and conceptions developed. Based on these relationships, it is then possible to conceive the linkages between the models and types of information useful for interior design tasks. (Fig. 2)

Interior design, in general, is a professional field which deals with the designing of indoor environments, which may cover various aspects including formal design of spatial enclosures (walls, floors and ceilings), arrangement of objects (furniture, fixtures and appliances), lighting, use of materials and textures, underlying wiring and other technical managements. To support such tasks through the use of AR visualization based on smart devices, it is necessary to examine the three SDAR models according to their capabilities against aspects of interior design since a particular model might be more suitable than the others for a particular aspect of interior design. In Table 2, a cross-comparison of the three models of SDAR versus aspects of interior design is made accordingly in order to analyze their capabilities.

Objects in interior space are presumably visualized the best based on the Filtered Reality model. Although visualization based on the Parallel Reality is also able to show virtual objects, it does not create a clear contrast between the simulated objects and the existing physical environment. In addition, the Projective Reality model does not provide the best quality of images for simulated objects considering the rather insufficient illumination from a micro projector.

Spatial enclosures are visualized the best based on the Parallel Reality model. It is the nature of Parallel Reality model, by definition, that virtual representations of spatial enclosures are displayed in full inside a portable screen, which otherwise cannot be done according to the Filtered Reality model. Displaying spatial enclosures in the Filter Reality model goes against the model itself for being qualified as augment reality. Projective Reality model may not be the most suitable option for this task due to same reason stated above.

Lighting in space generally refers to the distribution of light over spatial enclosures. For this reason, it is visualized the best based on the Parallel Reality model. The Filtered Reality model is unable to provide the visualization of spatial enclosures required. Spatial projection based on the Projective Reality model, limited by its illumination, cannot provide ideal lighting simulation. Moreover, a lighting simulation often deals with lighting not design for the timing the simulation is performed — e.g. a simulation for lighting during the night may be conducted during the day, with undesirable natural light which may be preventable. The Parallel Reality model is, therefore, more suitable than the Projective Reality model in this case.

Wiring for interior design is an underlying part which is normally hidden beneath the surfaces of spatial enclosures. With AR, it is possible to visualize locations of wirings. Visualizations based on the three models all seem to be capable feasible for this task. However, considering that in actual interior design practice, people would need to find out exact locations of certain wirings, The Projective Reality model seem to be the best option among the three for such a purpose. Projected virtual images

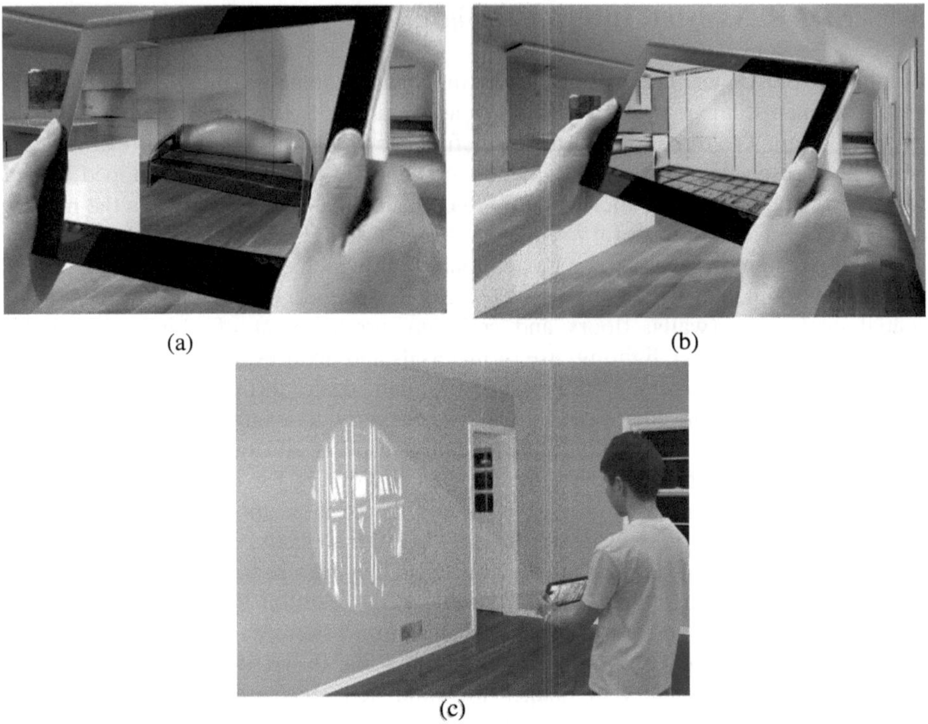

Fig. 2. Visualizations based on the three SDAR models and their applications on interior design: (a) Filtered Reality model and virtual objects; (b) Parallel Reality model and spatial enclosures; (c) Projective Reality model and projected images on the wall

allow the locations of wirings to be seen by multiple people while the user is operating a micro-projector-integrated SDAR system, which consequently enables the wiring locations to be marked down physically. This, in comparison, is difficult to be done based on other SDAR models.

The analysis on the visualization of wirings also points out an important difference between the three models. While visualizations based on the Filtered Reality model or the Parallel Reality model are more suitable for the "single-user" situation, visualization based

Table 2. Three SDAR models and there capabilities to display information. Symbols to distinguish between capabilities of each model (strengths of linkages between a model and a specific aspect): (○: strong Δ: moderate ×: weak)

Model	Object	Spatial Enclosure	Lighting	Wiring
Filtered Reality	○	Δ	×	Δ
Parallel Reality	Δ	○	○	Δ
Projective Reality	Δ	Δ	×	○

on the Projective Reality model provides video projections that can be shared by people in the same physical space, and this can be valuable in certain cases. To sum up, the above analyses are centered on tasks/aspects of interior design. Relationships described in this way tell the priorities of these three models for the purpose of using SDAR-based visualization for each aspect of interior design. The same set of relationships can be re-described with a center on the three models. Thus, it is possible to make descriptions for the capabilities of each visualization model against aspects of interior design.

Since there are clear distinctions between the three models in terms of the screen-body relationships, it is then possible to develop a SDAR-based system capable of automatically switching between designed operation modes corresponding to the three SDAR models. In each of the operation modes, information of certain types is shown or hidden according to the capability of the corresponding SDAR model, as described in the analyses above. A key technical issue involved is to detect the status of screen-body relationship (Fig. 3). This may be achieved by using sensors (e.g. infrared or ultrasonic sensors) or computer visions with designed algorithm. In addition to the filtering of information display, graphical interface should be designed according to the metaphors/conceptual models. Each model may have a particular set of operational logic and graphical style in order to support the communication of conceptions involved.

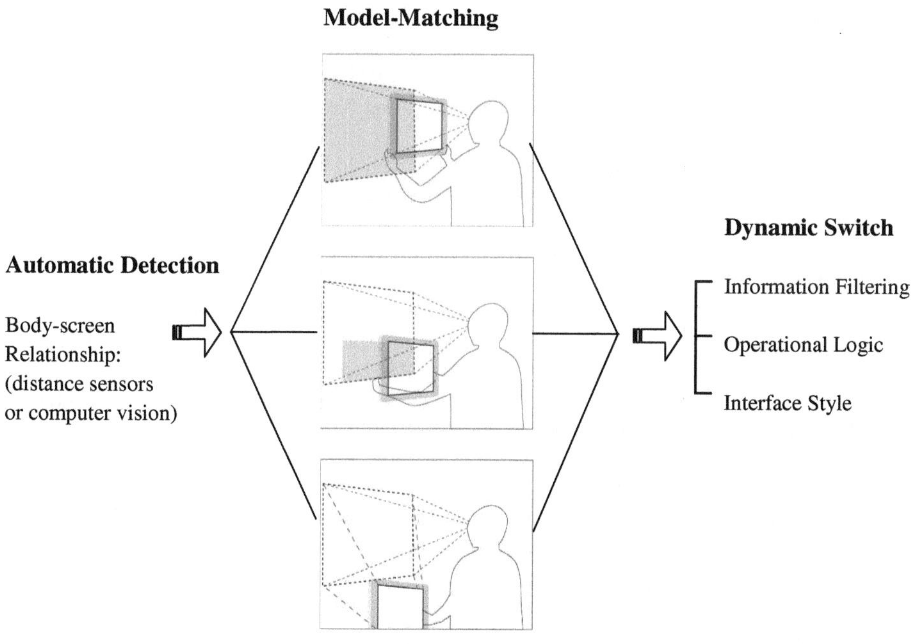

Fig. 3. Dynamically switching between modes of SDAR operation based on automatic detection of body-screen relationship

4 Conclusion and Future Work

Augmented Reality is not just a technology, but a specific way for us to look at our world, which is a complex amalgamation of both physical and virtual entities. As the viewing devices for AR change from head-mounted display to smart devices, the viewing experience and associated conceptions become different. The three models of SDAR, which is at the core of this paper, are developed in response to such a difference. However, they do not point to new technologies, nor do they seek to define a phenomenon that should be regarded as a new member for the AR/VR/Mixed Reality family.

Throughout this paper, we present a framework for the rethinking of smart-device-based augmented reality and their applications in the field of interior design. Metaphors and conceptual models described in the three models do not lead to ultimate answers to the designing of applications based on SDAR. Instead, they point out the importance and possible benefits of re-examining factors of augmented reality based on the new context. They also aim to show that, with such a re-examination, design guidelines for a SDAR-assisted application may be established, so can design possibilities be explored.

Based on the framework that has been set up in this paper, future work will go future into design implementations which cover information design, interface and associated technical issues. Design prototypes will be developed to test the concept and performance of SDAR-assisted interior design.

References

1. Manovich, L.: The Language of New Media. The MIT Press, London (1995)
2. Bolter, D., Grusin, R.: Remediation: Understanding New Media. The MIT Press, London (2000)
3. Phan, V.T., Choo, S.Y.: Interior Design in Augmented Reality Environment. International Journal of Computer Applications 5(5), 16–21 (2010)
4. Nóbrega, R., Correia, N.: Design your room: adding virtual objects to a real indoor scenario. In: ACM Human Factors in Computing Systems (CHI EA 2011), pp. 2143–2148. ACM, New York (2011)
5. Wei, D., Zhou, S.Z., Xie, D.: MTMR: A conceptual interior design framework integrating Mixed Reality with the Multi-Touch tabletop interface. In: 2010 9th IEEE International Symposium on Mixed and Augmented Reality (ISMAR), pp. 279–280 (2010)
6. Kruijff, E., Swan, J.E., Feiner, S.: Perceptual issues in augmented reality revisited. In: Mixed and Augmented Reality, pp. 3–12. IEEE Publishing (2010)
7. Azuma, R.T.: A Survey of Augmented Reality. Presence: Teleoperators and Virtual Environments 6(4), 355–385 (1997)
8. Choi, J., Kim, G.: Usability of one handed interaction methods for hand-held projection-based augmented reality. Personal and Ubiquitous Computing 17(2), 399–409 (2013)
9. Schöning, J., Rohs, M., Kratz, S., Löchtefeld, M., Krüger, A.: Map torchlight: a mobile augmented reality camera projector unit. In: ACM: Human Factors in Computing Systems: CHI 2009 Extended Abstracts (CHI EA 2009), pp. 3841–3846 (2009)
10. Raskar, R., Low, K.L.: Interacting with Spatially Augmented Reality. In: AFRIGRGH 2001 International Conference on Computer Graphics, Virtual Reality and Visualisation, pp. 101–108. ACM, New York (2001)
11. Bimber, O., Raskar, R.: Spatial Augmented Reality: Merging Real and Virtual Worlds. A K Peters, Wellesley (2005)

Incorporating Learning Management System with Social Network Sites to Support Online Collaborative Learning: Preliminary Analysis

Sharifah Nadiyah Razali[1], Faaizah Shahbodin[2], Norasiken Bakar[2], Hanipah Hussin[2], Mohd. Hafiez Ahmad[3], and Normala Sulaiman[4]

[1,2] Faculty of Information and Communication Technology
Malaysia Technical University Malacca
Hang Tuah Jaya, 76100, Durian Tunggal, Melaka, Malaysia
[2] Centre of Language and Islamic
Malaysia Technical University Malacca
Hang Tuah Jaya, 76100, Durian Tunggal, Melaka, Malaysia
[3] Electrical Technology Department
Masjid Tanah Community College,
Paya Rumput, 78300, Malacca, Malaysia
[4] Hospitality and Tourism Department
Merlimau Polytechnic,
Merlimau, 77300, Malacca, Malaysia
{shnadiyah,hafiezamani}@yahoo.com, {faaizah,hanipah, norasiken}@utem.edu.my,
normal@pmm.edu.my

Abstract. In 21st Century Learning, students use educational technologies to apply knowledge to new situations, to analyse information, to collaborate, to solve problems, and to make decisions. Utilising emerging technologies to provide expanded learning opportunities is critical to the success of future generations. In this paper, the author aims to discover if the 21st century's skills (collaboration, communication, problem solving, and critical thinking) can be discovered through integration of Learning Management System with Social Network Sites. In this preliminary study, two sets of questionnaires were distributed to 84 diploma students and 41 lecturers from Politeknik Ibrahim Sultan, Politeknik Merlimau, Politeknik Tuanku Syed Sirajuddin and Politeknik Sultan Idris Shah. This paper shares the preliminary findings on the perceptions of the students and lecturers on the use of Learning Management System, Social Network Sites and Collaborative Learning in the teaching and learning process. All collected data had been analyse using SPPS 19 software and the results of the study showed the existence of difficulties in communication and interaction in existing LMS and the need to assess students' engagement in group projects. Incorporating LMS with Facebook to support Online Collaborative Learning as recommendation for future research is suggested.

Keywords: 21st century learning, learning management system, social network sites, online collaborative learning.

H. Badioze Zaman et al. (Eds.): IVIC 2013, LNCS 8237, pp. 549–557, 2013.

1 Introduction

The benefits of collaboration in learning have been proven by Social Constructivism [1]. According to [2], learning tends to be most effective when students are in the position to work collaboratively in expressing their thoughts, discussing and challenging the ideas with others, and working together towards a group solution to the given problem. Collaborative learning, which in the online environment is typically referred to as online teams or online groups, refers to instructional activities for getting students to work together online to achieve common educational goals. Interest in collaboration is a natural outgrowth of the trend in education toward active learning, whereby students become involved in constructing their own knowledge through discovery, discussion, and expert guidance. Research by [3] shows that undergraduates improve their academic performance by interacting with their peers in an online collaborative learning (OCL).

To support collaborative learning environment, educator must track their student learning process. Therefore, [4] suggests that educators including teachers and lecturers should closely monitor how their students work together in a collaborative learning process for effective learning to take place. By monitoring the collaborative learning process, it can help the educators to keep track on students' on-going performance [5]. But, in online collaborative learning, it is difficult for educators to monitor and evaluate students' participation in group project [6]. Therefore, certain strategies must be applied to monitor the learning process.

Even though many researchers in education field have looked into the potential of adapting Social Network Sites (SNSs) in their teaching and learning process [7], [8] and [9], there are a few studies on integration of conventional Learning Management System (LMS) such as Moodle with SNSs. This has left a gap in body of knowledge on how LMS can integrate with SNSs platform to effectively facilitate learning especially in an OCL environment. Therefore, the researcher aims to incorporate LMS and SNSs to support OCL.

This paper shares the preliminary findings on the perceptions of the students and lecturers on the use of LMS, SNSs, and CL in the teaching and learning process. Discussion and future research are provided based on the findings of this study.

2 Materials and Methods

There were two survey instruments used in this study: student and lecturer survey. The purposes of the survey were to gather information about the current problem in teaching and learning using e-learning Curriculum Information Document Online System (CIDOS) at Malaysia Polytechnic. The lecturer survey instrument was a 23-item questionnaire and the student survey was a 19-item questionnaire. Both questionnaires consisted of three parts: LMS, SNSs, and CL. For LMS and SNSs sections, both instruments were adapted and modified from [10], and for CL section, it was adapted and modified from [11].

The respondents were randomly selected in order to collect information for this research. The questionnaires were distributed were given to 84 diploma students and 41 lecturers and participation was voluntary. The questionnaires were personally administered to respondents from Politeknik Ibrahim Sultan, Politeknik Merlimau, Politeknik Tuanku Syed Sirajuddin and Politeknik Sultan Idris Shah.

3 Finding

This section presents the findings based on the focus of this study, which is to discover the respondents' perceptions on LMS, SNSs, and CL environment. Therefore, only the items relevant to the focus are presented in this section. In this study, the Cronbach alpha was 0.863 for the student survey instrument and 0.832 for the lecturer survey instrument. [12] indicates that a questionnaire has high reliability if the Cronbach alpha is above 0.80. Therefore, it can be concluded that the internal consistency of the data was achieved.

In terms of the trends in LMS usage, Fig. 1 shows that the two main LMS features most frequently used by lecturers were Assessment (95.12%) and Course Management (80.49%). On the other hand, the least used features by lecturer were Communication (48.78%) and Productivity (68.29%). Next, as shown in Fig. 2, the two main LMS features most frequently used by students were Assessment (82.14%) and Course Management (73.81%) while the least used features in LMS the by students were Productivity (20.24%) and Communication (16.67%).

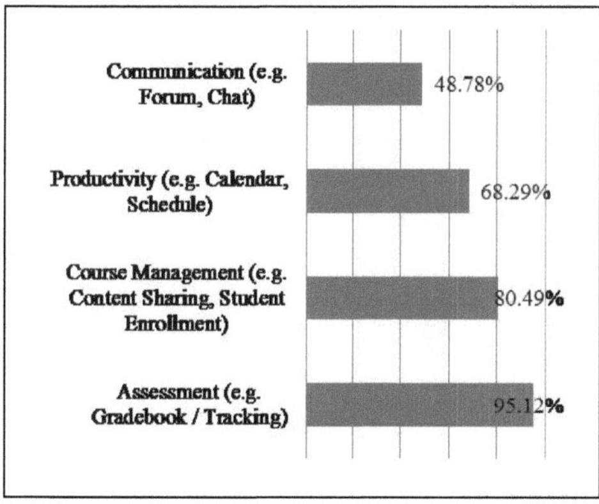

Fig. 1. Percentage of LMS access by lecturer

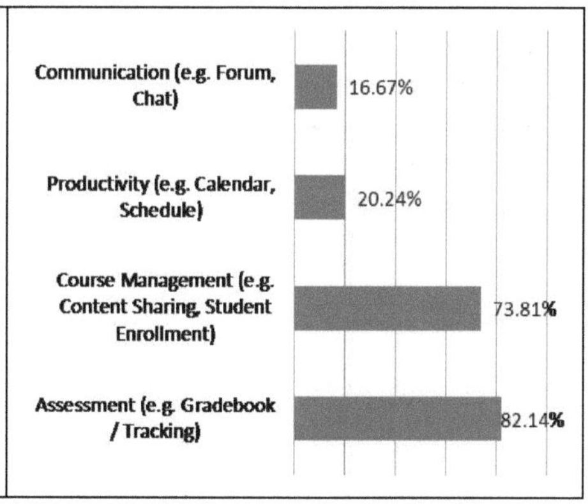

Fig. 2. Percentage of LMS access by student

As shown by Fig. 3, Social Networking such as Facebook, MySpace, and Twitter was the most commonly used alternative application by lecturers to complement the LMS provided by their institutions (39.02%) followed by Content Sharing (21.95%).

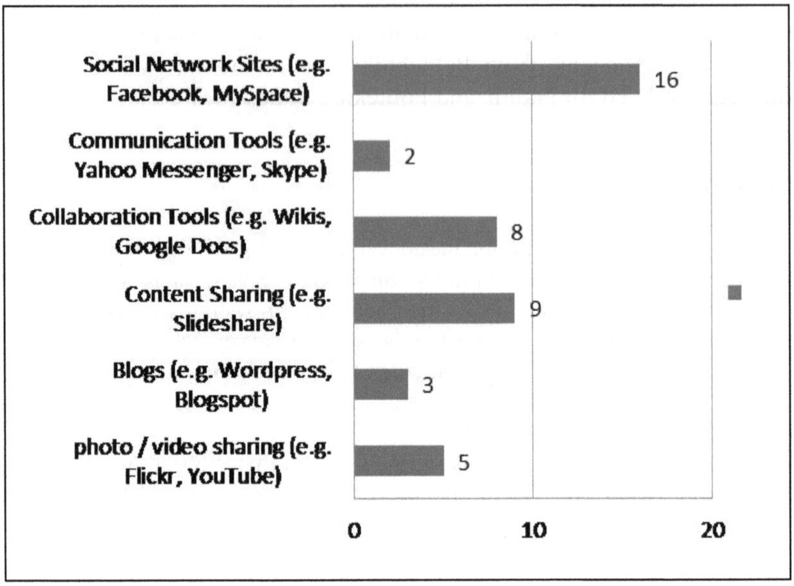

Fig. 3. Lecturer's alternative application to complement LMS

Fig. 4 and Fig. 5 show the percentage of SNSs based on lecturers' and students' preferences. 95.12% of lecturers and 95.24% of students preferred Facebook as their favourite SNS.

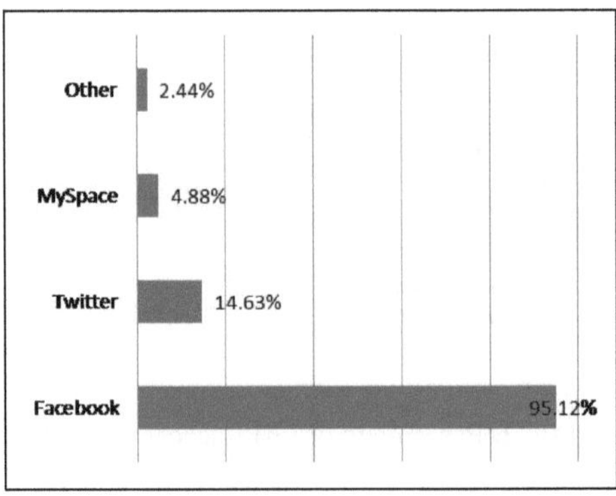

Fig. 4. Social Network Sites based on Lecturers Preferences

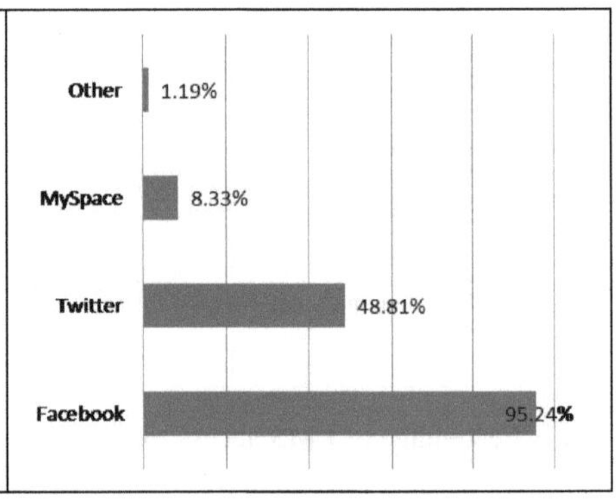

Fig. 5. Social Network Sites based on Students Preferences

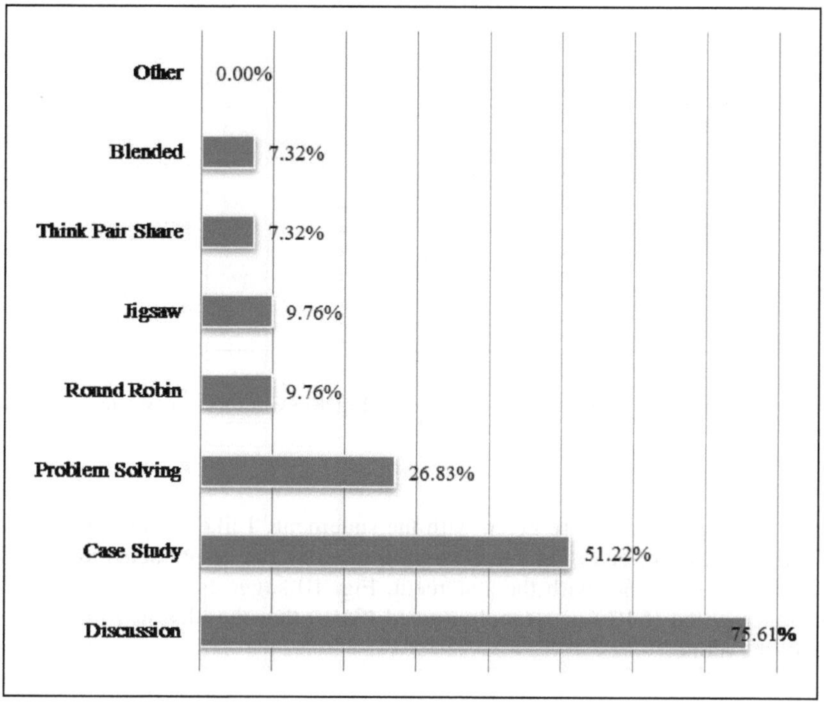

Fig. 6. Collaborative Learning activities implemented by lecturers

As shown in Fig. 6, it is clear that 75.61% of lecturers implemented discussion activity in their collaborative learning process compared to other Collaborative Learning activities. Fig. 7 showed that 88% of lecturers were aware of the free rider issues, but only 46.3% of lecturers assessed their students' projects based on output and student contribution. 27% of lecturers measured only the output and other 27% of lecturers did not measure anything (see Fig. 8).

In order to identify students' perceptions on the CL environment, the following items were given: (1.) Students' Group Work Experiences; (2.) Students' Attitude towards Working in Group; (3.) Students' Opinion about Lecturers' Measuring Strategy; (4.) Students' View about the Marks of Group Project; and (5.) Students' Preferences on Group Marks Evaluation. A series of questions measured with four-point Likert scale were designed to measure levels of agreement, with 1 = strongly disagree, 2 = disagree, 3 = agree, and 4 = strongly agree. The author used four-point Likert scale to eliminate possible misinterpretation of mid-point. Use of five-point Likert scale could make the respondents prefer not to take side between agree and disagree by always marking the most neutral answer [13]. Therefore, in cases in which specific respondents' opinions are essential such as opinion on services or products, a four-point Likert-scale can be employed.

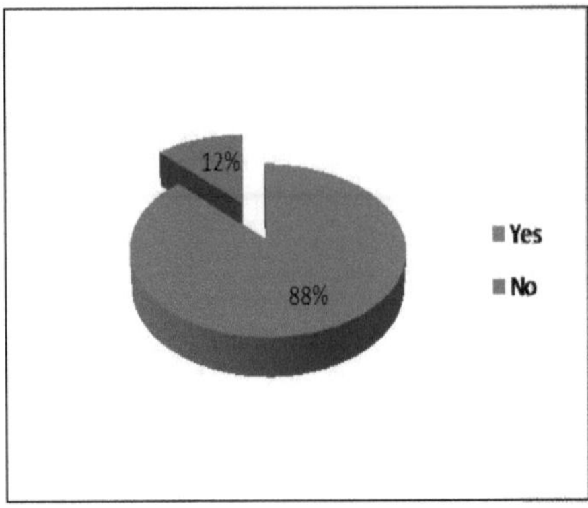

Fig. 7. Lecturers' perceptions on free rider issues

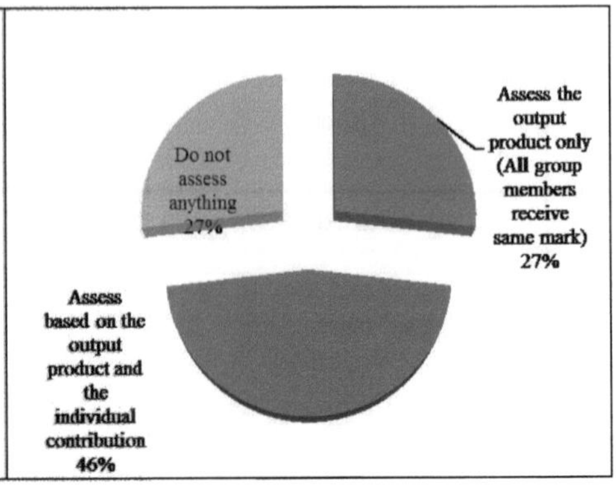

Fig. 8. Lecturers' measuring strategy

When the respondents were given with the statement "I like to participate in group work experiences" (refer to Fig. 9), a large number of the respondents agreed (76%) or strongly agreed (20%) with the statement. Fig. 10 suggests a large number of the respondents agreed (54%) or strongly agreed (31%) that they learned more in group than learning alone.

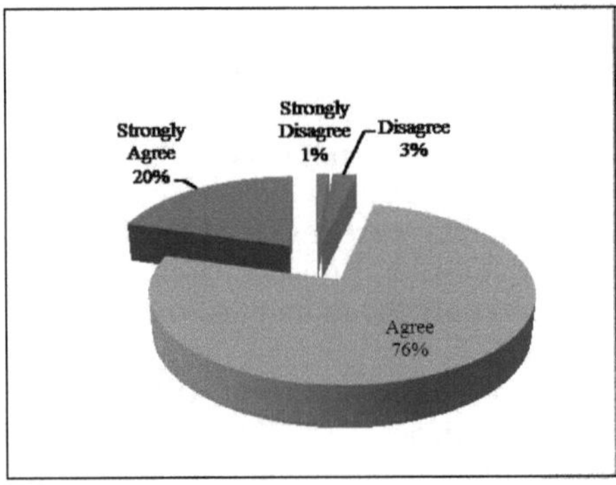

Fig. 9. Students' group work experiences

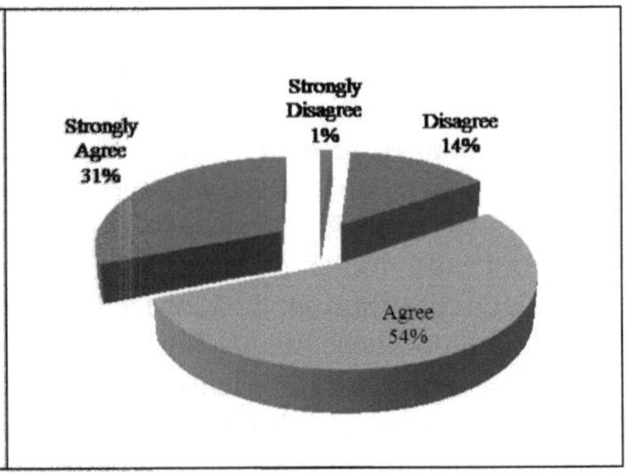

Fig. 10. Students' attitude towards working in group

70% of the respondents agreed and 12% of the respondents strongly agreed with the statement that lecturers only evaluated the output and the respondents will get equal marks in their group (refer to Fig. 11). Fig. 12 shows that more than half of the respondents (57%) strongly agreed and 33% of the respondents agreed with the statement "It is unfair for all members to get same marks". 57% of the respondents agreed and 41% of the respondents strongly agreed that lecturer should evaluate the group work based on student contributions (refer to Fig. 13).

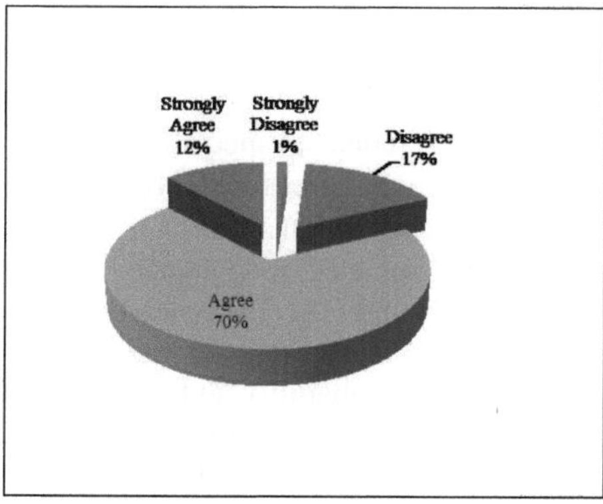

Fig. 11. Students' opinion on lecturers' measuring method

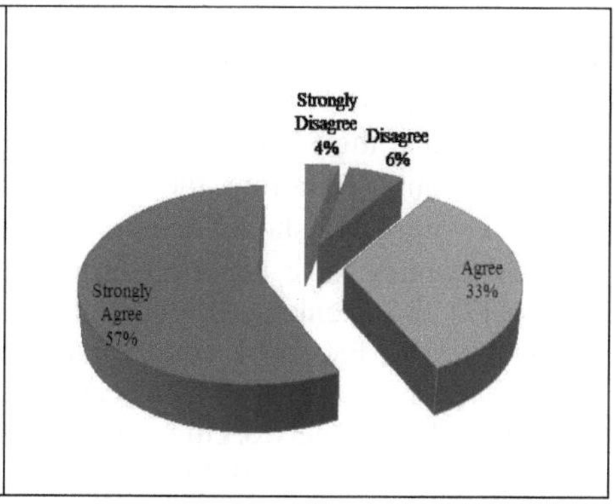

Fig. 12. Students' perceptions on the marks of group project

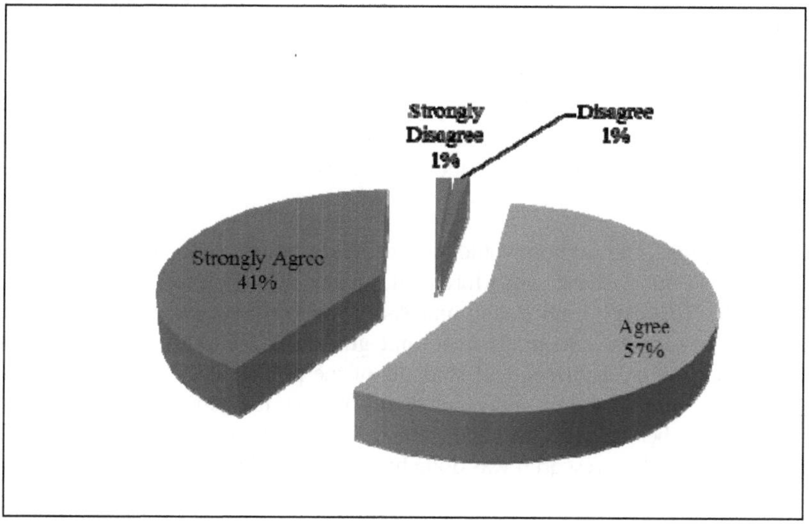

Fig. 13. Students' preferences on group marks evaluation

4 Discussion and Conclusion

Most educational institutions have implemented LMS to centralise the contents, learning, and assessment activities in one single learning environment. The educators and learners use forum and discussion boards to facilitate their communication and collaboration work. However, from the results, it was found that the lecturers preferred to employ Social Network Sites to facilitate their communication than using

LMS. This result showed that there were weaknesses in LMS in the field of communication and collaboration among users. Moreover, this results is similar with the result by [14]. The authors use other applications as a replacement for built-in discussion forum in LMS. However, this is different from the result reported by [15], who believe that the SNSs may cause distraction to the students, especially the newly enrolled students. Therefore, the author of this present study agrees with [10] and [16] that the existing LMS should be upgraded with social network function.

Recent studies have reported how Facebook can be used to enhance learning process [17] and to enhance collaboration activities [14] and [18]. In contrast with the findings by [19], Facebook simply cannot be successful in meeting the needs of the students; it can only be used as a supplement due to the incapability and limitation of the LMS such as in networking and communication. The findings from the survey in this present study indicated that 95% of students and 98% of lecturers have their own SNSs account, and 95.24% of students and 95.12% of lecturers were Facebook subscribers.

In each collaborative activity, evaluation must also emerge. It was difficult for the lecturers to monitor and evaluate the student participation in group project [6]. According to [20], a detailed evaluation on collaborative processes will help students achieve the desired goals. Therefore, lecturers had to apply certain instrument to record and monitor student discussion and to assess student contribution from the discussion. [21] find that students prefer to use tool that they are familiar with. Therefore, on the next stage of this present research, the author will incorporate Learning Management System (LMS) with Facebook to enable students and lecturers communicate on Moodle through Facebook. This will be used as an instrument to support OCL.

Acknowledgments. The author would like to thank people who have been supportive throughout this study. First and foremost, Associate Professor Dr. Faaizah binti Shahbodin, Dr. Norasiken binti Bakar, and Associate Professor Dr. Hanipah binti Hussin for their advice, support, encouragement, and guidance. The author would also like to thank the management, lecturers, and students of the polytechnics for their involvement, cooperation, and support in this study. Last but not least, the author would like to express an infinite love to her beloved husband, family, and colleagues for giving much support and encouragement. This research was done by a PhD candidate from UTeM.

References

1. Vygotsky, L.S.: Mind in Society. Harvard University Press, Cambridge (1978)
2. Johnson, R.T., Johnson, D.W.: Cooperation and competition: Theory and research. Interaction Book Company, Edina (1989)
3. Chen, Y.: Learning styles and adopting Facebook technology. In: Technology Management in the Energy Smart World, pp. 1–9 (2011)
4. Wang, Q.: Design and evaluation of a collaborative learning environment. Computers & Education 53(4), 1138–1146 (2009)
5. Wang, Q.: Using online shared workspaces to support group collaborative learning. Computers & Education 55(3), 1270–1276 (2010)

6. Ellis, T., Hafner, W., Harman, K.: Building a framework to support project-based collaborative learning experiences in an asynchronous learning network. International Journal of Doctoral Studies 4 (2009)
7. Al-Zoube, M.: E-Learning on the Cloud. International Arab Journal of e-Technology 1(2), 58–64 (2009)
8. McCarthy, J.: Utilising Facebook: immersing Generation-Y students into first year university. The Journal of the Education Research Group of Adelaide 1(2), 39–49 (2009)
9. Marijana, D.-Z., Aleksandra, B.L., Aleksandar, R.M.: Fostering engineering e-learning courses with social network services. In: 19th Telecommunications Forum (TELFOR), pp. 1–4 (2011)
10. Embi, M.A.: e-learning in Malaysian Higher Education: Status, Trends and Challeges. Department of Higher Education Ministry of Higher Education 2011 (2011)
11. Capdeferro, N., Romero, M.: Are online learners frustrated with collaborative learning experiences? The International Review of Research in Open and Distance Learning 13(2) (2012)
12. Ghaffar, M.N.A.: Penyelidikan Pendidikan. Penerbit Universiti Teknologi Malaysia, Skudai (1999)
13. Green, K., Lam, T.: Likert Scale the Same as 'Don't Know' for Informed and Uninformed Respondents? Effects of Serial Position and Labeling on Selection of Response Options, vol. 6641 (May 2010), http://portfolio.du.edu
14. Hernández, R., Amado-Salvatierra, H.R., Guetl, C., Smadi, M.: Facebook for CSCL, Latin-American Experience for Professors. In: 2012 IEEE 12th International Conference on Advanced Learning Technologies, pp. 327–328 (2012)
15. Li, C., Dong, Z., Untch, R.: Peerspace-an online collaborative learning environment for computer science students. Advanced Learning ..., 409–411 (2011)
16. Marijana, D., Aleksandar, M., Zorica, B., Dušan, B., Krčo, S.: Providing Adaptivity in Moodle LMS Courses Adaptive e-learning systems. Educational Technology & Society 15, 326–338 (2012)
17. Ractham, P., Firpo, D.: Using Social Networking Technology to Enhance Learning in Higher Education: A Case Study Using Facebook. In: 44th Hawaii International Conference on System Sciences, pp. 1–10 (2011)
18. Cerdà, F.L., Planas, N.C.: Facebook' s Potential for Collaborative e-Learning. Revista de Universidad y Sociedad del Conocimiento (RUSC) 8(2), 197–210 (2011)
19. Ishan Sudeera, A., Tham, C.Y.: Implementation of Facebook Study Groups as Supplements for Learning Management Systems (LMS) in Adult ODL Environments. Asian Association of Open Universities Journal 7(1), 1–11 (2011)
20. Swan, K., Shen, J., Hiltz, S.: Assessment and collaboration in online learning. Journal of Asynchronous Learning ..., 45–62 (2006)
21. Suthathip, M., Songrit, M.: Can Facebook be a New Communicative Channel in a Student-Centered LMS? In: The Asian Conference on Technology in the Classroom 2012 Official Conference Proceedings, Osaka, pp. 115–129 (2012)

Student's Behavioral Intention to Use Online Discussion Site (ODS) Scale: Investigating Unidimensionality of the Measurement Model

Prasanna Ramakrisnan[1,2], Azizah Jaafar[2], and Noor Faezah Binti Mohd. Yatim[3]

[1] Faculty Computer and Mathematical Sciences (FSKM), University Technology MARA (UiTM), 40450 Shah Alam, Selangor, Malaysia
[2] Institute of Visual Informatics, National University of Malaysia (UKM), 43600 Bangi, Selangor, Malaysia
[3] Faculty Infomation Science and Technology (FTSM), National University of Malaysia (UKM), 43600 Bangi, Selangor, Malaysia
prasanna@fskm.uitm.edu.my, aj@ftsm.ukm, my noor_yatim@yahoo.com

Abstract. The primary purpose of this study was to investigate unidimensionality of scale used to understand student's behavior towards an Online Discussion Site (ODS). The extended Technology Acceptance Model (TAM) model was adapted and examined for unidimensionality using Rasch analysis. Seven factors was used to model the student's intention to use ODS. There are Online Course Design (OCD), User-interface Design (UID), Previous Online Learning Experience (POLE), Perceived Usefulness (PU), Perceived Ease of Use (PEOU), Perceived Interaction (PI) and Intention to Use an Online Discussion Site (IUODS). Item fit statistics and principle component analysis (PCA) suggested that unidimensionality assessment can be achieved after removal of one item from User-interface Design (UID) factor. Our result reports that after removal the misfitting item, the 23 item instrument might provide a unidimensionality assessment of student's intention to use ODS ability.

Keywords: intention to use, rasch analysis, online discussion site.

1 Introduction

Online Discussion Sites (ODS) are widely being used in many universities as a medium to assist in the teaching and learning process. The message board or internet forum are example of ODS where students have conversations with their peers or instructors to discuss subject related topics. There are many ODS available over internet. Some of the popular ODS are related with technology, games, sports, politics, entertainments and etc. The educational based ODS are usually embedded in an e-learning platform.

In Universiti Teknologi MARA (UiTM), students are connected to each other in the ODS system using the i-Learn Portal (e-learning platform). They are able to

H. Badioze Zaman et al. (Eds.): IVIC 2013, LNCS 8237, pp. 558–568, 2013.

discuss tutorial and subject related questions anytime online regardless of their location. As one of the largest university in Malaysia, UiTM has the highest enrolment of students every semester. With the increase in the number of students, many generic courses are now being partially conducted online to reduce classroom utilization hours. For successful utilization of ODS for learning purpose, the ODS discussion platform needs to be used by the students to address subject related questions. There are many factors that influence the students' usage of the ODS. But the interest of this study is to identify factors that influence students' intention to use the ODS.

The technology acceptance assessment is increasingly being used in system and website design. Understanding the outcome of the assessment can assist in improving the current ODS design. The extended TAM model was proposed for studying intention to use an online learning community [1]. This model was originally developed with 24 items. The structural validity was examined using structural equation modeling (SEM). An exploratory factor analysis revealed there were seven factors that affect student's intention to use an online learning community. The analysis of the instrument demonstrated good level of reliability and validity. Hence we adapted the extended TAM model to understand the unidimensionality of the scale using Rasch analysis.

2 Applying Rasch Model in Intention to Use ODS

An individual's intention and usage of technology is commonly studied using the Technology Acceptance Model (TAM). TAM was developed and validated by Davis based on the Theory of Reasoned Action (TRA) [2] and [3]. This model suggests that an individual's attitude towards using a particular system is influenced by its perceived ease of use and perceived usefulness.

Davis [3] defined perceived ease of use (PEU) as "the degree to which an individual believes that using a particular system would be free of physical and mental effort" and perceived usefulness (PU) as "the degree of which a person believes that using a particular system would enhance his or her job performance".

There are many previous studies which have applied the TAM model to investigate students' intention to use e-learning technologies [4], [5], [6], [7], [8], [9], [10], [11], [12], [13], [14], [15] and [16]. Examples of technologies that support e-learning are the learning management system, blogs, the internet forum, social networking sites, wikis, instant messaging and etc. However most of studies used the TAM to examine the concept of e-learning systems. Our interest was to study student's behavioral intention to use current ODS design for learning purpose. Recent study showed that the extended TAM model can be used to investigate student's intention to use ODS [1].

Rasch analysis allows the distribution of person and item on a same interval scale. This allows characterization of person along a continuum and concurrently link the person to items reflecting a relative ordering of latent variable [17]. The person is placed on the scale based on their abilities to endorse to the items while items are scaled based on their difficulty.

Lately, Rasch model has been used for validation of a measurement model. The purpose of using Rasch analysis in validating a measurement model is due to the idea of fundamental measurement [18]. The Rasch model determines the extent actual data satisfy the modelled requirement. The estimation of person ability and item difficulty are used to determine respondent's responses towards items in the instrument. The Rasch model allows estimation of item location and person measure to be made along one single scale. The advantage using this model is the estimation of items and persons is independent of sample and instrument used [19].

Location of items and person along the measurement scale is estimated by the model from the proportion of response of each person to each item. Item location reports how difficult it is to be endorsed agree by the sample group. While the person measure states the ability of the person to endorse agree or disagree to the set of items distributed.

The scale resulting from the Rasch analysis of ordinal response of each person to each item has the properties of an interval scale. Interval level scaling results in residual which is used to assess unidimensionality [20]. Thus this study adopted Rasch model to investigate the unidimensionality of the measurement model.

3 Methods

3.1 Participants

The data was collected from full time undergraduate students at University Teknologi MARA (UiTM) who use the i-learn portal, the e-learning portal for their academic discussions. Seventy seven responses were collected from the survey questionnaires distributed manually and online.

3.2 Instrument

An instrument adopted for this study were designed by Liu et al [1]. It consist of seven factors, Online Course Design (OCD), User-interface Design (UID), Previous Online Learning Experience (POLE), Perceived Usefulness (PU), Perceived Ease of Use (PEOU), Perceived Interaction (PI) and Intention to Use an Online Discussion Site (IUODS). This are rated on a four-point Likert scale. The response categories used were (1) strongly disagree, (2) disagree, (3) agree, and (4) strongly agree. Table 1 summarizes the instrument used for this study.

3.3 Data Analysis

The instrument consisting of 24 items was administered manually and online to the students. The data collected was analysed using the Rasch analysis software

(WINSTEP 3.68.2). The purpose of this study was to scrutinize the instrument constructs and identify whether all the 24 items are required for investigating intention to use the ODS. This study will show all the required procedure to examine unidimensionality of the measurement model.

Table 1. The Items of the Instrument (adapted from [1])

Item	Statement
Online Course Design (OCD)	
OCD1	The course content is interesting
OCD2	The course content level is mid-range
OCD3	The course content meets my needs
OCD4	In general, I am satisfied with the design of the course content and quality
User-interface Design (UID)	
UID1	The layout design of the Online Discussion Site (ODS) makes it easy to read.
UID2	The font style, colour and layout of the interface make it comfortable for me to read.
UID3	In general, I am satisfied with the design of the Online Discussion Site (ODS) interface.
Previous Online Learning Experience (POLE)	
POLE1	I feel it would easier to operate the Online Discussion Site (ODS) if I had previous experience of using it.
POLE2	I will have a better understanding of how to use the Online Discussion Site (ODS) if it has a function for online guidance.
POLE3	I will have a better understanding of how to use the Online Discussion Site (ODS) if a lecturer or peer operates it first.
Perceived Usefulness (PU)	
PU1	I could improve my learning performance by using the Online Discussion Site (ODS).
PU2	I could improve my learning by using the Online Discussion Site (ODS).
PU3	I could increase my learning productivity by using the Online Discussion Site (ODS).
PU4	I think using the Online Discussion Site (ODS) helps me learn.
Perceived Ease of Use (PEOU)	
PEOU1	I feel that the interface design and information delivery in Online Discussion Site (ODS) are clear and easy to understand.
PEOU2	It is easy for me to do the things that I want to do by operating this Online Discussion Site (ODS).
PEOU3	I feel the Online Discussion Site (ODS) is easy to handle when I encounter a problem.
PEOU4	In general, I feel it is easy for me to use the Online Discussion Site (ODS).
Perceived Interaction (PI)	
PI1	I discuss relevant learning topics with other members on the Online Discussion Site (ODS).
PI2	I'm able to send e-mails to other members as a way of communicating.
PI3	I'm able to engage in real-time learning interaction with other members in the Online Discussion Site (ODS).

Table 1. *(Continued)*

Item	Statement
PI4	In general, I think this Online Discussion Site (ODS) provides good opportunities for interaction with other users.
Intention to Use an Online Discussion Site (IUODS)	
IUODS1	I intend to use this Online Discussion Site (ODS) for activities that involve learning.
IUODS2	I will reuse this Online Discussion Site (ODS) for relevant learning activities.

4 Unidimensionality of the Measurement Model

Measurement model represents the relationship between the observable variables and the underlying construct [21]. Traditionally the development and evaluation of measurement models are based on analysis from coefficient alpha, item-total correlations, exploratory factor analysis and confirmatory factor analysis. Our study proposes Rasch analysis for further understanding unidimensionality of the measurement model.

Dimensionality is defined as the total number of abilities required to satisfy the assumption of local independence [22]. Local independence assumes that given any particular level of ability, responses to different items are independent. Thus the measurement model is said to be unidimensional when the items of a test measure a single ability [23] which is there is only one ability affecting the responses of a set of items. The Rasch model assumes that item responses are unidimensional and locally independent [24].

The requirement of unidimensionality is to measure one attribute at a time. There are few approaches used in literature to assess unidimensionality. The approaches are: (1) classical method [25] and [26], (2) item fit analysis [27], (3) residual analysis [28] and investigation of the hierarchy of item calibrations [29]. But this study focuses on detecting the unidimensionality using item fit and principle component analysis (PCA) of standardized residuals from Rasch analysis.

Item fit is used to understand how well each item fits within the underlying construct [18]. The item fit is measured by the mean square fit statistics. There are two types of mean square fit statistics; infit and outfit. The infit statistics (weighted) report patterns of responses to items targeted on the estimated person abilities while outfit statistics (un-weighted) give the response pattern to items with difficulty far from estimated person abilities. The value of item mean square fit statistics is standardized to z-standard (Zstd) to show the size of randomness in the measurement.

Item fit statistics was assesses for the seven factors as well as for the total extended TAM model. The recommended range for mean square fit (infit / outfit) is from 0.50 to 1.5 while the standardized mean square ranges of -2.0 to 2.00. This range was used to identify the misfit items with variance in the response pattern. These misfit items usually lead to overfitting or underfitting to the model. The overfitting items have a lower mean square fit and z-standard value. These items also have predictable responses and are too good to be true, while underfitting items have a higher value of mean square fit and z-standard value with unpredictable responses. Hence, if any item with a poor fit statistics value was identified, it was considered for removal from the instrument. This process is iterated until no further misfit item was detected.

After removal of poorly fitting items, the unidimensionality was assessed again using the principal components analysis of standardized residuals using Rasch analysis. The principal component analysis (PCA) of standardized residuals was used to assess the dimensionality of the measurement model. The correlated items in the instrument were transformed into principle component by principal component analysis (PCA). Supposedly the residuals for pairs of item or person should be normally distributed and uncorrelated after removal of Rasch measures from the data [20]. If any pairs of item with a high residual correlation were detected, those items share more than half their random variance. Thus, large correlation would mean local dependency between pairs of items [30] and [31].

The PCA measures were used to examine the dimensionality of the measurement model [32]. For the dimensionality analysis, concern was on "variance explained by the first construct in residuals". If the value of "variance explained by the first construct in residuals" is big, there is existence of second dimension. If more than one dimension exists it can be detected through the measures of PCA in Table 2.

Table 2. PCA Measures used for Dimensionality Analysis

No	Test	Measures	Guidelines	References
1	Measurement Dimension	Variance Explained by the Measure	≥ 40% : Strong ≥ 30% : Moderate ≥ 20% : Minimal	[33]
2	Unidimensionality	Variance Explained by the First Construct	< 10%	[17]
3	Unidimensionality	Variance Explained by the Measure to Variance in the First Contrast	Ratio 3 to 1	[33]
4	Unidimensionality	Eigenvalue of the First Construct	< 3.0	[34]

5 Finding

Two criteria used to measure unidimensionality of the measurement model. It is based on the measures obtain from (1) item fit statistics and (2) principal component analysis (PCA) of standardized residuals.

5.1 Fit Statistics

Table 3 fit statistics of the items used in this study. There were four items with values out of the expected fit statistics range. The recommended range for mean square fit (infit / outfit) is from 0.50 to 1.5 while the standardized mean square ranges of

-2.0 to 2.00. The items were OCD4, UID2, PI4 and IUODS1. Item OCD4, IUODS1 and PI4 are identified as items over fitting to the model and might be a redundant measurement for this study. The responses for these 3 items are overly predictable from other responses and might not provide any new information. Thus, further analysis was conducted to detect redundancy of items in the study.

Table 3. Item Fit Statistics

Construct	**Items**	**Infit Statistics**		**Outfit Statistics**	
		MnSq	**Zstd**	**MnSq**	**Zstd**
Online Course Design (OCD)	OCD1	0.82	-0.80	0.88	-0.30
	OCD2	0.93	-0.30	1.29	1.10
	OCD3	1.12	0.70	0.96	-0.10
	OCD4	0.65	-2.20	0.52	-2.50
User-interface Design (UID)	UID1	0.97	-0.10	1.04	0.30
	UID2	1.62	2.50	1.62	2.10
	UID3	1.14	0.80	1.08	0.40
Previous Online Learning Experience (POLE)	POLE1	0.80	-0.90	0.73	-1.10
	POLE2	1.18	0.80	1.23	0.90
	POLE3	1.21	1.10	1.22	0.90
Perceived Usefulness (PU)	PU1	0.69	-1.60	0.61	-1.70
	PU2	1.11	0.60	1.04	0.30
	PU3	0.76	-1.10	0.70	-1.10
	PU4	0.73	-1.40	0.65	-1.50
Perceived Ease of Use (PEOU)	PEOU1	1.22	1.20	1.12	0.60
	PEOU2	1.25	1.20	1.28	1.10
	PEOU3	1.21	1.20	1.14	0.60
	PEOU4	0.77	-1.20	0.67	-1.40
Perceived Interaction (PI)	PI1	1.24	1.20	1.21	0.90
	PI2	0.78	-1.10	0.74	-1.00
	PI3	1.38	1.90	1.40	1.60
	PI4	0.51	-2.70	0.42	-2.60
Intention to Use an Online Discussion Site (IUODS)	IUODS1	0.65	-2.00	0.53	-2.20
	IUODS2	0.97	-0.10	0.85	-0.50

Note: MnSq = Mean Square, Zstd = Z-Standard

Redundant items have a high inter-item dependency and can be detected in response-residual analysis [35]. High dependency among items can the effect the reliability and quality of the instrument. The dependency between pairs of items can be seen in residual correlation in Table 4.

High positive correlation of residuals between pairs of items indicates that the items may be locally dependent. It specifies that the pairs of items are duplicative or are dominated by a shared dimension. Based on the finding from Table 4, the items in this study were found to be locally independence (Residual Correlation < +0.70) and there are no redundancy of items in this study.

Another way to detect redundancy is when items identified at the same difficulty level. If items are at the same difficulty level, we are testing same task and same domain. Thus, the items need to be eliminated from the instrument based on lower point measure correlation value.

Table 4. Largest Standardized Residual Correlation

Residual Correlation	Item	Item
0.38	UID3	OCD4
0.37	PU1	PU3
0.36	POLE1	PU4
0.33	POLE2	PEOU2
0.32	PEOU2	PI2
-0.44	POLE1	UID2
-0.42	PI2	PI3
-0.41	POLE2	UID3
-0.34	PI2	UID3
-0.32	PEOU1	POLE2

Table 5 provides items that detected at same difficulty level. There were 5 pairs of items identified at same difficulty level. But the responses for 10 items are independent and testing on different domain. Hence, those items will not be eliminated from the instrument. It is because those items will not contribute to redundant in the measurement and do not affect the measures.

Table 5. Item with Same Difficulty Level

Difficulty (logits)	Items	Domain / Construct
0.71	PEOU3	Perceived Ease of Use
	OCD4	Online Course Design
0.63	OCD3	Online Course Design
	UID3	User-interface Design
0.10	PEOU2	Perceived Ease of Use
	PI2	Perceived Interaction
-0.32	PU1	Perceived Usefulness
	OCD2	Online Course Design
-0.66	IUODS2	Intention to Use an ODS
	PU3	Perceived Usefulness

After the investigation of item redundancy, the overfitting item OCD4, IUODS1 and PI4 were not eliminated from the instruments because it does not indicate any redundancy in the same domain.

Earlier item UID2 was identified as an underfit item because it was out of the expected fit statistics range. Item UID2 had a high mean square and z-standard value (Table 3). Hence it has a too unpredictable response pattern. It is confirmed by looking at the scalogram for the responses pattern towards the item UID2. It was recognized that students with higher ability to endorse agree, disagreeing to the easy item (UID2) while students with lower ability agreeing to item UID2.

Besides that, from the finding the largest negative correlation (-0.44) between UID2 and POLE1 detected in Table 4. Large negative correlation between pairs of items indicates one of the items is likely to have a large misfit. This is proven that UID2 is a underfitting item and need to be eliminated from the instrument for successful implementation of Rasch measurement.

5.2 Principle Components Analysis (PCA)

The result of principle component analysis (PCA) of standardized residual suggested that no additional dimension were present in extended TAM measurement model (see Table 6). The Rasch model explained 41.7% of the variance in the instrument, which is nearly identical to the variance expected by the model (41.9%). The variance explained by the measures was ≥ 40% therefore indicates a strong principal measurement dimension [33].

The PCA resulted in a first component eigenvalue of 2.9 represents only 7.4% of the residual variance. An eigenvalue < 3.0 is considered good [17]. 12.7% of the unexplained variance is explained by the first residual variance. This is a ratio of 3 to 1. Thus, the variance explained by the first factor of residuals supports unidimensionality.

The PCA of the Rasch Model residual indicated that the underlying items in the instrument are assessing a unidimensional measurement model. The unidimensionality provides the operational definition of meaningful activities found in intention to use ODS measurement.

Table 6. Principle Component Analysis (PCA) of Standardized Residual

	Eigenvalue	Empirically (%)	Modelled (%)
Total raw variance in observations	39.4	100.0	100.0
Raw variance explained by measures	16.4	41.7	41.9
Raw variance explained by persons	13.8	34.9	35.1
Raw variance explained by items	2.7	6.8	6.8
Raw unexplained variance (total)	23.0	58.3	58.1
Unexplained variance in 1st contrast	2.9	7.4	

6 Conclusion

This study conducted a unidimensional analysis to identify if all the items in the instrument measuring a single latent trait (intention to use). In previous study, the principle component analysis (PCA) resulted a seven factor structure for factor analysis [1]. Our study based on Rasch analysis demonstrated that only one item (UID2) from the User-interface Design (UID) factor had misfit and showed as a redundant measurement. Thus item UID2 was removed from the instrument to improve the quality of the instrument. Once the item eliminated, Rasch analysis indicated the measurement model was unidimensional. The 23 items in the instrument now can be used to study overall student's intention to use ODS. This may facilitate the interpretation of intention to use score within ODS design.

References

1. Liu, I.-F., Chen, M.C., Sun, Y.S., Wible, D., Kuo, C.-H.: Extending the TAM model to explore the factors that affect Intention to Use an Online Learning Community. Computers & Education 54, 600–610 (2010)
2. Davis, F.D., Bagozzi, R.P., Warshaw, P.R.: User acceptance of computer technology: a comparison of two theoretical models. Management Science 35, 982–1003 (1989)
3. Davis, F.D.: A technology acceptance model for empirically testing new end-user information systems: Theory and results (1985)
4. Liu, S.-H., Liao, H.-L., Peng, C.-J.: Applying The Technology Acceptance Model and Flow Theory to Online e-Learning Users' Acceptance Behavior. E-learning 4, H8 (2005)
5. Park, S.Y.: An analysis of the technology acceptance model in understanding university students' behavioral intention to use e-learning. Educational Technology & Society 12, 150–162 (2009)
6. Roca, J.C., Chiu, C.-M., Martínez, F.J.: Understanding e-learning continuance intention: An extension of the Technology Acceptance Model. International Journal of Human-Computer Studies 64, 683–696 (2006)
7. Masrom, M.: Technology acceptance model and e-learning (2007)
8. Ong, C.-S., Lai, J.-Y.: Gender differences in perceptions and relationships among dominants of e-learning acceptance. Computers in Human Behavior 22, 816–829 (2006)
9. Saadé, R.G., Nebebe, F., Tan, W.: Viability of the'Technology Acceptance Model' in Multimedia Learning Environments: A Comparative Study. Interdisciplinary Journal of Knowledge and Learning Objects 3, 175–184 (2007)
10. Van Raaij, E.M., Schepers, J.J.L.: The acceptance and use of a virtual learning environment in China. Computers & Education 50, 838–852 (2008)
11. Ngai, E.W.T., Poon, J.K.L., Chan, Y.H.C.: Empirical examination of the adoption of WebCT using TAM. Computers & Education 48, 250–267 (2007)
12. Pituch, K.A., Lee, Y.: The influence of system characteristics on e-learning use. Computers & Education 47, 222–244 (2006)
13. Lee, B.-C., Yoon, J.-O., Lee, I.: Learners' acceptance of e-learning in South Korea: Theories and results. Computers & Education 53, 1320–1329 (2009)
14. Sanchez-Franco, M.J.: WebCT–The quasimoderating effect of perceived affective quality on an extending Technology Acceptance Model. Computers & Education 54, 37–46 (2010)
15. Lee, Y.-C.: An empirical investigation into factors influencing the adoption of an e-learning system. Online Information Review 30, 517–541 (2006)
16. Liaw, S.-S.: Investigating students' perceived satisfaction, behavioral intention, and effectiveness of e-learning: A case study of the Blackboard system. Computers & Education 51, 864–873 (2008)
17. Eakman, A.M.: Measurement characteristics of the Engagement in Meaningful Activities Survey in an age-diverse sample. The American Journal of Occupational Therapy 66, e20–e29 (2012)
18. Bond, T., Fox, C.: Applying the Rasch model: Fundamental measurement in the human sciences. Lawrence Erlbaum (2007)
19. Smith, A., Wright, P., Selby, P., Velikova, G.: A Rasch and factor analysis of the Functional Assessment of Cancer Therapy-General (FACT-G). Health and Quality of Life Outcomes, 5, 19 (2007)

20. Chien, C.W., Bond, T.G.: Measurement properties of fine motor scale of Peabody developmental motor scales-: A Rasch analysis. American Journal of Physical Medicine & Rehabilitation, 376, 88 (2009)
21. Götz, O., Liehr-Gobbers, K., Krafft, M.: Evaluation of structural equation models using the partial least squares (PLS) approach. In: Handbook of Partial Least Squares, pp. 691–711. Springer (2010)
22. Lord, F.M., Novick, M.R., Birnbaum, A.: Statistical theories of mental test scores. Addison-Wesley Reading, MA (1968)
23. Bejar, I.I.: A procedure for investigating the unidimensionality of achievement tests based on item parameter estimates. Journal of Educational Measurement 17, 283–296 (1980)
24. Reise, S.P., Widaman, K.F., Pugh, R.H.: Confirmatory factor analysis and item response theory: Two approaches for exploring measurement invariance. Psychological Bulletin 114, 552–566 (1993)
25. Lai, J.-S., Crane, P.K., Cella, D.: Factor analysis techniques for assessing sufficient unidimensionality of cancer related fatigue. Quality of Life Research 15, 1179–1190 (2006)
26. Reeve, B.B., Hays, R.D., Bjorner, J.B., Cook, K.F., Crane, P.K., Teresi, J.A., Thissen, D., Revicki, D.A., Weiss, D.J., Hambleton, R.K.: Psychometric evaluation and calibration of health-related quality of life item banks: plans for the Patient-Reported Outcomes Measurement Information System (PROMIS). Medical Care 45, S22–S31 (2007)
27. Tennant, A., Hillman, M., Fear, J., Pickering, A., Chamberlain, M.A.: Are we making the most of the Stanford Health Assessment Questionnaire? Rheumatology 35, 574–578 (1996)
28. Donovan, N.J., Rosenbek, J.C., Ketterson, T.U., Velozo, C.A.: Adding meaning to measurement: Initial Rasch analysis of the ASHA FACS Social Communication Subtest. Aphasiology 20, 362–373 (2006)
29. Prieto, L., Alonso, J., Lamarca, R.: Classical test theory versus Rasch analysis for quality of life questionnaire reduction. Health and Quality of Life Outcomes 1, 27 (2003)
30. Yen, W.M.: Scaling performance assessments: Strategies for managing local item dependence. Journal of Educational Measurement 30, 187–213 (1993)
31. Yen, W.M.: Effects of local item dependence on the fit and equating performance of the three-parameter logistic model. Applied Psychological Measurement 8, 125–145 (1984)
32. Smith Jr, E.V.: Understanding Rasch measurement: Detecting and evaluating the impact of multidimenstionality using item fit statistics and principal component analysis of residuals. Journal of Applied Measurement (2002)
33. Conrad, K.J.: Validation of the Substance Problem Scale to the Rasch Measurement Model GAIN Methods
34. Yen, W.K.S., Lan, O.S.: Validating Student-Parent Actions Model (SPA) of Consistency using the Rasch Measurement Model. Asia Pacific Journal of Educators and Education 27, 119–138 (2012)
35. Linacre, J.M.: Redundant items, overfit and measure bias. Rasch Measurement Transactions 14, 755 (2000)

A Rewritable Data Embedding in JPEG-XR Compressed Image with File Size Preservation

Kazuki Minemura and KokSheik Wong

Faculty of Computer Science and Information Technology, University of Malaya, 50603 Kuala Lumpur, Malaysia
kazuki.minemura@siswa.um.edu.my, koksheik@um.edu.my

Abstract. In this paper, we propose a rewritable data embedding method in the JPEG-XR compressed domain. Our proposed method is based on modifying the sign of the selected FCT (Forward Core Transform) coefficients. Specifically, the last coefficient, with respect to the conventional zigzag scanning order, in a 4×4 HP block is selected to embed data. Af- ter extracting the embedded data, the proposed method can restore the image quality by using the proposed simple majority vote method. Al- though the restoration does not perfectly regenerate the original image, the proposed data embedding method is rewritable. To evaluate the pro- posed method, four criteria including quality of the output image (i.e., embedded with data), file size of the output image, available payload and reconstructed image quality, are considered. Experiments are carried out to verify the basic performance of the proposed method. In the best case scenario, the proposed method can embed up to 15954 bits into an 8-bit grayscale image of dimension 512×512 pixels with a reconstructed image of SSIM = 0.9919.

Keywords: Rewritability, Data embedding, Sign modulation, FCT (Forward core transform), JPEG-XR.

1 Introduction

With the proliferation of smart devices with high quality capturing capability, multimedia contents including image, audio, and video can be effortlessly gener- ated. The captured content can be easily edited using the built-in user-friendly yet powerful software and broadcasted through the ever improving social net- working services. However, the conveniences enjoyed by the users also lead to the problems related to organization, retrieval, authentication of the contents, and other security issues. To address these problems, data hiding can be considered as an one of the possible solutions. For example, metadata describing the content can be embedded for efficient retrieval; fragile watermark can be embedded into a content to rise alarm for any act to forgery, etc. [1, 2].

With the advancement of display and capturing technology, HDR (high dy- namic range) imaging is increasingly utilized in a broad spectrum of applications, including, satellite imaging, medical diagnosis, military, photography, etc. In ad- dition, although the current consumer cameras are not equipped with the HDR photo

H. Badioze Zaman et al. (Eds.): IVIC 2013, LNCS 8237, pp. 569–580, 2013.

sensor, a HDR image can be artificially generated through the blending technology [3] using three images captured at different levels of exposure. As its name implies, a HDR image is of higher bit-depth and hence it requires a larger storage space when compared to the legacy 8-bit image. Therefore, there is an urgent need to efficiently compress these HDR images. As a result, the JPEG-XR [4] compression algorithm is standardized to compress HDR image. JPEG-XR takes a block-transform approach using FCT (forward core transfor- mation) that is derived from LBT (lapped orthogonal transform) [5]. It utilizes adaptive scanning and adaptive variable length coding to further enhance the compression efficiency.

Since JPEG-XR is recently finalized in year 2009, to the best of our knowl- edge, there are only two papers [6, 7] related to data embedding in the LBT (FCT) domain. The former method [6] focuses mainly on robustness against var- ious watermark attacks, but it causes file size expansion after data embedding by modifying the LBT components. In particular, the LBT coefficients are modified by adjusting their quantization step sizes and data embedding is achieved while sacrificing compression efficiency when applied to JPEG-XR compressed image. On the other hand, the latter method [7] studied on embedding data in JPEG- XR compressed image using only coefficients of value '1' and '-1' in the complex blocks. This method achieves high payload (i.e., the number of bits embeddable into the image) and high output image quality while preserving the original file size. However, [7] is irreversible and offers low payload in image of low spatial activity (i.e., smooth).

Among the desired features for a data embedding method in the compressed domain, file size preservation and rewritability are two important ones to achieve. In particular, if data embedding leads to severe file size expansion, it defeats the very purposes of compression as well as not being able to fit into the original storage device. Hence, data embedding method in the compressed domain should strike to minimize file size expansion. On the other hand, rewritability is a feature that allows an image to be *recycled* as the host without incurring further quality degradation in succeeding embedding. This feature is particularly useful when the embedded data (e.g., meta data) needs to be updated frequently.

In this work, we extend the work in [7] to realize rewritable data hiding in JPEG-XR compressed image while maintaining its original file size. In particular, we focus on the performances in terms of file size expansion, rewritability, output image quality, and payload. Experiments are carried out using the standard test images of USC-SIPI image database to verify the basic performance of the proposed method.

2 JPEG-XR Compression Standard

The JPEG-XR compression standard is invented by ISO/ITU community to efficiently compress HDR image. The standard was approved recently in year 2009 and it is still being improved by additional appendices and parts. Similar to the legacy JPEG compression standard, JPEG-XR is a block transform compression

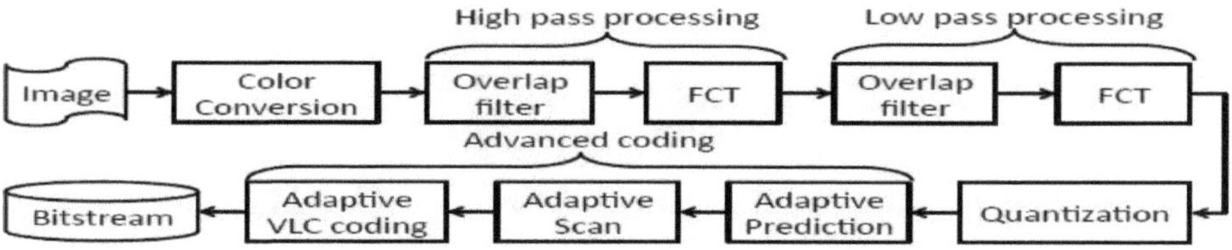

Fig. 1. Process flow of JPEG-XR compression

algorithm and Fig. 1 summarizes its main components. First, the input image g is converted from RGB to YCbCr channels where Y denotes the luminance channel, and Cb and Cr are the blue-difference and red-difference chrominance channels, respectively. Here, the chrominance channels are possibly sub-sampled (e.g., 4:2:2, 4:1:1, etc.). The resulting channels are then divided into non-overlapping 16 × 16 pixel blocks and each of these blocks is referred to as MB (macroblock) as adopted from video compression.

Each MB is further divided into sixteen 4 × 4 blocks and transformed using FCT to capture the response of each subband component. Fig. 2 shows the relationship among various components in a MB. In particular, the upper left element from all sixteen transformed blocks are grouped to form a new 4 × 4 block and then transformed using FCT. The upper left element in the output of this process (i.e., second transformation) is called the DC component of the MB while the rest (i.e., 15 of them) are called the LP (Low Pass) components. The remaining components (i.e., 15 coefficients) in each of the sixteen 4 × 4 block after the first FCT are named the HP (High Pass) components. An overlap filter is applied prior to each FCT transformation for suppressing the blocking effect and the overlap filter operations in JPEG-XR are reversible.

The coefficients are then quantized by using QT (quantization table), which has the respective divisors $QT[u][v]$ $(1 \leq u, v \leq 4)$ determined by QP (quan-tization parameter), where smaller QP implies higher image quality, and vice versa. Next, the quantized coefficients are predicted depending on their features. The prediction errors are encoded to further improve compression efficiency. Furthermore, an adaptive scanning order is applied to the prediction errors to generate the ZRV (zero-run value) pairs where the scanning order is consistently updated after encoding a 4 × 4 block. Finally, the ZRV pairs are entropy coded by using adaptive Huffman tables. For decoding, it is almost the reverse of the aforementioned processes and the details are omitted here.

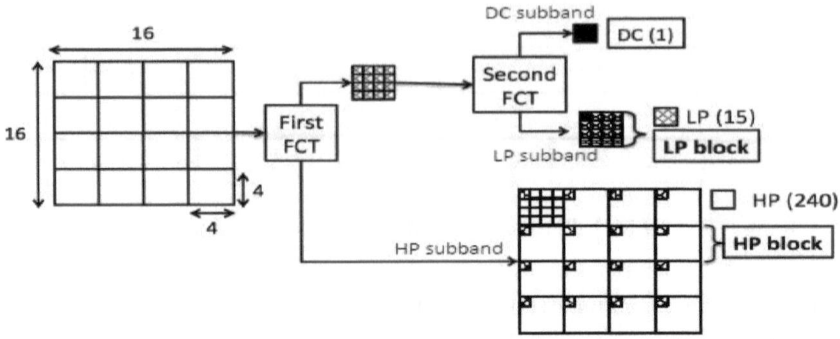

Fig. 2. Arrangement of DC, LP, and HP components in a JPEG-XR macroblock

3 Proposed Data Hiding Method

A JPEG-XR compressed image is first partially decoded to access to the pre- dicted HP components for data embedding purposes. Here, the predicted HP components are selected to suppress quality degradation in the output image. Each HP coefficient in the 4×4 block is scanned in zigzag order to locate the position of the last coefficient with magnitude of unity (denoted as LO) for data embedding. Next, external information is embedded into the sign of the located last coefficient with magnitude of unity. These selection and estimating processes are detailed in Section 3.1 and 3.2, respectively, while the embedding process is discussed in Section 3.3. Finally, the extracting and rewriting processes (i.e., restoring image quality) are detailed in Section 3.4.

3.1 HP Component Selection

In order to minimize distortion, the effect of data embedding on each of the 15 possible positions in a 4×4 block is investigated. In the JPEG compressed domain, Huang et al. [8] reported that the traditional data hiding methods tend to select the middle frequency DCT components to suppress visible distortion. However, when considering FCT components in the JPEG-XR compressed domain, the perceptual effect due to data embedding will differ because different basis functions are considered. Hence, we investigate the distortion effect of each FCT components in detail. Fig. 3 shows the average SSIM of nine standard test images (i.e., Elaine, F-16, Boat, House, Lenna, Mandrill, Lake, Peppers and Splash) [9] after flipping the sign of FCT coefficients with magnitude of unity (i.e., '1' or '-1') at increasing position with respect to the zigzag scanning order. It is observed that the first five components cause more distortion than other components, because low frequency components represent the general apperance of the image. Therefore, we restrict data embedding to the sixth coefficient onwards, i.e., the first five coefficients are not considered for data embedding purposes.

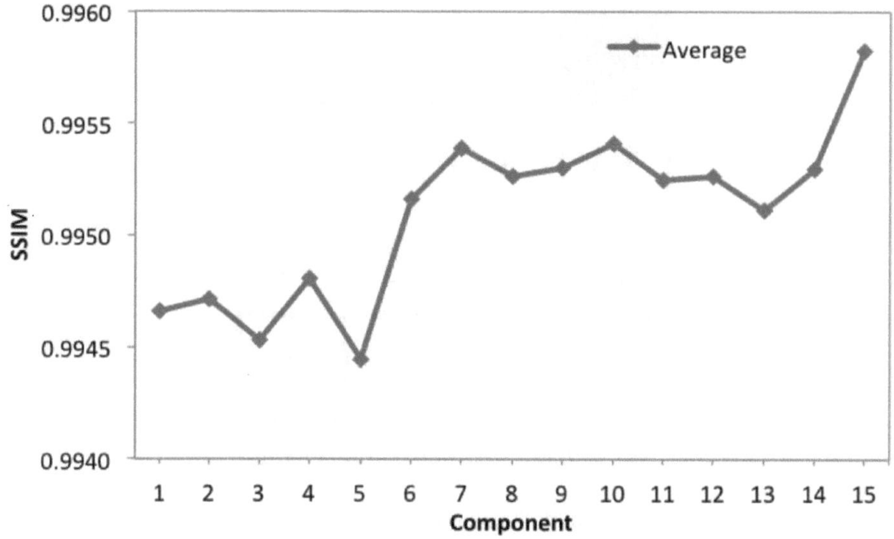

Fig. 3. Average SSIM of nine standard test images for $QP = 10$ after flipping the sign of '-1' and '1' at increasing position with respect to zigzag scanning order

3.2 Sign Estimation

Our previous work [7] is also based on modulating the sign of nonzero FCT coefficients for data embedding purposes. However, it is not able to reconstruct the original image after extracting the embedded data. Hence, in this work, we investigate the estimation of sign (i.e., positive or negative) for the last coefficient in each 4 × 4 blocks in detail. First, the coefficient(s) with magnitude of unity is (are) scanned in zigzag order from the sixth coefficient until the location of the second last coefficient with magnitude of unity in the current block. Then, the number of positive coefficients (denoted as $PS_{i,j}$) and negative coefficients (denoted as $NS_{i,j}$) with magnitude of unity are counted. In other words, we only focus on coefficients with magnitude of unity. Finally, the sign of the last coefficient with magnitude of unity in the (i, j)-th block (denoted as $LO_{i,j}$) is estimated using majority vote and it is formulated as follows:

Fig. 4 shows a 4 × 4 block and the zigzag scanning order. In this example, $PS_{i,j} = 2$ and $NS_{i,j} = 3$ although there are 9 nonzero positive coefficients and 3 nonzero negative coefficients. Here, we do not consider the last nonzero coefficient, i.e., -1, because its sign is to be estimated. Table 1 shows the estimation accuracy of the sign for the last coefficient with magnitude of unity for various QP values. The minimum

$$LO_{i,j} = \begin{cases} 1 & \text{if } PS_{i,j} \geq NS_{i,j}; \\ -1 & \text{otherwise.} \end{cases} \tag{1}$$

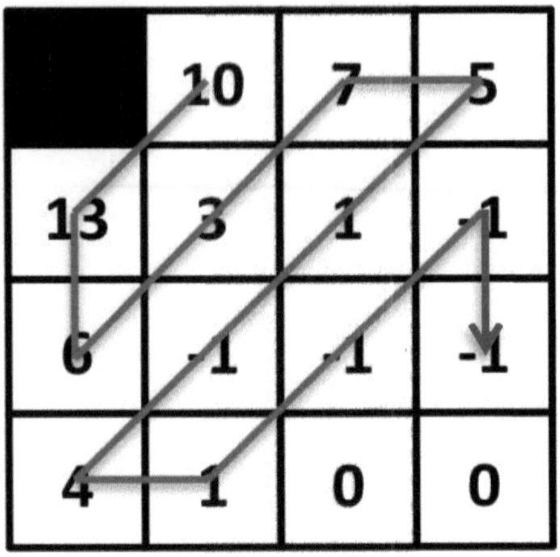

Fig. 4. Zigzag scan order in 4 × 4 block

Table 1. Estimation accuracy [%]

QP	Eliane	F-16	Boat	House	Lenna	Mandrill	Pepeprs	Lake	Splash	Average
10	56.3	70.9	58.6	70.9	65.6	60.0	55.1	57.7	69.7	62.8
20	58.1	74.9	64.8	75.7	72.5	63.5	62.8	62.6	77.0	68.7
30	61.2	77.8	70.3	77.2	76.7	65.6	68.0	67.7	79.5	71.6
40	67.9	82.1	78.5	78.6	80.6	68.2	72.6	72.8	84.2	76.2
50	74.1	77.5	86.6	82.5	84.4	70.3	77.3	76.7	86.7	79.6
60	75.3	73.1	90.4	85.0	83.7	72.8	85.6	74.6	62.5	78.1
70	100	70.6	91.9	90.6	92.9	76.8	87.5	75.0	33.3	79.8
80	N/A	66.7	91.3	88.9	100	76.5	100	50.3	100	84.2
90	N/A	N/A	100	100	N/A	75.2	N/A	N/A	N/A	91.7
100	N/A	N/A	N/A	N/A	N/A	N/A	N/A	N/A	N/A	N/A

N/A indicates that there is no coefficient in the image with magnitude of unity

estimation accuracy is 33.3%[1], but the average accuracy is over 60% regardless of QP, which is relatively higher than that of replacing the sign by using a random sequence (i.e., the average accuracy of ran- dom flipping is 50%). The results also indicate that, on average, the estimation accuracy increases as QP increases. Therefore, our proposed estimation is viable and hence we utilize this feature for embedding and reconstruction purposes.

3.3 Data Embedding

We propose a data embedding method for JPEG-XR compressed image to achieve the following objectives: (a) zero variation in output file size, i.e., file size

[1] The only exceptionally low value is obtained in the test image Splash at QP = 70, but all the estimated signs can be negated in this case to achieve an accuracy of 66.7% by using a 1-bit flag in the payload.

preserving; (b) rewritability, and; (c) high output image quality. Since FCT coefficients follow the Laplacian distribution with peak and mean both located at zero, changing the zero value to non-zero value or increasing the magnitude of a nonzero coefficient will cause file size increment due the entropy coding designed for JPEG-XR. Therefore, we decided to use only the '1' and '-1' coefficients. The proposed embedding algorithm is expressed as follows:

$$G_{i,j}(LO) = \begin{cases} 1 & \text{if} \quad w_{i,j} = 0; \\ -1 & \text{otherwise}, \end{cases} \tag{2}$$

where $G_{i,j}(LO)$ denotes the last coefficient with magnitude of unity in the (i, j)- th block and $w_{i,j} \in \{0, 1\}$ denotes the external information to be embedded. To avoid unauthorized viewing of the embedded data, the external information can be first encrypted.

3.4 Data Extracting and Rewriting Process

To extract the embedded data, each 4×4 block is visited and the last coefficient with magnitude of unity is located. Its polarity is then considered as follows to obtain the embedded data:

$$w'_{i,j} = \begin{cases} 0 \text{ if } G_{i,j}(LO) = 1; \\ 1 \quad \text{otherwise}. \end{cases} \tag{3}$$

Next, the estimation algorithm is invoked to approximate the original image. In particular, $LO_{i,j}$ is calculated by using Eq. 1 and $G^{0}_{i,j}(LO)$ is estimated using Eq. (1). The decryption process will follow if the external data was encrypted prior to data embedding.

4 Experimental Results and Discussions

As a proof of concept, the proposed method is implemented using the JPEG-XR reference software [10]. Nine standard grayscale test images from [9], each with the size of 512×512 pixels (i.e., Elaine, F-16, Boat, House, Lenna, Mandrill, Peppers, Lake and Splash) are considered. First, it is verified that the embedded data can be extracted without the need of the original image and the output images resemble their original counterparts.

Next, we measured the file size variation due to data embedding. Since only the '1' and '-1' coefficients are utilized to embed external information, the file size is exactly the same for the original, embedded, and reconstructed images. In other words, the proposed method maintains the file size of the original JPEG- XR compressed image while embedding external information into it at the ex-pense of slight degradation in image quality, which can be further improved by the proposed reconstruction process using majority vote.

Secondly, the effect of data embedding on visual distortion for various QP values are quantified using SSIM [11]. Fig. 5 shows the SSIM values for nine test images when we embedded at the maximum length, i.e., the last coefficient with magnitude of unity in each 4×4 block is considered. It is observed that all images embedded with external data exhibit high SSIM value, i.e., greater than 0.92. In general, the quality decreases then increases again (i.e., resembling a convex function) as QP increases. It is because many HP coefficients are quan- tized to zero when QP increases and hence the payload decreases accordingly as shown in Fig. 9. Consequently, the distortion also reduces since there are less coefficients to modify for data embedding, resulting in higher SSIM values. As the representative example, Fig. 6 shows the set of output images of Elaine com- pressed using JPEG-XR standard and embedded with external data. By visual inspection, in general, the output images resemble their original counterparts without visible artifacts. It should be noted that the visible artifact in Fig. 6(f), i.e., QP = 90, is due mainly to the coarse quantization of coefficients to achieve high compression ratio.

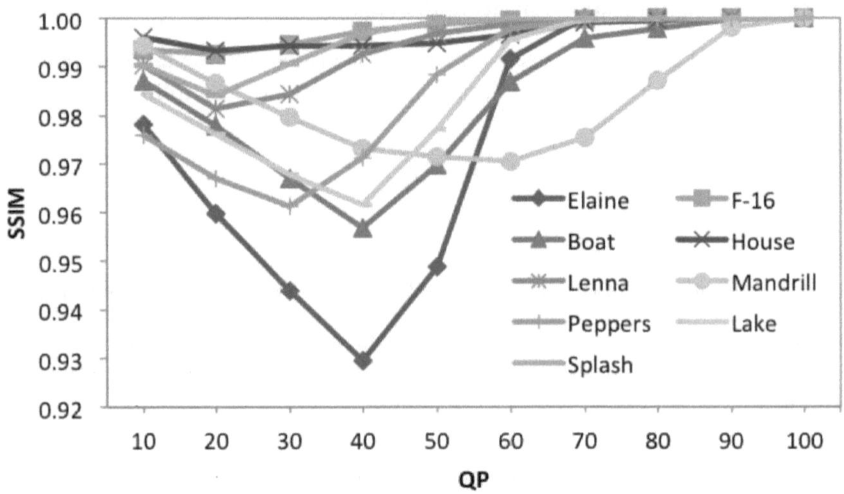

Fig. 5. SSIM for images embedded with external data for various QP values

Thirdly, quality of the reconstructed images using the proposed majoring vote method are recorded in Fig. 7 for various QP values. The results from Fig. 5 and Fig. 7 verified that the proposed method can restore the quality of the original image up to a certain level, hence the proposed method can serve as a rewritable data embedding method. Furthermore, to show the superiority of the proposed method, we compare our proposed rewriting method with three simple guessing methods, namely: (a) set all signs to positive; (b) set all signs to negative, and; (c) randomly set all signs to positive or negative. Fig. 8 shows the results of the aforementioned four ways to assign the sign information. Results indicate that the average SSIM of our proposed method is better than other simple rewriting methods. Hence, our proposed rewriting method reconstructs the original sign information (and hence the image quality) more accurately when compared to the simple rewriting processes considered.

(a) QP = 10

(b) QP = 20

(c) QP = 30

(d) QP = 50

(e) QP = 70

(f) QP = 90

Fig. 6. Output images embedded with external data for various QP values

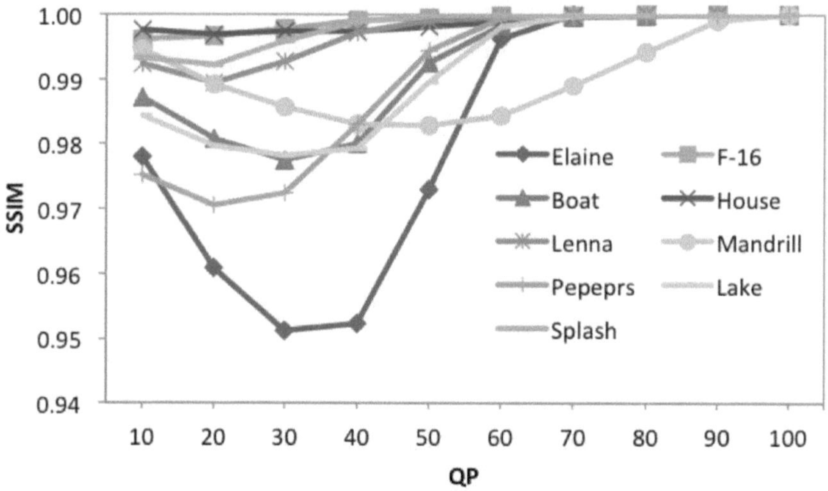

Fig. 7. SSIM after applying the proposed rewriting method

Last but not least, the payload (i.e., number of embeddable bits) of each image is depicted in Fig. 9 for various QP values. Results suggest that, in general, the payload decreases as QP increases (i.e., when quality factor decreases). This is because most of the components are quantized to zero when QP is large. Also, it is observed that image of

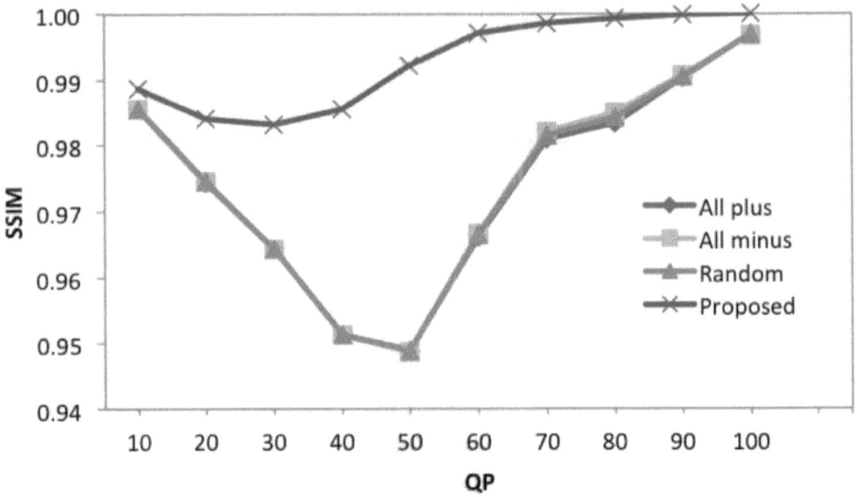

Fig. 8. Comparison SSIM for four rewriting methods

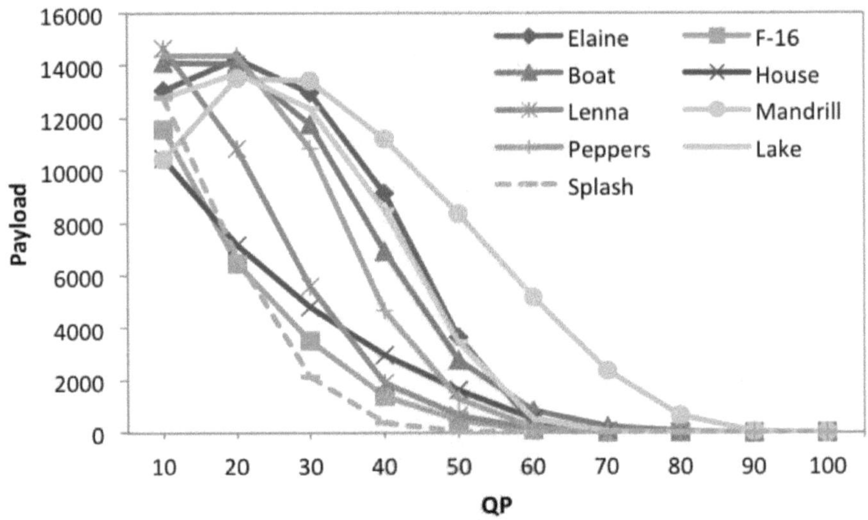

Fig. 9. Graph of QP versus payload

higher complexity (e.g., Baboon) offers higher payload, and vice versa, because it is more probable to find a nonzero coefficient in each 4 × 4 block and hence more probable to find coefficients with magnitude of unity. On average, 14689 and 12911 bits can be embedded into an JPEG- XR image compressed at QP = 10 and 20, respectively. However, our previous work [7] can embed up 17191 and 17840 bits on average for QP= 10 and 20, respectively. Hence, this work is inferior to [7] in terms of payload but [7] is not equipped with the rewritable feature. In addition, [7] also suffers from low payload when the input host image is of low spatial activity. Fig. 10 shows the average payload achieved in the proposed method and [7] for Peppers and Splash. It clearly shows that the proposed method has higher payload, especially for QP ≤ 40. Therefore, the proposed method offers more stable performance when compared to [7].

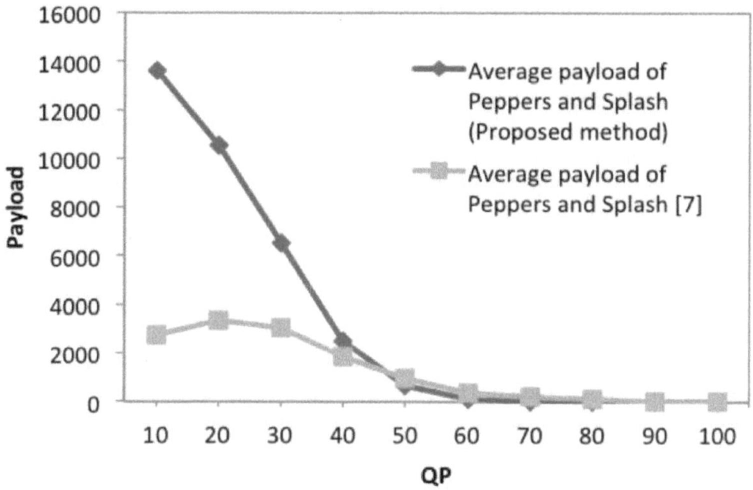

Fig. 10. Comparison of the proposed method and [7] in terms of average payload

5 Conclusions

In this work, we proposed a rewritable data embedding method in the JPEG-XR compressed image. A simple verification were carried out to investigate the effect of changing the sign of each FCT subband component on image quality and it was concluded that the first five coefficients should remain unmodified to ensure high image quality. The last coefficients of value '1' or '-1' from each 4 × 4 HP blocks were then utilized for data embedding. Experimental results demonstrated that our proposed method: (a) preserves file size, (b) offers rewritable feature, and (c) offers comparable payload against existing method, and (d) produces high quality output image.

As future work, we will further suppress distortion while maintaining the embedding capacity, improving the rewriting algorithm to achieve higher SSIM, and also improve the proposed method to a reversible data embedding method in the JPEG-XR compressed domain.

References

[1] Katzenbeisser, S., Petitcolas, F.A. (eds.): Information Hiding Techniques for Steganography and Digital Watermarking, 1st edn. Artech House, Inc., Norwood (2000)

[2] Kondo, K.: Multimedia Information Hiding Technologies and Methodologies for Controlling Data. IGI Global (2012)

[3] Sun, N., Mansour, H., Ward, R.: HDR image construction from multi-exposed stereo LDR images. In: 2010 17th IEEE International Conference on Image Processing (ICIP), pp. 2973–2976 (2010)
[4] ISO/IEC: ISO/IEC 29199-2:2009 Information technology - JPEG XR image coding system - Part 2: Image coding specification (2009)
[5] Malvar, H.: Biorthogonal and nonuniform lapped transforms for transform coding with reduced blocking and ringing artifacts. IEEE Transactions on Signal Processing 46(4), 1043–1053 (1998)
[6] Wei, W.: Robust image watermarking scheme using lapped biorthogonal transform. In: 2nd International Congress on Image and Signal Processing, CISP 2009, pp. 1–4 (2009)
[7] Minemura, K., Wong, K.: A preliminary study on data hiding into JPEG-XR compressed image. ITE Technical Report 37(35), 43–46 (2013)
[8] Huang, J., Shi, Y.Q., Shi, Y.: Embedding image watermarks in DC components. IEEE Transactions on Circuits and Systems for Video Technology 10(6), 974–979 (2000)
[9] University of Southern Califonia Signal Processing Institute: USC-SIPI Image Database, http://sipi.usc.edu/database/
[10] ISO/IEC: ISO/IEC FCD 29199-5: Information technology - JPEG XR image coding system - Part 5: Reference software, http://www.itscj.ipsj.or.jp/sc29/open/29view/29n10430c.htm/
[11] Wang, Z., Bovik, A., Sheikh, H., Simoncelli, E.: Image quality assessment: from error visibility to structural similarity. IEEE Transactions on Image Processing 13(4), 600–612 (2004)

Evaluation of Augmented Reality Remedial Worksheet Based on AVCTP Algorithm for Negative Numbers (AR^{2}WN^2)

Halimah Badioze Zaman, Elango a/l Periasamy, Azlina Ahmad, Riza Sulaiman, Mei Choo Ang, and Norshita Mat Nayan

Institute of Visual Informatics,
Universiti Kebangsaan Malaysia

Abstract. The original work on development of Augmented Reality Remedial Worksheet System for Negative Numbers Subtraction Operation (AR2WN2),which is a system designed to assist remedial learners visualize correct thinking process (CTP) on negative numbers subtraction operation, using visualization of correct thinking process (AVCTP) via an animated step-by-step algorithm involved five stages: i) to identifying incorrect steps taken by respondents for items tested; ii) to predict incorrect thinking process (ITP) of respondents based on incorrect solution identified at stage (i); iii) to scaffold respondents based on the ITP predicted towards a CTP based on AVCTP that can be emulated by remedial learners; iv) to create a flowchart algorithm for negative numbers subtraction operation involving two integers based on the AVCTP identified from stage (iii) and v) evaluation of AR2WN2 through a usability testing. Thus, a Usability Testing on AR2WN2 involving two integers based on AVCTP, was conducted on the five (5) selected constructs: ease of use, learnability, effectiveness, flexibility and attitude of users on the AR2WN2 system. The respondents of this study involved 124 students aged 14 years old and six (6) Mathematics teachers from two secondary schools in Malaysia. However, this paper highlights only the Effectiveness and Ease of use constructs based on the five (5) components/modules: History, Thematic (Job), Diagnostic Assessment, Hybrid and Learning Game. The Ease of use construct and its components were measured based on the Data Analysis Model 1 (DAM1). Generally, findings of the usability testing on the 'Effectiveness' and 'Ease of use' constructs of the AR2WN2 system based on the components mentioned earlier, indicated either highly or moderately accepted or both respectively, by the remedial learners and Mathematics teachers.

1 Introduction

The use of Augmented Reality (AR) technology in education is beginning to attract interests of many educators and unlike other computing technologies in education, AR interfaces offer seamless interaction between the real and virtual world, a tangible interface metaphor and a means for transitioning between real and virtual worlds. More collaborative work should be conducted between educators and researchers in the field of AR in education, to explore how AR characteristics can best be applied

H. Badioze Zaman et al. (Eds.): IVIC 2013, LNCS 8237, pp. 581–594, 2013.

in the learning environment [1]. AR interfaces can range from traditional approach (AR as information browser), spatial (3D AR interfaces), augmented surfaces and tangible interfaces, tangible AR interfaces or transitional AR interfaces [2]. It has also been recognised that AR interfaces are preferred for co-located collaboration, tangible object interaction or enhanced interaction in the real world [1].

AR is a technology by which the user's view of the real world is augmented with additional information from a computer model [3]. This means that learners can see the real world around them, with computer graphics superimposed with the real world, and instead of replacing the real world, it is supplemented and ideally, it would seem to the user that the real and virtual objects coexisted [4] and the information is presented three-dimensionally integrated into the real world [4] and [3], which can be either in 2D images or 3D objects [4] and [5]. Nevertheless, research in the area of AR in education is beginning to mature and applied in many subject domains, particularly in the areas of science and mathematics [1] and [6].

Based on the report by the Malaysian Examination Board [7], the achievement of the Lower Secondary Examination (PMR) students showed that they were unable to master the skills and understand the abstract concepts of negative numbers operation in fraction, transformation and algebra. In the 2002 PMR examination, 47% of the students showed clear weaknesses in operation involving negative numbers such as (-17+14), (-17+22+8), (-17-14) and (-17+30) [8]. Thus, a study was conducted on samples comprising of 124 students aged 14 years from two secondary schools in Malaysia [9], which revealed that they had difficulties in solving negative numbers subtraction operation involving two integers. Naylor [10] and [11] explained that such phenomenon as situations whereby negative numbers extend our number line and greatly simplify our calculations, but sometimes students struggle with the concepts. Nevertheless, it is also important for students to determine what things are and what they are not, to avoid incorrect assumptions, thought processes, generalizations and conclusions, which very often created misconceptions.

Therefore, this study was conducted to narrow the gap in school remedial learning environment by introducing an AR^2WN^2 subtraction operation system involving single and double digit integers. AR^2WN^2 is a useful remedial learning system on

Table 1. lgorithm Visualization of Correct Thinking Process (AVCTP)

Step	AVCTP
1	Identify any continues symbols and solve it, such as (– , – = +) or (–, + = –) in between two numbers, then rewrite the sentence question.
2	Identify and draw circle onto the negative number.
3	Identify and draw square onto the positive number.
4	Make a negative/ positive number group table as shown. 
5	Move magnitude value of negative numbers into the negative group.
6	Move magnitude value of positive numbers into the positive group.
7	Sum all number in each group if more than one numbers in each group.
8	Move the smaller number into the bigger number group. Then, subtract the smaller number from the bigger number.
9	Write the answer and put the positive/negative symbol with reference to the group where the answer is.

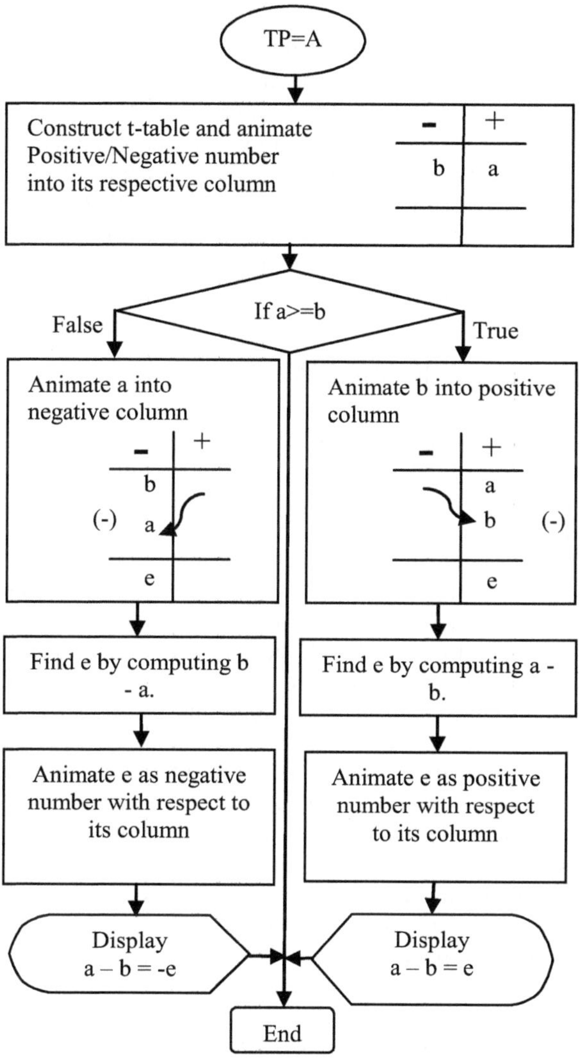

Fig. 1. Part of the Flowchart of AVCTP

negative numbers subtraction operation, through animated visualizations of correct thinking process (CTP), via an algorithm visualization of correct thinking process (AVCTP), which was created based on the meta-cognitive study conducted [9], [12] and [13]. These studies predicted an expert thinking process when confronted with sentence or word questions to help remedial learners overcome some of their misconceptions. This paper highlights the creation of the Algorithm Visualisation of Correct Thinking Process (AVCTP), in guiding remedial learners to undergo tasks on negative numbers subtraction operation involving two integers and its flowchart, so that an appropriate software engineering process with augmented reality technology to be integrated into a system to be developed to help in visualization of correct thinking process-based remedial works to be called AR^{2}WN^2. This paper also highlights an evaluation through a usability testing conducted on AR^{2}WN^2 based on two (2) of the five constructs selected: effectiveness and ease of use of AR^{2}WN^2. These constructs were measured based on the Data Analysis model (DAM1-DAM2). Table 1 shows the AVCTP and Figure 1 shows part of the flowchart incorporated into AR^{2}WN^2.

The usability testing conducted on the remedial learners and Mathematics teachers were after they had experienced the use of the AR2WN2 system for subtraction operation system involving single and double digit integers, through animated visualizations of correct thinking process (CTP), via an algorithm visualization of correct thinking process (AVCTP).

2 Background and Related Works

The integration of AR into an educational tool can make it powerful with its main advantage, being the use of virtual objects that can be animated, respond to the users' actions, and are not constrained by cost, practical or physical limitations of real objects which include 2D images, 3D objects, animated 2D images (i.e. videos), animated 3D objects and sound (both background sound and narration) [5].

On the other hand, a study conducted by [14], observed children reading an augmented book aimed at early literacy education. They explored how children aged six to seven experienced and interacted with these novel instructional new virtual media. They focused on issues arising from the tangibility of interface elements; the integration of physical and digital elements, on-screen and paper elements, and of text and interactive sequences. With an interactive book, a range of factors contributed to the user experience: the story itself, the visuals, the interactive sequences and how the user interacts with these, how 3D elements, interactive sequences and traditional text related to each other and the handling of the overall augmented book. Nevertheless, the children repeatedly had issues navigating from page to page and sequence to sequence, especially when switching between text pages (on the computer screen and navigated by mouse) and interactive sequences (physical pages, sometimes in sequence). Although most children did learn how to handle this, it required close assistance in the beginning and there were episodes of insecurity of how to go on. Children often attempted to use the wrong button or continued to flip physical pages waiting for something to happen. Added complexity was created by sometimes having two buttons for 'next' and 'close window' to start interactive sequences.

Thus, it was recommended to keep navigation as simple, explicit and consistent as possible. An on-screen button might simply say 'next' and *always* continue to whatever is the next logical element (if linear sequence). Added complexity is introduced by different navigation styles when on screen and paper. Making use of the AR technology, this could be simplified by providing a paper sheet for each screen page and flipping pages (showing markers) telling the system to move on, using the book metaphor for navigating through the story. In this case, the creators of the stories deemed pattern recognition to be too unreliable in uncontrolled lighting conditions, running the risk of the system jumping to the wrong page or starting a scene all over again. Careful consideration should furthermore be given to visibility of instructions and additional visual cues when the book is distributed across screen and paper. Children that looked to the screen often did not notice additional cues on the paper pages (e.g. 'hot spots' for putting the paddle). Thus, according to them navigation turned out to be an important issue when combining paper and on-screen elements, in particular if these are not integrated in one visual area and deployed tangible and desktop-based input devices.

The concept adopted in the design and development of AR^2WN^2 was constructivism. Thus, previous work on systems designed based on this concept indicated that constructivism promotes learning which allows students to construct new phenomenon. For example, students may have problems understanding the physical concepts of mechanics. It could be that physics in the traditional sense is sometimes taught in an abstract, jejune way and is therefore not motivating for the remedial students. The result is that theoretical models behind physical phenomena are often misunderstood. Conveying these concepts correctly is of utmost importance since they are fundamental to physics. Many theoretical models are based on Newton's laws of motion. For example, an educational AR application called PhysicsPlayground [15] and [16], was designed and developed to help remedial learners understand the concepts of mechanics. In this three-dimensional virtual environment, learners and educators in remedial, were able to create physical experiments that can be simulated in real time. They considered the analyzing functionality an important strength of a virtual laboratory like PhysicsPlayground. It offers possibilities that was far superior to what can be done in a real physics laboratory. A direct connection between simulated reality and physical data helped remedial learners grasp the theoretical basics of mechanics. To establish a direct link to learner's prior knowledge, physical data that can be acquired through the application was presented in a way that was closely related to formulas and equations of school mechanics. As AR^2WN^2 also included 3D in its design, it was essential to review previous works on the use of 3D in three dimensional dynamic geometry construction tools, that can be used in high school education.

The study on Construct3D used AR to provide a natural setting for face-to-face collaboration of teachers and students[17]. AR can also be integrated with Virtual Reality environment. The main advantage of using AR and VR is that learners can see the three dimensional objects similar to real life which otherwise, have to be calculated and construct, using traditional methods (pen and paper). By working directly in 3D space, complex spatial problems and spatial relationships may be comprehended better compared with traditional methods.

Three usability studies conducted with more than 100 students since 2000 [18] had resulted in the formulation of guidelines on how to design AR applications for geometry education [19] and [20]. For example, the evidence to support their claim is that the system Construct3D combined four domain areas: geometry, pedagogy, psychology and Augmented Reality. This combination had made the system easy to learn, encouraged experimentation with geometric constructions, and improved spatial skills [17], [21], [23] and [24]. Although usability of Construct3D was high and teachers as well as learners were highly motivated to use the system, practical usage in schools was hindered by hardware costs, support of a low number of users and technical complexity of the whole setup (requiring dedicated personnel for maintenance).

Designing an AR system is equivalent to interface design which uses different input and output technologies [2]. The important aspects in designing AR Interfaces include: i) goal that makes the computer invisible and enhance the user experience ii) a high quality of user experience in terms of appropriateness to tasks and applications or ease of use; iii) learning of interface and performance as well as satisfaction and iv) usability evaluation necessary to measure quality of the experience [2]. Therefore, in designing an AR system, there is a need to consider various aspects such as its navigational, interface, pedagogical and content aspects and how these would compliment each other in achieving the final goal. In order to ensure the achievement of this final goal, there is a need to measure the system through a usability testing.

3 Methodology

This research involved 124 respondents aged 14 years old, comprised of 53 boys and 71 girls. The number of respondents that achieved Grade A were 26 (20.97%), Grade B were 58 (46.77%) and Grade C were 40(32.26%), for their Primary School Evaluation Examination (UPSR) in the subject of mathematics. As this paper focuses on the creation of AVCTP in guiding negative numbers subtraction operation involving two integers and its flowchart in the AR^2WN^2 system, and its usability, therefore the methodology was divided into five stages as follows: First stage: to identify the incorrect solution produced by respondent for each items tested is found in [10];Second stage: to predict the ITP based on the incorrect solution from the first stage in [9];Third stage: to create a scaffolding process to analyze and synthesize the ITP predicted from second stage with CTP by learners and teachers for each item with respect to its frequencies. Then, to identify an AVCTP to help remedial learners emulate CTP and develop their expertise in negative numbers subtraction operation of two integers;Fourth stage: to create a specific flowchart for negative numbers subtraction operation involving two integers based on the AVCTP from the third stage; and Fifth stage: to conduct a usability testing on the AR^2WN^2 system.

The evaluation conducted based on usability testing was to examine whether each component in AR^2WN^2 which had incorporated the animated visualizations of correct thinking process (CTP), via an algorithm visualization of correct thinking process (AVCTP),is usable and acceptable by users. Two (2) constructs were selected from the five (5) usability constructs : Effectiveness and Ease of use. The items in the instrument according to the constructs were built based on the five (5) components/modules in the system namely: history (13 items), thematic (represented by selected jobs) (23 items), diagnostic assessment (28 items), hybrid learning environment (32 items), and learning game component (26 items). The items for the constructs were verified for reliability test using alpha Cronbach coefficient values: 0.8956 for Effectiveness, 0.9158 for Ease of use and 0.9701 for the overall instrument. Data collected through the questionnaires and observational check lists were analysed based on the 5 Likert scale: the highest value was 5 and the lowest value was 1. The mean score interval interpretation was based on the mean interval interpretation table as indicated in Table 2.

Table 2. Mean Interval Interpretation

Mean class interval	Interpretation
1.00-2.33	Low
2.34-3.66	Moderate
3.67-5.00	High

The full constructs: Effectiveness and Ease of use, Learnability, Flexibility and Attitude were measured based on the Data Analysis Model (DAM1-DAM11). However, this paper will highlight only findings of the Effectiveness and Ease of use constructs on all five (5) components based on Data Analysis Model 1-Model 2 (DAM1-DAM2).

4 Findings

The usability mean average result of each item of the construct Effectiveness : History component can be observed in Table 3. Based in this table, it can be observed that the remedial learners and Mathematics teachers' mean average scores obtained for item EfH7 (*History component/module can help motivate to learn negative numbers operation*) were 3.72 and 2.83 respectively, which were interpreted as 'high' and 'moderate'. Thus, the History component/module of the AR^2WN^2 system, was highly and moderately accepted as a suitable module in fulfilling the needs of effectiveness by the respondents. Based on the same table, the respondents' mean average scores obtained for item EfH8 (*Knowledge of how negative numbers was discovered from the 17th -19th century encourages one to learn negative numbers*) were 3.63 and 3.33 respectively, which were interpreted as moderate.

Table 3. Item Mean Result of Effectiveness Construct: History Component

No Item	Remedial Learners		Mathematics Teachers	
	Mean	Int.	Mean	Int.
EfH7	3.72	H	2.83	M
EfH8	3.63	H	3.33	M

L=Low M=Moderate H=High

This means that based on item EfH8 of the History component of AR^2WN^2, was moderately accepted as suitable in fulfilling the needs of effectiveness of the system by the respondents.

Table 4 shows the mean average result of each of the item of the effectiveness construct: Thematic Job component. As can be observed, item EfJ8 *(Knowledge on how negative numbers are related to the selected jobs encourages one to learn negative numbers*) shows an average scores of 3.81 and 3.67 by the remedial learners and Mathematics teachers respectively; and item EfJ12 (*Jobs like accountants and auditors makes one sees the relevance of learning negative numbers*) shows an average mean scores of 3.72 and 3.67 by the remedial learners and mathematics teachers, respectively. Thus, for these two items, the thematic job component of the system was highly accepted by both respondents as suitable in fulfilling the effectiveness construct of the system. Based on the table too, item EfJ14(*one is familiar with fire fighting job-relating it to negative numbers makes learning easy*) shows an average scores of 3.00 and 3.50 by the remedial learners and mathematics teachers respectively; and item EfJ15 (*Relating the job of computer engineers with negative numbers makes one sees the relevance of learning this topic*) shows an average scores of 3.53 and 3.33 by the remedial learners and mathematics teachers, respectively. Therefore, for these two items, the thematic job component of the system was moderately accepted by both respondents as suitable in fulfilling the effectiveness construct of the system. However, for the items EfJ7 (*the thematic job component/module motivates to learn negative numbers)*, EfJ16(*Familiarity with the jobs of police and detectives and relating them to negative numbers helps in learning the topic easier*), EfJ17(*Familiarity with the jobs of accountants and auditors and relating them to negative numbers make learning easy*) and EfJ18(*Familiarity with the jobs of aircraft pilots and flight engineers and their relevance to the topic makes learning easy*), the mean average scores were between 3.72-3.84 interpreted as high and between 3.33-3.50 interpreted as moderate by both the remedial learners and mathematics teachers.

Table 4. Item Mean Result of Effectiveness Construct: Thematic Job Component

No Item	Remedial Learners		Mathematics Teachers	
	Mean	Int.	Mean	Int.
EfJ7	3.84	H	3.50	M
EfJ8	3.81	H	3.67	H
EfJ12	3.72	H	3.67	H
EfJ14	3.00	M	3.50	M
EfJ15	3.53	M	3.33	M
EfJ16	3.78	H	3.50	M
EfJ17	3.72	H	3.33	M
EfJ18	3.75	H	3.33	M

L=Low M=Moderate H=High

Therefore, items EfJ7, EfJ16, EfJ17 and EfJ18 were highly and moderately accepted respectively, as suitable in fulfilling the effectiveness construct of the system by the remedial learners and mathematics teachers, respectively.

The usability mean average result of each item of the effectiveness construct: Diagnostic Assessment component is as indicated in Table 5. As can be observed, the mean average scores of the remedial learners and mathematics teachers for items EfD13 (*the reports inform the type of sentence questions that need remediation*); EfD14(*Diagnostic assessment allows one to identify own weakness in negative numbers subtraction operation involving two integers independently*);EfD15 (*The type: A,B,C&D categories of remediation report helps one to focus better on their weaknesses*); EfD16 (*the diagnostic assessment is accurate and can be repeated;* and item *EfD17(the diagnostic assessment answering sequence is self controlled*) ranged from 3.83 to 4.56 which were interpreted as highly accepted in fulfilling the needs of the effectiveness construct by the remedial learners and mathematics teachers.

Table 5. Item Mean Result of Effectiveness Construct: Diagnostic Assessment Component

No Item	Remedial Learners		Mathematics Teachers	
	Mean	Int.	Mean	Int.
EfD13	4.56	H	4.00	H
EfD14	4.44	H	4.17	H
EfD15	4.22	H	4.17	H
EfD16	4.25	H	4.00	H
EfD17	4.28	H	4.17	H

L=Low M=Moderate H=High

Table 6 shows the usability mean average result of each item of the effectiveness construct: Hybrid component. As can be observed from the table, the remedial learners and the Mathematics teachers' mean average scores obtained for items EH18 to EfHY18 through EfHY21 were from 3.84 to 4.44 which were interpreted as high, respectively. Thus, the Hybrid component of the AR^2WN^2 system was highly accepted as suitable in fulfilling the needs of the Effectiveness construct of the usability testing based on the items EfHY18 through EfHY21.

Table 6. Item Mean Result of Effectiveness Construct: Hybrid Component

No Item	Remedial Learners		Mathematics Teachers	
	Mean	Int.	Mean	Int.
EfHY18	4.25	H	4.17	H
EfHY19	3.84	H	4.17	H
EfDY20	4.25	H	4.33	H
EfDY21	4.44	H	4.33	H

L=Low M=Moderate H=High

The usability mean average result of each item of the effectiveness construct : Learning game component/module is as indicated in Table 7. As can be observed, the remedial learners and Mathematics teachers' mean average scores obtained for the items: EfG14 through EfG17 were from 3.83 to 4.69. Therefore, the Learning game component/module of the AR^2WN^2system was highly accepted as suitable in fulfilling the needs of effectiveness construct by the remedial learners and Mathematics teachers.

Table 7. Item Mean Result of Effectiveness Construct: Learning Game Component

No Item	Remedial Learners		Mathematics Teachers	
	Mean	Int.	Mean	Int.
EfG14	4.56	H	4.33	H
EfG15	4.56	H	4.17	H
EfG16	4.50	H	4.00	H
EfG17	4.38	H	3.83	H

L=Low M=Moderate H=High

Figure 2 shows the Data Analysis Model 1 (DAM 1) of how the Ease of use construct was measured on all five components. The usability mean average result of each item for the construct Ease of use : History component can be observed in Table 8. Based on the Table, the learners' and Mathematics teachers' mean average scores obtained for the EH1, EH2 and EH4 items were from 3.67 to 4.34, which were interpreted as high. Thus, the History component of the AR^2WN^2 system, was highly accepted as suitable in fulfilling the needs of the three items for the ease of use construct in this study by the respondents. As also indicated in Table 8, the learners' and Mathematics teachers' mean average scores obtained for item EH3 were 3.84 and 3.50, which were

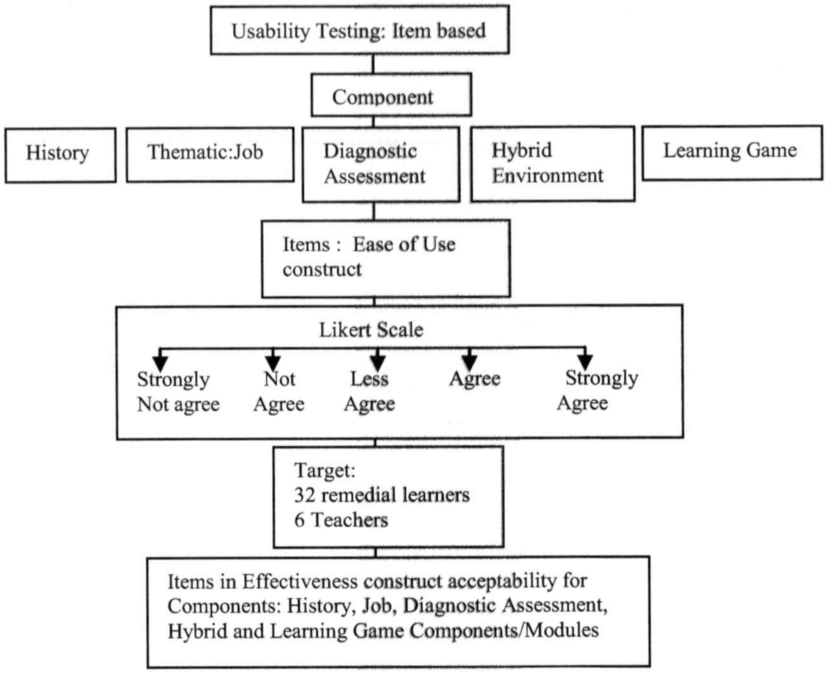

Fig. 2. Data Analysis Model 2 (DAM2)

Table 8. Item Mean Result of Ease of Use Construct: History Component

No Item	Remedial Learners		Mathematics Teachers	
	Mean	Int.	Mean	Int.
EH1	4.34	H	4.17	H
EH2	4.19	H	3.67	H
EH3	3.84	H	3.50	M
EH4	3.91	H	4.00	H

L=Low M=Moderate H=High

interpreted as high and moderate, respectively. Therefore, the History component of $AR^2WN^2$was highly and moderately accepted respectively, as suitable in fulfilling the needs of the item EH3 for the Ease of use construct by the respondents.

The usability mean average result of each item for the construct Ease of use : Job component can be observed in Table 9. Based on the Table, the learners' and Mathematics teachers' mean average scores obtained for items EJ1, EJ2 and EJ4 were from 3.83 to 4.47, which were interpreted as high. Thus, the AR^2WN^2: Job component was highly accepted as suitable in fulfilling the needs of the three items for the Ease of use construct in this study by the learners and Mathematics teachers.

Table 9. Item Mean Result of Ease of Use Construct: Job Component

No Item	Remedial Learners		Mathematics Teachers	
	Mean	Int.	Mean	Int.
EJ1	4.41	H	4.00	H
EJ2	4.22	H	4.17	H
EJ3	4.22	H	3.33	M
EJ4	4.47	H	3.83	H

L=Low M=Moderate H=High

It can also be observed from Table 9, that the learners' and Mathematics teachers' mean average scores obtained for item EJ3 were 4.22 and 3.33, which were interpreted as high and moderate, respectively. Thus, the AR^2WN^2: Job component was highly and moderately accepted respectively, as suitable in fulfilling the needs of the item EJ3 for the Ease of use construct in this study by the respondents.

Table 10. Item Mean Result of Ease of Use Construct: Diagnostic Component

No Item	Remedial Learners		Mathematics Teachers	
	Mean	Int.	Mean	Int.
ED1	4.53	H	4.00	H
ED2	4.34	H	3.67	H
ED3	4.47	H	3.83	H
ED4	4.56	H	4.00	H

L=Low M=Moderate H=High

The usability mean average result of each item for the construct Ease of use: Diagnostic Assessment component can be observed in Table 10. Based on the Table, the learners' and Mathematics teachers' mean average scores obtained for items ED1, ED2, ED3 and ED4 were from 3.67 to 4.56, which were interpreted as high. Therefore, the Diagnostic Assessment component of AR^2WN^2 was highly accepted as suitable in fulfilling the needs of the four items of the ease of use construct in this study by the respondents.

Table 11. Item Mean Result of Ease of Use Construct: Hybrid Component

No Item	Remedial Learners		Mathematics Teachers	
	Mean	Int.	Mean	Int.
EHY1	4.25	H	4.17	H
EHY2	4.16	H	3.17	H
EHY3	4.19	H	4.00	H
EHY4	4.19	H	3.83	H
EHY5	4.09	H	4.00	H
EHY6	4.13	H	4.17	H
EHY7	3.97	H	4.17	H

L=Low M=Moderate H=High

The usability mean average result of each item for the construct Ease of use: Hybrid component can be observed in Table11. Based on the Table, the learners' and Mathematics teachers' mean average scores obtained for the items EHY1, EHY2, EHY3 EHY4, EHY5, EHY6, and EHY7, were from 3.83 to 4.25, which were interpreted as high. Thus, the Hybrid component of AR^2WN^2 was highly accepted as suitable in fulfilling the needs of the seven items of the ease of use construct in this study by the respondents.

Table 12. Item Mean Result of Ease of Use Construct : Learning Game Component

No Item	Remedial Learners		Mathematics Teachers	
	Mean	Int.	Mean	Int.
EG1	4.63	H	4.17	H
EG2	4.59	H	3.83	H
EG3	4.53	H	3.33	M
EG4	4.56	H	3.67	H
EG5	4.59	H	4.17	H

L=Low M=Moderate H=High

The usability mean average result of each item for the construct Ease of use : Learning Game component can be observed in Table 12. Based on the Table, the learners' and Mathematics teachers' mean average scores obtained for the EG1, EG2, EG4, and EG5 items were from 3.67 to 4.63, which were interpreted as high. Thus, the Learning Game component of the AR^2WN^2 was highly accepted as suitable in fulfilling the needs of these four items of the ease of use construct in this study by the respondents. Meanwhile, based on Table 12, the learners' and Mathematics teachers' mean average scores obtained for item EG3 item was 4.53 and 3.33 respectively, which were interpreted as high and moderate. Therefore, the Learning Game component of the AR^2WN^2 was highly and moderately accepted respectively, as suitable in fulfilling the needs of this item of the ease of use construct in this study by the respondents.

5 Conclusions

The AVCTP in AR^2WN^2 was created to help remedial students be aware of the mental analysis and synthesis process needed when they are confronted with negative numbers subtraction operation involving two integers, and to help guide the software engineering process of incorporating AVCTP within the system. The ultimate goal of the educational algorithm visualization created in the AR^2WN^2 system was to aid remedial learners learn more effectively.

The success of the system can only be proved through an evaluation test. Thus, a usability testing was conducted to see the usefulness of the system based on the constructs: effectiveness, ease of use, learnability, flexibility and attitude of the users towards the system. The constructs were analysed based on the items built using the 5-Likert scale. All the constructs were measured based on the Data Analysis Models.

However, this paper highlighted only findings of the 'Effectiveness' and 'Ease of use' constructs on all five (5) components: History, Thematic (Job), Diagnostic Assessment, Hybrid Environment and Learning Game, based on Data Analysis Model 1-2(DAM1-DAM2). Generally, findings of the usability testing revealed that AR^2WN^2 was highly and moderately or both, suitable in meeting the needs of the 'Effectiveness' and 'Ease of use' constructs, respectively, based on all five components tested by the respondents. Therefore, generally, the findings revealed that AR^2WN^2 is practically accepted as suitable in meeting the needs of the usability constructs in this study by the remedial learners and Mathematics teachers involved in remedial education.

Acknowledgement. We would like to thank the Ministry of Higher Education (MOHE) and Universiti Kebangsaan Malaysia (UKM) for the Research University Grant (UKM-GUP-TMK-07-030036) and Arus Perdana Grant (UKM-AP-ICT-16-2009) that made it possible for us to conduct the research successfully.

References

1. Billinghurst, M.: Augmented Reality in Education. New Horizons for Learning (2002)
2. http://www.newhorizons.org/strategies/technology/billinghurst.htm (January 20, 2009)
3. Billinghurst, M., Grasset, R., Looser, J.: Designing augmented reality interfaces. SIGGRAPH Comput. Graph. 39(1), 17–22 (2005)
4. Bauer, M.A.: AR Forum - Discussion on Augmented and Virtual Reality Technology: What is augmented reality (2006), http://campar.in.tum.de/ARForum/AugmentedReality (retrieved from September 27, 2008)
5. Azuma Ronald, T.: NSF/ARPA Science and Technology Centre for Computer Graphics and Scientific Visualization: Registration Errors in Augmented Reality (1995), http://www.cs.unc.edu/~azuma/azuma_AR.html (retrieved from September 27, 2008)
6. Woods, E., Billinghurst, M., Looser, J., Aldridge, G., Brown, D., Garrie, B., Nelles, C.: Augmenting the science centre and museum experience. In: Spencer, S.N. (ed.) Proceedings of the 2nd International Conference on Computer Graphics and Interactive Techniques in Australasia and South East Asia, GRAPHITE 2004, Singapore, June 15-18, pp. 230–236. ACM, New York (2004)
7. Kaufmann, H., Schmalstieg, D.: Mathematics and geometry education with collaborative augmented reality. In: ACM SIGGRAPH 2002 Conference Abstracts and Applications, SIGGRAPH 2002, San Antonio, Texas, July 21-26, pp. 37–41. ACM, New York (2002)
8. Lembaga Peperiksaan Malaysia. Laporan Prestasi PMR. Kementerian Pendidikan Malaysia, Kuala Lumpur (1993)
9. Lembaga Peperiksaan Malaysia. Laporan Prestasi PMR. Kementerian Pendidikan Malaysia, Kuala Lumpur (2002)

10. Periasamy, E., Badioze Zaman, H.: Augmented Reality as a Remedial Paradigm for Negative Numbers: Content Aspect. In: Badioze Zaman, H., Robinson, P., Petrou, M., Olivier, P., Schröder, H., Shih, T.K. (eds.) IVIC 2009. LNCS, vol. 5857, pp. 371–381. Springer, Heidelberg (2009)
11. Naylor, M.: Integrating Math in Your Classroom. Accentuate the Negative. Teaching Pre K-8. ERIC 36(4), 34–35 (2006)
12. Brumbaugh, K.D., Rock, D.: Teaching secondary Mathematics. Lawrence Erlbaum, New Jersey (2006)
13. Periasamy, E., Zaman, H.B.: Predict Incorrect Thinking Process: Negative Numbers Subtraction Operation Second Category. International Journal on Advanced Science, Engineering and Information Technology 1(2), 145–149 (2011)
14. Periasamy, E., Zaman, H.B.: Augmented Reality Remedial Paradigm for Negative Numbers: AVCTP. In: Mohamad Zain, J., Wan Mohd, W.M.b., El-Qawasmeh, E. (eds.) ICSECS 2011, Part I. CCIS, vol. 179, pp. 188–198. Springer, Heidelberg (2011)
15. Dunser, A., Hornecker, E.: Lessons from an Ar Book Study. In: Proceedings of the 1st International Conference on Tangible and Embedded Interaction. ACM, Baton Rouge (2007)
16. Kaufmann, H., Meyer, B.: Simulating Educational Physical Experiments in Augmented Reality. In: ACM SIGGRAPH ASIA 2008 Educators Programme. ACM, Singapore (2008)
17. Meyer, B.: Physics Education in the Field of Mechanics with Virtual Reality. Master's thesis, University of Applied Sciences Deggendorf and Vienna University of Technology (2007)
18. Kaufmann, H., Schmalstieg, D.: Mathematics and geometry education with collaborative augmented reality. Computers & Graphics 27(3), 339–345 (2003)
19. Kaufmann, H., Dünser, A.: Summary of usability evaluations of an educational augmented reality application. In: Shumaker, R. (ed.) HCII 2007 and ICVR 2007. LNCS, vol. 4563, pp. 660–669. Springer, Heidelberg (2007)
20. Kaufmann, H., Schmalstieg, D.: Designing immersive virtual reality for geometry education. In: Proceedings of IEEE Virtual Reality Conference 2006, pp. 51–58 (2006)
21. Jensen, E.: Brain-Based Learning: The New Paradigm of Teaching, 2nd edn. Corwin Press, California (2008)
22. Badioze Zaman, H., Bakar, N., Ahmad, A., Sulaiman, R., Arshad, H., Mohd. Yatim, N.F.: Virtual Visualisation Laboratory for Science and Mathematics Content (Vlab-SMC) with Special Reference to Teaching and Learning of Chemistry. In: Badioze Zaman, H., Robinson, P., Petrou, M., Olivier, P., Schröder, H., Shih, T.K. (eds.) IVIC 2009. LNCS, vol. 5857, pp. 356–370. Springer, Heidelberg (2009)
23. Sollervall, H.: Collaborative Mathematical Enquiry with Augmented Reality. Research and Practice in Technology Enhanced Learning 7(3), 153–173 (2012)
24. Bujak, K., Radu, L., Catrambone, R., Macintyre, B., Zheng, R., Golubski, G.: A psychological per-spective on augmented reality in the mathematics classroom. Computers & Education 68, 536–544 (2013)

Advocating Green Technology Solutions for Sustainable Transport Efficiency: A Preliminary Investigation on Cab Providers and Users in Melaka

Maizam Alias[1], Sazilah Salam[2], Edna Buyong[2], Norasiken Bakar[2], and Riduwan Mohd. Nawawi[2]

[1] Universiti Tun Hussein Onn Malaysia, 86400 Parit Raja, Batu Pahat, Johor Malaysia
[2] Universiti Teknikal Malaysia Melaka, Hang Tuah Jaya, 76100 Durian Tunggal, Melaka, Malaysia
{sazilah,edna,norasiken,riduwan}@utem.edu.my, maizam@uthm.edu.my

Abstract. Reduced carbon footprints and sustainable public transportation including cab services can be achieved with the applications of suitable green technology. However, to promote the usage of green technology, the technology must not only meet public needs but the public must also appreciate the benefits of adopting green technology in the form of ICT solutions in their routines. Using a theoretical model based on the theory of Technology Acceptance Model (TAM), this study determines the needs for prompt delivery from cab operators as one of the most important modes of public transportation and to develop the appropriate technology applications that would best fulfill these needs. Twenty five cab drivers and users from the state of Malacca were surveyed on their perceptions of existing services as well as suggestions for actions to improve the services. Potential characteristics of green technology for meeting these needs were also identified which will be used for the development of the new technology. Initial findings from this research indicate that ascertaining availability of cab services is an issue that can be alleviated by employing appropriate applications. Important attributes of the ICT solution identified included ease of payment and ease of use.

Keywords: public transportation, sustainable environment, green technology, ICT application.

1 Introduction

Malaysia aspires to be a high income nation by the year 2020 and emphasizes sustainability development as one of its core values. Thus, green technology has been identified as one of the key elements in the process of achieving the high income goal status. To spearhead the achievement of the vision, the Ministry of Energy, Water and Communications was established in March 2004 (which was later renamed as Ministry of Energy, Green Technology and Water in April 2009) formulated the

H. Badioze Zaman et al. (Eds.): IVIC 2013, LNCS 8237, pp. 595–604, 2013.

National Green Technology Policy (NGTP) that provides national guidelines to improve the four (4) key sectors namely, *energy*, buildings, water *& waste water management* and *transportation*.

Meanwhile, the New Economic Model (NEM) has recognized sustainability as one of the three goals of the economic transformation programs and aspires to place Malaysia as a green hub all the way along the business development continuum; from research to design to manufacturing to commercialization. The Ministry of Energy, Green Technology and Water has elaborated on the vision for the energy sector for 2020, which stipulates that by the year 2020, every member of Malaysian society should have access to high quality, secure electrical power and other convenient forms of energy supplied in a sustainable, efficient and cost-effective manner, and to use them efficiently and responsibly to propel economic activities and maintain a high quality of life, having regard to the need to minimize the negative impacts of their supply and use on the environment (Ministry of Energy, Green Technology and Water, 2013).

To ensure proper planning, regulating and enforcement of public land transportation related matters and operations, The Land Public Transport Commission (SPAD), was established in June 2010 and began operations in September 20120 (SPAD, 2012). It is also responsible for providing guidelines that lead to safe and reliable services public transport at reasonable fares to encourage more people to use public transport (Tenth Malaysia Plan, 2010). The establishment of SPAD supports the high income nation agenda as public transportation is related to high productivity; a key factor in the high income nation agenda. Efficient public transportation encourages the use of public transportation; discourage the use of private transportation leading to reduced traffic congestion [15]. Public transportation thus, should become the preferred services for the people of Malaysia in the urban area, as one of the effort to support the sustainable environment.

However, as it is now, public transportation is not the preferred choice for commuters in Malaysia as compared to other developed countries. For example, a typical urban area such as the Klang Valley records only 17% of public transport users in 2010 compared to around 60% in Singapore and 89% in Hong Kong [13]. The low usage of public transportation according to [13] is due to the fact that public transportation system in Malaysia is still below the standard of other developed countries and thus is unsatisfactory in meeting public needs. These figures indicate that improvement is needed in some aspects of management and implementation of public transport services in Malaysia.

Malaysia recognises the need to upgrade the existing public transportation services nationwide and by creating more reliable, efficient and integrated public transportation system and has taken appropriate measures towards it [12]. Effective public transportation system will increase public transportation users and indirectly reduce private vehicles and their associated problems such as high accidents occurrences, traffic congestion and air pollution. Ineffective public transportation system will not only affect the economy, but also affect the environment from greenhouse gas emission. For that reason, reduced carbon footprints and sustainable public transportation including cab services is necessary and can be achieved with the applications of suitable green technology.

Previous study has proven that ICT application has significantly decreased the total number of trips made by users [10]. Thus, ICT system can be applied to increase the effectiveness of management and implementation of public transportations system, especially cab services. Past study also indicate that public transportation will be the preferred choice of commuters if it is efficient as commuters can avoid from paying high petrol prices and tolls and being stuck in traffic jams when using private transport [14]. Therefore, the purpose of this study is to seek greater understanding of the public transportation issues and potential green technology solutions. The specific objectives are to identify needs of public relating to cab providers services, to identify attributes of the green technology that may fulfil the needs of public (operators, drivers and users), and to determine public awareness of green technology.

2 Methodology

2.1 Research Design

The survey design was used in this study, as it can be used to make descriptive assertions about large population [1]. A random sample of 25 cab drivers and 25 cab users in Melaka were surveyed on their perceptions of existing services and possible steps to be undertaken to improve the services. Melaka was selected as the location of the study as Melaka is a tourist state that is expected to benefit most from the immediate establishment of efficient public transport.

Potential characteristics of green technology for meeting these needs were also identified which will be used for the development of the new technology. To strengthen the findings, interview was conducted to support the quantitative data. Of all participants, ten drivers and nine users were randomly selected for semi-structured interview. All the drivers are male participants with ranges from 28 to 65 years old, while six female and three male users with ranges from 17 to 58 years old.

2.2 Instruments

The study uses questionnaire for data collection, which comprises of 3 parts: Part A = satisfaction of cab services, Part B = intention to use of green technology, and Part C = public awareness of green technology. In part B and C, the Technology Acceptance Model (TAM) was used to guide the researchers in the identifications of green technology attributes to increase users' acceptance of the yet to- be- developed technology. Based on TAM, two components are crucial in influencing users' intention to use a new technology namely, perceive usefulness and ease of use. Thus, the questionnaire on characteristics of green technology has two main components, perceived usefulness and ease of use. An example of item for perceived usefulness is "Driver's profile permitting consumers to choose drivers as necessary to increase passenger's safety" and an example of item for ease of use is "Can implement mode of payment online (MB2u)". Respondents were asked to give their agreements to given statements based on the five point Likert Scale, "1" for strongly disagree and "5" for strongly agree.

Instrument was tested for reliability. A high reliability coefficient indicates a highly reliable instrument. The reliability coefficient based on the Cronbach Alpha method for the instrument as a whole is 0.73, which is acceptable being above 0.6 (Perera et al., 2008). The reliability estimates for each questionnaire components are shown in Table 1.

Table 1. Cronbach Alpha reliability coefficients

Part	Reliability
A	0.63
B	0.81
C	0.61

Quantitative data from the questionnaires were analysed using frequencies, percentage and mean scores. For the qualitative data, the interviewed participants were asked a series of thematic questions regarding the uses and satisfaction of cab services, their intention to use green technology, and awareness of green technology. The qualitative data were recorded in written formats. They were then classified according to thematic groups and arranged into matrix form.

3 Results

3.1 Demography

The gender of the participants is not split equally, with 72% female and 28% male for the users. It was found that 96% (24) respondents use cab services at least 3 times for a week and only 4.0% (1) travels by cab on the average between 4 to 6 times for a week. The highest proportion of users demonstrates that 80% (20) travel by cabs for private purposes. Another 12% (3) use cab services to travel to work and 8% (2) stated other reasons for travelling by cabs. Other reasons for using cab services include for a safe journey 12% (3), 72% (18) because they travel faster thus enabling them to reach their destinations on time, 12% (3), for comfort (12%), and only 4.0% (1) uses cabs for other reasons (e.g.: travel to school and to hometown). The majority of users , 60%(15) secures the service of cabs from the designated cab stations , 36% (9) by calling directly to the cab drivers and only 4% (1) through the call centre.

3.2 Issues Related to Public Transportation

Means and standard deviations (SD) were used to determine issues and problems related to public transportation services. The data is based on Part A, regarding users' satisfaction of cab services. Of all respondents, 16% (4) users had spent more than 30 minutes waiting for a cab services. When asked regarding users' satisfaction, 40% (10) rated low or dissatisfaction on the item "Cab service is easily available" with mean score 3.24 (SD = .93). Only 4% (1) perceived dissatisfaction of cab interior comfort (Mean = 3.64; SD = .57) and also 4% (1) perceived dissatisfaction on the punctuality of the cab services (Mean = 3.56; SD = .96). The mean scores for the other items are indicated in Table 2.

Based on the interview data, respondents highlighted that the cab services were regularly prompt and fast, with the majority of respondents interviewed waiting less than 30 minutes. However, according to interview with the cab drivers, the participants raised issues– on disgruntled passengers who complain that cab drivers are overcharging and users who often disagreed with the specified fare. The participants also believed that this issue is due to the conventional payment system, that is using cash. Other issues include nagging passengers.

Table 2. Users satisfaction of cab services

Item	Bus Users	
	Min	**SD**
Services are available on time	3.56	.96
Drivers are courteous	3.52	.82
Reasonable rate	2.72	1.17
Feel secured using cab	3.32	.80
Interior comfort is satisfactory	3.64	.57
Cab service is easily available	3.24	.93

3.3 Attributes of Green Technology

48% users of cab services perceived that information regarding the cost and payments is useful with mean score 3.96 (SD = .73). 40% of users perceived usefulness on the item "Proof of payment and reimbursement" with mean score 4.16 (SD = .80). Also, 64% of users perceived usefulness on the item "Travel map to be introduced enabling consumers to choose their travel routes" with mean score 3.96 (SD = .61). The other items were also rated useful in regards to the information of current traffic condition 60% (Mean =3.96; SD = .73) and the information of driver profiles 64% (mean = 4.04; SD = .61).

For cab drivers, 32% of the respondents agreed that proof of payment and reimbursement–are very important for ICT application (Mean = 3.80; SD = 1.08). However, the respondents perceived that the consumer's acknowledgement was of lesser importance with mean score 2.92 (SD = .70). The details of information are shown in Table 3.

Table 3. Preceived usefulness of ICT application

Item	Cab Users		Cab Drivers	
	Min	SD	Min	SD
Travel map to be introduced enabling consumers to choose their travel routes	3.96	.61	352	1.19
Driver's profile permitting consumers to choose drivers as necessary to increase passenger's safety	4.04	.61	3.92	1.22
Current traffic conditions and related activities that can influence traffic flow, hence enabling consumers to plan their journey	3.96	.73	3.36	1.12
The cost and payment enabling consumers to plan their budget	3.96	.73	3.16	1.25
Consumer's acknowledgement enabling them to plan their journe efficienly	3.68	.75	2.92	.70
Proof of payment and reimbursement	4.16	.80	3.80	1.08

Equally pertinent to this research is the ease of use of ICT application. The result indicated 56% of the users agreed that the ICT application should display information in dual languages (Bahasa Melayu and English) with the highest mean score 4.36 (SD = .57). 32% of the users are agreeable that the ICT application is easily accessible using all types of smart phones (Mean = 2.56; SD = 1.45).

Among the cab drivers, it was found that 64% of the respondents agreed that the ICT application should display information in dual languages (Bahasa Melayu and English) with the highest mean score 4.20 (SD = .58). It was most interesting to note that, only 1% of the cab drivers disagreed on the item "Can implement mode of payment online (e.g.maybank2u)". The details of the mean score and standard deviation on each item are illustrated in Table 4.

Based on users' interview, most comments highlighted on the application of ICT. The comments were "implementing touch N go and online payment system", "introducing mobile and internet application", and "using better website application".

Table 4. Attributes of ICT application

Item	Cab Users		Cab Drivers	
	Min	SD	Min	SD
Consumer can register online	2.48	1.29	3.96	.54
Easily accessible using all types of smart phones	2.56	1.45	4.12	.67
Online access 24/7	4.04	.98	3.84	.75
Interface that is consumer-friendly	3.04	.79	4.00	.71
Display both Bahasa Melayu and English	4.36	.57	4.20	.58
Can implement mode of payment online (MB2u)	1.80	1.04	3.60	.96

The cab drivers interviewed also stressed on the importance of implementing mobile application system that is aligned with the opinion of users. Interestingly, the drivers highlighted their interests on the implementation of touch and go system, and online payment method.

3.4 Public Awareness on Green Technology

Table 5 provides an illustration on public awareness of green technology. Of all respondents, 52% of the users acknowledged that green technology has been practiced in Melaka with the highest mean score 4.24 (SD = .88). The lowest mean score is 3.60 (SD = .76) on the item "I understand the meaning of green technology".

Among the cab drivers surveyed, it was found that 52% of the respondents are interested in green technology (Mean = 4.08; SD = .70) and 48% acknowledge that green technology is used in Melaka (Mean = 3.88; SD = .73). Similar to cab users, the lowest mean score was on the item "I use green technology in my daily routine" with a mean score 3.32 (SD = .80). Descriptive statistics with their details are shown in Table 5.

Table 5. Public awareness on green technology

Item	Cab Users		Cab Drivers	
	Min	SD	Min	SD
I understand the meaning of green tehcnology	3.96	.79	3.60	.76
I understand the purpose of using green technology	4.16	.70	3.96	1.02
I know that Melaka practices green technology	3.88	.73	4.24	.88
I am interested in green technology	4.08	.70	4.40	.76
I use green technology in my daily routine	3.32	.80	3.84	1.07
Green technology improves the quality of work life	4.12	.73	4.36	.76

Based on the qualitative data , users' suggestions on ways and means of using green technology include "using website application", "using mobile internet application", and "implementing touch N go and online payment system". Other suggestions from cab drivers include several ways of green technology practices such as "applying mobile, touch N go, and online payment system", and "the application of mobile system", including the uses of Natural Gas Vehicle (NGV) for green technology.

4 Discussion

Public transport plays an important role in the economic development of the country by creating employment opportunities and sustaining economic activities and also the channel of social and economic interaction involving the physical movement of people and goods [7].

Dealing with public transport services, users' satisfaction is one of the main concerns to be achieved by providers. The public transport efficiency and service quality that people are concern mostly are less waiting time and the reliability of the system [3].

The first contact a tourist gets with locals is often during airport transits to hotels and it creates a very strong first impression, either be good or bad. Flat rate, no metre," one driver may insists as the tourists try to find a cab to take them to their hotel, less than two kilometres away. Cab drivers have an outsize impact on a nation's image. In this study, users voiced dissatisfaction towards cab services in the Melaka city. Amongst the main issues is the delay in service delivery by the cab provideers. It is perceived that prompt services are associated with most issues raised by users. These include the time for waiting a cab, which posed difficulty to users to catch a cab at the cab station or at the designated pick-up points, quality, courtesy, availability and expertise as well as unkempt and hostile drivers. Other complaints from users include long waiting time, overcharging, and pick-and-choose which destinations they will travel to. Cab drivers on the other hand' often had to deal with disgruntled passengers who complain that cab drivers are overcharging and users often disagreed with the fare specified. The respondents also believed that this issue is due to the conventional payment system that is using cash. Other issues include nagging passengers.

[10]Study found positive impact of ICT application on time use and travel behaviour of public transport users, which might be solving similar issues above. Therefore, users and drivers' intention to use ICT application were first investigated that is based on three main components of TAM model: perceived usefulness, ease of use, and awareness. According to the result, ICT application that supports green technology for cab services must provide information regarding the cost and payment, provides proof of payment and reimbursement, display travel map, information of current traffic condition, as well as the information of driver's profiles. The drivers also agreed with users in terms of proof of payment and reimbursement as these are very important for ICT application.On the contrary, the respondents perceived that consumer's acknowledgement was less important.

For the second component, in term of ease of use of ICT application, users and drivers highlight on the need of the ICT application to display information in dual languages; Bahasa Melayu and English.Users also agreed that the ICT application should be accessible from any types of smart phone. It is more interesting to note that cab drivers disagreed on the item "Payment can be made online (e.g.maybank2u)". This finding shows that drivers are still sceptical on the online payment system. Users do not feel safe since security is an essential condition for the payment system using ICT application [3] and [4].

Based on the users' interview, most comments highlighted the application of ICT. The comments were ""uses touch N go and online payment method", "introduces mobile and internet application", and "uses of better website application". The users and drivers also stressed on the usage of mobile application. Cab drivers highlighted the usage of online ticketing, the usage of touch N go, and the online payment method. Additionally, previous study suggests the availability of technical support is another attribute that enhances users' perceived ease of use of ICT application [8].

For the third component of TAM model, in regards to awareness of green technology (all aspects including the uses of ICT application), the majority of users acknowledged that green technology has been practiced in Melaka. Although, some cab users and drivers suggest several ways of green technology practices such as, "using website application", "using mobile internet application", and "implementing touch N go and online payment system".Cab drivers, on the other hand, green technology for sustainable environment such as "using of NGV for green technology". However, this does not mean that users and drivers are well informed of green technology, as the majority of them has yet to understand the purpose and meaning of green technology being practiced in Melaka. This is because, understanding must include a capacity to have knowledge in helping to solve environmental problems and practices relating environmental protection, conservation, as well as values [2]. For that reason, both cab users and drivers therefore do not practice green technology in their daily routines.

5 Conclusion

TAM model is used in evaluating users and drivers intention to use technology, including perceived usefulness, ease of use, and awareness of green technology. The data indicate that public transport users have needs that can be alleviated with the use of technology and the technology suggested is an ICT application. These findings support the need to develop an online system that can help to alleviate some of the problems facing public transportation, especially drivers and users. Ease of use of the ICT application however must fulfil essential requirements including high security level for online payment and the availability of technical support.

From the findings, the research concludes that competitive advantage from technology can be created when certain conditions exist. Innovation— the foresight to see how the technology could be used. Opportunity— the technology is able to exploit a condition in the public transport industry that makes a competitive advantage possible. Timing— to exploit a window of opportunity between the technology becoming economically viable and mainstream.

References

1. Dantzker, M.L., Hunter, R.D.: Research Methods for Criminology and Criminal Justice, Jones & Bartlett Learning, Canada (2012)
2. Ganai, M.Y., Zargar, S.S.: Assessment Of Environmental Knowledge, Awareness and Practices of College Students in Government, Sheikhul Alam Degree College Budgam, J&K. Academia Arena 5(1) (2013)
3. Hung, S.Y., Chang, C.M., Yu, T.J.: Determinants of User Acceptance of the e-Government Services: The Case of Online Tax Filling and Payment System. Government Information Quarterly 23(1), 97–122 (2006)

4. Linck, K., Pousttchi, K., Wiedemann, D.G.: Security Issues in Mobile Payment from the Customer Viewpoint. In: Ljungberg, J. (Hrsg.) Proceedings of the 14th European Conference on Information Systems (ECIS 2006), Göteborg, Schweden, pp. S.1–S.11 (2006)
5. Ministry of Energy, Green Technology and Water (2013), `http://www.kettha.gov.my/content/sejarah-kementerian` (achieved on May 22, 2013)
6. Perera, R., Heneghan, C., Badenoch, D.: Statistics Toolkit. Blackwell Publishing, Massachusetts (2008)
7. SPAD (2012), `http://www.spad.gov.my/about-us/profile`
8. Thompson, R., Higgins, C., Howell, J.: Personal Computing: Towards a Conceptual Model of Utilization. MIS Quarterly 15(1), 125–143 (1991)
9. Wall, G., McDonald, M.: Improving Bus Service Quality and Information in Winchester. Transport Policy 14(2) (2007)
10. Wang, D., Law, F.Y.T.: Impacts of Information and Communication Technologies on Time Use and Travel Behaviour: A Structural Equation Analysis. Transportation 34, 513–527 (2007)
11. Yazici, M.A., Ilicali, M., Camkesen, N., Kamga, C.: A Bus Rapid Transit Line Case Study: Istanbul's Metrobus System. Journal of Public Transportation 16(1) (2013)
12. Tenth Malaysia Plan, Tenth Malaysia Plan 2011-2015, Speech by the Prime Minister in The Dewan Rakyat (June 10, 2010)
13. Yaakub, N., Napiah, M.: Public Bus Passenger Demographic and Travel Characteristics- A Study of Public Bus Passenger Profile in Kota Bharu, Kelantan. IEEE (2011)
14. Kambala, A.N., Atiq, R., Rahmat, O.K., Ismail, A.: Why Do People Use Their Cars: A Case Study in Malaysia. Journal of Social Sciences 3(3), 117–122 (2007)
15. Kamaruddin, R., Osman, I., Che Pei, C.A.: Public Transport Services in Klang Valley: Customer Expectations and Its Relationship Using SEM. Social and Behavioral Sciences 36, 431–438 (2012)

Analytical Comparison of Factors Affecting EHR Visualization for Physicians in Public Health Care Units

Muhammad Sheraz Arshad Malik* and Suziah Sulaiman

Department of Computer & Information Sciences
Universiti Teknologi PETRONAS
Bandar Seri Iskandar, 31750, Tronoh, Perak, Malaysia
sheraz_awan@hotmail.com, suziah@petronas.com.my

Abstract. Information visualization is a significant, measured and potential advantage of Electronic Health Records (EHR) for understanding patient data to physicians. Doctors take primarily interest in understanding a complete knowledge from different portions of visualization that is comprised of numbers, pictures, texts and colored icons. However, complex presentation due to non-identification of different knowledge driven factors in EHR tools results in lesser attraction for its daily use in public health care units. Understanding and analysis of these factors that affect the utilization and sole understanding of visualization in EHR by physicians is main issue. Based on previous work by different researchers in same domain, these factors are shortlisted and compared to analyze the use of such tools by doctors. A survey based questionnaire study with a group of doctors is conducted using a approach to understand the deficiency areas for EHR tools. This figure out the requirements and expectations of doctors with EHR that may also assist other stakeholders like database professionals and visualization designers to align the tools based upon physician's requirements. Results are analyzed based on feedback of doctors from emergency and outdoor departments of hospitals as they are first to deal with patients and their data in daily routine. Facts are represented in two different categories where first is mentioning the rate of knowledge skills of physicians about visualization and second is mentioning future expectations from such tools. Results concluded that EHR tools should facilitate in more insight about multiple patients history and more skills improvement is required for doctors to use such tools. This research paper is also an integral part of our ongoing effort for developing an integrated model, CARE1.0 that has been proposed in one of the previous work.

Keywords: Visualization factors,EHR visualization tools semiotic knowledge, decision support systems symbols, patient data representation, multiple information visualization, CARE1.0.

1 Introduction

Different health care units such as public hospitals are using different kind of Electronic Health Record (EHR) systems or sometimes called as Electronic Medical

* Corresponding author.

H. Badioze Zaman et al. (Eds.): IVIC 2013, LNCS 8237, pp. 605–614, 2013.

Records (EMR). Information visualization in these systems is carried out to facilitate physicians and paramedical staff in addition to organizational stakeholders to provide better health care practices to patients. Single or multiple patients entries are carried out normally with the help of nursing or administrative staff while medication recommendations, doctors' comments or other details are sometimes keyed-in by doctors.. Various types of data are embedded normally in a structured database format in these systems from brain images to textual form of doctor's prescription as well as numerical form of blood pressure to cyclic graphs of heart rate. This makes the information visualization an interesting area for physicians to particularly take interest in single or multiple patient records based on different scenarios and facing situations from emergency to outdoor patient departments [1][2][3].

Various EHR systems present a different kind of visualization for single or multiple patient based query for the physicians based on their requirement parameters. Perceptual concept of a visualization makes the analysis part easier for doctors and physicians in different perspectives with reference to its pictorial shapes [4][5]. Semiotic perception of complex integration of symbols often dissipates the content of information within its end users due to mismatching of colors, non linkage of data as well as poor understanding of similar knowledge traits. Different hospitals are using different EHR systems based on their sources availability, local trademark of medicines and basic IT infrastructure provision even within the same country based on the number of capacity of beds. The type of data set availability is also different and complex based on their patients and facilities type. Larger hospitals have more facilities and handle more patients and complex diseases as compared to town based health care units, so patient data is also varying for doctors. This results in a difference in representation of visualization tools and representation structure for physicians. The visualization tools, either local or internationally developed, tend to physicians in order to possess more knowledge with respect to their use and understanding [6][7][12].

There are many research and commercial visualization tools that attempt to encompass the needs of doctors based on their different schematic representations, and the complex data understanding needs of doctors. Some of the examples are PreFuse [9], TimeLine [10], Fusion Ware [13], ProtoVis [15], Life Line [17], LifeFlow [18], and TURF [19]. These tools are probably good in representation of different data sets but the use and meaning inferences of information are randomly different. Interfaces, operational method and representation of visualization are different with reference to information intern linkage for patients' tests, history and doctor's notes in each application. Each tool handles data differently and this result in a more confusion to doctors and physicians who want to interpret the data at the same level of grounds rather than using a different technique for each set of data at different hospitals. Resultant visualization always tries to attract the significance and novelty of information from complex and difficult scenarios. But complicated methods of operating the applications, complex information in understanding knowledge, and varied interface structure to obtain pertinent patient information result in lesser use and weaker attraction to such applications. These applications are designed mostly to keep the complexity of data visualization rather than the basic requirement of physicians' complexity to understand the level of information from such tools.

Physicans normally possess different levels of IT knowledge to operate various tools and in larger health care units, patient(s) information such as personal details, past visits to hospitals, previous doctors recommendations or notes as well as test results are coming from different resources to single point of query. In the case of multiple patients visualization, data become more complex and more interesting but lose its meaning when it is not easy to understand based on complex inter connections of links, difficult terms for operation of application, lesser knowledge availability and training for concerned medical professional. These have resulted in lesser adaptability trend towards its practical implementation in daily patient doctor interaction processes. This also results in physicians hesitation and ignorance to avoid such systems based on more time consumption, lesser knowledge derivation and more efforts input as compared to per patient time distribution[7][11][24].

The core focus in this manuscript is to identify the areas of interest, influential factors, and personal likings of doctors that can influence on better use of visualization tools and their future versions development process. The more the visualization knowledge availability is, the easier the use of an application and its frequency will be on the adaptation procedure for an EHR visualization tool in daily health care practices. There is also a psychological trend in the patients that doctors are using more time to computers than attending to put their personal interaction efforts and vice versa. A better understanding about the current and future needs of expectations and their areas of interest related to operation, understanding, and knowledge derivation can lead to develop a better systematic application for visualization by developers, database professionals and visualization specialists as per their needs. So a visualization should not only encompass the symbols, pictures, texts or other temporal information merely but it should exhibit its true meanings to its primary stakeholders that is its real objective [17][20].

This work focuses on addressing the combined analysis of different factors affecting the use of doctors in improvement of an EHR system visualization that can help to improve its future use. This analysis also highlights the areas of deficiency with respect to visualization among doctors as well as their expectations and future requirements perception from a visualization tool. Based on an ongoing proposed work on a model CARE 1.0 [3], this research paper is one of the predecessor steps for analyzing the current level of knowledge and future development areas as per physicians' requirement in an EHR visualization tool. The rest of this paper is organized as follows: Section 2 presents the relevant and previously performed similar work in the domain. More focus is towards the requirements, and areas for future work of past researchers information visualization (IV) for EHR. Section 3 presents the methodology of the study conducted as well as the comparison of factors. Section 4 describes the results and conclusion while Section 5 proposes for future work.

2 Past Work for EHR Visualization

Various EHR Information Visualization (IV) systems work quite similar to implicit Intelligent Decision Support Systems when schematizing different facts out of patient's data[3][5][8][9][11]. Previous work done is mostly related to representing the data of patients in different manner either in the form of naming conventions with different colors, diseases with different shape bars, and use of medicines and test results with different color lines. Some of these IV tools utilize gathering of particular information only from data pool and represent it in a separate form of sections on the same interface [8][22][23].

LifeLine versions 1 and 2 along with Life Flow are some of the nominated past work within this domain for IV particularly to patient based records. A slighter glimpse of Life Flow is shown in Figure 1, representing different time and action panes to address the problem of data segregation on Shneiderman's mantra-- "Overview first, zoom and filter, then details on demand" [4][17][18][23]. But still it is quite complicated for a number of doctors in order to understand the representation due to event capturing interests as well as based on their general understanding knowledge in IV domains. Research work is still ongoing to address different issues and improvements in these areas and tools to apprehend further achievements. For complex situation query, resulting visualization becomes more complicated as it utilizes both time and attention factor to understand.

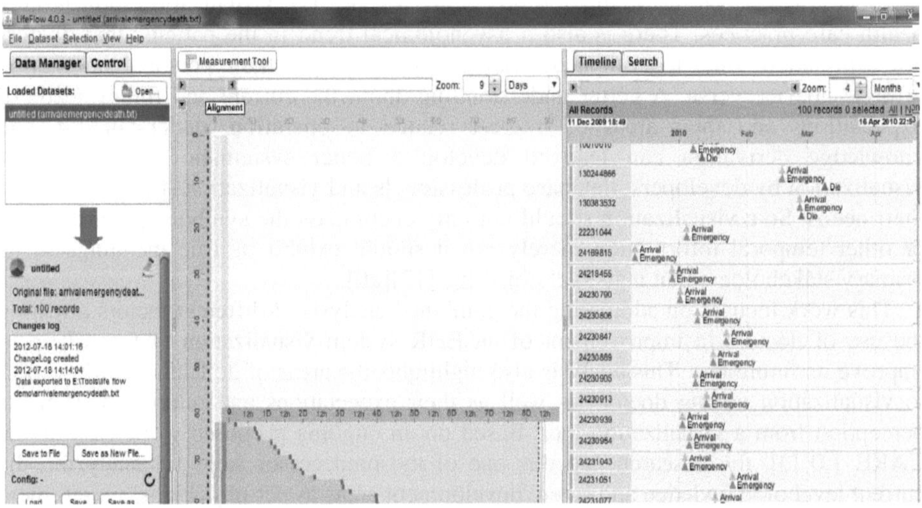

Fig. 1. Screenshot of Life Flow (K. Wongsuphasawat, et al., 2011)

A few other markable milestones were covered in the past with different researchers focusing on information collaboration and segregating similar problem set pertaining to simplicity of information to doctors using organ based or section based approach in temporal data elements within EHR. TimeLine, FusionViewer and Prefuse are some markable tools that tried to assimilate similar events and type of data in different segments, sections or proposed on the basis of collaboration of information using patient history, ID, name and pictorial form of tests in single dialogue box but that too, complicate the extraction of to the point information for fresh and less experience doctors [9][10][13]. Figure 2 also shows a brief overview of Timeline.

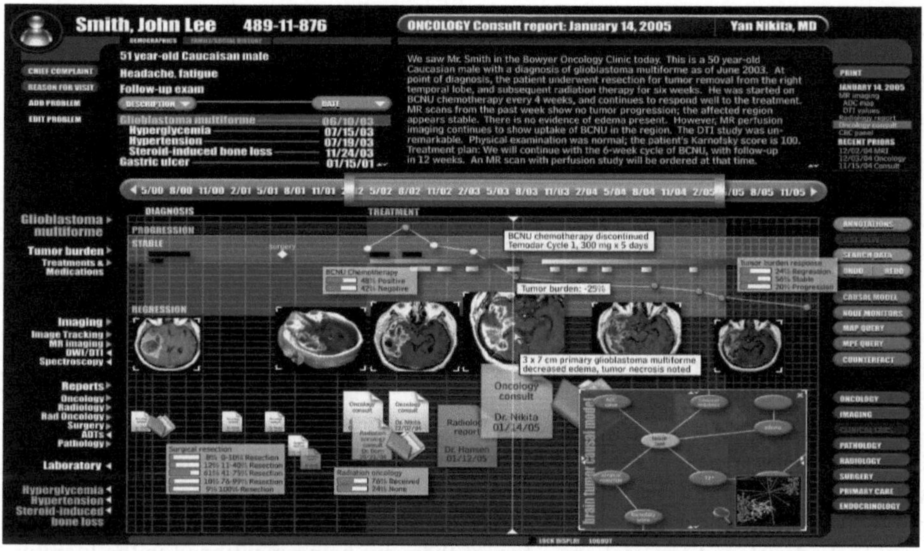

Fig. 2. Screenshot of TimeLine (Bui *et al.*, 2007)

These visualization tools may be excellently presenting the temporal information but the problem with them is related to factors affecting the easy understanding and frequent utilization in daily health care practices. These tools have been implemented either to a local laboratory area or with smaller data set with less complicated information set. While in hospitals, where the number of patients are more, and the number of queries are on different ground set, it is more important to understand the potential IV knowledge needs of those medical professionals. Addressing such a need is lacking as there is no or less work done towards the IV knowledge understanding level about such tools among physicians.

Understanding and information inference is the key role for visualization within EHR, more than data representation in an IV tool. The sole possibility for this objective is only based on the factors that influence the knowledge set of doctors and their understanding behavior about a visualization of single or multiple patient records. The research work presented in this paper is in fact focusing on the basis of pre-adapted study procedures using survey development and observation at the hospitals that is already being used in the development and improvement of information visualization tools [3][5][12][15][16].

3 Methodology

A sample study of 18 participant doctors were involved with a questionnaire based interview and survey as adopted in many previously implemented applications and tests in IV [3][5][14][21][24]. Normally in previous studies 6-8 doctors group was selected because of busy schedules and availability of medical doctors. Here in this work 18 participants were involved as due to availability of professionals in emergency and range of work experience from junior doctors to middle level experience holders. Normally all the participants have experience of 2-4 years in emergency and outdoor departments. These participants were selected from different experience range and age group but mostly from emergency and outdoor department of hospitals as that are the first entry points for most of the patients. Every participant is considered as possessing either average or lower average knowledge set about EHR applications based on daily patient chart use experience.

The questionnaire used in the study comprised of 32 different factors divided in two main categories. One is covering the factors related to doctor's knowledge about EHR tools and second is related to future perspective and expectations from such applications. Questions are generated based on literature review and taking guide line from the standardized doctor's feedback strategy adapted by HCI experts in the same domain [5][17][21].

The structure of conducting research work is also described in details within CARE1.0 primary proposal [25]. EHR systems use acquaintance and feature options within IV applications for handling multiple EHR data. These factors have been highlighted and considered as important salient features based on current and previously developed applications a few of them are being mentioned in the literature review. Nearly all researchers focused on either few or some of them in their resulting applications and mentioned to work on others as future work scope. A 5 point Likert scale based was used to associate with the questionnaire options for selection of the factors in which "1" denotes for "less" or "poor knowledge" whereas "5" signifies "experienced" or "more expert level knowledge". These survey questions were distributed to the participants.

Figure 3 and Figure 4 as mentioned in result section represent graphically the complete analysis of these factors with reference to doctors enlisted as knowledge about EHR tools, features information, information visualization seeking data, application interface understanding, icons and other signs understanding , patient history visualization, comparison of multiple visualization, data administration, patient satisfaction notes or details, detailed insight into patient medical background or past medical details, knowledge sharing capability of tool, analysis of available data based on query, user friendly behavior of application, representation of complex temporal data, ease in sharing of information with different other applications and doctors and database limitations due to complex forms of data.

Data has been gathered from these participants based on their experience and information provided and then compiled in excel sheet in enumerated form. Figure 3 and Figure 4 show the factors as listed earlier presented on X-axis and input of participants' population on a particular factor on Y-axis. Color scheme is used to represent the identification of choice and experience details in a simplified form [5]. Data is segregated on the basis of temporal information clarity and understanding of doctor's perception about knowledge of IV applications in specific use of multiple EHR tools.

4 Results and Discussion

With reference to the information presented in Figure 3, it is shown that in most factors, doctors considered themselves as having lesser experience with ratings in

Level 1 or less in areas relating to information visualization data, comparison of different patients data, icons understandability, application limitations to encompass in depth previous history information, detailed level of information, and visualization understanding convenience. The findings reveal that most of the doctors have average knowledge and given medium level importance to information about different prevailing EHR visualization tools, data gathering and updating facility, interface understanding, user friendly GUI, and database integration in future applications. These imply that doctors still have an average level of knowledge about certain areas in existing EHR tools and still need more help and guidance.

4.1 Visualization Knowledge Factors

Despite considering as having an average level knowledge, most of the doctors emphasized on the importance of EHR tools and their resulting visualization. This is evident from the results shown in Figure 3. Unfortunately, very few of them are expert in patients satisfaction using such tools, data controlling techniques such as deletion and updating of information within such applications, as well as inferring multiple visualizations, and complex operational procedures of such applications.

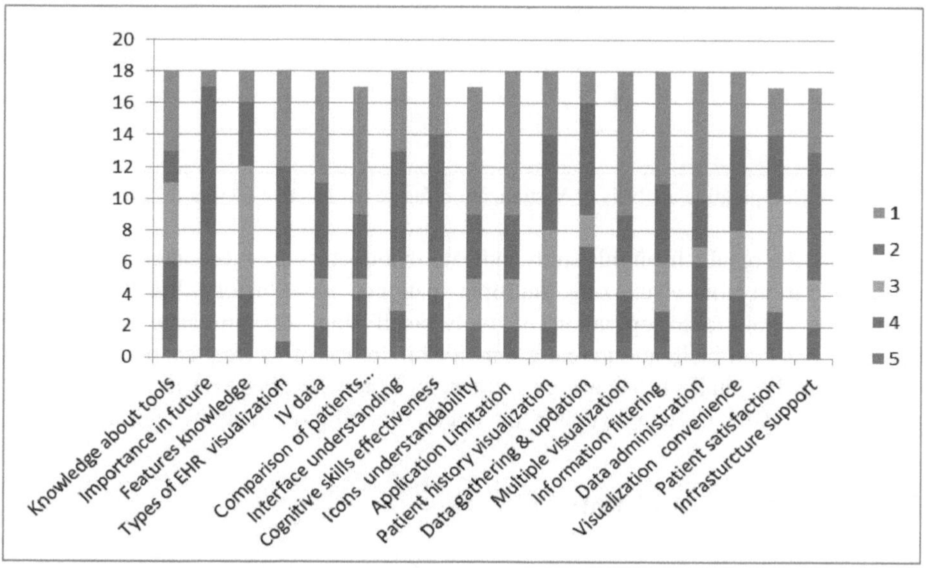

Fig. 3. Comparative analysis of Visualization knowledge factors for Physicians

The representation in Figure 3 depicts a perception of highest level of interest of doctors towards icons understanding to accelerate the process of EHR visualization applications, as well as patient history visualization. Multiple patients past data comparison with visualization and user friendly attitude of tool in addition to detailed insight of previous historical information are other same scale factors.

4.2 Future Perspective Factors

Figure 4 is representing that around 50 percent of doctors have interest in improving database limitations, increase knowledge understanding about complex temporal data and more useful GUI. They also expect that weakness in determining such operations and patient history detailed insight should be provided within later versions of such tools.

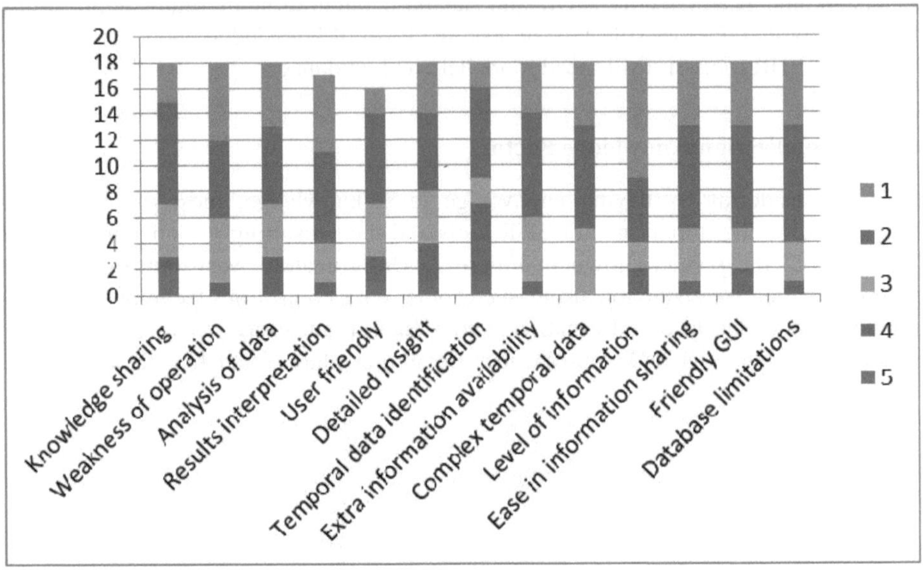

Fig. 4. Comparative analysis of Visualization future perspective factors for Physicians

Overall, the results from this study indicate that doctors are more interested in EHR tools operation for visualizing multiple patients past history but have lesser knowledge about auto operation of tools itself due less guidance and support provided. Such an inclination creates a major hindrance of its frequent adaptation and daily use in hospitals. In such a case, there is a need to focus on developing EHR visualization tools that could support the doctors based on their new requirements.

5 Conclusion and Future Work

Information visualization factors influencing the use of EHR visualization tools in daily routine hospitals are directly associated with doctors and medical professionals associated with them. Since there are a massive number of patients and data variations, this area becomes more complex due to variation in data type and applicability of a single application to fulfill the demands of its end users with multitude aspect of analysis of information. A lot of applications are in the way and also ongoing works to formalize the requirements flow in the form of query in an organized manner to better address the results in an understandable visualization for multiple patients that are a cumbersome task with relation to fully cover the needs.

The study presented in this paper encompassed the needs of doctors and their shortcomings and influence in handling the data but still more work is also required with reference to form and type of data, its behavior with these needs and creation of application handling flow with respect to its primary users that are physicians. But such applications cannot rely on single stakeholders' perception alone as they are associated with other stakeholders such as database professionals input as well as limitation of database with such applications as well as feedback from visualization experts and creation of a standard, unified and simple graphical representation.

This research work is a premier phase of our ongoing project CARE1.0 for with reference to doctor's case study. More input is still required from different research hospitals from different resources to standardize the data in this area. Similarly, more database end and visualization limitations ends need to be addressed in the future with collaboration of other stakeholders associated with information visualization for better and more sophisticated form of a visualization in this domain.

Acknowledgment. The authors would like to thank Universiti Teknologi PETRONAS for providing technical and financial supports for this research work. Special thanks to The Government Civil Hospital Emergency Ward, Faisalabad, Pakistan and Sir Ganga RAM Hospital outdoor patients Unit, Lahore, Pakistan for providing feedback with the help of doctors.

References

[1] Wilcox, L., Lu, J., Lai, J., Feiner, S., Jordan, D.: Physician- driven management of patient progress notes in an intensive care unit. Presented at the Proceedings of the 28th International Conference on Human Factors in Computing Systems, Atlanta, Georgia, USA (2010)

[2] Mane, K.K., Bizon, C., Schmitt, C., Owen, P., Burchett, B., Pietrobon, R., Gersing, K.: VisualDecisionLinc: A visual analytics approach for comparative effectiveness-based clinical decision support in psychiatry. Journal of Biomedical Informatics 45, 101–106 (2012)

[3] Malik, M.S.A., Sulaiman, S.: An Integrated Modular approach for Visual Analytic Systems in Electronic Health Records. International Journal of Advanced Computer Science and Applications 3, 246–250 (2012)

[4] Krist, W., Monroe, M., Plaisant, C., Shneiderman, B., Millstein, J., Gold, S.: Exploring Point and Interval Event Patterns: Display Methods and Interactive Visual Query Available (2012), http://www.cs.umd.edu/hcil/eventflow/

[5] Ware, C.: Information Visualization Perception for Design, 3rd edn., pp. 6–8. Morgan Kaufmann Publishers (2013)

[6] Jitao, Z., Ting, W.: A general framework for medical data mining. In: 2010 International Conference on Future Information Technology and Management Engineering (FITME), pp. 163–165 (2010)

[7] Ofri, D.: The Doctor vs. the Computer (2010), http://well.blogs.nytimes.com/2010/12/30/the-doctor-vs-the-computer

[8] Bade, R., Schelchweg, S., Miksch, S.: Connecting timeoriented data and information to a coherent interactive visualization. In: Proc. 22nd ACM Int. Conf. on Human Factors in Comp. Syst., New York, NY, USA, pp. 105–112 (2004)
[9] Heer, J., Card, K.S., Landay, J.A.: Prefuse: A toolkit for interactive information visualization. Presented at the Proceedings of the SIGCHI Conference on Human Factors in Computing Systems, Portland, Oregon, USA (2005)
[10] Bui, A.A.T., Aberle, D.R., Hooshang, K.: TimeLine: Visualizing Integrated Patient Records. IEEE Transactions on Information Technology in Biomedicine 11, 462–473 (2007)
[11] Pieczkiewicz, D.S., Finkelstine, S.M., Hertz, M.I.: Design and evaluation of a web-based interactive visualization system for lung transplant home monitoring data. In: Proc. Am. Med. Inform. Assoc. Ann. Symp., pp. 598–602 (2007)
[12] Pohl, M., Rester, M., Wiltner, S.: Usability and transferability of a visualization methodology for medical data. In: Holzinger, A. (ed.) USAB 2007. LNCS, vol. 4799, pp. 171–184. Springer, Heidelberg (2007)
[13] Helguera, M., Baum, K.G., Krol, A.: Fusion Viewer: A New Tool for Fusion and Visualization of Multimodal
[14] Medical Data Sets. Journal of Digital Imaging 21, S59–S68 (2008)
[15] Bostock, M., Heer, J.: Protovis: A Graphical Toolkit for Visualization. IEEE Transactions on Visualization and Computer Graphics 15, 1121–1128 (2009)
[16] Horsky, J., Macolgan, K., Pang, E.J., Melnikas, A.J., Linder, A.J., Schnipper, J.L., Middelton, B.: Complementary methods of system usability evaluation: Surveys and observations during software design and development cycles. Journal of Biomedical Informatics 43, 782–790 (2010)
[17] Wongsuphasawat, K., Wang, T.D., Plaisant, C., Shneiderman, B.: Visual information seeking in multiple electronic health records: Design recommendations and a process model. Presented at the Proceedings of the 1st ACM International Health Informatics Symposium, Arlington, Virginia, USA (2010)
[18] Wongsuphasawat, K., Gomez, J.A.G., Plaisant, C., Schneiderman, B., Wang, T.D., Maimon, M.T.: LifeFlow: Visualizing an overview of event sequences. Presented at the Proceedings of the 2011 Annual Conference on Human Factors in Computing Systems, Vancouver, BC, Canada (2011)
[19] Zhang, J., Walji, M.F.: TURF: Toward a unified framework of EHR usability. Journal of Biomedical Informatics 44, 1056–1067 (2011)
[20] Wang, H.-Q., Li, J.S., Zhang, Y., Suzuki, M., Araki, K.: Creating personalised clinical pathways by semantic interoperability with electronic health records. Artificial Intelligence in Medicine (2013)
[21] Malik, M.S.A., Sulaiman, S.: Towards the development of an interface model for information visualization in multiple electronic health records. Presented at the International Conference on Computer Medical Applications (ICCMA), Tunisia (2013)
[22] Hastreiter, P., Ertl, T.: Integrated registration and visualization of medical image data. In: Proceedings of the Computer Graphics International, pp. 78–85 (1998)
[23] Plaisant, C., Mushlin, R., Snyder, A., Li, J., Heller, D., Shneiderman, B.: Using visualization to enhance navigation and analysis of patient records. In: Proc. Am. Med. Inform Assoc., pp. 76–80 (1998)
[24] Taylor, P.: From Patient Data to Medical Knowledge the principles and practice of health informatics, 1st edn. Blackwell Publishing, Oxford (2006)
[25] Malik, M.S.A., Sulaiman, S.: An Integrated Modular approach for Visual Analytic Systems in Electronic Health Records. International Journal of Advanced Computer Science and Applications 3, 246–250 (2012)

"SynMax": A Mathematics Application Tool for Down Syndrome Children

Afza Shafie[1,*], Wan Fatimah Wan Ahmad[1], Nadhrah Mohd.[1], Josefina Janier Barnachea[1], M. Faisal Taha[1], and Rahmah Lob Yusuff[2]

[1] Universiti Teknologi PETRONAS, Bandar Sri Iskandar, Tronoh, 31750 Perak, Malaysia
[2] Universiti Teknologi MARA Kampus Kuantan, 25200 Pahang, Malaysia
{afza,fatimhd,josefina,mfaisal}@petronas.com.my, rahmah128@pahang.uitm.edu.my

Abstract. Research has shown that the number skills delayed relative to reading skills for Down Syndrome (DS) children. The DS children use the same learning strategy as the normal children, but their learning stages develop more slowly. A possible solution using computer based application, which the children can interact with material that have the integration of visual information and auditory. This paper describes the design, implementation and evaluation of a computer application for learning basic numeracy skills for DS. This application consists of three modules; learning identifying numbers, matching and counting. Dual Coding theory, Schema learning theory and Rapid Application Development (RAD) is employed in the design. Initial user acceptance test of the prototype has shown positive results.

Keywords: down syndrome, numeracy, computer, learning skills.

1 Introduction

Down Syndrome (DS) is a well known genetic disorder and it is caused by a chromosome abnormality that occurs before birth. In normal cell development there are 46 chromosomes but for DS, there are 47. There is an additional number 21 chromosome, resulting in the medical diagnosis of Trisomy 21. With this extra genetic material it causes changes in the orderly development of the body, brain including the physical characteristics and delayed physical, intellectual, and language development [1]. DS children do suffer from learning problems and most are classified as mildly or moderately disabled [2]. It is the most common cause of mental retardation and malformation in a newborn. Research carried out by British Medical Journal (BMJ) has shown that number of diagnoses of DS in England and Wales has increased by 71% from 1989 to 2008, whereas that of live births decreased by 1% [3]. For Malaysia, there are about 52 cases every year.

* Corresponding author.

H. Badioze Zaman et al. (Eds.): IVIC 2013, LNCS 8237, pp. 615–626, 2013.

Despite their distinct features, there is great diversity in terms of personality, intelligence, appearance, humor, learning style, compassion, compliance and attitude. DS will have a full range of emotions, are creative, imaginative in play, and can grow up in varying degrees of support and accommodation [1]. They can be friendly and can be included in community activities and by the time they become adults, they usually have some level of independence. They must therefore benefit from the same care, attention, inclusion in the community and opportunities for education which are needed in order to develop their social and academic skills needed in life. According to [4], different types of specialized therapies, counseling, and training can help them learn the necessary skills and manage emotional issues.

Most children with DS have mild to moderate retardation (IQ 30 to 60). Persons with DS at the upper end of the IQ range might attain 4th to 6th grade reading skill. They can provide for basic self–help needs, and have varying degrees of educational achievement and social and occupational skills. They need special education, training facilities, and frequently sheltered living and work situations [5]. With the advancement of technology and the internet, people with DS must be given the opportunity to access information and communication technology (ICT) in order to be fully included in the society. Research has shown that ICT would be a useful tool for DS to differentiate the curriculum and promote inclusion as well as to promote areas of development such as number skills and social development. Computer-assisted learning offers particular benefits for children with Down syndrome and for people with learning disabilities in general such as visual presentation, self-paced learning, highly motivating graphics and sound, immediate feedback and the opportunity to be in control of their own learning. It is easy to obtain many characteristics of computer-assisted learning that would reflect the specific learning style of children with DS and computers can often sustain a child's interest for much longer periods than traditional teaching. Although detailed evidence to support this view is limited, there is a growing body of research in this field. A study conducted by [7] has indicated that children with DS started to use computer as early as 3 years old and 80% of them use computer for educational purposes. This research showed that people with DS are being exposed to computer and using computer might help them in their learning.

Researchers in special education are to some extent informed of the potential of computer technology in helping individuals with DS. They claimed that computer technology can help people with DS increase confidence and motivation through creative activities and Web browsing. This can achieved if educational software programs are age appropriate and are able to reach educational goals for individuals with DS. For example, study conducted by [6] showed that virtual reality using Wii gaming technology is potentially effective intervention to enhance sensory motor functions in children with DS. They claimed that repetitive training and the observation, practice, and representation on the screen of task-specific can facilitate brain plasticity of children that engaged the mirror neuron system or long-term effects [7] and [8].

Mandy Wood, a psychologist, has indentified the advantages of computer assisted learning for children with Down syndrome such as visual learning style, non-verbal mode of response, being in control, opportunities for practice and immediate rewards, errorless learning, self-paced learning, improving motivation, clutter free working environment and fear of failure. For instance, in the case of improving motivation, a child's attention span may be increased as the learning experience is enhanced with pictures, sounds and animations. One study using interactive commercial software suggested that attention span could be increased from less than 3 minutes to more than 15 minutes in children mild to moderate learning difficulties. Also, the child is able to proceed as quickly or as slowly as he/she wishes as the computer will 'wait' for the child to respond without prompting them before he/she has had time to fully process the information and construct his/her response [9] and [10].

A study conducted by [11], suggested that technological tool must be incorporated in the teaching and learning process. It was emphasized that teaching the elementary concepts in Mathematics represents a long term process with individual's with DS where mastering could take years. For this reason, the system has to be rich in the variety of media and tasks presented, because it is necessary to avoid the repetition of activities. In addition, chronological and cognitive ages of the children must be considered hence the presentation should be in stages, i.e., from childhood to adulthood.

Since children with DS experience cognitive delays that cause them to have slower physical and mental development, it is crucial to ensure that the mismatch between learning and teaching methods are minimized. A possible solution using computer based application, which the children can interact with material that have the integration of visual information and auditory. A study is conducted to identify the suitable learning theory (s) to be adapted in designing the application, develop the application and conduct a user acceptance test for the developed application.

This paper describes the design, implementation and evaluation of a computer application for learning basic numeracy skills for DS. This application consists of three modules; learning identifying numbers, matching and counting. The application was developed in collaboration with the Ipoh Kiwanis Down Syndrome Foundation Centre. The center was established on September, 2006 by Kiwanis Club of Bandaraya Ipoh for Down Syndrome children ages 2 months old to 6 years old. Currently the centre has nineteen (19) Down Syndrome (DS) children between 1—13 years old.

2 SynMax

A study exploring the extent to which computer-assisted teaching facilities assisted children with DS in learning basic mathematical concepts and skills was conducted by [12]. The results showed that the group of children with DS that was taught using multimedia teaching method showed a higher performance than the paper and pencil assisted teaching group on a variety of tasks and measures. This result suggests a clear relation between teaching method and mathematical learning in DS children. Since children with DS have the same educational goals as those of other learners but have a slower learning pace, computer software can be carefully programmed to meet individual needs and teaching activities can be achieved in very small stages [7] and [13], providing the opportunity for Artificial Intelligent (AI) be incorporated in the design to allow for personalized teaching. The AI agent will act as the agent for transition between progression (moving forward), regression (moving backward) and permanency (no change in phase).

Study by Gonzalez proposed the following to be considered in designing education programs for children with learning difficulties:

- Operations, instructions, and verbal content must be structured in levels
- The content must also be in a simple format for early learners to access
- Feedback sequences must be incorporated which can explain the causes of error to the learner
- Learner must be guided towards getting the correct answer.
- Reinforcement techniques need to be incorporated

They went on to suggest that mathematics software for DS need to incorporate activities related with their experiences from their environment, their lexical deficits and to avoid repetition of presentation.

SynMax is mathematics computer application software that is developed to assist DS to learn the number concepts. The acquisition of number concept will help the learner to know numerical series and the order of numbers. The initial stage of the development involves only single numbers from 1 to 10. The problems and learning environment is designed to be as close as possible to the experiences of the learners. Three modules were considered; identifying numbers, matching and learn.

The development of SynMax has also taken into consideration of some learning theories such as behaviorism, cognitivism and constructivism together with the Dual Coding theory (Clark & Paivo, 1991). Dual-coding theory postulates that both visual and verbal information is used to represent information The ability to code a stimulus two different ways increases the chance of remembering an item compared to if the stimulus was only coded one way. For instance, there will be both written and verbal instructions to assist the children in using the application.

Schema theory is about concepts: objects and the relationships they have with other objects, situations, events, sequences of events. The focus of the application is on numbers from 1 to 10. These are the numbers that had been taught by the teachers. The design of the prototype is based on the methodology as shown in Fig. 1.

Rapid Application Development (RAD) was considered in the development of the prototype. The tools used in the development of the prototype are Adobe Flash CS5.5, Action Script 2.0, Photo editing and Sound Recorder. Suggestions from staff of Ipoh Kiwanis Down Syndrome Foundation (DSF), Center are (a) use bright colors in the presentation; (b) font size must be big enough for the DS to recognize; (c) use of familiar objects to represent numbers. The application was developed to accommodate Bahasa Melayu and English Language users. The objective of SynMax is to teach children with DS to recognize number from 1 to 10 There are mainly 3 activities which are "Learning ", "Counting" and "Matching" and users can choose whether to do the activities starting from 1 until 5 or 1 to 10. Phases involved in the RAD are; Requirement Planning, User Design, Construction and Cutover. The brief description for the phases is as follows:

- Requirement Planning

In this phase, interview and survey had been done. An interview with the staff of Kiwanis Down Syndrome Foundation Center (KDSFC) , Ipoh were done to get

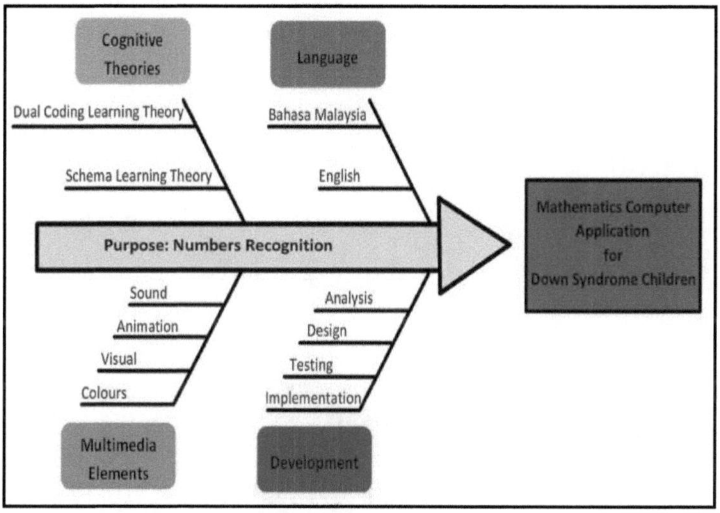

Fig. 1. Methodology for the development of SynMax

feedback regarding what should be included in the mathematics application tool to specify area or requirement needed by the DS children in learning mathematics. Also, a survey using a set questionnaire was done to gather data from parents and teacher at KDSC

- User Design

During this time, the instructors of the DS children will give some opinion on how the application should work to ensure that it will successfully assist DS children in learning mathematics. Instructors and developer will work closely to create prototypes that capture systems requirements and that become the basis for the physical design of the system being developed. The outcome is the preliminary draft of the interface.

- Construction

Here is where the development of the application will take place. The outcomes from this activity are finalized number skill conceptual framework and the application.

- Cutover

Cutover is the delivery of the application to its end users. Cutover involves implementation, testing and training users. The outcome from this activity is that the new application will be implemented

2.1 The Prototype

The main page of the application allows the user to choose whether they want to do the activities in English or Malay Language by clicking either one of the buttons, This is then followed by the e level page. At this page users can choose to do the activities from number 1 to 5 or from number 1 to 10. User is then directed to the 3 modules which are the "Learning" Module, "Match" Module and "Count" Module. A series of animation, text, images and are incorporated in the application but is kept at minimum. The screenshots of the application are shown in Fig. 2, 3 and 4. The prototype was developed for numbers from 1 to 5 only.

Fig. 2. Screenshot of the main page

Fig. 3. Screenshot of the level

Fig. 4. Screenshot of the main page

The screenshots for the modules are shown in Fig. 5, 6 and 7. In the "learn identification" Module, the user will be introduced to numbers. The digits will appear one by one and in sequence together with the pronunciation. The objective of the module is to introduce the numbers and for the user to recognize the digit. Each of the digits is repeated three times.

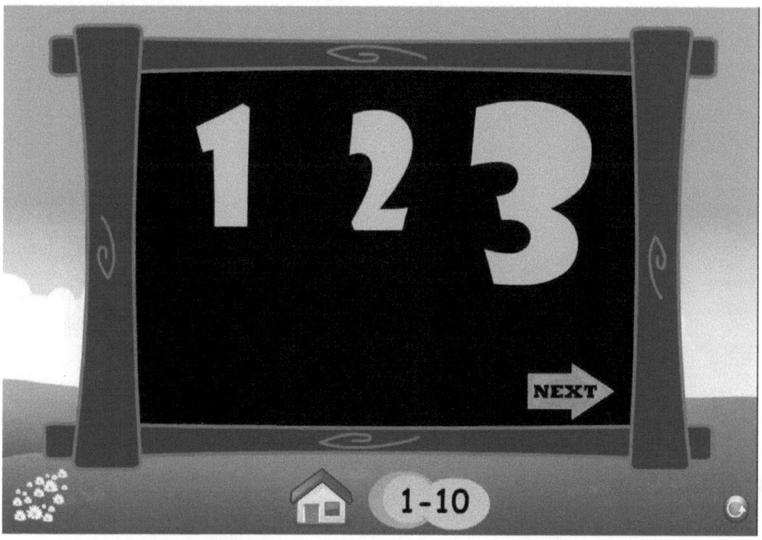

Fig. 5. Screenshot of the Learn Module

The user is required to match the number that appears on the board with that in the given shape in the "Match" .Module. User will have to draw a line to match the items.

Besides numeracy skill, the module will help with the development of fine motor skills. Finally, the Count modules require the user to pop the number of balloons as shown on the screen.

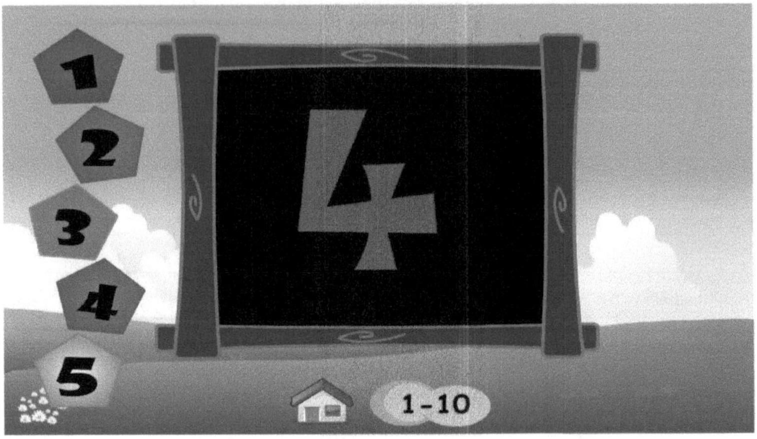

Fig. 6. Screenshot of the Match Module

Fig. 7. Screenshot of the Count Module

3 Methodology

Due to limited number of DS students at the center, a one stage sampling method was used. This prototype was tested with three (3) children aged between 8 – 13 years of age. One of them had followed the intervention programme that was held by the center in his early years there. The main requirement that the children had to fulfill is their ability to respond to instructions that are given by their teachers. The teacher is present throughout the evaluation session. The evaluation was carried out for 45 minutes for each student.

Two observation checklists8 items were prepared for the survey. The teacher and parents will answer the survey in order for the researchers to have a basic understanding about the DS children by observing the activities performed by them at the center and at home. The checklist is composed of 34 items. These items include observable learning skills (cognitive, affective , psychomotor) and occurrence of observable behavioral problems of the DS child.

Another instrument is the user acceptance test to be filled up by the teacher by rating the DS child according to his performance in using the SYNMAX-the mathematics application tool. It is composed of 8 items were each item need to be answered by either 'YES" or "NO" using different levels from 0 "NO" (not done at all) to 4, "YES" (well done). The aim of the evaluation is to test users acceptance to the application and also to find out whether users can connect or recall their prior knowledge with the information in the application. Only three (3) children with DS aged between 8-13 participated in the testing process.

4 Results and Discussion

4.1 Survey Findings

The questionnaires serve the purpose of having a basic understanding about the children by observing the activities performed by them during class session at the center and at home. Nineteen (19) DS children aged between 1 to 13 years old were observed and the respondents of the questionnaire consist of 10 mothers and 1 teacher from KDSC. In the questionnaire, mean is used to determine the occurrence of activities performed by the children during the session and behavior of the children at the center and at home. The results are given in Table 1 and Table 2.

Table 1. Response from the Teachers

Category	Age		
	7 - 9	**4 - 6**	**1 - 3**
Cognitive	1.45	2.61	1.74
Affective	2	3.02	2.54
Psychomotor	1.9	2.43	1.7
Behavioral Problem	2.0	1.75	1.29

Table 2. Parents' Resonses

Category	Age		
	7 - 9	**4 - 6**	**1 - 3**
Cognitive	2.65	1.68	2.03
Affective	2.66	2.82	2.56
Psychomotor	2.4	2.67	2.27
Behavioral Problem	2.7	1.88	1.67

From the results in Table 1 and Table 2, it showed the children show their anxiety (nervous) with repetitive behavior, they tend to withdraw from peers or family members and they have many intellectual challenges. Therefore, it is necessary for the teacher to find strategies so that they will progressively move up and never assume that the child is not capable of doing things. They could be helped using the right tools that are appropriate for their learning capabilities. It is hoped that the application that is being developed will help them in learning Mathematics more effectively.

In addition, some of the inputs gathered from interviewing the staff are; the children's attention span increases when they use the computer, DS kids like colours, sound and direct manipulation of objects while learning and the preferred language is either English or Bahasa Malaysia.

4.2 User Acceptance Test for Prototype

These user interfaces was developed using Adobe Flash CS5.5. The application tool "SynMAX" was developed to accommodate Bahasa Melayu and English Language users. The main idea is to teach children with DS to recognize number from 1 to 10. There are mainly 3 activities which are "Learning", "Counting" and "Matching" and users can choose whether to do the activities starting from 1 until 5 or 1 to 10.

The user acceptance results are shown in Fig. 8.

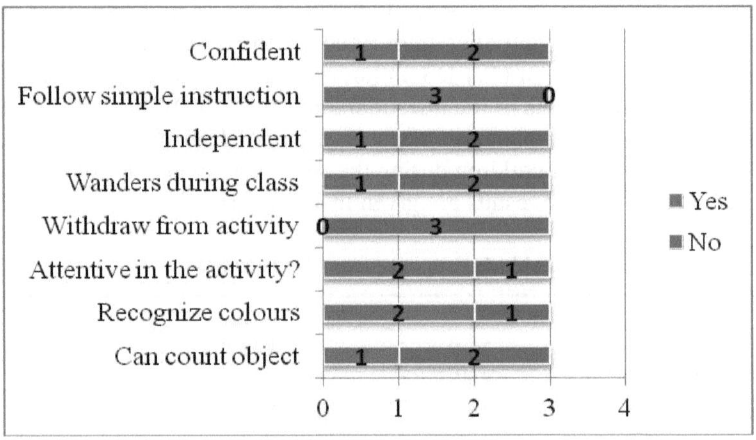

Fig. 8. The User Acceptance Results

On the whole, the results indicate that the students seem to be able to accept the application The results has shown that the students are able to follow the instructions given in the application even though the teacher sometimes need to repeat the instructions to them. It is also positive to note that they do not withdraw from the activity and were attentive to the animation and the images on the screen. These seem to imply that the students are receptive towards using computers as a learning tool, consistent with the results of some of the studies that had been carried out. However, only one of them managed to complete the "Learn" module. It is also interesting to observe that this is the student that had been exposed to the intervention plan. Even though there was a child that always wanders during the activity, he will continue to do the activity once instructed by the teacher and was eager to use the computer.

Some of the positive feedback that was given by the instructors are;

- The colours, font size and animations are suitable for the students.
- The level of content is satisfactory
- The activities are suitable for the students.
- DS children learn better when the information are given in small amount.

While the recommendations for improvements include:

- Replace the existing background music with nursery rhymes or songs that the students are familiar with. This will provide a familiar environment to them.
- Include a "teacher kind of figure" in each of the modules, and this figure be used to show the examples.
- Repeat the activities for at least a few times but with different scenarios and animation.
- More animation and interactivity added in this application since DS are very fond of interactivity in their learning. Interactivity will allow them to explore the knowledge by themselves and it can expand their attention span that will assist them in learning.
- Consideration to integrate application with handheld devices such as smart phones and tablets to allow simultaneous development of motor skills.

5 Conclusion

The paper has discussed on the design and development of an initial prototype of a mathematics software , SYNMAX for Down Syndrome children. This design, based on dual coding learning theory, schema learning theory, is the first initiative of development of a learning tool for DS children in Malaysia aimed at enhancing their numeracy skills. Positive feedback and suggestions for improvement of the prototype have been obtained from the user acceptance evaluation. Enhancement of the prototype is currently being carried out. The application is currently extended to mobile applications in keeping up with the advancement of technology.

Acknowledgments. The research is funded by the Ministry of Higher Education (MOHE) under Fundamental Research Grant Scheme (FRGS Fasa 1/2012). The authors would also like to acknowledge the staff and students of Kiwanis Down Syndrome Foundation (DSF), Ipoh Center, Perak.

References

1. Public Awareness Language Guidelines National Down Syndrome Congress, `http://www.ndscenter.org/resources/packages4.php` (accessed Date: October 7, 2010)

2. Trix, Victoria, Teaching tips for children with Down Syndrome. JEN (2008), http://www.brighthub.com/education/special/articles/29680.aspx (2009) (accessed Date: October 7, 2010)
3. Morris, J.K., Alberman, E.: Trends in Down's syndrome live births and antenatal diagnoses in England and Wales from 1989 to 2008: analysis of data from the National Down Syndrome Cytogenetic register. BMJ2009-339-b3794do:10.1136/bmj.b3794 (2009)
4. Sexton, M.J., Dolan, S.M., Smith, D.: Common therapies, counseling and training for young people with Down Syndrome. Health & Fitness (2009), http://wrondiagnosis.pubs.righthealth.com/topic/People%20Down%syndrome?as=clink&ac+1437&afc=21686466&p=&dqp.cache.mode+PMBypass#xzz11jtmHk8 (accessed on October 8, 2010)
5. Leshin, L.H.: Down Syndrome, Trisomy 21. Encyclopedia Index, http://www.drhull.com/EncyMaster/D/Down_syndrome.html (accessed on: November 18, 2010)
6. Wuang, Y.P., Chinag, C.S., Su, C.Y., Wang, C.C.: Research in Development Diasabilities (2010), doi:10.1016/j.ridd.2010.10.002
7. Feng, J., Lazar, J.: Computer Usage by Children with Down Syndrome: Challenges and Future Research ACM Transactions on Accessible Computing 2 (3), Article 13, 13– 44 (2010)
8. Bird, G., Buckley, S.: Down Syndrome News and Update, 1 (4), 159–174 (2000)
9. Wood, M.: Down Syndrome News and Update 1 (4), 2–10 (2004)
10. Black, B.: Down Syndrome News and Update 2 (6), 66–68 (2006)
11. Bruno, A., Gonzales, L., Moreno, L., Noda, M., Aguilar, R., Munoz, V.: Teaching Mathematics to Children with Down's Syndrome. Universidad de La Laguna, Tenerife, Spain (2003)
12. Ortega–Tudela, J.M., Gomez– Ariza, C.J.: Computer-assisted teaching and mathematical learning in Down Syndrome children. Journal of Computer Assisted Learning 22, 298–307 (2006)
13. Garcia, J., Ipina, K.L., Irigoyen, E., Elorriaga, J., Garay, N., Zulueta, E., Rubio, J., Vaquero, C., Penagarikano, M., Lopez, J.M., Ezeiza, A., Ipina, J.M.L. (2006), http://www.iadat.org/iadat-e2006/abstracts_web/IADAT-e2006_32.pdf
14. Clark, J.M., Paivo, A.: Dual coding theory and education. Educational Psychology Review 3(3), 149–170 (1971)

Presence in Visual Mental Imagery

Jayesh S. Pillai[1], Uday A. Athavankar[2], Colin T.A. Schmidt[3,4], and Simon Richir[4]

[1] Indian Institute of Information Technology, Design & Manufacturing, Jabalpur, India
jayesh@iiitdmj.ac.in
[2] IDC, Indian Institute of Technology Bombay, India
uaa@iitb.ac.in
[3] Le Mans University, Le Mans, France
[4] LAMPA, Arts et Metiers ParisTech, Angers, France
{colin.schmidt,simon.richir}@ensam.eu

Abstract. 'Presence', the sense of being inside a virtual environment evoked with the help of computer mediation, has come to be a subject well explored in the field of virtual reality. Studies on mental imagery confirm that we can intuitively evoke objects and spaces in our minds and interact with them temporally. We believe that a sense of presence could be experienced in such self-evoked reality as well. This paper explores the experience of presence in visual mental imagery. We studied verbal expressions, physical movements and gestures, exhibited during mental imagery experiences in two scenarios - a guiding task and a mental walk exercise. A 'protocol analysis' was performed followed by analysis of time taken and mapping of physical movements. The results evidently point to this spatio-temporal phenomenon of experiencing presence. Furthermore, we present a comparative review on the sense of presence experienced during mental imagery and virtual reality.

Keywords: presence, mental imagery, mental walk, spatial attention, protocol analysis, virtual reality.

1 Introduction

Research on how we experience a sense of presence in computer generated immersive virtual environments, has been going on for years. In fact the ultimate aim of virtual reality would be to be able to evoke a strong sense of presence almost similar to our presence in the real world [1], [2], [3] and [4]. But as the research on presence progressed it became clear that presence could be evoked not only by computer mediated virtual spaces, but also be evoked endogenously in immersive mental imagery spaces. According to Sanchez-Vives & Slater [5], presence research should be opened up, beyond the domain of computer science and other technologically oriented disciplines, as the concept of presence is sufficiently similar to consciousness and it may help to transform research within domains outside virtual reality. Pillai et al. [6] and Pillai [7] suggested that the sense of presence is not confined to such media-evoked reality but could be experienced in self-evoked reality as well. Biocca

H. Badioze Zaman et al. (Eds.): IVIC 2013, LNCS 8237, pp. 627–639, 2013.

[8] rightly pointed out that research on presence in virtual reality often failed to adequately incorporate the roles of mental imagery and spatial attention.

Findings of Shepard & Metzler [9] and Kosslyn [10] in the area of mental imagery provided empirical evidence of our wonderful ability to evoke images or imagine stimuli without actually perceiving them. In addition, Kosslyn's [11] and [12] work demonstrated that there are considerable similarities between the neural mappings for imagined stimuli and perceived stimuli. Recent experiments conducted by Athavankar et al. [13] on blindfolded architects to study how they efficiently used movements and hand gestures to interact with objects and spaces around in mental imagery, clearly indicate a sense of presence similar to the physical world. Being immersed in the mental imagery space (whether visually faint or highly vivid), they reacted as if they were in a real-world space that was continuously being shaped. Thus we decided to investigate directly into this sense of presence evoked by mental imagery with the help of mental walk exercises. Lately, the term 'presence' has come to have multiple meanings [14], as a result of being observed from different fields of communication media. So, it should be noted that we will use the term 'sense of presence' for what we experience in the virtual world, as opposed to presence we experience in the real (physical) world. The term 'presence' would mean presence in general.

2 Background

2.1 The Sense of Presence

Virtual reality researchers have attempted to define presence in many ways. Presence, as Steuer [4] describes, is the key to defining virtual reality in terms of human experience rather than technological hardware. He adds that presence refers not to one's surroundings as they exist in the physical world, but to the perception of those surroundings as mediated by both automatic and controlled mental processes. Witmer & Singer [15] defined presence as the subjective experience of being in one environment (there) when physically in another environment (here). Presence induced by computer applications or interactive simulations was believed to be what gave people the sensation of, as Sheridan called it, 'being there'. Although beginning with what was called 'telepresence' [2], the idea evolved over time with the slow realization that the sense of presence is beyond just the 'being there' quality. Lombard & Ditton [1] described presence as an 'illusion of non-mediation' that occurs when a person fails to perceive or acknowledge the existence of a medium in his/her communication environment and responds as he/she would if the medium were not there. They explained how the concept of presence is derived from multiple fields like communication, computer science, engineering, science, psychology, philosophy, and the arts. As we can see clearly, almost all the definitions above correspond to the sense of presence induced by different kinds of mediation. Presently this sense of presence that we experience (different from physical reality) is being studied from various disciplines associated with cognitive science (for instance, film theory and art, television and media [16], literature theory [17], teleoperation [3] and [18], communication media [1], video games and serious games [19] and [20], virtual reality [5], [14] and [21]).

2.2 Mental Imagery

Although the best way to examine mental imagery is through 'introspection', research on mental imagery required objective methods of analysis to support its evidence. It indeed took many years for researchers to come up with a method, which Kosslyn called 'the quantification of introspection'. This method attempted to externalize mental events and tried to detect and measure the behavioural consequences, often in terms of performance time of internal processing. One of the best examples in this direction was Shepard and Metzler's [8] experiment on the mental rotation of geometric shapes. Presently mental imagery is studied extensively, through various methods of externalization of mental activities. One such method is protocol analysis with the help of thinking aloud process where the externalization is through real time verbal expressions and associated physical gestures and movements. We attempt to study the sense of presence in mental imagery. To begin with, Athavankar et al. [13] and [22] had earlier found the indication of a sense of presence in mental imagery in the experiments conducted with blindfolded architects, although the objectives of those experiments were to explore design possibilities. It was observed that, even though the architects used different strategies as part of their design process, they remained immersed in the (simultaneously being designed) mentally evoked spaces. They acted in the mental space with certain similarities corresponding to the physical world. This led us to conduct an experiment to study how people experienced mental imagery, with their sense of presence as our primary focus.

2.3 Analyzing Presence

Analysing and measuring the sense of presence is still an ongoing debate, in the fields of communication media [23]. Different questionnaires and methods have been proposed in order to break down this subjective experience into objective parameters. In the area of mental imagery, experiments were devised to objectively study the properties of mental processes through behaviour analysis [24] or the process of thinking aloud [25]. In our experiment we chose a verbal descriptive task, thus ensuring availability of protocols and thus used 'protocol analysis'. Its effectiveness has been seen in previous experiments conducted on designers and architects [26]. Study of gestures and movements along with verbal transcriptions took protocol analysis method one step further, helping in the efficient mapping of various elements of mentally evoked spaces [13] and [27]. Studies show that although mental transformations could involve the visual system, the operations may perhaps be guided by inputs from the motor system as well (certainly in some situations, according to Zacks [28]), and thus it may not be difficult to convert them into corresponding physical movements [12] and [29].

Research Questions. The two main questions that we try to address in this paper are:

1. Does one experience a ‘sense of presence’ in mental imagery?
2. Can this sense of presence be objectively identified by analysing verbal expressions, gestures and movements?

3 Experimental Procedure

3.1 Mental Tasks

To objectively study presence, we chose to have two scenarios for the experiment - an indirect and a direct task. The tasks concentrated particularly on imagery spaces evoked from memory. As we were interested in presence in particular, we chose tasks that would not necessarily require design thinking or creativity. We decided on ‘way finding’ as the means of indirectly studying presence, as it did not impose additional mental load on the participants and they could rely principally on their long term memory. The tasks were defined as follows:

Scenario-1 - Guiding Task: The participants were asked to guide a friend verbally on mobile phone, from point A to B, while they were themselves at point B. The given locations (namely IDC and Nescafe Stall) were well known to the participants.
Scenario-2 - Mental Walk: The participants were asked to imagine that they were at point A and were going to point B. They were asked to think aloud while doing so.

In both cases, the subjects were blindfolded and were in a sound proof experiment hall in order to completely depend on their mental imagery and have minimum interference from external perception during the mental tasks. They had enough space to physically move around. In addition, the order of the tasks was alternatively changed with each subsequent participant.

3.2 Experimental Setup

For both the scenarios, there were mainly 3 stages in the experiment process.

Stage 1: The task was given to the participant in writing. They were asked to recall the task once, just before the experiment started.

Stage 2: In the hall, they were given the freedom to choose where to stand and to orient themselves however they preferred to, before starting the experiment. As soon as they did so, they were blindfolded.

Stage 3: They were cued to begin the task. From beginning to the end of the task, Stage 3 session was recorded on video for transcription of verbal expressions and study of gestures and movements.

In case the participants preferred to move around during the experiment (Scenario-2), the floor was marked with grids of 50cm by 50cm size, to map their physical movements. After Stage 3, post-experiment discussions also took place, which in fact helped us clarify certain aspects of their mental imagery experiences. Although such clarifications are introspective and subjective, they were used only to compare the remarks with what we could objectively deduct from the transcripts and the videos.

Subjects. For each task, there were eight subjects (five male and three female). All the participants had a fair knowledge of the locations mentioned in the tasks and had often been using the given route. They had no knowledge of the primary objectives of our study, and only knew that the experiments were regarding mental imagery.

Methodology. The contents of the protocols (from the externalised think aloud data) helped us decode the various elements they encountered during the imagery experience. From the recorded videos, data was later transcribed and logged in data sheets for analysis. The information was organized in a tabular form under - Timestamp, Transcripts (Verbal Data), Gestures and Movements (Physical Data). Verbal data provided direct information on various aspects such as self-positioning and elements of the evoked imagery space, while physical movements and gestures helped us in comparing and analyzing those. In Scenario-2, the floor-grids helped us plot outlines of the physical movements made by them with respect to their mental movements. In Scenario-1, as there were no (or inconsiderable) physical changes in positions we had to rely on verbal data and gestures (with orientation) for the analysis.

4 Analysis

4.1 Scenario-1: Guiding Task

Protocol Analysis. Based on the analysis method the protocols were classified into two main information categories - 'Verbal Expressions' and 'Physical Expressions'. Both were transcribed from the videos so as to analyze them with their simultaneity in time. Verbal Expressions were divided into the sub categories - Body and External Space, while Physical Expressions into - Orientation and Gestures. The sub categories

Table 1. Information categories, sub categories and codes from the protocols for Scenario-1

Information Categories (Scenario-1)		
Analysis Method	**Sub Category**	**Codes (Elements of Sense of Presence in Mental Imagery, based on the protocols)**
Verbal Expressions	Body	Position Action Direction Orientation
	External Space	Distance Specific Location / Space / Building Elements / Things Relative position of elements with respect to other elements Properties Visual Sense
Physical Expressions	Orientation	Rotation / Orientation with respect to cognitive map
	Gestures	Self Position Relative position of elements with respect to self position Shapes and forms of elements Direction

were further broken down into different codes, denoting various elements of mental imagery that pointed towards the sense of presence (Table 1). In Scenario-1, verbal data analysis was difficult, as the sense of presence was to be detected indirectly. Although certain aspects of verbal data provided direct references to the locations and movements in the imagery, as we studied the corresponding gestures, the way they positioned themselves in the imagery space became clearer. Mainly two strategies were observed in guiding techniques: (1) the participant guided the friend in real time, through every point between starting and the ending locations, or (2) the participant guided the friend such that after his guidance, the friend would take that route.

Time and Distance. We analysed the time taken by the participants for different segments of the mental task. It was then compared to the average time that one would take to walk (at constant speed) from the locations A to B in a real-world scenario. Two intermediate landmark points were identified from the protocols, depending on the locations that every participant had encountered. It was interesting to find (as we can see in Fig. 1) that the time taken by them to mentally go through each part of the route correlated with the average real-world walking time. To confirm this, we compared their speed of mental movement at each interval. The graph in Fig. 2 shows their speed, with the value of speed in the real-world as 1. This showed a positive correlation between the time and the distance taken mentally to reach from one point to another (Pearson correlation coefficient between average time taken during Physical Walk (real-world scenario) and Mental Guiding Task $r = 0.999$, $p = 0.010$).

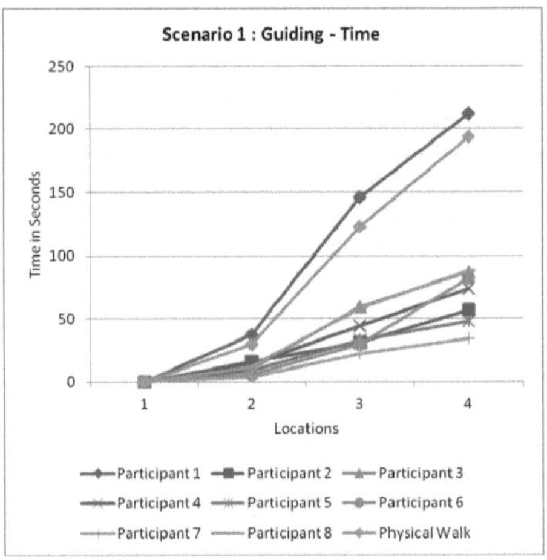

Fig. 1. Time taken to reach the locations mentally (Scenario-1), compared to the avg. walking time in real-world scenario

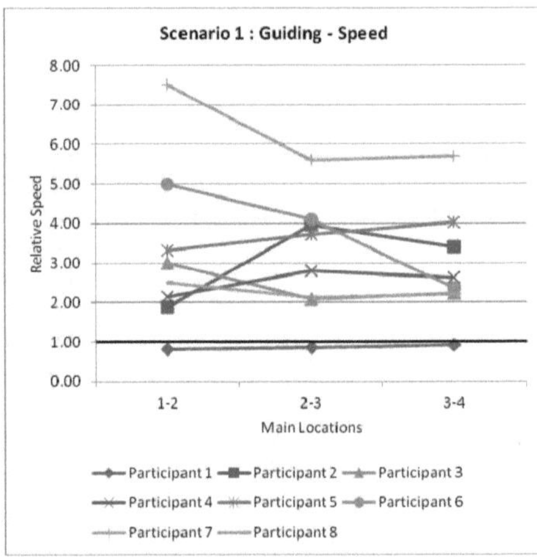

Fig. 2. Relative speed at the intervals (Scenario-1) compared to the avg. walking speed in real-world scenario (taken as 1)

Orientation Strategies. When the verbal expressions and the physical movements were correlated, two strategies seemed to emerge. The participant performed mental movement either (1) with physical orientation, or (2) without physical orientation.

At times the participants naturally oriented themselves while imagining turns or pointing to landmarks on their sides, while other times they did not move at all. They constantly shifted between the two strategies. In both cases, the hand gestures, or subtle upper body and head movements were very helpful in unravelling where they were present in the mental space during that time.

4.2 Scenario-2: Mental Walk

Protocol Analysis. In this case, the main analysis methods remained same, while some subcategories differed. Verbal Expressions were categorised into - Body (Self) and External Space, while Physical Expressions into - Movement, Orientation and Gestures. The sub categories were again broken down into different codes representing the elements of sense of presence in mental imagery (Table. 2). In this case, the participants naturally evoked the mental space to be experienced from their own perspective. We found that while the participants moved in the mental space, their corresponding physical movements occurred naturally. We believe that physical movements may have in fact helped them to navigate in the mental space better and with ease of orientation. An example of how these physical movements corresponding to the mental walk were mapped with the help of transcripts can be seen in Fig. 3 below (the starting, intermediate and ending points are marked on the route map).

Table 2. Information categories, sub categories and codes from the protocols for Scenario-2

Information Categories (Scenario-2)		
Analysis Method	**Sub Category**	**Codes (Elements of Sense of Presence in Mental Imagery, based on the protocols)**
Verbal Expressions	Body (Self)	Position
		Action
		Direction
		Orientation
	External Space	Distance
		Specific Location / Space / Building
		Elements / Things
		Relative position of elements with respect to other elements
		Properties
		Visual Sense
		Other Senses
Physical Expressions	Movement	Location
		Direction of movement
	Orientation	Rotation / Orientation with respect to cognitive map
	Gestures	Self Position
		Relative position of elements with respect to self position
		Shapes and forms of elements
		Direction

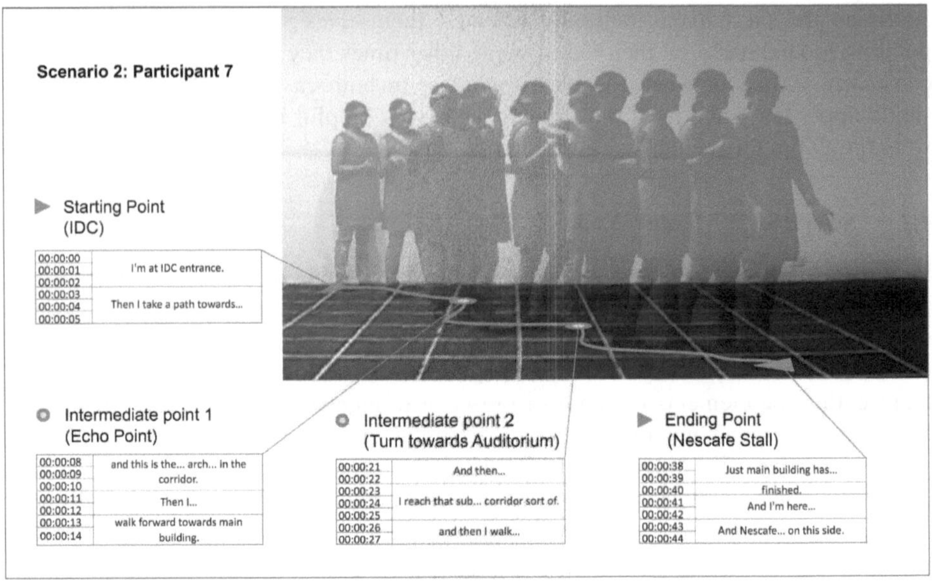

Fig. 3. Example showing how the physical movements of a participant (in Scenario-2) were mapped with the help of transcripts and the floor grid

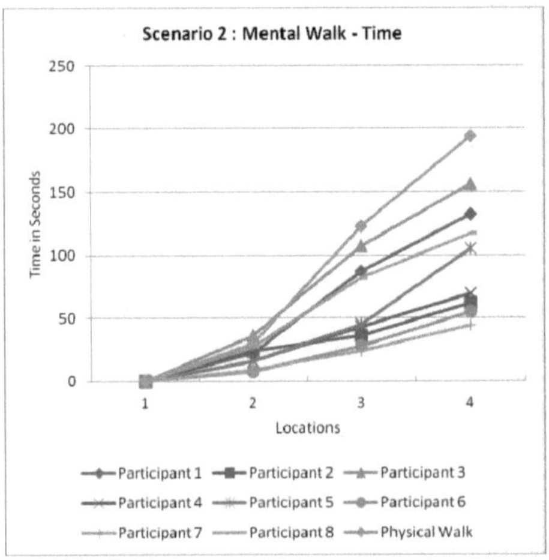

Fig. 4. Time taken to reach the locations mentally (Scenario-2), compared to the avg. walking time in real-world scenario

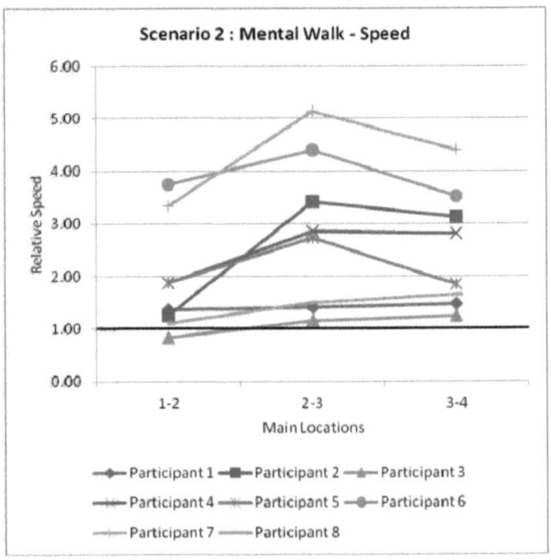

Fig. 5. Relative speed at the intervals (Scenario-2) compared to the avg. walking speed in real-world scenario (taken as 1)

Time and Distance. On exploring the mental walk time, this case also showed considerable correlations with time that one would take in a real situation. As we can see in Fig. 4, all the participants performed the task faster than the average time to walk in the real-world scenario. Although the time taken was shorter, it shows considerable correlations (Pearson correlation coefficient between average time taken during Physical Walk (real-world scenario) and Mental Walk $r = 0.997$, $p = 0.045$), which can also be observed from their relative speeds at different intervals (Fig. 5). In order to maintain the speed of the mental movements they at times omitted verbal details (even a simple right or a left turn). However, several of those details were often noticeably reflected in the associated physical movements (particularly in Scenario-2).

Movement and Orientation Strategies. During the task, almost all the participants moved physically, corresponding to their mental walk. Although a few did not intend to, they ended up taking few steps at times as there was enough space to move. There was also a participant who did not move at all, but his upper body and head movements often indicated directions and properties of his mental space.

So, in this scenario, three strategies seemed to evolve. The participant performed mental movement (1) with corresponding physical movement and orientation, or (2) with partial physical movement or orientation, or (3) without any physical movement or orientation (although with faint upper body responses). While one participant adopted the third strategy consistently, the rest of the participants seemed to adopt mainly the first strategy (although shifting at times to the second strategy).

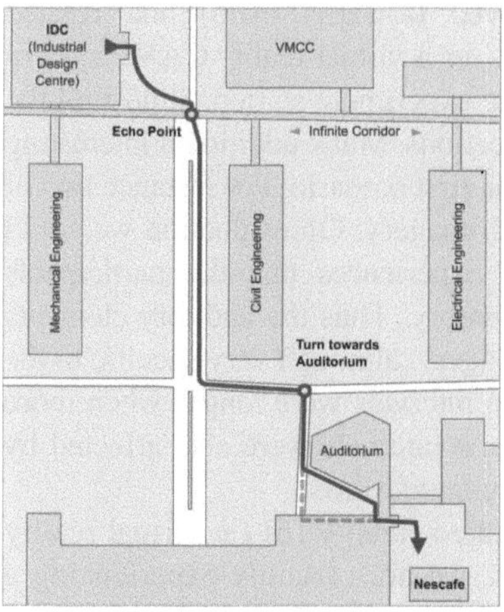

Fig. 6. Map showing the original path, from point A (IDC) to point B (Nescafe stall) and the two main landmark points

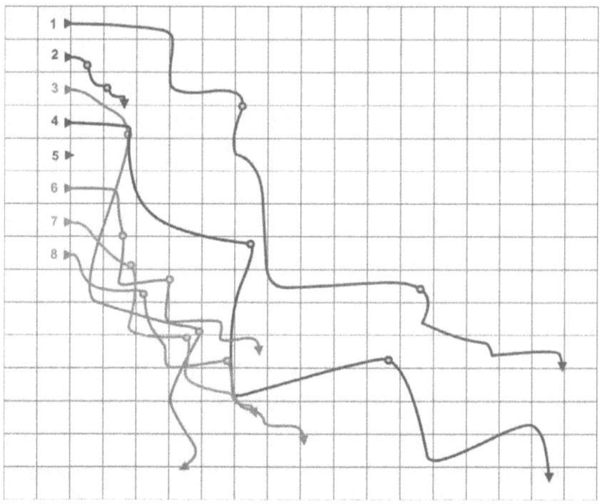

Fig. 7. Physical movements of the participants in relation to their mental walk (arranged according to the initial orientation) and their respective positions of the two intermediate landmark points

To study the physical movements corresponding to the mental task, we plotted them on a graph. Fig. 6 shows the actual path that one would take from point A (IDC) to point B (Nescafe) in a real-world scenario. In Fig. 7 we can see the physical movements of each participant with respect to their mental walk (note that the plotted movements on the grid were in fact extremely disordered, however in the figure they are arranged according to their initial orientations facing the same direction, to make it comprehensible). The intermediate points were also plotted with reference to the protocols. We can clearly see spatial correlations in the movements of participants. Although the scales of their movements differ notably, we can't deny their remarkable similarity with the actual path. As the experiment was related to way finding, this plotting of movements turned out to be an excellent approach to efficiently mapping and thus confirming the mental path they took during the task.

5 Inference and Discussion

5.1 Indication of Presence in Mental Imagery

In Scenario-1, on carefully analyzing the gestures and upper body movements with respect to verbal data, we found that the (guiding) participants naturally put themselves in the (guided) friend's perspective. Although they did not physically move, it was noticed that whenever they reached a point where a turn was required, their hand gestures or head movements indicated the direction. And after they took the turn their point of view intuitively took that direction in such a way that the same direction which was few seconds ago to their left or right, became straight ahead. It shows that the spatial imagery was constantly updating in order to give the illusion of movement. While they did not take steps to physically move, the imagery moved (towards them) and rotated accordingly (similar to a first-person video game view, or a virtual reality CAVE system with changing surroundings). In Scenario-2, before the experiment started, almost all the participants wanted to orient themselves in certain directions. Many additional interesting elements were also noticed which did not turn up in the first scenario. For instance two of the participants imagined sounds in addition to visual imagery. On evaluation we could see that auditory imagery was a result of certain experiences that the participants previously had, which were well embedded in the memory. Thus the auditory elements too contributed to their sense of presence in mental imagery, although very specific to the individual participants. In both the scenarios, the time intervals were longer when more verbal details were reported. It may imply that the time intervals were also affected by the ability of the participants to put those details into suitable words.

If we find similarities in an experience of an Evoked Reality [6] (in virtual reality or mental imagery) with the real world experiences, we are certainly experiencing a sense of presence. The concept of self, being in a place, is the first step towards the signs of evidence of presence (the subsequent steps being the vividness of experience, levels of presence, spatial attention characteristics, multisensory experiences etc). The illusion of perceiving a spatio-temporal reality validates presence [7]. Every participant expressed a sense of moving in a mentally evoked space for a certain amount of time. Similar to the phenomenon of visual selective attention in a real-world scenario [30], the elements of mental imagery spaces were selective as well and this played a major role in their subjective experiences. The mental load was balanced by evoking only the relevant details required for the task. However, sometimes extremely non task-related elements were also evoked, if they were well set in their memory of the path.

5.2 Similarities with Presence in Virtual Reality (or Media-Evoked Reality)

The evoked sense of presence in mental imagery clearly shows much resemblance with the experience of presence in virtual reality and associated media. Here we provide a comprehensible account of the comparisons between presence in mental imagery and media experiences.

After the experiments it was intriguing to note that the participants referred to the mental imagery space as a place they just visited and the mental events as something that happened a few minutes before, which also strongly implied their experience of presence. It is similar to the case of post-virtual reality experience of the sense of 'being there' [16, 31]. There was also the element of 'suspension of disbelief', that normally occurs among the users of media, by which they believe that they are in a world other than where their real bodies are located [1, 32]. This helped the participants move and interact well with the mental imagery environment, although they knew on a sub-conscious plane that they were in the experiment hall. Our ability to project our point of view into another person at another location was observed especially in the first experiment scenario. Buckner & Carroll [33] identified four related forms of self-projection and suggested that they may share a common functional anatomy. They illustrated how the phenomenon of self-projection relies on a personal mental simulation of another time, place or perspective. This attribute is comparable to one of the primary characteristics of a virtual reality illusion that gives us the feeling of 'telepresence' [3, 18] or a sense of 'transportation' to a virtual world [17] or what Rheingold [21] called 'a form of out-of-body experience'.

And most of all, mental imagery elements are evoked internally without the requirement of any external perception. Although this illusion of reality evoked in the mind is entirely endogenous, due to the presence thus evoked, we interact with the imagery environment as if it may have been real. This phenomenon is comparable to the sense of presence due to external mediation, which is often referred to as 'perceptual illusion of non-mediation' [1] or 'mediated presence' [34]. Although we found evidence of presence, its properties have to be further explored. The experience of presence is often referred to as a psychological state or a subjective perception [35]. So, various aspects of mental imagery like the imagery itself (for instance, its vividness compared to physical reality) may be still indefinable. We expect that further research on mental imagery would help us probe into this sense of presence and consequently contributing to our knowledge on internal perception and cognition.

6 Conclusion

We had two main research questions, and we were able to coherently answer both.

1. Yes, one surely experiences a sense of presence in mental imagery, similar to being in a virtual reality environment. In the case of virtual reality, presence is evoked since our external perception is mediated, leading to an illusion of reality similar to our physical world. In mental imagery the spaces are evoked endogenously by our mind without the help of any external perception, bringing about an experience of presence. Because in the case of a media evoked reality (like virtual reality), the illusion of a different reality is created by forcing our external sense organs to perceive the computer generated world in an intuitive manner, our perception is very

much similar to how it would be in the real-world situation. In the case of self evoked reality like mental imagery, even though the perceptual elements are evoked internally by our mind, there are remarkable similarities to the real-world scenarios.

2. Yes, this sense of presence can be detected by analysing verbal expressions, gestures and movements. In fact the verbal and physical expressions complemented each other and helped us putting together the externalization of the mental experience. It became clear how the participants experienced the imagery from their perspectives by evoking the task related mental space around them. The experiments were rather successful in providing evidence of presence in mental imagery. Thus, we strongly believe that presence study should be opened up further, and not be confined to virtual reality or mediated virtual environments.

Acknowledgments. This study was made possible through a collaboration between the laboratories of Arts et Métiers ParisTech and Indian Institute of Technology Bombay as part of the IIT-ParisTech mobility programme.

References

1. Lombard, M., Ditton, T.: At the Heart of It All: The Concept of Presence, `http://jcmc.indiana.edu/vol3/issue2/lombard.html`
2. Minsky, M.: Telepresence. Omni 2, 45–52 (1980)
3. Sheridan, T.B.: Musings on telepresence and virtual presence. Presence: Teleoperators and Virtual Environments 1, 120–126 (1992)
4. Steuer, J.: Defining virtual reality: Dimensions determining telepresence. Journal of Communication 42, 73–93 (1992)
5. Sanchez-Vives, M.V., Slater, M.: From presence to consciousness through virtual reality. Nature Reviews Neuroscience 6, 332–339 (2005)
6. Pillai, J.S., Schmidt, C.T.A., Richir, S.: Achieving Presence through Evoked Reality. Frontiers in Psychology (Frontiers in Consciousness Research) 4 (2013)
7. Pillai, J.S.: Evoked Reality: From Dreams to Simulations - A conceptual framework of Reality referring to Presence (Doctoral Thesis) Angers: Arts et Métiers ParisTech (2013)
8. Biocca, F.: Can we resolve the book, the physical reality, and the dream state problems? From the two-pole to a three-pole model of shifts in presence. In: EU Future and Emerging Technologies, Presence Initiative Meeting (2003)
9. Shepard, R.N., Metzler, J.: Mental rotation of three-dimensional objects. Science 171, 701–703 (1971)
10. Kosslyn, S.M.: Image and Mind. Harvard University Press, Cambridge (1980)
11. Kosslyn, S.M.: Mental images and the brain. Cognitive Neuropsychology 22, 333–347 (2005)
12. Kosslyn, S.M.: Image and Brain: The Resolution of the Imagery Debate. MIT Press, Cambridge (1994)
13. Athavankar, U.A., Bokil, P., Guruprasad, K., Patsute, R., Sharma, S.: Reaching Out in the Mind's Space. In: Design Computing and Cognition 2008, pp. 321–340 (2008)
14. Slater, M.: Place Illusion and Plausibility Illusion can lead to realistic behaviour in immersive virtual environments. Philosophical Transactions of the Royal Society B: Biological Sciences 364, 3549–3557 (2009)

15. Witmer, B.G., Singer, M.F.: Measuring presence in virtual environments. In: ARI Technical Report, pp. 783-784. Army Research Inst For The, Behavioral Social Sciences (1994)
16. Reeves, B.: Being there: Television as symbolic versus natural experience. Institute for Communication Research. Stanford University (1991) (unpublished manuscript)
17. Gerrig, R.J.: Experiencing narrative worlds: On the psychological activities of reading. Yale University Press (1993)
18. Schloerb, D.W.: A quantitative measure of telepresence. Presence: Teleoperators and Virtual Environments 4, 64–80 (1995)
19. Geslin, E., Bouchard, S., Richir, S.: Gamers' versus non-gamers' emotional response in virtual reality. Journal of CyberTherapy & Rehabilitation 4, 489–493 (2011)
20. Ravaja, N., Saari, T., Turpeinen, M., Laarni, J., Salminen, M., Kivikangas, M.: Spatial presence and emotions during video game playing: does it matter with whom you play? Presence: Teleoperators and Virtual Environments 15, 381–392 (2006)
21. Rheingold, H.: Virtual reality. Summit Books, New York (1991)
22. Athavankar, U.A., Mukherjee, A.: Blindfolded classroom getting design students to use mental imagery. In: Human Behaviour in Design, pp. 111–120. Springer (2003)
23. Slater, M.: A note on presence terminology, `http://publicationslist.org/data/melslater/ref-201/a%20note%20on%20presence%20terminology.pdf`
24. Austin, J., Delaney, P.F.: Protocol analysis as a tool for behavior analysis. The Analysis of verbal behavior 15, 41 (1998)
25. Ericsson, K.A., Simon, H.A.: Verbal reports on thinking. Introspection in Second Langauge Research, 24–53 (1987)
26. Suwa, M., Tversky, B.: What do architects and students perceive in their design sketches? A protocol analysis. Design Studies 18, 385–403 (1997)
27. Athavankar, U.: Gestures, Imagery and Spatial Reasoning. In: Garo, J.S., T.B. (eds.) Visual and Spatial Reasoning, Preprints of the International Conference on Visual and Spatial Reasoning, pp. 103–128. MIT, Cambridge (1999)
28. Zacks, J.M.: Neuroimaging studies of mental rotation: A meta-analysis and review. Journal of Cognitive Neuroscience 20, 1–19 (2008)
29. Reisberg, D., Logie, R.: The ins and outs of working memory: Overcoming the limits on learning from imagery. Advances in Psychology: Imagery Creativity and Discovery 98, 39–76 (1993)
30. Duncan, J.: Selective attention and the organization of visual information. Journal of Experimental Psychology: General 501, 113 (1984)
31. Slater, M., Steed, A.: A Virtual Presence Counter. Presence: Teleoperators and Virtual Environments 9, 413–434 (2000)
32. Slater, M., Usoh, M.: Representations systems, perceptual position, and presence in immersive virtual environments. Presence: Teleoperators and Virtual Environments 2, 221–233 (1993)
33. Buckner, R.L., Carroll, D.C.: Self-projection and the brain. Trends in Cognitive Sciences 11, 49–57 (2007)
34. Biocca, F., Burgoon, J., Harms, C., Stoner, M.: Criteria and scope conditions for a theory and measure of social presence. Presence: Teleoperators and Virtual Environments (2001)
35. ISPR - International Society for Presence Research: The Concept of Presence: Explication Statement, `http://ispr.info/about-presence-2/about-presence/`

Usability Evaluation of the Agile Software Process

Wan Fatimah Wan Ahmad, Saad Masood Butt, and Lukman Rahim

Computer and Information Sciences Department
Universiti Teknologi PETRONAS
Tronoh, Perak, Malaysia
{fatimhd,lukmanrahim}@petronas.com.my,
saadmasoodbutt668@yahoo.com

Abstract. Agile development methods are most flexible approach for software development where the development team keeps on improving the software with ongoing involvement of user. Despite its flexibility approach in software development, agile methods are still lacking usability evaluation approaches in their development, and integration of usability evaluation into agile development methods is not adequately addressed. In Agile software development, emphasis on requirement gathering and development of comprehensive feasibility reports is not considered in detail. Traditional software development considered this documentation as a quality attribute for the success of the project. Rapid solutions provided by agile software methods leads to the deficiency of good design and architecture which renders the project as expensive. As a remedy, a proposed life cycle for agile software development has been designed. The proposed life cycle outlined in this paper integrates usability evaluation concepts and agile software methodologies for the development of interactive software. To achieve the results, a survey form was formulated and carried out. The results show a greater interest of usability at the initial stage of software development along with user participation and involvement at each stage. The experiment was conducted in the software company by developing an interactive desktop-based application to evaluate the proposed life cycle and IEEE Std. 12207-2008, ISO 9241:210 was used to validate the proposed software model.

Keywords: software development, usability evaluation, agile software.

1 Introduction

A high-level of usability is recognized as an important feature for software products. The software products are not successful in the market due to a very common failure in effective usability design. Thus, one of the complications involved in software development is to observe users and analyse the user participation in the design and development stages, their behaviour and efficiency, then gather ideas for the ensuing development.

It is quite apparent that the development of better systems needs the collaboration of different subject matter experts (SME) from the Human Computer Interaction

H. Badioze Zaman et al. (Eds.): IVIC 2013, LNCS 8237, pp. 640–651, 2013.

(HCI), Software Engineering (SE), Stakeholder, Usability experts and User experience experts. Software Engineers, HCI experts and end-users are the most important key players of the software development life cycle. Involving users in the software development is an important thought-provoking task. Neglecting HCI approaches from software development will affect the role of usability in the software and make the software difficult to learn and to use which results in the dissatisfaction of the users. Software engineers, HCI experts and users need to cooperate with each other to create a software product that is usable and useful for the target audience. Unfortunately, in reality, these three key players (Software Engineers, HCI experts and Users) do not cooperate as smoothly as they should.

By the time this lack of cooperation is released, big software projects may fail to deliver what they promised; therefore, such projects often fall short [1]. Their failure can be in various forms; such as (a) the delivered system is not able to offer considerable specifications to the conventional system which is top quality that would make it possible to actually set up the system, (b) involvement of the user is introduced too late which produces a high impact on the software efficiency , (c) the cost, time and resources are exceeded by large factors and (d) the product is difficult to understand due to the lack of usability role in the development. The agreed upon factors for which software projects fail are many with variety of types [2]. In this paper, a new agile software process is proposed where usability evaluation has been integrated into an agile software development method.

2 Literature Review

Symon [3] the author claimed that user contribution at the design stage has a smaller footprint size because it contains specific or functional matters. Due to this purpose, software designers normally avoid user's participation in the level.

On the contrary, Olsson [4], in his research, claimed that users should be engaged in the design and development of systems. User's engagement in the application development process is an important responsibility towards the result of the application item [5]. Furthermore, Carrol [6] strengthened that user participation is an important factor in the success of a project and is the best choice for many projects.

Pessagno [7] elaborated further on the importance of usability in developing interactive software. The results of the survey and usability test mentioned in his study has shown that design is an important factor in determining a site's success because it creates its identity while simultaneously facilitating its usability.

As mentioned in [8], the modified heuristics are more efficient and capture more defects then the one proposed by Nielsen 10 heuristics. Also the research [9] shows that the pitfalls of the Heuristics Evaluation (HE) and it seems useful to follow more than one method for software usability evaluation.

The methodology mentioned in [10] is to improve the problems with the agile process and focus on the software design approach. Agile software development is the most widely used software models in the software Industry. Its efficiency to handle rapid change in the requirement handling and involving user at every stage of development is valued. However, agile based projects fail due to insufficient quality attributes.

The word agile means fast, light and more nimble. Agile process is also considered as a light weight process [11]. One major catastrophe in many software projects was the time it took for development exceeded the deadline. To develop systems faster with its limited time, agile software methods were developed. These methods develop systems faster by less focus on analysis and designing [12].

U-SCRUM methodology [13] is proposed by Singh to improve the usability. Unlike SCRUM having one product owner, U-SRUM has two product owners, one focused on the functionality and other focused on the usability. Result shows U-SRUM improve usability in the product then traditional SCRUM.

McInerney and Maurer mentioned in [14], the possibility of integrating software engineers and usability experts in agile software development. As both are from different backgrounds having different domain knowledge that helps to solve the problem that mostly occurred in software development in their own ways and most importantly agile methods only focus in functional requirements and neglect usability issues.

3 Current Gaps in Software Models

At present various software projects are being developed using different software models. However, there are some loopholes which persist in the software development such as documentation, total cost of the project, time to complete the project, resources required for the project and usability of the software. Research and market report shows 70 to 80% effort is done for the development of feasibility report and SRS (software requirements specification) document of the software project. The requirements of the software keeps on changing with time which greatly impact the development of software.

Usability does not focus on software projects as the role of usability experts are not defined properly in the development of software. In order to handle this issue huge amount is spent on users in the training of software. Still many software fails due to lack of user understanding and poor software interface. Table 1 shows the various factor leads to the failure of software.

Table 1. Major factors persist in software models

Factors	Details
Software Documentation	A lot of paperwork is done to make SRS (software requirements specification) document and gather the requirement before the development starts.
Cost	Non agile software project sometimes over exceed the project cost due to the unclear gathered requirement.
Time	If the SRS (software requirements specification) document keeps on changing it takes more time to complete the project before the deadline.
Resources	Resources can be hardware or software. So depends on the requirement client is giving you.
Usability	Many companies spend a lot of money on the training of particular software to train their users. Because real users were not involved in the design phase hence software designer design interface which is not easy for the user to understand or sometime make the whole software failed. The role of usability expert is also not clear at any stage of software development

Hedberg discussed about the Integration of HCI specialist in Open Source Software (OSS) Development [15]. Typical OSS development projects are organized around developers whose interaction is based on specialized technical aspects and source code. It seems very difficult to communicate with end users who have no technical knowledge. Hedberg proposed a model (as shown in Fig.1) that intergrade HCI in OSS and makes the existence of HCI professionals noticeable in the projects, and encourages connections between designers and the HCI specialists in the course of a project.

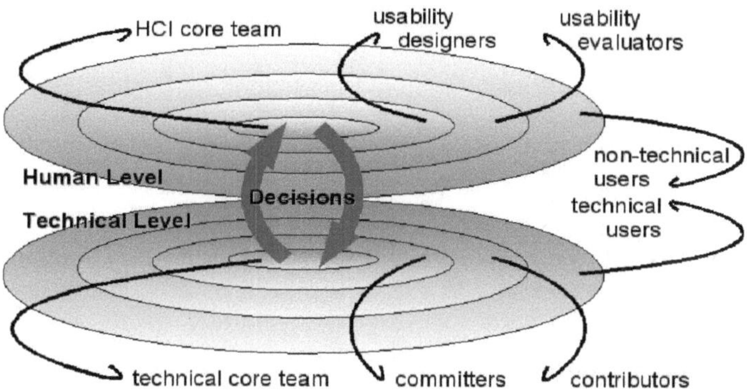

Fig. 1. The proposed model with the technical level and the human level roles

In 2007, Memmel et al. from Human-Computer Interaction Lab Germany proposed a software development life cycle in his paper "Agile Human Centered Software Engineering" later published by British Computer Society [16]. The authors of this paper confess that they did not implement this development lifecycle practically. But the proposed lifecycle is based on the facts of industry and research experience. His proposed lifecycle CRUISER shown in Fig.2, helps to bridge HCI and SE based on common features of both fields. CRUISER is very close to XP but don't have agile aspects. The author tried to integrate the important discipline in one lifecycle and increased the involvement of user and stakeholder by using prototype and scenarios.

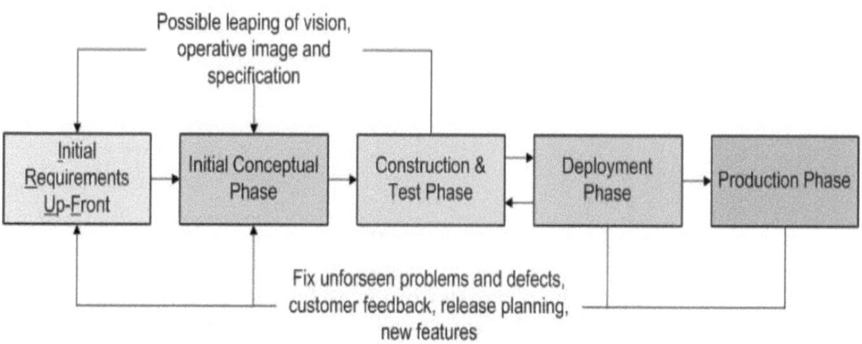

Fig. 2. Phases of CRUISER

Pardha proposed a model as shown in Fig.3, which provides a development infrastructure which accommodate Usability Engineering and SDLC. The proposed model have some potential downfall such as resource overhead and need expert for documentation entry into the design representation model.

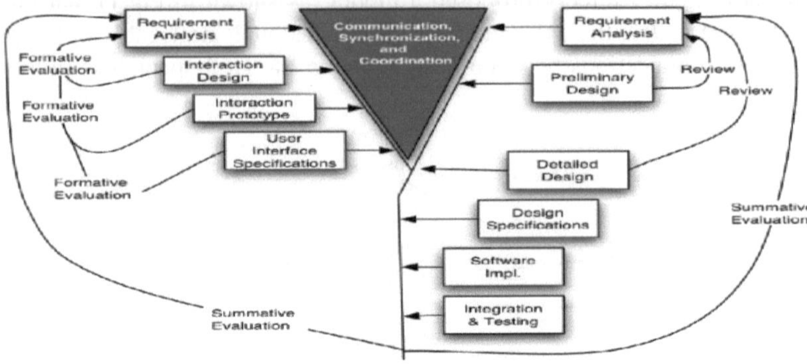

Fig. 3. Proposed Model-Based Framework for Integrating Usability and Software Engineering Life Cycles

4 Proposed Lifecycle

Figure 4 shows the agile life cycle starts from Flex REQ [17] and ends at a final product. Passing through various processes helps agile software experts, usability experts to work together. Flex REQ [17] is a process to develop product feasibility documents in a small amount of time unlike traditional soft model spends a considerable amount of time in documentation to achieve product quality at the end.

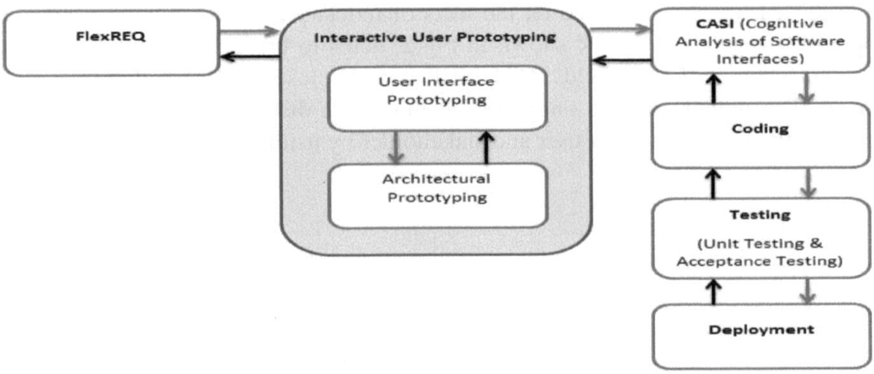

Fig. 4. Agile Usability Software Engineering Lifecycle

Interactive User Prototyping consists of two further process user interface prototyping and architectural prototyping as shown in Fig. 4. The final requirements gathered from the Flex REQ phase are now in the phase of designing (IUP) where interface and architecture prototypes are refined according to the specified requirement.

The resulted prototypes from the IUP phase will further tested for the Usability by using CASI [19]. CASI is a Usability evaluation method helps to improve the usability of software interfaces. Involvement of user and usability expert is highly important in this phase to find the usability defects. CASI keeps on the evaluating the interface until user fully satisfied. After CASI phase the coding starts and later unit and acceptance testing will be conducted to check final product satisfies all specifications and useful for the customer.

5 Survey and Experiment

For this analysis, a survey has been conducted randomly with 45 selected IT professionals. The purpose of the study is to create an "Agile Usability Software Engineering Life Cycle" that could comprehend the influence of the users in the software development process. The purpose is to make software development process reliable and finally integrate the Usability Evaluation to make the software more usable. The distribution of the survey targeted IT experts, researchers, software users and stakeholders. The questionnaire is divided into four sections. Section A is about demographic information of all those people who will answer the survey questions.

Section B is on the software process particularly focusing agile process in software industry. Section C looks into the Usability Evaluation in the agile software process. Section D is focused on developing a process that able to do the things that normally require human intelligence to perform that task in software development. All questions mentioned in every section were rated using the scale of 1 to 5 (1= strongly disagree, 2= disagree, 3= fair, 4= agree, and 5= strongly agree).

Fig.5 shows 81% respondents agreed on the active participation of users in software development. Software interfaces also play a magnificent role in product success and failure but also prefer less documentation in software development process. Rest 5% disagree with the active participation of users in software development, role of software interfaces in product quality and also disagree on less document in software development.

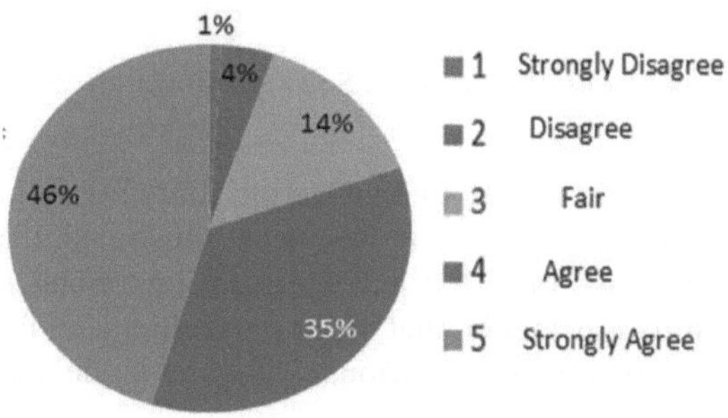

Fig. 5. Active participation of users in software development

From Fig.6, 78% of the respondents agreed on the Usability Evaluation methods to be considered in software development. Some prefer to consider it in evaluation methods in agile software development. Remaining 6% disagree to consider in agile software development.

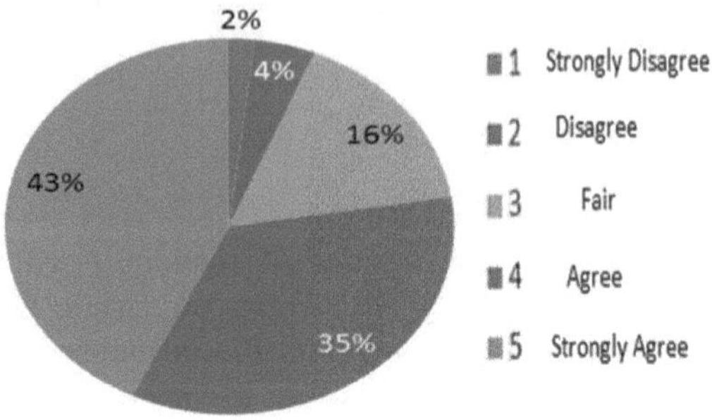

Fig. 6. Usability Evaluation in the agile software process

Fig.7 shows 82% respondents agreed on a development of process that is the part of the software model to make the development faster. The other 4% disagrees with such model used in software process.

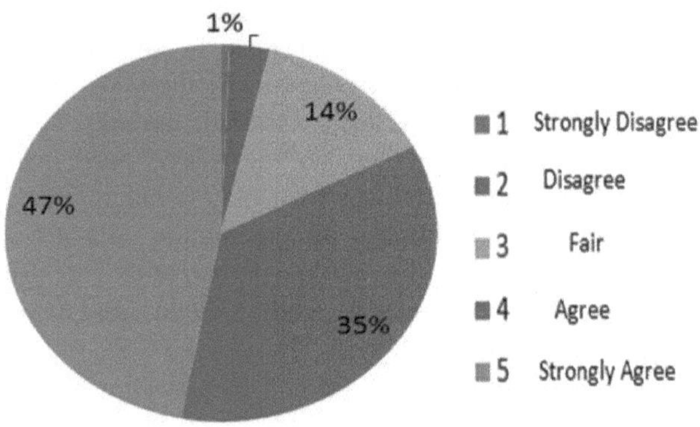

Fig. 7. Use various processes in an Agile Software Model for faster development

The focus of this paper is mainly to analyze the role of usability and users in the software model. From the research, it has been illustrated that in the software development, the parts played by HCI and users are important. In addition, role of helping process in software model that makes development faster and effective. Table 2 shows the comparison of various software models based on different features.

Table 2. Comparison with other Models

Features	SDLC	Prototyping Model	Agile Model	Spiral Model
User Involvement	Beginning	High	High	High
Adaptation of Usability	No	Intermediate	No	No
Development and Integration of helping process	No	No	No	No
Interface Evaluation using UE	No	No	No	No
Cost	Low	High	Intermediate	Expensive

After analysis of various software models through numerous factors and keeping survey analysis report that was discussed, it has been found that all models except agile model to be expensive to use (in term of cost, time and resources), used for big projects and having lack of Usability approaches. Whereas agile software model is a renowned model and is followed by many companies for small medium and large project. Hence introducing usability approaches in agile model increase the efficiency and usability of software. The project subsequently was developed using the most popular methodologies such as Scrum, Waterfall Model and OSSD and was rated using the scale of 0 to 4 (0= No, 1= fair, 2= Normal 3= Good, 4= Excellent). The results shown in Fig.8 are based on three important features; Usability, User Involvement in software development and Time taken to meet the deadline of the project deployment. From the outcomes it indicates that Usability concentrated more in AUSEL as compared to other models. On the other hand, "User Involvements" was observed more in AUSEL and Scrum. The "Time" for completion outcome shows that by using OSSD the time of completion will be lesser as compared to other software models.

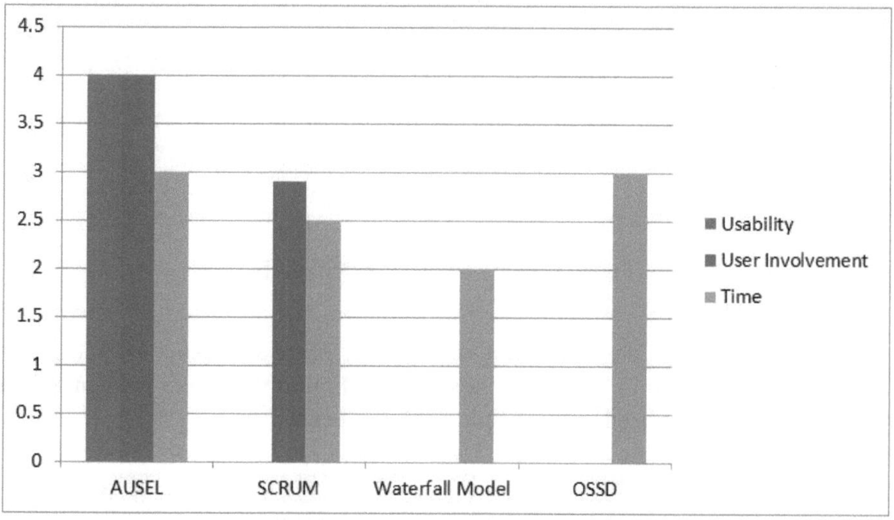

Fig. 8. Comparison with other Models

6 Validation

There are some essential features that are mostly considered in validation of the software model. In the proposed AUSEL, Industry Standards should be followed to validate every process and make the processes of AUSEL standardize.

To validate AUSEL, ISO 9241:210 [21] (Usability standards) and IEEE Std. 12207-2008 (System Context Processes) are followed. The International Standards (ISO 9241:210 and IEEE Std 12207-2008) determine a common model for software life cycle process, having a well-defined terminology that can be recommended by the software industry [20]. Fig.9 shows the most common processes of system set by the International Standards Group that may be performed during the lifecycle of software system. The outcomes mentioned in each process need to be achieved to standardize the process. Few standard processes are used in order to validate and standardize the Agile Usability Software Engineering Lifecycle (AUSEL).

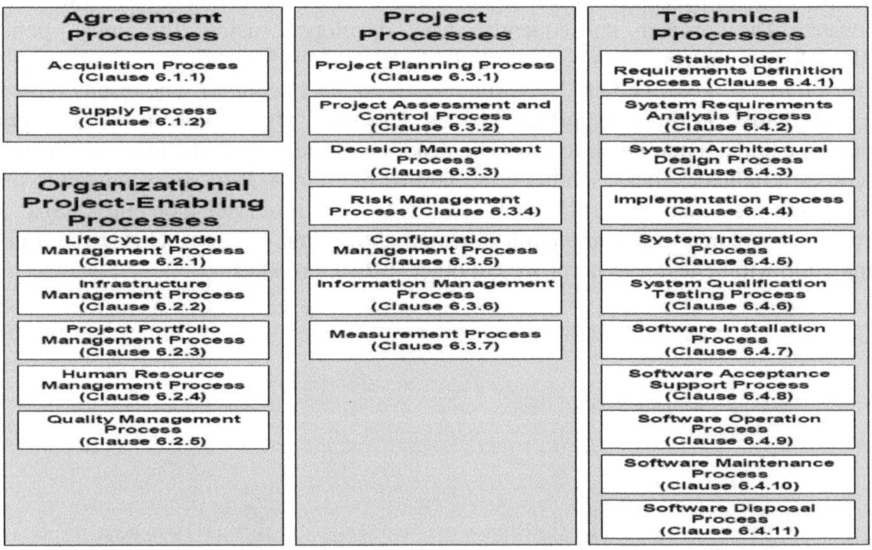

Fig. 9. System Context Processes [20]

The Table 3 shows the validation of AUSEL processes using ISO Usability Standards. The outcome of each process shown in Figure 9 has its own benchmark. The model shall be validated only when it meets the benchmark.

Table 3. ISO 9241-210 (Usability Standards)

ISO 9241-210 (Usability Standards)	AUSEL
The design is based upon an explicit understanding of users, tasks and environments.	AUSEL understand user, user requirements and design such interface that help user to perform its task easily.
The design is driven and refined by user-centered evaluation.	In AUSEL the interface usability evaluation is carried out by CASI.
Users are involved throughout design and development.	Active user participation is observed in whole lifecycle.
The process is iterative.	AUSEL have iteration between every process.
The design addresses the whole user experience.	IUP process of AUSEL focus on Usability and User Experience at software designing stage.
The design team includes multidisciplinary skills and perspectives.	AUSEL involves software developers, designer and Usability expert in software development.

7 Future Work

In this paper various models are discussed in each section; with literature review and gaps within software models inclusive. Several models which are discussed and proposed, are either having weakness or not yet practically tested. Nevertheless, all of these models do have their significance in terms of usability in the software development.

At present Open Source Software Development is a most widely used technique in software development. However, as per discussion, Open Source Software Development fails when user involvement is considered. In few of the proposed models, it has been indicated that the importance of HCI for software development is not only just for improvement in product usability but also to increase the market value of their product. The standards used to validate the proposed model will be endorsed by the software companies. A survey technique will be carried out in order to be validated by the software companies.

8 Conclusion

Agile development methods are most flexible approach for software development where the development team keeps on improving the software with ongoing involvement of user. Despite its flexibility approach in software development, agile methods are not integrated with usability approaches, whereas it is crucial to integrate in order to achieve software usability. It is essential to incorporate usability process in the agile software method. This paper has produced a variety of contributions: literature review, current gaps in software models, survey, proposed agile software model, experiments and results. From the literature and proposed life cycle we derived that there are many benefits that can be achieved by integrating usability in the Agile software model. A few major loopholes were succinctly explained under the section of current gaps in software models. A survey was conducted among IT professionals to analyse Usability Evaluation in Agile software development. After getting the survey results, a proposed Agile model i.e. Agile Usability Software Engineering Lifecycle is proposed. The proposed model is then tested with a software company to evaluate it. Meanwhile the AUSE life cycle was validated by IEEE Std 12207-2008 and ISO 9241-210 (Usability standards).

References

1. Kikuno: Why do software projects fail? Reasons and a solution using a Bayesian classifier to predict potential risk. In: 11th IEEE Pacific Rim International Symposium (2005)
2. Belengueret, J.: HCI Designers and Engineers: It is possible to work together, `http://citeseerx.ist.psu.edu/viewdoc/summary?doi=10.1.1.11.1728`
3. Symon, G.: The work of IT system developers in context: an organizational case study. Human–Computer Interaction 13(1), 37–71 (2007)
4. Gasson: User involvement in decision-making in information systems development. In: Conference Proceeding of 18th IRIS. IRIS Association, Gjern Denmark (2005)
5. Ollson, E.: What active users and designers contribute in the design process. Interacting with Computers 16, 377–400 (2004), `http://www.elsevierComputerScience.com`
6. Carroll, M.: Introduction: The Scenario Perspective on System Development in Scenario-Based Design: Envisioning Work and Technology in System Development. IEEE Transactions on Software Engineering 24(12), 1156–1170 (1995)
7. Pessagno, R.: Design and usability of social networking web sites. In: California Polytechnic State University (2011), doi:digitalcommons.calpoly.edu/grcsp/23
8. Ivory, M.Y., Hearst, M.A.: The state of the art in automating usability evaluation of user interfaces. ACM Comput. Surv. 33, 470–516 (2007)
9. Polson, P.G., Lewis, C., Rieman, J., Wharton, C.: Cognitive walk- throughs: a method for theory-based evaluation of user interfaces. J. Man-Mach. Stud. 36, 741–773 (2002)
10. Akbari, F.: A Review to the Usage of Concepts of Software Architecture in Agile methods. In: International Symposium on Instrumentation & Measurement, Sensor Network and Automation, IEEE Software, vol. 2, pp. 389–392 (2012)
11. What is agile software development (May 14, 2008), `http://www.agilealliance.org/show/2`
12. Koskela: Software configuration management in agile methods. VTT publication 5 14, ESPOO, pp –54 (2003)
13. Singh, M.: U-SCRUM: An agile methodology for promoting usability. In: Proc. AGILE 2009 Conference (Agile 2009), pp. 555–560. IEEE Press (2009)
14. Mcinerney, P., Maurer, F.: UCD in agile projects: dream team or odd couple? Interactions 12(6), 19–23 (2007)
15. Hedberg, H., Iivari, N.: Integrating HCI Specialists into Open Source Software Development Projects. In: Boldyreff, C., Crowston, K., Lundell, B., Wasserman, A.I. (eds.) OSS 2009. IFIP AICT, vol. 299, pp. 251–263. Springer, Heidelberg (2009)

16. Memmel, T., Gundelsweiler, F., Reiterer, H.: CRUISER: A Cross-Discipline User Interface and Software Engineering Lifecycle. In: Jacko, J.A. (ed.) HCI 2007. LNCS, vol. 4550, pp. 174–183. Springer, Heidelberg (2007)
17. Pyla, P.S., Pérez-Quiñones, M.A., Arthur, J.D., Hartson, H.R.: Towards a model-based framework for integrating usability and software engineering life cycles. Arxiv Preprint cs/0402036 (2008)
18. Masood Butt, S., Ahmad, W.F.W.: Handling requirements using FlexREQ model. In: 2012 IEEE 3rd International Conference on Software Engineering and Service Science (ICSESS), pp. 661–664. IEEE (2012)
19. Butt, S.M., Ahmad, W.F.W.: Analysis and Evaluation of Cognitive Behavior in Software Interfaces using an Expert System. International Journal 5 (2012)
20. IEEE Standards Association, 12207-2008-IEEE System and Software Engineering-Software life cycle processes, `https://standards.ieee.org/findstds/standard/12207-2008.html`
21. ISO 9241-210:2010 Ergonomics of human-system interaction -Part 210: Human-centred design for interactive systems, `http://www.iso.org/iso/catalogue_detail.htm?csnumber=52075`

The Effects of Icon Characteristics on Users' Perception

Syed Ghayas[1,*], Suziah Sulaiman[1], Muzafar Khan[2], and Jafreezal Jaafar[1]

[1] Computer and Information Sciences Department, Universiti Teknologi PETRONAS, Tronoh, Perak, Malaysia

[2] Department of Computer Science, COMSATS Institute of Information Technology, Islamabad, Pakistan

syedghayas@ciit.net.pk, {suziah,jafreez}@petronas.com.my, muzafar_khan@comsats.edu.pk

Abstract. Modern mobile phone application interfaces have potential to support various age group users. Among the different age groups, older adults have been quite slow in adopting mobile phone applications and its interfaces. Limited research work has been carried out to investigate the graphical icons and examine its ease of use for various age group users. This paper presents an experimental study to determine the recognition rates of icons from two sets of users with different age groups i.e. younger adults (20 – 40 years) and older adults (+50 years). Users responded to a set of questions consisting of 40 icons obtained from two different brands of mobile phones. The findings reveal that recognition rates vary depending on how familiar the icons are to the users. The results from this study could be useful to support application developers to develop mobile phone applications interfaces that are more suitable for various age group users.

Keywords: interfaces, icons, icons characteristics, usability, familiarity, recognition.

1 Introduction

Mobile devices such as cell phones and tablet computers are very common today. A study has reported that 4.7 billion people used mobile phones in 2009 as compared to 1.4 billion in 2003. These mobile phone users range from children to elderly people. The diversity of mobile phones users creates a challenge in designing the mobile phone interfaces. Various usability issues exist due to the declining in users' vision, motor skills and coordination and interface complexity that hinder the adoption of mobile phones in elderly people as compared to younger adults [25], [28] and [29].

In addressing the interface complexity, the research in [28-29] focus on improving the initial usability of mobile phone application interfaces graphical icons for various age group users. There are a few features in which the design of an icon is greatly affected: those are when these icons are being interpreted, the initial usability of these icons and the initial usability of the application in which those icons are found.

* Corresponding author.

H. Badioze Zaman et al. (Eds.): IVIC 2013, LNCS 8237, pp. 652–663, 2013.

Correctly interpreted icons are particularly important in learning to perform tasks on a mobile phone. Mobile phones have many varieties of functionalities and features which cannot be found on ordinary laptop computers or desktop based computers, for example data entry methods and connecting the mobile phone to the Internet. If there is a need for those functions on the mobile phones, it can only be utilized through special icons and some buttons. While mobile devices have specialized operating systems such as Android based, iPhone based, and Symbian based, the desktop personal computers have the Windows, Macintosh, and Linux based operating system. Each operating system normally uses its own unique set of designed icons. Interpreting icons initially may be more complex for mobile phones users because of the rapid growth in mobile phones and applications. It is common for users replacing their mobile phones more frequently than their computers systems.

Despite the prevalence of icons, very little research has been carried out on investigating the effect of graphical icons on various age groups using either ordinary desktop-based computers or mobile phones. It has been experienced that a decrease in energy level, vision and memory abilities that all accompanies normal aging might effect on various age group's users ability in interpreting graphical icons. It also will help in identifying the visual objects which are present in that icon. As there is a decrease in energy level, vision and memory abilities of older adults, so if we compare older adults with younger adults this step may be more challenging. In research work carried out by Hawthorn, many questions were raised on whether older adults, as compared to younger adults, are able to benefit as much from the cues provided by icons for interpreting the icon's function. Interpreting an icon also depends on several factors. As an example, the environment supplied by the software platform which is using icon, and how many users are familiar with the icons and its application context [4].

According to research work, a comparison is made between various age group users while using mobile devices, results of the research shows that older adults have less experience with those devices and existing icons and applications. The reason is the natural decrease in vision and verbal abilities, and decrease in the overall ability to learn and find new associations. We speculated that some icons may be more difficult for users to initially use, and that there are opportunities to design icons that are easier for various age group users to initially use those icons [5].

Our earlier qualitative exploratory study has identified which icon characteristics helps initial icon usability for various age group users [6]. A summary of this work is presented in Section 3. The findings indicate that older adults have more difficulties using modern mobile phone application interfaces. The specific icon characteristics- semantic distance (natural close link between icon object and its function), familiarity (referring to the frequency with which images are encountered), complexity (referring to the level of difficulty to interpret the image) – improve initial icon usability for older adults. The findings motivate us to conduct an experimental study to determine the recognition rates of icons from two different age groups i.e. younger adults (20 – 40 years) and older adults (+50 years). The methodology used for this study is presented in Section 4. Section 5 reports the study result that involves users' response to survey questions consisting of 40 icons obtained from two different brands of mobile phones. We present a discussion on the findings in Section 6 and conclude the research work in Section 7.

2 Related Work

An icon is a picture object that represents objects, concept or functionality [7]. Before interpreting a new icon, we need to understand the relationship between that item and the icon's functionality [8]. When an icon is used, it brings many graphical properties that need to be processed such as the icon visual details and the way it shows resemblance to a real object.

In the past research work many icon characteristics were found to have an effect on icon usability. Some of the examples are physical characteristics (e.g. visual detail, colour, and size), choice of icon object in the association with the intended icon meaning, and how that object is described (e.g. dots versus calendar) [8]. Researchers also pointed out various user-related characteristics (such as intelligence, experience, and culture) and the context in which icon is found as factors that influence icon usability [5].

There are a few research studies which have exploited in detail the overall effects on icon initial usability of few of these characteristics, such as animation [1], and spacing and size [2]. These studies are very closely related to our work presented in this paper.

In a research work on icons [9], all the icons characteristics are described. According to the research, icon concreteness and visual complexity are two distinct dimensions. The icons used in the experiment include graphics shown for road signs, electronic symbols, and computer based icons. The icon characteristics discussed are concreteness, complexity, meaningfulness, familiarity, and semantic distance.

Another study [10] is conducted on desktop email programme which has icons and labels. Participants' perceptions for the ease of use and usefulness of the software are measured. Results of the study show that participants of the study have better performance with text labels than icons which are not labelled during initial use of icons.

In another research work [11], a series of experiments is conducted to investigate the effects of icon concreteness and visual complexity on tasks involving visual search and matching icons with labels. Results of the experiment show that concrete icons have more visual detail than abstract icons.

A few researchers have chosen three icon characteristics which are concreteness, semantic distance, and labeling in designing their mobile phone interfaces for elderly users [12]. From the experiments, the researchers had determined that the elderly users were able in interpreting very few existing mobile phones icons than younger users, especially in the semantically far icons. It is seen from the research results that it is very hard for elderly users when identifying objects in an abstract and semantically far icons.

3 Experimental Study on Icon Interpretability

Our earlier study findings [26] provided a basis for us to conduct an in-depth study on the icon characteristics for mobile phone users in a quantitative manner. This is to investigate the extent to which semantic distance, complexity and familiarity effect icon usability in various age group users. The objective of the experimental study is to determine the recognition rates of icons from two different age groups of users i.e. younger adults (20 – 40 years) and older adults (+50 years).

3.1 Familiarity and Recognition

Familiarity refers to the frequency with which images are encountered. It is the degree to which user identify components in user interface and see how much familiar they are with interface with that in the past. Other definition of familiarity includes the experience of users interacting with product [13]. In such a case, familiarity is the knowledge users have of a product, which is based on their experiences [14]. According to a research work on icons it is found that familiarity is an important predictor of user performance with icons ([15] and [16]). When applied to interface design, familiarity minimizes learning time and thus results in enhancing user satisfaction. On the other hand, the lack of familiarity with interface needs one to learn the meanings of the icons [17]. Once learning is established, one could recognize and become familiar with the icons. This is supported by the dual process theories of recognition memory, which proposes two processes underlying recognition: recollection process and familiarity [18].

3.2 Methodology

There are several criteria an icon needs to meet before it could be effectively selected. Those criteria are legibility, distinctiveness, comprehension and the reaction time [19]. There are also a few issues involved when evaluating icons which are icons designs and modification [20]. An appropriate testing technique should be carefully chosen in order to obtain an accurate result.

In general, the method used to evaluate symbols and icons is named 'comprehension test' or a 'recognition test' [21]. There are many research works conducted that have used 'matching tests' in order to evaluate graphic symbols ([22] and [23]). Using 'matching method', icons are evaluated in relation to other icon variables to see how suitable a particular icon is. Another method called 'icon intuitiveness test', involves an icon without label that could be presented to a relatively small group of users (e.g. up to five users). The test participants are asked to interpret what an icon is representing [24]. According to the Organization for International Standardization (ISO 3864), an icon could be considered as acceptable if its recognition rate is at least 66 % [25].

In this paper, the recognition rate of the icons is calculated with the help of the following formula:

$$\text{Recognition rate (\%)} = (\text{No. of correct answers/No. of respondents})*100 \qquad (1)$$

In our experimental study the following hypothesis are tested. The hypotheses are tested for three dependent variables to assess icon interpretability. Two primary dependent variables are the degree of accuracy in identifying mobile phone icon object and the degree of accuracy in mobile phone icon meaning. Third dependent variable, secondary to the other two, is the degree of test participants' confidence in their icons interpretations. The hypotheses are given below:

Hypothesis 1 (overall icon interpretation): Elderly users encounter more difficulties than younger adults with mobile phone icons.
Hypothesis 2 (complexity): Elderly users encounter more difficulties than younger adults with mobile phone icons.
Hypothesis 3 (semantic distance): Elderly users encounter more difficulties than younger adults with mobile phone icons.
Hypothesis 4 (familiarity): Elderly users encounter more difficulties than younger adults with mobile phone icons.

3.3 Equipment Used

The mobile phones used were chosen from five different vendors on the basis of its popularity. We selected a set of icons from the main menu functions of the mobile phones. It was quite difficult to represent each function by a certain standard number of icons since the icons differ from each other in their appearance. It is our intention in this study to find out whether the visual representation offered by a particular icon does help users to understand the functionality of the icon in question.

3.4 Study Material

We selected 40 icons from different mobile phones that are popular in year 2013. Mobile phones brands selected were Samsung Galaxy S3 and Samsung Nexus. All these icons are presented in a list shown in Fig. 1 (sample icons list). We enlarged most of the icons to minimize effects of icons sizes due to differences in vision capabilities among the participants. All icons were displayed on the computer screen when presenting them to the test participants.

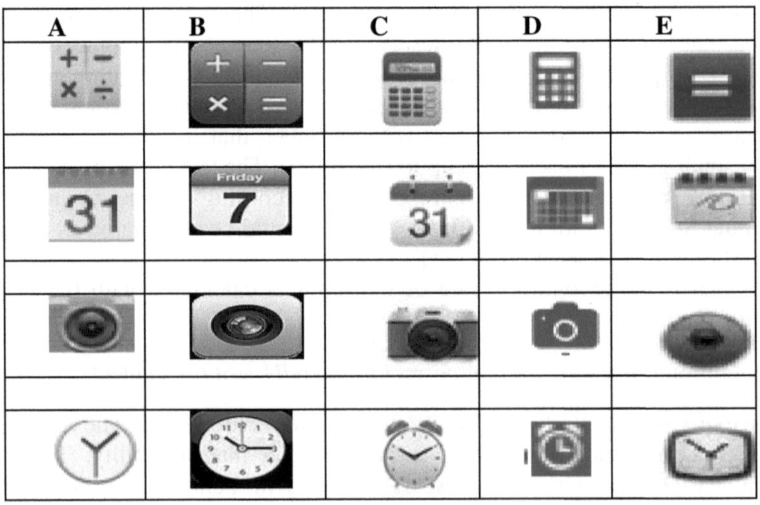

Fig. 1. Sample Icons List

3.5 Participants

Two groups of equal numbers were formed, consisting of 30 test participants in total. The first group consists of those participants ranging from 20 to 49 years old (younger adults) while the second from 50+ years of age (elderly). Two of the younger adults (male) and one elderly (female) participants were replaced because from their expressions it was evident that they were unable to understand the experimental study tasks. Test participants were invited through departmental advertisement boards. It was a pre-requisite for all the participants that they should have some experience with usage of computers, correct eyesight, no color blindness and fluency in English. We were interested in those who were unfamiliar with the mobile phone icons used in the experimental study. Before conducting the study a few tests were conducted on to the test users, such as vision test and verbal fluency. The test mechanism used was Snellen eye test and the FAS test [3], respectively. The results confirmed that the test users had normal vision, and meeting verbal fluency levels as required for conducting the study.

3.6 Study Setup

The study was mainly carried out in the HCI-testing lab located at Computer and Information Sciences Department, Universiti Teknologi PETRONAS while a few of the sessions were conducted at the participants' places. A consent form was given before conducting the study. All participants were requested to carefully read the consent form before signing it. The first ten minutes was given to familiarize test users with the functionalities of existing modern mobile phones (e.g. MMS and SMS options).

In the main study session, each participant was shown the icons list and was given the questions for each single icon that was presented (40 icons in total). The participant has to rate each icon with regards to the question prepared. The following are the sample questions asked from the test participants pertaining to the icons:

1. Identification of the icon objects - (example: What can you see in the icon?)
2. Interpreting the icon's functionality - (example: How can we use the icon?)
3. Level of familiarity with the icon - (example: Have you seen this icon before?)
4. Confidence level while interpreting icons - (example: Are you sure on the functionality of the icon?)

3.7 Study Measures

Data were collected to test our hypothesis. Each icon tested was given a score. This is in association with the responses from questions in Section 3.6. The score is obtained for the following dependent variables.

1. The degree on how accurate the icon is while identification procedure of icons is taking place. (values to be used: 0 or 1)
2. The degree of accuracy in interpreting the icons. (values to be used: 0 or 1)
3. The confidence level of the participants in interpreting the icons meaning (values to be used : scale 1-5; 1= no sure; 5= very much assure)
4. The degree of familiarity with the icons (values from 1-5)

In our experimental study, we focused on the initial usability required for mobile phone interfaces. For this reason, we have as much as possible recruited participants who were not very familiar with the mobile phone icons presented. Familiarity scores of the test users with icons in our study were measured in order to assess and control the effect of the icons on the initial usability measures.

4 Results and Analysis

We calculated the recognition rate for 40 icons from two different brands of mobile phones i.e. Samsung Galaxy and Samsung Nexus mobile phones. Only these two brands of mobile phones were chosen because they are very popular in Malaysia and we are only interested in exploring and comparing the icon recognition of two different models. From the main experimental study, 20 Samsung Galaxy phone icons were selected which is shown in Fig. 2. Keeping in view of the ISO standard as mentioned in section 4, we awarded two numbers to the icons tested: '1', for a correct answer rate above 66%, and '0', for rate less than 66%.

Using the ISO guidelines, fifteen (15) icons from Fig. 2 are considered suitable for mobile phone usage while the rest of the icons achieved low recognition rate. With the recognition rate of 66%, then the most best suited icons are:

- F and P with the recognition rate of 95%
- C and R with the recognition rate of 86%
- A, B, and N with the recognition rate of 81%

A detailed analysis is presented in Fig. 3, for icons with very low recognition rates and suggested factors which may be responsible for poor performance. As an example, icon number 'I' that is meant for Gmail has been misunderstood as normal messages because of the symbol 'M' on it. In another example, icon number 'O', meant for search function has been assumed as 'Google' application due to the 'g' symbol which is normally used on the Internet.

Similarly, Fig. 4 details out the recognition rates when using Samsung Nexus phone. Recognition rates are calculated for 20 icons. Out of 20 icons, 11 icons achieved low recognition rate. Nine (9) icons fulfill the ISO standard requirements which is 66% +. Fig. 5 presents the analysis for icons (Samsung Nexus) with very low recognition rates and the suggested factors which may be responsible for poor performance.

Fig. 6 presents the analysis for difference of recognition rates among both age groups (younger vs. older). From the research findings it is evident that older participants were less accurate in recognizing and interpreting the icon meanings.

From the icon recognition test, 15 of 20 icons from Samsung galaxy phone enjoying recognition rate of more than 66 %. 9 out of 20 icons from Samsung nexus phone enjoying recognition rate of more than 66 %. Comparing both models recognition rates (i.e. Fig 2 & 4), most of the icons differ in terms of their recognition rate. It is suggesting that there is no consistency in designing interfaces among same phones from same vendors. The complexity of graphics minimizes the ease with which the icon is correctly interpreted. If we use the familiar metaphors, it enhances the likelihood that an icon will be interpreted correctly.

In the study, our main focus was upon anyone who owns mobile phone regardless of their experience and professional career. They were not much experienced with the technology. The factors that need to be taken into account when conducting this study are the medium in which the icons were presented and examined and, most importantly, the age groups involved.

Calculator A	Calendar B	Camera C	Clock D	Add book E
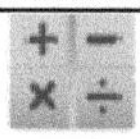				
81	81	86	71	67
Download F	Email G	Gallery H	Gmail I	Internet J
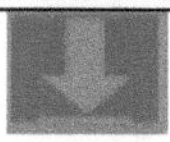		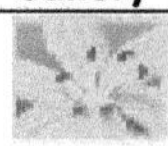		
95	76	38	19	71
Map K	Message L	Music M	Phone N	Search O
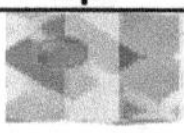				
71	67	86	81	24
Settings P	Voice Mail Q	Battery R	Miss Call S	Synchronize T
	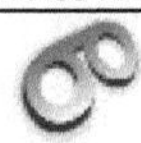			
95	10	76	90	20

Fig. 2. Recognition rates of icons (Samsung Galaxy)

Icons	Reco/rate	Function	Expected reasons for not understanding
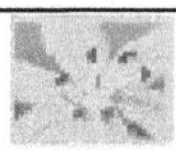	38 %	Gallery	It denotes only a flower so most of users replied picture
	19 %	Gmail	Resemble with email due to word M
	24 %	Search	Most users replied with google due to word 'g' on icon
	10 %	Voice mail	Confusing -no match with voice mail

Fig. 3. Icons with low recognition rates (Samsung Galaxy)

Calculator A	Calendar B	Camera C	Clock D	Add book E
20	44	48	76	35
Download F	Email G	Gallery H	Gmail I	Internet J
90	70	62	15	50
Map K	Message L	Music M	Phone N	Search O
30	67	25	86	95
Settings P	Voice Mail Q	Battery R	Miss Call S	Synchronize T
30	10	72	90	20

Fig. 4. Recognition rates of icons (Samsung Nexus)

Icons	Reco/rate	Function	Expected reasons for not understanding
	20 %	Calculator	Most users replied with equal sign
	44 %	Calendar	Sign on the top is difficult to identify
	24 %	Address Book	Image on the icon is confusing
	15 %	Gmail	Resemble with email due to word 'M'
	30 %	Maps	Most of users replied with pictures.
	25 %	Music	Users answers speaker icon
	30 %	Settings	Unfamiliar icon. Users replied camera and speaker icon
	10 %	Voice Mail	Recorder
	20 %	Synchronize	Icon replied with refresh icons

Fig. 5. Icons with low recognition (Samsung Nexus)

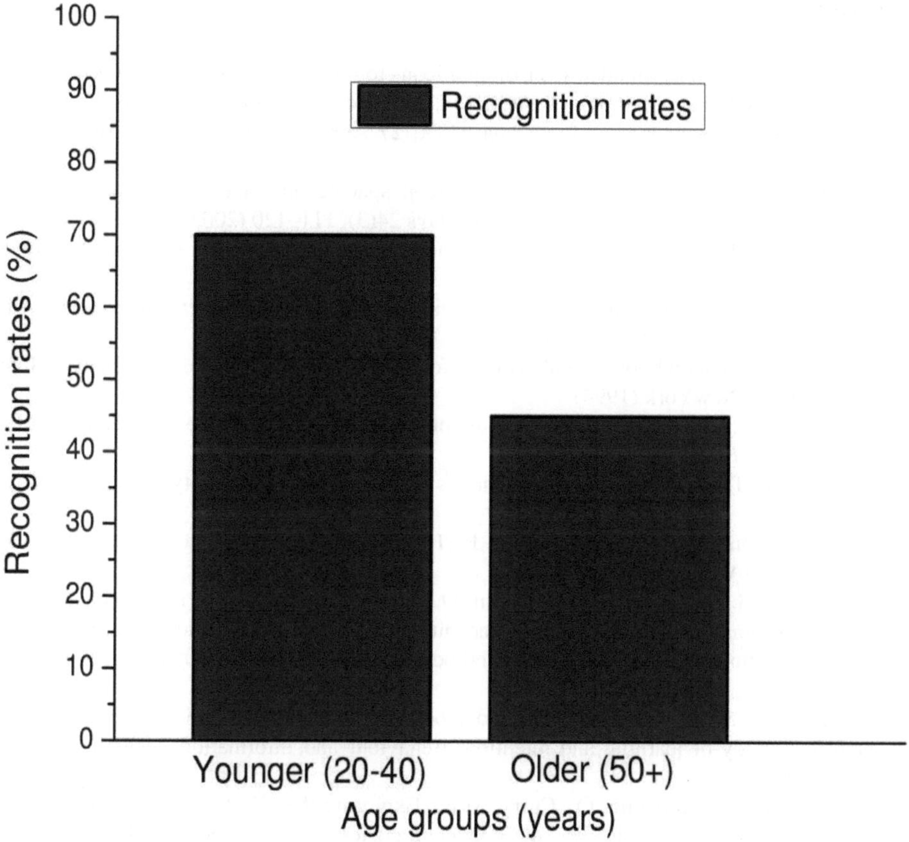

Fig. 6. Recognition rates of younger and older adults

5 Conclusion and Future Work

This paper presents the study about the representation and recognition of the mobile phone icons. It is investigated that how users of different age group use mobile phones application interfaces and icons. The recognition rate of the icons is calculated based on the participants' feedback for icons familiarity. The limitations of the existing mobile phone interfaces in terms of familiarity and recognition are highlighted. The reasons for the low recognizable icons are highlighted; there is no consistency in designing interfaces among phones (even from the same vendor). The complexity of graphics minimizes the ease with which the icon is correctly interpreted. If the familiar metaphors are used, it enhances the likelihood that an icon will be interpreted correctly. These findings could contribute in terms of providing guidelines to improve the mobile phone interfaces.

In the future, the structure of menus and different color combinations employed in the icons will be studied in detail.

References

1. Baecker, R., Small, I., Mander, R.: Bringing icons to life. In: Robertson, S.P., Olson, G.M., Olson, J.S. (eds.) Proceedings of SIGCHI Conference on Human Factors in Computing Systems (CHI), NewOrleans, Louisiana, USA, 27 April – 2 May, pp. 1–6. ACM Press, New York (1991)
2. Lindberg, T., Nasanen, R.: The effect of icon spacing and size on the speed of icon processing in the human visual system. Displays 24(3), 111–120 (2003)
3. Benton, A.L., Hamsher, K.: Multilingual aphasia examination manual. University of Iowa, Iowa City (1978)
4. Hawthorn, D.: Possible implications of aging for interface designers. Interacting with Computers 12(5), 507–528 (2000)
5. Horton, W.: The icon book: visual symbols for computer systems and documentation. John Wiley&Sons, NewYork (1994)
6. Seaman, C.B.: Qualitative methods in empirical studies of software engineering. IEEE Trans. Softw. Eng. 25, 557–572 (1999)
7. Peirce, C.S.: The collected papers of Charles Sanders Peirce. University Press, Cambridge (1932)
8. Heim, S.: Icons.The resonant interface: HCI foundations for interaction design, pp. 407–451. Addison Wesley, Boston (2007)
9. McDougall, S.J., Curry, M.B., de Bruijn, O.: Measuring symbol and icon characteristics: Norms for concreteness, complexity, meaningfulness, familiarity, and semantic distance for 239 symbols. Behavior Research Methods. Instruments, & Computers 31(3), 487–519 (1999)
10. Wiedenbeck, S.: The use of icons and labels in an end user application program: an empirical study of learning and retention. Behaviour and Information Technology 18(2), 68–82 (1999)
11. McDougall, S.J., de Brujin, O., Curry, M.B.: Exploring the effects of icon characteristics on user performance: The role of icon concreteness, complexity, and distinctiveness. Journal of Experimental Psychology Applied 6(4), 291–306 (2000)
12. Leung, R., McGrenere, J., Graf, P.: Age-related Differences in the Initial Usability of mobile Device Icons. Behavior & Information Technology 30(5), 629–642 (2009)
13. Alba, J.W., Hutchinson, J.W.: Dimensions of consumer expertise. Journal of Consumer Research 13(1), 411–454 (1987)
14. Luhmann, N.: Familiarity, confidence, trust: problems and alternatives. In: Gambetta, D.G. (ed.) Trust, pp. 94–107. Basil Blackwell, New York (1988)
15. Isherwood, S.J., McDougall, S.J.P., Curry, M.: Icon Identification in Context: The changing role of icon characteristics with user experience. Human Factors 49(3), 465–476 (2007)
16. Isherwood, S.: Graphics and Semantics: The Relationship between What Is Seen and What Is Meant in Icon Design. In: Harris, D. (ed.) EPCE 2009. LNCS (LNAI), vol. 5639, pp. 197–205. Springer, Heidelberg (2009)
17. Galitz, W.G.: The Essential Guide to User Interface Design:An Introduction to GUI Design Principles and Techniques. Wiley Publishing, Indianapolis (2007)
18. Gardiner, J.M.: Functional aspects of recollective experience. Memory & Cognition 16, 309–318 (1988)
19. Dewar, R.: Design and evaluation of public information symbols. In: Zwaga, H.J.G., Boersema, T., Hoonhout, H.C.M. (eds.) Visual Information for Everyday Use: Design and Research Perspectives, pp. 285–304. Taylor & Francis, London (1999)

20. Blankenberger, S., Hainj, K.: Effects of icon design on human-computer interaction. Int.J. Man-Machine Studies 35, 363–377 (1991)
21. Howell, W., Fuchs, A.: Population stereotypy in code design. Organisational Behavior in Human Performance 3, 310–339 (1968)
22. Heard, E.: A symbol study-1972, Paper No 740304. Society of Automotive Engineers, New York (1974)
23. Easterby, R.S., Zwaga, H.: Information design. The design and evaluation of signs and printed material, pp. 277–297. J. Wiley & Sons, New York (1984)
24. Nielsen, J., Sano, D.: SunWeb: User Interface Design for Sun Microsystem's Internal Web. In: Proc. 2nd World Wide eb Conf.: Mosaic and the Web, Chicago, IL, pp. 547–557 (1994)
25. Piamonte, D.P.T., Abeysekera, J.D.A., Ohlsson, K.: Understanding small graphical symbols: a cross-cultural study. International Journal of Industrial Ergonomics 27(6), 399–404 (2000)
26. Ghayas, S., Sulaiman, S., Jafaar, J., Khan, M.: Mobile Phone Icons Recognition: a comparative study. In: ICT-2013, Singapore (2013)
27. Jacko, J.A., et al.: Macular degeneration and visualicon use: deriving guidelines for improvedaccess. Universal Access in the Information Society 1(3), 197–206 (2002)
28. Moor, K.A., Connelly, K.H., Rogers, Y.: A comparative study of elderly, younger, and chronically ill novice PDA users. Bloomington, IN: Indiana University. Technical Report TR 595 (2004)
29. Ziefle, M., Bay, S.: How older adults meet complexity: aging effects on the usability of different mobile phones. Behavior& Information Technology 24(5), 375–389 (2005)

Knowledge Preservation Framework for University's Intellectual Output

Zatul Amilah Shaffiei, Saidatul Rahah Hamidi,
Haryani Haron, and Andra Israh Ab. Halim

Faculty of Computer and Mathematical Sciences,
Universiti Teknologi MARA,
40450 Shah Alam, Selangor Malaysia
{zatul,rahah,haryani}@tmsk.uitm.edu.my,
andraisrah.abhalim@gmail.com

Abstract. Intellectual Output (IO) of a university is often neglected by society whereas it actually possesses a great capacity of university's knowledge produced by researchers. Knowledge preservation is important for community to be able to access, utilize and improve the knowledge at the same time. Thus, Institutional Repository (IR) of an institution is essential to ensure the knowledge is stored and accessible at anytime. There is no specific technique to preserve knowledge, but with the existence of ontological and taxonomy model can help in modeling the knowledge. The scope of IO in this paper is University's IO gained by UiTM Research Innovation Business Unit (RIBU). Taxonomy presented in this paper is derived from RIBU's intellectual output which is expected to help the search and retrieval mechanism for an IR.

Keywords: Intellectual Output, Institutional Repository, Knowledge Preservation Framework, RIBU and taxonomy.

1 Introduction

In the past few decades, there is an increasing research on transforming the tacit knowledge into explicit knowledge in organizations [1]. In academic institutions, the producers of intellectual property which are lecturers and faculties have an inspiration to communicate and deliver their ever-growing and diverse body of work to the society. Some of their works are known as Intellectual output (IO). IO can be defined as sincere and systematic research done by researchers that have been observed and reviewed by professional supervisors, and other expertise (i.e examiners, reviewers and journal editors) especially when reporting research results etc [2]. IO consists of teaching, research, innovation, and achievement of the IO producer. It is essential for these IO to be properly recorded and made available to the nation and abroad as well; this is where, Institutional Repository (IR) role takes place.

IR enables resources to be accessed on and off campus which will benefit user without time constraint. Other than that, by having IR, an institution can avoid

H. Badioze Zaman et al. (Eds.): IVIC 2013, LNCS 8237, pp. 664–670, 2013.

information scattered and ensure the effective usage of knowledge owned by institution itself so that it can be reused and applied for future works[3, 4].

In the real-world application, information is often fuzzy or confusing[5]. There are numerous proposals to widen database model that maintains the ambiguity and vagueness of real-world application[6]. Hence, the needs of taxonomy to manage the knowledge are essential to an organization. Therefore, this study has been proposed to RIBU, UiTM in order to solve the current issues.

2 Literature Review

2.1 Intellectual Output (IO)

Intellectual is defined as a person who uses thoughts, able to reasons by using critical and analytical thinking, intelligence in distributing ideas[7] whereas output defined by Random House Webster's College Dictionary as the end product or yield. By combining these two definitions Intellectual Output (IO) can be defined as an end product by academician in visualizing their ideas on any field of studies after going through critical and analytical thinking. IO is basically produced by institutional members such as faculty, research staff, and even students of an institution [8, 9] that consists of teaching, research, innovation, and achievement. It is estimated around 80 to 85% university's IO is never made public and unable the user to access it [10]. University digital IO consists of various types of data such as annual reports, computer programs, conference paper, data sets, learning/complex objects, lecture series materials, models, pre-prints/post-prints, proceedings, research reports, working papers, web pages, and white papers[11].

To preserve the IO, there is a need of Institutional Repository (IR). IR is considered as a service that collect, organize, save and retrieve[12] any kind of digital materials created by institutional and its members[4] which includes pre-prints, post-prints, books, theses, conference proceedings, teaching material and so on[13]. It is intended to break the individual belonging of digital content into a public access by installing a common store[14]. IO of a laboratory, departments, university and other entities basically are preserved by an IR of an organizations[15]. Thus making the main purpose of IR is to preserve IO of single or multi institutions[16].

2.2 Knowledge Modeling and Taxonomy

Knowledge preservation is a process of ensuring the knowledge from getting loss. It is important to preserve the knowledge as it is an asset to organizations. According to a blog entitled "How to preserve Institutional Knowledge" there are three strategies in order to preserve knowledge [17] which are 1) build an explicit strategy to maintain the institutional memory, 2) identify important key things everyone should know and 3) able to do and make use of technology for creating a process that is used to capture institutional knowledge. In knowledge modeling, a knowledge representation is a simple yet suitable way in representing a complex knowledge into explicit knowledge [18]. Nowadays, there are many kinds of knowledge representation that exists such as production rules, fuzzy Petri nets-revisited, hierarchical representation of procedural knowledge, semantic networks, description logic, neural networks, ontology, knowledge webs, knowledge networks and other various field [19].

In general, a real system is very large to understand, and it consists of many components that connected to each other which make them to work in complex manners. Knowledge representation is a good idea to be used. By having models, it helps people from different field to understand it and view them in a unified manner[20].

There are many arguments arises regarding the terms taxonomy and ontology which both are actually knowledge representation. Ontology is known as knowledge map that made up from various assumptions, perceptions on the same field which have been developed to represent knowledge in order to improve information organization, management and understanding[21]. In terms of computer and information sciences, ontology is a representation used to model a domain of knowledge where it is actually a general conceptualization[22]. Meanwhile, taxonomy is defined by Cambridge Advanced Learner's Dictionary as categorizing and naming things by a system such as plants, animals, into groups of similarities[23]. Taxonomy is a hierarchical tree-like classification that shows relationship between terms[21]. The following Fig.1 shows the idea of taxonomy structure.

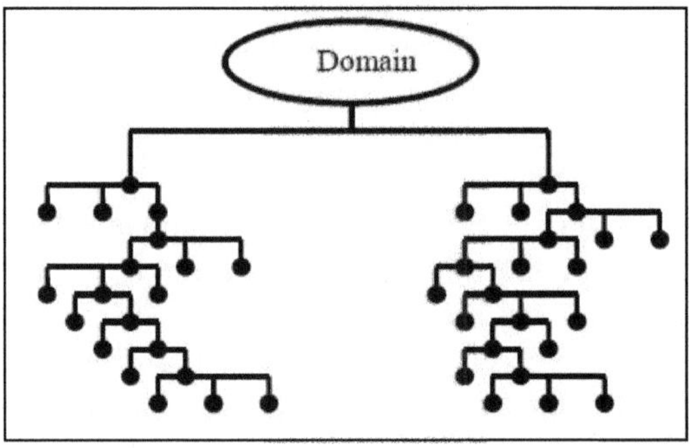

Fig. 1. Taxonomy Structure[21]

2.3 Research Innovation Business Units (RIBU), UiTM

RIBU is a Research Innovation Business Unit in UiTM which provides a central platform to researcher in handling and monitoring commercialization activities. RIBU[1] consists of three main units that are Innovation Creativity Unit, Intellectual Property Application Unit and Commercialization Unit. RIBU has been chosen as a case study due to some issues in organizing and managing data. RIBU has been introduced since 2011; therefore, there are numerous data that have been stored here.

[1] Research Innovation Business Unit, RIBU `http://ribu.uitm.edu.my/`

In current practice, there is no specific method of organizing data in RIBU. The data is managed by using traditional filing which leads to unorganized data. Thus, this study introduced a suitable taxonomy to RIBU and it is hoped that the currents issues can be solved. For this study, the focus is only on Innovation Creativity Unit that has been divided into three sections which are innovation, invention and design.

3 Research Methodology

A research methodology is supposed to support the overall of research development. In this paper, the phases of research method are shown in Fig.2.

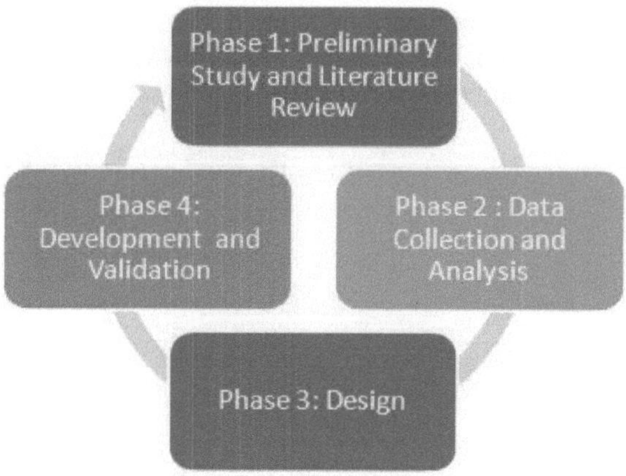

Fig. 2. Research Methodology

The research started with preliminary study to justify the research problem, research questions, objectives and scopes. While literature reviews supported the problems by giving evidence from journals, articles besides to have a deep understanding on IO, IR, KM and taxonomy. Then, the data collection started where the interview method had been used to obtain the data. As the scope for the project was the Research Innovation Business Unit (RIBU) of UiTM, therefore, one of the publication officers had been interviewed. The purpose of the interview was to know the type of IO produced by UiTM members, how the current IO is stored and how the current system works. The interview session is an essential step as later it can justify the candidates of the taxonomy. Next is data analysis which is to identify the possible candidates of the taxonomy.

Next is the design phase. In this phase, the candidates of taxonomy had been categorized based on decided criteria. Then, the development phase took place where the taxonomy model for knowledge preservation framework had been developed.

Protégé had been chosen as the taxonomy modeling and development tool as it has a lot of benefits which includes ontology visualization, project management, software engineering and modeling tasks. Finally is the validation phase to complete the whole process where the proposed taxonomy framework will be validated by the experts in RIBU. Currently, the validation phase is in progress.

4 Proposed Taxonomy Framework

Currently, according to interview session with RIBU officer, the collection of University's IO is unorganized and unstructured. The data obtained from RIBU were in the form of user manuals and excel files. The data from user manuals and excel files have been studied to perform a suitable taxonomy to RIBU.

From the user manual, a major class was attained. The model of IO is obtained from the current categories specified by RIBU itself. There are two main taxonomies are produced as the product can inherit or categorize under one of the three categories that are innovation, invention and design. Fig. 3 below shows the proposed main class of RIBU framework and the overall RIBU taxonomies.

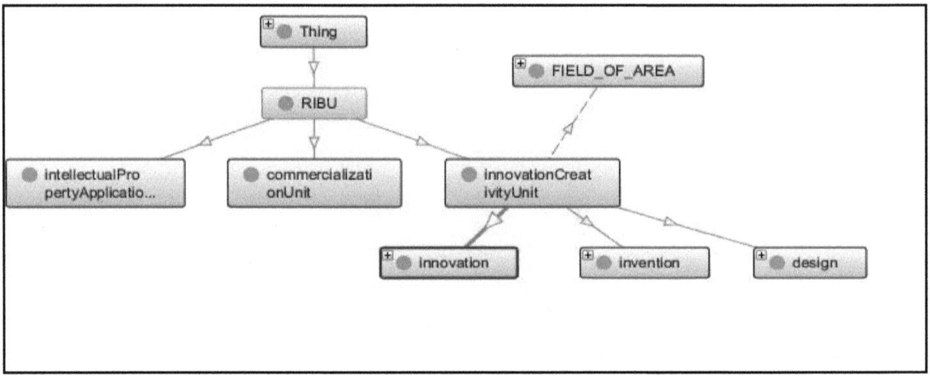

Fig. 3. Overall RIBU Framework

In Fig. 3, field of area will inherit the subclasses in Innovation Creativity Unit, which means field of area is belongs to any of innovation, invention and design.

From the data collection and analysis, the framework for preserving University's IO can be done by classifying all the possible candidates by faculties defined by UiTM. UiTM divides its faculties into three major fields which are 1) Science & Technology, 2) Science & Humanities and 3) Management & Business. The 23 faculties then were classified into these three fields. For Science and Technology, the field then is divided into three sub-areas that made up of Engineering, Applied Studies and Health Studies. Science and Humanities is also divided into three sub-units which are Creative, Education and Social Studies. The last field is Management and Business that has only one sub-unit that is Management Studies. The division is done by referring to the suitability of the faculties with their similar characteristics.

The possible taxonomy candidates are obtained from manual given by RIBU. First, the candidates are mapped to the suitable fields, and then mapped to the suitable faculties. If the candidates are having the same characteristics or properties, it will be grouped under the same name. The final candidates of each category are all cannot be divided anymore such as watches, alarm and clocks. Hence, once the candidate is no longer having possible sub-classes, mapping process will stop. Fig. 4 below shows the final level of taxonomy with no possible sub-classes.

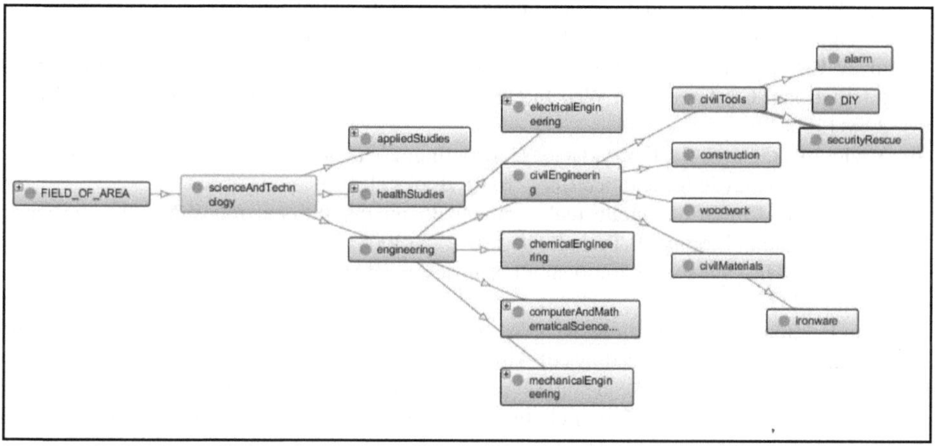

Fig. 4. Taxonomy Sub-Classes

5 Discussion and Conclusion

Knowledge preservation is very important for the dissemination within an organization. Among the important knowledge that needs to be preserved is the University's IO. This study proposes taxonomy to be incorporated in the Knowledge Preservation Framework for University's Intellectual Output in the case study of RIBU, UiTM. The practical contribution of the proposed taxonomy includes serving as a guideline in the creation of an institutional repository for RIBU. The taxonomy guides the users or researchers to categorize their product based on hierarchy. The knowledge preservation framework contributes towards an organized university's IO for an improved retrieval.

Acknowledgement. The authors gratefully acknowledge the financial grant given by Research Management Institute (RMI), Universiti Teknologi MARA (UiTM) for this study. A special thanks to the Centre of Information Technology, Faculty of Computer and Mathematical Sciences, UiTM, for all the supports and resources.

References

1. Haron, H., Noordin, S.A., Alias, R.A.: An Interpretive Exploration on Tacit Knowledge Dimensions in Academia. Paper Presented at International Conference on Information Retrieval and Knowledge Management, CAMP 2010 (2010)

2. Gobinda, G.: How to make best use of the intellectual output of the country? A simple approach to the design of a digital library of theses and dissertations in Indian universities (2001)
3. Ioannidis, Y.: Digital libraries at a crossroads. International Journal on Digital Libraries 5(4), 255–265 (2005)
4. Lynch, C.A.: Institutional repositories: essential infrastructure for scholarship in the digital age. Portal: Libraries and the Academy 3(2), 327–336 (2003)
5. Zhang, F., Ma, Z.M., Lv, Y., Wang, X.: Formal semantics-preserving translation from fuzzy ER model to fuzzy OWL DL ontology. Paper Presented at the IEEE/WIC/ACM International Conference on Web Intelligence and Intelligent Agent Technology, WI-IAT 2008 (2008)
6. Yazici, A., George, R.: Fuzzy database modeling, 26th edn. Physica-Verlag HD (1999)
7. Sowell, T.: Knowledge and decisions. Basic Books (1996)
8. Doctor, G.: Capturing intellectual capital with an institutional repository at a business school in India. Library Hi Tech 26(1), 110–125 (2008)
9. Crow, R.: The case for institutional repositories: a SPARC position paper. ARL Bimonthly Report 223 (2002)
10. Jain, P., Bentley, G., Oladiran, M.: The role of institutional repository in digital scholarly communications. In: Proceedings of African Digital Scholarship & Curation (2009)
11. Walters, T.O.: The New Academic Library—Building Institutional Repositories to Support Changing Scholarly and Research Processes. In: Sailing into the Future: Charting our Destiny: Proceedings of the Thirteenth National Conference of the Association of College and Research Libraries, March 29-April 1, Amer Library Assn., Baltimore (2007)
12. Naiwen, L., Xin, Z.: The Study on Constructing Institutional Repository of University. Paper Presented at the 2012 Fourth International Conference on Multimedia Information Networking and Security, MINES (2012)
13. Doctor, G., & Ramachandran, S.: Enabling knowledge sharing with an institutional repository. Paper Presented at the Seventh IEEE International Conference on Advanced Learning Technologies, ICALT (2007).
14. Hayes, H.: Digital Repositories: Helping universities and colleges. JISC Briefing Paper (2005)
15. Drake, M.A.: Institutional Repositories: Hidden Treasures (2004)
16. Dhanabalan, A., Ponnudurai, R.: Design and Development of Institutional Repository at Annamalai University. Journal of Advances in Library and Information Science 1(4), 160–164 (2012)
17. Ashkenas, R.: How to Preserve Institutional Knowledge. Harvard Business Review (2013)
18. McCalla, G., Cercone, N.: Guest Editors' Introduction: Approaches to Knowledge Representation. Computer 16(10), 12–18 (1983)
19. Yan, H.-S.: A new complicated-knowledge representation approach based on knowledge meshes. IEEE Transactions on Knowledge and Data Engineering 18(1), 47–62 (2006)
20. Abdullah, M.S., et al.: Knowledge modelling techniques for developing knowledge management systems. In: 3rd European Conference on Knowledge Management, Dublin, Ireland (2002)
21. Jashapara, A.: Knowledge management: an integrated approach. Pearson Education (2004)
22. Gruber, T.: What is an Ontology. Encyclopedia of Database Systems (2008)
23. Shaw, T.R., Pawlowski, S.D., Davis, J.B.: Building theory about IT professionals: is a taxonomy or typology the answer? In: Proceedings of the 2005 ACM SIGMIS CPR Conference on Computer Personnel Research. ACM (2005)

Heuristics Evaluation of Preschool Cognitive Skills Learning System

Muhammad Azeem Abbas, Wan Fatimah Wan Ahmad, and Khairul Shafee Kalid

Computer & Information Sciences Department,
Universiti Teknologi PETRONAS,
Bandar Seri Iskandar,
31750 Tronoh, Perak, Malaysia
azeem.abbas@uaar.edu.pk,
{fatimhd,khairulshafee_kalid}@petronas.com.my

Abstract. The ubiquitous use of computer by children is highly perceptible in current research. Therefore, providing the increasing interaction to computer technologies demands a careful designing of these technologies keeping in view the pedagogical aspects, psychology, abilities and interests of the children. These requirements make development of such applications a very complex job. Therefore, existing applications follow the content delivery model i.e. previously crafted contents are stored to deliver to a user. This limits the effective learning of the children. The present work proposed a rule-based system utilizing semantic web technologies (Ontologies) as a domain knowledge and semantic web rule language (SWRL) for rules representation. The proposed system overcomes the complexity of developing the intelligent and interactive applications for children. Evaluation is performed by using formal usability evaluation heuristics over an application developed using our proposed system for preschool cognitive skills tutoring. Results provided here demonstrates that the underlying knowledge modeled through the use of Ontologies is highly supported to flexible and child-friendly interfaces and pedagogical and playability activities (motor, reasoning) for cognitive skills tutoring.

Keywords: Semantic Web, Ontology, Intelligent Tutoring System.

1 Introduction

It is well understood now that Information and Communication Technologies (ICT) contributes to interactive learning environment in several ways. Such as, ICT provides a ways to access information from different sources and it can depict this information in multiple perspectives. Same concept if taught through different perspectives provides deeper and better understanding [1]. Complex concepts or processes become easier to understand with simulations, visual presentations or animations. In current educational environment, ICT plays a role of facilitator to both teachers and students. Individualized learning is possible through ICT i.e. it provides curriculum differentiation based on student's understanding and capabilities. Finally tailored

H. Badioze Zaman et al. (Eds.): IVIC 2013, LNCS 8237, pp. 671–682, 2013.

feedback for individual student is possible through ICT. Researchers expect that in future modern education will be dominated by ICT [2].

Advantages of ICT are countless. Yet, the benefits quoted in theory are not experienced by audience because development of a flexible application following psychology, intelligence, interactivity, creativity and pedagogy for any real domain is highly complex. From technical aspects, the traditional way of close-ended application development techniques are one of the major hurdles in overcoming this complexity. Traditional applications follow the close-ended models (e.g. relational databases or content delivery) for domain modeling that seriously lacks the capacity of modeling semantics of the data. The goal of the proposed work is to utilize the semantics of data i.e. modeled through the use of Ontologies to develop an intelligent (dynamic content creation) and interactive application for preschool cognitive skills tutoring. Researchers generally consider Ontologies as the best way for modeling reality because of their semantic modeling ability. Ontologies can represent complex concepts of any domain using classes, properties, instances, aggregation relations, generalization relations and axioms. Axioms are represented formally using some logic languages, such as description logic (DL) or first order logic (FOL) that represent true semantics to the models. Above all Ontologies are implementation-independent and can be used or reused with several different applications. The primary contribution of this work is to show that semantic enabled modeling approach provides ease to both software development activities and usability aspects of the child friendly application.

ICT has shown its integral part in the psychology of education and related cognitive strategies such as problem solving and reasoning skills, memorize and understanding concepts and to create new knowledge from the current knowledge. Several studies suggest a positive impact of cognitive skills teaching to achieve better performance even from less-succeeding students. Such benefits from cognitive skills tutoring through ICT are motivational force behind present work. In present work the proposal of a child-friendly computer software program to develop the early cognitive skills of preschoolers are addressed.

Pre-school children are divided into two groups; the first group consists of children aged 3 and 4 years old, and the second group consists of children from 5 to 7 years old. Children belonging to the first group, in general, still do not have the skills to read and write; they can only listen, speak and draw lines. Curriculum for this group is composed of motor activities and cognitive skills only. Coloring, drawing and sketching are the motor activities while cognitive skills contain classification, relatedness, ordering (later become mathematics) and spatial skills. The former group has the same components in their curriculum with language, mathematics, problem solving and science.

Perry and Dockett [3] reported that much of the learning is accomplished only by children's own interest and excitement during learning, without the use of formal contents. Interaction with mobile applications provides interest and excitement to the children and it is very much clear that learning gain is high with the use of technological resources [4] and [5]. Similarly Afza & Fatimah W. [6] addressed that only those computer games that follow educational objectives, curriculum items and exploratory nature are thought to hold potential for effective learning. But the existing applications lack these items in a way that they claims educational goals but they either are a mean of information display only (previously stored contents for delivery) or target a single objective (motor activity, memory building, sounds and words pronunciation etc.) with static contents. This static nature of existing application limits the performance of children. These limitation has been overcome by our proposed application that is dynamic, reckon with pedagogical aspects and specially take into account the abilities and interests of the children.

The dynamic nature of proposed application is developed by a rule-based system using semantic web rule language (SWRL). The knowledge underlying rule-based system is modeled using Ontologies. Ontology is an essential component of semantic web technologies that provides a common and formally defined vocabulary of concepts of a domain, along with the meaning of each concept, their properties and the relationships among them. During the last decade, areas such as knowledge management, intelligent information systems and education [7] received high attention on Ontologies and their use in applications.

Presentation of learning contents also affects modeling complexity of the domain knowledge [1]. Some applications use sophisticated graphical user interfaces or some operates over shell to reduce the knowledge burden. From a developer's perspective, manipulating domain knowledge to a presentable learning content is itself a complex activity. The present work introduces a Reasoner (details are given in Section 3.3) within application that fetch the knowledge from domain model and manipulate it under respective rules to get the final list of items for a learning content. Above that, presentation module is simply a template based structure that display list of items provided by Reasoner in a respective template in accordance with selected cognitive skill. Section 3 provides further details.

The rest of the paper is organized as follows. Section 2 provides analysis and discussion of related works. The details of proposed rule-based system are presented in Sections 3. Section 4 describes the evaluation results of the implemented prototype application based on proposed system. Conclusion of the work is provided in Section 5 with directions of our future research.

2 Related Work

Analyzing existing work reveals that the primary need to overcome shortcoming identified in previous sections is the domain models, that is, domain knowledge represented in a way that allows the system to generate dynamic contents and support pedagogical theories. A similar work with the present work was done by Abbas et.al.[1]. An application named Self Learner Tutor (SLT) was proposed for preschool children. SLT is based on Resource Description Framework (RDF) a component of semantic web technologies. Present work uses Ontology that is a component of semantic web but it is at a higher level in semantic web layered architecture than RDF. Ontology support complex and dense knowledge modeling as compared to RDF model. Similarly SLT designed for PC workstations while present work addresses mobile applications.

A software application named Epilist was proposed by Ming & Quek [8] and [9]. Sets are used by Epilist to model the domain knowledge. Related objects are grouped together based on their related property into one set called semantic network. A semantic network is applicable only if it is complete and unique i.e. a set with containing all items are classified correctly is called complete. For example grouping items in male and female is a complete semantic network. Similarly a profession set is not unique because several items can hold different professions at a same time. In a sematic network different properties are used to make such classification complete and unique. Epilist is a list-making game. We have achieved conceptualization of complete and consistent reality of the domain by using the advanced technology named Ontology. Ontologies natively provide a way to model complex domain knowledge completely and consistently.

Abbas et al. [10] proposed a content authoring tool named MySekolah for teachers and parents to create or generate learning contents. A framework for development of intelligent tutoring system was provided. Since semantic technologies are utilized for creation of learning content but the true semantic utilization of domain knowledge has not yet achieved. Also MySekolah does not have a formal assessment model.

A survey was conducted to investigate Malaysian preschool curriculum for modeling it to a mobile application [1]. Preschool curriculum in general is concept understanding [11]. Students at age of 3 to 5 years are primarily taught about concepts of the real world around them. These concepts range from color recognition to science processes. At the initial level children are introduced to objects followed by their properties and later classification of objects for example animals and birds, fruits and vegetables etc. Classification is one of the cognitive skills found in preschool curriculum. Relatedness is another cognitive skills found in preschool curriculum that is knowledge about things that are related through some property or relationship for example Fireman with Fire, Bee with honey, Frog with insects etc. Classification and relatedness both make reasoning skills that is child can reason about implicit things such as match box and danger, deep water and drowning etc.

The practices used to teach cognitive skills in current school environment are through the use of textbooks and worksheets. The hardcopy learning materials mainly follow match the column, circle an object and mark a tick or cross for conducting classification and relatedness cognitive skills exercises. We follow the same in our proposed application.

Authors in the work [12] and [6] had proposed an interactive way for teaching mathematics. This application is based on textual and animated representation of concepts. This visualization of mathematical concepts in a step by step way give good understanding to the students as claimed by the authors. But this is not an interactive way in a true sense. To make students understand any concept, three examples along with their solutions are presented. Student can navigate back and forward between each step of the solution. But student cannot varies or alter the numeric values with in the provided problems to see what happens if values exceed too large or decreased to too small. Examples visualized here are hard coded restricting the true definition of interactivity. Similarly the game like mobile application named SPELL IT! was designed for children to build English vocabulary [5]. The application follows the traditional content delivery model i.e. limited number of words along with their English translation was stored for practice and exercise. Botzer & Yerushalmy [13] highlighted the learning experiences of children through mobile learning. Two mathematics applications mainly for 2-d graph creation are used for evaluation. Results of this work identified the potential and benefits of mobile learning only.

Some problems related to the interface designing of software for kids were identified by Karuovic & Radosav [14]. These problems are limited usage of electronic devices and difficulties while interviewing the end users about their demand. Interface designer must design the interface to clearly show the child's work tasks which he/she has to perform. Software designer must also understand the mental system of the child (children psychology) while performing some tasks and tools required to accomplish underlying activities. In our proposed work we followed the same interfaces found in hardcopy learning materials because children as users are very much familiar with those interfaces. Tools provided to accomplish an activity are tapping the screen and drawing a line with the finger between two objects.

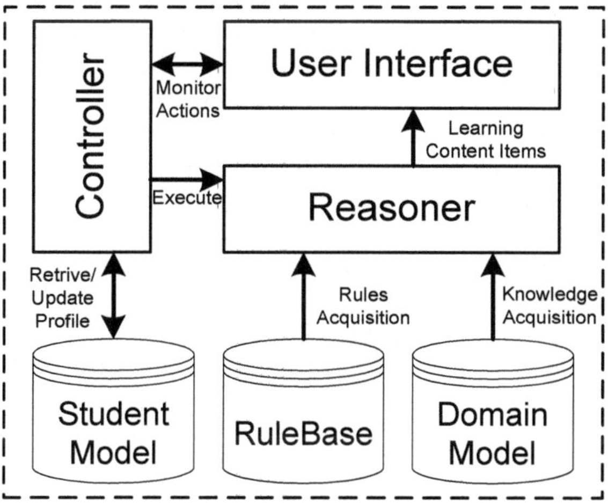

Fig. 1. Proposed System Architecture

3 Proposed System

The following section presents the system features, describing each component of the system and the interaction among them. Figure 1 shows the proposed system that is built on basic building blocks of a rule-based system. Domain model contains the domain knowledge modeled using semantic technologies i.e. Ontologies. Rulebase contain list of rules for generation of cognitive skills learning contents. Rules are defined using semantic web rule language (SWRL). Student model holds the students profile that is required for navigation among different contents. Reasoner infers the logical consequences from the list of rules provided in the Rulebase. The user interface module is responsible to display learning contents according to different cognitive skills representations defined by educationists. Finally, Controller module is main driver program that controls all communication among other components of the system. Details of each system component are provided in the next subsections.

3.1 Domain Model

Ontologies an essential part of semantic web technologies is a knowledge representation or modeling approach. Generally, Ontologies are defined as representation of shared conceptualization of a particular domain. In our case here the domain is preschool cognitive skills. The primary reason for using Ontologies for the present work is because Ontologies by definition provide a way to formally specify the vocabulary of terms and their semantics.

Table 1. Domain Ontology

Preschool Cognitive Skills Ontology	
Thing⊑Concrete_Objects	Abstract_Objects⊑Spatial
Thing⊑Abstract_Objects	Abstract_Objects⊑Mathematics
Concrete_Objects⊑Animal	Abstract_Objects⊑Science
Concrete_Objects⊑Plant	Mathematics⊑Measurement
Concrete_Objects⊑Food	Measurement⊑Weight
Concrete_Objects⊑Artifact	Measurement⊑Size
Concrete_Objects⊑Place	Measurement⊑Speed
Animal⊑Vertebrate	Science⊑Pet_Animal
Animal⊑Invertebrate	Science⊑Wild_Animal
Vertebrates⊑Mammal	Science⊑Carnivorous
Vertebrates⊑Bird	Science⊑Herbivorous
Mammal⊑Human	Carnivorous⊑(Animal∪Bird)⊓∀eats.Animal
Mammal⊑Cow	Herbivorous⊑(Animal∪Bird)⊓∀eats.Plant
Food⊑Meat	Science⊑Pet
Meat⊑∀partOf.Animal	Science⊑Wild
Milk⊑Food⊓∀produceBy.Cow	Pet⊑(Animal∪Bird)∀livesIn.Farm
Milk⊑Food⊓∀produceBy.Goat	Wild⊑(Animal∪Bird)∀livesIn.Jungle
Milk⊑Liquid	....
....	....
....	....

The same methodology is used for teaching cognitive skills i.e. a concept and its associated semantics formally specified in an Ontology are taught through using some representations of objects or text. More specifically, Ontologies provide a way to represent formally and explicitly concepts of a domain, their associated properties and relationships [15]. Cognitive skills of classification and relatedness are highly dependent on properties and relationship of things.

Ontologies natively provides solution to all requirements for modeling of our domain i.e. conceptualization, classification, relatedness, early mathematics concepts, spatial and science. Concepts are represented by classes in Ontologies [15]. For example, a class of Mammals represents all mammals. More specifically animals that are mammals become instances of this class. A class can have subclasses that represent concepts that are more specific than the superclass. For example, we can divide Animal concept into Vertebrate and Invertebrate. Properties of classes and their instances are called slots. For example Cow is an Animal and it produces Milk. In this example there are two slots: the slot isA with the value Anmial and the slot Produce with value Milk. In this case, all the instances of Cow have slots isA and Produce.

All concepts are formally defined as classes in Ontologies. Similarly the hierarchical structure (superclass-subclass) provides single as well as multiple classifications of concepts. Concepts/classes in Ontologies are connected to each other with properties that provide relatedness among concepts. In Ontologies, concepts or classes at top level hierarchy are more generalized than the lower ones such as Animal. These generalized concepts are split into more specialized concepts at lower levels in hierarchy such as Vertebrates and Invertebrates. Table 1 shows snapshot of domain Ontology.

3.2 RuleBase

Ontologies along with rule-based systems are also opening new horizons in artificial intelligence domain. Basic rules support here in this work is gained through axioms representation within OWL. OWL (Web Ontology Language) is a knowledge representation language used to author Ontologies. OWL provides support to represent axioms such as concept *PET* shown in Table 1. Rule is defined as a statement that expressed in the IF (antecedent) and THEN (consequent) form. If the antecedent is true, then the consequent is also true. While, rule base is the knowledge system whose knowledge base contains a set of production rules. Meanwhile, rule-based expert system is an expert system whose knowledge base contains a set of production rules [16].

3.3 Reasoner

Reasoning is a way of formal manipulation of the facts to produce new ones [15] or take actions against provided input and underlying rules. The proposed system perform reasoning to generate new learning contents that are aligned with the belief and understanding of the child using the application, as opposed to just presenting static contents in a linear way. Here the Reasoner works in a way, that when a user understood a basic concept, the Reasoner brings the same basic concept to another more abstract concept to validate the understanding of the child. For example if a child knows a *Horse* is an *Animal* then Reasoner will test the concept *Horse* under *Pet Animals* subsequently to *Herbivorous*. This sequence is given as an example rather Reasoner is allowed to select concept of its own choice. Reasoner performs reasoning based on subsumption analysis through finding implication and contradictions.

3.4 User Interface Module

Interface designing for children keeping account of their abilities and interest along with ensuring the pedagogical theories is an important issue in the field of human computer interaction. The practices used to teach cognitive skills in current school environment are through the use of textbooks and worksheets. The contents found in textbooks contain limited number of concepts. Also a concept is available in a single context that limits the deeper understanding. The proposed application evaluates any concepts in all possible contexts (represented in RuleBase and Domain Model) to give deeper and more effective understanding about the selected concept. The hardcopy learning materials mainly follow match the column, circle an object and mark a tick or cross for conducting classification and relatedness cognitive skills exercises. With the advent of technology new ways of interactions are now available to conduct exercises. The proposed application uses match the columns, drag and drop, tap the screen and scroll a list for interaction.

Fig. 2. Same concepts with different classification skills and results

Figure 2 shows the learning contents for classification skills. Iconic representation is used for concept visualization as at this age the children do not have the ability to read and write. But textual annotation is used with icons to familiarize students with words. Our domain model contains several categories of concepts ranging from animals to artifacts. At the start of the application, a student can select his/her preference of objects from domain model categories that give individualized learning and align the interest of a child. In example shown in Fig. 2, the user has selected plants as his/her choice.

Fig. 3. Same concepts with different ordering skills

As discussed in Section 1, presenting a same concept from different perspective gives better understanding. Figure 3 shows an example of brining same concepts under different characteristics (animal running speed, animal weight carrying capacity, animal size, etc). Answering correctly to all these exercises shows clear understanding by students. Learning contents shown in Figure 3 follows the ordering cognitive skill under mathematics. From usability aspect, user uses the drag and drop methods to fulfill this exercise. Showing a video related to speed and weight carrying capacity of animals etc before conducting the learning contents gives a very effective learning for the children. This proposal is a future work for our application and it can be easily accommodated by annotating the domain model concepts with video streams.

Fig. 4. Same concepts with different classification skills

Figure 4 provides examples of classification using the same objects. User can solve these contents by drawing a line from the object to the related iconic representations. Disambiguation is a cognitive skill. Figure 5 shows an example of learning content for disambiguation. In this content user has to identify/disambiguate the object that does not fall under provided classification. The example shown here is an advance learning content where all classifications appears in the example are not provided to the user. In earlier examples, user is clearly informs about all appearing classifications to make it easy to perform disambiguation. Children user can perform circle the object or color the not-belonging object methods that follow the motor skills.

Fig. 5. Disambiguation skills

The proposed application is dynamic because the learning content in Figure 5 is either through *Pet and Wild* or *Carnivorous and Herbivorous* classification. It depends on application self-reasoning to generate such learning contents.

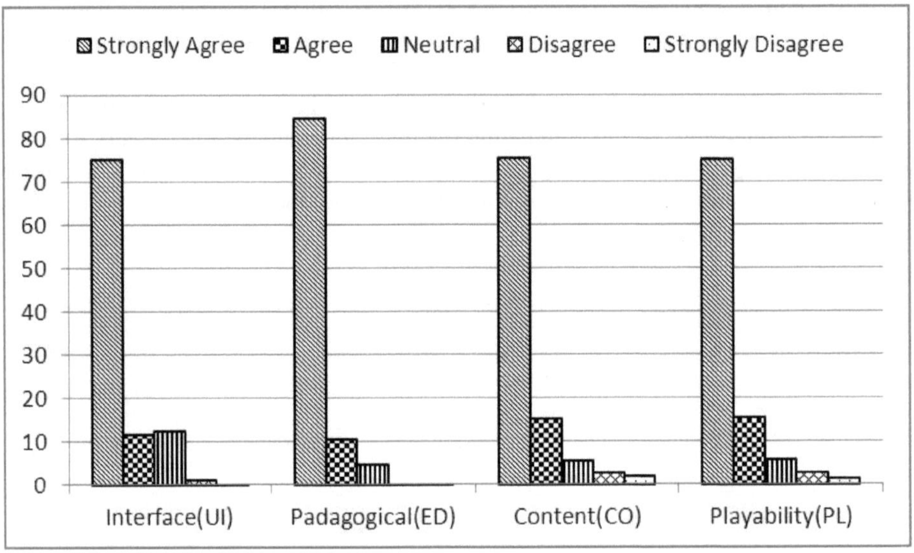

Fig. 6. Evaluation results

4 Results and Discussion

The evaluation of proposed application is conducted through the use of formative usability evaluation heuristics proposed by Hasiah et. al. [17]. These usability evaluation heuristics were proposed for evaluation of educational games for children. These heuristics encompasses evaluation of pedagogical issues, user interfaces, learning content and multimedia items. The evaluation is conducted by three teachers of three preschools (called Tadika) in state of Perak, Malaysia. These teachers are provided with a Likert scale survey containing items of usability evaluation heuristics.

The survey is filled by teachers after observing/experimenting their two students (aged between 3 to 5) using our proposed application. The technical aspects of application are evaluated by two PhD students mainly working in usability research at Universiti Teknologi PETRONAS. An associate professor is also involved as an expert in evaluation experiment. Figure 6 depict the results of our experiments conducted. Evaluation items are borrowed from [17]. The Figure 6 shows the cumulative results of all heuristics evaluation questions [17] in percentage of acceptance. X-axis of the graph in Figure 6 reflects the categories of educational game heuristics evaluation whereas Y-axis shows the percentage of acceptance. The graph depicts participants agreement is mostly toward "Agree" or "Strongly Agree" with respect to software interface, educational and pedagogical objectives, learning contents generated by our proposed application, and its playability.

5 Conclusion

Cognitive skill learning has a major part in preschool curriculum. Traditional method for cognitive skill teaching is through the use of text books and worksheets. These traditional methods inhibit several shortcomings such as they limit the interactivity, interest and individualized learning. Current environment is an instructive way where contents are just dispense to students. In contrast the constructive pedagogical model provides exploratory and individualized way of teaching. The proposed work here provides a proposal of a system to implement an application for preschool cognitive skills teaching following constructive pedagogical model. Above fulfilling the pedagogical requirements, the proposed application highly considers the child-friendly visual interfaces issues to enhance motor and reasoning abilities along with cognitive skills.

Acknowledgments. The researchers would like to thank the Management of Universiti Teknologi PETRONAS for their support to this research work. Appreciative thanks for the teachers and PhD students who helped in evaluation study. This work is a part of research project "Intelligent Tutoring System (ITS) Framework for Cognitive Skills Tutoring in Pre-School Children" funded by Ministry of Higher Education Malaysia under Exploratory Research Grant Scheme (ERGS).

References

1. Abbas, M.A., Ahmad, W.F.W., Kalid, K.S.: Resource Description Framework based intelligent tutoring system. In: 2012 International Conference on Computer & Information Science (ICCIS), June 12-14, vol. 1, pp. 324–328 (2012)
2. Aburas, A.A., Shreef, R.: On-line homeschooling learning management system using intelligent tutoring system. In: 2010 International Symposium in Information Technology (ITSim), vol. 2, pp. 967–971 (2010)

3. Perry, B., Dockett, S.: Young children's access to powerful mathematical ideas. In: English, L. (ed.) Handbook of International Research in Mathematics Education, pp. 81–111. Lawrence Erlbaum Associates, Mahwah (2002)
4. Sivapalan, S., Ahmad, W.F.W.: A Web-Based Multimedia Approach to Literature in Malaysian Secondary Schools: Learner's Preferences. European Journal of Social Sciences 12(3) (2010)
5. Ahmad, W.F.W., Shaarani, A.R.S., Afrizal, S.: Mobile Language Translation Game. In: Intl Conference on Computer and Information Science, ICCIS (2012)
6. Shafie, A., Ahmad, W.F.W.: Design and Heuristic Evaluation of MathQuest: A Role-Playing Game for Numbers. Procedia - Social and Behavioral Sciences, 8, 620–625 (2010), doi:10.1016/j.sbspro.2010.12.086, ISSN 1877-0428
7. Devedzic, V.: Semantic Web and Education. Integrated Series in Information Systems (2006)
8. Goh, G.M., Quek, C.: EpiList: An Intelligent Tutoring System Shell for Implicit Development of Generic Cognitive Skills That Support Bottom-Up Knowledge Construction. IEEE Transactions on Systems, Man, and Cybernetics 37(1) (January 2007)
9. Goh, G.M., Quek, C., Maskell, D.L.: EpiList II: Closing the Loop in the Development of Generic Cognitive Skills. IEEE Transactions on Systems, Man, and Cybernetics 40(4) (July 2010)
10. Abbas, M.A., Ahmad, W.F.W., Kalid, K.S.: Semantic Web Technologies for Preschool Cognitive Skills Tutoring System. Journal of Information Science and Engineering (accepted, 2013)
11. MOEM. National Pre-School Curriculum Ministry of Education Malaysia (2001), `http://www.moe.gov.my/bpk/sp_hsp/pra/sp_prasekolah.pdf` (viewed December 2012)
12. Bt Shafie, A., Barnachea Janier, J., Bt Wan Ahmad, W.F.: Visual Learning in Application of Integration. In: Badioze Zaman, H., Robinson, P., Petrou, M., Olivier, P., Schröder, H., Shih, T.K. (eds.) IVIC 2009. LNCS, vol. 5857, pp. 832–843. Springer, Heidelberg (2009)
13. Botzer, G., Yerushalmy, M.: Mobile Application for Mobile Learning. In: International Conference on Cognition and Exploratory Learning in Digital Age (CELDA 2007), pp. 313–316 (2007)
14. Karuovic, D., Radosav, D.: Educational Software for preschool children. In: 7th International Symposium on Intelligent Systems and Informatics, SISY 2009 (2009)
15. Antoniou G., H. F. V.: A Semantic Web Primer. MIT Press (2004)
16. Noh, N.M., Ahmad, A., Halim, S.A., Ali, A.M.: Intelligent Tutoring System using Rule-based And Case-based: A Comparison. Procedia - Social and Behavioral Sciences 67(10), 454–463 (2012), doi:10.1016/j.sbspro.2012.11.350, ISSN 1877-0428
17. Hasiah, M.O., Jaafar, A.: Challenges in the evaluation of educational computer games. In: 2010 International Symposium in Information Technology (ITSim), June 15-17, vol. 1, pp. 1–6 (2010)

Effectiveness of Concept Map Approach in Teaching History Subject

Siti Salwa Salleh and Rashedah Ismail

Faculty of Computer and Mathematical Sciences, University Technology MARA, Shah Alam, Selangor, Malaysia
ssalwa@tmsk.uitm.edu.my

Abstract. Concept map is a technique that arranges knowledge in a form of connected nodes. In our hypothesis, applying a concept map approach in teaching and learning History as a courseware can improve students' understanding and cognitive development. Therefore, we developed a courseware to complement the text book and were distributed to students in a Secondary School. For the purpose of this study, an experimental assessment was conducted among students where twenty students responded and went through the courseware assessment session. They filled in a form which was purposely designed to assess the effectiveness of the concept map instructional delivery and learner-friendliness of the design interface. In particular, the study looked at the effectiveness of a simulated learning experience, interface design as well as the technical aspects of the courseware. The findings from the study suggested that, in general, an implementation of concept map has been effective and useful. The outcome of the study concluded that concept map is one of the promising methods that can be effectively used to teach history in secondary students.

Keywords: concept map, concept of knowledge, teaching and learning, visualization, history subject.

1 Introduction

Visualizing knowledge is an approach where a subject with non-visual content is represented by graphics, diagrams or other readable/recognizable forms [1]. These visuals can be illustrated either two dimensionally (2D) or three dimensionally (3D). One of the popular techniques that can be used to visualize knowledge is by adopting a concept map approach.

Concept map is an easily understood tool [2]. It is a technique where concepts of knowledge are presented by graphical display that facilitates knowledge management and exchange. This also helps to personalize the learning process [3].

The concept map has become a useful instrument for teachers to aid student in understanding various subjects as it combines scientific rigidity with simplicity and flexibility. It also assists those who intend to generate, transmit, store and spread information and knowledge [3]. Alhberg [4] mentioned that teachers can monitor and promote students' learning and thinking through the use of concept maps.

H. Badioze Zaman et al. (Eds.): IVIC 2013, LNCS 8237, pp. 683–693, 2013.

Having acknowledged the concept map's capability of presenting knowledge, this study aimed to investigate its effectiveness in a multimedia courseware. This courseware offers modalities like interaction, animation, auditory and other features, which are advantageous to a learning environment and knowledge representation.

This paper presents a summary of an experimental assessment process and findings regarding the effectiveness of applying a concept map approach to a courseware. In particular, it looks into the application of the tool in teaching History to secondary school students under the Malaysian Curriculum.

Content wise, students' learning styles are described in Section 2. Section 3 explains research motivation and Section 4 presents knowledge representation and concept map. Section 5 describes research methodology and experimentation while Section 6 presents the results and discussion.

2 Learning Styles

Conventional teaching can be passive as instructors transmit information in sequence and textual forms. This teaching method, which is devoid of visualization, can hinder students' cognitive development. As shown in Table 1, students capture knowledge either by auditory, visual or tactile-kinesthetic style[5]:

Table 1. Sensory Learning Styles

Modalities	Descriptions
Auditory	• Auditory type of learners prefer and focus more when learning using voice over or sound. • They prefer verbal instructions or verbal communication to assist them in learning.
Visual	• Visual type learner prefers to have visualized information which combines text, graphical or images. • Diagrams, charts and graph, blackboard are those valuable tools for demonstration in their learning process. • Global visual learners will process iconic (pictorial) information before proceed reading the printed text. • Analytic visual learners will process the printed word before iconic (pictorial) information.
Tactile/ Kinaesthetic	• Tactile-kinaesthetic learners remember best the learning content by actively physical engagement. • Kinaesthetic learners tend to have a good memorizing what they are experience such as interaction with physical engagement, playing. • The learners enjoy learning process by manipulating and touching, such as drawing, touch on touch screen applications, tracing and pointing, writing. • They actively engage in the content through the movement and focusing by hear and visual the information presented.

Cognitive development was the major focus in the courseware prototype design of the present study. Under this prototype, visual modality approach that supported the concept map approach is pointed in Table 2.

Table 2. Area of Cognitive

Area	Description
Perception and Attention	• Visual representation of data example font, color and placement. • Information must easy to receive. • Positioning information examples important information place in the center for easiest perceive.

3 Research Motivation

Identifying appropriate lesson content was imperative to serve the purpose of the present study. Hence, the History subject, which commonly requires effective delivery methods, was chosen.

In the Malaysian curriculum, History is a core and compulsory subject for the first three years of secondary schooling [6]. The subject is highly factual in nature. Despite many inexperienced History teachers considering it as one of the easiest subjects to teach [9], the truth has been contradictory. Sustaining students' attention in a History class has been a difficult process and this becomes a rising problem among school teachers. Delivering definite facts is equally challenging, and yet to help students understand that they are studying a scene in a great drama of human life. Moreover, it is difficult to encourage student's imagination particularly when they are trying to develop their reasoning skills and judgment.

According to Nor Azan and Wong [10], many students perceived History as a difficult and boring subject as they had to memorize and understand facts, concepts, dates and historical events. Specifically, the researchers found that 79% of secondary students had problems memorizing facts when learning History. Teaching media in the form of text books also caused students to lose interest, which further promoted problems of learning History [7].

From the researcher's viewpoint, the challenge of educating history is not only shouldered by students, but by History's teachers as well. History teachers are compelled to make their teaching method creative and interesting to young generations.

Following the factors mentioned above, this study attempted to apply the concept map approach in teaching and learning History. In particular, it aimed:

a) To apply the concept map approach in teaching and learning module in the multimedia prototype courseware; and b) To evaluate the courseware's effectiveness and usability.

4 Knowledge Representation and Concept Map

4.1 Knowledge Representation

Knowledge is a theoretical or practical understanding of a subject which consists of relationships between information and facts [8]. It is commonly represented by symbols to facilitate inference from the knowledge elements before creating new ones [9]. Therefore, the representation of knowledge must be in the form understandable by humans [9].

4.2 Concept Map as Knowledge Representation Tool

Concept map is a graphical tool that enables human to express their knowledge in a form easily understood by others [2]. It offers a framework for capturing experts' internal knowledge and making it explicit in a visual, graphical form that can be easily examined and shared [3]. With regards to artificial intelligence, the concept map is known as Semantic Networks that attempts to reproduce cognition [9]. According to Canas *et al.* [2], concept maps are usually presented in boxes or circles, which represent the concept of certain subject matter. All boxes or circles are connected by directed arcs, which encode brief relationships between them. These relationships usually consist of verbs, forming proposition or a certain conceptual phrase [2].

Canas *et al.* also mentioned that the structure of a concept map is dependent on its context. Consequently, maps having similar concepts can vary from one context to another and are highly idiosyncratic [2]. The strength of a concept map hinges on its ability to measure a person's knowledge on a given topic within a specific context [2]. Therefore, concept maps constructed by different persons on the same topic may not be similar, as each depicts its creator's personal knowledge [2]. To further elaborate the tool, the concept map's characteristics are simplified in Table 3 [3].

Table 3. Concept Map Characteristics

Characteristic	Description
Hierarchical structure	• General concepts are presented at the top, specific concepts at the bottom. • The root node is a good representative of the topic.
Proposition	• Every two concepts with their linking phrase. Short as possible, possibly single words. Forms a 'unit of meaning'. Provides semantics to the relationship between concepts.
Context	• Present particular domain of knowledge. • All concepts and propositions are to be interpreted within a context.

Fig. 1 shows the characteristics of a concept map. The structure is arranged hierarchically with general knowledge at the top and specific knowledge at the bottom. Inclusive concepts are found at the highest levels, and progress downwards to a more specific, less inclusive ones.

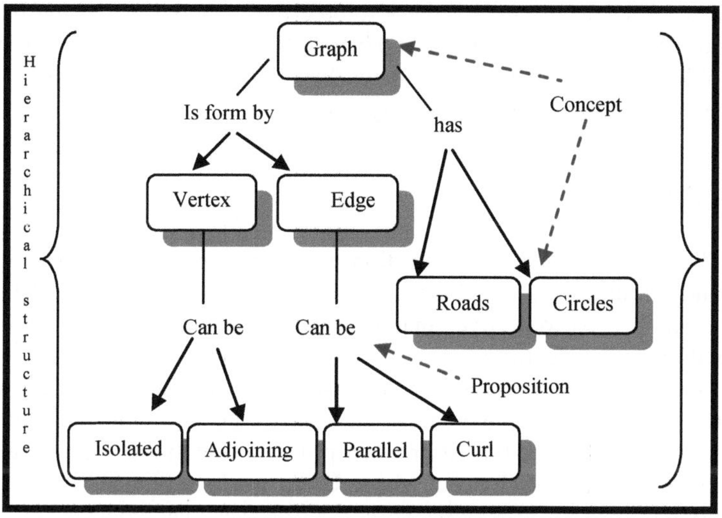

Fig. 1. Characteristics of concept maps [6]

According to Farrand *et al.* as stated by Alhberg [4], mind mapping helps a little, but significant factual recall of memory. This recall of facts is one of the main points stressed by Buzan in his book. The downside of mind mapping is that it does not represent precise presentation of facts, as it merely mentions and hits [4].

4.3 Related Researches: Concept Maps Technique

Few researches were conducted to investigate the concept map's effectiveness and usability. Espinosa et al. [3] for instance, have presented a new approach to elaborate the Intelligent Teaching-Learning Systems that combined a concept map with case-based reasoning to elaborate the intelligent teaching-learning system. This model was implemented in a computational system, and was later applied successfully in a teaching-learning process of Computer Science.

The systems were created with particular features. Few of its nodes appeared as questionnaire through the interface, and they were capable of getting a cognitive and affective state from student as well as able to guide user's navigation.

Another researcher, Jeng [11], has developed a Computer-Based Customizable Self-Contained Concept Map for Taiwanese History Education. This interactive learning environment has allowed users to customize both the degree of complexity and the selection of needed concepts to best fit their individual teaching and learning needs [11]. Jeng particularly developed an interactive concept map which linked high school history instruction to the digitized historical materials.

Another research undertaken by Emilio and Artacho [12] concerned the use of collaborative concept maps for coordination and knowledge-sharing in learning communities for science subject. They explored the potential of reusing the learning output within the virtual community both as a knowledge-building process and as learning object itself. Ultimately, they formed a family of tools to generate collaborative concept maps when teaching practical Science.

5 Methodology

To fulfill the research aims, an application prototype consisting of two modules i.e. teaching and learning was developed. This prototype followed the ADDIE model approach, which involved five major phases: analysis, design, development, implementation and evaluation.

Three chapters of Secondary School History Curriculum were covered in the courseware. A first time user would use the courseware in a sequence manner. After completing the teaching module, users then proceeded with the quizzes, which were represented in the form of Concept Maps. Users were facilitated with features like 'drag and drop' in order to choose the correct answer. The concept map approach designed in the courseware was replicated from that of Espinosa *et al.*'s [3]. Generally, it presented a form of hierarchical structure as shown is Figure 1.

As mentioned earlier, the structure of multimedia objects were arranged in a hierarchical form with general knowledge positioned at the top. The horizontal axis expresses this structure in hierarchical flow. The following Figure 2 shows how the concept is applied in the prototype courseware.

In the learning module (see Fig. 3), the quizzes applied similar concept and design. To add to the interactivity, users were required to drag and drop an object to answer a question.

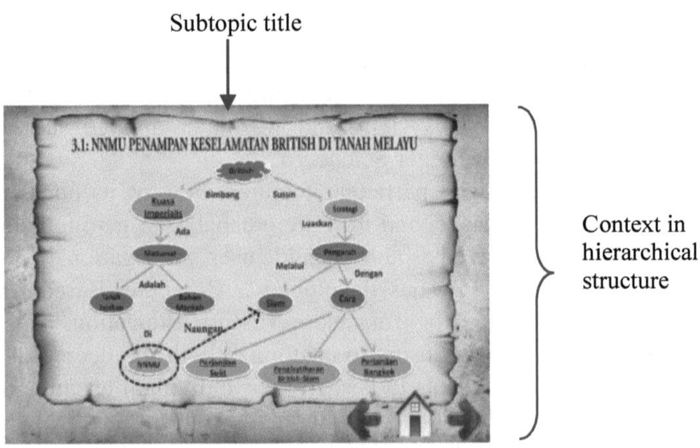

Fig. 2. Concept Map Structure in Teaching Module

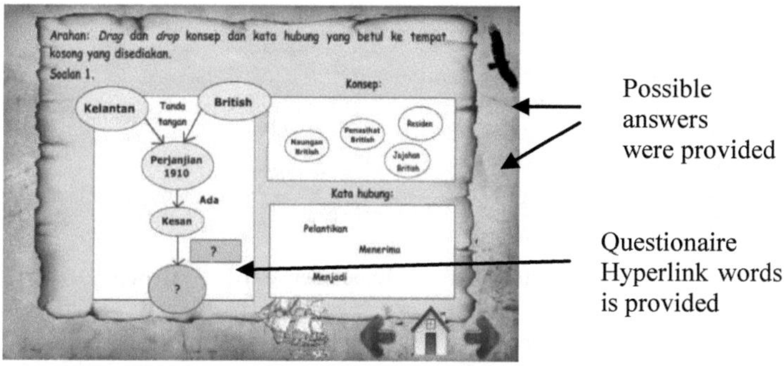

Fig. 3. Concept Map Structure in Learning Module (Quiz)

6 Result and Discussion

An experiment was conducted to measure the concept map's effectiveness and usability. 40 respondents participated in the experiment. They were divided randomly into two groups. The control group was made up of 12 boys and 8 girls. The experimental group was made up of the remaining 20 students which consisted of 10 boys and 10 girls. All respondents were 14-year-old students selected from one of the secondary schools in Malaysia.

6.1 Effectiveness Evaluation

According to Rogers *et al.* [13], effectiveness is defined by how good a product is at delivering what it claims to do. Based on this definition, identifying the goal of a particular subject is the first step to evaluate effectiveness. Within the education context, the prototype application or other aided learning tools are intended to enhance students' understanding as well as their performance in a particular subject [14]. Therefore, an application is considered effective when it can produce students' good results [14]. This outcome can be evaluated by comparing students' scores before and after using the prototype application [13].

The two groups were labelled as group A and B. Group A stood as Control Group while Group B stood as Experimental Group. Respondents from both groups attended the tests individually.

Two sets of multiple choice questions were used as instruments in both pre-test and post-test to obtain students' comparative score values. The same questions were used in both tests, but were ordered differently. In order to control students' memorization or experience during pre-test, similar questions were designed with different response order [16]. Figure 4 shows the average test scores obtained by the students for pre-test and post-test.

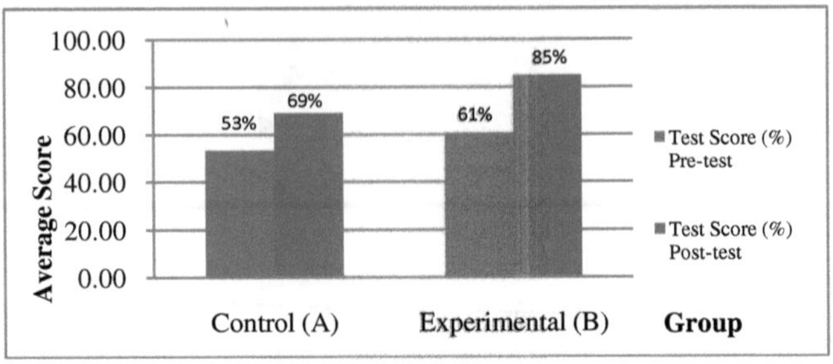

Fig. 4. Average score between control and experimental group

Table 4 shows the pre-test results obtained by the students. This data was used to obtain students' baseline performance before the process of teaching and learning History subject.

Table 4. Pre-test Analysis

Group	No of Student	Mean	Std Dev	t	P-value
Control (A)	20	53.33	12.54		
Experimental(B)	20	60.83	14.72	-1.23	0.25

In general, both groups of students had the same level of understanding on the selected chapter of History subject. This was evident from the mean score difference (7.50) between Group A and Group B. From the data, the value of P is 0.25 which was greater than 0.05 (P > 0.05). Therefore, there was no significant difference in the mean scores of pre-test for both groups.

The post-test data is shown in Table 5. The result was obtained after both groups involved in the learning process. Group A went through the learning process by adopting the conventional method (textbook and notes). Group B went through the process by using the prototype courseware.

Table 5. Post-Test Analysis

Group	No of Student	Mean	Std dev	t	P-value
Control (A)	20	69.17	11.81		
Experimental (B)	20	85.00	15.11	-2.61	0.03

In post-test, Group A scored comparatively lower (mean 69.16) compared to group B (mean 85.00). The value of P is 0.03, which is less than 0.05 (P < 0.05). This is considered to be statistically significant. It indicated that there were some improvements in the students' performance after using the multimedia prototype application. This led to the conclusion that the prototype courseware using the concept maps have been effective in improving the teaching and learning process of the History subject.

6.2 Usability Evaluation

A five-point Likert Scale questionnaire was adopted, where each response to a question received a value from one to five. A score of 1 indicated the statement as least favorable while a score of 5 indicated it as most favorable. Each student from the experimental group filled in the questionnaire individually.

Several criteria were evaluated pertaining to students' perception towards multimedia prototype application (interface design, sound, interactivity, animation, content and general perception). 4 out of 6 scored a mean value above 4.0 except for the interface design and the animation criteria. This means that all criteria were acceptable as they scored above 3.0. Conclusively, students gave a positive perception toward the new Concept Map approach.

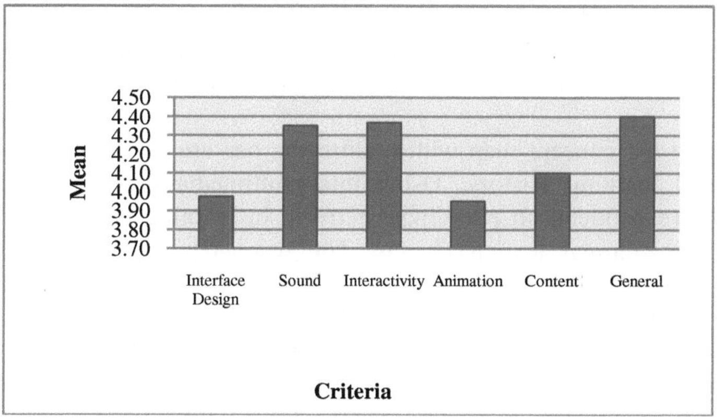

Fig. 5. Perception towards the prototype courseware

Criteria evaluated pertaining to students' perception towards the concept map included their understanding, interest, difficulty and general perception. It showed that only difficulty criteria scored a mean value lower than 4.0. This indicated that all criteria were acceptable since they all scored a mean above 3.0. Hence, students appeared positive in their perception towards the concept map approach.

Several criteria were adopted to evaluate the concept map approach: expression, time taken, association and categorization. The association and the categorization criteria were tested because they were the essential skills in building concept maps.

The mean value for time taken criterion is 2.65, which was lower than 3.0. This indicated that students took time to understand and answer the question. The small standard deviation also indicated that all students had the same standard behaviors. The 'expressions' criterion scored a mean value of 3.15, indicating that it was accepted. From a general viewpoint, the criterion 'time taken' scored lower than other criteria because the students took some time to understand and answer the question, despite having possessed association and categorization skills necessary for building concept maps. In conclusion, students reacted positively to the concept map approach.

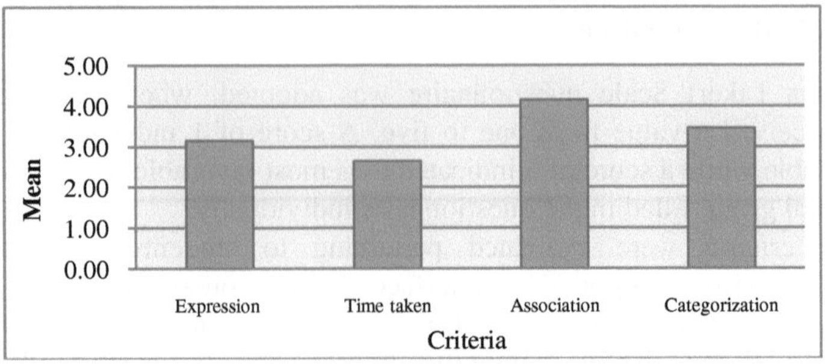

Fig. 6. Direct observation

The pre-test, post-test and usability evaluation (questionnaires and direct observation) showed that courseware prototype that was supported by some modalities e.g. visual, auditory and tactile, have enhanced the teaching and learning process effectively. It has also gained positive perception and observation from the respondents.

Integrating the concept map with multimedia has created a new environment for teaching and learning History. Using this multimedia prototype courseware has allowed the respondents to participate actively in learning the subject since it was supported by minimal textual objects. The respondents were able to develop a structural flow of events that consisted of certain detailed understanding of historical events. Thus, the concept map was considered successful in presenting history facts in a visual form that could easily be applied by respondents in a computer-based application. The tool has evidently outperformed the conventional approach.

7 Conclusion

Teaching and learning History is not simple, thus, including multimedia such as concept maps is necessary to increase students' performance significantly. Results from the post-test showed that students who used the prototype courseware scored higher than those who learned by conventional means. This indirectly reflected the effectiveness of the prototype courseware for educational purposes. In addition, the usability of the multimedia prototype application was also found to yield positive perception and observation. This research concluded that applying the concept map approach has been effective in improving students' performance and understanding. Overall, this study contributed much to the understanding that some parts of multimedia and knowledge representation techniques applied in multimedia prototype application are able to make a significant difference in students' cognitive development.

Acknowledgment. This research is sponsored by faculty internal grant of University Technology MARA, Shah Alam, Selangor, Malaysia.

References

1. Kosara, R.: What is Visualization (2011), `http://eagereyes.org/criticism/`
2. Cañas, A.J., Carff, R., Hill, G., Carvalho, M., Arguedas, M., Eskridge, T.C., Lott, J., Carvajal, R.: Concept Maps: Integrating Knowledge and Information Visualization. In: Tergan, S.-O., Keller, T. (eds.) Knowledge and Information Visualization. LNCS, vol. 3426, pp. 205–219. Springer, Heidelberg (2005)
3. Espinosa, M.L., Sánchez, N.M., Valdivia, Z.Z.G.: Concept Maps Combined with Case-Based Reasoning to Elaborate Intelligent Teaching-Learning Systems. In: Proceeding of the 7th International Conference on Intelligent Systems Design and Applications, pp. 205–210 (2007)
4. Alhberg, M.: Practical Method and Techniques of Knowledge Representation in Particular those Related to Concept Mapping and Mind Mapping. History, Theoretical, Background, Software and Comparison Table. In: Invited Discussion Paper in Instructional Technology Forum, ITForum, the Univ, Georgia, (2008)
5. Graf, S., Kinshuk, P.: An Approach for Detecting Learning Styles in Learning Management Systems. In: Proceeding of the 6 th International Conference on Advanced Learning Technologies, pp. 161–163 (2006)
6. Mohamad, R.: Design, Development and Evaluation of an Adaptive Multimedia Learning Environment Courseware among History Teachers. In: Proceeding of the 2nd World Conference on Information Technology, pp. 18–23 (2011)
7. Nor Azan, M.Z., Wong, S.Y.: Game Based Learning Model for History Courseware: a Preliminary Analysis. In: Proceeding of the International Symposium on Information Technology, pp. 1–8 (2008)
8. Davis, R., Shrobe, H., Szolovits, P.: What is a Knowledge Representation? AI Magazine 14, 17–33 (1993)
9. Gasevic, D.: Knowledge Representation. In: Model Driven Engineering and Ontology Development, 2nd edn., pp. 10–19. Springer, Heidelberg (2009)
10. Farrand, P., Hussain, F., Hennessy, E.: The Efficacy of the Mind Map Study Technique. Journal of Medical Education 36, 426–431 (2002)
11. Jeng, Y.T.: Developing a Computer-based Customizable Self-Contained Concept Mapping for Taiwanese History Education. In: Proceeding of the 5 th IEEE Int. Conference on Advanced Learning Technologies (ICALT), pp. 341–343 (2005)
12. Emilio, L., Artacho, M.R.: Using Collaborative Concept maps for Coordination and Knowledge-Sharing in Learning Communities for Science. In: Proceeding of the 11 th IEEE Int. Conference on Advanced Learning Technologies (ICALT), pp. 558–562 (2011)
13. Rogers, Y., Sharp, H., Preece, J.: Interaction Design: Beyond Human-Computer Interaction, 2nd edn. John Wiley & Sons, New York (2007)
14. Bayram, S., Nous, A.P.: Evolution of Educational Software Evaluation: Instructional Software Assessment. The Turkish Online Journal of Educational Technology 3, 21–27 (2004)
15. Sekaran, U., Bougie, R.: Research Methods for Business: A Skill-Building Approach, 5th edn. John Wiley and Sons, New York (2010)
16. Wang, T.J.: Educational Benefits of Multimedia Skills Training. Technology Trends 54, 47–57 (2010)

An AHP-Based Approach in the Early Design Evaluation via Usability Goals

Meei Hao Hoo[1] and Azizah Jaafar[2]

[1] Universiti Tunku Abdul Rahman, Kuala Lumpur, Malaysia
[2] Universiti Kebangsaan Malaysia, Bangi, Malaysia
hoomh@utar.edu.my,
aj@ftsm.ukm.my

Abstract. The usability engineering process has indicated the importance of setting usability criteria and a measureable level for important goals. Without goal-oriented practice, novice or inexperienced designers do not know how to deliver usable and quality system and would unreasonably follow what they have seen or used before. This paper presents a quantitative basis for selecting and prioritizing design goals or usability goals, thereafter selecting the best prototype relative to the usability goals. The proposed method consists of two main phase, namely: the prioritizing goals phase and the user evaluation phase. The objective of the prioritizing goal phase is to set priorities of the usability goals using analytic hierarchy process (AHP). The second phase involves users in the quantitative and qualitative evaluation methods to evaluate the prototypes using quantitative criteria and thereafter select the best prototype. The level of importance of usability goals assists designers to decide which alternative designs meet the most important usability goals. A case study of prototype selection in students' design assignment is presented, and the proposed approach is applied to facilitate their design decision during prototype development and evaluation.

Keywords: usability goal, early design evaluation, usability evaluation, quantitative approach, analytic hierarchy process.

1 Introduction

Usability goal setting and assessment are critically important in usability engineering [1] as well as in the user experience quality. Identifying and specifying a usability goal can lead to production of a quality, interactive product. Prior to producing a usable product, it is important to determine the criteria and attributes related to usability. In specifying a usability goal, usability attributes or criteria to be used in achieving the goals need to be identified. There is no clear method on how the usability criteria are to be achieved along the design practice. Conflict of design criteria or attributes could occur in a more complicated design situation. Most experienced designers would depend on their own experience to make decisions. In the midst of design complexity, our proposed method is targeted to junior designers in

H. Badioze Zaman et al. (Eds.): IVIC 2013, LNCS 8237, pp. 694–706, 2013.

order to help them to have a clear usability criterion while designing the prototypes. It would also assist in quantifying the result before a final decision is made. When a conflict in design situation arises, the prioritization of the usability goal could act as a guide to decide which goal is more important than the others. Furthermore, a decision based on the quantified data is strong and convincing, rather than depending on the individual intuitive feelings.

An analysis study conducted by [2] discovered that AHP is the most reliable research approach for conducting software quality trade-offs. This comprised 13% of 168 publications. Their analysis results showed that AHP was mostly applied for or proposed for use related to development artifacts. [3] showed that adopting the AHP method in the quantitative usability evaluation is reliable. [4] showed that the quantitative method using AHP efficiently evaluates the user interface designs as an alternative method to user testing.

In this paper, we present the application of a decision making method called analytic hierarchy process developed by Saaty [5],[6] in the design decision, specifically in determining the priority of usability goals of a designed system and subsequently to select the best prototype to fulfill the important goal. The decision framework proposed in this paper consists of two phases, which are namely: prioritizing the goal phase and the user evaluation phase. The proposed decision-making method in the design practice aims to help a designer to determine a clear and consensus design goal, thereafter choosing the best design prototype before moving on to further development. The approach would guide designers to deliver a good-quality product and avoid having to use their intuition to make a judgement.

This paper is structured as follows. First, the paper gives an overview of related work on the design for usability, usability evaluation and application of AHP in the user interface design. This is followed by a description of the methodology of the case study and a description of the case method applied. In the next section, findings are presented and discussed. Finally, we provide the conclusion and future work.

2 Design for Usability

Previous studies in [7] and [8] reported that usability is a quality attribute of the whole system. Numerous quality standards have included usability attribute in their documentations as a tool to guide the managers to employ usability in their work or organization such as in [9] and [10]. There are also several standards in place relating to usability which can be categorized as in the following: being related to context of use (examples such as [11],[12],[13]), interface and interaction (examples such as [14],[15],[16]), user centered process (examples such as [17]),[18]) and usability capability (with example [19]).

Identifying usability criteria is one of the common design practices. Usability can be measured with the following usage indicators, namely: learnability, memorability, speed of performance, error rate, satisfaction, and task completion [20]. Results of the comparison and evaluation of all usability criteria by [21] showed that learnability, efficiency in use, reliability in use and subjective satisfaction were the most commonly cited. A determined usability criterion acts as a design goal in design-related work in order to increase usability. This is shown in the studies of [22], [23] and [24], respectively.

An initial survey study in [25] found out that 75% of the respondents (who were industry practitioners in Malaysia) agreed with having usability goals in the project. In another related survey on the usability engineering methods, [26] revealed that the activity of having a clear priority in usability parameters to determine the levels on important goals has an impact on improving the usability. Thus, it is important to identify and select a usability goal before a particular design work or project starts. Another survey in [27] reported that knowledge in the usability is an obstacle in deploying usability in the software development organization. Therefore, novice designer may have problem in implementing the usability goals during the design and development of a system if their understanding is not clear.

There are techniques, methods, guidelines and processes on how to design for a usable system. Keinonen [28] has classified approaches to design for usability into product-oriented design and process-oriented design. Product-oriented design is capturing the design knowledge. Techniques and method used in getting requirements, analyzing tasks, design and testing are all in process-oriented design approach. All these techniques support the three principles of user-centered design approach as asserted in [29] that believed is able to deliver a usable product. Furthermore, user-centered design approach was endorsed as the best practice in leading to product usefulness and usability. These can be seen when the approach defined in ISO documents in [17] and [19].

Conducting usability test is costly and time consuming. Hence a lot of practitioners in industries failed to adapt the usability methods to evaluate their product development. A survey by [27] had shown two significant obstacles in deploying the usability evaluation. They were resource allocation and developer's mindset. Another similar survey in [30] also identified developer's mindset and resource demands as the major barriers to deploy the usability evaluation.

Accordingly, we suggest looking at another evaluation method of quantitative usability measurement to use in the preliminary evaluation and directly leading the prospect developer or designer to think of how to design for usability of the system before implementation comes.

3 Application of AHP

AHP has gained widespread attention as a decision making tool in various applications. To name a few, some applications of AHP had contributed in the area of education ([31], [32]); in computers ([33], [34]), in technology ([35], [36], [37]) etc.

Previous studies showed two purposes of applications of AHP in the user interface design, namely: (i) to weight the usability criteria and evaluate the interfaces based on these criteria([4],[38]) and (ii) to prioritize the usability problems during heuristics evaluation ([39],[40],[41]).

Even though our goal is similar to the goal in the study from [4] which is finding the best prototype, our approaches and implementation are different in ways as follows: (i) the rank and weight of importance goals is to drive the designer in implementing the design to achieve the targeted goals, (ii) involvement of user in the judgement of prototype preferences for all selected usability goals and (iii) aggregate individual judgement to determine the factor weights in order to determine the best prototype.

4 Methodology

The study proposed the approach of early design evaluation using Analytic Hierarchy Process [5] to select the best prototype. The approach consists of two main phases, namely: prioritizing usability goals and user evaluation phase. Both phases used AHP to perform the pair-wise comparison. The pair-wise comparisons of criteria and alternatives are performed whilst applying comparative judgement. The comparisons are made using a scale of absolute judgement to reflect the relative preference of one criterion (or one alternative) over another. Preferences are derived from the calculation of composite weight for each alternative using criteria or sub-criteria matrix. The alternative with the highest overall rating is usually chosen.

The stepwise procedure used to prioritize the usability goal and to evaluate the design prototypes using AHP, in detail, is shown below:

1. A brief description of the usability goals (as in Table 1) was given to the decision makers before they make their decision on the pair-wise comparison. Decision maker in setting usability goals employs the pair-wise comparison method on the four main usability goals. Recommended by Saaty ([6], [42], [43]), a nine-point scale as described in Table 2 is in the pair-wise comparison. An approximate weight vector is then calculated to determine the weight factor for each usability goal.
2. Consistency measures on the responses in the pair-wise comparison are carried out to ensure the responses to the pair-wise comparison matrix are consistent. If the consistency ratio is greater than 0.10, the decision-makers should consider re-evaluating his or her responses in the pair-wise comparison again.
3. Each user involved in the testing employs the pair-wise comparison method for all prototypes with respect to the usability goals in order to determine the factor evaluations for all prototypes in all usability goals. Similar in Table 2, the preferences between design alternatives are quantified by using a nine-point scale.
   - 3.1 Consistency measures on the responses in the pair-wise comparison of user preferences in all usability goals are carried out.
   - 3.2 Get geometric mean of all preferences consistent judgement. Following [44], [45] and has been proved in [42] that the geometric mean is an appropriate rule for combining judgements because it preserves the reciprocal property in the combined pair-wise combination matrices.
   - 3.3 Calculate the factor evaluation for each usability goals.
4. An overall ranking should be obtained. This is achieved by multiplying the factor weight for each usability goal (result from step 1) with the factor evaluations for each usability goals in all prototypes (result from step 3). This will give the total weighted score or overall ranking for all prototypes. A prototype receiving the highest total weighted score or highest ranking is recommended as the optimal user-interface prototype.

Table 1. Description of usability goals/ attributes (adopted from [21])

Usability goals	*Description*
Efficiency of use	The number of tasks per unit time that the user can perform when using the system or the duration to complete given specific tasks.
Learnability	Users can quickly and easily begin to do productive work with a system that is new to them, with the ease of remembering the way the system operates.
Reliability in use	User error rate when using the system and the time it takes to recover from errors.
Satisfaction	Subjective opinions of the users of the system

Table 2. Scale of importance between usability goals (adapted from [6])

Preference level of importance	*Definition*	*Explanation*
1	Equal important	Two attributes or goals are equally important
3	Moderate important	Experience or judgement slightly important over another.
5	Strong important	Experience or judgement strongly important over another.
7	Very strong important	An attribute or a goal is strongly important over another. Its dominance is demonstrated in practice.
9	Extreme important	The evidence of favouring one goal or attribute over another is of the highest possible order of affirmation.
2,4,6,8	Intermediate values	Used to represent compromise between the ranks listed above.
reciprocal	Reciprocals for inverse comparison	

5 Case Study

In the case study with the students' assignments, six teams were formed with each team consisting of three to four members. The method was evaluated in the user interface design assignment allocated to six groups of students. They were required to design user interfaces for student's society community system based on the given general description. The general purposes of the system is to help students' societies, clubs or organizations communicate with their members, keep up-to-date- rosters and received regular communications from the department of student's affair in the university. The students or novice designers, in this context of paper, were free to add in any possible functions that could support the best usage of the system. They were required to have some transaction processing in their designed system. The team was required to design the application to three different interactive prototypes. The prototypes must be possible to be interacted on the web or the desktop to give to users to evaluate. They were also required to arrange the potential users to provide their feedbacks on their design.

For demonstration purposes, a team was used in the discussion. There were four students involved in this project design assignment. The main functions that the team designed are, namely: creating, updating, editing society and committee members; creating events and activities, media uploading, and forum.

5.1 Prioritizing Goal Phase

Following the above mentioned procedure, data on prioritizing the goal in designing the specify system were collected from the expert. The expert has about 7-9 years of experience in software development specifically in developing education software and system software in a private university.

In order to ensure the reliability of the collected judgement, they were briefed on the purpose of the judgement, were explained the usability goals and were guided in deciding the weight of importance. They were guided in the following two questions in each comparison: (i) The first question to ask is of the following kind: in designing user interfaces for Student Society community system, compare between the efficiency of use and learnability, which usability attribute/ goal is more importance? (ii) The next question is of the following kind: based on the given table scale (in Table 2), what is your weight of importance?

The results of the pair-wise comparison judgement matrices with respect to usability goals for expert are shown in Table 3. The judgement result of the expert was taken into the next phase to determine the best prototype fulfilling the goals.

Table 3. Pair-wise comparison judgement matrix and relative weights with respect to usability goal

Usability goal	*Efficiency*	*Learnability*	*Reliability*	*Satisfaction*	*Factor weights (level of importance)*
Efficiency	1	7	1	3	0.4050 (1)
Learnability	1/7	1	1/3	1/3	0.0741 (4)
Reliability	1	3	1	5	0.3871 (2)
Satisfaction	1/3	3	1/5	1	0.1338 (3)

Consistency Ratio = 0.0879

5.2 User Evaluation Phase

In user testing phase, 3 users from each category of novice, knowledge-intermittent and expert were invited for the usability test. Previous reviews demonstrated that a total of 5 users in usability testing are sufficient to identify the most prevalent usability problems in a design ([46], [47]). Many professionals recommend between 5 to 12 users is sufficient [48].

In this study, a total of 9 users, comprising 3 from each categories of novice, knowledge-intermittent and expert were selected for the test. As selecting an alternative design occurs in the early design phase, and further designs and tests are practiced in an iterative design process, it is sufficient to have 3-5 users in this test. Moreover, the test is supported with appropriate qualitative measures in order to understand the design flaw and improvement for each prototype. Each user took about 20-25 minutes to complete all 3 prototypes evaluation. Table 4 shows the summary of user profile involved in the user evaluation phase.

Table 4. User profile

Type of users	Novice	Knowledge-intermittent	Expert-frequent
Age	20-23	22-24	21-23
Involvement in societies/ club	- Member of a society; - not active to slightly active.	- Committee member of a society - slightly active to active.	- Secretary or chairperson in a society - Very active.
Skill	- Experience in using computer for 7-8 years.	- Experience in using computer for 9 -10 years.	- Experience in using computer for 10-13 years.
Task goal	To check for society community's activities or updates	To check and update society community's activities, financial report; and reply feedback of members	To check society community's meeting reports; update activities and committee documentation; and reply feedback of members.

In testing the efficiency and reliability, the users were given 5 task scenarios which included: new member registration, changing committee member's details, creating event and activities, media approval and making announcement. While users were performing the test scenario, the other team members acted as observers to record the time taken to complete the tasks given, observe users' expressions and listen to users' comments. The result shows that prototype 3 was better than prototype 2 in terms of efficiency. Prototype 2 and 3 had shown similar number of errors but prototype 2 seems to be better than prototype 3 as it has more positive feedbacks. A general user satisfaction survey is adapted from system usability scale (SUS) [49] consisted of 10 items questionnaires that gives the overview of satisfaction for the evaluated software. Responses from all 9 users showed that prototype 1 and prototype 2 has about the same average SUS score 65.6 and 65.3 respectively, while prototype 3 has lesser satisfaction score 57.5. The result for the comparison of three different designs is shown in Table 5.

Table 5. Average measurement for efficiency, reliability and satisfaction test

Average	*Prototype 1*	*Prototype 2*	*Prototype 3*
Duration to complete all 5 tasks (estimation in seconds)	5 min 56 sec	4 min 26 sec	4 min 15 sec
Number of errors	2	1	1
User feedbacks and observation	3 positive 8 negative	6 positive 7 negative	4 positive 7 negative
SUS score	65.6	65.3	57.5

Nevertheless, given the result above, novice designers may not know which particular prototype need to be chosen for further improvement. The above result was further examined when users were asked to weigh their preferences for each of the prototypes according to four usability attributes. However, only users who were given the preference relations were of acceptable consistency (consistency ratio <=0.1) and their judgement were considered in the selection of the best prototype. Thus, 3 users were considered for efficiency in use, 4 users for learnability, 3 users for reliability and 3 users for satisfaction.

We further analyzed the prototype selection by aggregating all users' judgement of their preferences (only users who were in the range of acceptable consistent judgement) by calculating the row geometric mean for all usability goals. As all users were using the system to achieve similar goal, which was to communicate with their members in the society effectively and efficiently using the system, we chose the aggregation of individual judgement as we assumed that the group is to act together as an individual. This group of users becomes an individual decision maker. The result of the aggregate individual judgement on the efficiency in use, reliability, learnability and satisfaction are shown in Table 6, Table 7, Table 8 and Table 9, respectively.

Table 6. Aggregate individual judgement matrix for efficiency in use

Efficiency in use	Prototype 1	Prototype 2	Prototype 3
Prototype 1	1	1.5874	0.4149
Prototype 2	0.62996	1	0.3293
Prototype 3	2.41014	3.0366	1

Consistency Ratio = 0.0051

Table 7. Aggregate individual judgement matrix for reliability

Reliability	Prototype 1	Prototype 2	Prototype 3
Prototype 1	1	2	0.6586
Prototype 2	0.5	1	0.3029
Prototype 3	1.5183	3.3019	1

Consistency Ratio = 0.0007

Table 8. Aggregate individual judgement matrix for learnability

Learnability	Prototype 1	Prototype 2	Prototype 3
Prototype 1	1	1.5651	1.7321
Prototype 2	0.6389	1	1
Prototype 3	0.5774	1	1

Consistency Ratio = 0.0010

Table 9. Aggregate individual judgement matrix for satisfaction

Satisfaction	Prototype 1	Prototype 2	Prototype 3
Prototype 1	1	2.7144	1.5183
Prototype 2	0.3684	1	1
Prototype 3	0.6586	1	1

Consistency Ratio = 0.0325

Based on the result shown in Table 10, the proposed evaluation method using AHP recommended that prototype 3 is the best choice as it has the highest score. After consideration, the factor weights of both efficiency in use and reliability is very high in prototype 3 compare to other prototypes. It is reasonable that prototype 3 is the best due to the higher priority goal placed on both efficiency and reliability (approximately 40%) than satisfaction and learnability. The result is affirmed when we compare the result of the average duration to complete tasks. Prototype 3 has faster duration compare with other prototypes.

Table 10. The factor evaluation of 3 prototypes for aggregated individual judgement in all four usability goals and total weighted evaluation for each prototype

	Efficiency in use	Reliability	Learnability	Satisfaction	Total weighted evaluation (rank order of preference)
Prototype 1	0.256	0.328	0.451	0.500	0.3310 (2)
Prototype 2	0.174	0.160	0.279	0.226	0.1832 (3)
Prototype 3	0.570	0.512	0.270	0.274	0.4858 (1)

6 Discussion

The suggested quantitative analysis method using AHP would assist the designers to measure all opinions from the decision-makers in the decision made. We focused on the usability goal prioritization and user evaluation. We had made some improvements on the methodology of this proposed practice based on our previous work in [50]. In the usability goal prioritization, common usability goals were given to the experts to make the decision, instead of designers. Setting the usability goal should come from an expert. Expert has a wide experience with users and designs. They are often knowledgeable about standards and guidelines. Thus, the result from the expert is more reliable and should be taken into the next judgement phase. We involved more users' decisions in the user evaluation so that the selection of the best prototype is encompassing all related users from different skill level and usage. As been discussed earlier, the numbers of respondent involved in the usability testing was 9 persons in all three different skill level categories and this is sufficient when considering the duration of the test and the purpose of the test. However, respondents who were having consistent judgement on their preferences of the pair-wise comparison were between 3-4 users in each evaluated usability goal.

As there are 6 individual comparison matrices in an acceptable consistency, we combined their judgement in this group decision making process. There are two main aggregation methods, namely: aggregation of individual priorities and aggregation of individual judgement. Following the reviews, we used the common method of geometric mean in [5] to employ in the aggregation procedures. In earlier discussion, we chose the aggregation of individual judgement as we assumed that the group is to act together as an individual.

We also had enquired on our procedures and the proposed practices of usability goal prioritization and user evaluation using AHP to the industry-experts. Both experts from a public university agreed that this proposed practice would be appropriate to a new system proposed to the users in order to convince them and in the circumstance where designers and developers are unclear of the task or requirements of the system design. In their practice, there is no clear discussion or formal discussion on which particular usability goal is important and will need to focus as they believed that their co-workers understand what needs to be achieved. In an enquiry session with the novice designers after the completion of their assignment, three groups were asked on a question – "Without knowing and following the steps and procedures as in the assignment, how would you design the prototypes that contain usability features?". All of them unhesitantly answered to just follow the existing or relevant application in the internet or system. We can confirmed that without a goal and guide in helping their design decision, novice designers would just follow unreasonably what they have seen or used the application previously.

7 Conclusion

We believe that this suggested approach works well in determining the right design solution. The approach involves users in the early stage to test the design solution before further design and development work is performed. It follows the approaches to design for usability that consists of product-oriented design and process-oriented design. It begins with quantified usability goals to determine the rank of importance for the design. The proposed method is neither replacing nor improved any usability evaluation method. It is another quick discounted evaluation method to provide a clear idea of how much a particular prototype had achieved the targeted usability goals and which prototype is the best among others. It serves as a guide to direct novice designer to employ usability engineering in their software design in order to minimize the possibility of having usability problems that need to rectify in the later iteration. Further detail enquiries need to be made from the practitioners on the possibility to adopt the proposed method in order to give us more thoughtful idea for the establishment of the best method and practices in leading the novice designers to deliver a quality system that is in par with the industry standard and expectation.

Acknowledgements. The authors would like to thank all the software engineering students in Year 2 who had taken the subject User Interface Design in semester 2 (2012/2013) as well as relevant experts for their feedbacks throughout the study. Without their collaboration, the study would have been impossible. We also convey our appreciation to Dr Ong Poh Hwa to review the application of the formula in the calculations of the judgement result.

References

1. Leventhal, L., Barnes, J.: Usability Engineering: process, products and examples. Pearson Prentice Hall, New Jersey (2008)
2. Barney, S., Petersen, K., Svahnberg, M., et al.: Software quality trade-offs: A systematic map. Information and Software Technology 54(7), 651–662 (2012)

3. Fukuzumi, S., Ikegami, T., Okada, H.: Development of Quantitative Usability Evaluation Method. In: Jacko, J.A. (ed.) HCI International 2009, Part I. LNCS, vol. 5610, pp. 252–258. Springer, Heidelberg (2009)
4. Park, K.S., Lim, C.H.: A structured methodology for comparative evaluation of user interface designs using usability criteria and measures. International Journal of Industrial Ergonomics 23(5), 379–389 (1999)
5. Saaty, T.L.: AHP: The Analytic Hierarchy Process. McGraw-Hill (1980)
6. Saaty, T.L.: Decision making with the analytic hierarchy process. International Journal of Services Sciences 1(1), 83–98 (2008)
7. Seffah, A., Metzker, E.: On Usability and Usability Engineering. In: Adoption-centric Usability Engineering, Part I, pp. 3–13 (2009)
8. Bevan, N.: International standards for HCI and usability. International Journal of Human-Computer Studies 55, 533–552 (2001)
9. ISO DIS 9241-10: Dialogue Principles (1994a)
10. ISO DIS 9241-14: Menu Guidelines (1994b)
11. ISO/IEC FDIS 9126-1: Software Engineering – Product Quality- Part 1: Quality Model (2000)
12. ISO/IEC DTR 9126-4: Software Engineering – Product Quality- Part 4: Quality in Use Metrics (2001)
13. ISO 9241-11: Guidance on Usability (1998)
14. ISO/IEC 9126: Information Technology - Software quality characteristics and metrics (1991)
15. ISO14915: Software Ergonomics for multimedia user interfaces (2000)
16. IEC TR 61997: Guidelines for the user interfaces in multimedia equipment for general purpose use (2000)
17. ISO Std 13407: Human-Centred Design Processes for Interactive Systems (1999)
18. ISO DTR 16982: Usability methods supporting human centred design (2001)
19. ISO TR 18529: Ergonomics of human-system interaction – human-centred lifecycle process descriptions (2000)
20. van Welie, M., van der Veer, G.C., Eliens, A.: Breaking down Usability. In: Proceedings of Interact 1999, Edinburgh, Scotland (1999)
21. Folmer, E., van Gurp, J., Bosch, J.: A framework for capturing the relationship between usability and software architecture. Software Process: Improvement and Practice 8(2), 67–87 (2003)
22. Michael Pearson, J., Pearson, A., Green, D.: Determining the importance of key criteria in web usability. Management Research News 30(11), 816–828
23. Gonzalez, R., Martin, M., Arteaga, J., et al.: Web Service-Security Specification based on Usability Criteria and Pattern Approach. Journal of Computers 4 (August 2009)
24. Ozok, A.A., Fan, Q., Norcio, A.F.: Design guidelines for effective recommender system interfaces based on a usability criteria conceptual model: results from a college student population. Behaviour & Information Technology 29, 57–83 (2009)
25. Hoo, M.H., Jaafar, A.: Usability in practice: Perception and practicality of management and practitioners. In: International Conference on Pattern Analysis and Intelligent Robotics (ICPAIR), vol. 2, pp. 211–216 (2011)
26. Nielsen, J.: The usability engineering life cycle. Computer 25(3), 12–22 (1992)
27. Bak, J.O., Nguyen, K., Risgaard, P., Stage, J.: Obstacles to usability evaluation in practice: a survey of software development organizations. In: Proceedings of the 5th Nordic Conference on Human-Computer Interaction: Building Bridges (NordiCHI 2008), pp. 23–32. ACM, New York (2008)

28. Keinonen, T.: One dimensional usability – influence of usability on consumers product preference. University of Art and Design (1998)
29. Gould, J.D., Lewis, C.: Designing for usability: key principles and what designers think. Communications of the ACM 28(3), 300–311 (1985)
30. Ardito, C., Buono, P., Caivano, D., Costabile, M.F., Lanzilotti, R., Bruun, A., Stage, J.: Usability Evaluation: A Survey of Software Development Organizations. In: Proc. SEKE, Knowledge Systems, Institute Graduate School, Skokie, IL, USA (2011)
31. Saaty, T.L., Rogers, P.C.: Higher education in the United States (1985-2000): Scenario construction using a hierarchical framework with eigenvector weighting. Socio-Economic Planning Science 10, 251–263 (1976)
32. Saaty, T.L., Ramanujam, V.: An objective approach to facility promotion and tenure by the analytic hierarchy process. Research in Higher Education 18, 311–331 (1983)
33. Vellore, R.C., Olson, D.L.: An AHP Application to Computer System Selection. Mathematical and Computer Modelling 15(7), 83–93 (1991)
34. Hokey, M.: Selection of software: The analytic Hierarchy Process. International Journal of Physical Distribution and Logistic Management 22, 42–52 (1992)
35. Ramanujam, V., Saaty, T.L.: Technological Choice in Less Developing Countries. Technological Forecasting and Social Change 19(1), 81–98 (1981)
36. Arbel, A.: Venturing into new technological markets. Mathematical Modeling 9, 293–298 (1987)
37. Chang, P.L., Chen, Y.C.: A fuzzy multi-criteria decision making method for technology transfer strategy selection in Biotechnology. Fuzzy Sets and Systems 63, 31–139 (1984)
38. Mitta, D.A.: An application of the analytic hierarchy process: A rank-ordering of computer interfaces. Human Factors: The Journal of the Human Factors and Ergonomics Society 35(1) (1993)
39. Hasiah, O.M., Rohana, Y., Azizah, J.: Quantitative analysis in a heuristic evaluation for usability of Educational Computer Game (UsaECG). In: International Conference on Information Retrieval & Knowledge Management (CAMP), Kuala Lumpur, Malaysia, pp. 187–192 (2012)
40. Hasiah, O.M., Azizah, J.: AHP_HeGES: Tools to evaluate usability of educational computer game (UsaECG). In: International Conference on User Science and Engineering (i-USEr), Shah Alam, Selangor, pp. 73–76 (2011)
41. Delice, E.K., Gungor, Z.: The usability analysis with heuristic evaluation and analytic hierarchy process. International Journal of Industrial Ergonomics 39(6) (2009)
42. Saaty, T.L.: Priority setting in complex problems. IEEE Transactions on Engineering Management 30(3), 140–155 (1983)
43. Saaty, T.L., Vargas, L.G.: The logic of priorities: applications in business, energy, health, and transportation. Kluwer-Nijhoff, Boston (1982)
44. Saaty, T.L.: Group Decision Making and the AHP. In: Golden, B.L., Wasil, E.A., Harker, P.T. (eds.) The Analytic Hierarchy Process: Application and Studies, pp. 59–67. Springer (1989)
45. Saary, T.L.: The Analytic Hierarchy Process: Planning, Priority Setting, and Resource Allocation. RWS Publication, Pittsburgh (1990)
46. Virzi, R.A.: Refining the Test Phase of Usability Evaluation: How many subjects is enough? Human Factors: The Journal of the Human Factors and Ergonomics Society 34(4), 457–468 (1992)

47. Nielsen, J.: How many test users in a Usability study? Alertbox, http://www.useit.com/alertbox/number-of-test-users.html
48. Dumas, J.S., Redish, J.C.: A practical guide to usability testing. Intellect Ltd. (1999)
49. Brooke, J.: SUS-A quick and dirty usability scale. Usability Evaluation in Industry 189 (1996)
50. Hoo, M.H., Jaafar, A.: Quantitative Approach in a Preliminary Study of Evaluating User Interface Designs Using Usability Goal. In: Proceedings of the Visual Informatics International Seminar 2012 (VIIS 2012), pp. 128–136. Institute of Visual Informatics. UKM and Working Group on Visual Informatics, MyRen, Malaysia (2012)

Engendering Trust through Emotion in Designing Persuasive Application

Wan Nooraishya Wan Ahmad and Nazlena Mohamad Ali

Institute of Visual Informatics, Universiti Kebangsaan Malaysia,
43600 UKM, Bangi, Selangor Darul Ehsan, Malaysia
wanaishya@gmail.com, nazlena@ivi.ukm.my

Abstract. Attitudinal theory from the social psychology has been widely used in developing persuasive information technology and services in conjunction to shape or change user's attitude or behavior. Persuasion is the essence in building trust. The nature of this article is conceptual-theoretical where it discusses how emotion approach can be used to make people trust persuasive application. This article describes the three components; persuasive technology, trust, and emotion individually and the relation between them. Moreover, a conceptual model with related elements is proposed to show the relationship between those components.

Keywords: trust, emotion, persuasive technology, persuasion.

1 Introduction

Trust is important to persuasive technology as it gives confidence to users regarding the information and benefits that they will gain from an application. Without trust, users will not have the courage to use persuasive technology or application and even if they try, they may have doubts on the credibility of the provided information or the technique delivered by the application with regards to shaping or changing their attitude or behavior. This was demonstrated in a study by McGraa [22] which showed that persuasive messages are most effective when coming from a known and trusted source.

Recently, the study of emotion has grown in importance as research in Human-Computer Interaction (HCI) focuses on the need to incorporate emotion into the design of computer applications [3, 32, 4, 27]. In addition, there has been an increasing interest in studying the influence or impact of emotion on trust [17, 30, 6, 11, 31]. Therefore, the main concern of this paper is to discuss the role of emotion in persuasive applications in generating and increasing users' trust. The guru of persuasive technology and also the founder of Stanford Persuasive Technology Lab defined persuasive technology as *"technology that is designed to change attitudes or behavior through persuasion and social influence, but not through coercion"* [1]. Since coercion is not the means or goal of persuasion, emotion may be able to bridge the gap. Emotion plays an important part in transacting the effect of 'feeling' from the computer to the user in a process to persuade people to change their attitudes or

H. Badioze Zaman et al. (Eds.): IVIC 2013, LNCS 8237, pp. 707–717, 2013.

behaviors. This research is motivated by the view that a system that is deemed as trustworthy will have higher powers of persuasion [20, 21] and that emotion could have a powerful influence over cognition and decision-making, as suggested by a number of research studies and and theoretical models [29]. Hence, with the presence of emotion, trust can be obtained through the sense of feeling that users have when they interact with an application.

This paper describes a preliminary theoretical construction of emotion, trust and persuasive technology, and how these concepts should be understood together. The paper is divided into four sections: Section 1 gives a brief introduction about the importance of trust and emotion in the area of HCI. Section 2 explains the challenges and findings from previous research regarding persuasive technology, trust and emotion as the mediator in stimulating trust. We also present the relation between these three elements in the review. Section 3 in this paper explains the issues identified from the literature review and it proposes a conceptual framework that integrates the three elements, trust, emotion, and persuasive technology, to solve the issues. Finally, Section 4 describes the pilot study or initial experiments that we will conduct as future work related to this research.

2 Background

This section discusses related terms such as persuasive technology, trust, and emotion, their definitions and their relationship to each other. It is critical to understand and establish an integrated perspective of these terms to position the direction of this research.

2.1 Persuasive Technology

Persuasive technology is the study of how people are persuaded when interacting with computer technology [1]. It differs from other persuasion types in that it is not always clear who the persuader is. Synthesizing the diverse definitions offered in the domain psychology, Fogg defined persuasion as *"an attempt to shape, reinforce, or change behaviors, feelings or thoughts about an issue, object or action"* [10].

True persuasion requires intentionality. The intentionality does not come from the computer or any mobile devices that a user uses as computers do not have intentions of their own. The intention to affect someone's attitudes or behavior comes from the designer, distributor, and the people who adopt the technology [1, 10]. Intention has been divided into three types which are:

- Exogenous - An intention/attempt to change a person's attitude or behavior by providing them the technology
- Endogenous - A technology is created with the intention of persuading people in some way
- Autogenous - Self intention of a person in using technology to change his/her own attitude or behavior

In indirect interaction, communication transaction is done through Computer-Mediated Communication (CMC) where computers act as mediators with two or more computers being used by a person to transact communication. Through the use of email, social networking websites, and instant messengers, social constraints are eliminated [11]. This kind of interaction structure has allowed people to interact without sharing the same physical space. In indirect persuasion, the persuasive intent is not obvious: it does not condemn or confront a person's attitude nor does it espouse the attitudes of others who have already accepted the given message or idea [34].

For direct interaction, communication is transacted between the user and the technology itself. The user's intent is transferred into the application as the user interacts with the technology [5]. This type of interaction is the focal point in the field of Human Computer Interaction (HCI). In HCI, the transaction of communication is limited to the user and the technology since HCI is only concerned with the interface levels of the software and hardware of the technology. Oinas-Kukkonen and Harjumaa [35] in their study outlined that the emphasis of HCI is placed on the elements of *"argument, consistency and credibility"*. In the case of direct persuasion, persuasion has clear and apparent intentions. It provides clear directions to a person with goal-setting included in the process and clear instructions to achieve that person's goal regardless of whether the person agrees or not [34].

2.2 Trust

The perception of trust is unique to each individual, and thus trust is a subjective notion. In any situation, different individuals will have different perceptions of trust based on their assumptions, experience or knowledge and will reach different conclusions on whether to trust or not to trust something or someone. Trust is based on expectation. Hence, it is connected to emotion as expectation is a major source of emotions [14]. Trust is supposed to build from interaction, either human-to-human, human with technology or human-between-human mediated by technology. In addition, when expectation is not fulfilled by the other party in the interaction, regardless of whether it is human or technology, the criteria of ability or competence of that party is used to assess the trustworthiness of the interaction partner [18]. Benevolence [28] – a good deed from another party in the interaction to trustors, and integrity or honesty [8] - a set of principles that trustors consider acceptable are two criteria which can also be used to do reliable assessments on trust.

Today, an ever-increasing number of first time encounters are mediated by technology, as when people find business partners in online discussion or social media (e.g. LinkedIn) and when people sign up for weight management plans through online portals or websites such as MyHealth Penilaian Risiko (http://hra.moh.gov.my/), a health portal developed by the Ministry of Health Malaysia. First time encounters, especially those that are mediated through technology, will turn into repetitive encounters if elements of trust exist in the interactions. These interactions will only happen if users trust the systems they use to meet and interact.

Particularly, trust in human-computer interaction is often focused on cognitive trust in increasing the perceived trustworthiness of technology [33, 26] rather than on emotional trust that is motivated by strong positive feelings towards that which is trusted [33]. Some of the cognitive trust focuses on trustworthiness of perception design and interface elements [37], perceived credibility [7], and good use of visual design elements [2]. Most studies in trust that have been carried out are related to online websites such as e-commerce [9] and e-government [13]. However, far too little attention has been paid to other persuasive applications or technology such as games, health or exercise applications and mobile applications [33]. There are studies [9, 36] that have defined trust as being able to make users express their confidence towards the creators of persuasive applications or technologies and to anticipate that the technology would do what it is supposed to do without causing any harm to the user. Others [1] view trust cognitively as credibility that is associated with trust in the information provided, trust in the advice, and believe in the output. With trust, the credibility of an application or technology is not questioned as it accepts that the application or technology is reliable.

Nevertheless, Wang and Emurian [37] have argued that trust in both online and offline contexts share similar characteristics which include trustor and trustee, vulnerability, produced actions and subjective matters. However, according to these researchers there are some unique distinctions in the online environment context.

Several researchers have also recognized the need for a model of trust that is independent from specific technologies and domains. Tan and Thoen [15] have presented a generic model of trust specifically for e-commerce that illustrates that individuals will only engage in transactions if their level of trust exceeds their personal threshold which will depend on the type of transaction and the other parties involved. Fogg [1] introduced a computer credibility model for websites while Riegelsberger et. al. [9] created an independent trust model that allows users to have the ability to make correct trust decisions to differentiate between trustworthy and less trustworthy actors which can be applied across mediated interactions in organizations and in technology, e-commerce vendors and human advisors for health application.

In conjunction with trust research and personal differences, empirical evidence from personality records of 1940 to 1992 studies found that females scored consistently higher on the scales of trust [39]. On the other hand, in an experimental study using the Investment Game, Buchan et. al. [42] found that men trust more than women by sending more money through interactions in the game as they expected to receive more from their responders. The notion was set out in an earlier study [43] which showed that expected returns reflect the decision to extend trust. This implies that people, specifically according to gender, vary in terms of their willingness to trust.

2.3 Emotion

Emotions affect how people feel as they deal with their daily activities including interactions with the people they meet and with their surroundings. Studies [17] show that emotion is triggered by three appraisal controls: self-control – a state of emotion that is triggered by the user personally, personal control by others – a state of emotion that is triggered by another person, and situational control – a state of emotion that is triggered by situations or environments. Each appraisal control will produce different emotional states. However, one of the limitations in this study is that it did not explain interactions between humans and computer applications. In relation to persuasive technology, appraisal controls of emotion seems to be have different impacts on users depending on the persuasion technique or functionality used to persuade the users. Norman [4] categorized emotion into three levels: visceral, behavioral and reflective. The visceral level of emotion refers to the emotional response that is triggered by visual and tactile modalities like the appearances of a product (i.e. colors, type of font, layout design); the behavioral level of emotion is reflected by the functionality and usability of a product; whereas, the reflective level refers to the emotional response produced by cues that bring confidence to a person, such as a brand name. These levels of emotion proposed by Norman, has lead to the development of interactive applications that focus on designs at these various levels.

Scaffer [19], therefore, believes that another important component towards the establishment of trust is to understand the user's emotions. He argues that just throwing persuasive tools may work initially, but in time, it creates 'persuasion clutter', weaken trust, and is not effective. Thus, it is imperative for designers to carefully select appropriate persuasion tools based on a deep understanding of the user's emotions.

A study by Griskevicius et. al. [16] show how different users' emotions influenced the processing of persuasive messages. Their study found that four of the positive emotions tested: anticipatory, enthusiasm, amusement, and attachment love, facilitated greater acceptance of weak persuasive messages, whereas another two positive emotions, awe and nurturant love, reduced persuasion by weak messages.

Research by Dunn and Schweitzer [17], on the other hand, highlighted the influence of users' emotional states on trust. Through a series of five experiments, they found that trust levels increased as users experienced emotions with positive valence (eg: happiness and gratitude), and decreased as users experienced emotion with negative valence (eg: anger). Recent study [31] discovered that the impact of emotion on trust decisions varies on individual differences to the following factors: attention to emotion, motivation to use and watch over against emotion, or regulation of emotion.

In addition, a study by Myers and Tingley [30] found that emotions have an effect on trusting behavior. Anxiety slightly reduces trusting behavior, while others, including anger and guilt, showed no effect on trusting behavior. Although a number of researchers have maintained that emotions are critical considerations in understanding the development of trust and its changes, others [23, 25] have suggested that emotions influence how people evaluate others' trust, and still others [12, 24] have noted that emotions influence trust repair, and other [6] emphasized that the rationale of human choices and decision could be understand by understanding emotions, in particular. These findings indicate that emotions can influence a user's acceptance of persuasive technology and hence, it should become an important component for consideration in creating and leveraging a sense of trust [19].

Interaction design is an essential part of designing for emotion. It has been shown in a study [32] that interactivity is an important factor of affective quality and also a dynamic aspect of interaction, and has a strong influence on the user's emotional experience with an interactive product. The study on emotion also relates affective quality which refers to the feel and impression of an artifact [27] or features of an artifact that influence a person's emotion [41] with user interface. Interactivity as reported by Svanaes [38] is an important factor of affective quality that relates to the feel dimension of interactive media. He also uses the term ''look and feel'' to describe interactivity. The ''look'' is conveyed by the visual elements that make up a user interface while the ''feel'' refers to its interactivity.

Both studies [38, 32] prove that interactivity is an important element of affective quality in user interface design and it strongly influences the user's emotional experience with an interactive application. Thus, there is a connection between emotion and interaction in engendering trust. With the occurence of emotion through the exchange of interaction between the user and the application, it will be easier for users to make decisions about whether to trust the application and to rely on it to achieve their goal.

3 Conceptual Framework

This section discusses in detail the goal of this paper: the integration between trust, emotion and persuasive applications. The framework in Figure 1 is an illustration derived from the previous research mentioned in Section 2.

From the review groundwork that we did, we identified three issues that need to be solved: (1) the level of users' trust that determines the success of a persuasive system design, (2) the element of emotion that may influence trust in using a persuasive application and (3) signal or cues of trustworthiness that an interaction can provide to encourage the use of the persuasive application. Trust is an element that is important to persuasive applications because it relates to the shaping of behavior. When trust exists, competence and delight are felt; people are willing to try new behaviors [22, 40]. To integrate the three issues and clarify them better, we have outlined several research questions:

Q1. What kinds of emotion affective qualities influence users' trust when using persuasive computer systems?
Q2. How do the affective qualities affect users' emotions and motivate them to trust the computer system?
Q3. What kinds of interaction methods signal trustworthiness to the user to use the persuasive computer system?
Q4. What is the degree of trust when users are being persuaded?

Thus, to address the issues identified, we devised a conceptual framework that integrates the three elements, trust, emotion, and persuasive technology, as shown in Figure 1.

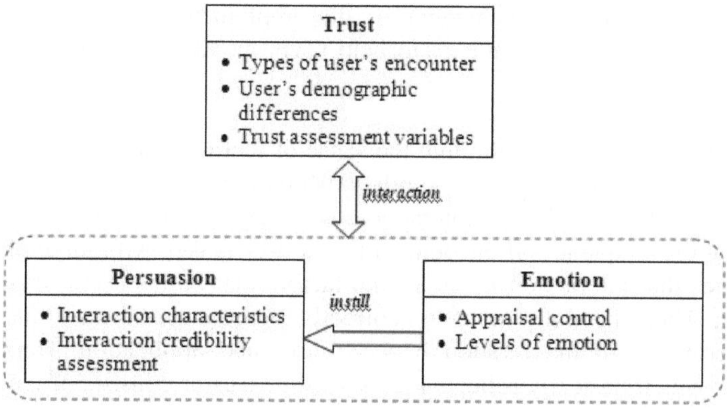

Fig. 1. Conceptual framework

Emotion: This component plays an important role in contributing to trust towards the application. The emotion component can become a spark or a trigger that makes users realize a wrong habit, attitude or behavior they own; it can also motivate them to change their attitude or behavior. The emotions can be triggered through appraisal controls, and levels of emotion. By instilling elements of emotion of different appraisal controls (personal, situational and others control), perhaps different impacts and outcomes of persuasion can be triggered. The level of emotions that may be implemented for interaction design in persuasive applications can be derived from the visceral, behavioral and reflective types of emotion elements. As emotion is also the key element to user experience, it can improve the persuasion process in order to ensure successfully designed persuasive applications.

Persuasion: The approach to be investigated in instilling emotions into persuasive application is through the interaction. Studying trust through interaction has not been investigated much by researchers. Trust provides the opportunity for advantageous interactions and therefore it works as an incentive for the agents of the system to interact with other agents. Thus, the component of persuasion process to be examined in this dimension is the characteristics of interaction and the interaction's credibility assessment. When a user interacts with a persuasive application, the interaction is aimed at accomplishing a particular task to achieve the user's goal. The context of the interaction may depend on the user's ability, skills or knowledge and the application features such as the functionality and the interface design. The context and features will affect and determine the characteristics of the interaction. On the users' part, they may have their own set of assessment criteria that they will use to assess a successful interaction. For example, the success of an interaction with an application that uses gesture communication such as eyeToy Sony Playstation and Wii is determined by how precisely the camera is able to capture the gesture. If a user keeps doing the required gesture needed to interact with the application but the camera does not work well in capturing the motion, the user might feel frustrated with the technology. A few dimensions of interaction design will be investigated (i.e. visual representation, physical space, time and behavior) in the implementation of dialogue support principles of persuasive technology to help users move towards their goal or target behavior.

Trust: Trust can be attained through the sense of feeling when users interact with an application or technology. When the relationship between the user's emotion and the application is developed, the interaction between the user and the computer is assessed by the frequency of encounters that a user makes with an application. This demonstrates that interaction is one of the factors that builds users' trust towards an application. Thus, the ability to assess correctly the trustworthiness of the trustee is of major importance in the relation between user and application. Hence, the trust component which basically reflects the user as the trustor consists of the type of user encounter (first-time or repetitive), the gender of the user who interacts with the application and the trust assessment quality as judged by the users during their interaction with the application.

It is important to frame the relationship in this particular way as it clearly shows the direction of each dimension and how they interact with each other. This framework could help designers to design better persuasive applications as it allows designers to not only design applications that are trusted by users by merely invoking functionality and usability, but also by the sense of feeling evoked when interacting with the applications. Once the key emotional responses of users are understood, designers can develop content and applications to amplify users' motivations and minimize their concerns while using the persuasive application by strengthening the persuasion strategies.

This framework will help to enhance trust in information systems by providing a new avenue in research related to persuasive technology in interaction design and Human Computer Interaction as it is important to provide more reliable and trusted applications for communities. Apart from viewing trust from the cognitive perspective through user interface design and elements, trust needs to be felt by users who use the information systems since trust is fragile and can dissolve quickly through negative experiences. This is where emotion plays an important role in contributing to the trust component as it is a key aspect of user experience.

In conclusion, the integration of the three components will contribute to the success of designing a persuasive application as the persuasion process itself should have an impact on users' feelings; only then can it affect the users themselves in changing their attitude or behavior.

4 Discussion and Future Works

This paper has briefly discussed the importance of emotion on trust decisions and how emotion can contribute towards designing trusted persuasive applications. Thus, the next step of this research is to investigate the relationship between emotion in engendering trust towards persuasive applications in different domains (e.g. education, health) and applications. The research work will first start with a small pilot study to examine the user's trust when they interact with persuasive applications such as games, mobile applications and health or exercise applications. From the pilot study, an analysis to determine the elements of trust integrated in these types of persuasive applications will be conducted. This initial experiment will help to shed light on the characteristics or variables necessary for the modeling of an emotion-trust model, the natural setting in which the persuasive applications are being used, and the rules of interaction.

References

1. Fogg, B.J.: Persuasive Technology Using Computers to Change What We Think and Do. Morgan Kaufmann, San Francisco (2003)
2. Briggs, P., de Angeli, A., Simpson, B.: Personalisation and Trust: A Reciprocal Relationship? In: Karat, M.C., Blom, J., Karat, J. (eds.) Designing Personalized User Experiences for E-Commerce, pp. 39–55. Kluwer (2004)
3. Norman, D.: Emotional Design: Why We Love (or Hate) Everyday Things. Basic Books, New York (2004)
4. Gutica, M., Petrina, S.: Emotional design: Perspectives of IT Designers. In: Proceedings of the Technological Learning and Thinking: Culture, Design, Sustainability, Human Ingenuity Conference, Vancouver, BC, pp. 17–21 (2010)
5. Oinas-Kukkonen, H., Harjumaa, M.: A Systematic Framework for Designing and Evaluating Persuasive Systems. In: Oinas-Kukkonen, H., Hasle, P., Harjumaa, M., Segerståhl, K., Øhrstrøm, P. (eds.) PERSUASIVE 2008. LNCS, vol. 5033, pp. 164–176. Springer, Heidelberg (2008)
6. Sardo, F.: Emotions and Decision Making in Trust Games (2011) (unpublished)
7. Corritore, C.L., Kracher, B., Wiedenbeck, S.: Online Trust: Concepts, Evolving Themes, a Model. International Journal of Human Computer Studies 58(6), 737–758 (2003)
8. Bhattacherjee, A.: Individual Trust in Online Firms: Scale Development and Initial Test. Journal of Management Information Systems 19, 211–241 (2002)
9. Riegelsberger, J., Sasse, M.A., McCarthy, J.D.: The Mechanics of Trust: A Framework for Research and Design. International Journal of Human-Computer Studies 62(3), 381–422 (2005)
10. Fogg, B.J.: Persuasive Computers: Perspectives and Research Directions. In: Proceedings of the SIGCHI Conference on Human Factors in Computing Systems, pp. 225–232. ACM Press/Addison-Wesley Publishing Co., Los Angeles, California (1998)
11. Wiafe, I.: A Framework for Designing persuasive Technology Based on Levels of Cognitive Dissonance (2010), `http://reading.academia.edu/IsaacWiafe/Papers/509281/PhD_Transfer_Report`
12. Wu, J.J., Shu, H.C., Ying, H.C., Hsin, T.C.: The Role of Positive Emotion in Trust Repair. In: International Conference on Financial Management and Economics IPEDR, vol. 11. IACSIT Press, Singapore (2011)
13. Colesca, S.E.: Understanding Trust in e-Government. Inzinerine Ekonomika-Engineering Economics, 3 (2009)
14. Jones, G., George, J.M.: The Experience and Evolution of Trust: Implications for Cooperation and Teamwork. Academy of Management Review 23(3), 531–546 (1998)
15. Tan, Y., Thoen, W.: Toward a Generic Model of Trust for Electronic Commerce. International Journal of Electronics Commerce 5, 61–74 (2000)

16. Griskevicius, V., Shiota, M.N., Neufeld, S.L.: Influence of Different Positive Emotions on Persuasion Processing: A Functional Evolutionary Approach. Emotion 10, 190–206 (2010)
17. Dunn, J.R., Schweitzer, M.E.: Feeling and Believing: The Influence of Emotion on Trust. Journal of Personality and Social Psychology 88(5), 736–748 (2005)
18. Beldad, A., De Jong, M., Steehouder, M.: How Shall I Trust the Faceless and the Intangible? A Literature Review on the Antecedents of Online Trust. Computers in Human Behavior 26(5), 857–869 (2010)
19. Scaffer, E.: PET Research: Looking Deeper to Understand Motivations. A White Paper published by Human Factors International Inc. (2010)
20. Janssen, R.: Persuasive Technology to Support Self-directed Learning in Adult Learning Programs (Master thesis). Available from University of Utrect Master Thesis database (2012)
21. Jimison, H., Gorman, P., Wood, S., Nygren, P., Walker, M., Norris, S., Hersh, W.: Barriers and Drivers of Health Information Technology Use for the Elderly, Chronically Ill and Underserved. Evidence Report/Technology Assessment No. 175 (Prepared by the Oregon Evidence-based Practice Center under Contract No. 290-02-0024). AHRQ Publication No. 09-E004, Agency for Healthcare Research and Quality, Rockville, MD (November 2008)
22. McGraa, K.L.: The Effects of Persuasive Motivational Text Messaging on Adherence to Diet and Exercise Programs Across Different Personality Traits (Doctoral Dissertation). Available from ProQuest Dissertation and Thesis Database (2010)
23. Williams, M.: In Whom We Trust: Group membership as an Affective Context for Trust Development. The Academy of Management Review 26(3), 377–396 (2001)
24. Tomlinson, E.C., Mayer, R.C.: The Role of Causal Attribution Dimensions in Trust Repair. The Academy of Management Review 34(1), 85–104 (2009)
25. Andersen, P.H., Kumar, R.: Emotions, Trust and Relationship Development in Business Relationships: A Conceptual Model for Buyer–Seller Dyads. Industrial Marketing Management 35(4), 522–535 (2006)
26. Ou, C.X., Sia, C.L.: Consumer Trust and Distrust: An Issue of Website Design. International Journal of Human Computer-Studies 68, 913–934 (2010)
27. Park, D., Lee, J.H., Kim, S.: Investigating the Affective Quality of Interactivity by Motion Feedback in Mobile Touch Screen User Interfaces. International Journal of Human-Computer Studies 69, 839–853 (2011)
28. Mayer, R.C., Davis, J.H., Schoorman, F.F.: An Integrative Model of Organizational Trust. Academy of Management Review 20(3), 709–734 (1995)
29. Lewis, M., Haviland-Jones, J.M., Barrett, L.F.: Handbook of Affective Sciences. Oxford University Press, Oxford (2009)
30. Myers, D., Tingley, D.: The Influence of Emotion on Trust (2011), `http://scholar.harvard.edu/files/dtingley/files/emotionmanipulationm11.pdf`
31. Lee, W.S., Selart, M.: The Impact of Emotions on Trust Decisions. In: Moore, K.O., Gonzalez, N.P. (eds.) Handbook on Psychology of Decision-Making, pp. 1–16. Nova Science Publishers, Inc. (2011)
32. Lim, Y.-K., Donaldson, J., Jung, H., Kunz, B., Royer, D., Ramalingam, S., Thirumaran, S., Stolterman, E.: Emotional Experience and Interaction Design. In: Peter, C., Beale, R. (eds.) Affect and Emotion in HCI. LNCS, vol. 4868, pp. 116–129. Springer, Heidelberg (2008)

33. Riegelsberger, J.: Trust in Mediated Interactions. University College London (Doctoral Thesis) (2005), http://hornbeam.cs.ucl.ac.uk/hcs/publications/Riegelsberger_Trust%20in%20Mediated%20Interactions_PhDThesis2005.pdf
34. Aleahmad, T., Balakrishnan, A.D., Wong, J., Fussell, S.R., Kiesler, S.: Fishing for Sustainability?: The Effects of Indirect and Direct Persuasion. In: Proceedings of CHI 2008, pp. 1–6. ACM, Florence (2008)
35. Oinas-Kukkonen, H., Harjumaa, M.: Towards Deeper Understanding of Persuasion in Software and Information Systems. In: 1st International Conference on Advances in Computer-Human Interaction, pp. 200–205. IEEE (2008)
36. Verbeek, P.: Persuasive Technology and Moral Responsibility Toward an Ethical Framework for Persuasive Technologies. In: Persuasive 2006, pp. 1–15. Eindhoven University of Technology (2006)
37. Wang, Y.D., Emurian, H.H.: An Overview of Online Trust: Concepts, Elements and Implications. Journal of Computers in Human Behavior 21, 105–125 (2005)
38. Svanaes, D.: Understanding Interactivity: Steps to a Phenomenology of Human-Computer Interaction. (Doctoral Thesis) Norges Teknisk-naturvitenskapelige Universitet (2000)
39. Feingold, A.: Gender Differences in Personality: A Meta-Analysis. Psychological Bulletin 116(3), 429–456 (1994), http://www.ncbi.nlm.nih.gov/pubmed/7809307
40. Fogg, B.J., Eckles, D.: The Behavior Chain for Online Participation: How Successful Web Services Structure Persuasion. In: de Kort, Y.A.W., IJsselsteijn, W.A., Midden, C., Eggen, B., Fogg, B.J. (eds.) PERSUASIVE 2007. LNCS, vol. 4744, pp. 199–209. Springer, Heidelberg (2007)
41. Russell, J.A.: Core Affect and the Psychological Construction of Emotion. Psychological Review 110, 145–172 (2003)
42. Buchan, N.R., Croson, R.T.A., Solnick, S.: Trust and Gender: An Examination of Behavior and Beliefs in the Investment Game. Journal of Economic Behavior & Organization 68(3-4), 466–476 (2008)
43. Eckel, C., Wilson, R.: Attractiveness and Trust: Does Beauty Confound Intuition? Virginia Tech University Department of Economics. Working Paper (2005)

A Study on the Naturalness of Gesture-Based Interaction for Children

Mohd. Salihan Ab. Rahman[1], Nazlena Mohamad Ali[1], and Masnizah Mohd.[2]

[1] Institute Visual Informatics, Universiti Kebangsaan Malaysia, Bangi, 43600, Malaysia
[2] Faculty of Information Science & Technology,
Universiti Kebangsaan Malaysia, Bangi, 43600, Malaysia
salihan@yahoo.com, nazlena@ivi.ukm.my, mas@ftsm.ukm.my

Abstract. The emergence of new gesture-technologies that use bare-hands without any remote control or tools to hold is a good indicator that the technology is implementing naturalness in an input control system. However, the concept of naturalness that is commonly applied is interpreted from the adult user's perspective without realizing that the equally importance users of gesture-based technology are children. For this reason, this study was undertaken to describe the natural elements of gesture-based interaction in terms of how they influence the behavior of children using gesture-based technology devices, and to what extent the children benefit from their use. This includes the identification of issues and opportunities related to naturalness in using the latest gesture-based technologies, Kinect and iPad. Our observations show that the naturalness in gesture-control devices enabled children to reflect real world situations into the interaction, thus, aiding them to call back (recall and demonstrate) the gesture command easily and sparking positive feelings during the interaction. We conclude that understanding naturalness from a children's perspective can offer potential benefits to children in the utilization of gesture-based technologies.

Keywords: gesture-based interaction, children's technology, interaction design.

1 Introduction

The recent introduction of gesture-based technology offers a natural way of interaction, thus, contributing to the key area of engagement [1] in any gesture-based system or device use, as pointed out by many researchers [2], [3], [4], [5] and [6]. Several studies successfully point to the importance of natural gesture interaction such as controlling robotic devices [7], enabling the natural control of wheelchairs for the disabled and aiding the elderly in memorizing [8]. However, a question that still remains unanswered is how natural gesture interaction can benefit young users, who are still developing their cognitive abilities and fine motor skills. Does natural gesture interaction enable children to control devices as found in the study by Peters et al. [7] or aid them in memorizing as shown in Stößel et al. [8]

H. Badioze Zaman et al. (Eds.): IVIC 2013, LNCS 8237, pp. 718–728, 2013.

Often the terms of natural gesture-based interaction are misinterpreted. Gesture-based interaction is actually interaction that contains information such as waving to indicate goodbye. Meanwhile, natural interactions refer to mutual or reciprocal actions that the user operates through intuitive actions that are related to or are as close as possible to natural everyday human behavior. By 'intuitive', we mean a device or an interactive system that is not just easy to use, but is used based on what one feels to be true even without conscious reasoning. Many researchers claim that natural gesture-based interaction should be easy to learn without using any tools attached to the user's body such as a remote control or glove [9], [10], [11] and [12].

Based on these claims, Kinect and tablet technology are the most common types of natural user interface (NUI) [13]. Related to this matter, children are the users that should be focused on, since they will be the main users of these technologies in the near future. Therefore, we aim to obtain a deep understanding of gesture-based interactions relating to children by exploring the naturalness of gestures in the most recent gesture-based technology available publicly. The user study is done to find out how children with no or little early experience or training can use and interact with the technologies by making the correct gestures; we also study their ability to remember the gesture commands.

In the next section, we summarize the work related to our study. In section 3, we present the study methods, the results in section 4 and the conclusion in the final section.

2 Related Work

The review of previous work is presented in three (3) areas, reflecting the goals of this study: natural gesture-based technology, naturalness and children, and the measurement of naturalness.

2.1 Natural Gesture-Based Technology

Gesture-based technology is becoming more and more natural. Kinect for example provides the user with free-form interaction that allows the user to interact through body motions, gestures and spoken words. Similarly, tablet technology, such as the iPad which is currently popular, allows for bare handed touch-form interaction. This kind of technologies are being said to be the most natural gesture technology known as NUI [13]. The goal of NUI is to create smooth interaction without seams or obvious joints such as wires. In addition, devices that use attachments or markers (attachment that sticks on the human body to amplify gesture detection by reflecting the infra red) limit the sense of reality and immersion; thus, the markers should be removed [14]. Several research studies [9], [10], [11], and [12] have also agreed that, in natural gesture-based interaction, no attachment should be on the user's physical hand. According to them, gesture recognition interaction that uses camera-based methods to capture body movement but uses attachments such as gloves puts too much restriction on users, resulting in much discomfort and unnaturalness.

2.2 Naturalness and Children

In gesture-based interaction, a number of studies have looked at the interaction itself, either its manipulation or its control. While computer vision gesture research claims that it provides a more natural style of interaction, there is no method to define or describe the characteristics of the interaction, or how they affect the user's perception of natural interaction [9] and [15]. However, it is clear that many gesture-based applications are being designed for children, and it is becoming a crucial field of research [16]. Studies of usage mostly tend to consider issues of performance and task efficiency rather than the experiences of users and their attitudes towards the naturalness of the devices or the technologies [17].

According to the world's largest organization working on behalf of young children, The National Association for the Education of Young Children (NAEYC), desktops provided in the classroom may attract the children initially but these are unable to hold the engagement level and are left unused in the corner after some time. The main reason for this engagement issue is that the desktop does not offer natural interaction with natural activities or an environment beneficial for digital learning [18]. Natural gesture-based interaction is believed to have the ability to engage children in the virtual learning process; unfortunately, this is not yet been proven.

In a philosophical view of embodied cognition, it is reasonable to conjecture that youngsters can adjust their responses if given more time, space and training and if a device does not make greater demands on their capacity throughout the whole process [19]. This considers the ways that are better tuned to children's developing abilities and how they construct meaning through action. Cognition and action working together can be seen in how children exploit physical action to dynamically offload parts of mental operations to physical action in the environment. Cognitive performance is enhanced through physical strategies that simplify the cognitive aspects of task. Furthermore, through natural interaction, children can build abstract knowledge through metaphor [20]. One of the quality factors of gesture as constructed by Barclay is the property of naturalness [21]. He further recommends conducting research to investigate the impact of naturalness not just on general users but on more focused user groups.

2.3 The Measurement of Naturalness

Since naturalness contributes to the effectiveness of a gesture [22], it has been claimed to be one of the quality factors of a gesture [21]. Naturalness can be achieved through the use of symbols [23]; for instance, stretching two fingers to double the size of an image or nodding one's head to indicate a 'yes' command. If a gesture is not natural enough, more time is spent trying to recall it. Therefore, it can be said that naturalness influences the time spent on recalling the gesture. The problem is that if the measurement is taken during the use of a device, the time taken might include the additional time taken to think of which function the user wants to select, and if the user is a child, there is a possibility of the child being distracted by the user interface. For example, a child might take some time to watch a font flashing or wonder how an image is rotating. Therefore, it is suggested that the time taken to call-back a gesture be taken out of the system/device use [21].

3 Initial Study

This section explains the methodology of the study. It covers the participants and materials, the procedures, and the tasks.

3.1 Participants and Materials

Participants comprised 16 pre-school children aged between 5 and 6 years. Initially 20 children agreed to participate but 4 of the participants withdrew. 'Within-subjects design' approach was applied for this study where each participant used two forms of technology under the same conditions and in the same place. This experiment did not intend to investigate the differences of the technologies used, but since the study sample was quite small, this design approach was able to reduce error variance (although this was a qualitative experiment) associated with individual differences. The two forms of natural technologies are free-form and touch-form; in this study, Microsoft Kinect represents the free-form technology and the iPad tablet represents touch-form technology. In this study, a multi-platform game called Kinectimals was chosen, as it allows the user to nurture, interact and play with the cub virtually. Note that despite the game's title that sounds biased towards Kinect, this game was chosen because of its relevant multi-platform game for pre-school children. Other multi-platform games available (at the time this experiment was undertaken) were not suitable (based on local market) for testing because of the complex gesture manipulations required, the huge vocabulary of gesture commands to be remembered, and the unsuitable content for presentation to children. Complex gestures here mean that the gestures required are difficult for children since they involve more complex ergonomics of motion. Unsuitable content refers to content that might disturb children such as violence and pornography.

3.2 The Procedure

Since the goal of this study was to observe the naturalness of children's gesture-based technology, the participants took turns using the technology. Each participant was assigned a number between 1 and 16. Odd-numbered participants used Kinect first and then the iPad tablet. Even-numbered participant used the iPad tablet first and then Kinect. This grouping was made because there was a question and answer session that required participants to call-back selected obvious gestures in the study. For the record, all participants were given 10 minutes (for each gesture-form) to use the device with guidance and an extra 10 minutes to try the device by themselves before the actual experiment was done. All the behaviors and interactions were recorded by video recorders. The recording session was analyzed to note any issues related to naturalness during the device use. The behavioral analysis was also done by four PhD students who were experienced in qualitative studies. This step was taken to increase the confidence level of behavioral data gathered.

3.3 The Tasks

Before the question and answer session was carried out, the participants were assigned three tasks. These tasks were given to highlight the most obvious gestures performed by the participants. The tasks were:

- *Care* – Select a brush and brush / towel the tiger cub.
- *Skills* – Teach skills to the cub such as jumping, barrel-rolling and sitting.
- *Throw game* – Choose a ball and throw the ball towards the objects around the cub.

Since there were three tasks assigned, three call-back gestures were investigated as well. The gestures were 'brush/wash' (brush and wash were regarded as the same function and gesture), 'jump', and 'throw'. For other gestures apart from these three gestures, the call-back times were not taken; however, they were observed and annotated to study the children's behavior.

4 The Findings

In this section, the findings are reported in three subsections: natural in the real world, natural gestures and positive feelings, and call-back times.

4.1 Natural to Reflect the Real World

From the analysis of video recordings, we identified some issues related to natural gesture interactions. When the participants used the free-form technology, gesture commands were easily remembered and called back. One of the most obvious natural gesture commands was 'throw' which is the same as throw in the real world. It starts initially by getting the hand ready at the back position, and then moving the hand forward. The 'throw' also permitted participants to do the gesture in a lower position, as shown in Fig. 1, or higher up which again echoes the real world situation. Most of the gesture commands were similar to natural gesturing except for a few gestures like 'select'. 'Select' in free-form requires participants to hold their hands for about two to three seconds. It was observed that this gesture was confusing to the children, and many of them slowed down their interaction and hesitated to perform the gesture. Perhaps, a gesture that would better reflect the real world would be to point with the forefinger.

Fig. 1. A participant gesturing a ball throw

Gesturing with the touch-form iPad was logically easier to do, but in our observation, some gestures seemed unnatural when it did not reflect the real world. One example was gesture commands that required the performing of complex gestures. For example, as shown in Fig. 2, the participant had difficulty gesturing in a half circle clockwise direction to command the cub to 'roll over'. (This gesture would command the virtual cub to acrobatically roll his body 360°). This gesture is easy for adults, but for the children, it was different as they had to repeat the gesture many times to get the job done. In some cases, participants disengaged with the process and decided to go back to the main menu.

Fig. 2. A gesture to command the cub to 'roll over' failed

4.2 Natural Gesture Leads to Positive Feelings

Natural gesture commands have the potential to kindle and influence participants' feelings. In many video sessions that we observed, participants exhibited positive body language and expression when they were doing natural gestures. These behaviors usually occurred during the use of free-form technology. For instance, the participants smiled while gesturing a throw, laughed while jumping and even talked to the cub while brushing it. These behaviors were less apparent during the use of touch-form technology.

During the interview session, we also asked all the participants about their feelings after each technology use session. The question was based on a 5-point Likert scale smileyometer [24] where we asked them to choose which option best described their feelings, as shown in Fig. 3.

Fig. 3. Smileyometer

For touch-form gestures, 11 participants were 'happy' to use the touch-form iPad and 4 participants were 'very happy' and 1 participant felt 'OK' (see Fig. 4). Results from the use of free-form gestures showed that 8 participants felt 'very happy', 2 participants felt 'happy', and the remaining 6 participants felt 'OK'. From our observations, the results in the touch-form (mainly 'happy') indicated participants' preference for fast and direct interaction. However, free-form interaction was able to elicit more 'very happy' responses than touch-form interaction. We believe, if the system can be improved to avoid gesture misinterpretation, more 'very happy' results can be obtained. This is because, as observed, natural interactions lead to positive feelings, but this was thwarted by many unintended gestures that were interpreted as command gestures. For instance, when participants were adjusting their pants, or clapping their hands in excitement, the body gesture was interpreted as a throw or a swipe. These incidents indirectly affected participants' feelings as the system registered something that they had not intended to do. In worse cases, the participants were afraid to gesture and hid their hands close to their bodies or mouths (in a gesture that indicated that they were afraid). The problem can be solved by either upgrading the detection and interpretation system, or by introducing mechanisms to avoid the misinterpretation of gestures. We plan to implement and evaluate this in the development of a prototype in the future.

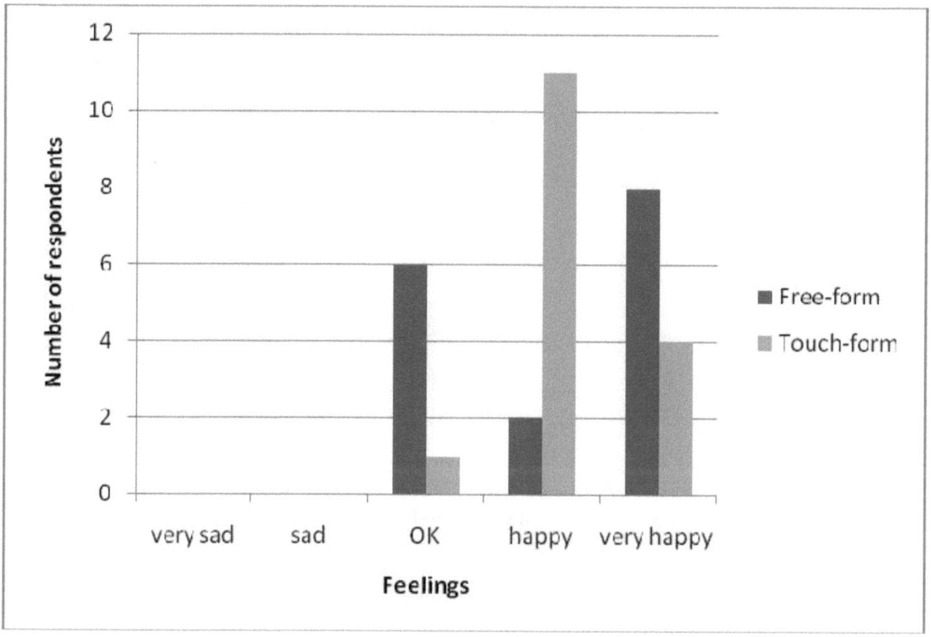

Fig. 4. Participants' feelings after gesture technology use

4.3 Call-Back Times

Since the time taken to call-back a gesture is suggested to be taken out of the system/device use as mentioned earlier in section 2.3, a question and answer session was carried out after the participants completed the activities using the gesture-based technology. Each participant was asked to demonstrate the most obvious gesture in each task. The gestures were 'brush-wash', 'jump' and 'throw ball'. The duration taken for each participant's attempt to answer the question was recorded. The time taken started after each question was asked and the time was stopped when the participant started his/her demonstration. A stopwatch was used, and the time (t) was recorded and logged. The results are shown in Fig. 5.

The graph shows the obvious differences between free-form and touch-form. In free-form device usage, the participants were able to call-back the gestures faster than the call-back in touch-form gestures. Even though data from consent forms showed that more than 90% of participants had touch-form tablets at home and less than 10% of them had free-form console devices at home, the touch-form gestures took about two to five times longer to remember compared to free-form gestures. This showed that children can easily remember natural gestures even though they still young and have little experience about the real world.

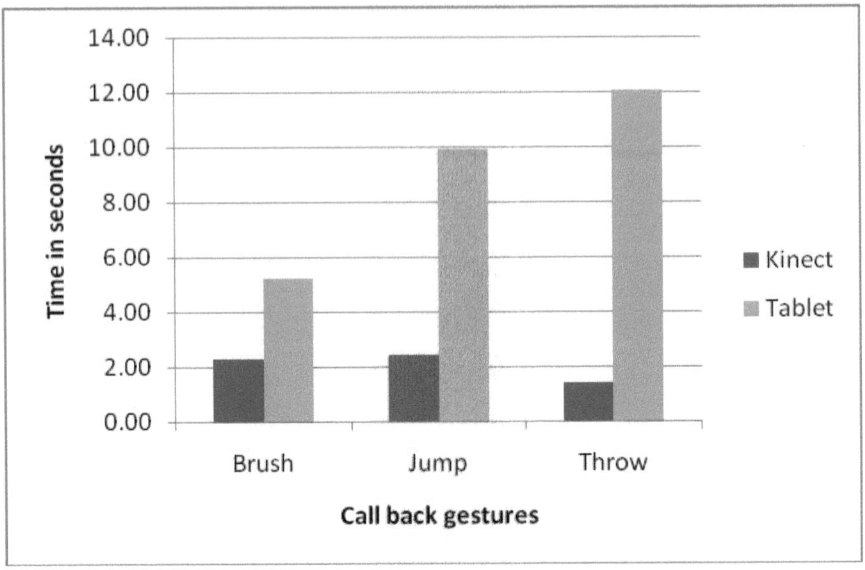

Fig. 5. Time taken to call back the gestures

5 Conclusion

In this paper, we explored the naturalness of recent gesture-based technology and its influence on children's interaction. This study has shown that natural gesture-based interaction benefited the children by enriching their cognitive abilities. Naturalness in gesturing also helped them to reflect gestures in the real-world, and at the same time it made the children happy. The findings of this study suggest that the more natural the gestures implemented for a gesture system, the greater the benefit to children. Natural gestures helped the children engage in gesture interaction by speeding up the interaction; they required less effort to call-back, and eliminated engagement issues such as hesitation and fear when gesturing. These findings add substantially to our understanding of naturalness in gesture-based interaction and can contribute towards better gesture utilization for children.

Acknowledgements. We would like to thank all participants and their parents for participating in the study.

References

1. O'Brien, H.L., Toms, E.G.: What is user engagement? A conceptual framework for defining user engagement with technology. Journal of the American Society for Information Science and Technology 59, 938–955 (2008)
2. Broaders, S.C., Cook, S.W., Mitchell, Z., Goldin-Meadow, S.: Making children gesture brings out implicit knowledge and leads to learning. Journal of Experimental Psychology: General 136, 539 (2007)

3. Rosenfeld, M.C.: All Fingers and Thumbs: Multitouch Interface Design and Implementation. In: Bennett, G., Ante, W., Ash, M., Jackson, B., Mix, N., Peterson, S., Rosenfeld, M.C. (eds.) iPhone Cool Projects, pp. 81–104. Apress, Berkeley (2009)
4. Lee, J.C.: Hacking the Nintendo Wii Remote. IEEE Pervasive Computing 7, 39–45 (2008)
5. Donker, A., Reitsma, P.: Young children's ability to use a computer mouse. Computers & Education 48, 602–617 (2007)
6. Höysniemi, J., Hämäläinen, P., Turkki, L., Rouvi, T.: Children's intuitive gestures in vision-based action games. Communications of the ACM 48, 44–50 (2005)
7. Peters, C., Castellano, G., de Freitas, S.: An exploration of user engagement in HCI. In: Proceedings of the International Workshop on Affective-Aware Virtual Agents and Social Robots, pp. 1–3. ACM, Boston (2009)
8. Stößel, C., Wandke, H., Blessing, L.: Gestural interfaces for elderly users: Help or hindrance? In: Kopp, S., Wachsmuth, I. (eds.) GW 2009. LNCS, vol. 5934, pp. 269–280. Springer, Heidelberg (2010)
9. Karam, M.: A taxonomy of Gestures in Human Computer Interaction. ACM Transactions on Computer Human Interactions, 1–45 (2005)
10. Wang, X., Zhang, X., Dai, G.: Tracking of deformable human hand in real time as continuous input for gesture-based interaction, pp. 235–242. ACM (2007)
11. Pavlovic, V.I., Sharma, R., Huang, T.S.: Visual interpretation of hand gestures for human-computer interaction: A review. IEEE Transactions on Pattern Analysis and Machine Intelligence 19, 677–695 (1997)
12. Shi, J., Zhang, M., Pan, Z.: A real-time bimanual 3D interaction method based on bare-hand tracking. In: Proceedings of the 19th ACM International Conference on Multimedia, pp. 1073–1076. ACM, Scottsdale (2011)
13. Wigdor, D., Wixon, D.: Brave NUI world: designing natural user interfaces for touch and gesture. Morgan Kaufmann (2011)
14. Doe-Hyung, L., Kwang-Seok, H.: Game interface using hand gesture recognition, pp. 1092–1097. IEEE (2010)
15. Xie, L., Antle, A.N., Motamedi, N.: Are tangibles more fun?: Comparing children's enjoyment and engagement using physical, graphical and tangible user interfaces, pp. 191–198. ACM (2008)
16. Druin, A.: The role of children in the design of new technology. Behaviour and Information Technology 21, 1–25 (2002)
17. McKnight, L., Fitton, D.: Touch-screen technology for children: giving the right instructions and getting the right responses. In: Proceedings of the 9th International Conference on Interaction Design and Children, pp. 238–241. ACM, Barcelona (2010)
18. Naeyc, Fred Rogers Center.: Technology and Interactive Media as Tools in Early Childhood Programs (2012)
19. Agudo, J.E., Sánchez, H., Rico, M.: Playing Games on the Screen: Adapting Mouse Interaction at Early Ages. In: IEEE 10th International Conference on Advanced Learning Technologies (ICALT), pp. 493–497 (2010)
20. Antle, A.N., Fernaeus, Y., Marshall, P.: Children and embodied interaction: seeking common ground. In: Proceedings of the 8th International Conference on Interaction Design and Children, pp. 306–308. ACM (2009)
21. Barclay, K., Wei, D., Lutteroth, C., Sheehan, R.: A quantitative quality model for gesture based user interfaces. In: Proceedings of the 23rd Australian Computer-Human Interaction Conference, pp. 31–39. ACM (2011)

22. Lenman, S., Bretzner, L., Thuresson, B.: Computer vision based hand gesture interfaces for human-computer interaction. Royal Institute of Technology, Sweden (2002)
23. Stern, H.I., Wachs, J.P., Edan, Y.: Human factors for design of hand gesture Human-Machine Interaction. In: IEEE International Conference on Systems, Man and Cybernetics (SMC 2006), pp. 4052–4056. IEEE (2006)
24. Read, J.C., MacFarlane, S.: Using the fun toolkit and other survey methods to gather opinions in child computer interaction. In: Proceedings of the 2006 Conference on Interaction Design and Children, pp. 81–88. ACM, Tampere (2006)

Developing Architecture of Haptik Visual Jawi (HV-Jawi)

Maizan Mat Amin[1], Halimah Badioze Zaman[2], and Azlina Ahmad[2]

[1] Faculty of Informatics and Computing, University of Sultan Zainal Abidin (UniSZA), Gong Badak Campus, 21300, Kuala Terengganu, Terengganu, Malaysia; Institute of Visual Informatics, Universiti Kebangsaan Malaysia (UKM), 43600 Bangi, Selangor, Malaysia
maizan@unisza.edu.my

[2] Institute of Visual Informatics, Universiti Kebangsaan Malaysia (UKM), 43600 Bangi, Selangor, Malaysia
{hbz,aa}@ftsm.ukm.my

Abstract. The characteristics of the visual haptic approach complement the need in teaching and learning of proper Jawi handwriting skills in Malaysian educational setting. This paper explores literatures and previous studies on the visual haptic applications focusing on handwriting. The advantages, limitations and possible solutions for each stage will be taken into consideration in designing and developing Haptik Visual-Jawi (HV-Jawi). The development of the HV-Jawi architecture also has been proposed based on the review and findings of the relevant literatures, previous studies, and our preliminary analysis results.

Keywords: haptic, handwriting, jawi, architecture.

1 Introduction

Jawi is a script derived from Arabic alphabets and adopted for the use of Malay language writing. Jawi has been taught as one of the subjects under the Islamic Education in the Malaysian educational setting. Jawi handwriting skills are essential to be properly written by pupils to enable them to read and study in Islamic Education, as well in learning the language of the Al-Quran. Pupils must to master writing and reading Jawi, as the textbooks and examinations in the Islamic Education are constructed using Jawi script [1]. According Muzni [2], pupils are most weak in Jawi writing compared to reading. A review by Nik Rosila has verified that the mastery of writing and reading Jawi skills among pupils are weak and it is significantly correlated with pupils' achievement in Islamic Education [3].

Nik Rosila [3] also reported that the method used in teaching Jawi is not motivating. The situation is very worrying because the pupils will experience the drop-out and it will be difficult for them to understand the syllabus in the higher Islamic Education. The failure or inability of primary school pupils in acquiring basic skills in Jawi especially in handwriting is among the challenges in education today.

H. Badioze Zaman et al. (Eds.): IVIC 2013, LNCS 8237, pp. 729–741, 2013.

Thus, it is important to have an effective learning aid to help the pupils to write proper Jawi and at the same time, build up their interest to master Jawi.

The use of computers and Information and Communication Technology (ICT) have brought a great influence and potential to the world of education. Innovative teaching using various methods, such as multimedia courseware, online teaching and learning resources, the Internet, virtual reality [4], haptic technology, and many others, are important for pupils to learn more intensively and to attract them to keep learning. Visual haptic technology is part of visual informatics that have been explored in improving the teaching and learning process [5]. The combination of haptic technology with visual displays can be exploited in learning or training that requires visual motor integration or hand eye coordination, such as handwriting [6] and [7], surgical operations, and learning [8] and [9]. Our focus will be more on the adaptation in learning cursive Jawi handwriting skills. Several visual haptic applications have been developed for training or teaching and learning handwriting of various language characters such as for cursive Latin, Japanese, Chinese, Arabic, Tamil and Persian, but not in Jawi script so far.

Hence, the aim of our study is to develop a visual haptic learning aid for a proper writing Jawi character called *Haptik Visual-Jawi* (HV-Jawi). This article will highlight the potential of the visual haptic approach which complements the need in learning proper Jawi handwriting skills in Malaysian educational setting. The next section presents the related works on learning cursive Jawi handwriting skills and previous studies on the visual haptics application in handwriting. The suitable solutions from the review and findings will be proposed in developing HV-Jawi.

2 Related Works

2.1 Learning Cursive Jawi Handwriting Skill

Handwriting is an activity of writing by using hand. Hand movements involved in handwriting to support the visual recognition of letters and contributed to the low level of reading skills. The handwriting was part of an important experience for each student. Handwriting mainly involves 30 to 60 percent of the time allocated to primary schools and writing fine motor activities of students [10]. In handwriting, the pupil has to graphomotorically form each letter. Pupils need to produce a graphic shape similar to as much as possible the standard shapes of specific letters [11]. Mastery of writing skills is important to allow children to write neatly, beautiful and organized; a chance to learn proper techniques and writing; ability to understand what was written by them and be able to read what is written.

The learning process of Jawi handwriting has similar learning stages with other languages. As pupils have gone the pre-writing stages, they will have the capacity to start writing on letters. Consequently the early education on handwriting will affect pupils for many years to come. Writing skills should be controlled by emphasizing standards or basic aspects of writing, as early as possible. Trajectory or the movement of the letter is very important as it emphasized the dynamic aspects of letters such as way letters are formed, their point of entry and direction of stroke, than their static shape [12].

Pupils tend to make mistakes in learning Jawi writing as most of the characters in Jawi have various curvatures and forms as shown in Table 1. Moreover, Jawi script which consists of 37 letters [13] are written right to left and based on distinct shapes that vary according to their connection to preceding or following letters [14]. For most of the letter, there are four different shapes. Table 2 depicted Jawi letter letter ڠ (nga) with four different shapes depends on its position. The shape is used depends on the position of letters within its word or subword. According to Sassoon, when we are concentrating on letter forms, writing ceases to be automatic [12]. The learning of correct movement and sequences of writing basic Jawi letters is essential before moving on for further lesson.

Table 1. Various curvatures and forms of cursive Jawi characters

ج	ث	ة	ت	ب	ا
ر	ذ	د	خ	ح	چ
ط	ض	ص	ش	س	ز
ق	ف	ڠ	غ	ع	ظ
ن	م	ل	ݢ	ک	ڤ
ى	ي	ء	ه	ۏ	و
					ڽ

Table 2. Jawi letter ڠ (nga) with different shapes depends on its position

Letter (name)	Isolated	Start	Middle	End
ڠ (nga)	ڠ	ڠـ	ـڠـ	ـڠ

Motor skills refer to skills in which both the movement and the outcome of action are emphasized [16]. Learning to write Jawi characters by hand is difficult task for pupils to learn. Various skills are involved in order to coordinate motor output with sensory (visual and haptic) feedback for producing perfect strokes. The sensory-motor skills of wrist and fingers need to be trained over a long period before the structure and sequence of strokes become familiar. Pupil learn handwriting in different ways: in visual information, extra kinaesthetic feedback and actions to be described orally [40]. All these methods will be benificial and should be employed with a certain amount of repetition and reinforcement to make sure pupil understand what it is being taught. Somehow, the kinaesthetic feedback is essential in handwriting because it is a motor skill and not depend exclusively on visual feedback.

The fine motor skills required in Jawi handwriting also involve good hand-eye coordination and movement [17]. These Jawi handwriting skills can be developed through various pencil activities such scribbling, colouring, channeling, tracing and copying [18]. Scribbling involves drawing continuous lines such wavy or zigzag patterns and colouring activity through shading using different colours in horizontal, vertical or oblique direction within the boundaries. Channeling requires drawing a line between two boundaries and tracing entail joining lines between adjacent points. Copying involves writing or drawing the given letter or pattern. Bennette [15]reported tracing is important because it almost as the teacher is there to guide student's hand to show how to write correctly. Besides that he also suggested to alternates practice exercises between tracing and copying to aids in seeing any mistakes done.

In addition, hands-on learning or training method with the teachers will lead to the reliance on teachers' skills [19] and [20] and the learning process will obviously consume time [21[and [22]. These conventional methods need a new approach to enhance the learning process and to reduce the reliance on teachers. It is vital to explore ways to aid the learning process. Therefore, the visual haptic approach is proposed as the capability of haptic force feedback in guiding and controlling the hand movement of pupils to learn to write proper handwriting of Jawi characters.

2.2 Visual Haptic Approach in Learning Handwriting

Visual haptic technology is part of visual informatics that can be explored to be used by pupils in improving teaching and learning process [5]. Haptic can enhance the virtual environment by allowing pupils to touch and feel. Hayward et al. [23] defined the haptic as the ability to feel natural or synthetic mechanical environment through touch. According to Eid [21], a touch on the object and / or the environment can be done by humans, machines, or a combination of both; where objects and environments can either be real, virtual, or a combination of both, and, the interaction is not necessarily accompanied with other sensory modalities such as vision or hearing.

Haptics can be implemented in four interdisciplinary of research branches as shown in Fig. 1 [21]. The study of human haptic refers to the tactile senses human sensing and manipulation through tactile and kinaesthetic sensations with four subsystems: mechanical, sensory, motor and cognitive functions. Machine haptic involves the process of designing, building and developing mechanical devices that replace or augment the human sense of touch. Meanwhile, computer haptic associated with developing computer algorithms and software to generate and produce a "touch" of the virtual environment and objects. Multimedia haptic involves the process of integrating and coordinating haptic interface data presentations, and other media types in multimedia applications to gain benefit of gesture recognition (gesture), tactile, and force feedback. Each area focuses on different aspects, yet somehow can be interrelated to each other.

Haptic systems are new additions to multimodal systems with a great prospective. There are two types of haptic feedback: tactile feedback and force feedback. Tactile or touch feedback is the term applied to the sensations felt by the skin such as the texture of surfaces, temperature and vibration. Force feedback reproduces directional forces that can result from solid boundaries, the weight of grasped virtual objects, mechanical compliance of an object and inertia. Haptic feedbacks have been applied in many fields such as simulation, teaching and learning aids, medical procedures and training, assistive and rehabilitative devices, and scientific visualisations. The integration of haptic technology with visual displays is very useful and can be explored in learning or training involved with visual motor integration or hand eye coordination.

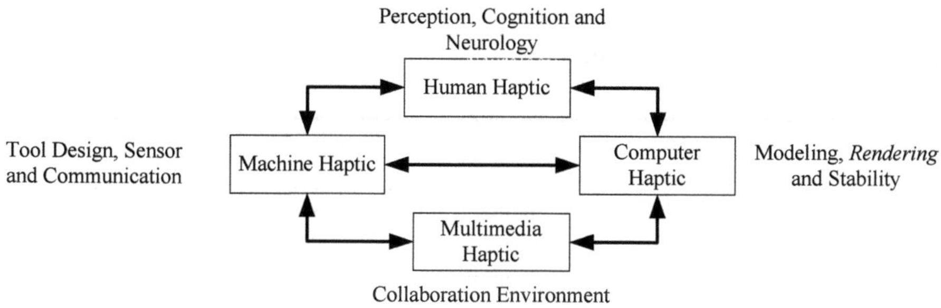

Fig. 1. Interdisciplinary of haptic research branches

Our focus will be more on the adaptation in learning cursive Jawi handwriting skills by utilizing the guidance and control from visual haptic technology. While a computer is an effective environment in which to practice as the user doesn't need to be supervised but can be still monitored, visual haptic technology also can be a strategic tool to learn and practice handwriting. Pupils can keep practicing without or less supervision from the teacher as the haptic application can be developed to guide and evaluate the learning of Jawi handwriting skill. With the haptic technology, teacher's skills can be replicated. Not only pupils can learn the correct formation and movement of Jawi handwriting, yet haptic technology will also decrease the time consumed and provide the equivalent opportunity for all pupils or trainees to learn under the same instructions [24].

3 Developing *Haptik Visual-Jawi* (HV-Jawi) for Learning Jawi Handwriting Skills

The aim of our study is to develop a visual haptic learning aid for a proper writing Jawi character called *Haptik Visual-Jawi* (HV-Jawi). Previous works on visual haptic applications for handwriting and the summary results of our preliminary analysis were presented as input in developing architecture of HV-Jawi.

3.1 Visual Haptic Applications for Handwriting

The potential of haptic force feedback in guiding and controlling the hand movement in learning handwriting has been proven [21] and [25]. Several visual haptic applications have been devoted to training or teaching and learning handwriting of various language characters such as for cursive Latin [22], [26], [27] and [28],

Japanese [29], [30], [31], [32] and [33], Chinese [19] and [34], Arabic [30], Tamil [35] and Persian [24]. Yet, none study had been done to Jawi script. The area is still open to be studied because cursive letters characteristics are different and difficult for new beginner like pupil to learn how to write. Table 3 summarized visual haptic applications or tools that had been developed for handwriting learning or training purposes.

Table 3. Summary of the visual haptic applications or tools developed for handwriting learning or training

Applications / Tools	Language / Script	Details / Findings
Visual Haptic Tool-Telemaque [7, 22, 27]	Cursive Latin Letters	Built a handwriting font based on control points, elliptic arcs and straight lines. Use the beginning of the strokes, the end of the strokes, the vertical tangent points, the horizontal tangent points, the inflexion points and the turn back points as control points. Exercises designed to develop phonemic awareness, knowledge of letters and related letter/sound of children aged 5 years on the understanding and application of the principle characters
Motor rehabilitation training after stroke using haptic handwriting and games [36]	Chinese	As stroke rehabilitation tools to stroke patients to practice motor trainings and improve rehabilitation process, haptic handwriting and Ten Pin Bowling game with the Novint Falcon device Motor rehabilitation using haptic applications is encouraging and motivating, and the effectiveness of the proposed motor training method is confirmed via experiments.
Multimodal Handwriting Instructions for Young Students [37]	English letters	A multimodal system for improving a student's ability to efficiently write printed English letters. The system, overall, provides information from multiple sources a) a visual cue rendered on a computer screen to simulate letters, b) haptic force-feedback (PHANToM Omni), and c) auditory and visual instructions from a teacher
Persian Calligraphy Hand Writing Learning System [24]	Persian	Two different modes of learning : full guidance and partial guidance Hardware: Phantom Omni; Software: OpenGL, Openhaptics, Microsoft Visual C++, MATLAB; Curve fitting: Cubic spline
Visual-Manual Tracking Of trajectories [30]	Japanese and Arabic	Conducted an experiment involving two Japanese alphabets and two Arabic alphabets to compare three training techniques of haptic guidance to analyse the criteria of speed (kinematic) and shape. Findings showed that haptic guidance force feedback generally improved the smoothness of the trajectory tracking of a visual-manual.

Table 3. (*Continued*)

Applications / Tools	Language / Script	Details / Findings
Hand Writing and Multimedia Learning Assessment Tools [21, 38]	English, Chinese, Japanese, French and Arabic	Combining haptic sensory modalities to enhance the ability to learn and a smooth writing letters: English, Chinese, Japanese, French and Arabic; Used XML-based schema (easy to introduce new characters) Learning and assessment mode; Guidance mode and the aid may be adjusted by the user; Assessment - Dynamic Time Warping (DTW)
Chinese Calligraphy Simulation System [19]	Chinese	Modeled Chinese characters based on the combination of sequential strokes. Characters classified into combination of basic (described by third order Bezier curves) and complex strokes Simulation with/without force feedback has been compared and the results indicate using haptic feedback in Chinese calligraphy training system is helpful to reduce writing error and to improve writing speed.
Robotic Teachers of Chinese handwriting [34]	Chinese	Introduce a virtual teaching system for Chinese ideograms Guides movement by haptic and visual with a powerful 6DOF haptic interface and the reflection of the image ensure transparent virtual manipulation with undistorted hand-eye coordination. Learning process : motion guidance and path constraining. Guidance mode and assistance levels can be adapted to the user and optimized for learning. Users performance and progress is quantitatively evaluated: shape, motion, force and smoothness.
Interactive System for improving Japanese handwriting [32]	Japanese	Deals with an application of Reactive Robot System implementation using Haptic interaction as a skill transfer system to teach people to write Japanese characters Implemented a modeling system based on discrete Hidden Markov Models.
Virtual Japanese Calligraphy System [33]	Japanese	Developed a system for teaching Japanese calligraphy using a record and play strategy, primarily utilizing force information. After the system proven highly effective, they use a position based control method.

Based on previous works, visual haptic applications can be a good learning medium to support the learning of handwriting skills. Most of the visual haptic applications that have been developed enhanced conventional methods, practices and assessments in training or teaching and learning handwriting skills. These applications experimented the learning with full guidance, half guidance and no guidance of haptic device. These studies also have shown that the visual haptic approach is proven to reduce mistakes and improve handwriting skills. Performance and progress of users are evaluated based on various criteria such as shape, motion, force, speed and smoothness. The development method used in character modeling phase is diverse depends on the focus and scope of the research. Beziers, Splines and mathematical models used to accomplish their research purposes.

3.2 Results of Preliminary Analysis

An effort to help pupils in learning Jawi handwriting skills has prompted the researchers to develop a visual haptic application called *Haptik-Visual Jawi* (HV-Jawi). A preliminary study has been conducted to determine the current approach of teaching and learning Jawi handwriting skills in Malaysian educational setting, and the potential of the haptic visual approach in the process [20]. The study involved the teachers, pupils and the experts in Jawi. The study has explored current problems, teaching and learning methods used, frequent mistakes done by pupils, and related issues in learning Jawi handwriting skills. Fig. 2 presents the methods used in this preliminary analysis. The study was done throughout questionnaires for teacher, interview with experts and observations. The details of the method used in this preliminary study had been reported in [20].

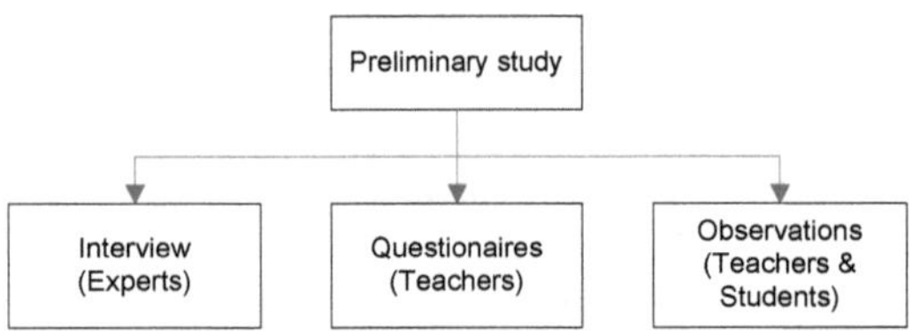

Fig. 2. Methods used in preliminary study

The results show that lack of emphasize of the basic Jawi character formation in the beginning process of learning handwriting will create more mistakes in further lesson. It is important for the pupils to have the right basic Jawi handwriting skill on the early stage. It also shows that the current approach is too reliant on skills and presence of teachers either in the learning or/and assessment process. The results of the preliminary analysis are summarized in Table 4.

Table 4. Summary of the preliminary analysis results [20] based on conventional approach in Jawi teaching and learning; and potential offers by the haptic approach

	Conventional approach	Haptic approach
Practices	With the help from teachers	With the help of haptic devices
Teaching methods	Teacher-reliant	Visual-haptic application tool and self-reliant
Learning methods	Teachers hold pupils' hands, tracing and copying	Full guidance Half guidance No guidance

Table 4. (*Continued*)

Assessment of mistakes	Teachers' assessment Assessment by output	Haptic application's evaluation Assessment by output or/and process of writing
Instructions	Teachers concentrate more to weak pupils	The haptic application provides an equivalent opportunity for all pupils to learn under the same instructions
Advancement	Group advancement	Individual advancement

This research highlighted on learning proper Jawi handwriting. It is one of the important learning outcomes of Jawi lessons in Malaysian educational setting. The application will emphasize on the sequences, direction and standard shape of proper writing cursive Jawi letters. We believe the abundance of process in producing Jawi letters lead pupils to make mistakes. It's become worse if they repeat the same mistakes in further lesson. As our concern is the process in writing, as well as the output, the application will utilize dynamic data for learning and assessment purposes. Fig. 3 depicts the conventional and the visual haptic approach in learning Jawi handwriting skills. Our goal is to develop a teaching and learning aid that will result in improving Jawi handwriting skills taking advantage of the force feedback provided by the haptic device.

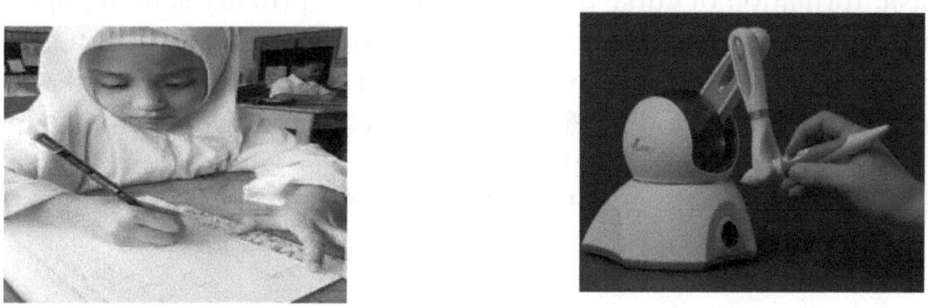

a) Conventional Approach b) Visual Haptic Approach

Fig. 3. (a) Conventional approach and (b) Visual Haptic approach in learning cursive Jawi

3.3 Developing Architecture of Haptik-Visual Jawi (HV-Jawi)

It is expected that the visual haptic application able to enhance the process of teaching and learning in Jawi handwriting skills in Malaysian educational setting. Our study will use a visual haptic approach and apply to conventional methods and process in Jawi learning handwriting skills. The application will improve the conventional learning and the assessment process. The content will engross copying and tracing activities with the guidance and control of force feedback haptic. Full guidance guides the user to follow a pre-recorded trajectory by applying proper force to the pupil's hand in representing how teacher's hold pupil's hand in teaching how to write. Partial guidance offers the combination of haptics and visual feedback guides the pupil and prevents deviation from the desired trajectory, in place of tracing or channeling activity. Meanwhile copying activity will be done with no haptic guidance but maybe with visual guidance instruction. The elements of acquisition model in theories of learning and scaffolding approach also will be employed in this application.

Visual haptic technology and force feedback capabilities also can be a strategic tool to learn and practice handwriting. Pupils can keep practicing without or less supervision from the teacher as the haptic application can be developed to guide and evaluate the learning of Jawi handwriting skill. The teachers' guide will be replicated using a haptic device as teachers cannot assess the correct stroke order, unless they are present during the process of writing. In this case, haptic technology can mimic the role played by teachers in teaching and evaluating the correct way of writing. This application will employ online handwriting recognition for the assessment purpose. It is because the learning in handwriting is happening during the process not as the product only. It is also important to pupil to know their mistakes during the process of writing. In addition the application will provide visualisation part to show the trajectory done by the pupil.

Haptic device named Phantom Omni will be used in different level of guidance and control during the learning. Phantom Omni is a serial 6-DOF (x,y,z and pitch, roll, yaw) input, 3-DOF (x,y,z) output device. This application will use OpenGL, C++ and OpenHaptics software to support haptic device used. The lesson scope will be on the learning basic formation of cursive Jawi character for primary school pupils. Based on the review and findings of the relevant literatures, previous studies and our preliminary analysis results, development life cycle model and development architecture have been proposed. Fig. 4 shows the Interactive-Evolution-Involvement HV-Jawi (IEPHV-Jawi) Life Cycle Model that has been adapted from Iterative-Evolution-Involvement MEL-SindD (IEP-MEL-SindD) Life Cycle Model [39].

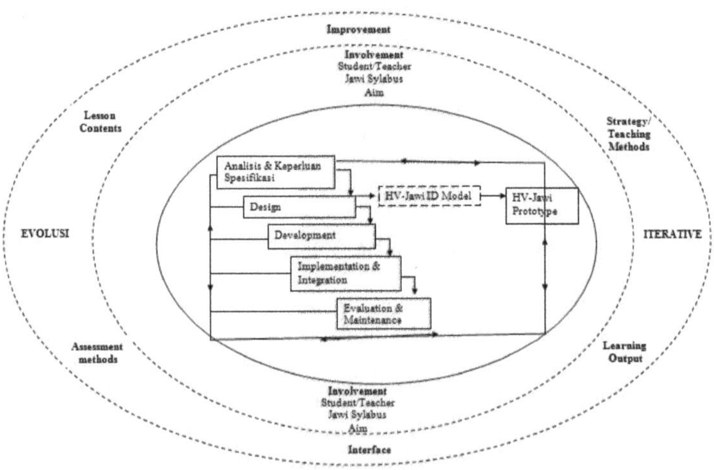

Fig. 4. Interactive-Evolution-Involvement HV-Jawi (IEPHV-Jawi) Development Life Cycle Model

While, Fig. 5 illustrates the development architecture of HV-Jawi that consists of task planning and simulation engine. The task-planning part is essential component to ensure realistic force interaction and to decompose the skills into important control commands during Jawi handwriting process for a haptic device. The simulation engine part involves Jawi character modelling, collision detection and force model.

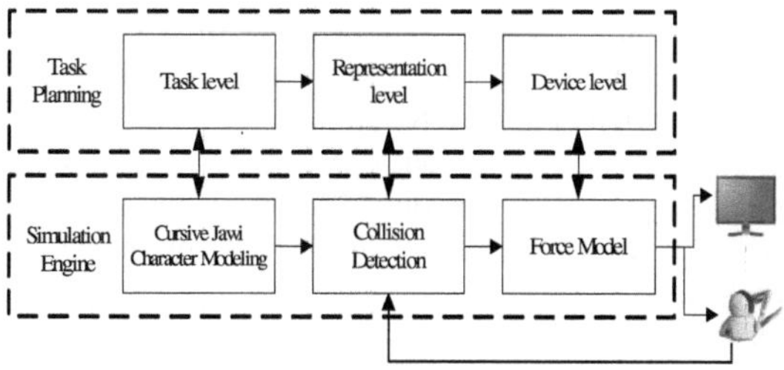

Fig. 5. Development architecture of HV-Jawi

4 Conclusion and Future Works

The visual haptic approach offers a big potential in helping pupils in learning Jawi handwriting skills. It is expected that the visual haptic application can enhance the conventional process of teaching and learning in Jawi handwriting skills with the help of guidance and control of force feedback haptic. The application also aimed to help primary school pupils in learning proper Jawi handwriting skills. The development architecture of HV-Jawi is proposed based on reviews and findings of the relevant literatures and works; and also our preliminary analysis results. The elements of acquisition model in theories of learning and scaffolding approach also will be employed in this application. The advantages, limitations and possible solutions will take into consideration in designing and developing HV-Jawi.

References

1. Nordin, A.L., Ahmad, M.Y.: Penilaian Dalam Pendidikan Islam. In: Seminar Penyelidikan Jangka Pendek 2003, Kuala Lumpur, Malaysia, March 11-12. Universiti Malaya (2003) (unpublished)
2. Borhan, M.: Penguasaan Pelajaran Jawi Di Kalangan Murid Tahun Lima Di Sekolah-sekolah Rendah Daerah Tampin, Negeri Sembilan Darul Khusus, Bangi, Universiti Kebangsaan Malaysia (1995)
3. Yaacob, N.R.N.: Penguasaan Jawi dan Hubungannya dengan Minat dan Pencapaian Pelajar dalam Pendidikan Islam. Malaysian Journal of Educators and Education 22, 161–172 (2007)
4. Parhizkar, B., Badioze Zaman, H.: Development of an Augmented Reality Rare Book and Manuscript for Special Library Collection (AR Rare-BM). In: Badioze Zaman, H., Robinson, P., Petrou, M., Olivier, P., Schröder, H., Shih, T.K. (eds.) IVIC 2009. LNCS, vol. 5857, pp. 344–355. Springer, Heidelberg (2009)

5. Zaman, H.B.: Simbiosis Seni, Sains dan Teknologi Berasingan ke Multimedia-Fusion. Penerbit UKM, Bangi (2009) ISBN 978-967-942-896-4
6. Mullins, J., Mawson, C., Nahavandi, S.: Haptic handwriting aid for training and rehabilitation. In: IEEE International Conference on Systems, Man and Cybernatics. IEEE (2006)
7. Bara, F., Gentaz, E.: Haptics in teaching handwriting: The role of perceptual and visuo-motor skills. Human Movement Science (2011)
8. Gillenwater, C., et al.: Running Head: HAPTICS, PRESENCE, & HCI (2008)
9. Williams II, R.L., Chen, M.Y., Seaton, J.M.: Haptics-augmented high school physics tutorials. International Journal of Virtual Reality 5(1) (2002)
10. Marr, D., Windsor, M., Cermak, S.: Handwriting readiness: Locatives and visuo-motor skills in the kindergarten year. Early Childhood Research and Practice 3(1), 1–16 (2006)
11. Mangen, A., Velay, J.L.: Digitizing literacy: Reflections on the haptics of writing. Journal of Advances in Haptics, 385–401 (2006)
12. Sassoon, R.: Handwriting problems in the secondary school. Sage Publications Limited (2006)
13. dan Pustaka, D.B.: Daftar kata bahasa Melayu: Rumi-Sebutan-Jawi. Dewan Bahasa dan Pustaka (2008)
14. Rahman, H.A.: Panduan menulis dan mengeja Jawi. Dewan Bahasa dan Pustaka (1999)
15. Bennette, J.: Calligraphy for Dummies. Wiley Publishing (2007)
16. Newell, K.: Motor skill acquisition. Annual Review of Psychology 42(1), 213–237 (1991)
17. Man, C.S.C.: Pendekatan Pengajaran Jawi, pp. xvi–225. Dewan Bahasa dan Pustaka (2006)
18. Saad, C.M., Hamid, Z.A.: Lancar Jawi 1. Al-Ameen (2008)
19. Wang, D., Zhang, Y., Yao, C.: Stroke-based modeling and haptic skill display for Chinese calligraphy simulation system. Virtual Reality 9(2), 118–132 (2006)
20. Mat Amin, M., Badioze Zaman, H., Ahmad, A.: Preliminary study on haptic approach in learning jawi handwriting skills. In: Badioze Zaman, H., Robinson, P., Petrou, M., Olivier, P., Shih, T.K., Velastin, S., Nyström, I. (eds.) IVIC 2011, Part II. LNCS, vol. 7067, pp. 168–179. Springer, Heidelberg (2011)
21. Eid, M., Orozco, M., El Saddik, A.: A guided tour in haptic audio visual environments and applications. International Journal of Advanced Media and Communication 1(3), 265–297 (2007)
22. Palluel-Germain, R., et al.: A Visuo-haptic device-Telemaque-increases kindergarten children's handwriting acquisition. In: Proceedings of IEEE World Haptics, pp. 72–77 (2007)
23. Hayward, V., et al.: Haptic interfaces and devices. Sensor Review 24(1), 16–29 (2004)
24. Boroujeni, M.M., Meghdari, A.: Haptic Device Application in Persian Calligraphy. In: International Conference on Computer and Automation Engineering (2009)
25. Morris, D., et al.: Haptic feedback enhances force skill learning. In: Second Joint EuroHaptics Conference and Symposium on Haptic Interfaces for Virtual Environment and Teleoperator Systems, World Haptics 2007. IEEE (2007)
26. Steinherz, T., et al.: Offline loop investigation for handwriting analysis. IEEE Transactions on Pattern Analysis and Machine Intelligence 31(2), 193–209 (2008)
27. Hennion, B., et al.: Telemaque, a new visuo-haptic interface for remediation of dysgraphic children. IEEE (2005)
28. Wang, J., et al.: Learning-based cursive handwriting synthesis (2002)
29. Nishino, H., et al.: A Japanese Calligraphy Trainer Based on Skill Acquisition Through Haptization. IEEE (2010)

30. Bluteau, J., et al.: Haptic guidance improves the visuo-manual tracking of trajectories. PLoS ONE 3(3) (2008)
31. Bayart, B., Pocheville, A., Kheddar, A.: An adaptive haptic guidance software module for I-Touch: example through a handwriting teaching simulation and a 3D maze. In: Proceedings of the Haptic Audio Visual Environments and their Applications, Ottawa, Canada (2005)
32. Solis, J., Avizzano, C.A., Bergamasco, M.: Teaching to write Japanese characters using a haptic interface. IEEE Computer Society (2002)
33. Henmi, K., Yoshikawa, T.: Virtual lesson and its application to virtual calligraphy system. In: Proceedings of the IEEE International Conference on Robotics and Animations. IEEE Press (1998)
34. Teo, C.L., Burdet, E., Lim, H.P.: A robotic teacher of Chinese handwriting. In: Proceedings of 10th Haptic Interfaces for Virtual Environment and Teleoperator Systems (2002)
35. Li, X., et al.: A novel and robust algorithm to model handwriting skill for haptic applications. IEEE (2009)
36. Xu, Z., Yu, H., Yan, S.: Motor rehabilitation training after stroke using haptic handwriting and games. In: Proceedings of the 4th International Convention on Rehabilitation Engineering & Assistive Technology. Singapore Therapeutic, Assistive & Rehabilitative Technologies (START) Centre (2010)
37. Fisackerly, S., Zadeh, M.H.: Haptic-enabled virtual handwriting: Multimodal handwriting instructions for young students. IEEE (2010)
38. Mansour, M., Eid, M., El Saddik, A.: A Multimedia Handwriting Learning and Evaluation Tool. In: Proc. Intelligent Interactive Learning Object Repositories (I2LOR), Montreal, QC, Canada (2007)
39. Yussof, R.L.: Metodologi Pembangunan Perisian Kursus Bacaan untuk Murid Sindrom Down (MELb-SindD). Universiti Kebangsaan Malaysia (2009)
40. Sassoon, R.: Handwriting the way to teach it. Pat Savage Publications (2003)

An Investigation of the Factors That Influence Students' Intention to Adopt E-Learning

Mohamed Hussain Thowfeek[1] and Azizah Jaafar[2]

[1] Faculty of Management and Commerce, South Eastern University of Sri Lanka (SEUSL), University Park, Oluvil 32360, Sri Lanka
thowfeek@seu.ac.lk
[2] Institute of Visual Informatics, Universiti Kebangsaan Malaysia (UKM), 43600 UKM Bangi, Malaysia
azizah@ivi.ukm.my

Abstract. Universities and other educational institutions around the world are increasingly using e-learning technology to more efficiently and effectively deliver the education to their students. Successful implementation of e-learning system is determined by the acceptance of such system by students. Therefore this study was undertaken to explore the factors that influence the intention of students to adopt e-learning at the South Eastern University of Sri Lanka (SEUSL) and the investigation was carried out by using UTAUT model. It was found that, performance expectancy, effect expectancy and facilitation conditions are the important factors, that are influencing students' intention to adopt e-learning, and the results are contributory for the development of a strategy for implementing e-learning system at this university. It was also found that, both, the university and students are capable of adopting e-learning system.

Keywords: e-learning, adoption, utuat, technology acceptance.

1 Introduction

Information and communication technology (ICT) has created better prospects for education. Today, most of the universities and education organizations are using e-learning technology to deliver the education to their students, more efficiently and effectively. In the recent years, there is a significant growth in the design and implementation of e-learning systems [1]. The advent of digital network technologies has altered the way of conducting educational program and offered totally new opportunities [2]. E-learning, which is considered as a useful method and an innovative approach for better teaching and learning, enhances the learner's knowledge, skills, or other performance [3]. The e-learning method enables the paradigm shift of the education, from teacher centered to learner-centered [4], and provides many advantages, such as, cost reduction, elimination of time restriction and physical barrier, and provides an alternative way for improving the traditional classroom instructions [5]. In addition to these, e-learning is also regarded as an alternative tool for those students who are having some social restriction to attend

H. Badioze Zaman et al. (Eds.): IVIC 2013, LNCS 8237, pp. 742–752, 2013.

campus programs [6] and [7]. Further, it provides students with increased information accessibility, improved content delivery, customized instruction, accountability, on-demand availability, self-pacing, interactivity, confidence, and better convenience [8].

Students, faculties, educational administrators and employers are the main stakeholders of e-learning [9]. The benefits brought by the e-learning system inspire all the stakeholders to accept e-learning system around the globe. A large number of studies have been carried out by researchers on e-learning acceptance. When an institution introduces an e-learning system, it has to consider different factors that influence the decision of the users on how and when they use the particular system. Most of the studies on e-learning adoption have focused on students, and have explored the factors influencing their adoption behavior [10].

Technology acceptance model (TAM) is the widely used theory to study the technology adoption behavior. In a critical review and meta-analysis of TAM, it was found that, the TAM was a useful and powerful model [11] and [12]. It is also confirmed in a meta-analysis of e-learning technology acceptance studied by Sumak et al. [10] that,_TAM was widely used. However, the confusion created by the expansions of TAM by many researchers [11] and the exclusion of mandatory situation of real-life organization in the TAM [12], let researchers to comprehend the need of discovering a robust theory to study technology adoption behavior. Consequently, the unified theory of acceptance and use of technology (UTAUT) was presented by Venkatesh et al. [13]. The UTAUT model is widely used to study technology acceptance behavior in various fields. However, Sumak et al. [10] have further asserted in their meta-analysis of e-learning technology acceptance that, UTAUT was used in one single research in the context of student acceptance of e-learning.

Though UTUAT is considered as a superior, explanatory and predictive theory, it has not been commonly used to study e-learning adoption behavior of students. Therefore the primary objective of this study is to use UTAUT to investigate students' intention to adopt e-learning and to find out the factors influencing their adoption behavior.

2 Theoretical Background

The research on technology adoption has drawn considerable attention of researchers all over the world, and many researchers have embarked on experimental researches and investigated the factors influencing acceptance of technologies.

The first principle theory evolved to study the individual technology acceptance behavior is the theory of reasoned action (TRA) [14]. Attitudes and subjective norms are the two key constructs in TRA that determine behavioral intention to perform the behavior. Technology acceptance model (TAM), which was developed by Davis [15] based on TRA, is the mostly used theory in a number of studies relevant to technology acceptance. TAM uses two beliefs, perceived usefulness and perceived ease of use, to predict technology acceptance. Perceived usefulness is defined as "the degree to which a person believes that, using a particular system would enhance his/her job performance"; and perceived ease of use is defined as "the degree to which a person believes that, using a particular system would be free of effort" [15]. These two key beliefs influence the attitude of individuals to use a particular technology.

Theory of planned behavior (TPB) is another extension of TRA [16]. This theory added an additional construct, perceived behavioral control to TRA. It is a theory that predicts deliberate behavior, because, behavior can be deliberative and planned, it is not always voluntary or under control. Motivation was found as a key determinant of behavior in a variety of studies that resulted in the formation of the model, called motivational model (MM) [17], which uses two border classes of motivation, intrinsic and extrinsic motivation. Taylor and Todd [18] have argued that, TAM is unclear in predicting behavior of inexperienced users, therefore they have combined TAM and TPB to form a hybrid model called combined TAM and TPB (C-TAM-TPB). Many researchers have tested TRA in sociological and psychological research settings, and found it to be lacking in certain respect [19], and it was proposed to modify and redefine many of the same concepts and constructs [20]. Consequently, the model of PC utilization (MPCU) was introduced [19, 20]. The other important model is social cognitive theory (SCT), developed by Bandura [21], and extended by Compeau and Higgins [22]. The SCT postulates that, human functioning results from interactions among personal factors, behaviors, and environmental conditions. Innovation diffusion theory (IDT) is another frequently cited theory. This theory explores and helps to explain the adoption of an innovation [23] and [24]. Innovation, communication channels, time, and social system are the four key components of the diffusion of innovations.

2.1 The UTAUT Model

The comparison of conceptual and empirical similarities of the eight major technological acceptance theories is the foundation for the formation of the refined theory, called 'UTAUT'.

The use of information systems in organizations is often mandatory, but most of the studies on information systems had been conducted in voluntary contexts, and theories were formulated based on the findings [13]. Venkatesh et al. [13] have identified a number of limitations in the previous studies, and formulated this unified model. The UTAUT aims to explain user intentions to use an information system (IS) and subsequent usage behavior. It was evidenced that the UTAUT model can explain up to 70% of the variance of usage intention, which is a very a higher prediction ability and a major improvement [25] and [26].

This theory was formulated with four core determinants of IT acceptance, and other four variables that moderate the key relationships.

Performance expectancy is defined as "the degree to which an individual believes that using the system will help him or her to attain gains in job performance" [13, p. 447]. UTUAT explains that, performance expectancy is equivalent to perceived usefulness from TAM, extrinsic motivation from MM, Job-fit from MPCU, relative advantage from IDT, and outcome expectations from ICT.

Effort expectancy is defined as "the degree of ease associated with the use of the system" [13, p. 450]. Effort expectancy is an inclusion of perceived ease of use from TAM, complexity from MPCU and ease of use from IDT.

Social influence is defined as "the degree to which an individual perceives that important others believe he or she should use the new system" [13, p. 451]. UTUAT warrants the social influence is similar construct like subjective norm from TRA, TAM and C-TAM-TPB, social factors from MPCU, and Image from IDT.

Facilitating conditions are defined as "the degree to which an individual believes that an organizational and technical infrastructure exists to support use of the system" [13, p. 453]. The root constructs for facilitating conditions are perceived behavioral control (TBP, C-TAM-TBP), facilitating conditions (MPCU), and compatibility (IDT).

The variables gender, age, experience and voluntariness of use moderate the effects on the acceptance of IT.

2.2 Research Model and Hypotheses

The objective of this study is to use UTUAT model to investigate students' intention to adopt e-learning. The main constructs of UTAUT, such as, performance expectancy, effect expectancy, social influence and facilitating conditions were taken into account to structure the research model (see fig. 1). The moderating variables, such as, gender, age, experience and voluntariness of use have been dropped from the model, due to the fact that, these were assumed not having moderating impact on the main constructs.

It was found in a research conducted among relatively same age and young work force, the moderating variable, age, has not moderated the influence of performance expectancy on behavioral intentions to use computers [27]. In an another study of e-government adoption, Barua [28] found that, nearly all the employees have similar experience, and it was mandatory for them to use the applications, therefore, he has removed all the moderating variables, as they are controlled in the study.

This present research was also conducted among the students of same age group and relatively same level experiences in relation to use of IT. A situation of voluntary use of e-learning will not normally exist in the universities here in Sri Lanka. If the management plans to introduce the system, every student will have to use it compulsorily. In UTUAT, for example, it was theorized that, the influence of performance expectancy on behavioral intention will be moderated by gender and age [13]. As there is always a mandatory situation exists in current research setting, the gender differences and voluntariness of use also cannot have moderating impact on the adoption of e-learning. Thus, by excluding the moderating variables, we have derived the following hypotheses:

H_1: Performance expectancy will positively influence the students' behavioral intention to adopt e-learning.

H_2: Effort expectancy will positively influence the students' behavioral intention to adopt e-learning.

H_3: Social influence will positively influence the students' behavioral intention to adopt e-learning.

H_4: Facilitating condition will positively influence the students' behavioral intention to adopt e-learning.

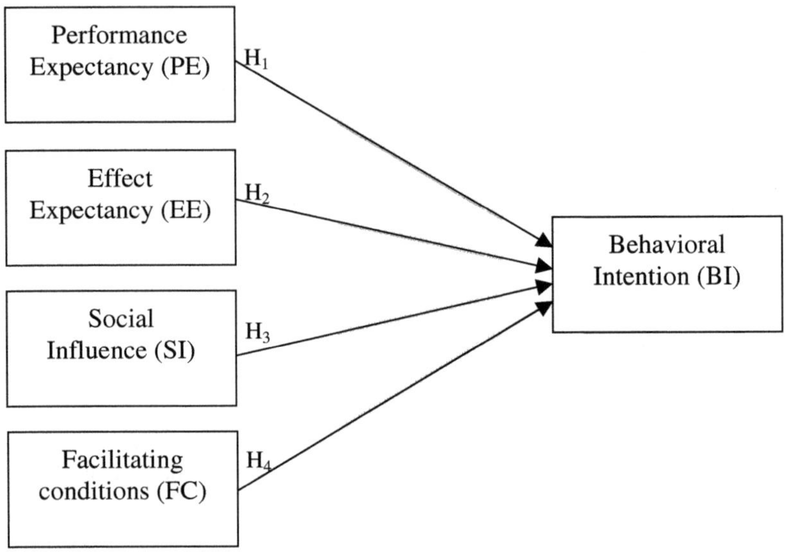

Fig. 1. Research Model

3 Research Methodology

This survey was conducted among the final year students of South Eastern University of Sri Lanka (SEUSL), representing three faculties: Faculty of Management and Commerce, Faulty of Arts and Culture, and Faculty of Islamic Studies & Arabic Languages.

The survey instrument consisted of two parts. The first part used nominal scales to collect the demographic information of the respondents. The second part used subjective measures to evaluate respondents' intention with regards to the adoption of e-learning. Since this study is based on UTUAT theory, the items for the survey instrument to measure the behavioral intention, performance expectancy, effort expectancy, social influence, and facilitating conditions were adapted from the UATUT, and measured using a five-point Likert scale, ranging from 1- strongly disagree to 5 - strongly agree, with the mid-point (3) representing the state of uncertain or neutral.

Convenience sampling is thought to be appropriate to conduct study among people or other units that are readily available [29]. Students are busy with their studies and assignments, and sometimes they are reluctant to participate in survey. Therefore, the students who were readily available in their lecture halls after their lectures were approached to conduct this study. Those who voluntarily agreed to take part in the survey were requested to remain in the hall, and the survey questionnaires were distributed among them. In order to make sure that the sample should be representative of the whole population, three consecutive surveys at their relevant faculties were conducted in the same manner, and totally 112 questionnaires were distributed and collected successfully, and it was found that, all questionnaires were in usable state.

4 Result and Discussion

The respondents' demographic information collected as part of the survey has been illustrated in the table 1. Possessing a personal computer and the availability of Internet connection would facilitate and enhance learning activities carried out via the e-learning mode. About 88 percent of students of SEUSL have got their own computer, either laptop or desktop, and around 71 percent of them have Internet connection at their homes. Though 29 percent of them did not have the Internet connection at home, they have free access to computer and the Internet at university. While, 33 percent of them said that, they access the Internet at home, majority of them (around 55 percent) said that, they browse the Internet at university very frequently. The reasons for majority of the students access the Internet at university can be attributed to their availability and staying inside the campus. Further, about 13 percent of the students have their own device (dongle) to access the Internet, at anytime and anywhere. All of the students access the Internet every day, and majority of them (above 76 percent) allocate more than one hour to browse the Internet for various purposes.

Table 1. Demographic information of respondents

Item	Categories	Sample size	Percentage
Gender	Male	66	58.9
	Female	46	41.1
Own a personal computer	Yes	99	88.4
	No	13	11.6
Internet connection at home	Yes	80	71.4
	No	32	28.6
Frequent Internet access	Home	37	33.0
	University	61	54.5
	Other	14	12.5
Hours of Internet access per day	Less than 1 hour	38	33.9
	Between 1 to 3 hours	58	51.8
	More than 3 hours	16	14.3

The analysis of demographic information exhibits that, a very optimistic scenario exists for the implementation of an e-learning system at SEUSL, and the capability of the students, in terms of knowledge and facilities to embark on the e-learning mode is also optimal. However, it is necessary to examine other important factors that influence their intention to adopt e-learning system.

The items for the survey instrument to measure the behavioral intention, such as, performance expectancy (PE), effort expectancy (EE), social influence (SI), and facilitating conditions (FC) were adapted from the UATUT, and the reliability analyses were conducted to know patterns of internal consistency of the items in the instrument. The Cronbach's α reliability test, shown in table 2 indicates that, the Alpha values for all constructs are above the recommended scores of 0.6 [30]. This shows that, the survey instrument can be used to measure what is supposed to measure.

Table 2. Cronbach's α reliability test

Construct	No. of items	Cronbach's Alpha
PE	4	0.826
EE	3	0.715
SI	3	0.627
FC	4	0.684

The data reduction technique, factor analysis, to reduce a large number of variables to a smaller set of underlying factors was also done, using principle component analysis method and varimax method. The table 3 illustrates the factor loading analysis of the surveys items used to measure the constructs. The items which fall within the each construct surpassing the ceiling value of 0.5 [31] have been exhibited in the table. All the items used to measure the performance expectancy (PE) and facilitating conditions (FC) have been extracted; whereas the item no.4 to measure effect expectancy (EE) and the item no.1 to measure social influence (SI) were removed from the analysis, since these two items had achieved a lower value than the recommended value of 0.5.

Table 3. Factor loading analysis of survey items

	1	2	3	4
PE 1	0.778			
PE 2	0.604			
PE 3	0.794			
PE 4	0.811			
EE 1		0.672		
EE 2		0.845		
EE 3		0.812		
SI 2			0.557	
SI 3			0.802	
SI 4			0.748	
FC 1				0.764
FC 2				0.814
FC 3				0.680
FC 4				0.505

Following the factor analysis, we had performed correlation analyses to investigate the relationship between the independent variables (performance expectancy, effect expectancy, social influences, and facilitating condition) and dependent variable (behavioral intention to adopt e-learning). Subsequently bivariate liner regression analyses were also separately executed between each independent variables and dependent variable, to examine the strength of the relations, and thereby hypotheses are tested and proved.

Table 4 shows correlation coefficient (r) and the associated significant values (p). The performance expectancy, which is explained by the perception of a person using e-learning system would enhance his/her, learning performances and would influence their behavioral intention to adopt e-learning. The correlation coefficient of the performance expectancy (PE) (r=0.781, p=0.000) confirmed that, there is a strong positive relationship with behavioral intention (BI) to adopt e-learning.

Effort expectancy is the degree of ease associated with the use of the system. If a person believes that, using e-learning system is easy, then he or she tends to use it. The correlation coefficient of the Effort expectancy (EE) (r=0.660, p=0.004) also confirmed in this study that, there is a positive correlation between EE and BI to adopt e-learning.

The correlation coefficient of social influence (SI) (r=0.379) indicates the positive correlation with BI, but it is statistically not a significant correlation, because p value (0.072) is grater the 0.05. Here the students perceive that, important people do not believe that, he or she should use e-learning new system.

If the facilitating conditions (FC), such as, organizational and technical infrastructure exists to support use of e-learning system, then students' intention to use e-learning will be stimulated, thereby, they would adopt it. The correlation coefficient of FC (r=0.692, p=0.000) exhibits that, there is a positive and significant correlation between FC and BI.

Table 4. Correlation Analysis

		BI
PE	Correlation Coefficient	0.781
	Sig. (2-tailed)	0.000
EE	Correlation Coefficient	0.660
	Sig. (2-tailed)	0.004
SI	Correlation Coefficient	0.379
	Sig. (2-tailed)	0.072
FC	Correlation Coefficient	0.692
	Sig. (2-tailed)	0.000

Table 5 summarizes the hypotheses test. Except the hypothesis H_4 (social influence will positively influence the students' behavioral intention to adopt e-learning), all other three hypothesized associations were strongly significant at $p<0.05$. The behavioral intention to adopt e-learning is determined by performance expectancy

(β=0.533, p<0.000), effort expectancy (β=0.245, p<0.004) and facilitating conditions (β= 0.309, p<0.000). Therefore, three hypotheses (H_1: performance expectancy will positively influence the students' behavioral intention to adopt e-learning, H_2: effort expectancy will positively influence the students' behavioral intention to adopt e-learning and H_4: facilitating condition will positively influence the students' behavioral intention to adopt e-learning) are supported in the regression analysis and accepted.

Table 5. Summary of hypotheses test

	Hypotheses	β	p-value	Support
H_1	PE → BI	0.533	0.000	Yes
H_2	EE → BI	0.245	0.004	Yes
H_3	SI → BI	0.045	0.072	No
H_4	FC → BI	0.309	0.000	Yes

5 Conclusion

This empirical study was conducted among the students of South Eastern University of Sri Lanka (SEUSL) in order to investigate their intention to adopt e-learning, and to find out the factors influencing their adoption behavior. The investigation was based on UTAUT model, but the moderating variables of the model have been excluded in the study, as they do not have moderating impact, particularly in the context of current research settings.

The analysis of demographic information depicts that, both, the university and students are competent to embark on e-learning system. Majority of the students are with the basic facilities and internet experience, to have proper access to e-learning system. The basic infrastructure facilities are also readily available at this university to implement e-learning system.

Hypotheses were formulated to test whether there are any significant relationships between the main constructs of UTUAT (such as, performance expectancy, effect expectancy, social influences, and facilitating conditions) and the behavioral intention to adopt e-learning.

The study has found that, performance expectancy, effect expectancy, and facilitation conditions were significant, and influence the behavioral intention to adopt e-learning among the student of SEUSL. The social influence, one of the main constructs of UTAUT did not yield significant results in the analysis of the data obtained from the students. The findings clearly indicate that, the students' intention to adopt e-learning at this university has not been influenced by 'social influence' factor, i.e. by the people who are important for the student. The reasons for this may be related to the facts that, either the students are always self-motivated, or they are obligated to accept a new system. However, it could be ascertained that, there is always a mandatory situation in the public universities in Sri Lanka and the top level decisions coming in the form of circulars or other official documents are accepted by relevant parties. However, the findings have implication for accepting e-learning system and developing e-learning implementation strategy at this university. Students perceive that, the performance expectancy, effect expectancy, and facilitation conditions are the important factors that influence their intention to adopt e-learning.

References

1. Hogo, M.A.: Evaluation of E-learning systems based on fuzzy clustering models and statistical tools. Expert Systems with Applications 37(10), 6891–6903 (2010)
2. Martin, W., Anderson, T.: Digital resilience in higher education. European Journal of Open, Distance and Elearning (EURODL) 16(1), 53–66 (2013)
3. Siritongthaworn, S., Krairit, D., Dimmitt, N.J., Paul, H.: The study of e-learning technology implementation: A preliminary investigation of universities in Thailand. Education and Information Technologies 11(2), 137–160 (2006)
4. Lee, B.C., Yoon, J.O., Lee, I.: Learners' acceptance of E-Learning in South Korea: Theories and results. Computers & Education 53(4), 1320–1329 (2009)
5. Chao, R.J., Chen, Y.H.: Evaluation of the criteria and effectiveness of distance e-learning with consistent fuzzy preference relations. Expert Systems with Applications 36(7), 10657–10662 (2009)
6. Appana, S.: A review of benefits and limitations of online learning in the context of the student, the instructor and the tenured faculty. International Journal on E-Learning 7, 5–22 (2008)
7. Vaughan, N.: Perspectives on blended learning in higher education. International Journal on E-Learning 6, 81–94 (2007)
8. Bhuasiri, W., Xaymoungkhoun, O., Zo, H., Rho, J.J., Ciganek, A.P.: Critical success factors for e-learning in developing countries: A comparative analysis between ICT experts and faculty. Computers & Education 58(2), 843–855 (2012)
9. Ozkan, S., Koseler, R.: Multi-dimensional students' evaluation of e-learning systems in the higher education context: An empirical investigation. Computers & Education 53(4), 1285–1296 (2009)
10. Sumak, B., Hericko, M., Pusnik, M.: A meta-analysis of e-learning technology acceptance: The role of user types and e-learning technology types. Computers in Human Behavior 27(6), 2067–2077 (2011)
11. Legris, P., Ingham, J., Collerette, P.: Why do people use Information Technology? A critical review of the technology acceptance mode. Information & Management 40, 191–204 (2003)
12. King, W., He, J.: A meta-analysis of the technology acceptance model. Information & Management 43(6), 740–755 (2006)
13. Venkatesh, V., Morris, M., Davis, G.B., Davis, F.D.: User Acceptance of information technology: Toward a unified view. MIS Quarterly 27(3), 425–478 (2003)
14. Fishbein, M., Ajzen, I.: Belief, attitude, intention and behavior: An Introduction to theory and research. Addison-Wesley, Reading (1975)
15. Davis, F.D.: Perceived usefulness, perceived ease of use, and user acceptance of information technology. MIS Quarterly 13, 319–340 (1989)
16. Ajzen, I.: The theory of planned behavior. Organizational Behavior and Human Decision Processes 50, 179–211 (1991)
17. Davis, F.D., Bagozzi, R.P., Warshaw, P.R.: Extrinsic and intrinsic motivation to use computers in the workplace. Journal of Applied Social Psychology 22, 1111–1132 (1992)

18. Taylor, S., Todd, P.A.: Understanding information technology usage: A test of competing models. Information Systems Research 6(2), 144–176 (1995)
19. Thompson, R.L., Higgins, C.A., Howell, J.M.: Personal computing: Toward a conceptual model of utilization. MIS Quarterly 15(1), 124–143 (1991)
20. Triandis, H.C.: Interpersonal Behaviour. Brooke/Cole, Monterey (1977)
21. Bandura, A.: Social Foundations of Thought and action: A social cognitive theory. Prentice Hall, Englewood Cliffs (1986)
22. Compeau, D.R., Higgins, C.A.: Computer self-efficacy: Development of a measure and Initial test. MIS Quarterly 19(2), 189–211 (1995)
23. Moore, G.C., Benbasat, I.: Development of an instrument to measure the perceptions of adopting an information technology innovation. Information Systems Research 2(3), 192–222 (1991)
24. Rogers, E.M.: Diffusion of innovation. Free Press, New York (2003)
25. Schaper, L.K., Pervan, G.P.: A model of information and communication technology acceptance and utilization by occupational therapists. International Journal of Medical Informatics 76, 790–800 (2007)
26. Fusilier, M., Durlabhji, S., Cucchi, A.: An investigation of the integrated model of user technology acceptance: Internet user samples in four countries. Journal of Educational Computing Research 38, 155–182 (2008)
27. Al-Gahtani, S.S., Hubona, G.S., Wang, J.: Information technology (IT) in Saudi Arabia: Culture and the acceptance and use of IT. Information & Management 44(8), 681–691 (2007)
28. Barua, M.: E-governance adoption in government organization of India. International Journal of Managing Public Sector Information and Communication Technologies 3(1), 1–20 (2012)
29. Leedy, P.D., Ormrod, J.E.: Practical Research: Planning and Design. Pearson Prentice Hall, New Jersey (2005)
30. Nunnally, J.: Psychometric Theory. McGraw-Hill, New York (1978)
31. Hair, J.F., Anderson, R.E., Tatham, R.L., Black, W.C.: Multivariate data analysis. Prentice-Hall, Englewood Cliffs (1998)

Cultural Differences in Interface Preferences

Zurida Ishak and Azizah Jaafar

Institute Visual Informatics
Universiti Kebangsaan Malaysia
Bangi, Malaysia
zuridaishak@gmail.com, aj@ftsm.ukm.my

Abstract. This study aims to examine the reliability of five cultural dimensions of Power Distance, Individualism, Uncertainty Avoidance, Masculinity and Long-Term Orientation towards interface tendency among university students. The second purpose of this study was to test whether there are differences in the pattern of utilization of the interface according to culture. The third purpose of this study was to determine whether there are differences for each of the cultural dimensions of religion and thus has a distinct tendency to interface components. A total of 100 population samplings were collected from the respondents. The questionnaire was adapted from the study of Reinecke (2010), which includes questions for dimension of Power Distance, Individualism, Uncertainty Avoidance, Masculinity and Long-Term Orientation. Data were analyzed using the Cronbach alpha test.

Keywords: adaptive interface, cultural interface preferences, cultural dimensions.

1 Introduction

A multicultural country like Malaysia will have issues in cultural interface due to the existence of people with different religions, races and cultures that live together and utilize computer interface in their daily tasks such as social network communications, online shopping and online bill payment.

Even though the interface preferences are just a matter of sense and it varies from one person to another, the commonalities could still be found deeply-rooted in culture [5]. Research from [12] shown that people from the same cultural group will perceive and process information in similar ways. There are studies about interface preferences that conclude that Asian web sites tend to offer more colorful and often come with animated user interface [4]. However, the result and conclusion of the studies was so general where the preferences of users were taken collectively regardless the differences of cultures and lifestyles in every Asian country.

There are different races, religions, cultures and lifestyles in Asian countries. Thus, preferences in the interface will also be different. For example, a Chinese user who lived half of his life in the USA will choose USA as country of residence, but he will use a better interface according to the Chinese design, or a combination of both [13].

H. Badioze Zaman et al. (Eds.): IVIC 2013, LNCS 8237, pp. 753–764, 2013.

Therefore, this is one of the things that need to be studied and discussed and to see if the user interface could be adapted to culture, country, or continent.

There have been studies done that connect one with a national culture [7], [16] and [3]. The study aims to compare and analyze website among the countries involved. Yet, the study could not show a significant difference in the interface design as there are different types of designs that have been implemented. Therefore, this study will look into two aspects of interface preferences, which are from the users (students) and also from the religions perspective.

2 Related Work

Antropologists such as Trompenaar and Hampden-Turner [15], Hofstede [9], or Hall [8] have made cultural classification to facilitate researchers from other fields including interface designers. One of the most comprehensive studies was conducted by Hofstede. He has classified culture into five categories: *Power Distance, Individualism vs Collectivism, Masculinity vs Feminity, Uncertainty Avoidance* and *Short- vs Long Term Orientation.* This category is the result of a study carried out on IBM employees in 53 countries. The scores from each country will represent a kind of cultural dimensions, for example, Malaysia is a country with the highest score in *Power Distance.*

Each dimension of culture produced by Hofstede has the following definition:

- *Power Distance :* Related to the hierarchy of society as well as in organization.
- *Individualism:* Societies are more individualistic and tend to mind their own business
- *Collectivism:* Communities have a strong bond, care and protect each other regardless of any resistance.
- *Masculinity:* focus on the masculine role as assertiveness, competition and toughness.
- *Feminity*: focus on feminine roles such as caring for the household, their children and tenderness.
- *Uncertainty Avoidance:* is associated with feelings of anxiety with regard to something that is not sure or unknown caused by known or unknown treats.
- *Short- vs Long Term Orientation:* is related to the way of life, faith and the search for truth to balance the everyday life.

Based on the definition of these cultural dimensions, [10] have conducted a study to analyze the issues, needs, preferences and expectations based on the Hofstede's cross-cultural theory. They have issued guidelines for interface design to meet the demands and needs of users from different cultures around the world. These guidelines constitute a starting point and catalyst for culture-based interface researchers to produce a more efficient interface according to the requirements of the users.

One of the interface researchers who adopted these guidelines is Reinecke [13]. She has defined the culture according to the definition of citizenship and identified the characteristics of the culture needed to build the interface adaptation or localization sites. Instead of making use of the specific cultural elements, Reinecke has used variables that can be used to refine a cultural group or community that can connect to associate the different cultural backgrounds. The factors that she has used for interface adaptation process were nationality (space and place), country of current residence, former residence(s), language, religion, education level, most familiar form of instruction of education, political norms and social structure, computer literacy, main reading/writing direction, second language, mother tongue, father's nationality, mother's nationality, age and gender [14]. Out of these factors, language, age and gender are cultural not related. These are the variables and aspects used to build user's cultural background in user model in order to perform preferable interface.

Combining the effort of defining the culture based on user's nationality and referring to the guideline from Marcus, she has come out with cultural localization guidelines based on nationality. The adaptation of the user interface is based on the scores obtained as a result of the calculation which can be found from [13]. Therefore, based on this calculation, the interface adaptation by country or continent can be avoided and Chinese users who lived in America may not get the interface designed for the Western.

3 Interface Design for Multi-cultural Country

Every country in the world has people of different backgrounds. The background of the people closely associated with the history of conquest, colonization and migration. The culture and religion in each country are different and unique according to their history. What has happened thousands or even hundreds of years ago occurs back now. The society in these days is now moving to a different country because they want to change and have better lives.

Technology has obviously facilitated information sharing and therefore strong social influence occurs. Intermarriage and cultural exchange also occur. Changing lifestyles can take place where the Western lifestyle practiced in Asian countries or vice-versa. Among the obvious cultural exchange are like eating, speech and apparel. Information technology is also playing a role, in accordance with [2], has changed the framework and mindset (Weltanschauung) community, a friendly relationship devalue their fellow members in the community, reducing familiar feeling in the family, resulting in a sense of quiet and alone and many other negative values to the community.

ICT developments have changed the values of the society as the diversity political views, sexual activity, social activity and the displacement of time. With the use of the Internet, more people are exposed to this valid or invalid information without boundaries and to some extent able to influence their thinking. Social transformation in society may change the definition and culture score performed by Hofstede.

Hofstede study implemented in 1967-1973 for IBM employees in 50 countries may have changed in terms of the culture definition in this age where in that era computers or ICT did not exist in the workplace or everyday life. The index score which was determined by Hofstede for each country may have changed. He also added in his web site that the score for each country may be different and it is proven by a research conducted by K.B. Mediwake in an unpublished study, comparing Chinese and Sri Lankans where the results differ.

The influence of ICT and borderless world may lead to changing one's lifestyle which eventually involved the local community too. However, a person's strong beliefs and faith will lead to a successful life even there were too many influences from ICT. A person with strong spiritual belief should be able to differentiate between good or evil behavior. Therefore, he or she would be able to make more rational decisions and succeed in their education or career [6].

This study aims to examine the reliability of five cultural dimensions of Power Distance, Individualism, Uncertainty Avoidance, Masculinity and Long-Term Orientation towards interface tendency among university students. The second purpose of this study was to determine whether there are differences for each of the cultural dimensions of religion and thus has a distinct tendency to interface components.

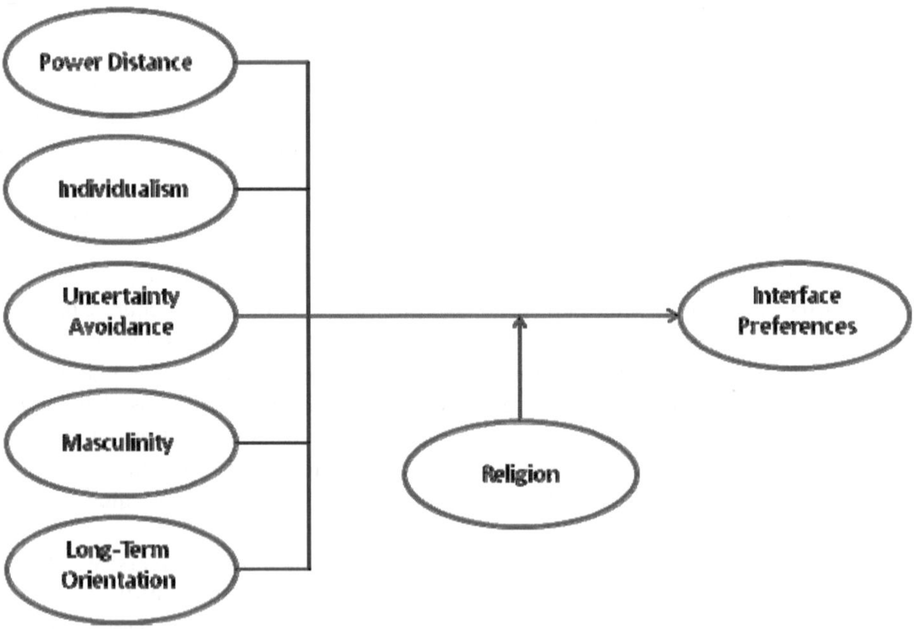

Fig. 1. Theoretical Model

4 Research Method

4.1 Method

A survey has been conducted to search for answers that aligned with the research questions. This study is a descriptive and inferential study which examines the relationship between the independent variables of Power Distance, Individualism, Uncertainty Avoidance, Masculinity and Long-Term Orientation with interface preferences. A total of 100 students from two universities, namely Universiti Kebangsaan Malaysia and Management and Science University were selected and information obtained from them were gender, religion, race, age and level of educational attainment. The survey was distributed to the students by the researcher and each student will return the completed questionnaires to the researcher.

Subject characteristics include gender, race, age, religion and level of education of respondents. Out of 100 respondents selected, consisting of 50% men and 50% are women. In this study Muslim respondents are 53 people (53%), 15 Buddhist (15%), 21 Hindu (21%), and Christian 11 (11%).

4.2 Research Tool

The survey questions were developed by [13] was adapted to be used to find the dimensions of a religious culture and their preferences towards interface design. This survey is not divided into parts, but contains questions that represent five dimensions of Power Distance (PDI), Uncertainty Avoidance (UAI), Individualism (IDV), Masculinity (MAS) and Long-term orientation (LTO).

Power Distance (PDI)

This section aims to measure culture dimension of Power Distance. There are 20 questions and there are two types of questions. 12 items represented the interface preferences and 8 items embodied the attitude towards teaching and learning. Each question uses the 5-point Likert scale where 5 is strongly Disagree, 4 is Disagree, 3 is Neutral, 2 is Agree and 1 is Strongly Agree. Items in the questionnaire contain both positive and negative items.

Example of positive item: I normally organize my files hierarchically in folders. (PDI)
Example of negative item: I rarely organize my files in folder hierarchies with subfolders. (PDI)

Table 1. Factor of Power Distance By Item

No.	*Culture Dimension*	*Positive Item No.*	*Negative Item No.*
1	Internet Preferences	1,2,3,5,11,12,13,	6,7,14,15,16
2	Attitude Towards Teaching and Learning	20,21,22,28,	29,31,35

Individualism (IDV)

This section aims to measure culture dimension of Individualism. There are 12 questions with two types of questions. Six items represent the interface preferences and the rest of them represent attitude towards teaching and learning. Each question uses the 5-point Likert scale where 5 is strongly Disagree, 4 is Disagree, 3 is Neutral, 2 is Agree and 1 is Strongly Agree. Items in the questionnaire contain both positive and negative items.

Example of positive item: I like colorful interfaces. (IDV)
Example of negative item: I prefer plain-colored interfaces to colorful interfaces. (IDV)

Table 2. Factor of Individualism (IDV) by Item

No	*Culture Dimension*	*Positive Item No.*	*Negative Item No.*
1	Internet Preferences	4,8,9,10,19	18
2	Attitude Towards Teaching and Learning	23,24,25	27,36,41

Uncertainty Avoidance (UAI)

This section aims to assess the culture dimension of Uncertainty Avoidance. There are 9 questions that include two types of questions. One item represents the interface preferences and another eight items represent attitude towards teaching and learning. Each question uses the 5-point Likert scale where 5 is strongly Disagree, 4 is Disagree, 3 is Neutral, 2 is Agree and 1 is Strongly Agree. Items in the questionnaire contain both positive and negative items.

Example of positive item: In a learning situation, the objectives should always be clearly stated. (UAI)
Example of negative item: I like learning situations where I do not have to work towards fixed objectives. (UAI)

Table 3. Factor of Uncertainty Avoidance (UAI) by Item

No.	*Culture Dimension*	*Positive Item No.*	*Negative Item No.*
1	Internet Preferences	17	
2	Attitude Towards Teaching and Learning	26,32,37,42,	34,38,39,43

Masculinity (MAS)

This section aims to measure culture dimension of Masculinity (MAS). There are 2 questions which represent attitude towards teaching and learning. Each question using a 5-point Likert scale where 5 is strongly Disagree, 4 is Disagree, 3 is Neutral, 2 is Agree and 1 is Strongly Agree. Items in the questionnaire have depicted positive items only.

Table 4. Factor of MAS by Item

No.	*Culture Dimension*	*Positive Item No.*	*Negative Item No.*
1	Attitude Towards Teaching and Learning	30,44	

Long-Term Orientation (LTO)

This section aims to measure culture dimension of LTO. There are 2 questions which represent attitude towards teaching and learning. Each question uses the 5-point Likert scale where 5 is strongly Disagree, 4 is Disagree, 3 is Neutral, 2 is Agree and 1 is Strongly Agree. Items in the questionnaire contain positive and negative item.

Table 5. Factor of LTO by Item

No.	*Culture Dimension*	*Positive Item No.*	*Negative Item No.*
1	Attitude Towards Teaching and Learning	33	40

4.3 Scoring System

Power Distance (PDI)

This section will measure the culture dimension of PDI, the Likert scale has been used and all items are measured based on the type of items (which is the interface preferences and attitude towards teaching and learning). Maximum score for this section is 100 and minimum is 20. Therefore, subjects that obtained scores from 60 to 100 were considered as the high score dimension. Whereas subjects that had obtained scores in between 20 and 59 were considered to have a low score dimension. The negative items were coded before data processing. Distribution of scores is as Error! Reference source not found.

Individualism (IDV)

This section will measure the culture dimension of IDV, where the 5-point Likert scale has been used. All items are measured based on the types of items (which is the interface preferences and attitude towards teaching and learning). Maximum score for this section is 60 and minimum is 12. Therefore, subject who obtained scores in between 30 to 60 is considered as high score dimension. Subjects who scored 12 to 29 were considered to have low score dimensions. The negative items were coded before data processing. Distribution of scores is as Table 6.

Uncertainty Avoidance (UAI)

This section will measures culture dimension of UAI, where the 5-point Likert scale has been distributed and all items were measured based on the type of items (which was the interface preferences and attitude towards teaching and learning). Maximum score for this section is 45 and minimum is 9. Therefore, the subject who scored from 27 to 45 is considered as the high score dimension. While the subject who obtained scores in between 9 and 26 is considered to have a low score dimension. The negative items were coded before data processing. Distribution of scores is as Table 6.

Masculinity (MAS)

This section will measure culture dimension of MAS, where the 5-point Likert scale were distributed and all items were measured based on the types of items (which are the interface preferences and attitude towards teaching and learning). Maximum score for this section is 10 and minimum is 2. Therefore, subject who obtained scores of 6 to 10 is considered as a high score dimension. While subject who obtained scores of 2 to 5 is considered to have a low score dimension. The negative items were coded before data processing. Distribution of scores is as Table 6.

Long-Term Orientation (LTO)

This section will measures culture dimension of LTO, given 5 Likert scale choices of answers and all items are measured based on the type of items (which is the interface preferences and attitude towards teaching and learning). Maximum score for this section is 10 and minimum is 2. Therefore, subject who obtained scores between 6 to 10 is considered as high score dimension. While subjects who obtained scores in between 2 and 5 is considered to have low score dimension. The negative items were coded before data processing. Distribution of scores is as Table 6.

Table 6. Scoring Scale for Culture Dimensions

Degree of Consensus	*Positive Item Scores*	*Negative Item Scores*
Strongly Agree	1	5
↑	2	4
	3	3
↓	4	2
Strongly Disagree	5	1

4.4 Reliability of the Instrument

Cronbach alpha method was used to evaluate the reliability of the test instrument in order to measure Power Distance, Individualism, Uncertainty Avoidance, Masculinity and Long-Term Orientation. Alpha coefficient values are as Table 7.

Table 7. Pre-test reliability coefficient values by measurement

Variable	*No. of Item*	*Item deleted*	*Alpha Value*
Power Distance	20	-	.77
Individualism	12	-	.70
Uncertainty Avoidance	9	-	.72
Masculinity	2	-	.86
Long-Term Orientation	2	-	.88

From Table 7, it can be seen that the value of the coefficient α for measuring Masculinity and Long-Term Orientation is above .80. This indicates that this measurement tool can distinguish between individuals and it is in line with the statement of Anastasi (1982) who stated that 0.8 is reliable. To measure Power Distance, Individualism and Uncertainty Avoidance, the alpha coefficient was more than .7. These results are consistent with Kaplan and Saccuzzo opinion (2001) that suggested the value of α is from .7 to .8.

5 Results

5.1 Cultural Dimensions of Student

The survey results obtained from the students have determined the mean value for the type of cultural dimensions of interest in the use of the interface. Table 8 shows the obtained values.

Table 8. The mean value for each culture dimension

Culture Dimension	*Mean*
PDI	58.35 (Low PDI)
IDV	34.90 (High IDV)
UAI	26.21 (Low UAI)
MAS	5.97 (Low MAS)
LTO	5.96 (Low LTO)

From Table 8, the mean value of the PDI dimension is 58.35. This value lies in between 20-59 in the scoring scale value. Therefore, it is evident that the cultural dimension of the students is in low PDI. The next dimension is IDV. The mean value obtained was at 34.90. This value is from 30-60 in scoring scale. Therefore, the cultural dimension of the students is on a high IDV. UAI dimension on the other hand has a mean value of 26.21. This value is less than 27. Therefore, the cultural dimension of the students is in low UAI. Next, the MAS dimension can be seen to have a mean value of 5.97. This value is less than 6 in scoring scale. Therefore, the cultural dimension of the students is low MAS. The final one is the LTO which has the mean value of 5.96. This value is less than 6 in the scoring scale. Therefore, the cultural dimension of the students is low LTO.

5.2 Cultural Dimensions of Different Religions

The study also assesses the cultural dimensions of each religion in Malaysia. Every religion may have different cultural dimensions. Table 9 shows the results of this study.

Table 9. Mean culture dimensions for each religious

Dimensions/Religions	*Muslim*	*Buddha*	*Hindu*	*Cristian*
PDI	62.28 (High PDI)	49.67 (Low PDI)	57.05 (Low PDI)	53.73 (High PDI)
IDV	37.25 (High IDV)	28.87 (Low IDV)	34.29 (High IDV)	33 (High IDV)
UAI	27.94 (High UAI)	22.13 (Low UAI)	25.71 (Low UAI)	26.21 (Low UAI)
MAS	6.11 (High MAS)	5.47 (Low MAS)	6.14 (High MAS)	5.64 (Low MAS)
LTO	6.28 (High LTO)	5.60 (Low LTO)	5.95 (Low LTO)	4.90 (Low LTO)

Result shows that different races and religions will contain more than one cultural dimension. This is because each races who profess different religion have different thought, management style and way of life [1].

6 Discussion

6.1 Culture Dimension of Student

Based on the results obtained from the analysis of the survey, students tend to have low PDI dimensions, high IDV, low UAI, low MAS and LTO. This revealed that the culture at the level of the students is different and cannot be equated by a country's cultural dimensions. Table 10 elicits the user interface design for this group of students.

6.2 Culture Dimension of Different Religion

The results also have shown that different believers of religions have specific cultural dimensions. Lifestyles, characters and someone's way of thinking will be formed according to their role based on the situation in which they are located. For example, if a person is in a place where he or she is studying (university), he or she would automatically play a role as a student. During the study, students may have a different view and a different learning culture.

On the other hand, if a person is viewed from the point of his religion, he would have a different culture and attitudes as a believer of a religion. Thus, differences in

Table 10. Interface design for respected culture dimension (Adapted from [13])

Culture Dimension	*Interface Design*
Low PDI	- Different access and navigation possibilities; nonlinear - Data does not have to be structured - Many functionalities - Most information at interface level, hierarchy of information less deep - Friendly error messages suggesting how to proceed - Support is only rarely needed - Websites often contain images showing the country's leader or the whole nation
High IDV	- Use color to encode information - High text-to-image ratio - Low multimodality - Monotoriously colored interface
Low UAI	- Most information at interface level, complex interfaces - Non-linear navigation - Code colors, typography and sound to maximize information
Low MAS	- Little saturation, pastel colors - Allow for exploration and different paths to navigate - Personal presentation of content and friendly communication with the user
Low LTO	- Reduced information density - Content highly structured into small units

the individual will influenced them while using computer interface. Most users rely on a lot of Internet applications in order to communicate, learn, shop, pay bills and information searching. These activities are daily activities that they do and their intermediaries are virtual computer interface.

Thus, the interface should be tailored according to a users' culture. Each user will not get the same interface as studies have shown that different cultures have different designs preferences. Further studies are needed to refine the definition of culture and determine the factors that contribute to individual differences according to culture.

References

1. Aziz, A.B.: Seminar Nilai dalam Komuniti (SIVIC) anjuran Jabatan Pengajian Umum, pp. 1–13. Universiti Utara Malaysia (September 2004)
2. Basri, M.: Teknologi maklumat dan komunikasi (ICT) dan nilai dalam masyarakat. In: Seminar Antarabangsa Nilai dalam Komuniti Pasca Modenisme (SIVIC 2004), Hotel City Bayview Langkawi, September 4-6 (2004) (unpublished)

3. Burgmann, I., Kitchen, P., Williams, R.: Does Culture Matter on the Web? Marketing Intelligence & Planning 24(1), 6–73 (2006)
4. Callahan, E.: Cultural Similarities and Differences in the Design of University Websites. Journal of Computer-Mediated Communication 11(1) (2005)
5. Dormann, C., Chisalita, C.: Cultural Values in Web Site Design. In: European Conference on Cognitive Ergonomics (2002)
6. Fagan, P.F.: Religious Practice and Educational Attainment. Research Synthesis. Family Research Council (2010)
7. Gould, E., Zakaria, N., Yusof, S.: Applying Culture to Website Design: A Comparison of Malaysian and US Websites. In: Joint IEEE International and 18th Annual Conference on Computer Documentation, pp. 161–171 (2000)
8. Hall, E., Hall, M.: Understanding Cultural Differences. Intercultural Press, Maine (1990)
9. Hofstede, G.: Culture's Consequences: Comparing Values, Behaviours and Organisations across nations. Sage Publications (2003)
10. Marcus, A., Gould, E.W.: Crosscurrents: Cultural Dimensions and Global Web User-Interface Design. ACM Interactions 7(4), 32–46 (2000)
11. Ramli, N.H.: Memprofil Mangsa Bunuh Diri. Bernama.com (March 17, 2009)
12. Nisbett, R.: The Geography of Thought. Free Press, New York (2003)
13. Reinecke, K.: Culturally Adaptive User Interface. PhD Thesis (2010)
14. Reinecke, K., Bernstein, A.: Improving Performance, Perceived Usability, and Aesthetics with Culturally Adaptive User Interfaces. Working Paper (2010a)
15. Trompenaars, F., Hampden-Turner, C.: Riding the Waves of Culture: Understanding Cultural Diversity in Business. Nicholas Brealey Publishing Ltd. (1997)
16. Zhao, W., Massey, B., Murphy, J., Lui, F.: Cultural dimensions of web site design and content. Prometheus 21, 75–84 (2003)

Preliminary Study of Eye Tracking Evaluation on Product Label Design

Mohd. Hafiz Faizal Mohamad Kamil and Azizah Jaafar

Faculty of Information Science and Technology
National University of Malaysia, 43600 Bangi, Selangor, Malaysia
hafizfaizal@umk.edu.my, aj@ftsm.ukm.my

Abstract. There are various techniques to determine the usability of a design such as product label. One of them is the employment of eye movement measurement technique which takes into account a more natural setting and actual user involvement. While previous studies have explained the definition of eye movement and in the usability of a design, this preliminary research was study the eye movement characteristics through the theory of eye tracking on product label that was choose by student, before the research will be further on expert validation on product label through interview. It combining several aspects in eye movement measurements comprises fixation count, fixation duration, cumulative proportion of respondent fixation count and cumulative proportion of respondents for fixation duration on area of interest (AOI) of product label design. The findings reveal that AOI for text design has the highest cumulative proportion of respondent in fixation count and fixation duration. However, AOI for text design also indicates that there was a lack of attention in eye movement. In conclusion, the characteristics of the design elements for each AOI can be determined by the proportion results of eye movement.

Keywords: eye tracking, product label design, fixation count, fixation duration.

1 Introduction

The usability of design elements such as text, image and colour could not be known without being validated through a study. There are a lot of usability guidelines which have been developed based on consumers' perception survey, experience or experts' knowledge of design and testing. However, this paper aims at determining the usability aspects in terms of effectiveness and efficiency of design elements of text, image and colour on product labels released in market. The assessment was conducted by measuring the eye movement when consumers were going through the process of making a purchase selection. The measurement aspects accounting for this study were the numbers and duration of fixation on design elements found on the area of interest (AOI). The advantage of this assessment is that it is able to explain usability aspects and thus able to understand how a label design can have an impact on consumers.

H. Badioze Zaman et al. (Eds.): IVIC 2013, LNCS 8237, pp. 765–775, 2013.

2 Product Label Design Elements

Product label belongs to the category of multimedia elements for designs printed by computing technology because it has some of the characteristics of multimedia elements such as text and image. Each design element has its own effect on consumers. Image for instance, is able to stimulate response from consumers more than the use of sentences. Besides, it increases and facilitates consumers' information processing of a particular product. In addition, it has an advantage of attracting the consumer attention and also evokes the memory to the product if properly used [18].

Colour also compliments to the elements of text and image on a product label to make it more visually appealing. The use of colour particularly a unique one or of different density which is sometimes associated with a particular product as a sign or symbol on a product label can potentially help in consumers' purchasing activities. Studies have shown that the use of colour is often associated with various consumers' background or related aspects in a particular community. The use of colour for logo designs, labels or packaging to be marketed should take into account the understanding and acceptance of consumers in the area about colour and its combinations [1]. In addition, colour is also connected to the identity of a product that can integrate with users' perception about the quality or type of products such as flavour, nutrition and satisfaction. More positive effects can be achieved through a combination of several factors including colour, packaging projecting the colour the product content, lighting environment and brand appearance.

Based on a study by [13], product label design can be classified into two major parts, namely the visual elements and information. These two elements also can be further categorized into sub-elements which are graphics, colour, size, shape and arrangement of materials for visual elements. Meanwhile, information elements are divided into producing factors, producing countries as well as brand. The label design concepts are applied to the study of marketing in order to identify their importance and impacts on consumer behaviour in driving and during the purchase decision. In the study, the role of design elements could be determined. This is evidenced by the findings in respect to the design of verbal elements on the package labels of dairy and detergent products carried out in the study. What matters most to the consumers are the size, visual materials, product information and producing countries [13]. Evidently, a good product design is manifested by an appropriate visual design and a clear message about a particular product [19].

In addition, a parallel study on label design was conducted by [4], in which they also claim that label design consists of visual elements and information including five sub-items namely the size, shape, colour, and information technology. The objectives of their study is similar to that of [13] in which it intends to find the different effects of design elements on purchasing decisions in different phases with different research methods.. This study focuses in depth on the design elements for three different phase called pre-purchase, purchase and post-purchase. The findings show that the impact of product label design on the packaging is higher in purchase phase compared with the post-purchase phase. In relation to information design, Scoot [19], asserts that too much content information on a label product will likely confuse consumers and make it difficult for them to get the actual information they need. This is because they only use about five to seven seconds to observe a product label, depending on the total number of messages appearing on the label. He also suggests that useful and key messages be combined in one location.

3 Purpose of Eye Tracking Evaluation Study

Eye movement is a more consistent performance assessment technique compared with the one conducted in a traditional way. Studies have found that a design complying with the appropriate design principles affects the consumers in term of time taken for completing tasks, accuracy and satisfaction. [6] have employed eye tracking as methods of measuring visual design relationship with eye movement to study human understanding through visual attention. Besides, [3] and [7] have studied visual design of text and image using eye movement measurement methods as usability evaluation research techniques. The study has found that that users complete tasks more quickly with texts as compared to images.

Stanford Poynter Project [3] has studied about online and offline newspapers reading techniques. The study has found that more readers look at the images when reading newspapers on-line and text when they do it off-line. The study is extended by adding research control on news reading through website. The findings have revealed that there are more fixations on a small sized text than a large text size. However there are more fixations on a large text size than a small one for the headlines [17].

[7] identify that consumers will use their experience of using the specific design features that have the oft-used characteristics of most designs to be applied to the other designs. Therefore, they need a time for adaptation in the use of designs uncommon for them [6] and among the factors that affect visual search behaviour are gender, methods of design display, etc. [10]

4 Advantages of Eye Tracking Method

Eye tracking technique is suitable for the assessment of usability because it does not depend on user memory in the data collection process. Eye tracking technique is dependent on eye movement recordings made for certain activities naturally determined by the researcher or by using a special tool of eye tracking during the process of information collection. Therefore, eye movement tracking techniques are not meant to burden the consumers particularly in the thinking process that may have an impact on the outcome of usability evaluation [6].

Tracking the eye movement is a visual performance evaluation of consumer attitudes to accomplish certain tasks. Eye tracking technique is independent and can combine with the other assessment techniques in order to obtain a more accurate survey result and achieve the objectives of the study. Expectations and user experience can be accessed through a combination of measurement techniques of tracking eye movement, interviews and questionnaires [1].

5 Research Method

This paper is a preliminary research to study the eye movement characteristics through the theory of eye tracking on product label that was choose by student, before the research will be further on expert validation of product label design through interview. An observational study was conducted on product label design with six AOI. A total of eight final year students (respondents that choose Jacob HI-Fibre biscuit product) that was registered for multimedia class from the Faculty of Technology and Information Science (FTSM), National University of Malaysia (UKM) were selected as respondents. The final year students were selected as a respondent is based on their experiences in expenses on food items during their study [2] and [15]. They are also considered as an expert in the field of multimedia (3 years in a multimedia course) and the amount is already sufficient for usability evaluation [16]. Four eye movement measurement elements observed and recorded were fixation count, fixation duration, cumulative proportion of respondent fixation count and cumulative proportion of respondents for fixation duration on AOI of a product label design.

Fig. 1. AOI on product label

Eye tracker device from SMI RED-4 desk-based model was utilized to record the number and duration of respondent's fixation on the product label design. Respondents were asked to look at the products label on the shelves of supermarkets in the form of image using Dell monitors sized 23 inch LCD. The respondents needed to look at the products label design image based on the situation when they had to choose to make the selection of product purchase. Jacobs Hi-fibre biscuit (Fig. 1) was used for the study based on the most selected by students among the products on shelve. The results of the fixation and duration counts of the design elements of text, image and colour on the area of interest were then displayed via Be Gaze software version 2. These AOI design elements are illustrated in the table 1.

Table 1. AOI for the label design of product

AOI	Label design
1	Imej 1
2	Teks 1
3	Teks 2
4	Teks 3
5	Teks 4
6	Teks 5

6 Research Analysis

Table 2. Fixation count on AOI for each respondent

	AOI1	AOI2	AOI3	AOI4	AOI5	AOI6
R1	5	2	3	0	0	2
R2	1	1	0	0	0	0
R3	0	11	2	0	0	0
R4	10	7	1	3	0	0
R5	1	3	0	0	0	0
R6	0	3	1	0	0	0
R7	0	4	1	0	0	0
R8	2	0	0	0	0	0

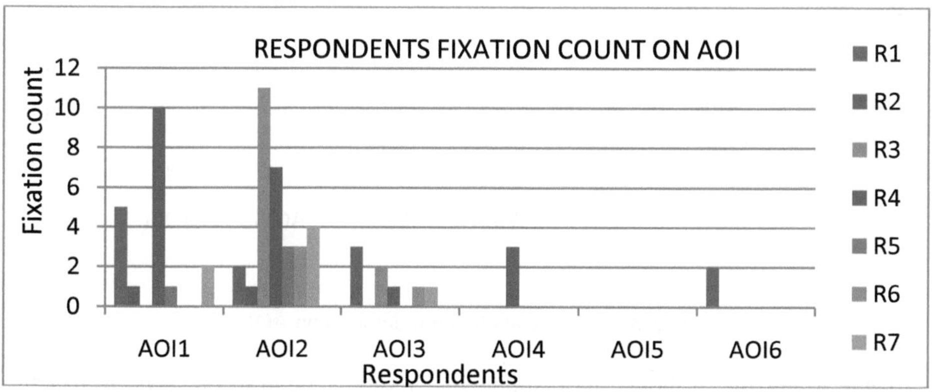

Fig. 2. Respondent's fixation count on AOI

Table 2 and fig. 2 show the number of respondent's fixation on AOI. AOI 2 records eleven fixations, which is the highest number of fixation by the third respondent. The highest fixation number for AOI 1 is ten which is by the fourth respondent. Three fixations show the highest number of fixation on AOI 3 by the first respondent. Meanwhile, one respondent records his/her fixation on AOI 4 with three fixation counts and AOI 6 with two fixation counts. AOI 5 does not record any number of fixations.

Table 3. Fixation count on AOI for each respondent

	AOI1	AOI2	AOI3	AOI4	AOI5	AOI6
R1	508.13	391.44	258.32	0	0	200.05
R2	91.7	216.57	0	0	0	0
R3	0	2766.45	291.62	0	0	0
R4	1666.03	1350.04	199.09	758.18	0	0
R5	166.61	583.23	0	0	0	0
R6	0	391.65	133.21	0	0	0
R7	0	741.7	191.77	0	0	0
R8	266.73	0	0	0	0	0
Total	2699.2	6441.08	1074.01	758.18	0	200.05

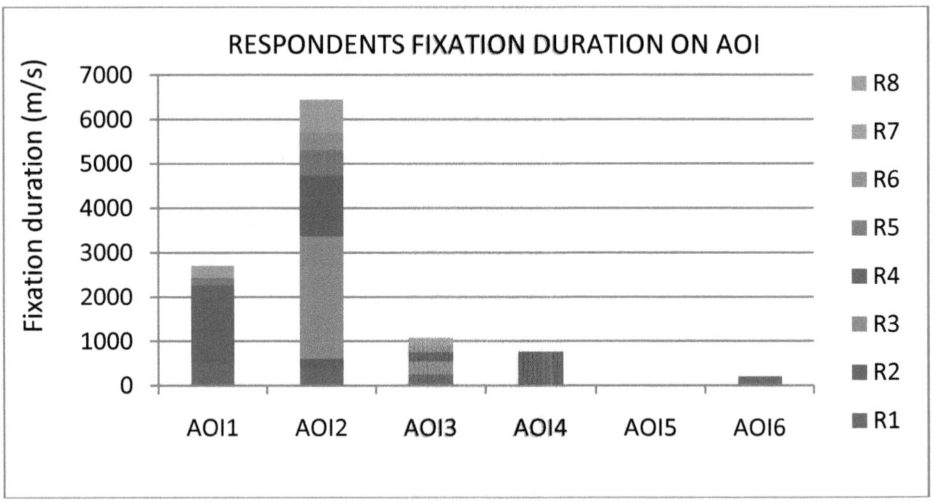

Fig. 3. Respondents fixation duration on AOI

Table 3 and fig. 3 shows the respondents' fixation duration on AOI. AOI 2 has attracted the respondents' attention with 6441.08 millisecond, the highest fixation duration compared with other AOIs. It also records, which is the largest numbers of respondents of all. While, AOI 5 is the only AOI which has not been seen by the respondents and thus no fixation duration could be identified. AOI 4 and AOI 6 have been seen by one respondents only namely the fourth respondent for AOI 4 and the first respondents for AOI 6. AOI 4 records 1074.01 millisecond, the third lowest of fixation duration and AOI 6 records 200.05 millisecond, the second lowest of fixation duration. Meanwhile, AOI 1 and AOI 3 have been seen by five respondents of the study. Fixation duration for AOI 1 is 2699.2 millisecond, the second highest of fixation duration recorded. While AOI 3 is the third highest of fixation duration with 1074.01 millisecond.

Table 4. Proportion and cumulative proportion of respondent (%) for fixation count

Fixation count	Proportion AOI 1	C. P. AOI1	Proportion AOI 2	C. P. AOI2	Proportion AOI 3	C. P. AOI3	Proportion AOI 4	C. P. AOI4	Proportion AOI 5	C. P. AOI5	Proportion AOI 6	C. P. AOI6
0	38	38	13	13	38	38	88	88	100	100	88	88
2	38	38	25	25	50	50	13	13	0	0	13	13
4	0	38	38	63	13	63	0	13	0	0	0	13
6	13	50	0	63	0	63	0	13	0	0	0	13
8	0	50	13	75	0	63	0	13	0	0	0	13
10	13	63	0	75	0	63	0	13	0	0	0	13
12	0	63	13	88	0	63	0	13	0	0	0	13
TOTAL	63		88		63		13		0		13	

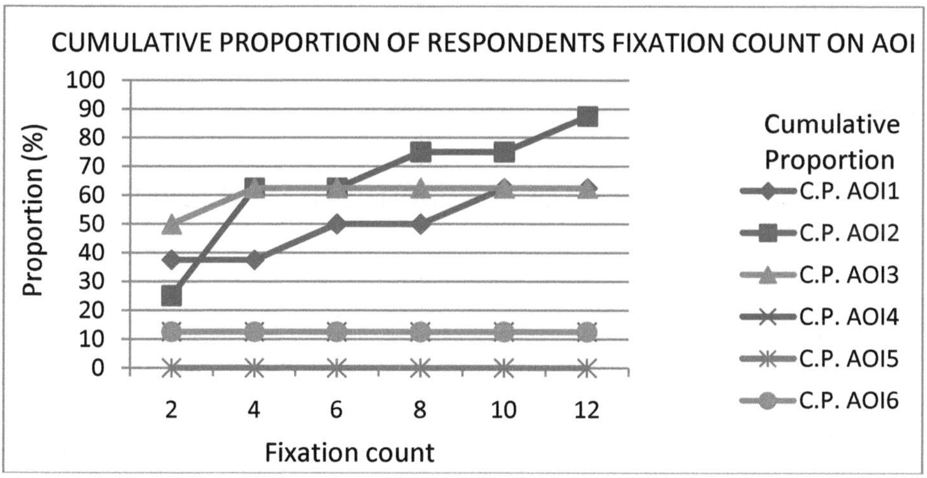

Fig. 4. Cumulative proportion of respondents fixation count on AOI

The graph shown in fig. 4 and fig.5 are derived from the data in fig. 1 and fig.2. Fig. 4 indicates the cumulative proportion of respondents fixation count on AOI. Cumulative proportion for 0 fixation count is not included. AOI 2 was seen by 88% of respondents with 12 fixation counts which makes it the highest cumulative proportion of respondents fixation count on AOI. AOI 1 and 3 have same cumulative proportion when they have been seen by 63% of respondents with fixation count of 12. With the same fixation count, 13% of respondents have seen AOI 4 and 6. Meanwhile no respondent has seen AOI 5 in the study.

Table 5. Proportion and cumulative proportion of respondent (%) for fixation duration

Fixation Duration (m/s)	Proportion AOI 1	C. P. AOI 1	Proportion AOI 2	C. P. AOI 2	Proportion AOI 3	C. P. AOI 3	Proportion AOI 4	C. P. AOI 4	Proportion AOI 5	C. P. AOI 5	Proportion AOI 6	C. P. AOI 6
0	37.5	37.5	12.5	12.5	37.5	37.5	87.5	87.5	0	0	87.5	87.5
1000	50	50	62.5	62.5	62.5	62.5	12.5	12.5	0	0	12.5	12.5
2000	12.5	62.5	12.5	75	0	62.5	0	12.5	0	0	0	12.5
3000	0	62.5	12.5	87.5	0	62.5	0	12.5	0	0	0	12.5
4000	0	62.5	0	87.5	0	62.5	0	12.5	0	0	0	12.5
5000	0	62.5	0	87.5	0	62.5	0	12.5	0	0	0	12.5
6000	0	62.5	0	87.5	0	62.5	0	12.5	0	0	0	12.5
7000	0	62.5	0	87.5	0	62.5	0	12.5	0	0	0	12.5
TOTAL	62.5		87.5		62.5		12.5		0		12.5	

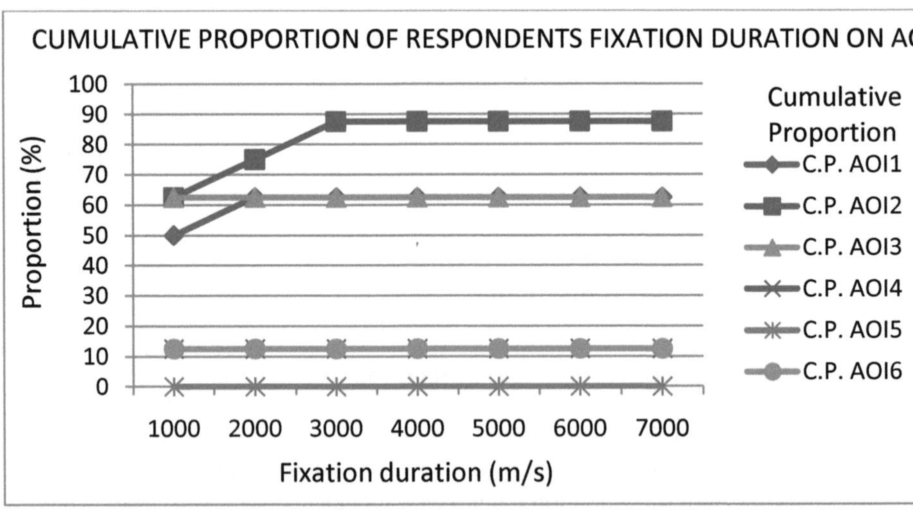

Fig. 5. Cumulative proportion of respondent fixation duration on AOI

Graph in fig. 5 shows the cumulative proportion of respondents' fixation duration on the AOI. Cumulative proportion is not accounted for 0 fixation duration. The graph clearly shows that AOI 2 is the most notable by respondents. It starts with 63% of respondents for 1000 milliseconds and increases to 88% for 3000 milliseconds. AOI 1 and 3 have same cumulative proportion when it seen by 63% of respondents for 2000 milliseconds until 7000 millisecond. 13% respondents have seen AOI 4 and 6 with fixation duration from 1000 until 7000 milliseconds. There is no respondent at AOI 5, therefore, no fixation duration recorded in the graph.

7 Discussion

The findings show that there is a difference in consumer eye movement in terms of the number of fixation and fixation duration. This study has evaluated the number of fixation on AOI according to [17] and has confirmed that more fixations on a particular area indicate that it is more noticeable, or more important, to the viewer than other areas. For fixation duration aspect, [8] confirms that longer fixation duration means that the object is more engaging in some way and time is needed for extracting the information. Meanwhile, the assessment on the number of respondents is based on [1], if a low proportion of participants is fixating on an area that is important to the task, it may need to be highlighted or moved.

According to the four aspects of eye tracking analysis, the study finds that AOI 2 is the best and it is the design element of text on the label design. It is based on the highest cumulative proportion of respondents for fixation count on AOI at 75% of respondents with 8 and 10 fixation counts, and 88% with12 fixation count. While for fixation duration, AOI 2 also records the highest cumulative proportion of respondent's fixation duration by 75% with 2000 millisecond and 88% of respondents with 3000 milliseconds until 7000 milliseconds. AOI 2 is the text design features consisting of roman, bold, expanded, uppercase, large and serif. Meanwhile, the colour is light blue, dark blue and white.

8 Conclusion

Eye movement measurement is one of the methods that can determine how people interact and thus can determine the effectiveness of the design aspects in terms of usability. Based on references from previous studies, research in the field of multimedia field can also employ eye movement measurement methods in the marketing environment. However, there are more interpretations of eye movement especially in usability evaluation that need to be referred and reviewed in order to get more accurate findings.

Label design evaluation studies based on consumer eye movement have considered four aspects which consist of the fixation count, fixation duration, the cumulative proportion of respondent for fixation count and cumulative proportion of respondents for fixation duration. This study has been carried out on eight respondents consisting of final year of multimedia students from the faculties of science and information technology, National University of Malaysia. They are representing consumer that choose the Jacob Hi-Fibre biscuit product. The assessment based on eye movement is able to determine the AOI that becomes consumers' point of attention and thus able to determine the design elements. This study has found that the characteristics of the design elements that have recorded highest proportion of the four aspects of eye movement assessment are text designs with design characteristics of roman, bold, expanded, uppercase, and large and serif. Meanwhile, for colours they are light blue, dark blue and white. While, for the characteristics of design elements that do not get the consumers' attention are text designs that have the design characteristics of italic, light, condensed, uppercase, small, san-serif. While for colour it is dark yellow. However, the attention of consumers is also likely to be influenced by other factors such as the position of the design on the label design, size design and the type of information conveyed product. Therefore, further studies need to be extended with the addition of other possible factors so that attempts to create designs based on interaction could be materialized.

References

1. Crowe, E.C., Narayanan, N.H.: Comparing interfaces based on what users watch and do. In: Proceedings Eye Tracking Research and Applications Symposium 2000, pp. 29–36. Association for Computing Machinery, New York (2000)
2. Paulin, G.D.: Expenditures of college-age students and nonstudents. Monthly Labor Review (2011)
3. Ellis, S., Candrea, R., Misner, J., Craig, C.S., Lankford, C.P., Hutshinson, T.E.: Windows to the soul? What eye movements tell us about software usability. In: Proceedings of the Usability Professionals' Association Conference 1998, pp. 151–178 (1998)
4. Estiri, M., Hasangholipour, T., Hazdani, H., Nejad, H.J., Rayej, H.: Food product consumer behaviours: The role of packaging elements. J. Applied Sciences 10, 535–543 (2010)
5. Holmqvist, K., Nystrom, M., Andersson, R., Dewhurst, R., Jarodzka, H., Weijer, J.V.D.: Eye tracking: A comprehensive guide to methods and measures (2001)
6. Jacob, R.J.K., Karn, K.S.: Eye tracking in human computer interaction and usability research: Ready to deliver the promise. In: Radach, R., Hyona, J., Deubel, H. (eds.) The Mind's eye: Cognitive and Applied Aspects of Eye Movement Research, pp. 573–605. North-Holland/Elsevier, Boston (2003)
7. Josepshson, S., Holmes, M.E.: Visual attention to repeated internet images: testing the scan path theory on world wide web. In: Proceeding of the Eye Tracking Research & Applications Symposium 2002. ACM, New York (2002)
8. Just, M.A., Carpenter, P.A.: Eye Fixations and Cognitive Processes. Cognitive Psychology 8, 441–480 (1976)
9. Just, M.A., Carpenter, P.A.: The role of eye-fixation research in cognitive psychology. Behavior Research Methods & Instrumentation 8, 139–143 (1976)
10. Karn, K., Ellis, S., Juliano, C.: The hunt for usability: Tracking eye movements (2000)
11. SIGCHI Bulletin, p. 11. Association for Computing Machinery, New York (November/December 2000), `http://www.acm.org/sigchi/bulletin/2000.5/eye.html`

12. Kotval, X.P., Goldberg, J.H.: Eye movements and interface components grouping: An evaluation method. In: Proceedings of the 42nd Annual Meeting of the Human Factors and Ergonomics Society, pp. 486–490. Human Factors and Ergonomics Society, Santa Monica (1998)
13. Kuvykaite, R., Dovaliene, A., Navickiene, L.: Impact of package elements on consumer's purchase decision. Economics and Management 19, 441–447 (2009)
14. Mohamad Kamil, M.H.F., Jaafar, A.: Usability of Package and Label Designs Using Eye Tracking. In: IEEE Conference on Open Systems (ICOS 2011), Langkawi, Malaysia, September 25-28 (2011)
15. Mohd, J.R., Mohamed, N., Muhamad, D.F.: Kajian impak UiTM 2007 kampus Pulau Pinang. UiTM (2007)
16. Nielsen, J.: Finding usability problems through heuristic evaluation. Human-Computer Interaction Conference (1992)
17. Tzanidou, E.: Eye Tracking as a complementary usability evaluation technique for E-Commerce sites (2005)
18. Underwood, R.L., Klein, N.M., Burke, R.R.: Packaging communication: Attentional effect of product imagery. Journal of Product and Brand Management 10(7), 403–422 (2001)
19. Young, S.: Winning at retail: research insights to improve the packaging of children's products. Advertising & Marketing to Children, 17–22 (2003)

Visual Interaction Patterns of Students' Feedback: Reliability and Usability of Teaching and Supervision Evaluation System (TESES)

Uswatun Bakar* and Azizah Jaafar

Faculty of Information Science and Technology,
Universiti Kebangsaan Malaysia,
43600 UKM Bangi, Malaysia
us_alang@yahoo.com.my, aj@ftsm.ukm.my

Abstract. Teaching and Supervision Evaluation System (TESES), is a system to evaluate the quality of teaching and supervision from students' perspective. It is an official student feedback system used to evaluate efficiency and effectiveness of the Quality Management System (QMS) MS ISO 9001:2008 for management of undergraduate and graduate studies. In addition, the input obtained from the students will be used to continually improve and enhance the quality of teaching and learning at Universiti Kebangsaan Malaysia. Although the feedback from the system can contribute to improving the quality of the programs but the usability issues in terms of effectiveness and efficiency of the system design along with the reliability of the inputs and feedbacks from the students are disputable. Subsequently, these issues are studied in order to improve the system. This study use a triangulation method which is an integration of the three techniques; namely survey, observation through eye tracking technique and interviews, carried out on a sample consists of 30 students from the Faculty of Information Science and Technology. The visual interaction patterns, usability problems and the reliability level of student feedback are identified at the end of the study.

Keywords: eye tracking, usability, reliability, teaching and supervision evaluation system and triangulation method.

1 Introduction

Teaching and Supervision Evaluation System (TESES), is a system to evaluate the quality of course teaching and supervision from students' perspective. It is one of the official user feedback systems used to evaluate the efficiency and effectiveness of the Quality Management System (QMS) of MS ISO 9001:2008 for management of undergraduate and graduate studies. In addition, the input obtained from the students will be used to continually improve and enhance the quality of teaching and learning at Universiti Kebangsaan Malaysia. The TESES are divided into two sections namely Course Delivery

* Corresponding author.

H. Badioze Zaman et al. (Eds.): IVIC 2013, LNCS 8237, pp. 776–787, 2013.

Assessment and Supervision Assessment. Course delivery assessment section divided into three categories; i. General (7 questions for course content, infrastructure and equipment), ii. Faculty/Centre/Institute (3 – 10 questions for every teaching mode) and iii. Lecturer Evaluation (5 questions for every lecturer who handles the course).

The General and Lecturer Evaluation sections are used to evaluate the achievements of learning quality based on the Quality Management System (QMS) MS ISO 9001:2008, as well as to continuously improve the quality of teaching and course delivery. The Faculty/Centre/Institute section is use for internal quality improvement and to enhance the quality of teaching designing and revising the curriculum. Supervisory evaluation sections are divided into five categories; i. Supervisor Sensitivity (3 questions for supervisor sensitivity), ii. Interpersonal Relation (3 questions for interpersonal relation), iii. Interpersonal Relation (3 questions for interpersonal relation), iv. Conformance to Policy and Regulation (3 questions for conformance to policy and regulation), v. Transfer of Skills (3 questions for transfer of skills) and vi. Remarks.

In UKM's effort to improving the quality of teaching and learning, the commitment from students is needed to complete the questionnaire on Teaching and Supervision Evaluation System (TESES). Therefore, students are required to answer all the listed questions based on the likert scale 1-5 as stated in each part.

In this study, the students are required to complete the questionnaire on Teaching and Supervision Evaluation System (TESES) by online, while the student's eye movement was recorded by the Eye Tracker technology. The students are required to log in on the TESES and then complete the given task. This study is done to determine the validity and reliability of student feedback input on the system. In addition, the Eye Tracker also can help the researchers to identify usability problems encountered by users when interacting with the system. This is because the output produced by the eye tracker can be used as a guide to researchers to design a user-friendly interface.

1.1 Eye Tracking

Research related to eye movement has been done nearly 100 years ago when researcher doing an observation on the role of the eye movement in reading (Alex Poole et al. 2005). The recording of eye movement was done by using eye tracking technology. Eye tracking refers to recording eye movements while participants examine the visual stimulus (Agnieszka et al. 1990). This process allows researchers to understand of what a student searching and reading before they complete the task. Besides, eye trackers can tell where someone's eyes focus and interest (Louis Emile Javal 1978). This is because, what is fixated by the eye could be considered as the thinking of the user's cognitive processes (Just & Carpenter 1980).

According to Andrew Duchowski (2007), Eye Trackers use reflection of infrared rays to detect human pupils. Infrared rays are responsible to stimulate human pupils and help system for tracking user's eyes from the video image (Crane 1994). Besides, infrared rays would produce the corneal reflection and causes the bright pupil effect as showed in figure 1 below. According to Abdallahi Ould Mohamed et al. (2007), the reflections of objects from structure of the eye are known as Purkinje image.

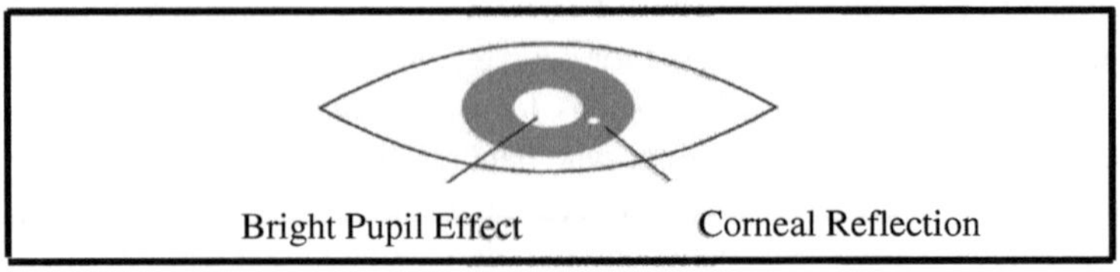

Fig. 1. The example of bright pupil effect and corneal reflection in Purkinje image
Source: Alex Poole et al. 2005

1.2 Reading Process

Reading is defined as observing the written or printed contents and followed by understanding the meaning of its contents (Dewan Dictionary Fourth Edition). During reading, our eyes doing a movement in a sequence called saccades, followed by fixation (Dodge 1903). Saccades are quick and rapid eye movements occurring between fixations and there is no information are recorded when the saccade occurred (Ahmed Emam et al. 2012). According to Barrios et al. (2005), fixation is the eye's focus, which requires 300 to 400 ms for the human understand and process the information. During fixation, information from the fixated area is usually extracted and encoded.

Lufting in 1987 state that the reading process refers to identify and converting printed symbols into sound pronunciation (decoding) and later translate it to the appropriate meaning according to the language they have learned. As showed in figure 2 below, Baharuddin et al. (2002) found that the eye's movement started from the left-top of the screen computer and then turn horizontally toward the right side of the computer screen. After that the user will be crosswise down to the bottom-left of the computer screen and eventually moved sideways to the right side of the computer screen as in the figure below.

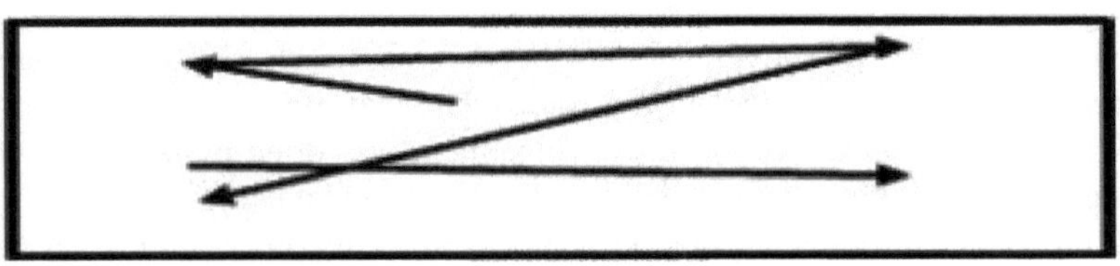

Fig. 2. User eye movements during reading on a computer screen
Source: Baharuddin et al. 2002

1.3 Usability

Definition of acceptance is very wide, implicitly including not only utility, but also usability, likeability and cost (Brian Shackel 1991; Chapanis 1991; Booth 1989). According to (Brian Shackel 1991), usability refers to users' ability to utilize the system functionality in practice. Usability measures the quality of the user experience when interacting with a product or system (Brooke et al. 1990). ISO 9241-11 defines usability as the extent to which a product can be used by specified users to achieve specified goals with efficiency, effectiveness and satisfaction in a specified context of use (Azizah Jaafar et al. 2010).

Besides, usability testing supports the activities of students in aspect of; speed and efficiency while completing the tasks, the effectiveness of the task and satisfaction and comfort of the system while completing the tasks. In this study, effectiveness of TESES can be obtained by completion of questionnaires given to students. The efficiency can be measured by the time that required by students to complete the task. While, satisfaction refers to the comfort and acceptability of use, it's requiring student's assessment on TESES concerning how pleasant it is to use.

1.4 Triangulation Method

Usability testing is a research technique to assess ease of a product where the users can use the products to perform the desired tasks efficiently and enjoy it (Rubin 1993). In usability tests, the samples representing the real users will be asked to test and complete typical tasks while observers watch, listen and take notes. To enhance the credibility and validity of data; for confirmatory and completeness purposes, the triangulation techniques will be applied in the process of data collection (Ashatu Hussein 2009; Alexander Jakob 2001; Shih 1998). Triangulation is defined as the use of multiple methods', mainly qualitative and quantitative methods in studying the same phenomenon for the purpose of increasing study credibility, accuracy and validity of the research findings (Sabina Yeasmin et al. 2012; Hunt 1991; Denzin 1978). This approach consists of two or more methodological approaches, theoretical perspectives, data sources, investigators and analysis methods to study the same phenomenon in order to enhance confidence of findings (Denzin 1970).

2 Research Aim and Objective

The main purpose of this research is to examine the usability and reliability of student feedback on TESES. The general objectives of the study are as following; i. Identify reliability of student input on TESES feedback, ii. Conduct usability testing on TESES interface by using Eye Tracking Technology and iii. Analyze and comparing data collected.

3 Research Methodology

In this research, the whole process of data collection will be conducted in the usability laboratory where 30 students from the Faculty of Information Science and Technology were selected as the research sample. The triangulation method is used which consist of an observation through eye tracking, survey and interviews that is showed by the research framework in figure 3.

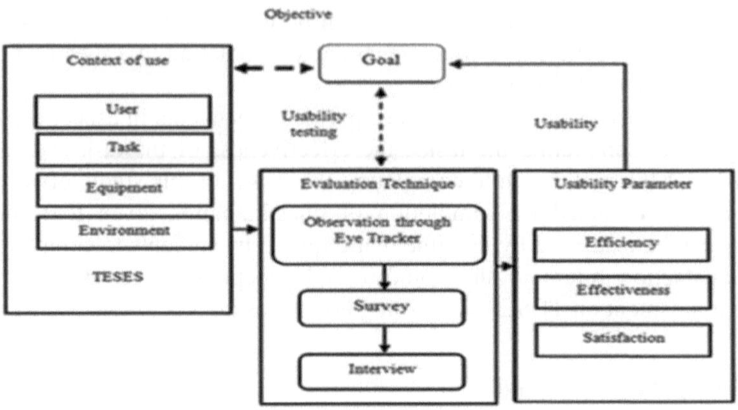

Fig. 3. Research framework

The combination of eye tracking techniques with other evaluation techniques can contribute to a better data collection. The students are required to log in into Teaching and Supervision Evaluation System (TESES) and complete all given questions in each section as show in the flow chart in figure 4 below. The feedback input obtained from students is used to continuously improve the quality of the program. During the testing, student's eye movements are recorded by the Eye Tracker technology. Once testing is completed, the students are required to complete the distributed questionnaire and later the interviews' session will be conducted between the testers and the respondents. The students are allowed to express their opinion, giving suggestion or criticism freely on Teaching and Supervision Evaluation System (TESES).

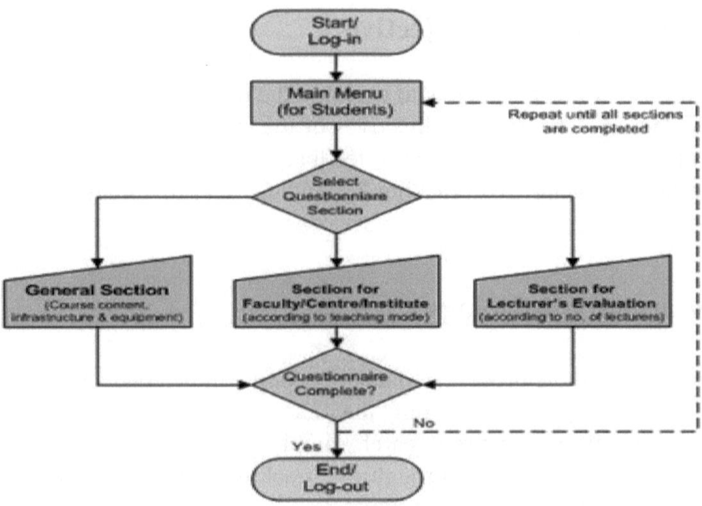

Fig. 4. The flow chart for answering the feedback questions

4 Research Results

The research was conducted on 30 students. The findings of the personal details of respondents showed that 83.3% of respondents are female and 16.7% of the respondents were male. More than 60% of participants involved this study were postgraduate students where about 83.3% of respondents had been in the UKM for more than one year or in other words, that have experienced in using TESES.

4.1 Reliability and Validity of Student Input

Based on the survey of finding, the result showed that the level of validity and reliability of student's input on TESES were not sure with an average 3.03 (as showed in table 1). In other words, 16.67% of the students agreed that the TESES input unreliable and about 20% of the students agreed that the TESES input can be trusted. Instead, 63.33% of the students are not sure whether the TESES results are reliable or not to help improving teaching and learning at the Universiti Kebangsaan Malaysia.

Table 1. The performance of student

Average Score	Performance
1.00-1.80	Extremely Not Agree
1.81-2.60	Not Agree
2.61-3.40	Not Sure
3.41-4.20	Agree
4.21-5.00	Extremely Agree

During identifying the validity and reliability of student input, there are two research questions need to be answered in order to solve the problem statement. These questions are either; i) the students read the question before answering questions; ii) the student thinks and makes judgments before answering questions. To ensure the validity and reliability of student input, the respondents were asked to complete the TESES questionnaire by online. This is because, an admission of students in the survey and interview only are very difficult to determine validity and reliability on TESES. During a testing was ongoing, the eye of the respondent will be recorded by using Eye Tracker in the usability laboratory. The output from the Eye Tracker can help the researcher to disengage all the doubts and questions that arise in this research.

To identifying the first question, whether the students read the question or not before answering questions, the analysis of eye tracker output must be done thoroughly. The indicator of eye movement from left to right with fixations and saccades from one word to another word in the questionnaire can be a guide to knowing whether students actually read the questionnaire or not. The figure 5 showed an example of eye movement patterns during reading the questions.

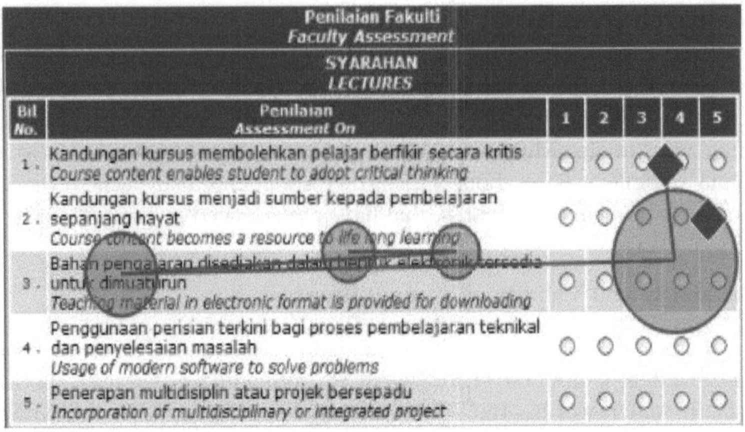

Fig. 5. Eye movements from the left to the right with fixations and saccades from one word to another word

While, figure 6 shows the patterns of student eye movement who did not read the question when completing the assessment questionnaire. This figure below showed that there no student's eye movements recorded in figure 6.

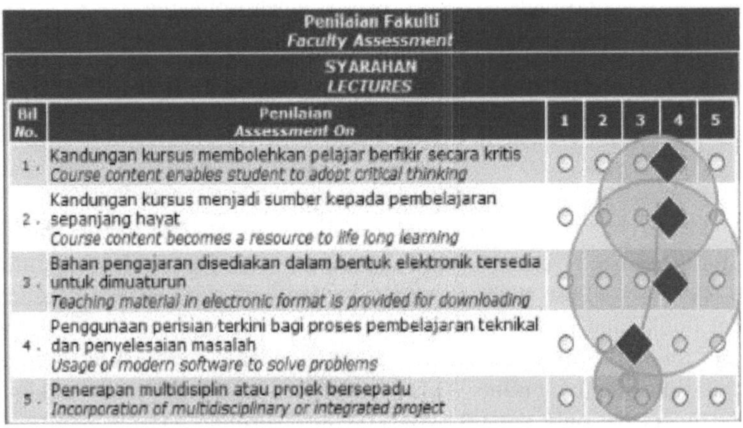

Fig. 6. There are no eye movements recorded

To answer the second question, an indicator of eye movements on a scale before answering question will determine the validity of the feedback input to the evaluation system. This is because, the information processing only happening when the eye is in a static position. Hence, the scanned of the eye on the question and guide scale can be interpreted as the student thinking in the cognitive process as showed in figure 7 and figure 8 below.

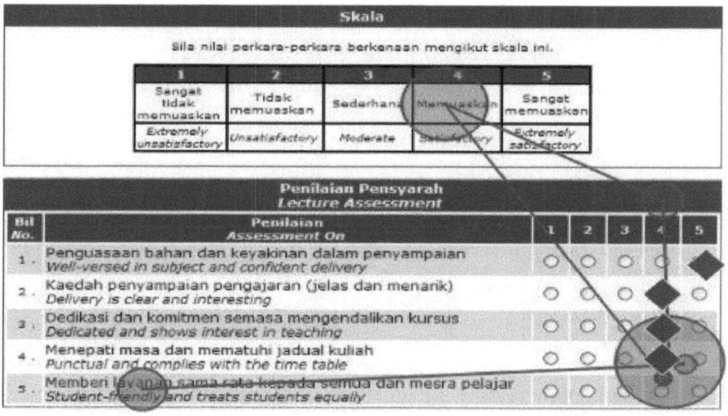

Fig. 7. Examples of eye movement patterns on reference scale

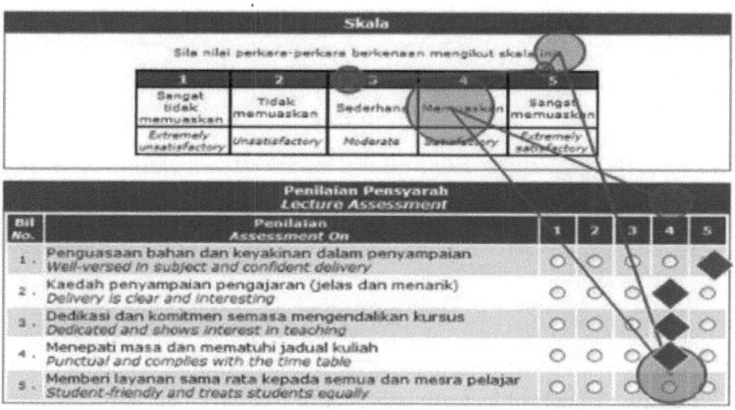

Fig. 8. The scan path shows the students are thinking and doing consideration before giving a rating

However, not all the respondents refer to scale guide before answering the question. This is because, about 30% of students admitted give opinions and evaluation with carefully during completing the questionnaire with an average 3.13 and 43.33% of the students are familiar with TESES and admitted using memory and an experience during answering the questionnaires. Therefore, the observation on the number or size of fixation circles appearing on the answer scale will be used as another indicator to answering the second question (as showed in figure 9 and 10).

Based on the finding, the result showed that 30% of the respondents read every TESES question before filling in answers and 16.67% of students read the question between 50% to 75% of questions. Besides, the finding revealed about 20% of the students did not read the question before answering questionnaires on TESES. In conclusion, the level of the validity and reliability of student input on Teaching and Supervision Evaluation System (TESES) is at the weak level as showed in table 2.

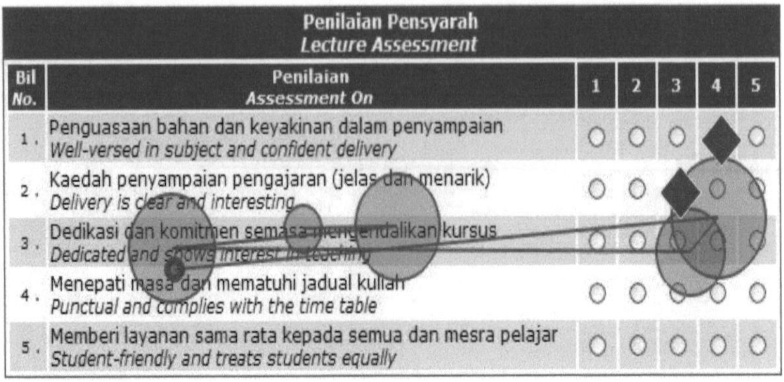

Fig. 9. Example of increasing the number of fixation circle on the answer scale

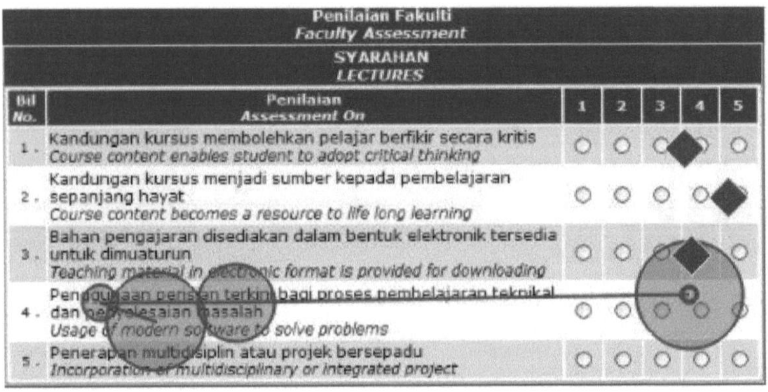

Fig. 10. Example of increasing the size of fixation on the answer scale

Table 2. The level of performance

Percentages (%)	Performance Level
80-100	Very Good
60-79	Good
40-59	Moderate
20-39	Weak
0-19	Very Weak

4.2 Usability Problems Based on Survey

Based on the finding, 73.34% of the students agreed that Teaching Evaluation and Supervision System (TESES) are required to enhance the learning process while 70% of students agreed that the TESES provides an opportunity for students to express their views or criticism on teaching and learning at the Universiti Kebangsaan Malaysia with average 3.9. However, about 63.33% of students admitted that TESES would burden the students because it was made a condition for registration of a semester. This is because, the Teaching and Supervision Evaluation system are compulsory for all students before registration of the new semester. These prerequisites can contribute to usability problems on Teaching and Supervision Evaluation System with the highest score (mean=3.73). In another word; about 60% of the students have negative emotions on Teaching and Supervision Evaluation System with a mean 3.67.

The usability problem was identified are the TESES interface was so boring (mean=3.40), followed by less of link (mean=3.23) and inefficiency of the interface with an average mean of 3.20. However, about 86.67% of students agree that TESES needed to be improve (mean=4.07). The improvements should be done are reducing the number of questions (mean=3.97), reducing the number of clicks (mean=3.93), uploading the guide video to facilitate the students answer the questions and creating more interesting interface (mean=3.3).

Based on the observation of eye tracker output, most of the students who were first time used the evaluation system felt uncomfortable and fail to handle properly. This is because, most students do not realize the instruction given below. Besides, most of the students click on the name of the lecturer and not on the lecturer's number button. In addition, the observation through the eye tracker also shows that most students do backtracking readings while completed the task.

5 Conclusions

In conclusion, the validity and reliability of student feedback of the TESES are at the weak level. This is shown by the analysis of survey, Eye Tracker and interview output where 30% of the students read the questions, about 16.67% of students read between 50% to 75% of the questions and 20% of the students did not read the question before answering questionnaires. Based on the finding on the usability problem, the interfaces of TESES were unattractive, confusing, quite boring, unfriendly, inefficient and there are too many questions, which can cause the students to have negative perception on Teaching and Supervision Evaluation System. Based on the findings, a new interface design of the system is introduced together with the design guidelines are proposed. The proposal is expected to help the university to improve the usability of the available Teaching and Supervision Evaluation System.

References

1. Hussein, A.: The use of Triangulation in Social Sciences Research: can qualitative and quantitative methods be combined? Journal of Comparative Social Work 2009(1) (2009)
2. Jaafar, A., Abdullah, S., Latif, A.A., Paraidathathu, T., Ahmad, W.N.W., Abdullah, N., Daud, S., Salima, J., Lee, C.S.: Reliability of student feedback on the course teaching evaluation system (CTES) and system usability. Procedia Social and Behavioral Sciences 18(2011), 24–32 (2010)
3. Mohamed, A.O., Da Silva, M.P., Courboulay, V.: A history of eye gaze tracking (2007)

4. Andrews, D.H., Goodson, L.A.: A comparative analysis of model of instructional design. Journal of Instructional Development 3(4), 2–16 (1980)
5. ACM SIGCHI Curricula for Human-Computer Interaction, http://www.acm.org/sigchi/cdg/cdg3.html (November 23, 2012)
6. Emam, A., Youssef, A.E.: Do Females Read Faster than Males? An Empirical Study Using Eye Tracking Systems (2012)
7. Byrne, M.D., Anderson, J.R., Douglass, S., Matessa, M.: Eye Tracking the Visual Search of Click-Down Menus. In: Human Factors In Computing Systems CHI 1999 Conference Proceedings, pp. 402–409 (1999)
8. Bevan, N.: Human-Computer Interaction Standards. In: Anzai, Y., Ogawa (eds.) Proceedings of the 6th International Conference on Human Computer Interaction. Elsevier, United Kingdom (1995)
9. Bednarik, R.: Methods to Analyze Visual Attention Strategies: Applications in the Studies of Programming (2007)
10. Duchowski, A.T.: Eye Tracking Methodology. Theory and Practice (2007)
11. Eivazi, S., Bednarik, R.: Predicting Problem-Solving Behavior and Performance Levels from Visual Attention Data. In: 2nd Workshop on Eye Gaze in Intelligent Human Machine Interaction, pp. 9–16 (2011)
12. Zenga, F., Hub, Z., Chenb, R., Yang, Z.: Determinants of online service satisfaction and their impacts on behavioural intentions. Total Quality Management 20(9), 953–969 (2009)
13. Gommans, M., Krishnan, K.S., Scheffold, K.B.: From Brand Loyalty to E-Loyalty: A Conceptual Framework. Journal of Economic and Social Research 3(1), 43–58 (2001)
14. Holmqvist, K., Nystrom, M., Andersson, R., Dewhurst, R., Jarodzka, H., Weijer, J.V.D.: Eye Tracking: A Comprehensive Guide to Methods and Measures, New York (2011)
15. Jeng, J.: Usability Assessment of Academic Digital Libraries: Effectiveness, Efficiency, Satisfaction, and Learnability. Libri 55, 96–121 (2005)
16. Just, M.A., Carpenter, P.A.: A Theory of Reading: From Eye Fixations to Comprehension (1980)
17. Just, M.A., Carpenter, P.A.: Eye Fixations and Cognitive Processes. Cognitive Psychology 8, 441–480 (1979)
18. Kuutti, K.: HCI and design: uncomfortable bedfellows (Re)searching the Digital Bauhaus, 43–59 (2009)
19. Shahzad, M.I., Mehmood, S.: Control of Articulated Robot Arm by Eye Tracking, Sweden (2010)
20. Macdonald, N.: what is web design? Switzerland (2003)
21. Omar, M.H.: Proses Pengajaran-Pembelajaran dimantapkan Menerusi Penggabungan SPK Prasiswazah dan Siswazah. Buletin Pembangunan Akademik Bil Julai – Dis. 1.24 (2009)
22. Mansour, J.K., Flowe, H.D.: Eye tracking and Eyewitness Memory (2010)
23. Mansour, J.K., Flowe, H.D.: Eye tracking and eyewitness memory. Forensic Update 101 – Autumn, 11-15 (2010)
24. Neilsen, J., Pernice, K.: Eye Tracking Web Usability, USA (2010)
25. Poole, A., Ball, L.J.: Eye tracking in HCI and usability research, United Kingdom (2006)
26. Poole, A., Ball, L.J.: Eye Tracking in Human-Computer Interaction and Usability Research: Current Status and Future Prospects, United Kingdom (2005)
27. Melayu, P.R.P.: http://prpm.dbp.gov.my/Search.aspx?k=reading
28. Review and Analysis of Human Computer Interaction (HCI) Principles 1-13, http://arxiv.org/ftp/arxiv/papers/0707/0707.3638.pdf
29. Radach, R., Hyona, J., Deube, J.: The Mind's Eye: Cognitive and Applied Aspects of Eye Movement Research, Holland (2003)

30. Rayner, K.: Eye Movements in Reading and Information Processing: 20 Years of Research. Psychological Bulletin 1998 124(3), 372–422 (1998)
31. Sensomotoric Instrument. Experiment Center 2 Manual Version 2.1, Germany (2008)
32. Sensomotoric Instrument. 2008. BeGaze 2 Manual. Version 2.2, Germany (2008)
33. Sensomotoric Instrument. 2008. I View X System Manual. Version 2.2, Germany (2008)
34. Szymanski, D.M., Hise, R.T.: E-satisfaction: An initial examination. Journal of Retailing 76(3), 309–322 (2000)
35. Salvucci, D.D., Goldberg, J.H.: Identifying fixations and saccades in eye-tracking protocols. In: Proceedings of the Eye Tracking Research and Applications Symposium, pp. 71–78 (2000)
36. Salvucci, D.D.: An Interactive Model-Based Environment for Eye-Movement Protocol Analysis and Visualization. In: Eye Tracking Research & Applications Symposium, pp. 57–63 (2000)
37. Shelly, G.B., Nappier, H.A., Rivers, O.N.: Web Design: Introductory Concepts and Techniques, USA (2008)
38. Sistem Penilaian Pengajaran dan Penyeliaan, https://smp.ukm.my/sppk/
39. Yeasmin, S., Rahman, K.F.: Triangulation' Research Method as the Tool of Social Science Research. Bup Journal 1(1) (September 2012) ISSN: 2219-4851
40. Usability of Interactive Products, http://www2.uiah.fi/projekti/metodi/158.htm
41. Usability Testing: Developing Useful and Usable Products, http://www.units.muohio.edu/mtsc/usabilitytestingrevisedFINAL.pdf
42. Usability.gov, http://www.usability.gov/how-to-and-tools/methods/usability-testing.html
43. Wang, Y.D., Emurian, H.H.: An overview of online trust: Concepts, elements, and implications. Computers in Human Behavior 21(1), 105–125 (2005)
44. Wedel, M., Pieters, R.: Eye Tracking For Visual Marketing, USA (2006)
45. Zambarbieri, D., Carniglia, E., Robino, C.: Eye Tracking Analysis in Reading Online Newspapers. Journal of Eye Movement Research 2(4):7, 1–8 (2008)

Visually Impaired User's Navigation Experiences in Facebook

Bavani Ramayah[1], Azizah Jaafar[2], and Noor Faezah Mohd. Yatim[3]

[1] Faculty of Science, The University of Nottingham (Malaysia Campus), Selangor, Malaysia
[2] Institut of Visual Informatics (IVI)
[3] Faculty of Information Science and Technology,
University Kebangsaan Malaysia (UKM)
bavani.ramayah@nottingham.edu.my,
{aj,nfmy}@ftsm.ukm.my

Abstract. Social networking is a platform to build social relation among people around the world. Facebook is one of the applications widely used by everyone. Now we can share information, ideas, knowledge through social networking sites (SNS). These activities are enjoyed by everyone without any barriers. In this paper we discuss the navigation issues in Facebook by visually impaired (VI) user who using screen reader. Our study focuses on important navigation activities by VI user, explaining navigation barriers and suggesting solutions.

Keywords: facebook, usability, accessibility, visually impaired user.

1 Introduction

The Web is a place to connect millions of people around the world. Web 2.0 is the second generation of the World Wide Web, which increases the ability of people to share information via online. Social Networks like Facebook, Twitter are the components of Web 2.0 which allow people to interact, make friends and post information. Social networking sites(SNS), particularly Facebook, have become hugely popular in the last few years. According to GlobalWebIndex [1], Facebook remained the top social network worldwide; over half of Internet users logging on to the site at least once a month in 2013. Based on GlobalWebIndex's count, Facebook has almost 700-million active users worldwide. Facebook is clearly evolving and is used by a majority of people. Therefore, is it important for the application to be accessible and usable for all, including people with special needs.

Accessibility and usability play an important role in the use of social network because this always being considered when designing a user interface to provide universal access. An accessible and usable page allows users to focus on content and continue their Web "journey" without any barrier. VI users easily will be frustrated if encountered problems continuously and wasting too much time on the perception of interface. Accessibility allows users to reach on-line applications and content, while usability provides simple, efficient and satisfying navigation and interaction[2].

H. Badioze Zaman et al. (Eds.): IVIC 2013, LNCS 8237, pp. 788–796, 2013.

Web Content Accessibility Guidelines (WCAG) 2.0 covers a wide range of recommendations for making Web content more accessible[3]. Following these guidelines will make content accessible to a wider range of people with disabilities, including blindness and low vision, deafness and hearing loss, learning disabilities, cognitive limitations, limited movement, speech disabilities, photosensitivity and combinations of these. Following these guidelines will also often make your Web content more usable to users in general [3].

2 Viewing Web Page via Screen Reader

There are software programs that convert text into synthesized speech and VI people are able to listen to web content. These software programs are generally called as screen reader. Screen reader is the most popular assistive technology utilized by users with visual impairment. The most popular screen readers are JAWS (Freedom Scientific, St. Petersburg, FL) and Window-Eyes (GW-Micro, Ft. Wayne, IN) [4], [5] and [6]. There are also simple versions of screen readers built into some operating systems [7]. Most VI users type into a keyboard, as they have the keyboard layout memorized and do not need to see the keyboard to use it. Therefore, output is more challenging compared to input for VI users. Screen readers allow users to navigate Web content in many ways. The user can simply let the screen reader read everything from top to bottom, one line at a time, or the user can use the tab key to navigate from link to link. The user can also navigate from one heading to the next (if the web content has headings), from one frame to the next (if there are frames), or by other methods [4]. Although a Web site might be accessible to a VI user, it still might be very hard to use. For instance, the information on the Web page may be arranged in a layout that makes VI users become frustrated in attempting to access the information [7]. Many pages contain multiple columns or redundant links, which require a VI user to read each Web page in a line-by-line. With each selection of a link, users must start from the top of the next page in reading until they either reach the bottom of the page or find a desired link. The selection of a new link refreshes the screen, which generally forces screen readers to move focus to the top left-hand corner of the screen. The frustration occurs when users must listen to the same information each time they choose a new link [7].

The sighted users visualize web content by looking at the monitor and they view a page of elements like a map located at top-right, top-center, top-left, middle-right, center, bottom, right and etc. For the VI user, the screen reader as audio mediated software read the information for them directly from source code. As we know, source code only has one column with information one after another line. Therefore, the sighted users view the page as three columns. However, for VI users, a screen reader will read the source code starts from heading followed by navigation bar, body text and images. Therefore, sometime sighted users may think that images appear first, but to the VI users the images are the last item on a page. Although the use of screen readers is common, VI users can use a Web page only when it is designed to be flexible; that is, to be used in conjunction with various forms of assistive technology [7].

3 Related Work

The World Wide Web Consortium (W3C) was founded by Tim Berners-Lee in 1994. The mission of W3C is to lead the World Wide Web in developing protocols and guidelines that ensure the long-term growth of the Web[8].Web for all is one of the design principle of W3C's work. This is to make Web available to all people, whatever their hardware, software, network infrastructure, native language, culture, geographical location, or physical or mental ability[8]. Since there is increased attention on accessibility issues for the VI user, Section 508 of the Rehabilitation Act was amended in 1998 in United States[9] and [6].

In spite of these efforts, we find accessibility and usability issues still exist in web pages even some are compliant with basic regulation and guidelines. This is due to the focusing on compliance and guidelines without looking into real usability[10]. By designing web pages accessible to visually impaired user, we are making a contribution to universal access. There are number of studies addressing on web accessibility and usability issues for VI users[10], [11], [12], [13], [14] and [6]. Several proposals have been presented in previous studies. There are several studies in SNS which address issues for VI users who interact web pages via screen reader. There is a study on understanding perception and current use of SNS when VI user asking for help while accessing the web pages. In order to understand VI users' navigation behavior in more detail, observation was done on their web activities in SNS. Facebook and Twitter are the two sites were used to understand VI users' navigation activities[2] and [15].The researchers tested some of the features in social network to observed and to addressed issues when VI users interact with web page via screen reader. There is a study found that Twitter is more accessible and usable compare to Facebook due to page complexity[2].

Since there are more problems in Facebook, more studies must be carried out to understand VI users' interaction with Facebook via screen reader. Since there is a relationship between VI users' navigation behavior and their mental model[16], it is important to understand their perception via screen reader of Web pages in social network. There will be some additional features observed in this study which are not included in previous studies on Twitter and Facebook[2] and [15]. This study is part of ongoing research of VI user navigation behavior in social network sites. Based on the results of this analysis, the authors will attempt to outline detail research on cognitive behavior and task analysis with more number of participants (VI users) by focusing accessibility and usability of social network for people interacting via screen reader.

In this paper we discuss the navigation activities and the barriers involved in interacting via screen reader with Facebook. Specifically we focus on communication-related features and will analyze the following functionalities:

- New user registration and log-in
- Finding and Adding friend
- Reading updates posted by others
- Log out

4 Interaction with Facebook

4.1 Evaluation Methodology

To evaluate the Facebook user interface, we used the screen reader JAWS and Internet Explorer version 7 browser. The test was carried out by a VI user; her name is Anna. She has been totally blind since childhood and skilled at using JAWS. She is a web programmer. The observation was performed in April 2013. Equipment such as computer and audio recorder were used for the observation. The observation took two hours and conducted in naturalistic environment. There was no formal training given to the user before begin with observation on her navigation. Training is inapplicable because in reality people use the Web on a daily basis without any formal training [17].

4.2 Registration and Log In

The user did not have any difficulties in log-in procedure. Since the page just required two fields to login, the screen reader easily detects two required fields. The user moves to username and password edit box via arrow key and tab key. They are some issues when typing an incorrect username and password. The user needs to read or listen to the audio error message carefully to know the error messages are for incorrect password and username.

The main problem occur when the user begin the process with registration. The whole process took more than fifteen minutes. The text box or text field labels can be detected by the VI user. However, there was some difficulty which occurred when the user name or the email were already registered or invalid. In order to detect the error messages the user needs to read all the content sequentially. Whenever the user used the tab key to move, it jumped to the hyperlink by ignoring other text in the error message. For example, the user type email id which is belongs to an existing account. Instead of reading whole message as "*Sorry it looks like meera1115@yahoo.com belongs to an existing account. Would you like to claim this email address*?" but the screen just read as "*claim this email address*" which is coded as a hyperlink (Fig. 1 shows an example).

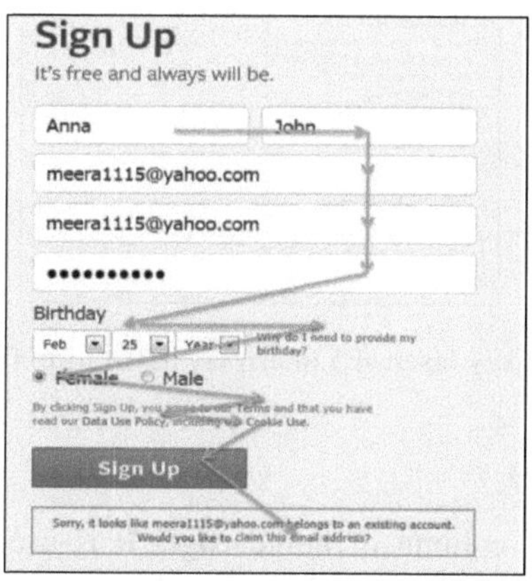

Fig. 1. Movement of cursor when using tab key in keyboard

However, the good news for the registration page is that there is no CAPTCHA since it gave lot of problems for VI user. Previous studies found that VI users stay away from social network sites due to the complexity of CAPTCHA [18]. . CAPTCHA is an abstract rendering of random characters that ask users to retype the word they see on the screen [19]. CAPTCHA is meant to keep spam programs out of the system, but unfortunately they also keep out people with vision loss because they are essentially jumbled text embedded in an unlabeled graphic[19].

4.3 Searching and Adding Friend

After logging into Facebook page, we requested Anna to search for her friend's name in Facebook and add her by clicking to "add friend" button. She could search for friend's name by typing the name in text box. When she reached to the friend's individual page, she spent quite long time to find for "add friends" option. The virtual cursor was moving to page content without reaching the option button for "add friend". Anna uses many types of shortcut keys such as Insert+F5, Insert+F6, Insert+F7 and tab keys. These shortcut keys uses in screen reader where it gives voice to computers through applications that synthesize written words and keyboard commands into human sounding speech[20]. JAWS key command in a screen reader equivalent to mouse functions in order for VI computer users to launch programs, navigate their desktop, read documents, and surf the web. For example, the arrow keys enable users to quickly cycle around desktop items or section headings on a website[20]. Pressing Insert + F7 displays a list of all links on that page[20].Since she did not know that the "add friend" is in "button" form, she had to use various type of shortcut keys. At last she found "Add Friend" by using Insert+F5 because this shortcut key could display list of form field in active page (Fig. 2 shows an example).

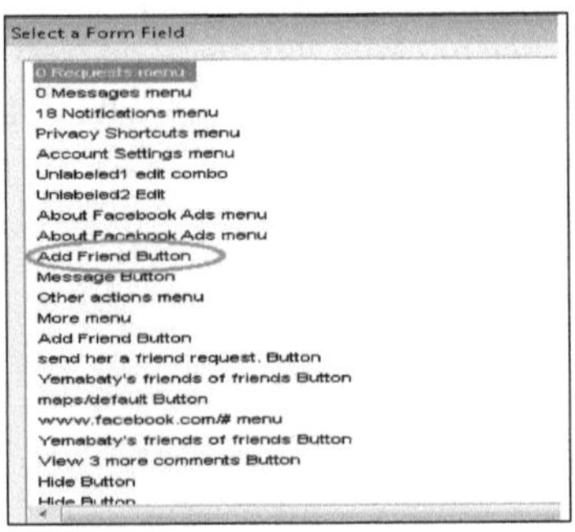

Fig. 2. Shortcut key Insert+F5 to display list of form field in web page

4.4 Checking Updates

News Feed is the center column of home page. It is a constantly updating list of stories from people and pages that you follow on Facebook. News feed stories include status updates, photos, videos, links, app activity and likes. This is the most complicated page since there is a lot of information posted by other friends. We asked Anna to check updates and wall posts sent by her friend. She took fifteen minutes to get overview of entire page. She used keyboard shortcut keys such as INSERT+F6, where these navigation methods able to list down all the headings consist in the web page (Fig. 3 shows an example). In the end, she found the messages and updates in her timeline page.

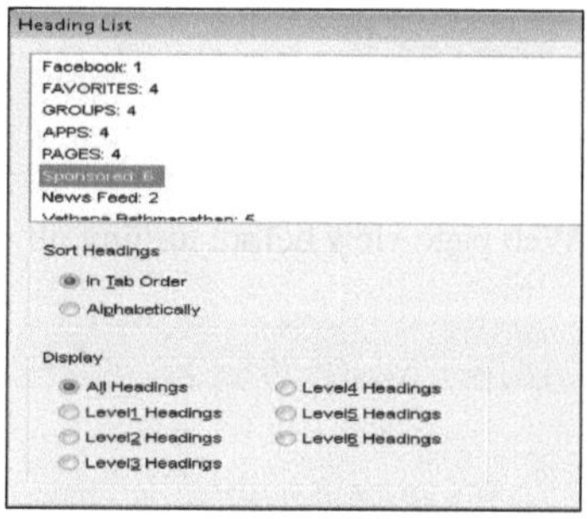

Fig. 3. Shortcut key Insert+F6 to display list of heading in a web page

4.5 Logging Out from User Account

Login or logon refers to the credentials required to access a computer system or other restricted area. Logging in (or on) and signing in (or on) is the process by which individual access to a computer system is controlled by identifying and authenticating the user through the credentials presented by the user[21].

Once a user has logged in, they can then log out when access is no longer required. To log out is to close off one's access to a computer system after having previously logged in. If an account gets accessed by strangers, this could open up a large can of worms, so we should seriously prevent unwanted access to our account. However, logging out from the Facebook account was the most frustrating aspect experienced by the VI user. She spent almost fifteen minutes to find the log out button. She moved from top to bottom and tried to locate the log out button. She used various navigation methods to detect the log out option. Although the researcher as an observer (sighted user), sitting next to VI user could not view or locate the log out button. At last we found that the graphic button that link to log out option disappear once turn off images in web browser. Since images are not useful for VI users, the first thing she did once logging on to the Facebook page was turning off images (refer to Fig. 4 and Fig. 5). VI users could "visualize" images by referring to Alternate (ALT) text, which conveys the meaning of the image. Turning off images also useful for mobile users who have lower bandwidth, or people in a rural area with low bandwidth, to speed downloads [3].

Fig. 4. Web page view before turning off images

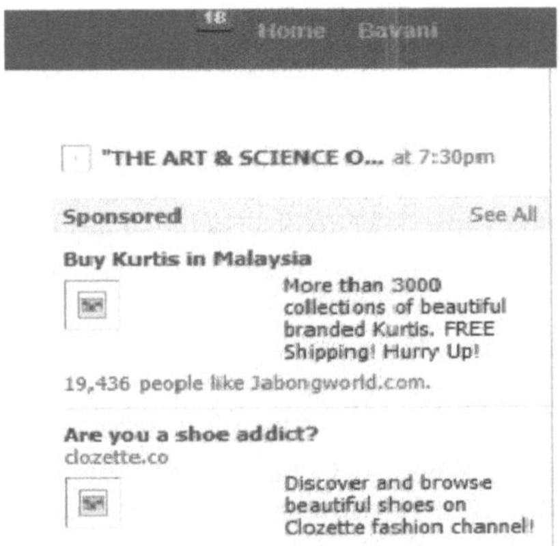

Fig. 5. Web page view before turning off the images

5 Discussion

SNS have changed user behavior to socialize better with people around the world. It is important to ensure everyone participate into social world without any problem even they have various types of physical disabilities. Regarding Web accessibility and usability, several studies have been presented as well as guidelines and principles and some of them already applied and tested. However, users who interact through assistive technologies still facing problems and difficulties. Therefore, social network sites such as Facebook should not only be accessible but should be easy to use through technologies such as screen reader.

Overall, Facebook is not easy to navigate by VI users who using screen readers for web interaction. Although accessibility guidelines and criteria are often applied to web pages in Facebook, unfortunately there are still certain barriers that exist between users and the application. The main problems encountered by the VI user are summarized. General observed issues include:

- Adding friend: the search for a person is not usable because there are too many steps and clicks before reaching the "add" button
- Wall content: difficult to detect the "wall text" in the sequential
- Wall navigation: difficult to navigate among the wall post

Even a web page is designed including accessible and usable elements; it must easily reach by VI users who depend on screen readers. In order to make any system to have universal access, the system should be simple and allow the user to focus on content. Comparing the accessibility and usability issues raised for Facebook with those observed in Twitter[2], we found that Facebook having more issues compare to Twitter. The environment and user interface for Twitter are simpler compare to Facebook. In previous study on Facebook[15], similar issues were found such as messages, related to form element. However, based on our finding we found additional issue where problem occur when user log out from her Facebook account. Same time we notice that there is no CAPTCHA (security checker) as mentioned in previous study[15]. Besides, the web guidelines recommend that web developers or designers test their web pages by accessing their pages by using screen reader[22]. The web checkers only rely on syntactical checking techniques to detect accessibility issues. Therefore the detected errors are limited to the level of the tag description layer[10].

When designing and developing a system, such as social networks like Facebook, some basic concepts should be taken into account:-

- User Interface should be simple and easy to find the web page content
- The home page should be easily access and able to move from one section to another section
- Avoid from using graphics as navigation buttons
- Focus on accessibility as well as usability guidelines in designing user interface

6 Conclusion

Social networks are the new way to stay in touch and share information with others. Today many services rely on this kind of new media even it's become famous among teenagers at the beginning. Government, business, and education sectors use social network as medium to transfer information to public. We able to keep ourselves up-to-date by getting latest information and news through Facebook. The issues in Facebook could make the VI users to stay away from social network. This is totally unfair to them who have interest to socialize and keep themselves up to date with current information. In this paper we carried out a study to investigate VI users' navigation behavior in Facebook. The results from our observation via JAWS screen reader clearly indicate that there are several usability issues in Facebook. Lastly, some basic suggestions have been proposed to improve the navigation activities of VI user with Facebook and related platforms.

Acknowledgment. The author would like to thank the participant who volunteered in this study and special thanks to Malaysian Blind Association (MAB), National Council of Blind Malaysia (NCBM) for their tremendous supports.

References

1. ZDNet-Google+ moves up to second place in social networks, http://www.zdnet.com/google-moves-up-to-second-place-in-social-networks-7000010372/
2. Buzzi, M.C., Buzzi, M., Leporini, B.: Web 2.0: Twitter and the blind. In: Proceedings of the 9th ACM SIGCHI Italian Chapter International Conference on Computer-Human Interaction: Facing Complexity, pp. 151–156 (2011)
3. Web Content Accessibility Guidelines (WCAG) 2_0, http://www.w3.org/TR/WCAG/
4. WebAIM Visual Disabilities - Blindness, http://webaim.org/articles/visual/blind
5. Calder, M., Cohen, R.F., Lanzoni, J., Landry, N., Skaff, J.: Teaching data structures to students who are blind. ACM SIGCSE Bulletin 39(3), 87 (2007)
6. Sierkowski, B.: Achieving Web Accessibility 1990, 288–291 (1990)
7. Lazar, J., Allen, A., Kleinman, J., Malarkey, C.: What Frustrates Screen Reader Users on the Web: A Study of 100 Blind Users. International Journal of Human-Computer Interaction 22(3), 247–269 (2007)
8. World Wide Consortium- Mission, http://www.w3.org/Consortium/mission
9. An Official Website of The United States Government-Section 508, https://www.section508.gov/
10. Takagi, H., Asakawa, C.: Accessibility Designer: Visualizing Usability for the Blind. SIGACCESS Access. Comput., 177–184 (2004)
11. Michailidou, E., Harper, S., Bechhofer, S.: Investigating sighted users' browsing behaviour to assist web accessibility. In: Proceedings of the 10th International ACM SIGACCESS Conference on Computers and Accessibility (Assets 2008), p. 121 (2008)
12. Richards, J.T., Hanson, V.L.: Web accessibility: a broader view. In: Proceedings of the 13th International Conference on World Wide Web, pp. 72–79 (2004)
13. Di Blas, N., Paolini, P., Speroni, M.: Usable Accessibility to the Web for blind Users (2003)
14. Mankoff, J., Fait, H., Tran, T.: Is Your Web Page Accessible? A Comparative Study of Methods for Assessing Web Page Accessibility for the Blind. In: Proceedings of the SIGCHI Conference on Human Factors in Computing Systems, pp. 41–50 (2005)
15. Buzzi, M.C., Buzzi, M., Leporini, B., Akhter, F.: Is Facebook really 'open' to all? In: 2010 IEEE International Symposium on Technology and Society, pp. 327–336 (2010)
16. Ramayah, B.: Human Computer Interface: Visually Impaired Users' Mental Model and Navigation Behavior on News Web Site. GSTF Journal on Computing 2(2), 36–40 (2012)
17. Zhang, Y.: The influence of mental models on undergraduate students' searching behavior on the Web. Information Processing & Management 44(3), 1330–1345 (2008)
18. Ramayah, B., Jaafar, A., Yatim, N.F.M.: Accessibility Issues of Social Networking Sites to Blind Users in Malaysia. In: Visual Informatics International Seminar 2012 (VIIS 2012) (2012)
19. Are Social Networking Sites Accessible to People with Vision Loss, AFB, http://www.afb.org/section.aspx?sectionid=57&topicid=167&documentid=3153
20. WebAIM Using JAWS to Evaluate Web Accessibility, http://webaim.org/articles/jaws/
21. Login - Wikipedia, the free encyclopedia, https://en.wikipedia.org/wiki/Login
22. Asakawa, C., Itoh, T.: User interface of a Home Page Reader. In: Proceedings of the Third International ACM Conference on Assistive Technologies (Assets 1998), pp. 149–156 (1998)

Author Index

MIX
Papier aus verantwortungsvollen Quellen
Paper from responsible sources
FSC® C105338

If you have any concerns about our products,
you can contact us on
ProductSafety@springernature.com

In case Publisher is established outside the EU,
the EU authorized representative is:
Springer Nature Customer Service Center GmbH
Europaplatz 3, 69115 Heidelberg, Germany

Printed by Libri Plureos GmbH
in Hamburg, Germany